# BARRON'S

# AP®

# Computer Science A

## WITH 6 PRACTICE TESTS

### NINTH EDITION

**Roselyn Teukolsky, M.S.**

Formerly, Ithaca High School
Ithaca, New York

**About the Author:**

Roselyn Teukolsky has an M.S. degree from Cornell University, and has been teaching programming and computer science since 1980. She has published articles in *The Mathematics Teacher* and in the National Council of Teachers of Mathematics Yearbook. She is the author of Barron's *ACT Math and Science Workbook* and co-author of Barron's *SAT 1600: Aiming for the Perfect Score*. She has received the Edyth May Sliffe Award for Distinguished Mathematics Teaching and the Alfred Kalfus Distinguished Coach Award from the New York State Math League (NYSML).

© Copyright 2020, 2018, 2015, 2013, 2010 by Kaplan, Inc.,
d/b/a Barron's Educational Series
Previous editions © copyright 2007 under the title
*AP Computer Science Levels A and AB*, 2003 under the title
*How to Prepare for the AP Computer Science Advanced
Placement Examination, JAVA Version*, and 2001
under the title *How to Prepare for the AP Computer
Science Advanced Placement Examination*
by Kaplan, Inc., d/b/a Barron's Educational Series

Published by Kaplan, Inc.,
d/b/a Barron's Educational Series
750 Third Avenue
New York, NY 10017
**www.barronseduc.com**

ISBN: 978-1-4380-1289-6

10 9 8 7 6 5 4 3 2 1

Kaplan, Inc., d/b/a Barron's Educational
Series print books are available at special
quantity discounts to use for sales
promotions, employee premiums, or
educational purposes. For more information
or to purchase books, please call the
Simon & Schuster special sales department
at 866-506-1949.

# Contents

**Preface** . . . . . . . . . . . . . . . . . . . . . . . . . . . . . . . . . . . . . . xi

**Introduction** . . . . . . . . . . . . . . . . . . . . . . . . . . . . . . . . . xiii
    **General Information About the Exam** . . . . . . . . . . . . . . xiii
    **How to Use This Book** . . . . . . . . . . . . . . . . . . . . . . . xiii

**Diagnostic Test** . . . . . . . . . . . . . . . . . . . . . . . . . . . . . . . . 1
    **Computer Science A Section I** . . . . . . . . . . . . . . . . . . 5
    **Computer Science A Section II** . . . . . . . . . . . . . . . . . . 35
    **Answer Key (Section I)** . . . . . . . . . . . . . . . . . . . . . . . 45
    **Diagnostic Chart** . . . . . . . . . . . . . . . . . . . . . . . . . . . 45
    **Answers Explained** . . . . . . . . . . . . . . . . . . . . . . . . . . 47

**1 Strategies for Taking the Exam** . . . . . . . . . . . . . . . . 58
    **The Multiple-Choice Section** . . . . . . . . . . . . . . . . . . . . 58
        What Is Tested? . . . . . . . . . . . . . . . . . . . . . . . . . . . 58
        Time Issues . . . . . . . . . . . . . . . . . . . . . . . . . . . . . 58
        Guessing . . . . . . . . . . . . . . . . . . . . . . . . . . . . . . . 59
        The Java Quick Reference . . . . . . . . . . . . . . . . . . . 59
        An Active Pencil . . . . . . . . . . . . . . . . . . . . . . . . . . 59
        Troubleshooting—What's Wrong with This Code? . . . . 60
        Loop Tracing . . . . . . . . . . . . . . . . . . . . . . . . . . . . 60
        Java Exceptions . . . . . . . . . . . . . . . . . . . . . . . . . . 60
        Matrix Manipulation . . . . . . . . . . . . . . . . . . . . . . . 61
        Comparing Algorithms . . . . . . . . . . . . . . . . . . . . . 61
        Mechanics of Answering Questions . . . . . . . . . . . . . 61
    **The Free-Response Section** . . . . . . . . . . . . . . . . . . . . 61
        What Is the Format? . . . . . . . . . . . . . . . . . . . . . . . 61
        What Is Tested? . . . . . . . . . . . . . . . . . . . . . . . . . . 62
        What Types of Questions? . . . . . . . . . . . . . . . . . . . 62
        Skill Focus in Free-Response Questions . . . . . . . . . . 62
        The Java Quick Reference . . . . . . . . . . . . . . . . . . . 63
        Time Issues . . . . . . . . . . . . . . . . . . . . . . . . . . . . . 63
        Grading the Free-Response Questions . . . . . . . . . . . 63
        Coding Issues . . . . . . . . . . . . . . . . . . . . . . . . . . . 64
        Maximizing Your Score . . . . . . . . . . . . . . . . . . . . . 65

**2 Introductory Java Language Features** . . . . . . . . . . . . . . . . . 66

**Packages and Classes** . . . . . . . . . . . . . . . . . . . . . . . . . . . 66
    Javadoc Comments . . . . . . . . . . . . . . . . . . . . . . . . . . 68
**Types and Identifiers** . . . . . . . . . . . . . . . . . . . . . . . . . . . 68
    Identifiers . . . . . . . . . . . . . . . . . . . . . . . . . . . . . . . 68
    Built-in Types . . . . . . . . . . . . . . . . . . . . . . . . . . . . . 68
    Storage of Numbers . . . . . . . . . . . . . . . . . . . . . . . . . 69
    Hexadecimal and Octal Numbers . . . . . . . . . . . . . . . . . . 70
    Final Variables . . . . . . . . . . . . . . . . . . . . . . . . . . . . 70
**Operators** . . . . . . . . . . . . . . . . . . . . . . . . . . . . . . . . . 71
    Arithmetic Operators . . . . . . . . . . . . . . . . . . . . . . . . 71
    Relational Operators . . . . . . . . . . . . . . . . . . . . . . . . . 72
    Logical Operators . . . . . . . . . . . . . . . . . . . . . . . . . . 73
    Assignment Operators . . . . . . . . . . . . . . . . . . . . . . . . 74
    Increment and Decrement Operators . . . . . . . . . . . . . . . . 74
    Operator Precedence . . . . . . . . . . . . . . . . . . . . . . . . 75
**Input/Output** . . . . . . . . . . . . . . . . . . . . . . . . . . . . . . . 75
    Input . . . . . . . . . . . . . . . . . . . . . . . . . . . . . . . . . 75
    Output . . . . . . . . . . . . . . . . . . . . . . . . . . . . . . . . 75
    Escape Sequences . . . . . . . . . . . . . . . . . . . . . . . . . . 76
**Control Structures** . . . . . . . . . . . . . . . . . . . . . . . . . . . . 77
    Decision-Making Control Structures . . . . . . . . . . . . . . . . 77
    Iteration . . . . . . . . . . . . . . . . . . . . . . . . . . . . . . . 79
**Errors and Exceptions** . . . . . . . . . . . . . . . . . . . . . . . . . . 83
**Multiple-Choice Questions on Introductory Java Language Features** . . . . . 85
**Answer Key** . . . . . . . . . . . . . . . . . . . . . . . . . . . . . . . . 96
**Answers Explained** . . . . . . . . . . . . . . . . . . . . . . . . . . . . 96

**3 Classes and Objects** . . . . . . . . . . . . . . . . . . . . . . . . . . 100

**Objects** . . . . . . . . . . . . . . . . . . . . . . . . . . . . . . . . . . 100
**Classes** . . . . . . . . . . . . . . . . . . . . . . . . . . . . . . . . . . 100
**Public, Private, and Static** . . . . . . . . . . . . . . . . . . . . . . . . 101
**Methods** . . . . . . . . . . . . . . . . . . . . . . . . . . . . . . . . . . 102
    Headers . . . . . . . . . . . . . . . . . . . . . . . . . . . . . . . 102
    Types of Methods . . . . . . . . . . . . . . . . . . . . . . . . . . 103
    Method Overloading . . . . . . . . . . . . . . . . . . . . . . . . 107
**Scope** . . . . . . . . . . . . . . . . . . . . . . . . . . . . . . . . . . . 107
    The this Keyword . . . . . . . . . . . . . . . . . . . . . . . . . . 108
**References** . . . . . . . . . . . . . . . . . . . . . . . . . . . . . . . . . 109
    Reference vs. Primitive Data Types . . . . . . . . . . . . . . . . . 109
    The Null Reference . . . . . . . . . . . . . . . . . . . . . . . . . 110
    Method Parameters . . . . . . . . . . . . . . . . . . . . . . . . . 111
**Multiple-Choice Questions on Classes and Objects** . . . . . . . . . . . . 119
**Answer Key** . . . . . . . . . . . . . . . . . . . . . . . . . . . . . . . . 134
**Answers Explained** . . . . . . . . . . . . . . . . . . . . . . . . . . . . 134

**4  Inheritance and Polymorphism** . . . . . . . . . . . . . . . . . . . . . . . 139

**Inheritance** . . . . . . . . . . . . . . . . . . . . . . . . . . . . . . . . . 139

   Superclass and Subclass . . . . . . . . . . . . . . . . . . . 139

   Inheritance Hierarchy . . . . . . . . . . . . . . . . . . . . . . 139

   Implementing Subclasses . . . . . . . . . . . . . . . . . . . 140

   Declaring Subclass Objects . . . . . . . . . . . . . . . . . . 145

**Polymorphism** . . . . . . . . . . . . . . . . . . . . . . . . . . . . . . . 146

   Dynamic Binding (Late Binding) . . . . . . . . . . . . . . 146

   Using super in a Subclass . . . . . . . . . . . . . . . . . . . 148

**Type Compatibility** . . . . . . . . . . . . . . . . . . . . . . . . . . . . 149

   Downcasting . . . . . . . . . . . . . . . . . . . . . . . . . . . . 149

**Abstract Classes** . . . . . . . . . . . . . . . . . . . . . . . . . . . . . . 150

**Interfaces** . . . . . . . . . . . . . . . . . . . . . . . . . . . . . . . . . . . 150

**Multiple-Choice Questions on Inheritance and Polymorphism** . . . . . . . 151

**Answer Key** . . . . . . . . . . . . . . . . . . . . . . . . . . . . . . . . . . 164

**Answers Explained** . . . . . . . . . . . . . . . . . . . . . . . . . . . . 164

**5  Some Standard Classes** . . . . . . . . . . . . . . . . . . . . . . . . . . . 167

**The Object Class** . . . . . . . . . . . . . . . . . . . . . . . . . . . . . . 167

   The Universal Superclass . . . . . . . . . . . . . . . . . . . 167

   Methods in Object . . . . . . . . . . . . . . . . . . . . . . . . 167

**The String Class** . . . . . . . . . . . . . . . . . . . . . . . . . . . . . . 169

   String Objects . . . . . . . . . . . . . . . . . . . . . . . . . . . 169

   Constructing String Objects . . . . . . . . . . . . . . . . . 170

   The Concatenation Operator . . . . . . . . . . . . . . . . . 170

   Comparison of String Objects . . . . . . . . . . . . . . . . 171

   Other String Methods . . . . . . . . . . . . . . . . . . . . . . 172

**Wrapper Classes** . . . . . . . . . . . . . . . . . . . . . . . . . . . . . . 173

   The Integer Class . . . . . . . . . . . . . . . . . . . . . . . . 173

   The Double Class . . . . . . . . . . . . . . . . . . . . . . . . . 174

   Autoboxing and Unboxing . . . . . . . . . . . . . . . . . . 174

**The Math Class** . . . . . . . . . . . . . . . . . . . . . . . . . . . . . . . 176

   Random Numbers . . . . . . . . . . . . . . . . . . . . . . . . 178

**Multiple-Choice Questions on Some Standard Classes** . . . . . . . 180

**Answer Key** . . . . . . . . . . . . . . . . . . . . . . . . . . . . . . . . . . 195

**Answers Explained** . . . . . . . . . . . . . . . . . . . . . . . . . . . . 195

**6  Program Design and Analysis** . . . . . . . . . . . . . . . . . . . . . . 201

**Software Development** . . . . . . . . . . . . . . . . . . . . . . . . . . 201

   Program Specification . . . . . . . . . . . . . . . . . . . . . 201

   Program Design . . . . . . . . . . . . . . . . . . . . . . . . . . 201

   Program Implementation . . . . . . . . . . . . . . . . . . . 202

   Testing and Debugging . . . . . . . . . . . . . . . . . . . . . 202

   Program Maintenance . . . . . . . . . . . . . . . . . . . . . 203

**Object-Oriented Program Design** . . . . . . . . . . . . . . . . . . . 203

   Identifying Classes . . . . . . . . . . . . . . . . . . . . . . . . 203

   Identifying Behaviors . . . . . . . . . . . . . . . . . . . . . . 204

   Determining Relationships Between Classes . . . . . . . . . . . 204

UML Diagrams . . . . . . . . . . . . . . . . . . . . . . . . . . . . 205

Implementing Classes . . . . . . . . . . . . . . . . . . . . . . . 205

Implementing Methods . . . . . . . . . . . . . . . . . . . . . . 206

Vocabulary Summary . . . . . . . . . . . . . . . . . . . . . . . . 211

**Program Analysis** . . . . . . . . . . . . . . . . . . . . . . . . . . 212

Program Correctness . . . . . . . . . . . . . . . . . . . . . . . . 212

Assertions . . . . . . . . . . . . . . . . . . . . . . . . . . . . . . . 212

Efficiency . . . . . . . . . . . . . . . . . . . . . . . . . . . . . . . . 213

**Multiple-Choice Questions on Program Design and Analysis** . . . . . . . . 214

**Answer Key** . . . . . . . . . . . . . . . . . . . . . . . . . . . . . . 223

**Answers Explained** . . . . . . . . . . . . . . . . . . . . . . . . . 223

**7  Arrays and Array Lists** . . . . . . . . . . . . . . . . . . . . . 226

**One-Dimensional Arrays** . . . . . . . . . . . . . . . . . . . . . . 226

Initialization . . . . . . . . . . . . . . . . . . . . . . . . . . . . . . 226

Length of Array . . . . . . . . . . . . . . . . . . . . . . . . . . . . 227

Traversing a One-Dimensional Array . . . . . . . . . . . . . . 228

Arrays as Parameters . . . . . . . . . . . . . . . . . . . . . . . . 228

Array Variables in a Class . . . . . . . . . . . . . . . . . . . . . 231

Array of Class Objects . . . . . . . . . . . . . . . . . . . . . . . 232

Analyzing Array Algorithms . . . . . . . . . . . . . . . . . . . . 233

**Array Lists** . . . . . . . . . . . . . . . . . . . . . . . . . . . . . . . 234

The ArrayList Class . . . . . . . . . . . . . . . . . . . . . . . . . 235

The Methods of ArrayList<E> . . . . . . . . . . . . . . . . . . 235

Autoboxing and Unboxing . . . . . . . . . . . . . . . . . . . . . 236

Using ArrayList<E> . . . . . . . . . . . . . . . . . . . . . . . . . 236

**Two-Dimensional Arrays** . . . . . . . . . . . . . . . . . . . . . . 242

Declarations . . . . . . . . . . . . . . . . . . . . . . . . . . . . . . 242

Matrix as Array of Row Arrays . . . . . . . . . . . . . . . . . . 243

Processing a Two-Dimensional Array . . . . . . . . . . . . . . 243

Two-Dimensional Array as Parameter . . . . . . . . . . . . . . 246

**Multiple-Choice Questions on Arrays and Array Lists** . . . . . . . . . . 249

**Answer Key** . . . . . . . . . . . . . . . . . . . . . . . . . . . . . . 280

**Answers Explained** . . . . . . . . . . . . . . . . . . . . . . . . . 280

**8  Recursion** . . . . . . . . . . . . . . . . . . . . . . . . . . . . . 286

**Recursive Methods** . . . . . . . . . . . . . . . . . . . . . . . . . 286

**General Form of Simple Recursive Methods** . . . . . . . . . . . . . 287

**Writing Recursive Methods** . . . . . . . . . . . . . . . . . . . . . 289

**Analysis of Recursive Methods** . . . . . . . . . . . . . . . . . . . 290

**Sorting Algorithms That Use Recursion** . . . . . . . . . . . . . . . 291

**Recursive Helper Methods** . . . . . . . . . . . . . . . . . . . . . 291

**Recursion in Two-Dimensional Grids** . . . . . . . . . . . . . . . . 294

Sample Free-Response Question 1 . . . . . . . . . . . . . . . 296

Sample Free-Response Question 2 . . . . . . . . . . . . . . . 299

**Multiple-Choice Questions on Recursion** . . . . . . . . . . . . . . 303

**Answer Key** . . . . . . . . . . . . . . . . . . . . . . . . . . . . . . 314

**Answers Explained** . . . . . . . . . . . . . . . . . . . . . . . . . 314

**9 Sorting and Searching** . . . . . . . . . . . . . . . . . . . . . . . . . . . . 319

   **Sorts: Selection and Insertion Sorts** . . . . . . . . . . . . . . . . . 319

      Selection Sort . . . . . . . . . . . . . . . . . . . . . . . . . . . . . . . . 319

      Insertion Sort . . . . . . . . . . . . . . . . . . . . . . . . . . . . . . . . 320

   **Recursive Sorts: Merge Sort and Quicksort** . . . . . . . . . . . 320

      Merge Sort . . . . . . . . . . . . . . . . . . . . . . . . . . . . . . . . . . 320

      Quicksort . . . . . . . . . . . . . . . . . . . . . . . . . . . . . . . . . . . 322

   **Sorting Algorithms in Java** . . . . . . . . . . . . . . . . . . . . . . . . 323

   **Sequential Search** . . . . . . . . . . . . . . . . . . . . . . . . . . . . . . 324

   **Binary Search** . . . . . . . . . . . . . . . . . . . . . . . . . . . . . . . . . 324

      Analysis of Binary Search . . . . . . . . . . . . . . . . . . . . . . . 326

   **Multiple-Choice Questions on Sorting and Searching** . . . 328

   **Answer Key** . . . . . . . . . . . . . . . . . . . . . . . . . . . . . . . . . . . 340

   **Answers Explained** . . . . . . . . . . . . . . . . . . . . . . . . . . . . . . 340

**10 The AP Computer Science A Labs** . . . . . . . . . . . . . . . . . . 345

   **The Magpie Lab** . . . . . . . . . . . . . . . . . . . . . . . . . . . . . . . . 345

      Special Emphasis . . . . . . . . . . . . . . . . . . . . . . . . . . . . . . 345

   **The Elevens Lab** . . . . . . . . . . . . . . . . . . . . . . . . . . . . . . . . 347

      Special Emphasis . . . . . . . . . . . . . . . . . . . . . . . . . . . . . . 348

   **The Picture Lab** . . . . . . . . . . . . . . . . . . . . . . . . . . . . . . . . 350

      Special Emphasis . . . . . . . . . . . . . . . . . . . . . . . . . . . . . . 350

   **Multiple-Choice Questions on the Lab Concepts** . . . . . . . 353

   **Answer Key** . . . . . . . . . . . . . . . . . . . . . . . . . . . . . . . . . . . 366

   **Answers Explained** . . . . . . . . . . . . . . . . . . . . . . . . . . . . . . 366

## PRACTICE TESTS

**Practice Test 1** . . . . . . . . . . . . . . . . . . . . . . . . . . . . . . . . . . . 371

   **Computer Science A Section I** . . . . . . . . . . . . . . . . . . . . . 373

   **Computer Science A Section II** . . . . . . . . . . . . . . . . . . . . . 400

   **Answer Key (Section I)** . . . . . . . . . . . . . . . . . . . . . . . . . . . 409

   **Answers Explained** . . . . . . . . . . . . . . . . . . . . . . . . . . . . . . 409

**Practice Test 2** . . . . . . . . . . . . . . . . . . . . . . . . . . . . . . . . . . . 421

   **Computer Science A Section I** . . . . . . . . . . . . . . . . . . . . . 423

   **Computer Science A Section II** . . . . . . . . . . . . . . . . . . . . . 449

   **Answer Key (Section I)** . . . . . . . . . . . . . . . . . . . . . . . . . . . 459

   **Answers Explained** . . . . . . . . . . . . . . . . . . . . . . . . . . . . . . 459

**Appendix: Glossary of Useful Computer Terms** . . . . . . . . . 470

**Index** . . . . . . . . . . . . . . . . . . . . . . . . . . . . . . . . . . . . . . . . . . 473

 **Barron's Essential**

As you review the content in this book to work toward earning that **5** on your AP Computer Science A exam, here are five things that you **MUST** know above everything else:

**1**

**The Basics.** Every AP exam question uses at least one of these:
- Types and identifiers (p. 68)
- Operators (p. 71)
- Control structures (p. 77)

**2**

**Objects, Classes, and Inheritance.** You may have to write your own class. You'll definitely need to interpret at least one class that's given.
- Methods (p. 102)
- Superclasses (p. 139)
- Subclasses (p. 139)

**3**

**Lists and Arrays.** Learn to manipulate a list. Search, delete an item, insert an item. It seems as if every second question on the AP exam uses a list!
- One-dimensional arrays (p. 226)
- ArrayLists (p. 234)

**4**

**Two-Dimensional Arrays.** Learn to manipulate a matrix. This topic has become more prominent on the AP exam in recent years.
- Two-dimensional arrays (p. 242)
- Row-column traversal (p. 243)
- For-each loop traversal (p. 243)
- Row-by-row array processing (p. 244)

**5**

**Sorting and Searching.** Know these algorithms!
- Selection sort (p. 319)
- Insertion sort (p. 320)
- Merge sort (p. 320)
- Sequential search (p. 324)
- Binary search (p. 324)

# Preface

This book is aimed at students reviewing for the AP Computer Science A exam. It would normally be used at the completion of an AP course. However, it contains a complete summary of all topics for the exam, and it can be used for self-study if accompanied by a suitable textbook.

The book provides a review of object-oriented programming, algorithm analysis, and data structures. It can therefore be used as a supplement to a first-semester college course where Java is the programming language, and as a resource for teachers of high school and introductory college courses.

New to this ninth edition are

- Updated practice tests that conform to the requirements of the Fall 2019 Course and Exam Description for AP Computer Science A.

- Many new multiple-choice and free-response questions.

- Many streamlined free-response questions that closely follow the style and numbering conventions of recent and future AP exams.

- An updated section on analyzing the binary search algorithm.

- Updated scoring rubrics for the free-response questions.

This edition covers all features of Java that will be tested on the AP exam, including topics that are emphasized on the exam: arrays, two-dimensional arrays, strings, list-processing, and inheritance in object-oriented programming. There are multiple questions on enhanced `for` loops (using a for-each loop traversal), and treating a matrix as an array of arrays. Additionally, there's a chapter that covers the AP Computer Science A labs that were developed to satisfy the lab requirement for AP Computer Science A. There are no questions on the AP exam that test the specific content of the labs, but there are questions that test the concepts developed in the labs. Chapter 10 is exclusively devoted to these concepts.

Changes that go into effect for the May 2020 exam are marked with a "lightning" symbol in the margin, as shown here.

Note that the ninth edition has been updated to reflect the facts that abstract classes, interfaces, `List<E>`, and number systems other than base 10 are no longer part of the AP Java subset, but autoboxing and `ConcurrentModificationException` are new to the subset.

The style of all questions and examples in the book continues to reflect the style of recent exams.

There are six complete practice tests. The practice tests follow the format of the AP exam, with multiple-choice and free-response sections. One practice test is presented after the introduction to the book for possible use as a diagnostic test. A diagnostic chart accompanies this test. There are two practice tests at the end of the book. Detailed solutions with explanations and scoring rubrics are provided for all tests. There is no overlap of questions between the practice tests.

Note that the scoring worksheets that accompany each test have been updated to reflect the College Board policy of not penalizing students for wrong answers on the multiple-choice section.

## ACKNOWLEDGMENTS

Many people helped in the creation of this book.

I would like to thank my editor, Annie Bernberg, for her kindness, expertise, and assurance in taking the reins of the project. Thanks also to Christine Ricketts, production editor, and Mary Behr, copyeditor, as well as Jeff Batzli, Alison Maresca, Jalisa Valladares, Mandy Luk, and all the other members of the Kaplan staff who worked on the production of the book and online tests.

I am most grateful to my former editor, Linda Turner, of Barron's, for her friendly guidance and moral support over many years.

A very special thank you to Judy Hromcik and Richard Kick who went above and beyond in checking content and making valuable suggestions.

Thank you to all of the computer science teachers throughout the country who took time to write to me with suggestions.

My husband, Saul, continues to be my partner in this project—typesetting the manuscript, producing the figures, and giving advice and moral support. This book is dedicated to him.

*Roselyn Teukolsky*
*Ithaca, NY*
*September 2019*

# Introduction

*Computer Science: The boring art*
*of coping with a large number of trivialities.*
—*Stan Kelly-Bootle*, The Devil's DP Dictionary *(1981)*

## GENERAL INFORMATION ABOUT THE EXAM

The AP Computer Science A exam is a three-hour written exam. No books, calculators, or computers are allowed! The exam consists of two parts that have equal weight:

- Section I: 40 multiple-choice questions in 1 hour and 30 minutes.
- Section II: 4 free-response questions in 1 hour and 30 minutes.

Section I is scored by machine—you will bubble your answers with a pencil on a mark-sense sheet. Each question correctly answered is worth 1 point. There are no deductions for incorrect answers, and a question left blank is ignored.

> There is no penalty for wrong answers on the multiple-choice section.

Section II is scored by human readers—you will write your answers in a booklet provided. Free-response questions typically involve writing methods in Java to solve a given problem. Sometimes there are questions analyzing algorithms or designing and modifying data structures. You may be asked to write or design an entire class. To ensure consistency in the grading, each grader follows the same rubric, and each of your four answers may be examined by more than one reader. Each question is worth 9 points, with partial credit awarded where applicable. Your name and school are hidden from the readers.

Your raw score for both sections is converted to an integer score from 1 to 5, where 1 represents "Not at all qualified" and 5 represents "Extremely well qualified." Be aware that the awarding of AP credit varies enormously from college to college. The exam covers roughly a one-semester introductory college course.

The language of the AP exam is Java. Only a subset of the Java language will be tested on the exam. In writing your solutions to the free-response questions, however, you may use any Java features, including those that are not in the AP subset. For a complete description of this subset, see the College Board website at *https://apstudent.collegeboard.org/courses/ap-computer-science-a.* **Every language topic in this review book is part of the AP Java subset unless explicitly stated otherwise. Note that the entire subset is covered in the book.**

For both the multiple-choice and free-response sections of the exam, there will be a quick reference in the appendix. You can look at this ahead of time by selecting About the Exam and then clicking on quick reference on the College Board website.

## HOW TO USE THIS BOOK

Chapter 1 provides detailed information about the content and format of the AP exam, as well as strategies and tips for tackling the multiple-choice and free-response questions on the exam.

Starting with Chapter 2, each chapter in the book contains a comprehensive review of a topic, multiple-choice questions that focus on the topic, and detailed explanations of answers. These focus questions help you to review parts of the Java subset that you should know. A few questions are not typical AP exam questions—for example, questions that test low-level details of syntax. Most of the focus questions, however, and all the multiple-choice questions in the practice tests are representative of actual exam questions.

You should also note that several groups of focus questions are preceded by a single piece of code to which the questions refer. Be aware that the AP exam will usually restrict the number of questions per code example to two.

In both the text and questions/explanations, a special code font is used for parts of the text that are Java code.

```
//This is an example of code font
```

A different font is used for pseudo-code.

*< Here is pseudo-code font. >*

A small number of optional topics that are not part of the AP Java subset are included in the book because they are useful in the free-response questions. Sections in the text and multiple-choice questions that are optional topics are clearly marked as such. Some sections are marked by a lightning bolt, as shown here in the margin. This means wake up! Here is something new about the AP Java subset.

Before the AP exam, you should study the strategies in Chapter 1 and attempt as many of the practice tests as you can. Three complete practice tests are provided in the book and three more are available online. One practice test is at the start of the book and may be used as a diagnostic test. It is accompanied by a diagnostic chart that refers you to related topics in the review book. The other two practice tests are at the end of the book. You can find the link to the three online practice tests on the card at the front of this book.

Each of the six practice tests has complete solutions and scoring rubrics for the free-response questions, and an answer key and detailed explanations for the multiple-choice questions. There is no overlap in the questions.

An answer sheet is provided for the Section I questions of each test. When you have completed an entire test, and have checked your answers, you may wish to calculate your approximate AP score. Use the scoring worksheet provided on the back of the answer sheet.

An appendix at the end of the book provides a glossary of computer terms that occasionally crop up on the exam.

A final hint about the book: Try the questions before you peek at the answers. Good luck!

# Diagnostic Test

The test that follows has the same format as that used on the actual AP exam. There are two ways you may use it:

1. As a diagnostic test before you start reviewing. A diagnostic chart that relates each question to sections that you should review follows the answer key.
2. As a practice test when you have completed your review.

Complete explanations are provided for each solution for both the multiple-choice and free-response questions.

# ANSWER SHEET
## Diagnostic Test

**Section I**

1. Ⓐ Ⓑ Ⓒ Ⓓ Ⓔ
2. Ⓐ Ⓑ Ⓒ Ⓓ Ⓔ
3. Ⓐ Ⓑ Ⓒ Ⓓ Ⓔ
4. Ⓐ Ⓑ Ⓒ Ⓓ Ⓔ
5. Ⓐ Ⓑ Ⓒ Ⓓ Ⓔ
6. Ⓐ Ⓑ Ⓒ Ⓓ Ⓔ
7. Ⓐ Ⓑ Ⓒ Ⓓ Ⓔ
8. Ⓐ Ⓑ Ⓒ Ⓓ Ⓔ
9. Ⓐ Ⓑ Ⓒ Ⓓ Ⓔ
10. Ⓐ Ⓑ Ⓒ Ⓓ Ⓔ
11. Ⓐ Ⓑ Ⓒ Ⓓ Ⓔ
12. Ⓐ Ⓑ Ⓒ Ⓓ Ⓔ
13. Ⓐ Ⓑ Ⓒ Ⓓ Ⓔ
14. Ⓐ Ⓑ Ⓒ Ⓓ Ⓔ

15. Ⓐ Ⓑ Ⓒ Ⓓ Ⓔ
16. Ⓐ Ⓑ Ⓒ Ⓓ Ⓔ
17. Ⓐ Ⓑ Ⓒ Ⓓ Ⓔ
18. Ⓐ Ⓑ Ⓒ Ⓓ Ⓔ
19. Ⓐ Ⓑ Ⓒ Ⓓ Ⓔ
20. Ⓐ Ⓑ Ⓒ Ⓓ Ⓔ
21. Ⓐ Ⓑ Ⓒ Ⓓ Ⓔ
22. Ⓐ Ⓑ Ⓒ Ⓓ Ⓔ
23. Ⓐ Ⓑ Ⓒ Ⓓ Ⓔ
24. Ⓐ Ⓑ Ⓒ Ⓓ Ⓔ
25. Ⓐ Ⓑ Ⓒ Ⓓ Ⓔ
26. Ⓐ Ⓑ Ⓒ Ⓓ Ⓔ
27. Ⓐ Ⓑ Ⓒ Ⓓ Ⓔ
28. Ⓐ Ⓑ Ⓒ Ⓓ Ⓔ

29. Ⓐ Ⓑ Ⓒ Ⓓ Ⓔ
30. Ⓐ Ⓑ Ⓒ Ⓓ Ⓔ
31. Ⓐ Ⓑ Ⓒ Ⓓ Ⓔ
32. Ⓐ Ⓑ Ⓒ Ⓓ Ⓔ
33. Ⓐ Ⓑ Ⓒ Ⓓ Ⓔ
34. Ⓐ Ⓑ Ⓒ Ⓓ Ⓔ
35. Ⓐ Ⓑ Ⓒ Ⓓ Ⓔ
36. Ⓐ Ⓑ Ⓒ Ⓓ Ⓔ
37. Ⓐ Ⓑ Ⓒ Ⓓ Ⓔ
38. Ⓐ Ⓑ Ⓒ Ⓓ Ⓔ
39. Ⓐ Ⓑ Ⓒ Ⓓ Ⓔ
40. Ⓐ Ⓑ Ⓒ Ⓓ Ⓔ

# How to Calculate Your (Approximate) AP Computer Science A Score

**Multiple Choice**

Number correct (out of 40)  =  _____     ⟸  Multiple-Choice Score

**Free Response**

Question 1  _____
          (out of 9)

Question 2  _____
          (out of 9)

Question 3  _____
          (out of 9)

Question 4  _____
          (out of 9)

Total  _____  ×  1.11  =  _____     ⟸  Free-Response Score
                                              (Do not round.)

**Final Score**

_____  +  _____  =  _____
Multiple-           Free-             Final Score
Choice            Response     (Round to nearest
Score             Score         whole number.)

## Chart to Convert to AP Grade
## Computer Science A

| Final Score Range | AP Grade[a] |
|---|---|
| 62–80 | 5 |
| 47–61 | 4 |
| 37–46 | 3 |
| 29–36 | 2 |
| 0–28 | 1 |

[a]The score range corresponding to each grade varies from exam to exam and is approximate.

# Diagnostic Test

## COMPUTER SCIENCE A
## SECTION I

Time—1 hour and 30 minutes
Number of questions—40
Percent of total grade—50

**DIRECTIONS:** Determine the answer to each of the following questions or incomplete statements, using the available space for any necessary scratchwork. Then decide which is the best of the choices given and fill in the corresponding oval on the answer sheet. Do not spend too much time on any one problem.

**NOTES:**
- Assume that the classes in the Quick Reference have been imported where needed.
- Assume that variables and methods are declared within the context of an enclosing class.
- Assume that method calls that have no object or class name prefixed, and that are not shown within a complete class definition, appear within the context of an enclosing class.
- Assume that parameters in method calls are not `null` unless otherwise stated.

1. Consider this inheritance hierarchy, in which `Novel` and `Textbook` are subclasses of `Book`.

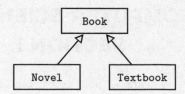

Which of the following is a false statement about the classes shown?

(A) The `Textbook` class can have private instance variables that are in neither `Book` nor `Novel`.

(B) Each of the classes—`Book`, `Novel`, and `Textbook`—can have a method `computeShelfLife`, whose code in `Book` and `Novel` is identical, but different from the code in `Textbook`.

(C) If the `Book` class has private instance variables `title` and `author`, then `Novel` and `Textbook` cannot directly access them.

(D) Both `Novel` and `Textbook` inherit the constructors in `Book`.

(E) If the `Book` class has a private method called `readFile`, this method may not be accessed in either the `Novel` or `Textbook` classes.

**GO ON TO THE NEXT PAGE.**

2. A programmer is designing a program to catalog all books in a library. She plans to have a `Book` class that stores features of each book: `author`, `title`, `isOnShelf`, and so on, with operations like `getAuthor`, `getTitle`, `getShelfInfo`, and `setShelfInfo`. Another class, `LibraryList`, will store an array of `Book` objects. The `LibraryList` class will include operations such as `listAllBooks`, `addBook`, `removeBook`, and `searchForBook`. What is the relationship between the `LibraryList` and `Book` classes?

   (A) Composition
   (B) Inheritance
   (C) Independent classes
   (D) Polymorphism
   (E) `ArrayList`

3. Consider the following code segment, which is intended to add zero to the end of `list` every time a certain condition is met. You may assume that `list` is an `ArrayList<Integer>` that contains at least one element.

```
for (Integer num : list)
{
    if (< condition >)
        list.add(0);
}
```

   Which of the following errors is most likely to occur?

   (A) `ArrayIndexOutOfBoundsException`
   (B) `IndexOutOfBoundsException`
   (C) `NullPointerException`
   (D) `ConcurrentModificationException`
   (E) `IllegalArgumentException`

**GO ON TO THE NEXT PAGE.**

Questions 4 and 5 refer to the Card and Deck classes shown below.

```java
public class Card
{
    private String suit;
    private int value;       //0 to 12

    public Card(String cardSuit, int cardValue)
    { /* implementation */ }

    public String getSuit()
    { return suit; }

    public int getValue()
    { return value; }

    public String toString()
    {
        String faceValue = "";
        if (value == 11)
            faceValue = "J";
        else if (value == 12)
            faceValue = "Q";
        else if (value == 0)
            faceValue = "K";
        else if (value == 1)
            faceValue = "A";
        if (value >= 2 && value <= 10)
            return value + " of " + suit;
        else
            return faceValue + " of " + suit;
    }
}

public class Deck
{
    private Card[] deck;
    public final static int NUMCARDS = 52;

    public Deck()
    { ...

    /** Simulate shuffling the deck. */
    public void shuffle()
    { ...

    //Other methods are not shown.
}
```

GO ON TO THE NEXT PAGE.

4. Which of the following represents correct /* *implementation* */ code for the constructor in the Card class?

(A) ```
suit = cardSuit;
value = cardValue;
```

(B) ```
cardSuit = suit;
cardValue = value;
```

(C) ```
Card = new Card(suit, value);
```

(D) ```
Card = new Card(cardSuit, cardValue);
```

(E) ```
suit = getSuit();
value = getValue();
```

5. Consider the implementation of a writeDeck method that is added to the Deck class.

```
/** Write the cards in deck, one per line. */
public void writeDeck()
{
    /* implementation code */
}
```

Which of the following is correct /* *implementation code* */?

I ```
System.out.println(deck);
```

II ```
for (Card card : deck)
      System.out.println(card);
```

III ```
for (Card card : deck)
      System.out.println((String) card);
```

(A) I only
(B) II only
(C) III only
(D) I and III only
(E) II and III only

**GO ON TO THE NEXT PAGE.**

6. Refer to the following method that finds the smallest value in an array.

```
/** Precondition: arr is an array of nonzero length
 *                and is initialized with int values.
 * @param arr the array to be processed
 * @return the smallest value in arr
 */
public static int findMin(int[] arr)
{
    int min = /* some value */;
    int index = 0;
    while (index < arr.length)
    {
        if (arr[index] < min)
            min = arr[index];
        index++;
    }
    return min;
}
```

Which replacement(s) for /* *some value* */ will always result in correct execution of the findMin method?

  I  `Integer.MIN_VALUE`

 II  `Integer.MAX_VALUE`

III  `arr[0]`

(A) I only
(B) II only
(C) III only
(D) I and III only
(E) II and III only

**GO ON TO THE NEXT PAGE.**

7. Consider the following loop, where n is some positive integer.

```
for (int i = 0; i < n; i += 2)
{
    if (/* test */)
        /* perform some action */
}
```

In terms of n, which Java expression represents the maximum number of times that /* *perform some action* */ could be executed?

(A) n / 2

(B) (n + 1) / 2

(C) n

(D) n - 1

(E) (n - 1) / 2

8. A method is to be written to search an array for a value that is larger than a given item and return its index. The problem specification does not indicate what should be returned if there are several such values in the array. Which of the following actions would be best?

(A) The method should be written on the assumption that there is only one value in the array that is larger than the given item.

(B) The method should be written so as to return the index of every occurrence of a larger value.

(C) The specification should be modified to indicate what should be done if there is more than one index of larger values.

(D) The method should be written to output a message if more than one larger value is found.

(E) The method should be written to delete all subsequent larger items after a suitable index is returned.

GO ON TO THE NEXT PAGE.

9.  When will method `whatIsIt` cause a stack overflow (i.e., cause computer memory to be exhausted)?

    ```
    public static int whatIsIt(int x, int y)
    {
        if (x > y)
            return x * y;
        else
            return whatIsIt(x - 1, y);
    }
    ```

    (A)  Only when x < y
    (B)  Only when x ≤ y
    (C)  Only when x > y
    (D)  For all values of x and y
    (E)  The method will never cause a stack overflow.

10.  The boolean expression `a[i] == max || !(max != a[i])` can be simplified to
    (A)  `a[i] == max`
    (B)  `a[i] != max`
    (C)  `a[i] < max || a[i] > max`
    (D)  `true`
    (E)  `false`

11.  Consider the following code segment.

    ```
    int[][] mat = {{3,4,5},
                   {6,7,8}};

    int sum = 0;
    for (int[] arr: mat)
    {
        for (int n = 0; n < mat.length; n++)
            sum += arr[n];
    }
    ```

    What is the value of `sum` as a result of executing the code segment?
    (A)  9
    (B)  11
    (C)  13
    (D)  20
    (E)  33

**GO ON TO THE NEXT PAGE.**

12. Consider a `Clown` class that has a default constructor. Suppose a list `ArrayList<Clown> list` is initialized. Which of the following will not cause an `IndexOutOfBoundsException` to be thrown?

(A) `for (int i = 0; i <= list.size(); i++)`
      `list.set(i, new Clown());`

(B) `list.add(list.size(), new Clown());`

(C) `Clown c = list.get(list.size());`

(D) `Clown c = list.remove(list.size());`

(E) `list.add(-1, new Clown());`

GO ON TO THE NEXT PAGE.

Refer to the following class for Questions 13 and 14.

```java
public class Tester
{
    private int[] testArray = {3, 4, 5};

    /** @param n an int to be incremented by 1 */
    public void increment (int n)
    { n++; }

    public void firstTestMethod()
    {
        for (int i = 0; i < testArray.length; i++)
        {
            increment(testArray[i]);
            System.out.print(testArray[i] + " ");
        }
    }

    public void secondTestMethod()
    {
        for (int element : testArray)
        {
            increment(element);
            System.out.print(element + " ");
        }
    }
}
```

13. What output will be produced by invoking `firstTestMethod` for a `Tester` object?
    (A) 3 4 5
    (B) 4 5 6
    (C) 5 6 7
    (D) 0 0 0
    (E) No output will be produced. An `ArrayIndexOutOfBoundsException` will be thrown.

14. What output will be produced by invoking `secondTestMethod` for a `Tester` object, assuming that `testArray` contains 3,4,5?
    (A) 3 4 5
    (B) 4 5 6
    (C) 5 6 7
    (D) 0 0 0
    (E) No output will be produced. An `ArrayIndexOutOfBoundsException` will be thrown.

**GO ON TO THE NEXT PAGE.**

Questions 15–17 refer to the following `Point`, `Quadrilateral`, and `Rectangle` classes.

```
public class Point
{
    private int xCoord;
    private int yCoord;

    //constructor
    public Point(int x, int y)
    {
        ...
    }

    //accessors

    public int get_x()
    {
        ...
    }

    public int get_y()
    {
        ...
    }

    //Other methods are not shown.

}

public class Quadrilateral
{
    private String labels;     //e.g., "ABCD"

    //constructor
    public Quadrilateral(String quadLabels)
    { labels = quadLabels; }

    public String getLabels()
    { return labels; }

    public int perimeter()
    { return 0; }

    public int area()
    { return 0; }
}
```

**GO ON TO THE NEXT PAGE.**

```
public class Rectangle extends Quadrilateral
{
    private Point topLeft;    //coords of top left corner
    private Point botRight;   //coords of bottom right corner

    //constructor
    public Rectangle(String theLabels, Point theTopLeft, Point theBotRight)
    { /* implementation code */ }

    public int perimeter()
    { /* implementation not shown */ }

    public int area()
    { /* implementation not shown */ }

    //Other methods are not shown.
}
```

15. Which of the following statements about the `Point`, `Quadrilateral`, and `Rectangle` classes are false?

    I  `Point` is a subclass of `Quadrilateral`.

    II  `Point` is a subclass of `Rectangle`.

    III  The `Rectangle` class inherits the constructor of `Quadrilateral`.

(A) I only
(B) II only
(C) III only
(D) I and II only
(E) I, II, and III

16. Which represents correct /* *implementation code* */ for the `Rectangle` constructor?

    I  `super(theLabels);`

    II  `super(theLabels, theTopLeft, theBotRight);`

    III  `super(theLabels);`
         `topLeft = theTopLeft;`
         `botRight = theBotRight;`

(A) I only
(B) II only
(C) III only
(D) I and II only
(E) II and III only

**GO ON TO THE NEXT PAGE.**

17. Refer to the `Parallelogram` and `Square` classes below.

```
public class Parallelogram extends Quadrilateral
{
    //Private instance variables and constructor are not shown.
        ...

    public int perimeter()
    { /* implementation not shown */ }

    public int area()
    { /* implementation not shown */ }
}

public class Square extends Rectangle
{
    //Private instance variables and constructor are not shown.
        ...

    public int perimeter()
    { /* implementation not shown */ }

    public int area()
    { /* implementation not shown */ }
}
```

Consider an `ArrayList<Quadrilateral>` quadList whose elements are of type Rectangle, Parallelogram, or Square.

Refer to the following method, `writeAreas`:

```
/** Precondition:  quadList contains Rectangle, Parallelogram, or
 *                 Square objects in an unspecified order.
 */
public static void writeAreas(ArrayList<Quadrilateral> quadList)
{
    for (Quadrilateral quad : quadList)
        System.out.println("Area of " + quad.getLabels()
            + " is " + quad.area());
}
```

What is the effect of executing this method?
(A) The area of each `Quadrilateral` in `quadList` will be printed.
(B) A value of 0 will be printed for each element of `quadList`.
(C) A compile-time error will occur, stating that there is no `getLabels` method in classes Rectangle, Parallelogram, or Square.
(D) A `NullPointerException` will be thrown.
(E) A `ConcurrentModificationException` will occur.

**GO ON TO THE NEXT PAGE.**

18. Refer to the doSomething method below.

```
// postcondition
public static void doSomething(ArrayList<SomeType> list, int i, int j)
{
    SomeType temp = list.get(i);
    list.set(i, list.get(j));
    list.set(j, temp);
}
```

Which best describes the *postcondition* for doSomething?

(A) Removes from list the objects indexed at i and j.

(B) Replaces in list the object indexed at i with the object indexed at j.

(C) Replaces in list the object indexed at j with the object indexed at i.

(D) Replaces in list the objects indexed at i and j with temp.

(E) Interchanges in list the objects indexed at i and j.

GO ON TO THE NEXT PAGE.

19. Consider the `NegativeReal` class below, which defines a negative real number object.

```
public class NegativeReal
{
    private Double negReal;

    /** Constructor. Creates a NegativeReal object whose value is num.
     *  @param num  a negative real number
     */
    public NegativeReal(double num)
    { /* implementation not shown */ }

    /** @return the value of this NegativeReal */
    public double getValue()
    { /* implementation not shown */ }

    /** @return this NegativeReal rounded to the nearest integer */
    public int getRounded()
    { /* implementation */ }
}
```

Here are some rounding examples:

| Negative real number | Rounded to nearest integer |
| :---: | :---: |
| −3.5 | −4 |
| −8.97 | −9 |
| −5.0 | −5 |
| −2.487 | −2 |
| −0.2 | 0 |

Which /* *implementation* */ of getRounded produces the desired postcondition?

(A) `return (int) (getValue() - 0.5);`

(B) `return (int) (getValue() + 0.5);`

(C) `return (int) getValue();`

(D) `return (double) (getValue() - 0.5);`

(E) `return (double) getValue();`

**GO ON TO THE NEXT PAGE.**

20. Consider the following method.

```
public static void whatsIt(int n)
{
    if (n > 10)
        whatsIt(n / 10);
    System.out.print(n % 10);
}
```

What will be output as a result of the method call whatsIt(347)?

(A) 74
(B) 47
(C) 734
(D) 743
(E) 347

21. A large list of numbers is to be sorted into ascending order. Assuming that a "data movement" is a swap or reassignment of an element, which of the following is a true statement?

(A) If the array is initially sorted in descending order, then insertion sort will be more efficient than selection sort.
(B) The number of comparisons for selection sort is independent of the initial arrangement of elements.
(C) The number of comparisons for insertion sort is independent of the initial arrangement of elements.
(D) The number of data movements in selection sort depends on the initial arrangement of elements.
(E) The number of data movements in insertion sort is independent of the initial arrangement of elements.

**GO ON TO THE NEXT PAGE.**

22. Refer to the definitions of ClassOne and ClassTwo below.

```java
public class ClassOne
{
    public void methodOne()
    {
        ...
    }

    //Other methods are not shown.
}

public class ClassTwo extends ClassOne
{
    public void methodTwo()
    {
        ...
    }

    //Other methods are not shown.
}
```

Consider the following declarations in a client class. You may assume that ClassOne and ClassTwo have default constructors.

```java
ClassOne c1 = new ClassOne();
ClassOne c2 = new ClassTwo();
```

Which of the following method calls will cause an error?

  I  c1.methodTwo();

 II  c2.methodTwo();

III  c2.methodOne();

(A) None
(B) I only
(C) II only
(D) III only
(E) I and II only

**GO ON TO THE NEXT PAGE.**

23. Consider the code segment

```
if (n == 1)
    k++;
else if (n == 4)
    k += 4;
```

Suppose that the given segment is rewritten in the form

```
if (/* condition */)
    /* assignment statement */;
```

Given that n and k are integers and that the rewritten code performs the same task as the original code, which of the following could be used as

(1) */* condition */*   and   (2) */* assignment statement */*?

(A)  (1)   n == 1 && n == 4        (2)   k += n

(B)  (1)   n == 1 && n == 4        (2)   k += 4

(C)  (1)   n == 1 || n == 4        (2)   k += 4

(D)  (1)   n == 1 || n == 4        (2)   k += n

(E)  (1)   n == 1 || n == 4        (2)   k = n - k

24. Which of the following will execute *without* throwing an exception?

```
I  String s = null;
   String t = "";
   if (s.equals(t))
       System.out.println("empty strings?");
```

```
II  String s = "holy";
    String t = "moly";
    if (s.equals(t))
        System.out.println("holy moly!");
```

```
III  String s = "holy";
     String t = s.substring(4);
     System.out.println(s + t);
```

(A) I only
(B) II only
(C) III only
(D) I and II only
(E) II and III only

**GO ON TO THE NEXT PAGE.**

25. Three numbers *a*, *b*, and *c* are said to be a *Pythagorean Triple* if and only if the sum of the squares of two of the numbers equals the square of the third. A programmer writes a method `isPythTriple` to test if its three parameters form a Pythagorean Triple:

```
//Returns true if a * a + b * b == c * c; otherwise returns false.
public static boolean isPythTriple(double a, double b, double c)
{
    double d = Math.sqrt(a * a + b * b);
    return d == c;
}
```

When the method was tested with known Pythagorean Triples, `isPythTriple` sometimes erroneously returned `false`. What was the most likely cause of the error?
(A) Round-off error was caused by calculations with floating-point numbers.
(B) Type `boolean` was not recognized by an obsolete version of Java.
(C) An overflow error was caused by entering numbers that were too large.
(D) `c` and `d` should have been cast to integers before testing for equality.
(E) Bad test data were selected.

26. Refer to the following class containing the `mystery` method.

```
public class SomeClass
{
    private int[] arr;

    /** Constructor. Initializes arr to contain nonnegative
     *  integers k such that 0 <= k <= 9.
     */
    public SomeClass()
    { /* implementation not shown */ }

    public int mystery()
    {
        int value = arr[0];
        for (int i = 1; i < arr.length; i++)
            value = value * 10 + arr[i];
        return value;
    }
}
```

Which best describes what the `mystery` method does?
(A) It sums the elements of `arr`.
(B) It sums the products `10*arr[0] + 10*arr[1] + ··· + 10*arr[arr.length-1]`.
(C) It builds an integer of the form $d_1 d_2 d_3 \ldots d_n$, where $d_1 = $ `arr[0]`, $d_2 = $ `arr[1]`, $\ldots$, $d_n = $ `arr[arr.length-1]`.
(D) It builds an integer of the form $d_1 d_2 d_3 \ldots d_n$, where $d_1 = $ `arr[arr.length-1]`, $d_2 = $ `arr[arr.length-2]`, $\ldots$, $d_n = $ `arr[0]`.
(E) It converts the elements of `arr` to base-10.

**GO ON TO THE NEXT PAGE.**

Questions 27 and 28 refer to the search method in the Searcher class below.

```java
public class Searcher
{
    private int[] arr;

    /** Constructor. Initializes arr with integers. */
    public Searcher()
    { /* implementation not shown */ }

    /** Precondition: arr[first]...arr[last] sorted in ascending order.
     *  Postcondition: Returns index of key in arr. If key not in arr,
     *                 returns -1.
     */
    public int search(int first, int last, int key)
    {
        int mid;
        while (first <= last)
        {
            mid = (first + last) / 2;
            if (arr[mid] == key)        //found key, exit search
                return mid;
            else if (arr[mid] < key)  //key to right of arr[mid]
                first = mid + 1;
            else                        //key to left of arr[mid]
                last = mid - 1;
        }
        return -1;                      //key not in list
    }
}
```

27. Which assertion is true just before each execution of the while loop?

    (A) arr[first] < key < arr[last]
    (B) arr[first] ≤ key ≤ arr[last]
    (C) arr[first] < key < arr[last] or key is not in arr
    (D) arr[first] ≤ key ≤ arr[last] or key is not in arr
    (E) key ≤ arr[first] or key ≥ arr[last] or key is not in arr

28. Consider the array a with values

    4, 7, 19, 25, 36, 37, 50, 100, 101, 205, 220, 271, 306, 321

    where 4 is a[0] and 321 is a[13]. Suppose that the search method is called with first = 0 and last = 13 to locate the key 205. How many iterations of the while loop must be made in order to locate it?

    (A) 3
    (B) 4
    (C) 5
    (D) 10
    (E) 13

GO ON TO THE NEXT PAGE.

29. Consider the following `RandomList` class.

```java
public class RandomList
{
    private int[] ranList;

    public RandomList()
    { ranList = getList(); }

    /** @return array with random Integers from 0 to 100
     *     inclusive */
    public int[] getList()
    {
        System.out.println("How many integers? ");
        int listLength = ...;      //read user input
        int[] list = new int[listLength];
        for (int i = 0; i < listLength; i++)
        {
            /* code to add integer to list */
        }
        return list;
    }

    /** Print all elements of this list. */
    public void printList()
    { ...
}
```

Which represents correct /* *code to add* integer *to* list */?

(A) `list[i] = (int) (Math.random() * 101);`

(B) `list.add((int) (Math.random() * 101));`

(C) `list[i] = (int) (Math.random() * 100);`

(D) `list.add(new Integer(Math.random() * 100))`

(E) `list[i] = (int) (Math.random() * 100) + 1;`

**GO ON TO THE NEXT PAGE.**

30. Refer to method `insert` described here. The `insert` method has two string parameters and one integer parameter. The method returns the string obtained by inserting the second string into the first starting at the position indicated by the integer parameter `pos`. For example, if `str1` contains `xy` and `str2` contains `cat`, then

```
insert(str1, str2, 0)   returns   catxy
insert(str1, str2, 1)   returns   xcaty
insert(str1, str2, 2)   returns   xycat
```

Method `insert` follows:

```
/** Precondition:   0 <= pos <= str1.length().
 *  Postcondition:  If str1 = a₀a₁...aₙ₋₁ and str2 = b₀b₁...bₘ₋₁,
                    returns a₀a₁...a_pos-1 b₀b₁...b_m-1 a_pos a_pos+1...aₙ₋₁
public static String insert(String str1, String str2, int pos)
{
    String first, last;
        /* more code */
    return first + str2 + last;
}
```

Which of the following is a correct replacement for /* *more code* */?

(A) ```
first = str1.substring(0, pos);
last = str1.substring(pos);
```

(B) ```
first = str1.substring(0, pos - 1);
last = str1.substring(pos);
```

(C) ```
first = str1.substring(0, pos + 1);
last = str1.substring(pos + 1);
```

(D) ```
first = str1.substring(0, pos);
last = str1.substring(pos + 1, str1.length());
```

(E) ```
first = str1.substring(0, pos);
last = str1.substring(pos, str1.length() + 1);
```

**GO ON TO THE NEXT PAGE.**
```

31. A matrix (two-dimensional array) is declared as

```
int[][] mat = new int[2][3];
```

Consider the following method.

```
public static void changeMatrix(int[][] mat)
{
    for (int r = 0; r < mat.length; r++)
        for (int c = 0; c < mat[r].length; c++)
            if (r == c)
                mat[r][c] = Math.abs(mat[r][c]);
}
```

If mat is initialized to be

```
-1 -2 -6
-2 -4  5
```

which matrix will be the result of a call to changeMatrix(mat)?

(A)  1 -2 -6
    -2  4  5

(B) -1  2 -6
     2 -4  5

(C) -1 -2 -6
    -2 -4 -5

(D)  1  2 -6
     2  4  5

(E)  1  2  6
     2  4  5

GO ON TO THE NEXT PAGE.

Use the following program description for Questions 32–34.

A programmer plans to write a program that simulates a small bingo game (no more than six players). Each player will have a bingo card with 20 numbers from 0 to 90 (no duplicates). Someone will call out numbers one at a time, and each player will cross out a number on his card as it is called. The first player with all the numbers crossed out is the winner. In the simulation, as the game is in progress, each player's card is displayed on the screen.

The programmer envisions a short driver class whose `main` method has just two statements:

```
BingoGame b = new BingoGame();
b.playBingo();
```

The `BingoGame` class will have several objects: a `Display`, a `Caller`, and a `PlayerGroup`. The `PlayerGroup` will have a list of `Players`, and each `Player` will have a `BingoCard`.

32. The relationship between the `PlayerGroup` and `Player` classes is an example of
    (A) procedural abstraction.
    (B) data encapsulation.
    (C) composition.
    (D) inheritance.
    (E) independent classes.

33. Which is a reasonable data structure for a `BingoCard` object? Recall that there are 20 integers from 0 to 90 on a `BingoCard`, with no duplicates. There should also be mechanisms for crossing off numbers that are called, and for detecting a winning card (i.e., one where all the numbers have been crossed off).

```
    I  int[] bingoCard;    //will contain 20 integers
                     //bingoCard[k] is crossed off by setting it to -1.
       int numCrossedOff;   //player wins when numCrossedOff reaches 20.

    II boolean[] bingoCard;  //will contain 91 boolean values, of which
                         //20 are true. All the other values are false.
                         //Thus, if bingoCard[k] is true, then k is
                         //on the card, 0 <= k <= 90. A number k is
                         //crossed off by changing the value of
                         //bingoCard[k] to false.
       int numCrossedOff;  //player wins when numCrossedOff reaches 20.

    III ArrayList<Integer> bingoCard;  //will contain 20 integers.
            //A number is crossed off by removing it from the ArrayList.
            //Player wins when bingoCard.size() == 0.
```

    (A) I only
    (B) II only
    (C) III only
    (D) I and II only
    (E) I, II, and III

**GO ON TO THE NEXT PAGE.**

34. The programmer decides to use an `ArrayList<Integer>` to store the numbers to be called by the `Caller`, but there is an error in the code.

```
public class Caller
{
    private ArrayList<Integer> numbers;

    public Caller()
    {
        numbers = getList();
        shuffleNumbers();
    }

    /** Returns the numbers 0...90 in order. */
    private ArrayList<Integer> getList()
    { /* implementation not shown */ }

    /** Shuffle the numbers. */
    private void shuffleNumbers()
    { /* implementation not shown */ }
}
```

When the programmer tests the constructor of the `Caller` class, she gets a `NullPointerException`. Which could be the cause of this error?

(A) The `Caller` object in the driver class was not created with `new`.

(B) The programmer forgot the `return` statement in `getList` that returns the list of `Integers`.

(C) The declaration of `numbers` is incorrect. It needed to be

```
private ArrayList<Integer> numbers = null;
```

(D) In the `getList` method, an attempt was made to add an `Integer` to an `ArrayList` that had not been created with `new`.

(E) The `shuffleNumbers` algorithm went out of range, causing a `null Integer` to be shuffled into the `ArrayList`.

**GO ON TO THE NEXT PAGE.**

35. Consider method findSomething below.

```java
/** Precondition:  a.length is equal to b.length. */
public static boolean findSomething(int[] a, int[] b)
{
    for (int aValue: a)
    {
        boolean found = false;
        for (int bValue: b)
        {
            if (bValue == aValue)
                found = true;
        }
        if (!found)
            return false;
    }
    return true;
}
```

Which best describes what method findSomething does?  Method findSomething returns true only if

(A)  arrays a and b contain identical elements in the same order.

(B)  arrays a and b contain identical elements in reverse order.

(C)  arrays a and b are permutations of each other.

(D)  array a contains at least one element that is also in b.

(E)  every element of array a is also in b.

**GO ON TO THE NEXT PAGE.**

36. Consider a program that has a two-dimensional array `mat` of `int` values. The program has several methods that change `mat` by reflecting elements of `mat` across a mirror placed symmetrically on the matrix. Here are five such methods:

```
                                              2 4 6        2 4 2
mirrorVerticalLeftToRight    transforms       1 3 5   to   1 3 1
                                              8 9 0        8 9 8


                                              2 4 6        6 4 6
mirrorVerticalRightToLeft    transforms       1 3 5   to   5 3 5
                                              8 9 0        0 9 0


                                              2 4 6        2 4 6
mirrorHorizontalTopToBottom  transforms       1 3 5   to   1 3 5
                                              8 9 0        2 4 6


                                              2 4 6        8 9 0
mirrorHorizontalBottomToTop  transforms       1 3 5   to   1 3 5
                                              8 9 0        8 9 0


                                              2 4 6        2 4 6
mirrorDiagonalRightToLeft    transforms       1 3 5   to   4 3 5
                                              8 9 0        6 5 0
```

Consider the following method that transforms the matrix in one of the ways shown above.

```java
public static void someMethod(int[][] mat)
{
    int height = mat.length;
    int numCols = mat[0].length;
    for (int col = 0; col < numCols; col++)
        for (int row = 0; row < height/2; row++)
            mat[height - row - 1][col] = mat[row][col];
}
```

Which method described above corresponds to `someMethod`?
(A) `mirrorVerticalLeftToRight`
(B) `mirrorVerticalRightToLeft`
(C) `mirrorHorizontalTopToBottom`
(D) `mirrorHorizontalBottomToTop`
(E) `mirrorDiagonalRightToLeft`

**GO ON TO THE NEXT PAGE.**

Refer to the following for Questions 37 and 38.

A word creation game uses a set of small letter tiles, all of which are initially in a tile bag. A partial implementation of a `TileBag` class is shown below.

```
public class TileBag
{
    //tiles contains all the tiles in the bag
    private List<Tile> tiles;
    //size is the number of not-yet-used tiles
    private int size;

    //Constructors and other methods are not shown.
}
```

Consider the following method in the `TileBag` class that allows a player to get a new tile from the `TileBag`.

```
public Tile getNewTile()
{
    if (size == 0)  //no tiles left
        return null;
    int index = (int) (Math.random() * size);
    size--;
    Tile temp = tiles.get(index);
    /* code to swap tile at position size with tile at position index */
    return temp;
}
```

37. Which /* *code to swap tile at position* `size` *with tile at position* `index` */ performs the swap correctly?

  (A) `tiles.set(size, temp);`
      `tiles.set(index, tiles.get(size));`

  (B) `tiles.set(index, tiles.get(size));`
      `tiles.set(size, temp);`

  (C) `tiles.swap(index, size);`

  (D) `tiles.get(size, temp);`
      `tiles.get(index, tiles.set(size));`

  (E) `tiles.get(index, tiles.set(size));`
      `tiles.get(size, temp);`

38. Which is true about the `getNewTile` algorithm?
  (A) The algorithm allows the program to keep track of both used and unused tiles.
  (B) The `tiles` list becomes one element shorter when `getNewTile` is executed.
  (C) The algorithm selects a random `Tile` from all tiles in the list.
  (D) The `tiles` list has used tiles in the beginning and unused tiles at the end.
  (E) The `tiles` list contains only tiles that have not been used.

**GO ON TO THE NEXT PAGE.**

39. Consider the following two classes.

```java
public class Bird
{
    public void act()
    {
        System.out.print("fly ");
        makeNoise();
    }

    public void makeNoise()
    {
        System.out.print("chirp ");
    }
}

public class Dove extends Bird
{
    public void act()
    {
        super.act();
        System.out.print("waddle ");
    }

    public void makeNoise()
    {
        super.makeNoise();
        System.out.print("coo ");
    }
}
```

Suppose the following declaration appears in a class other than Bird or Dove.

```java
Bird pigeon = new Dove();
```

What is printed as a result of the call pigeon.act()?

(A) fly
(B) fly chirp
(C) fly chirp waddle
(D) fly chirp waddle coo
(E) fly chirp coo waddle

**GO ON TO THE NEXT PAGE.**

40. Consider a method `partialProd` that returns an integer array `prod` such that for all `k`, `prod[k]` is equal to `arr[0]` * `arr[1]` * ⋯ `arr[k]`. For example, if `arr` contains the values {2,5,3,4,10}, the array `prod` will contain the values {2,10,30,120,1200}.

```
public static int[] partialProd(int[] arr)
{
    int[] prod = new int[arr.length];
    for (int j = 0; j < arr.length; j++)
        prod[j] = 1;
    /* missing code */
    return prod;
}
```

Consider the following two implementations of /* *missing code* */.

**Implementation 1**

```
for (int j = 1; j < arr.length; j++)
{
    prod[j] = prod[j - 1] * arr[j];
}
```

**Implementation 2**

```
for (int j = 0; j < arr.length; j++)
    for (int k = 0; k <= j; k++)
    {
        prod[j] = prod[j] * arr[k];
    }
```

Which of the following statements is true?
(A) Both implementations work as intended but Implementation 1 is faster than Implementation 2.
(B) Both implementations work as intended but Implementation 2 is faster than Implementation 1.
(C) Both implementations work as intended and are equally fast.
(D) Implementation 1 doesn't work as intended because the elements of `prod` are incorrectly assigned.
(E) Implementation 2 doesn't work as intended because the elements of `prod` are incorrectly assigned.

**END OF SECTION I**

# COMPUTER SCIENCE A
## SECTION II

Time—1 hour and 30 minutes
Number of questions—4
Percent of total grade—50

DIRECTIONS:  SHOW ALL YOUR WORK. REMEMBER THAT
PROGRAM SEGMENTS ARE TO BE WRITTEN IN JAVA.

Write your answers in <u>pencil only</u> in the booklet provided.

**NOTES:**

- Assume that the classes in the Quick Reference have been imported where needed.

- Unless otherwise noted in the question, assume that parameters in method calls are not `null` and that methods are called only when their preconditions are satisfied.

- In writing solutions for each question, you may use any of the accessible methods that are listed in classes defined in that question. Writing significant amounts of code that can be replaced by a call to one of these methods will not receive full credit.

**GO ON TO THE NEXT PAGE.**

1. In this question you will write two methods of an `Experiment` class that handles chemical solutions.

   A chemical solution is said to be acidic if it has a pH integer value from 1 to 6 inclusive. The lower the pH, the more acidic the solution.

   An experiment has three chemical solutions, numbered 0, 1, and 2, arranged in a line, and a mechanical arm that moves back and forth along the line, stopping at any of the solutions.

   A chemical solution is specified by a `Solution` class shown as follows.

```
public class Solution
{
    private int PH;
    private int positionLabel;

    /** Returns the PH of the solution, an
     * integer ranging from 1 (very acidic) to 14.
     */
    int getPH()
    { return PH; }

    /** Returns the position label of the solution, an
     * integer ranging from 0 to 2, inclusive.
     */
    int getPos()
    { return positionLabel; }

    //Constructors and other methods not shown.
}
```

   The experiment keeps track of the solutions and the mechanical arm. The figure below represents the solutions and mechanical arm in an experiment. The arm, indicated by the arrow, is currently at the solution whose position is at 2. The integers in the boxes represent the pH values of the solutions.

| position | 0 | 1 | 2 |
|----------|---|---|----|
| pH | 7 | 4 | 10 |

←

   In this experiment, the most acidic solution is at position 1, since its pH value is the lowest. The mechanical arm, which is specified by a position and a direction, is at position 2 and facing left.

**GO ON TO THE NEXT PAGE.**

The `MechanicalArm` class is shown below.

```
public class MechanicalArm
{
    private int currentPos;
    private boolean facesRight;

    /** Returns the current position of the mechanical arm.
     */
    public int getCurrentPos()
    { return currentPos; }

    /** Returns true if the mechanical arm is facing
     *  right (toward higher position numbers);
     *  false if it is facing left.
     */
    public boolean isFacingRight()
    { /* implementation not shown */ }

    /** Changes direction of the mechanical arm.
     */
    public void changeDirection()
    { /* implementation not shown */ }

    /** Moves the mechanical arm forward numLocs
     *  positions in its current direction.
     *  Precondition: numLocs >= 0.
     *  Postcondition: 0 <= currentPos <=2.
     */
    public void moveForward (int numLocs)
    { /* implementation not shown */ }

    //Constructors and other methods not shown.
}
```

An experiment is represented by the `Experiment` class shown below.

```
public class Experiment
{
    private MechanicalArm arm;
    private Solution s0, s1, s2;

    /** Resets the experiment, such that the mechanical arm has
     *  a current position of 0 and is facing right.
     */
    public void reset()
    { /* to be implemented in part(a) */ }

    /** Returns the position of the most acidic solution,
     *  or -1 if there are no acidic solutions, as
     *  described in part(b).
     */
    public int mostAcidic()
    { /* to be implemented in part(b) */ }
}
```

**GO ON TO THE NEXT PAGE.**

(a) Write the Experiment method reset that places the mechanical arm facing right, at index 0.

For example, suppose the experiment contains the solutions with pH values shown. The arrow represents the mechanical arm.

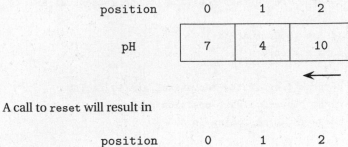

A call to reset will result in

| position | 0 | 1 | 2 |
|----------|---|---|----|
| pH | 7 | 4 | 10 |

$\longrightarrow$

---

Class information for this question

```
public class Solution

private int PH
private int positionLabel
int getPH()
int getPos()

public class MechanicalArm

private int currentPos
private boolean facesRight
int getCurrentIndex()
boolean isFacingRight()
void changeDirection()
void moveForward(int numLocs)

public class Experiment

private MechanicalArm arm
private Solution s0, s1, s2
public void reset()
public int mostAcidic()
```

**GO ON TO THE NEXT PAGE.**

Complete method `reset` below.

```
/** Resets the experiment, such that the mechanical arm has
 *  a current position of 0 and is facing right.
 */
public void reset()
```

(b) Write the `Experiment` method `mostAcidic` that returns the `position` of the most acidic solution and places the mechanical arm facing right at the location of the most acidic solution. A solution is acidic if its pH is less than 7. The lower the pH, the more acidic the solution. If there are no acidic solutions in the experiment, the `mostAcidic` method should return -1, and place the mechanical arm at position 0, facing right.

For example, suppose the experiment has this state:

| position | 0 | 1 | 2 |
|----------|---|---|---|
| pH | 7 | 4 | 10 |

←

A call to `mostAcidic` should return the value 1 and result in the following state for the experiment:

| position | 0 | 1 | 2 |
|----------|---|---|---|
| pH | 7 | 4 | 10 |

→

If the experiment has this state,

| position | 0 | 1 | 2 |
|----------|---|---|---|
| pH | 7 | 9 | 8 |

←

a call to `mostAcidic` should return the value -1 and result in the following state for the experiment:

| position | 0 | 1 | 2 |
|----------|---|---|---|
| pH | 7 | 9 | 8 |

→

**GO ON TO THE NEXT PAGE.**

Complete method `mostAcidic` below.

```
/** Returns the position of the most acidic solution,
 *  or -1 if there are no acidic solutions, as
 *  described in part(b).
 */
public int mostAcidic()
```

2. This question involves keeping track of details for a world cruise, using a `Cruise` class. A `Cruise` object is created with two parameters, the number of people currently signed up for the cruise, and the current price.

The `Cruise` class provides a constructor and the following methods.

- `setPrice`, which can change the price of the cruise.
- `checkResponse`, which increments the count of people if someone has requested the cruise using a phrase that includes the word "cruise". You may assume all lowercase letters.
- `calculateRevenue`, which returns the number of signups so far multiplied by the current price. Note that if more than 300 people have signed up for the cruise, everyone will receive a $500 discount off the current price. If between 200 and 300 (including 200) people have signed up, everyone will receive a $350 discount off the current price.

The following table contains sample code and corresponding results.

| Statements and Expressions | Comments |
| --- | --- |
| `Cruise cr = newCruise(78, 4000);` | There are 78 signups so far, and the cruise price is $4,000. |
| `cr.setPrice(5000);` | Changes the price to $5,000. |
| `cr.checkResponse("world cruise");` | Increments signup number to 79. |
| `cr.checkResponse("ship trip");` | Does not change number. It is still 78. |
| `cr.calculateRevenue();` | With 79 signups and price $5,000, returns $79 \times 5000$. |
| `Cruise cr1 = newCruise(200, 2000);` | |
| `cr1.calculateRevenue();` | Returns $200 \times 1650$ |
| `Cruise cr2 = newCruise(397, 6000);` | |
| `cr2.calculateRevenue();` | Returns $397 \times 5500$ |

Write the complete `Cruise` class, including the constructor and any required instance variables and methods. Your implementation must meet all specifications and be consistent with the examples shown above.

**GO ON TO THE NEXT PAGE.**

3. A text-editing program uses a `Sentence` class that manipulates a single sentence. A sentence contains letters, blanks, and punctuation. The first character in a sentence is a letter, and the last character is a punctuation mark. Any two words in the sentence are separated by a single blank. A partial implementation of the `Sentence` class is as follows.

```java
public class Sentence
{
    /** The sentence to manipulate */
    private String sentence;

    /**  Returns an ArrayList of integer positions containing a
     *   blank in this sentence. If there are no blanks in the
     *   sentence, returns an empty list.
     */
    public ArrayList<Integer> getBlankPositions()
    { /* to be implemented in part (a) */ }

    /**  Returns the number of words in this sentence
     *   Precondition:  Sentence contains at least one word.
     */
    public int countWords()
    { /* implementation not shown */ }

    /** Returns the array of words in this sentence.
     *  Precondition:
     *     - Any two words in the sentence are separated by one blank.
     *     - The sentence contains at least one word.
     *  Postcondition: String[] contains the words in this sentence.
     */
    public String[] getWords()
    { /* to be implemented in part (b) */ }

    //Constructor and other methods are not shown.
}
```

(a) Write the `Sentence` method `getBlankPositions`, which returns an `ArrayList` of integers that represent the positions in a sentence containing blanks. If there are no blanks in the sentence, `getBlankPositions` should return an empty list.

Some results of calling `getBlankPositions` are shown below.

| Sentence | Result of call to getBlankPositions |
|---|---|
| I love you! | [1, 6] |
| The cat sat on the mat. | [3, 7, 11, 14, 18] |
| Why? | [ ] |

**GO ON TO THE NEXT PAGE.**

Complete method `getBlankPositions` below.

```
/** Returns an ArrayList of integer positions containing a
 *  blank in this sentence. If there are no blanks in the
 *  sentence, returns an empty list.
 */
public ArrayList<Integer> getBlankPositions()
```

(b) Write the `Sentence` method `getWords`, which returns an array of words in the sentence. A word is defined as a string of letters and punctuation, and does not contain any blanks. You may assume that a sentence contains at least one word.

Some examples of calling `getWords` are shown below.

| Sentence | Result returned by `getWords` |
|---|---|
| The bird flew away. | {The, bird, flew, away.} |
| Wow! | {Wow!} |
| Hi! How are you? | {Hi!, How, are, you?} |

In writing method `getWords`, you *must* use methods `getBlankPositions` and `countWords`.

Complete method `getWords` below.

```
/** Returns the array of words in this sentence.
 *  Precondition:
 *    - Any two words in the sentence are separated by one blank.
 *    - The sentence contains at least one word.
 *  Postcondition: String[] contains the words in this sentence.
 */
public String[] getWords()
```

4. This question manipulates a two-dimensional array. In parts (a) and (b) you will write two methods of a `Matrix` class.

In doing so, you will use the `reverseArray` method shown in the class below.

```
public class ArrayUtil
{
    /** Reverses elements of array arr.
     *  Precondition: arr.length > 0.
     *  Postcondition: The elements of arr have been reversed.
     */
    public static void reverseArray(int[] arr)
    { /* implementation not shown */ }

    //Other methods are not shown.
}
```

**GO ON TO THE NEXT PAGE.**

Consider the following incomplete `Matrix` class, which represents a two-dimensional matrix of integers. Assume that the matrix contains at least one integer.

```
public class Matrix
{
    private int[][] mat;

    /** Constructs a matrix of integers. */
    public Matrix (int[][] m)
    {  mat = m; }

    /** Reverses the elements in each row of mat.
     *  Postcondition: The elements in each row have been reversed.
     */
    public void reverseAllRows()
    { /* to be implemented in part (a) */ }

    /** Reverses the elements of mat, as described in part (b).
     */
    public void reverseMatrix()
    { /* to be implemented in part (b) */ }

    //Other instance variables, constructors and methods are not shown.
}
```

(a) Write the `Matrix` method `reverseAllRows`. This method reverses the elements of each row. For example, if `mat1` refers to a `Matrix` object, then the call `mat1.reverseAllRows()` will change the matrix as shown below.

**Before call**

|   | 0 | 1 | 2 | 3 |
|---|---|---|---|---|
| 0 | 1 | 2 | 3 | 4 |
| 1 | 5 | 6 | 7 | 8 |
| 2 | 9 | 10 | 11 | 12 |

**After call**

|   | 0 | 1 | 2 | 3 |
|---|---|---|---|---|
| 0 | 4 | 3 | 2 | 1 |
| 1 | 8 | 7 | 6 | 5 |
| 2 | 12 | 11 | 10 | 9 |

In writing `reverseAllRows`, you *must* call the `reverseArray` method in the `ArrayUtil` class.

Complete method `reverseAllRows` below.

```
/** Reverses the elements in each row of mat.
 *  Postcondition: The elements in each row have been reversed.
 */
public void reverseAllRows()
```

**GO ON TO THE NEXT PAGE.**

(b) Write the `Matrix` method `reverseMatrix`. This method reverses the elements of a matrix such that the final elements of the matrix, when read in row-major order, are the same as the original elements when read from the bottom corner, right to left, going upward. Again let `mat1` be a reference to a `Matrix` object. The call `mat1.reverseMatrix()` will change the matrix as shown below.

**Before call**

| | 0 | 1 |
|---|---|---|
| 0 | 1 | 2 |
| 1 | 3 | 4 |
| 2 | 5 | 6 |

**After call**

| | 0 | 1 |
|---|---|---|
| 0 | 6 | 5 |
| 1 | 4 | 3 |
| 2 | 2 | 1 |

In writing `reverseMatrix`, you *must* call the `reverseAllRows` method in part (a). Assume that `reverseAllRows` works correctly regardless of what you wrote in part (a).

Complete method `reverseMatrix` below.

```
/** Reverses the elements of mat, as described in part (b).
 */
public void reverseMatrix()
```

**STOP**

**END OF EXAM**

# ANSWER KEY
## Diagnostic Test

### Section I

| | | |
|---|---|---|
| 1. **D** | 15. **E** | 29. **A** |
| 2. **A** | 16. **C** | 30. **A** |
| 3. **D** | 17. **A** | 31. **A** |
| 4. **A** | 18. **E** | 32. **C** |
| 5. **B** | 19. **A** | 33. **E** |
| 6. **E** | 20. **E** | 34. **D** |
| 7. **B** | 21. **B** | 35. **E** |
| 8. **C** | 22. **E** | 36. **C** |
| 9. **B** | 23. **D** | 37. **B** |
| 10. **A** | 24. **E** | 38. **A** |
| 11. **D** | 25. **A** | 39. **E** |
| 12. **B** | 26. **C** | 40. **D** |
| 13. **A** | 27. **D** | |
| 14. **A** | 28. **B** | |

## DIAGNOSTIC CHART

Each multiple-choice question has a complete explanation (p. 47).

The following table relates each question to sections that you should review. For any given question, the topic(s) in the chart represent the concept(s) tested in the question. These topics are explained on the corresponding page(s) in the chart and should provide further insight into answering that question.

| Question | Topic | Page |
|---|---|---|
| 1 | Inheritance | 142 |
| 2 | Relationship between classes | 204 |
| 3 | `ConcurrentModificationException` | 239 |
| 4 | Constructors | 103 |
| 5 | The `toString` method | 169 |
| 6 | `Integer.MIN_VALUE` and `Integer.MAX_VALUE` | 70 |
| 7 | `for` loop | 79 |
| 8 | Program specification | 201 |
| 9 | Recursion | 287 |
| 10 | Boolean expressions | 73 |
| 11 | 2D arrays | 242 |
| 12 | `IndexOutOfBoundsException` for `ArrayList` | 236 |
| 13 | Passing parameters | 229 |
| 14 | Passing parameters | 229 |
| 15 | Subclasses | 139 |
| 16 | Subclass constructors and `super` keyword | 143 |
| 17 | Polymorphism | 146 |
| 18 | `swap` method | 230 |
| 19 | Rounding real numbers | 69 |
| 20 | Recursion | 290 |
| 21 | Selection and insertion sort | 319 |
| 22 | Subclass method calls | 150 |
| 23 | Compound boolean expressions | 73 |
| 24 | String class `equals` method | 171 |
|  | String class `substring` method | 172 |
| 25 | Round-off error | 70 |
| 26 | Array processing | 228 |
| 27 | Assertions about algorithms | 212 |
|  | Binary search | 324 |
| 28 | Binary search | 324 |
| 29 | Random integers | 178 |
| 30 | String class `substring` method | 172 |
| 31 | Two-dimensional arrays | 242 |
| 32 | Relationships between classes | 209 |
| 33 | Array of objects | 232 |
|  | `ArrayList` | 234 |
| 34 | `NullPointerException` | 111 |
| 35 | Traversing an array | 228 |
|  | The `if` statement | 77 |
| 36 | Processing a 2D array | 243 |
|  | Mirror images | 351 |
| 37 | Using `ArrayList` | 236 |
| 38 | Using `ArrayList` | 236 |
| 39 | Using `super` in a subclass | 148 |
| 40 | One-dimensional arrays | 226 |

DIAGNOSTIC TEST

# ANSWERS EXPLAINED

## Section I

1. **(D)** Constructors are never inherited. If a subclass has no constructor, the default constructor for the superclass is generated. If the superclass does not have a default constructor, a compile-time error will occur.

2. **(A)** The relationship between `LibraryList` and `Book` is: A `LibraryList` *has-a* `Book`. (It has a list of books.) The *has-a* relationship is a composition relationship. Choice B is wrong: An inheritance relationship is the *is-a* relationship between a subclass and superclass. A `Book` is not a `LibraryList`. Choice C is wrong: `LibraryList` and `Book` are not independent, since a `LibraryBook` has a list of `Book` objects. Choice D is wrong: Polymorphism is not a relationship between classes. It's a mechanism for selecting which subclass method to implement during run time of a program. Choice E is wrong: `ArrayList` is not a relationship between classes. It is a data structure that contains a list of object references.

3. **(D)** Changing the size of an `ArrayList` while traversing it with an enhanced `for` loop can result in a `ConcurrentModificationException` being thrown. Therefore, you should not add or remove elements during traversal of an `ArrayList` with an enhanced `for` loop. Choices A and B are wrong because you are not using indexes in the traversal. Choice C, a `NullPointerException`, would only be thrown if the `list` object had not been initialized. Choice E, an `IllegalArgumentException`, occurs when a parameter doesn't satisfy a precondition of a method. There's no information in the question that suggests this is the case.

4. **(A)** In the constructor, the private instance variables `suit` and `value` must be initialized to the appropriate parameter values. Choice A is the only choice that does this.

5. **(B)** Implementation II invokes the `toString` method of the `Card` class. Implementation I fails because the default `toString` method for an array won't print individual elements of the array, just `classname@hashcode`. Implementation III will cause an error because you cannot cast a `Card` to a `String`.

6. **(E)** Since the values in `arr` cannot be greater than `Integer.MAX_VALUE`, the test in the `while` loop will be true at least once and will lead to the smallest element being stored in `min`. (If *all* the elements of the array are `Integer.MAX_VALUE`, the code still works.) Similarly, initializing `min` to `arr[0]`, the first element in the array, ensures that all elements in `arr` will be examined and the smallest will be found. Choice I, `Integer.MIN_VALUE`, fails because the test in the loop will always be false! There is no array element that will be less than the smallest possible integer. The method will (incorrectly) return `Integer.MIN_VALUE`.

7. **(B)** The maximum number will be achieved if /* *test* */ is true in each pass through the loop. So the question boils down to: How many times is the loop executed? Try one odd and one even value of `n`:

$$\text{If } n = 7, \quad i = 0, 2, 4, 6 \quad \text{Ans} = 4$$
$$\text{If } n = 8, \quad i = 0, 2, 4, 6 \quad \text{Ans} = 4$$

Notice that choice B is the only expression that works for both $n = 7$ and $n = 8$.

8. **(C)** Here is one of the golden rules of programming: Don't start planning the program until every aspect of the specification is crystal clear. A programmer should never make unilateral decisions about ambiguities in a specification.

9. **(B)** When x ≤ y, a recursive call is made to `whatIsIt(x-1, y)`. If x decreases at every recursive call, there is no way to reach a successful base case. Thus, the method never terminates and eventually exhausts all available memory.

10. **(A)** The expression `!(max != a[i])` is equivalent to `max == a[i]`, so the given expression is equivalent to `a[i] == max || max == a[i]`, which is equivalent to `a[i] == max`.

11. **(D)** In this problem, `mat.length` equals 2, the number of rows in the matrix. Each row is an array of `int`. Note that `arr.length`, which isn't used in the code, is 3. Here's what the code does: For each array `arr` in `mat`, add `arr[0]` and `arr[1]` to the sum. Note that when n is 2, the inner `for` loop terminates, so `arr[2]`, the elements of the third column, are not included in the sum, which equals $3 + 4 + 6 + 7 = 20$.

12. **(B)** The index range for `ArrayList` is $0 \le \text{index} \le \text{size()}-1$. Thus, for methods `get`, `remove`, and `set`, the last in-bounds index is `size()-1`. The one exception is the `add` method—to add an element to the end of the list takes an index parameter `list.size()`.

13. **(A)** The array will not be changed by the `increment` method. Here are the memory slots:

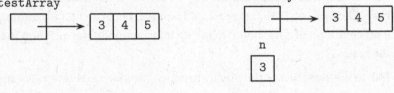

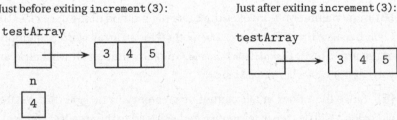

The same analysis applies to the method calls `increment(4)` and `increment(5)`.

14. **(A)** As in the previous question, the array will not be changed by the `increment` method. Nor will the local variable `element`! What *will* be changed by `increment` is the copy of the parameter during each pass through the loop.

15. **(E)** Statements I and II are false because `Point` is neither a `Quadrilateral` nor is it a `Rectangle`. (Notice that the `Point` class does not have the `extends` keyword.) Statement III is false because subclasses never inherit the constructors of their superclass. The code for a subclass constructor must be explicitly written; otherwise, the compiler slots in code for the superclass's default constructor.

16. **(C)** Segment I starts correctly but fails to initialize the additional private variables of the `Rectangle` class. Segment II is wrong because by using `super` with `theTopLeft` and `theBotRight`, it implies that these values are used in the `Quadrilateral` superclass. This is false—there isn't even a constructor with three arguments in the superclass.

17. **(A)** During execution the appropriate `area` method for each `quad` in `quadList` will be determined (polymorphism or dynamic binding). Choice B is wrong because the overridden method in the appropriate subclass is selected at run time—not the superclass method. Choice C is wrong because each of those subclasses inherit the `getLabels` method of `Quadrilateral`. Choice D would occur if `quadList` had a `null` value; but the precondition states that `quadList` is initialized. Choice E would occur if an attempt were made to alter `quadList` by adding or removing elements in the enhanced `for` loop.

18. **(E)** The algorithm has three steps:

    1. Store the object at `i` in `temp`.
    2. Place at location `i` the object at `j`.
    3. Place `temp` at location `j`.

    This has the effect of swapping the objects at `i` and `j`. Notice that choices B and C, while incomplete, are not incorrect. The question, however, asks for the *best* description of the postcondition, which is found in choice E.

19. **(A)** Subtracting 0.5 from a negative real number and then truncating it produces the number correctly rounded to the nearest integer. Note that casting to an `int` truncates a real number. The expression in choice B is correct for rounding a *positive* real number. Choice C won't round correctly. For example, −3.7 will be rounded to −3 instead of −4. Choices D and E don't make sense. Why cast to `double` if you're rounding to the nearest integer?

20. **(E)** The method call `whatsIt(347)` puts on the stack `System.out.print(7)`.
    The method call `whatsIt(34)` puts on the stack `System.out.print(4)`.
    The method call `whatsIt(3)` is a base case and writes out 3.
    Now the stack is popped from the top, and the 3 that was printed is followed by 4, then 7. The result is 347.

21. **(B)** Recall that insertion sort takes each element in turn and (a) finds its insertion point and (b) moves elements to insert that element in its correct place. Thus, if the array is in reverse sorted order, the insertion point will always be at the front of the array, leading to the maximum number of comparisons and data moves—very inefficient. Therefore choices A, C, and E are false.

    Selection sort finds the smallest element in the array and swaps it with `a[0]` and then finds the smallest element in the rest of the array and swaps it with `a[1]`, and so on. Thus, the same number of comparisons and moves will occur, irrespective of the original arrangement of elements in the array. So choice B is true, and choice D is false.

22. **(E)** Method call I fails because `ClassOne` does not have access to the methods of its subclass. Method call II fails because `c2` needs to be cast to `ClassTwo` to be able to access `methodTwo`. Thus, the following would be OK:

    ```
    ((ClassTwo) c2).methodTwo();
    ```

    Method call III works because `ClassTwo` inherits `methodOne` from its superclass, `ClassOne`.

23. **(D)** Notice that in the original code, if `n` is 1, `k` is incremented by 1, and if `n` is 4, `k` is incremented by 4. This is equivalent to saying "if `n` is 1 or 4, `k` is incremented by `n`."

24. **(E)** Segment I will throw a `NullPointerException` when `s.equals...` is invoked, because `s` is a null reference. Segment III looks suspect, but when the `startIndex` parameter of the `substring` method equals `s.length()`, the value returned is the empty string. If, however, `startIndex > s.length()`, a `StringIndexOutOfBoundsException` is thrown.

25. **(A)** Since results of calculations with floating-point numbers are not always represented exactly (round-off error), direct tests for equality are not reliable. Instead of the boolean expression `d == c`, a test should be done to check whether the difference of `d` and `c` is within some acceptable tolerance interval (see the Box on comparing floating-point numbers, p. 73).

26. **(C)** If `arr` has elements 2, 3, 5, the values of `value` are

```
2                      //after initialization
2*10 + 3 = 23          //when i = 1
23*10 + 5 = 235        //when i = 2
```

27. **(D)** The point of the binary search algorithm is that the interval containing `key` is repeatedly narrowed down by splitting it in half. For each iteration of the `while` loop, if `key` is in the list, `arr[first] ≤ key ≤ arr[last]`. Note that (i) the endpoints of the interval must be included, and (ii) `key` is not necessarily in the list.

28. **(B)**

|                       | first | last | mid | a[mid] |
|-----------------------|-------|------|-----|--------|
| After first iteration | 0     | 13   | 6   | 50     |
| After second iteration| 7     | 13   | 10  | 220    |
| After third iteration | 7     | 9    | 8   | 101    |
| After fourth iteration| 9     | 9    | 9   | 205    |

29. **(A)** The data structure is an array, not an `ArrayList`, so you cannot use the `add` method for inserting elements into the list. This eliminates choices B and D. The expression to return a random integer from 0 to `k-1` inclusive is

```
(int) (Math.random() * k)
```

Thus, to get integers from 0 to 100 requires `k` to be 101, which eliminates choice C. Choice E fails because it gets integers from 1 to 100.

30. **(A)** Suppose `str1` is `strawberry` and `str2` is `cat`. Then `insert(str1, str2, 5)` will return the following pieces, concatenated:

```
straw + cat + berry
```

Recall that `s.substring(k, m)` (a method of `String`) returns a substring of `s` starting at position `k` and ending at position `m-1`. String `str1` must be split into two parts, `first` and `last`. Then `str2` will be inserted between them. Since `str2` is inserted starting at position 5 (the "b"), `first = straw`, namely `str1.substring(0,pos)`. (Start at 0 and take all the characters up to and including location `pos-1`, which is 4.) Notice that `last`, the second substring of `str1`, must start at the index for "b", which is `pos`, the index at which `str2` was inserted. The expression `str1.substring(pos)` returns the substring of `str1` that starts at `pos` and continues to the end of the string, which was required. Note that you don't need any "special case" tests. In the cases where `str2` is inserted at the front of `str1` (i.e., `pos` is 0) or the back of `str1` (i.e., `pos` is `str1.length()`), the code for the general case works.

31. **(A)** Method `changeMatrix` examines each element and changes it to its absolute value if its row number equals its column number. The only two elements that satisfy the condition `r == c` are `mat[0][0]` and `mat[1][1]`. Thus, –1 is changed to 1 and –4 is changed to 4, resulting in the matrix in choice A.

32. **(C)** Composition is the *has-a* relationship. A `PlayerGroup` *has-a* `Player` (several of them, in fact). Inheritance (choice D) is the *is-a* relationship, which doesn't apply here. None of the choices A, B, or E apply in this example: Procedural abstraction is the use of separate methods to encapsulate each task (see p. 206); data encapsulation is combining the data and methods of an object in a class so that the data can be hidden (see p. 101); and `PlayerGroup` and `Player` are clearly dependent on each other since `PlayerGroup` contains several `Player` objects (see p. 205).

33. **(E)** All of these data structures are reasonable. They all represent 20 bingo numbers in a convenient way and provide easy mechanisms for crossing off numbers and recognizing a winning card. Notice that data structure II provides a very quick way of searching for a number on the card. For example, if 48 is called, `bingoCard[48]` is inspected. If it is `true`, then it was one of the 20 original numbers on the card and gets crossed out. If `false`, 48 was not on that player's card. Data structures I and II require a linear search to find any given number that is called. (Note: There is no assumption that the array is sorted, which would allow a more efficient binary search.)

34. **(D)** A `NullPointerException` is thrown whenever an attempt is made to invoke a method with an object that hasn't been created with `new`. Choice A doesn't make sense: To test the `Caller` constructor requires a statement of the form

```
Caller c = new Caller();
```

Choice B is wrong: A missing `return` statement in a method triggers a compile-time error. Choice C doesn't make sense: In the declaration of `numbers`, its default initialization is to `null`. Choice E is bizarre. Hopefully you eliminated it immediately!

35. **(E)** For each element in `a`, `found` is switched to `true` if that element is found anywhere in `b`. Notice that for any element in `a`, if it is not found in `b`, the method returns `false`. Thus, to return `true`, every element in `a` must also be in `b`. Notice that this doesn't necessarily mean that `a` and `b` are permutations of each other. For example, consider the counterexample of `a=[1,1,2,3]` and `b=[1,2,2,3]`. Also, not every element in `b` needs to be in `a`. For example, if `a=[3,3,5]` and `b=[3,5,6]`, the method will return `true`.

36. **(C)** In the example given, `height = 3`, `height/2 = 1`, and `numCols = 3`. Notice that in each pass through the loop, `row` has value 0, while `col` goes from 0 through 2. So here are the assignments:

```
mat[2][0] = mat[0][0]
mat[2][1] = mat[0][1]
mat[2][2] = mat[0][2]
```

From this you should see that row 2 is being replaced by row 0.

37. **(B)** Eliminate choices D and E immediately, since assignment of new values in an `ArrayList` is done with the `set` method, not `get`. Eliminate choice C since you do not know that the `TileBag` class has a swap method. Choice A fails because it replaces the element at position `size` before storing it. Choice B works because the element at position `index` has been saved in `temp`.

38. **(A)** The `size` variable stores the number of unused tiles, which are in the `tiles` list from position 0 to position `size`. A random `int` is selected in this range, giving the index of the `Tile` that will be swapped to the end of the unused part of the `tiles` list. Note that the length of the `tiles` `ArrayList` stays constant. Each execution of `getNewTile` decreases the "unused tiles" part of the list and increases the "already used" part at the end of the list. In this way, both used and unused tiles are stored.

39. **(E)** When `pigeon.act()` is called, the act method of `Dove` is called. (This is an example of polymorphism.) The `act` method of `Dove` starts with `super.act()` which goes to the `act` method of `Bird`, the superclass. This prints `fly`, then calls `makeNoise()`. Using polymorphism, the `makeNoise` method in `Dove` is called, which starts with `super.makeNoise()`, which prints `chirp`. Completing the `makeNoise` method in `Dove` prints `coo`. Thus, so far we've printed `fly chirp coo`. But we haven't completed Dove's `act` method, which ends with printing out `waddle`! The rule of thumb is: When `super` is used, find the method in the superclass. But if that method calls a method that's been overridden in the subclass, go back there for the overridden method. You also mustn't forget to check that you've executed any pending lines of code in that superclass method!

40. **(D)** In Implementation 1, the first element assigned is `prod[1]`, and it multiplies `arr[1]` by `prod[0]`, which was initialized to 1. To fix this implementation, you need a statement preceding the loop, which correctly assigns `prod[0]`: `prod[0]=arr[0];`

# Section II

1. (a)
```java
public void reset()
{
    if(arm.isFacingRight())
        arm.changeDirection();
    arm.moveForward(arm.getCurrentPos());
    arm.changeDirection();
}
```

(b)
```java
public int mostAcidic()
{
    reset();
    int minPH = Integer.MAX_VALUE, minPos = 0;
    if (s0.getPH() < s1.getPH())
    {
        minPH = s0.getPH();
        minPos = s0.getPos();
    }
    else
    {
        minPH = s1.getPH();
        minPos = s1.getPos();
    }
    if (s2.getPH() < minPH)
    {
        minPH = s2.getPH();
        minPos = s2.getPos();
    }
    if (minPH >= 7)
        return -1;
    else
    {
        arm.moveForward(minPos);
        return minPos;
    }
}
```

**NOTE**

- In part (b), notice that resetting the mechanical arm causes the arm to face right.
- In part (b), you could initialize minPH to any integer greater than or equal to 7 for this algorithm to work. You just must be careful not to set it to an "acidic" number—namely, 1 to 6.

## Scoring Rubric: Chemical Solutions

| Part (a) | reset | 3 points |
|---|---|---|
| +1 | get arm to face left | |
| +1 | move arm forward to position 0 | |
| +1 | turn to face right | |

| Part (b) | mostAcidic | 6 points |
|---|---|---|
| +1 | initialize minPH and indexes | |
| +1 | reset | |
| +1 | test all solutions | |
| +1 | test each solution and adjust minPos and minPH | |
| +1 | test at the end if minPH is greater than 7 | |
| +1 | else part at end: move arm forward and return minPos | |

2.
```java
public class Cruise
{
    private int numPassengers;
    private double price;

    public Cruise(int num, double thePrice)
    {
        numPassengers = num;
        price = thePrice;
    }

    public void setPrice (double newPrice)
    { price = newPrice;}

    public void checkResponse(String response)
    {
        if (response.indexOf("cruise") != -1)
            numPassengers++;
    }

    public double calculateRevenue()
    {
        if (numPassengers >= 300)
            return numPassengers * (price - 500);
        else if (numPassengers >= 200)
            return numPassengers * (price - 350);
        else return numPassengers * price;
    }
}
```

## Scoring Rubric: Cruise

| class Cruise | 9 points |
|---|---|
| +1 | private instance variables |
| +1 | constructor |
| +1 | setPrice |
| +1 | checkResponse |
| +1 | indexOf |
| +1 | numPassengers++ |
| +1 | calculateRevenue |
| +1 | correct if...else statements |
| +1 | correct return values |

3. (a)
```
public ArrayList<Integer> getBlankPositions()
{
    ArrayList<Integer> posList = new ArrayList<Integer>();
    for (int i = 0; i < sentence.length(); i++)
    {
        if (sentence.substring(i, i + 1).equals(" "))
            posList.add(i);
    }
    return posList;
}
```

(b)
```
public String[] getWords()
{
    ArrayList<Integer> posList = getBlankPositions();
    int numWords = countWords();
    String[] wordArr = new String[numWords];
    for (int i = 0; i < numWords; i++)
    {
        if (i == 0)
        {
            if (posList.size() != 0)
                wordArr[i] = sentence.substring(0, posList.get(0));
            else
                wordArr[i] = sentence;
        }
        else if (i == posList.size())
            wordArr[i] = sentence.substring(posList.get(i - 1) + 1);
        else
            wordArr[i] = sentence.substring(posList.get(i - 1) + 1,
                    posList.get(i));
    }
    return wordArr;
}
```

- In part (a), it would also work to have the test

  ```
  i < sentence.length() - 1;
  ```

  in the for loop. But you don't need the -1 because the last character is a punctuation mark, not a blank.
- In part (b), you have to be careful when you get the first word. If there's only one word in the sentence, there are no blanks, which means posList is empty, and you can't use posList.get(0) (because that will throw an IndexOutOfBoundsException!).
- Also in part (b), the second test deals with getting the last word in the sentence. You have to distinguish between the cases of more than one word in the sentence and exactly one word in the sentence. Note that adding 1 to the start index of substring extracts the last word without the blank that precedes it.

## Scoring Rubric: Sentence Manipulation

| Part (a) | getBlankPositions | 4 points |
|---|---|---|
| +1 | create temporary ArrayList | |
| +1 | traverse sentence | |
| +1 | test a character for a blank | |
| +1 | update and return posList | |

| Part (b) | getWords | 5 points |
|---|---|---|
| +1 | get list of blank positions and word count | |
| +1 | get first and last words of sentence | |
| +1 | get a middle word of sentence | |
| +1 | get the last word of sentence | |
| +1 | declaration and return of wordArr | |

4. (a)
```
public void reverseAllRows()
{
    for (int[] row: mat)
        ArrayUtil.reverseArray (row);
}
```

(b)
```
public void reverseMatrix()
{
    reverseAllRows();
    int mid = mat.length/2;
    for (int i = 0; i < mid; i++)
    {
        for (int col = 0; col < mat[0].length; col++)
        {
            int temp = mat[i][col];
            mat[i][col] = mat[mat.length - i - 1][col];
            mat[mat.length - i - 1][col] = temp;
        }
    }
}
```

Alternative solution:

```
public void reverseMatrix()
{
    reverseAllRows();
    int mid = mat.length/2;
    for (int i = 0; i < mid; i++)
    {
        int[] temp = mat[i];
        mat[i] = mat[mat.length - i - 1];
        mat[mat.length - i - 1] = temp;
    }
}
```

**NOTE**

- The alternative solution in part (b) swaps the first and last elements, then the second and second last, etc., moving toward the middle. In this case, each element is a row. If there is an odd number of rows, the middle row does not move.
- In the first solution of part (b), start by reversing all rows. Then for each column, swap the elements in the first and last rows, then the second and second last, and so on, moving toward the middle.
- The alternative solution in part (b) is more elegant. It is not, however, part of the AP subset to replace one row of a matrix with a different array.

## Scoring Rubric: Reverse Matrix

| Part (a) | reverseAllRows | 3 points |
|---|---|---|
| +1 | traverse mat | |
| +1 | call to reverseArray | |
| +1 | correct parameter for reverseArray | |

| Part (b) | reverseMatrix | 6 points |
|---|---|---|
| +1 | call to reverseAllRows | |
| +1 | assign mid | |
| +1 | outer for loop | |
| +1 | inner for loop | |
| +2 | swap matrix elements | |

# Strategies for Taking the Exam

1

*Take time to deliberate, but when the time for action comes,*
*stop thinking and go in.*
—*Napoléon Bonaparte*

→ **Strategies for Multiple-Choice**
  **Questions**

→ **Strategies for Free-Response**
  **Questions**

## THE MULTIPLE-CHOICE SECTION

### What Is Tested?

The questions in the multiple-choice section span the entire AP Java subset, and the types of questions are classified according to the type of content. The table below shows the weighting of various topics on the multiple-choice section, as described in the College Board's AP Computer Science A Course and Exam Description of 2019. Note that categories can overlap in a given question (for example, a question can compare a recursive algorithm with a fundamental loop implementation), so the percentage total is greater than 100%.

| Topic | Exam Weighting |
|-------|----------------|
| Primitive Types | 2.5 – 5% |
| Using Objects | 5 – 7.5% |
| Boolean Expressions and `if` statements | 15 – 17.5% |
| Iteration | 17.5 – 22.5% |
| Writing Classes | 5 – 7.5% |
| Array | 10 – 15% |
| `ArrayList` | 2.5 – 7.5% |
| 2D Array | 7.5 – 10% |
| Inheritance | 5 – 10% |
| Recursion | 5 – 7.5% |

### Time Issues

You have 90 minutes for 40 questions, which means a little more than 2 minutes per question. There are, however, several complicated questions that need to be hand traced, which may take longer than 2 minutes. The bottom line is that you don't have time to waste.

Don't let yourself become bogged down on a question. You know how it goes: You're so close to getting the answer, and you've already put in the time to trace the code, and maybe you made an error in your trace and should do it again ... meanwhile the clock is ticking. If a given question stymies you, circle it and move on. You can always come back to it if you have time at the end.

## Guessing

There's no penalty for guessing. If you don't know the answer to a question and are ready to move on, eliminate the answer choices that are clearly wrong, and guess one of the remaining choices.

When time is almost up, bubble in an answer for each of your unanswered questions. Remember, you should make random guesses rather than leaving blanks.

## The Java Quick Reference

You will have access to the Java Quick Reference for both the multiple-choice and free-response sections of the AP exam. You should familiarize yourself with it ahead of time (see p. xiii on how to find it), so that you don't waste time searching for something that isn't in it.

The quick reference contains specifications for methods and constants from the Java library for the `Object`, `Integer`, `Double`, `String`, `Math`, and `ArrayList` classes. Each of the methods provided may appear in multiple-choice questions on the AP exam.

## An Active Pencil

You will not be given scratch paper but you may write on the exam booklet. Don't trace tricky algorithms in your head. Here are some active-pencil tips:

- For each iteration of a loop, write down the values of the loop variables and other key variables. Often, just a few values on the page will reveal a pattern and clarify what an algorithm is doing.

- When you trace an algorithm that has a method with parameters, draw memory slots to visualize what's happening to the values. Remember, when a method is called, copies are made of the actual parameters. It's not possible to alter actual values, unless the parameters are references. (See p. 112.)

- To find a value returned by a recursive algorithm, write down the multiple method calls to keep track. (See, e.g., Question 5 on p. 304.)

- In a complicated question about inheritance, sketch a quick UML (inheritance) diagram to reinforce the relationships between classes. (See p. 205.)

- In the multiple-choice section, questions like the following occur frequently:

  - What does this algorithm do?
  - Which could be a postcondition for ...?
  - Which array will result from ...?
  - Which string will be returned?

The key to solving these easily is to think *small*. Give yourself a 3-element array, or a 2 × 2 matrix, or a 3-character string, and hand execute the code on your manageable little data structure. Write down values. Keep track of the loop variables. And the answer will be revealed.

## Troubleshooting—What's Wrong with This Code?

Some multiple-choice questions tell you that the code doesn't work as intended. You are to identify the incorrect replacement for `/* more code */`, or simply find the error. Here are some quick details you can check:

- If it's a recursive algorithm, does it have a base case?
- Does the base case in a recursive algorithm actually lead to termination?
- In an array algorithm, can the index equal `arr.length`? If so, it is out of bounds.
- Does the algorithm contain `arr[i]` and `arr[i + 1]`? Often `arr[i + 1]` goes out of bounds.
- In a string algorithm that has `str.substring[start]`, is `start` greater than `str.length()`? If so, it is out of bounds.
- In a string algorithm that has `str.substring[start, end]`, is `start` greater than or equal to `end`? If so, it will cause an error. Is `end` greater than `str.length()`? If so, it is out of bounds.
- In an `ArrayList` method other than `add`, is the index value greater than or equal to `list.size()`? If so, it is out of bounds.
- Is a client program of `SomeClass` trying to directly access the private instance variables or private methods of `SomeClass`? It will cause an error.
- Is the keyword `super` being used in a constructor? If so, it had better be in the first line of code; otherwise, it will cause a compile-time error.
- If a value is being inserted into a sorted list, is there a range check to make sure that the algorithm doesn't sail off the end of the list?

## Loop Tracing

Here are some tips:

- There are several questions that will ask how many times a loop is executed. This can be phrased in different ways: How many times will a word or phrase be printed? How many times will a method in the loop body be executed? If the numbers are small, write down all of the values of the loop variable for which the loop will be executed, and count them! That's the answer.
- If the answer to a question with a loop depends on a parameter $n$, try setting $n$ to 2 or 3 to see the pattern.
- Be sure to pay attention to whether the loop test uses < or <= (or > or >=).
- Watch out for how the loop variable is being changed. It is not always `i++` (increment by 1) or `i--` (decrement by 1).

## Java Exceptions

Occasionally, one of the answer choices is the following:

> The code throws `<some kind of run-time exception>`.

Run your eye down the algorithm and check for:

- An array, `ArrayList`, or `String` going out of bounds. Each situation will throw an `ArrayIndexOutOfBoundsException` or `IndexOutOfBoundsException`. If you find it, you can move on without even glancing at the other answer choices.

- Integer division by zero. If division by zero occurs in the first part of a compound test, an `ArithmeticException` will always be thrown. If the division is in the second part of the test, you won't get the exception if the value of the whole test is already known (short-circuit evaluation). (See p. 74.)

## Matrix Manipulation

Suppose you are given a matrix and an algorithm that changes the matrix in some way. These algorithms are often hard to trace, and, to complicate the problem, you don't have much time.

Assume that `row` and `col` are loop variables in the algorithm. For a quick solution, try looking at the element that corresponds to the first `row` value and first `col` value of the loop. Often this is the element in the top left-hand corner. Does it change? Can you eliminate some of the answer choices, based on this one element? Repeat the process for the final `row` and `col` values. Often this is the element in the bottom right-hand corner. Can you eliminate other answer choices?

In other words, you don't always need to trace all of the values to find the answer.

## Comparing Algorithms

Several questions may ask you to compare two algorithms that supposedly implement the same algorithm. They may ask you which algorithm is more efficient. Factors that affect efficiency are the number of comparisons and the number of data moves. Check out the body of each loop. Count the comparisons and data movements. Multiply the total by the number of iterations of the loop. The algorithm with the lower answer is the more efficient algorithm.

You may be asked to compare data structures. These are the questions to ask yourself:

- Which involves the least number of comparisons to locate a given element?

- Which involves the least number of data moves to insert or remove an element?

- Does the structure store the entire state of the object?

## Mechanics of Answering Questions

Here are three final tips:

- Take care that you bubble in the answer that corresponds to the number of the question you just solved!

- Since the mark-sense sheet is scored by machine, make sure that you erase completely if you change an answer.

- Take a moment at the end to check that you have provided an answer for every question.

## THE FREE-RESPONSE SECTION

## What Is the Format?

- You will have 90 minutes for 4 free-response questions.

- Each question is worth 9 points. Note that the free-response and multiple-choice sections carry equal weight in determining your AP score.

- The code that you write must be in Java.

- Write your solutions to the questions on the test booklet provided, underneath the specification for each part of a question.

- You should use a No. 2 pencil for your solutions.

## What Is Tested?

In theory, the entire AP Java subset is fair game for free-response questions. But you should pay special attention to each of the following:

- List manipulation using both arrays and `ArrayLists`
- String manipulation
- Two-dimensional arrays
- Classes and subclasses

## What Types of Questions?

You may be asked to do each of the following:

- Write the body of a specified method
- Write the bodies of methods using code from previous parts of the question
- Write an overloaded method (p. 107)
- Write a constructor (p. 143)
- Provide an overridden method in a subclass (p. 143)
- Write a complete class or subclass

## Skill Focus in Free-Response Questions

As in past exams, all of the questions will test your ability to use expressions, conditional statements, and loops, according to various specifications.

Additionally, starting with the May 2020 AP exam, each free-response question will have a particular skill focus.

**QUESTION 1: METHODS AND CONTROL STRUCTURES**  This tests your ability to call methods, write code for methods, and write code to create objects of a class.

The question may include String manipulation, or expressions that use div (`/`) and mod (`%`), or sequences of `if...else` statements.

**QUESTION 2: CLASS WRITING**  This tests your ability to write code for a class or subclass according to various specifications.

Brush up on writing constructors, use of `super`, and overridden and inherited methods.

**QUESTION 3: ARRAY AND ARRAYLIST MANIPULATION**  This tests your ability to create, traverse, and manipulate elements in a 1D array or `ArrayList` of objects.

Review the rules for using enhanced `for` loops in traversals, and the specific methods of `ArrayList` for manipulating lists of objects.

**QUESTION 4: 2D ARRAY MANIPULATION** This tests your ability to create, traverse, and manipulate elements in a 2D array of objects.

Brush up on row-by-row traversals, using the fact that a 2D array is an array of 1D arrays. Review the rules for using enhanced `for` loops in 2D array traversals.

## The Java Quick Reference

You will continue to have access to the Java Quick Reference for the free-response section of the AP exam. Here are tips for using it in the code you write:

- When you use a library method from the `ArrayList` interface, or from the `Object`, `String`, or `Math` classes, a glance at the quick reference will confirm that you're using the correct method name and also the correct format and ordering of parameters.

- The correct format of the constants for the smallest and largest `Integer` values (`Integer.MIN_VALUE` and `Integer.MAX_VALUE`) are shown on the first page.

- Again, use the quick reference throughout the year. Do not study it for the first time during the AP exam!

- When you write code that uses methods of the `String` class, the quick reference will help ensure that you use the correct type and order of parameters.

## Time Issues

Here are some tips for managing your time:

- Just 90 minutes for 4 questions means fewer than 23 minutes per question. Since many of the questions involve up to two pages of reading, you don't have much time. Nevertheless, you should take a minute to read through the whole section so that you can start with a question you feel confident about. It gives you a psychological boost to have a solid question in the bag.

- When you tackle a free-response question, underline key words in the problem as well as return types and parameters. This kind of close reading will help you to process the question quickly without inadvertently missing important information.

- Take a minute to circle the methods that you are given to implement other methods. If you write code that reimplements those given methods, you won't get full credit.

- Work steadily through the questions. If you get stuck on a question, move on. If you can answer only one part of a question, do it and leave the other parts blank. You can return to them if there's time at the end.

- Don't waste time writing comments: the graders generally ignore them. The occasional comment that clarifies a segment of code is OK. I know this because I graded AP Computer Science exams for many years.

## Grading the Free-Response Questions

Be aware that this section is graded by humans. It's in your interest to have graders understand your solutions. With this in mind:

- Use a sharp pencil, write legibly, space your answers, and indent correctly.
- Use self-documenting names for variables, methods, and so on.

- Use the identifiers that are used in the question.

- Write clear, readable code. Avoid obscure, convoluted code.

The graders have a rubric that allocates each of the 9 points for solving the various parts of a problem. If your solution works, you will get full credit. This is irrespective of whether your code is efficient or elegant. You should never, ever take time to rewrite a working piece of code more elegantly.

You will be awarded partial credit if you used the right approach for a question, but didn't quite nail the solution. Each valid piece of your code that is included in the rubric will earn you some credit.

There are certain errors that are not penalized. For example, the graders will look the other way if you omit semicolons, or misspell identifiers, or use keywords as identifiers, or confuse `length` with `length()`, or use = instead of ==, or use the wrong kind of brackets for an array element.

They will, however, deduct points for each of the following types of errors:

- Including output statements in methods that don't require it.

- Including an output statement in a method, instead of returning a value. (Are you clear on this? No `System.out.print()` or `System.out.println()` statements in methods that didn't ask for output!)

- Using local variables that aren't declared.

- Returning the wrong type of value in a method, or returning a value in a `void` method, or having a constructor return a value.

- Using incorrect syntax for traversing and processing arrays and `ArrayLists`.

Take heart: On any given question, you won't receive a negative score!

## Coding Issues

Here are important reminders for the code that you write:

- It's worth repeating: You must use Java for your solutions. No pseudo-code, or C++, or any other programming language.

- If the statement of the question provides an algorithm, you should say thank you and use it. Don't waste time trying to reinvent the wheel.

- Don't omit a question just because you can't come up with a complete solution. Remember, partial credit is awarded. Also, don't omit part (b) of a question just because you couldn't do part (a)—the various parts of a question are graded independently.

- In writing solutions to a question, you must use the public methods of classes provided in that question wherever possible. If you write a significant chunk of code that can be replaced by a call to one of those methods, you will probably not receive full credit for the question.

- If you're writing a subclass of a given superclass, don't rewrite the public methods of that class unless you are overriding them. All public methods are inherited.

- It is fine to use methods from the Java library that are not in the AP Java subset. You will receive full credit if you use those methods correctly. If your usage, however, is incorrect, your solution will be penalized. Note that there is always a solution that uses the subset, and you should try to find it.

- It is fine to write a helper method for your solution. But be aware that usually you can solve the question using methods that are already provided.

## Maximizing Your Score

Here are some final general tips for maximizing your free-response score:

- At the start of the free-response section, clear the decks! The multiple-choice section is over, and whether you killed it or it killed you, it is past history. Take a deep breath and psych yourself up for the code-writing part of the exam. Now is the time to strut your stuff.

- Don't ever erase a solution. Cross it out. You want to avoid a situation in which you erased some code, but don't have time to write the replacement code.

- If you can't see a solution to a question, but have some understanding of what is required to solve it, write something down. Just showing that you understand that you must loop through all of the elements in a list, for example, may earn you a point from the rubric.

- Don't provide more than one solution for a given part. The exam readers are instructed to grade the first attempt only, and to ignore all subsequent ones. Not even the most warm-hearted among us will go wading through the marshes of your various solutions, searching for the one that solves the problem correctly. This means that you must choose one solution and cross out the others with firm, legible lines.

- One final reminder: Use clear, readable code from the AP Java subset. Avoid obscure, opaque brilliancies. The AP exam is not the place to show the world you're a genius.

Good luck!

# Introductory Java Language Features

2

*Fifty loops shalt thou make ...*
—Exodus 26:5

- → **Packages and classes**
- → **Types and identifiers**
- → **Operators**

- → **Input/output**
- → **Control structures**
- → **Errors and exceptions**

The AP Computer Science course includes algorithm analysis, data structures, and the techniques and methods of modern programming, specifically, object-oriented programming. A high-level programming language is used to explore these concepts. Java is the language currently in use on the AP exam.

Java was developed by James Gosling and a team at Sun Microsystems in California; it continues to evolve. The AP exam covers a clearly defined subset of Java language features that are presented throughout this book. A complete listing of this subset can be found at the College Board website, *https://apstudent.collegeboard.org/courses/ap-computer-science-a*.

Java provides basic control structures such as the `if-else` statement, `for` loop, enhanced `for` loop, and `while` loop, as well as fundamental built-in data types. But the power of the language lies in the manipulation of user-defined types called objects, many of which can interact in a single program.

## PACKAGES AND CLASSES

A typical Java program has user-defined classes whose objects interact with those from Java class libraries. In Java, related classes are grouped into *packages*, many of which are provided with the compiler. For example, the package `java.util` contains the collections classes. Note that you can put your own classes into a package—this facilitates their use in other programs.

The package `java.lang`, which contains many commonly used classes, is automatically provided to all Java programs. To use any other package in a program, an `import` statement must be used. To import all of the classes in a package called `packagename`, use the form

```
import packagename.*;
```

Note that the package name is all lowercase letters. To import a single class called `ClassName` from the package, use

```
import packagename.ClassName;
```

Java has a hierarchy of packages and subpackages. Subpackages are selected using multiple dots:

```
import packagename.subpackagename.ClassName;
```

For example,

```
import java.util.ArrayList;
```

The `import` statement allows the programmer to use the objects and methods defined in the designated package. You will not be expected to write any `import` statements.

A Java program must have at least one class, the one that contains the *main method.* The Java files that comprise your program are called *source files.*

A *compiler* converts source code into machine-readable form called *bytecode.*

Here is a typical source file for a Java program:

```
/*  Program FirstProg.java
    Start with a comment, giving the program name and a brief
    description of what the program does.
 */
import package1.*;
import package2.subpackage.ClassName;

public class FirstProg  //note that the file name is FirstProg.java
{
    public static type1 method1(parameter list)
    {
        < code for method 1 >
    }
    public static type2 method2(parameter list)
    {
        < code for method 2 >
    }
        ...

    public static void main(String[] args)
    {
        < your code >
    }
}
```

## NOTE

1. All Java methods must be contained in a class.
2. The words `class`, `public`, `static`, and `void` are *reserved words*, also called *keywords.* (This means they have specific uses in Java and may not be used as identifiers.)
3. The keyword `public` signals that the class or method is usable outside of the class, whereas `private` data members or methods (see Chapter 3) are not.
4. The keyword `static` is used for methods that will not access any objects of a class, such as the methods in the `FirstProg` class in the example above. This is typically true for all methods in a source file that contains no *instance variables* (see Chapter 3). Most methods in Java do operate on objects and are not static. The `main` method, however, must always be static.
5. The program shown above is a Java *application.*

6. There are three different types of comment delimiters in Java:

- /* ... */, which is the one used in the program shown, to enclose a block of comments. The block can extend over one or more lines.
- //, which generates a comment on one line.
- /** ... */, which generates Javadoc comments. These are used to create API documentation of Java library software.

## Javadoc Comments

The Javadoc comments @param and @return are no longer part of the AP Java subset.

## TYPES AND IDENTIFIERS

### Identifiers

An *identifier* is a name for a variable, parameter, constant, user-defined method, or user-defined class. In Java, an identifier is any sequence of letters, digits, and the underscore character. Identifiers may not begin with a digit. Identifiers are case-sensitive, which means that age and Age are different. Wherever possible identifiers should be concise and self-documenting. A variable called area is more illuminating than one called a.

By convention, identifiers for variables and methods are lowercase. Uppercase letters are used to separate these into multiple words, for example getName, findSurfaceArea, preTaxTotal, and so on. Note that a class name starts with a capital letter. Reserved words are entirely lowercase and may not be used as identifiers.

### Built-in Types

Every identifier in a Java program has a type associated with it. The *primitive* or *built-in* types that are included in the AP Java subset are

| | |
|---|---|
| int | An integer. For example, 2, -26, 3000 |
| boolean | A boolean. Just two values, true or false |
| double | A double precision floating-point number. For example, 2.718, -367189.41, 1.6e4 |

(Note that primitive type char is not included in the AP Java subset.)

Integer values are stored exactly. Because there's a fixed amount of memory set aside for their storage, however, integers are bounded. If you try to store a value whose magnitude is too big in an int variable, you'll get an *overflow error*. (Java gives you no warning. You just get a wrong result!)

An identifier, for example a *variable*, is introduced into a Java program with a *declaration* that specifies its type. A variable is often initialized in its declaration. Some examples follow:

```
int x;
double y,z;
boolean found;
int count = 1;              //count initialized to 1
double p = 2.3, q = 4.1;    //p and q initialized to 2.3 and 4.1
```

One type can be cast to another compatible type if appropriate. For example,

```
int total, n;
double average;
    ...
average = (double) total/n;    //total cast to double to ensure
                               //real division is used
```

Alternatively,

```
average = total/(double) n;
```

Assigning an `int` to a `double` automatically casts the `int` to `double`. For example,

```
int num = 5;
double realNum = num;    //num is cast to double
```

Assigning a `double` to an `int` without a cast, however, causes a compile-time error. For example,

```
double x = 6.79;
int intNum = x;    //Error. Need an explicit cast to int
```

Note that casting a floating-point (real) number to an integer simply truncates the number. For example,

```
double cost = 10.95;
int numDollars = (int) cost;    //sets numDollars to 10
```

If your intent was to round `cost` to the nearest dollar, you needed to write

```
int numDollars = (int) (cost + 0.5);  //numDollars has value 11
```

To round a negative number to the nearest integer:

```
double negAmount = -4.8;
int roundNeg = (int) (negAmount - 0.5);   //roundNeg has value -5
```

The strategy of adding or subtracting 0.5 before casting correctly rounds in all cases.

## Storage of Numbers

The details of storage are not tested on the AP exam. They are, however, useful for understanding the differences between types `int` and `double`.

### INTEGERS

Integer values in Java are stored exactly, as a string of bits (binary digits). One of the bits stores the sign of the integer, 0 for positive, 1 for negative.

The Java built-in integral type, `byte`, uses one byte (eight bits) of storage.

The picture represents the largest positive integer that can be stored using type `byte`: $2^7 - 1$.

Type `int` in Java uses four bytes (32 bits). Taking one bit for a sign, the largest possible integer stored is $2^{31} - 1$. In general, an $n$-bit integer uses $n/8$ bytes of storage, and stores integers from $-2^{n-1}$ to $2^{n-1} - 1$. (Note that the extra value on the negative side comes from not having to store $-0$.) There are two Java constants that you should know. `Integer.MAX_VALUE` holds the maximum value an `int` can hold, $2^{31} - 1$. `Integer.MIN_VALUE` holds the minimum value an `int` can hold, $-2^{31}$.

Built-in integer types in Java are `byte` (one byte), `short` (two bytes), `int` (four bytes), and `long` (eight bytes). Of these, only `int` is in the AP Java subset.

**FLOATING-POINT NUMBERS**

There are two built-in types in Java that store real numbers: `float`, which uses four bytes, and `double`, which uses eight bytes. A *floating-point number* is stored in two parts: a *mantissa*, which specifies the digits of the number, and an exponent. The JVM (Java Virtual Machine) represents the number using scientific notation:

$$\text{sign} * \text{mantissa} * 2^{\text{exponent}}$$

In this expression, 2 is the *base* or *radix* of the number. In type `double`, 11 bits are allocated for the exponent, and (typically) 52 bits for the mantissa. One bit is allocated for the sign. This is a *double-precision* number. Type `float`, which is *single-precision,* is not in the AP Java subset.

When floating-point numbers are converted to binary, most cannot be represented exactly, leading to *round-off error.* These errors are compounded by arithmetic operations. For example,

$$0.1*26 \neq 0.1+0.1+\cdots+0.1 \quad \text{(26 terms)}$$

In Java, no exceptions are thrown for floating-point operations. There are two situations you should be aware of:

- When an operation is performed that gives an undefined result, Java expresses this result as `NaN`, "not a number." Examples of operations that produce `NaN` are: taking the square root of a negative number, and 0.0 divided by 0.0.

- An operation that gives an infinitely large or infinitely small number, like division by zero, produces a result of `Infinity` or `-Infinity` in Java.

## Hexadecimal and Octal Numbers

Base 2, base 8, and base 16 are no longer part of the AP Java subset. Only base 10 will be used on the AP exam.

## Final Variables

A *final variable* or *user-defined constant*, identified by the keyword `final`, is a quantity whose value will not change. Here are some examples of `final` declarations:

```
final double TAX_RATE = 0.08;
final int CLASS_SIZE = 35;
```

1. Constant identifiers are, by convention, capitalized.
2. A `final` variable can be declared without initializing it immediately. For example,

```
final double TAX_RATE;
if (<some condition>)
    TAX_RATE = 0.08;
else
    TAX_RATE = 0.0;
// TAX_RATE can be given a value just once: its value is final!
```

3. A common use for a constant is as an array bound. For example,

```
final int MAXSTUDENTS = 25;
int[] classList = new int[MAXSTUDENTS];
```

4. Using constants makes it easier to revise code. Just a single change in the `final` declaration need be made, rather than having to change every occurrence of a value.

## OPERATORS

## Arithmetic Operators

| Operator | Meaning | Example |
|----------|---------|---------|
| + | addition | `3 + x` |
| − | subtraction | `p - q` |
| * | multiplication | `6 * i` |
| / | division | `10 / 4  //returns 2, not 2.5!` |
| % | mod (remainder) | `11 % 8  //returns 3` |

NOTE

1. These operators can be applied to types `int` and `double`, even if both types occur in the same expression. For an operation involving a `double` and an `int`, the `int` is promoted to `double`, and the result is a `double`.
2. The mod operator `%`, as in the expression `a % b`, gives the remainder when `a` is divided by `b`. Thus `10 % 3` evaluates to `1`, whereas `4.2 % 2.0` evaluates to `0.2`.
3. Integer division `a/b` where both `a` and `b` are of type `int` returns the integer quotient only (i.e., the answer is truncated). Thus, 22/6 gives 3, and 3/4 gives 0. If at least one of the operands is of type `double`, then the operation becomes regular floating-point division, and there is no truncation. You can control the kind of division that is carried out by explicitly casting (one or both of) the operands from `int` to `double` and vice versa. Thus

```
3.0 / 4        →    0.75
3 / 4.0        →    0.75
(int) 3.0 / 4  →    0
(double) 3 / 4 →    0.75
```

You must, however, be careful:

$$(\texttt{double}) \ (3 \ / \ 4) \quad \rightarrow \quad 0.0$$

since the integer division 3/4 is computed first, before casting to `double`.

4. The arithmetic operators follow the normal precedence rules (order of operations):

  (1) parentheses, from the inner ones out (highest precedence)

  (2) `*, /, %`

  (3) `+, –` (lowest precedence)

Here operators on the same line have the same precedence, and, in the absence of parentheses, are invoked from left to right. Thus, the expression `19 % 5 * 3 + 14 / 5` evaluates to `4 * 3 + 2 = 14`. Note that casting has precedence over all of these operators. Thus, in the expression `(double) 3/4`, 3 will be cast to `double` before the division is done.

## Relational Operators

| Operator | Meaning | Example |
|----------|---------|---------|
| `==` | equal to | `if (x == 100)` |
| `!=` | not equal to | `if (age != 21)` |
| `>` | greater than | `if (salary > 30000)` |
| `<` | less than | `if (grade < 65)` |
| `>=` | greater than or equal to | `if (age >= 16)` |
| `<=` | less than or equal to | `if (height <= 6)` |

**NOTE**

1. Relational operators are used in *boolean expressions* that evaluate to `true` or `false`.

   ```
   boolean x = (a != b);     //initializes x to true if a != b,
                             // false otherwise
   return p == q;   //returns true if p equals q, false otherwise
   ```

2. If the operands are an `int` and a `double`, the `int` is promoted to a `double` as for arithmetic operators.

3. Relational operators should generally be used only in the comparison of primitive types (i.e., `int`, `double`, or `boolean`). Strings are compared using the `equals` and `compareTo` methods (see p. 171).

> Do not routinely use == to test for equality of floating-point numbers.

4. Be careful when comparing floating-point values! Since floating-point numbers cannot always be represented exactly in the computer memory, a round-off error could be introduced, leading to an incorrect result when `==` is used to test for equality.

### Comparing Floating-Point Numbers

Because of round-off errors in floating-point numbers, you can't rely on using the == or != operators to compare two double values for equality. They may differ in their last significant digit or two because of round-off error. Instead, you should test that the magnitude of the difference between the numbers is less than some number about the size of the machine precision. The machine precision is usually denoted $\epsilon$ and is typically about $10^{-16}$ for double precision (i.e., about 16 decimal digits). So you would like to test something like $|x - y| \leq \epsilon$. But this is no good if $x$ and $y$ are very large. For example, suppose $x = 1234567890.123456$ and $y = 1234567890.123457$. These numbers are essentially equal to machine precision, since they differ only in the 16th significant digit. But $|x - y| = 10^{-6}$, not $10^{-16}$. So in general you should check the *relative* difference:

$$\frac{|x - y|}{\max(|x|, |y|)} \leq \epsilon$$

To avoid problems with dividing by zero, code this as

$$|x - y| \leq \epsilon \max(|x|, |y|)$$

## Logical Operators

A *logical operator* (sometimes called a *boolean operator*) is one that returns a boolean result that is based on the boolean result(s) of one or two other boolean expressions. The three logical operators are shown in the table below.

| Operator | Meaning | Example |
|---|---|---|
| ! | NOT | if (!found) |
| && | AND | if (x < 3 && y > 4) |
| \|\| | OR | if (age < 2 \|\| height < 4) |

**NOTE**

1. Logical operators are applied to boolean expressions to form *compound boolean expressions* that evaluate to true or false.
2. Values of true or false are assigned according to the truth tables for the logical operators.

| && | T | F |
|---|---|---|
| T | T | F |
| F | F | F |

| \|\| | T | F |
|---|---|---|
| T | T | T |
| F | T | F |

| ! | |
|---|---|
| T | F |
| F | T |

For example, F && T evaluates to F, while T \|\| F evaluates to T.

3. *Short-circuit evaluation.* The subexpressions in a compound boolean expression are evaluated from left to right, and evaluation automatically stops as soon as the value of the entire expression is known. For example, consider a boolean OR expression of the form A || B, where A and B are some boolean expressions. If A is true, then the expression is true irrespective of the value of B. Similarly, if A is false, then A && B evaluates to false irrespective of the second operand. So in each case the second operand is not evaluated. For example,

```
if (numScores != 0 && scoreTotal/numScores > 90)
```

will not cause a run-time ArithmeticException (division-by-zero error) if the value of numScores is 0. This is because numScores != 0 will evaluate to false, causing the entire boolean expression to evaluate to false without having to evaluate the second expression containing the division.

## Assignment Operators

| Operator | Example | Meaning |
|----------|---------|---------|
| = | x = 2 | simple assignment |
| += | x += 4 | x = x + 4 |
| -= | y -= 6 | y = y - 6 |
| *= | p *= 5 | p = p * 5 |
| /= | n /= 10 | n = n / 10 |
| %= | n %= 10 | n = n % 10 |

NOTE

1. All these operators, with the exception of simple assignment, are called *compound assignment operators.*
2. *Chaining* of assignment statements is allowed, with evaluation from right to left. (This is not tested on the AP exam.)

```
int next, prev, sum;
next = prev = sum = 0;   //initializes sum to 0, then prev to 0
                         //then next to 0
```

## Increment and Decrement Operators

| Operator | Example | Meaning |
|----------|---------|---------|
| ++ | i++ or ++i | i is incremented by 1 |
| -- | k-- or --k | k is decremented by 1 |

Note that i++ (postfix) and ++i (prefix) both have the net effect of incrementing i by 1, but they are not equivalent. For example, if i currently has the value 5, then System.out.println(i++) will print 5 and then increment i to 6, whereas System.out.println(++i) will first increment i to 6 and then print 6. It's easy to remember: If the ++ is first, you first increment. A similar distinction occurs between k-- and --k. (Note: You do not need to know these distinctions for the AP exam.)

## Operator Precedence

$$
\begin{array}{lll}
\text{highest precedence} \;\rightarrow & (1) & !, \;++, \;-- \\
& (2) & *, \;/, \;\% \\
& (3) & +, \;- \\
& (4) & <, \;>, \;<=, \;>= \\
& (5) & ==, \;!= \\
& (6) & \&\& \\
& (7) & || \\
\text{lowest precedence} \;\rightarrow & (8) & =, \;+=, \;-=, \;*=, \;/=, \;\%=
\end{array}
$$

Here operators on the same line have equal precedence. The evaluation of the operators with equal precedence is from left to right, except for rows (1) and (8) where the order is right to left. It is easy to remember: The only "backward" order is for the unary operators (row 1) and for the various assignment operators (row 8).

### ➡ Example _____

What will be output by the following statement?

```
System.out.println(5 + 3 < 6 - 1);
```

Since + and - have precedence over <, 5 + 3 and 6 - 1 will be evaluated before evaluating the boolean expression. Since the value of the expression is false, the statement will output `false`.

## INPUT/OUTPUT

### Input

Since there are so many ways to provide input to a program, user input is not a part of the AP Java subset. If reading input is a necessary part of a question on the AP exam, it will be indicated something like this:

```
double x = call to a method that reads a floating-point number
```

or

```
double x = ...;    //read user input
```

**NOTE**

The Scanner class simplifies both console and file input. It will not, however, be tested on the AP exam.

### Output

Testing of output will be restricted to System.out.print and System.out.println. Formatted output will not be tested.

System.out is an object in the System class that allows output to be displayed on the screen. The println method outputs an item and then goes to a new line. The print method outputs an item without going to a new line afterward. An item to be printed can be a string, or a number, or the value of a boolean expression (true or false). Here are some examples:

```
System.out.print("Hot");
System.out.println("dog");
```
} prints  Hotdog

```
System.out.println("Hot");
System.out.println("dog");
```
prints  Hot
dog

```
System.out.println(7 + 3);
```
} prints  10

```
System.out.println(7 == 2 + 5);
```
} prints  true

```
int x = 27;
System.out.println(x);
```
} prints  27
```
System.out.println("Value of x is " + x);
```
prints  Value of x is 27

In the last example, the value of x, 27, is converted to the string "27", which is then concatenated to the string "Value of x is ".

To print the "values" of user-defined objects, the toString() method is invoked (see p. 167).

## Escape Sequences

An *escape sequence* is a backslash followed by a single character. It is used to print special characters. The three escape sequences that you should know for the AP exam are

| Escape Sequence | Meaning |
|---|---|
| \n | newline |
| \" | double quote |
| \\ | backslash |

Here are some examples:

```
System.out.println("Welcome to\na new line");
```

prints

```
Welcome to
a new line
```

The statement

```
System.out.println("He is known as \"Hothead Harry\".");
```

prints

```
He is known as "Hothead Harry".
```

The statement

```
System.out.println("The file path is d:\\myFiles\\..");
```

prints

```
The file path is d:\myFiles\..
```

## CONTROL STRUCTURES

Control structures are the mechanism by which you make the statements of a program run in a nonsequential order. There are two general types: decision-making and iteration.

### Decision-Making Control Structures

These include the `if`, `if...else`, and `switch` statements. They are all selection control structures that introduce a decision-making ability into a program. Based on the truth value of a boolean expression, the computer will decide which path to follow. The `switch` statement is not part of the AP Java subset.

#### THE `if` STATEMENT

```
if (boolean expression)
{
    statements
}
```

Here the *statements* will be executed only if the *boolean expression* is `true`. If it is `false`, control passes immediately to the first statement following the `if` statement.

#### THE `if...else` STATEMENT

```
if (boolean expression)
{
    statements
}
else
{
    statements
}
```

Here, if the *boolean expression* is `true`, only the *statements* immediately following the test will be executed. If the *boolean expression* is `false`, only the *statements* following the `else` will be executed.

#### NESTED `if` STATEMENT

If the statement in an `if` statement is itself an `if` statement, the result is a *nested `if` statement*.

➡️ **Example 1** _____

```
if (boolean expr1)
    if (boolean expr2)
        statement;
```

This is equivalent to

```
if (boolean expr1 && boolean expr2)
    statement;
```

Beware the dangling `else`! Suppose you want to read in an integer and print it if it's positive and even. Will the following code do the job?

```java
int n = ...;          //read user input
if (n > 0)
    if (n % 2 == 0)
        System.out.println(n);
else
    System.out.println(n + " is not positive");
```

A user enters 7 and is surprised to see the output

```
7 is not positive
```

The reason is that `else` always gets matched with the *nearest* unpaired `if`, not the first `if` as the indenting would suggest.

There are two ways to fix the preceding code. The first is to use {} delimiters to group the statements correctly.

```java
int n = ...;          //read user input
if (n > 0)
{
    if (n % 2 == 0)
        System.out.println(n);
}
else
    System.out.println(n + " is not positive");
```

The second way of fixing the code is to rearrange the statements.

```java
int n = ...;          //read user input
if (n <= 0)
    System.out.println(n + " is not positive");
else
    if (n % 2 == 0)
        System.out.println(n);
```

### EXTENDED `if` STATEMENT

For example,

```java
String grade = ...;          //read user input
if (grade.equals("A"))
    System.out.println("Excellent!");
else if (grade.equals("B"))
    System.out.println("Good");
else if (grade.equals("C") || grade.equals("D"))
    System.out.println("Poor");
else if (grade.equals("F"))
    System.out.println("Egregious!");
else
    System.out.println("Invalid grade");
```

If any of A, B, C, D, or F are entered, an appropriate message will be written, and control will go to the statement immediately following the extended if statement. If any other string is entered, the final else is invoked, and the message Invalid grade will be written.

## Iteration

Java has three different control structures that allow the computer to perform iterative tasks: the for loop, while loop, and do...while loop. The do...while loop is not in the AP Java subset.

### THE for LOOP

The general form of the for loop is

```
for (initialization; termination condition; update statement)
{
    statements          //body of loop
}
```

The termination condition is tested at the top of the loop; the update statement is performed at the bottom.

### ➡ Example 1

```
//outputs 1 2 3 4
for (i = 1; i < 5; i++)
    System.out.print(i + " ");
```

Here's how it works. The *loop variable* i is initialized to 1, and the termination condition i < 5 is evaluated. If it is true, the body of the loop is executed, and then the loop variable i is incremented according to the update statement. As soon as the termination condition is false (i.e., i >= 5), control passes to the first statement following the loop.

### ➡ Example 2

```
//outputs 20 19 18 17 16 15
for (k = 20; k >= 15; k--)
    System.out.print(k + " ");
```

### ➡ Example 3

```
//outputs 2 4 6 8 10
for (j = 2; j <= 10; j += 2)
    System.out.print(j + " ");
```

**NOTE**

1. The loop variable should not have its value changed inside the loop body.
2. The initializing and update statements can use any valid constants, variables, or expressions.
3. The scope (see p. 107) of the loop variable can be restricted to the loop body by combining the loop variable declaration with the initialization. For example,

```
for (int i = 0; i < 3; i++)
{
    ...
}
```

4. The following loop is syntactically valid:

```
for (int i = 1; i <= 0; i++)
{
    ...
}
```

The loop body will not be executed at all, since the exiting condition is true before the first execution.

## ENHANCED for LOOP (FOR-EACH LOOP)

This is used to iterate over an array or collection. The general form of the loop is

```
for (SomeType element : collection)
{
    statements
}
```

(Read the top line as "For each element of type SomeType in collection ...")

## ➡ Example _____

```
//Outputs all elements of arr, one per line.
for (int element : arr)
    System.out.println(element);
```

## NOTE

1. The enhanced for loop should be used for accessing elements in the data structure, not for replacing or removing elements as you traverse.
2. The loop hides the index variable that is used with arrays.

## THE while LOOP

The general form of the while loop is

```
while (boolean test)
{
    statements            //loop body
}
```

The *boolean test* is performed at the beginning of the loop. If true, the loop body is executed. Otherwise, control passes to the first statement following the loop. After execution of the loop body, the test is performed again. If true, the loop is executed again, and so on.

## ➡ Example 1 _____

```java
int i = 1, mult3 = 3;
while (mult3 < 20)
{
    System.out.print(mult3 + " ");
    i++;
    mult3 *= i;
}                   //outputs 3 6 18
```

**NOTE**

1. It is possible for the body of a while loop never to be executed. This will happen if the test evaluates to false the first time.
2. Disaster will strike in the form of an infinite loop if the test can never be false. Don't forget to change the loop variable in the body of the loop in a way that leads to termination!

> The body of a while loop must contain a statement that leads to termination.

## ➡ Example 2 _____

```java
int power2 = 1;
while (power2 != 20)
{
    System.out.println(power2);
    power2 *= 2;
}
```

Since power2 will never exactly equal 20, the loop will grind merrily along eventually causing an integer overflow.

## ➡ Example 3 _____

```java
/* Screen out bad data.
 * The loop won't allow execution to continue until a valid
 * integer is entered.
 */
System.out.println("Enter a positive integer from 1 to 100");
int num = ...;          //read user input
while (num < 1 || num > 100)
{
    System.out.println("Number must be from 1 to 100.");
    System.out.println("Please reenter");
    num = ...;
}
```

**Example 4** _____

```
/* Uses a sentinel to terminate data entered at the keyboard.
 * The sentinel is a value that cannot be part of the data.
 * It signals the end of the list.
 */
final int SENTINEL = -999;
System.out.println("Enter list of positive integers," +
    " end list with " + SENTINEL);
int value = ...;        //read user input
while (value != SENTINEL)
{
    process the value
    value = ...;        //read another value
}
```

## NESTED LOOPS

You create a *nested loop* when a loop is a statement in the body of another loop.

**Example 1** _____

```
for (int k = 1; k <= 3; k++)
{
    for (int i = 1; i <= 4; i++)
        System.out.print("*");
    System.out.println();
}
```

Think:

```
for each of 3 rows
{
    print 4 stars
    go to next line
}
```

Output:

```
****
****
****
```

**Example 2** _____

This example has two loops nested in an outer loop.

```
for (int i = 1; i <= 6; i++)
{
    for (int j = 1; j <= i; j++)
        System.out.print("+");
    for (int j = 1; j <= 6 - i; j++)
        System.out.print("*");
    System.out.println();
}
```

Output:

```
+*****
++****
+++***
++++**
+++++*
++++++
```

## ERRORS AND EXCEPTIONS

An *exception* is an error condition that occurs during the execution of a Java program. For example, if you divide an integer by zero, an `ArithmeticException` will be thrown. If you use a negative array index, an `ArrayIndexOutOfBoundsException` will be thrown.

An *unchecked exception* is one that is automatically handled by Java's standard exception-handling methods, which terminate execution. It is thrown if an attempt is made to divide an integer by 0, or if an array index goes out of bounds, and so on. The exception tells you that you now need to fix your code!

A *checked exception* is one where you provide code to handle the exception, either a `try/catch/finally` statement, or an explicit `throw new...Exception` clause. These exceptions are not necessarily caused by an error in the code. For example, an unexpected end-of-file could be due to a broken network connection. Checked exceptions are not part of the AP Java subset.

The following unchecked exceptions are in the AP Java subset:

| Exception | Discussed on page |
|---|---|
| ArithmeticException | this page |
| NullPointerException | 111 |
| ArrayIndexOutOfBoundsException | 226 |
| IndexOutOfBoundsException | 236 |
| IllegalArgumentException | next page |
| ConcurrentModificationException | 239 |

Java allows you to write code that throws a standard unchecked exception. Here are typical examples:

### ➡ Example 1 _____

```
if (numScores == 0)
    throw new ArithmeticException("Cannot divide by zero");
else
    findAverageScore();
```

## ➡ Example 2 _____

```
public void setRadius(int newRadius)
{
    if (newRadius < 0)
        throw new IllegalArgumentException
                ("Radius cannot be negative");
    else
        radius = newRadius;
}
```

**NOTE**

1. `throw` and `new` are both reserved words. (The keywords `throw` and `throws` are not in the AP Java subset.)

2. The error message is optional: The line in Example 1 could have read

   ```
   throw new ArithmeticException();
   ```

   The message, however, is useful, since it tells the person running the program what went wrong.

3. An `IllegalArgumentException` is thrown to indicate that a parameter does not satisfy a method's precondition.

## Chapter Summary

Be sure that you understand the difference between primitive and user-defined types and between the following types of operators: arithmetic, relational, logical, and assignment. Know which conditions lead to what types of errors.

You should be able to work with numbers—know how to compare them and be aware of the conditions that can lead to round-off error.

You should know the `Integer` constants `Integer.MIN_VALUE` and `Integer.MAX_VALUE`.

Be familiar with each of the following control structures: conditional statements, `for` loops, `while` loops, and enhanced `for` loops.

Be aware of the AP exam expectations concerning input and output.

Learn the unchecked exceptions that are part of the AP Java subset.

# MULTIPLE-CHOICE QUESTIONS ON INTRODUCTORY JAVA LANGUAGE FEATURES

1. Which of the following pairs of declarations will cause an error message?

   ```
   I  double x = 14.7; ✓
      int y = x;          no cost
   ```

   *(handwritten: double → int not ok / int → double ok)*

   ```
   II double x = 14.7;
      int y = (int) x;
   ```

   ```
   III int x = 14;
       double y = x;
   ```

   (A) None
   (B) I only  *(circled)*
   (C) II only
   (D) III only
   (E) I and III only

2. What output will be produced by the following?

   *(handwritten: \\ → one backslash)*

   ```
   System.out.print("\\* This is not\n a comment *\\");
   ```

   *(handwritten: newline)*

   (A) * This is not a comment *

   (B) \* This is not a comment *\

   (C) * This is not
       a comment *

   (D) \\* This is not
       a comment *\\

   (E) \* This is not
       a comment *\   *(circled)*

3. Consider the following code segment.

   ```
   if (n != 0 && x / n > 100)   → so 1%
       statement1;
   else
       statement2;
   ```

   If n is of type int and has a value of 0 when the segment is executed, what will happen?
   (A) An ArithmeticException will be thrown.
   (B) A syntax error will occur.
   (C) *statement1*, but not *statement2*, will be executed.
   (D) *statement2*, but not *statement1*, will be executed.  *(circled)*
   (E) Neither *statement1* nor *statement2* will be executed; control will pass to the first
       statement following the if statement.

4. Refer to the following code fragment.

```java
double answer = 13 / 5;
System.out.println("13 / 5 = " + answer);
```

The output is

```
13 / 5 = 2.0
```

The programmer intends the output to be

```
13 / 5 = 2.6
```

Which of the following replacements for the first line of code will not fix the problem?

(A) `double answer = (double) 13 / 5;`
(B) `double answer = 13 / (double) 5;`
(C) `double answer = 13.0 / 5;`
(D) `double answer = 13 / 5.0;`
(E) `double answer = (double) (13 / 5);`

5. What value is stored in `result` if

```java
int result = 13 - 3 * 6 / 4 % 3;
```

(A) −5
(B) 0
(C) 13
(D) −1
(E) 12

6. Suppose that addition and subtraction had higher precedence than multiplication and division. Then the expression

```
2 + 3 * 12 / 7 - 4 + 8
```

would evaluate to which of the following?

(A) 11
(B) 12
(C) 5
(D) 9
(E) −4

7. Which is true of the following boolean expression, given that `x` is a variable of type `double`?

```
3.0 == x * (3.0 / x)
```

(A) It will always evaluate to false.
(B) It may evaluate to false for some values of x.
(C) It will evaluate to false only when x is zero.
(D) It will evaluate to false only when x is very large or very close to zero.
(E) It will always evaluate to true.

8. Let `x` be a variable of type `double` that is positive. A program contains the boolean expression (`Math.pow(x,0.5)` `==` `Math.sqrt(x)`). Even though $x^{1/2}$ is mathematically equivalent to $\sqrt{x}$, the above expression returns the value `false` in a student's program. Which of the following is the most likely reason?

(A) `Math.pow` returns an `int`, while `Math.sqrt` returns a `double`.
(B) `x` was imprecisely calculated in a previous program statement.
(C) The computer stores floating-point numbers with 32-bit words.
(D) There is round-off error in calculating the `pow` and `sqrt` functions.
(E) There is overflow error in calculating the `pow` function.

9. What will the output be for the following poorly formatted program segment, if the input value for `num` is 22?

```
int num =  call to a method that reads an integer;
if (num > 0)
if (num % 5 == 0)
System.out.println(num);
else System.out.println(num + " is negative");
```

(A) `22`
(B) `4`
(C) `2 is negative`
(D) `22 is negative`
(E) Nothing will be output.

10. What values are stored in `x` and `y` after execution of the following program segment?

```
int x = 30, y = 40;
if (x >= 0)
{
    if (x <= 100)
    {
        y = x * 3;
        if (y < 50)
            x /= 10;
    }
    else
        y = x * 2;
}
else
    y = -x;
```

(A) `x = 30 y = 90`
(B) `x = 30 y = -30`
(C) `x = 30 y = 60`
(D) `x = 3  y = -3`
(E) `x = 30 y = 40`

11. Which of the following will evaluate to true only if boolean expressions A, B, and C are all false?

    (A) !A && !(B && !C)
    (B) !A || !B || !C
    (C) !(A || B || C)
    (D) !(A && B && C)
    (E) !A || !(B || !C)

12. Assume that a and b are integers. The boolean expression

    !(a <= b) && (a * b > 0)

will always evaluate to true given that

    (A) a = b.
    (B) a > b.
    (C) a < b.
    (D) a > b and b > 0.
    (E) a > b and b < 0.

13. Given that a, b, and c are integers, consider the boolean expression

    (a < b) || !((c == a * b) && (c < a))

Which of the following will guarantee that the expression is true?

    (A) c < a is false.
    (B) c < a is true.
    (C) a < b is false.
    (D) c == a * b is true.
    (E) c == a * b is true, and c < a is true.

14. In the following code segment, you may assume that a, b, and n are all type int.

```
if (a != b && n / (a - b) > 90)
{
    /* statement 1 */
}
else
{
    /* statement 2 */
}
/* statement 3 */
```

What will happen if a == b is false?

    (A) /* statement 1 */ will be executed.
    (B) /* statement 2 */ will be executed.
    (C) Either /* statement 1 */ or /* statement 2 */ will be executed.
    (D) A compile-time error will occur.
    (E) An exception will be thrown.

15. Given that n and `count` are both of type `int`, which statement is true about the following code segments?

```
 I for (count = 1; count <= n; count++)
       System.out.println(count);

II count = 1;
   while (count <= n)
   {
       System.out.println(count);
       count++;
   }
```

   (A) I and II are exactly equivalent for all input values n.
   (B) I and II are exactly equivalent for all input values n ≥ 1, but differ when n ≤ 0.
   (C) I and II are exactly equivalent only when n = 0.
   (D) I and II are exactly equivalent only when n is even.
   (E) I and II are not equivalent for any input values of n.

16. The following fragment intends that a user will enter a list of positive integers at the keyboard and terminate the list with a sentinel.

```
int value = 0;
final int SENTINEL = -999;
while (value != SENTINEL)
{
    //code to process value
      ...
    value = ...;        //read user input
}
```

The fragment is not correct. Which is a true statement?
   (A) The sentinel gets processed.
   (B) The last nonsentinel value entered in the list fails to get processed.
   (C) A poor choice of SENTINEL value causes the loop to terminate before all values have been processed.
   (D) The code will always process a value that is not on the list.
   (E) Entering the SENTINEL value as the first value causes a run-time error.

17. Consider this code segment.

```
int x = 10, y = 0;
while (x > 5)
{
    y = 3;
    while (y < x)
    {
        y *= 2;
        if (y % x == 1)
            y += x;
    }
    x -= 3;
}
System.out.println(x + " " + y);
```

What will be output after execution of this code segment?

(A) 1    6
(B) 7    12
(C) -3    12
(D) 4    12
(E) -3    6

Questions 18 and 19 refer to the following method, `checkNumber`, which checks the validity of its four-digit integer parameter.

```java
/** Returns true if the 4-digit integer n is valid,
 *  false otherwise.
 */
boolean checkNumber(int n)
{
    int d1,d2,d3,checkDigit,nRemaining,rem;
    //strip off digits
    checkDigit = n % 10;
    nRemaining = n / 10;
    d3 = nRemaining % 10;
    nRemaining /= 10;
    d2 = nRemaining % 10;
    nRemaining /= 10;
    d1 = nRemaining % 10;
    //check validity
    rem = (d1 + d2 + d3) % 7;
    return rem == checkDigit;
}
```

A program invokes method `checkNumber` with the statement

```java
boolean valid = checkNumber(num);
```

18. Which of the following values of `num` will result in `valid` having a value of `true`?
    (A) 6143
    (B) 6144
    (C) 6145
    (D) 6146
    (E) 6147

19. What is the purpose of the local variable `nRemaining`?
    (A) It is not possible to separate `n` into digits without the help of a temporary variable.
    (B) `nRemaining` prevents the parameter `num` from being altered.
    (C) `nRemaining` enhances the readability of the algorithm.
    (D) On exiting the method, the value of `nRemaining` may be reused.
    (E) `nRemaining` is needed as the left-hand side operand for integer division.

20. What output will be produced by this code segment? (Ignore spacing.)

```
for (int i = 5; i >= 1; i--)
{
    for (int j = i; j >= 1; j--)
        System.out.print(2 * j - 1);
    System.out.println();
}
```

(A) 9 7 5 3 1
    9 7 5 3
    9 7 5
    9 7
    9

    *97531*

(B) 9 7 5 3 1
    7 5 3 1
    5 3 1
    3 1
    1

(C) 9 7 5 3 1
    7 5 3 1 -1
    5 3 1 -1 -3
    3 1 -1 -3 -5
    1 -1 -3 -5 -7

(D) 1
    1 3
    1 3 5
    1 3 5 7
    1 3 5 7 9

(E) 1 3 5 7 9
    1 3 5 7
    1 3 5
    1 3
    1

21. Which of the following program fragments will produce this output? (Ignore spacing.)

```
2 - - - - -
- 4 - - - -
- - 6 - - -
- - - 8 - -
- - - - 10 -
- - - - - 12
```

I
```
for (int i = 1; i <= 6; i++)
{
    for (int k = 1; k <= 6; k++)
        if (k == i)
            System.out.print(2 * k);
        else
            System.out.print("-");
    System.out.println();
}
```

II
```
for (int i = 1; i <= 6; i++)
{
    for (int k = 1; k <= i - 1; k++)
        System.out.print("-");
    System.out.print(2 * i);
    for (int k = 1; k <= 6 - i; k++)
        System.out.print("-");
    System.out.println();
}
```

III
```
for (int i = 1; i <= 6; i++)
{
    for (int k = 1; k <= i - 1; k++)
        System.out.print("-");
    System.out.print(2 * i);
    for (int k = i + 1; k <= 6; k++)
        System.out.print("-");
    System.out.println();
}
```

(A) I only
(B) II only
(C) III only
(D) I and II only
(E) I, II, and III

22. Consider this program segment.

```java
int newNum = 0, temp;
int num = k;              //k is some predefined integer value ≥ 0
while (num > 10)
{
    temp = num % 10;
    num /= 10;
    newNum = newNum * 10 + temp;
}
System.out.print(newNum);
```

Which is a true statement about the segment?

I  If 100 ≤ num ≤ 1000 initially, the final value of newNum must be in the range 10 ≤ newNum ≤ 100.

II There is no initial value of num that will cause an infinite while loop.

III If num ≤ 10 initially, newNum will have a final value of 0.

(A) I only
(B) II only
(C) III only
(D) II and III only
(E) I, II, and III

23. Consider the method reverse.

```
/** Returns n with its digits reversed.
 *   - Example: If n = 234, method reverse returns 432.
 *   Precondition:  n > 0.
 */
int reverse(int n)
{
    int rem, revNum = 0;

    /* code segment */

    return revNum;
}
```

Which of the following replacements for /* *code segment* */ would cause the method to work as intended?

```
I for (int i = 0; i <= n; i++)
  {
      rem = n % 10;
      revNum = revNum * 10 + rem;
      n /= 10;
  }

II while (n != 0)
   {
       rem = n % 10;
       revNum = revNum * 10 + rem;
       n /= 10;
   }

III for (int i = n; i != 0; i /= 10)
    {
        rem = i % 10;
        revNum = revNum * 10 + rem;
    }
```

(A) I only
(B) II only
(C) I and II only
(D) II and III only
(E) I and III only

## ANSWER KEY

| | | |
|---|---|---|
| 1. **B** | 9. **D** | 17. **D** |
| 2. **E** | 10. **A** | 18. **B** |
| 3. **D** | 11. **C** | 19. **C** |
| 4. **E** | 12. **D** | 20. **B** |
| 5. **E** | 13. **A** | 21. **E** |
| 6. **C** | 14. **C** | 22. **D** |
| 7. **B** | 15. **A** | 23. **D** |
| 8. **D** | 16. **D** | |

## ANSWERS EXPLAINED

1. **(B)** When x is converted to an integer, as in segment I, information is lost. Java requires that an explicit cast to an `int` be made, as in segment II. Note that segment II will cause x to be truncated: The value stored in y is 14. By requiring the explicit cast, Java doesn't let you do this accidentally. In segment III, y will contain the value 14.0. No explicit cast to a `double` is required since no information is lost.

2. **(E)** The string argument contains two escape sequences: '\\', which means print a backslash (\), and '\n', which means go to a new line. Choice E is the only choice that does both of these.

3. **(D)** Short-circuit evaluation of the boolean expression will occur. The expression (n != 0) will evaluate to `false`, which makes the entire boolean expression `false`. Therefore the expression (x / n > 100) will not be evaluated. Hence no division by zero will occur, causing an `ArithmeticException` to be thrown. When the boolean expression has a value of `false`, only the `else` part of the statement, *statement2*, will be executed.

4. **(E)** For this choice, the integer division 13/5 will be evaluated to 2, which will then be cast to 2.0. The output will be 13/5 = 2.0. The compiler needs a way to recognize that real-valued division is required. All the other options provide a way.

5. **(E)** The operators \*, /, and % have equal precedence, all higher than -, and must be performed first, from left to right.

```
    13 - 3 * 6 / 4 % 3
=   13 - 18 / 4 % 3
=   13 - 4 % 3
=   13 - 1
=   12
```

6. **(C)** The expression must be evaluated as if parenthesized like this:

```
(2 + 3) * 12 / (7 - 4 + 8)
```

This becomes 5 \* 12 / 11 = 60 / 11 = 5.

7. **(B)** Although the expression is always algebraically true for nonzero x, the expression may evaluate to false. This could occur because of round-off error in performing the division and multiplication operations. Whether the right-hand side of the expression evaluates to exactly 3.0 depends on the value of x. Note that if x is zero, the expression will be evaluated to `false` because the right-hand side will be assigned a value of `Infinity`.

8. **(D)** Any time arithmetic operations are done with floating-point numbers, round-off error occurs. The `Math` class methods (see p. 176) such as `pow` and `sqrt` use various approximations to generate their answers to the required accuracy. Since they do different internal arithmetic, however, the round-off will usually not result in exactly the same answers. Note that choice A is not correct because both `Math.pow` and `Math.sqrt` return type `double`. Choice B is wrong because no matter how x was previously calculated, the same x is input to `pow` and `sqrt`. Choice C is wrong since round-off error occurs no matter how many bits are used to represent numbers. Choice E is wrong because if x is representable on the machine (i.e., hasn't overflowed), then its square root, $x^{1/2}$, will not overflow.

9. **(D)** Each `else` gets paired with the nearest unpaired `if`. Thus when the test (22 % 5 == 0) fails, the `else` part indicating that 22 `is` `negative` will be executed. This is clearly not the intent of the fragment, which can be fixed using delimiters:

```
int num = call to a method that reads an integer;
if (num > 0)
{
    if (num % 5 == 0)
        System.out.println(num);
}
else
    System.out.println(num + " is negative");
```

10. **(A)** Since the first test (x >= 0) is `true`, the matching `else` part, y = -x, will not be executed. Since (x <= 100) is `true`, the matching `else` part, y = x * 2, will not be executed. The variable y will be set to x * 3 (i.e., 90) and will now fail the test y < 50. Thus, x will never be altered in this algorithm. Final values are x = 30 and y = 90.

11. **(C)** In order for !(A || B || C) to be true, (A || B || C) must evaluate to false. This will happen only if A, B, and C are *all* false. Choice A evaluates to true when A and B are false and C is true. In choice B, if any *one* of A, B, or C is false, the boolean expression evaluates to true. In choice D, if any one of A, B, or C is false, the boolean expression evaluates to true since we have !(false). All that's required for choice E to evaluate to true is for A to be false. Since true||(any) evaluates to true, both B and C can be either true or false.

12. **(D)** To evaluate to `true`, the expression must reduce to `true && true`. We therefore need !(false) && true. Choice D is the only condition that guarantees this: a > b provides !(false) for the left-hand expression, and a > b and b > 0 implies both a and b positive, which leads to `true` for the right-hand expression. Choice E, for example, will provide true for the right-hand expression only if a < 0. You have no information about a and can't make assumptions about it.

13. **(A)** If `(c < a)` is false, `((c == a*b) && (c < a))` evaluates to `false` irrespective of the value of `c == a*b`. In this case, `!(c == a*b && c < a)` evaluates to `true`. Then `(a < b) || true` evaluates to `true` irrespective of the value of the test `(a < b)`. In all the other choices, the given expression *may* be `true`. There is not enough information given to guarantee this, however.

14. **(C)** If `a == b` is false, then `a != b` is true. Thus, the second piece of the compound test must be evaluated before the value of the whole test is known. Since `a == b` is false, `a - b` is not equal to zero. Thus, there is no division by zero, and no exception will be thrown. Also, since the relative values of `a`, `b`, and `n` are unknown, the value of the test `n / (a - b) > 90` is unknown, and there is insufficient information to determine whether the compound test is true or false. Thus, either /* *statement 1* */ or /* *statement 2* */ will be executed.

15. **(A)** If $n \geq 1$, both segments will print out the integers from 1 through n. If $n \leq 0$, both segments will fail the test immediately and do nothing.

16. **(D)** The `(value != SENTINEL)` test occurs before a value has been read from the list. This will cause `0` to be processed, which may cause an error. The code must be fixed by reading the first value before doing the test:

```
final int SENTINEL = -999;
int value = ...;           //read user input
while (value != SENTINEL)
{
    //code to process value
    value = ...;           //read user input
}
```

17. **(D)** Here is a trace of the values of `x` and `y` during execution. Note that the condition `(y % x == 1)` is never `true` in this example.

| x | 10 |  |  |  | 7 |  |  |  | 4 |
|---|----|---|---|---|---|---|---|----|---|
| y |  | 3 | 6 | 12 |  | 3 | 6 | 12 |  |

The `while` loop terminates when `x` is 4 since the test `while (x > 5)` fails.

18. **(B)** The algorithm finds the remainder when the sum of the first three digits of `n` is divided by 7. If this remainder is equal to the fourth digit, `checkDigit`, the method returns `true`, otherwise `false`. Note that `(6+1+4) % 7` equals 4. Thus, only choice B is a valid number.

19. **(C)** As `n` gets broken down into its digits, `nRemaining` is the part of `n` that remains after each digit is stripped off. Thus, `nRemaining` is a self-documenting name that helps describe what is happening. Choice A is false because every digit can be stripped off using some sequence of integer division and mod. Choice B is false because `num` is passed by value and therefore will not be altered when the method is exited (see p. 112). Eliminate choice D: When the method is exited, all local variables are destroyed. Choice E is nonsense.

20. **(B)** The outer loop produces five rows of output. Each pass through the inner loop goes from `i` down to 1. Thus five odd numbers starting at 9 are printed in the first row, four odd numbers starting at 7 in the second row, and so on.

21. **(E)** All three algorithms produce the given output. The outer `for (int i ...)` loop produces six rows, and the inner `for (int k ...)` loops produce the symbols in each row.

22. **(D)** Statement I is false, since if $100 \leq num \leq 109$, the body of the `while` loop will be executed just once. (After this single pass through the loop, the value of `num` will be 10, and the test `if (num > 10)` will fail.) With just one pass, `newNum` will be a one-digit number, equal to `temp` (which was the original `num % 10`). Note that statement II is true: There cannot be an infinite loop since `num /= 10` guarantees termination of the loop. Statement III is true because if $num \leq 10$, the loop will be skipped, and `newNum` will keep its original value of 0.

23. **(D)** The algorithm works by stripping off the rightmost digit of `n` (stored in `rem`), multiplying the current value of `revNum` by 10, and adding that rightmost digit. When `n` has been stripped down to no digits (i.e., `n == 0` is true), `revNum` is complete. Both segments II and III work. Segment I fails to produce the right output whenever the input value `n` has first digit less than (number of digits – 1). For these cases, the output has the first digit of the original number missing from the end of the returned number.

# Classes and Objects

3

*Work is the curse of the drinking classes.*
—*Oscar Wilde*

→ **Objects and classes**          → **Keywords** public, private, **and** static
→ **Data encapsulation**           → **Methods**
→ **References**                    → **Scope of variables**

## OBJECTS

Most programs that you write involve at least one thing that is being created or manipulated by the program. This thing, together with the operations that manipulate it, is called an *object*.

Consider, for example, a program that must test the validity of a four-digit code number for accessing a photocopy machine. Rules for validity are provided. The object is a four-digit code number. Some of the operations to manipulate the object could be readNumber, getSeparateDigits, testValidity, and writeNumber.

Any given program can have several different types of objects. For example, a program that maintains a database of all books in a library has at least two objects:

1. A Book object, with operations like getTitle, getAuthor, isOnShelf, isFiction, and goOutOfPrint.
2. A ListOfBooks object, with operations like search, addBook, removeBook, and sortByAuthor.

An object is characterized by its *state* and *behavior*. For example, a book has a state described by its title, author, whether it's on the shelf, and so on. It also has behavior, like going out of print.

Notice that an object is an idea, separate from the concrete details of a programming language. It corresponds to some real-world object that is being represented by the program.

All object-oriented programming languages have a way to represent an object as a variable in a program. In Java, a variable that represents an object is called an *object reference*.

## CLASSES

A *class* is a software blueprint for implementing objects of a given type. In object-oriented programming, an object is a single *instance* of the class.

The current state of a given object is maintained in its *data fields* or *instance variables*, provided by the class. The *methods* of the class provide both the behaviors exhibited by the object

.and the operations that manipulate the object. Combining an object's data and methods into a single unit called a class is known as *data encapsulation*.

Here is the framework for a simple bank account class:

```
public class BankAccount
{
    private String password;
    private double balance;
    public static final double OVERDRAWN_PENALTY = 20.00;

  //constructors
    /** Default constructor.
     *  Constructs bank account with default values. */
    public BankAccount()
    { /* implementation code */ }

    /** Constructs bank account with specified password and balance. */
    public BankAccount(String acctPassword, double acctBalance)
    { /* implementation code */ }

    //accessor
    /** Returns balance of this account. */
    public double getBalance()
    { /* implementation code */ }

    //mutators
    /** Deposits amount in bank account with given password.
     */
    public void deposit(String acctPassword, double amount)
    { /* implementation code */ }

    /** Withdraws amount from bank account with given password.
     *  Assesses penalty if balance is less than amount.
     */
    public void withdraw(String acctPassword, double amount)
    { /* implementation code */ }
}
```

## PUBLIC, PRIVATE, AND STATIC

The keyword `public` preceding the class declaration signals that the class is usable by all *client programs*, namely, pieces of code that are outside the class and use that class. If a class is not public, it can be used only by classes in its own package. In the AP Java subset, all classes are public.

Similarly, *public methods* are accessible to all client programs. Clients, however, are not privy to the class implementation and may not access the private instance variables and private methods of the class. In Java, restriction of access is implemented by using the keyword `private`. *Private methods and variables in a class can be accessed only by methods of that class.* Even though Java allows public instance variables, in the AP Java subset all instance variables are private.

A *static variable* (class variable) contains a value that is shared by all instances of the class. "Static" means that memory allocation happens once.

Typical uses of a static variable are to

- keep track of statistics for objects of the class.
- accumulate a total.
- provide a new identity number for each new object of the class.

For example,

```
public class Employee
{
    private String name;
    private static int employeeCount = 0; //number of employees

    public Employee(< parameter list >)
    {
        < initialization of private instance variables >
        employeeCount++; //increment count of all employees
    }
    ...
}
```

Notice that the static variable was initialized outside the constructor and that its value can be changed.

*Static final variables* (constants) in a class cannot be changed. They are often declared public (see some examples of Math class constants on p. 176). The variable OVERDRAWN_PENALTY is an example in the BankAccount class. Since the variable is public, it can be used in any client method. The keyword static indicates that there is a single value of the variable that applies to the whole class, rather than a new instance for each object of the class. A client method would refer to the variable as BankAccount.OVERDRAWN_PENALTY. In its own class it is referred to as simply OVERDRAWN_PENALTY.

See p. 105 for static methods.

## METHODS

## Headers

All method headers, with the exception of constructors (see on the next page) and static methods (p. 105), look like this:

```
public     void     withdraw (String password, double amount)
```

access specifier    return type    method name      parameter list

**NOTE**

1. The *access specifier* tells which other methods can call this method (see the "Public, Private, and Static" section on the previous page).
2. A *return type* of void signals that the method does not return a value.
3. Items in the *parameter list* are separated by commas.

The implementation of the method directly follows the header, enclosed in a {} block.

# Types of Methods

## CONSTRUCTORS

A *constructor* creates an object of the class. You can recognize a constructor by its name—always the same as the class. Also, a constructor has no return type.

Having several constructors provides different ways of initializing class objects. For example, there are two constructors in the BankAccount class.

1. The *default constructor* has no arguments. It provides reasonable initial values for an object. Here is its implementation:

```
/** Default constructor.
 *  Constructs a bank account with default values. */
public BankAccount()
{
    password = "";
    balance = 0.0;
}
```

In a client method, the declaration

```
BankAccount b = new BankAccount();
```

constructs a BankAccount object with a balance of zero and a password equal to the empty string. The new operator returns the address of this newly constructed object. The variable b is assigned the value of this address—we say "b is a *reference* to the object." Picture the setup like this:

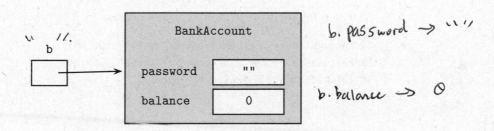

2. The constructor with parameters sets the instance variables of a BankAccount object to the values of those parameters.
   Here is the implementation:

```
/** Constructor. Constructs a bank account with
 *  specified password and balance. */
public BankAccount(String acctPassword, double acctBalance)
{
    password = acctPassword;
    balance = acctBalance;
}
```

In a client program a declaration that uses this constructor needs matching parameters:

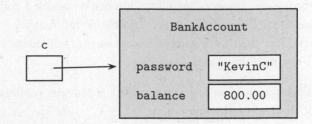

```
BankAccount c = new BankAccount("KevinC", 800.00);
```

*Password    Balance* (handwritten)

**NOTE**

b and c are *object variables* that store the *addresses* of their respective `BankAccount` objects. They do not store the objects themselves (see "References" on p. 109).

**ACCESSORS**

An *accessor method* is a public method that accesses a class object without altering the object. An accessor returns some information about the object, and it allows other objects to get the value of a private instance variable.

The `BankAccount` class has a single accessor method, `getBalance()`. Here is its implementation:

```
/** Returns the balance of this account. */
public double getBalance()
{ return balance; }
```

A client program may use this method as follows:

```
BankAccount b1 = new BankAccount("MattW", 500.00);
BankAccount b2 = new BankAccount("DannyB", 650.50);
if (b1.getBalance() > b2.getBalance())
    ...
```

**NOTE**

1. The *. operator* (dot operator) indicates that `getBalance()` is a method of the class to which b1 and b2 belong, namely the `BankAccount class`.
2. A non-void method returns a single value, whose type is specified in the header of the method.

**MUTATORS**

A *mutator method* changes the state of an object by modifying at least one of its instance variables. It is often a void method (i.e., has no return type). A mutator can be a private helper method within its class, or a public method that allows other objects to change a private instance variable.

Here are the implementations of the `deposit` and `withdraw` methods, each of which alters the value of `balance` in the `BankAccount` class:

```
/** Deposits amount in a bank account with the given password.
 */
public void deposit(String acctPassword, double amount)
{
    if (!acctPassword.equals(password))
        /* throw an exception */
    else
        balance += amount;
}


/** Withdraws amount from bank account with given password.
 *  Assesses penalty if balance is less than amount.
 */
public void withdraw(String acctPassword, double amount)
{
    if (!acctPassword.equals(password))
        /* throw an exception */
    else
    {
        balance -= amount;        //allows negative balance
        if (balance < 0)
            balance -= OVERDRAWN_PENALTY;
    }
}
```

*"void function".*
*applicable*

A mutator method in a client program is invoked in the same way as an accessor: using an object variable with the dot operator. For example, assuming valid `BankAccount` declarations for `b1` and `b2`:

```
b1.withdraw("MattW", 200.00);
b2.deposit("DannyB", 35.68);
```

## STATIC METHODS

**STATIC METHODS VS. INSTANCE METHODS**  The methods discussed in the preceding sections—constructors, accessors, and mutators—all operate on individual objects of a class. They are called *instance methods.* A method that performs an operation for the entire class, not its individual objects, is called a *static method* (sometimes called a *class method*).

The implementation of a static method uses the keyword `static` in its header. There is no implied object in the code (as there is in an instance method). Thus, if the code tries to call an instance method or invoke a private instance variable for this nonexistent object, a syntax error will occur. A static method can, however, use a static variable in its code. For example, in the `Employee` example on p. 102, you could add a static method that returns the `employeeCount`:

```
public static int getEmployeeCount()
{ return employeeCount; }
```

Here's an example of a static method that might be used in the `BankAccount` class. Suppose the class has a static variable `intRate`, declared as follows:

```
private static double intRate;
```

*Changes all static methods in class.*

The static method `getInterestRate` may be as follows:

```
public static double getInterestRate()
{
    System.out.println("Enter interest rate for bank account");
    System.out.println("Enter in decimal form:");
    intRate = ...;          // read user input
    return intRate;
}
```

Since the rate that's read in by this method applies to all bank accounts in the class, not to any particular `BankAccount` object, it's appropriate that the method should be static.

Recall that an instance method is invoked in a client program by using an object variable followed by the dot operator followed by the method name:

```
BankAccount b = new BankAccount();   //invokes the deposit method for
b.deposit(acctPassword, amount);     //BankAccount object b
```

A static method, by contrast, is invoked by using the *class name* with the dot operator:

```
double interestRate = BankAccount.getInterestRate();
```

**STATIC METHODS IN A DRIVER CLASS**   Often a class that contains the `main()` method is used as a driver program to test other classes. Usually such a class creates no objects of the class. So all the methods in the class must be static. Note that at the start of program execution, no objects exist yet. So the `main()` method must *always* be static.

For example, here is a program that tests a class for reading integers entered at the keyboard:

```
import java.util.*;
public class GetListTest
{
    /** Returns a list of integers from the keyboard. */
    public static ArrayList<Integer> getList()
    {
        ArrayList<Integer> a = new ArrayList<Integer>();
        < code to read integers into a>
        return a;
    }

    /** Write contents of ArrayList a.
     */
    public static void writeList(ArrayList<Integer> a)
    {
        System.out.println("List is : " + a);
    }

    public static void main(String[] args)
    {
        ArrayList<Integer> list = getList();
        writeList(list);
    }
}
```

**NOTE**

1. The calls to `writeList(list)` and `getList()` do not need to be preceded by `GetListTest` plus a dot because `main` is not a client program: It is in the same class as `getList` and `writeList`.

2. If you omit the keyword `static` from the `getList` or `writeList` header, you get an error message like the following:

```
Can't make static reference to method getList()
in class GetListTest
```

The compiler has recognized that there was no object variable preceding the method call, which means that the methods were static and should have been declared as such.

## Method Overloading

*Overloaded methods* are two or more methods in the same class (or a subclass of that class) that have the same name but different parameter lists. For example,

```
public class DoOperations
{
    public int product(int n) { return n * n; }
    public double product(double x) { return x * x; }
    public double product(int x, int y) { return x * y; }
    ...
```

The compiler figures out which method to call by examining the method's *signature*. The signature of a method consists of the method's name and a list of the parameter types. Thus, the signatures of the overloaded `product` methods are

```
product(int)
product(double)
product(int, int)
```

Note that for overloading purposes, the return type of the method is irrelevant. You can't have two methods with identical signatures but different return types. The compiler will complain that the method call is ambiguous.

Having more than one constructor in the same class is an example of overloading. Overloaded constructors provide a choice of ways to initialize objects of the class.

## SCOPE

The *scope* of a variable or method is the region in which that variable or method is visible and can be accessed.

The instance variables, static variables, and methods of a class belong to that class's scope, which extends from the opening brace to the closing brace of the class definition. Within the class all instance variables and methods are accessible and can be referred to simply by name (no dot operator!).

A *local variable* is defined inside a method. It can even be defined inside a statement. Its scope extends from the point where it is declared to the end of the block in which its declaration occurs. A *block* is a piece of code enclosed in a {} pair. When a block is exited, the memory for a local variable is automatically recycled.

Local variables take precedence over instance variables with the same name. (Using the same name, however, creates ambiguity for the programmer, leading to errors. You should avoid the practice.)

## The this Keyword

An instance method is always called for a particular object. This object is an *implicit parameter* for the method and is referred to with the keyword this. You are expected to know this vocabulary for the exam.

In the implementation of instance methods, all instance variables can be written with the prefix this followed by the dot operator.

➡️ **Example 1** _____

In the method call obj.doSomething("Mary",num), where obj is some class object and doSomething is a method of that class, "Mary" and num, the parameters in parentheses, are *explicit* parameters, whereas obj is an *implicit* parameter.

➡️ **Example 2** _____

Here's an example where this is used as a parameter:

```
public class Person
{
    private String name;
    private int age;

    public Person(String aName, int anAge)
    {
        name = aName;
        age = anAge;
    }

    /** Returns the String form of this person. */
    public String toString()
    { return name + " " + age; }

    public void printPerson()
    { System.out.println(this); }

    //Other variables and methods are not shown.
}
```

Suppose a client class has these lines of code:

```
Person p = new Person("Dan", 10);
p.printPerson();
```

The statement

```
System.out.println(this);
```

in the printPerson method means "print the current Person object." The output should be Dan 10. Note that System.out.println invokes the toString method of the Person class.

## Example 3 _____

The `deposit` method of the `BankAccount` class can refer to `balance` as follows:

```java
public void deposit(String acctPassword, double amount)
{
    this.balance += amount;
}
```

The use of `this` is unnecessary in the above example.

## Example 4 _____

Consider a rational number class called `Rational`, which has two private instance variables:

```java
private int num;          //numerator
private int denom;        //denominator
```

Now consider a constructor for the `Rational` class:

```java
public Rational(int num, int denom)
{
    this.num = num;
    this.denom = denom;
}
```

It is definitely *not* a good idea to use the same name for the explicit parameters and the private instance variables. But if you do, you can avoid errors by referring to `this.num` and `this.denom` for the current object that is being constructed. (This particular use of `this` will not be tested on the exam.)

## REFERENCES

## Reference vs. Primitive Data Types

Simple built-in data types, like `double` and `int`, as well as types `char` and `boolean`, are *primitive* data types. All objects and arrays are *reference* data types, such as `String`, `Random`, `int[]`, `String[][]`, `Cat` (assuming there is a `Cat` class in the program), and so on. The difference between primitive and reference data types lies in the way they are stored.

Consider the statements

```java
int num1 = 3;
int num2 = num1;
```

The variables `num1` and `num2` can be thought of as memory slots, labeled `num1` and `num2`, respectively:

num1       num2

[3]       [3]

If either of the above variables is now changed, the other is not affected. Each has its own memory slot.

Contrast this with the declaration of a reference data type. Recall that an object is created using `new`:

```
Date d = new Date(2, 17, 1948);
```

This declaration creates a reference variable d that refers to a Date object. The value of d is the address in memory of that object:

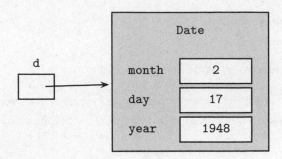

Suppose the following declaration is now made:

```
Date birthday = d;
```

This statement creates the reference variable birthday, which contains the same address as d:

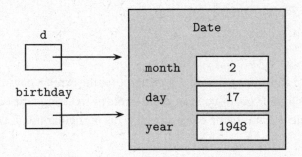

Having two references for the same object is known as *aliasing*. Aliasing can cause unintended problems for the programmer. The statement

```
d.changeDate();
```

will automatically change the object referred to by birthday as well.

What the programmer probably intended was to create a second object called birthday whose attributes exactly matched those of d. This cannot be accomplished without using new. For example,

```
Date birthday = new Date(d.getMonth(), d.getDay(), d.getYear());
```

The statement d.changeDate() will now leave the birthday object unchanged.

## The Null Reference

The declaration

```
BankAccount b;
```

defines a reference b that is uninitialized. (To construct the object that b refers to requires the new operator and a BankAccount constructor.) An uninitialized object variable is called a *null reference* or *null pointer*. You can test whether a variable refers to an object or is uninitialized by using the keyword null:

```
    if (b == null)
```

If a reference is not null, it can be set to null with the statement

```
    b = null;
```

An attempt to invoke an instance method with a null reference may cause your program to terminate with a `NullPointerException`. For example,

```
    public class PersonalFinances
    {
        BankAccount b;                    //b is a null reference
           ...
        b.withdraw(acctPassword, amt);    //throws a NullPointerException
           ...                            //if b not constructed with new
```

**NOTE**

If you fail to initialize a local variable in a method before you use it, you will get a compile-time error. If you make the same mistake with an instance variable of a class, the compiler provides reasonable default values for primitive variables (0 for numbers, `false` for booleans), and the code may run without error. However, if you don't initialize *reference* instance variables in a class, as in the above example, the compiler will set them to `null`. Any method call for an object of the class that tries to access the null reference will cause a run-time error: The program will terminate with a `NullPointerException`.

> Do not make a method call with an object whose value is `null`.

## Method Parameters

**FORMAL VS. ACTUAL PARAMETERS**

The header of a method defines the *parameters* of that method. For example, consider the `withdraw` method of the `BankAccount` class:

```
    public class BankAccount
    {  ...
        public void withdraw(String acctPassword, double amount)
           ...
```

This method has two explicit parameters, `acctPassword` and `amount`. These are *dummy* or *formal parameters*. Think of them as placeholders for the pair of *actual parameters* or *arguments* that will be supplied by a particular method call in a client program.

For example,

```
    BankAccount b = new BankAccount("TimB", 1000);
    b.withdraw("TimB", 250);
```

Here `"TimB"` and 250 are the actual parameters that match up with `acctPassword` and `amount` for the `withdraw` method.

**NOTE**

1. The number of arguments in the method call must equal the number of parameters in the method header, and the type of each argument must be compatible with the type of each corresponding parameter.

2. In addition to its explicit parameters, the `withdraw` method has an implicit parameter, `this`, the `BankAccount` from which money will be withdrawn. In the method call

```
b.withdraw("TimB", 250);
```

the actual parameter that matches up with `this` is the object reference `b`.

## PASSING PRIMITIVE TYPES AS PARAMETERS

Parameters are *passed by value*. For primitive types this means that when a method is called, a new memory slot is allocated for each parameter. The value of each argument is copied into the newly created memory slot corresponding to each parameter.

During execution of the method, the parameters are local to that method. *Any changes made to the parameters will not affect the values of the arguments in the calling program.* When the method is exited, the local memory slots for the parameters are erased.

Here's an example. What will the output be?

```java
public class ParamTest
{
    public static void foo(int x, double y)
    {
        x = 3;
        y = 2.5;
    }

    public static void main(String[] args)
    {
        int a = 7;
        double b = 6.5;
        foo(a, b);
        System.out.println(a + "   " + b);
    }
}
```

The output will be

```
7   6.5
```

The arguments `a` and `b` remain unchanged, despite the method call!

This can be understood by picturing the state of the memory slots during execution of the program.

Just before the `foo(a, b)` method call:

```
  a         b
+---+     +-----+
| 7 |     | 6.5 |
+---+     +-----+
```

At the time of the `foo(a, b)` method call:

```
  a         b
+---+     +-----+
| 7 |     | 6.5 |
+---+     +-----+

  x         y
+---+     +-----+
| 7 |     | 6.5 |
+---+     +-----+
```

Just before exiting the method: (Note that the values of x and y have been changed.)

a        b

| 7 | | 6.5 |

x        y

| 3 | | 2.5 |

After exiting the method: (Note that the memory slots for x and y have been reclaimed. The values of a and b remain unchanged.)

a        b

| 7 | | 6.5 |

## PASSING OBJECTS AS PARAMETERS

In Java both primitive types and object references are passed by value. When an object's reference is a parameter, the same mechanism of copying into local memory is used. The key difference is that the *address* (reference) is copied, not the values of the individual instance variables. As with primitive types, changes made to the parameters will not change the values of the matching arguments. What this means in practice is that it is not possible for a method to replace an object with another one—you can't change the reference that was passed. It is, however, possible to change the state of the object to which the parameter refers through methods that act on the object.

### ➡ Example 1 _____

A method that changes the state of an object:

```
/** Subtracts fee from balance in b if current balance too low. */
public static void chargeFee(BankAccount b, String password,
        double fee)
{
    final double MIN_BALANCE = 10.00;
    if (b.getBalance() < MIN_BALANCE)
        b.withdraw(password, fee);
}

public static void main(String[] args)
{
    final double FEE = 5.00;
    BankAccount andysAccount = new BankAccount("AndyS", 7.00);
    chargeFee(andysAccount, "AndyS", FEE);
        ...
}
```

Here are the memory slots before the chargeFee method call:

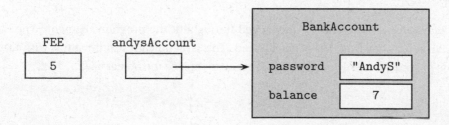

At the time of the `chargeFee` method call, copies of the matching parameters are made:

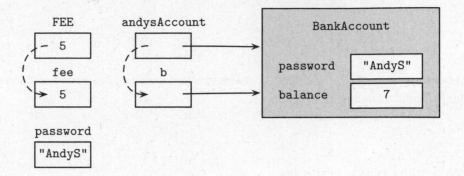

Just before exiting the method: (The `balance` field of the `BankAccount` object has been changed.)

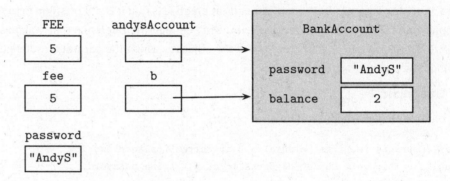

After exiting the method: (All parameter memory slots have been erased, but the object remains altered.)

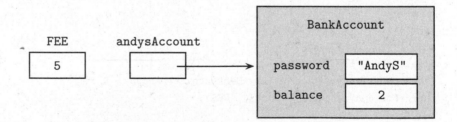

**NOTE**

The `andysAccount` reference is unchanged throughout the program segment. The object to which it refers, however, has been changed. This is significant. Contrast this with Example 2 on the next page in which an attempt is made to replace the object itself.

## ➥ Example 2 _____

A `chooseBestAccount` method attempts—erroneously—to set its `betterFund` parameter to the `BankAccount` with the higher balance:

```
public static void chooseBestAccount(BankAccount better,
            BankAccount b1, BankAccount b2)
{
    if (b1.getBalance() > b2.getBalance())
        better = b1;
    else
        better = b2;
}


public static void main(String[] args)
{
    BankAccount briansFund = new BankAccount("BrianL", 10000);
    BankAccount paulsFund = new BankAccount("PaulM", 90000);
    BankAccount betterFund = null;

    chooseBestAccount(betterFund, briansFund, paulsFund);
    ...
}
```

The intent is that `betterFund` will be a reference to the `paulsFund` object after execution of the `chooseBestAccount` statement. A look at the memory slots illustrates why this fails.

Before the `chooseBestAccount` method call:

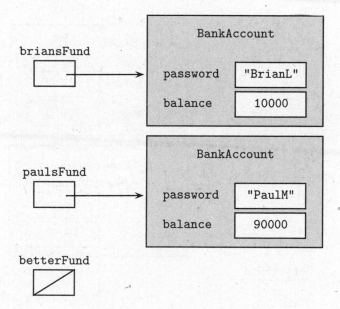

At the time of the `chooseBestAccount` method call, copies of the matching references are made:

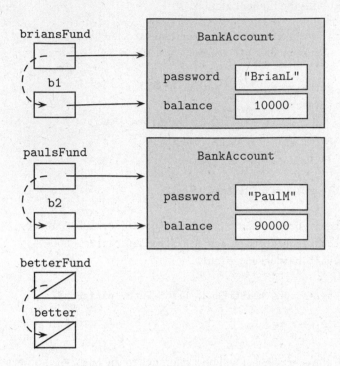

Just before exiting the method, the value of `better` has been changed; `betterFund`, however, remains unchanged:

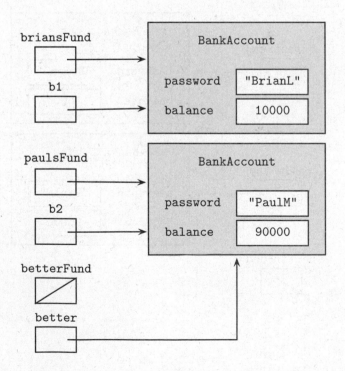

**After** exiting the method, all parameter slots have been erased:

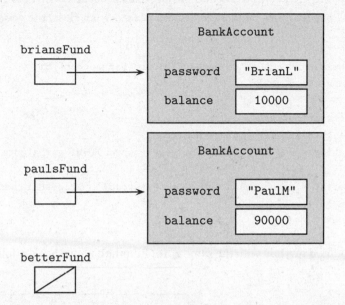

Note that the betterFund reference continues to be null, contrary to the programmer's intent.

The way to fix the problem is to modify the method so that it returns the better account. Returning an object from a method means that you are returning the address of the object.

```
public static BankAccount chooseBestAccount(BankAccount b1,
        BankAccount b2)
{
    BankAccount better;
    if (b1.getBalance() > b2.getBalance())
        better = b1;
    else
        better = b2;
    return better;
}

public static void main(String[] args)
{
    BankAccount briansFund = new BankAccount("BrianL", 10000);
    BankAccount paulsFund = new BankAccount("PaulM", 90000);
    BankAccount betterFund = chooseBestAccount(briansFund, paulsFund);
        ...
}
```

**NOTE**

The effect of this is to create the betterFund reference, which refers to the same object as paulsFund:

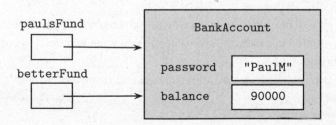

What the method does *not* do is create a new object to which `betterFund` refers. To do that would require the keyword `new` and use of a `BankAccount` constructor. Assuming that a `getPassword()` accessor has been added to the `BankAccount` class, the code would look like this:

```
public static BankAccount chooseBestAccount(BankAccount b1,
        BankAccount b2)
{
    BankAccount better;
    if (b1.getBalance() > b2.getBalance())
        better = new BankAccount(b1.getPassword(), b1.getBalance());
    else
        better = new BankAccount(b2.getPassword(), b2.getBalance());
    return better;
}
```

Using this modified method with the same `main()` method above has the following effect:

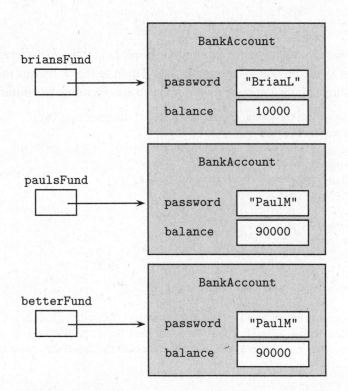

Modifying more than one object in a method can be accomplished using a *wrapper class* (see p. 173).

## Chapter Summary

By now you should be able to write code for any given object, with its private data fields and methods encapsulated in a class. Be sure that you know the various types of methods—static, instance, and overloaded.

You should also understand the difference between storage of primitive types and the references used for objects.

Questions 1–3 refer to the Time class declared below.

```java
public class Time
{
    private int hrs;
    private int mins;
    private int secs;

    public Time()
    { /* implementation not shown */ }

    public Time(int h, int m, int s)
    { /* implementation not shown */ }

    /** Resets time to hrs = h, mins = m, secs = s. */
    public void resetTime(int h, int m, int s)
    { /* implementation not shown */ }

    /** Advances time by one second. */
    public void increment()
    { /* implementation not shown */ }

    /** Returns true if this time equals t, false otherwise. */
    public boolean equals(Time t)
    { /* implementation not shown */ }

    /** Returns true if this time is earlier than t, false otherwise. */
    public boolean lessThan(Time t)
    { /* implementation not shown */ }

    /** Returns a String with the time in the form hrs:mins:secs. */
    public String toString()
    { /* implementation not shown */ }
}
```

1. Which of the following is a false statement about the methods?
   (A) equals, lessThan, and toString are all accessor methods.
   (B) increment is a mutator method.
   (C) Time() is the default constructor.
   (D) The Time class has three constructors.
   (E) There are no static methods in this class.

2. Which of the following represents correct *implementation code* for the constructor with parameters?

    (A)  `hrs = 0;`
           `mins = 0;`
           `secs = 0;`

    (B)  `hrs = h;`
           `mins = m;`
           `secs = s;`

    (C)  `resetTime(hrs, mins, secs);`

    (D)  `h = hrs;`
           `m = mins;`
           `s = secs;`

    (E)  `Time = new Time(h, m, s);`

3. A client class has a `display` method that writes the time represented by its parameter:

```
/** Outputs time t in the form hrs:mins:secs.
 */
public void display (Time t)
{
    /* method body */
}
```

Which of the following are correct replacements for /* *method body* */?

    I  `Time T = new Time(h, m, s);`
        `System.out.println(T);`

    II  `System.out.println(t.hrs + ":" + t.mins + ":" + t.secs);`

    III  `System.out.println(t);`

    (A)  I only
    (B)  II only
    (C)  III only
    (D)  II and III only
    (E)  I, II, and III

4. Which statement about parameters is false?
    (A)  The scope of parameters is the method in which they are defined.
    (B)  Static methods have no implicit parameter this.
    (C)  Two overloaded methods in the same class must have parameters with different names.
    (D)  All parameters in Java are passed by value.
    (E)  Two different constructors in a given class can have the same number of parameters.

Questions 5–11 refer to the following `Date` class declaration.

```java
public class Date
{
    private int day;
    private int month;
    private int year;

    public Date()                         //default constructor
    {
        ...
    }

    public Date(int mo, int da, int yr)    //constructor
    {
        ...
    }

    public int month()        //returns month of Date
    {
        ...
    }

    public int day()          //returns day of Date
    {
        ...
    }

    public int year()          //returns year of Date
    {
        ...
    }

    //Returns String representation of Date as "m/d/y", e.g. 4/18/1985.
    public String toString()
    {
        ...
    }
}
```

5. Which of the following correctly constructs a `Date` object in a client class?

    (A) `Date d = new (2, 13, 1947);`

    (B) `Date d = new Date(2, 13, 1947);`

    (C) `Date d;`
        `d = new (2, 13, 1947);`

    (D) `Date d;`
        `d = Date(2, 13, 1947);`

    (E) `Date d = Date(2, 13, 1947);`

6. Which of the following will cause an error message?

```
 I  Date d1 = new Date(8, 2, 1947);
    Date d2 = d1;

II  Date d1 = null;
    Date d2 = d1;

III Date d = null;
    int x = d.year();
```

(A) I only
(B) II only
(C) III only
(D) II and III only
(E) I, II, and III

7. A client program creates a Date object as follows.

```
Date d = new Date(1, 13, 2002);
```

Which of the following subsequent code segments will cause an error?
(A) String s = d.toString();
(B) int x = d.day();
(C) Date e = d;
(D) Date e = new Date(1, 13, 2002);
(E) int y = d.year;

8. Consider the implementation of a write() method that is added to the Date class.

```
/** Write the date in the form m/d/y, for example 2/17/1948. */
public void write()
{
    /* implementation code */
}
```

Which of the following could be used as /* *implementation code* */?

```
 I System.out.println(month + "/" + day + "/" + year);

II System.out.println(month() + "/" + day() + "/" + year());

III System.out.println(this);
```

(A) I only
(B) II only
(C) III only
(D) II and III only
(E) I, II, and III

9. Here is a client program that uses Date objects:

```
public class BirthdayStuff
{
    public static Date findBirthdate()
    {
        /* code to get birthDate */
        return birthDate;
    }

    public static void main(String[] args)
    {
        Date d = findBirthdate();
            ...
    }
}
```

Which of the following is a correct replacement for
/* code to get birthDate */?

```
 I System.out.println("Enter birthdate: mo, day, yr: ");
   int m = ...;                    //read user input
   int d = ...;                    //read user input
   int y = ...;                    //read user input
   Date birthDate = new Date(m, d, y);

 II System.out.println("Enter birthdate: mo, day, yr: ");
   int birthDate.month() = ...;       //read user input
   int birthDate.day() = ...;         //read user input
   int birthDate.year() = ...;        //read user input
   Date birthDate = new Date(birthDate.month(), birthDate.day(),
       birthDate.year());

 III System.out.println("Enter birthdate: mo, day, yr: ");
   int birthDate.month = ...;         //read user input
   int birthDate.day = ...;           //read user input
   int birthDate.year = ...;          //read user input
   Date birthDate = new Date(birthDate.month, birthDate.day,
       birthDate.year);
```

(A) I only
(B) II only
(C) III only
(D) I and II only
(E) I and III only

10. A method in a client program for the Date class has the following declaration.

```
Date d1 = new Date(mo, da, yr);
```

Here, mo, da, and yr are previously defined integer variables. The same method now creates a second Date object d2 that is an exact copy of the object d1 refers to. Which of the following code segments will not do this correctly?

I Date d2 = d1;

II Date d2 = new Date(mo, da, yr);

III Date d2 = new Date(d1.month(), d1.day(), d1.year());

(A) I only
(B) II only
(C) III only
(D) II and III only
(E) I, II, and III

11. The Date class is modified by adding the following mutator method:

```
public void addYears(int n)    //add n years to date
```

Here is part of a poorly coded client program that uses the Date class:

```
public static void addCentury(Date recent, Date old)
{
    old.addYears(100);
    recent = old;
}

public static void main(String[] args)
{
    Date oldDate = new Date(1, 13, 1900);
    Date recentDate = null;
    addCentury(recentDate, oldDate);
        . . .
}
```

Which will be true after executing this code?
(A) A NullPointerException is thrown.
(B) The oldDate object remains unchanged.
(C) recentDate is a null reference.
(D) recentDate refers to the same object as oldDate.
(E) recentDate refers to a separate object whose contents are the same as those of oldDate.

12. Here are the private instance variables for a `Frog` object:

```
public class Frog
{
    private String species;
    private int age;
    private double weight;
    private Position position;     //position (x,y) in pond
    private boolean amAlive;
        ...
```

Which of the following methods in the `Frog` class is the best candidate for being a static method?

(A) swim                    //frog swims to new position in pond

(B) getPondTemperature      //returns temperature of pond

(C) eat                     //frog eats and gains weight

(D) getWeight               //returns weight of frog

(E) die                     //frog dies with some probability based
                            //on frog's age and pond temperature

13. What output will be produced by this program?

```
public class Mystery
{
    public static void strangeMethod(int x, int y)
    {
        x += y;
        y *= x;
        System.out.println(x + " " + y);
    }

    public static void main(String[] args)
    {
        int a = 6, b = 3;
        strangeMethod(a, b);
        System.out.println(a + " " + b);
    }
}
```

(A) 36
    9

(B) 3 6
    9

(C) 9 27
    9 27

(D) 6 3
    9 27

(E) 9 27
    6 3

Questions 14–17 refer to the following definition of the Rational class.

```java
public class Rational
{
    private int numerator;
    private int denominator;

    /** default constructor */
    Rational()
    { /* implementation not shown */ }

    /** Constructs a Rational with numerator n and
     *  denominator 1. */
    Rational(int n)
    { /* implementation not shown */ }

    /** Constructs a Rational with specified numerator and
     *  denominator. */
    Rational(int numer, int denom)
    { /* implementation not shown */ }

    /** Returns numerator. */
    int numerator()
    { /* implementation not shown */ }

    /** Returns denominator. */
    int denominator()
    { /* implementation not shown */ }

    /** Returns (this + r). Leaves this unchanged.
     */
    public Rational plus(Rational r)
    { /* implementation not shown */ }

    //Similarly for times, minus, divide
        ...
    /** Ensures denominator > 0. */
    private void fixSigns()
    { /* implementation not shown */ }

    /** Ensures lowest terms. */
    private void reduce()
    { /* implementation not shown */ }
}
```

14. The method reduce() is not a public method because
    (A) methods whose return type is void cannot be public.
    (B) methods that change this cannot be public.
    (C) the reduce() method is not intended for use by objects outside the Rational class.
    (D) the reduce() method is intended for use only by objects outside the Rational class.
    (E) the reduce() method uses only the private data fields of the Rational class.

15. The constructors in the `Rational` class allow initialization of `Rational` objects in several different ways. Which of the following will cause an error?

    (A) `Rational r1 = new Rational();`
    (B) `Rational r2 = r1;`
    (C) `Rational r3 = new Rational(2,-3);`
    (D) `Rational r4 = new Rational(3.5);`
    (E) `Rational r5 = new Rational(10);`

16. Here is the implementation code for the `plus` method:

```
/** Returns (this + r). Leaves this unchanged.
 */
public Rational plus(Rational r)
{
    fixSigns();
    r.fixSigns();
    int denom = denominator * r.denominator;
    int numer = numerator * r.denominator
                + r.numerator * denominator;
    /* more code */
}
```

Which of the following is a correct replacement for `/* more code */`?

    (A) 
```
Rational rat(numer, denom);
rat.reduce();
return rat;
```
    (B) `return new Rational(numer, denom);`
    (C) 
```
reduce();
Rational rat = new Rational(numer, denom);
return rat;
```
    (D) 
```
Rational rat = new Rational(numer, denom);
Rational.reduce();
return rat;
```
    (E) 
```
Rational rat = new Rational(numer, denom);
rat.reduce();
return rat;
```

17. Assume these declarations:

```
Rational a = new Rational();
Rational r = new Rational(numer, denom);
int n = value;
//numer, denom, and value are valid integer values
```

Which of the following will cause a compile-time error?

    (A) `r = a.plus(r);`
    (B) `a = r.plus(new Rational(n));`
    (C) `r = r.plus(r);`
    (D) `a = n.plus(r);`
    (E) `r = r.plus(new Rational(n));`

Questions 18–20 refer to the `Temperature` class shown below.

```java
public class Temperature
{
    private String scale;   //valid values are "F" or "C"
    private double degrees;

    /** constructor with specified degrees and scale */
    public Temperature(double tempDegrees, String tempScale)
    { /* implementation not shown */ }

    /** Mutator. Converts this Temperature to degrees Fahrenheit.
     *  Returns this temperature in degrees Fahrenheit.
     *  Precondition: Temperature is a valid temperature
     *                in degrees Celsius.
     */
    public Temperature toFahrenheit()
    { /* implementation not shown */ }

    /** Mutator. Converts this Temperature to degrees Celsius.
     *  Returns this temperature in degrees Celsius.
     *  Precondition: Temperature is a valid temperature
     *                in degrees Fahrenheit.
     */
    public Temperature toCelsius()
    { /* implementation not shown */ }

    /** Mutator.
     *  Returns this temperature raised by amt degrees.
     */
    public Temperature raise(double amt)
    { /* implementation not shown */ }

    /** Mutator.
     *  Returns this temperature lowered by amt degrees.
     */
    public Temperature lower(double amt)
    { /* implementation not shown */ }

    /** Returns true if tempDegrees is a valid temperature
     *  in the given temperature scale, false otherwise.
     */
    public static boolean isValidTemp(double tempDegrees,
                                      String tempScale)
    { /* implementation not shown */ }

    //Other methods are not shown.
}
```

**18.** A client method contains this code segment:

```
Temperature t1 = new Temperature(40, "C");
Temperature t2 = t1;
Temperature t3 = t2.lower(20);
Temperature t4 = t1.toFahrenheit();
```

Which statement is true following execution of this segment?

(A) t1, t2, t3, and t4 all represent the identical temperature, in degrees Celsius.

(B) t1, t2, t3, and t4 all represent the identical temperature, in degrees Fahrenheit.

(C) t4 represents a Fahrenheit temperature, while t1, t2, and t3 all represent degrees Celsius.

(D) t1 and t2 refer to the same Temperature object; t3 refers to a Temperature object that is 20 degrees lower than t1 and t2, while t4 refers to an object that is t1 converted to Fahrenheit.

(E) A NullPointerException was thrown.

**19.** Consider the following code.

```
public class TempTest
{
    public static void main(String[] args)
    {
        System.out.println("Enter temperature scale: ");
        String tempScale = ...;      //read user input
        System.out.println("Enter number of degrees: ");
        double tempDegrees = ...;    //read user input
        /* code to construct a valid temperature from user input */
    }
}
```

Which is the best replacement for /* *code to construct...*   */?

(A) `Temperature t = new Temperature(tempDegrees, tempScale);`

(B) `Temperature t = new Temperature(tempDegrees, tempScale);`
    `if (Temperature.isNotValidTemp(tempDegrees, tempScale))`
        /* *error message and exit program* */

(C) `Temperature t = new Temperature(tempDegrees, tempScale);`
    `if (!t.isValidTemp(tempDegrees,tempScale))`
        /* *error message and exit program* */

(D) `if (isValidTemp(tempDegrees,tempScale))`
        `Temperature t = new Temperature(tempDegrees, tempScale);`
    `else`
        /* *error message and exit program* */

(E) `if (Temperature.isValidTemp(tempDegrees,tempScale))`
        `Temperature t = new Temperature(tempDegrees, tempScale);`
    `else`
        /* *error message and exit program* */

20. The formula to convert degrees Celsius $C$ to Fahrenheit $F$ is

$$F = 1.8C + 32$$

For example, 30° C is equivalent to 86° F.

An `inFahrenheit()` accessor method is added to the `Temperature` class. Here is its implementation:

```
/** Returns an equivalent temperature in degrees Fahrenheit.
 *  Precondition:  The temperature is a valid temperature
 *                 in degrees Celsius.
 *  Postcondition:
 *   - An equivalent temperature in degrees Fahrenheit has been
 *     returned.
 *   - Original temperature remains unchanged.
 */
public Temperature inFahrenheit()
{
    Temperature result;
    /* more code */
    return result;
}
```

Which of the following correctly replaces /* *more code* */ so that the postcondition is achieved?

I  `result = new Temperature(degrees * 1.8 + 32, "F");`

II  `result = new Temperature(degrees * 1.8, "F");`
    `result = result.raise(32);`

III  `degrees *= 1.8;`
     `this = this.raise(32);`
     `result = new Temperature(degrees, "F");`

(A) I only
(B) II only
(C) III only
(D) I and II only
(E) I, II, and III

21. Consider this program.

```java
public class CountStuff
{
    public static void doSomething()
    {
        int count = 0;
        ...
        //code to do something - no screen output produced
        count++;
    }

    public static void main(String[] args)
    {
        int count = 0;
        System.out.println("How many iterations?");
        int n = ...;       //read user input
        for (int  i = 1; i <= n; i++)
        {
            doSomething();
            System.out.println(count);
        }
    }
}
```

If the input value for n is 3, what screen output will this program subsequently produce?

(A)  0
     0
     0

(B)  1
     2
     3

(C)  3
     3
     3

(D)  ?
     ?
     ?

where ? is some undefined value.

(E)  No output will be produced.

22. This question refers to the following class.

```
public class IntObject
{
    private int num;

    public IntObject()          //default constructor
    { num = 0; }

    public IntObject(int n)   //constructor
    { num = n; }

    public void increment()   //increment by 1
    { num++; }
}
```

Here is a client program that uses this class:

```
public class IntObjectTest
{
    public static IntObject someMethod(IntObject obj)
    {
        IntObject ans = obj;
        ans.increment();
        return ans;
    }

    public static void main(String[] args)
    {
        IntObject x = new IntObject(2);
        IntObject y = new IntObject(7);
        IntObject a = y;
        x = someMethod(y);
        a = someMethod(x);
    }
}
```

Just before exiting this program, what are the object values of x, y, and a, respectively?

(A) 9, 9, 9
(B) 2, 9, 9
(C) 2, 8, 9
(D) 3, 8, 9
(E) 7, 8, 9

23. Consider the following program.

```java
public class Tester
{
    public void someMethod(int a, int b)
    {
        int temp = a;
        a = b;
        b = temp;
    }
}

public class TesterMain
{
    public static void main(String[] args)
    {
        int x = 6, y = 8;
        Tester tester = new Tester();
        tester.someMethod(x, y);
    }
}
```

Just before the end of execution of this program, what are the values of x, y, and temp, respectively?

(A) 6, 8, 6

(B) 8, 6, 6

(C) 6, 8, ?, where ? means undefined

(D) 8, 6, ?, where ? means undefined

(E) 8, 6, 8

## ANSWER KEY

| | | |
|---|---|---|
| 1. **D** | 9. **A** | 17. **D** |
| 2. **B** | 10. **A** | 18. **B** |
| 3. **C** | 11. **C** | 19. **E** |
| 4. **C** | 12. **B** | 20. **D** |
| 5. **B** | 13. **E** | 21. **A** |
| 6. **C** | 14. **C** | 22. **A** |
| 7. **E** | 15. **D** | 23. **C** |
| 8. **E** | 16. **E** | |

## ANSWERS EXPLAINED

1. **(D)** There are just two constructors. Constructors are recognizable by having the same name as the class, and no return type.

2. **(B)** Each of the private instance variables should be assigned the value of the matching parameter. Choice B is the only choice that does this. Choice D confuses the order of the assignment statements. Choice A gives the code for the *default* constructor, ignoring the parameters. Choice C would be correct if it were `resetTime(h, m, s)`. As written, it doesn't assign the parameter values `h`, `m`, and `s` to `hrs`, `mins`, and `secs`. Choice E is wrong because the keyword `new` should be used to create a new object, not to implement the constructor!

3. **(C)** Replacement III will automatically print time `t` in the required form since a `toString` method was defined for the `Time` class. Replacement I is wrong because it doesn't refer to the parameter, `t`, of the method. Replacement II is wrong because a client program may not access private data of the class.

4. **(C)** The parameter names can be the same—the *signatures* must be different. For example,

```
public void print(int x)       //prints x
public void print(double x)    //prints x
```

The signatures (method name plus parameter types) here are `print(int)` and `print(double)`, respectively. The parameter name `x` is irrelevant. Choice A is true: All local variables and parameters go out of scope (are erased) when the method is exited. Choice B is true: Static methods apply to the whole class. Only instance methods have an implicit `this` parameter. Choice D is true even for object parameters: Their references are passed by value. Note that choice E is true because it's possible to have two different constructors with different signatures but the same number of parameters (e.g., one for an `int` argument and one for a `double`).

5. **(B)** Constructing an object requires the keyword `new` and a constructor of the `Date` class. Eliminate choices D and E since they omit `new`. The class name `Date` should appear on the right-hand side of the assignment statement, immediately following the keyword `new`. This eliminates choices A and C.

6. **(C)** Segment III will cause a `NullPointerException` to be thrown since `d` is a null reference. You cannot invoke a method for a null reference. Segment II has the effect of assigning `null` to both `d1` and `d2`—obscure but not incorrect. Segment I creates the object reference `d1` and then declares a second reference `d2` that refers to the same object as `d1`.

7. **(E)** A client program cannot access a private instance variable.

8. **(E)** All are correct. Since `write()` is a `Date` instance method, it is OK to use the private data members in its implementation code. Segment III prints `this`, the current `Date` object. This usage is correct since `write()` is part of the `Date` class. The `toString()` method guarantees that the date will be printed in the required format (see p. 167).

9. **(A)** The idea here is to read in three separate variables for month, day, and year and then to construct the required date using `new` and the `Date` class constructor with three parameters. Code segment II won't work because `month()`, `day()`, and `year()` are accessor methods that access existing values and may not be used to read new values into `bDate`. Segment III is wrong because it tries to access private instance variables from a client program.

10. **(A)** Segment I will not create a second object. It will simply cause `d2` to refer to the *same* object as `d1`, which is not what was required. The keyword `new` *must* be used to create a new object.

11. **(C)** When `recentDate` is declared in `main()`, its value is null. Recall that a method is not able to replace an object reference, so `recentDate` remains null. Note that the intent of the program is to change `recentDate` to refer to the updated `oldDate` object. The code, however, doesn't do this. Choice A is false: No methods are invoked with a null reference. Choice B is false because `addYears()` is a mutator method. Even though a method doesn't change the address of its object parameter, it can change the contents of the object, which is what happens here. Choices D and E are wrong because the `addCentury()` method cannot change the value of its `recentDate` argument.

12. **(B)** The method `getPondTemperature` is the only method that applies to more than one frog. It should therefore be static. All of the other methods relate directly to one particular `Frog` object. So `f.swim()`, `f.die()`, `f.getWeight()`, and `f.eat()` are all reasonable methods for a single instance `f` of a `Frog`. On the other hand, it doesn't make sense to say `f.getPondTemperature()`. It makes more sense to say `Frog.getPondTemperature()`, since the same value will apply to all frogs in the class.

13. **(E)** Here are the memory slots at the start of `strangeMethod(a, b)`:

| a | b |
|---|---|
| 6 | 3 |

| x | y |
|---|---|
| 6 | 3 |

Before exiting `strangeMethod(a, b)`:

| a | b |
|---|---|
| 6 | 3 |

| x | y |
|---|---|
| 9 | 27 |

Note that 9  27 is output before exiting. After exiting `strangeMethod(a, b)`, the memory slots are

The next step outputs 6  3.

14. **(C)** The `reduce()` method will be used only in the implementation of the instance methods of the `Rational` class. It's a private helper method.

15. **(D)** None of the constructors in the `Rational` class takes a real-valued parameter. Thus, the real-valued parameter in choice D will need to be converted to an integer. Since in general truncating a real value to an integer involves a loss of precision, it is not done automatically—you have to do it explicitly with a cast. Omitting the cast causes a compile-time error.

16. **(E)** A new `Rational` object must be created using the newly calculated `numer` and `denom`. Then it must be reduced before being returned. Choice A is wrong because it doesn't correctly create the new object. Choice B returns a correctly constructed object, but one that has not been reduced. Choice C reduces the current object, `this`, instead of the new object, `rat`. Choice D is wrong because it invokes `reduce()` for the `Rational` class instead of the specific `rat` object.

17. **(D)** The `plus` method of the `Rational` class can only be invoked by `Rational` objects. Since n is an `int`, the statement in choice D will cause an error.

18. **(B)** This is an example of *aliasing*. The keyword `new` is used just once, which means that just one object is constructed. Here are the memory slots after each declaration:

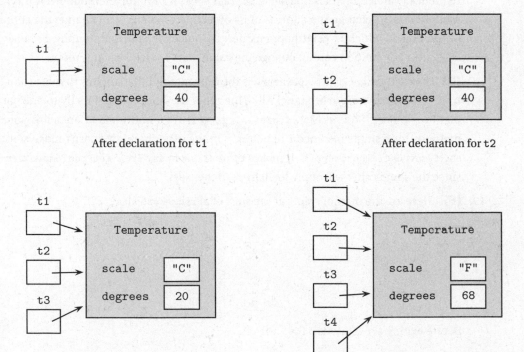

After declaration for t1

After declaration for t2

After declaration for t3

After declaration for t4

19. **(E)** Notice that `isValidTemp` is a static method for the `Temperature` class, which means that it should be invoked with the class name, `Temperature`, as in choice E. The method

should not be invoked with `t`, a `Temperature` object, as is done in choice C. (Even though `t.isValidTemp` may work, its use is discouraged. A good compiler will give you a warning.) Choice A is not a good choice because it is not robust: It allows the program to proceed with data that may be invalid. Choice B fails because it uses `isNotValidTemp`, a method that is not in the program. Choice D fails because `isValidTemp` is not a method of the `TempTest` class.

20. **(D)** A new `Temperature` object must be constructed to prevent the current `Temperature` from being changed. Segment I, which applies the conversion formula directly to `degrees`, is the best way to do this. Segment II, while not the best algorithm, does work. The statement

```
result = result.raise(32);
```

has the effect of raising the `result` temperature by 32 degrees, and completing the conversion. Segment III fails because

```
degrees *= 1.8;
```

alters the `degrees` instance variable of the current object, as does

```
this = this.raise(32);
```

To be correct, these operations must be applied to the `result` object.

21. **(A)** This is a question about the scope of variables. The scope of the `count` variable that is declared in `main()` extends up to the closing brace of `main()`. In `doSomething()`, `count` is a local variable. After the method call in the `for` loop, the local variable `count` goes out of scope, and the value that's being printed is the value of the `count` in `main()`, which is unchanged from 0.

22. **(A)** Here are the memory slots before the first `someMethod` call:

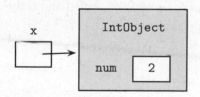
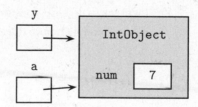

Just before exiting `x = someMethod(y)`:

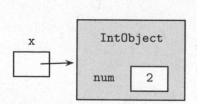
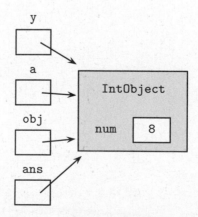

After exiting

```
x = someMethod(y);
```

x has been reassigned, so the object with num = 2 has been recycled:

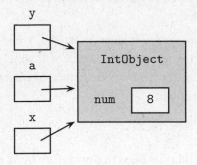

After exiting a = someMethod(x):

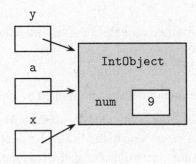

23. **(C)** Recall that when primitive types are passed as parameters, copies are made of the actual arguments. All manipulations in the method are performed on the copies, and the arguments remain unchanged. Thus x and y retain their values of 6 and 8. The local variable temp goes out of scope as soon as someMethod is exited and is therefore undefined just before the end of execution of the program.

# Inheritance and Polymorphism

4

*Say not you know another entirely,
till you have divided an inheritance with him.*
—*Johann Kaspar Lavatar,* Aphorisms on Man

→ **Superclasses and subclasses**     → **Polymorphism**
→ **Inheritance hierarchy**

## INHERITANCE

### Superclass and Subclass

*Inheritance* defines a relationship between objects that share characteristics. Specifically it is the mechanism whereby a new class, called a *subclass*, is created from an existing class, called a *superclass*, by absorbing its state and behavior and augmenting these with features unique to the new class. We say that the subclass *inherits* characteristics of its superclass.

Don't get confused by the names: a subclass is bigger than a superclass—it contains more data and more methods!

Inheritance provides an effective mechanism for code reuse. Suppose the code for a superclass has been tested and debugged. Since a subclass object shares features of a superclass object, the only new code required is for the additional characteristics of the subclass.

### Inheritance Hierarchy

A subclass can itself be a superclass for another subclass, leading to an *inheritance hierarchy* of classes.

For example, consider the relationship between these classes: `Person`, `Employee`, `Student`, `GradStudent`, and `UnderGrad`.

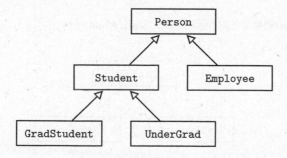

For any of these classes, an arrow points to its superclass. The arrow designates an inheritance relationship between classes, or, informally, an *is-a* relationship. Thus, an Employee *is-a* Person; a Student *is-a* Person; a GradStudent *is-a* Student; an UnderGrad *is-a* Student. Notice that the opposite is not necessarily true: A Person may not be a Student, nor is a Student necessarily an UnderGrad.

Note that the *is-a* relationship is transitive: If a GradStudent *is-a* Student and a Student *is-a* Person, then a GradStudent *is-a* Person.

Every subclass inherits the public or protected variables and methods of its superclass (see p. 142). Subclasses may have additional methods and instance variables that are not in the superclass. A subclass may redefine a method it inherits. For example, GradStudent and UnderGrad may use different algorithms for computing the course grade, and need to change a computeGrade method inherited from Student. This is called *method overriding*. If part of the original method implementation from the superclass is retained, we refer to the rewrite as *partial overriding* (see p. 143).

## Implementing Subclasses

### THE extends KEYWORD

The inheritance relationship between a subclass and a superclass is specified in the declaration of the subclass, using the keyword extends. The general format looks like this:

```
public class Superclass
{
    //private instance variables
    //other data members
    //constructors
    //public methods
    //private methods
}

public class Subclass extends Superclass
{
    //additional private instance variables
    //additional data members
    //constructors  (Not inherited!)
    //additional public methods
    //inherited public methods whose implementation is overridden
    //additional private methods
}
```

For example, consider the following inheritance hierarchy:

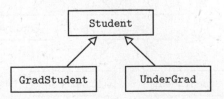

The implementation of the classes may look something like this (discussion follows the code):

```java
public class Student
{
    //data members
    public final static int NUM_TESTS = 3;
    private String name;
    private int[] tests;
    private String grade;

    //constructor
    public Student()
    {
        name = "";
        tests = new int[NUM_TESTS];
        grade = "";
    }


    //constructor
    public Student(String studName, int[] studTests, String studGrade)
    {
        name = studName;
        tests = studTests;
        grade = studGrade;
    }

    public String getName()
    { return name; }

    public String getGrade()
    { return grade; }

    public void setGrade(String newGrade)
    { grade = newGrade; }

    public void computeGrade()
    {
        if (name.equals(""))
            grade = "No grade";
        else if (getTestAverage() >= 65)
            grade = "Pass";
        else
            grade = "Fail";
    }

    public double getTestAverage()
    {
        double total = 0;
        for (int score : tests)
            total += score;
        return total/NUM_TESTS;
    }
}
```

```
public class UnderGrad extends Student
{
    public UnderGrad()    //default constructor
    { super(); }

    //constructor
    public UnderGrad(String studName, int[] studTests, String studGrade)
    { super(studName, studTests, studGrade); }

    public void computeGrade()
    {
        if (getTestAverage() >= 70)
            setGrade("Pass");
        else
            setGrade("Fail");
    }
}

public class GradStudent extends Student
{
    private int gradID;

    public GradStudent()        //default constructor
    {
        super();
        gradID = 0;
    }

    //constructor
    public GradStudent(String studName, int[] studTests,
            String studGrade, int gradStudID)
    {
        super(studName, studTests, studGrade);
        gradID = gradStudID;
    }

    public int getID()
    { return gradID; }

    public void computeGrade()
    {
        //invokes computeGrade in Student superclass
        super.computeGrade();
        if (getTestAverage() >= 90)
            setGrade("Pass with distinction");
    }
}
```

## INHERITING INSTANCE METHODS AND VARIABLES

A subclass inherits all the public and protected methods of its superclass. It does not, however, inherit the private instance variables or private methods of its parent class, and therefore does not have direct access to them. To access private instance variables, a subclass must use the accessor or mutator methods that it has inherited.

In the `Student` example, the `UnderGrad` and `GradStudent` subclasses inherit all of the methods of the `Student` superclass. Notice, however, that the `Student` instance variables `name`, `tests`, and `grade` are private and are therefore not inherited or directly accessible to the methods in the `UnderGrad` and `GradStudent` subclasses. A subclass can, however, directly invoke the public accessor and mutator methods of the superclass. Thus, both `UnderGrad` and `GradStudent` use `getTestAverage`. Additionally, both `UnderGrad` and `GradStudent` use `setGrade` to access indirectly—and modify—`grade`.

If, instead of `private`, the access specifier for the instance variables in `Student` were public or `protected`, then the subclasses could directly access these variables. The keyword `protected` is not part of the AP Java subset.

Classes on the same level in a hierarchy diagram do not inherit anything from each other (for example, `UnderGrad` and `GradStudent`). All they have in common is the identical code they inherit from their superclass.

## METHOD OVERRIDING AND THE super KEYWORD

Any public method in a superclass can be overridden in a subclass by defining a method with the same return type and signature (name and parameter types). For example, the `compute-Grade` method in the `UnderGrad` subclass overrides the `computeGrade` method in the `Student` superclass.

Sometimes the code for overriding a method includes a call to the superclass method. This is called *partial overriding*. Typically this occurs when the subclass method wants to do what the superclass does, plus something extra. This is achieved by using the keyword `super` in the implementation. The `computeGrade` method in the `GradStudent` subclass partially overrides the matching method in the `Student` class. The statement

```
super.computeGrade();
```

signals that the `computeGrade` method in the superclass should be invoked here. The additional test

```
if (getTestAverage() >= 90)
    ...
```

allows a `GradStudent` to have a grade `Pass with distinction`. Note that this option is open to `GradStudents` only.

## NOTE

Private methods cannot be overridden.

## CONSTRUCTORS AND super

Constructors are never inherited! If no constructor is written for a subclass, the superclass default constructor with no parameters is generated. If the superclass does not have a default (zero-parameter) constructor, but only a constructor with parameters, a compiler error will occur. If there is a default constructor in the superclass, inherited data members will be initialized as for the superclass. Additional instance variables in the subclass will get a default initialization—0 for primitive types and `null` for reference types.

> Be sure to provide at least one constructor for a subclass. Constructors are never inherited from the superclass.

A subclass constructor can be implemented with a call to the super method, which invokes the superclass constructor. For example, the default constructor in the UnderGrad class is identical to that of the Student class. This is implemented with the statement

```
super();
```

The second constructor in the UnderGrad class is called with parameters that match those in the constructor of the Student superclass.

```
public UnderGrad(String studName, int[] studTests, String studGrade)
{ super(studName, studTests, studGrade); }
```

For each constructor, the call to super has the effect of initializing the instance variables name, tests, and grade exactly as they are initialized in the Student class.

Contrast this with the constructors in GradStudent. In each case, the instance variables name, tests, and grade are initialized as for the Student class. Then the new instance variable, gradID, must be explicitly initialized.

```
public GradStudent()
{
    super();
    gradID = 0;
}
```

```
public GradStudent(String studName, int[] studTests,
            String studGrade, int gradStudID)
{
    super(studName, studTests, studGrade);
    gradID = gradStudID;
}
```

**NOTE**

1. If super is used in the implementation of a subclass constructor, it *must* be used in the first line of the constructor body.
2. If no constructor is provided in a subclass, the compiler provides the following default constructor:

   ```
   public SubClass()
   {
       super();        //calls default constructor of superclass
   }
   ```

3. If the superclass has at least one constructor with parameters, the code in Note 2 above will cause a compile-time error if the superclass does not also contain a default (no parameter) constructor.

## claring Subclass Objects

n a superclass object is declared in a client program, that reference can refer not only
n object of the superclass, but also to objects of any of its subclasses. Thus, each of the
wing is legal:

```
Student s = new Student();
Student g = new GradStudent();
Student u = new UnderGrad();
```

This works because a GradStudent *is-a* Student, and an UnderGrad *is-a* Student.

Note that since a Student is not necessarily a GradStudent nor an UnderGrad, the following
declarations are *not* valid:

```
GradStudent g = new Student();
UnderGrad u = new Student();
```

Consider these valid declarations:

```
Student s = new Student("Brian Lorenzen", new int[] {90,94,99},
        "none");
Student u = new UnderGrad("Tim Broder", new int[] {90,90,100},
        "none");
Student g = new GradStudent("Kevin Cristella",
        new int[] {85,70,90}, "none", 1234);
```

Suppose you make the method call

```
s.setGrade("Pass");
```

The appropriate method in Student is found and the new grade assigned. The method calls

```
g.setGrade("Pass");
```

and

```
u.setGrade("Pass");
```

achieve the same effect on g and u since GradStudent and UnderGrad both inherit the set(
method from Student. The following method calls, however, won't work:

```
int studentNum = s.getID();
int underGradNum = u.getID();
```

Neither Student s nor UnderGrad u inherit the getID method from the GradStudent cl
superclass does not inherit from a subclass.

Now consider the following valid method calls:

```
s.computeGrade();
g.computeGrade();
u.computeGrade();
```

Since s, g, and u have all been declared to be of type Student, will the appropriate meth
executed in each case? That is the topic of the next section, *polymorphism*.

**NOTE**

The initializer list syntax used in constructing the array parameters—for exa
new int[] {90,90,100}— will not be tested on the AP exam.

## POLYMORPHISM

A method that has been overridden in at least one subclass is said to be *polymorphic*. An
example is computeGrade, which is redefined for both GradStudent and UnderGrad.

*Polymorphism* is the mechanism of selecting the appropriate method for a particular object in a class hierarchy. The correct method is chosen because, in Java, method calls are
always determined by the type of the *actual object*, not the type of the object reference.
For example, even though s, g, and u are all declared as type Student, s.computeGrade(),
g.computeGrade(), and u.computeGrade() will all perform the correct operations for their particular instances. In Java, the selection of the correct method occurs *during the run of the*
*program*.

### Dynamic Binding (Late Binding)

Making a run-time decision about which instance method to call is known as *dynamic binding*
or *late binding*. Contrast this with selecting the correct method when methods are *overloaded*
(see p. 107) rather than overridden. The compiler selects the correct overloaded method at
compile time by comparing the methods' signatures. This is known as *static binding*, or *early*
*binding*. In polymorphism, the actual method that will be called is not determined by the
compiler. Think of it this way: The compiler determines *if* a method can be called (i.e., is it legal?), while the run-time environment determines *how* it will be called (i.e., which overridden
form should be used?).

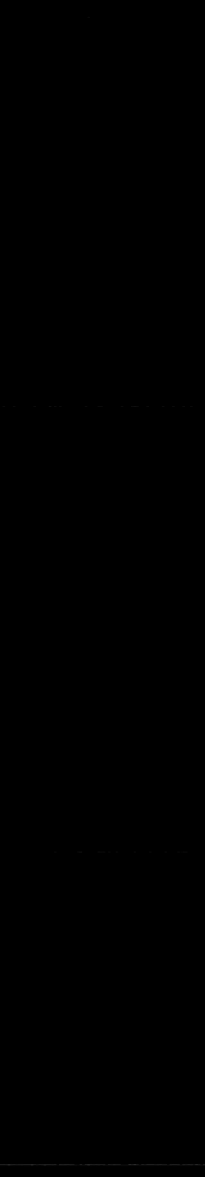

## ➡ Example 1

```
Student s = null;
Student u = new UnderGrad("Tim Broder", new int[] {90,90,100},
        "none");
Student g = new GradStudent("Kevin Cristella",
        new int[] {85,70,90}, "none", 1234);
System.out.print("Enter student status: ");
System.out.println("Grad (G), Undergrad (U), Neither (N)");
String str = ...;        //read user input
if (str.equals("G"))
    s = g;
else if (str.equals("U"))
    s = u;
else
    s = new Student();
s.computeGrade();
```

When this code fragment is run, the computeGrade method used will depend on the type of the actual object s refers to, which in turn depends on the user input.

## ➡ Example 2

```
public class StudentTest
{
    public static void computeAllGrades(Student[] studentList)
    {
        for (Student s : studentList)
            if (s != null)
                s.computeGrade();
    }

    public static void main(String[] args)
    {
        Student[] stu = new Student[5];
        stu[0] = new Student("Brian Lorenzen",
                    new int[] {90,94,99}, "none");
        stu[1] = new UnderGrad("Tim Broder",
                    new int[] {90,90,100}, "none");
        stu[2] = new GradStudent("Kevin Cristella",
                    new int[] {85,70,90}, "none", 1234);
        computeAllGrades(stu);
    }
}
```

> Polymorphism applies only to overridden methods in subclasses.

Here an array of five Student references is created, all of them initially null. Three of these references, stu[0], stu[1], and stu[2], are then assigned to actual objects. The computeAllGrades method steps through the array invoking for each of the objects the appropriate computeGrade method, using dynamic binding in each case. The null test in computeAllGrades is necessary because some of the array references could be null.

## Using super in a Subclass

A subclass can call a method in its superclass by using super. Suppose that the superclass method then calls another method that has been overridden in the subclass. By polymorphism, the method that is executed is the one in the subclass. The computer keeps track and executes any pending statements in either method.

**➡ Example** _____

```java
public class Dancer
{
    public void act()
    {
        System.out.print (" spin ");
        doTrick();
    }

    public void doTrick()
    {
        System.out.print (" float ");
    }
}

public class Acrobat extends Dancer
{
    public void act()
    {
        super.act();
        System.out.print (" flip ");
    }

    public void doTrick()
    {
        System.out.print (" somersault ");
    }
}
```

Suppose the following declaration appears in a class other than Dancer or Acrobat:

```java
Dancer a = new Acrobat();
```

What is printed as a result of the call a.act()?

When a.act() is called, the act method of Acrobat is executed. This is an example of polymorphism. The first line, super.act(), goes to the act method of Dancer, the superclass. This prints spin, then calls doTrick(). Again, using polymorphism, the doTrick method in Acrobat is called, printing somersault. Now, completing the act method of Acrobat, flip is printed. So what all got printed?

```java
spin somersault flip
```

**NOTE**

Even though there are no constructors in either the Dancer or Acrobat classes, the declaration

```
Dancer a = new Acrobat();
```

compiles without error. This is because Dancer, while not having an explicit superclass, has an implicit superclass, Object, and gets its default (no-argument) constructor slotted into its code. Similarly the Acrobat class gets this constructor slotted into its code.

The statement Dancer a = new Acrobat(); will not compile, however, if the Dancer class has at least one constructor with parameters but no default constructor.

## TYPE COMPATIBILITY

## Downcasting

Consider the statements

```
Student s = new GradStudent();
GradStudent g = new GradStudent();
int x = s.getID();          //compile-time error
int y = g.getID();          //legal
```

Both s and g represent GradStudent objects, so why does s.getID() cause an error? The reason is that s is of type Student, and the Student class doesn't have a getID method. At compile time, only nonprivate methods of the Student class can appear to the right of the dot operator when applied to s. Don't confuse this with polymorphism: getID is not a polymorphic method. It occurs in just the GradStudent class and can therefore be called only by a GradStudent object.

The error shown above can be fixed by casting s to the correct type:

```
int x = ((GradStudent) s).getID();
```

Since s (of type Student) is actually representing a GradStudent object, such a cast can be carried out. Casting a superclass to a subclass type is called a *downcast*.

**NOTE**

1. The outer parentheses are necessary, so

   ```
   int x = (GradStudent) s.getID();
   ```

   will still cause an error, despite the cast. This is because the dot operator has higher precedence than casting, so s.getID() is invoked before s is cast to GradStudent.

2. The statement

   ```
   int y = g.getID();
   ```

   compiles without problem because g is declared to be of type GradStudent, and this is the class that contains getID. No cast is required.

3. Class casts will not explicitly be tested on the AP exam. You should, however, understand why the following statement will cause a compile-time error:

   ```
   int x = s.getID(); //No getID method in Student class
   ```

   And the following statement will compile without error:

   ```
   int y = g.getID(); //getID method is in GradStudent class
   ```

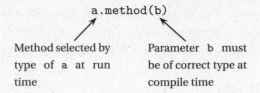

**Type Rules for Polymorphic Method Calls**

$$a.method(b)$$

Method selected by type of a at run time

Parameter b must be of correct type at compile time

- For a declaration like

    ```
    Superclass a = new Subclass();
    ```

    the type of a at compile time is Superclass; at run time it is Subclass.

- At compile time, method must be found in the class of a, that is, in Superclass. (This is true whether the method is polymorphic or not.) If method cannot be found in the class of a, you need to do an explicit cast on a to its actual type.

- For a polymorphic method, at run time the actual type of a is determined—Subclass in this example—and method is selected from Subclass. This could be an inherited method if there is no overriding method.

- The type of parameter b is checked at compile time. It must pass the *is-a* test for the type in the method declaration. You may need to do an explicit cast to a subclass type to make this correct.

## ABSTRACT CLASSES

Abstract classes are no longer part of the AP Java subset.

## INTERFACES

Interfaces are no longer part of the AP Java subset.

## Chapter Summary

You should be able to write your own subclasses, given any superclass.

Be sure you understand the use of the keyword super, both in writing constructors and calling methods of the superclass.

You should understand what polymorphism is: Recall that it only operates when methods have been overridden in at least one subclass. You should also be able to explain the difference between the following concepts:

- An overloaded method and an overridden method.

- Dynamic binding (late binding) and static binding (early binding).

Questions 1–9 refer to the BankAccount, SavingsAccount, and CheckingAccount classes defined below.

```
public class BankAccount
{
    private double balance;

    public BankAccount()
    { balance = 0; }

    public BankAccount(double acctBalance)
    { balance = acctBalance; }

    public void deposit(double amount)
    { balance += amount; }

    public void withdraw(double amount)
    { balance -= amount; }

    public double getBalance()
    { return balance; }
}

public class SavingsAccount extends BankAccount
{
    private double interestRate;

    public SavingsAccount()
    { /* implementation not shown */ }

    public SavingsAccount(double acctBalance, double rate)
    { /* implementation not shown */ }

    public void addInterest()    //Add interest to balance
    { /* implementation not shown */ }
}

public class CheckingAccount extends BankAccount
{
    private static final double FEE = 2.0;
    private static final double MIN_BALANCE = 50.0;

    public CheckingAccount(double acctBalance)
    { /* implementation not shown */ }

    /** FEE of $2 deducted if withdrawal leaves balance less
     *  than MIN_BALANCE. Allows for negative balance. */
    public void withdraw(double amount)
    { /* implementation not shown */ }
}
```

1. Of the methods shown, how many different nonconstructor methods can be invoked by a SavingsAccount object?
   (A) 1
   (B) 2
   (C) 3
   (D) 4
   (E) 5

2. Which of the following correctly implements the default constructor of the SavingsAccount class?

   I   interestRate = 0;
       super();

   II  super();
       interestRate = 0;

   III super();

   (A) II only
   (B) I and II only
   (C) II and III only
   (D) III only
   (E) I, II, and III

3. Which is a correct implementation of the constructor with parameters in the SavingsAccount class?

   (A) balance = acctBalance;
       interestRate = rate;

   (B) getBalance() =  acctBalance;
       interestRate = rate;

   (C) super();
       interestRate = rate;

   (D) super(acctBalance);
       interestRate = rate;

   (E) super(acctBalance, rate);

4. Which is a correct implementation of the CheckingAccount constructor?

   I   super(acctBalance);

   II  super();
       deposit(acctBalance);

   III deposit(acctBalance);

   (A) I only
   (B) II only
   (C) III only
   (D) II and III only
   (E) I, II, and III

5. Which is correct implementation code for the `withdraw` method in the `CheckingAccount` class?

    (A)  `super.withdraw(amount);`
         `if (balance < MIN_BALANCE)`
           `super.withdraw(FEE);`

    (B)  `withdraw(amount);`
         `if (balance < MIN_BALANCE)`
           `withdraw(FEE);`

    (C)  `super.withdraw(amount);`         → ∴ *balance* δ *private*
         `if (getBalance() < MIN_BALANCE)`
           `super.withdraw(FEE);`

    (D)  `withdraw(amount);`
         `if (getBalance() < MIN_BALANCE)`
           `withdraw(FEE);`

    (E)  `balance -= amount;`
         `if (balance < MIN_BALANCE)`
           `balance -= FEE;`

6. Redefining the `withdraw` method in the `CheckingAccount` class is an example of
    (A)  method overloading.
    (B)  method overriding.
    (C)  downcasting.
    (D)  dynamic binding (late binding).
    (E)  static binding (early binding).

Use the following for Questions 7 and 8.

A program to test the `BankAccount`, `SavingsAccount`, and `CheckingAccount` classes has these declarations:

```
BankAccount b = new BankAccount(1400);
BankAccount s = new SavingsAccount(1000, 0.04);
BankAccount c = new CheckingAccount(500);
```

7. Which method call will cause an error?
    (A)  `b.deposit(200);`
    (B)  `s.withdraw(500);`
    (C)  `c.withdraw(500);`
    (D)  `s.deposit(10000);`
    (E)  `s.addInterest();`

8. In order to test polymorphism, which method must be used in the program?
    (A)  Either a `SavingsAccount` constructor or a `CheckingAccount` constructor
    (B)  `addInterest`
    (C)  `deposit`
    (D)  `withdraw`
    (E)  `getBalance`

9. A new method is added to the `BankAccount` class.

```
/** Transfer amount from this BankAccount to another BankAccount.
 *  Precondition:  balance > amount
 *  @param another a different BankAccount object
 *  @param amount the amount to be transferred
 */
public void transfer(BankAccount another, double amount)
{
    withdraw(amount);
    another.deposit(amount);
}
```

A program has these declarations:

```
BankAccount b = new BankAccount(650);
SavingsAccount timsSavings = new SavingsAccount(1500, 0.03);
CheckingAccount daynasChecking = new CheckingAccount(2000);
```

Which of the following will transfer money from one account to another without error?

I  `b.transfer(timsSavings, 50);`

II  `timsSavings.transfer(daynasChecking, 30);`

III  `daynasChecking.transfer(b, 55);`

(A) I only
(B) II only
(C) III only
(D) I, II, and III
(E) None

→ all bank account subclass

10. Consider these class declarations.

```
public class Person
{
    ...
}

public class Teacher extends Person
{
    ...
}
```

Which is a true statement?

I   Teacher inherits the constructors of Person.
II  Teacher can add new methods and private instance variables.
III Teacher can override existing private methods of Person.

(A) I only
(B) II only
(C) III only
(D) I and II only
(E) II and III only

11. Which statement about subclass methods is false?

(A) Writing two subclass methods with the same name but different parameters is called method overriding.
(B) A public method in a subclass that is not in its superclass is not accessible by the superclass.
(C) A private method in a superclass is not inherited by its subclass.
(D) Two different subclasses of the same superclass inherit the same methods of the superclass.
(E) If Class1 is a superclass of Class2, and Class2 is a superclass of Class3, and Class2 has no overridden methods, Class3 inherits all the public methods of Class1.

12. Consider the following hierarchy of classes.

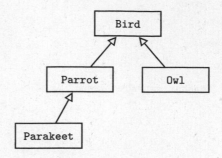

A program is written to print data about various birds:

```
public class BirdStuff
{
    public static void printName(Bird b)
    { /* implementation not shown */ }

    public static void printBirdCall(Parrot p)
    { /* implementation not shown */ }

    //several more Bird methods

    public static void main(String[] args)
    {
        Bird bird1 = new Bird();
        Bird bird2 = new Parrot();
        Parrot parrot1 = new Parrot();
        Parrot parrot2 = new Parakeet();
        /* more code */
    }
}
```

Assuming that all of the given classes have default constructors, which of the following segments of /* *more code* */ will cause an error?

(A) printBirdCall(bird2);

(B) printName(parrot2);

(C) printName(bird2);

(D) printBirdCall(parrot2);

(E) printBirdCall(parrot1);

Refer to the classes below for Questions 13 and 14.

```java
public class ClassA
{
    //default constructor not shown ...

    public void method1()
    { /* implementation of method1 */ }

    public void method2()
    { /* implementation of method2 */ }
}

public class ClassB extends ClassA
{
    //default constructor not shown ...

    public void method1()
    { /* different implementation from method1 in ClassA*/ }

    public void method3()
    { /* implementation of method3 */ }
}
```

13. The `method1` method in `ClassB` is an example of
    - (A)  method overloading.
    - (B)  method overriding.
    - (C)  polymorphism.
    - (D)  data encapsulation.
    - (E)  procedural abstraction.

14. Consider the following declarations in a client class.

```java
ClassA ob1 = new ClassA();
ClassA ob2 = new ClassB();
ClassB ob3 = new ClassB();
```

Which of the following method calls will cause an error?

I  `ob1.method3();`

II  `ob2.method3();`

III  `ob3.method2();`

    - (A)  I only
    - (B)  II only
    - (C)  III only
    - (D)  I and II only
    - (E)  I, II, and III

Use the declarations below for Questions 15 and 16.

```java
public class Solid
{
    private String name;

    //constructor
    public Solid(String solidName)
    { name = solidName; }

    public String getName()
    { return name; }

    public double volume()
    { /* implementation not shown */ }
}

public class Sphere extends Solid
{
    private double radius;

    //constructor
    public Sphere(String sphereName, double sphereRadius)
    {
        super(sphereName);
        radius = sphereRadius;
    }

    public double volume()
    { return (4.0/3.0) * Math.PI * radius * radius * radius; }
}

public class RectangularPrism extends Solid
{
    private double length;
    private double width;
    private double height;

    //constructor
    public RectangularPrism(String prismName, double l, double w,
            double h)
    {
        super(prismName);
        length = l;
        width = w;
        height = h;
    }

    public double volume()
    { return length * width * height; }
}
```

15. A program that tests these classes has the following declarations and assignments:

```
Solid s1, s2, s3, s4;
s1 = new Solid("blob");
s2 = new Sphere("sphere", 3.8);
s3 = new RectangularPrism("box", 2, 4, 6.5);
s4 = null;
```

How many of the above lines of code are incorrect?
(A) 0
(B) 1
(C) 2
(D) 3
(E) 4

16. Here is a program that prints the volume of a solid:

```
public class SolidMain
{
    /** Output volume of Solid s. */
    public static void printVolume(Solid s)
    {
        System.out.println("Volume = " + s.volume() +
                " cubic units");
    }

    public static void main(String[] args)
    {
        Solid sol;
        Solid sph = new Sphere("sphere", 4);
        Solid rec = new RectangularPrism("box", 3, 6, 9);
        int flipCoin = (int) (Math.random() * 2);   //0 or 1
        if (flipCoin == 0)
            sol = sph;
        else
            sol = rec;
        printVolume(sol);
    }
}
```

Which is a true statement about this program?
(A) It will output the volume of the sphere or box, as intended.
(B) It will output the volume of the default Solid s, which is neither a sphere nor a box.
(C) It will randomly print the volume of sphere or a box.
(D) A run-time error will occur because it is not specified whether s is a sphere or a box.
(E) A run-time error will occur because of parameter type mismatch in the method call printVolume(sol).

17. Consider these class declarations.

```
public class Player
{
    public Player()
    { /* implementation not shown */ }

    public int getMove()
    { /* implementation not shown */ }

    //Other constructors and methods not shown.
}

public class ExpertPlayer extends Player
{
    public int compareTo(ExpertPlayer expert)
    { /* implementation not shown */ }

    //Constructors and other methods not shown.
}
```

Which code segment in a client program will cause an error?

```
  I Player p1 = new ExpertPlayer();
    int x1 = p1.getMove();

 II int x;
    ExpertPlayer c1 = new ExpertPlayer();
    ExpertPlayer c2 = new ExpertPlayer();
    if (c1.compareTo(c2) < 0)
        x = c1.getMove();
    else
        x = c2.getMove();

III int x;
    Player h1 = new ExpertPlayer();
    Player h2 = new ExpertPlayer();
    if (h1.compareTo(h2) < 0)
        x = h1.getMove();
    else
        x = h2.getMove();
```

(A) I only
(B) II only
(C) III only
(D) I and II only
(E) I, II, and III

18. Consider the following class definitions.

```
public class Animal
{
    private String type;

    public Animal(String theType)
    {
        type = theType;
    }

    public String getType()
    {
        return type;
    }
}


public class Dog extends Animal
{
    public Dog(String theType)
    {
        super(theType);
    }
}
```

The following code segment appears in a class other than Animal or Dog.

```
Animal d1 = new Animal("poodle");
Animal d2 = new Dog("shnauzer");
Dog d3 = new Dog("yorkie");

public static void display(Animal a)
{
    System.out.println("This dog is a " + a.getType(););
}
```

Which of the following method calls will compile without error?

I display(d1);

II display(d2);

III display(d3);

(A) I only
(B) II only
(C) III only
(D) I and II only
(E) I, II, and III

19. Consider the following class definitions.

```java
public class StrStuff1
{
    public void printSub(String str)
    {
        String s = str.substring(2);
        System.out.print(s);
    }
}


public class StrStuff2 extends StrStuff1
{
    public void printSub(String str)
    {
        String s = str.substring(1);
        super.printSub(s);
        System.out.print(s);
    }
}
```

The following code segment appears in a class other than StrStuff1 and StrStuff2.

```java
StrStuff1 p = new StrStuff2();
p.printSub("crab");
```

What is printed as a result of executing the code segment?

(A) crabab
(B) brab
(C) rabb
(D) abb
(E) ab

20. Consider the following class definitions.

```
public class Class1
{
    public void doSomething(int n)
    {
        n -= 4;
        System.out.print(n);
    }
}

public class Class2 extends Class1
{
    public void doSomething(int n)
    {
        super.doSomething(n + 3);
        n *= 2;
        System.out.print(n);
    }
}
```

The following code segment appears in a class other than Class1 and Class2.

```
Class1 c = new Class2();
c.doSomething(8);
```

What is printed as a result of executing the code segment?

(A) 416
(B) 422
(C) 714
(D) 716
(E) 722

## ANSWER KEY

| | | |
|---|---|---|
| 1. **D** | 8. **D** | 15. **A** |
| 2. **C** | 9. **D** | 16. **A** |
| 3. **D** | 10. **B** | 17. **D** |
| 4. **E** | 11. **A** | 18. **E** |
| 5. **C** | 12. **A** | 19. **B** |
| 6. **B** | 13. **B** | 20. **D** |
| 7. **E** | 14. **D** | |

## ANSWERS EXPLAINED

1. **(D)** The methods are `deposit`, `withdraw`, and `getBalance`, all inherited from the `BankAccount` class, plus `addInterest`, which was defined just for the class `SavingsAccount`.

2. **(C)** Implementation I fails because `super()` *must* be the first line of the implementation whenever it is used in a constructor. Implementation III may appear to be incorrect because it doesn't initialize `interestRate`. Since `interestRate`, however, is a primitive type—`double`—the compiler will provide a default initialization of 0, which was required.

3. **(D)** First, the statement `super(acctBalance)` initializes the inherited private variable `balance` as for the `BankAccount` superclass. Then the statement `interestRate = rate` initializes `interestRate`, which belongs uniquely to the `SavingsAccount` class. Choice E fails because `interestRate` does not belong to the `BankAccount` class and therefore cannot be initialized by a `super` method. Choice A is wrong because the `SavingsAccount` class cannot directly access the private instance variables of its superclass. Choice B assigns a value to an accessor method, which is meaningless. Choice C is incorrect because `super()` invokes the *default* constructor of the superclass. This will cause `balance` of the `SavingsAccount` object to be initialized to 0, rather than `acctBalance`, the parameter value.

4. **(E)** The constructor must initialize the inherited instance variable `balance` to the value of the `acctBalance` parameter. All three segments achieve this. Implementation I does it by invoking `super(acctBalance)`, the constructor in the superclass. Implementation II first initializes `balance` to 0 by invoking the *default* constructor of the superclass. Then it calls the inherited `deposit` method of the superclass to add `acctBalance` to the account. Implementation III works because `super()` is automatically called as the first line of the constructor code if there is no explicit call to `super`.

5. **(C)** First the `withdraw` method of the `BankAccount` superclass is used to withdraw `amount`. A prefix of `super` must be used to invoke this method, which eliminates choices B and D. Then the balance must be tested using the accessor method `getBalance`, which is inherited. You can't test `balance` directly since it is private to the `BankAccount` class. This eliminates choices A and E, and provides another reason for eliminating choice B.

6. **(B)** When a superclass method is redefined in a subclass, the process is called *method overriding*. Which method to call is determined at run time. This is called *dynamic binding* (p. 146). *Method overloading* is two or more methods with different signatures

in the same class (p. 107). The compiler recognizes at compile time which method to call. This is *early binding*. The process of *downcasting* is unrelated to these principles (p. 149).

7. **(E)** The `addInterest` method is defined only in the `SavingsAccount` class. It therefore cannot be invoked by a `BankAccount` object. The error can be fixed by casting `s` to the correct type:

```
((SavingsAccount) s).addInterest();
```

The other method calls do not cause a problem because `withdraw` and `deposit` are both methods of the `BankAccount` class.

8. **(D)** The `withdraw` method is the only method that has one implementation in the superclass and a *different* implementation in a subclass. Polymorphism is the mechanism of selecting the correct method from the different possibilities in the class hierarchy. Notice that the `deposit` method, for example, is available to objects of all three bank account classes, but it's the *same* code in all three cases. So polymorphism isn't tested.

9. **(D)** It is OK to use `timsSavings` and `daynasChecking` as parameters since each of these *is-a* `BankAccount` object. It is also OK for `timsSavings` and `daynasChecking` to call the `transfer` method (statements II and III), since they inherit this method from the `BankAccount` superclass.

10. **(B)** Statement I is false: A subclass must specify its own constructors. Otherwise the default constructor of the superclass will automatically be invoked. Note that statement III is false: Private instance methods cannot be overridden.

11. **(A)** What is described in choice A is an example of overloaded methods. A key point is that one method is in the same class as the other method, and therefore cannot be an overridden method. An overridden method in a subclass has the same header as a method in its superclass, but different implementation.

12. **(A)** There is a quick test you can do to find the answer to this question: Test the *is-a* relationship—namely, the parameter for `printName` *is-a* `Bird`? and the parameter for `printBirdCall` *is-a* `Parrot`? Note that to get the type of the actual parameter, you must look at its left-hand-side declaration. Choice A fails the test: `bird2` *is-a* `Parrot`? The variable `bird2` is declared a `Bird`, which is not necessarily a `Parrot`. Each other choice passes the test: Choice B: `parrot2` *is-a* `Bird`. Choice C: `bird2` *is-a* `Bird`. Choice D: `parrot2` *is-a* `Parrot`. Choice E: `parrot1` *is-a* `Parrot`.

13. **(B)** Method overriding occurs whenever a method in a superclass is redefined in a subclass. Method overloading is a method in the same class that has the same name but different parameter types. Polymorphism is when the correct overridden method is called for a particular subclass object during run time. Data encapsulation is when data and methods of an object are combined in a class so that the data can be hidden. Procedural abstraction is using separate methods to encapsulate each task in a class.

14. **(D)** Both method calls I and II will cause errors.
    I: An object of a superclass does not have access to a new method of its subclass.
    II: `ob2` is declared to be of type `ClassA`, so a compile-time error will occur with a message indicating that there is no `method2` in `ClassA`. Casting `ob2` to `ClassB` would correct the problem. (Note: Class casting is no longer included in the AP Java subset.)
    III is correct because a subclass inherits all the public methods of its superclass.

15. **(A)** All are correct! They all pass the *is-a* test: (a `Solid` *is-a* `Solid`, a `Sphere` *is-a* `Solid`, a `RectangularPrism` *is-a* `Solid`); and the parameters all match the constructors. Note that the default value for `s4` is `null`, so the assignment `s4 = null` is redundant (but correct).

16. **(A)** This is an example of polymorphism: The correct `volume` method is selected at run time. The parameter expected for `printVolume` is a `Solid` reference, which is what it gets in `main()`. The reference `sol` will refer either to a `Sphere` or a `RectangularPrism` object depending on the outcome of the coin flip. Since a `Sphere` is a `Solid` and a `RectangularPrism` is a `Solid`, there will be no type mismatch when these are the actual parameters in the `printVolume` method. (Note: The `Math.random` method is discussed in Chapter 5.)

17. **(D)** Segment III won't work because `Player` doesn't have a `compareTo` method. The method call `h1.compareTo...` will cause a compile-time error. Also, the `compareTo` method requires an `ExpertPlayer` parameter, but `h2` is a `Player`, which isn't necessarily an `ExpertPlayer`. Segment II avoids both of these pitfalls. Segment I works because the `Player` class has a `getMove` method.

18. **(E)** All compile without error. For the method call `display(arg)`, the compiler checks that the parameter `arg` *is-a* `Animal`, the type in the method's signature. Each of the objects `d1`, `d2`, and `d3` passes the *is-a* test.

19. **(B)** Since the actual type of `p` is `StrStuff2`, the `printSub` method of `StrStuff2`, the subclass, will be called first. This is polymorphism, which calls the method of the actual object during run time. The `String s` is set equal to `"rab"`, and the `printSub` method of the superclass, `StrStuff1`, will be called, namely `printSub("rab")`. This gets the substring of `"rab"` starting at position 2, which is `"b"`. Then `"b"` is printed. At this point, only `"b"` has been printed. But recall that execution of the subclass method was halted for `super.printSub(s)`, so this method must now be completed by executing `System.out.print("rab")`.

    Whew!

    To recap, here is the order of execution of the statements:

    - Set local `String s` to `"rab"`.
    - Call the superclass `printSub("rab")`.
    - Set local `s` variable in superclass method to `"b"`.
    - Print `"b"`.
    - Print the value of `s` in the subclass method, namely `"rab"`.
    - So, the output is `"brab"`.

20. **(D)** As in the previous question, the method in the subclass will be executed first. Here is the order of execution of the statements:

    - `super.doSomething(11)`
    - `n` is set equal to 7.
    - Print 7.
    - Go back to finish `doSomething` in `Class2`. (Note that the parameter in this method is 8.)
    - `n` is set equal to 16.
    - Print 16.

    Therefore, what gets printed is 716.

# Some Standard Classes

5

*Anyone who considers arithmetical methods of producing*
*random digits is, of course, in a state of sin.*
*—John von Neumann (1951)*

→ **The** `Object` **class**
→ **The** `String` **class**
→ **Wrapper classes**

→ **The** `Math` **class**
→ **Random numbers**

## THE `Object` CLASS

## The Universal Superclass

Think of `Object` as the superclass of the universe. Every class automatically extends `Object`, which means that `Object` is a direct or indirect superclass of every other class. In a class hierarchy tree, `Object` is at the top:

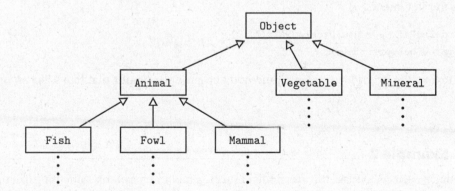

## Methods in `Object`

There are many methods in `Object`, all of them inherited by every other class. The expectation is that these methods will be overridden in any class where the default implementation is not suitable. The methods of `Object` in the AP Java subset are `toString` and `equals`.

**THE toString METHOD**

```
public String toString()
```

This method returns a version of your object in `String` form.

When you attempt to print an object, the inherited default `toString` method is invoked, and what you will see is the class name followed by an @ followed by a meaningless number (the address in memory of the object). For example,

```
SavingsAccount s = new SavingsAccount(500);
System.out.println(s);
```

produces something like

```
SavingsAccount@fea485c4
```

To have more meaningful output, you need to override the `toString` method for your own classes. Even if your final program doesn't need to output any objects, you should define a `toString` method for each class to help in debugging.

## ➡ Example 1 _____

```java
public class OrderedPair
{
    private double x;
    private double y;

    //constructors and other methods ...

    /** Returns this OrderedPair in String form. */
    public String toString()
    {
        return "(" + x + "," + y + ")";
    }
}
```

Now the statements

```java
OrderedPair p = new OrderedPair(7,10);
System.out.println(p);
```

will invoke the overridden `toString` method and produce output that looks like an ordered pair:

```
(7,10)
```

## ➡ Example 2 _____

For a `BankAccount` class the overridden `toString` method may look something like this:

```java
/** Returns this BankAccount in String form. */
public String toString()
{
    return "Bank Account: balance = $" + balance;
}
```

The statements

```java
BankAccount b = new BankAccount(600);
System.out.println(b);
```

will produce output that looks like this:

```
Bank Account: balance = $600
```

1. The + sign is a concatenation operator for strings (see p. 170).
2. Array objects are unusual in that they do not have a `toString` method. To print the elements of an array, the array must be traversed and each element must explicitly be printed.

### THE `equals` METHOD

```
public boolean equals(Object other)
```

All classes inherit this method from the `Object` class. It returns `true` if this object and `other` are the same object, `false` otherwise. Being the same object means referencing the same memory slot. For example,

```
Date d1 = new Date("January", 14, 2001);
Date d2 = d1;
Date d3 = new Date("January", 14, 2001);
```

> Do not use == to test objects for equality. Use the equals method.

The test `if (d1.equals(d2))` returns `true`, but the test `if (d1==d3)` returns `false`, since `d1` and `d3` do not refer to the same object. Often, as in this example, you may want two objects to be considered equal if their *contents* are the same. In that case, you have to override the `equals` method in your class to achieve this. Some of the standard classes described later in this chapter have overridden `equals` in this way. You will not be required to write code that overrides `equals` on the AP exam.

### NOTE

1. The default implementation of `equals` is equivalent to the `==` relation for objects: In the `Date` example above, the test `if (d1 == d2)` returns `true`; the test `if (d1 == d3)` returns `false`.
2. The operators `<`, `>`, and so on are not used for objects (reference types) in Java. To compare objects, you must use either the `equals` method or define a `compareTo` method for the class.

## THE `String` CLASS

## `String` Objects

An object of type `String` is a sequence of characters. All *string literals*, such as `"yikes!"`, are implemented as instances of this class. A string literal consists of zero or more characters, including escape sequences, surrounded by double quotes. (The quotes are not part of the `String` object.) Thus, each of the following is a valid string literal:

```
""              //empty string
"2468"
"I must\n go home"
```

`String` objects are *immutable*, which means that there are no methods to change them after they've been constructed. You can, however, always create a new `String` that is a mutated form of an existing `String`.

## Constructing String Objects

A String object is unusual in that it can be initialized like a primitive type:

```
String s = "abc";
```

This is equivalent to

```
String s = new String("abc");
```

in the sense that in both cases s is a reference to a String object with contents "abc" (see Box on p. 172).

It is possible to reassign a String reference:

```
String s = "John";
s = "Harry";
```

This is equivalent to

```
String s = new String("John");
s = new String("Harry");
```

Notice that this is consistent with the immutable feature of String objects. "John" has not been changed; he has merely been discarded! The fickle reference s now refers to a new String, "Harry". It is also OK to reassign s as follows:

```
s = s + " Windsor";
```

s now refers to the object "Harry Windsor".

Here are other ways to initialize String objects:

```
String s1 = null;            //s1 is a null reference
String s2 = new String();    //s2 is an empty character sequence

String state = "Alaska";
String dessert = "baked " + state;  //dessert has value "baked Alaska"
```

## The Concatenation Operator

The dessert declaration above uses the *concatenation operator*, +, which operates on String objects. Given two String operands lhs and rhs, lhs + rhs produces a single String consisting of lhs followed by rhs. If either lhs or rhs is an object other than a String, the toString method of the object is invoked, and lhs and rhs are concatenated as before. If one of the operands is a String and the other is a primitive type, then the non-String operand is converted to a String, and concatenation occurs as before. If neither lhs nor rhs is a String object, an error occurs. Here are some examples:

```
int five = 5;
String state = "Hawaii-";
String tvShow = state + five + "-0";  //tvShow has value
                                      //"Hawaii-5-0"
int x = 3, y = 4;
String sum = x + y;          //error: can't assign int 7 to String
```

Suppose a Date class has a toString method that outputs dates that look like this: 2/17/1948.

```
Date d1 = new Date(8, 2, 1947);
Date d2 = new Date(2, 17, 1948);
String s = "My birthday is " + d2;  //s has value
                                    //"My birthday is 2/17/1948"
String s2 = d1 + d2;    //error: + not defined for objects
String s3 = d1.toString() + d2.toString();  //s3 has value
                                    //8/2/19472/17/1948
```

## Comparison of String Objects

There are two ways to compare String objects:

1. Use the equals method that is inherited from the Object class and overridden to do the correct thing:

   ```
   if (string1.equals(string2)) ...
   ```

   This returns true if string1 and string2 are identical strings, false otherwise.

2. Use the compareTo method. The String class has a compareTo method:

   ```
   int compareTo(String otherString)
   ```

   It compares strings in dictionary (lexicographical) order:

   - If string1.compareTo(string2) < 0, then string1 precedes string2 in the dictionary.
   - If string1.compareTo(string2) > 0, then string1 follows string2 in the dictionary.
   - If string1.compareTo(string2) == 0, then string1 and string2 are identical. (This test is an alternative to string1.equals(string2).)

Be aware that Java is case-sensitive. Thus, if s1 is "cat" and s2 is "Cat", s1.equals(s2) will return false.

Characters are compared according to their position in the ASCII chart. All you need to know is that all digits precede all capital letters, which precede all lowercase letters. Thus "5" comes before "R", which comes before "a". Two strings are compared as follows: Start at the left end of each string and do a character-by-character comparison until you reach the first character in which the strings differ, the $k$th character, say. If the $k$th character of s1 comes before the $k$th character of s2, then s1 will come before s2, and vice versa. If the strings have identical characters, except that s1 terminates before s2, then s1 comes before s2. Here are some examples:

```
String s1 = "HOT", s2 = "HOTEL", s3 = "dog";
if (s1.compareTo(s2) < 0))    //true, s1 terminates first
    ...
if (s1.compareTo(s3) > 0))    //false, "H" comes before "d"
```

## Other String Methods

The Java String class provides many methods, only a small number of which are in the AP Java subset. In addition to the constructors, comparison methods, and concatenation operator + discussed so far, you should know the following methods:

```
int length()
```

Returns the length of this string.

```
String substring(int startIndex)
```

Returns a new string that is a substring of this string. The substring starts with the character at startIndex and extends to the end of the string. The first character is at index zero. The method throws an IndexOutOfBoundsException if startIndex is negative or larger than the length of the string. Note that if you're using Java 7 or above, you will see the error StringIndexOutOfBoundsException. However, the AP Java subset lists only IndexOutOfBoundsException, which is what they will use on the AP exam.

```
String substring(int startIndex, int endIndex)
```

Returns a new string that is a substring of this string. The substring starts at index startIndex and extends to the character at endIndex-1. (Think of it this way: startIndex is the first character that you want; endIndex is the first character that you *don't* want.) The method throws a StringIndexOutOfBoundsException if startIndex is negative, or endIndex is larger than the length of the string, or startIndex is larger than endIndex.

```
int indexOf(String str)
```

Returns the index of the first occurrence of str within this string. If str is not a substring of this string, -1 is returned. The method throws a NullPointerException if str is null.

Here are some examples:

```
"unhappy".substring(2)        //returns "happy"
"cold".substring(4)           //returns "" (empty string)
"cold".substring(5)           //StringIndexOutOfBoundsException
"strawberry".substring(5,7)   //returns "be"
"crayfish".substring(4,8)     //returns "fish"
"crayfish".substring(4,9)     //StringIndexOutOfBoundsException
"crayfish".substring(5,4)     //StringIndexOutOfBoundsException

String s = "funnyfarm";
int x = s.indexOf("farm");    //x has value 5
x = s.indexOf("farmer");      //x has value -1
int y = s.length();           //y has value 9
```

## WRAPPER CLASSES

A *wrapper class* takes either an existing object or a value of primitive type, "wraps" or "boxes" it in an object, and provides a new set of methods for that type. The point of a wrapper class is to provide extended capabilities for the boxed quantity:

- It can be used in generic Java methods that require objects as parameters.
- It can be used in Java container classes like ArrayList that require the items be objects.

In each case, the wrapper class allows:

1. Construction of an object from a single value (wrapping or boxing the primitive in a wrapper object).
2. Retrieval of the primitive value (unwrapping or unboxing from the wrapper object).

Java provides a wrapper class for each of its primitive types. The two that you should know for the AP exam are the Integer and Double classes.

### The Integer Class

The Integer class wraps a value of type int in an object. An object of type Integer contains just one instance variable whose type is int.

Here are the Integer methods and constants you should know for the AP exam. These are part of the Java Quick Reference.

```
Integer(int value)
```

Constructs an `Integer` object from an `int`. (Boxing.)

```
int intValue()
```

Returns the value of this `Integer` as an `int`. (Unboxing.)

```
Integer.MIN_VALUE
```

A constant equal to the minimum value represented by an `int` or `Integer`.

```
Integer.MAX_VALUE
```

A constant equal to the maximum value represented by an `int` or `Integer`.

## The `Double` Class

The `Double` class wraps a value of type `double` in an object. An object of type `Double` contains just one instance variable whose type is `double`.

The methods you should know for the AP exam are analogous to those for type `Integer`. These, too, are part of the Java Quick Reference.

```
Double(double value)
```

Constructs a `Double` object from a `double`. (Boxing.)

```
double doubleValue()
```

Returns the value of this `Double` as a `double`. (Unboxing.)

**NOTE**

1. The `compareTo` and `equals` methods for the `Integer` and `Double` classes are no longer part of the AP Java subset. This is probably because the later versions of Java make extensive use of autoboxing and auto-unboxing.
2. `Integer` and `Double` objects are immutable. This means there are no mutator methods in the classes.

## Autoboxing and Unboxing

This topic is now part of the AP Java subset.

*Autoboxing* is the automatic conversion that the Java compiler makes between primitive types and their corresponding wrapper classes. This includes converting an `int` to an `Integer` and a `double` to a `Double`.

Autoboxing is applied when a primitive value is assigned to a variable of the corresponding wrapper class. For example,

```
Integer intOb = 3;   //3 is boxed
```

```
ArrayList<Integer> list = new ArrayList<Integer>();
list.add(4); //4 is boxed
```

Autoboxing also occurs when a primitive value is passed as a parameter to a method that expects an object of the corresponding wrapper class. For example,

```
public String stringMethod(Double d)
{ /* return string that has d embedded in it */ }


double realNum = 4.5;
String str = stringMethod(realNum);    //realNum is boxed
```

*Unboxing* is the automatic conversion that the Java compiler makes from the wrapper class to the primitive type. This includes converting an `Integer` to an `int` and a `Double` to a `double`.

Unboxing is applied when a wrapper class object is passed as a parameter to a method that expects a value of the corresponding primitive type. For example,

```
Integer intOb1 = 9;
Integer intOb2 = 8;


public static int sum (int num1, int num2)
{ return num1 + num2; }


System.out.println(sum(intOb1, intOb2)); //intOb1 and intOb2 are unboxed
```

Unboxing is also applied when a wrapper class object is assigned to a variable of the corresponding primitive type. For example,

```
int p = intOb1; //intOb1 is unboxed
```

### COMPARISON OF WRAPPER CLASS OBJECTS

Unboxing is often used in the comparison of wrapper objects of the same type. But it's trickier than it sounds. Don't use == to test `Integer` objects! You may get surprising results. The expression if `(intOb1 == intOb2)` tests whether `intOb1` and `intOb2` are the same *reference*. It does not test the actual values.

➡ **Example 1** _____

```
Integer intOb1 = 4; //boxing
Integer intOb2 = 4; //boxing
if (intOb1 == intOb2)...
```

The test returns `true`, but not for the reason you might expect. The reason is that for efficiency Java creates only one Integer object if the `int` values are the same. So the references are the same. This is safe because an `Integer` cannot be altered. (It's immutable.)

➡ **Example 2** _____

```
Integer intOb1 = 4;                  //boxing
Integer intOb2 = new Integer(4);  //boxing
if (intOb1 == intOb2)...
```

This test returns `false` because use of `new` creates a new object. `intOb1` and `intOb2` are different references in this example. See the analogous situation for `String` objects in the Box on p. 172.

```
Integer intOb1 = 4;   //boxing
int n = 4;
if (intOb1 == n)...
```

This test returns `true` because if the comparison is between an `Integer` object and a primitive integer type, the object is automatically unboxed.

➥ **Example 4** _____

```
Integer intOb1 = 4;               //boxing
Integer intOb2 = new Integer(4);  //boxing
if (intOb1.intValue() == intOb2.intValue())...
```

This test returns `true` because the values of the objects are being tested. This is the correct way to test `Integer` objects for equality.

The relational operators less than (<) and greater than (>) do what you may expect when testing `Integer` and `Double` objects.

➥ **Example 5** _____

```
Integer intOb1 = 4;    //boxing
Integer intOb2 = 8;    //boxing
if (intOb1 < intOb2)...
```

This test returns `true` because the compiler unboxes the objects as follows:

```
if (intOb1.intValue() < intOb2.intValue())
```

➥ **Example 6** _____

```
Integer intOb1 = 4; //boxing
int n = 8;
if (intOb1 < n)...
```

This test will return `true` because, again, if one of the operands is a primitive type, the object will be unboxed.

## THE `Math` CLASS

This class implements standard mathematical functions such as absolute value, square root, trigonometric functions, the log function, the power function, and so on. It also contains mathematical constants such as $\pi$ and $e$.

Here are the functions you should know for the AP exam:

```
static int abs(int x)
```

Returns the absolute value of integer $x$.

```
static double abs(double x)
```

Returns the absolute value of real number $x$.

```
static double pow(double base, double exp)
```

Returns base$^{\text{exp}}$. Assumes base > 0, or base = 0 and exp > 0, or base < 0 and exp is an integer.

```
static double sqrt(double x)
```

Returns $\sqrt{x}$, $x \geq 0$.

```
static double random()
```

Returns a random number $r$, where $0.0 \leq r < 1.0$. (See the next section, "Random Numbers".)

All of the functions and constants are implemented as static methods and variables, which means that there are no instances of Math objects. The methods are invoked using the class name, Math, followed by the dot operator.

Here are some examples of mathematical formulas and the equivalent Java statements.

1. The relationship between the radius and area of a circle is

$$r = \sqrt{A/\pi}$$

   In code:

```
   radius = Math.sqrt(area / Math.PI);
```

2. The amount of money $A$ in an account after ten years, given an original deposit of $P$ and an interest rate of 5% compounded annually, is

$$A = P(1.05)^{10}$$

   In code:

```
   a = p * Math.pow(1.05, 10);
```

3. The distance $D$ between two points $P(x_P, y)$ and $Q(x_Q, y)$ on the same horizontal line is

$$D = |x_P - x_Q|$$

   In code:

```
   d = Math.abs(xp - xq);
```

**NOTE**

The static import construct allows you to use the static members of a class without the class name prefix. For example, the statement

```
import static java.lang.Math.*;
```

allows use of all Math methods and constants without the Math prefix. Thus, the statement in formula 1 above could be written

```
radius = sqrt(area / PI);
```

Static imports are not part of the AP subset.

## Random Numbers

### RANDOM REALS

The statement

```
double r = Math.random();
```

produces a random real number in the range 0.0 to 1.0, where 0.0 is included and 1.0 is not.

This range can be scaled and shifted. On the AP exam you will be expected to write algebraic expressions involving `Math.random()` that represent linear transformations of the original interval $0.0 \leq x < 1.0$.

### ➡ Example 1

Produce a random real value $x$ in the range $0.0 \leq x < 6.0$.

```
double x = 6 * Math.random();
```

### ➡ Example 2

Produce a random real value $x$ in the range $2.0 \leq x < 3.0$.

```
double x = Math.random() + 2;
```

### ➡ Example 3

Produce a random real value $x$ in the range $4.0 \leq x < 6.0$.

```
double x = 2 * Math.random() + 4;
```

In general, to produce a random real value in the range `lowValue` $\leq x <$ `highValue`:

```
double x = (highValue - lowValue) * Math.random() + lowValue;
```

### RANDOM INTEGERS

Using a cast to `int`, a scaling factor, and a shifting value, `Math.random()` can be used to produce random integers in any range.

### ➡ Example 1

Produce a random integer from 0 to 99.

```
int num = (int) (Math.random() * 100);
```

In general, the expression

```
(int) (Math.random() * k)
```

produces a random `int` in the range $0, 1, \ldots, k - 1$, where $k$ is called the scaling factor. Note that the cast to `int` truncates the real number `Math.random()` * k.

### ➡ Example 2

Produce a random integer from 1 to 100.

```
int num = (int) (Math.random() * 100) + 1;
```

In general, if $k$ is a scaling factor, and $p$ is a shifting value, the statement

```
int n = (int) (Math.random() * k) + p;
```

produces a random integer $n$ in the range $p, p + 1, \ldots, p + (k - 1)$.

## ➡ Example 3 _____

Produce a random integer from 5 to 24.

```
int num = (int) (Math.random() * 20) + 5;
```

Note that there are 20 possible integers from 5 to 24, inclusive.

**NOTE**

There is further discussion of strings and random numbers, plus additional questions, in Chapter 10 (The AP Computer Science A Labs).

## Chapter Summary

All students should know about overriding the `equals` and `toString` methods of the `Object` class and should be familiar with the `Integer` and `Double` wrapper classes.

Know the AP subset methods of the `Math` class, especially the use of `Math.random()` for generating random numbers. Learn the `String` methods `substring` and `indexOf`, including knowing where exceptions are thrown in the `String` methods.

1. Consider the following declarations in a program to find the quantity $base^{exp}$.

```
double base = <a double value>
double exp = <a double value>
/* code to find power, which equals base^exp */
```

Which is a correct replacement for
/* **code to find** power, **which equals** $base^{exp}$ */?

```
I  double power;
   Math m = new Math();
   power = m.pow(base, exp);

II  double power;
    power = Math.pow(base, exp);

III  int power;
     power = Math.pow(base, exp);
```

(A) I only
(B) II only
(C) III only
(D) I and II only
(E) I and III only

2. Consider the squareRoot method defined below.

```
/** Returns a Double whose value is the square root
 *  of the value represented by d.
 */
public Double squareRoot(Double d)
{
    /* implementation code */
}
```

Which /* **implementation code** */ satisfies the postcondition?

```
I  double x = d;
   x = Math.sqrt(x);
   return x;

II  return new Double(Math.sqrt(d.doubleValue()));

III  return Double(Math.sqrt(d.doubleValue()));
```

(A) I only
(B) I and II only
(C) I and III only
(D) II and III only
(E) I, II, and III

3. Here are some examples of negative numbers rounded to the nearest integer:

| Negative real number | Rounded to nearest integer |
| --- | --- |
| −3.5 | −4 |
| −8.97 | −9 |
| −5.0 | −5 |
| −2.487 | −2 |
| −0.2 | 0 |

Refer to the following declaration.

```
double d = -4.67;
```

Which of the following correctly rounds d to the nearest integer?

(A) `int rounded = Math.abs(d);`

(B) `int rounded = (int) (Math.random() * d);`

(C) `int rounded = (int) (d - 0.5);`

(D) `int rounded = (int) (d + 0.5);`

(E) `int rounded = Math.abs((int) (d - 0.5));`

4. A program is to simulate plant life under harsh conditions. In the program, plants die randomly according to some probability. Here is part of a `Plant` class defined in the program:

```
public class Plant
{
    /** Probability that plant dies is a real number between 0 and 1. */
    private double probDeath;

    public Plant(double plantProbDeath, < other parameters >)
    {
        probDeath = plantProbDeath;
        < initialization of other instance variables >
    }

    /** Plant lives or dies. */
    public void liveOrDie()
    {
        /* statement to generate random number */
        if (/* test to determine if plant dies */)
            < code to implement plant's death >
        else
            < code to make plant continue living >
    }

    //Other variables and methods are not shown.
}
```

Which of the following are correct replacements for
(1) /* *statement to generate random number* */ and
(2) /* *test to determine if plant dies* */?

(A)  (1) `double x = Math.random();`
     (2) `x == probDeath`

(B)  (1) `double x = (int) (Math.random());`
     (2) `x > probDeath`

(C)  (1) `double x = Math.random();`
     (2) `x < probDeath`

(D)  (1) `int x = (int) (Math.random() * 100);`
     (2) `x < (int) probDeath`

(E)  (1) `int x = (int) (Math.random() * 100) + 1;`
     (2) `x == (int) probDeath`

5. A program simulates 50 slips of paper, numbered 1 through 50, placed in a bowl for a raffle drawing. Which of the following statements stores in `winner` a random integer from 1 to 50?

```
(A) int winner = (int) (Math.random() * 50) + 1;
(B) int winner = (int) (Math.random() * 50);
(C) int winner = (int) (Math.random() * 51);
(D) int winner = (int) (Math.random() * 51) + 1;
(E) int winner = (int) (1 + Math.random() * 49);
```

6. Consider the following code segment.

```
Integer i = new Integer(20);
/* more code */
```

Which of the following replacements for /* *more code* */ correctly sets `i` to have an `Integer` value of 25?

```
  I  i = new Integer(25);

 II  i.intValue() = 25;

III  Integer j = new Integer(25);
        i = j;
```

(A) I only
(B) II only
(C) III only
(D) I and III only
(E) II and III only

7. Refer to these declarations.

```
Integer k = new Integer(8);
Integer m = new Integer(4);
```

Which test(s) will generate a compile-time error?

```
  I  if (k == m)...

 II  if (k.intValue() == m.intValue())...

III  if ((k.intValue()).equals(m.intValue()))...
```

(A) I only
(B) II only
(C) III only
(D) I and II only
(E) II and III only

8. Consider the following code fragment.

```
Object intObj = new Integer(9);
System.out.println(intObj);
```

You may assume that the Integer class has a toString method. What will be output as a result of running the fragment?

(A) No output. An IllegalArgumentException will be thrown.

(B) No output. An ArithmeticException will be thrown.

(C) 9

(D) "9"

(E) An address in memory of the reference IntObj

9. Consider these declarations.

```
String s1 = "crab";
String s2 = new String("crab");
String s3 = s1;
```

Which expression involving these strings evaluates to true?

I  s1 == s2

II  s1.equals(s2)

III  s3.equals(s2)

(A) I only

(B) II only

(C) II and III only

(D) I and II only

(E) I, II, and III

10. Suppose that strA = "TOMATO", strB = "tomato", and strC = "tom". Given that "A" comes before "a" in dictionary order, which is true?

(A) strA.compareTo(strB) < 0 && strB.compareTo(strC) < 0

(B) strB.compareTo(strA) < 0 || strC.compareTo(strA) < 0

(C) strC.compareTo(strA) < 0 && strA.compareTo(strB) < 0

(D) !(strA.equals(strB)) && strC.compareTo(strB) < 0

(E) !(strA.equals(strB)) && strC.compareTo(strA) < 0

11. This question refers to the following declaration.

```
String line = "Some more silly stuff on strings!";
//the words are separated by a single space
```

What string will `str` refer to after execution of the following?

```
int x = line.indexOf("m");
String str = line.substring(10, 15) + line.substring(25, 25 + x);
```

  (A) `"sillyst"`

  (B) `"sillystr"`

  (C) `"silly st"`

  (D) `"silly str"`

  (E) `"sillystrin"`

12. A program has a `String` variable `fullName` that stores a first name, followed by a space, followed by a last name. There are no spaces in either the first or last names. Here are some examples of `fullName` values: `"Anthony Coppola"`, `"Jimmy Carroll"`, and `"Tom DeWire"`. Consider this code segment that extracts the last name from a `fullName` variable, and stores it in `lastName` with no surrounding blanks:

```
int k = fullName.indexOf(" ");     //find index of blank
String lastName = /* expression */
```

Which is a correct replacement for /* *expression* */?

  I `fullName.substring(k);`

  II `fullName.substring(k + 1);`

  III `fullName.substring(k + 1, fullName.length());`

  (A) I only

  (B) II only

  (C) III only

  (D) II and III only

  (E) I and III only

13. One of the rules for converting English to Pig Latin states: If a word begins with a consonant, move the consonant to the end of the word and add "ay". Thus "dog" becomes "ogday," and "crisp" becomes "rispcay". Suppose s is a String containing an English word that begins with a consonant. Which of the following creates the correct corresponding word in Pig Latin? Assume the declarations

```
String ayString = "ay";
String pigString;
```

(A) `pigString = s.substring(0, s.length()) + s.substring(0,1)`
              `+ ayString;`

(B) `pigString = s.substring(1, s.length()) + s.substring(0,0)`
              `+ ayString;`

(C) `pigString = s.substring(0, s.length()-1) + s.substring(0,1)`
              `+ ayString;`

(D) `pigString = s.substring(1, s.length()-1) + s.substring(0,0)`
              `+ ayString;`

(E) `pigString = s.substring(1, s.length()) + s.substring(0,1)`
              `+ ayString;`

14. This question refers to the getString method shown below.

```
public static String getString(String s1, String s2)
{
    int index = s1.indexOf(s2);
    return s1.substring(index, index + s2.length());
}
```

Which is true about getString? It may return a string that

  I  Is equal to s2.
  II  Has no characters in common with s2.
  III  Is equal to s1.

(A) I and III only
(B) II and III only
(C) I and II only
(D) I, II, and III
(E) None is true.

15. Consider this method.

```
public static String doSomething(String s)
{
    final String BLANK = " ";    //BLANK contains a single space
    String str = "";             //empty string
    String temp;
    for (int i = 0; i < s.length(); i++)
    {
        temp = s.substring(i, i + 1);
        if (!(temp.equals(BLANK)))
            str += temp;
    }
    return str;
}
```

Which of the following is the most precise description of what doSomething does?

(A) It returns s unchanged.

(B) It returns s with all its blanks removed.

(C) It returns a String that is equivalent to s with all its blanks removed.

(D) It returns a String that is an exact copy of s.

(E) It returns a String that contains s.length() blanks.

Questions 16 and 17 refer to the classes `Position` and `PositionTest` below.

```java
public class Position
{
    /** row and col are both >= 0 except in the default
     *  constructor where they are initialized to -1.
     */
    private int row, col;

    public Position()            //constructor
    {
        row = -1;
        col = -1;
    }

    public Position(int r, int c)        //constructor
    {
        row = r;
        col = c;
    }

    /** Returns row of Position. */
    public int getRow()
    { return row; }

    /** Returns column of Position. */
    public int getCol()
    { return col; }

    /** Returns Position north of (up from) this position. */
    public Position north()
    { return new Position(row - 1, col); }

    //Similar methods south, east, and west
            ...

    /** Compares this Position to another Position object.
     *  Returns -1 (less than), 0 (equals), or 1 (greater than).
     */
    public int compareTo(Position p)
    {
        if (this.getRow() < p.getRow() || this.getRow() == p.getRow()
            && this.getCol() < p.getCol())
                return -1;
        if (this.getRow() > p.getRow() || this.getRow() == p.getRow()
            && this.getCol() > p.getCol())
                return 1;
        return 0;            //row and col both equal
    }

    /** Returns String form of Position. */
    public String toString()
    { return "(" + row + "," + col + ")"; }
}
```

```
public class PositionTest
{
    public static void main(String[] args)
    {
        Position p1 = new Position(2, 3);
        Position p2 = new Position(4, 1);
        Position p3 = new Position(2, 3);

        //tests to compare positions
            ...
    }
}
```

16. Which is true about the value of `p1.compareTo(p2)`?
    (A) It equals `true`.
    (B) It equals `false`.
    (C) It equals `0`.
    (D) It equals `1`.
    (E) It equals `-1`.

17. Which boolean expression about p1 and p3 is true?

    I   `p1 == p3`

    II  `p1.equals(p3)`

    III `p1.compareTo(p3) == 0`

    (A) I only
    (B) II only
    (C) III only
    (D) II and III only
    (E) I, II, and III

Questions 18 and 19 deal with the problem of swapping two integer values. Three methods are proposed to solve the problem, using primitive `int` types, `Integer` objects, and `IntPair` objects, where `IntPair` is defined as follows.

```java
public class IntPair
{
    private int firstValue;
    private int secondValue;

    public IntPair(int first, int second)
    {
        firstValue = first;
        secondValue = second;
    }

    public int getFirst()
    { return firstValue; }

    public int getSecond()
    { return secondValue; }

    public void setFirst(int a)
    { firstValue = a; }

    public void setSecond(int b)
    { secondValue = b;}
}
```

18. Here are three different swap methods, each intended for use in a client program.

```
 I public static void swap(int a, int b)
   {
       int temp = a;
       a = b;
       b = temp;
   }

II public static void swap(Integer obj_a, Integer obj_b)
   {
       Integer temp = new Integer(obj_a.intValue());
       obj_a = obj_b;
       obj_b = temp;
   }

III public static void swap(IntPair pair)
    {
        int temp = pair.getFirst();
        pair.setFirst(pair.getSecond());
        pair.setSecond(temp);
    }
```

When correctly used in a client program with appropriate parameters, which method will swap two integers, as intended?

(A) I only

(B) II only

(C) III only

(D) II and III only

(E) I, II, and III

19. Consider the following program that uses the `IntPair` class.

```
public class TestSwap
{
    public static void swap(IntPair pair)
    {
        int temp = pair.getFirst();
        pair.setFirst(pair.getSecond());
        pair.setSecond(temp);
    }

    public static void main(String[] args)
    {
        int x = 8, y = 6;
        /* code to swap x and y */
    }
}
```

Which is a correct replacement for /* *code to swap* x *and* y */?

```
 I IntPair iPair = new IntPair(x, y);
   swap(x, y);
   x = iPair.getFirst();
   y = iPair.getSecond();

 II IntPair iPair = new IntPair(x, y);
    swap(iPair);
    x = iPair.getFirst();
    y = iPair.getSecond();

III IntPair iPair = new IntPair(x, y);
    swap(iPair);
    x = iPair.setFirst();
    y = iPair.setSecond();
```

(A) I only
(B) II only
(C) III only
(D) II and III only
(E) None is correct.

Refer to the Name class below for Questions 20 and 21.

```java
public class Name
{
    private String firstName;
    private String lastName;

    public Name(String first, String last)  //constructor
    {
        firstName = first;
        lastName = last;
    }

    public String toString()
    { return firstName + " " + lastName; }

    public boolean equals(Object obj)
    {
        Name n = (Name) obj;
        return n.firstName.equals(firstName) &&
                n.lastName.equals(lastName);
    }

    public int compareTo(Name n)
    {
        /* more code */
    }
}
```

20. The `compareTo` method implements the standard name-ordering algorithm where last names take precedence over first names. Lexicographic or dictionary ordering of `Strings` is used. For example, the name Scott Dentes comes before Nick Elser, and Adam Cooper comes before Sara Cooper.

Which of the following is a correct replacement for /* *more code* */?

```
  I int lastComp = lastName.compareTo(n.lastName);
    if (lastComp != 0)
        return lastComp;
    else
        return firstName.compareTo(n.firstName);

 II if (lastName.equals(n.lastName))
        return firstName.compareTo(n.firstName);
    else
        return 0;

III if (!(lastName.equals(n.lastName)))
        return firstName.compareTo(n.firstName);
    else
        return lastName.compareTo(n.lastName);
```

(A) I only
(B) II only
(C) III only
(D) I and II only
(E) I, II, and III

21. Which statement about the `Name` class is false?
(A) `Name` objects are immutable.
(B) It is possible for the methods in `Name` to throw a `NullPointerException`.
(C) If `n1` and `n2` are `Name` objects in a client class, then the expressions `n1.equals(n2)` and `n1.compareTo(n2) == 0` must have the same value.
(D) The `compareTo` method throws a run-time exception if the parameter is null.
(E) Since the `Name` class has a `compareTo` method, it *must* provide an implementation for an `equals` method.

## ANSWER KEY

| | | |
|---|---|---|
| 1. **B** | 8. **C** | 15. **C** |
| 2. **B** | 9. **C** | 16. **E** |
| 3. **C** | 10. **D** | 17. **C** |
| 4. **C** | 11. **A** | 18. **C** |
| 5. **A** | 12. **D** | 19. **B** |
| 6. **D** | 13. **E** | 20. **A** |
| 7. **C** | 14. **A** | 21. **E** |

## ANSWERS EXPLAINED

1. **(B)** All the `Math` class methods are static methods, which means you can't use a `Math` object that calls the method. The method is invoked using the class name, `Math`, followed by the dot operator. Thus segment II is correct, and segment I is incorrect. Segment III will cause an error: Since the parameters of `pow` are of type `double`, the result should be stored in a `double`.

2. **(B)** The `Math.sqrt` method must be invoked on a primitive type `double`, but auto-unboxing takes care of that in the line

   ```
   double x = d;
   ```

   The return type of the method is `Double`, and autoboxing takes care of that in the statement

   ```
   return x;
   ```

   Segment III fails because you can't use the `Double` constructor to create a new object without using the keyword `new`.

3. **(C)** The value −4.67 must be rounded to −5. Subtracting 0.5 gives a value of −5.17. Casting to `int` truncates the number (chops off the decimal part) and leaves a value of −5. None of the other choices produces −5. Choice A gives the absolute value of d: 4.67. Choice B is an incorrect use of `Random`. The parameter for `nextInt` should be an integer $n$, $n \geq 2$. The method then returns a random `int` $k$, where $0 \leq k < n$. Choice D is the way to round a *positive* real number to the nearest integer. In the actual case it produces −4. Choice E gives the absolute value of −5, namely 5.

4. **(C)** The statement `double x = Math.random();` generates a random `double` in the range $0 \leq x < 1$. Suppose `probDeath` is 0.67, or 67%. Assuming that random doubles are uniformly distributed in the interval, one can expect that 67% of the time x will be in the range $0 \leq x < 0.67$. You can therefore simulate the probability of death by testing if $x$ is between 0 and 0.67, that is, if x < 0.67. Thus, x < `probDeath` is the desired condition for plant death, eliminating choices A and B. Choices D and E fail because `(int) probDeath` truncates `probDeath` to 0. The test x < 0 will always be false, and the test x == 0 will only be true if the random number generator returned exactly 0, an extremely unlikely occurrence! Neither of these choices correctly simulates the probability of death.

5. **(A)** The expression

```
(int) (Math.random() * 50);
```

returns an int from 0 to 49. Therefore, adding 1 shifts the range to be 1 to 50, which was required.

6. **(D)** The `Integer` class has no methods that can change the contents of `i`. However, `i` can be reassigned so that it refers to another object. This happens in both segments I and III. Segment II is wrong because `intValue` is an *accessor*—it cannot be used to change the value of object `i`.

7. **(C)** Tests I and II both get past the compiler. Test I compiles because `==` tests the *references* for equality. To test the values, use `intValue`, which Test II does correctly. Test III fails because you can't invoke a method (in this case `equals`) with an `int`.

8. **(C)** The `toString` method of the `Integer` class is invoked, which returns a string representing the value of `intObj`:

```
System.out.println(intObj.toString());     //outputs 9
```

9. **(C)** Here are the memory slots:

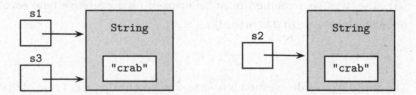

Statements II and III are true because the contents of `s1` and `s2` are the same, and the contents of `s3` and `s2` are the same. Statement I is false because `s1` and `s2` are not the same reference. Note that the expression `s1 == s3` would be true since `s1` and `s3` *are* the same reference.

10. **(D)** Note that `"TOMATO"` precedes both `"tomato"` and `"tom"`, since `"T"` precedes `"t"`. Also, `"tom"` precedes `"tomato"` since the length of `"tom"` is less than the length of `"tomato"`. Therefore each of the following is true:

```
strA.compareTo(strB) < 0
strA.compareTo(strC) < 0
strC.compareTo(strB) < 0
```

So

Choice A is T and F which evaluates to F
Choice B is F or F which evaluates to F
Choice C is F and T which evaluates to F
Choice D is T and T which evaluates to T
Choice E is T and F which evaluates to F

11. **(A)** `x` contains the index of the first occurrence of `"m"` in `line`, namely 2. (Remember that `"S"` is at index 0.) The method call `line.substring(10,15)` returns `"silly"`, the substring starting at index 10 and extending though index 14. The method call `line.substring(25,27)` returns `"st"` (don't include the character at index 27!). The concatenation operator, +, joins these.

12. **(D)** The first character of the last name starts at the first character after the space. Thus, `startIndex` for `substring` must be `k+1`. This eliminates expression I. Expression II takes all the characters from position `k+1` to the end of the `fullName` string, which is correct. Expression III takes all the characters from position `k+1` to position `fullName.length()-1`, which is also correct.

13. **(E)** Suppose `s` contains `"cat"`. You want `pigString = "at" + "c" + "ay"`. Now the string `"at"` is the substring of `s` starting at position 1 and ending at position `s.length()-1`. The correct substring call for this piece of the word is `s.substring(1,s.length())`, which eliminates choices A, C, and D. (Recall that the first parameter is the starting position, and the second parameter is one position past the last index of the substring.) The first letter of the word—`"c"` in the example—starts at position 0 and ends at position 0. The correct expression is `s.substring(0,1)`, which eliminates choice B.

14. **(A)** Statement I is true whenever `s2` occurs in `s1`. For example, if strings `s1 = "catastrophe"` and `s2 = "cat"`, then `getString` returns `"cat"`. Statement II will never happen. If `s2` is not contained in `s1`, the `indexOf` call will return `-1`. Using a negative integer as the first parameter of `substring` will cause a `StringIndexOutOfBoundsException`. Statement III will be true whenever `s1` equals `s2`.

15. **(C)** The `String temp` represents a single-character substring of `s`. The method examines each character in `s` and, if it is a nonblank, appends it to `str`, which is initially empty. Each assignment `str += temp` assigns a new reference to `str`. Thus, `str` ends up as a copy of `s` but without the blanks. A reference to the final `str` object is returned. Choice A is correct in that `s` is left unchanged, but it is not the *best* characterization of what the method does. Choice B is not precise because an object parameter is never modified: Changes, if any, are performed on a copy. Choices D and E are wrong because the method removes blanks.

16. **(E)** The `compareTo` method returns an `int`, so eliminate choices A and B. In the implementation of `compareTo`, the code segment that applies to the particular example is

```
if (this.getRow() < p.getRow() || ...
    return -1;
```

Since 2 < 4, the value `-1` is returned.

17. **(C)** Expression III is true: The `compareTo` method is implemented to return 0 if two `Position` objects have the same row and column. Expression I is false because `object1 == object2` returns `true` only if `object1` and `object2` are the *same reference*. Expression II is tricky. You would like `p1` and `p3` to be equal since they have the same row and column values. This is not going to happen automatically, however. The `equals` method must explicitly be overridden for the `Position` class. If this hasn't been done, the default `equals` method, which is inherited from class `Object`, will return true only if `p1` and `p3` are the same reference, which is not true.

18. **(C)** Recall that primitive types and object references are passed by value. This means that copies are made of the actual arguments. Any changes that are made are made to the *copies*. The actual parameters remain unchanged. Thus, in methods I and II, the parameters will retain their original values and remain unswapped.

   To illustrate, for example, why method II fails, consider this piece of code that tests it:

```
public static void main(String[] args)
{
    int x = 8, y = 6;
    Integer xObject = new Integer(x);
    Integer yObject = new Integer(y);
    swap(xObject, yObject);
    x = xObject.intValue();      //surprise! still has value 8
    y = yObject.intValue();      //surprise! still has value 6
        ...
}
```

Here are the memory slots before swap is called:

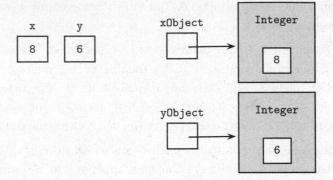

Here they are when swap is invoked:

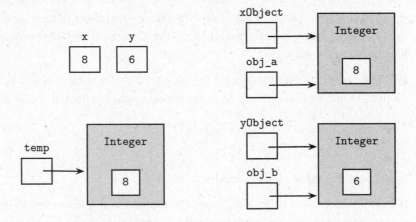

Just before exiting the swap method:

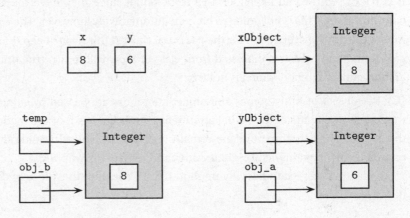

After exiting, xObject and yObject have retained their original values:

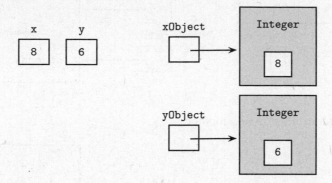

The reason method III works is that instead of the object references being changed, the object *contents* are changed. Thus, after exiting the method, the IntPair reference is as it was, but the first and second values have been interchanged. (See the explanation of the next question for diagrams of the memory slots.) In this question, IntPair is used as a wrapper class for a pair of integers whose values need to be swapped.

19. **(B)** The swap method has just a single IntPair parameter, which eliminates segment I. Segment III fails because setFirst and setSecond are used incorrectly. These are mutator methods that change an IntPair object. What is desired is to return the (newly swapped) first and second values of the pair: Accessor methods getFirst and getSecond do the trick. To see why the swap code in segment II works, look at the memory slots.

Before the swap method is called:

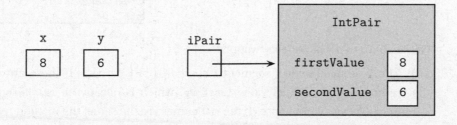

Just after the swap method is called:

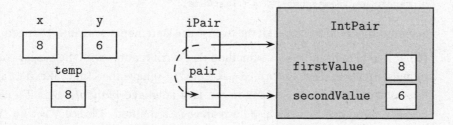

Just before exiting the swap method:

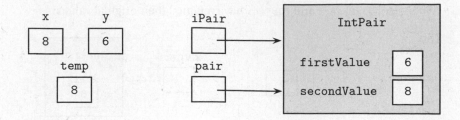

Just after exiting the swap method:

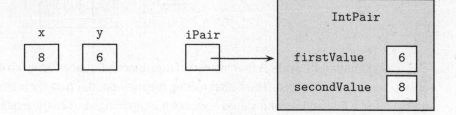

After the statements:

```
x = iPair.getFirst();
y = iPair.getSecond();
```

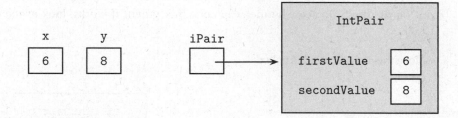

Notice that x and y have been swapped!

20. **(A)** The first statement of segment I compares last names. If these are different, the method returns the `int` value `lastComp`, which is negative if `lastName` precedes `n.lastName`, positive otherwise. If the last names are the same, the method returns the `int` result of comparing first names. Segments II and III use incorrect algorithms for comparing names. Segment II would be correct if the `else` part were

    ```
    return lastName.compareTo(n.lastName);
    ```

    Segment III would be correct if the two `return` statements were interchanged.

21. **(E)** It is *wise* to have an `equals` method that is compatible with the `compareTo` method, namely, `n1.equals(n2)` and `n1.compareTo(n2)==0` have the same value if `n1` and `n2` are `Name` objects. However, nothing in the Java language *mandates* that if a class has a `compareTo` method, it must also have an `equals` method. Choice A is true. You know this because the `Name` class has no mutator methods. Thus, `Name` objects can never be changed. Choice B is true: If a `Name` is initialized with null references, each of the methods will throw a `NullPointerException`. Choice C is true: If `n1.equals(n2)` is true, then `n1.compareTo(n2) == 0` is true, because both are conditions for equality of `n1` and `n2` and should therefore be consistent. Choice D is true: If the parameter is null, the `compareTo` method will throw a `NullPointerException`.

# Program Design and Analysis 6

*Weeks of coding can save you hours of planning.*
*—Anonymous*

→ **Software development, including design and testing**

→ **Object-oriented program design**

→ **Relationships between classes**

→ **Program analysis**

→ **Efficiency**

Students of introductory computer science typically see themselves as programmers. They no sooner have a new programming project in their heads than they're at the computer, typing madly to get some code up and running. (Is this you?)

To succeed as a programmer, however, you have to combine the practical skills of a software engineer with the analytical mindset of a computer scientist. A software engineer oversees the life cycle of software development: initiation of the project, analysis of the specification, and design of the program, as well as implementation, testing, and maintenance of the final product. A computer scientist (among other things!) analyzes the implementation, correctness, and efficiency of algorithms. All these topics are tested on the AP exam.

## SOFTWARE DEVELOPMENT

### Program Specification

The *specification* is an explicit written description of the project. Typically it is based on a customer's (or a teacher's!) requirements. The first step in writing a program is to analyze the specification. Make sure you understand it, and clarify with the customer anything that is unclear.

### Program Design

Even for a small-scale program a good design can save programming time and enhance the reliability of the final program. The design is a fairly detailed plan for solving the problem outlined in the specification. It should include all objects that will be used in the solution, the data structures that will implement them, plus a detailed list of the tasks to be performed by the program.

A good design provides a fairly detailed overall plan at a glance, without including the minutiae of Java code.

## Program Implementation

Program implementation is the coding phase. Design and implementation are discussed in more detail on the next page.

## Testing and Debugging

### TEST DATA

Not every possible input value can be tested, so a programmer should be diligent in selecting a representative set of *test data*. Typical values in each part of a domain of the program should be selected, as well as endpoint values and out-of-range values. If only positive input is required, your test data should include a negative value just to check that your program handles it appropriately.

**➡ Example** _____

A program must be written to insert a value into its correct position in this sorted list:

    2    5    9

Test data should include:

- A value less than 2
- A value between 2 and 5
- A value between 5 and 9
- A value greater than 9
- 2, 5, and 9
- A negative value

### TYPES OF ERRORS (BUGS)

- A *compile-time error* occurs during compilation of the program. The compiler is unable to translate the program into bytecode and prints an appropriate error message. A *syntax error* is a compile-time error caused by violating the rules of the programming language. Some examples are omitting semicolons or braces, using undeclared identifiers, using keywords inappropriately, having parameters that don't match in type and number, and invoking a method for an object whose class definition doesn't contain that method.

- A *run-time error* occurs during execution of the program. The Java run-time environment *throws an exception*, which means that it stops execution and prints an error message. Typical causes of run-time errors include attempting to divide an integer by zero, using an array index that is out of bounds, attempting to open a file that cannot be found, and so on. An error that causes a program to run forever ("infinite loop") can also be regarded as a run-time error. (See also "Errors and Exceptions," p. 83.)

- An *intent* or *logic error* is one that fails to carry out the specification of the program. The program compiles and runs but does not do the job. These are sometimes the hardest types of errors to fix.

**ROBUSTNESS**

Always assume that any user of your program is not as smart as you are. You must therefore aim to write a *robust* program, namely one that:

- Won't give inaccurate answers for some input data.
- Won't crash if the input data are invalid.
- Won't allow execution to proceed if invalid data are entered.

Examples of bad input data include out-of-range numbers, characters instead of numerical data, and a response of "maybe" when "yes" or "no" was asked for.

Note that bad input data that invalidates a computation won't be detected by Java. Your program should include code that catches the error, allows the error to be fixed, and allows program execution to resume.

## Program Maintenance

Program maintenance involves upgrading the code as circumstances change. New features may be added. New programmers may come on board. To make their task easier, the original program must have clear and precise documentation.

## OBJECT-ORIENTED PROGRAM DESIGN

Object-oriented programming has been the dominant programming methodology since the mid 1990s.

Here are the steps in object-oriented design:

- Identify classes to be written.
- Identify behaviors (i.e., methods) for each class.
- Determine the relationships between classes.
- Write the public method headers for each class.
- Implement the methods.

## Identifying Classes

Identify the objects in the program by picking out the nouns in the program specification. Ignore pronouns and nouns that refer to the user. Select those nouns that seem suitable as classes, the "big-picture" nouns that describe the major objects in the application. Some of the other nouns may end up as attributes of the classes.

Many applications have similar object types: a low-level basic component; a collection of low-level components; a controlling object that puts everything together; and a display object that could be a GUI (graphical user interface) but doesn't have to be.

### ➡ Example 1 _____

Write a program that maintains an inventory of stock items for a small store.

Nouns to consider: inventory, item, store.

| | |
|---|---|
| Basic Object: | `StockItem` |
| Collection: | `Inventory` (a list of `StockItems`) |
| Controller: | `Store` (has an `Inventory`, uses a `StoreDisplay`) |
| Display: | `StoreDisplay` (could be a GUI) |

**➥ Example 2** _____

Write a program that simulates a game of bingo. There should be at least two players, each of whom has a bingo card, and a caller who calls the numbers.

Nouns to consider: game, players, bingo card, caller.

| | |
|---|---|
| Basic Objects: | `BingoCard, Caller` |
| Collection: | `Players` (each has a `BingoCard`) |
| Controller: | `GameMaster` (sets up the `Players` and `Caller`) |
| Display: | `BingoDisplay` (shows each player's card and displays winners, etc.) |

**➥ Example 3** _____

Write a program that creates random bridge deals and displays them in a specified format. (The specification defines a "deal" as consisting of four hands. It also describes a deck of cards, and shows how each card should be displayed.)

Nouns to consider: deal, hand, format, deck, card.

| | |
|---|---|
| Basic Object: | `Card` |
| Collection: | `Deck` (has an array of `Cards`) |
| | `Hand` (has an array of `Cards`) |
| | `Deal` (has an array of `Hands`) |
| | `Dealer` (has a `Deck`, or several `Decks`) |
| Controller: | `Formatter` (has a `Deal` and a `TableDisplay`) |
| Display: | `TableDisplay` (could be a GUI) |

## Identifying Behaviors

Find all verbs in the program description that help lead to the solution of the programming task. These are likely behaviors that will probably become the methods of the classes. Now decide which methods belong in which classes. Recall that the process of bundling methods and data fields into a class to enable its data to be hidden is called *data encapsulation*.

Think carefully about who should do what. Do not ask a basic object to perform operations for the group. For example, a `StockItem` should keep track of its own details (price, description, how many on the shelf, etc.) but should not be required to search for another item. A `Card` should know its value and suit but should not be responsible for keeping track of how many cards are left in a deck. A `Caller` in a bingo game should be responsible for keeping track of the numbers called so far and for producing the next number but not for checking whether a player has bingo: That is the job of an individual player (element of `Players`) and his `BingoCard`.

You will also need to decide which data fields each class will need and which data structures should store them. For example, if an object represents a list of items, consider an array or `ArrayList` as the data structure.

## Determining Relationships Between Classes

### INHERITANCE RELATIONSHIPS

Look for classes with common behaviors. This will help identify *inheritance relationships*. Recall the *is-a* relationship—if `object1` *is-a* `object2`, then `object2` is a candidate for a superclass.

**COMPOSITION RELATIONSHIPS**

Composition relationships are defined by the *has-a* relationship. For example, a `Nurse` *has-a* `Uniform`. Typically, if two classes have a composition relationship, one of them contains an instance variable whose type is the other class.

Note that a wrapper class always implements a *has-a* relationship with any objects that it wraps.

## UML Diagrams

An excellent way to keep track of the relationships between classes and show the inheritance hierarchy in your programs is with a UML (Unified Modeling Language) diagram. This is a standard graphical scheme used by object-oriented programmers. Although it is not part of the AP subset, on the AP exam you may be expected to interpret simple UML diagrams and inheritance hierarchies.

Here is a simplified version of the UML rules:

- Represent classes with rectangles.
- Show the *is-a* relationship between classes with an open up-arrow.
- Show the *has-a* relationship with a down arrow or sideways arrow (indicates composition).

### ➡ Example _____

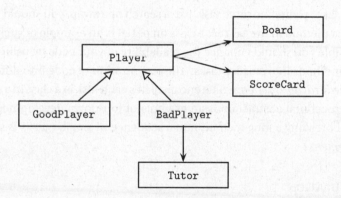

From this diagram you can see at a glance that `GoodPlayer` and `BadPlayer` are subclasses of a class `Player`, and that every `Player` has a `Board` and a `ScoreCard`, while only the `BadPlayer` has a `Tutor`.

## Implementing Classes

### BOTTOM-UP DEVELOPMENT

For each method in a class, list all of the other classes needed to implement that particular method. These classes are called *collaborators*. A class that has no collaborators is *independent*.

To implement the classes, often an incremental, *bottom-up* approach is used. This means that independent classes are fully implemented and tested before being incorporated into the overall project. Typically, these are the basic objects of the program, like `StockItem`, `Card`, and `BingoCard`. Unrelated classes in a programming project can be implemented by different programmers.

Note that a class can be tested using a dummy `Tester` class that will be discarded when the methods of the class are working. Constructors, then methods, should be added, and tested, one at a time. A *driver class* that contains a `main` method can be used to test the program as you go. The purpose of the driver is to test the class fully before incorporating it as an object in a new class.

When each of the independent classes is working, classes that depend on just one other class are implemented and tested, and so on. This may lead to a working, bare bones version of the project. New features and enhancements can be added later.

Design flaws can be corrected at each stage of development. Remember, a design is never set in stone: It simply guides the implementation.

**TOP-DOWN DEVELOPMENT**

In a top-down design, the programmer starts with an overview of the program, selecting the highest-level controlling object and the tasks needed. During development of the program, subsidiary classes may be added to simplify existing classes.

## Implementing Methods

### PROCEDURAL ABSTRACTION

A good programmer avoids chunks of repeated code wherever possible. To this end, if several methods in a class require the same task, like a search or a swap, you should use *helper methods*. The `reduce` method in the `Rational` class on p. 126 is an example of such a method. Also, wherever possible you should enhance the readability of your code by using helper methods to break long methods into smaller tasks. The organization of code into different methods is known as *procedural abstraction*, which encapsulates each task in a class in a separate method of the class. Procedural abstraction is an example of top-down development within a class. The process of breaking a long method into a sequence of smaller tasks is sometimes called *stepwise refinement*.

### DATA ENCAPSULATION

Instance variables and helper methods are generally declared as `private`, which prevents client classes from accessing them. *Data encapsulation* is when the data and methods of an object are combined in a class so that the data can be hidden.

### STUB METHOD

Sometimes it makes more sense in the development of a class to test a calling method before testing a method it invokes. A *stub* is a dummy method that stands in for a method until the actual method has been written and tested. A stub typically has an output statement to show that it was called in the correct place, or it may return some reasonable values if necessary.

### ALGORITHM

An *algorithm* is a precise step-by-step procedure that solves a problem or achieves a goal. Don't write any code for an algorithm in a method until the steps are completely clear to you.

## ➡ Example 1

A program must test the validity of a four-digit code number that a person will enter to be able to use a photocopy machine. The number is valid if the fourth digit equals the remainder when the sum of the first three digits is divided by seven.

Classes in the program may include an `IDNumber`, the four-digit code; `Display`, which would handle input and output; and `IDMain`, the driver for the program. The data structure used to implement an `IDNumber` could be an instance variable of type `int`, or an instance variable of type `String`, or four instance variables of type `int`—one per digit, and so on.

A top-down design for the program that tests the validity of the number is reflected in the steps of the `main` method of `IDMain`:

Create `Display`
Read in `IDNumber`
Check validity
Print message

Each method in this design is tested before the next method is added to `main`. If the display will be handled in a GUI (graphical user interface), stepwise refinement of the design might look like this:

Create `Display`

    Construct a `Display`
    Create window panels
    Set up text fields
    Add panels and fields to window

Read in `IDNumber`

    Prompt and read

Check validity of `IDNumber`
    Check input
        Check characters
        Check range
    Separate into digits
    Check validity property

Print message
    Write number
    State if valid

**NOTE**

    1. The `IDNumber` class, which contains the four-digit code, is responsible for the following operations:
        Split value into separate digits
        Check condition for validity
    The `Display` class, which contains objects to read and display, must also contain an `IDNumber` object. It is responsible for the following operations:

Set up display

Read in code number

Display validity message

Creating these two classes with their data fields (instance variables) and operations (methods) is an example of data encapsulation.

2. The `Display` method `readCodeNumber` needs private helper methods to check the input: `checkCharacters` and `checkRange`. This is an example of procedural abstraction (the use of separate methods to implement each task) and data encapsulation (making the data private within the class).

3. Initially the programmer had just an `IDNumber` class and a driver class. The `Display` class was added as a refinement, when it was realized that handling the input and message display was separate from checking the validity of the `IDNumber`. This is an example of top-down development (adding an auxiliary class to clarify the code).

4. The `IDNumber` class contains no data fields that are objects. It is therefore an independent class. The `Display` class, which contains an `IDNumber` data member, has a composition relationship with `IDNumber` (`Display` *has-a* `IDNumber`).

5. When testing the final program, the programmer should be sure to include each of the following as a user-entered code number: a valid four-digit number, an invalid four-digit number, an $n$-digit number, where $n \neq 4$, and a "number" that contains a nondigit character. A robust program should be able to deal with all these cases.

## ➡ Example 2

A program must create a teacher's grade book. The program should maintain a class list of students for any number of classes in the teacher's schedule. A menu should be provided that allows the teacher to:

- Create a new class of students.

- Enter a set of scores for any class.

- Correct any data that's been entered.

- Display the record of any student.

- Calculate the final average and grade for all students in a class.

- Print a class list, with or without grades.

- Add a student, delete a student, or transfer a student to another class.

- Save all the data in a file.

### IDENTIFYING CLASSES

> Use nouns in the specification to identify possible classes.

Use the nouns in the specification as a starting point for identifying classes in the program. The nouns are: program, teacher, grade book, class list, class, student, schedule, menu, set of scores, data, record, average, grade, and file.

Eliminate each of the following:

| | |
|---|---|
| program | (Always eliminate "program" when used in this context.) |
| teacher | (Eliminate, because he or she is the user.) |
| schedule | (This will be reflected in the name of the external file for each class, e.g., `apcs_period3.dat`.) |
| data, record | (These are synonymous with student name, scores, grades, etc., and will be covered by these features.) |
| class | (This is synonymous with class list.) |

The following seem to be excellent candidates for classes: GradeBook, ClassList, Student, and FileHandler. Other possibilities are Menu, ScoreList, and a GUI_Display.

On further thought: Basic independent objects are Student, Menu, Score, and FileHandler. Group objects are ClassList (collection of students), ScoreList (collection of scores), and AllClasses (collection of ClassLists). The controlling class is the GradeBook. A Display class is essential for many of the grade book operations, like showing a class list or displaying information for a single student.

## RELATIONSHIPS BETWEEN CLASSES

There are no inheritance relationships. There are many composition relationships between objects, however. The GradeBook *has-a* Menu, the ClassList *has-a* Student (several, in fact!), a Student *has-a* name, average, grade, list_of_scores, etc. The programmer must decide whether to code these attributes as classes or data fields.

## IDENTIFYING BEHAVIORS

Use the verbs in the specification to identify required operations in the program. The verbs are: maintain <list>, provide <menu>, allow <user>, create <list>, enter <scores>, correct <data>, display <record>, calculate <average>, calculate <grade>, print <list>, add <student>, delete <student>, transfer <student>, and save <data>.

You must make some design decisions about which class is responsible for which behavior. For example, will a ClassList display the record of a single Student, or will a Student display his or her own record? Who will enter scores—the GradeBook, a ClassList, or a Student? Is it desirable for a Student to enter scores of other Students? Probably not!

> Use verbs in the specification to identify possible methods.

## DECISIONS

Here are some preliminary decisions. The GradeBook will provideMenu. The menu selection will send execution to the relevant object.

The ClassList will maintain an updated list of each class. It will have these public methods: addStudent, deleteStudent, transferStudent, createNewClass, printClassList, printScores, and updateList. A good candidate for a helper method in this class is search for a given student.

Each Student will have complete personal and grade information. Public methods will include setName, getName, enterScore, correctData, findAverage, getAverage, getGrade, and displayRecord.

Saving and retrieving information is crucial to this program. The FileHandler will take care of openFileForReading, openFileForWriting, closeFiles, loadClass, and saveClass. The FileHandler class should be written and tested right at the beginning, using a small dummy class list.

Score, ScoreList, and Student are easy classes to implement. When these are working, the programmer can go on to ClassList. Finally, the Display GUI class, which will have the GradeBook, can be developed. This is an example of bottom-up development.

## ➡ Example 3 _____

A program simulates a game of Battleships, which is a game between two players, each of whom has a grid where ships are placed. Each player has five ships:

```
battleship  o o o o o
cruiser     o o o o
submarine   o o o
destroyer   o o
frigate     o
```

The grids of the players' fleets may look like this. Any two adjacent squares that are taken must belong to the same ship, i.e., different ships shouldn't "touch."

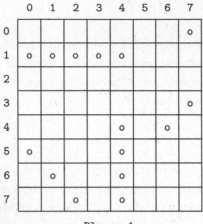

Player 1

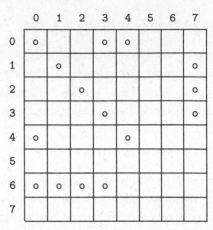

Player 2

Each player's grid is hidden from the other player. Players alternate "shooting" at each other's ships by calling out a position, a row and column number. A player must make an honest response, "hit" or "miss." If it's a hit, a player gets another turn. If the whole ship has been hit, the owner must say something like, "You sank my cruiser." Each player must keep track of hits and misses. The first player to sink his opponent's fleet is the winner.

**IDENTIFYING CLASSES**

The nouns in the specification are program, game, players, grid, ship, battleship, cruiser, submarine, destroyer, frigate, square, position, opponent, row, column, turn, hits, misses, fleet, winner.

Eliminate each of the following:

| | |
|---|---|
| program | Always eliminate. |
| row, col | These are parts of a given position or square, more suitable as instance variables for a position or square object. |
| hits, misses | These are simply marked positions and probably don't need their own class. |
| turn | Taking a turn is an action and will be described by a method rather than a class. |
| opponent | This is another word for player. |

The following seem to be good candidates for classes: `Player`, `Grid`, `Position`, `Ship`, `Battleship`, `Cruiser`, `Submarine`, `Destroyer`, and `Frigate`. Additionally, it seems there should be a `GameManager` and `Display`.

**RELATIONSHIP BETWEEN CLASSES**

This program provides two examples of inheritance relationships. Each of the five ships *is-a* `Ship`, and shares common features, like `isHit`, `isSunk`, and array of positions. However, each has a unique name, length, and position in the grid. This means that `Ship` is a good candidate for an abstract class with abstract methods like `getLength`, `getName`, and `getPositions`, which depend on the kind of ship.

The second inheritance relationship is between the grids. There are two types of grids for each player: his own `FleetGrid` (the current state of his own ships) and his opponent's `HitGrid`, which keeps track of his hits and misses. Each of these grids *is-a* `Grid`. A grid is a candidate for an interface, with a list of methods like `getAdjacentNeighbors`, `getRightNeighbor`, etc. Each of `FleetGrid` and `HitGrid` would implement `Grid`.

There are several composition relationships in this program. A `Player` *has-a* `HitGrid` and a `FleetGrid` and also has five ships. The `GameManager` has each of the two `Player` objects and also *has-a* `Display`. The `Display` has each of the grids.

### IDENTIFYING BEHAVIORS

Use the verbs to identify key methods in the program: simulate <game>, place <ships>, shoot <at position>, call out <position>, respond <hit or miss>, sink <ship>, inform that <ship was sunk>, keep track of <hits or misses>, sink <opponent's fleet>, win <game>.

You need to decide who will do what. There's no definitive way of implementing the program, but it seems clear that the `GameManager` should run the game and declare the winner. Should the `GameManager` also be in charge of announcing if a ship is sunk? It makes sense because the game manager can see both players' grids. Each player should keep track of his calls, so that he can make an intelligent next call and also respond "hit" or "miss." Will each player have a display? Or will the `Display` have both players? You have to set it up so that a player can't see his opponent's `FleetGrid`, but he can see his own and also a grid showing the state of the calls he has made. Should each player have a list of his ships, so he can keep track of the state of his fleet? And what about each ship in the fleet? Should a ship have a list of its positions, and should it keep track of if it's hit or sunk?

Saving and retrieving updated information is crucial to this program. It seems a bit overwhelming. Where should you start? The `Ship` classes are low-level classes, independent of the players and grids. Start with these and test that you can get accurate information about each ship. In your driver program create an `ArrayList<Ship>`. Have a loop that prints information about each ship. Polymorphism will take care of getting the correct information about each ship.

Now try the `Grid` classes. This is a complicated program where each small piece should be coded and tested with simple output. For example, a `Grid` can be displayed with a two-dimensional array of 0's and 1's to show the positions of ships. Other symbols can be used to show what's been hit and what's been sunk.

When everything is working with the grids, you could add a `Display` class that has `Grid` variables and a `display` method.

Try a `Player`. Give him a list of ships, two grids and a `Display`.

Then create a `GameManager`. Give her two `Player` variables and be sure she has a `playGame` method.

The program development shown above is an example of bottom-up development.

## Vocabulary Summary

Know these terms for the AP exam:

| Vocabulary | Meaning |
| --- | --- |
| software development | Writing a program |
| object-oriented program | Uses interacting objects |
| program specification | Description of a task |
| program design | A written plan, an overview of the solution |
| program implementation | The code |
| test data | Input to test the program |
| program maintenance | Keeping the program working and up to date |
| top-down development | Implement main classes first, subsidiary classes later |
| independent class | Doesn't use other classes of the program in its code |
| bottom-up development | Implement lowest level, independent classes first |
| driver class | Used to test other classes; contains `main` method |
| inheritance relationship | *is-a* relationship between classes |
| composition relationship | *has-a* relationship between classes |
| inheritance hierarchy | Inheritance relationship shown in a tree-like diagram |
| UML diagram | Tree-like representation of relationship between classes |
| data structure | Java construct for storing a data field (e.g., array) |
| data encapsulation | Hiding data fields and methods in a class |
| stepwise refinement | Breaking methods into smaller methods |
| procedural abstraction | Using separate methods to encapsulate each task |
| algorithm | Step-by-step process that solves a problem |
| stub method | Dummy method called by another method being tested |
| debugging | Fixing errors |
| robust program | Screens out bad input |
| compile-time error | Usually a syntax error; prevents program from compiling |
| syntax error | Bad language usage (e.g., missing brace) |
| run-time error | Occurs during execution (e.g., `int` division by 0) |
| exception | Run-time error thrown by Java method |
| logic error | Program runs but does the wrong thing |

## PROGRAM ANALYSIS

### Program Correctness

Testing that a program works does not prove that the program is correct. After all, you can hardly expect to test programs for every conceivable set of input data. Computer scientists have developed mathematical techniques to prove correctness in certain cases, but these are beyond the scope of the AP course. Nevertheless, you are expected to be able to make assertions about the state of a program at various points during its execution.

### Assertions

An *assertion* is a precise statement about a program at any given point. The idea is that if an assertion is proved to be true, then the program is working correctly at that point.

An informal step on the way to writing correct algorithms is to be able to make different kinds of assertions about your code.

**PRECONDITION**

The *precondition* for any piece of code, whether it is a method, loop, or block, is a statement of what is true immediately before execution of that code.

**POSTCONDITION**

The *postcondition* for a piece of code is a statement of what is true immediately after execution of that code.

## Efficiency

An efficient algorithm is one that is economical in the use of:

- CPU time. This refers to the number of machine operations required to carry out the algorithm (arithmetic operations, comparisons, data movements, etc.).
- Memory. This refers to the number and complexity of the variables used.

Some factors that affect run-time efficiency include unnecessary tests, excessive movement of data elements, and redundant computations, especially in loops.

Always aim for early detection of output conditions: Your sorting algorithm should halt when the list is sorted; your search should stop if the key element has been found.

In discussing efficiency of an algorithm, we refer to the *best case*, *worst case*, and *average case*. The best case is a configuration of the data that causes the algorithm to run in the least possible amount of time. The worst case is a configuration that leads to the greatest possible run time. Typical configurations (i.e., not specially chosen data) give the average case. It is possible that best, worst, and average cases don't differ much in their run times.

For example, suppose that a list of distinct random numbers must be searched for a given key value. The algorithm used is a sequential search starting at the beginning of the list. In the best case, the key will be found in the first position examined. In the worst case, it will be in the last position or not in the list at all. On average, the key will be somewhere in the middle of the list.

## Chapter Summary

There's a lot of vocabulary that you are expected to know in this chapter. Learn the words!

Never make assumptions about a program specification, and always write a design before starting to write code. Even if you don't do this for your own programs, these are the answers you will be expected to give on the AP exam. You are certain to get questions about program design. Know the procedures and terminology involved in developing an object-oriented program.

Be sure you understand what is meant by best case, worst case, and average case for an algorithm. There will be questions about efficiency on the AP exam.

By now you should know what a precondition and postcondition are.

# MULTIPLE-CHOICE QUESTIONS ON PROGRAM DESIGN AND ANALYSIS

1. A program that reads in a five-digit identification number is to be written. The specification does not state whether zero can be entered as a first digit. The programmer should
   (A) write the code to accept zero as a first digit since zero is a valid digit.
   (B) write the code to reject zero as a first digit since five-digit integers do not start with zero.
   (C) eliminate zero as a possibility for any of the digits.
   (D) treat the identification number as a four-digit number if the user enters a number starting with zero.
   (E) check with the writer of the specification whether zero is acceptable as a first digit.

2. Refer to the following three program descriptions.

   I  Test whether there exists at least one three-digit integer whose value equals the sum of the squares of its digits.
   II Read in a three-digit code number and check if it is valid according to some given formula.
   III Passwords consist of three digits and three capital letters in any order. Read in a password, and check if there are any repeated characters.

   For which of the preceding program descriptions would a `ThreeDigitNumber` class be suitable?
   (A) I only
   (B) II only
   (C) III only
   (D) I and II only
   (E) I, II, and III

3. Top-down programming is illustrated by which of the following?
   (A) Writing a program from top to bottom in Java
   (B) Writing an essay describing how the program will work, without including any Java code
   (C) Using driver programs to test all methods in the order that they're called in the program
   (D) Writing and testing the lowest level methods first and then combining them to form appropriate abstract operations
   (E) Writing the program in terms of the operations to be performed and then refining these operations by adding more detail

4. Which of the following should influence your choice of a particular algorithm?

    I  The run time of the algorithm
    II  The memory requirements of the algorithm
    III  The ease with which the logic of the algorithm can be understood

  (A)  I only
  (B)  III only
  (C)  I and III only
  (D)  I and II only
  (E)  I, II, and III

5. A list of numbers is stored in a sorted array. It is required that the list be maintained in sorted order. This requirement leads to inefficient execution for which of the following processes?

    I  Summing the five smallest numbers in the list
    II  Finding the maximum value in the list
    III  Inserting and deleting numbers

  (A)  I only
  (B)  III only
  (C)  II and III only
  (D)  I and III only
  (E)  I, II, and III

6. Which of the following is not necessarily a feature of a robust program?
  (A)  Does not allow execution to proceed with invalid data
  (B)  Uses algorithms that give correct answers for extreme data values
  (C)  Will run on any computer without modification
  (D)  Will not allow division by zero
  (E)  Will anticipate the types of errors that users of the program may make

7. A certain freight company charges its customers for shipping overseas according to this scale.

    $80 per ton for a weight of 10 tons or less
    $40 per ton for each additional ton over 10 tons but
        not exceeding 25 tons
    $30 per ton for each additional ton over 25 tons

For example, to ship a weight of 12 tons will cost 10(80) + 2(40) = $880. To ship 26 tons will cost 10(80) + 15(40) + 1(30) = $1430.

    A method takes as parameter an integer that represents a valid shipping weight and outputs the charge for the shipment. Which of the following is the smallest set of input values for shipping weights that will adequately test this method?
  (A)  10, 25
  (B)  5, 15, 30
  (C)  5, 10, 15, 25, 30
  (D)  0, 5, 10, 15, 25, 30
  (E)  5, 10, 15, 20, 25, 30

8. A code segment calculates the mean of values stored in integers n1, n2, n3, and n4 and stores the result in average, which is of type double. What kind of error is caused with this statement?

```
double average = n1 + n2 + n3 + n4 / (double) 4;
```

(A) Logic
(B) Run-time
(C) Overflow
(D) Syntax
(E) Type mismatch

9. A program evaluates binary arithmetic expressions that are read from an input file. All of the operands are integers, and the only operators are +, -, *, and /. In writing the program, the programmer forgot to include a test that checks whether the right-hand operand in a division expression equals zero. When will this oversight be detected by the computer?
   (A) At compile time
   (B) While editing the program
   (C) As soon as the data from the input file is read
   (D) During evaluation of the expressions
   (E) When at least one incorrect value for the expressions is output

10. A programmer plans to write a program that simulates various games. In the program, there is a Player class that has a getMove method. Method getMove returns an int value to simulate a move in a game.

    Which of the games described below are suitable candidates for using the getMove method as specified above?

    I   High-Low Guessing Game: The computer thinks of a number and the player who guesses it with the least number of guesses wins. After each guess, the computer tells whether its number is higher or lower than the player's guess.

    II  Chips: Start with a pile of chips. Each player, in turn, removes some number of chips, but not all of them. The winner is the one who removes the final chip.

    III Tic-Tac-Toe: Two players alternate placing "X" or "O" on a 3 × 3 grid. The first player to get three in a row, where a row can be horizontal, vertical, or diagonal, wins.

    (A) I only
    (B) II only
    (C) III only
    (D) I and II only
    (E) I, II, and III

11. Which best describes the precondition of a method? It is an assertion that
    (A) describes precisely the conditions that must be true at the time the method is called.
    (B) initializes the parameters of the method.
    (C) describes the effect of the method on its postcondition.
    (D) explains what the method does.
    (E) states what the initial values of the local variables in the method must be.

12. Consider the following code fragment.

```
/** Precondition:  a1, a2, a3 contain 3 distinct integers.
 *   Postcondition: max contains the largest of a1, a2, a3.
 */
//first set max equal to larger of a1 and a2
if (a1 > a2)
    max = a1;
else
    max = a2;
//set max equal to larger of max and a3
if (max < a3)
    max = a3;
```

For this algorithm, which of the following initial setups for a1, a2, and a3 will cause
    (1) the least number of computer operations (best case) and
    (2) the greatest number of computer operations (worst case)?

    (A)   (1) largest value in a1 or a2     (2) largest value in a3
    (B)   (1) largest value in a2 or a3     (2) largest value in a1
    (C)   (1) smallest value in a1          (2) largest value in a2
    (D)   (1) largest value in a2           (2) smallest value in a3
    (E)   (1) smallest value in a1 or a2    (2) largest value in a3

13. Refer to the following code segment.

```
/** Compute the mean of integers 1 .. N.
 *  N is an integer >= 1 and has been initialized.
 */
int k = 1;
double mean, sum = 1.0;
while (k < N)
{
    /* loop body */
}
mean = sum / N;
```

What is the precondition for the while loop?
    (A) k $\geq$ N,  sum = 1.0
    (B) sum = 1 + 2 + 3 + ... + k
    (C) k < N,  sum = 1.0
    (D) N $\geq$ 1,  k = 1,  sum = 1.0
    (E) mean = sum / N

14. The sequence of Fibonacci numbers is 1, 1, 2, 3, 5, 8, 13, 21, .... The first two Fibonacci numbers are each 1. Each subsequent number is obtained by adding the previous two. Consider this method.

```
/** Precondition:  n >= 1.
 *  Postcondition: The nth Fibonacci number has been returned.
 */
public static int fib(int n)
{
    int prev = 1, next = 1, sum = 1;
    for (int i = 3; i <= n; i++)
    {
        /* assertion */
        sum = next + prev;
        prev = next;
        next = sum;
    }
    return sum;
}
```

Which of the following is a correct /* *assertion* */ about the loop variable i?

(A) $1 \le i \le n$

(B) $0 \le i \le n$

(C) $3 \le i \le n$

(D) $3 < i \le n$

(E) $3 < i < n+1$

15. Refer to the following method.

```
/** Precondition:  a and b are initialized integers.
 */
public static int mystery(int a, int b)
{
    int total = 0, count = 1;
    while (count <= b)
    {
        total += a;
        count++;
    }
    return total;
}
```

What is the postcondition for method mystery?

(A) total $= a + b$

(B) total $= a^b$

(C) total $= b^a$

(D) total $= a * b$

(E) total $= a/b$

16. A program is to be written that prints an invoice for a small store. A copy of the invoice will be given to the customer and will display:

   ■ A list of items purchased.

   ■ The quantity, unit price, and total price for each item.

   ■ The amount due.

   Three candidate classes for this program are `Invoice`, `Item`, and `ItemList`, where an `Item` is a single item purchased and `ItemList` is the list of all items purchased. Which class is a reasonable choice to be responsible for the `amountDue` method, which returns the amount the customer must pay?

   I  `Item`

   II  `ItemList`

   III  `Invoice`

   (A) I only
   (B) III only
   (C) I and II only
   (D) II and III only
   (E) I, II, and III


17. Which is a false statement about classes in object-oriented program design?
   (A) If a class `C1` has an instance variable whose type is another class, `C2`, then `C1` *has-a* `C2`.
   (B) If a class `C1` is associated with another class, `C2`, then `C1` depends on `C2` for its implementation.
   (C) If classes `C1` and `C2` are related such that `C1` *is-a* `C2`, then `C2` *has-a* `C1`.
   (D) If class `C1` is independent, then none of its methods will have parameters that are objects of other classes.
   (E) Classes that have common methods do not necessarily define an inheritance relationship.

18. A Java program maintains a large database of vehicles and parts for a car dealership. Some of the classes in the program are Vehicle, Car, Truck, Tire, Circle, SteeringWheel, and AirBag. The declarations below show the relationships between classes. Which is a poor choice?

(A) ```
    public class Vehicle
    {   ...
        private Tire[] tires;
        private SteeringWheel sw;
        ...
    }
    ```

(B) ```
    public class Tire extends Circle
    {   ...
        //inherits methods that compute circumference
        //and center point
    }
    ```

(C) ```
    public class Car extends Vehicle
    {   ...
        //inherits private Tire[] tires from Vehicle class
        //inherits private SteeringWheel sw from Vehicle class
        ...
    }
    ```

(D) ```
    public class Tire
    {   ...
        private String rating;      //speed rating of tire
        private Circle boundary;
    }
    ```

(E) ```
    public class SteeringWheel
    {   ...
        private AirBag ab;  //AirBag is stored in SteeringWheel
        private Circle boundary;
    }
    ```

19. A Java programmer has completed a preliminary design for a large program. The programmer has developed a list of classes, determined the methods for each class, established the relationships between classes, and written an outline for each class. Which class(es) should be implemented first?

(A) Any superclasses
(B) Any subclasses
(C) All collaborator classes (classes that will be used to implement other classes)
(D) The class that represents the dominant object in the program
(E) All independent classes (classes that have no references to other classes)
    ```

Use the program description below for Questions 20–22.

A program is to be written that simulates bumper cars in a video game. The cars move on a square grid and are located on grid points $(x, y)$, where $x$ and $y$ are integers between $-20$ and 20. A bumper car moves in a random direction, either left, right, up, or down. If it reaches a boundary (i.e., $x$ or $y$ is $\pm 20$), then it reverses direction. If it is about to collide with another bumper car, it reverses direction. Your program should be able to add bumper cars and run the simulation. One step of the simulation allows each car in the grid to move. After a bumper car has reversed direction twice, its turn is over and the next car gets to move.

20. To identify classes in the program, the nouns in the specification are listed:

> program, bumper car, grid, grid point, integer, direction, boundary, simulation

How many nouns in the list should immediately be discarded because they are unsuitable as classes for the program?

(A) 0
(B) 1
(C) 2
(D) 3
(E) 4

A programmer decides to include the following classes in the program. Refer to them for Questions 21 and 22.

- Simulation will run the simulation.

- Display will show the state of the game.

- BumperCar will know its identification number, position in the grid, and current direction when moving.

- GridPoint will be a position in the grid. It will be represented by two integer fields, x_coord and y_coord.

- Grid will keep track of all bumper cars in the game, the number of cars, and their positions in the grid. It will update the grid each time a car moves. It will be implemented with a two-dimensional array of BumperCar.

21. Which operation should not be the responsibility of the GridPoint class?

    (A)   isEmpty      returns false if the grid point contains a BumperCar, true otherwise

    (B)   atBoundary   returns true if $x$ or $y$ coordinate $= \pm 20$, false otherwise

    (C)   left         if not at left boundary, change the grid point to 1 unit left of current point

    (D)   up           if not at top of grid, change the grid point to 1 unit above current point

    (E)   get_x       return $x$-coordinate of this point

22. Which method is not suitable for the BumperCar class?

    (A) public boolean atBoundary()
        //Returns true if BumperCar at boundary, false otherwise.

    (B) public void selectRandomDirection()
        //Select random direction (up, down, left, or right)
        // at start of turn.

    (C) public void reverseDirection()
        //Move to grid position that is in direction opposite to
        // current direction.

    (D) public void move()
        //Take turn to move. Stop move after two changes
        // of direction.

    (E) public void update()
        //Modify Grid to reflect new position after each stage
        // of move.

# ANSWER KEY

| | | |
|---|---|---|
| 1. **E** | 9. **D** | 17. **C** |
| 2. **D** | 10. **D** | 18. **B** |
| 3. **E** | 11. **A** | 19. **E** |
| 4. **E** | 12. **A** | 20. **C** |
| 5. **B** | 13. **D** | 21. **A** |
| 6. **C** | 14. **C** | 22. **E** |
| 7. **C** | 15. **D** | |
| 8. **A** | 16. **D** | |

# ANSWERS EXPLAINED

1. **(E)** A programmer should never make unilateral decisions about a program specification. When in doubt, check with the person who wrote the specification.

2. **(D)** In I and II a three-digit number is the object being manipulated. For III, however, the object is a six-character string, suggesting a class other than a `ThreeDigitNumber`.

3. **(E)** Top-down programming consists of listing the methods for the main object and then using stepwise refinement to break each method into a list of subtasks. Eliminate choices A, C, and D: Top-down programming refers to the design and planning stage and does not involve any actual writing of code. Choice B is closer to the mark, but "top-down" implies a list of operations, not an essay describing the methods.

4. **(E)** All three considerations are valid when choosing an algorithm. III is especially important if your code will be part of a larger project created by several programmers. Yet even if you are the sole writer of a piece of software, be aware that your code may one day need to be modified by others.

5. **(B)** A process that causes excessive data movement is inefficient. Inserting an element into its correct (sorted) position involves moving elements to create a slot for this element. In the worst case, the new element must be inserted into the first slot, which involves moving every element up one slot. Similarly, deleting an element involves moving elements down a slot to close the "gap." In the worst case, where the first element is deleted, all elements in the array will need to be moved. Summing the five smallest elements in the list means summing the first five elements. This requires no testing of elements and no excessive data movement, so it is efficient. Finding the maximum value in a sorted list is very fast—just select the element at the appropriate end of the list.

6. **(C)** "Robustness" implies the ability to handle all data input by the user and to give correct answers even for extreme values of data. A program that is not robust may well run on another computer without modification, and a robust program may need modification before it can run on another computer.

7. **(C)** Eliminate choice D because 0 is an invalid weight, and you may infer from the method description that invalid data have already been screened out. Eliminate choice E because it tests two values in the range 10–25. (This is not wrong, but choice C is better.) Eliminate choice A since it tests only the endpoint values. Eliminate B because it tests *no* endpoint values.

8. **(A)** The statement is syntactically correct, but as written it will not find the mean of the integers. The bug is therefore an intent or logic error. To execute as intended, the statement needs parentheses:

```
double average = (n1 + n2 + n3 + n4) / (double) 4;
```

9. **(D)** The error that occurs is a run-time error caused by an attempt to divide by zero (`ArithmeticException`). Don't be fooled by choice C. Simply reading an expression 8/0 from the input file won't cause the error. Note that if the operands were of type `double`, the correct answer would be E. In this case, dividing by zero does not cause an exception; it gives an answer of `Infinity`. Only on inspecting the output would it be clear that something was wrong.

10. **(D)** Games I and II are perfect games for using an integer value to describe the next move. For the High-Low Guessing Game, `getMove()` will return the next guess, and for Chips, `getMove()` will return the number of chips removed at the player's turn. Game III, Tic-Tac-Toe, requires a location on a $3 \times 3$ grid as a player's next move: a simple integer value isn't a suitable return type for the `getMove` method.

11. **(A)** A precondition does not concern itself with the action of the method, the local variables, the algorithm, or the postcondition. Nor does it initialize the parameters. It simply asserts what must be true directly before execution of the method.

12. **(A)** The best case causes the fewest computer operations, and the worst case leads to the maximum number of operations. In the given algorithm, the initial test `if (a1 > a2)` and the assignment to `max` will occur irrespective of which value is the largest. The second test, `if (max < a3)`, will also always occur. The final statement, `max = a3`, will occur only if the largest value is in `a3`; thus, this represents the worst case. So the best case must have the biggest value in `a1` or `a2`.

13. **(D)** The precondition is an assertion about the variables in the loop just before the loop is executed. Variables `N`, `k`, and `sum` have all been initialized to the values shown in choice D. Choice C is wrong because `k` may equal `N`. Choice A is wrong because `k` may be less than `N`. Choice E is wrong because `mean` is not defined until the loop has been exited. Choice B is wrong because it omits the assertions about `N` and `k`.

14. **(C)** Eliminate choices A and B, since `i` is initialized to 3 in the `for` loop. Choices D and E are wrong because `i` is equal to 3 the first time through the loop.

15. **(D)** The quantity `a` is being added to `total` `b` times, which means that at the end of execution `total = a*b`.

16. **(D)** It makes sense for an `Item` to be responsible for its name, unit price, quantity, and total price. It is *not* reasonable for it to be responsible for other `Items`. Since an `ItemList`, however, will contain information for all the `Items` purchased, it is reasonable to have it also compute the total `amountDue`. It makes just as much sense to give an `Invoice` the responsibility for displaying information for the items purchased, as well as providing a final total, `amountDue`.

17. **(C)** The *is-a* relationship defines inheritance, while the *has-a* relationship defines association. These types of relationships are mutually exclusive. For example, a graduate student *is-a* student. It doesn't make sense to say a student *has-a* graduate student!

18. **(B)** Even though it's convenient for a `Tire` object to inherit `Circle` methods, an inheritance relationship between a `Tire` and a `Circle` is incorrect: It is false to say that a `Tire` *is-a* `Circle`. A `Tire` is a car part, while a `Circle` is a geometric shape. Notice that there is an *association* relationship between a `Tire` and a `Circle`: A `Tire` *has-a* `Circle` as its boundary.

19. **(E)** Independent classes do not have relationships with other classes and can therefore be more easily coded and tested.

20. **(C)** The word "program" is never included when it's used in this context. The word "integer" describes the type of coordinates $x$ and $y$ and has no further use in the specification. While words like "direction," "boundary," and "simulation" may later be removed from consideration as classes, it is not unreasonable to keep them as candidates while you ponder the design.

21. **(A)** A `GridPoint` object knows only its $x$ and $y$ coordinates. It has no information about whether a `BumperCar` is at that point. Notice that operations in all of the other choices depend on the $x$ and $y$ coordinates of a `GridPoint` object. An `isEmpty` method should be the responsibility of the `Grid` class that keeps track of the status of each position in the grid.

22. **(E)** A `BumperCar` is responsible for itself—keeping track of its own position, selecting an initial direction, making a move, and reversing direction. It is not, however, responsible for maintaining and updating the grid. That should be done by the `Grid` class.

# Arrays and Array Lists 7

*Should array indices start at 0 or 1?*
*My compromise of 0.5 was rejected,*
*without, I thought, proper consideration.*
*—S. Kelly-Bootle*

→ **One-dimensional arrays**  → **Two-dimensional arrays**
→ **The `ArrayList<E>` class**

## ONE-DIMENSIONAL ARRAYS

A one-dimensional array is a data structure used to implement a list object, where the elements in the list are of the same type; for example, a class list of 25 test scores, a membership list of 100 names, or a store inventory of 500 items.

For an array of $N$ elements in Java, index values ("subscripts") go from 0 to $N-1$. Individual elements are accessed as follows: If `arr` is the name of the array, the elements are `arr[0]`, `arr[1]`, ..., `arr[N-1]`. If a negative subscript is used, or a subscript $k$ where $k \geq N$, an `ArrayIndexOutOfBoundsException` is thrown.

## Initialization

In Java, an array is an object; therefore, the keyword `new` must be used in its creation. The one exception is an initializer list (discussed on the next page). The size of an array remains fixed once it has been created. As with `String` objects, however, an array reference may be reassigned to a new array of a different size.

➡ **Example** _____

All of the following are equivalent. Each creates an array of 25 `double` values and assigns the reference `data` to this array.

1.  `double[] data = new double[25];`

2.  `double data[] = new double[25];`

3.  `double[] data;`
    `data = new double[25];`

A subsequent statement like

```
data = new double[40];
```

reassigns `data` to a new array of length 40. The memory allocated for the previous `data` array is recycled by Java's automatic garbage collection system.

When arrays are declared, the elements are automatically initialized to zero for the primitive numeric data types (`int` and `double`), to `false` for boolean variables, or to `null` for object references.

It is possible to declare several arrays in a single statement. For example,

```
int[] intList1, intList2;   //declares intList1 and intList2 to
                            //contain int values
int[] arr1 = new int[15], arr2 = new int[30];  //reserves 15 slots
                                               //for arr1, 30 for arr2
```

### INITIALIZER LIST

Small arrays whose values are known can be conveniently declared with an *initializer list*. For example, instead of writing

```
int[] coins = new int[4];
coins[0] = 1;
coins[1] = 5;
coins[2] = 10;
coins[3] = 25;
```

you can write

```
int[] coins = {1, 5, 10, 25};
```

This construction is the one case where `new` is not required to create an array.

## Length of Array

A one-dimensional array in Java has a final public instance variable (i.e., a constant), `length`, which can be accessed when you need the number of elements in the array. For example,

```
String[] names = new String[25];
< code to initialize names >

//loop to process all names in array
for (int i = 0; i < names.length; i++)
    < process names >
```

**NOTE**

1. The array subscripts go from 0 to `names.length-1`; therefore, the test on `i` in the `for` loop must be strictly less than `names.length`.
2. `length` is not a method and therefore is not followed by parentheses. Contrast this with `String` objects, where `length` *is* a method and *must* be followed by parentheses. For example,

```
String s = "Confusing syntax!";
int size = s.length();    //assigns 17 to size
```

## Traversing a One-Dimensional Array

Use an enhanced `for` loop whenever you need access to every element in an array without replacing or removing any elements. Use a `for` loop in all other cases: to access the index of any element, to replace or remove elements, or to access just some of the elements.

Note that if you have an array of objects (not primitive types), you can use the enhanced `for` loop and mutator methods of the object to modify the fields of any instance (see the `shuffleAll` method on p. 233).

### ➥ Example 1

```
/** Returns the number of even integers in array arr of integers. */
public static int countEven(int[] arr)
{
    int count = 0;
    for (int num : arr)
        if ( num % 2 == 0)   //num is even
            count++;
    return count;
}
```

### ➥ Example 2

```
/** Change each even-indexed element in array arr to 0.
 *  Precondition:  arr contains integers.
 *  Postcondition: arr[0], arr[2], arr[4], ... have value 0.
 */
public static void changeEven(int[] arr)
{
    for (int i = 0; i < arr.length; i += 2)
        arr[i] = 0;
}
```

## Arrays as Parameters

Since arrays are treated as objects, passing an array as a parameter means passing its object reference. No copy is made of the array. *Thus, the elements of the actual array can be accessed—and modified.*

### ➥ Example 1

Array elements accessed but not modified:

```
/** Returns index of smallest element in array arr of integers. */
public static int findMin (int[] arr)
{
    int min = arr[0];
    int minIndex = 0;
    for (int i = 1; i < arr.length; i++)
        if (arr[i] < min)    //found a smaller element
        {
            min = arr[i];
            minIndex = i;
        }
    return minIndex;
}
```

To call this method (in the same class that it's defined):

```
int[] array;
< code to initialize array >
int min = findMin(array);
```

## ➡ Example 2

Array elements modified:

```
/** Add 3 to each element of array b. */
public static void changeArray(int[] b)
{
    for (int i = 0; i < b.length; i++)
        b[i] += 3;
}
```

To call this method (in the same class):

```
int[] list = {1, 2, 3, 4};
changeArray(list);
System.out.print("The changed list is ");
for (int num : list)
    System.out.print(num + " ");
```

The output produced is

```
The changed list is 4 5 6 7
```

> When an array is passed as a parameter, it is possible to alter the contents of the array.

Look at the memory slots to see how this happens:

Before the method call:

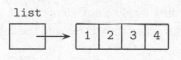

At the start of the method call:

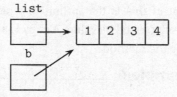

Just before exiting the method:

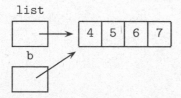

After exiting the method:

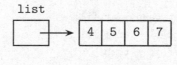

## ➡ Example 3

Contrast the changeArray method with the following attempt to modify one array element:

```
/** Add 3 to an element. */
public static void changeElement(int n)
{ n += 3; }
```

Here is some code that invokes this method:

```
int[] list = {1, 2, 3, 4};
System.out.print("Original array: ");
for (int num : list)
    System.out.print(num + " ");
changeElement(list[0]);
System.out.print("\nModified array: ");
for (int num : list)
    System.out.print(num + " ");
```

Contrary to the programmer's expectation, the output is

```
Original array: 1 2 3 4
Modified array: 1 2 3 4
```

A look at the memory slots shows why the list remains unchanged.

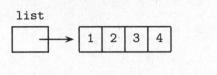

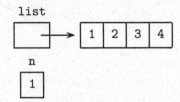

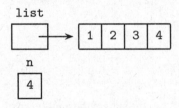

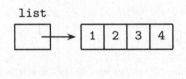

The point of this is that primitive types—including single array elements of type `int` or `double`—are passed by value. A copy is made of the actual parameter, and the copy is erased on exiting the method.

### ➡ Example 4

```
/** Swap arr[i] and arr[j] in array arr. */
public static void swap(int[] arr, int i, int j)
{
    int temp = arr[i];
    arr[i] = arr[j];
    arr[j] = temp;
}
```

To call the swap method:

```
int[] list = {1, 2, 3, 4};
swap(list, 0, 3);
System.out.print("The changed list is: ");
for (int num : list)
    System.out.print(num + " ");
```

The output shows that the program worked as intended:

```
The changed list is: 4 2 3 1
```

```
/** Returns array containing NUM_ELEMENTS integers read from the keyboard.
 *  Precondition:  Array undefined.
 *  Postcondition: Array contains NUM_ELEMENTS integers read from
 *                 the keyboard.
 */
public int[] getIntegers()
{
    int[] arr = new int[NUM_ELEMENTS];
    for (int i = 0; i < arr.length; i++)
    {
        System.out.println("Enter integer: ");
        arr[i] = ...;          //read user input
    }
    return arr;
}
```

To call this method:

```
int[] list = getIntegers();
```

## Array Variables in a Class

Consider a simple Deck class in which a deck of cards is represented by the integers 0 to 51.

```
public class Deck
{
    private int[] deck;
    public static final int NUMCARDS = 52;

    /** constructor */
    public Deck()
    {
        deck = new int[NUMCARDS];
        for (int i = 0; i < NUMCARDS; i++)
            deck[i] = i;
    }

    /** Write contents of Deck. */
    public void writeDeck()
    {
        for (int card : deck)
            System.out.print(card + " ");
        System.out.println();
        System.out.println();
    }

    /** Swap arr[i] and arr[j] in array arr. */
    private void swap(int[] arr, int i, int j)
    {
        int temp = arr[i];
        arr[i] = arr[j];
        arr[j] = temp;
    }
```

```
/** Shuffle Deck: Generate a random permutation by picking a
 *     random card from those remaining and putting it in the
 *     next slot, starting from the right.
 */
public void shuffle()
{
    int index;
    for (int i = NUMCARDS - 1; i > 0; i--)
    {
        //generate an int from 0 to i
        index = (int) (Math.random() * (i + 1));
        swap(deck, i, index);
    }
}
```

Here is a simple driver class that tests the Deck class:

```
public class DeckMain
{
    public static void main(String args[])
    {
        Deck d = new Deck();
        d.shuffle();
        d.writeDeck();
    }
}
```

**NOTE**

There is no evidence of the array that holds the deck of cards—deck is a private instance variable and is therefore invisible to clients of the Deck class.

## Array of Class Objects

Suppose a large card tournament needs to keep track of many decks. The code to do this could be implemented with an array of Deck:

```
public class ManyDecks
{
    private Deck[] allDecks;
    public static final int NUMDECKS = 500;

    /** constructor */
    public ManyDecks()
    {
        allDecks = new Deck[NUMDECKS];
        for (int i = 0; i < NUMDECKS; i++)
            allDecks[i] = new Deck();
    }
```

```
/** Shuffle the Decks. */
public void shuffleAll()
{
    for (Deck d : allDecks)
        d.shuffle();
}

/** Write contents of all the Decks. */
public void printDecks()
{
    for (Deck d : allDecks)
        d.writeDeck();
}
}
```

**NOTE**

1. The statement

   ```
   allDecks = new Deck[NUMDECKS];
   ```

   creates an array, allDecks, of 500 Deck objects. The default initialization for these Deck objects is null. In order to initialize them with actual decks, the Deck constructor must be called for each array element. This is achieved with the for loop of the ManyDecks constructor.

2. In the shuffleAll method, it's OK to use an enhanced for loop to modify each deck in the array with the mutator method shuffle.

## Analyzing Array Algorithms

➡️ **Example 1** _____

Discuss the efficiency of the countNegs method below. What are the best and worst case configurations of the data?

```
/** Returns the number of negative values in arr.
 * Precondition:   arr[0],...,arr[arr.length-1] contain integers.
 */
public static int countNegs(int[] arr)
{
    int count = 0;
    for (int num : arr)
        if (num < 0)
            count++;
    return count;
}
```

Solution:

This algorithm sequentially examines each element in the array. In the best case, there are no negative elements, and count++ is never executed. In the worst case, all the elements are negative, and count++ is executed in each pass of the for loop.

## ➤ Example 2 _____

The code fragment below inserts a value, `num`, into its correct position in a sorted array of integers. Discuss the efficiency of the algorithm.

```
/** Precondition:
 *    - arr[0],...,arr[n-1] contain integers sorted in increasing order.
 *    - n < arr.length.
 * Postcondition: num has been inserted in its correct position.
 */
{
    //find insertion point
    int i = 0;
    while (i < n && num > arr[i])
        i++;
    //if necessary, move elements arr[i]...arr[n-1] up 1 slot
    for (int j = n; j >= i + 1; j--)
        arr[j] = arr[j-1];
    //insert num in i-th slot and update n
    arr[i] = num;
    n++;
}
```

Solution:

In the best case, `num` is greater than all the elements in the array: Because it gets inserted at the end of the list, no elements must be moved to create a slot for it. The worst case has `num` less than all the elements in the array. In this case, `num` must be inserted in the first slot, `arr[0]`, and every element in the array must be moved up one position to create a slot.

This algorithm illustrates a disadvantage of arrays: Insertion and deletion of an element in an ordered list is inefficient, since, in the worst case, it may involve moving all the elements in the list.

## ARRAY LISTS

An `ArrayList` provides an alternative way of storing a list of objects and has the following advantages over an array:

- An `ArrayList` shrinks and grows as needed in a program, whereas an array has a fixed length that is set when the array is created.

- In an `ArrayList` list, the last slot is always `list.size()-1`, whereas in a partially filled array, you, the programmer, must keep track of the last slot currently in use.

- For an `ArrayList`, you can do insertion or deletion with just a single statement. Any shifting of elements is handled automatically. In an array, however, insertion or deletion requires you to write the code that shifts the elements.

- It is easier to print the elements of an `ArrayList` than those of an array. For an `ArrayList` `list` and an array `arr`, the statement

    ```
    System.out.print(list);
    ```

will output the elements of `list`, nicely formatted in square brackets, with the elements separated by commas. Whereas to print the elements of `arr`, an explicit piece of code that accesses and prints each element is needed. The statement

```
System.out.print(arr);
```

will produce weird output that includes an @ symbol—not the elements of the array.

## The `ArrayList` Class

The `ArrayList` class is part of the `java.util` package. An `import` statement makes this class available in a program. Java allows the generic type `ArrayList<E>`, where `E` is the type of the elements in the `ArrayList`. When a generic class is declared, the type parameter is replaced by an actual object type. For example,

```
private ArrayList<Clown> clowns;
```

**NOTE**

The `clowns` list must contain only `Clown` objects. An attempt to add an `Acrobat` to the list, for example, will cause a compile-time error.

## The Methods of `ArrayList<E>`

Here are the methods you should know:

`ArrayList()`

Constructor constructs an empty list.

`int size()`

Returns the number of elements in the list.

`boolean add(E obj)`

Appends `obj` to the end of the list. Always returns `true`. If the specified element is not of type `E`, throws a run-time exception.

`void add(int index, E element)`

Inserts `element` at specified `index`. Elements from position `index` and higher have 1 added to their indices. Size of list is incremented by 1.

`E get(int index)`

Returns the element at the specified `index` in the list.

`E set(int index, E element)`

Replaces item at specified `index` in the list with specified `element`. Returns the element that was previously at `index`. If the specified element is not of type `E`, throws a run-time exception.

`E remove(int index)`

Removes and returns the element at the specified `index`. Elements to the right of position `index` have 1 subtracted from their indices. Size of list is decreased by 1.

Each of these methods that has an index parameter—add, get, remove, and set—throws an IndexOutOfBoundsException if index is out of range. For get, remove, and set, index is out of range if

```
index < 0 || index >= size()
```

For add, however, it is OK to add an element at the end of the list. Therefore index is out of range if

```
index < 0 || index > size()
```

## Autoboxing and Unboxing

An ArrayList cannot contain a primitive type like double or int: It must only contain *objects*. (It actually contains the references to those objects.) Numbers must therefore be boxed—placed in wrapper classes like Integer and Double—before insertion into an ArrayList.

*Autoboxing* is the automatic wrapping of primitive types in their wrapper classes (see p. 174).

To retrieve the numerical value of an Integer (or Double) stored in an ArrayList, the intValue() (or doubleValue()) method must be invoked (unwrapping). *Unboxing* is the automatic conversion of a wrapper class to its corresponding primitive type. This means that you don't need to explicitly call the intValue() or doubleValue() methods. Be aware that if a program tries to auto-unbox null, the method will throw a NullPointerException.

Note that while autoboxing and unboxing cut down on code clutter, these operations must still be performed behind the scenes, leading to decreased run-time efficiency. It is much more efficient to assign and access primitive types in an array than an ArrayList. You should therefore consider using an array for a program that manipulates sequences of numbers and does not need to use objects.

**NOTE**
1. Autoboxing and unboxing is now a part of the AP Java subset.
2. The List<E> interface and the methods of List<E> are no longer part of the AP Java subset.

## Using ArrayList<E>

### ➡ Example 1

```
//Create an ArrayList containing 0 1 4 9.
ArrayList<Integer> list = new ArrayList<Integer>();
for (int i = 0; i < 4; i++)
    list.add(i * i);  //example of autoboxing
                      //i*i wrapped in an Integer before insertion

Integer intOb = list.get(2); //assigns Integer with value 4 to intOb.
                             //Leaves list unchanged.

int n = list.get(3);   //example of auto-unboxing
                       //Integer is retrieved and converted to int
                       //n contains 9

Integer x = list.set(3, 5);  //list is 0 1 4 5
                             //x contains Integer with value 9
```

```
x = list.remove(2);          //list is 0 1 5
                             //x contains Integer with value 4

list.add(1, 7);              //list is 0 7 1 5

list.add(2, 8);              //list is 0 7 8 1 5
```

## ➡ Example 2 _____

```
/** Swap two values in list, indexed at i and j. */
public static void swap(ArrayList<E> list, int i, int j)
{
    E temp = list.get(i);
    list.set(i, list.get(j));
    list.set(j, temp);
}
```

## ➡ Example 3 _____

```
/** Returns an ArrayList of random integers from 0 to 100. */
public static ArrayList<Integer> getRandomIntList()
{
    ArrayList<Integer> list = new ArrayList<Integer>();
    System.out.print("How many integers? ");
    int length = ...;      //read user input
    for (int i = 0; i < length; i++)
    {
        int newNum = (int) (Math.random() * 101);
        list.add(newNum);   //autoboxing
    }
    return list;
}
```

### TRAVERSING AN ArrayList

To traverse an ArrayList means to access all of the elements of the list using an iteration statement (for loop, while loop, or enhanced for loop).

Here are several examples to illustrate different types of traversals.

For simple accessing—for example, printing each element or adding each element to a running total, etc.—an enhanced for loop is a convenient method of traversal.

## ➡ Example 4 _____

```
/** Print all negatives in list.
 * Precondition: list contains Integer values.
 */
public static void printNegs(ArrayList<Integer> list)
{
    System.out.println("The negative values in the list are: ");
    for (Integer i : list)
        if (i < 0)              //auto-unboxing
            System.out.println(i);
}
```

**NOTE**

Here's how to think of this algorithm: For each `Integer i` in `ArrayList list`, create a local copy of the element, test if it's negative, and print it if negative.

To access an element with a specific index—for example, to replace the element at that index, or insert an element at that index—use an index traversal. Since the indices for an `ArrayList` start at `0` and end at `list.size()-1`, trying to access an element with an index value outside of this range will cause an `IndexOutOfBoundsException` to be thrown.

➡ **Example 5** _____

```
/** Precondition: ArrayList list contains Integer values sorted in increasing order.
 *  Postcondition: value inserted in its correct position in list.
 */
public static void insert(ArrayList<Integer> list, Integer value)
{
    int index = 0;
    //find insertion point
    while (index < list.size() &&
            value > list.get(index)        //unboxing
        index++;
    //insert value
    list.add(index, value);
}
```

**NOTE**

Suppose `value` is larger than all the elements in `list`. Then the `insert` method will throw an `IndexOutOfBoundsException` if the first part of the test is omitted, that is, `index < list.size()`.

➡ **Example 6** _____

```
/** Change every even-indexed element of strList to the empty string.
 *  Precondition: strList contains String values.
 */
public static void changeEvenToEmpty(ArrayList<String> strList)
{
    boolean even = true;
    int index = 0;
    while (index < strList.size())
    {
        if (even)
            strList.set(index, "");
        index++;
        even = !even;
    }
}
```

**NOTE**

Deleting elements during the traversal of an `ArrayList` requires special care to avoid skipping elements.

```
/* Remove all occurrences of value from list. */
public static void removeAll(ArrayList<Integer> list, int value)
{
    int index = 0;
    while (index < list.size())
    {
        if (list.get(index) == value)
            list.remove(index);
        else
            index++;
    }
}
```

**NOTE**

1. The statement

   ```
   list.remove(index);
   ```

   causes the elements to the right of the removed element to be shifted left to fill the "hole." In this case, if index is incremented, the current element will be skipped, and if two consecutive elements are equal to value, one will be missed and (mistakenly) remain in the list.

2. Trying to add or delete an element during a traversal with an enhanced for loop may result in a ConcurrentModificationException being thrown. Therefore, if you want to add or delete elements, don't use an enhanced for loop to traverse the ArrayList.

➥ **Example 8**

```
ArrayList<Integer> list = new ArrayList<Integer>();
< code to initialize list >

for (Integer num : list)
{
    if (num < 0)
        list.add(0);        //WRONG!
}
```

**NOTE**

This code segment throws a ConcurrentModificationException.

It is okay, however, to use an enhanced for loop to *modify* objects that have a mutator method in their class definition.

➥ **Example 9**

Consider a Clown class that has a changeAct method, and an ArrayList<Clown> that has been initialized with Clown objects. The following code is fine.

```
for (Clown c : clownList)
{
    if ( <some condition on Clown c > )
        clownList.changeAct();
}
```

## SIMULTANEOUS TRAVERSAL OF AN ArrayList AND AN ARRAY

In the traversal of a list, if it's important to keep track of indices (positions) in the list, you must use an index traversal. Sometimes an algorithm requires the simultaneous traversal of an array and an ArrayList. Try your hand at writing code for the following problems.

## ➡ Example 1

Consider an ArrayList<Integer> list, and an array arr of int that have both been initialized. A method getProductSum returns the sum of products of the values of corresponding elements. Thus, prodArr[0] will be the product of arr[0] and the first Integer value in list; prodArr[1] will be the product of arr[1] and the second Integer value in list; and so on. The algorithm stops when the end of the shorter list is reached.

Here are some examples:

| list | arr | getProductSum |
|------|-----|---------------|
| [2,1,4] | {5,0,3} | 22 |
| [1,3,5,7,9] | {2,4} | 14 |
| [7,6,5] | {1,2,3,4,5} | 34 |
| [] | {2,3,7} | 0 |

The method getProductSum, whose header is given below, returns the sum of products as described above. Write code for the method.

```
public static int getProductSum(ArrayList<Integer> list, int[] arr)
```

Solution:

```
public static int getProductSum(ArrayList<Integer> list, int[] arr)
{
    int sum = 0;
    int index = 0;

    //Traverse both arr and list, until the end of
    //one of the lists is reached.
    while(index < arr.length && index < list.size())
    {
        sum += arr[index] * list.get(index);      //auto-unboxing;
        index++;
    }
    return sum;
}
```

**NOTE**

Beware of going off the end of either list!

Here is a trickier example.

Consider an `ArrayList<Integer>` `list` and an array `arr` of `int` that have both been initialized. An array called `productArr` is to be created that contains the products of the values of corresponding elements. Thus, `prodArr[0]` will be the product of `arr[0]` and the first `Integer` value in `list`; `prodArr[1]` will be the product of `arr[1]` and the second `Integer` value in `list`; and so on. When the end of the shorter list is reached, the algorithm should copy the remaining elements of the longer list into `productArr`.

Here are some examples:

| list | arr | productArr |
|------|-----|------------|
| [2,1,4] | {5,0,3} | {10, 0, 12} |
| [1,3,5,7,9] | {2,4} | {2,12,5,7,9} |
| [7,6,5] | {1,2,3,4,5} | {7,12,15,4,5} |
| [] | {2,3,7} | {2,3,7} |

The method `getProducts`, whose header is given below, returns an array of products as described above. Write code for the method.

```
public static int[] getProducts(ArrayList<Integer> list, int[] arr)
```

Solution:

```
public static int[] getProducts(ArrayList<Integer> list, int[] arr)
{
    int prodArrSize, smallerCount;
    boolean arrayIsLonger;
    //Determine length of prodArray.
    if (list.size() < arr.length)
    {
        prodArrSize = arr.length;
        smallerCount = list.size();
        arrayIsLonger = true;
    }
    else
    {
        prodArrSize = list.size();
        smallerCount = arr.length;
        arrayIsLonger = false;
    }
    int [] prodArray = new int[prodArrSize];
    //Place all products in prodArray.
    for (int i = 0; i < smallerCount; i++)
        prodArray[i] = arr[i] * list.get(i);
    //How many elements must be transferred to prodArray?
    int numExtra = Math.abs(arr.length - list.size());
```

```
    //Transfer those final elements to prodArray.
    for (int i = 0; i <= numExtra - 1; i++)
    {
        if (arrayIsLonger)
            prodArray[prodArrSize - numExtra + i] =
                    arr[prodArrSize - numExtra + i];
        else
            prodArray[prodArrSize - numExtra + i] =
                    list.get(prodArrSize - numExtra + i);
    }
    return prodArray;
}
```

**NOTE**

1. Use Math.abs to get a positive value for the number of extra elements to be copied.
2. prodArray already has slots for the leftover elements that must be copied. But you must be careful in the indexes for these elements that are taken from the end of the longer list and placed in the end slots of the prodArray.

## TWO-DIMENSIONAL ARRAYS

A two-dimensional array (matrix) is often the data structure of choice for objects like board games, tables of values, theater seats, and mazes.

Look at the following 3 × 4 matrix:

$$
\begin{array}{cccc}
2 & 6 & 8 & 7 \\
1 & 5 & 4 & 0 \\
9 & 3 & 2 & 8
\end{array}
$$

If mat is the matrix variable, the row subscripts go from 0 to 2 and the column subscripts go from 0 to 3. The element mat[1][2] is 4, whereas mat[0][2] and mat[2][3] are both 8. As with one-dimensional arrays, if the subscripts are out of range, an ArrayIndexOutOfBoundsException is thrown.

## Declarations

Each of the following declares a two-dimensional array:

```
int[][] table;      //table can reference a 2D array of integers
                    //table is currently a null reference
double[][] matrix = new double[3][4];  //matrix references a 3 × 4
                                       //array of real numbers.
                                       //Each element has value 0.0
String[][] strs = new String[2][5]; //strs references a 2 × 5
                                    //array of String objects.
                                    //Each element is null
```

An *initializer list* can be used to specify a two-dimensional array:

```
int[][] mat = { {3, 4, 5},          //row 0
                {6, 7, 8} };        //row 1
```

This defines a 2 × 3 *rectangular* array (i.e., one in which each row has the same number of elements). All two-dimensional arrays on the AP exam are rectangular.

The initializer list is a list of lists in which each inside list represents a row of the matrix.

## Matrix as Array of Row Arrays

A matrix is implemented as an array of rows, where each row is a one-dimensional array of elements. Suppose mat is the 3 × 4 matrix

```
2 6 8 7
1 5 4 0
9 3 2 8
```

Then mat is an array of three arrays:

| | | |
|---|---|---|
| mat[0] | contains | {2, 6, 8, 7} |
| mat[1] | contains | {1, 5, 4, 0} |
| mat[2] | contains | {9, 3, 2, 8} |

The quantity mat.length represents the number of rows. In this case it equals 3 because there are three row-arrays in mat. For any given row k, where 0 ≤ k < mat.length, the quantity mat[k].length represents the number of elements in that row, namely the number of columns. (Java allows a variable number of elements in each row. Since these "jagged arrays" are not part of the AP Java subset, you can assume that mat[k].length is the same for all rows k of the matrix, i.e., that the matrix is rectangular.)

## Processing a Two-Dimensional Array

There are three common ways to traverse a two-dimensional array:

- row-column (for accessing elements, modifying elements that are class objects, or replacing elements)
- enhanced for loop (for accessing elements or modifying elements that are class objects, but no replacement)
- row-by-row array processing (for accessing, modifying, or replacement of elements)

**NOTE**

A row-by-row traversal, starting in the top, leftmost corner and going from left to right is called a *row-major traversal*:

```
for (row = 0; row < mat.length; row++)
    for (col = 0; col < mat[0].length; col++)
        processElements();
```

A column-by-column traversal, starting in the top, leftmost corner and going from top to bottom is less common and is called a *column-major traversal*:

```
for (col = 0; col < mat[0].length; col++)
    for (row = 0; row < mat.length; row++)
        processElements();
```

Find the sum of all elements in a matrix mat. Here is a row-column traversal:

```
/** Precondition: mat is initialized with integer values. */
int sum = 0;
for (int r = 0; r < mat.length; r++)
    for (int c = 0; c < mat[r].length; c++)
        sum += mat[r][c];
```

**NOTE**

1. mat[r][c] represents the rth row and the cth column.
2. Rows are numbered from 0 to mat.length-1, and columns are numbered from 0 to mat[r].length-1. Any index that is outside these bounds will generate an ArrayIndexOutOfBoundsException.

Since elements are not being replaced, nested enhanced for loops can be used instead:

```
for (int[] row : mat)        //for each row array in mat
    for (int element : row)  //for each element in this row
        sum += element;
```

**NOTE**

You also need to know how to process a matrix as shown below, using a third type of traversal, row-by-row array processing. This traversal

■ assumes access to a method that processes an array;

■ passes a one-dimensional array reference as a parameter to a method that processes each row;

■ traverses the rows using either a regular loop or an enhanced for loop.

So, continuing with the example to find the sum of all elements in mat: In the class where mat is defined, suppose you have the method sumArray.

```
/** Returns the sum of integers in arr. */
public int sumArray(int[] arr)
{ /* implementation not shown */ }
```

You could use this method to sum all the elements in mat as follows:

```
int sum = 0;
for (int row = 0; row < mat.length; row++) //for each row in mat,
    sum += sumArray(mat[row]);              //add that row's total to sum
```

Note how, since mat[row] is an array of int for 0 ≤ row < mat.length, you can use the sumArray method for each row in mat. Alternatively, you can use an enhanced for loop traversal:

```
for (int [] rowArr: mat)          //for each row array in mat
    sum += sumArray(rowArr);      //add that row's total to sum
```

## Example 2

Add 10 to each element in row 2 of matrix `mat`.

```
for (int c = 0; c < mat[2].length; c++)
    mat[2][c] += 10;
```

**NOTE**

1. In the `for` loop, you can use `c < mat[k].length`, where $0 \le k < mat.length$, since each row has the same number of elements.
2. You should not use an enhanced `for` loop here because elements are being replaced.
3. You can, however, use row-by-row array processing. Suppose you have method `addTen` shown below.

   ```
   /** Add 10 to each int in arr */
   public void addTen(int[] arr)
   {
       for (int i = 0; i < arr.length; i++)
           arr[i] += 10;
   }
   ```

   You could add 10 to each element in row 2 with the single statement

   ```
   addTen(mat[2]);
   ```

   You could also add 10 to every element in `mat`:

   ```
   for (int row = 0; row < mat.length; row++)
       addTen(mat[row]);
   ```

## Example 3

Suppose `Card` objects have a mutator method `changeValue`:

```
public void changeValue(int newValue)
{ value = newValue; }
```

Now consider the following declaration.

```
Card[][] cardMatrix;
```

Suppose `cardMatrix` is initialized with `Card` objects. A piece of code that traverses the `cardMatrix` and changes the value of each `Card` to `v` is

```
for (Card[] row : cardMatrix)   //for each row array in cardMatrix,
    for (Card c : row)          //for each Card in that row,
        c.changeValue(v);       //change the value of that card
```

Alternatively:

```
for (int row = 0; row < cardMatrix.length; row++)
    for (int col = 0; col < cardMatrix[0].length; col++)
        cardMatrix[row][col].changeValue(v);
```

**NOTE**

The use of the nested enhanced `for` loop is OK. Modifying the objects in the matrix with a mutator method is fine. What you shouldn't do is *replace* the `Card` objects with new `Cards`.

## ➥ Example 4

The major and minor diagonals of a square matrix are shown below:

**Major diagonal**

**Minor diagonal**

You can process the diagonals as follows:

```
int[][] mat = new int[SIZE][SIZE];  //SIZE is a constant int value
for (int i = 0; i < SIZE; i++)
    Process mat[i][i];                 //major diagonal
        OR
    Process mat[i][SIZE - i - 1];   //minor diagonal
```

## Two-Dimensional Array as Parameter

## ➥ Example 1

Here is a method that counts the number of negative values in a matrix:

```
/** Returns count of negative values in mat.
 *  Precondition:  mat is initialized with integers.
 */
public static int countNegs (int[][] mat)
{
    int count = 0;
    for (int[] row : mat)
        for (int num : row)
            if (num < 0)
                count++;
    return count;
}
```

A method in the same class can invoke this method with a statement such as

```
int negs = countNegs(matrix);
```

Reading elements into a matrix:

```java
/** Returns matrix containing rows × cols integers
 *  read from the keyboard.
 *  Precondition: Number of rows and columns known.
 */
public static int[][] getMatrix(int rows, int cols)
{
    int[][] mat = new int[rows][cols];   //initialize slots
    System.out.println("Enter matrix, one row per line:");
    System.out.println();

    //read user input and fill slots
    for (int r = 0; r < rows; r++)
        for (int c = 0; c < cols; c++)
            mat[r][c] = ...;   //read user input
    return mat;
}
```

To call this method:

```java
//prompt for number of rows and columns
int rows = ...;        //read user input
int cols = ...;        //read user input
int[][] mat = getMatrix(rows, cols);
```

**NOTE**

You should not use an enhanced `for` loop in `getMatrix` because elements in `mat` are being replaced. (Their current value is the initialized value of `0`. The new value is the input value from the keyboard.)

There is further discussion of arrays and matrices, plus additional questions, in Chapter 10 (The AP Computer Science A Labs).

## Chapter Summary

Manipulation of one-dimensional arrays, two-dimensional arrays, and array lists should be second nature to you by now. Know the Java subset methods for the `ArrayList<E>` class. You must also know when these methods throw an `IndexOutOfBoundsException` and when an `ArrayIndexOutOfBoundsException` can occur.

When traversing an `ArrayList`:

- Use an enhanced `for` loop to access each element without changing it, or to modify each object in the list using a mutator method.
- Take special care with indices when removing multiple elements from an `ArrayList`.

A two-dimensional array is an array of row arrays. The number of rows is `mat.length`. The number of columns is `mat[0].length`.

When traversing a two-dimensional array:

- Use a row-column traversal to access, modify, or replace elements. Know the difference between row-major order and column-major order.

- Use a nested `for` loop to access or modify elements, but not replace them.

- Know how to do row-by-row array processing if you have an appropriate method that takes an array parameter.

1. Which of the following correctly initializes an array `arr` to contain four elements each with value 0?

   I  `int[] arr = {0, 0, 0, 0};`

   II  `int[] arr = new int[4];`

   III  `int[] arr = new int[4];`
   ```
   for (int i = 0; i < arr.length; i++)
       arr[i] = 0;
   ```

   (A) I only
   (B) III only
   (C) I and III only
   (D) II and III only
   (E) I, II, and III


2. The following program segment is intended to find the index of the first negative integer in `arr[0] ... arr[N-1]`, where `arr` is an array of N integers.

   ```
   int i = 0;
   while (arr[i] >= 0)
   {
       i++;
   }
   location = i;
   ```

   This segment will work as intended
   (A) always.
   (B) never.
   (C) whenever `arr` contains at least one negative integer.
   (D) whenever `arr` contains at least one nonnegative integer.
   (E) whenever `arr` contains no negative integers.

3. Refer to the following code segment. You may assume that `arr` is an array of `int` values.

```
int sum = arr[0], i = 0;
while (i < arr.length)
{
    i++;
    sum += arr[i];
}
```

Which of the following will be the result of executing the segment?

(A) Sum of `arr[0]`, `arr[1]`, ..., `arr[arr.length-1]` will be stored in `sum`.

(B) Sum of `arr[1]`, `arr[2]`, ..., `arr[arr.length-1]` will be stored in `sum`.

(C) Sum of `arr[0]`, `arr[1]`, ..., `arr[arr.length]` will be stored in `sum`.

(D) An infinite loop will occur.

(E) A run-time error will occur.

4. Refer to the following code segment. You may assume that array `arr1` contains elements `arr1[0]`, `arr1[1]`, ..., `arr1[N-1]`, where N = `arr1.length`.

```
int count = 0;
for (int i = 0; i < N; i++)
    if (arr1[i] != 0)
    {
        arr1[count] = arr1[i];
        count++;
    }
int[] arr2 = new int[count];
for (int i = 0; i < count; i++)
    arr2[i] = arr1[i];
```

If array `arr1` initially contains the elements 0, 6, 0, 4, 0, 0, 2 in this order, what will `arr2` contain after execution of the code segment?

(A) 6, 4, 2

(B) 0, 0, 0, 0, 6, 4, 2

(C) 6, 4, 2, 4, 0, 0, 2

(D) 0, 6, 0, 4, 0, 0, 2

(E) 6, 4, 2, 0, 0, 0, 0

5. Consider this program segment.

```
for (int i = 2; i <= k; i++)
    if (arr[i] < someValue)
        System.out.print("SMALL");
```

What is the maximum number of times that SMALL can be printed?

(A) 0

(B) 1

(C) k - 1

(D) k - 2

(E) k

6. What will be output from the following code segment, assuming it is in the same class as the doSomething method?

```
int[] arr = {1, 2, 3, 4};
doSomething(arr);
System.out.print(arr[1] + " ");
System.out.print(arr[3]);
    ...
public void doSomething(int[] list)
{
    int[] b = list;
    for (int i = 0; i < b.length; i++)
        b[i] = i;
}
```

(A) 0 0

(B) 2 4

(C) 1 3

(D) 0 2

(E) 0 3

7. Consider writing a program that reads the lines of any text file into a sequential list of lines. Which of the following is a good reason to implement the list with an ArrayList of String objects rather than an array of String objects?

(A) The get and set methods of ArrayList are more convenient than the [] notation for arrays.

(B) The size method of ArrayList provides instant access to the length of the list.

(C) An ArrayList can contain objects of any type, which leads to greater generality.

(D) If any particular text file is unexpectedly long, the ArrayList will automatically be resized. The array, by contrast, may go out of bounds.

(E) The String methods are easier to use with an ArrayList than with an array.

8. Consider writing a program that produces statistics for long lists of numerical data. Which of the following is the best reason to implement each list with an array of `int` (or `double`), rather than an `ArrayList` of `Integer` (or `Double`) objects?

(A) An array of primitive number types is more efficient to manipulate than an `ArrayList` of wrapper objects that contain numbers.

(B) Insertion of new elements into a list is easier to code for an array than for an `ArrayList`.

(C) Removal of elements from a list is easier to code for an array than for an `ArrayList`.

(D) Accessing individual elements in the middle of a list is easier for an array than for an `ArrayList`.

(E) Accessing all the elements is more efficient in an array than in an `ArrayList`.

Refer to the following classes for Questions 9–12.

```java
public class Address
{
    private String name;
    private String street;
    private String city;
    private String state;
    private String zip;

    //constructors
        ...

    //accessors
    public String getName()
    { return name; }
    public String getStreet()
    { return street; }
    public String getCity()
    { return city; }
    public String getState()
    { return state; }
    public String getZip()
    { return zip; }
}

public class Student
{
    private int idNum;
    private double gpa;
    private Address address;

    //constructors
        ...

    //accessors
    public Address getAddress()
    { return address; }
    public int getIdNum()
    { return idNum; }
    public double getGpa()
    { return gpa; }
}
```

9. A client method has this declaration, followed by code to initialize the list.

```
Address[] list = new Address[100];
```

Here is a code segment to generate a list of *names only*.

```
for (Address a : list)
    /* line of code */
```

Which is a correct /* **line of code** */?
- (A) `System.out.println(Address[i].getName());`
- (B) `System.out.println(list[i].getName());`
- (C) `System.out.println(a[i].getName());`
- (D) `System.out.println(a.getName());`
- (E) `System.out.println(list.getName());`

10. The following code segment is to print out a list of addresses.

```
for (Address addr : list)
{
    /* more code */
}
```

Which is a correct replacement for /* **more code** */?

```
 I  System.out.println(list[i].getName());
    System.out.println(list[i].getStreet());
    System.out.print(list[i].getCity() + ", ");
    System.out.print(list[i].getState() + " ");
    System.out.println(list[i].getZip());
```

```
II  System.out.println(addr.getName());
    System.out.println(addr.getStreet());
    System.out.print(addr.getCity() + ", ");
    System.out.print(addr.getState() + " ");
    System.out.println(addr.getZip());
```

```
III System.out.println(addr);
```

- (A) I only
- (B) II only
- (C) III only
- (D) I and II only
- (E) I, II, and III

11. A client method has this declaration.

```
Student[] allStudents = new Student[NUM_STUDS];  //NUM_STUDS is
                                     //an int constant
```

Here is a code segment to generate a list of Student names only. (You may assume that allStudents has been initialized.)

```
for (Student student : allStudents)
    /* code to print list of names */
```

Which is a correct replacement for /* *code to print list of names* */?

(A) `System.out.println(allStudents.getName());`

(B) `System.out.println(student.getName());`

(C) `System.out.println(student.getAddress().getName());`

(D) `System.out.println(allStudents.getAddress().getName());`

(E) `System.out.println(student[i].getAddress().getName());`

12. Here is a method that locates the `Student` with the highest `idNum`.

```
/** Returns Student with highest idNum.
 * Precondition: Array stuArr of Student is initialized.
 */
public static Student locate(Student[] stuArr)
{
    /* method body */
}
```

Which of the following could replace /* *method body* */ so that the method works as intended?

```
I  int max = stuArr[0].getIdNum();
   for (Student student : stuArr)
       if (student.getIdNum() > max)
       {
           max = student.getIdNum();
           return student;
       }
   return stuArr[0];
```

```
II Student highestSoFar = stuArr[0];
   int max = stuArr[0].getIdNum();
   for (Student student : stuArr)
       if(student.getIdNum() > max)
       {
           max = student.getIdNum();
           highestSoFar = student;
       }
   return highestSoFar;
```

```
III int maxPos = 0;
    for(int i = 1; i < stuArr.length; i++)
        if(stuArr[i].getIdNum() > stuArr[maxPos].getIdNum())
            maxPos = i;
    return stuArr[maxPos];
```

(A) I only
(B) II only
(C) III only
(D) I and III only
(E) II and III only

Questions 13–15 refer to the Ticket and Transaction classes below.

```java
public class Ticket
{
    private String row;
    private int seat;
    private double price;

    //constructor
    public Ticket(String aRow, int aSeat, double aPrice)
    {
        row = aRow;
        seat = aSeat;
        price = aPrice;
    }

    //accessors getRow(), getSeat(), and getPrice()
        ...
}

public class Transaction
{
    private int numTickets;
    private Ticket[] tickList;

    //constructor
    public Transaction(int numTicks)
    {
        numTickets = numTicks;
        tickList = new Ticket[numTicks];
        String theRow;
        int theSeat;
        double thePrice;
        for (int i = 0; i < numTicks; i++)
        {
            < read user input for theRow, theSeat, and thePrice >
                ...

            /* more code */
        }
    }

    /** Returns total amount paid for this transaction. */
    public double totalPaid()
    {
        double total = 0.0;
        /* code to calculate amount */
        return total;
    }
}
```

13. Which of the following correctly replaces /* *more code* */ in the Transaction constructor to initialize the tickList array?

    (A) `tickList[i] = new Ticket(getRow(), getSeat(), getPrice());`

    (B) `tickList[i] = new Ticket(theRow, theSeat, thePrice);`

    (C) `tickList[i] = new tickList(getRow(), getSeat(), getPrice());`

    (D) `tickList[i] = new tickList(theRow, theSeat, thePrice);`

    (E) `tickList[i] = new tickList(numTicks);`

14. Which represents correct /* *code to calculate amount* */ in the totalPaid method?

    (A)
```
for (Ticket t : tickList)
    total += t.price;
```

    (B)
```
for (Ticket t : tickList)
    total += tickList.getPrice();
```

    (C)
```
for (Ticket t : tickList)
    total += t.getPrice();
```

    (D)
```
Transaction T;
for (Ticket t : T)
    total += t.getPrice();
```

    (E)
```
Transaction T;
for (Ticket t : T)
    total += t.price;
```

15. Suppose it is necessary to keep a list of all ticket transactions. Assuming that there are NUMSALES transactions, a suitable declaration would be

    (A) `Transaction[] listOfSales = new Transaction[NUMSALES];`

    (B) `Transaction[] listOfSales = new Ticket[NUMSALES];`

    (C) `Ticket[] listOfSales = new Transaction[NUMSALES];`

    (D) `Ticket[] listOfSales = new Ticket[NUMSALES];`

    (E) `Transaction[] Ticket = new listOfSales[NUMSALES];`

16. The following code fragment is intended to find the smallest value in
    arr[0] ... arr[n-1], but does not work as intended.

```
/** Precondition:
 *    - arr is an array, arr.length = n.
 *    - arr[0]...arr[n-1] initialized with integers.
 *  Postcondition: min = smallest value in arr[0]...arr[n-1].
 */
int min = arr[0];
int i = 1;
while (i < n)
{
    i++;
    if (arr[i] < min)
        min = arr[i];
}
```

For the segment to work as intended, which of the following modifications could be
made?

  I  Change the line

     `int i = 1;`

     to

     `int i = 0;`

     Make no other changes.

  II  Change the body of the while loop to

```
{
    if (arr[i] < min)
        min = arr[i];
    i++;
}
```

     Make no other changes.

  III  Change the test for the while loop as follows.

     `while (i <= n)`

     Make no other changes.

(A) I only
(B) II only
(C) III only
(D) I and II only
(E) I, II, and III

17. Refer to method `match` below.

```
/** Returns true if there is an integer k that occurs
 *  in both arrays; otherwise returns false.
 *  Precondition:
 *    - v is an array of int sorted in increasing order
 *    - w is an array of int sorted in increasing order
 *    - N is the number of elements in array v
 *    - M is the number of elements in array w
 *    - v[0]..v[N-1] and w[0]..w[M-1] is initialized with integers.
 *    - v[0] < v[1] < .. < v[N-1] and w[0] < w[1] < .. < w[M-1].
 */
public static boolean match(int[] v, int[] w, int N, int M)
{
    int vIndex = 0, wIndex = 0;
    while (vIndex < N && wIndex < M)
    {
        if (v[vIndex] == w[wIndex])
            return true;
        else if (v[vIndex] < w[wIndex])
            vIndex++;
        else
            wIndex++;
    }
    return false;
}
```

Assuming that the method has not been exited, which assertion is true at the end of every execution of the `while` loop?

(A) `v[0]..v[vIndex-1]` and `w[0]..w[wIndex-1]` contain no common value, `vIndex` ≤ N and `wIndex` ≤ M.

(B) `v[0]..v[vIndex]` and `w[0]..w[wIndex]` contain no common value, `vIndex` ≤ N and `wIndex` ≤ M.

(C) `v[0]..v[vIndex-1]` and `w[0]..w[wIndex-1]` contain no common value, `vIndex` ≤ N-1 and `wIndex` ≤ M-1.

(D) `v[0]..v[vIndex]` and `w[0]..w[wIndex]` contain no common value, `vIndex` ≤ N-1 and `wIndex` ≤ M-1.

(E) `v[0]..v[N-1]` and `w[0]..w[M-1]` contain no common value, `vIndex` ≤ N and `wIndex` ≤ M.

18. Consider this class.

```
public class Book
{
    private String title;
    private String author;
    private boolean checkoutStatus;

    public Book(String bookTitle, String bookAuthor)
    {
        title = bookTitle;
        author = bookAuthor;
        checkoutStatus = false;
    }

    /** Change checkout status. */
    public void changeStatus()
    { checkoutStatus = !checkoutStatus; }

    //Other methods are not shown.
}
```

A client program has this declaration.

```
Book[] bookList = new Book[SOME_NUMBER];
```

Suppose bookList is initialized so that each Book in the list has a title, author, and checkout status. The following piece of code is written, whose intent is to change the checkout status of each book in bookList.

```
for (Book b : bookList)
    b.changeStatus();
```

Which is true about this code?
(A) The bookList array will remain unchanged after execution.
(B) Each book in the bookList array will have its checkout status changed, as intended.
(C) A NullPointerException may occur.
(D) A run-time error will occur because it is not possible to modify objects using the enhanced for loop.
(E) A logic error will occur because it is not possible to modify objects in an array without accessing the indexes of the objects.

Consider this class for Questions 19 and 20.

```
public class BingoCard
{
    private int[] card;

    /** Default constructor: Creates BingoCard with
     *  20 random digits in the range 1 - 90.
     */
    public BingoCard()
    { /* implementation not shown */ }

    /* Display BingoCard. */
    public void display()
    { /* implementation not shown */ }
        ...
}
```

A program that simulates a bingo game declares an array of BingoCard. The array has NUMPLAYERS elements, where each element represents the card of a different player. Here is a code segment that creates all the bingo cards in the game.

```
/* declare array of BingoCard */
/* construct each BingoCard */
```

19. Which of the following is a correct replacement for

    /* *declare array of* BingoCard */?

    (A) int[] BingoCard = new BingoCard[NUMPLAYERS];

    (B) BingoCard[] players = new int[NUMPLAYERS];

    (C) BingoCard[] players = new BingoCard[20];

    (D) BingoCard[] players = new BingoCard[NUMPLAYERS];

    (E) int[] players = new BingoCard[NUMPLAYERS];

20. Assuming that players has been declared as an array of BingoCard, which replacement for /* *construct each* BingoCard */ is correct?

    I   for (BingoCard card : players)
            card = new BingoCard();

    II  for (BingoCard card : players)
            players[card] = new BingoCard();

    III for (int i = 0; i < players.length; i++)
            players[i] = new BingoCard();

    (A) I only
    (B) II only
    (C) III only
    (D) I and III only
    (E) I, II, and III

21. Consider these declarations.

```
ArrayList<String> strList = new ArrayList<String>();
String ch = " ";
Integer intOb = new Integer(5);
```

Which statement will cause an error?
- (A) `strList.add(ch);`
- (B) `strList.add(new String("handy andy"));`
- (C) `strList.add(intOb.toString());`
- (D) `strList.add(ch + 8);`
- (E) `strList.add(intOb + 8);`

22. Let `list` be an `ArrayList<Integer>` containing these elements.

```
2 5 7 6 0 1
```

Which of the following statements would not cause an error to occur? Assume that each statement applies to the given list, independent of the other statements.
- (A) `Object ob = list.get(6);`
- (B) `Integer intOb = list.add(3.4);`
- (C) `list.add(6, 9);`
- (D) `Object x = list.remove(6);`
- (E) `Object y = list.set(6, 8);`

23. Refer to method `insert` below.

```
/** Inserts element in its correct sorted position in list.
 *  Precondition: list contains String values sorted
 *                in decreasing order.
 */
public void insert(ArrayList<String> list, String element)
{
    int index = 0;
    while (element.compareTo(list.get(index)) < 0)
        index++;
    list.add(index, element);
}
```

Assuming that the type of `element` is compatible with the objects in the list, which is a true statement about the `insert` method?
- (A) It works as intended for all values of `element`.
- (B) It fails for all values of `element`.
- (C) It fails if `element` is greater than the first item in `list` and works in all other cases.
- (D) It fails if `element` is smaller than the last item in `list` and works in all other cases.
- (E) It fails if `element` is either greater than the first item or smaller than the last item in `list` and works in all other cases.

24. Consider the following code segment, applied to `list`, an `ArrayList` of `Integer` values.

```
int len = list.size();
for (int i = 0; i < len; i++)
{
    list.add(i + 1, new Integer(i));
    Object x = list.set(i, new Integer(i + 2));
}
```

If `list` is initially 6  1  8, what will it be following execution of the code segment?

(A) 2 3 4 2 1 8
(B) 2 3 4 6 2 2 0 1 8
(C) 2 3 4 0 1 2
(D) 2 3 4 6 1 8
(E) 2 3 3 2

Questions 25 and 26 are based on the Coin and Purse classes given below.

```java
/* A simple coin class */
public class Coin
{
    private double value;
    private String name;

    //constructor
    public Coin(double coinValue, String coinName)
    {
        value = coinValue;
        name = coinName;
    }

    /** Returns the value of this coin. */
    public double getValue()
    { return value; }

    /** Returns the name of this coin. */
    public String getName()
    { return name; }

    /** Returns true if this coin equals obj; false otherwise. */
    public boolean equals(Object obj)
    { return name.equals(((Coin) obj).name); }

    //Other methods are not shown.
}


/* A purse holds a collection of coins */
public class Purse
{
    private ArrayList<Coin> coins;

    /** Creates an empty purse. */
    public Purse()
    { coins = new ArrayList<Coin>(); }

    /** Adds aCoin to the purse. */
    public void add(Coin aCoin)
    { coins.add(aCoin); }

    /** Returns the total value of coins in purse. */
    public double getTotal()
    { /* implementation not shown */}

}
```

25. Here is the getTotal method from the Purse class.

```
/** Returns the total value of coins in purse. */
public double getTotal()
{
    double total = 0;
    /* more code */
    return total;
}
```

Which of the following is a correct replacement for /* *more code* */?

(A) 
```
for (Coin c : coins)
{
    c = coins.get(i);
    total += c.getValue();
}
```

(B) 
```
for (Coin c : coins)
{
    Coin value = c.getValue();
    total += value;
}
```

(C) 
```
for (Coin c : coins)
{
    Coin c = coins.get(i);
    total += c.getValue();
}
```

(D) 
```
for (Coin c : coins)
{
    total += coins.getValue();
}
```

(E) 
```
for (Coin c : coins)
{
    total += c.getValue();
}
```

26. Two coins are said to *match* each other if they have the same name or the same value. You may assume that coins with the same name have the same value and coins with the same value have the same name. A boolean method `find` is added to the `Purse` class.

```
/** Returns true if the purse has a coin that matches aCoin,
 *  false otherwise.
 */
public boolean find(Coin aCoin)
{
    for (Coin c : coins)
    {
        /* code to find match */
    }
    return false;
}
```

Which is a correct replacement for /* *code to find match* */?

```
 I  if (c.equals(aCoin))
        return true;
```

```
 II  if ((c.getName()).equals(aCoin.getName()))
         return true;
```

```
III  if ((c.getValue()).equals(aCoin.getValue()))
         return true;
```

(A) I only
(B) II only
(C) III only
(D) I and II only
(E) I, II, and III

27. Which of the following initializes an 8 × 10 matrix with integer values that are perfect squares? (0 is a perfect square.)

```
 I  int[][] mat = new int[8][10];
```

```
 II  int[][] mat = new int[8][10];
     for (int r = 0; r < mat.length; r++)
         for (int c = 0; c < mat[r].length; c++)
             mat[r][c] = r * r;
```

```
III  int[][] mat = new int[8][10];
     for (int c = 0; c < mat[r].length; c++)
         for (int r = 0; r < mat.length; r++)
             mat[r][c] = c * c;
```

(A) I only
(B) II only
(C) III only
(D) I and II only
(E) I, II, and III

28. Consider the following code segment.

```
int[][] mat = {{1,3,5},
               {2,4,6},
               {0,7,8},
               {9,10,11}}

for (int col = 0; col < mat[0].length; col++)
    for (int row = mat.length - 1; row > col; row--)
        System.out.println(mat[row][col]);
```

When this code is executed, which will be the fifth element printed?

(A) 3

(B) 4

(C) 5

(D) 6

(E) 7

29. Consider a class that has this private instance variable.

```
private int[][] mat;
```

The class has the following method, alter.

```
public void alter(int c)
{
    for (int i = 0; i < mat.length; i++)
        for (int j = c + 1; j < mat[0].length; j++)
            mat[i][j-1] = mat[i][j];
}
```

If a 3 × 4 matrix mat is

```
1 3 5 7
2 4 6 8
3 5 7 9
```

then alter(1) will change mat to

(A) 1 5 7 7
    2 6 8 8
    3 7 9 9

(B) 1 5 7
    2 6 8
    3 7 9

(C) 1 3 5 7
    3 5 7 9

(D) 1 3 5 7
    3 5 7 9
    3 5 7 9

(E) 1 7 7 7
    2 8 8 8
    3 9 9 9

30. Consider the following method that will alter the matrix mat.

```
public static void matStuff(int[][] mat, int row)
{
    int numCols = mat[0].length;
    for (int col = 0; col < numCols; col++)
        mat[row][col] = row;
}
```

Suppose mat is originally

```
1  4  9  0
2  7  8  6
5  1  4  3
```

After the method call matStuff(mat,2), matrix mat will be

(A)  1  4  9  0
       2  7  8  6
       2  2  2  2

(B)  1  4  9  0
       2  2  2  2
       5  1  4  3

(C)  2  2  2  2
       2  2  2  2
       2  2  2  2

(D)  1  4  2  0
       2  7  2  6
       5  1  2  3

(E)  1  2  9  0
       2  2  8  6
       5  2  4  3

31. Assume that a square matrix mat is defined by

```
int[][] mat = new int[SIZE][SIZE];
//SIZE is an integer constant >= 2
```

What does the following code segment do?

```
for (int i = 0; i < SIZE - 1; i++)
    for (int j = 0; j < SIZE - i - 1; j++)
        swap(mat, i, j, SIZE - j - 1, SIZE - i - 1);
```

You may assume the existence of this swap method.

```
/** Interchange mat[a][b] and mat[c][d]. */
public void swap(int[][] mat, int a, int b, int c, int d)
```

(A)  Reflects mat through its major diagonal. For example,

$$\begin{matrix} 2 & 6 \\ 4 & 3 \end{matrix} \longrightarrow \begin{matrix} 2 & 4 \\ 6 & 3 \end{matrix}$$

(B)  Reflects mat through its minor diagonal. For example,

$$\begin{matrix} 2 & 6 \\ 4 & 3 \end{matrix} \longrightarrow \begin{matrix} 3 & 6 \\ 4 & 2 \end{matrix}$$

(C)  Reflects mat through a horizontal line of symmetry. For example,

$$\begin{matrix} 2 & 6 \\ 4 & 3 \end{matrix} \longrightarrow \begin{matrix} 4 & 3 \\ 2 & 6 \end{matrix}$$

(D)  Reflects mat through a vertical line of symmetry. For example,

$$\begin{matrix} 2 & 6 \\ 4 & 3 \end{matrix} \longrightarrow \begin{matrix} 6 & 2 \\ 3 & 4 \end{matrix}$$

(E)  Leaves mat unchanged.

32. Consider a class `MatrixStuff` that has a private instance variable.

```
private int[][] mat;
```

Refer to method `alter` below that occurs in the `MatrixStuff` class. (The lines are numbered for reference.)

```
Line 1:  /** Precondition:
Line 2:   *    - the matrix mat is initialized with integers.
Line 3:   *  Postcondition:
Line 4:   *    - Column c has been removed.
Line 5:   *    - The last column is filled with zeros.
Line 6:   */
Line 7:  public void alter(int[][] mat, int c)
Line 8:  {
Line 9:      for (int i = 0; i < mat.length; i++)
Line 10:         for (int j = c; j < mat[0].length; j++)
Line 11:             mat[i][j] = mat[i][j+1];
Line 12:     //code to insert zeros in rightmost column
Line 13:         . . .
Line 14: }
```

The intent of the method `alter` is to remove column c. Thus, if the input matrix `mat` is

$$
\begin{array}{cccc}
2 & 6 & 8 & 9 \\
1 & 5 & 4 & 3 \\
0 & 7 & 3 & 2
\end{array}
$$

the method call `alter(mat, 1)` should change `mat` to

$$
\begin{array}{cccc}
2 & 8 & 9 & 0 \\
1 & 4 & 3 & 0 \\
0 & 3 & 2 & 0
\end{array}
$$

The method does not work as intended. Which of the following changes will correct the problem?

  I  Change line 10 to

```
for (int j = c; j < mat[0].length - 1; j++)
```

and make no other changes.

 II  Change lines 10 and 11 to

```
for (int j = c + 1; j < mat[0].length; j++)
    mat[i][j-1] = mat[i][j];
```

and make no other changes.

III  Change lines 10 and 11 to

```
for (int j = mat[0].length - 1; j > c; j--)
    mat[i][j-1] = mat[i][j];
```

and make no other changes.

(A) I only

(B) II only

(C) III only

(D) I and II only

(E) I, II, and III

33. This question refers to the following method.

```
public static boolean isThere(String[][] mat, int row, int col,
    String symbol)
{
    boolean yes;
    int i, count = 0;
    for (i = 0; i < SIZE; i++)
        if (mat[i][col].equals(symbol))
            count++;
    yes = (count == SIZE);
    count = 0;
    for (i = 0; i < SIZE; i++)
        if (mat[row][i].equals(symbol))
            count++;
    return (yes || count == SIZE);
}
```

Now consider this code segment.

```
public final int SIZE = 8;
String[][] mat = new String[SIZE][SIZE];
```

Which of the following conditions on a matrix mat of the type declared in the code segment will by itself guarantee that

```
isThere(mat, 2, 2, "$")
```

will have the value true when evaluated?

  I  The element in row 2 and column 2 is "$"
 II  All elements in both diagonals are "$"
III  All elements in column 2 are "$"

(A) I only
(B) III only
(C) I and II only
(D) I and III only
(E) II and III only

34. The method changeNegs below should replace every occurrence of a negative integer in its matrix parameter with 0.

```java
/** Replaces all negative values in mat with 0.
 * Precondition: mat is initialized with integers.
 */
public static void changeNegs(int[][] mat)
{
    /* code */
}
```

Which is a correct replacement for /* *code* */?

```java
  I for (int r = 0; r < mat.length; r++)
        for (int c = 0; c < mat[r].length; c++)
            if (mat[r][c] < 0)
                mat[r][c] = 0;

 II for (int c = 0; c < mat[0].length; c++)
        for (int r = 0; r < mat.length; r++)
            if (mat[r][c] < 0)
                mat[r][c] = 0;

III for (int[] row : mat)
        for (int element : row)
            if (element < 0)
                element = 0;
```

(A) I only
(B) II only
(C) III only
(D) I and II only
(E) I, II, and III

35. A two-dimensional array `rainfall` that contains `double` values will be used to represent the daily rainfall for a given year. In this scheme, `rainfall[month][day]` represents the amount of rain on the given day and month. For example,

   `rainfall[1][15]`     is the amount of rain on Jan. 15
   `rainfall[12][25]`    is the amount of rain on Dec. 25

The array can be declared as follows.

```
double[][] rainfall = new double[13][32];
```

This creates 13 rows indexed from 0 to 12 and 32 columns indexed from 0 to 31, all initialized to 0.0. Row 0 and column 0 will be ignored. Column 31 in row 4 will be ignored, since April 31 is not a valid day. In years that are not leap years, columns 29, 30, and 31 in row 2 will be ignored since Feb. 29, 30, and 31 are not valid days.

Consider the method `averageRainfall` below.

```
/** Precondition:
 *    - rainfall is initialized with values representing amounts
 *      of rain on all valid days.
 *    - Invalid days are initialized to 0.0.
 *    - Feb 29 is not a valid day.
 * Postcondition: Returns average rainfall for the year.
 */
public double averageRainfall(double rainfall[][])
{
    double total = 0.0;
    /* more code */
}
```

Which of the following is a correct replacement for /* *more code* */ so that the postcondition for the method is satisfied?

```
 I for (int month = 1; month < rainfall.length; month++)
        for (int day = 1; day < rainfall[month].length; day++)
            total += rainfall[month][day];
    return total / (13 * 32);
```

```
 II for (int month = 1; month < rainfall.length; month++)
        for (int day = 1; day < rainfall[month].length; day++)
            total += rainfall[month][day];
    return total / 365;
```

```
III for (double[] month : rainfall)
        for (double rainAmt : month)
            total += rainAmt;
    return total / 365;
```

(A) None
(B) I only
(C) II only
(D) III only
(E) II and III only

36. This question is based on the `Point` class below.

```
public class Point
{
    /** The coordinates. */
    private int x;
    private int y;

    public Point (int xValue, int yValue)
    {
        x = xValue;
        y = yValue;
    }

    /** Returns the x-coordinate of this point. */
    public int getx()
    { return x; }

    /** Returns the y-coordinate of this point. */
    public int gety()
    { return y; }

    /** Sets x and y to new_x and new_y. */
    public void setPoint(int new_x, int new_y)
    {
        x = new_x;
        y = new_y;
    }

    //Other methods are not shown.
}
```

The method `changeNegs` below takes a matrix of `Point` objects as parameter and replaces every `Point` that has as least one negative coordinate with the `Point` (0, 0).

```
/** Replaces every point that has at least one negative coordinate
 *  with Point(0,0).
 *  Precondition:  pointMat is initialized with Point objects.
 */
public static void changeNegs (Point [][] pointMat)
{
    /* code */
}
```

Which is a correct replacement for /* *code* */?

```
 I for (int r = 0; r < pointMat.length; r++)
       for (int c = 0; c < pointMat[r].length; c++)
           if (pointMat[r][c].getx() < 0
               || pointMat[r][c].gety() < 0)
                   pointMat[r][c].setPoint(0, 0);

II for (int c = 0; c < pointMat[0].length; c++)
       for (int r = 0; r < pointMat.length; r++)
           if (pointMat[r][c].getx() < 0
               || pointMat[r][c].gety() < 0)
                   pointMat[r][c].setPoint(0, 0);

III for (Point[] row : pointMat)
       for (Point p : row)
           if (p.getx() < 0 || p.gety() < 0)
                   p.setPoint(0, 0);
```

(A) I only
(B) II only
(C) III only
(D) I and II only
(E) I, II, and III

37. A simple Tic-Tac-Toe board is a 3 × 3 array filled with either X's, O's, or blanks. Here is a class for a game of Tic-Tac-Toe.

```
public class TicTacToe
{
    private String[][] board;
    private static final int ROWS = 3;
    private static final int COLS = 3;

    /** Construct an empty board. */
    public TicTacToe()
    {
        board = new String[ROWS][COLS];
        for (int r = 0; r < ROWS; r++)
            for (int c = 0; c < COLS; c++)
                board[r][c] = " ";
    }

    /** Places symbol on board[r][c].
     *  Precondition: The square board[r][c] is empty.
     */
    public void makeMove(int r, int c, String symbol)
    {
        board[r][c] = symbol;
    }

    /** Creates a string representation of the board, e.g.
     *    |o  |
     *    |xx |
     *    |  o|
     *  Returns the string representation of board.
     */
    public String toString()
    {
        String s = "";       //empty string
        /* more code */
        return s;
    }
}
```

Which segment represents a correct replacement for /* *more code* */ for the `toString` method?

```
(A) for (int r = 0; r < ROWS; r++)
    {
        for (int c = 0; c < COLS; c++)
        {
            s = s + "|";
            s = s + board[r][c];
            s = s + "|\n";
        }
    }

(B) for (int r = 0; r < ROWS; r++)
    {
        s = s + "|";
        for (int c = 0; c < COLS; c++)
        {
            s = s + board[r][c];
            s = s + "|\n";
        }
    }

(C) for (int r = 0; r < ROWS; r++)
    {
        s = s + "|";
        for (int c = 0; c < COLS; c++)
            s = s + board[r][c];
    }
    s = s + "|\n";

(D) for (int r = 0; r < ROWS; r++)
        s = s + "|";
    for (int c = 0; c < COLS; c++)
    {
        s = s + board[r][c];
        s = s + "|\n";
    }

(E) for (int r = 0; r < ROWS; r++)
    {
        s = s + "|";
        for (int c = 0; c < COLS; c++)
            s = s + board[r][c];
        s = s + "|\n";
    }
```

# ANSWER KEY

| | | | | | |
|---|---|---|---|---|---|
| 1. **E** | | 14. **C** | | 27. **D** | |
| 2. **C** | | 15. **A** | | 28. **E** | |
| 3. **E** | | 16. **B** | | 29. **A** | |
| 4. **A** | | 17. **A** | | 30. **A** | |
| 5. **C** | | 18. **B** | | 31. **B** | |
| 6. **C** | | 19. **D** | | 32. **D** | |
| 7. **D** | | 20. **C** | | 33. **B** | |
| 8. **A** | | 21. **E** | | 34. **D** | |
| 9. **D** | | 22. **C** | | 35. **E** | |
| 10. **B** | | 23. **D** | | 36. **E** | |
| 11. **C** | | 24. **A** | | 37. **E** | |
| 12. **E** | | 25. **E** | | | |
| 13. **B** | | 26. **D** | | | |

# ANSWERS EXPLAINED

1. **(E)** Segment I is an initializer list which is equivalent to

    ```
    int[] arr = new int[4];
    arr[0] = 0;
    arr[1] = 0;
    arr[2] = 0;
    arr[3] = 0;
    ```

    Segment II creates four slots for integers, which by default are initialized to 0. The `for` loop in segment III is therefore unnecessary. It is not, however, incorrect.

2. **(C)** If `arr` contains no negative integers, the value of `i` will eventually exceed `N-1`, and `arr[i]` will cause an `ArrayIndexOutOfBoundsException` to be thrown.

3. **(E)** The intent is to sum elements `arr[0]`, `arr[1]`, ..., `arr[arr.length-1]`. Notice, however, that when `i` has the value `arr.length-1`, it is incremented to `arr.length` in the loop, so the statement `sum += arr[i]` uses `arr[arr.length]`, which is out of range.

4. **(A)** The code segment has the effect of removing all occurrences of 0 from array `arr1`. The algorithm copies the nonzero elements to the front of `arr1`. Then it transfers them to array `arr2`.

5. **(C)** If `arr[i] < someValue` for all `i` from 2 to `k`, SMALL will be printed on each iteration of the `for` loop. Since there are `k - 1` iterations, the maximum number of times that SMALL can be printed is `k - 1`.

6. **(C)** Array `arr` is changed by `doSomething`. Here are the memory slots:

Just before `doSomething` is called:

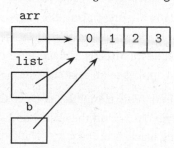

Just after `doSomething` is called, but before the `for` loop is executed:

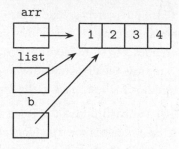

Just before exiting `doSomething`:

arr

| 0 | 1 | 2 | 3 |

list

b

Just after exiting `doSomething`:

arr

| 0 | 1 | 2 | 3 |

7. **(D)** Arrays are of fixed length and do not shrink or grow if the size of the data set varies. An `ArrayList` automatically resizes the list. Choice A is false: The [] notation is compact and easy to use. Choice B is not a valid reason because an array `arr` also provides instant access to its length with the quantity `arr.length`. Choice C is invalid because an array can also contain objects. Also, generality is beside the point in the given program: The list *must* hold `String` objects. Choice E is false: Whether a `String` object is `arr[i]` or `list.get(i)`, the `String` methods are equally easy to invoke.

8. **(A)** In order for numerical elements to be added to an `ArrayList`, each element must be wrapped in a wrapper class before insertion into the list. Then, to retrieve a numerical value from the `ArrayList`, the element must be unboxed using the `intValue` or `doubleValue` methods. Even though these operations can be taken care of with autoboxing and unboxing, there are efficiency costs. In an array, you simply use the [] notation for assignment (as in `arr[i] = num`) or retrieval (`value = arr[i]`). Note that choices B and C are false statements: Both insertion and deletion for an array involve writing code to shift elements. An `ArrayList` automatically takes care of this through its `add` and `remove` methods. Choice D is a poor reason for choosing an array. While the `get` and `set` methods of `ArrayList` might be slightly more awkward than using the [] notation, both mechanisms work pretty easily. Choice E is false: Efficiency of access is roughly the same.

9. **(D)** For each `Address` object a in `list`, access the name of the object with `a.getName()`.

10. **(B)** Since the `Address` class does not have a `toString` method, each data field must explicitly be printed. Segment III would work if there *were* a `toString` method for the class (but there isn't, so it doesn't!). Segment I fails because of incorrect use of the enhanced `for` loop: The array index should not be accessed.

11. **(C)** Each `Student` name must be accessed via the `getName()` accessor of the `Address` class. The expression `student.getAddress()` accesses the entire address of that student. The `name` field is then accessed using the `getName()` accessor of the `Address` class.

12. **(E)** Both correct solutions are careful not to lose the student who has the highest `idNum` so far. Segment II does it by storing a reference to the student, `highestSoFar`. Segment III does it by storing the array index of that student. Code segment I is incorrect because it returns the first student whose `idNum` is greater than `max`, not necessarily the student with the highest `idNum` in the list.

13. **(B)** For each `i`, `tickList[i]` is a new `Ticket` object that must be constructed using the `Ticket` constructor. Therefore eliminate choices C, D, and E. Choice A is wrong because `getRow()`, `getSeat()`, and `getPrice()` are accessors for values *that already exist* for some `Ticket` object. Note also the absence of the dot member construct.

14. **(C)** To access the price for each `Ticket` in the `tickList` array, the `getPrice()` accessor in the `Ticket` class must be used, since `price` is private to that class. This eliminates choices A and E. Choice B uses the array name incorrectly. Choices D and E incorrectly declare a `Transaction` object. (The method applies to an existing `Transaction` object.)

15. **(A)** An array of type `Transaction` is required. This eliminates choices C and D. Additionally, choices B and D incorrectly use type `Ticket` on the right-hand side. Choice E puts the identifier `listOfSales` in the wrong place.

16. **(B)** There are two problems with the segment as given:

    1. `arr[1]` is not tested.
    2. When `i` has a value of `n-1`, incrementing `i` will lead to an out-of-range error for the `if(arr[i] < min)` test.

    Modification II corrects both these errors. The change suggested in III corrects neither of these errors. The change in I corrects (1) but not (2).

17. **(A)** Notice that either `vIndex` or `wIndex` is incremented at the end of the loop. This means that, when the loop is exited, the current values of `v[vIndex]` and `w[wIndex]` have not been compared. Therefore, you can only make an assertion for values `v[0]..v[vIndex-1]` and `w[0]..w[wIndex-1]`. Also, notice that if there is no common value in the arrays, the exiting condition for the `while` loop will be that the end of one of the arrays has been reached, namely `vIndex` equals `N` or `wIndex` equals `M`.

18. **(B)** Objects in an array can be changed in an enhanced `for` loop by using mutator methods of the objects' class. The `changeStatus` method, a mutator in the `Book` class, will work as intended in the given code. Choice C would be true if it were not given that each `Book` in `bookList` was initialized. If any given `b` had a value of `null`, then a `NullPointerException` would be thrown.

19. **(D)** The declaration must start with the type of value in the array, namely `BingoCard`. This eliminates choices A and E. Eliminate choice B: The type on the right of the assignment should be `BingoCard`. Choice C is wrong because the number of slots in the array should be `NUMPLAYERS`, not 20.

20. **(C)** Segment III is the only segment that works, since the enhanced `for` loop should not be used to replace elements in an array. After the declaration

    ```
    BingoCard[] players = new BingoCard[NUMPLAYERS];
    ```

    each element in the `players` array is `null`. The intent in the given code is to replace each null reference with a newly constructed `BingoCard`.

21. **(E)** All elements added to `strList` must be of type `String`. Each choice satisfies this except choice E. Note that in choice D, the expression `ch + 8` becomes a `String` since `ch` is a `String` (just one of the operands needs to be a `String` to convert the whole expression to a `String`). In choice E, neither `intOb` nor 8 is a `String`.

22. **(C)** The effect of choice C is to adjust the size of the list to 7 and to add the `Integer` 9 to the last slot (i.e., the slot with index 6). Choices A, D, and E will all cause an `IndexOutOfBoundsException` because there is no slot with index 6: the last slot has index 5. Choice B will cause a compile-time error, since it is attempting to add an element of type `Double` to a list of type `Integer`.

23. **(D)** If `element` is smaller than the last item in the list, it will be compared with every item in the list. Eventually `index` will be incremented to a value that is out of bounds. To avoid this error, the test in the `while` loop should be

```
while(index < list.size() && element.compareTo(list.get(index)) < 0)
```

Notice that if `element` is greater than or equal to at least one item in list, the test as given in the problem will eventually be false, preventing an out-of-range error.

24. **(A)** Recall that `add(index, obj)` shifts all elements, starting at `index`, one unit to the right, then inserts `obj` at position `index`. The `set(index, obj)` method replaces the element in position `index` with `obj`. So here is the state of `list` after each change:

```
i = 0     6 0 1 8
          2 0 1 8
i = 1     2 0 1 1 8
          2 3 1 1 8
i = 2     2 3 1 2 1 8
          2 3 4 2 1 8
```

25. **(E)** The value of each `Coin c` in `coins` must be accessed with `c.getValue()`. This eliminates choice D. Eliminate choices A and B: The loop accesses each `Coin` in the `coins` `ArrayList`, which means that there should not be any statements attempting to get the next `Coin`. Choice B would be correct if the first statement in the loop body were

```
double value = c.getValue();
```

26. **(D)** Code segment III is wrong because the `equals` method is defined for objects only. Since `getValue` returns a `double`, the quantities `c.getValue()` and `aCoin.getValue()` must be compared either using `==`, or as described in the box on p. 73 (better).

27. **(D)** Segment II is the straightforward solution. Segment I is correct because it initializes all slots of the matrix to 0, a perfect square. (By default, all arrays of `int` or `double` are initialized to 0.) Segment III fails because `r` is undefined in the condition `c < mat[r].length`. In order to do a column-by-column traversal, you need to get the number of columns in each row. The outer `for` loop could be

```
for (int c = 0; c < mat[0].length; c++)
```

Now segment III works. Note that since the array is rectangular, you can use any index k in the conditional `c < mat[k].length`, provided that k satisfies the condition $0 \le k < mat.length$ (the number of rows).

28. **(E)** When `col` is 0: `row` is 3, then 2, then 1.

When `col` is 1: `row` is 3, then 2.

When `col` is 2: `row` is 3.

Here are the corresponding elements, in order, that are printed:

`mat[3][0]`, `mat[2][0]`, `mat[1][0]`,
`mat[3][1]`, `mat[2][1]`,
`mat[3][2]`

The fifth element in the list is `mat[2][1]`, which is 7.

29. **(A)** Method `alter` shifts all the columns, starting at column `c+1`, one column to the left. Also, it does it in a way that overwrites column `c`. Here are the replacements for the method call `alter(1)`:

```
mat[0][1] = mat[0][2]
mat[0][2] = mat[0][3]
mat[1][1] = mat[1][2]
mat[1][2] = mat[1][3]
mat[2][1] = mat[2][2]
mat[2][2] = mat[2][3]
```

30. **(A)** `matStuff` processes the row selected by the row parameter, 2 in the method call. The row value, 2, overwrites each element in row 2. Don't make the mistake of selecting choice B—the row labels are 0, 1, 2.

31. **(B)** Hand execute this for a $2 \times 2$ matrix. `i` goes from 0 to 0, `j` goes from 0 to 0, so the only interchange is swap `mat[0][0]` with `mat[1][1]`, which suggests choice B. Check with a $3 \times 3$ matrix:

```
i = 0   j = 0   swap mat[0][0] with mat[2][2]
        j = 1   swap mat[0][1] with mat[1][2]
i = 1   j = 0   swap mat[1][0] with mat[2][1]
```

The elements to be interchanged are shown paired in the following figure. The result will be a reflection through the minor diagonal.

32. **(D)** The method as given will throw an `ArrayIndexOutOfBoundsException`. For the matrix in the example, `mat[0].length` is 4. The call `mat.alter(1)` gives `c` a value of 1. Thus, in the inner `for` loop, `j` goes from 1 to 3. When `j` is 3, the line `mat[i][j] = mat[i][j+1]` becomes `mat[i][3] = mat[i][4]`. Since columns go from 0 to 3, `mat[i][4]` is out of range. The changes in segments I and II both fix this problem. In each case, the correct replacements are made for each row `i`: `mat[i][1] = mat[i][2]` and `mat[i][2] = mat[i][3]`. Segment III makes the following incorrect replacements as `j` goes from 3 to 2: `mat[i][2] = mat[i][3]` and `mat[i][1] = mat[i][2]`. This will cause both columns 1 and 2 to be overwritten. Before inserting zeros in the last column, `mat` will be

```
2   9   9   9
1   3   3   3
0   2   2   2
```

This does not achieve the intended postcondition of the method.

33. **(B)** For the method call isThere(mat, 2, 2, "$"), the code counts how many times "$" appears in row 2 and how many times in column 2. The method returns true only if count == SIZE for either the row or column pass (i.e., the whole of row 2 or the whole of column 2 contains the symbol "$"). This eliminates choices I and II.

34. **(D)** Segment I is a row-by-row traversal; segment II is a column-by-column traversal. Each achieves the correct postcondition. Segment III traverses the matrix but does not alter it. All that is changed is the local variable element. You cannot use this kind of loop to replace elements in an array.

35. **(E)** Since there are 365 valid days in a year, the divisor in calculating the average must be 365. It may appear that segments II and III are incorrect because they include rainfall for invalid days in total. Since these values are initialized to 0.0, however, including them in the total won't affect the final result.

36. **(E)** This is similar to the previous question, but in this case segment III is also correct. This is because instead of *replacing* a matrix element, you are *modifying* it using a mutator method.

37. **(E)** There are three things that must be done in each row:

- Add an opening boundary line:

```
s = s + "|";
```

- Add the symbol in each square:

```
for (int c = 0; c < COLS; c++)
    s = s + board[r][c];
```

- Add a closing boundary line and go to the next line:

```
s = s + "|\n";
```

All of these statements must therefore be enclosed in the outer for loop, that is,

```
for (int r = ...)
```

# Recursion

8

> recursion *n. See* recursion.
> —*Eric S. Raymond,* The New Hacker's Dictionary *(1991)*

→ **Understanding recursion**          → **Recursive helper methods**

→ **Recursive methods**               → **Analysis of recursive algorithms**

→ **Recursion in two-dimensional grids**   → **Tracing recursive algorithms**

## RECURSIVE METHODS

> In the multiple-choice section of the AP exam, you will be asked to understand and trace recursive methods. You will not, however, be asked to come up with code for recursive methods in the free-response part of the exam.

A *recursive method* is a method that calls itself. For example, here is a program that calls a recursive method stackWords:

```
public class WordPlay
{
    public static void stackWords()
    {
        String word = ...;      //read user input
        if (word.equals("."))
            System.out.println();
        else
            stackWords();
        System.out.println(word);
    }

    public static void main(String args[])
    {
        System.out.println("Enter list of words, one per line.");
        System.out.println("Final word should be a period (.)");
        stackWords();
    }
}
```

Here is the output if you enter

```
hold
my
hand
.
```

You get

```
.
hand
my
hold
```

The program reads in a list of words terminated with a period, and prints the list in reverse order, starting with the period. How does this happen?

Each time the recursive call to `stackWords()` is made, execution goes back to the start of a new method call. The computer must remember to complete all the pending calls to the method. It does this by stacking the statements that must still be executed as follows: The first time `stackWords()` is called, the word `"hold"` is read and tested for being a period. No, it's not, so `stackWords()` is called again. The statement to output `"hold"` (which has not yet been executed) goes on a stack, and execution goes to the start of the method. The word `"my"` is read. No, it's not a period, so the command to output `"my"` goes on the stack. And so on. You should picture the stack as looking something like this before the recursive call in which the period is read:

```
|                                    |
|                                    |
|                                    |
| System.out.println("hand");        |
| System.out.println("my");          |
| System.out.println("hold");        |
```

Imagine that these statements are stacked like plates. In the final `stackWords()` call, `word` has the value `"."`. Yes, it *is* a period, so the `stackWords()` line is skipped, the period is printed on the screen, and the method call terminates. The computer now completes each of the previous method calls in turn by "popping" the statements off the top of the stack. It prints `"hand"`, then `"my"`, then `"hold"`, and execution of method `stackWords()` is complete.[1]

**NOTE**

1. Each time `stackWords()` is called, a new local variable `word` is created.
2. The first time the method actually terminates, the program returns to complete the most recently invoked previous call. That's why the words get reversed in this example.

## GENERAL FORM OF SIMPLE RECURSIVE METHODS

Every recursive method has two distinct parts:

- A base case or termination condition that causes the method to end.
- A nonbase case whose actions move the algorithm toward the base case and termination.

---

[1]Actually, the computer stacks the pending statements in a recursive method call more efficiently than the way described. But *conceptually* this is how it is done.

Here is the framework for a simple recursive method that has no specific return type:

```
public void recursiveMeth( ... )
{
    if (base case)
        < Perform some action >
    else
    {
        < Perform some other action >
        recursiveMeth( ... );     //recursive method call
    }
}
```

The base case typically occurs for the simplest case of the problem, such as when an integer has a value of 0 or 1. Other examples of base cases are when some key is found, or an end-of-file is reached. A recursive algorithm can have more than one base case.

In the `else` or nonbase case of the framework shown, the code fragment < *Perform some other action* > and the method call `recursiveMeth` can sometimes be interchanged without altering the net effect of the algorithm. Be careful though, because what *does* change is the order of executing statements. This can sometimes be disastrous. (See the `eraseBlob` example on p. 295.)

## ➡ Example 1 _____

```
public void drawLine(int n)
{
    if (n == 0)
        System.out.println("That's all, folks!");
    else
    {
        for (int i = 1; i <= n; i++)
            System.out.print("*");
        System.out.println();
        drawLine(n - 1);
    }
}
```

The method call `drawLine(3)` produces this output:

```
***
**
*
That's all, folks!
```

**NOTE**

1. A method that has no pending statements following the recursive call is an example of *tail recursion*. Method `drawLine` is such a case, but `stackWords` is not.
2. The base case in the `drawLine` example is n == 0. Notice that each subsequent call, `drawLine(n - 1)`, makes progress toward termination of the method. If your method has no base case, or if you never reach the base case, you will create *infinite recursion*. This is a catastrophic error that will cause your computer eventually to run out of memory and give you heart-stopping messages like `java.lang.StackOverflowError....`

## ➥ Example 2

```
//Illustrates infinite recursion.
public void catastrophe(int n)
{
    System.out.println(n);
    catastrophe(n);
}
```

Try running the case `catastrophe(1)` if you have lots of time to waste!

## WRITING RECURSIVE METHODS

You will not be required to write recursive methods on the AP exam. The sections "Recursive Helper Methods," "Recursion in Two-Dimensional Grids," and "Sample Free-Response Questions 1 and 2" are optional topics. They are included to deepen your understanding of recursion, and to show how recursion is used to solve various coding problems. Recursive algorithms in two-dimensional grids show up often in programming contests, but not on the AP exam. To practice recursion for the exam, you should try all of the multiple-choice questions at the end of this chapter.

To come up with a recursive algorithm, you have to be able to frame a process *recursively* (i.e., in terms of a simpler case of itself). This is different from framing it *iteratively*, which repeats a process until a final condition is met. A good strategy for writing recursive methods is to first state the algorithm recursively in words.

**Optional topic**

## ➥ Example 1

Write a method that returns *n*! (*n* factorial).

| *n*! defined iteratively | *n*! defined recursively |
|---|---|
| 0! = 1 | 0! = 1 |
| 1! = 1 | 1! = (1)(0!) |
| 2! = (2)(1) | 2! = (2)(1!) |
| 3! = (3)(2)(1) | 3! = (3)(2!) |
| ... | ... |

The general recursive definition for *n*! is

$$n! = \begin{cases} 1 & n = 0 \\ n(n-1)! & n > 0 \end{cases}$$

The definition seems to be circular until you realize that if 0! is defined, all higher factorials are defined. Code for the recursive method follows directly from the recursive definition:

```
/** Compute n! recursively.
 * Precondition: n is a nonnegative integer.
 */
public static int factorial(int n)
{
    if (n == 0)      //base case
        return 1;
    else
        return n * factorial(n - 1);
}
```

## ➥ Example 2

Write a recursive method `revDigs` that outputs its integer parameter with the digits reversed. For example,

| | | |
|---|---|---|
| revDigs(147) | outputs | 741 |
| revDigs(4) | outputs | 4 |

First, describe the process recursively: Output the rightmost digit. Then, if there are still digits left in the remaining number `n/10`, reverse its digits. Repeat this until `n/10` is `0`. Here is the method:

```
/** Returns n with its digits reversed.
 *  Precondition: n is a nonnegative integer.
 */
public static void revDigs(int n)
{
    System.out.print(n % 10);  //rightmost digit
    if (n / 10 != 0)               //base case
        revDigs(n / 10);
}
```

**NOTE**

On the AP exam, you are expected to "understand and evaluate" recursive methods. This means that you would not be asked to come up with the code for methods such as `factorial` and `revDigs` (as shown above). You could, however, be asked to identify output for any given call to `factorial` or `revDigs`.

## ANALYSIS OF RECURSIVE METHODS

Recall the Fibonacci sequence 1, 1, 2, 3, 5, 8, 13, … . The $n$th Fibonacci number equals the sum of the previous two numbers if $n \geq 3$. Recursively,

$$\text{Fib}(n) = \begin{cases} 1, & n = 1, 2 \\ \text{Fib}(n-1) + \text{Fib}(n-2), & n \geq 3 \end{cases}$$

Here is the method:

```
/** Returns the nth Fibonacci number.
 *  Precondition: n is a positive integer.
 */
public static int fib(int n)
{
    if (n == 1 || n == 2)
        return 1;
    else
        return fib(n - 1) + fib(n - 2);
}
```

Notice that there are two recursive calls in the last line of the method. So to find Fib(5), for example, takes eight recursive calls to `fib`!

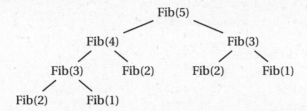

In general, each call to `fib` makes two more calls, which is the tipoff for an exponential algorithm (i.e., one that is *very* inefficient). This is *much* slower than the run time of the corresponding iterative algorithm (see Chapter 6, Question 14).

You may ask: Since every recursive algorithm can be written iteratively, when should programmers use recursion? Bear in mind that recursive algorithms can incur extra run time and memory. Their major plus is elegance and simplicity of code.

---

**General Rules for Recursion**

1. Avoid recursion for algorithms that involve large local arrays—too many recursive calls can cause memory overflow.
2. Use recursion when it significantly simplifies code.
3. Avoid recursion for simple iterative methods like factorial, Fibonacci, and the linear search on p. 293.
4. Recursion is especially useful for

   - Branching processes like traversing trees or directories.
   - Divide-and-conquer algorithms like merge sort and binary search.

---

## SORTING ALGORITHMS THAT USE RECURSION

Merge sort and quicksort are discussed in Chapter 9.

## RECURSIVE HELPER METHODS

A common technique in designing recursive algorithms is to have a public nonrecursive driver method that calls a private *recursive helper method* to carry out the task. The main reasons for doing this are:

> **Optional topic**

- To hide the implementation details of the recursion from the user.
- To enhance the efficiency of the program.

## ➥ Example 1

Consider the simple example of recursively finding the sum of the first *n* positive integers.

```
/** Returns 1 + 2 + 3 + ... + n.
 *  Precondition:  n is a positive integer.
 */
public static int sum(int n)
{
    if (n == 1)
        return 1;
    else
        return n + sum(n - 1);
}
```

Notice that you get infinite recursion if $n \le 0$. Suppose you want to include a test for $n > 0$ before you execute the algorithm. Placing this test in the recursive method is inefficient because if *n* is initially positive, it will remain positive in subsequent recursive calls. You can avoid this problem by using a driver method called getSum, which does the test on *n just once*. The recursive method sum becomes a private helper method.

```
public class FindSum
{
    /** Private recursive helper method.
     *  Returns 1 + 2 + 3 + ... + n.
     *  Precondition:  n is a positive integer.
     */
    private static int sum(int n)
    {
        if (n == 1)
            return 1;
        else
            return n + sum(n - 1);
    }

    /* Driver method */
    public static int getSum(int n)
    {
        if (n > 0)
            return sum(n);
        else
        {
            throw new IllegalArgumentException
                    ("Error: n must be positive");
        }
    }
}
```

**NOTE**

This is a trivial method used to illustrate a private recursive helper method. In practice, you would never use recursion to find a simple sum!

Consider a recursive solution to the problem of doing a sequential search for a key in an array of strings. If the key is found, the method returns `true`, otherwise it returns `false`.

The solution can be stated recursively as follows:

- If the key is in `a[0]`, then the key is found.

- If not, recursively search the array starting at `a[1]`.

- If you are past the end of the array, then the key wasn't found.

Here is a straightforward (but inefficient) implementation:

```
public class Searcher
{
    /** Recursively search array a for key.
     * Returns true if a[k] equals key for 0 <= k < a.length;
     * false otherwise.
     */
    public boolean search(String[] a, String key)
    {
        if (a.length == 0)  //base case. key not found
            return false;
        else if (a[0].compareTo(key) == 0) //base case
            return true;                    //key found
        else
        {
            String[] shorter = new String[a.length-1];
            for (int i = 0; i < shorter.length; i++)
                shorter[i] = a[i+1];
            return search(shorter, key);
        }
    }

    public static void main(String[] args)
    {
        String[] list = {"Mary", "Joe", "Lee", "Jake"};
        Searcher s = new Searcher();
        System.out.println("Enter key: Mary, Joe, Lee or Jake.");
        String key = ...;  //read user input
        boolean result = s.search(list, key);
        if (!result)
            System.out.println(key + " was not found.");
        else
            System.out.println(key + " was found.");
    }
}
```

Notice how horribly inefficient the `search` method is: For each recursive call, a new array `shorter` has to be created! It is much better to use a parameter, `startIndex`, to keep track of where you are in the array. Replace the `search` method above with the following one, which calls the private helper method `recurSearch`:

```
/** Driver method. Searches array a for key.
 *  Return trues if a[k] equals key for 0 <= k < a.length;
 *  false otherwise.
 *  Precondition: a contains at least one element.
 */
public boolean search(String[] a, String key)
{
    return recurSearch(a, 0, key);
}


/** Recursively searches array a for key, starting at startIndex.
 *  Returns true if a[k] equals key for 0 <= k < a.length;
 *  false otherwise.
 *  Precondition:
 *    - a contains at least one element.
 *    - 0 <= startIndex <= a.length.
 */
private boolean recurSearch(String[] a, int startIndex,
    String key)
{
    if(startIndex == a.length)    //base case. key not found
        return false;
    else if(a[startIndex].compareTo(key) == 0) //base case
        return true;                           //key found
    else
        return recurSearch(a, startIndex+1, key);
}
```

Use a recursive helper method to hide private coding details from a client.

**NOTE**

1. Using the parameter startIndex avoids having to create a new array object for each recursive call. Making startIndex a parameter of a helper method hides implementation details from the user.

2. The helper method is private because it is called only by search within the Searcher class.

3. It's easy to modify the search method to return the index in the array where the key is found: Make the return type int and return startIndex if the key is found, −1 (say) if it isn't.

## RECURSION IN TWO-DIMENSIONAL GRIDS

Here is a commonly used technique: using recursion to traverse a two-dimensional array. The problem comes in several different guises, for example,

1. A game board from which you must remove pieces.
2. A maze with walls and paths from which you must try to escape.
3. White "containers" enclosed by black "walls" into which you must "pour paint."

In each case, you will be given a starting position (row, col) and instructions on what to do.

The recursive solution typically involves these steps:

**(continued)**

*Check that the starting position is not out of range:*
    *If (starting position satisfies some requirement)*
        *Perform some action to solve problem*
        *RecursiveCall(row + 1, col)*
        *RecursiveCall(row − 1, col)*
        *RecursiveCall(row, col + 1)*
        *RecursiveCall(row, col − 1)*

## ➥ Example

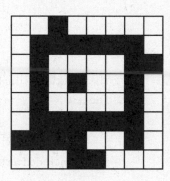

On the right is an image represented as a square grid of black and white cells. Two cells in an image are part of the same "blob" if each is black and there is a sequence of moves from one cell to the other, where each move is either horizontal or vertical to an adjacent black cell. For example, the diagram represents an image that contains two blobs, one of them consisting of a single cell.

Assuming the following `Image` class declaration, you are to write the body of the `eraseBlob` method, using a recursive algorithm.

```
public class Image
{
    private final int BLACK = 1;
    private final int WHITE = 0;
    private int[][] image;   //square grid
    private int size;        //number of rows and columns


    public Image()   //constructor
    { /* implementation not shown */ }


    public void display()   //displays Image
    { /* implementation not shown */ }

    /** If 0 <= row < size, 0 <= col < size, and image[row][col] is
     *  BLACK, sets all cells in the same blob to WHITE.
     *  Otherwise, image is unchanged.
     *  Precondition:  Image is defined with either BLACK or WHITE cells.
     */
    public void eraseBlob(int row, int col)
    /* your code goes here */
}
```

*(continued)*

Solution:

```
public void eraseBlob(int row, int col)
{
    if (row >= 0 && row < size && col >= 0 && col < size)
        if (image[row][col] == BLACK)
        {
            image[row][col] = WHITE;
            eraseBlob(row - 1, col);
            eraseBlob(row + 1, col);
            eraseBlob(row, col - 1);
            eraseBlob(row, col + 1);
        }
}
```

**NOTE**

1. The ordering of the four recursive calls is irrelevant.
2. The test

   ```
   if (image[row][col] == BLACK)
   ```

   can be included as the last piece of the test in the first line:

   ```
   if (row >= 0 && ...
   ```

   If `row` or `col` is out of range, the test will short-circuit, avoiding the dreaded `ArrayIndexOutOfBoundsException`.
3. If you put the statement

   ```
   image[row][col] = WHITE;
   ```

   *after* the four recursive calls, you get infinite recursion if your blob has more than one cell. This is because, when you visit an adjacent cell, one of its recursive calls visits the original cell. If this cell is still BLACK, yet more recursive calls are generated, *ad infinitum*.

A final thought: Recursive algorithms can be tricky. Try to state the solution recursively *in words* before you launch into code. Oh, and don't forget the base case!

## Sample Free-Response Question 1

Here is a sample free-response question that uses recursion in a two-dimensional array. See if you can answer it before looking at the solution.

A *color grid* is defined as a two-dimensional array whose elements are character strings having values "b" (blue), "r" (red), "g" (green), or "y" (yellow). The elements are called pixels because they represent pixel locations on a computer screen. For example,

|   |   |   |   |
|---|---|---|---|
| b | b | g | r |
| g | r | g | r |

```
r r r r
```

|   |   |   |
|---|---|---|
| y | g | r |
| b | y | g |
| g | r | b |
| b | b | g |

A *connected region* for any pixel is the set of all pixels of the same color that can be reached through a direct path along horizontal or vertical moves starting at that pixel. A connected region can consist of just a single pixel or the entire color grid. For example, if the two-dimensional array is called `pixels`, the connected region for `pixels[1][0]` is as shown here for three different arrays.

```
                  y g r b
b b g r           g g y g          b b
g r g r           b g r g          b b
```

The class `ColorGrid`, whose declaration is shown below, is used for storing, displaying, and changing the colors in a color grid.

```
public class ColorGrid
{
    private String[][] pixels;
    private int rows;
    private int cols;

    /** Creates numRows × numCols ColorGrid from String s. */
    public ColorGrid(String s, int numRows, int numCols)
    { /* to be implemented in part (a) */ }

    /* If 0 <= row < rows and 0 <= col < cols, paints the
     * connected region of pixels[row][col] the newColor.
     * Does nothing if oldColor is the same as newColor.
     *   Precondition:
     *     - pixels[row][col] is oldColor, one of "r", "b","g", or "y".
     *     - newColor is one of "r","b","g", or "y".
     */
    public void paintRegion(int row, int col, String newColor,
        String oldColor)
    { /* to be implemented in part (b) */ }

    //Other methods are not shown.
}
```

(a) Write the implementation code for the `ColorGrid` constructor. The constructor should initialize the `pixels` matrix of the `ColorGrid` as follows: The dimensions of `pixels` are numRows × numCols. String s contains numRows × numCols characters, where each character is one of the colors of the grid—"r", "g", "b", or "y". The characters are contained in s row by row from top to bottom and left to right. For example, given that numRows is 3, and numCols is 4, if s is "brrygrggyyyr", `pixels` should be initialized to be

```
b r r y
g r g g
y y y r
```

Complete the following constructor:

```
/** Creates numRows × numCols ColorGrid from String s. */
public ColorGrid(String s, int numRows, int numCols)
```

(b) Write the implementation of the `paintRegion` method as started below. **Note: You must write a recursive solution.** The `paintRegion` paints the connected region of the given pixel, specified by `row` and `col`, a different color specified by the `newColor` parameter. If `newColor` is the same as `oldColor`, the color of the given pixel, `paintRegion` does nothing. To visualize what `paintRegion` does, imagine that the different colors surrounding the connected region of a given pixel form a boundary. When paint is poured onto the given pixel, the new color will fill the connected region up to the boundary.

For example, the effect of the method call `c.paintRegion(2, 3, "b", "r")` on the `ColorGrid` `c` is shown here. (The starting pixel is shown in a frame, and its connected region is shaded.)

|  | before |  |  |  |  |  |  | after |  |  |  |  |
|---|---|---|---|---|---|---|---|---|---|---|---|---|
| r | r | b | g | y | y |  | r | r | b | g | y | y |
| b | r | b | y | r | r |  | b | r | b | y | b | b |
| g | g | r | r | r | b |  | g | g | b | b | b | b |
| y | r | r | y | r | b |  | y | b | b | y | b | b |

Complete the method `paintRegion` below. **Note: Only a recursive solution will be accepted.**

```
/* If 0 <= row < rows and 0 <= col < cols, paints the
 * connected region of pixels[row][col] the newColor.
 * Does nothing if oldColor is the same as newColor.
 *   Precondition:
 *    - pixels[row][col] is oldColor, one of "r", "b","g", or "y".
 *    - newColor is one of "r","b","g", or "y".
 */
public void paintRegion(int row, int col, String newColor,
    String oldColor)
```

## Solution

```
(a) public ColorGrid(String s, int numRows, int numCols)
    {
        rows = numRows;
        cols = numCols;
        pixels = new String[numRows][numCols];
        int stringIndex = 0;
        for (int r = 0; r < numRows; r++)
            for (int c = 0; c < numCols; c++)
            {
                pixels[r][c] = s.substring(stringIndex,
                    stringIndex + 1);
                stringIndex++;
            }
    }
```

```
(b)  public void paintRegion(int row, int col, String newColor,
            String oldColor)
    {
        if (row >= 0 && row < rows && col >= 0 && col < cols)
            if (!pixels[row][col].equals(newColor) &&
                pixels[row][col].equals(oldColor))
            {
                pixels[row][col] = newColor;
                paintRegion(row + 1, col, newColor, oldColor);
                paintRegion(row - 1, col, newColor, oldColor);
                paintRegion(row, col + 1, newColor, oldColor);
                paintRegion(row, col - 1, newColor, oldColor);
            }
    }
```

**NOTE**

- In part (a), you don't need to test if `stringIndex` is in range: The precondition states that the number of characters in s is numRows × numCols.
- In part (b), each recursive call must test whether `row` and `col` are in the correct range for the `pixels` array; otherwise, your algorithm may sail right off the edge!
- Don't forget to test if `newColor` is different from that of the starting pixel. Method `paintRegion` does nothing if the colors are the same.
- Also, don't forget to test if the current pixel is `oldColor`—you don't want to overwrite *all* the colors, just the connected region of `oldColor`!
- The color-change assignment `pixels[row][col] = newColor` must precede the recursive calls to avoid infinite recursion.

## Sample Free-Response Question 2

Here is another sample free-response question that uses recursion.

This question refers to the `Sentence` class below. Note: A *word* is a string of consecutive nonblank (and nonwhitespace) characters. For example, the sentence

"Hello there!" she said.

consists of the four words

"Hello      there!"      she      said.

```
public class Sentence
{
    private String sentence;
    private int numWords;

    /** Constructor. Creates sentence from String str.
     *               Finds the number of words in sentence.
     *  Precondition:  Words in str separated by exactly one blank.
     */
    public Sentence(String str)
    { /* to be implemented in part (a) */ }
```

```
        public int getNumWords()
        { return numWords; }

        public String getSentence()
        { return sentence; }

        /** Returns a copy of String s with all blanks removed. */
        private static String removeBlanks(String s)
        { /* implementation not shown */ }

        /** Returns a copy of String s with all letters in lowercase.
         *  Postcondition: Number of words in returned string equals
         *                 number of words in s.
         */
        private static String lowerCase(String s)
        { /* implementation not shown */ }

        /** Returns a copy of String s with all punctuation removed.
         *  Postcondition: Number of words in returned string equals
         *                 number of words in s.
         */
        private static String removePunctuation(String s)
        { /* implementation not shown */ }
    }
```

(a) Complete the `Sentence` constructor as started below. The constructor assigns `str` to `sentence`. You should write the subsequent code that assigns a value to `numWords`, the number of words in `sentence`.

Complete the constructor below:

```
/** Constructor. Creates sentence from String str.
 *              Finds the number of words in sentence.
 *  Precondition: Words in str separated by exactly one blank.
 */
public Sentence(String str)
{
    sentence = str;
```

(b) Consider the problem of testing whether a string is a palindrome. A *palindrome* reads the same from left to right and right to left, ignoring spaces, punctuation, and capitalization. For example,

> A Santa lived as a devil at NASA.
> Flo, gin is a sin! I golf.
> Eva, can I stab bats in a cave?

A public method `isPalindrome` is added to the `Sentence` class. Here is the method and its implementation:

(continued)

```
/** Returns true if sentence is a palindrome, false otherwise. */
public boolean isPalindrome()
{
    String temp = removeBlanks(sentence);
    temp = removePunctuation(temp);
    temp = lowerCase(temp);
    return isPalindrome(temp, 0, temp.length() - 1);
}
```

The overloaded isPalindrome method contained in the code is a private recursive helper method, also added to the Sentence class. You are to write the implementation of this method. It takes a "purified" string as a parameter, namely one that has been stripped of blanks and punctuation and is all lowercase letters. It also takes as parameters the first and last index of the string. It returns true if this "purified" string is a palindrome, false otherwise.

A recursive algorithm for testing if a string is a palindrome is as follows:

- If the string has length 0 or 1, it's a palindrome.
- Remove the first and last letters.
- If those two letters are the same, and the remaining string is a palindrome, then the original string is a palindrome. Otherwise it's not.

Complete the isPalindrome method below:

```
/** Private recursive helper method that tests whether a substring of
 *  string s, starting at start and ending at end, is a palindrome.
 *  Returns true if the substring is a palindrome, false otherwise.
 *  Precondition:  s contains no spaces, punctuation, or capitals.
 */
private static boolean isPalindrome(String s, int start, int end)
```

## Solution

```
(a) public Sentence(String str)
    {
        sentence = str;
        numWords = 1;
        int k = str.indexOf(" ");
        while (k != -1)    //while there are still blanks in str
        {
            numWords++;
            str = str.substring(k + 1); //substring after blank
            k = str.indexOf(" ");        //get index of next blank
        }
    }
```

```
(b)  private static boolean isPalindrome(String s, int start,
          int end)
     {
         if (start >= end)  //substring has length 0 or 1
             return true;
         else
         {
             String first = s.substring(start, start + 1);
             String last = s.substring(end, end + 1);
             if (first.equals(last))
                 return isPalindrome(s, start + 1, end - 1);
             else
                 return false;
         }
     }
```

**NOTE**

- In part (a), for every occurrence of a blank in `sentence`, `numWords` must be incremented. (Be sure to initialize `numWords` to 1!)
- In part (a), the code locates all the blanks in `sentence` by replacing `str` with the substring that consists of the piece of `str` directly following the most recently located blank.
- Recall that `indexOf` returns −1 if its `String` parameter does not occur as a substring in its `String` calling object.
- In part (b), the `start` and `end` indexes move toward each other with each subsequent recursive call. This shortens the string to be tested in each call. When `start` and `end` meet, the base case has been reached.
- Notice the private static methods in the `Sentence` class, including the helper method you were asked to write. They are static because they are not invoked by a `Sentence` object (no dot member construct). The only use of these methods is to help achieve the postconditions of other methods in the class.

## Chapter Summary

On the AP exam you will be expected to calculate the results of recursive method calls. Recursion becomes second nature when you practice a lot of examples. For the more difficult questions, untangle the statements with either repeated method calls (like that shown in the solution to Question 5 on p. 314), or box diagrams (as shown in the solution to Question 12 on p. 315).

You should understand that recursive algorithms can be *very* inefficient.

1. Which of the following statements about recursion are true?

    I  Every recursive algorithm can be written iteratively.

    II  Tail recursion is always used in "divide-and-conquer" algorithms.

    III  In a recursive definition, a process is defined in terms of a simpler case of itself.

  (A)  I only

  (B)  III only

  (C)  I and II only

  (D)  I and III only

  (E)  II and III only

2. Which of the following, when used as the /* *body* */ of method sum, will enable that method to compute $1 + 2 + \cdots + n$ correctly for any $n > 0$?

```
/** Returns 1 + 2 + ... + n.
 *  Precondition:  n is a positive integer.
 */
public int sum(int n)
{
    /* body */
}
```

```
 I  return n + sum(n - 1);

II  if (n == 1)
        return 1;
    else
        return n + sum(n - 1);

III if (n == 1)
        return 1;
    else
        return sum(n) + sum(n - 1);
```

  (A)  I only

  (B)  II only

  (C)  III only

  (D)  I and II only

  (E)  I, II, and III

3. Refer to the method `stringRecur`.

```java
public void stringRecur(String s)
{
    if (s.length() < 15)
        System.out.println(s);
    stringRecur(s + "*");
}
```

When will method `stringRecur` terminate without error?
(A) Only when the length of the input string is less than 15
(B) Only when the length of the input string is greater than or equal to 15
(C) Only when an empty string is input
(D) For all string inputs
(E) For no string inputs

4. Refer to method `strRecur`.

```java
public void strRecur(String s)
{
    if (s.length() < 15)
    {
        System.out.println(s);
        strRecur(s + "*");
    }
}
```

When will method `strRecur` terminate without error?
(A) Only when the length of the input string is less than 15
(B) Only when the length of the input string is greater than or equal to 15
(C) Only when an empty string is input
(D) For all string inputs
(E) For no string inputs

Questions 5 and 6 refer to method `result`.

```java
public int result(int n)
{
    if (n == 1)
        return 2;
    else
        return 2 * result(n - 1);
}
```

5. What value does `result(5)` return?
(A) 64
(B) 32
(C) 16
(D) 8
(E) 2

6. If $n > 0$, how many times will result be called to evaluate result(n) (including the initial call)?

    (A) 2

    (B) $2^n$

    (C) $n$

    (D) $2n$

    (E) $n^2$

7. Refer to method mystery.

```
public int mystery(int n, int a, int d)
{
    if (n == 1)
        return a;
    else
        return d + mystery(n - 1, a, d);
}
```

What value is returned by the call mystery(3, 2, 6)?

    (A) 20

    (B) 14

    (C) 10

    (D) 8

    (E) 2

8. Refer to method f.

```
public int f(int k, int n)
{
    if (n == k)
        return k;
    else
        if (n > k)
            return f(k, n - k);
        else
            return f(k - n, n);
}
```

What value is returned by the call f(6, 8)?

    (A) 8

    (B) 4

    (C) 3

    (D) 2

    (E) 1

9. What does method recur do?

```
/** x is an array of n integers.
 * n is a positive integer.
 */
public int recur(int[] x, int n)
{
    int t;
    if (n == 1)
        return x[0];
    else
    {
        t = recur(x, n - 1);
        if (x[n-1] > t)
            return x[n-1];
        else
            return t;
    }
}
```

(A) It finds the largest value in x and leaves x unchanged.

(B) It finds the smallest value in x and leaves x unchanged.

(C) It sorts x in ascending order and returns the largest value in x.

(D) It sorts x in descending order and returns the largest value in x.

(E) It returns x[0] or x[n-1], whichever is larger.

10. Which best describes what the printString method below does?

```
public void printString(String s)
{
    if (s.length() > 0)
    {
        printString(s.substring(1));
        System.out.print(s.substring(0, 1));
    }
}
```

(A) It prints string s.

(B) It prints string s in reverse order.

(C) It prints only the first character of string s.

(D) It prints only the first two characters of string s.

(E) It prints only the last character of string s.

11. Refer to the method power.

```
/** Returns base raised to the expo power.
 *  Precondition:
 *    - base is a nonzero real number.
 *    - expo is an integer.
 */
public double power(double base, int expo)
{
    if (expo == 0)
        return 1;
    else if (expo > 0)
        return base * power(base, expo - 1);
    else
        return /* code */;
}
```

Which /* *code* */ correctly completes method power?
(Recall that $a^{-n} = 1/a^n$, $a \neq 0$; for example, $2^{-3} = 1/2^3 = 1/8$.)

(A) (1 / base) * power(base, expo + 1)

(B) (1 / base) * power(base, expo - 1)

(C) base * power(base, expo + 1)

(D) base * power(base, expo - 1)

(E) (1 / base) * power(base, expo)

12. Consider the following method.

```
public void doSomething(int n)
{
    if (n > 0)
    {
        doSomething(n - 1);
        System.out.print(n);
        doSomething(n - 1);
    }
}
```

What would be output following the call doSomething(3)?

(A) 3211211

(B) 1121213

(C) 1213121

(D) 1211213

(E) 1123211

13. A user enters several positive integers at the keyboard and terminates the list with a sentinel (-999). A `writeEven` method reads those integers and outputs the even integers only, in the reverse order that they are read. Thus, if the user enters

```
3 5 14 6 1 8 -999
```

the output for the `writeEven` method will be

```
8 6 14
```

Assume that the user enters at least one positive integer and terminates the list with −999. Here is the method.

```
/** Postcondition: All even integers in the list are output in
 *                  reverse order.
 */
public static void writeEven()
{
    int num = ...;     //read user input
    if (num != -999)
    {
        /* code */
    }
}
```

Which /* code */ satisfies the postcondition of method `writeEven`?

```
 I  if (num % 2 == 0)
        System.out.print(num + " ");
    writeEven();

II  if (num % 2 == 0)
        writeEven();
    System.out.print(num + " ");

III writeEven();
    if (num % 2 == 0)
        System.out.print(num + " ");
```

(A) I only
(B) II only
(C) III only
(D) I and II only
(E) I, II, and III

14. Refer to the following recursive method.

```
public int mystery(int n)
{
    if (n < 0)
        return 2;
    else
        return mystery(n - 1) + mystery(n - 3);
}
```

What value is returned by the call mystery(3)?

(A) 12
(B) 10
(C) 8
(D) 6
(E) 4

Questions 15 and 16 refer to method t.

```java
/** Precondition: n is a positive integer. */
public int t(int n)
{
    if (n == 1 || n == 2)
        return 2 * n;
    else
        return t(n - 1) - t(n - 2);
}
```

15. What will be returned by t(5)?
    (A) 4
    (B) 2
    (C) 0
    (D) −2
    (E) −4

16. For the method call t(6), how many calls to t will be made, including the original call?
    (A) 6
    (B) 7
    (C) 11
    (D) 15
    (E) 25

17. This question refers to methods f1 and f2 that are in the same class.

```java
public int f1(int a, int b)
{
    if (a == b)
        return b;
    else
        return a + f2(a - 1, b);
}

public int f2(int p, int q)
{
    if (p < q)
        return p + q;
    else
        return p + f1(p - 2, q);
}
```

What value will be returned by a call to f1(5, 3)?
    (A) 5
    (B) 6
    (C) 7
    (D) 12
    (E) 15

18. Consider method `foo`.

```
public int foo(int x)
{
    if (x == 1 || x == 3)
        return x;
    else
        return x * foo(x - 1);
}
```

Assuming no possibility of integer overflow, what will be the value of z after execution of the following statement? Note that $n! = (n)(n-1)(n-2)\ldots(2)(1)$.

```
int z = foo(foo(3) + foo(4));
```

(A) $(15!)/(2!)$

(B) $3! + 4!$

(C) $(7!)!$

(D) $(3! + 4!)!$

(E) 15

Questions 19 and 20 refer to the `IntFormatter` class below.

```
public class IntFormatter
{
    /** Write 3 digits adjacent to each other.
     *  Precondition: n is a nonnegative integer.
     */
    public static void writeThreeDigits(int n)
    {
        System.out.print(n / 100);
        System.out.print((n / 10) % 10);
        System.out.print(n % 10);
    }

    /** Insert commas in n, every 3 digits starting at the right.
     *  Precondition: n is a nonnegative integer.
     */
    public static void writeWithCommas(int n)
    {
        if (n < 1000)
            System.out.print(n);
        else
        {
            writeThreeDigits(n % 1000);
            System.out.print(",");
            writeWithCommas(n / 1000);
        }
    }
}
```

19. The method `writeWithCommas` is supposed to print its nonnegative `int` argument with commas properly inserted (every three digits, starting at the right). For example, the integer 27048621 should be printed as 27,048,621. Method `writeWithCommas` does not always work as intended, however. Assuming no integer overflow, which of the following integer arguments will not be printed correctly?

   (A)  896
   (B)  251462251
   (C)  365051
   (D)  278278
   (E)  4

20. Which change in the code of the given methods will cause method `writeWithCommas` to work as intended?

   (A)  Interchange the lines `System.out.print(n / 100)` and `System.out.print(n % 10)` in method `writeThreeDigits`.
   (B)  Interchange the lines `writeThreeDigits(n % 1000)` and `writeWithCommas(n / 1000)` in method `writeWithCommas`.
   (C)  Change the test in `writeWithCommas` to if `(n > 1000)`.
   (D)  In the method `writeWithCommas`, change the line `writeThreeDigits(n % 1000)` to `writeThreeDigits(n / 1000)`.
   (E)  In the method `writeWithCommas`, change the recursive call `writeWithCommas(n / 1000)` to `writeWithCommas(n % 1000)`.

21. Consider the following method.

```java
public static void sketch(int x1, int y1, int x2, int y2, int n)
{
    if (n <= 0)
        drawLine(x1, y1, x2, y2);
    else
    {
        int xm = (x1 + x2 + y1 - y2) / 2;
        int ym = (y1 + y2 + x2 - x1) / 2;
        sketch(x1, y1, xm, ym, n - 1);
        sketch(xm, ym, x2, y2, n - 1);
    }
}
```

Assume that the screen looks like a Cartesian coordinate system with the origin at the center, and that drawLine connects (x1,y1) to (x2,y2). Assume also that x1, y1, x2, and y2 are never too large or too small to cause errors. Which picture best represents the sketch drawn by the method call

```
sketch(a, 0, -a, 0, 2)
```

where a is a positive integer?

(A)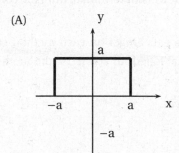

(B)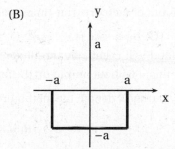

(C)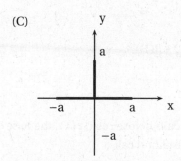

(D)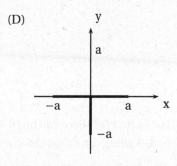

(E)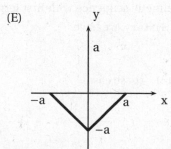

## ANSWER KEY

| | | |
|---|---|---|
| 1. **D** | 8. **D** | 15. **E** |
| 2. **B** | 9. **A** | 16. **D** |
| 3. **E** | 10. **B** | 17. **E** |
| 4. **D** | 11. **A** | 18. **A** |
| 5. **B** | 12. **C** | 19. **C** |
| 6. **C** | 13. **C** | 20. **B** |
| 7. **B** | 14. **A** | 21. **B** |

## ANSWERS EXPLAINED

1. **(D)** Tail recursion is when the recursive call of a method is made as the last executable step of the method. Divide-and-conquer algorithms like those used in merge sort or quicksort have recursive calls *before* the last step. Thus, statement II is false.

2. **(B)** Code segment I is wrong because there is no base case. Code segment III is wrong because, besides anything else, sum(n) prevents the method from terminating—the base case n == 1 will not be reached.

3. **(E)** When stringRecur is invoked, it calls itself irrespective of the length of s. Since there is no action that leads to termination, the method will not terminate until the computer runs out of memory (run-time error).

4. **(D)** The base case is s.length() $\geq$ 15. Since s gets longer on each method call, the method will eventually terminate. If the original length of s is $\geq$ 15, the method will terminate without output on the first call.

5. **(B)** Letting $R$ denote the method result, we have

$$R(5) = 2 * R(4)$$
$$= 2 * (2 * (R(3)))$$
$$= \cdots$$
$$= 2 * (2 * (2 * (2 * R(1))))$$
$$= 2^5$$
$$= 32$$

6. **(C)** For result(n) there will be $(n-1)$ recursive calls before result(1), the base case, is reached. Adding the initial call gives a total of $n$ method calls.

7. **(B)** This method returns the $n$th term of an arithmetic sequence with first term a and common difference d. Letting $M$ denote method mystery, we have

$$M(3,2,6) = 6 + M(2,2,6)$$
$$= 6 + (6 + M(1,2,6)) \quad \text{(base case)}$$
$$= 6 + 6 + 2$$
$$= 14$$

8. **(D)** Here are the recursive calls that are made, in order: $f(6,8) \rightarrow f(6,2) \rightarrow f(4,2) \rightarrow f(2,2)$, base case. Thus, 2 is returned.

9. **(A)** If there is only one element in x, then `recur` returns that element. Having the recursive call at the beginning of the `else` part of the algorithm causes the `if` part for each method call to be stacked until t eventually gets assigned to x[0]. The pending `if` statements are then executed, and t is compared to each element in x. The largest value in x is returned.

10. **(B)** Since the recursive call is made directly following the base case, the `System.out.print...` statements are stacked up. If `printString("cat")` is called, here is the sequence of recursive calls and pending statements on the stack:

| printString("at") | → | print "c" |
| printString("t") | → | print "a" |
| printString("") | → | print "t" |

```
print "t"
print "a"
print "c"
```
Execution stack

When `printString("")`, the base case, is called, the `print` statements are then popped off the stack in reverse order, which means that the characters of the string will be printed in reverse order.

11. **(A)** The required code is for a negative `expo`. For example, `power(2, -3)` should return $2^{-3} = 1/8$. Notice that

$$2^{-3} = \tfrac{1}{2}\left(2^{-2}\right)$$
$$2^{-2} = \tfrac{1}{2}\left(2^{-1}\right)$$
$$2^{-1} = \tfrac{1}{2}\left(2^{0}\right)$$

In general:
$$2^{n} = \tfrac{1}{2}(2^{n+1}) \quad \text{whenever} \quad n < 0$$

This is equivalent to `(1 / base) * power(base, expo + 1)`.

12. **(C)** Each box in the diagram below represents a recursive call to `doSomething`. The numbers to the right of the boxes show the order of execution of the statements. Let D denote `doSomething`.

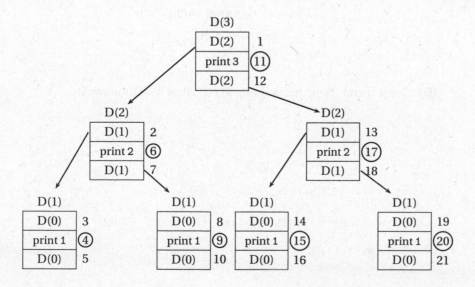

The numbers in each box refer to that method call only. D(0) is the base case, so the statement immediately following it is executed next. When all statements in a given box (method call) have been executed, backtrack along the arrow to find the statement that gets executed next. The circled numbers represent the statements that produce output. Following them in order, statements 4, 6, 9, 11, 15, 17, and 20 produce the output in choice C.

13. **(C)** Since even numbers are printed *before* the recursive call in segment I, they will be printed in the order in which they are read from the keyboard. Contrast this with the correct choice, segment III, in which the recursive call is made before the test for even-ness. These tests will be stacked until the last number is read. Recall that the pending statements are removed from the stack in reverse order (most recent recursive call first), which leads to even numbers being printed in reverse order. Segment II is wrong because all numbers entered will be printed, irrespective of whether they are even or not. Note that segment II would work if the input list contained only even numbers.

14. **(A)** Let `mystery(3)` be denoted $m(3)$. Picture the execution of the method as follows:

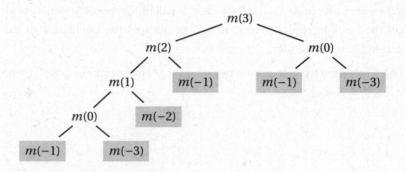

The base cases are shaded. Note that each of the six base case calls returns 2, resulting in a total of 12.

15. **(E)** The method generates a sequence. The first two terms, $t(1)$ and $t(2)$, are 2 and 4. Each subsequent term is generated by subtracting the previous two terms. This is the sequence: 2, 4, 2, −2, −4, −2, 2, 4, .... Thus, $t(5) = −4$. Alternatively,

$$t(5) = t(4) − t(3)$$
$$= [t(3) − t(2)] − t(3)$$
$$= −t(2)$$
$$= −4$$

16. **(D)** Count them! (Note that you stop at $t(2)$ since it's a base case.)

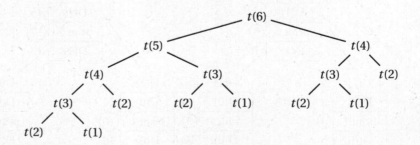

17. **(E)** This is an example of *mutual recursion*, where two methods call each other.

$$f_1(5,3) = 5 + f_2(4,3)$$
$$= 5 + (4 + f_1(2,3))$$
$$= 5 + (4 + (2 + f_2(1,3)))$$
$$= 5 + (4 + (2 + 4))$$
$$= 15$$

Note that $f_2(1,3)$ is a base case.

18. **(A)** foo(3) = 3 (This is a base case). Also, foo(4) = 4 × foo(3) = 12. So you need to find foo(foo(3) + foo(4)) = foo(15).

$$\text{foo}(15) = 15 \times \text{foo}(14)$$
$$= 15 \times (14 \times \text{foo}(13))$$
$$= \cdots$$
$$= 15 \times 14 \times \cdots \times 4 \times \text{foo}(3)$$
$$= 15 \times 14 \times \cdots \times 4 \times 3$$
$$= (15)!/(2!)$$

19. **(C)** Suppose that $n = 365051$. The method call `writeWithCommas(365051)` will write 051 and then execute the call `writeWithCommas(365)`. This is a base case, so 365 will be written out, resulting in 051,365. A number like 278278 (two sets of three identical digits) will be written out correctly, as will a "symmetrical" number like 251462251. Also, any $n < 1000$ is a base case and the number will be written out correctly as is.

20. **(B)** The cause of the problem is that the numbers are being written out with the sets of three digits in the wrong order. The problem is fixed by interchanging `writeThreeDigits(n % 1000)` and `writeWithCommas(n / 1000)`. For example, here is the order of execution for `writeWithCommas(365051)`.

> `writeWithCommas(365)` → Base case. Writes 365
> `System.out.print(",");` → 365,
> `writeThreeDigits(051)` → 365,051 which is correct

21. **(B)** Here is the "box diagram" for the recursive method calls, showing the order of execution of statements. Notice that the circled statements are the base case calls, the only statements that actually draw a line. Note also that the first time you reach a base case (see circled statement 6), you can get the answer: The picture in choice B is the only one that has a line segment joining (a,0) to (a,-a).

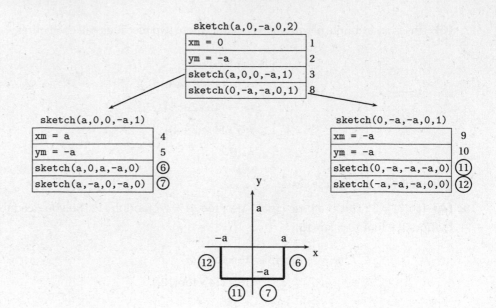

# Sorting and Searching 9

*Critics search for ages for the wrong word, which,*
*to give them credit, they eventually find.*
—*Peter Ustinov (1952)*

→ **Sorting algorithms in Java**   → **Merge sort**
→ **Selection and insertion sorts**   → **Sequential search and binary search**

For each of the following sorting algorithms, assume that an array of $n$ elements, a[0],
a[1], ..., a[n-1], is to be sorted in ascending order.

## SORTS: SELECTION AND INSERTION SORTS

### Selection Sort

This is a "search-and-swap" algorithm. Here's how it works.

Find the smallest element in the array and exchange it with a[0], the first element. Now
find the smallest element in the subarray a[1] ...a[n-1] and swap it with a[1], the second
element in the array. Continue this process until just the last two elements remain to be
sorted, a[n-2] and a[n-1]. The smaller of these two elements is placed in a[n-2]; the larger,
in a[n-1]; and the sort is complete.

Trace these steps with a small array of four elements. The unshaded part is the subarray
still to be searched.

```
8   1   4   6

1   8   4   6      after first pass

1   4   8   6      after second pass

1   4   6   8      after third pass
```

**NOTE**

1. For an array of $n$ elements, the array is sorted after $n-1$ passes.
2. After the $k$th pass, the first $k$ elements are in their final sorted position.

## Insertion Sort

Think of the first element in the array, a[0], as being sorted with respect to itself. The array can now be thought of as consisting of two parts, a sorted list followed by an unsorted list. The idea of insertion sort is to move elements from the unsorted list to the sorted list one at a time; as each item is moved, it is inserted into its correct position in the sorted list. In order to place the new item, some elements may need to be moved to the right to create a slot.

Here is the array of four elements. In each case, the boxed element is "it," the next element to be inserted into the sorted part of the list. The shaded area is the part of the list sorted so far.

| 8 | 1 | 4 | 6 |

| 1 | 8 | 4 | 6 |    after first pass

| 1 | 4 | 8 | 6 |    after second pass

| 1 | 4 | 6 | 8 |    after third pass

**NOTE**

1. For an array of $n$ elements, the array is sorted after $n - 1$ passes.
2. After the $k$th pass, a[0], a[1], ..., a[k] are sorted with respect to each other but not necessarily in their final sorted positions.
3. The worst case for insertion sort occurs if the array is initially sorted in reverse order, since this will lead to the maximum possible number of comparisons and moves.
4. The best case for insertion sort occurs if the array is already sorted in increasing order. In this case, each pass through the array will involve just one comparison, which will indicate that "it" is in its correct position with respect to the sorted list. Therefore, no elements will need to be moved.

> Both insertion and selection sorts are inefficient for large $n$.

## RECURSIVE SORTS: MERGE SORT AND QUICKSORT

Selection and insertion sorts are inefficient for large $n$, requiring approximately $n$ passes through a list of $n$ elements. More efficient algorithms can be devised using a "divide-and-conquer" approach, which is used in both the sorting algorithms that follow. Quicksort is not in the AP Java subset.

### Merge Sort

Here is a recursive description of how merge sort works:

If there is more than one element in the array,
        Break the array into two halves.
        Merge sort the left half.
        Merge sort the right half.
        Merge the two subarrays into a sorted array.

Merge sort uses a `merge` method to merge two sorted pieces of an array into a single sorted array. For example, suppose array `a[0]` ... `a[n-1]` is such that `a[0]` ... `a[k]` is sorted and `a[k+1]` ... `a[n-1]` is sorted, both parts in increasing order. Example:

| a[0] | a[1] | a[2] | a[3] | a[4] | a[5] |
|------|------|------|------|------|------|
| 2    | 5    | 8    | 9    | 1    | 6    |

In this case, `a[0]` ...`a[3]` and `a[4]` ...`a[5]` are the two sorted pieces. The method call `merge(a,0,3,5)` should produce the "merged" array:

| a[0] | a[1] | a[2] | a[3] | a[4] | a[5] |
|------|------|------|------|------|------|
| 1    | 2    | 5    | 6    | 8    | 9    |

The middle numerical parameter in `merge` (the 3 in this case) represents the index of the last element in the first "piece" of the array. The first and third numerical parameters are the lowest and highest index, respectively, of array a.

Here's what happens in merge sort:

1. Start with an unsorted list of $n$ elements.
2. The recursive calls break the list into $n$ sublists, each of length 1. Note that these $n$ arrays, each containing just one element, are sorted!
3. Recursively merge adjacent pairs of lists. There are then approximately $n/2$ lists of length 2; then, approximately $n/4$ lists of approximate length 4, and so on, until there is just one list of length $n$.

An example of merge sort follows:

> The main disadvantage of merge sort is that it uses a temporary array.

Analysis of merge sort:

1. The major disadvantage of merge sort is that it needs a temporary array that is as large as the original array to be sorted. This could be a problem if space is a factor.
2. Merge sort is not affected by the initial ordering of the elements. Thus, best, worst, and average cases have similar run times.

## Quicksort

Optional topic

For large $n$, quicksort is, on average, the fastest known sorting algorithm. Here is a recursive description of how quicksort works:

If there are at least two elements in the array,
       Partition the array.
       Quicksort the left subarray.
       Quicksort the right subarray.

The `partition` method splits the array into two subarrays as follows: a *pivot* element is chosen at random from the array (often just the first element) and placed so that all items to the left of the pivot are less than or equal to the pivot, whereas those to the right are greater than or equal to it.

For example, if the array is 4, 1, 2, 7, 5, −1, 8, 0, 6, and `a[0]` = 4 is the pivot, the `partition` method produces

$$\begin{array}{ccccccccc} -1 & 1 & 2 & 0 & \boxed{4} & 5 & 8 & 7 & 6 \end{array}$$

Here's how the partitioning works: Let `a[0]`, 4 in this case, be the pivot. Markers `up` and `down` are initialized to index values 0 and $n-1$, as shown. Move the `up` marker until a value less than the pivot is found, or `down` equals `up`. Move the `down` marker until a value greater than the pivot is found, or `down` equals `up`. Swap `a[up]` and `a[down]`. Continue the process until `down` equals `up`. This is the pivot position. Swap `a[0]` and `a[pivotPosition]`.

Notice that the pivot element, 4, is in its final sorted position.

Analysis of quicksort:

1. For the fastest run time, the array should be partitioned into two parts of roughly the same size.

(continued)

2. If the pivot happens to be the smallest or largest element in the array, the split is not much of a split—one of the subarrays is empty! If this happens repeatedly, quicksort degenerates into a slow, recursive version of selection sort and is very inefficient.

3. The worst case for quicksort occurs when the partitioning algorithm repeatedly divides the array into pieces of size 1 and $n-1$. An example is when the array is initially sorted in either order and the first or last element is chosen as the pivot. Some algorithms avoid this situation by initially shuffling up the given array (!) or selecting the pivot by examining several elements of the array (such as first, middle, and last) and then taking the median.

> The main disadvantage of quicksort is that its worst case behavior is very inefficient.

**NOTE**

For both quicksort and merge sort, when a subarray gets down to some small size $m$, it becomes faster to sort by straight insertion. The optimal value of $m$ is machine-dependent, but it's approximately equal to 7.

## SORTING ALGORITHMS IN JAVA

Unlike the container classes like `ArrayList`, whose elements must be objects, arrays can hold either objects or primitive types like `int` or `double`.

A common way of organizing code for sorting arrays is to create a sorter class with an array private instance variable. The class holds all the methods for a given type of sorting algorithm, and the constructor assigns the user's array to the private array variable.

➡ **Example**

Selection sort for an array of `int`.

```
/* A class that sorts an array of ints from
 * largest to smallest using selection sort. */

public class SelectionSort
{
    private int[] a;

    public SelectionSort(int[] arr)
    { a = arr; }

    /** Swap a[i] and a[j] in array a. */
    private void swap(int i, int j)
    {
        int temp = a[i];
        a[i] = a[j];
        a[j] = temp;
    }
```

```
/** Sort array a from largest to smallest using selection sort.
 *  Precondition: a is an array of ints.
 */
public void selectionSort()
{
    int maxPos, max;

    for (int i = 0; i < a.length - 1; i++)
    {
        //find max element in a[i+1] to a[a.length-1]
        max = a[i];
        maxPos = i;
        for (int j = i + 1; j < a.length; j++)
            if (max < a[j])
            {
                max = a[j];
                maxPos = j;
            }
        swap(i, maxPos); //swap a[i] and a[maxPos]
    }
}
```

## SEQUENTIAL SEARCH

Assume that you are searching for a key in a list of $n$ elements. A sequential search starts at the first element and compares the key to each element in turn until the key is found or there are no more elements to examine in the list. If the list is sorted, in ascending order, say, stop searching as soon as the key is less than the current list element. (If the key is less than the current element, it will be less than all subsequent elements.)

Analysis:

1. The best case has the key in the first slot.
2. The worst case occurs if the key is in the last slot or not in the list. In the worst case, all $n$ elements must be examined.
3. On average, there will be $n/2$ comparisons.

## BINARY SEARCH

Binary search works only if the array is sorted on the search key.

If the elements are in a *sorted* array, a divide-and-conquer approach provides a much more efficient searching algorithm. The following recursive pseudo-code algorithm shows how the *binary search* works.

Assume that a[low] ... a[high] is sorted in ascending order and that a method binSearch returns the index of key. If key is not in the array, it returns −1.

```
if (low > high)    //Base case. No elements left in array.
    return -1;
else
{
    mid = (low + high)/2;
    if (key is equal to a[mid])    //found the key
        return mid;
    else if (key is less than a[mid])  //key in left half of array
        <binSearch for key in a[low] to a[mid-1]>
    else    //key in right half of array
        <binSearch for key in a[mid+1] to a[high]>
}
```

Note that this algorithm can also be described iteratively. There are no recursive calls, just an adjustment of mid so that the algorithm searches to the left or the right.

Again, assume that a[low]...a[high] is sorted in ascending order and that the method will return the index of key. If key is not in the array, the method will return −1.

```
while (low is less than or equal to high)
{
    int mid = (low + high)/2;
    if (key is equal to a[mid])  //found the key
        return mid;
    else if (key is less than a[mid]) //key in left half of array
        high = mid - 1;
    else  //key in right half of array
        low = mid + 1;
}
//If we get to here, then key is not in array.
return -1;
```

**NOTE**

1. After just one comparison, the binary search algorithm ignores one half of the array elements. This is true for both the iterative and recursive versions.

2. When low and high cross, there are no more elements to examine, and key is not in the array.

For example, suppose 5 is the key to be found in the following array:

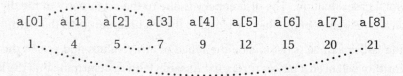

```
    a[0]  a[1]  a[2]  a[3]  a[4]  a[5]  a[6]  a[7]  a[8]
     1     4     5     7     9    12    15    20    21
```

First pass: low is 0, high is 8.     mid = (0+8)/2 = 4.    Check a[4].
Second pass: low is 0, high is 3.    mid = (0+3)/2 = 1.    Check a[1].
Third pass: low is 2, high is 3.     mid = (2+3)/2 = 2.    Check a[2]. Yes! Key is found.

## Analysis of Binary Search

1. In the best case, the key is found on the first try (i.e., `(low + high)/2` is the index of `key`).

2. In the worst case, the key is not in the array or is at an endpoint of the array. Here, the $n$ elements must be divided by 2 until there is just one element, and then that last element must be compared with the key. An easy way to find the number of comparisons in the worst case is to round $n$ up to the next power of 2 and take the exponent. For example, in the array above, $n$ is 9. Suppose 21 were the key. Round 9 up to 16, which is $2^4$. Thus you would need 4 comparisons with the key to find it. If $n$ is an exact power of 2, the number of comparisons in the worst case equals the exponent plus one. For example, if the number of elements $n = 32 = 2^5$, then the number of comparisons in the worst case is $5 + 1 = 6$. Note that in this discussion, the number of comparisons refers to the number of passes through the search loop of the above algorithm, namely, the outer `else` piece of code.

3. There's an interesting wrinkle when discussing the worst case of a binary search that uses the above algorithm. The worst case (i.e., the maximum number of comparisons) will either have the key at an endpoint of the array, or be equal to a value that's not in the array. The opposite, however, is not necessarily true: If the key is at an endpoint, or a value not in the array, it is not necessarily a worst case situation.

> The number of comparisons for binary search in the worst case depends on whether $n$ is a power of 2 or not.

As a simple example, consider the array 3, 7, 9, 11, where `a[0]` is 3 and `a[3]` is 11. The number of elements $n$ equals 4, which is $2^2$, an exact power of 2. The worst case for searching for a given key will be 3 comparisons, the exponent plus one.

- If the key is 11 (an endpoint of the array), the algorithm will need 3 passes through the search loop to find the key. This is a worst case. Here's how it works:

  1st pass: `low = 0 high = 3 mid = 1`
  2nd pass: `low = 2 high = 3 mid = 2`
  3rd pass: `low = 3 high = 3 mid = 3`

  The key is found during the 3rd pass when you examine `a[3]`. Thus a key of 11 represents a worst case.

- If the key is 3 (the other endpoint of the array), the algorithm will need 2 passes through the search loop to find the key. Here's how it works:

  1st pass: `low = 0 high = 3 mid = 1`
  2nd pass: `low = 0 high = 0 mid = 0`

  The key is found during the 2nd pass when you examine `a[0]`. Thus a key of 3 is not a worst case situation. The discrepancy is due to the asymmetry of the div operation, which gives values of `mid` that are closer to the left endpoint than the right.

- If the key is 1 or 20, say (outside the range of array values and not in the array), the algorithm will need 3 passes through the search loop to determine that the key is not in the array, a worst case.

- If the key is 8, say (not in the array but inside the range of array values), the algorithm will need just 2 passes through the search loop to determine that the key is not in the array. This is therefore not a worst case situation.

- If the key is 10, say (not in the array but between `a[2]` and `a[3]` in this example), the algorithm will need 3 passes through the search loop to determine that the key is not in the array, a worst case! Here is how it works:

1st pass: `low = 0 high = 3 mid = 1`

2nd pass: `low = 2 high = 3 mid = 2`

3rd pass: `low = 3 high = 3 mid = 3`

When `a[3]` is found to be greater than `key`, the value of `low` becomes 4, while `high` is still 3, which means that the test `if (low > high)` becomes true and is a base case that terminates the algorithm. There are no further comparisons with `key`.

Here is another example, where $n$ is not a power of 2.

Suppose the array is 1, 3, 5, 7, 9. Here $n$ is 5. To find the number of passes in the worst case, round up to the nearest power of 2, which is 8 or $2^3$. In the worst case, the number of passes through the search loop will be 3:

If the key is 1, there will be 2 passes to find it, which is not a worst case.

If the key is 9, there will be 3 passes to find it, which is a worst case.

If the key is 8, there will be 3 passes to find it, which is a worst case.

If the key is 4, there will be 2 passes to find it, which is not a worst case.

If the key is any value outside the range of 1 – 9, there will be 3 passes to find it, which is a worst case.

The lessons from these examples is that not every key that is not in the array represents a worst case.

Here are some general rules for calculating the maximum number of loop passes in different binary search situations. In each case it's assumed that the algorithm given in this book is used.

- If $n$, the number of elements, is not a power of 2, round $n$ up to the nearest power of 2. The number of passes in the worst case equals the exponent.

- If $n$ is a power of 2, the number of passes in the worst case equals the exponent plus one.

- Irrespective of $n$, the worst case will always involve a key that is either at the right endpoint or not in the array.

- Irrespective of $n$, any key that is not in the array and is less than `a[0]` or greater than `a[n-1]` will be a worst case situation.

- Irrespective of $n$, any key that is between `a[0]` and `a[n-1]`, but is not in the array may or may not be a worst case situation.

## Chapter Summary

You should not memorize any sorting code. You must, however, be familiar with the mechanism used in each of the sorting algorithms. For example, you should be able to explain how the merge method of merge sort works, or how many elements are in their final sorted position after a certain number of passes through the selection sort loop. You should know the best and worst case situations for each of the sorting algorithms.

Be familiar with the sequential and binary search algorithms. You should know that a binary search is more efficient than a sequential search, and that a binary search can only be used for an array that is sorted on the search key.

1. The decision to choose a particular sorting algorithm should be made based on which of the following?

    I  Run-time efficiency of the sort
    II  Size of the array
    III  Space efficiency of the algorithm

  (A) I only
  (B) II only
  (C) III only
  (D) I and II only
  (E) I, II, and III

2. The following code fragment does a sequential search to determine whether a given integer, value, is stored in an array a[0] ... a[n-1].

```
int i = 0;
while (/* boolean expression */)
{
    i++;
}
if (i == n)
    return -1;     //value not found
else
    return i;      // value found at location i
```

Which of the following should replace /* boolean expression */ so that the algorithm works as intended?
  (A) value != a[i]
  (B) i < n && value == a[i]
  (C) value != a[i] && i < n
  (D) i < n && value != a[i]
  (E) i < n || value != a[i]

3. A feature of data that is used for a binary search but not necessarily used for a sequential search is
  (A) length of list.
  (B) type of data.
  (C) order of data.
  (D) smallest value in the list.
  (E) median value of the data.

4. Array `unsortedArr` contains an unsorted list of integers. Array `sortedArr` contains a list of integers sorted in increasing order. Which of the following operations is more efficient for `sortedArr` than `unsortedArr`? Assume the most efficient algorithms are used.

    I  Inserting a new element

    II  Searching for a given element

    III  Computing the mean of the elements

  (A)  I only

  (B)  II only

  (C)  III only

  (D)  I and II only

  (E)  I, II, and III

5. An algorithm for searching a large sorted array for a specific value $x$ compares every third item in the array to $x$ until it finds one that is greater than or equal to $x$. When a larger value is found, the algorithm compares $x$ to the previous two items. If the array is sorted in increasing order, which of the following describes all cases when this algorithm uses fewer comparisons to find $x$ than would a binary search?

  (A)  It will never use fewer comparisons.

  (B)  When $x$ is in the middle position of the array

  (C)  When $x$ is very close to the beginning of the array

  (D)  When $x$ is very close to the end of the array

  (E)  When $x$ is not in the array

6. Assume that `a[0] ... a[N-1]` is an array of $N$ positive integers and that the following assertion is true.

$$\texttt{a[0]} > \texttt{a[k]} \text{ for all } k \text{ such that } 0 < k < N$$

Which of the following *must* be true?

  (A)  The array is sorted in ascending order.

  (B)  The array is sorted in descending order.

  (C)  All values in the array are different.

  (D)  `a[0]` holds the smallest value in the array.

  (E)  `a[0]` holds the largest value in the array.

7. The following code is designed to set `index` to the location of the first occurrence of `key` in array `a` and to set `index` to $-1$ if `key` is not in `a`.

```
index = 0;
while (a[index] != key)
    index++;
if (a[index] != key)
    index = -1;
```

In which case will this program *definitely* fail to perform the task described?

  (A)  When `key` is the first element of the array

  (B)  When `key` is the last element of the array

  (C)  When `key` is not in the array

  (D)  When `key` equals 0

  (E)  When `key` equals `a[key]`

8. Consider the following class.

```java
/** A class that sorts an array of Integer objects from
 *  largest to smallest using a selection sort.
 */
public class Sorter
{
    private Integer[] a;

    public Sorter(Integer[] arr)
    { a = arr; }

    /** Swap a[i] and a[j] in array a. */
    private void swap(int i, int j)
    { /* implementation not shown */ }

    /** Sort array a from largest to smallest using selection sort.
     *  Precondition: a is an array of Integer objects.
     */
    public void selectionSort()
    {
        for (int i = 0; i < a.length - 1; i++)
        {
            //find max element in a[i+1] to a[n-1]
            Integer max = a[i];
            int maxPos = i;
            for (int j = i + 1; j < a.length; j++)
                if (max.compareTo(a[j]) < 0) //max less than a[j]
                {
                    max = a[j];
                    maxPos = j;
                }
            swap(i, maxPos);    //swap a[i] and a[maxPos]
        }
    }
}
```

If an array of Integer contains the following elements, what would the array look like after the third pass of selectionSort, sorting from high to low?

89  42  −3  13  109  70  2

| | | | | | | | |
|---|---|---|---|---|---|---|---|
| (A) | 109 | 89 | 70 | 13 | 42 | −3 | 2 |
| (B) | 109 | 89 | 70 | 42 | 13 | 2 | −3 |
| (C) | 109 | 89 | 70 | −3 | 2 | 13 | 42 |
| (D) | 89 | 42 | 13 | −3 | 109 | 70 | 2 |
| (E) | 109 | 89 | 42 | −3 | 13 | 70 | 2 |

9. Refer to method search.

```
/** Returns value k such that -1 <= k <= v.length-1.
 * If k >= 0 then v[k] == key.
 * If k == -1, then key != any of the elements in v.
 */
public static int search(int[] v, int key)
{
    int index = 0;
    while (index < v.length && v[index] < key)
        index++;
    if (v[index] == key)
        return index;
    else
        return -1;
}
```

Assuming that the method works as intended, which of the following should be added to the precondition of search?

(A) v is sorted smallest to largest.

(B) v is sorted largest to smallest.

(C) v is unsorted.

(D) There is at least one occurrence of key in v.

(E) key occurs no more than once in v.

Questions 10–14 are based on the binSearch method and the private instance variable a for some class.

```java
private int[] a;

/** Does binary search for key in array a[0]...a[a.length-1],
 *  sorted in ascending order.
 *  Returns index such that a[index]==key.
 *  If key is not in a, returns -1.
 */
public int binSearch(int key)
{
    int low = 0;
    int high = a.length - 1;
    while (low <= high)
    {
        int mid = (low + high) / 2;
        if (a[mid] == key)
            return mid;
        else if (a[mid] < key)
            low = mid + 1;
        else
            high = mid - 1;
    }
    return -1;
}
```

A binary search will be performed on the following list.

| a[0] | a[1] | a[2] | a[3] | a[4] | a[5] | a[6] | a[7] |
|------|------|------|------|------|------|------|------|
| 4    | 7    | 9    | 11   | 20   | 24   | 30   | 41   |

10. To find the key value 27, the search interval *after* the first pass through the `while` loop will be
    (A) a[0]...a[7]
    (B) a[5]...a[6]
    (C) a[4]...a[7]
    (D) a[2]...a[6]
    (E) a[6]...a[7]

11. How many iterations will be required to determine that 27 is not in the list?
    (A) 1
    (B) 3
    (C) 4
    (D) 8
    (E) 16

12. What will be stored in y after executing the following?

```
int y = binSearch(4);
```

    (A) 20
    (B) 7
    (C) 4
    (D) 0
    (E) -1

13. If the test for the while loop is changed to

```
while (low < high)
```

the binSearch method does not work as intended. Which value in the given list will not be found?

    (A) 4
    (B) 7
    (C) 11
    (D) 24
    (E) 30

14. For binSearch, which of the following assertions will be true following every iteration of the while loop?

    (A) key = a[mid] or key is not in a.
    (B) a[low] ≤ key ≤ a[high]
    (C) low ≤ mid ≤ high
    (D) key = a[mid], or a[low] ≤ key ≤ a[high]
    (E) key = a[mid], or a[low] ≤ key ≤ a[high], or key is not in array a.

15. A large sorted array containing about 30,000 elements is to be searched for a value key using an iterative binary search algorithm. Assuming that key is in the array, which of the following is closest to the smallest number of iterations that will guarantee that key is found? Note: $10^3 \approx 2^{10}$.

    (A) 15
    (B) 30
    (C) 100
    (D) 300
    (E) 3000

For Questions 16–19 refer to the `insertionSort` method and the private instance variable `a`, both in a `Sorter` class.

```
private Integer[] a;

/** Precondition:  a[0],a[1]...a[a.length-1] is an unsorted array
 *                 of Integer objects.
 * Postcondition: Array a is sorted in descending order.
 */
public void insertionSort()
{
    for (int i = 1; i < a.length; i++)
    {
        Integer temp = a[i];
        int j = i - 1;
        while (j >= 0 && temp > a[j])   //temp and a[j] are unboxed
        {
            a[j+1] = a[j];
            j--;
        }
        a[j+1] = temp;
    }
}
```

16. An array of `Integer` is to be sorted biggest to smallest using the `insertionSort` method. If the array originally contains

$$1 \quad 7 \quad 9 \quad 5 \quad 4 \quad 12$$

what will it look like after the third pass of the `for` loop?
    (A) 9 7 1 5 4 12
    (B) 9 7 5 1 4 12
    (C) 12 9 7 1 5 4
    (D) 12 9 7 5 4 1
    (E) 9 7 12 5 4 1

17. When sorted biggest to smallest with `insertionSort`, which list will need the fewest changes of position for individual elements?
    (A) 5, 1, 2, 3, 4, 9
    (B) 9, 5, 1, 4, 3, 2
    (C) 9, 4, 2, 5, 1, 3
    (D) 9, 3, 5, 1, 4, 2
    (E) 3, 2, 1, 9, 5, 4

18. When sorted biggest to smallest with `insertionSort`, which list will need the greatest number of changes in position?
    (A) 5, 1, 2, 3, 4, 7, 6, 9
    (B) 9, 5, 1, 4, 3, 2, 1, 0
    (C) 9, 4, 6, 2, 1, 5, 1, 3
    (D) 9, 6, 9, 5, 6, 7, 2, 0
    (E) 3, 2, 1, 0, 9, 6, 5, 4

19. While typing the `insertionSort` method, a programmer by mistake enters

    ```
    while (temp >  a[j])
    ```

    instead of

    ```
    while (j >= 0 && temp > a[j])
    ```

    Despite this mistake, the method works as intended the first time the programmer enters an array to be sorted in descending order. Which of the following could explain this?

    I  The first element in the array was the largest element in the array.
    II  The array was already sorted in descending order.
    III  The first element was less than or equal to all the other elements in the array.

    (A) I only
    (B) II only
    (C) III only
    (D) I and II only
    (E) II and III only

20. The elements in a long list of integers are roughly sorted in decreasing order. No more than 5 percent of the elements are out of order. Which of the following is a valid reason for using an insertion sort rather than a selection sort to sort this list into decreasing order?

    I  There will be fewer comparisons of elements for insertion sort.
    II  There will be fewer changes of position of elements for insertion sort.
    III  There will be less space required for insertion sort.

    (A) I only
    (B) II only
    (C) III only
    (D) I and II only
    (E) I, II, and III

21. Which of the following is a valid reason why merge sort is a better sorting algorithm than insertion sort for sorting long, randomly ordered lists?

    I  Merge sort requires less code than insertion sort.
    II  Merge sort requires less storage space than insertion sort.
    III  Merge sort runs faster than insertion sort.

    (A) I only
    (B) II only
    (C) III only
    (D) I and II only
    (E) II and III only

22. A large array of lowercase characters is to be searched for the pattern "pqrs." The first step in a very efficient searching algorithm is to look at characters with index
    (A) 0, 1, 2, ... until a "p" is encountered.
    (B) 0, 1, 2, ... until any letter in "p" ... "s" is encountered.
    (C) 3, 7, 11, ... until an "s" is encountered.
    (D) 3, 7, 11, ... until any letter in "p" ... "s" is encountered.
    (E) 3, 7, 11, ... until any letter other than "p" ... "s" is encountered.

23. The array `names[0], names[1], ..., names[9999]` is a list of 10,000 name strings. The list is to be searched to determine the location of some name `X` in the list. Which of the following preconditions is necessary for a binary search?
    (A) There are no duplicate names in the list.
    (B) The number of names $N$ in the list is large.
    (C) The list is in alphabetical order.
    (D) Name `X` is definitely in the list.
    (E) Name `X` occurs near the middle of the list.

24. Consider the following method.

```
/** Precondition: a[0],a[1]...a[n-1] contain integers. */
public static int someMethod(int[] a, int n, int value)
{
    if (n == 0)
        return -1;
    else
    {
        if (a[n-1] == value)
            return n - 1;
        else
            return someMethod(a, n - 1, value);
    }
}
```

The method shown is an example of
    (A) insertion sort.
    (B) merge sort.
    (C) selection sort.
    (D) binary search.
    (E) sequential search.

25. The `partition` method for quicksort partitions a list as follows.

**Optional topic**

    (i) A pivot element is selected from the array.

    (ii) The elements of the list are rearranged such that all elements to the left of the pivot are less than or equal to it; all elements to the right of the pivot are greater than or equal to it.

Partitioning the array requires which of the following?
(A) A recursive algorithm
(B) A temporary array
(C) An external file for the array
(D) A swap algorithm for interchanging array elements
(E) A merge method for merging two sorted lists

26. Assume that merge sort will be used to sort an array `arr` of n integers into increasing order. What is the purpose of the `merge` method in the merge sort algorithm?
(A) Partition `arr` into two parts of roughly equal length, then merge these parts.
(B) Use a recursive algorithm to sort `arr` into increasing order.
(C) Divide `arr` into n subarrays, each with one element.
(D) Merge two sorted parts of `arr` into a single sorted array.
(E) Merge two sorted arrays into a temporary array that is sorted.

27. A binary search is to be performed on an array with 600 elements. In the *worst* case, which of the following best approximates the number of iterations of the algorithm?
(A) 6
(B) 10
(C) 100
(D) 300
(E) 600

28. A worst case situation for insertion sort would be

    I A list in correct sorted order.
    II A list sorted in reverse order.
    III A list in random order.

(A) I only
(B) II only
(C) III only
(D) I and II only
(E) II and III only

29. Consider a binary search algorithm to search an ordered list of numbers. Which of the following choices is closest to the maximum number of times that such an algorithm will execute its main comparison loop when searching a list of 1 million numbers?
(A) 6
(B) 20
(C) 100
(D) 120
(E) 1000

30. Consider these three tasks.

    I  A sequential search of an array of $n$ names

    II  A binary search of an array of $n$ names in alphabetical order

    III  An insertion sort into alphabetical order of an array of $n$ names that are initially in random order

For large $n$, which of the following lists these tasks in order (from least to greatest) of their average case run times?

(A)    II    I    III
(B)    I    II    III
(C)    II    III    I
(D)    III    I    II
(E)    III    II    I

Questions 31–33 refer to the Hi-Lo game described below.

Consider the problem of writing a Hi-Lo game in which a user thinks of an integer from 1 to 100 inclusive and the computer tries to guess that number. Each time the computer makes a guess, the user makes one of three responses.

- "lower" (i.e., the number is lower than the computer's guess)
- "higher" (i.e., the number is higher than the computer's guess)
- "you got it in *< however many >* tries!"

31. Suppose the game is programmed so that the computer uses a binary search strategy for making its guesses. What is the maximum number of guesses the computer could make before guessing the user's number?
    (A) 50
    (B) 25
    (C) 10
    (D) 7
    (E) 6

32. Suppose the computer used a *sequential search* strategy for guessing the user's number. What is the maximum number of guesses the computer could make before guessing the user's number?
    (A) 100
    (B) 99
    (C) 50
    (D) 25
    (E) 10

33. Using a sequential search strategy, how many guesses *on average* would the computer need to guess the number?
    (A) 100
    (B) Between 51 and 99
    (C) 50
    (D) 25
    (E) Fewer than 25

## ANSWER KEY

| | | |
|---|---|---|
| 1. **E** | 12. **D** | 23. **C** |
| 2. **D** | 13. **A** | 24. **E** |
| 3. **C** | 14. **E** | 25. **D** |
| 4. **B** | 15. **A** | 26. **D** |
| 5. **C** | 16. **B** | 27. **B** |
| 6. **E** | 17. **B** | 28. **B** |
| 7. **C** | 18. **A** | 29. **B** |
| 8. **A** | 19. **D** | 30. **A** |
| 9. **A** | 20. **A** | 31. **D** |
| 10. **C** | 21. **C** | 32. **B** |
| 11. **B** | 22. **D** | 33. **C** |

## ANSWERS EXPLAINED

1. **(E)** The time and space requirements of sorting algorithms are affected by all three of the given factors, so all must be considered when choosing a particular sorting algorithm.

2. **(D)** Choice B doesn't make sense: The loop will be exited as soon as a value is found that does *not* equal a[i]. Eliminate choice A because, if value is not in the array, a[i] will eventually go out of bounds. You need the i < n part of the boolean expression to avoid this. The test i < n, however, must precede value != a[i] so that if i < n fails, the expression will be evaluated as false, the test will be short-circuited, and an out-of-range error will be avoided. Choice C does not avoid this error. Choice E is wrong because both parts of the expression must be true in order to continue the search.

3. **(C)** The binary search algorithm depends on the array being sorted. Sequential search has no ordering requirement. Both depend on choice A, the length of the list, while the other choices are irrelevant to both algorithms.

4. **(B)** Inserting a new element is quick and easy in an unsorted array—just add it to the end of the list. Computing the mean involves finding the sum of the elements and dividing by $n$, the number of elements. The execution time is the same whether the list is sorted or not. Operation II, searching, is inefficient for an unsorted list, since a sequential search must be used. In sortedArr, the efficient binary search algorithm, which involves fewer comparisons, could be used. In fact, in a sorted list, even a sequential search would be more efficient than for an unsorted list: If the search item were not in the list, the search could stop as soon as the list elements were greater than the search item.

5. **(C)** Suppose the array has 1000 elements and $x$ is somewhere in the first 8 slots. The algorithm described will find $x$ using no more than five comparisons. A binary search, by contrast, will chop the array in half and do a comparison six times before examining elements in the first 15 slots of the array (array size after each chop: 500, 250, 125, 62, 31, 15).

6. **(E)** The assertion states that the first element is greater than all the other elements in the array. This eliminates choices A and D. Choices B and C are incorrect because you have no information about the relative sizes of elements `a[1]...a[N-1]`.

7. **(C)** When `key` is not in the array, `index` will eventually be large enough that `a[index]` will cause an `ArrayIndexOutOfBoundsException`. In choices A and B, the algorithm will find `key` without error. Choice D won't fail if 0 is in the array. Choice E will work if `a[key]` is not out of range.

8. **(A)**

| | | | | | | | |
|---|---|---|---|---|---|---|---|
| After 1st pass: | 109 | 42 | −3 | 13 | 89 | 70 | 2 |
| After 2nd pass: | 109 | 89 | −3 | 13 | 42 | 70 | 2 |
| After 3rd pass: | 109 | 89 | 70 | 13 | 42 | −3 | 2 |

9. **(A)** The algorithm uses the fact that array `v` is sorted smallest to largest. The `while` loop terminates—which means that the search stops—as soon as `v[index] >= key`.

10. **(C)** The first pass uses the interval `a[0]...a[7]`. Since `mid = (0+7)/2 = 3`, `low` gets adjusted to `mid+1 = 4`, and the second pass uses the interval `a[4]...a[7]`.

11. **(B)** First pass: Compare 27 with `a[3]`, since `low = 0 high = 7 mid = (0+7)/2 = 3`. Second pass: Compare 27 with `a[5]`, since `low = 4 high = 7 mid = (4+7)/2 = 5`. Third pass: Compare 27 with `a[6]`, since `low = 6 high = 7 mid = (6+7)/2 = 6`. The fourth pass doesn't happen, since `low = 6`, `high = 5`, and therefore the test (`low <= high`) fails. Using the general rule for finding the number of iterations when `key` is not in the list: If $n$ is the number of elements, round $n$ up to the nearest power of 2, which is 8 in this case. Note that $8 = 2^3$. Since 27 lies between 4 and 41, there will be 3 iterations of the "divide-and-compare" loop.

12. **(D)** The method returns the index of the `key` parameter, 4. Since `a[0]` contains 4, `binSearch(4)` will return 0.

13. **(A)** Try 4. Here are the values for `low`, `high`, and `mid` when searching for 4:

$$\text{1st pass:} \quad low = 0, \quad high = 7, \quad mid = 3$$
$$\text{2nd pass:} \quad low = 0, \quad high = 2, \quad mid = 1$$

After this pass, `high` gets adjusted to `mid −1`, which is 0. Now `low` equals `high`, and the test for the `while` loop fails. The method returns −1, indicating that 4 wasn't found.

14. **(E)** When the loop is exited, either `key = a[mid]` (and `mid` has been returned) or `key` has not been found, in which case either `a[low]` ≤ `key` ≤ `a[high]` or `key` is not in the array. The correct assertion must account for all three possibilities.

15. **(A)** $30{,}000 = 1000 \times 30 \approx 2^{10} \times 2^5 = 2^{15}$. Since a successful binary search in the worst case requires $\log_2 n$ iterations, 15 iterations will guarantee that `key` is found. (Note that $30{,}000 < 2^{10} \times 2^5 = 32{,}768$.) Shortcut: $30{,}000 < 2^{15}$. Therefore, the maximum (worst case) number of comparisons that guarantees the key is found is equal to the exponent, 15.

16. **(B)** Start with the second element in the array.

| | | | | | | |
|---|---|---|---|---|---|---|
| After 1st pass: | 7 | 1 | 9 | 5 | 4 | 12 |
| After 2nd pass: | 9 | 7 | 1 | 5 | 4 | 12 |
| After 3rd pass: | 9 | 7 | 5 | 1 | 4 | 12 |

17. **(B)** An insertion sort compares `a[1]` and `a[0]`. If they are not in the correct order, `a[0]` is moved and `a[1]` is inserted in its correct position. `a[2]` is then inserted in its correct position, and `a[0]` and `a[1]` are moved if necessary, and so on. Since B has only one element out of order, it will require the fewest changes.

18. **(A)** This list is almost sorted in reverse order, which is the worst case for insertion sort, requiring the greatest number of comparisons and moves.

19. **(D)** `j >= 0` is a stopping condition that prevents an element that is larger than all those to the left of it from going off the left end of the array. If no error occurred, it means that the largest element in the array was `a[0]`, which was true in situations I and II. Omitting the `j >= 0` test will cause a run-time (out-of-range) error whenever `temp` is bigger than all elements to the left of it (i.e., the insertion point is `0`).

20. **(A)** Look at a small array that is almost sorted:

    10 8 9 6 2

    For <u>insertion sort</u>, you need four passes through this array.
    The first pass compares 8 and 10—one comparison, no moves.
    The second pass compares 9 and 8, then 9 and 10. The array becomes
    10 9 8 6 2—two comparisons, two moves.
    The third and fourth passes compare 6 and 8, and 2 and 6—no moves.
    In summary, there are approximately one or two comparisons per pass and no more than two moves per pass.
    For <u>selection sort</u>, there are four passes too.
    The first pass finds the biggest element in the array and swaps it into the first position. The array is still 10 8 9 6 2—four comparisons. There are two moves if your algorithm makes the swap in this case, otherwise no moves.
    The second pass finds the biggest element from `a[1]` to `a[4]` and swaps it into the second position: 10 9 8 6 2—three comparisons, two moves.
    For the third pass there are two comparisons, and one for the fourth. There are zero or two moves each time.
    Summary: $4+3+2+1$ total comparisons and a possible two moves per pass.
    Notice that reason I is valid. Selection sort makes the same number of comparisons irrespective of the state of the array. Insertion sort does far fewer comparisons if the array is almost sorted. Reason II is invalid. There are roughly the same number of data movements for insertion and selection. Insertion may even have more changes, depending on how far from their insertion points the unsorted elements are. Reason III is wrong because insertion and selection sorts have the same space requirements.

21. **(C)** Reject reason I. Merge sort requires both a `merge` and a `mergeSort` method—*more* code than the relatively short and simple code for insertion sort. Reject reason II. The `merge` algorithm uses a temporary array, which means *more* storage space than insertion sort. Reason III is correct. For long lists, the "divide-and-conquer" approach of merge sort gives it a faster run time than insertion sort.

22. **(D)** Since the search is for a four-letter sequence, the idea in this algorithm is that if you examine every fourth slot, you'll find a letter in the required sequence very quickly. When you find one of these letters, you can then examine adjacent slots to check if you have the required sequence. This method will, on average, result in fewer comparisons than the strictly sequential search algorithm in choice A. Choice B is wrong. If you encounter a "q," "r," or "s" without a "p" first, you can't have found "pqrs." Choice C is wrong because you may miss the sequence completely. Choice E doesn't make sense.

23. **(C)** The main precondition for a binary search is that the list is ordered.

24. **(E)** This algorithm is just a recursive implementation of a sequential search. It starts by testing if the last element in the array, `a[n-1]`, is equal to `value`. If so, it returns the index $n - 1$. Otherwise, it calls itself with `n` replaced by $n - 1$. The net effect is that it examines `a[n-1]`, `a[n-2]`, .... The base case, `if (n == 0)`, occurs when there are no elements left to examine. In this case, the method returns $-1$, signifying that `value` was not in the array.

25. **(D)** The `partition` algorithm performs a series of swaps until the pivot element is swapped into its final sorted position (see p. 322). No temporary arrays or external files are used, nor is a recursive algorithm invoked. The `merge` method is used for merge sort, not quicksort.

Optional topic

26. **(D)** Recall the merge sort algorithm:

> Divide `arr` into two parts.
> Merge sort the left side.
> Merge sort the right side.
> Merge the two sides into a single sorted array.

The `merge` method is used for the last step of the algorithm. It does not do any sorting or partitioning of the array, which eliminates choices A, B, and C. Choice E is wrong because `merge` starts with a *single* array that has two sorted parts.

27. **(B)** Round 600 up to the next power of 2, which is $1024 = 2^{10}$. Recall the shortcut: $600 < 2^{10}$, so the worst case equals the exponent, 10.

28. **(B)** If the list is sorted in reverse order, each pass through the array will involve the maximum possible number of comparisons and the maximum possible number of element movements if an insertion sort is used.

29. **(B)** 1 million $= 10^6 = (10^3)^2 \approx (2^{10})^2 = 2^{20}$. Thus, there will be on the order of 20 comparisons.

30. **(A)** A binary search, on average, has a smaller run time than a sequential search. All of the sorting algorithms have greater run times than a sequential search. This is because a sequential search looks at each element once. A sorting algorithm, however, processes *other* elements in the array for each element it looks at.

31. **(D)** The computer should find the number in no more than seven tries. This is because the guessing interval is halved on each successive try:

$$
\begin{array}{lll}
(1) & 100 \div 2 = 50 & \text{numbers left to try} \\
(2) & 50 \div 2 = 25 & \text{numbers left to try} \\
(3) & 25 \div 2 = 13 & \text{numbers left to try} \\
(4) & 13 \div 2 = 7 & \text{numbers left to try} \\
(5) & 7 \div 2 = 4 & \text{numbers left to try} \\
(6) & 4 \div 2 = 2 & \text{numbers left to try} \\
(7) & 2 \div 2 = 1 & \text{number left to try}
\end{array}
$$

Seven iterations of the loop leaves just 1 number left to try! Don't forget the shortcut. The algorithm is a binary search of 100 possible elements. Rounding 100 up to the next power of 2 gives $128 = 2^7$. The exponent, 7, is the number of guesses in the worst case.

32. **(B)** The maximum number of guesses is 99. A sequential search means that the computer starts at the first possible number, namely 1, and tries each successive number until it gets to 99. If the user's number is 100, the computer will know that when it tests 99.

33. **(C)** On average the computer will make 50 guesses. The user is equally likely to pick any number between 1 and 100. Half the time it will be less than 50; half the time, greater than 50. So on the average, the distance of the number from 1 is 50.

# The AP Computer Science A Labs 10

→ **The Magpie Lab**          → **The Picture Lab**

→ **The Elevens Lab**

The AP Computer Science A labs were developed to satisfy the 20-hour lab requirement for the AP course. There will be no specific questions on the AP exam that require knowledge of the content of the labs. There are, however, questions that focus on concepts from the AP Java subset that are emphasized in the labs.

What follows below is a brief summary of the labs, the concepts they illustrate, and some sample multiple-choice questions based on these concepts.

## THE MAGPIE LAB

In this lab, students modify a chatbot, which is a computer program designed to simulate an intelligent conversation between a computer and a human user. Students enter phrases, the computer searches for keywords, and then it comes up with an intelligent-seeming response.

Student activities include:

- Working through the Magpie code (`if` statements)

- Using `Magpie` and `String` methods (`while` loops and strings)

- Using an array of possible responses in generating a random response from the computer (arrays, `ArrayLists`, and random integers)

- Improving the search to find keywords that are complete words, not substrings buried in other strings (`String` methods)

- Transforming a computer response based on the format of the statement entered by the user (`String` methods)

### Special Emphasis

#### STRING METHODS

The `String` methods `substring` and `indexOf` are used continually in this lab. Be sure that you recall:

- The first index of a `String` is 0.

- The method call s.substring(start, end) returns the substring of s starting at index start but ending at index end-1.

- The method call s.indexOf(sub) returns the index of the first occurrence of substring sub in s.

- s.indexOf(sub) returns -1 if sub is not in s.

you should be nimble and well practiced in processing strings.

The following type of code is used repeatedly in the lab to look for multiple occurrences of a substring in a given string

```
int pos = s.indexOf(someSubstring);
while (pos >= 0)                     //the substring was found
{
    doSomething();
    s = s.substring(pos + 1);  //throw away all characters of s
                               //up to and including someSubstring

    pos = s.indexOf(someSubstring);  //Is there another occurrence
                                     //of someSubstring?
}
```

A modified version of the above code, using some combination of a loop, indexOf, and substring, can be used to

- count number of occurrences of substring in str.

- replace all occurrences of substring in str with replacementStr.

- remove all occurrences of substring in str.

On the AP exam, there will almost certainly be at least one free-response question that requires you to manipulate strings.

### RANDOM ELEMENT SELECTION

Another skill that is demonstrated in this lab is returning a random element from an array or ArrayList. For example, suppose responses is an ArrayList<String> of surprised responses the computer may make to a user's crazy input. If the contents of responses are currently

| 0 | 1 | 2 | 3 | 4 | 5 |
|---|---|---|---|---|---|
| Oh my! | Say what? | No! | Heavens! | You're kidding me. | Jumping Jellybeans! |

you should be able to randomly return one of these responses. The key is to select a random index from 0 to 5, inclusive, and then return the string in the responses list that is at that index.

Recall that the expression (int)(Math.random()*howMany) generates a random int in the range 0...howMany-1. In the given example, howMany is 6. The piece of code that returns a random response is:

```
int randIndex = (int) (Math.random() * 6);
String response = responses.get(randIndex);
```

## CONDITIONALS: `if...else` STATEMENT

The Magpie lab is loaded with conditionals, searching for keywords that will trigger different responses from the chatbot (computer). Using `if` and `if...else` should be second nature to you.

### ➡ Example

The user will enter a `sentence` and the chatbot will produce a `chatBotReply`.

```
if (sentence.indexOf ("love") != -1)
{
    if (sentence.indexOf ("you") != -1)
        chatBotReply = "I'm in heaven!";
    else
        chatBotReply = "But do you love me?";
}
else
    chatBotReply = "My heart is in pieces on the floor.";
```

Here are some possible sentences that the user may enter, with the corresponding chatBoxReply:

| Sentence | chatBoxReply |
|---|---|
| I love chocolate cake. | But do you love me? |
| I love chocolate cake; do you? | I'm in heaven. |
| I hate fudge. | My heart is in pieces on the floor. |

If the substring `"love"` isn't in the sentence, the opening test will be `false`, and execution skips to the `else` outside the braces, producing the `chatBotReply` "My heart is in pieces on the floor". If sentence contains both `"love"` and `"you"`, the first test in the braces will be `true`, and the `chatBotReply` will be "I'm in heaven!" The middle response "But do you love me?" will be triggered by a sentence that contains `"love"` but doesn't contain `"you"`, causing the first test in the braces to be `false`, and the `else` part in the braces to be executed.

## THE ELEVENS LAB

In this lab, students simulate a game of solitaire, Elevens, and a related game, Thirteens. A GUI is provided for the labs to make the game interesting and fun to play. You are not required to know about GUIs.

Student activities include:

- Creating a `Card` class (objects, classes, and `Strings`)
- Creating a `Deck` class (arrays, `ArrayLists`, conditionals, loops)
- Shuffling the deck (`Math.random`, list manipulation)
- Writing an `ElevensBoard` class, using an abstract `Board` class (inheritance, abstract classes)
  Note that abstract classes are no longer part of the AP Java subset.
- Testing and debugging
- Playing the game

## Special Emphasis

### SHUFFLING

Several different algorithms are discussed for shuffling an array of elements. A key ingredient of a good shuffle is generation of random integers. For example, to shuffle a deck of 52 cards in an array may require a random int from 0 to 51:

```
int cardNum = (int) (Math.random() * 52);
```

(Recall that the multiplier in parentheses is the number of possible random integers.)

The following code for shuffling an array of Type elements is used often:

```
for (int k = arr.length - 1; k > 0; k--)
{
    //Pick a random index in the array from 0 to k
    int index = (int) (Math.random() * (k + 1));
    //Swap randomly selected element with element at position k
    Type temp = arr[k];
    arr[k] = arr[index];
    arr[index] = temp;
}
```

### WRITING SUBCLASSES

On the AP exam, you will probably be asked to write a subclass of a given class. Don't forget the extends keyword:

```
public class Subclass extends Superclass
```

Recall that constructors are not inherited, and if you use the keyword super in writing a constructor for your subclass, the line containing it should precede any other code in the constructor.

### ➡ Example _____

```
public class Dog
{
    private String name;
    private String breed;

    public Dog (String aName, String aBreed)
    {
        name = aName;
        breed = aBreed;
    }
        ...
}
```

```
public class Poodle extends Dog
{
    private boolean needsGrooming;

    public Poodle (String aName, String aBreed, boolean grooming)
    {
        super(aName, aBreed);
        needsGrooming = grooming;
    }
        ...
}
```

## POLYMORPHISM

Consider this hierarchy of classes, and the declarations that follow it:

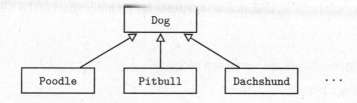

Suppose the `Dog` class has this method:

```
public void eat()
{ /* implementation not shown */ }
```

And each of the subclasses, `Poodle`, `PitBull`, `Dachshund`, etc., has a different, overridden `eat` method. Now suppose that `allDogs` is an `ArrayList<Dog>` where each `Dog` declared above has been added to the list. Each `Dog` in the list will be processed to eat by the following lines of code:

```
for (Dog d: allDogs)
    d.eat();
```

Polymorphism is the process of selecting the correct `eat` method, during run time, for each of the different dogs.

## TESTING AND DEBUGGING

In the Elevens lab, a lot of emphasis is placed on testing and debugging code as you write it. Here are some general principles:

- Start simple. For example, if writing a `Deck` class, start with a deck that contains just two or three cards.

- Always have a driver class (one with a `main` method) to test the current class you're writing.

- In your class, start with a constructor. You want to be sure you can create your object.

- After the constructor, write a `toString` method for clear and easy display. You want to be able to "see" the results of running your code.

### SIMULATING RANDOM EVENTS

Flipping a coin, tossing a die, or picking a random card from a deck. Those random numbers again! If there are k possible outcomes, each of them equally likely, be sure you can generate a random `int` from 0 to k-1.

## THE PICTURE LAB

In this lab, students manipulate digital pictures using two-dimensional arrays. Code for the GUI is provided in the lab.

The main concept emphasized is traversal of two-dimensional arrays. Other concepts used are UML diagrams, binary numbers, inheritance, interfaces, abstract methods, constants, and program analysis.

### NOTE

Binary numbers, interfaces, and abstract methods are no longer part of the AP Java subset.

Student activities include:

- Learning how colors are stored in a program
- Modifying a picture
- Creating a mirror image of a picture
- Mirroring part of a picture
- Creating a collage
- Detecting the edge of a picture

## Special Emphasis

### PROCESSING A TWO-DIMENSIONAL ARRAY

A matrix is stored as an array of rows, each of which is also an array. In the lab, an enhanced `for` loop is often used for traversal. Here is an example that traverses an array of `int`:

```
for (int[] row : matrix)      //for each row array in the matrix
    for (int num : row)       //for each int element in the current row
        doSomething();
```

Here is what `doSomething` can do:

- Access each element in the matrix (count, add, compare, etc.)

Here is what `doSomething` should not do:

- Replace an element with another.

Suppose the matrix is an array of objects that can be changed with mutator methods. The enhanced `for` loop can be used not only to access elements, but also to modify them. (No replacing with new elements, however.) The following code is OK.

```
for (Clock[] row : clockMatrix)
    for (Clock c : row)
        c.setTime(t);
```

**MIRROR IMAGES**

A large part of the lab is spent coming up with algorithms that create some kind of mirror image of a matrix. Students are asked to reflect across mirrors placed somewhere in the center of the matrix, horizontally, vertically, or diagonally.

Note that if a vertical mirror is placed down the center of a matrix, so that all elements to the left of the mirror are reflected across it, the element `mat[row][col]` reflects across to element `mat[row][numCols-col-1]`.

You should teach yourself to trace the following type of code:

```
public static void matrixMethod(int[][] mat)
{
    int height = mat.length;
    int numCols = mat[0].length;
    for (int col = 0; col < numCols; col++)
        for (int row = 0; row < height/2; row++)
            mat[height - row - 1][col] = mat[row][col];
}
```

What does it do? How does it transform the matrix below?

```
2 3 4
5 6 7
8 9 0
1 1 1
```

Solution: The algorithm reflects the matrix from top to bottom across a horizontal mirror placed at its center.

```
height = 4, numCols = 3
col takes on values 0, 1, and 2
row takes on values 0 and 1
```

Here are the replacements that are made:

```
col = 0, row = 0: mat[3][0] = mat[0][0]
        row = 1: mat[2][0] = mat[1][0]

col = 1, row = 0: mat[3][1] = mat[0][1]
        row = 1: mat[2][1] = mat[1][1]

col = 2, row = 0: mat[3][2] = mat[0][2]
        row = 1: mat[2][2] = mat[1][2]
```

This transforms the matrix into

```
2 3 4
5 6 7
5 6 7
2 3 4
```

Note that an enhanced `for` loop was not used in the traversal, because elements in the matrix are being replaced.

**BASE 2, BASE 8, BASE 16**

Binary (base 2) and hexadecimal (base 16) numbers are discussed in the Picture lab as they apply to storage of colors.

**NOTE**

Multi-base conversions are no longer part of the AP Java subset.

## Chapter Summary

String manipulation and matrix processing are the two big topics you should master. Review the meanings and boundary conditions of the parameters in the `String` methods `substring` and `indexOf`. For matrices, you should nail down both the row-column and enhanced `for` traversals. Remember, you should not use an enhanced `for` loop for the replacement of elements.

Be sure you can hand-execute tricky matrix algorithms, like those used for modifying matrices using mirror images.

A matrix is an array of row-arrays, so familiarize yourself with the use of a method with an array parameter to process the rows of a matrix.

Array manipulation is another big topic. Be sure you know how to shuffle the elements of an array.

Other concepts emphasized in the labs are inheritance and polymorphism, writing subclasses, simulation of events using random numbers, and conditional (`if...else`) statements. You should have all of these at your fingertips.

1. For ticket-selling purposes, there are three categories at a certain theater.

| Age | Category |
|---|---|
| 65 or above | Senior |
| From 18 to 64 inclusive | Adult |
| Below 18 | Child |

Which of the following code segments will assign the correct string to `category` for a given integer age?

```
 I if (age >= 65)
        category = "Senior";
    if (age >= 18)
        category = "Adult";
    else
        category = "Child";
```

```
 II if (age >= 65)
        category = "Senior";
    if (18 <= age <= 64)
        category = "Adult";
    else
        category = "Child";
```

```
III if (age >= 65)
        category = "Senior";
    else if (age >= 18)
        category = "Adult";
    else
        category = "Child";
```

(A) I only

(B) II only

(C) III only

(D) II and III only

(E) I, II, and III

2. What is the output of the following code segment?

```
String s = "How do you do?";
int index = s.indexOf("o");
while (index >= 0)
{
    System.out.print(index + " ");
    s = s.substring(index + 1);
    index = s.indexOf("o");
}
```

(A) 1 3 2 3

(B) 2 4 3 4

(C) 1 5 8 12

(D) 1 5 8 11

(E) No output because of an IndexOutOfBoundsException

3. Consider the following method `removeAll` that creates and returns a string that has stripped its input phrase of all occurrences of its single-character `String` parameter `ch`.

```
Line 1:  public static String removeAll(String phrase, String ch)
Line 2:  {
Line 3:      String str = "";
Line 4:      String newPhrase = phrase;
Line 5:      int pos = phrase.indexOf(ch);
Line 6:      if (pos == -1)
Line 7:          return phrase;
Line 8:      else
Line 9:      {
Line 10:         while (pos >= 0)
Line 11:         {
Line 12:             str = str + newPhrase.substring(0, pos - 1);
Line 13:             newPhrase = newPhrase.substring(pos + 1);
Line 14:             pos = newPhrase.indexOf(ch);
Line 15:             if (pos == -1)
Line 16:                 str = str + newPhrase;
Line 17:         }
Line 18:         return str;
Line 19:     }
Line 20: }
```

The method doesn't work as intended. Which of the following changes to the `removeAll` method will make it work as specified?

(A) Change Line 10 to

```
while (pos >= -1)
```

(B) Change Line 12 to

```
str = str + newPhrase.substring(0, pos);
```

(C) Change Line 13 to

```
newPhrase = newPhrase.substring(pos);
```

(D) Change Line 14 to

```
pos = phrase.indexOf(ch);
```

(E) Change Line 16 to

```
str = str + newPhrase.substring(pos + 1);
```

4. A programmer has written a program that "chats" to a human user based on statements that the human inputs. The program contains a method findKeyWord that searches an input statement for a given keyword. The findKeyWord method contains the following line of code.

```
pos = statement.indexOf(word);
```

Suppose pos has a value >= 0, that is, word was found. The programmer now wants to test that an actual word was found, not part of another word. For example, if "cat" is the keyword, the programmer needs to check that it's not part of "catch" or "category." Here is the code that tests if word is a stand-alone word. (You may assume that statement is all lowercase and contains only letters and blanks.)

```
pos = statement.indexOf(word);
//Check for first or last word
if (pos == 0 || pos + word.length() == statement.length())
{
    before = " ";
    after = " ";
}
else
{
    before = statement.substring(pos - 1, pos);
    after = statement.substring(pos + word.length(),
            pos + word.length() + 1);
    if (/* test */)
        //then a stand-alone word was found ...
    else
        //word was part of a larger word
}
```

Which replacement for /* *test* */ will give the desired result?
(A) (before < "a" || before > "z") && (after < "a" || after > "z")
(B) (before > "a" || before < "z") && (after > "a" || after < "z")
(C) (before.compareTo("a") < 0 && before.compareTo("z") > 0) || (after.compareTo("a") > 0 && after.compareTo("z") < 0)
(D) (before.compareTo("a") > 0 && before.compareTo("z") < 0) && (after.compareTo("a") > 0 && after.compareTo("z") < 0)
(E) (before.compareTo("a") < 0 || before.compareTo("z") > 0) && (after.compareTo("a") < 0 || after.compareTo("z") > 0)

5. A program that simulates a conversation between a computer and a human user generates a random response to a user's comment. All possible responses that the computer can generate are stored in an array of `String` called `allResponses`. The method given below, `getResponse`, returns a random response string from the array.

```
/** Precondition:  array allResponses is initialized with strings.
 *  Postcondition: returns a random response from allResponses.
 */
public String getResponse();
{ /* implementation */ }
```

Which is a correct /* *implementation* */?

(A) `int i = (int) (Math.random() * allResponses.length);`
    `return allResponses[i];`

(B) `return (String) (Math.random() * allResponses.length);`

(C) `int i = Math.random() * allResponses.length;`
    `return allResponses[i];`

(D) `int i = (int) (Math.random() * (allResponses.length - 1));`
    `return allResponses[i];`

(E) `return (int) (Math.random() * allResponses.length);`

Questions 6 and 7 refer to the `Deck` class described below.

A `Deck` class contains an array `cards` with an even number of `Card` values and a `final` variable `NUMCARDS`, which is an odd integer.

6. Here are two possible algorithms for shuffling the deck.

    **Algorithm 1**

    Initialize an array of `Card` called `shuffled` of length `NUMCARDS`.

    Set k to 0.

    For j=0 to NUMCARDS/2-1

    - Copy `cards[j]` to `shuffled[k]`
    - Set k to k+2

    Set k to 1.

    For j=NUMCARDS/2 to NUMCARDS-1

    - Copy `cards[j]` to `shuffled[k]`
    - Set k to k+2

    **Algorithm 2**

    Initialize an array of `Card` called `shuffled` containing `NUMCARDS` slots.

    For k=0 to NUMCARDS-1

    - Repeatedly generate a random integer j from 0 to `NUMCARDS-1`,
       until `cards[j]` contains a card not marked as empty
    - Copy `cards[j]` to `shuffled[k]`
    - Set `cards[j]` to empty

    Which is a false statement concerning Algorithms 1 and 2?

    (A) A disadvantage of Algorithm 1 is that it won't generate all possible deck permutations.

    (B) For Algorithm 2, to determine the last element shuffled requires an average of `NUMCARDS` calls to the random number generator.

    (C) Algorithm 2 will lead to more permutations of the deck than Algorithm 1.

    (D) In terms of run time, Algorithm 2 is more efficient than Algorithm 1.

    (E) If Algorithm 1 is repeated several times, it may return the deck to its original state.

7. The following `shuffle` method is used to shuffle the cards in the `Deck` class.

```
Line 1: public void shuffle()
Line 2: {
Line 3:     for (int k = NUMCARDS; k > 0; k--)
Line 4:     {
Line 5:         int randPos = (int) (Math.random() * (k + 1));
Line 6:         //swap randomly selected card with card at position k
Line 7:         Card temp = cards[k];
Line 8:         cards[k] = cards[randPos];
Line 9:         cards[randPos] = temp;
Line 10:    }
Line 11: }
```

The method does not work as intended. Which of the following changes should be made to correct the method?

(A) Replace Line 3 with

```
for (int k = NUMCARDS; k >= 0; k--)
```

(B) Replace Line 3 with

```
for (int k = NUMCARDS - 1; k > 0; k--)
```

(C) Replace Line 3 with

```
for (int k = 1; k <= NUMCARDS; k++)
```

(D) Replace Line 5 with

```
int randPos = (int) (Math.random() * k);
```

(E) Replace Lines 7 – 9 with

```
Card temp = cards[randPos];
cards[randPos] = cards[k];
cards[k] = temp;
```

Questions 8 and 9 refer to the following.

A word creation game uses letter tiles, where each tile has a letter and a point value for scoring purposes. A `Tile` class is used to represent a letter tile.

```
public class Tile
{
    private String letter;
    private int pointValue;

    //Constructors and other methods are not shown.
}
```

8. The `Tile` class contains a `toString` method that creates a `String` containing the letter and point value of a `Tile`. The string should be in the following format.

```
Letter letter (point value = pointValue)
```

For example,

```
Letter A (point value = 1)
Letter Z (point value = 10)
```

Consider the `toString` method below.

```
public String toString()
{
    return /* code */
}
```

Which /* code */ leads to correct output?

(A) `Letter + "letter " + "(point value = " + pointValue + ")";`

(B) `"Letter " + letter + ("point value = " + pointValue);`

(C) `Letter + this.letter + " (point value = " + pointValue + ")";`

(D) `"Letter " + letter + " (point value = " + (String) pointValue + ")";`

(E) `"Letter " + letter + " (point value = " + pointValue + ")";`

9. Any two tiles in the word game that have the same letter also have the same point value, but the opposite is not necessarily true. For example, all the vowels have a point value of 1. Two tiles are said to match if they have the same letter. Consider the following `matches` method for the `Tile` class.

```
/** Returns true if the letter on this tile equals the letter
 *  on otherTile. */
public boolean matches(Tile otherTile)
{ return /* code */; }
```

Which replacements for /* *code* */ return the desired result? Note: You may not assume that the `Tile` class has its own `equals` method.

```
I letter == otherTile.letter

II this.equals(otherTile)

III letter.equals(otherTile.letter)
```

(A) I only

(B) II only

(C) III only

(D) II and III only

(E) I and III only

10. Consider the following method.

```
public static void alterArray(int[] arr)
{
    int mid = arr.length/2;
    for (int i = 0; i < mid; i++)
    {
        int temp = arr[i];
        arr[i] = arr[arr.length - i - 1];
        arr[arr.length - i - 1] = temp;
    }
}
```

If the current state of a matrix mat is

```
2 7 9 5
8 1 4 3
6 5 0 9
```

which matrix will result from the method call alterArray(mat[2])?

(A) 2 7 9 5
    3 4 1 8
    6 5 0 9

(B) 2 7 0 5
    8 1 4 3
    6 5 9 9

(C) 5 9 7 2
    3 4 1 8
    9 0 5 6

(D) 2 7 9 5
    8 1 4 3
    9 0 5 6

(E) 5 9 7 2
    8 1 4 3
    6 5 0 9

11. Consider a program to manipulate digital images. The inheritance hierarchy is as follows.

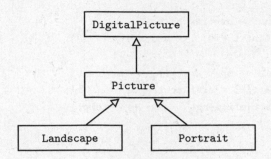

You may assume that `DigitalPicture` and `Picture` have default (no-argument) constructors, but that `Landscape` and `Portrait` do not have any constructors. Which of the following declarations will compile?

I `DigitalPicture p = new Portrait();`

II `Landscape p = new Picture();`

III `DigitalPicture p = new DigitalPicture();`

(A) I only
(B) II only
(C) III only
(D) I and II only
(E) I and III only

12. A `Pixel` class has several mutator methods that allow the color of a `Pixel` to be changed. For example,

```
/* Sets amount of red in Pixel to value. */
public void setRed(int value)
{ /* implementation not shown */ }
```

Consider a `Picture` class that has a private instance variable `pixels`, which is a 2D array of `Pixel` objects. There are also `int` variables `rows` and `cols` that contain the number of rows and columns in the `pixels` array.

A method `removeRed` in the `Picture` class sets the red value of every pixel to zero.

```
public void removeRed()
{
    for (int row = 0; row < numRows; row++)
        for (int col = 0; col < numCols; col++)
        {
            /* code to set red value to 0 */
        }
}
```

Which is a correct replacement for /* *code to set red value to 0* */?

   I  `Pixel p = pixels[row][col];`
      `p.setRed(0);`

  II  `pixels[row][col].setRed(0);`

 III  `pixels[row][col] = 0;`

(A) I only
(B) II only
(C) III only
(D) I and II only
(E) I, II, and III

13. Consider a class `MatrixStuff` that has a private instance variable `mat`.

```
private int[][] mat;
```

The following method uses a vertical mirror down the center of a matrix to reflect the left half of the matrix onto the right. The following two examples show the result of mirroring a two-dimensional array of numbers from left to right vertically. (Another way of saying this is that the right half of the matrix is replaced by a vertical mirror image of the left half.)

**Example 1:**

| | mat | | | | | | mat after mirroring | | |
|---|---|---|---|---|---|---|---|---|---|
| 1 | 2 | 3 | 4 | 5 | 1 | 2 | 3 | 2 | 1 |
| 6 | 7 | 8 | 9 | 10 | 6 | 7 | 8 | 7 | 6 |
| 11 | 12 | 13 | 14 | 15 | 11 | 12 | 13 | 12 | 11 |

**Example 2:**

| | mat | | | | mat after mirroring | | |
|---|---|---|---|---|---|---|---|
| 1 | 2 | 3 | 4 | 1 | 2 | 2 | 1 |
| 5 | 6 | 7 | 8 | 5 | 6 | 6 | 5 |
| 9 | 10 | 11 | 12 | 9 | 10 | 10 | 9 |

```
public static void mirrorVerticalLeftToRight(int[][] mat)
{
    int width = mat[0].length;
    int numRows = mat.length;
    for (int row = 0; row < numRows; row++)
        for (int col = 0; col < width/2; col++)
            /* element assignments */
}
```

Which replacement for /* *element assignments* */ will make the method work as intended?

(A) `mat[row][col] = mat[row][width - col];`

(B) `mat[row][width - col] = mat[row][col];`

(C) `mat[row][width - 1 - col] = mat[row][col];`

(D) `mat[row][col] = mat[row][width - 1 - col];`

(E) `mat[row][width - 1 - col] = mat[col][row];`

14. Consider a square matrix in a class that has a private instance variable `mat`.

```
private int[][] mat;
```

Method `alter` in the class changes `mat`.

```
public void alter()
{
    for (int row = 1; row < mat.length; row++)
        for (int col = 0; col < row; col++)
            mat[col][row] = mat[row][col];
}
```

If `mat` has current value

```
{{1, 2, 3},
 {4, 5, 6},
 {7, 8, 9}}
```

what are the contents of `mat` after method `alter` has been executed?

(A)  {{1, 4, 7},
     {4, 5, 8},
     {7, 8, 9}}

(B)  {{1, 4, 7},
     {2, 5, 8},
     {3, 6, 9}}

(C)  {{1, 2, 3},
     {2, 5, 6},
     {3, 6, 9}}

(D)  {{9, 6, 3},
     {8, 5, 6},
     {7, 8, 9}}

(E)  {{1, 2, 3},
     {4, 5, 2},
     {7, 4, 1}}

## ANSWER KEY

| | | |
|---|---|---|
| 1. **C** | 6. **D** | 11. **E** |
| 2. **A** | 7. **B** | 12. **D** |
| 3. **B** | 8. **E** | 13. **C** |
| 4. **E** | 9. **C** | 14. **A** |
| 5. **A** | 10. **D** | |

## ANSWERS EXPLAINED

1. **(C)** Segment III works because if you enter an age of 90, say, `category` will correctly be assigned "Senior", and none of the other `else` pieces of code will be executed. Similarly, if you enter an age corresponding to an adult or a child, only the correct assignment is made. Segment I fails because if you enter an age of 90, `category` will be assigned "Senior", but then will be changed to "Adult" when the age passes the second test. Segment II uses incorrect syntax. The segment will work if you change the second test to

   ```
   if (age >= 18 && age <= 64)
   ```

2. **(A)** The algorithm prints the current index of "o" in the string, and then creates a new substring containing all remaining characters following that "o". Here is the series of substrings and the corresponding output for each (the symbol ␣ denotes a blank character):

   | | |
   |---|---|
   | How␣do␣you␣do? | 1 |
   | w␣do␣you␣do? | 3 |
   | ␣you␣do? | 2 |
   | u␣do? | 3 |

3. **(B)** Here is a description of the algorithm:

   Make a copy of `phrase` in `newPhrase`.
   Find the first occurrence of `ch` in `newPhrase` (`pos` is the index).
   If you found it, concatenate to `str` the characters in `newPhrase` from 0 to `pos-1`.
   Change `newPhrase` to contain all characters from `ch` to the end, excluding `ch`.
   Repeat the process until there are no more occurrences of `ch` in `newPhrase`.

   So Line 12 is wrong because `newPhrase.substring(0,pos-1)` will not include the character at `pos-1`, which means that the string returned will lose a character that is *not* equal to `ch`.

4. **(E)** The program has found a stand-alone word if the characters `before` and `after` are both blank. Choice E tests that they are not letters between "a" and "z", i.e., they must be blank. Choices A and B fail because you must use `compareTo` for inequality tests on strings. Choices C and D allow at least one of `before` and `after` to be a letter, which would mean that `word` was not a stand-alone word.

5. **(A)** The first line in choice A returns a random integer that lies between 0 and `allResponses.length-1`. This range corresponds to the range of the array indexes and so it is correct. Choice B is garbage—you cannot cast a real number to a string. Choice C fails because `Math.random()` is type `double` and you require an `int`; you must do the cast to `int` shown in choice A. Choice D fails because the element `allResponses[allResponses.length-1]` will never be returned: i will contain a random `int` from 0 to `allResponses.length-2`. Choice E returns an `int`, not a `String`.

6. **(D)** The big defect of Algorithm 2 is that it eventually slows down. This is because every time it selects an empty element, it has to loop again. Each of the other choices is true. In choice A, for example, the element `cards[0]` always moves to `shuffled[0]`, eliminating all permutations that have `cards[0]` in a different slot. For choice B, by the time you get to assign the last element, all but two slots of the `cards` array are marked empty. So, on average, you will need to go through `NUMCARDS` tries to find one of those two nonempty slots. For choice C, even though Algorithm 2 is slow, in theory every element in `cards` could land in any given slot in `shuffled`. This is not true for Algorithm 1, where the first element never budges out of the first slot. For choice E, because of the precise ordering of elements in Algorithm 1, the array will always eventually return to its original state, assuming there are sufficient iterations.

7. **(B)** If k starts with the value `NUMCARDS`, the method encounters `cards[NUMCARDS]` on Line 7 and throws an `ArrayIndexOutOfBoundsException`.

8. **(E)** The actual letter and its point value must not be in quotes because their *values* must be printed. Everything else, including the parentheses, must be in quotes. (All text in quotes is printed literally, as is.) Choices A and C fail because they don't place the opening word, `Letter`, in quotes. Choice B doesn't have the parentheses in quotes. Choice D incorrectly tries to cast an `int` to a `String`.

9. **(C)** Segment I will only be true if an object and its parameter are the same reference, which is not necessarily true for two matching tiles. Segment II fails similarly if the `Tile` class doesn't have its own `equals` method. (The inherited method from `Object` compares references.)

10. **(D)** The matrix `mat` consists of an array of rows, `mat[0]`, `mat[1]`, `mat[2]`, each of which is an array. The method `alterArray` swaps the first and last element of an array, then the second and second-last elements, and so on, until it reaches the middle of the array. The method call `alterArray(mat[2])` performs this series of swaps on row 2 of the matrix, the bottom row, resulting in the matrix in choice D.

11. **(E)** Declaration I works because a `Portrait` *is-a* `DigitalPicture`, and it will be assigned the default constructor from `Picture`, its superclass. Declaration II fails because a `Picture` is *not* a `Landscape`. Declaration III works because `DigitalPicture` *is-a* `DigitalPicture`.

12. **(D)** Segment I works because p is a reference to the element `pixels[row][col]`. Changing p with a mutator method will change the array. Segment II changes the two-dimensional array directly. Segment III fails because `pixels` is not an array of integers.

13. **(C)** Look at Example 2 for this question:

|  | mat |  |  |  |  | mat after mirroring |  |  |
|---|---|---|---|---|---|---|---|---|
| 1 | 2 | 3 | 4 |  | 1 | 2 | 2 | 1 |
| 5 | 6 | 7 | 8 |  | 5 | 6 | 6 | 5 |
| 9 | 10 | 11 | 12 |  | 9 | 10 | 10 | 9 |

Now consider one element, 12 say. It must be replaced by its vertical mirror image 9, i.e., `mat[2][3]=mat[2][0]`. The value of `width` is 4. See which expression in the answer choices correctly makes this assignment. Eliminate choices A and D right away because `col` can only have the values 0 and 1 in this algorithm, so `mat[2][3]` will not be assigned. In choice B, when `col` has value 1, `mat[2][3]=mat[2][1]`, an incorrect assignment. Choice C works: when `row` is 2 and `col` is 0, `mat[2][3]=mat[2][0]`. In choice E, when `row` is 2 and `col` is 0, the assignment `mat[2][3]=mat[0][2]` is incorrect.

14. **(A)** Method `alter` places a mirror along the major diagonal and reflects the elements from left to right across this diagonal.

In this algorithm, when `row` is 1, `col` can only be 0, and when `row` is 2, `col` takes on the values 0 and 1. Thus, only three elements are altered: `mat[0][1]`, `mat[0][2]`, and `mat[1][2]`. (Note that the method assigns values to `mat[col][row]`.) These elements are all to the right of the diagonal. Choice A is the only choice that leaves elements to the left of the diagonal unchanged.

# Practice Tests

# ANSWER SHEET
## Practice Test 1

**Section I**

1. Ⓐ Ⓑ Ⓒ Ⓓ Ⓔ
2. Ⓐ Ⓑ Ⓒ Ⓓ Ⓔ
3. Ⓐ Ⓑ Ⓒ Ⓓ Ⓔ
4. Ⓐ Ⓑ Ⓒ Ⓓ Ⓔ
5. Ⓐ Ⓑ Ⓒ Ⓓ Ⓔ
6. Ⓐ Ⓑ Ⓒ Ⓓ Ⓔ
7. Ⓐ Ⓑ Ⓒ Ⓓ Ⓔ
8. Ⓐ Ⓑ Ⓒ Ⓓ Ⓔ
9. Ⓐ Ⓑ Ⓒ Ⓓ Ⓔ
10. Ⓐ Ⓑ Ⓒ Ⓓ Ⓔ
11. Ⓐ Ⓑ Ⓒ Ⓓ Ⓔ
12. Ⓐ Ⓑ Ⓒ Ⓓ Ⓔ
13. Ⓐ Ⓑ Ⓒ Ⓓ Ⓔ
14. Ⓐ Ⓑ Ⓒ Ⓓ Ⓔ

15. Ⓐ Ⓑ Ⓒ Ⓓ Ⓔ
16. Ⓐ Ⓑ Ⓒ Ⓓ Ⓔ
17. Ⓐ Ⓑ Ⓒ Ⓓ Ⓔ
18. Ⓐ Ⓑ Ⓒ Ⓓ Ⓔ
19. Ⓐ Ⓑ Ⓒ Ⓓ Ⓔ
20. Ⓐ Ⓑ Ⓒ Ⓓ Ⓔ
21. Ⓐ Ⓑ Ⓒ Ⓓ Ⓔ
22. Ⓐ Ⓑ Ⓒ Ⓓ Ⓔ
23. Ⓐ Ⓑ Ⓒ Ⓓ Ⓔ
24. Ⓐ Ⓑ Ⓒ Ⓓ Ⓔ
25. Ⓐ Ⓑ Ⓒ Ⓓ Ⓔ
26. Ⓐ Ⓑ Ⓒ Ⓓ Ⓔ
27. Ⓐ Ⓑ Ⓒ Ⓓ Ⓔ
28. Ⓐ Ⓑ Ⓒ Ⓓ Ⓔ

29. Ⓐ Ⓑ Ⓒ Ⓓ Ⓔ
30. Ⓐ Ⓑ Ⓒ Ⓓ Ⓔ
31. Ⓐ Ⓑ Ⓒ Ⓓ Ⓔ
32. Ⓐ Ⓑ Ⓒ Ⓓ Ⓔ
33. Ⓐ Ⓑ Ⓒ Ⓓ Ⓔ
34. Ⓐ Ⓑ Ⓒ Ⓓ Ⓔ
35. Ⓐ Ⓑ Ⓒ Ⓓ Ⓔ
36. Ⓐ Ⓑ Ⓒ Ⓓ Ⓔ
37. Ⓐ Ⓑ Ⓒ Ⓓ Ⓔ
38. Ⓐ Ⓑ Ⓒ Ⓓ Ⓔ
39. Ⓐ Ⓑ Ⓒ Ⓓ Ⓔ
40. Ⓐ Ⓑ Ⓒ Ⓓ Ⓔ

# How to Calculate Your (Approximate) AP Computer Science A Score

**Multiple Choice**

Number correct (out of 40)   =   _____   ⟸   Multiple-Choice Score

**Free Response**

Question 1   _____
(out of 9)

Question 2   _____
(out of 9)

Question 3   _____
(out of 9)

Question 4   _____
(out of 9)

Total   _____   ×   1.11   =   _____   ⟸   Free-Response Score
(Do not round.)

**Final Score**

_____   +   _____   =   _____
Multiple-          Free-               Final Score
Choice            Response          (Round to nearest
Score              Score              whole number.)

### Chart to Convert to AP Grade
### Computer Science A

| Final Score Range | AP Grade[a] |
| --- | --- |
| 62–80 | 5 |
| 47–61 | 4 |
| 37–46 | 3 |
| 29–36 | 2 |
| 0–28 | 1 |

[a]The score range corresponding to each grade varies from exam to exam and is approximate.

# Practice Test 1
## COMPUTER SCIENCE A
## SECTION I

Time—1 hour and 30 minutes
Number of questions—40
Percent of total grade—50

---

**DIRECTIONS:** Determine the answer to each of the following questions or incomplete statements, using the available space for any necessary scratchwork. Then decide which is the best of the choices given and fill in the corresponding oval on the answer sheet. Do not spend too much time on any one problem.

**NOTES:**
- Assume that the classes in the Quick Reference have been imported where needed.
- Assume that variables and methods are declared within the context of an enclosing class.
- Assume that method calls that have no object or class name prefixed, and that are not shown within a complete class definition, appear within the context of an enclosing class.
- Assume that parameters in method calls are not `null` unless otherwise stated.

---

1. A large Java program was tested extensively, and no errors were found. What can be concluded?
   - (A) All of the preconditions in the program are correct.
   - (B) All of the postconditions in the program are correct.
   - (C) The program may have bugs.
   - (D) The program has no bugs.
   - (E) Every method in the program may safely be used in other programs.

**GO ON TO THE NEXT PAGE.**

Questions 2–4 refer to the Worker class below.

```java
public class Worker
{
    private String name;
    private double hourlyWage;
    private boolean isUnionMember;

    public Worker()
    { /* implementation not shown */ }

    public Worker(String aName, double anHourlyWage, boolean union)
    { /* implementation not shown */ }

    //Accessors getName, getHourlyWage, getUnionStatus are not shown.

    /** Permanently increase hourly wage by amt.
     * @param amt the amount of wage increase
     */
    public void incrementWage(double amt)
    { /* implementation of incrementWage */ }

    /** Switch value of isUnionMember from true to false and
     * vice versa.
     */
    public void changeUnionStatus()
    { /* implementation of changeUnionStatus */ }
}
```

2. Refer to the incrementWage method. Which of the following is a correct
   /* implementation of incrementWage */?
   (A) return hourlyWage + amt;
   (B) return getHourlyWage() + amt;
   (C) hourlyWage += amt;
   (D) getHourlyWage() += amt;
   (E) hourlyWage = amt;

**GO ON TO THE NEXT PAGE.**

3. Consider the method `changeUnionStatus`. Which is a correct
   /* *implementation of* `changeUnionStatus` */?

```
     I if (isUnionMember)
            isUnionMember = false;
        else
            isUnionMember = true;

    II isUnionMember = !isUnionMember;

   III if (isUnionMember)
            isUnionMember = !isUnionMember;
```

   (A) I only
   (B) II only
   (C) III only
   (D) I and II only
   (E) I, II, and III

4. A client method `computePay` will return a worker's pay based on the number of hours worked.

```
    /** Precondition:  Worker w has worked the given number of hours.
     *  @param w a Worker
     *  @param hours the number of hours worked
     *  @return amount of pay for Worker w
     */
    public static double computePay(Worker w, double hours)
    { /* code */ }
```

   Which replacement for /* *code* */ is correct?
   (A) `return hourlyWage * hours;`
   (B) `return getHourlyWage() * hours;`
   (C) `return w.getHourlyWage() * hours;`
   (D) `return w.hourlyWage * hours;`
   (E) `return w.getHourlyWage() * w.hours;`

5. Consider this program segment. You may assume that `wordList` has been declared as `ArrayList<String>`.

```
    for (String s : wordList)
        if (s.length() < 4)
            System.out.println("SHORT WORD");
```

   What is the maximum number of times that SHORT WORD can be printed?
   (A) 3
   (B) 4
   (C) `s.length()`
   (D) `wordList.size() - 1`
   (E) `wordList.size()`

**GO ON TO THE NEXT PAGE.**

6. Refer to the following method.

```
public static int mystery(int n)
{
    if (n == 1)
        return 3;
    else
        return 3 * mystery(n - 1);
}
```

What value does `mystery(4)` return?

(A) 3

(B) 9

(C) 12

(D) 27

(E) 81

7. Refer to the following declarations.

```
String[] colors = {"red", "green", "black"};
ArrayList<String> colorList = new ArrayList<String>();
```

Which of the following correctly assigns the elements of the `colors` array to `colorList`? The final ordering of colors in `colorList` should be the same as in the `colors` array.

```
 I for (String col : colors)
        colorList.add(col);
```

```
 II for (String col : colorList)
        colors.add(col);
```

```
III for (int i = colors.length - 1; i >= 0; i--)
        colorList.add(i, colors[i]);
```

(A) I only

(B) II only

(C) III only

(D) II and III only

(E) I, II, and III

**GO ON TO THE NEXT PAGE.**

8. Often the most efficient computer algorithms use a divide-and-conquer approach, for example, one in which a list is repeatedly split into two pieces until a desired outcome is reached. Which of the following use a divide-and-conquer approach?

    I  Merge sort
   II  Insertion sort
  III  Binary search

(A) I only
(B) II only
(C) III only
(D) I and III only
(E) I, II, and III

9. An `Insect` class is to be written, containing the following data fields.

`age`, which will be initialized to 0 when an `Insect` is constructed.

`nextAvailableID`, which will be initialized to 0 outside the constructor and incremented each time an `Insect` is constructed.

`idNum`, which will be initialized to the current value of `nextAvailableID` when an `Insect` is constructed.

`position`, which will be initialized to the location in a garden where the `Insect` is placed when it is constructed.

`direction`, which will be initialized to the direction the `Insect` is facing when placed in the garden.

    Which variable in the `Insect` class should be static?

(A) `age`
(B) `nextAvailableID`
(C) `idNum`
(D) `position`
(E) `direction`

**GO ON TO THE NEXT PAGE.**

Questions 10 and 11 refer to the classes `Address` and `Customer` given below.

```
public class Address
{
    private String street;
    private String city;
    private String state;
    private int zipCode;

    public Address(String aStreet, String aCity, String aState,
            int aZipCode)
    { /* implementation not shown */ }

    //Other methods are not shown.
}

public class Customer
{
    private String name;
    private String phone;
    private Address address;
    private int ID;

    public Customer(String aName, String aPhone, Address anAddr,
            int anID)
    { /* implementation not shown */ }

    public Address getAddress()
    { /* implementation not shown */ }

    public String getName()
    { /* implementation not shown */ }

    public String getPhone()
    { /* implementation not shown */ }

    public int getID()
    { /* implementation not shown */ }

    //Other methods are not shown.
}
```

**GO ON TO THE NEXT PAGE.**

10. Which of the following correctly creates a `Customer` object `c`?

```
  I Address a = new Address("125 Bismark St", "Pleasantville",
        "NY", 14850);
    Customer c = new Customer("Jack Spratt", "747-1674", a, 7008);

 II Customer c = new Customer("Jack Spratt", "747-1674",
        "125 Bismark St, Pleasantville, NY 14850", 7008);

III Customer c = new Customer("Jack Spratt", "747-1674",
        new Address("125 Bismark St", "Pleasantville", "NY", 14850),
        7008);
```

(A) I only
(B) II only
(C) III only
(D) I and II only
(E) I and III only

11. Consider an `AllCustomers` class that has the following private instance variable.

```
private Customer[] custList;
```

Given the ID number of a particular customer, a method of the class, `locate`, must find the correct `Customer` record and return the name of that customer. Here is the method `locate`:

```
/** Returns the name of the customer with the specified idNum.
 * Precondition: custList contains a complete list of Customer objects.
 */
public String locate(int idNum)
{
    for (Customer c : custList)
        if (c.getID() == idNum)
            return c.getName();
    return null;     //idNum not found
}
```

A more efficient algorithm for finding the matching `Customer` object could be used if
(A) `Customer` objects were in alphabetical order by name.
(B) `Customer` objects were sorted by phone number.
(C) `Customer` objects were sorted by ID number.
(D) the `custList` array had fewer elements.
(E) the `Customer` class did not have an `Address` data member.

**GO ON TO THE NEXT PAGE.**

12. The following shuffling method is used to shuffle an array arr of int values. The method assumes the existence of a swap method, where swap(arr,i,j) interchanges the elements arr[i] and arr[j].

```java
public static void shuffle (int[] arr)
{
    for (int k = arr.length - 1; k > 0; k--)
    {
        int randIndex = (int) (Math.random() * (k + 1));
        swap(arr, k, randIndex);
    }
}
```

Suppose the initial state of arr is 1 2 3 4 5, and when the method is executed the values generated for randIndex are 3, 2, 0, and 1, in that order. What will be the final state of arr?

(A) 5 2 1 3 4
(B) 1 2 5 3 4
(C) 5 4 1 3 2
(D) 4 5 1 3 2
(E) 2 5 1 3 4

**GO ON TO THE NEXT PAGE.**

13. Refer to method removeWord.

```
/** Removes all occurrences of word from wordList.
/** Precondition: wordList is an ArrayList of String objects.
 * Postcondition: All occurrences of word have been removed
 *                from wordList.
 */
public static void removeWord(ArrayList<String> wordList,
                                              String word)
{
    for (int i = 0; i < wordList.size(); i++)
        if ((wordList.get(i)).equals(word))
            wordList.remove(i);
}
```

The method does not always work as intended. Consider the method call

```
removeWord(wordList, "cat");
```

For which of the following lists will this method call fail?

(A) The cat sat on the mat
(B) The cat cat sat on the mat mat
(C) The cat sat on the cat
(D) cat
(E) The cow sat on the mat

14. A Clock class has hours, minutes, and seconds represented by int values. It also has each of the following methods: setTime to change the time on a Clock to the hour, minute, and second specified; getTime to access the time; and toString to return the time as a String. The Clock class has a constructor that allows a Clock to be created with three int parameters for hours, minutes, and seconds. Consider a two-dimensional array of Clock values called allClocks. A code segment manipulating allClocks is as follows.

```
for (Clock[] row : allClocks)
    for (Clock c : row)
        /* more code */
```

Assuming the Clock class works as specified, which replacement for /* more code */ will cause an error?

```
  I System.out.print(c);

 II c.setTime(0, 0, 0);

III c = new Clock(0, 0, 0);
```

(A) I only
(B) II only
(C) III only
(D) II and III only
(E) I and II only

**GO ON TO THE NEXT PAGE.**

15. Consider the following method that will access a square matrix mat.

```java
/** Precondition: mat is initialized and is a square matrix.
 */
public static void printSomething(int[][] mat)
{
    for (int r = 0; r < mat.length; r++)
    {
        for (int c=0; c<=r; c++)
            System.out.print(mat[r][c] + " ");
        System.out.println();
    }
}
```

Suppose mat is originally

```
0 1 2 3
4 5 6 7
3 2 1 0
7 6 5 4
```

After the method call printSomething(mat) the output will be

(A)  0 1 2 3
    4 5 6 7
    3 2 1 0
    7 6 5 4

(B)  0
    4 5
    3 2 1
    7 6 5 4

(C)  0 1 2 3
    4 5 6
    3 2
    7

(D)  0
    4
    3
    7

(E)  There will be no output. An ArrayIndexOutOfBoundsException will be thrown.

**GO ON TO THE NEXT PAGE.**

16. Consider two different ways of storing a set of nonnegative integers in which there are no duplicates.

Method One: Store the integers explicitly in an array in which the number of elements is known. For example, in this method, the set {6, 2, 1, 8, 9, 0} can be represented as follows.

| 0 | 1 | 2 | 3 | 4 | 5 |
|---|---|---|---|---|---|
| 6 | 2 | 1 | 8 | 9 | 0 |

6 elements

Method Two: Suppose that the range of the integers is 0 to MAX. Use a boolean array indexed from 0 to MAX. The index values represent the possible values in the set. In other words, each possible integer from 0 to MAX is represented by a different position in the array. A value of true in the array means that the corresponding integer is in the set, a value of false means that the integer is not in the set. For example, using this method for the same set above, {6, 2, 1, 8, 9, 0}, the representation would be as follows (T = true, F = false).

| 0 | 1 | 2 | 3 | 4 | 5 | 6 | 7 | 8 | 9 | 10 | ... | MAX |
|---|---|---|---|---|---|---|---|---|---|----|-----|-----|
| T | T | T | F | F | F | T | F | T | T | F | ... | F |

The following operations are to be performed on the set of integers.

   I  Search for a target value in the set.
   II  Print all the elements of the set.
   III  Return the number of elements in the set.

Which statement is true?
(A) Operation I is more efficient if the set is stored using Method One.
(B) Operation II is more efficient if the set is stored using Method Two.
(C) Operation III is more efficient if the set is stored using Method One.
(D) Operation I is equally efficient for Methods One and Two.
(E) Operation III is equally efficient for Methods One and Two.

17. An algorithm for finding the average of $N$ numbers is

$$\text{average} = \frac{\text{sum}}{N}$$

where $N$ and sum are both integers. In a program using this algorithm, a programmer forgot to include a test that would check for $N$ equal to zero. If $N$ is zero, when will the error be detected?
(A) At compile time
(B) At edit time
(C) As soon as the value of $N$ is entered
(D) During run time
(E) When an incorrect result is output

**GO ON TO THE NEXT PAGE.**

18. Consider an array arr of 64 distinct int values, which are sorted in increasing order. The first element of the array, arr[0], equals 5, and the last element, arr[63], equals 200. A binary search algorithm will be used to locate various key values. Which of the following is a true statement?

    I   If 5 is the key, it will take exactly 7 iterations of the search loop to locate it.

    II  If 2 is the key, it will take exactly 7 iterations of the search loop to determine that 2 is not in arr.

    III If 100 is the key, and 100 is equal to arr[62], it will take fewer than 7 iterations of the search loop to locate the key.

    (A)  I only
    (B)  II only
    (C)  III only
    (D)  I and II only
    (E)  II and III only

19. Consider method getCount below.

```java
public static int getCount(String s, String sub)
{
    int count = 0;
    int pos = s.indexOf(sub);
    while (pos >= 0)
    {
        s = s.substring(pos);
        count++;
        pos = s.indexOf(sub);
    }
    return count;
}
```

What will the method call getCount("a carrot and car", "car") return?
    (A)  0
    (B)  1
    (C)  2
    (D)  3
    (E)  No value returned. The method is in an infinite loop.

**GO ON TO THE NEXT PAGE.**

20. Consider a program that deals with various components of different vehicles. Which of the following is a reasonable representation of the relationships among some classes that may comprise the program? Note that an open up-arrow denotes an inheritance relationship and a down-arrow denotes a composition relationship.

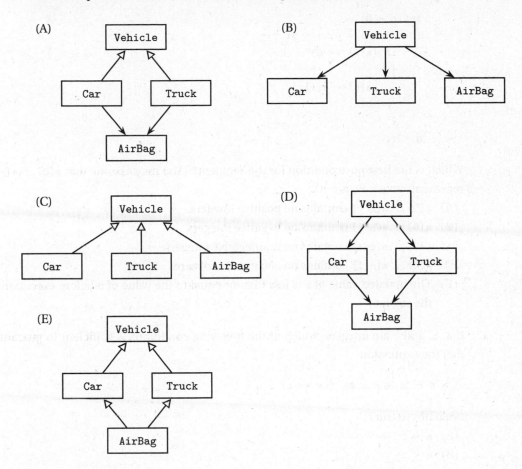

**GO ON TO THE NEXT PAGE.**

21. Consider the following program segment.

```
/** Precondition: a[0]...a[n-1] is an initialized array of integers,
 *                and 0 < n <= a.length.
 */
    int c = 0;
    for (int i = 0; i < n; i++)
        if (a[i] >= 0)
        {
            a[c] = a[i];
            c++;
        }
    n = c;
```

Which is the best postcondition for the segment? (You may assume that a[0]...a[-1] represents an empty array.)

(A) a[0]...a[n-1] contains no positive integers.

(B) a[0]...a[n-1] contains no negative integers.

(C) a[0]...a[n-1] contains no nonnegative integers.

(D) a[0]...a[n-1] contains no occurrences of zero.

(E) The updated value of n is less than or equal to the value of n before execution of the segment.

22. If a, b, and c are integers, which of the following conditions is sufficient to guarantee that the expression

```
a < c || a < b && !(a == c)
```

evaluates to true?

(A) a < c

(B) a < b

(C) a > b

(D) a == b

(E) a == c

23. Airmail Express charges for shipping small packages by integer values of weight. The charges for a weight $w$ in pounds are as follows.

$$0 < w \le 2 \qquad \$4.00$$
$$2 < w \le 5 \qquad \$8.00$$
$$5 < w \le 20 \qquad \$15.00$$

The company does not accept packages that weigh more than 20 pounds. Which of the following represents the best set of data (weights) to test a program that calculates shipping charges?

(A) 0, 2, 5, 20

(B) 1, 4, 16

(C) −1, 1, 2, 3, 5, 16, 20

(D) −1, 0, 1, 2, 3, 5, 16, 20, 22

(E) All integers from −1 through 22

**GO ON TO THE NEXT PAGE.**

24. Consider the following instance variable and methods in the same class.

```java
private int[][] matrix;

/** Precondition: array.length > 0.
  * @return the largest integer in array
  */
private int max(int[] array)
{  /* implementation not shown */  }

/** @return num1 if num1 >= num2; otherwise return num2
  */
public int max(int num1, int num2)
{  /* implementation not shown */  }
```

Suppose `matrix` has a current value of

```
2 1 4 8
6 0 3 9
5 7 7 6
1 2 3 4
```

What will be returned by the following method call in the same class?

```java
max(max(matrix[2]), max(matrix[3]))
```

(A) 9

(B) 8

(C) 7

(D) 4

(E) Compile-time error. No value returned.

**GO ON TO THE NEXT PAGE.**

Questions 25–26 are based on the following class declaration.

```
public class AutoPart
{
    private String description;
    private int partNum;
    private double price;

    public AutoPart(String desc, int pNum, double aPrice)
    { /* implementation not shown */ }

    public String getDescription()
    { return description; }

    public int getPartNum()
    { return partNum; }

    public double getPrice()
    { return price; }

    //Other methods are not shown.
    //There is no compareTo method.
}
```

**GO ON TO THE NEXT PAGE.**

25. This question refers to the `findCheapest` method below, which occurs in a class that has an array of `AutoPart` as one of its private data fields.

```
private AutoPart[] allParts;
```

The `findCheapest` method examines an array of `AutoPart` and returns the part number of the `AutoPart` with the lowest price whose description matches the `partDescription` parameter. For example, several of the `AutoPart` elements may have `"headlight"` as their description field. Different headlights will differ in both price and part number. If the `partDescription` parameter is `"headlight"`, then `findCheapest` will return the part number of the cheapest headlight.

```
/** Returns the part number of the cheapest AutoPart
 *  whose description matches partDescription.
 *  Precondition: allParts contains at least one element whose
 *                description matches partDescription.
 */
public int findCheapest(String partDescription)
{
    AutoPart part = null;       //AutoPart with lowest price so far
    double min = LARGE_VALUE;   //larger than any valid price
    for (AutoPart p : allParts)
    {
        /* more code */
    }
    return part.getPartNum();
}
```

Which of the following replacements for /* *more code* */ will find the correct part number?

```
I  if (p.getPrice() < min)
   {
       min = p.getPrice();
       part = p;
   }

II if (p.getDescription().equals(partDescription))
       if (p.getPrice() < min)
       {
           min = p.getPrice();
           part = p;
       }

III if (p.getDescription().equals(partDescription))
        if (p.getPrice() < min)
            return p.getPartNum();
```

(A) I only
(B) II only
(C) III only
(D) I and II only
(E) I and III only

**GO ON TO THE NEXT PAGE.**

26. Consider the following method.

```
/** Returns the smaller of st1 and st2.
 * Precondition:  st1 and st2 are distinct String objects.
 */
public static String min(String st1, String st2)
{
    if (st1.compareTo(st2) < 0)
        return st1;
    else
        return st2;
}
```

A method in the same class has these declarations.

```
AutoPart p1 = new AutoPart(< suitable values >);
AutoPart p2 = new AutoPart(< suitable values >);
```

Which of the following statements will cause an error?

I   `System.out.println(min(p1.getDescription(), p2.getDescription()));`

II  `System.out.println(min(p1.toString().getDescription(),`
    `p2.toString().getDescription()));`

III `System.out.println(min(p1, p2));`

(A) I only
(B) II only
(C) III only
(D) I and II only
(E) II and III only

27. This question is based on the following declarations.

```
String strA = "CARROT", strB = "Carrot", strC = "car";
```

Given that all uppercase letters precede all lowercase letters when considering alphabetical order, which is true?

(A) `strA.compareTo(strB) < 0 && strB.compareTo(strC) > 0`
(B) `strC.compareTo(strB) < 0 && strB.compareTo(strA) < 0`
(C) `strB.compareTo(strC) < 0 && strB.compareTo(strA) > 0`
(D) `!(strA.compareTo(strB) == 0) && strB.compareTo(strA) < 0`
(E) `!(strA.compareTo(strB) == 0) && strC.compareTo(strB) < 0`

**GO ON TO THE NEXT PAGE.**

28. A programmer has a file of names. She is designing a program that sends junk mail letters to everyone on the list. To make the letters sound personal and friendly, she will extract each person's first name from the name string. She plans to create a parallel file of first names only. For example,

| fullName | firstName |
| --- | --- |
| Ms.  Anjali DeSouza | Anjali |
| Dr.  John Roufaiel | John |
| Mrs.  Mathilda Concia | Mathilda |

Here is a method intended to extract the first name from a full name string.

```
/** Precondition:
 *   - fullName starts with a title followed by a period.
 *   - A single space separates the title, first name, and last name.
 *   @param fullName a string containing a title, period, blank,
 *   and last name
 *   @return the first name only in fullName
 */
public static String getFirstName(String fullName)
{
    final String BLANK = " ";
    String temp, firstName;

    /* code to extract first name */

    return firstName;
}
```

Which represents correct /* *code to extract first name* */?

```
 I  int k = fullName.indexOf(BLANK);
    temp = fullName.substring(k + 1);
    k = temp.indexOf(BLANK);
    firstName = temp.substring(0, k);

II  int k = fullName.indexOf(BLANK);
    firstName = fullName.substring(k + 1);
    k = firstName.indexOf(BLANK);
    firstName = firstName.substring(0, k);

III int firstBlank = fullName.indexOf(BLANK);
    int secondBlank = fullName.indexOf(BLANK);
    firstName = fullName.substring(firstBlank + 1, secondBlank + 1);
```

(A) I only
(B) II only
(C) III only
(D) I and II only
(E) I, II, and III

**GO ON TO THE NEXT PAGE.**

Questions 29–31 refer to the `ThreeDigitInteger` and `ThreeDigitCode` classes below.

```
public class ThreeDigitInteger
{
    private int hundredsDigit;
    private int tensDigit;
    private int onesDigit;
    private int value;

    public ThreeDigitInteger(int aValue)
    { /* implementation not shown */ }

    /** Returns the sum of digits for this ThreeDigitInteger. */
    public int digitSum()
    { /* implementation not shown */ }

    /** Returns the sum of the hundreds digit and tens digit. */
    public int twoDigitSum()
    { /* implementation not shown */ }

    //Other methods are not shown.
}

public class ThreeDigitCode extends ThreeDigitInteger
{
    private boolean isValid;

    public ThreeDigitCode(int aValue)
    { /* implementation code */ }

    /** A ThreeDigitCode is valid if and only if the remainder when
     *  the sum of the hundreds and tens digits is divided by 7 equals
     *  the ones digit. Thus 362 is valid while 364 is not.
     *  Returns true if ThreeDigitCode is valid, false otherwise.
     */
    public boolean isValid()
    { /* implementation not shown */ }
}
```

**GO ON TO THE NEXT PAGE.**

29. Which is a true statement about the classes shown?
    (A) The `ThreeDigitInteger` class inherits the `isValid` method from the class `ThreeDigitCode`.
    (B) The `ThreeDigitCode` class inherits all of the public accessor methods from the `ThreeDigitInteger` class.
    (C) The `ThreeDigitCode` class inherits the constructor from the class `ThreeDigitInteger`.
    (D) The `ThreeDigitCode` class can directly access all the private variables of the `ThreeDigitInteger` class.
    (E) The `ThreeDigitInteger` class can access the `isValid` instance variable of the `ThreeDigitCode` class.

30. Which is correct /* *implementation code* */ for the `ThreeDigitCode` constructor?

    ```
     I super(aValue);
       isValid = isValid();
    ```

    ```
     II super(value, valid);
    ```

    ```
    III super(value);
        isValid = twoDigitSum() % 7 == onesDigit;
    ```

    (A) I only
    (B) II only
    (C) III only
    (D) I and III only
    (E) I, II, and III

31. Refer to these declarations in a client program.

    ```
    ThreeDigitInteger code = new ThreeDigitCode(127);
    ThreeDigitInteger num = new ThreeDigitInteger(456);
    ThreeDigitCode newCode = new ThreeDigitCode(241);
    ```

    Which of the following subsequent tests will not cause an error?

    ```
     I if (code.isValid())
          ...
    ```

    ```
     II if (num.isValid())
          ...
    ```

    ```
    III if (newCode.isValid())
          ...
    ```

    (A) I only
    (B) II only
    (C) III only
    (D) I and II only
    (E) I and III only

**GO ON TO THE NEXT PAGE.**

32. Consider the following hierarchy of classes.

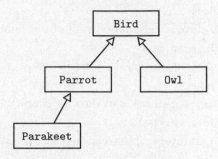

Assuming that each class has a valid default constructor, which of the following declarations in a client program are correct?

```
 I  Bird b1 = new Parrot();
    Bird b2 = new Parakeet();
    Bird b3 = new Owl();

 II Parakeet p = new Parrot();
    Owl o = new Bird();

III Parakeet p = new Bird();
```

(A) I only
(B) II only
(C) III only
(D) II and III only
(E) I, II, and III

33. Consider an array `arr` and a list `list` that is an `ArrayList<String>`. Both `arr` and `list` are initialized with string values. Which of the following code segments correctly appends all the strings in `arr` to the end of `list`?

```
 I  for (String s : arr)
        list.add(s);

 II for (String s : arr)
        list.add(list.size(), s);

III for (int i = 0; i < arr.length; i++)
        list.add(arr[i]);
```

(A) I only
(B) II only
(C) III only
(D) I and III only
(E) I, II, and III

**GO ON TO THE NEXT PAGE.**

34. Refer to the `nextIntInRange` method below.

```
/** Returns a random integer in the range low to high, inclusive. */
public int nextIntInRange(int low, int high)
{
    return /* expression */
}
```

Which /* *expression* */ will always return a value that satisfies the postcondition?

(A) `(int) (Math.random() * high) + low;`

(B) `(int) (Math.random() * (high - low)) + low;`

(C) `(int) (Math.random() * (high - low + 1)) + low;`

(D) `(int) (Math.random() * (high + low)) + low;`

(E) `(int) (Math.random() * (high + low - 1)) + low;`

35. Consider the following `mergeSort` method and the private instance variable a both in the same `Sorter` class.

```
private int[] a;

/** Sorts a[first] to a[last] in increasing order using merge sort. */
public void mergeSort(int first, int last)
{
    if (first != last)
    {
        int mid = (first + last) / 2;
        mergeSort(first, mid);
        mergeSort(mid + 1, last);
        merge(first, mid, last);
    }
}
```

Method `mergeSort` calls method `merge`, which has the following header.

```
/** Merge a[lb] to a[mi] and a[mi+1] to a[ub].
 * Precondition:  a[lb] to a[mi] and a[mi+1] to a[ub] both
 *                sorted in increasing order.
 */
private void merge(int lb, int mi, int ub)
```

If the first call to `mergeSort` is `mergeSort(0,3)`, how many *further* calls will there be to `mergeSort` before an array `b[0]...b[3]` is sorted?

(A) 2

(B) 3

(C) 4

(D) 5

(E) 6

**GO ON TO THE NEXT PAGE.**

36. A large hospital maintains a list of patients' records in no particular order. To find the record of a given patient, which represents the most efficient method that will work?
    (A) Do a sequential search on the name field of the records.
    (B) Do a binary search on the name field of the records.
    (C) Use insertion sort to sort the records alphabetically by name; then do a sequential search on the name field of the records.
    (D) Use merge sort to sort the records alphabetically by name; then do a sequential search on the name field of the records.
    (E) Use merge sort to sort the records alphabetically by name; then do a binary search on the name field of the records.

Use the following information for Questions 37 and 38.

Here is a diagram that shows the relationship between some of the classes that will be used in a program to draw a banner with block letters.

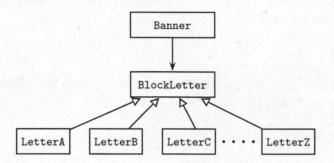

The diagram shows that the Banner class uses BlockLetter objects, and that the BlockLetter class has 26 subclasses, representing block letters from A to Z.

The BlockLetter class has a draw method

```
public void draw()
```

Each of the subclasses shown implements the draw method in a unique way to draw its particular letter. The Banner class gets an array of BlockLetter and has a method to draw all the letters in this array.

Here is a partial implementation of the Banner class.

```
public class Banner
{
    private BlockLetter[] letters;
    private int numLetters;

    /** Constructor. Gets the letters for the Banner. */
    public Banner()
    {
        numLetters = < some integer read from user input >
        letters = getLetters();
    }
```

**GO ON TO THE NEXT PAGE.**

```
/** Returns an array of block letters. */
public BlockLetter[] getLetters()
{
    String letter;
    letters = new BlockLetter[numLetters];
    for (int i = 0; i < numLetters; i++)
    {
        < read in capital letter >

        if (letter.equals("A"))
            letters[i] = new LetterA();
        else if (letter.equals("B"))
            letters[i] = new LetterB();
            ...                //similar code for C through Y
        else
            letters[i] = new LetterZ();
    }
    return letters;
}


/** Draw all the letters in the Banner. */
public void drawLetters()
{
    for (BlockLetter letter : letters)
        letter.draw();
}
}
```

37. You are given the information that `Banner` and `BlockLetter` are two classes used in the program. Which of the following can you conclude about the classes?

   I `BlockLetter` inherits all the methods of `Banner`.

   II `Banner` contains at least one `BlockLetter` object.

   III Each of the subclasses `LetterA`, `LetterB`, `LetterC`, ...`LetterZ` has an overridden `draw` method.

   (A) I only
   (B) II only
   (C) III only
   (D) II and III only
   (E) I, II, and III

38. Which is a true statement about method `drawLetters`?
   (A) It is an overloaded method in the `Banner` class.
   (B) It is an overridden method in the `Banner` class.
   (C) It uses polymorphism to draw the correct letters.
   (D) It will cause a logic error because the `draw` method of the `BlockLetter` class is different from the `draw` methods of its subclasses.
   (E) It will cause a run-time error because there is no `draw` method in the `Banner` class.

**GO ON TO THE NEXT PAGE.**

39. Consider `method1` and `method2` below, which are identical except for the second last line of code. Each method returns a new matrix based on the input matrix `mat`.

```
public static int[][] method1(int[][] mat)
{
    int numRows = mat.length;
    int numCols = mat[0].length;
    int[][] newMat = new int[numRows][numCols];
    for (int row = 0; row < numRows; row++)
        for (int col = 0; col < numCols; col++)
            newMat[numRows - row -1][col] = mat[row][col];
    return newMat;
}


public static int[][] method2(int[][] mat)
{
    int numRows = mat.length;
    int numCols = mat[0].length;
    int[][] newMat = new int[numRows][numCols];
    for (int row = 0; row < numRows; row++)
        for (int col = 0; col < numCols; col++)
            newMat[row][col] = mat[numRows - row - 1][col];
    return newMat;
}
```

Suppose the same input matrix is used for `method1` and `method2`, and the output for `method1` is `matrix1` while the output for `method2` is `matrix2`. Which is a true statement about `matrix1` and `matrix2`?

(A) `matrix1` is identical to `matrix2`.

(B) The rows of `matrix1` are the columns of `matrix2`.

(C) `matrix1` is a reflection of `matrix2` across a vertical line on the edge of either matrix.

(D) `matrix1` is a reflection of `matrix2` across a horizontal line on the bottom or top edge of either matrix.

(E) The rows of `matrix1` are the rows of `matrix2` in reverse order.

**GO ON TO THE NEXT PAGE.**

40. Consider an `ArrayList` cards of Card objects that needs to be shuffled. The following algorithm is used for shuffling.

> Create a temporary `ArrayList<Card>`
> Do the following `cards.size()` number of times
>> – Generate a random integer r that can index any card in `cards`
>> – Remove the card found at position r in `cards` and add it to the end
>>   of the temporary `ArrayList`
> Set `cards` to the temporary `ArrayList`

Here is the method that implements this algorithm.

```
Line 1:  public void shuffle()
Line 2:  {
Line 3:      int size = cards.size();
Line 4:      ArrayList<Card> temp = new ArrayList<Card>();
Line 5:      for (int j = 1; j < size; j++)
Line 6:      {
Line 7:          int index = (int) (Math.random() * size);
Line 8:          temp.add(cards.get(index));
Line 9:      }
Line 10:     cards = temp;
Line 11: }
```

The method does not work as intended. Which of the following changes to `shuffle` would ensure that it works correctly?

I Replace Line 5 with

```
for (int j = 0; j < size; j++)
```

II Replace Line 7 with

```
int index = (int) (Math.random() * cards.size());
```

III Replace Line 8 with

```
temp.add(cards.remove(index));
```

(A) I only
(B) II only
(C) III only
(D) I and III only
(E) I, II, and III

**END OF SECTION I**

# COMPUTER SCIENCE A
# SECTION II

Time—1 hour and 30 minutes
Number of questions—4
Percent of total grade—50

---

**DIRECTIONS:**   SHOW ALL YOUR WORK. REMEMBER THAT
PROGRAM SEGMENTS ARE TO BE WRITTEN IN JAVA.

Write your answers in pencil only in the booklet provided.

**NOTES:**

■ Assume that the classes in the Quick Reference have been imported where needed.

■ Unless otherwise noted in the question, assume that parameters in method calls are not `null` and that methods are called only when their preconditions are satisfied.

■ In writing solutions for each question, you may use any of the accessible methods that are listed in classes defined in that question. Writing significant amounts of code that can be replaced by a call to one of these methods will not receive full credit.

---

**GO ON TO THE NEXT PAGE.**

1. This question uses a password checker to report whether a given password is weak, medium, or strong. The PasswordChecker class is shown below. You will write two methods of the PasswordChecker class.

```java
public class PasswordChecker
{

    /** Returns the number of digits in s.
     * Precondition: s contains at least one character.
     */
    public static int numDigits(String s)
    { /* implementation not shown */ }

    /** Returns the number of letters in s.
     * Precondition: s contains at least one character.
     */
    public static int numLetters(String s)
    { /* implementation not shown */ }

    /** Returns the number of characters in s
     * that are neither letters nor digits.
     * Precondition: s contains at least one character.
     */
    public static int numSymbols(String s)
    { /* to be implemented in part (a) */ }

    /** Returns the strength of password p
     *   as described in part (b).
     * Precondition: p contains at least one character.
     */
    public static String passwordStrength(String p)
    { /* to be implemented in part (b) */ }

    // There may be instance variables, constructors and
    // methods not shown.
}
```

(a) Complete the numSymbols method, which finds how many characters in String s are neither letters or digits.

Two helper methods, numDigits and numLetters, have been provided.

- numDigits returns the number of digits in its String parameter.
- numLetters returns the number of letters in its String parameter.

The following are some examples showing the use of numDigits, numLetters, and numSymbols.

**GO ON TO THE NEXT PAGE.**

| Method Call | Return Value |
| --- | --- |
| numDigits("R2@n49") | 3 |
| numLetters("R2@n49") | 2 |
| numSymbols("R2@n49") | 1 |
| numDigits("!?!?") | 0 |
| numLetters("!?!?") | 0 |
| numSymbols("!?!?") | 4 |

Complete the numSymbols method below. You must use numDigits and numLetters appropriately to receive full credit.

```
/** Returns the number of characters in s
 *  that are neither letters nor digits.
 *  Precondition: s contains at least one character.
 */
public static int numSymbols(String s)
```

(b) Write the passwordStrength method. The method returns one of three String values: "strong", "medium", or "weak", depending on the characters of its String parameter p.

Here are the criteria for each type of password. (Assume that the word "symbol" refers to a character that is neither a digit nor a letter.)

- A strong password is one with at least 8 characters and at least one digit, one letter, and one symbol.
- A medium password has two possibilities:
  - Between 5 and 8 characters (5 inclusive), at least one of which is a symbol.
  - 8 or more characters, but is missing a digit, or letter or symbol, the second condition for being strong.
- A weak password has two possibilities:
  - Fewer than 5 characters
  - Between 5 and 8 characters 5 inclusive, in which none of the characters is a symbol.

Here are some examples.

| Method Call | Return Value |
| --- | --- |
| checkPassword("c@8") | weak |
| checkPassword("c1A2b3") | weak |
| checkPassword("c/A2b3") | medium |
| checkPassword("Two4two?") | strong |
| checkPassword("Hot3dog2019") | medium |

**GO ON TO THE NEXT PAGE.**

Complete method passwordStrength below. Assume that numSymbols works as specified, regardless of what you wrote in part (a).

```
/** Returns the strength of password p
 *       as described in part (b).
 * Precondition: p contains at least one character.
 */
public static String passwordStrength(String p)
```

2. In this question, you will write the implementation of a SnowyOwl class based on the hierarchy of classes shown below.

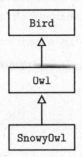

The Owl class is as follows.

```
public class Owl
{
    private String name;

    public Owl()
    { name = ""; }

    public Owl(String owlName)
    { name = owlName; }

    public String getName()
    { return name; }

    public String getFood()
    { return "furry animals, insects, or small birds"; }
}
```

Here are some features of a SnowyOwl.

- It's an Owl whose name is always "Snowy owl".
- If the owl is a male, its color is white.
- If it is a female, its color is speckled.
- Food for a SnowyOwl depends on what is available. A SnowyOwl will randomly eat a hare, a lemming, or a small bird, where each type of food is equally likely.

**GO ON TO THE NEXT PAGE.**

The SnowyOwl class should have a private instance variable of type boolean that stores true if the owl is male, false otherwise. It should also have a constructor and a getColor method that returns a string with the snowy owl's color.

Write the complete SnowyOwl class below. Your implementation should meet all specifications for a SnowyOwl.

3. Consider a system for processing names and addresses from a mailing list. A Recipients class will be used as part of this system. The lines in the mailing list are stored in an ArrayList<String>, a private instance variable in the Recipients class. The blank line that separates recipients in the mailing list is stored as the empty string in this list, and the final element in the list is an empty string.

A portion of the mailing list is shown below, with the corresponding part of the ArrayList.

```
Mr. J. Adams
6 Rose St.
Ithaca, NY 14850

Jack S. Smith
12 Posy Way
Suite 201
Glendale, CA 91203

Ms. M.K. Delgado
2 River Dr.
New York, NY 10013

    ...
```

| 0 | 1 | 2 | 3 | 4 |
|---|---|---|---|---|
| "Mr. J. Adams" | "6 Rose St." | "Ithaca, NY 14850" | "" | "Jack S. Smith" |

| 5 | 6 | 7 | 8 | 9 |
|---|---|---|---|---|
| "12 Posy Way" | "Suite 201" | "Glendale, CA 91023" | "" | "Ms. M.K. Delgado" |

| 10 | 11 | 12 | |
|---|---|---|---|
| "2 River Dr." | "New York, NY 10013" | "" | ... |

**GO ON TO THE NEXT PAGE.**

The Recipients class that processes this data is shown below.

```java
public class Recipients
{
    /** The list of lines in the mailing list */
    private ArrayList<String> lines;

    /** Constructor. Fill lines with mailing list data.
     *  Postcondition:
     *    - Each element in lines is one line of the mailing list.
     *    - Lines appear in the list in the same order
     *      that they appear in the mailing list.
     *    - Blank line separators in the mailing list are stored
     *      as empty strings.
     */
    public Recipients()
    { /* implementation not shown */ }

    /** Returns the city contained in the cityZip string of
     *  an address, as described in part (a).
     */
    public String extractCity(String cityZip)
    { /* to be implemented in part (a) */ }

    /** Returns the address of the recipient with the specified
     *  name, as described in part (b).
     */
    public String getAddress(String name)
    {/* to be implemented in part (b) */}

    //Other methods are not shown.
}
```

(a) Write the `extractCity` method of the `Recipients` class. In the `cityZip` parameter the city is followed by a comma, then one blank space, then two capital letters for a state abbreviation, then a space and 5-digit ZIP code. For example, if `cityZip` is `"Ithaca, NY 14850"`, the method call `extractCity(cityZip)` should return `"Ithaca"`.

---

Class information for this question

public class Recipients

private ArrayList<String> lines
public Recipients()
public String extractCity(String cityZip)
public String getAddress(String name)

---

**GO ON TO THE NEXT PAGE.**

Complete method `extractCity` below.

```
/** Returns the city contained in the cityZip string of
 *  an address, as described in part (a).
 */
public String extractCity(String cityZip)
```

(b) Write the `getAddress` method of the `Recipients` class. This method should return a string that contains only the address of the corresponding `name` parameter. For example, if `name` is `"Jack S. Smith"`, a string containing the three subsequent lines of his address should be returned. This string should contain line breaks in appropriate places, including after the last line of the address. This ensures that the address will have the proper address format when printed by a client class. In the given example of name `"Jack S. Smith"`, the printed version of his address string should look like this:

```
Jack S. Smith
12 Posy Way
Suite 201
Glendale, CA 91203
```

Complete method `getAddress` below.

```
/** Returns the address of the recipient with the specified
 *  name, as described in part (b).
 */
public String getAddress(String name)
```

4. A puzzle-solving competition is held in a large hall with a two-dimensional arrangement of contestants. Each rectangle below represents one contestant.

A contestant in the contest can be represented by a `Contestant` class, whose partial implementation is shown below.

**GO ON TO THE NEXT PAGE.**

```
public class Contestant
{
    private String name;
    private int score;

    /** Returns the name of this contestant. */
    public String getName()
    { return name; }

    /** Returns the score of this contestant. */
    public int getScore()
    { return score; }

    //Constructor and other methods are not shown.

}
```

In parts (a) and (b) you will write two methods of a ContestOrganizer class, whose partial implementation is shown below. A contest organizer keeps track of contestants in a two-dimensional array.

```
public class ContestOrganizer
{
    /** the number of rows of contestants */
    public static final int NUM_ROWS = <some integer>;

    /** the number of columns of contestants */
    public static final int CONTESTANTS_PER_ROW = <some integer>;

    /** The two-dimensional array of contestants */
    private Contestant[][] contestants;

    /** Sorts arr in increasing order by score. */
    private void sort(Contestant[] arr)
    { /* implementation not shown */ }

    /** Sorts each row of contestants into increasing order by score.
     *   Postcondition: Contestant with highest score in row[k] is
     *                  in the rightmost column of row[k], 0<=k<NUM_ROWS.
     */
    public void sortAllRows()
    { /* to be implemented in part(a) */ }

    /** Returns name of contestant with highest score.
     *   Precondition:
     *     - Contestants have not been sorted by score.
     *     - Top score is unique.
     *     - Only one contestant has the highest score.
     */
    public String findWinnerName()
    { /* to be implemented in part(b) */ }
}
```

**GO ON TO THE NEXT PAGE.**

(a) Write the `ContestOrganizer` method `sortAllRows`. This method should sort the contestants by score in each row, from lowest to highest.

Example: Suppose contestants are as shown below.

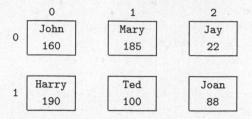

Here is what contestants will be after a call to `sortAllRows`.

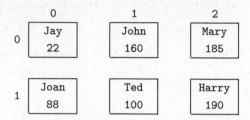

In writing `sortAllRows`, your method *must* use the `ContestOrganizer` method `sort`. You may assume that `sort` works as specified.

Complete method `sortAllRows` below.

```
/** Sorts each row of contestants into increasing order by score.
 *  Postcondition: Contestant with highest score in row[k] is
 *                 in the rightmost column of row[k], 0<=k<NUM_ROWS.
 */
public void sortAllRows()
```

(b) Write the `Contestant` method `findWinnerName`, which returns the name of the contestant with the highest score. For example, if the contestants are as shown above, a call to `findWinnerName` should return `"Harry"`.

When writing `findWinnerName`, you should assume that the contestants have not yet been sorted by score, and that there is only one contestant with the highest score. In writing your solution, you *must* use method `sortAllRows`. You may assume that `sortAllRows` works as specified, regardless of what you wrote in part (a).

Complete method `findWinnerName` below.

```
/** Returns name of contestant with highest score.
 *  Precondition:
 *     - Contestants have not been sorted by score.
 *     - Top score is unique.
 *     - Only one contestant has the highest score.
 */
public String findWinnerName()
```

## STOP

## END OF EXAM

# ANSWER KEY
## Practice Test 1

## Section I

| | | | | | |
|---|---|---|---|---|---|
| 1. **C** | | 15. **B** | | 29. **B** | |
| 2. **C** | | 16. **C** | | 30. **A** | |
| 3. **D** | | 17. **D** | | 31. **C** | |
| 4. **C** | | 18. **E** | | 32. **A** | |
| 5. **E** | | 19. **E** | | 33. **E** | |
| 6. **E** | | 20. **A** | | 34. **C** | |
| 7. **A** | | 21. **B** | | 35. **E** | |
| 8. **D** | | 22. **A** | | 36. **A** | |
| 9. **B** | | 23. **D** | | 37. **D** | |
| 10. **E** | | 24. **C** | | 38. **C** | |
| 11. **C** | | 25. **B** | | 39. **A** | |
| 12. **A** | | 26. **E** | | 40. **E** | |
| 13. **B** | | 27. **C** | | | |
| 14. **C** | | 28. **D** | | | |

## ANSWERS EXPLAINED

## Section I

1. **(C)** Testing a program thoroughly does not prove that a program is correct. For a large program, it is generally impossible to test every possible set of input data.

2. **(C)** The private instance variable `hourlyWage` must be incremented by `amt`. Eliminate choice E, which doesn't *increment* `hourlyWage`; it simply *replaces* it by `amt`. Choice D is wrong because you can't use a method call as the left-hand side of an assignment. Choices A and B are wrong because the `incrementWage` method is void and should not return a value.

3. **(D)** The value of the boolean instance variable `isUnionMember` must be changed to the opposite of what it currently is. Segments I and II both achieve this. Note that `!true` has a value of `false` and `!false` a value of `true`. Segment III fails to do what's required if the current value of `isUnionMember` is `false`.

4. **(C)** `computePay` is a client method and, therefore, cannot access the private variables of the class. This eliminates choices A and D. The method `getHourlyWage()` must be accessed with the dot member construct; thus, choice B is wrong, and choice C is correct. Choice E is way off base—`hours` is not part of the `Worker` class, so `w.hours` is meaningless.

5. **(E)** If `s.length() < 4` for all strings in `wordList`, then `SHORT WORD` will be printed on each pass through the `for` loop. Since there are `wordList.size()` passes through the loop, the maximum number of times that `SHORT WORD` can be printed is `wordList.size()`.

6. **(E)**
$$
\begin{aligned}
\text{mystery}(4) &= 3 * \text{mystery}(3) \\
&= 3 * 3 * \text{mystery}(2) \\
&= 3 * 3 * 3 * \text{mystery}(1) \\
&= 3 * 3 * 3 * 3 \\
&= 81
\end{aligned}
$$

7. **(A)** The declaration of the `colors` array makes the following assignments: `colors[0] = "red"`, `colors[1] = "green"`, and `colors[2] = "black"`. The loop in segment I adds these values to `colorList` in the correct order. Segment II fails because `colors` is an array and therefore can't use the `get` method. The code also confuses the lists. Segment III, in its first pass through the loop, attempts to add `colors[2]` to index position 2 of `colorList`. This will cause an `IndexOutOfBoundsException` to be thrown, since index positions 0 and 1 do not yet exist!

8. **(D)** Merge sort repeatedly splits an array of $n$ elements in half until there are $n$ arrays containing one element each. Now adjacent arrays are successively merged until there is a single merged, sorted array. A binary search repeatedly splits an array into two, narrowing the region that may contain the key. Insertion sort, however, does no array splitting. It takes elements one at a time and finds their insertion point in the sorted piece of the array. Elements are shifted to allow correct insertion of each element. Even though this algorithm maintains the array in two parts—a sorted part and yet-to-be-sorted part—this is not a divide-and-conquer approach.

9. **(B)** A static variable is shared by all instances of the class. "Static" means that there will be just one memory slot allocated, no matter how many `Insects` are constructed. All instances of `Insect` access the same information stored in that slot. When an `Insect` is created, it will get tagged with the current value of `nextAvailableID` for that memory slot, which will then be incremented for the next `Insect` created. All of the other variables—`age`, `idNum`, `position`, `direction`—are specific to one instance of `Insect` and should therefore be private instance variables in the class.

10. **(E)** A new `Address` object must be created, to be used as the `Address` parameter in the `Customer` constructor. To do this correctly requires the keyword `new` preceding the `Address` constructor. Segment II omits `new` and does not use the `Address` constructor correctly. (In fact, it inserts a new `String` object in the `Address` slot of the `Customer` constructor.)

11. **(C)** The algorithm used in method `locate` is a sequential search, which may have to examine all the objects to find the matching one. A binary search, which repeatedly discards a chunk of the array that does not contain the key, is more efficient. However, it can only be used if the values being examined—in this case customer ID numbers—are sorted. Note that it doesn't help to have the array sorted by name or phone number since the algorithm doesn't look at these values.

12. **(A)** The values of `k` are consecutively 4, 3, 2, and 1. The values of `randIndex` are consecutively 3, 2, 0, and 1. Thus, the sequence of swaps and corresponding states of `arr` will be:

```
swap arr[4] and arr[3]        1 2 3 5 4
swap arr[3] and arr[2]        1 2 5 3 4
swap arr[2] and arr[0]        5 2 1 3 4
swap arr[1] and arr[1]        5 2 1 3 4
```

13. **(B)** The `remove` method of `ArrayList` removes the indicated element, shifts the remaining elements one slot to the left (i.e., it does not leave gaps in the list), and adjusts the size of the list. Consider the list in choice B. The index values are shown:

```
The cat cat sat on the mat mat
 0   1   2   3   4  5   6   7
```

After the first occurrence of `cat` has been removed:

```
The cat sat on the mat mat
 0   1   2  3   4   5   6
```

The value of `i`, which was 1 when `cat` was removed, has now been incremented to 2 in the `for` loop. This means that the word to be considered next is `sat`. The second occurrence of `cat` has been missed. Thus, the given code will fail whenever occurrences of the word to be removed are consecutive. You fix it by not allowing the index to increment when a removal occurs:

```
int i = 0;
while (i < wordList.size())
{
    if ((wordList.get(i)).equals(word))
        wordList.remove(i);
    else
        i++;
}
```

14. **(C)** You should not use an enhanced `for` loop to replace elements, only to access (as in segment I) or modify using a mutator method (as in segment II). Note that segment III will compile and execute, but won't replace the clocks in `allClocks` as intended.

15. **(B)** When `r` is 0, `c` goes from 0 to 0, and just one element, `mat[0][0]`, will be printed. When `r` is 1, `c` goes from 0 to 1, and two elements, `mat[1][0]` and `mat[1][1]`, will be printed, and so on. When `r` is 3, all four elements of row 3 will be printed.

16. **(C)** To return the number of elements in the set for Method One requires no more than returning the number of elements in the array. For Method Two, however, the number of cells that contain true must be counted, which requires a test for each of the MAX values. Note that searching for a target value in the set is more efficient for Method Two. For example, to test whether 2 is in the set, simply check if `a[2] == true`. In Method One, a sequential search must be done, which is less efficient. To print all the elements in Method One, simply loop over the known number of elements and print. Method Two is less efficient because the whole array must be examined: Each cell must be tested for true before printing.

17. **(D)** An `ArithmeticException` will be thrown at run time. Note that if $N$ were of type `double`, no exception would be thrown. The variable `sum` would be assigned the value `Infinity`, and the error would only be detected in the output.

18. **(E)** Only statements II and III are true. Note that $n$, the number of elements in the array, is a power of 2: $n = 64 = 2^6$. A worst case takes (exponent $+ 1$) $= 7$ iterations of the search loop. Statement I is false, since the key is a left endpoint of the array, which does not represent a worst case. The key will be found in 6 iterations. Try it! Statement II, however, is true. It represents a worst case situation, in which the key is not in `arr` and is also outside the range of values of the array. So there will be 7 passes through the loop. Statement III is true because the key, 100, is an element of `arr` that is not an endpoint. It therefore does not represent a worst case, and the key will be found in fewer than 7 iterations.

19. **(E)** The first value of `pos` is 2, the index of the first occurrence of `"car"` in `"a carrot and car"`. Then `s` gets assigned `"carrot and car"` and `pos` is now 0. Since `pos` is not advanced, it is stuck with a value of 0 and the method has an infinite loop. Notice that you can fix this problem by changing `s=s.substring(pos);` to `s=s.substring(pos+1);`

20. **(A)** The correct diagram uses two up arrows to show that a `Car` *is-a* `Vehicle` and a `Truck` *is-a* `Vehicle` (inheritance relationship). The two down arrows indicate that a `Car` *has-a* `AirBag` and a `Truck` *has-a* `AirBag` (composition relationship). In each of the incorrect choices, at least one of the relationships does not make sense. For example, in choice B a `Vehicle` *has-a* `Truck`, and in choice E an `AirBag` *is-a* `Car`.

21. **(B)** The postcondition should be a true assertion about the major action of the segment. The segment overwrites the elements of array `a` with the nonnegative elements of `a`. Then `n` is adjusted so that now the array `a[0]...a[n-1]` contains just nonnegative integers. Note that even though choice E is a correct assertion about the program segment, it's not a good postcondition because it doesn't describe the main modification to array `a` (namely all negative integers have been removed).

22. **(A)** Note the order of precedence for the expressions involved: (1) parentheses, (2) `!`, (3) `<`, (4) `==`, (5) `&&`, (6) `||`. This means that `a < c`, `a < b`, and `!(a == b)` will all be evaluated before `||` and `&&` are considered. The given expression then boils down to `value1 || (value2 && value3)`, since `&&` has higher precedence than `||`. Notice that if `value1` is true, the whole expression is true since (`true || any`) evaluates to true. Thus, `a < c` will guarantee that the expression evaluates to true. None of the other conditions will guarantee an outcome of true. For example, suppose `a < b` (choice B). If `a == c`, then the whole expression will be false because you get `F || F`.

23. **(D)** Test data should always include a value from each range in addition to all boundary values. The given program should also handle the cases in which weights over 20 pounds or any negative weights are entered. Note that choice E contains redundant data. There is no new information to be gained in testing two weights from the same range—both 3 and 4 pounds, for example.

24. **(C)** The `max` methods shown are overloaded methods (same name but different parameter types). In the given statement, `matrix[2]` and `matrix[3]` refer to row 2 and row 3 of the matrix, respectively, each of which is an array of `int`. `max(matrix[2])` is the largest element in row 2, namely 7, and `max(matrix[3])` is the largest element in row 3, namely 4. The given statement is therefore equivalent to `max(7,4)`, which will return 7.

25. **(B)** Segment II correctly checks that the part descriptions match and keeps track of the current part with minimum price. If this is not done, the part whose number must be returned will be lost. Segment I is incorrect because it doesn't check that `partDescription` matches the description of the current part being examined in the array. Thus, it simply finds the `AutoPart` with the lowest price, which is not what was required. Segment III incorrectly returns the part number of the first part it finds with a matching description.

26. **(E)** Statement I is fine: The parameters are `String` objects and can be compared. Statement II shows incorrect usage of the `toString()` method, which returns strings representing the p1 and p2 objects. Using the dot operator and `getDescription()` following those strings is meaningless in this context, since `getDescription()` applies to the `AutoPart` class, not the `String` class. Statement III will fail because p1 and p2 are not `String` objects and `min` applies to strings. Also, the `AutoPart` class as currently written does not have a `compareTo` method, so `AutoPart` objects cannot be compared.

27. **(C)** Ordering of strings involves a character-by-character comparison starting with the leftmost character of each string. Thus, strA precedes strB (since "A" precedes "a") or `strA.compareTo(strB) < 0`. This eliminates choices B and D. Eliminate choices A and E since strB precedes strC (because "C" precedes "c") and therefore `strB.compareTo(strC) < 0`. Note that `string1.compareTo(string2) == 0` if and only if string1 and string2 are equal strings.

28. **(D)** Suppose `fullName` is Dr. John Roufaiel. In segment I, the expression `fullName.indexOf(BLANK)` returns 3. Then, `temp` gets assigned the value of `fullName.substring(4)`, which is John Roufaiel. Next, k gets assigned the value `temp.indexOf(BLANK)`, namely 4, and `firstName` gets assigned `temp.substring(0, 4)`, which is all the characters from 0 to 3 inclusive, namely John. Note that segment II works the same way, except `firstName` gets assigned John Roufaiel and then reassigned John. This is not good style, since a variable name should document its contents as precisely as possible. Still, the code works. Segment III fails because `indexOf` returns the *first* occurrence of its `String` parameter. Thus, `firstBlank` and `secondBlank` will both contain the same value, 3.

29. **(B)** `ThreeDigitCode` is a subclass of `ThreeDigitInteger` and therefore inherits all the public methods of `ThreeDigitInteger` except constructors. All of the statements other than B are false. For choice A, `ThreeDigitInteger` is the superclass and therefore cannot inherit from its subclass. For choice C, constructors are never inherited (see p. 143). For choice D, a subclass can access private variables of the superclass through accessor methods only (see p. 142). For choice E, a superclass cannot access any additional instance variables of its subclass.

30. **(A)** Implementation I works because it correctly calls the superclass constructor by using `super`, with the subclass parameter aValue, in its first line. Additionally, it correctly initializes the subclass's `isValid` private instance variable by calling the `isValid` method, which it inherits from the superclass. Implementation II is wrong because the constructor has no boolean validity parameter. Implementation III is wrong because a subclass cannot access a private instance variable of its superclass.

31. **(C)** Test III works because newCode is of type `ThreeDigitCode`, which has an `isValid` method. A compile-time error will occur for both tests I and II because at compile time the types of code and num are both `ThreeDigitInteger`, and the class `ThreeDigitInteger` does not have an `isValid` method. To avoid this error, the code object must be cast to `ThreeDigitCode`, its actual type.

32. **(A)** The *is-a* relationship must work from right-to-left: a `Parrot` *is-a* `Bird`, a `Parakeet` *is-a* `Bird`, and an `Owl` *is-a* `Bird`. All are correct. This relationship fails in declarations II and III: a `Parrot` is not necessarily a `Parakeet`, a `Bird` is not necessarily an `Owl`, and a `Bird` is not necessarily a `Parakeet`.

33. **(E)** All three segments traverse the array, accessing one element at a time, and appending it to the end of the `ArrayList`. In segment II, the first parameter of the `add` method is the position in `list` where the next string `s` will be added. Since `list.size()` increases by one after each insertion, this index is correctly updated in each pass through the enhanced `for` loop.

34. **(C)** Suppose you want random integers from 2 to 8, that is, `low = 2` and `high = 8`. This is 7 possible integers, so you need

    `(int) (Math.random() * 7)`

    which produces 0, 1, 2, …, or 6. Therefore the quantity

    `(int) (Math.random() * 7) + 2`

    produces 2, 3, 4, …, or 8. The only expression that yields the right answer with these values is

    `(int) (Math.random() * (high - low + 1)) + low;`

35. **(E)** Here is a "box diagram" for `mergeSort(0,3)`. The boldface numbers 1–6 show the order in which the `mergeSort` calls are made.

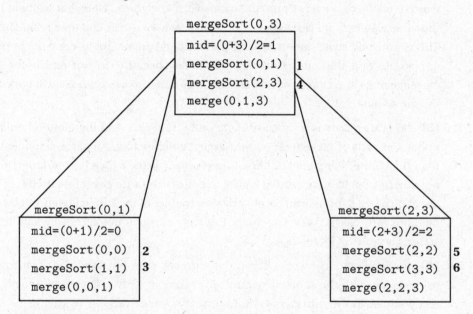

The `mergeSort` calls in which `first == last` are base case calls, which means that there will be no further method calls.

36. **(A)** Since the records are not sorted, the quickest way to find a given name is to start at the beginning of the list and sequentially search for that name. Choices C, D, and E will all work, but it's inefficient to sort and then search because all sorting algorithms take longer than simply inspecting each element. Choice B won't work: A binary search can only be used for a sorted list.

37. **(D)** Statement I is false because `BlockLetter` is not a subclass of `Banner`. Note that a `BlockLetter` is not a `Banner`. In the UML diagram, the down arrow indicates that a `Banner` *has-a* `BlockLetter`. Statement II is true: The down arrow of the UML diagram shows that one or more `BlockLetter` objects is used in the `Banner` code. Statement III is true: Each of the subclasses overrides the `draw` method of `BlockLetter`, the superclass. Without this feature, the program won't work as intended.

38. **(C)** The `draw` method is polymorphic, which means that it is a superclass (in this case `BlockLetter`) method that is overridden in at least one of its subclasses. During run time, there is dynamic binding between the calling object and the method, that is, the actual instance is bound to its particular overridden method. In the `drawLetters` method, the correct version of `draw` is called during each iteration of the `for` loop, and a banner with the appropriate letters is drawn.

39. **(A)** `method1` creates a mirror image of its parameter `mat` across a horizontal line placed under `mat`. If `mat` is the matrix

```
1 2 3
4 5 6
```

then the mirror image created below is

```
4 5 6
1 2 3
```

`method2` also creates a mirror image, this time with the mirror placed *above* its parameter `mat`. Note that the reflection across a horizontal line above

```
1 2 3
4 5 6
```

is also

```
4 5 6
1 2 3
```

A good general hint to solve a problem like this is to take a very simple matrix `mat` and generate some elements of `newMat`. It won't take long to see that the two methods produce the same matrix.

40. **(E)** All three changes must be made! In order to move all the `Card` elements to the temporary `ArrayList`, the `for` loop must be executed `size` times. If you start `j` at 1, the loop will be executed `size-1` times. The error in Line 7 is subtle. With each iteration of the loop, the size of the `cards` `ArrayList` is being reduced by 1, so the range of random indexes is getting smaller and smaller. This won't happen if you use `size`, the length of the *original* `cards` list. You must use `cards.size()`, which is the length of the current, shorter list. If you don't make correction III, the random element will not be removed from `cards`. It will (incorrectly) remain there while a copy of it will be added to `temp`. If this error isn't corrected, execution of the method is likely to cause the `temp` list to hold more than one copy of a given card!

## Section II

1. (a)
```
public static int numSymbols(String s)
{
    return s.length() - (numLetters(s) + numDigits(s));
}
```

(b)
```
public static String passwordStrength(String p)
{
    if (p.length() < 5)
        return "weak";
    else if (p.length() >= 5 && p.length() < 8)
    {
        if (numSymbols(p) > 0)
            return "medium";
        else
            return "weak";
    }
    else if (numSymbols(p) > 0 && numLetters(p) > 0 && numDigits(p) > 0)
        return "strong";
    else return "medium";
}
```

**NOTE**

- For part(b), by the first else if test, all passwords with fewer than 5 characters have been taken care of. By the second else if test, all passwords with fewer than 8 characters have been taken care of. Therefore, the second else if test deals only with passwords that have 8 or more characters, and you don't explicitly need to test for the number of characters.

## Scoring Rubric: Password Checker

| Part (a) | numSymbols | 2 points |
|---|---|---|
| +1 | use s.length() | |
| +1 | subtract (numDigits + numLetters) | |

| Part (b) | | 7 points |
|---|---|---|
| +1 | test length < 5 | |
| +1 | test length between 5 and 8 | |
| +1 | test numSymbols > 0 | |
| +1 | else return "weak" | |
| +1 | test for digit, letter, and symbol in long password | |
| +1 | return "strong" | |
| +1 | return "medium" | |

```
2.    public class SnowyOwl extends Owl
      {
          private boolean isMale;

          public SnowyOwl(boolean isAMale)
          {
              super("Snowy Owl");
              isMale = isAMale;
          }

          public String getColor()
          {
              if (isMale)
                  return "white";
              else
                  return "speckled";
          }

          public String getFood()
          {

              int num = (int) (Math.random() * 3);
              if (num == 0)
                  return "hare";
              else if (num == 1)
                  return "lemming";
              else
                  return "small bird";
          }
      }
```

**NOTE**

- The `Owl` getFood method is overridden to show the specific eating habits of a SnowyOwl.
- In the constructor, `super` must be used because there is no direct access to the private instance variables of the `Bird` class. The new variable is `isMale` must be initialized in the constructor.
- Note that the noise for `Owl` will always be "hoot". Thus, noise does not need to be provided as a parameter in the `SnowyOwl` constructor.

## Scoring Rubric: Snowy Owl

| | SnowyOwl class | 9 points |
|---|---|---|
| +1 | use of extends in declaration | |
| +1 | constructor declaration | |
| +1 | code using super | |
| +1 | "Snowy owl" parameter | |
| +1 | declaration of getFood | |
| +1 | getColor method | |
| +1 | get random int from 0 to 2 | |
| +1 | if...else statement | |
| +1 | return statements | |

3. (a)
```java
public String extractCity(String cityZip)
{
    int commaPos = cityZip.indexOf(",");
    return cityZip.substring(0, commaPos);
}
```

(b)
```java
public String getAddress(String name)
{
    int index = 0;
    while(index < lines.size() && !name.equals(lines.get(index)))
        index++;
    index++;
    String s = "";
    while (!(lines.get(index).equals("")))
    {
        s += lines.get(index) + "\n";
        index++;
    }
    return s;
}
```

**NOTE**

- Part (b) first finds the name that matches the parameter, and then builds a string out of the next two or three lines that comprise the address. Again, the empty string signals that the end of the address has been reached.
- The escape character string, "\n", inserts a line break into the string.

## Scoring Rubric: Mailing List

| Part (a) | extractCity | 3 points |
| --- | --- | --- |
| +1 | locate comma in ZIP code | |
| +1 | return substring that contains the city | |
| +1 | substring parameters | |

| Part (b) | getAddress | 6 points |
| --- | --- | --- |
| +1 | loop to search for name | |
| +1 | loop to traverse lines until end of address is reached | |
| +1 | check range of index | |
| +1 | concatenate lines of address | |
| +1 | newline characters | |
| +1 | return string containing address | |

4.  (a) 
```java
public void sortAllRows()
{
    for(Contestant[] row: contestants)
        sort(row);
}
```

(b) 
```java
public String findWinnerName()
{
    sortAllRows();
    int max = contestants[0][0].getScore();
    String winner = contestants[0][0].getName();
    for(int k = 0; k < NUM_ROWS; k++)
    {
        Contestant c = contestants[k][CONTESTANTS_PER_ROW - 1];
        if (c.getScore() > max)
        {
            winner = c.getName();
            max = c.getScore();
        }
    }
    return winner;
}
```

**NOTE**

- Part (a) uses the Java feature that a two-dimensional array is an array of arrays. Thus, each row, which is an array of Contestant, can be sorted using the helper method sort.
- Part (b) uses the fact that after you sort all the rows of contestants, the winning contestant will be in the last column of the matrix of contestants. When you go through the loop, searching for a score that's higher than the current max, be sure to store the name that goes with that score!

## Scoring Rubric: Two-Dimensional Contest Organizer

| Part (a) | sortAllRows | 2 points |
|---|---|---|
| +1 | loop over the rows of Contestants | |
| +1 | sort each row | |

| Part (b) | findWinnerName | 7 points |
|---|---|---|
| +1 | call sortAllRows | |
| +1 | get score of top scorer in first row | |
| +1 | get name of top scorer in first row | |
| +1 | loop over all rows | |
| +1 | accessing contestant in last column | |
| +1 | test for score higher than max | |
| +1 | adjust winner and max if higher score found | |

# ANSWER SHEET
## Practice Test 2

**Section I**

1. Ⓐ Ⓑ Ⓒ Ⓓ Ⓔ
2. Ⓐ Ⓑ Ⓒ Ⓓ Ⓔ
3. Ⓐ Ⓑ Ⓒ Ⓓ Ⓔ
4. Ⓐ Ⓑ Ⓒ Ⓓ Ⓔ
5. Ⓐ Ⓑ Ⓒ Ⓓ Ⓔ
6. Ⓐ Ⓑ Ⓒ Ⓓ Ⓔ
7. Ⓐ Ⓑ Ⓒ Ⓓ Ⓔ
8. Ⓐ Ⓑ Ⓒ Ⓓ Ⓔ
9. Ⓐ Ⓑ Ⓒ Ⓓ Ⓔ
10. Ⓐ Ⓑ Ⓒ Ⓓ Ⓔ
11. Ⓐ Ⓑ Ⓒ Ⓓ Ⓔ
12. Ⓐ Ⓑ Ⓒ Ⓓ Ⓔ
13. Ⓐ Ⓑ Ⓒ Ⓓ Ⓔ
14. Ⓐ Ⓑ Ⓒ Ⓓ Ⓔ

15. Ⓐ Ⓑ Ⓒ Ⓓ Ⓔ
16. Ⓐ Ⓑ Ⓒ Ⓓ Ⓔ
17. Ⓐ Ⓑ Ⓒ Ⓓ Ⓔ
18. Ⓐ Ⓑ Ⓒ Ⓓ Ⓔ
19. Ⓐ Ⓑ Ⓒ Ⓓ Ⓔ
20. Ⓐ Ⓑ Ⓒ Ⓓ Ⓔ
21. Ⓐ Ⓑ Ⓒ Ⓓ Ⓔ
22. Ⓐ Ⓑ Ⓒ Ⓓ Ⓔ
23. Ⓐ Ⓑ Ⓒ Ⓓ Ⓔ
24. Ⓐ Ⓑ Ⓒ Ⓓ Ⓔ
25. Ⓐ Ⓑ Ⓒ Ⓓ Ⓔ
26. Ⓐ Ⓑ Ⓒ Ⓓ Ⓔ
27. Ⓐ Ⓑ Ⓒ Ⓓ Ⓔ
28. Ⓐ Ⓑ Ⓒ Ⓓ Ⓔ

29. Ⓐ Ⓑ Ⓒ Ⓓ Ⓔ
30. Ⓐ Ⓑ Ⓒ Ⓓ Ⓔ
31. Ⓐ Ⓑ Ⓒ Ⓓ Ⓔ
32. Ⓐ Ⓑ Ⓒ Ⓓ Ⓔ
33. Ⓐ Ⓑ Ⓒ Ⓓ Ⓔ
34. Ⓐ Ⓑ Ⓒ Ⓓ Ⓔ
35. Ⓐ Ⓑ Ⓒ Ⓓ Ⓔ
36. Ⓐ Ⓑ Ⓒ Ⓓ Ⓔ
37. Ⓐ Ⓑ Ⓒ Ⓓ Ⓔ
38. Ⓐ Ⓑ Ⓒ Ⓓ Ⓔ
39. Ⓐ Ⓑ Ⓒ Ⓓ Ⓔ
40. Ⓐ Ⓑ Ⓒ Ⓓ Ⓔ

# How to Calculate Your (Approximate) AP Computer Science A Score

**Multiple Choice**

Number correct (out of 40)   =   _____   ⟸   Multiple-Choice Score

**Free Response**

Question 1   _____
                  (out of 9)

Question 2   _____
                  (out of 9)

Question 3   _____
                  (out of 9)

Question 4   _____
                  (out of 9)

Total   _____   ×   1.11   =   _____   ⟸   Free-Response Score
                                                              (Do not round.)

**Final Score**

_____   +   _____   =   _____
Multiple-              Free-                  Final Score
Choice                 Response            (Round to nearest
Score                  Score                whole number.)

### Chart to Convert to AP Grade
### Computer Science A

| Final Score Range | AP Grade[a] |
|---|---|
| 62–80 | 5 |
| 47–61 | 4 |
| 37–46 | 3 |
| 29–36 | 2 |
| 0–28 | 1 |

[a]The score range corresponding to each grade varies from exam to exam and is approximate.

# Practice Test 2

## COMPUTER SCIENCE A
## SECTION I

Time—1 hour and 30 minutes
Number of questions—40
Percent of total grade—50

---

**DIRECTIONS:** Determine the answer to each of the following questions or incomplete statements, using the available space for any necessary scratchwork. Then decide which is the best of the choices given and fill in the corresponding oval on the answer sheet. Do not spend too much time on any one problem.

**NOTES:**
- Assume that the classes in the Quick Reference have been imported where needed.
- Assume that variables and methods are declared within the context of an enclosing class.
- Assume that method calls that have no object or class name prefixed, and that are not shown within a complete class definition, appear within the context of an enclosing class.
- Assume that parameters in method calls are not `null` unless otherwise stated.

---

1. What output is produced by the following line of code?

    ```
    System.out.println("\"This is\n very strange\"");
    ```

    (A) \This is\n very strange\

    (B) "This is very strange"

    (C) This is
        very strange

    (D) \"This is
        very strange\"

    (E) "This is
        very strange"

**GO ON TO THE NEXT PAGE.**

2. A certain class, `SomeClass`, contains a method with the following header.

```
public int getValue(int n)
```

Suppose that methods with the following headers are now added to `SomeClass`.

```
  I  public int getValue()

 II  public double getValue(int n)

III  public int getValue(double n)
```

Which of the above headers will cause an error?
(A) I only
(B) II only
(C) III only
(D) I and II only
(E) I and III only

3. Consider the following statement.

```
int num = /* expression */;
```

Which of the following replacements for `/* expression */` creates in `num` a random integer from 2 to 50, including 2 and 50?
(A) `(int)(Math.random() * 50) - 2`
(B) `(int)(Math.random() * 49) - 2`
(C) `(int)(Math.random() * 49) + 2`
(D) `(int)(Math.random() * 50) + 2`
(E) `(int)(Math.random() * 48) + 2`

4. Consider the following code segment.

```
int num = 0, score = 10;
if (num != 0 && score / num > SOME_CONSTANT)
    statement1;
else
    statement2;
```

What is the result of executing this statement?
(A) An `ArithmeticException` will be thrown.
(B) A syntax error will occur.
(C) *statement1*, but not *statement2*, will be executed.
(D) *statement2*, but not *statement1*, will be executed.
(E) Neither *statement1* nor *statement2* will be executed; control will pass to the first statement following the `if` statement.

**GO ON TO THE NEXT PAGE.**

5. The following shuffle algorithm is used to shuffle an array of `int` values, `nums`.

```java
public void shuffle ()
{
    for (int k = nums.length - 1; k > 0; k--)
    {
        int randPos = (int) (Math.random() * (k + 1));
        int temp = nums[k];
        nums[k] = nums[randPos];
        nums[randPos] = temp;
    }
}
```

Suppose the initial state of `nums` is 8, 7, 6, 5, 4, and when the method is executed the values generated for `randPos` are 3, 2, 0, 0, in that order. What element will be contained in `nums[2]` after execution?

(A) 8

(B) 7

(C) 6

(D) 5

(E) 4

6. Consider the following instance variables and method `assignValues` in the same class.

```java
private int numRows;
private int numCols;
private int[][] mat;

/** arr has numCols elements */
private void assignValues(int[] arr, int value)
{
    for (int k = 0; k < arr.length; k++)
        arr[k] = value;
}
```

Which of the following code segments will correctly assign `mat` to have the value 100 in each slot? You may assume that the instance variables have all been correctly initialized.

```
 I for (int row = 0; row < numRows; row++)
        assignValues(mat[row], 100);

 II for (int col = 0; col < numCols; col++)
        assignValues(mat[col], 100);

III for (int[] row: mat)
        for (int num: row)
            num = 100;
```

(A) I only

(B) II only

(C) III only

(D) I and II only

(E) I and III only

**GO ON TO THE NEXT PAGE.**

7. Consider the following inheritance hierarchy.

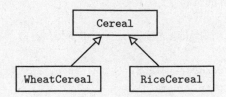

Which of the following declarations will not cause an error? You may assume that each of the classes above has a default constructor.

    I   WheatCereal w = new Cereal();

   II   Cereal c1 = new Cereal();

  III   Cereal c2 = new RiceCereal();

(A) I only
(B) II only
(C) III only
(D) II and III only
(E) I, II, and III

Questions 8 and 9 refer to the following class definitions.

```
public Class1
{
    public void method1()
    { /* implementation not shown */ }
}

public class Class2 extends Class1
{
    public void method2()
    { /* implementation not shown */ }

    //Private instance variables and other methods are not shown.
}

public class Class3 extends Class2
{
    public void method3(Class3 other)
    { /* implementation not shown */ }

    //Private instance variables and other methods are not shown.
}
```

8. Assuming that Class1, Class2, and Class3 have default constructors, which is (are) valid in a client class?

    I Class1 c1 = new Class2();

    II Class2 c2 = new Class3();

    III Class1 c3 = new Class3();

    (A) I only
    (B) II only
    (C) III only
    (D) I and II only
    (E) I, II, and III

9. Consider the following declarations in a client class.

    ```
    Class3 ob3 = new Class3();
    Class2 ob2 = new Class2();
    ```

    Which method calls would be legal?

    I ob3.method1();

    II ob2.method3(ob3);

    III ob3.method3(ob2);

    (A) I only
    (B) II only
    (C) III only
    (D) II and III only
    (E) I, II, and III

**GO ON TO THE NEXT PAGE.**

10. Refer to the following program segment.

```
for (int n = 50; n > 0; n = n / 2)
    System.out.println(n);
```

How many lines of output will this segment produce?

(A) 50
(B) 49
(C) 7
(D) 6
(E) 5

11. Let `list` be an `ArrayList<String>` containing only these elements.

```
"John", "Mary", "Harry", "Luis"
```

Which of the following statements will cause an error to occur?

```
 I list.set(2, "6");

 II list.add(4, "Pat");

 III String s = list.get(4);
```

(A) I only
(B) II only
(C) III only
(D) II and III only
(E) I, II, and III

12. Consider the following static method.

```
public static int compute(int n)
{
    for (int i = 1; i < 4; i++)
        n *= n;
    return n;
}
```

Which of the following could replace the body of `compute`, so that the new version returns the identical result as the original for all n?

(A) `return 4 * n;`
(B) `return 8 * n;`
(C) `return 64 * n;`
(D) `return (int) Math.pow(n, 4);`
(E) `return (int) Math.pow(n, 8);`

**GO ON TO THE NEXT PAGE.**

13. Consider the following instance variable and method.

```
private int[] nums;

/** Precondition: nums contains int values in no particular order.
 */
public int getValue()
{
    for (int k = 0; k < nums.length; k++)
    {
        if (nums[k] % 2 != 0)
            return k;
    }
    return -1;
}
```

Suppose the following statement is executed.

```
int j = getValue();
```

If the value returned in j is a positive integer, which of the following best describes the contents of nums?

(A) The only odd int in nums is at position j.
(B) All values in positions 0 through j-1 are odd.
(C) All values in positions 0 through j-1 are even.
(D) All values in positions nums.length-1 down to j+1 are odd.
(E) All values in positions nums.length-1 down to j+1 are even.

14. Consider the following method.

```
public int mystery (int n)
{
    if (n == 0)
        return 0;
    else if (n % 2 == 1)
        return n;
    else
        return n + mystery(n - 1);
}
```

What will be returned by a call to mystery(6)?

(A) 6
(B) 11
(C) 12
(D) 27
(E) 30

**GO ON TO THE NEXT PAGE.**

15. Consider the following code segment.

```
int num1 = value1, num2 = value2, num3 = value3;
while (num1 > num2 || num1 > num3)
{
    /* body of loop */
}
```

You may assume that value1, value2, and value3 are int values. Which of the following is sufficient to guarantee that /* *body of loop* */ will never be executed?

(A) There is no statement in /* *body of loop* */ that leads to termination.

(B) num1 < num2

(C) num1 < num3

(D) num1 > num2 && num1 > num3

(E) num1 < num2 && num1 < num3

16. Consider the following two classes.

```java
public class Performer
{
    public void act()
    {
        System.out.print(" bow");
        perform();
    }

    public void perform()
    {
        System.out.print(" act");
    }
}

public class Singer extends Performer
{
    public void act()
    {
        System.out.print(" rise");
        super.act();
        System.out.print(" encore");
    }

    public void perform()
    {
        System.out.print(" aria");
    }
}
```

Suppose the following declaration appears in a class other than Performer or Singer.

```java
Performer p = new Singer();
```

What is printed as a result of the call p.act();?

(A) rise bow aria encore

(B) rise bow act encore

(C) rise bow act

(D) bow act aria

(E) bow aria encore

**GO ON TO THE NEXT PAGE.**

Use the program description below for Questions 17–19.

A car dealer needs a program that will maintain an inventory of cars on his lot. There are four types of cars: sedans, station wagons, electric cars, and SUVs. The model, year, color, and price need to be recorded for each car, plus any additional features for the different types of cars. The program must allow the dealer to

- Add a new car to the lot.
- Remove a car from the lot.
- Correct any data that's been entered.
- Display information for any car.

17. The programmer decides to have these classes: `Car`, `Inventory`, `Sedan`, `SUV`, `ElectricCar`, and `StationWagon`. Which statement is true about the relationships between these classes and their attributes?

    I  There are no inheritance relationships between these classes.
    II  The `Inventory` class *has-a* list of `Car` objects.
    III  The `Sedan`, `SUV`, `ElectricCar`, and `StationWagon` classes are independent of each other.

(A) I only
(B) II only
(C) III only
(D) I and II only
(E) II and III only

18. Suppose that the programmer decides to have a `Car` class and an `Inventory` class. The `Inventory` class will maintain a list of all the cars on the lot. Here are some of the methods in the program.

```
addCar          //adds a car to the lot
removeCar       //removes a car from the lot
displayCar      //displays all the features of a given car
setColor        //sets the color of a car to a given color
                //   (may be used to correct data)
getPrice        //returns the price of a car
displayAllCars  //displays features for every car on the lot
```

In each of the following, a class and a method are given. Which is the least suitable choice of class to be responsible for the given method?
(A) `Car`, `setColor`
(B) `Car`, `removeCar`
(C) `Car`, `getPrice`
(D) `Car`, `displayCar`
(E) `Inventory`, `displayAllCars`

**GO ON TO THE NEXT PAGE.**

19. Suppose Car is a superclass and Sedan, StationWagon, ElectricCar, and SUV are sub-classes of Car. Which of the following is the most likely method of the Car class to be overridden by at least one of the subclasses (Sedan, StationWagon, ElectricCar, or SUV)?

    (A) setColor(newColor)   //sets color of Car to newColor
    (B) getModel()           //returns model of Car
    (C) displayCar()         //displays all features of Car
    (D) setPrice(newPrice)   //sets price of Car to newPrice
    (E) getYear()            //returns year of Car

20. Consider the following segment of code.

```
String word = "conflagration";
int x = word.indexOf("flag");
String s = word.substring(0, x);
```

    What will be the result of executing the above segment?
    (A) A syntax error will occur.
    (B) String s will be the empty string.
    (C) String s will contain "flag".
    (D) String s will contain "conf".
    (E) String s will contain "con".

21. A two-dimensional matrix mat with at least one row is initialized and will be traversed using a row-major (row-by-row, left-to-right) traversal. Which represents the last element accessed?

    (A) mat[mat.length][mat[0].length]
    (B) mat[mat[0].length][mat.length]
    (C) mat[mat.length - 1][mat[0].length - 1]
    (D) mat[mat[0].length - 1][mat.length - 1]
    (E) mat[mat.length - 1][mat.length - 1]

**GO ON TO THE NEXT PAGE.**

22. A class of 30 students rated their computer science teacher on a scale of 1 to 10 (1 means awful and 10 means outstanding). The `responses` array is a 30-element integer array of the student responses. An 11-element array `freq` will count the number of occurrences of each response. For example, `freq[6]` will count the number of students who responded 6. The quantity `freq[0]` will not be used.

Here is a program that counts the students' responses and outputs the results.

```
public class StudentEvaluations
{
    public static void main(String args[])
    {
        int[] responses = {6,6,7,8,10,1,5,4,6,7,
                           5,4,3,4,4,9,8,6,7,10,
                           6,7,8,8,9,6,7,8,9,2};
        int[] freq = new int[11];
        for (int i = 0; i < responses.length; i++)
            freq[responses[i]]++;
        //output results
        System.out.print("rating" + "  " + "frequency\n");
        for (int rating = 1; rating < freq.length; rating++)
            System.out.print(rating + "  " +
                freq[rating] + "\n");
    }
}
```

Suppose the last entry in the initializer list for the `responses` array was incorrectly typed as 12 instead of 2. What would be the result of running the program?
(A) A rating of 12 would be listed with a frequency of 1 in the output table.
(B) A rating of 1 would be listed with a frequency of 12 in the output table.
(C) An `ArrayIndexOutOfBoundsException` would be thrown.
(D) A `StringIndexOutOfBoundsException` would be thrown.
(E) A `NullPointerException` would be thrown.

GO ON TO THE NEXT PAGE.

Questions 23–25 are based on the three classes below.

```java
public class Employee
{
    private String name;
    private int employeeNum;
    private double salary, taxWithheld;

    public Employee(String aName, int empNum, double aSalary,
        double aTax)
    { /* implementation not shown */ }

    /** @return pre-tax salary */
    public double getSalary()
    { return salary; }

    public String getName()
    { return name; }

    public int getEmployeeNum()
    { return employeeNum; }

    public double getTax()
    { return taxWithheld; }

    public double computePay()
    { return salary - taxWithheld; }
}

public class PartTimeEmployee extends Employee
{
    private double payFraction;

    public PartTimeEmployee(String aName, int empNum, double aSalary,
        double aTax, double aPayFraction)
    { /* implementation not shown */ }

    public double getPayFraction()
    { return payFraction; }

    public double computePay()
    { return getSalary() * payFraction - getTax();}
}

public class Consultant extends Employee
{
    private static final double BONUS = 5000;

    public Consultant(String aName, int empNum, double aSalary,
        double aTax)
    { /* implementation not shown */ }

    public double computePay()
    { /* implementation code */ }
}
```

**GO ON TO THE NEXT PAGE.**

23. The `computePay` method in the `Consultant` class redefines the `computePay` method of the `Employee` class to add a bonus to the salary after subtracting the tax withheld. Which represents correct /* *implementation code* */ of `computePay` for `Consultant`?

    I  `return super.computePay() + BONUS;`

    II  `super.computePay();`
       `return getSalary() + BONUS;`

    III  `return getSalary() - getTax() + BONUS;`

  (A) I only
  (B) II only
  (C) III only
  (D) I and III only
  (E) I and II only

24. Consider these valid declarations in a client program.

```
Employee e = new Employee("Noreen Rizvi", 304, 65000, 10000);
Employee p = new PartTimeEmployee("Rafael Frongillo", 287, 40000,
    7000, 0.8);
Employee c = new Consultant("Dan Lepage", 694, 55000, 8500);
```

Which of the following method calls will cause an error?
  (A) `double x = e.computePay();`
  (B) `double y = p.computePay();`
  (C) `String n = c.getName();`
  (D) `int num = p.getEmployeeNum();`
  (E) `double g = p.getPayFraction();`

**GO ON TO THE NEXT PAGE.**

25. Consider the `writePayInfo` method.

```
/** Writes Employee name and pay on one line. */
public static void writePayInfo(Employee e)
{ System.out.println(e.getName() + " " + e.computePay()); }
```

The following piece of code invokes this method.

```
Employee[] empList = new Employee[3];
empList[0] = new Employee("Lila Fontes", 1, 10000, 850);
empList[1] = new Consultant("Momo Liu", 2, 50000, 8000);
empList[2] = new PartTimeEmployee("Moses Wilks", 3, 25000, 3750,
    0.6);
for (Employee e : empList)
    writePayInfo(e);
```

What will happen when this code is executed?
(A) A `NullPointerException` will be thrown.
(B) An `ArrayIndexOutOfBoundsException` will be thrown.
(C) A compile-time error will occur, with the message that the `getName` method is not in the `Consultant` class.
(D) A compile-time error will occur, with the message that an instance of an `Employee` object cannot be created.
(E) A list of employees' names and corresponding pay will be written to the screen.

**GO ON TO THE NEXT PAGE.**

26. Consider an array `arr` that is initialized with `int` values. The following code segment stores in `count` the number of positive values in `arr`.

```
int count = 0, index = 0;
while (index < arr.length)
{
    if (arr[index] > 0)
        count++;
    index++;
}
```

Which of the following is equivalent to the above segment?

```
 I  int count = 0;
    for (int num : arr)
    {
        if (arr[num] > 0)
            count++;
    }
```

```
 II  int count = 0;
     for (int num : arr)
     {
         if (num > 0)
             count++;
     }
```

```
 III  int count = 0;
      for (int i = 0; i < arr.length; i++)
      {
          if (arr[i] > 0)
              count++;
      }
```

(A) I only
(B) II only
(C) III only
(D) II and III only
(E) I and III only

GO ON TO THE NEXT PAGE.

27. A square matrix is declared as

```
int[][] mat = new int[SIZE][SIZE];
```

where SIZE is an appropriate integer constant. Consider the following method.

```
public static void mystery(int[][] mat, int value, int top, int left,
    int bottom, int right)
{
    for (int i = left; i <= right; i++)
    {
        mat[top][i] = value;
        mat[bottom][i] = value;
    }
    for (int i = top + 1; i <= bottom - 1; i++)
    {
        mat[i][left] = value;
        mat[i][right] = value;
    }
}
```

Assuming that there are no out-of-range errors, which best describes what method mystery does?

(A) Places value in corners of the rectangle with corners (top, left) and (bottom, right).
(B) Places value in the diagonals of the square with corners (top, left) and (bottom, right).
(C) Places value in each element of the rectangle with corners (top, left) and (bottom, right).
(D) Places value in each element of the border of the rectangle with corners (top, left) and (bottom, right).
(E) Places value in the topmost and bottommost rows of the rectangle with corners (top, left) and (bottom, right).

28. Consider the following declaration.

```
ArrayList<Integer> list = new ArrayList<Integer>();
```

Which of the following code segments will place the integers 1 to 10, in any order, in the empty list?

```
  I for (int i = 0; i < 10; i++)
        list.add(i + 1);
 II for (int i = 0; i < 10; i++)
        list.add(i, i + 1);
III for (int i = 9; i >= 0; i--)
        list.add(i, i + 1);
```

(A) I only
(B) II only
(C) III only
(D) I and II only
(E) I, II, and III

**GO ON TO THE NEXT PAGE.**

29. Assume that a Book class has a compareTo method in which, if b1 and b2 are Book objects, b1.compareTo(b2) is a negative integer if b1 is less than b2, a positive integer if b1 is greater than b2, and 0 if b1 equals b2. The following method is intended to return the index of the "smallest" book, namely the book that would appear first in a sorted list of Book objects.

```
/** Precondition:
 *    - books is initialized with Book objects.
 *    - books.length > 0.
 */
public static int findMin(Book[] books)
{
    int minPos = 0;
    for (int index = 1; index < books.length; index++)
    {
        if ( /* condition */ )
        {
            minPos = index;
        }
    }
    return minPos;
}
```

Which of the following should be used to replace /* *condition* */ so that findMin works as intended?

(A) books[index] < books[minPos]

(B) books[index] > books[minPos]

(C) books[index].compareTo(books[minPos]) > 0

(D) books[index].compareTo(books[minPos]) >= 0

(E) books[index].compareTo(books[minPos]) < 0

30. Refer to the static method `removeNegs` shown below.

```
/** Precondition: list is an ArrayList<Integer>.
 * Postcondition: All negative values have been removed from list.
 */
public static void removeNegs(ArrayList<Integer> list)
{
    int index = 0;
    while (index < list.size())
    {
        if (list.get(index).intValue() < 0)
        {
            list.remove(index);
        }
        index++;
    }
}
```

For which of the following lists will the method not work as intended?

(A) 6 -1 -2 5

(B) -1 2 -3 4

(C) 2 4 6 8

(D) -3

(E) 1 2 3 -8

**GO ON TO THE NEXT PAGE.**

31. A sorted list of 120 integers is to be searched to determine whether the value 100 is in the list. Assuming that the most efficient searching algorithm is used, what is the maximum number of elements that must be examined?

    (A) 7
    (B) 8
    (C) 20
    (D) 100
    (E) 120

32. Consider a sorted array arr of *n* elements, where *n* is large and *n* is even. Under which conditions will a sequential search of arr be faster than a binary search?

    I   The target is not in the list.

    II  The target is in the first position of the list.

    III The target is in arr[1 + n/2].

    (A) I only
    (B) II only
    (C) III only
    (D) I and III only
    (E) II and III only

GO ON TO THE NEXT PAGE.

33. Refer to the following data field and method.

```
private int[] arr;

/** Precondition:  arr.length > 0 and index < arr.length. */
public void remove(int index)
{
    int[] b = new int[arr.length - 1];
    int count = 0;
    for (int i = 0; i < arr.length; i++)
    {
        if (i != index)
        {
            b[count] = arr[i];
            count++;
        }
    }
    /* assertion */
    arr = b;
}
```

Which of the following assertions is true when the /* *assertion* */ line is reached during execution of remove?

(A) b[k] == arr[k] for 0 <= k < arr.length.

(B) b[k] == arr[k + 1] for 0 <= k < arr.length.

(C) b[k] == arr[k] for 0 <= k <= index, and
    b[k] == arr[k + 1] for index < k < arr.length - 1.

(D) b[k] == arr[k] for 0 <= k < index, and
    b[k] == arr[k + 1] for index <= k < arr.length - 1.

(E) b[k] == arr[k] for 0 <= k < index, and
    b[k] == arr[k + 1] for index <= k < arr.length.

34. Consider the following code segment.

```
for (int n = 25; n >= 0; n /= 2)
    System.out.println(n);
```

When the segment is executed, how many passes through the for loop will there be?

(A) Fewer than 5

(B) Between 5 and 12, inclusive

(C) Between 13 and 25, inclusive

(D) Between 26 and 100, inclusive

(E) More than 100

**GO ON TO THE NEXT PAGE.**

Questions 35–37 refer to the `TennisPlayer`, `GoodPlayer`, and `WeakPlayer` classes below. These classes are to be used in a program to simulate a game of tennis.

```java
public class TennisPlayer
{
    private String name;

    public TennisPlayer(String aName)
    { name = aName; }

    public boolean serve()
    { /* implementation not shown */ }
}

public class GoodPlayer extends TennisPlayer
{
    public GoodPlayer(String aName)
    { /* implementation not shown */ }

    public boolean serve()
    { /* implementation not shown */ }
}

public class WeakPlayer extends TennisPlayer
{
    public WeakPlayer(String aName)
    { /* implementation not shown */ }

    /** Returns true if serve is in (45% probability),
     *  false if serve is out (55% probability).
     */
    public boolean serve()
    { /* implementation not shown */ }
}
```

GO ON TO THE NEXT PAGE.

35. Which of the following declarations will cause an error? You may assume all the constructors are correctly implemented.

    (A) `WeakPlayer t = new TennisPlayer("Smith");`
    (B) `TennisPlayer g = new GoodPlayer("Jones");`
    (C) `TennisPlayer w = new WeakPlayer("Henry");`
    (D) `TennisPlayer p = null;`
    (E) `WeakPlayer q = new WeakPlayer("Grady");`

36. Refer to the `serve` method in the `WeakPlayer` class.

```
/** Returns true if serve is in (45% probability),
 *  false if serve is out (55% probability).
 */
public boolean serve()
{ /* implementation */ }
```

Which of the following replacements for /* *implementation* */ satisfy the postcondition of the serve method?

```
 I double value = Math.random();
   return value >= 0 || value < 0.45;
```

```
 II double value = Math.random();
    return value < 0.45;
```

```
III int val = (int) (Math.random() * 100);
    return val < 45;
```

    (A) I only
    (B) II only
    (C) III only
    (D) II and III only
    (E) I, II, and III

GO ON TO THE NEXT PAGE.

37. Consider the following class definition.

```
public class Beginner extends WeakPlayer
{
    private double costOfLessons;

    //methods of Beginner class
        ...
}
```

Refer to the following declarations and method in a client program.

```
TennisPlayer w = new WeakPlayer("Harry");
TennisPlayer b = new Beginner("Dick");
Beginner bp = new Beginner("Ted");

public void giveEncouragement(WeakPlayer t)
{ /* implementation not shown */ }
```

Which of the following method calls will cause an error?

I   giveEncouragement(w);

II  giveEncouragement(b);

III giveEncouragement(bp);

(A) I only
(B) II only
(C) III only
(D) I and II only
(E) I, II, and III

GO ON TO THE NEXT PAGE.

38. A matrix class that manipulates matrices contains the following declaration.

```
private int[][] mat = new int[numRows][numCols];
```

Consider the following method that alters matrix mat.

```
public void doSomething()
{
    int width = mat[0].length;
    int numRows = mat.length;
    for (int row = 0; row < numRows; row++)
        for (int col = 0; col < width/2; col++)
            mat[row][col] = mat[row][width - 1 - col];
}
```

If mat has current value

```
1 2 3 4 5 6
1 3 5 7 9 11
```

what will the value of mat be after a call to doSomething?

(A)  1 2 3 3 2 1
     1 3 5 5 3 1

(B)  6 5 4 4 5 6
     11 9 7 7 9 11

(C)  6 5 4 3 2 1
     11 9 7 5 3 1

(D)  1 2 3 4 5 6
     1 2 3 4 5 6

(E)  1 3 5 7 9 11
     1 3 5 7 9 11

Questions 39 and 40 refer to the following information.

Consider an array arr that is sorted in increasing order, and method findMost given below. Method findMost is intended to find the value in the array that occurs most often. If every value occurs exactly once, findMost should return –1. If there is more than one value that occurs the most, findMost should return any one of those. For example, if arr contains the values [1,5,7,7,10], findMost should return 7. If arr contains [2,2,2,7,8,8,9,9,9], findMost should return 2 or 9. If arr contains [1,2,7,8], findMost should return –1.

```
Line 1:  /** Precondition:  arr sorted in increasing order.
Line 2:  */
Line 3:  public static int findMost(int[] arr)
Line 4:  {
Line 5:      int index = 0;
Line 6:      int count = 1;
Line 7:      int maxCountSoFar = 1;
Line 8:      int mostSoFar = arr[0];
Line 9:      while (index < arr.length - 1)
Line 10:     {
Line 11:         while (index < arr.length - 1 &&
Line 12:                 arr[index] == arr[index + 1])
Line 13:         {
Line 14:             count++;
Line 15:             index++;
Line 16:         }
Line 17:         if (count > maxCountSoFar)
Line 18:         {
Line 19:             maxCountSoFar = count;
Line 20:             mostSoFar = arr[index];
Line 21:         }
Line 22:         index++;
Line 23:     }
Line 24:     if (maxCountSoFar == 1)
Line 25:         return -1;
Line 26:     else
Line 27:         return mostSoFar;
Line 28: }
```

39. The method findMost does not always work as intended. An *incorrect* result will be returned if arr contains the values

    (A) [1,2,3,4,5]
    (B) [6,6,6,6]
    (C) [1,2,2,3,4,5]
    (D) [1,1,3,4,5,5,5,7]
    (E) [2,2,2,4,5,5]

40. Which of the following changes should be made so that method findMost will work as intended?

    (A) Insert the statement count = 1; between Lines 20 and 21.
    (B) Insert the statement count = 1; between Lines 21 and 22.
    (C) Insert the statement count = 1; between Lines 16 and 17.
    (D) Insert the statement count = 0; between Lines 23 and 24.
    (E) Insert the statement count = 1; between Lines 23 and 24.

**END OF SECTION I**

# COMPUTER SCIENCE A
# SECTION II

Time—1 hour and 30 minutes
Number of questions—4
Percent of total grade—50

**DIRECTIONS:** SHOW ALL YOUR WORK. REMEMBER THAT
PROGRAM SEGMENTS ARE TO BE WRITTEN IN JAVA.

Write your answers in <u>pencil only</u> in the booklet provided.

**NOTES:**

- Assume that the classes in the Quick Reference have been imported where needed.

- Unless otherwise noted in the question, assume that parameters in method calls are not null and that methods are called only when their preconditions are satisfied.

- In writing solutions for each question, you may use any of the accessible methods that are listed in classes defined in that question. Writing significant amounts of code that can be replaced by a call to one of these methods will not receive full credit.

**GO ON TO THE NEXT PAGE.**

1. A WordSet, whose partial implementation is shown in the class declaration below, stores a set of String objects in no particular order and contains no duplicates. Each word is a sequence of capital letters only.

```java
public class WordSet
{
    /** Constructor initializes set to empty. */
    public WordSet()
    { /* implementation not shown */ }

    /** Returns the number of words in set. */
    public int size()
    { /* implementation not shown */ }

    /** Adds word to set.
     */
    public void insert(String word)
    { /* implementation not shown */ }

    /** Removes word from set if present, else does nothing.
     */
    public void remove(String word)
    { /* implementation not shown */ }

    /** Returns kth word in alphabetical order, where 1 <= k <= size().
     */
    public String findkth(int k)
    { /* implementation not shown */ }

    /** Returns true if set contains word, false otherwise. */
    public boolean contains(String word)
    { /* implementation not shown */ }

    //Other instance variables, constructors, and methods are not shown.
}
```

The findkth method returns the $k$th word in alphabetical order in the set, even though the implementation of WordSet may not be sorted. The number $k$ ranges from 1 (corresponding to first in alphabetical order) to $N$, where $N$ is the number of words in the set. For example, if WordSet s stores the words {"GRAPE", "PEAR", "FIG", "APPLE"}, here are the values when s.findkth(k) is called.

| k | values of s.findkth(k) |
|---|---|
| 1 | APPLE |
| 2 | FIG |
| 3 | GRAPE |
| 4 | PEAR |

**GO ON TO THE NEXT PAGE.**

```
public class WordSet

public WordSet()
public int size()
public void insert(String word)
public void remove(String word)
public String findkth(int k)
public boolean contains(String word)
```

(a) Write a client method `countA` that returns the number of words in `WordSet` s that begin with the letter "A." In writing `countA`, you may call any of the methods of the `WordSet` class. Assume that the methods work as specified.

Complete method `countA` below.

```
/**  Returns the number of words in s that begin with "A".
 */
public static int countA(WordSet s)
```

(b) Write a client method `removeA` that removes all words that begin with "A" from a non-null `WordSet`. If there are no such words in s, then `removeA` does nothing. In writing `removeA`, you may call method `countA` specified in part (a). Assume that `countA` works as specified, regardless of what you wrote in part (a).

Complete method `removeA` below.

```
/** Removes from WordSet s all words that begin with the letter "A".
 *  Precondition:  WordSet is not null.
 *  Postcondition: WordSet s contains no words that begin with
 *              "A", but is otherwise unchanged.
 */
public static void removeA(WordSet s)
```

**GO ON TO THE NEXT PAGE.**

2. A clothing store sells shoes, pants, and tops. The store also allows a customer to buy an "outfit," which consists of three items: one pair of shoes, one pair of pants, and one top.

Each clothing item has a description and a price. The four types of clothing items are represented by the four classes Shoes, Pants, Top, and Outfit. All four classes are subclasses of a ClothingItem class, shown below.

```java
public class ClothingItem
{
    private String description;
    private double price;

    public ClothingItem()
    {
        description = "";
        price = 0;
    }

    public ClothingItem(String descr, double aPrice)
    {
        description = descr;
        price = aPrice;
    }

    public String getDescription()
    { return description; }

    public double getPrice()
    { return price; }
}
```

The following diagram shows the relationship between the ClothingItem class and the Shoes, Pants, Top, and Outfit classes.

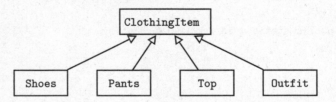

The store allows customers to create Outfit clothing items each of which includes a pair of shoes, pants, and a top. The description of the outfit consists of the description of the shoes, pants, and top, in that order, separated by "/" and followed by a space and "outfit". The price of an outfit is calculated as follows. If the sum of the prices of any two items equals or exceeds $100, there is a 25% discount on the sum of the prices of all three items. Otherwise there is a 10% discount.

For example, an outfit consisting of sneakers ($40), blue jeans ($50), and a T-shirt ($10) would have the name "sneakers/blue jeans/T-shirt outfit" and a price of $0.90(40 + 50 + 10) = \$90.00$. An outfit consisting of loafers ($50), cutoffs ($20), and dress-shirt ($60) would have the description `"loafers/cutoffs/dress-shirt outfit"` and price $0.75(50 + 20 + 60) = \$97.50$.

Write the `Outfit` subclass of `ClothingItem`. Your implementation must have just one constructor that takes three parameters representing a pair of shoes, pants, and a top, in that order.

A client class that uses the `Outfit` class should be able to create an outfit, get its description, and get its price. Your implementation should be such that the client code has the following behavior:

```
Shoes shoes;
Pants pants;
Top top;
/* Code to initialize shoes, pants, and top */

ClothingItem outfit =
    new Outfit (shoes, pants, top); //Compiles without error
ClothingItem outfit =
    new Outfit (pants, shoes, top); //Compile-time error
ClothingItem outfit =
    new Outfit (shoes, top, pants); //Compile-time error
```

Write your solution below.

3. Consider a note keeper object that is designed to store and manipulate a list of short notes. Here are some typical notes:

```
pick up drycleaning
special dog chow
car registration
dentist Monday
dog license
```

A note is represented by the following class.

```
public class Note
{
    /** Returns a one-line note. */
    public String getNote()
    { /* implementation not shown */ }

    //There may be instance variables, constructors, and methods
    //that are not shown.
}
```

**GO ON TO THE NEXT PAGE.**

A note keeper is represented by the `NoteKeeper` class shown below.

```
public class NoteKeeper
{
    /** The list of notes */
    private ArrayList<Note> noteList;

    /** Prints all notes in noteList, as described in part(a).
     */
    public void printNotes()
    { /* to be implemented in part (a) */}

    /** Removes all notes with specified string from noteList,
     *  as described in part (b).
     *  If none of the notes in noteList contains the given string,
     *  the list remains unchanged.
     */
    public void removeNotes(String str)
    { /* to be implemented in part (b) */ }

    //There may be instance variables, constructors, and methods
    //that are not shown.
}
```

(a) Write the `NoteKeeper` method `printNotes`. This method prints all of the notes in `noteList`, one per line, and numbers the notes, starting at 1. The output should look like this.

```
1. pick up drycleaning
2. special dog chow
3. car registration
4. dentist Monday
5. dog license
```

Complete method `printNotes` below.

```
/** Prints all notes in noteList, as described in part(a).
 */
public void printNotes()
```

GO ON TO THE NEXT PAGE.

(b) Write the `NoteKeeper` method `removeNotes`. Method `removeNotes` removes all notes from `noteList` that contain the string specified by the parameter. The ordering of the remaining notes should be left unchanged. For example, suppose that a `NoteKeeper` variable, `notes`, has a `noteList` containing the following.

```
[pick up drycleaning, special dog chow, car registration,
  dentist Monday, dog license]
```

The method call `notes.removeNotes("dog")` should modify the `noteList` of `notes` to be

```
[pick up drycleaning, car registration, dentist Monday]
```

The method call `notes.removeNotes("cow")` should leave the list shown above unchanged.

Here's another example. If `noteList` contains

```
[pick up car, buy carrots, dog license, carpet cleaning]
```

the method call `notes.removeNotes("car")` should modify the `noteList` of `notes` to be

```
[dog license]
```

Complete method `removeNotes` below.

```
/** Removes all notes with specified string from noteList,
 *  as described in part (b).
 *  If none of the notes in noteList contains the given string,
 *  the list remains unchanged.
 */
public void removeNotes(String str)
```

**GO ON TO THE NEXT PAGE.**

4. Consider the problem of keeping track of the available seats in a theater. Theater seats can be represented with a two-dimensional array of integers, where a value of 0 shows a seat is available, while a value of 1 indicates that the seat is occupied. For example, the array below shows the current seat availability for a show in a small theater.

|     | [0] | [1] | [2] | [3] | [4] | [5] |
|-----|-----|-----|-----|-----|-----|-----|
| [0] | 0   | 0   | 1   | 1   | 0   | 1   |
| [1] | 0   | 1   | 0   | 1   | 0   | 1   |
| [2] | 1   | 0   | 0   | 0   | 0   | 0   |

The seat at slot [1][3] is taken, but seat [0][4] is still available.

A show can be represented by the Show class shown below.

```
public class Show
{
    /** The seats for this show */
    private int[][] seats;

    private final int SEATS_PER_ROW = <some integer value>;
    private final int NUM_ROWS = <some integer value>;

    /** Reserve two adjacent seats and return true if this was
     *  successfully done, false otherwise, as described in part (a).
     */
    public boolean twoTogether()
    { /* to be implemented in part (a) */ }

    /** Return the lowest seat number in the specified row for a
     *  block of seatsNeeded empty adjacent seats, as described in part (b).
     */
    public int findAdjacent(int row, int seatsNeeded)
    { /* to be implemented in part (b) */ }

    //There may be instance variables, constructors, and methods
    //that are not shown.
}
```

GO ON TO THE NEXT PAGE.

(a) Write the Show method twoTogether, which reserves two adjacent seats and returns true if this was successfully done. If it is not possible to find two adjacent seats that are unoccupied, the method should leave the show unchanged and return false. For example, suppose this is the state of a show.

|       | [0] | [1] | [2] | [3] | [4] | [5] |
|-------|-----|-----|-----|-----|-----|-----|
| [0]   | 0   | 0   | 1   | 1   | 0   | 1   |
| [1]   | 0   | 1   | 0   | 1   | 0   | 1   |
| [2]   | 1   | 0   | 0   | 0   | 1   | 1   |

A call to twoTogether should return true, and the final state of the show could be any one of the following three configurations.

|       | [0] | [1] | [2] | [3] | [4] | [5] |
|-------|-----|-----|-----|-----|-----|-----|
| [0]   | 1   | 1   | 1   | 1   | 0   | 1   |
| [1]   | 0   | 1   | 0   | 1   | 0   | 1   |
| [2]   | 1   | 0   | 0   | 0   | 1   | 1   |

OR

|       | [0] | [1] | [2] | [3] | [4] | [5] |
|-------|-----|-----|-----|-----|-----|-----|
| [0]   | 0   | 0   | 1   | 1   | 0   | 1   |
| [1]   | 0   | 1   | 0   | 1   | 0   | 1   |
| [2]   | 1   | 1   | 1   | 0   | 1   | 1   |

OR

|       | [0] | [1] | [2] | [3] | [4] | [5] |
|-------|-----|-----|-----|-----|-----|-----|
| [0]   | 0   | 0   | 1   | 1   | 0   | 1   |
| [1]   | 0   | 1   | 0   | 1   | 0   | 1   |
| [2]   | 1   | 0   | 1   | 1   | 1   | 1   |

For the following state of a show, a call to twoTogether should return false and leave the two-dimensional array as shown.

|       | [0] | [1] | [2] | [3] | [4] | [5] |
|-------|-----|-----|-----|-----|-----|-----|
| [0]   | 0   | 1   | 0   | 1   | 1   | 0   |
| [1]   | 1   | 1   | 0   | 1   | 0   | 1   |
| [2]   | 0   | 1   | 1   | 1   | 1   | 1   |

**GO ON TO THE NEXT PAGE.**

```
Class information for this question

public class Show

private int[][] seats
private final int SEATS_PER_ROW
private final int NUM_ROWS
public boolean twoTogether()
public int findAdjacent(int row, int seatsNeeded)
```

Complete method twoTogether below.

```
/** Reserve two adjacent seats and return true if this was
 *  successfully done, false otherwise, as described in part (a).
 */
public boolean twoTogether()
```

(b) Write the Show method findAdjacent, which finds the lowest seat number in the specified row for a specified number of empty adjacent seats. If no such block of empty seats exists, the findAdjacent method should return -1. No changes should be made to the state of the show, irrespective of the value returned.

For example, suppose the diagram of seats is as shown.

|      | [0] | [1] | [2] | [3] | [4] | [5] |
|------|-----|-----|-----|-----|-----|-----|
| [0]  |  0  |  1  |  1  |  0  |  0  |  0  |
| [1]  |  0  |  0  |  0  |  0  |  1  |  1  |
| [2]  |  1  |  0  |  0  |  1  |  0  |  0  |

The following table shows some examples of calling findAdjacent for show.

| Method call | Return value |
|-------------|--------------|
| show.findAdjacent(0,3) | 3 |
| show.findAdjacent(1,3) | 0 or 1 |
| show.findAdjacent(2,2) | 1 or 4 |
| show.findAdjacent(1,5) | -1 |

Complete method findAdjacent below.

```
/** Return the lowest seat number in the specified row for a
 *  block of seatsNeeded empty adjacent seats, as described in part (b).
 */
public int findAdjacent(int row, int seatsNeeded)
```

**STOP**

**END OF EXAM**

PRACTICE TEST 2

# ANSWER KEY
## Practice Test 2

## Section I

| | | |
|---|---|---|
| 1. **E** | 15. **E** | 29. **E** |
| 2. **B** | 16. **A** | 30. **A** |
| 3. **C** | 17. **E** | 31. **A** |
| 4. **D** | 18. **B** | 32. **B** |
| 5. **A** | 19. **C** | 33. **D** |
| 6. **A** | 20. **E** | 34. **E** |
| 7. **D** | 21. **C** | 35. **A** |
| 8. **E** | 22. **C** | 36. **D** |
| 9. **A** | 23. **D** | 37. **D** |
| 10. **D** | 24. **E** | 38. **B** |
| 11. **C** | 25. **E** | 39. **E** |
| 12. **E** | 26. **D** | 40. **B** |
| 13. **C** | 27. **D** | |
| 14. **B** | 28. **D** | |

## ANSWERS EXPLAINED

## Section I

1. **(E)** The string parameter in the line of code uses two escape characters:
   \", which means print a double quote.
   \n, which means print a newline character (i.e., go to the next line).

2. **(B)** The intent of the programmer is to have overloaded `getValue` methods in `SomeClass`. Overloaded methods have different signatures, where the signature of a method includes the name and parameter types only. Thus, the signature of the original method is `getValue(int)`. The signature in header I is `getValue()`. The signature in header II is `getValue(int)`. The signature in header III is `getValue(double)`. Since the signature in header II is the same as that of the given method, the compiler will flag it and say that the method already exists in `SomeClass`. Note: The return type of a method is not included in its signature.

3. **(C)** The expression `(int)(Math.random() * 49)` produces a random integer from 0 through 48. (Note that 49 is the number of possibilities for `num`.) To shift this range from 2 to 50, add 2 to the expression.

4. **(D)** Short-circuit evaluation of the boolean expression will occur. The expression (num != 0) will evaluate to `false`, which makes the entire boolean expression `false`. Therefore the expression (score/num > SOME_CONSTANT) will not be evaluated. Hence no division by zero will occur, and there will be no `ArithmeticException` thrown. When the boolean expression has a value of `false`, only the `else` part of the statement, *statement2*, will be executed.

5. **(A)** The values of k are, consecutively, 4, 3, 2, and 1. The values of `randPos` are, consecutively, 3, 2, 0, and 0. Thus, the sequence of swaps and corresponding states of `nums` will be:

| | |
|---|---|
| swap nums[4] and nums[3] | 8 7 6 4 5 |
| swap nums[3] and nums[2] | 8 7 4 6 5 |
| swap nums[2] and nums[0] | 4 7 8 6 5 |
| swap nums[1] and nums[0] | 7 4 8 6 5 |

Thus, the element in `nums[2]` is 8.

6. **(A)** A matrix is stored as an array of arrays, that is, each row is an array. Therefore it is correct to call a method with an array parameter for each row, as is done in segment I. Segment II fails because `mat` is not an array of columns. The segment would cause an error, since `mat[col]` refers to a *row*, not a column. (If the number of rows were less than the number of columns, the method would throw an `ArrayIndexOutOfBoundsException`. If the number of rows were greater than the number of columns, the method would correctly assign the value 100 to the first n rows, where n is the number of columns. The rest of the rows would retain the values before execution of the method.) Segment III fails because this is incorrect usage of an enhanced `for` loop, which should not be used to assign new elements in the matrix. The matrix remains unchanged.

7. **(D)** Declaration I fails because it fails this test: Cereal *is-a* `WheatCereal`? No. Notice that declarations II and III pass this test: Cereal *is-a* `Cereal`? Yes. `RiceCereal` *is-a* `Cereal`? Yes.

8. **(E)** All satisfy the *is-a* test! `Class2` *is-a* `Class1`. `Class3` *is-a* `Class2`. `Class3` *is-a* `Class1`. Note: Since `Class3` is a subclass of `Class2`, it automatically implements any interfaces implemented by `Class2`, its superclass.

9. **(A)** Method call I works because `Class3` inherits all the methods of `Class1` and `Class2`. Method call II fails because `Class2` does not inherit the methods of `Class3`, its subclass. Method call III uses a parameter that fails the *is-a* test: ob2 is *not* a `Class3`, which the parameter requires.

10. **(D)** After each execution of the loop body, n is divided by 2. Thus, the loop will produce output when n is 50, 25, 12, 6, 3, and 1. The final value of n will be 1 / 2, which is 0, and the test will fail.

11. **(C)** Statement III will cause an `IndexOutOfBoundsException` because there is no slot 4. The final element, "Luis", is in slot 3. Statement I is correct: It replaces the string "Harry" with the string "6". It may look peculiar in the list, but the syntax is correct. Statement II looks like it may be out of range because there is no slot 4. It is correct, however, because you must be allowed to add an element to the end of the list.

12. **(E)** The effect of the given algorithm is to raise n to the 8th power.
When $i = 1$, the result is $n * n = n^2$.
When $i = 2$, the result is $n^2 * n^2 = n^4$.
When $i = 3$, the result is $n^4 * n^4 = n^8$.

13. **(C)** The method traverses `nums`, starting at position 0, and returns the current position the first time it finds an odd value. This implies that all values in positions 0 through the current index – 1 contained even numbers.

14. **(B)** Since `n == 6` fails the two base case tests, the method call `mystery(6)` returns `6 + mystery(5)`. Since 5 satisfies the second base case test, `mystery(5)` returns 5, and there are no more recursive calls. Thus, `mystery(6) = 6 + 5 = 11`.

15. **(E)** In order for /* *body of loop* */ not to be executed, the test must be false the first time it is evaluated. A compound OR test will be false if and only if both pieces of the test are false. Thus, choices B and C are insufficient. Choice D fails because it guarantees that both pieces of the test will be *true*. Choice A is wrong because /* *body of loop* */ may be executed many times, until the computer runs out of memory (an infinite loop!).

16. **(A)** When `p.act()` is called, the `act` method of `Singer` is executed. This is an example of polymorphism. The first line prints `rise`. Then `super.act()` goes to the `act` method of `Performer`, the superclass. This prints `bow` and then calls `perform()`. Again, using polymorphism, the `perform` method in `Singer` is called, which prints `aria`. Now, completing the `act` method of `Singer`, `encore` is printed. The result?

    ```
    rise bow aria encore
    ```

17. **(E)** Statement I is false: The `Sedan`, `StationWagon`, and `SUV` classes should all be subclasses of `Car`. Each one satisfies the *is-a* `Car` relationship. Statement II is true: The main task of the `Inventory` class should be to keep an updated list of `Car` objects. Statement III is true: A class is independent of another class if it does not require that class to implement its methods.

18. **(B)** The `Inventory` class is responsible for maintaining the list of all cars on the lot. Therefore methods like `addCar`, `removeCar`, and `displayAllCars` must be the responsibility of this class. The `Car` class should contain the `setColor`, `getPrice`, and `displayCar` methods, since all these pertain to the attributes of a given `Car`.

19. **(C)** Each subclass may contain additional attributes for the particular type of car that are not in the `Car` superclass. Since `displayCar` displays all features of a given car, this method should be overridden to display the original plus additional features.

20. **(E)** The expression `word.indexOf("flag")` returns the index of the first occurrence of `"flag"` in the calling string, `word`. Thus, x has value 3. (Recall that the first character in `word` is at index 0.) The method call `word.substring(0, x)` is equivalent to `word.substring(0, 3)`, which returns the substring in `word` from 0 to 2, namely `"con"`. The character at index 3 is not included.

21. **(C)** The number of rows in `mat` is given by `mat.length`. The indexes of the rows range from 0 to `mat.length - 1`. The number of columns in `mat` is given by `mat[0].length`. You can think of this as the length of the array represented by `mat[0]`, the first row. (Note that all the rows have the same length, but it is wise to use `mat[0]`, since you know that the matrix has at least one row. For example, `mat[1]` may be out of bounds.) The indexes of the columns range from 0 to `mat[0].length - 1`. The last element to be accessed in a row-by-row (or column-by-column) traversal is in the bottom right corner, namely, `mat[mat.length - 1][mat[0].length - 1]`.

22. **(C)** If the `responses` array contained an invalid value like 12, the program would attempt to add 1 to `freq[12]`. This is out of bounds for the `freq` array.

23. **(D)** Implementation I calls `super.computePay()`, which is equivalent to the `computePay` method in the `Employee` superclass. The method returns the quantity (`salary - taxWithheld`). The BONUS is then correctly added to this expression, as required. Implementation III correctly uses the public accessor methods `getSalary` and `getTax` that the `Consultant` class has inherited. Note that the `Consultant` class does not have direct access to the private instance variables `salary` and `taxWithheld`. Implementation II incorrectly returns the salary plus BONUS—there is no tax withheld. The expression `super.computePay()` returns a value equal to salary minus tax. But this is neither stored nor included in the `return` statement.

24. **(E)** Note that `p` is declared to be of type `Employee`, and the `Employee` class does not have a `getPayFraction` method. To avoid the error, `p` must be cast to `PartTimeEmployee` as follows:

```
double g = ((PartTimeEmployee) p).getPayFraction();
```

25. **(E)** The code does exactly what it looks like it should. The `writePayInfo` parameter is of type `Employee` and each element of the `empList` array *is-a* `Employee` and therefore does not need to be cast to its actual instance type. This is an example of polymorphism, in which the appropriate `computePay` method is chosen during run time. There is no `ArrayIndexOutOfBoundsException` (choice B) since the array is accessed using an enhanced `for` loop. None of the array elements is null; therefore, there is no `NullPointerException` (choice A). Choice C won't happen because the `getName` method is inherited by both the `Consultant` and `PartTimeEmployee` classes. Choice D would occur if the `Employee` superclass were abstract, but it's not.

26. **(D)** Segment I is incorrect because `num` is not an index in the loop: It is a value in the array. Thus, the correct test is `if (num > 0)`, which is correctly used in segment II. Segment III is a regular `for` loop, exactly equivalent to the given `while` loop.

27. **(D)** The first `for` loop places `value` in the top and bottom rows of the defined rectangle. The second `for` loop fills in the remaining border elements on the sides. Note that the `top + 1` and `bottom - 1` initializer and terminating conditions avoid filling in the corner elements twice.

28. **(D)** Segment I works because each `int` value, `i + 1`, is autoboxed in an `Integer`. Segment II works similarly using an overloaded version of the `add` method. The first parameter is the index and the second parameter is the element to be added. Segment III fails because an attempt to add an element to an empty list at a position other than 0 will cause an `IndexOutOfBoundsException` to be thrown.

29. **(E)** Eliminate choices A and B: When comparing `Book` objects, you cannot use simple inequality operators; you *must* use `compareTo`. For the calling object to be *less than* the parameter object, use the *less than* 0 test (a good way to remember this!).

30. **(A)** Method `removeNegs` will not work whenever there are consecutive negative values in the list. This is because removal of an element from an `ArrayList` causes the elements to the right of it to be shifted left to fill the "hole." The index in the given algorithm, however, always moves one slot to the right. Therefore in choice A, when –1 is removed, –2 will be passed over, and the final list will be 6 –2 5.

31. **(A)** If the list is sorted, a binary search is the most efficient algorithm to use. Binary search chops the current part of the array being examined in half, until you have found the element you are searching for, or there are no elements left to look at. In the worst case, you will need to divide by 2 seven times:

$$120/2 \rightarrow 60$$
$$60/2 \rightarrow 30$$
$$30/2 \rightarrow 15$$
$$15/2 \rightarrow 7$$
$$7/2 \rightarrow 3$$
$$3/2 \rightarrow 1$$
$$1/2 \rightarrow 0$$

Shortcut: Round 120 to the nearest power of 2, 128. Since $128 = 2^7$, the number of comparisons in the worst case equals the exponent, 7.

32. **(B)** For a sequential search, all $n$ elements will need to be examined. For a binary search, the array will be chopped in half a maximum of $\log_2 n$ times. When the target is in the first position of the list, a sequential search will find it in the first comparison. The binary search, which examines a middle element first, will not. Condition I is a worst case situation for the sequential search. It will require far more comparisons than a binary search. Condition III is approximately the middle of the list, but it won't be found on the first try of the binary search. (The first try examines `arr[n/2]`.) Still, the target *will* be located within fewer than $\log n$ tries, whereas the sequential search will need more than $n/2$ tries.

33. **(D)** The `remove` method removes from `arr` the element `arr[index]`. It does this by copying all elements from `arr[0]` up to but not including `arr[index]` into array `b`. Thus, `b[k] == arr[k]` for `0 <= k < index` is true. Then it copies all elements from `arr[index + 1]` up to and including `arr[arr.length - 1]` into `b`. Since no gaps are left in `b`, `b[k] == arr[k + 1]` for `index <= k < arr.length - 1`. The best way to see this is with a small example. If `arr` is 2, 6, 4, 8, 1, 7, and the element at `index` 2 (namely the 4) is to be removed, here is the picture:

```
b[0] == arr[0]
b[1] == arr[1]
b[2] == arr[3]
b[3] == arr[4]
b[4] == arr[5]
```

Notice that `arr.length` is 6, but `k` ends at 4.

34. **(E)** The segment is an example of an infinite loop. Here are successive values of `n`, which is updated with successive divisions by two using the `div` operator:

```
25, 12, 6, 3, 1, 0, 0, 0, ...
```

Note that 0/2 equals 0, which never fails the `n >= 0` test.

35. **(A)** Choice A is illegal because it fails this test: `TennisPlayer` *is-a* `WeakPlayer`? The answer is no, not necessarily.

36. **(D)** The statement

```
double value = Math.random();
```

generates a random `double` in the range $0 \le$ `value` $< 1$. Since random doubles are uniformly distributed in this interval, 45 percent of the time you can expect `value` to be in the range $0 \le$ `value` $< 0.45$. Therefore, a test for `value` in this range can be a test for whether the serve of a `WeakPlayer` went in. Since `Math.random()` never returns a negative number, the test in implementation II, `value < 0.45`, is sufficient. The test in implementation I would be correct if `||` were changed to `&&` ("or" changed to "and"—both parts must be true). Implementation III also works. The expression

```
(int) (Math.random() * 100)
```

returns a random integer from 0 to 99, each equally likely. Thus, 45 percent of the time, the integer `val` will be in the range $0 \le$ `val` $\le 44$. Therefore, a test for `val` in this range can be used to test whether the serve was in.

37. **(D)** Method calls I and II will each cause a compile-time error: The parameter must be of type `WeakPlayer`, but `w` and `b` are declared to be of type `TennisPlayer`. Each of these choices can be corrected by casting the parameter to `WeakPlayer`. Method call III works because `bp` *is-a* `WeakPlayer`.

38. **(B)** The method copies the elements from columns 3, 4, and 5 into columns 2, 1, and 0, respectively, as if there were a vertical mirror down the middle of the matrix. To see this, here are the values for the given matrix: `width = 6`, `width/2 = 3`, `numRows = 2`. The variable `row` goes from 0 to 1 and `column` goes from 0 to 2. The element assignments are

```
mat[0][0] = mat[0][5]
mat[0][1] = mat[0][4]
mat[0][2] = mat[0][3]
mat[1][0] = mat[1][5]
mat[1][1] = mat[1][4]
mat[1][2] = mat[1][3]
```

39. **(E)** In choice E, `findMost` returns the value 5. This is because `count` has not been reset to 1, so that when 5 is encountered, the test `count>maxCountSoFar` is `true`, causing `mostSoFar` to be incorrectly reassigned to 5. In choices A, B, and C, the outer `while` loop is not entered again, since a second run of equal values doesn't exist in the array. So `mostSoFar` comes out with the correct value. In choice D, when the outer loop is entered again, the test `count>maxCountSoFar` just happens to be `true` anyway and the correct value is returned. The algorithm fails whenever a new string of equal values is found whose length is shorter than a previous string of equal values.

40. **(B)** The `count` variable must be reset to 1 as soon as `index` is incremented in the outer `while` loop, so that when a new run of equal values is found, `count` starts out as 1.

# Section II

1. (a)
```
public static int countA(WordSet s)
{
    int count = 0;
    while (count < s.size() &&
            s.findkth(count + 1).substring(0, 1).equals("A"))
        count++;
    return count;
}
```

Alternatively,

```
public static int countA(WordSet s)
{
    boolean done = false;
    int count = 0;
    while (count < s.size() && !done)
    {
        String nextWord = s.findkth(count + 1);
        if (nextWord.substring(0,1).equals("A"))
            count++;
        else
            done = true;
    }
    return count;
}
```

(b)
```
public static void removeA(WordSet s)
{
    int numA = countA(s);
    for (int i = 1; i <= numA; i++)
        s.remove(s.findkth(1));
}
```

Alternatively,

```
public static void removeA(WordSet s)
{
    while (s.size() != 0 &&
            s.findkth(1).substring(0, 1).equals("A"))
        s.remove(s.findkth(1));
}
```

**NOTE**

- In part (a), to test whether a word starts with "A", you must compare the first letter of word, that is, word.substring(0,1), with "A".
- In part (a), you must check that your solution works if s is empty. For the given algorithm, count < s.size() will fail and short-circuit the test, which is desirable since s.findkth(1) will violate the precondition of findkth(k), namely that k cannot be greater than size().

- The parameter for s.findkth must be greater than 0. Hence the use of s.findkth(count+1) in part (a).
- For the first solution in part (b), you get a subtle intent error if your last step is s.remove(s.findkth(i)). Suppose that s is initially {"FLY", "ASK", "ANT"}. After the method call s.remove(s.findkth(1)), s will be {"FLY", "ASK"}. After the statement s.remove(s.findkth(2)), s will be {"ASK"}!! The point is that s is adjusted after each call to s.remove. The algorithm that works is this: If $N$ is the number of words that start with "A", simply remove the first element in the list $N$ times. Note that the alternative solution avoids the pitfall described by simply repeatedly removing the first element if it starts with "A." The alternative solution, however, has its own pitfall: The algorithm can fail if a test for s being empty isn't done for each iteration of the while loop.

## Scoring Rubric: Word Set

| Part (a) | countA | 6 points |
|---|---|---|
| +1 | use a count variable (declare, initialize, return) | |
| +1 | loop over the word set using findkth | |
| +1 | findkth(count + 1) | |
| +1 | substring(0, 1) | |
| +1 | equals("A") | |
| +1 | update count | |

| Part (b) | removeA | 3 points |
|---|---|---|
| +1 | call to countA | |
| +1 | for loop | |
| +1 | remove each word that starts with "A" | |

2.
```
public class Outfit extends ClothingItem
{
    private Shoes shoes;
    private Pants pants;
    private Top top;

    public Outfit (Shoes aShoes, Pants aPants, Top aTop)
    {
        shoes = aShoes;
        pants = aPants;
        top = aTop;
    }

    public String getDescription()
    {
        return shoes.getDescription() + "/" + pants.getDescription()
                + "/" + top.getDescription() + " outfit";
    }
```

```
        public double getPrice()
        {
            if (shoes.getPrice() + pants.getPrice() >= 100
                    ||shoes.getPrice() + top.getPrice() >= 100
                    ||top.getPrice() + pants.getPrice() >= 100)
                return 0.75 * (shoes.getPrice() + pants.getPrice() +
                        top.getPrice());
            else
                return 0.90 * (shoes.getPrice() + pants.getPrice() +
                        top.getPrice());
        }
    }
```

**NOTE**

- To access the price and descriptions of items that make up an outfit, your class needs to have variables of type Shoes, Pants, and Top.
- The private instance variables in the Outfit class should not be of type String! Note that in that case, the ordering of the parameters—shoes, pants, and top— becomes irrelevant, and your solution violates the specification that a compile-time error occurs with different ordering of the parameters.

## Scoring Rubric: Clothing Item

| | Outfit class | 9 points |
|---|---|---|
| +1 | class header with keyword extends | |
| +1 | private instance variables of types Shoes, Pants, and Top | |
| +1 | Outfit constructor with parameters of types Shoes, Pants, and Top | |
| +1 | assignment of instance variables in constructor | |
| +1 | getDescription header | |
| +1 | return concatenated string of outfit descriptions | |
| +1 | getPrice header | |
| +1 | test for amount of discount | |
| +1 | return corresponding price with 75% or 90% discount | |

3.  (a) 
```
public void printNotes()
{
    int count = 1;
    for (Note note: noteList)
    {
        System.out.println(count + ". " + note.getNote());
        count++;
    }
}
```

Alternative solution for part (a):

```
public void printNotes()
{
    for (int index = 0; index < noteList.size(); index++)
        System.out.println(index + 1 + ". "
            + noteList.get(index).getNote());
}
```

```
(b) public void removeNotes(String str)
    {
        int index = 0;
        while (index < noteList.size())
        {
            String note = noteList. get(index).getNote();
            if (note.indexOf(str) == -1)
                index++;
            else
                noteList.remove(index);
        }
    }
```

**NOTE**

- In part (b), you should increment the index only if you don't remove a note. This is because removing an element causes all notes following the removed item to shift one slot to the left. If, at the same time, the index moves to the right, you may miss elements that need to be removed.

## Scoring Rubric: Note Keeper

| Part (a) | printNotes | 4 points |
|---|---|---|
| +1 | initialize count of notes | |
| +1 | loop over notes in noteList | |
| +1 | print current number and corresponding note | |
| +1 | increment count | |

| Part (b) | removeNotes | 5 points |
|---|---|---|
| +1 | loop over notes in noteList | |
| +1 | get Note that corresponds to current index | |
| +1 | use getNote to access current note as string | |
| +1 | test whether parameter str is contained in current note | |
| +1 | remove note containing str | |

4.  (a) public boolean twoTogether()
    ```
    {
        for (int r = 0; r < NUM_ROWS; r++)
            for (int c = 0; c < SEATS_PER_ROW-1; c++)
                if (seats[r][c] == 0 && seats[r][c+1] == 0)
                {
                    seats[r][c] = 1;
                    seats[r][c+1] = 1;
                    return true;
                }
        return false;
    }
    ```

```
(b)  public int findAdjacent(int row, int seatsNeeded)
     {
         int index = 0, count = 0, lowIndex = 0;
         while (index < SEATS_PER_ROW)
         {
             while (index < SEATS_PER_ROW && seats[row][index] == 0)
             {
                 count++;
                 index++;
                 if (count == seatsNeeded)
                     return lowIndex;
             }
             count = 0;
             index++;
             lowIndex = index;
         }
         return -1;
     }
```

**NOTE**

- In part (a), you need the test c < SEATS_PER_ROW-1, because when you refer to seats[r][c+1], you must worry about going off the end of the row and causing an ArrayIndexOutOfBounds exception.
- In part (b), every time you increment index, you need to test that it is in range. This is why you need this test twice: index < SEATS_PER_ROW.
- In part (b), every time you reset the count, you need to reset the lowIndex, because this is the value you're asked to return.
- In parts (a) and (b), the final return statements are executed only if all rows in the show have been examined unsuccessfully.

## Scoring Rubric: Theater Seats

| Part (a) | twoTogether | 4 points |
|---|---|---|
| +1 | traverse all seats | |
| +1 | test for two adjacent empty seats | |
| +1 | assign seats as taken | |
| +1 | return false if two together not found | |

| Part (b) | findAdjacent | 5 points |
|---|---|---|
| +1 | nested loop to search for seats together | |
| +1 | range check for seats[row][index] | |
| +1 | update counts for inner and outer loops | |
| +1 | update indexes for inner and outer loops | |
| +1 | test count to see if number of seats needed has been found | |

# Appendix: Glossary of Useful Computer Terms

*I hate definitions.*
—*Benjamin Disraeli*, Vivian Grey *(1826)*

**API library:** Applications Program Interface library. A library of classes for use in other programs. The library provides standard interfaces that hide the details of the implementations.

**Applet:** A graphical Java program that runs in a web browser or applet viewer.

**Application:** A stand-alone Java program stored in and executed on the user's local computer.

**Binary number system:** Base 2.

**Bit:** From "binary digit." Smallest unit of computer memory, taking on only two values, 0 or 1.

**Buffer:** A temporary storage location of limited size. Holds values waiting to be used.

**Byte:** Eight bits. Similarly, megabyte (MB, $10^6$ bytes) and gigabyte (GB, $10^9$ bytes).

**Bytecode:** Portable (machine-independent) code, intermediate between source code and machine language. It is produced by the Java compiler and interpreted (executed) by the Java Virtual Machine.

**Cache:** A small amount of "fast" memory for the storage of data. Typically, the most recently accessed data from disk storage or "slow" memory is saved in the main memory cache to save time if it's retrieved again.

**Cloud computing:** A new form of Internet-based computing that shares data and computer processing resources on demand.

**Compiler:** A program that translates source code into object code (machine language).

**CPU:** The central processing unit (computer's brain). It controls the interpretation and execution of instructions. It consists of the arithmetic/logic unit, the control unit, and some memory, usually called "on-board memory" or cache memory. Physically, the CPU consists of millions of microscopic transistors on a chip.

**Cyberspace:** An abstract environment in which any communication with the Internet occurs.

**Debugger:** A program that helps find errors by tracing the values of variables in a program.

**Decimal number system:** Base 10.

**GUI:** Graphical user interface.

**Hardware:** The physical components of computers. These are the ones you can touch, for example, the keyboard, monitor, printer, CPU chip.

**Hertz (Hz):** One cycle per second. It refers to the speed of the computer's internal clock and gives a measure of the CPU speed. Similarly, megahertz (MHz, $10^6$ Hz) and gigahertz (GHz, $10^9$ Hz).

**Hexadecimal number system:** Base 16.

**High-level language:** A human-readable programming language that enables instructions that require many machine steps to be coded concisely, for example, Java, C++, Pascal, BASIC, FORTRAN.

**HTML:** Hypertext Markup Language. The instructions read by web browsers to format web pages, link to other websites, and so on.

**IDE:** Integrated Development Environment. Provides tools such as an editor, compiler, and debugger that work together, usually with a graphical interface. Used for creating software in a high-level language.

**Interpreter:** A program that reads instructions that are not in machine language and executes them one at a time.

**Javadoc:** A program that extracts comments from Java source files and produces documentation files in HTML. These files can then be viewed with a web browser.

**JavaScript:** (Not to be confused with Java, the programming language.) A dynamic programming language most commonly used as part of web browsers.

**JVM (Java Virtual Machine):** An interpreter that reads and executes Java bytecode on any local machine.

**Linker:** A program that links together the different modules of a program into a single executable program after they have been compiled into object code.

**Low-level language:** Assembly language. This is a human-readable version of machine language, where each machine instruction is coded as one statement. It is translated into machine language by a program called an assembler. Each different kind of CPU has its own assembly language.

**Mainframe computer:** A large computer, typically used by large institutions, such as government agencies and big businesses.

**Malware:** (Short for malicious software.) Any software designed to disrupt computer operation or gain access to private computer systems. For example, viruses, spyware, ransomware, etc.

**Microcomputer:** Personal computer.

**Minicomputer:** Small mainframe.

**Mobile app:** Software designed to run on smartphones and other mobile devices.

**Modem:** A device that connects a computer to a phone line or TV cable.

**Network:** Several computers linked together so that they can communicate with each other and share resources.

**Object code:** Machine language. Produced by compiling source code.

**Octal number system:** Base 8.

**Operating system:**  A program that controls access to and manipulation of the various files and programs on the computer.  It also provides the interface for user interaction with the computer. Some examples: Windows, MacOS, and Linux.

**Primary memory:**  RAM. This gets erased when you turn off your computer.

**RAM:**  Random Access Memory. This stores the current program and the software to run it.

**ROM:**  Read Only Memory.  This is permanent and nonerasable.  It contains, for example, programs that boot up the operating system and check various components of the hardware. In particular, ROM contains the BIOS (Basic Input Output System)—a program that handles low-level communication with the keyboard, disk drives, and so on.

**SDK:**  Sun's Java Software Development Kit. A set of tools for developing Java software.

**Secondary memory:**  Hard drive, disk, magnetic tapes, CD-ROM, and so on.

**Server:**  The hub of a network of computers. Stores application programs, data, mail messages, and so on, and makes them available to all computers on the network.

**Software:**  Computer programs written in some computer language and executed on the hardware after conversion to machine language.  If you can install it on your hard drive, it's software (e.g., programs, spreadsheets, word processors).

**Source code:**  A program in a high-level language like Java, C++, Pascal, or FORTRAN.

**Swing:**  A Java toolkit for implementing graphical user interfaces.

**Transistor:**  Microscopic semiconductor device that can serve as an on-off switch.

**URL:**  Uniform Resource Locator. An address of a web page.

**USB flash drive:**  A removable and rewritable device that fits into a USB port of a computer.

**Virus:**  A computer program that can replicate itself and spread from one computer to another. A form of malware.

**Web app:**  Software designed to run inside a web browser.

**Web browser:**  A software application for finding and presenting information on the web.

**Workstation:**  Desktop computer that is faster and more powerful than a microcomputer.

# Index

**Symbols**

! operator, 73

!= operator, 72

*= operator, 74

+ operator

   concatenation, 170

++ operator, 74

+= operator, 74

-- operator, 74

-= operator, 74

. operator, 104

/ operator, 71

/= operator, 74

< operator, 72

<= operator, 72

== operator, 72

> operator, 72

>= operator, 72

@param, 68

@return, 68

% operator, 71

%= operator, 74

&& operator, 73

|| operator, 73

**A**

abs method, 176

abstract class, 150

abstract method, 350

access specifier, 102

accessor, 104

actual parameter, 111

add method

   of ArrayList, 235

algorithm, 206, 212

   average case, 213

   best case, 213

   efficiency, 213, 233

   worst case, 213

aliasing, 110

AP exam, xiii

   free-response section, xiii, 61

   hints for taking, 58

   information, xiii

   mark-sense sheet, xiii

   multiple-choice section, xiii, 58

   raw score, xiii

   Section I, xiii

   Section II, xiii

AP Java subset, xiii, 68, 75, 83

APCS labs, *see* labs

API library, 470

applet, 470

application, 67, 470

argument, 111

arithmetic operators, 71

ArithmeticException, 83

array, 226–248

   as parameter, 228

   initialization, 227

   initializer list, 227, 242

   length, 227

   of objects, 232

   one-dimensional, 226

   shuffling, 348

   traversing, 228, 243, 350

   two-dimensional, 242, 350

ArrayIndexOutOfBoundsException, 83, 226, 242

ArrayList<E> class, 234

   methods of, 235

   vs. array, 234

assertion, 212

assignment operators, 74

autoboxing, xi, 174, 236

average case, 213

**B**

backslash \, 76

base case, 287

behavior, 100

best case, 213

binary number, 350, 352

binary search, 324

bit, 470

block, 107

boolean, 68

boolean expression, 72

   compound, 73

   short-circuit evaluation, 74

bottom-up development, 205, 212

buffer, 470

bug, 202

built-in type, 68

byte, 470

byte, 69

bytecode, 67, 470

**C**

cache, 470

casting, 68, 71, 149

chaining

   of assignment statements, 74

chatbot, *see* Magpie lab

class, 100 110

   abstract, 150, 350

   collaborator, 205

   independent, 205

   instance, 100

   wrapper, 118, 173

class method, 105

classes

   ArrayList<E>, 234

   Double, 174

   Integer, 173

   Math, 176

   Object, 167

   Position, 188

   String, 169, 173

client program, 101

cloud computing, 470

collaborator class, 205

College Board web site, 66

comment, 68

compareTo method, 72, 171

compile-time error, 202, 212

compiler, 67, 470

composition relationship, 205, 212

compound assignment operator, 74

compound boolean expression, 73

concatenation operator, 170

ConcurrentModificationException, xi, 83, 239

constant, 102

constructor, 103, 143, 348

   default, 103, 143, 144

control structures, 77–83

   decision-making, 77–79

   iteration, 79–83

CPU, 470

cyberspace, 470

**D**

dangling else, 78

data encapsulation, *see* encapsulation
data field, 100
data structure, 212
debugger, 470
debugging, 202
default constructor, 103, 143, 144
division
    floating-point, 71
    integer, 71
dot operator, 104
Double, 174
    methods of, 174
double, 68
double quote \", 76
doubleValue method, 174
downcasting, 149
driver class, 212
dummy parameter, 111
dynamic binding, 146

**E**
early binding, 146
efficiency, 213, 233
Elevens lab, 347–350
encapsulation, 101, 204, 206, 212
enhanced for loop, 80, 228, 243
    in 2D array, 243, 244, 350
    in array, 228
equals method, 169
equals vs. ==, 172
error, 83, 202
    checked exception, 83
    compile-time, 202
    intent, 202
    logic, 202
    overflow, 68
    round-off, 73
    run-time, 202
    syntax, 202
    unchecked exception, 83
escape sequence, 76
exam, *see* AP exam
exception, 83, 202, 212
    ArithmeticException, 83
    ArrayIndexOutOfBoundsException, 83, 226, 242
    checked, 83
    ConcurrentModificationException, xi, 83, 239
    IllegalArgumentException, 83
    IndexOutOfBoundsException, 83, 172, 236, 238
    NullPointerException, 83, 111, 173, 236
    StringIndexOutOfBoundsException, 172
    unchecked, 83
explicit parameter, 108
exponential run time, 291
extended if statement, 78, 345

extends, 140, 348

**F**
final variable, 70, 102
float, 70
floating-point division, 71
floating-point numbers
    comparison of, 73
    storage of, 70
for loop, 79
for-each loop , *see* enhanced for loop
formal parameter, 111

**G**
generics, 235
    ArrayList<E>, 235
    List<E>, 236
get method
    of ArrayList, 235
GUI, 470

**H**
hardware, 470
*has-a* relationship, 205
header, 102
helper method, 291
Hertz (Hz), 471
hexadecimal number, 70, 352, 471
high-level language, 471
hints
    for taking exam, 58
    for using this book, xiii
HTML, 471

**I**
IDE, 471
identifier, 68
if statement, 77
if...else statement, 77
if...else statement, 347
IllegalArgumentException, 83
immutable object, 169
implicit parameter, 108
import statement, 66
increment operator, 74
independent class, 205, 212
indexOf method, 173, 345
IndexOutOfBoundsException, 83, 172, 236, 238
infinite loop, 81
infinite recursion, 288
Infinity, 70
inheritance, 139–150, 350
inheritance hierarchy, 139, 212
inheritance relationship, 204, 212
inherited instance variable, 142
inherited method, 142
initialization, 111, 227
initializer list, 227, 242
input/output, 75
insertion sort, 320, 323

instance method, 105
instance variable, 67, 100
    inherited, 142
    protected, 143
int, 68
Integer, 173
    Integer.MAX_VALUE, 70, 174
    Integer.MIN_VALUE, 70, 174
    methods of, 173
integer division, 71
intent error, 202
interface, 150, 350
    List<E>, 236
interpreter, 471
intValue method, 174
*is-a* relationship, 140, 145, 204
iteration, 79–83
    enhanced for loop, 80, 228, 243, 350
    for loop, 79
    while loop, 80
iterative binary search, *see* binary search

**J**
Java
    enhanced for loop, 80, 228, 243
    static import, 177
Java application, 67
Java introductory language features, 66–84
Java subset, *see* AP Java subset
Java virtual machine, 471
java.lang, 66
Javadoc comments, 68, 471
JavaScript, 471

**K**
keyword, 67

**L**
lab
    Elevens, 347–350
    Magpie, 345–347
    Picture, 350–352
labs, 345–352
late binding, 146
length method, 172
linker, 471
List<E> interface, 236
local variable, 107
logic error, 202, 212
logical operators, 73
long, 70
loop
    enhanced for, 80, 228, 243, 350
    for, 79
    infinite, 81
    nested, 82
    while, 80
low-level language, 471

**M**
Magpie lab, 345–347

main method, 67, 106
mainframe computer, 471
malware, 471
mantissa, 70
Math class, 176
Math.PI, 177
matrix, 242
maximum int value, 70, 174
merge method, 321
merge sort, 320
method, 101
   accessor, 104
   class, 105
   constructor, 103, 143
   header, 102
   helper, 291
   inherited, 142
   instance, 105
   mutator, 104
   overloaded, 107, 146
   overriding, 140, 143
   partial overriding, 140, 143
   public, 101
   recursive, 286, 287
   signature, 107
   static, 67, 105
   stub, 206
method overriding, 140, 143
methods
   abs, 176
   add, 235
   compareTo, 72, 171
   doubleValue, 174
   equals, 169
   get, 235
   indexOf, 173, 345
   intValue, 174
   length, 172
   main, 67, 106
   merge, 321
   partition, 322
   pow, 177
   random, 177
   remove, 235
   set, 235
   size, 235
   sqrt, 177
   substring, 172, 345
   swap, 230
   toString, 167
microcomputer, 471
minicomputer, 471
minimum int value, 70, 174
mobile app, 471
mod, 71
modem, 471
mutator, 104

**N**

NaN, 70

nested if statement, 77
nested loop, 82
network, 471
new, 83, 226
newline \n, 76
null, 110
null reference, 110
NullPointerException, 83, 111, 173, 236

**O**

Object, 167
   methods of, 167
object, 100–118
   behavior, 100
   reference, 100, 103, 109
   state, 100
   variable, 104
object code, 471
object-oriented program, 212
object-oriented program design, 203, 350
octal number, 352
one-dimensional array, 226
operating system, 472
operator, 71–75
   arithmetic, 71
   assignment, 74
   concatenation, 170
   decrement, 74
   division, 71
   dot, 104
   increment, 74
   logical, 73
   mod, 71
   precedence, 72, 75
   relational, 72
output, 75
overflow error, 68
overloaded method, 107, 146

**P**

package, 66
parameter, 102
   actual, 111
   array, 228
   dummy, 111
   explicit, 108
   formal, 111
   implicit, 108
   pass by value, 112
   passing object as, 113
   passing primitive type as, 112
   two-dimensional array, 246
parameter list, 102
partial overriding, 140, 143
partition method, 322
PI ($\pi$), 177
Picture lab, 350–352
pivot element, 322
polymorphic method calls
   rules for, 150

polymorphism, 146–349
Position class, 188
postcondition, 213
pow method, 177
precondition, 213
primary memory, 472
primitive type, 68, 109
private, 67, 101
   method, 101
   variable, 101
procedural abstraction, 206, 212
program analysis, 212, 350
program correctness, 212
program design, 201–212, 350
   object-oriented, 203
program maintenance, 203, 212
program specification, 201, 212
protected, 143
public, 67, 101, 143
   method, 101
   variable, 101, 143

**Q**

Quick Reference, xiii, 59, 63
quicksort, 322

**R**

RAM, 472
random method, 177
random numbers, 178, 348
random selection, 346
ransomware, 471
recursion, 286–302
   base case, 287
   general rules, 291
   in 2D grids, 294
   infinite, 288
   stack overflow, 288
   tail, 288
recursive definition, 289
recursive helper method, 291
recursive method, 286, 287
   analysis of, 290
reference, 103, 109
relational operator, 72
remove method
   of ArrayList, 235
reserved word, 67
return type, 102
robust program, 203, 212
ROM, 472
round-off error, 73
rounding, 69
row-by-row array processing, 243
run-time error, 202, 212

**S**

scope, 107
   of loop variable, 79
SDK, 472

search
    binary, 324
    sequential, 324
secondary memory, 472
Section I answer sheet, xiv
selection sort, 319
sentinel, 82
sequential search, 324
server, 472
set method
    of ArrayList, 235
short, 70
short-circuit evaluation, 74
shuffle array, 348
signature, 107
size method
    of ArrayList, 235
software, 472
software development, 201, 212
sort
    insertion, 320, 323
    merge sort, 320
    quicksort, 322
    recursive, 320
    selection, 319
sorting, 319–324
    algorithms in Java, 323
source code, 472
source file, 67
specification, 201
spyware, 471
sqrt method, 177
stack overflow, 288
state, 100
static, 67, 102, 105
static binding, 146

static final variable, 102
static import, 177
static method, 105
static variable, 102
stepwise refinement, 206, 212
storage of numbers, 69
strategies, 58–65
String, 169, 173
    comparison, 171
    concatenation operator, 170
    in Magpie lab, 345
    initialization, 170
    methods of, 172, 345
string literal, 169
StringIndexOutOfBoundsException,
    172
stub method, 206, 212
subclass, 139, 348
    rules for, 145
subclass object
    declaration of, 145
subpackage, 66
substring method, 172, 345
super, 143, 148, 348
superclass, 139, 148
swap method, 230
Swing, 472
syntax error, 212

**T**
tail recursion, 288
test data, 202, 212
testing, 202
this, 108
throw, 83
top-down development, 206, 212

toString method, 167
transistor, 472
two-dimensional array, 242–248, 350
    as parameter, 246
    traversal, 243
type, 68
    boolean, 68
    built-in, 68
    double, 68
    int, 68
    primitive, 68, 109
type compatibility, 149

**U**
UML diagram, 205, 212, 350
URL, 472
USB flash drive, 472
user-defined constant, 70

**V**
variable, 68, 101
    final, 70, 102
    instance, 67, 100
    local, 107
    public, 101, 143
variable declaration, 68
virus, 471, 472
void, 102

**W**
web app, 472
web browser, 472
while loop, 80
workstation, 472
worst case, 213
wrapper class, 118, 173

# ¡Ya comprendo!

# ¡Ya comprendo!

## A Communicative Course in Spanish

## Matilde Olivella de Castells

California State University, Los Angeles

MACMILLAN PUBLISHING COMPANY

New York

Macmillan Publishing Company
866 Third Avenue, New York, New York 10022

Collier Macmillan Canada, Inc.

Library of Congress Cataloging-in-Publication Data
Castells, Matilde Olivella de.
   ¡Ya comprendo! / Matilde Olivella de Castells.
   Includes index. p.   cm.
   ISBN 0-02-320151-7
   1. Spanish language—Textbooks for foreign speakers—English.
I. Title.
PC4128.C37   1990
468.2′421—dc20                                                89-2601
                                                                CIP
Printing: 1 2 3 4 5 6 7   Year: 0 1 2 3 4 5 6

Illustration   acknowledgments appear on pages 514–515, which constitute
an extension of the copyright page.

Editor: Karen Davy
Production Supervisor: Lisa G. M. Chuck
Production Manager: Nick Sklitsis
Text Designer: Pat Smythe
Cover Designer: Brian Sheridan
Photo Researcher: Rona Tuccillo
Illustrations: Jerry McDaniel
End paper maps: Vantage Art, Inc.

This book was set in ITC Cheltenham by Ruttle, Shaw & Wetherill, Inc.,
printed by Von Hoffmann Press, Inc., and bound by Von Hoffmann Press,
Inc. The cover was printed by Von Hoffmann Press, Inc.

Student's Edition ISBN 0-02-320151-7

Instructor's Annotated Edition ISBN 0-02-439952-3

# *Preface*

*¡Ya comprendo!* is a new program for beginning college Spanish. It introduces the culture of the Hispanic world; helps students learn Spanish vocabulary and structure; and suggests a sequence of activities designed to lead students to develop the complete spectrum of language skills and a readiness to use Spanish for personally meaningful communication. It emphasizes interaction among students and identifies the purposes of using language in order to help students achieve the proficiency that most instructors have always hoped to see by the end of the first-year course.

## Characteristics of the Program

With the publication of its ACTFL Proficiency Guidelines in 1982, the American Council on the Teaching of Foreign Languages focused the attention of the language-teaching profession on a reorientation of objectives that had been gradually gaining support. Higher priority is now given to helping students develop communicative competence and language proficiency, that is, the ability to use language creatively and in culturally appropriate ways for authentic tasks in real-world settings. This orientation, discussed in conferences, articles, and books, represents a fundamental change in the way many universities and schools conduct language classes. It uses new sequences for presenting material so that it can be learned more efficiently. It reschedules the introduction of a few grammar structures, more important to written than to everyday spoken language, and supports them with appropriate activities, making room at the initial stages of instruction for more work with basic language functions.

The ACTFL Proficiency Guidelines significantly influenced the creation of this book, but so did the years of teaching experience of the author and her associates at California State University, Los Angeles. In addition, the author and one of her associates, Professor Hildebrando Villarreal, worked on the California Foreign Language Competency Project developing guidelines and materials for testing important skills at different levels of competency. A long-standing focus on teaching for communicative competence led the author team to devise numerous activities in which students practice communication in a variety of settings. Although the materials generally follow the sequences advocated in the Guidelines, they deviate slightly on occasion, reflecting classroom experience. While the number of grammatical structures presented for active oral mastery has been reduced, the textbook includes all the major structures traditionally taught. The emphasis of the program is on working with fewer structures and mastering those, rather than on tackling more and mastering fewer.

The dialogs and texts used in the book to present new language material are authentic but not overwhelming for students. Without compromising the authenticity of the material, the author team created or selected dialogs and texts in which new vocabulary and the number of new structures were controlled. These materials were written by native speakers or extracted from Spanish language sources such as magazines and newspapers. Native speakers from Argentina, Colombia, Mexico, Venezuela, and Spain have reviewed all of them for authenticity; particular selections were reviewed by speakers from other countries. The underlying goal of these texts, as of the other parts of the program, is to begin to familiarize students with the reality beyond the classroom, and to prepare them to use and comprehend Spanish as it is used by native speakers in a variety of situations.

*¡Ya comprendo!* does not attempt to present a systematic survey of the culture of the entire Hispanic world. It introduces selected material with the objective of acquainting students with various aspects of Hispanic behavior and attitudes and with important facts about the many different Hispanic countries. The text presents cultural material in limited quantities and at a pace intended to maintain interest in the Hispanic world, but not to distract from the program's primary focus on language acquisition.

In recent years language professionals have been refining their understanding of the role of listening in the acquisition of language. Listening is thought to play a major role in the communicative process. For many students, it is the primary way to internalize grammar and vocabulary. Accordingly, activities designed to promote the skills of listening comprehension now have a more prominent place in beginning language courses. This program specifies comprehension activities in the textbook itself and many more in the audio recordings and associated workbook/laboratory manual.

TPR, the total physical response technique, is one of the many ways to develop listening comprehension: The instructor gives commands in Spanish, and the students respond, not with words, but by carrying out the physical actions specified. The technique is based on the belief that understanding the spoken language should precede speaking and that physical movements in response to commands increase student comprehension and retention. *¡Ya comprendo!* begins with an optional section, **Actividades preliminares,** which relates TPR activities to classroom situations. Instructors may use the activities or not, adapt them to other settings, or use them in connection with vocabulary and structures presented elsewhere in the book. The Instructor's Manual that accompanies this program contains additional suggestions for implementing TPR activities.

Reading is another skill that receives special attention in *¡Ya comprendo!* Both the textbook and the workbook include comprehension activities that encourage students to practice skimming, scanning, extensive and intensive reading, and other strategies. The activities vary with the type of text and the purpose for reading it. After lesson 13, the reading selections, many taken from authentic Spanish language publications, serve to introduce and use certain tenses less frequent in the spoken language.

College students learning Spanish in a predominantly English-speaking country do not learn it the way children learn their first language, primarily because they are not immersed in Hispanic culture and do not dedicate sixteen hours a day to mastering the language of the community on which they depend for their every need. In addition, individuals of college age have developed a variety of personal learning styles. Some students are visually oriented, some hearing oriented, some need to order linguistic reality in terms of explicit grammatical concepts, some may work most efficiently with a computer, others may like to work as a team with a classmate. *¡Ya comprendo!* includes a wide range of options permitting students to adapt the materials to their individuality.

Starting with the textbook's **Actividades preliminares** and continuing with the varied activities and practical explanations in subsequent lessons, students can begin their acquisition of Spanish in a manner consistent with the ACTFL Proficiency Guidelines. As students progress, instructors can follow the text, supplement it with activities from the Instructor's Manual, or modify the program as required by the needs of each particular school. The program is suitable for instructors who want to teach a limited number of structures for greater mastery and proficiency, but at the same time it affords instructors who wish to teach additional structures ample opportunity to do so. Options within the program will help instructors to adapt the materials to a wide range of course designs.

## Textbook

*¡Ya comprendo!* has several components: student textbook, laboratory recordings, workbook/laboratory manual, videocassette, self-instructional (CAI) software, instructor's annotated edition of the textbook, instructor's manual, printed tapescript, testing program, and transparency masters.

The textbook begins with optional **Actividades preliminares** devoted to TPR activities. Four short **Pasos** follow which serve as an introduction to other aspects of the course. The **Pasos** help students familiarize themselves with the sound system of Spanish, listen to more examples of the language in context, and start communicating in situations they will encounter in everyday life in a Hispanic community or country. Language production for the students in this initial stage consists of one-word answers or short phrases that can be easily mastered. Students also start developing an awareness and appreciation for Hispanic culture. The **Pasos** introduce greetings, expressions of courtesy, and saying good-bye; introductions; cognates; numbers; time; days of the week; classroom objects and expressions useful in the classroom; the alphabet; and some Spanish sounds.

The seventeen **Lecciones** are different from the **Pasos** in many ways. They are longer and each revolves around a general semantic theme—for example, school activities, family, food, sports, shopping, traveling. Lessons start by presenting key vocabulary related to the lesson theme and useful for communicating in real-life situations. A variety of activities encourage students to become familiar with the vocabulary and to use it in meaningful ways. A cultural section then focuses on the same theme and draws attention to characteristics of the Hispanic world—for example, educational systems, family ties, typical foods. This section, together with the authentic materials from various countries distributed through the text, will help students understand and appreciate Hispanic culture.

Three sections of language practice and grammar, called **En contexto,** follow the vocabulary and cultural material. Each begins with a short text—a dialog, ad, postcard, comic strip, article—that introduces grammatical structures along with additional vocabulary related to the theme of the lesson. English translations of these texts appear at the bottom of the page in early lessons; later on, only selected words are glossed in the margin. Short activities give students additional opportunities to use the new vocabulary. Grammar explanations are short and concern themselves with structures needed for everyday communication. Exercises following the grammar presentations encourage students to use the words presented at the beginning of the lesson plus some of the new words from the introductory text; they also continuously recycle words from previous lessons. The exercises progress from skill-getting to skill-using activities. They are contextualized and personalized as appropriate to sustain student interest and motivation and to aid comprehension. The goal of each sequence of activities is to encourage communication in situations that emulate as closely as possible real-life situations encountered in the Hispanic world. The activities offer students ample opportunities to create with the language and to express personal interests and preferences.

Reading selections on the lesson theme and comprehension and discussion exercises follow the last skill-using activities. New words are either glossed in the margins or given before the passage to facilitate comprehension. Verb tenses intended for recognition and understanding (see "Scope and Sequence," next page) are presented in pre-reading sections beginning with lesson 13. Instructors who wish to actively practice these verb tenses will find additional exercises and activities in the Instructor's Manual and in the *Cuaderno de práctica,* the workbook/laboratory manual.

After the reading, a section of **Situaciones** invites students to participate in situations that involve two or more people communicating with each other in role playing, problem solving, information getting, and other activities. These situations help students practice genuine communication in circumstances similar to what they may encounter outside the classroom.

Each lesson ends with a vocabulary list that divides the active words introduced in the lesson into semantic fields. The textbook itself concludes with verb tables, a Spanish-English and an English-Spanish vocabulary, and a grammar index.

## Scope and Sequence

Since the 1950s, textbooks for beginning Spanish presented grammar structures—especially the verb tenses—in a certain order: the present indicative, then the preterit, leading on through to the present, imperfect, and compound subjunctives near the end of the book. Each new tense was supported in turn by a standard array of skill-getting drills. Since few classes completed all the textbook chapters in a single year, however, authors typically pared away more and more exercise material in successive editions, especially exercises supporting the tenses coming late in the sequence. This evolutionary shortening of textbooks meant that even in classes that did "cover the entire book," students would typically not achieve active control of most of the tenses studied. (The present subjunctive, sometimes held for teaching near the end of the book because it was complicated and potentially discouraging if presented for quick mastery, began to move forward in the sequence in response to the profession's recognition that it is critically important in Spanish and needs to be supported by an undiminished program of exercises.)

Not everyone was satisfied with the overall results achieved by the traditional grammar curriculum. Studies by government commissions and others concluded that language instruction in America was failing to produce widespread language competency of the sort required to ensure the country's success in international business and scientific competition. Criticism of this kind was one of the motivating factors leading to the publication of the ACTFL Proficiency Guidelines, intended as a contribution to the search for improved teaching results.

Universities throughout the world are eager to train students to speak on a more cultivated level, and Spanish departments naturally share in this aim. But beginning Spanish courses need to begin at the beginning, with the tenses most often used in real-life conversation.

The sequence of verb structures presented in *¡Ya comprendo!* begins with the present indicative, the present progressive, the commands and the present subjunctive, since talking about daily activities and plans for the future, as well as expressing wishes, needs, and desires are high-frequency items in everyday language. The past tenses, preterit and imperfect, and more uses of the subjunctive follow. Present and past perfect indicative and additional uses of the subjunctive complete the structures presented for active use. Having the subjunctive throughout several chapters in the book gives the students ample opportunity for using it in meaningful situations over several months. The remaining tenses are presented in pre-reading sections in the latter part of the book.

In *¡Ya comprendo!,* ample, but not excessive, amounts of exercise material support structures presented for active mastery, so that students do not feel overwhelmed or worry that they have missed some important activities. These exercises are organized in terms of language functions. Grammar explains the use of forms. Functions organize into broad general categories (like "asking permission") the purposes for which speakers use forms, that is, the behavioral applications of language to life. Losing sight of the possible uses of structures is probably an important reason so few of us can achieve active command of a second language in a short period of time. To master a structure, one needs to weave it extensively into a pattern of personally meaningful potential applications. By taking the time necessary to link classroom activities to a balanced array of language functions, *¡Ya comprendo!* aims to help learners apply what they learn in the classroom to the infinite variety of situations arising in real life.

The ACTFL Proficiency Guidelines reflect a realization that not everything can be learned at once, that is, in the first year. If anything is to be learned well, it must be practiced extensively, in a wide variety of formats and contexts. Time for this practice is gained by postponing some matters to more advanced levels of instruction. In *¡Ya comprendo!,* the future, imperfect subjunctive, conditional, and conditional perfect are presented for recognition. Some of these structures (for example, **me gustaría**) appear in *¡Ya comprendo!* as vocabulary in authentic dialogs and texts early in the book, but they are not formally treated until lesson 13 or later, where they are examined in connection with readings. They also appear in the verb tables at the back of the book, which show all verb tenses.

Few students emerging from traditional first-year Spanish courses are able to use in real-life conversations the structures presented for recognition in *¡Ya comprendo!* However, each language department has its own priorities. For classes that wish to teach some or all of these structures for active use, the Instructor's Manual and the *Cuaderno de práctica* include a wide array of skill-getting exercises. Students can reinforce classwork with these structures by regularly utilizing the *¡Ya comprendo!* CAI software supplement.

## Ancillary Components

A program of cassette recordings is available on loan for copying by institutions that adopt the textbook. A site license authorizes the adopting institution to produce cassette copies for student use at home. The recordings include listening comprehension passages and activities, sound discrimination and pronunciation exercises, and structured and open-ended production activities. Students have many opportunities to hear short interviews, weather reports, newscasts, descriptions, and other materials.

The *Cuaderno de práctica,* a workbook/laboratory manual, parallels the textbook. Part of each lesson is for use in conjunction with the laboratory recordings. Materials for the use of students at home help develop their writing skills; as the lessons progress, writing activities involve more and more real-life writing tasks. Activities and puzzles test their grasp of vocabulary. Another section is based on the cultural materials of the textbook chapter. New reading selections and authentic materials supplement those in the textbook.

As a complement to the listening comprehension activities of the textbook and audio recordings and as an extension of the cultural aspects of *¡Ya comprendo!,* a videocassette is available without charge to institutions that have adopted the textbook. The cassette includes authentic cultural materials from the TV systems of Spain, Hispanic America, and the Hispanic networks of the United States.

The self-instructional CAI software accompanying *¡Ya comprendo!* includes drill-and-practice exercises in several formats, guided cloze reading exercises, and gamelike rapid recognition exercises. Simple menus guide the user through the activities; messages acknowledge correct responses and comment on incorrect ones; hints and help are always a keystroke away. Scores are automatically recorded for the instructor. Like the audio and video components, the software is available without charge to institutions that adopt the textbook, and a license permits the institution to duplicate the disks for student use at home.

*¡Ya comprendo!* includes a variety of materials meant to assist instructors. An instructor's annotated edition of the textbook, prepared by Professor Carmen Salazar of Los Angeles Valley College, adds to the student text many marginal notes suggesting ways that the materials may be presented, used, or expanded upon. A separate instructor's manual prepared by Professors Ronald M. Harmon and María R. Montaño-Harmon of California State University, Fullerton, contains additional suggestions for implementing and expanding activities found in the textbook, a model syllabus, and sample lesson plans. A complete testing program, prepared by Professor Salazar and Nancy Anderson reflecting their extensive background in foreign language test administration and design, is also available to adopting schools.

## Acknowledgments

The author wishes to give special thanks to Professor Hildebrando Villarreal of California State University, Los Angeles, co-author of the *Cuaderno de práctica,* for his contribution to the preparation of activities, grammar explanations, and cultural notes in the textbook, as well as for having tested the material in pilot courses.

I also would like to express my gratitude to my colleague Professor Hugh

Kennedy for his contribution to the first lessons of the manuscript and to Mr. Roger Dorrell, Director of the Foreign Language Laboratory at California State University, Los Angeles, for his help in the preparation of the tapes for the pilot courses.

My thanks also to my former students and now colleagues, Ms. Mercedes Limón and Amanda Jiménez, for their refreshing ideas for activities in the various lessons, and to my son Ricardo Castells for his help in the preparation of the cultural sections, activities for the workbook, and classroom testing of some of the materials at Duke University.

I would like to acknowledge the following reviewers of the manuscript, whose comments and suggestions were extremely helpful in the preparation of the textbook: Margaret E. Beeson, Kansas State University; Brian Castronovo, California State University; Mary Lee Cozad, Northern Illinois University; Michelle A. Fuerch, Ripon College; Lynn Carbón Gorell, Pennsylvania State University; Carrie Grady, University of the District of Columbia; Barbara A. Johnson, Washington State University; John R. Kelly, North Carolina State University; Frederic W. Murray, Northern Illinois University; Michael Reider, West Virginia University; Renate Robinson, Northwestern University; Susan Schaffer, University of California, Los Angeles; Judith Strozer, University of Washington; Lourdes Torres, State University of New York, Stony Brook; Claudia María Vargas, University of Southern California.

My deepest appreciation to Professor Carmen Salazar, from Los Angeles Valley College, for the preparation of the Instructor's Annotated Edition of ¡Ya comprendo! and the development of the testing program. Her experience in the classroom and her expertise in testing proved invaluable in both areas.

As a final note, I am deeply indebted to the students whose interest and participation made this project a memorable experience.

**M.O.C.**

# Contents

*Actividades preliminares* ▪▪▪▪▪▪▪▪▪▪▪▪▪▪▪▪▪▪▪▪ *1*

**Optional total physical response (TPR) activities**

**Primer paso** 4

> ### *Functions*
> Greet people in formal and informal situations
> Use appropriate expressions to say good-bye
> Thank people and respond appropriately when
>   thanked
> Request permission and excuse yourself
> Express regret
> Ask for and give names
> Introduce yourself

Minidiálogos: **Saludos** 4
**Despedidas**
**Expresiones de cortesía**
Minidiálogos: **Presentaciones** 7
Pronunciación: **Las vocales** 7
El alfabeto
Expresiones útiles en la clase
Cultura: **General awareness, titles, and some social
customs** 10
Vocabulario

## Segundo paso                                                     12

> ### *Functions*
>
> Introduce people
> Identify people
> Describe yourself and others

Minidiálogos: **Más presentaciones**     12
Cognados
Identificación y descripción de personas
Pronunciación: **Las consonantes p, t, c, q, s, z**     15
Expresiones útiles en la clase
Cultura: **Social customs when greeting and body
language**     17
Vocabulario

## Tercer paso                                                     19

> ### *Functions*
>
> Identify objects
> Ask and answer questions about the location of
>    people and objects
> Describe objects

Un salón de clase     **19**
¿Dónde está?     **20**
¿Cómo es?     **22**
Pronunciación: **b, v, d**     23
Expresiones útiles en la clase
Cultura: **The Spanish language**     24
**Vocabulario**

## Cuarto paso                                                     26

> ### *Functions*
>
> Use numbers from 0 to 99
> Solve simple problems using those numbers
> Tell time
> Tell when an event takes place

Minidiálogo: **Las preguntas de Lupe** 26
Números 0–99
Días de la semana
La hora
Pronunciación: **g, j, r, rr** 33
Expresiones útiles en la clase
Cultura: **Attitudes concerning time in the Hispanic world** 34
Vocabulario

# Lección 1   La universidad ▬▬▬▬▬▬▬▬▬▬▬ 36

### Functions

Discuss daily activities
Ask for and provide information
Express needs
Ask about and express location

**Los estudios**

Cultura: **Education in the Hispanic world**
En contexto: **En la universidad** 40
Gramática: **Subject pronouns**
**Present tense of regular** -ar **verbs**
**The negative**
En contexto: **En la librería** 45
Gramática: **Noun gender**
**Articles (singular)**
**Noun plurals**
**Articles (plural)**
**Use of definite articles**
En contexto: **¿Dónde están los edificios?** 50
Gramática: **Present tense of the verb** estar
Pronunciación: **Linking** 52
Lectura: **Reading skills; La informática;**
**Una estudiante de informática** 53
Situaciones
Vocabulario

## *Lección 2   Los compañeros de clase* ■■■■■■ 58

> **Functions**
>
> Ask and answer questions concerning
> a. where people are from
> b. where and when events take place
> c. possessions
> d. descriptions of places, persons, and things

¿Quién es?

Cultura: **The Hispanics**
En contexto: **Un auto nuevo**    64
Gramática: **Adjectives**
**Position of adjectives**
En contexto: **El mundo hispano**    68
Gramática: **Present tense of the verb** ser; **uses of** ser
Ser **and** estar **with adjectives**
En contexto: **Preguntas y respuestas**    73
Gramática: **Question words**
Pronunciación: **l, m, n, ñ**    77
Lectura: **Los estereotipos**    78
Situaciones
Vocabulario

## *Lección 3   Las actividades de los estudiantes* ■■■■■ 82

> **Functions**
>
> Discuss and inquire about daily activities
> Order food
> Ask for and give addresses and telephone numbers
> Count from 100 to 1,000
> Solve simple problems using those numbers
> Make suggestions and future plans

Lugares y actividades:
**En la biblioteca; En el estadio; En una fiesta**

Cultura: **Student life in the Hispanic countries**
En contexto: **En un café**    86

Gramática: **Present tense of regular** -er **and** -ir **verbs**

En contexto: **En la Facultad de Ciencias**   90

Gramática: **Numbers 100 to 1,000**

En contexto: **La agenda de Laura**   92

Gramática: **Present tense of** ir

**Some ways to express the future: present;** ir
+ a + **infinitive**

Pronunciación: **ll, y, x**   95

Lectura: **¿Vas a dar una fiesta?; Los viajes de
estudio**   96

Situaciones

Vocabulario

# *Lección 4*   *La familia* ▬▬▬▬▬▬▬▬▬▬ *102*

### *Functions*

Identify and describe family members
Describe physical and emotional states
Provide information about a person's age and abilities
Ask about and express ownership
Express preferences and desires

**La familia de Eduardo**

Cultura: **Families in the Hispanic world**

En contexto: **Las vacaciones de la familia Villegas**   107

Gramática: **Present tense of** e ⟶ ie **and** o ⟶ ue
**stem-changing verbs**

En contexto: **¿Qué tienen estas personas?**   111

Gramática: **Special expressions with** tener

En contexto: **Una conversación entre dos niños**   114

Gramática: **Possessive adjectives**

Pronunciación: **Stress and the written accent mark**   116

Lectura: **Las familias hispanas; La tercera edad**   118

Situaciones

Vocabulario

## *Lección 5*  *La casa y los muebles* ▬▬▬▬▬ *122*

> ### *Functions*
>
> Ask about and describe living quarters
> Discuss daily activities in the home
> Ask about and discuss daily schedules
> Express and describe activities related to grooming

**La casa de la familia Estévez**

Cultura: **Housing in the Hispanic world**
En contexto: **A la hora de la cena    126**
Gramática: **Present tense of** hacer, poner, **and** salir
En contexto: **¿Qué hacen estas personas?    130**
Gramática: **Direct object nouns and pronouns;**
**the personal** a
En contexto: **Las actividades de Rafael    133**
Gramática: **Reflexive verbs and pronouns**
Pronunciación: **Stress and the written accent mark**
**(continuation)    138**
Lectura: **Buscando apartamento; Bueno, bonito y**
**barato; La división del trabajo en la**
**casa    140**
Situaciones
Vocabulario

## *Lección 6*  *Los deportes* ▬▬▬▬▬ *144*

> ### *Functions*
>
> Ask and answer questions concerning weather
>    conditions
> Express/describe physical abilities
> Express on-going actions
> Use numbers from 1,000 to 2,000,000
> Express sequence and order
> Express dates

**Las estaciones y los meses del año**

Cultura: **Sports in the Hispanic world**
En contexto: **Un partido de béisbol    150**

Gramática: **Present progressive:** estar + -ndo

En contexto: **Escuelas de deportes**    155

Gramática: **Numbers 1,000 to 2,000,000**

**Ordinal numbers**

**Dates**

En contexto: **Un partido muy importante**    160

Gramática: **Present tense of** e ⟶ i **stem-changing verbs**

Pronunciación: **Stress and the written accent mark (continuation)**    164

Lectura: **Un deporte muy popular entre la juventud; Dos deportes de origen hispano**    165

Situaciones

Vocabulario

## Lección 7   *De compras*                                  *170*

***Functions***

Talk about and describe clothing

Make and answer telephone calls

Ask for and tell prices

Express needs

Express likes and dislikes

Express satisfaction and dissatisfaction

**El escaparate de una tienda**

Cultura: **Shopping in the Hispanic world**

En contexto: **Una conversación por teléfono**    174

Gramática: **Indirect object nouns and pronouns**

**The verb** dar (***to give***)

En contexto: **En una tienda**    178

Gramática: **Demonstrative adjectives and pronouns**

En contexto: **En un almacén**    182

Gramática: **The verb** gustar

Lectura: **Unos regalos; La ropa**    187

Situaciones

Vocabulario

*Lección 8*   *El trabajo* ▬▬▬▬▬▬▬▬▬▬▬▬▬▬▬▬ *192*

| ***Functions*** |
| --- |
| Talk about the workplace and professions |
| Express opinions |
| Give orders |
| Give and follow directions |
| Express knowledge of facts |
| Express and ask for acquaintance of people |

**Las profesiones y los oficios**

Cultura: **Work and economic environment in the Hispanic countries**

En contexto: **Anuncios      197**

Gramática: Se **+ verb**

En contexto: **En la oficina del señor Macía      201**

Gramática: **Formal commands**

En contexto: **Una reunión de ventas      205**

Gramática: Saber **and** conocer

**Pronouns after prepositions**

Lectura: **Buscando trabajo; El empleado o empleada ideal; El trabajo      211**

Situaciones

Vocabulario


*Lección 9*   *El cuerpo y los ejercicios* ▬▬▬▬▬▬▬▬▬▬ *216*

| ***Functions*** |
| --- |
| Talk about and describe body movements |
| Give orders informally |
| Give advice informally |
| Give and follow instructions |
| Express weight and measurements |
| Make comparisons |

**Las partes del cuerpo**

Cultura: **Physical fitness and exercise in the Hispanic world**

En contexto: **El calentamiento y los ejercicios      220**

Gramática: **Informal commands**

En contexto: **El peso; La estatura** **225**

Gramática: **Comparisons of inequality**

En contexto: **En una clase de ejercicios aeróbicos** **229**

Gramática: **Comparisons of equality**

Lectura: **¿Existe el deporte ideal?; Algo más que un gimnasio** **233**

Situaciones

Vocabulario

## Lección 10   La comida ━━━━━━━━━━━━━ 238

### Functions

Plan menus
Order food
Express wishes and hope
Make requests
Express opinions
Express doubt
Express fear and worry
Express joy and satisfaction

**Supermercado La Cubanita**

Cultura: **Food in the Hispanic world**

En contexto: **Una invitación a cenar** **242**

Gramática: **Indicative versus subjunctive**
**Present subjunctive**
**The subjunctive used to express wishes and hope**
**The subjunctive used with verbs of emotion**

En contexto: **En un restaurante** **248**

Gramática: **The subjunctive used with verbs and expressions of doubt**

En contexto: **Miami** **252**

Gramática: **The superlative**
**Superlative with** -ísimo

Lectura: **Un verdadero banquete; Una fruta excelente** **256**

Situaciones

Vocabulario

## Lección 11 La salud y los médicos ══════════ 260

> ### Functions
>
> Describe health conditions
> Express opinions
> Express attitudes
> Express expectations and wishes

**El cuerpo humano por dentro**

Cultura: **Doctors, hospitals, and pharmacies in the Hispanic world**

En contexto: **En el consultorio de la doctora Suárez  264**

Gramática: **Indicative and subjunctive after impersonal expressions**

En contexto: **En el hospital  269**

Gramática: **The subjunctive after** ojalá
**The equivalents of English** *let's*

En contexto: **El campo y la ciudad  273**

Gramática: **Relative pronouns**

Lectura: **¿Lleva usted una forma de vida sana?; ¿Te quieres o no te quieres?  277**

Situaciones
Vocabulario

## Lección 12 Los viajes ══════════ 282

> ### Functions
>
> Make travel arrangements
> Ask about and discuss travel schedules
> Report past events
> Express denial
> Express uncertainty

**En el aeropuerto; En la estación de ferrocarril; En el puerto**

Cultura: **Los viajes en los países hispanos**

En contexto: **Un accidente  288**

Gramática: **Preterit tense**

En contexto: **En la agencia de viajes    294**
Gramática: **Affirmative and negative expressions**
En contexto: **La imaginación y la realidad    300**
Gramática: **Indicative and subjunctive in adjective clauses**
Lectura: **Evite accidentes; Puerto Rico; Al Andalus Expreso    306**
Situaciones
Vocabulario

## Lección 13  *Telegramas, tarjetas postales y cartas* ▬▬ *312*

### Functions

Interpret and compose telegraphic messages
Communicate by phone, postcard, and letter
Report past events
Describe actions

**Un telegrama**

Cultura: **El teléfono, las cartas y el servicio postal en los países hispanos**
En contexto: **Una conversación por teléfono    317**
Gramática: **Preterit of** ir **and** ser
**Preterit tense of stem-changing** -ir **verbs (e ⟶ i) (o ⟶ u)**
**Preterit of** -er **and** -ir **verbs whose stem ends in a vowel**
En contexto: **Una tarjeta postal    322**
Gramática: **Irregular preterits**
En contexto: **¿Cómo escriben y hablan?    327**
Gramática: **Adverbs**
**Comparison of adverbs**
Lectura: ***Antes de leer:* the future tense; Los horóscopos; Una carta    331**
Situaciones
Vocabulario

## Lección 14  De vacaciones ━━━━━━━━━━━ 340

**Functions**

Explain needs
Describe and get hotel accommodations
Report past events
Express possession (emphatic)

**La ciudad y la playa**

Cultura: **El turismo en los países hispanos**
En contexto: **En la recepción del hotel   346**
Gramática: **More irregular preterits**
En contexto: **En la taquilla   350**
Gramática: Hace **with expressions of time**
En contexto: **Un problema serio   353**
Gramática: **Stressed possessive adjectives**
**Possessive pronouns**
Lectura: *Antes de leer:* **the past subjunctive;**
**Unas vacaciones en Chile; Un hotel diferente;**
**Programa comercial   358**
Situaciones
Vocabulario


## Lección 15  Fiestas y tradiciones ━━━━━━━━ 364

**Functions**

Talk about and describe holiday activities
Express on-going actions in the past
Extend an invitation
Accept or decline an invitation
Express goals and purposes
Express intense reactions
Ask for and give a definition or an explanation

**Fechas importantes**

Cultura: **Días de fiesta y tradiciones en el mundo**
**hispano**
En contexto: **La abuela recuerda otros tiempos   369**
Gramática: **Preterit and imperfect**

Imperfect of regular and irregular verbs
Uses of the imperfect

En contexto: **El cumpleaños de Amparo**   **374**

Gramática: Por **and** para

Por **and** para **contrasted**

En contexto: **Una invitación para una fiesta**   **378**

Gramática: **Exclamatory** qué

**Interrogative** qué **and** cuál(es) **with** ser

Lectura: *Antes de leer:* **the conditional;**

**Un joven indeciso; Unos regalos para los novios; Las corridas de toros; El domingo se celebra la XI fiesta de la bicicleta**   **382**

Situaciones

Vocabulario

## *Lección 16   Problemas ambientales y catástrofes* ━━━━ *390*

---

**Functions**

Describe physical conditions and the environment
Report facts in the present and past
Express disappointment
Give opinions

---

**Los efectos de un terremoto; ¿Una ciudad moderna o un infierno?**

Cultura: **Catástrofes y problemas ambientales en el mundo hispano**

En contexto: **Las últimas noticias**   **395**

Gramática: **The past participle**

**The present perfect**

En contexto: **Los efectos de un huracán**   **400**

Gramática: **The past perfect**

**Past participles used as adjectives**

En contexto: **Peligro de incendio**   **403**

Gramática: **Direct and indirect object pronouns**

Lectura: *Antes de leer:* **the passive voice;**

**Murió víctima de un sabotaje; La ecología**

**The present perfect subjunctive**

**Los efectos de un terremoto**   **409**

Situaciones

Vocabulario

## *Lección 17 Los cambios de la sociedad* ▬▬▬▬▬ *416*

> **Functions**
>
> Talk about and describe social customs
> Describe customary actions
> Project goals and purposes
> Express conjecture
> Talk about and express unexpected occurrences

**¿Qué ha cambiado y qué no ha cambiado?**

Cultura: **Cambios en la sociedad hispana**
En contexto: **La mujer en la sociedad hispana    420**
Gramática: **Adverbial conjunctions that always require the subjunctive**
**Adverbial conjunctions that use the subjunctive or the indicative**
En contexto: **Problemas actuales en una ciudad grande    425**
Gramática: Se **for unplanned occurrences**
En contexto: **Letreros    427**
Gramática: **The infinitive as subject of a sentence**
**The infinitive as the object of a preposition**
Lectura: ***Antes de leer:* the conditional perfect; the pluperfect subjunctive;**
**Eusebio Manrique recuerda su vida;**
**Los hispanos en los Estados Unidos;**
**Los ángeles de la Guardia Civil marcan el paso en Baeza    430**
Situaciones
Vocabulario

**Verb Tables**                                                    **439**

**Spanish-English Vocabulary**                                     **453**

**English-Spanish Vocabulary**                                     **484**

**Index**                                                          **509**

# *Actividades preliminares*

## Optional total physical response (TPR) activities

The following drawings show activities that normally occur in the classroom. Your instructor may want to go over these **actividades** before beginning with the preliminary lessons, or **pasos.** Listening to these commands, observing your instructor and/or classmates acting them out, and performing them yourself will give you an excellent opportunity to hear and understand Spanish. Try to get the general meaning and react accordingly. Your instructor may want to combine several of these activities to see how much you can understand.

The more Spanish you hear in situations in which you understand most of what is being said, the sooner you will begin to communicate in Spanish.

Vaya a la puerta.

Vaya a su asiento.

Vaya a la pizarra.

Escriba su nombre.

Borre la pizarra.

Abra el libro.

Cierre la ventana.

Miren el reloj.

Escuche.

Salgan.

Entre.

Siéntese.

Levántese.

Levante la mano.

Tome la tiza.

Déme el lápiz.

**In the** Primer paso **you will**
a. **greet people in formal and informal situations.**
b. **use appropriate expressions to say good-bye.**
c. **thank people and respond appropriately when thanked.**
d. **request permission and excuse yourself.**
e. **express regret.**
f. **ask for and give names.**
g. **introduce yourself.**

## MINIDIÁLOGOS[1]

### Saludos

| | |
|---|---|
| **Señor Gómez** | Buenos días, señorita Mena. |
| **Señorita Mena** | Buenos días. ¿Cómo está usted, señor Gómez? |
| **Señor Gómez** | Bien, gracias. ¿Y usted? |
| **Señorita Mena** | Muy bien, gracias. |

| | |
|---|---|
| **Ana** | ¡Hola, Inés! ¿Qué tal? ¿Cómo estás? |
| **Inés** | Regular, ¿y tú? |
| **Ana** | Bastante bien, gracias. |

| | |
|---|---|
| **Señora Yanes** | Buenas tardes, Felipe. ¿Cómo estás? |
| **Felipe** | Bien, gracias. Y usted, ¿cómo está, señora? |
| **Señora Yanes** | Mal, Felipe, mal. |
| **Felipe** | Lo siento. |

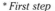

*\* First step*
[1] The English version of the dialogs is at the bottom of the page.

Greetings
MR. GÓMEZ: Good morning, Miss Mena. MISS MENA: Good morning. How are you, Mr. Gómez? MR. GÓMEZ: Fine, thanks. And you?
MISS MENA: Very well, thank you.

ANA: Hi, Inés. How's it going? How are you? INÉS: So-so. And you? ANA: Pretty well, thanks.

MRS. YANES: Good afternoon, Felipe. How are you? FELIPE: Fine, thanks. And how are you, ma'am? MRS. YANES: Not well, Felipe, not well. FELIPE: I'm sorry.

Dos estudiantes se dan la mano
en la Universidad de Panamá.

1. Spanish has more than one word meaning *you*. Use **usted** when you talk to someone you address respectfully as **señor, señora, señorita, doctor,** and so on. Use **tú** when you talk to someone on a first-name basis (close friend, relative, child). The verb form **está** goes with **usted,** and **estás** goes with **tú.**
2. **¿Qué tal?** is a more informal greeting. It is normally used with **tú,** but it may also be used with **usted.**
3. Use **buenas tardes** from noon until nightfall. After nightfall, use **buenas noches** *good evening, good night.* In the summer, especially in places where dinner is served rather late (after 9:00 P.M.), you may use **buenas tardes** even at 8:00 in the evening.

| **despedidas** | *saying good-bye* |
|---|---|
| adiós | *good-bye* |
| hasta luego | *see you later* |
| hasta mañana | *see you tomorrow* |

**Adiós** is generally used when you do not expect to see the other person for a while. It is also used meaning *hello* when people pass each other but have no time to stop and talk.

| **expresiones de cortesía** | *polite expressions* |
|---|---|
| por favor | *please* |
| gracias | *thanks, thank you* |
| de nada/por nada | *you're welcome* |
| con permiso | *pardon me, excuse me* |
| perdón | *pardon me, excuse me* |

**Con permiso** and **perdón** may be used before the fact, as when asking a person to allow you to go by or when asking for a person's attention. Only **perdón** is used after the fact, as when you have stepped on someone's foot.

5

## ACTIVIDADES

**A** You work at a hotel and have to greet people at different times of day. What greeting (**buenos días, buenas tardes, buenas noches**) would you use according to the following times?

9:00 A.M.     11:00 P.M.     4:00 P.M.     3:00 A.M.     10:00 A.M.     8:00 P.M.

**B** What expression (**perdón, con permiso**) will you use in the following situations?

1. You accidentally bump into someone.
2. You are trying to pass through a group of people.
3. You step on someone's foot at a store.
4. You stop someone to ask for directions.
5. You are at the movies and have to pass in front of someone to reach your seat.

**C** What expression (**gracias, de nada, por favor, adiós, hasta luego, lo siento**) will you use in the following situations?

1. Someone thanks you.
2. You are leaving a friend whom you are going to see later that evening.
3. You are asking a classmate for his notes.
4. You hear that your friend is sick.
5. You receive a present from a friend.
6. Your friend is going on a vacation to Spain.

**D** You meet the following people on the street. Greet them, ask how they are, and then say good-bye. One of your classmates will play the other role.

a classmate       your friend's little brother       an older lady
your history professor       your doctor       one of your cousins

Unas chicas se saludan en España.

# MINIDIÁLOGOS

## Presentaciones

| | |
|---|---|
| **Antonio** | Me llamo Antonio Mendoza. Y tú, ¿cómo te llamas? |
| **Benito** | Benito Sánchez. Mucho gusto. |
| **Antonio** | Igualmente. |
| | |
| **Profesor** | ¿Cómo se llama usted? |
| **Isabel** | Me llamo Isabel Mendoza. |
| **Profesor** | Mucho gusto. |
| **Isabel** | Encantada. |
| | |
| **Profesora** | Su nombre, por favor. |
| **José** | José Sánchez. |

**Mucho gusto** is used by both men and women when meeting someone for the first time. A man may also say **encantado** and a woman **encantada.** When responding to **mucho gusto,** both **encantado/a** and **igualmente** may be used.

# ACTIVIDADES

**A** You are an usher at a fund-raising banquet. Greet the guests formally and ask for their names. Your classmates will play the part of the guests.

**B** You meet some young people for the first time at commencement exercises. Introduce yourself and find out the other persons' names. Two of your classmates will play the other roles.

# PRONUNCIACIÓN

## Las vocales*

Spanish has five simple vowel sounds, represented in writing by the letters **a, e, i, o,** and **u.** These vowels are tense and short, and for all practical purposes, constant in length when pronounced in

---

Self-Introductions

ANTONIO: I'm Antonio Mendoza. And what's your name? BENITO: Benito Sánchez. Nice to meet you. ANTONIO: Likewise.

PROFESSOR: What's your name? ISABEL: My name is Isabel Mendoza. PROFESSOR: Pleased to meet you. ISABEL: Delighted.

PROFESSOR: Your name, please. JOSÉ: José Sánchez.

*\* The vowels*

both stressed and unstressed syllables. In order to avoid the glide sound of English stressed vowels (e.g., *no, same*), do not move your tongue, lips, or jaw. Avoid also the *uh* sound of English unstressed vowels (e.g., *opera, about*).

1. **a** is similar to the *a* in *father*, but shorter and tenser.

   llama   mañana   banana   Panamá   encantada

2. **e** is similar to the *e* in *they*, but without the glide sound.

   sé   nene   este   Sánchez   bastante

3. **i** is similar to the *i* in *machine*, but without the glide sound.

   sí   ni   Mimí   Inés   Felipe

4. **o** is similar to the *o* in *no*, but without the glide sound.

   no   con   Mónica   noches   profesor

5. **u** is similar to the *u* in *tuna*, but without the glide sound.

   su   tú   mucho   uno   usted

## EL ALFABETO

| | | | | | |
|---|---|---|---|---|---|
| **a** | a | **j** | jota | **r** | ere |
| **b** | be | **k** | ka | **rr** | erre |
| **c** | ce | **l** | ele | **s** | ese |
| **ch** | che | **ll** | elle | **t** | te |
| **d** | de | **m** | eme | **u** | u |
| **e** | e | **n** | ene | **v** | ve o uve |
| **f** | efe | **ñ** | eñe | **w** | doble ve, doble uve |
| **g** | ge | **o** | o | **x** | equis |
| **h** | hache | **p** | pe | **y** | i griega |
| **i** | i | **q** | cu | **z** | zeta |

The Spanish alphabet has more letters than the English alphabet. **Ch** and **ll** are considered single letters and are listed separately in most Spanish dictionaries and vocabularies. The letter **ñ** does not exist in English. Some Spanish grammars do not include **rr** in the alphabet, and words containing **rr** are alphabetized as in English.

Another name for **w** is **uve doble.** The letters **k** and **w** appear mainly in words of foreign origin.

Dos amigos se abrazan en México. El abrazo es muy común cuando los hombres se saludan.

## ACTIVIDADES

**A** Spell aloud the following names of cities in Mexico.

Puebla    Veracruz    Acapulco    Morelia    Guadalajara

**B** You will be asked your name. Give your name and then spell it to be sure it is understood.

*Modelo*    Su nombre, por favor.
**David Montoya. D-a-v-i-d M-o-n-t-o-y-a.**

### EXPRESIONES ÚTILES EN LA CLASE    *useful expressions in the classroom*

| | |
|---|---|
| Escuche(n). | *Listen.* |
| Conteste(n). | *Answer.* |
| Pregunte(n). | *Ask.* |
| Pregúntele a su compañero/a. | *Ask your classmate.* |
| Repita(n). | *Repeat.* |
| Abra(n) el libro. | *Open the book.* |
| Cierre(n) el libro. | *Close the book.* |
| Voy a pasar(la) lista. | *I'm going to call (the) roll.* |

When addressing just one person, Spanish uses a command form without **-n: escuche.** When addressing two or more people, the command form ends in **-n: escuchen.**

Although you may not have to use these expressions, you should recognize them and act accordingly. The following **Pasos** will present more **Expresiones útiles.**

# Cultura

## General awareness, titles, and some social customs

When you learn another language, you also learn about another culture—how people live, their family structure, their institutions, their social customs and attitudes, and so on. Gaining an understanding and appreciation for another culture enriches your own life, allowing an insight into your own language and culture.

Every lesson of this book will expose you to Hispanic culture through dialogs, readings, situations, and explanations. Cultural insights are further developed in the sections titled **Cultura.** In the **Primer paso** you have already learned about greetings, when to use them, and how to address people. In this corresponding cultural section, you will learn more about titles of respect and the ways in which people greet and address one another.

Other titles of respect besides **señor, señora,** and **señorita** are **don** and **doña.** Although the use of these titles may vary slightly from country to country, they all indicate formal relationships. The abbreviations for **señor, señora,** and **señorita** are **Sr., Sra.,** and **Srta.** They may be used with the first name, the last name, or both (**señora Mercedes, señor Martínez, señorita Berta Martínez**). There is no standard Spanish equivalent for *Ms.*; either **se-**ñora or **señorita** is used. The abbreviations for **don** and **doña** are **D.** and **Da.** They are used with the first name (**don Felipe, doña Marta**) and with the first and last name together (**don Felipe Sánchez, doña Marta Jiménez**).

When saying hello or good-bye and when being introduced, Hispanic men and women almost always shake hands. When greeting each other, young girls and women often place their cheeks together, kissing not each other's cheek but the air. This is also the custom for men and women who are close friends; sometimes the man kisses the women's cheek. In Spain this kissing is done on both cheeks. Men who are close friends normally embrace and pat each other on the back.

Children and young people stand up and greet adults individually. Girls usually kiss men and women, while boys may kiss them or shake hands. Adults generally address children and young people as **tú,** but children and young people address adults as **usted.** Nevertheless, in some countries, especially in cities, children and young people may address adults who are close friends of the family as **tú.** Parents and children usually address each other as **tú,** but in some areas children may use **usted** when speaking to their parents.

# VOCABULARIO

The vocabulary list that appears at the end of each **paso** and **lección** includes all the active words introduced in that chapter.

| | | | |
|---|---|---|---|
| **despedidas** | *saying good-bye* | muy bien | *very well* |
| adiós | *good-bye* | buenas noches | *good evening, night* |
| hasta luego | *see you later* | buenas tardes | *good afternoon* |
| hasta mañana | *see you tomorrow* | buenos días | *good morning* |
| | | ¿cómo está usted? | *how are you? (formal)* |
| **expresiones de cortesía** | *polite expressions* | | |
| | | ¿cómo estás? | *how are you? (familiar)* |
| con permiso | *excuse me* | | |
| de nada/por nada | *you're welcome* | hola | *hello, hi* |
| gracias | *thanks, thank you* | mal | *not well, ill* |
| lo siento | *I'm sorry* | ¿qué tal? | *how's it going?* |
| perdón | *excuse me* | regular | *so-so* |
| por favor | *please* | | |
| | | | |
| **presentaciones** | *introductions* | **personas** | *people* |
| ¿cómo se llama usted? | *what's your name? (formal)* | el profesor/la profesora | *professor, teacher* |
| ¿cómo te llamas? | *what's your name? (familiar)* | señor (Sr.) | *Mr.* |
| | | señora (Sra.) | *Mrs.* |
| encantado/a | *delighted* | señorita (Srta). | *Miss* |
| igualmente | *likewise* | tú | *you (familiar)* |
| me llamo... | *my name is. . .* | usted | *you (formal)* |
| mucho gusto | *pleased/nice to meet you* | | |
| | | **palabras útiles** | *useful words* |
| su nombre | *your name* | y | *and* |
| | | | |
| **saludos y contestaciones** | *greetings and answers* | | |
| | | **palabras interrogativas** | *question words* |
| bien | *well* | cómo | *how* |
| bastante bien | *pretty well, rather well* | | |

In the Segundo paso **you will**
a. **introduce people.**
b. **identify people.**
c. **describe yourself and others.**

## MINIDIÁLOGOS

### Más presentaciones

| | |
|---|---|
| **Carlos** | María, mi amigo José. |
| **José** | Mucho gusto. |
| **María** | Encantada. |

| | |
|---|---|
| **Sr. Gómez** | Doña Mirta, le presento a don José Flores. |
| **Don José** | Mucho gusto. |
| **Doña Mirta** | Igualmente. |

| | |
|---|---|
| **Ana** | Carlos, te presento a Marta. |
| **Carlos** | Mucho gusto. |
| **Marta** | Igualmente. |

In an introduction, use **le presento** if you address the person as **usted;** use **te presento** if you address the person as **tú.** A simpler form is to use only the names of the persons you are introducing (**Carlos Ríos, Marta Díaz**).

---

*\* Second step*

More introductions
CARLOS: María, my friend José. JOSÉ: Glad to meet you. MARÍA: Likewise.

MR. GÓMEZ: Doña Mirta, I'd like to introduce don José Flores to you. DON JOSÉ: Glad to meet you. DOÑA MIRTA: Likewise.

ANA: Carlos, I'd like to introduce Marta to you. CARLOS: Glad to meet you. MARTA: Likewise.

## *ACTIVIDAD*

Decide whether to use the **le** (formal) or **te** (familiar) to introduce persons in the following situations. Two of your classmates will assume the roles of the other persons.

1. Introduce two classmates.
2. You run into two of your professors in the Administration building.
3. You and a friend are downtown and you run into a former boss.
4. You are at the cafeteria having a snack with a friend when another friend comes over.

## COGNADOS

Cognates are words in English and Spanish that have the same origin and are similar in form and meaning. Since English shares so many words with Spanish, you will discover that you already know many words in Spanish. Here are some that are used to describe people.

The first group of cognates has only one form to describe a man or a woman.

| | | | |
|---|---|---|---|
| competente | inteligente | paciente | realista |
| eficiente | interesante | parcial | rebelde |
| elegante | liberal | persistente | sentimental |
| idealista | materialista | pesimista | terrible |
| importante | optimista | puntual | valiente |

The second group of cognates has two forms. The **o** form is used when describing a man and the **a** form when describing a woman.

| | | | |
|---|---|---|---|
| activo/a | extrovertido/a | introvertido/a | romántico/a |
| agresivo/a | fantástico/a | lógico/a | serio/a |
| ambicioso/a | generoso/a | moderno/a | sincero/a |
| creativo/a | impulsivo/a | pasivo/a | tímido/a |
| discreto/a | indiscreto/a | religioso/a | tranquilo/a |

You should be aware that there are some words that look like cognates, but do not have the same meaning in both languages. You will find some examples in future lessons.

Unos amigos conversan en una calle de Santiago de Chile.

## IDENTIFICACIÓN Y DESCRIPCIÓN DE PERSONAS

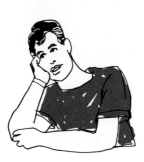

—¿Quién es ese chico?
—Es Julio.
—¿Cómo es Julio?
—Es romántico y sentimental.

—¿Quién es esa chica?
—Es Carmen.
—¿Cómo es Carmen?
—Es activa y muy seria.

| **ser** | *to be* |
|---|---|
| yo soy | *I am* |
| tú eres | *you are* |
| usted es | *you are* |
| él, ella es | *he/she is* |

## *ACTIVIDADES*

**A** Using positive characteristics, describe a student in your class.

*Modelo* **David es inteligente y sincero.**

**B** Think of an important person and then describe him/her.

*Modelo* **Woody Allen es liberal. Él no es elegante.**

---

Who's that boy?
It's Julio.
What's Julio like?
He's romantic and sentimental.

Who's that girl?
It's Carmen.
What's Carmen like?
She's active and very serious.

**C** Describe yourself to a classmate.

>  *Modelo*   **Yo soy optimista. No soy rebelde.**

**D** Find out if the person next to you has the following personality traits.

>  *Modelo*   **—¿Eres pesimista?**
>  **—No, no soy pesimista** o **—Sí, soy pesimista.**

> optimista      persistente      sincero/a      impulsivo/a

**E** **Entrevista** *Interview.* Get a student's attention and greet him/her; then find out who the person next to that student is, and what he/she is like.

**F** After hearing several students describe themselves, try to describe two of them from what you remember.

## PRONUNCIACIÓN

### Las consonantes

Some consonants are pronounced the same way in Spanish and English (e.g., **f, m**). Other consonants differ only slightly, while still others are completely different. In this section you will learn to pronounce some Spanish consonants that are slightly different from their English counterparts.

**1.** **p**

Spanish **p** is pronounced like English *p,* but it is never accompanied by a puff of air as the English *p* often is. Note the difference between these two words that your instructor will pronounce: **papá,** *papa.*

> Pepe      pino      pan      peso      poco      popular

**2.** **t**

Spanish **t** is pronounced by placing the tip of the tongue against the back of the upper front teeth, and it is never accompanied by a puff of air. English *t,* in contrast, is pronounced by placing the tip of the tongue against the gum ridge and it is often accompanied by a puff of air.

> te      tú      tomate      tono      está      optimista

**3.** **c, q, s, z**

Spanish **c** before a consonant or **a, o,** or **u** is pronounced like an English *c,* but without a puff of air. The Spanish letter combination **qu** before **e** or **i** is pronounced like an English *k,* but without a puff of air.

> como      café      cuna      típico      qué      quién

Spanish **c** before **e** or **i** is pronounced like English *c* before *e* or *i*.

cena    cita    cesto    once    gracias    cinco

Spanish **s** and **z** are pronounced like the English *s* in *some*. They are never pronounced like an English *z* when placed between vowels.

señora    está    ese    casa    zeta    tiza

## EXPRESIONES ÚTILES EN LA CLASE

| | |
|---|---|
| Escriba(n). | *Write.* |
| Lea(n). | *Read.* |
| Siga(n). | *Continue.* |
| Vaya(n) a la pizarra. | *Go to the chalkboard.* |
| Siénte(n)se. | *Sit down.* |
| Levánte(n)se. | *Stand up.* |
| La tarea, por favor. | *The homework, please.* |

Dos jóvenes españoles pasean por las calles de Madrid.

# Cultura

## Social customs when greeting and body language

People in the United States generally maintain a certain physical distance when speaking with each other. If someone should cross that invisible boundary and get too close, an American will start to back away. Hispanics, however, are more comfortable if they are close to the people with whom they are talking. Among friends and acquaintances, Hispanics tend to be more touch-oriented as well. It is not uncommon to see a young man with his hand or arm on a friend's shoulder at several points during a conversation. Young girls and women are often seen strolling arm in arm.

Hispanics also tend to be rather animated in conversation, frequently employing hand movements and gestures that are commonly understood. The following drawings illustrate some of these gestures:

no

un momentito *a moment*
un poquito *a little bit*

tacaño *stingy*

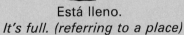

Está lleno.
*It's full. (referring to a place)*

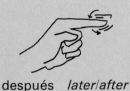

después *later/after*

inteligente

# VOCABULARIO

**personas**
el amigo/la amiga — *friend*
la chica — *girl*
el chico — *boy*
don — *title of respect for men*
doña — *title of respect for women*
él — *he*
ella — *she*
yo — *I*

**descripción** — *description*
activo — *active*
romántico — *romantic*
sentimental — *sentimental*
serio — *serious*

**presentaciones** — *introductions*
le presento a... — *I'd like you to meet ... (formal)*
te presento a... — *I'd like you to meet ... (fam.)*

**verbos** — *verbs*
eres — *you are (fam.)*
es — *he/she is, you are (formal)*
soy — *I am*

**palabras útiles**
ese/a — *that*
más — *more*
mi — *my*
no — *no*
sí — *yes*

**palabras interrogativas**
quién — *who*

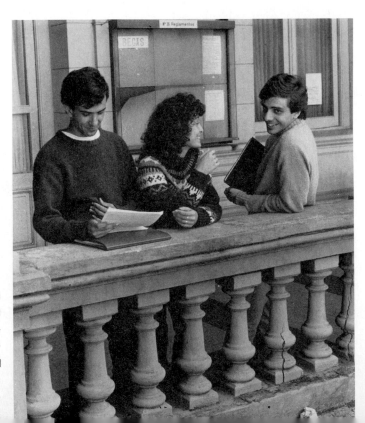

Unos estudiantes hablan sobre sus clases en la Universidad de la República, en Montevideo, Uruguay.

# *TERCER PASO**

In the Tercer paso you will
a. identify objects.
b. ask and answer questions about the location of people and objects.
c. describe objects.

## UN SALÓN DE CLASE¹

—¿Qué es esto?
—Es un bolígrafo.

—¿Qué es esto?
—Es una tiza.

Use **¿Qué es esto?** when asking for the identification of an object.

---

*\* Third step*

*¹ A classroom*

Unos estudiantes escuchan
atentamente la explicación de
su profesora en España.

## ACTIVIDADES

**A** Your instructor will mention the names of different objects in the classroom. Point or walk to where they are.

**B** Your instructor will point to some of the objects in the classroom and ask you to identify them by asking ¿**Qué es esto?**

**C** Enumerate the things you need for this class.

**D** Identify the items on the table to the right.

## ¿DÓNDE ESTÁ?[2]

**enfrente de** *in front of*
**detrás de** *behind*

**sobre** *on*
**debajo de** *underneath*

**al lado de** *beside*
**entre** *between*

¿Dónde está la profesora?
Está en la clase.

To ask for the location of a person or an object, use **dónde** + **está.**

---

[2] *Where is it?*

## ACTIVIDADES

**A** Complete the following sentences according to the relative position of people or objects in the drawing.

    1. La pizarra está ____ la profesora.
    2. El diccionario está ____ la mesa.
    3. Juan está ____ la profesora.
    4. Mercedes está ____ Juan y María.
    5. La mesa está ____ la ventana.
    6. María está ____ Mercedes.

**B** Identify where your classmates are in relation to each other.

    *Modelo*    **Profesor/a**  **¿Quién está al lado de Juan?**
                   **Estudiante**  **María (está al lado de Juan).**

**C** Your instructor will select several items from your classroom and ask you where they are. Answer by giving their location in relation to a person or another object.

    *Modelo*    **—¿Dónde está el libro?**
                 **—Está sobre el escritorio.**

**D** Look at the seating chart below. The X marks your location.

    1. Tell where Juan, Ángeles, Cristina, and Pedro are.
    2. With a partner, ask questions about the location of other students.

| María | Juan | Ester | Susana | Pedro |
|---|---|---|---|---|
| Carlos | Cristina | Ángeles | Alberto | Anita |
| Mercedes | Andrés | Roberto | Rocío | Pablo |

X

**E** Ask some of your classmates about the location of various students and objects in the classroom.

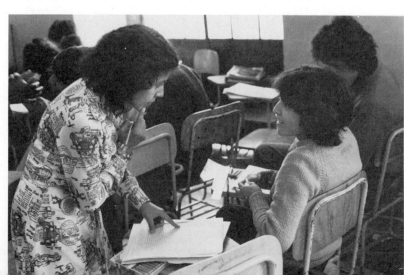

Una profesora escucha las preguntas de una estudiante en la UNAM (Universidad Nacional Autónoma de México), la universidad más importante de ese país.

## ¿CÓMO ES[3]?

El reloj es redondo.

La pizarra es rectangular.

See IM, **Tercer paso.**

La ventana es cuadrada.

—¿Cómo es el diccionario?
—Es grande.
—¿Y el cuaderno?
—Es pequeño.

—¿Cómo es la regla?
—Es larga.
—¿Y la tiza?
—Es corta.

---

[3] What is it like?
The clock is round. The window is square. The chalkboard is rectangular.

What's the dictionary like? It's big. And the notebook? It's small.

What's the ruler like? It's long. And the chalk? It's short.

# ACTIVIDADES

**A** **¿Verdadero o falso?** *True or false?* Tell whether each statement is true or false as your teacher or a classmate points to the item.

1. La puerta es cuadrada.
2. El escritorio es rectangular.
3. El salón de clase es pequeño.
4. La pizarra es redonda.

5. La ventana es rectangular.
6. El borrador es muy grande.
7. La tiza es pequeña.
8. El lápiz es largo.

**B** Describe the following objects in your classroom and tell where they are located in relation to a classmate.

| | | | | |
|---|---|---|---|---|
| la ventana | el cuaderno | el bolígrafo | la puerta | el escritorio |
| el pupitre | el reloj | el lápiz | la tiza | |

**C** **Adivinanzas** *Guessing game.* By giving a series of clues, have your classmates identify the object you have in mind. Your classmates will have to ask questions to find out what the object is.

| *Modelo* | Usted | **Es redondo.** |
|---|---|---|
| | Estudiante | **¿Dónde está?** |
| | Usted | **Está en la pared.** |
| | Estudiante | **Es el reloj.** |
| | Usted | **Sí.** |

# PRONUNCIACIÓN

## 1. b, v

In Spanish, the letters **b** and **v** are pronounced the same. At the beginning of an utterance or after an **m** or **n,** Spanish **b** and **v** sound like English *b.* In all other positions, Spanish **b** and **v** are pronounced by allowing the breath to pass between the lips, which are almost closed. This sound does not exist in English.

| | | | | | |
|---|---|---|---|---|---|
| bien | buenos | bonito | un vino | combate | vaca |
| sabe | Cuba | cabeza | uva | pavo | aviso |
| bebe | bebida | vive | bobo | babero | víbora |

## 2. d

Spanish **d,** like **t,** is pronounced by placing the tip of the tongue against the back of the upper teeth. It is pronounced in two ways, depending upon its position in a word or sentence. At the beginning of a sentence or after **l** or **n,** the air flow is interrupted until the tongue moves back. In all other positions, **d** is similar to the pronunciation of the English *th* in the word *father.*

| | | | | | |
|---|---|---|---|---|---|
| don | dónde | doña | doctor | día | dinero |
| adiós | comida | saludos | usted | médico | lado |

## EXPRESIONES ÚTILES EN LA CLASE

| | |
|---|---|
| ¿Comprende(n)? | *Do you understand?* |
| ¿Tiene(n) alguna pregunta? | *Do you have any questions?* |
| Levante(n) la mano. | *Raise your hand.* |

Other expressions that you may use in the classroom are:

| | |
|---|---|
| No comprendo. | *I don't understand.* |
| No sé. | *I don't know.* |
| Tengo una pregunta. | *I have a question.* |
| Más despacio, por favor. | *More slowly, please.* |
| ¿En qué página? | *On what page?* |
| ¿Cómo se dice... en español? | *How do you say . . . in Spanish?* |
| ¿Cómo se escribe...? | *How do you spell . . . ?* |
| presente | *here (present)* |
| ausente | *absent* |

# Cultura

## The Spanish language

Spanish, with some 300 million native speakers, is the fourth most widely used language. It is the official language of Spain and, in the New World, of Mexico, Cuba, Puerto Rico, the Dominican Republic, Guatemala, El Salvador, Honduras, Nicaragua, Costa Rica, Panama, Venezuela, Colombia, Ecuador, Peru, Bolivia, Paraguay, Uruguay, Chile, and Argentina.

Spanish is derived from Latin, the language spoken in the areas of Europe that were part of the Roman Empire. When Latin came in contact with the languages spoken in the various regions of the Iberian Peninsula, several dialects evolved. **Castilla** became the most important region in Spain (**España**), and eventually its language (**el castellano**) became the official language of Spain. When referring to the Spanish language, both **español** and **castellano** may be used.

The Arabs invaded Spain in 711 A.D. and remained there until 1492. During that time, many words of Arabic origin such as **álgebra, alcohol, cero** (*zero*), and **aceite** (*oil*) became part of the Spanish language.

When the Spaniards came to the New World, the languages spoken by the Indians contributed to the development of Spanish. Words such as **chocolate, tomate, coyote, maíz** (*corn*), and **aguacate** (*avocado*) are of Indian origin.

In the United States, especially in the West and Southwest, the influence of Spanish is evident in the names of cities (San Francisco, Las Vegas, San Agustin), states (Nevada, Montana), rivers (Colorado, Sacramento) and mountains (Sierra Nevada).

Una clase de computación en la ciudad de México. Para referirse a la capital y no al país, generalmente se escriben las letras D.F. (Distrito Federal) después de la palabra México.

# VOCABULARIO

**en el salón de clase** — *in the classroom*
el bolígrafo — *ballpoint pen*
el borrador — *eraser*
el cesto — *wastepaper basket*
el cuaderno — *notebook*
el diccionario — *dictionary*
el escritorio — *desk*
el lápiz — *pencil*
el libro — *book*
la mesa — *table*
la pared — *wall*
la pizarra — *chalkboard*
la puerta — *door*
el pupitre — *student's desk*
la regla — *ruler*
el reloj — *clock, watch*
la silla — *chair*
la tiza — *chalk*
la ventana — *window*

**personas**
el/la estudiante — *student*

**formas** — *shapes*
cuadrado — *square*
rectangular — *rectangular*
redondo — *round*

**tamaño** — *size*
corto — *short*
grande — *big*
largo — *long*
pequeño — *small*

**lugar** — *location*
al lado (de) — *next to*
debajo (de) — *under*
detrás (de) — *behind*
enfrente (de) — *in front of*
entre — *between*
sobre — *on, above*

**verbos**
está — *he/she is, you are (formal)*

**palabras útiles**
el/la — *the*
en — *in*
esto — *this*
un/una — *a, an*

**palabras interrogativas**
dónde — *where*
qué — *what*

# CUARTO PASO*

**In the** Cuarto paso **you will**
a. **use numbers from 0 to 99.**
b. **solve simple problems using those numbers.**
c. **tell time.**
d. **tell when an event takes place.**

## MINIDIÁLOGO

### Las preguntas de Lupe

| | |
|---|---|
| **Lupe** | Mamá, ¿cuántos días hay en una semana? |
| **Mamá** | Pues, hija, hay siete. |
| **Lupe** | ¿Y cuántas horas hay en un día? |
| **Mamá** | Hay veinticuatro. |
| **Lupe** | ¿Y cuántos días hay en un mes? |
| **Mamá** | Hay veintiocho, veintinueve, treinta o treinta y un días. Depende. |

## ACTIVIDAD

Complete the sentences with the appropriate expression.

1. En una semana hay ＿＿ días.
2. En un día hay ＿＿ horas.
3. En un mes hay ＿＿, ＿＿, ＿＿ o ＿＿ días.

## NÚMEROS 0–99

| | | | | | |
|---|---|---|---|---|---|
| 0 | cero | 5 | cinco | 10 | diez |
| 1 | uno | 6 | seis | 11 | once |
| 2 | dos | 7 | siete | 12 | doce |
| 3 | tres | 8 | ocho | 13 | trece |
| 4 | cuatro | 9 | nueve | 14 | catorce |

---

*\* Fourth step*

Lupe's questions
LUPE: Mom, how many days are there in a week? MOTHER: Well, dear (*literally, daughter*), there are seven. LUPE: And how many hours are there in a day? MOTHER: There are twenty-four. LUPE: And how many days are there in a month? MOTHER: There are twenty-eight, twenty-nine, thirty or thirty-one. It depends.

| | | | | |
|---|---|---|---|---|
| 15 | quince | 27 | veinte y siete (veintisiete) |
| 16 | diez y seis (dieciséis) | 28 | veinte y ocho (veintiocho) |
| 17 | diez y siete (diecisiete) | 29 | veinte y nueve (veintinueve) |
| 18 | diez y ocho (dieciocho) | 30 | treinta |
| 19 | diez y nueve (diecinueve) | 31 | treinta y uno |
| 20 | veinte | 40 | cuarenta |
| 21 | veinte y uno (veintiuno) | 50 | cincuenta |
| 22 | veinte y dos (veintidós) | 60 | sesenta |
| 23 | veinte y tres (veintitrés) | 70 | setenta |
| 24 | veinte y cuatro (veinticuatro) | 80 | ochenta |
| 25 | veinte y cinco (veinticinco) | 90 | noventa |
| 26 | veinte y seis (veintiséis) | | |

**1.** Numbers from 16 through 19 and 21 through 29 may be written as one word or as three words. Note the spelling changes and the written accent mark on some combined forms:

| | |
|---|---|
| diez y ocho | dieciocho |
| veinte y dos | veintidós |
| veinte y tres | veintitrés |

**2.** Beginning with 31, numbers are written as three words.

| | |
|---|---|
| 31 | treinta y uno |
| 45 | cuarenta y cinco |
| 58 | cincuenta y ocho |

**3.** The number *one* has three forms in Spanish: **uno, un,** and **una.** Use **uno** when counting: **uno, dos, tres.** Use **un** or **una** before nouns: **un borrador, una tiza; veintiún libros, veintiuna tizas.**[1]

**4.** Use **hay** for both *there is* and *there are*.

| | |
|---|---|
| **Hay** un libro sobre la mesa. | *There is a book on the table.* |
| **Hay** dos libros sobre la mesa. | *There are two books on the table.* |

## *ACTIVIDADES*

**A** Su profesor/a va a leer (*is going to read*) un número de cada (*each*) grupo. Indique cuál (*which one*) es el número.

| | | | | | | | | |
|---|---|---|---|---|---|---|---|---|
| 8 | 4 | 3 | 5 | | 54 | 38 | 76 | 95 |
| 12 | 9 | 16 | 6 | | 83 | 62 | 72 | 49 |
| 37 | 59 | 41 | 26 | | 47 | 14 | 91 | 56 |

---

[1] Gender of nouns is presented in **Lección 1.** For now, use **un** (meaning *one*) with nouns that take **el,** and **una** with nouns that take **la.**

**B** Lea los siguientes (*following*) números.

| | | | | | |
|---|---|---|---|---|---|
| 6 | 16 | 26 | 39 | 46 | 56 |
| 2 | 14 | 75 | 83 | 54 | 97 |

**C** Lea los números y las palabras.

| | | | |
|---|---|---|---|
| 1 cesto | 1 mesa | 1 lápiz | 1 silla |
| 21 ventanas | 41 libros | 51 señores | 81 chicas |

**D** Conteste las siguientes preguntas.

1. ¿Cuántos estudiantes hay en la clase?   2. ¿Cuántos profesores o cuántas profesoras hay?   3. ¿Cuántos borradores?   4. ¿Cuántas sillas hay?   5. ¿Cuántas puertas hay en la clase?   6. ¿Cuántas ventanas hay?

**E** Lea los siguientes problemas y dé (*give*) la solución. Use **y** ( + ), **menos** ( − ) y **son** ( = ).

*Modelo*   2 + 4 = 6     **dos y cuatro son seis**

| | | |
|---|---|---|
| 11 + 4 = | 20 − 6 = | 50 − 25 = |
| 8 + 2 = | 39 + 50 = | 26 + 40 = |
| 13 + 3 = | 80 − 1 = | |

**F** **¿Cuánto cuesta. . . ?** *how much is. . . ?* How much do you suppose the following items cost? Ask one of your classmates. ($$ = **dólares;** cents = **centavos**)

*Modelo*   una regla

**Usted**   ¿Cuánto cuesta una regla?
**Compañero/a**   Cuesta un dólar.

1. el libro de español
2. un lápiz
3. un bolígrafo

4. un diccionario
5. un cuaderno
6. un boleto (*ticket*) para un concierto

**G** **Números de teléfono y direcciones** *Addresses.* Lea la siguiente información:

| | | |
|---|---|---|
| Cafetería La Costa | General Páez 40 . . . . . . . . . . | 4-23-48-37 |
| Compañía La Nación | Avenida Cuarta 7. . . . . . . | 9-56-17-09 |
| Museo Colón | Calle Vigo 54 . . . . . . . . . . . . . . | 3-98-68-51 |
| Hotel Orfila | Chamberí 3 . . . . . . . . . . . . . . . . | 6-15-73-59 |

**H** **Adivinanzas.** You are "it"; choose a number from 0 to 99. Your classmates, in turn, try to guess your number. Tell them **más** if it is higher, **menos** if it is lower.

# DÍAS DE LA SEMANA

| | |
|---|---|
| lunes | *Monday* |
| martes | *Tuesday* |
| miércoles | *Wednesday* |
| jueves | *Thursday* |
| viernes | *Friday* |
| sábado | *Saturday* |
| domingo | *Sunday* |

## Septiembre

| LUNES | MARTES | MIÉRCOLES | JUEVES | VIERNES | SÁBADO | DOMINGO |
|---|---|---|---|---|---|---|
| 1 | 2 | 3 | 4 | 5 | 6 | 7 |
| 8 | 9 | 10 | 11 | 12 | 13 | 14 |
| 15 | 16 | 17 | 18 | 19 | 20 | 21 |
| 22 / 29 | 23 / 30 | 24 | 25 | 26 | 27 | 28 |

| | |
|---|---|
| ¿Qué día es hoy? | *What day is today?* |
| Hoy es... | *Today is . . .* |

**1.** Hispanic calendars generally begin the week with **lunes.** Days of the week are not capitalized in Spanish.

**2.** Express *on* + a day of the week as follows:

| | | | |
|---|---|---|---|
| el lunes | *on Monday* | los lunes | *on Mondays* |
| el domingo | *on Sunday* | los domingos | *on Sundays* |

# *ACTIVIDADES*

**A** **¿Qué día de la semana?** Según (*According to*) el calendario de septiembre, ¿qué día de la semana es el 2? ¿el 5? ¿el 30? ¿el 12? ¿el 23? ¿el 9?

**B** **Preguntas.** Conteste las siguientes preguntas.

1. ¿Qué día es hoy?
2. Si hoy es martes, ¿qué día es mañana (*tomorrow*)?
3. ¿Hay clase de español los domingos? ¿y los sábados?
4. ¿Qué días hay clase de español?

## LA HORA

1. Use **¿Qué hora es?** to inquire about the hour. To tell time, use **es la** from one o'clock to one thirty and **son las** with all other hours.

Es la una.

Son las tres.

2. To express the quarter hour, use **cuarto** or **quince.** To express the half hour use **media** or **treinta.**

Son las dos y cuarto.
Son las dos y quince.

Es la una y media.
Es la una y treinta.

3. For time after the half hour (3:50, for example) say the following hour (4:00) and use **menos** to express the minutes.

Son las cuatro menos diez.

There are several alternate ways to tell time in Spanish. For now, follow the model above.

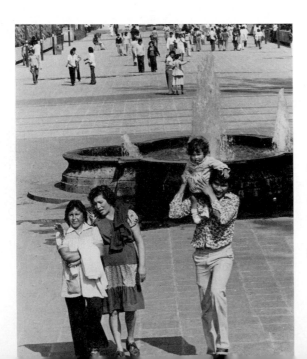

Una familia en el Parque de Chapultepec de la ciudad de México. Los sábados y los domingos este parque es el lugar de reunión de muchas familias mexicanas.

**4.** Add **en punto** for the exact time, **más o menos** for the approximate time.

> Es la una en punto.
> Son las cinco menos cuarto más o menos.

**5.** For A.M. and P.M., use the following:

| de la mañana | (from 1:00 A.M. to 11:59 A.M.) |
| de la tarde | (from noon to approximately 7:00 P.M.) |
| de la noche | (from about 7:00 P.M. to midnight) |

**6.** Use **¿A qué hora es?** to ask the hour at which something happens.

> —¿A qué hora es la clase?    —Es a las nueve y media.

## ACTIVIDADES

**A** **¿Qué hora es en. . . ?** Diga (*Say*) qué hora es en las siguientes ciudades (*cities*).

| 1 | 2 | 3 | 4 | 5 |
| LOS ÁNGELES | MÉXICO | SAN JUAN | BUENOS AIRES | MADRID |
| 11:00 AM | 1:00 PM | 2:00 PM | 5:00 PM | 8:00 PM |

**B** Add 15 minutes to each of the clock dials in Actividad A and reread. Give either exact or approximate time.

**C** **El horario de María** *María's Schedule.* Pregúntele a un/a compañero/a la hora de las clases y las actividades de María.

> *Modelo* —¿A qué hora es la clase de español?    —Es a las nueve.

lunes

| 9:00 | clase de español |
| 10:15 | receso |
| 10:30 | clase de matemáticas |
| 11:45 | laboratorio |
| 1:00 | almuerzo° | lunch |
| 2:00 | clase de física |
| 5:00 | partido de tenis° | tennis game |

**D ¿En qué página del libro está(n). . . ?**

el calendario      los relojes      los días de la semana      el Primer paso
el salón de clase      el alfabeto

Una pizarra con las salidas de los vuelos en el Aeropuerto de Barajas de Madrid, la capital de España.

Una de las estaciones de ferrocarril de la ciudad de Madrid.

# PRONUNCIACIÓN

## 1.  g, j

At the beginning of an utterance or after **n**, Spanish **g** followed by **l, r, a, o,** or **u** is pronounced like English *g* in *garden*. In all other positions, Spanish **g** followed by **l, r, a, o,** or **u** is pronounced with no interruption to the air flow, similar to the rapid and relaxed pronunciation of English *g* in *sugar*. Note the difference in the pronunciation of **g** in these words that your instructor will say: **gata, la gata.**

| gata | gusto | goma | gracias | grande | Domingo |
|------|-------|------|---------|--------|---------|
| amigo | lugar | regular | lechuga | agua | la gata |

In the syllables **gue** and **gui,** the letter **g** is pronounced as above, but the **u** is not pronounced.

guerra    guitarra    guía    Miguel    seguir    llegue

In Spanish, the pronunciation of the letter **g** in the syllables **ge** and **gi** and of the letter **j** is very similar to the pronunciation of English *h* in the word *heel*.

general    ligero    gigante    viaje    jugo    jueves

## 2.  r, rr

In Spanish, whenever the letter **r** occurs between vowels or after a consonant, its pronunciation is similar to English *d, dd, t,* or *tt* in words such as *matter, water* or *ladder,* pronounced rapidly by an American.

pero    señora    dinero    pared    tres    otro

Spanish **r** at the beginning of a word, after **n** or **l,** and **rr** is pronounced by placing the tip of the tongue on the upper gum ridge and tapping it several times. This sound does not exist in English.

perro    carro    rico    Roberto    Enrique    regalo    alrededor

## EXPRESIONES ÚTILES EN LA CLASE

| | |
|---|---|
| cuente(n) | *count* |
| diga(n) | *say* |
| Abran el libro en la página... | *Open the book on page . . .* |
| Más alto, por favor. | *Louder, please.* |
| otra vez | *again* |

# Cultura

## Attitudes concerning time in the Hispanic world

In Hispanic countries, events such as concerts, bullfights, and religious services begin on time. Normally, business meetings and medical appointments are also kept at the scheduled hour. However, informal social functions such as parties and private gatherings do not usually begin at a precise hour. In fact, guests are not expected to arrive until from one half to one full hour after the time indicated on an invitation. When in doubt, you may ask **¿hora americana?** or **¿hora inglesa?** (*precise time?*) to find out if you should be punctual.

Many countries use military time or the 24-hour clock, for train, bus, and plane schedules, as well as for television and radio programs.

Below is the bus schedule to the Ezeiza Airport, which is about one hour's drive from Buenos Aires, Argentina. If you were leaving on a flight at 8:00 P.M. on Tuesday, which bus would you take?

### HORARIO DE SALIDAS DE LOS ÓMNIBUS

DESDE CARLOS PELLEGRINI 509, CAPITAL A AEROPUERTO EZEIZA

| Lunes | Martes | Miercoles | Jueves | Viernes | Sabado | Domingo |
|-------|--------|-----------|--------|---------|--------|---------|
| 05.30 | 05.30 | 05.30 | 05.30 | 05.30 | 05.30 | 06.30 |
| 06.30 | 06.30 | 06.30 | 06.30 | 06.30 | 06.30 | 07.30 |
| 07.30 | 07.30 | 07.30 | 07.30 | 07.30 | 07.30 | 09.00 |
| 09.00 | 09.00 | 09.00 | 09.00 | 09.00 | 09.00 | 10.00 |
| 10.00 | 10.00 | 10.00 | 10.00 | 10.00 | 10.00 | 11.00 |
| 11.00 | 11.00 | 11.00 | 11.00 | 11.00 | 11.00 | 12.30 |
| 12.30 | 12.30 | 12.30 | 12.30 | 12.30 | 12.30 | 13.30 |
| 13.30 | 13.30 | 13.30 | 13.30 | 13.30 | 13.30 | 15.00 |
| 15.00 | 15.00 | 15.00 | 15.00 | 15.00 | 15.00 | 16.00 |
| 16.00 | 16.00 | 16.00 | 16.00 | 16.00 | 16.00 | 17.00 |
| 17.00 | 17.00 | 17.00 | 17.00 | 17.00 | 17.00 | 18.30 |
| 18.30 | 18.30 | 18.00 | 18.30 | 18.00 | 18.00 | 19.30 |
| 19.30 | 20.30 | 19.00 | 20.30 | 19.00 | 19.30 | 20.30 |
|       |       | 20.30 |        | 20.30 | 20.30 |         |

# VOCABULARIO²

**tiempo** — *time*
el día — *day*
la hora — *hour*
la mañana — *morning*
el mes — *month*
la semana — *week*
cuarto — *quarter*
en punto — *sharp*
hoy — *today*
media — *half*
menos — *minus, to* (in telling time)

**personas**
la hija — *daughter, dear*
la mamá — *mother*

**verbos**
depende — *it depends*
hay — *there is, there are*

**palabras interrogativas**
cuántos, cuántas — *how many*

**palabras útiles**
a — *at, to*
la pregunta — *question*
pues — *well*

**expresiones útiles**
¿A qué hora es...? — *At what time is ...?*
¿Qué hora es? — *What time is it?*
Es la.../Son las... — *It's ...*
más o menos — *more or less*

**palabras adicionales³**

**verbos**
dé — *give*
indique — *indicate*
va a... — *you are* / *he/she is* } *going to ...*

**otras palabras**
cada — *each*
cuál — *which one*
según — *according to*
siguiente — *following*

---

² See pages 26–27 and 29 for the numbers and the days of the week.
³ These words appear in the directions of the **Actividades.** You should recognize them since they will appear in future lessons. Cognates and words that were presented in **Expresiones útiles en la clase** have not been included in this list.

**In** Lección 1 **you will**
a. **discuss daily activities.**
b. **ask for and provide information.**
c. **express needs.**
d. **ask about and express location.**

# Los estudios

la computadora

el papel

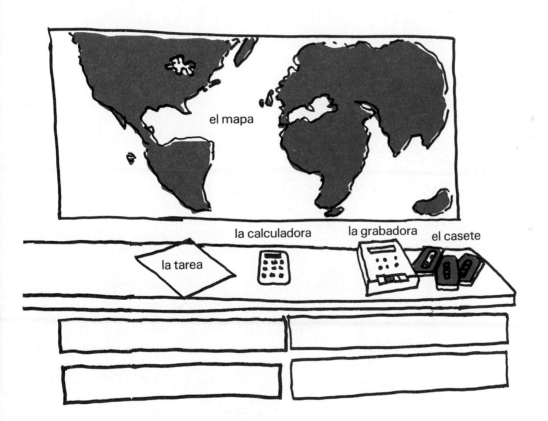

el mapa

la tarea

la calculadora

la grabadora

el casete

Juana estudia matemáticas.

Alfredo estudia español.

**otras materias** *other subjects*
economía
biología
historia
geografía
física
química
(p)sicología
contabilidad *accounting*

**otras lenguas** *other languages*
inglés
francés
chino
portugués
ruso
japonés
italiano
alemán *German*

Una clase en una escuela primaria de Isla Mujeres, México.

# ACTIVIDADES

**A** Complete las siguientes oraciones (*sentences*) de acuerdo con el dibujo (*drawing*)[1] de las páginas 36–37.

1. El chico está enfrente de la ____.
2. La computadora está entre el ____ y la ____.
3. La tarea está entre la ____ y la ____.
4. El ____ está en la pared.
5. El casete está al lado de la ____.

**B** Pregúntele a uno/a de sus (*your*) compañeros/as dónde está cada objeto en ese dibujo. Él/Ella debe contestar diciendo (*should answer saying*) dónde está en relación con otro objeto.

**C** Asocie las palabras de la columna de la izquierda (*left*) con las materias de la columna de la derecha (*right*).

1. diccionario        a. química
2. números           b. biología
3. oxígeno           c. español
4. animales          d. historia
5. Freud             e. economía
6. dólares           f. geografía
7. Napoleón          g. contabilidad
8. mapa              h. sicología

**D** Asocie las ciudades (*cities*) de la columna de la izquierda con las lenguas de la columna de la derecha.

1. París             a. portugués
2. Panamá            b. ruso
3. Moscú             c. italiano
4. Shanghai          d. inglés
5. Río de Janeiro    e. japonés
6. Roma              f. español
7. Tokio             g. alemán
8. Frankfurt         h. chino
9. Londres           i. francés

**E** Dígale a uno de sus compañeros qué materias estudia usted. Después (*Then*) pregúntele qué estudia él/ella.

| *Modelo* | **Usted** | **Yo estudio español, inglés y matemáticas. ¿Y tú?** |
|---|---|---|
| | **Compañero/a** | **Yo estudio física, contabilidad y español.** |

---

[1] From here on, directions for the **Actividades** will be given in Spanish. In cases where the directions involve new vocabulary, English equivalents will appear in parentheses.

# Cultura

## Education in the Hispanic World

Educational systems in the Hispanic countries are highly centralized and often controlled by the Ministry of Education.

All students begin their instruction in elementary school (**la escuela primaria**). At the secondary school level (**la escuela secundaria**), some students enter a technical or vocational school; others attend a **colegio, instituto,** or **liceo** to complete the program (**bachillerato**), which prepares them for university study. In some countries there is a requirement of a year or two of additional work (**la preparatoria**). And in most Hispanic countries, students must pass rigorous entrance examinations before acceptance by a university.

The majority of middle-class students attend private schools, most of which are Catholic. Some young people, especially those who already have a job, take courses such as languages or accounting in private institutions.

Those students who attend a university immediately begin a specialized program. In general, the course of study is quite rigid, with only limited electives. Since very few Spanish-American or Spanish universities have dormitories, students usually live in private homes or guest houses (**pensiones/casas de huéspedes**).

# EN CONTEXTO

## En la universidad

David, un estudiante norteamericano, habla con Olga, una estudiante española, en la Universidad de Málaga.

**Olga**   ¿Qué estudias este semestre, David?

**David**   Estudio historia del arte, literatura, antropología y gramática española. ¿Y tú?

**Olga**   Estudio informática. Además, trabajo con mi padre por las tardes.

**David**   Por eso estás tan ocupada siempre.

**Olga**   Un poco. Y tú, David, ya hablas español muy bien.

**David**   ¡Qué va! Escucho las cintas en el laboratorio, hablo con los alumnos, pero necesito practicar más.

---

David, an American student, chats with Olga, a Spanish student, at the University of Málaga.
OLGA: What are you studying this semester, David? DAVID: I am studying art history, literature, anthropology, and Spanish grammar. And you? OLGA: I'm studying computer science. Besides, I work with my father in the afternoons. DAVID: That's why you are always so busy. OLGA: A little. And David, you already speak Spanish very well. DAVID: Oh, no! I listen to the tapes in the lab, I talk with students, but I need to practice more.

**Para completar**

Complete las oraciones con la información que se da (*is given*) en el diálogo.

1. Este semestre David estudia. . .
2. Olga estudia. . .
3. Olga trabaja por las. . .
4. Olga está siempre muy. . .
5. David escucha las cintas en el. . .
6. David necesita. . .

## ACTIVIDADES

**A** Complete las siguientes oraciones sobre sus actividades en la universidad.

1. Este semestre estudio. . .   2. Mi clase favorita es. . .   3. El profesor/La profesora se llama. . .

**B** Complete el siguiente diálogo con su compañero/a.

**Usted** ¿Qué estudias este semestre/trimestre?
**Compañero/a** . . .
**Usted** ¿A qué hora es la clase de ____?
**Compañero/a** . . .
**Usted** ¿Quién es el profesor/la profesora?
**Compañero/a** . . .

Unos alumnos conversan frente a la Facultad de Derecho en la Universidad de la República, en Montevideo.

## GRAMÁTICA

### Subject pronouns

|  | SINGULAR |  |  | PLURAL |  |
|---|---|---|---|---|---|
| yo | *I* |  | nosotros, nosotras | *we* |  |
| tú | *you (familiar)* |  | vosotros, vosotras | *you (familiar)* |  |
| usted | *you (formal)* |  | ustedes | *you (formal)* |  |
| él | *he* |  | ellos ⎱ | *they* |  |
| ella | *she* |  | ellas ⎰ |  |  |

1. Spanish has many different equivalents for *you*: singular, plural, familiar, and formal. There are even regional variations. Your problem as a learner is to identify and select the right form from the various possibilities.

   Here are the forms used in Spain:

   | tú | vosotros/as |
   |---|---|
   | usted | ustedes |

   These are the forms used in Hispanic America:

   | tú |  |
   |---|---|
   | usted | ustedes |

   In both Spain and Hispanic America, **tú** and **usted** are not interchangeable. As explained in **Primer paso, tú** is used with close friends, relatives, and children, while **usted** is used when addressing someone as **señor, señora, doctor,** and so on. When you are in doubt whether to use **tú** or **usted,** use **usted.**
   In Spain, the plural of **tú** is **vosotros** or **vosotras.** In other Spanish-speaking countries, the plural of both **tú** and **usted** is **ustedes.**
   **Usted** and **ustedes** are abbreviated in writing as **Ud.** or **Vd.,** and **Uds.** or **Vds.,** respectively.

2. There is no Spanish equivalent for the English subject pronoun *it.*

   **Es redondo.**                         *It's round.*

3. Except for **ustedes,** the plural pronouns have masculine and feminine endings (**nosotros, nosotras, vosotros, vosotras, ellos, ellas**). Use the **-as** ending for a group composed only of females; use the **-os** ending for a mixed group or one composed only of males.

## ACTIVIDAD

¿Qué pronombre (*pronoun*) usa usted?

**1.** Usted habla de (*about*) las siguientes personas:

> Sr. Martínez    Alicia y Susana    usted (*yourself*)    Sra. Gómez
> Alfredo y Juana    Ana y usted

**2.** Usted habla con las siguientes personas:

> su profesor de historia    una azafata (*stewardess*)    su íntimo amigo
> dos compañeros    dos doctores    un niño (*child*)

## GRAMÁTICA

### Present tense of regular *-ar* verbs

|  | **hablar** *to speak* |  |  |
|---|---|---|---|
| yo | habl**o** | nosotros/as | habl**amos** |
| tú | habl**as** | vosotros/as | habl**áis** |
| él/ella, usted | habl**a** | ellos/as, ustedes | habl**an** |

**1.** The endings of Spanish **-ar** verbs (**-o, -as, -a, -amos, -áis, -an**) indicate the subject (who or what does the action). Therefore, subject pronouns are generally omitted, except for

| emphasis | **Yo estudio** español. | *I study Spanish.* |
|---|---|---|
| clarification | **Él practica** mucho. (*not* **ella** *or* **usted**) | *He practices a lot.* |
| contrast | **Ella habla** francés; **nosotros hablamos** español. | *She speaks French; we speak Spanish.* |

**2.** When you have two verbs in sequence, conjugate the first verb; the second verb is generally an infinitive (the form that ends in **-ar, -er,** or **-ir**).

> Ella **desea enseñar** aquí.    *She wants to teach here.*

**3.** The Spanish present tense has various English equivalents.

> Yo **trabajo** en la oficina.
> *I work in the office.*
> *I'm working in the office.*
> *I do work in the office.*
> *I'll work in the office.*

**4.** Some common **-ar** verbs are: desear, enseñar, escuchar, estudiar, hablar, necesitar, practicar, trabajar.

## The negative

**1.** Make sentences negative by placing the word **no** before the verb.

Ellos trabajan con mi padre. ⟶ Ellos **no** trabajan con mi padre.

**2.** When answering a question with a negative statement, say **no** twice.

—¿Enseñas francés? *"Do you teach French?"*
—**No,** (yo) **no** enseño francés. *"No, I don't teach French."*

## ACTIVIDADES

**A  En la clase de español.** Los estudiantes de la columna de la izquierda trabajan mucho en la clase. Los estudiantes de la columna de la derecha trabajan muy poco. Use la forma correcta de los siguientes verbos para expresar lo que hacen (*what they do*): **estudiar, trabajar, practicar, hablar, escuchar.**

|  | **mucho** | **poco** |
|---|---|---|
| *Modelos* | María | Alfredo |
|  | **María trabaja mucho.** | **Alfredo trabaja poco.** |
|  | Isabel | Pedro |
|  | Alicia y yo | tú |
|  | yo | Josefina y Marta |

**B  Un estudiante muy bueno.** David es un estudiante muy bueno. Dígale a su compañero/a lo que David hace (*does*) para sacar buenas notas (*to get good grades*). Después dígale lo que usted hace.

**C  Un estudiante muy malo.** Dígale a su compañero/a lo que ese estudiante no hace.

**D  Las clases de unos estudiantes.** Mire (*Look at*) la lista y dígale a un/a compañero/a lo que cada persona estudia. Después pregúntele a su compañero/a qué estudia él/ella.

1. Ana: inglés, matemáticas, contabilidad
2. Manuel: español, historia, química
3. José: antropología, geografía, economía
4. yo: . . .

**E  Mire el anuncio (*ad*) de la escuela Idiomas Serrano (*Serrano Language School*). Conteste las siguientes preguntas.**

1. ¿Qué enseñan en Idiomas Serrano?
2. ¿Dónde está Idiomas Serrano?
3. ¿Cuál es el teléfono?

**F En el salón de clase.**
Diga lo que hace cada
persona en la clase.

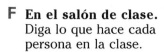

## EN CONTEXTO

### En la librería°                                                bookstore

| | |
|---|---|
| **Pablo** | Por favor, necesito comprar un diccionario de español. |
| **Dependiente** | ¿Un diccionario pequeño? |
| **Pablo** | No, es para mi clase de español. Yo busco°  *I'm looking for* |
| | un diccionario grande. |
| **Dependiente** | Este diccionario es excelente. Es muy popular |
| | entre los estudiantes. |
| **Pablo** | ¿Y cuánto cuesta°?  *¿y... And how much is it?* |
| **Dependiente** | Ochenta pesos. El precio° es muy bueno.  *price* |

### Para completar

Complete las oraciones con la información que se da en el diálogo.

1. Pablo está en la...
2. Él necesita comprar un...
3. Él habla con...

4. El diccionario grande es
   popular entre los...
5. El diccionario cuesta...

Unos clientes examinan
unos libros en una
librería de Montevideo,
Uruguay.

## *ACTIVIDADES* ▬▬▬▬▬▬▬▬

**A** ¿Qué necesita usted en estas clases? Asocie las materias de la columna de la izquierda con los objetos de las dos columnas de la derecha.

| | | |
|---|---|---|
| 1. matemáticas | a. un mapa | d. una grabadora |
| 2. geografía | b. una calculadora | e. un casete |
| 3. español | c. un diccionario | f. una regla |

**B** Usted necesita comprar un cuaderno para sus clases y va a la librería. Complete el siguiente diálogo con su compañero/a.

| | |
|---|---|
| **Usted** | Por favor, necesito... |
| **Dependiente/a** | ¿Grande o pequeño? |
| **Usted** | ... ¿Cuánto cuesta? |
| **Dependiente/a** | ... ¿Necesita algo más (*anything else*)? |
| **Usted** | ... |

## GRAMÁTICA

### Noun gender

Nouns are words that name a person, place, or thing. In English all nouns use the same definite article, *the,* and the indefinite articles *a* and *an.* In Spanish, however, nouns are divided into two types: those that use **un** or **el** and those that use **una** or **la.**

Traditionally, nouns that require **un** or **el** are called *masculine* while those requiring **una** or **la** are called *feminine.* These terms are used in a grammatical sense and have nothing to do with biological gender. Spanish speakers do not perceive objects as having biological gender. Only when nouns refer to males (masculine) and females (feminine) are the terms meaningful in a biological sense.

### Articles (singular)

| | MASCULINE | FEMININE |
|---|---|---|
| DEFINITE ARTICLES | el | la |
| INDEFINITE ARTICLES | un | una |

**1.** Usually nouns that end in **o** require **el** and those that end in **a** require **la.**

**el** libr**o**   **el** cuadern**o**   **el** diccionari**o**   **la** mes**a**   **la** sill**a**   **la** ventan**a**

**2.** Other nouns that are generally used with **un** or **el** end in the following letters: **e, l, n, r,** and **s.**

el/un pupitre   el/un papel   el/un salón   el/un borrador   el/un mes

**3.** Other nouns that require **una** or **la** end in the following letters: **-d, -ción, -sión.**

la/una actividad la/una lección la/una misión

**4.** Exceptions to these rules are few. Some common ones are

el/un día la/una clase la/una noche el/un mapa la/una tarde

Memorize the exceptions along with their article. You will come across others as you learn more Spanish.

**5.** With nouns referring to animate beings, biological gender determines whether to use **el/un** or **la/una.** Note that nouns ending in **o** change the **o** to **a** for the feminine, and that nouns that end in a consonant add **a** for the feminine.

el/un amigo la/una amiga el/un profesor la/una profesora

Nouns ending in **-e** may remain the same (**el/la estudiante**) or have a feminine form ending in **-a** (**el dependiente, la dependienta**).

La Universidad de Sevilla en España. Sevilla es la capital de Andalucía, la región del sur de España.

## *ACTIVIDADES*

**A** Dé el artículo indefinido; después el definido.

| mesa | tarea | lección | profesor | chica | libro | pupitre | actividad |
|---|---|---|---|---|---|---|---|
| museo | pared | acción | señora | lápiz | librería | amigo | |

**B** Complete este pequeño párrafo con artículos definidos.

María está en ____ clase de ____ profesora Sánchez. Ella trabaja en ____ laboratorio por ____ tarde. Por ____ noche ella estudia mucho.

**C** Complete estas oraciones con artículos indefinidos.

Susana necesita comprar ____ bolígrafo, ____ diccionario, ____ regla y ____ calculadora. Su amiga necesita ____ cuaderno y ____ casete. Ellas hablan con ____ dependiente.

**D** Pregúntele a su compañero/a cuánto cuesta cada uno de los siguientes objetos.

| *Modelo* | **Usted** | ¿Cuánto cuesta la calculadora? |
|---|---|---|
| | **Compañero/a** | Cuesta diez dólares. |

## GRAMÁTICA

### Noun plurals

1. Add **-s** to form the plural of nouns ending in a vowel (**silla/sillas**). Add **-es** to nouns ending in a consonant (**pared/paredes; señor/señores**). If a noun ends in **z,** change the **z** to **c** and add **-es** (**lápiz/lápices**).
2. Masculine plural forms (e.g., **amigos, profesores**) are used to refer to men and also to groups that include both men and women.

## Articles (plural)

Definite and indefinite articles also have plural forms. The indefinite articles **unos/unas** have the meaning *some* in English.

|  |  | SINGULAR | PLURAL |
|---|---|---|---|
| DEFINITE | MASCULINE | el libro | los libros |
|  | FEMININE | la chica | las chicas |
| INDEFINITE | MASCULINE | un libro | unos libros |
|  | FEMININE | una chica | unas chicas |

## Use of definite articles

Spanish and English often use definite articles with nouns in similar ways, but in certain contexts the two languages differ. Use the definite article

**1.** before a title of respect (except **don** and **doña**) when you are talking *about* the person.

¿Cómo está **el** señor Romero?      *How is Mr. Romero?*
**La** Srta. Ortiz estudia economía.      *Miss Ortiz studies economics.*

Do not use the definite article when you are talking directly *to* the person.

¿Cómo está usted, señor Romero?      *How are you, Mr. Romero?*

**2.** to express *on* with the days of the week.

Hablo con Arturo **el** lunes.      *I'll talk to Arturo on Monday.*
Estudiamos **los** jueves.      *We study on Thursdays.*

**3.** with names of languages except when they immediately follow **de, en, hablar,** and **estudiar.**

**El** español no es difícil.      *Spanish isn't difficult.*
Estudio español.      *I study Spanish.*

## *ACTIVIDADES*

**A** **¿Qué hay en la librería?**
Su compañero/a y usted deben hacer una lista de los objetos y personas que generalmente hay en una librería. Después comparen su lista con la de otros estudiantes.

*Modelo* **Hay una mesa.**

**B** **¿Sabe** (*Do you know*) **el plural?**

| | | | | | |
|---|---|---|---|---|---|
| el precio | una clase | la tarea | el professor | una mesa | el reloj |
| el borrador | un papel | un estudiante | la pizarra | una tiza | la chica |

**C** Complete este párrafo con artículos definidos. En algunos (*some*) casos no se necesita un artículo.

Nosotros estudiamos ___ español en ___ universidad. ___ clases son ___ lunes, miércoles y viernes. ___ español es muy interesante. Yo hablo ___ español con ___ profesor y con ___ estudiantes.

**D** **Saludos.** Haga las preguntas necesarias (*Ask the necessary questions*) para completar el siguiente diálogo. Salude al Sr. Chávez y pregúntele por (*about*) la Sra. Chávez. Su compañero debe hacer el papel (*should play the part*) del Sr. Chávez.

| | |
|---|---|
| **Usted** | ¿Cómo ___, Sr. Chávez? |
| **Sr. Chávez** | Muy bien, gracias. ¿Y tú? |
| **Usted** | ___. ¿Cómo ___ Sra. Chávez? |
| **Sr. Chávez** | Está bien, gracias. |

## EN CONTEXTO

**¿Dónde están los edificios (*buildings*)?**

## ACTIVIDADES

**A** Pregúntele a su compañero/a dónde están los diferentes (*various*) edificios de la universidad en el dibujo.

**B** Complete las siguientes oraciones con la palabra adecuada.

1. Compramos los libros en ____.
2. Escuchamos las cintas en ____.
3. Practicamos gimnasia en ____.
4. Estudiamos y consultamos libros en ____.
5. Hablamos con los compañeros en ____.

## GRAMÁTICA

**Present tense of the verb *estar***

| **estar** *to be* | |
|---|---|
| yo estoy | *I am* |
| tú estás | *you are* |
| él, ella, usted está | *he/she is, you are* |
| nosotros/as estamos | *we are* |
| vosotros/as estáis | *you are* |
| ellos, ellas, ustedes están | *they are, you are* |

**1.** Use **estar** to express the location of persons or objects.

—¿Dónde está el gimnasio?  —Está al lado de la cafetería.
—¿Dónde está Pedro?  —Está en la biblioteca.

**2.** Use **estar** to talk about states of health.

—¿Cómo estás?  —Estoy muy mal.

## ACTIVIDADES

**A** Pregúntele a su compañero/a dónde están los diferentes edificios de su universidad. Su compañero/a debe ser (*should be*) muy específico/a en su respuesta (*answer*).

**B** **Hora y lugares** *places*. Pregúntele a su compañero/a dónde está él/ella a las siguientes horas.

*Modelo*  8:00 A.M.  **Usted**  **¿Dónde estás a las ocho de la mañana?**
  **Compañero/a**  **Estoy en la clase de física.**

9:00 A.M.    1:00 P.M.    4:00 P.M.    11:00 A.M.    3:00 P.M.    10:00 P.M.

**C** Pregúnteles a dos de sus compañeros/as dónde están a) por la mañana, b) por la tarde, c) por la noche.

    *Modelo*        **Usted**   **¿Dónde están ustedes por la tarde?**
                **Compañeros/as**  **Estamos en la biblioteca.**

**D** Mire los siguientes dibujos. Pregúntele a su compañero/a dónde están las personas y cómo están.

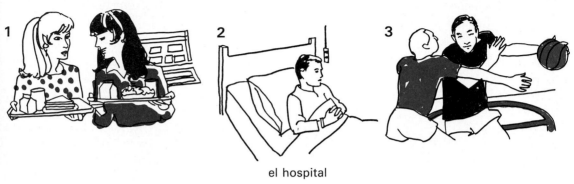

el hospital

## Linking

One of the characteristics of spoken Spanish is that words are linked together, while in spoken English they are generally separated by a slight pause.

If a Spanish word ends in a consonant and the next word begins with a vowel sound, the consonant forms a syllable with the following vowel.

    Nosotros hablamos español.

If a word ends in **a, e,** or **o** and the next word begins with another of these vowels, but not the same one, the resulting combination is linked.

    Ana es    Paco está    no habla

If a word ends in a vowel and the next word begins with the same vowel sound, the two vowels are linked in careful speech. In rapid speech, the two vowels are pronounced as one.

    una amiga ⟶ unamiga    ocho horas ⟶ ochoras

When two words are linked by any combination of **a, e,** or **o** with **i** or **u,** the vowels form a diphthong which is pronounced as one syllable.

    mi amigo ⟶ miamigo        la universidad ⟶ launiversidad
    la historia ⟶ lahistoria        habla inglés ⟶ hablainglés

# LECTURA*

## Reading skills

Reading skills are as important as the ability to converse, especially as you begin and advance in the study of a language.

In real life we read for two reasons: for pleasure and to get information. There is such a great variety in the written information we read that a competent reader has to use different techniques to extract meaning from a text. The following are some important ideas, especially for persons beginning to read a second language.

Reading depends on more than just knowing words. Your previous experiences and knowledge of the world are assets you bring to the text that will help you comprehend many concepts. Many students feel they must understand every single word in order to understand the text. This is not so. Sometimes understanding key words—nouns and verbs—is all you really need in order to get the gist of what you are reading. Remember to read the title and subtitles, and to pay close attention to visual clues, such as pictures, charts, or print size. Use these aids to make educated guesses about the meaning of a text. Guessing the meaning of unknown words by using the context is an effective reading technique. You will be surprised how often your guesses are correct.

Once you have determined the general meaning of a text, you may want to go back and look for specific details. Remember that these techniques are not mutually exclusive and that we use several at the same time when we read.

Look at the following ad and read it, trying to get the general meaning. The size of the word **inglés** at the beginning, the use of cognates such as **programa, cursos, profesores, teléfono, nativos,** and the numbers will help you get the gist of the ad.

You knew that the ad referred to a language school before you read the last line, which is in English. Now read it a second time looking for specific details (e.g., the word **empresas** *businesses*). This second reading will give you additional information.

The **lecturas** *readings* at the end of each lesson have glosses on the side. Try to read the following **lectura** to get the gist of it, making educated guesses without looking at the glosses. Then read it a second time looking for specific details and consulting the glosses when necessary.

---

* reading

## La informática

Éste es el programa oficial de la Facultad de Informática de la Universidad de Málaga para los alumnos de primer año. A la izquierda está el código o números que identifican cada materia y a la derecha está el nombre de las materias.

---

# FACULTAD DE INFORMATICA

| CÓD. | PRIMER CURSO |
|------|--------------|
| 001 | -Cálculo Infinitesimal |
| 002 | -Algebra |
| 003 | -Física |
| 004 | -Tecnología de los Computadores |
| 005 | -Laboratorio de Tecnología de Computadores |
| 006 | -Elementos de Programación |
| 007 | -Laboratorio de Programación I |

---

Las materias son difíciles° y los alumnos deben estudiar mucho para poder aprobar°. Sin embargo°, la informática es una carrera muy popular y hay muchos alumnos en las clases por la importancia de las computadoras en el mundo° actual y en el futuro. Además los estudiantes saben° que hay muchas posibilidades do obtener trabajo después° de la graduación.

son... *are difficult*
pass Sin... *Nevertheless*

*world*
*know*
*after*

## PREGUNTAS ▬▬▬▬▬▬▬▬▬▬▬▬▬▬▬▬▬▬▬▬▬▬▬▬▬▬▬▬▬▬▬▬▬▬

**A** La idea central de esta lectura es

    a. los estudios de informática en la Universidad de Málaga.
    b. los precios de las computadoras.
    c. las actividades de los estudiantes de informática.

**B** Diga si las siguientes oraciones son verdaderas o falsas, de acuerdo con la lectura.

    1. Hay cuatro materias en el programa de primer año.
    2. Los alumnos de informática estudian muy poco.
    3. Muchos alumnos estudian informática en la universidad.
    4. Es difícil obtener trabajo después de la graduación.

## Una estudiante de informática

Olga Marchena es una chica costarricense que estudia el primer año de informática en la Universidad de Costa Rica. Ella siempre está muy ocupada. Por las mañanas, de lunes a viernes, va a la universidad. Su primera clase empieza° a las nueve de la mañana. A las once más o menos Olga se reúne° con algunos compañeros en un café que está muy cerca° de la facultad. Allí° conversan y comen algo antes° de la siguiente clase.

Las clases terminan° a la una y media y Olga va a su casa° para almorzar° con su familia.

Por la tarde Olga ayuda° a su padre en la oficina donde trabaja con la computadora. Esta práctica es excelente para ella. Por las noches estudia, mira televisión o sale° con sus amigos.

*begins*
*se... gets together*
*near / There / comen. . .*
*they eat something before*
*end / home*
*para... to have lunch*
*helps*

*goes out*

## Preguntas

**A** La idea central de esta lectura es

    a. las actividades de Olga.
    b. la familia de Olga.
    c. los estudiantes de informática.

**B** Diga si las siguientes oraciones son verdaderas o falsas, de acuerdo con la lectura.

    1. Olga es una estudiante norteamericana.
    2. Ella va a la universidad por las tardes.
    3. Sus clases empiezan a las once.
    4. Ella va a un café para almorzar con sus compañeros.
    5. Olga trabaja en la oficina de su padre.
    6. Olga siempre estudia por las noches.

**C** Complete el siguiente diálogo con su compañero/a.

    **Usted** ¿A qué hora llegas a la universidad?
    **Compañero/a** . . .
    **Usted** ¿A qué hora es tu primera clase?
    **Compañero/a** . . .
    **Usted** ¿A qué hora es tu última (*last*) clase?
    **Compañero/a** . . .
    **Usted** ¿Cuál es tu clase favorita?
    **Compañero/a** . . .

## SITUACIONES

Read the information for each of the situations and role-play them with a partner.

1. You are talking about your job. Tell your partner (a) where you work, (b) the days of the week and the hours you work. Try to get the same information from him/her.

2. You need to buy some things (e.g., a book, some pencils, a calculator) for one of your classes; (a) tell your partner what you need, (b) ask where the bookstore is, (c) thank him/her, and (d) say good-bye.

3. You are at the bookstore: (a) ask the clerk for the location of what you want to buy, (b) ask how much it is, (c) pay the clerk, (d) count your change (**cambio**), and (e) thank him/her.

4. **Una entrevista.** Try to ask as many questions as possible of your partner (e.g., his/her name, what he/she studies). Share the information with your classmates.

5. Draw a university campus locating the buildings and places given below. Your partner will ask you for the location of these buildings and places, and will draw his/her own version of where they are, according to the information you give. When you finish, compare the two drawings.

| | | |
|---|---|---|
| cafetería | librería | gimnasio |
| biblioteca | Facultad de Ciencias | Facultad de Humanidades |

# VOCABULARIO

**en la clase**

| | |
|---|---|
| la calculadora | *calculator* |
| el casete | *cassette* |
| la cinta | *tape* |
| la computadora | *computer* |
| la grabadora | *tape recorder* |
| el mapa | *map* |
| el papel | *paper* |
| la tarea | *homework* |

**en la universidad** — *at the university*

| | |
|---|---|
| la biblioteca | *library* |
| la cafetería | *cafeteria* |
| el edificio | *building* |
| la facultad | *college, school* |
| el gimnasio | *gymnasium* |
| el laboratorio | *laboratory* |
| la librería | *bookstore* |

**lenguas** — *languages*

| | |
|---|---|
| el alemán | *German* |
| el chino | *Chinese* |
| el español | *Spanish* |
| el francés | *French* |
| el inglés | *English* |
| el italiano | *Italian* |
| el japonés | *Japanese* |
| el portugués | *Portuguese* |
| el ruso | *Russian* |

**materias** — *subjects*

| | |
|---|---|
| la antropología | *anthropology* |
| la biología | *biology* |
| las ciencias | *sciences* |
| la contabilidad | *accounting* |
| la economía | *economics* |
| la física | *physics* |

la geografía — *geography*
la gramática — *grammar*
la historia — *history*
  historia del arte — *art history*
las humanidades — *humanities*
la informática — *computer science*
la literatura — *literature*
las matemáticas — *mathematics*
la (p)sicología — *psychology*
la química — *chemistry*

**personas**
el alumno/la alumna — *student*
el dependiente/la
  dependienta — *clerk*
el padre — *father*
nosotros/nosotras — *we*
ellos/ellas — *they*
ustedes — *you (plural)*

**tiempo** — *time*
el semestre — *semester*
siempre — *always*

**descripciones**
excelente — *excellent*
ocupado — *busy*
popular — *popular*

**nacionalidad**
español/a — *Spanish*
norteamericano/a — *American*

**verbos**
buscar — *to look for*
comprar — *to buy*
desear — *to wish, to want*
enseñar — *to teach*
escuchar — *to listen to*
estar — *to be*
estudiar — *to study*
hablar — *to speak*
necesitar — *to need*
practicar — *to practice*
trabajar — *to work*

**de compras** — *shopping*
¿cuánto cuesta? — *how much is it?*
el dólar — *dollar*
el peso — *peso*
el precio — *price*

**palabras útiles**
además — *besides*
con — *with*
entre — *among*
este — *this*
los/las — *the*
otro(s)/otra(s) — *other*
para — *for, to*
pero — *but*
tan — *so*
unos/unas — *some*
ya — *already*

**expresiones útiles**
un poco — *a little*
por eso — *that's why*
¡qué va! — *of course not! no way!*

**palabras adicionales**
**verbos**
asocie — *match*
complete — *complete, fill in*

**otras palabras**
la derecha — *right*
el dibujo — *drawing*
la izquierda — *left*
la oración — *sentence*
el párrafo — *paragraph*
falso — *false*
verdadero — *true*

In Lección 2 you will ask and answer questions concerning
a. where people are from.
b. where and when events take place.
c. possessions.
d. descriptions of places, persons, and things.

Me llamo Luis López.
Soy de México. Soy bajo
y delgado, pero fuerte.
Yo estudio mucho
y saco buenas notas.

Me llamo Marta Chávez.
Soy española. Soy rubia.
Tengo el pelo corto. Soy
joven y alegre. Soy
soltera y muy trabajadora.

LUIS: My name is Luis López.
I'm from Mexico. I'm short and thin,
but strong. I study a lot and
get good grades.

MARTA: My name is Marta Chávez.
I'm Spanish. I'm blond. I have
short hair. I'm young and cheerful.
I'm single and a very hard worker.

# Lección 2
# Los compañeros de clase

## ¿Quién es?

Me llamo Arturo Mejía.
Soy boliviano. Soy
muy hablador, pero
simpático. También
soy alto. Tengo bigote,
ojos verdes y pelo castaño.

Me llamo Lupe Villegas.
Soy de Perú. No soy
alta ni baja. Tengo el
pelo largo. Soy callada,
pero inteligente.

ARTURO: My name is Arturo Mejía.
I'm Bolivian. I'm talkative but
nice. I'm also tall. I have a
moustache, green eyes, and
brown hair.

LUPE: My name is Lupe Villegas.
I'm from Perú. I'm neither tall
nor short. I have long hair.
I'm quiet, but intelligent.

# ACTIVIDADES

**A** Asocie las siguientes características con la persona apropiada.

1. Tiene el pelo largo.
2. Saca buenas notas.
3. Es de España.
4. Es fuerte.
5. Tiene bigote.
6. Es inteligente.
7. Es alegre.
8. Tiene ojos verdes.

a. Luis López
b. Marta Chávez
c. Arturo Mejía
d. Lupe Villegas

**B** Complete las siguientes oraciones de acuerdo con los dibujos y las descripciones.

1. Lupe es de...
2. Marta es...
3. Arturo tiene (*has*)...
4. Luis es..., pero...
5. Marta es de...
6. Lupe tiene...

## Descripción de personas

débil          fuerte

joven          viejo

bonita           fea
guapa

bueno          malo

listo

tonto

alegre

triste

simpático

antipático

gordo

delgado

rubia

morena

trabajador

perezoso

rica

pobre

casada

José

Juan

Miguel

soltera

## ACTIVIDADES

**A** Complete las siguientes oraciones con opuestos (*opposites*).

*Modelo*  Yo no soy vieja, soy **joven.**

1. Yo no soy malo/a, soy...
2. No soy perezoso/a, soy...
3. No soy antipático/a, soy...

4. Él no es tonto, es...
5. Ella no es pobre, es..
6. Él no es guapo, es...

**B** Complete las siguientes oraciones para describir a sus compañeros de clase.

1. ___ es alto.
2. ___ es hablador.
3. ___ es delgada y simpática.

4. ___ es alto y moreno.
5. ___ soltera y rubia.
6. ___ es trabajadora y lista.

**C Autodescripción**

1. Me llamo...
2. Soy... y...
3. No soy...

4. Trabajo en...
5. Deseo...

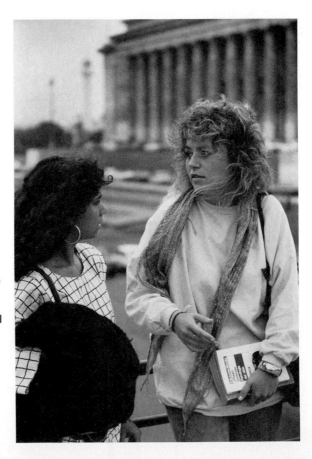

Dos estudiantes cerca de la Facultad de Derecho de la Universidad de Buenos Aires.

# Cultura

## The Hispanics

Even though the Hispanic nations share the same language, a common historical background, and similar traditions, customs, and values, they differ in many ways. Some of these differences are based on geography and on their economies, while others stem from the influence of ethnic subgroups unevenly distributed among them.

The Hispanic countries are located in Europe (Spain), North America (Mexico), and Central and South America. This vast territory includes nearly every imaginable type of geography and climate: cold, windswept lands; high mountains; deserts; fertile valleys and plains; jungles and tropical forests. Such differences affect the economy and culture of each country.

Most nations and races in the world have contributed to the present-day makeup of the populations of the Spanish-speaking countries. In Mexico and many parts of Central and South America, **mestizos** (people of mixed Indian and white ancestry) constitute a high percentage of the inhabitants. In the Caribbean, the original Indian population has practically disappeared, but the influence of blacks and mulattos (people of mixed black and white ancestry) is strong. Still other countries are conglomerates of immigrants from many sources, much like the United States. In Argentina, for example, waves of English, German, and especially Italian immigrants mixed with the Hispanic settlers who had arrived earlier.

Hispanics from various countries have profoundly influenced the development of the United States. Spaniards discovered and settled Louisiana and Florida, where in 1565 they founded Saint Augustine, the oldest city in this country. Spaniards and Mexicans conquered and settled the Southwest. They founded the first city west of the Mississippi, Santa Fe de Nuevo México, in 1609, eleven years before the Pilgrims landed on Plymouth Rock. With the Catholic missions in the states of Arizona, Texas, and California, Hispanic culture spread through the Southwest.

According to official government figures, there are some 19.4 million Hispanics in the United States. Unofficial figures put the number closer to 25 million, taking into account many undocumented workers who come to this country for economic or political reasons. Some experts believe that by the year 2000, Hispanics will total 30 to 35 million, which would make them the largest minority in this country.

Juan Ponce de León (¿1460?–1521), el primer gobernador de Puerto Rico y el descubridor de la Florida.

# EN CONTEXTO

## Un auto nuevo

**Lucía**   Rafael tiene un auto nuevo.

**Amparo**   ¿Y qué auto es?

**Lucía**   No estoy segura. Sólo sé que es pequeño, pero muy cómodo.

**Amparo**   ¿De qué color es?

**Lucía**   Es amarillo y los asientos son negros. Es muy bonito. Mira, allí, está Rafael.

## Preguntas

Conteste las siguientes preguntas sobre el diálogo.

1. ¿Quién tiene un auto nuevo?
2. ¿Es grande el auto?
3. ¿De qué color es el auto?
4. ¿De qué color son los asientos?
5. ¿De qué marca (*brand*) es el auto?

## más colores

| | | | |
|---|---|---|---|
| anaranjado | *orange* | rojo | *red* |
| azul | *blue* | rosado | *pink* |
| blanco | *white* | café | *brown* |
| gris | *gray* | claro | *light* |
| morado | *purple* | oscuro | *dark* |

## ACTIVIDADES

**A  Asociaciones.** ¿Qué colores asocia usted con estas palabras?

1. la noche
2. un dólar
3. Estados Unidos
4. Superman
5. un limón
6. las plantas
7. Drácula
8. las rosas
9. un elefante
10. una cebra
11. el autobús
12. un tigre

**B**  Dígale a su compañero/a cuál es su auto favorito. Después escoja (*choose*) entre las características que aparecen más abajo (*appear below*) o use otras para describirlo (*to describe it*).

1. Marca
2. Color exterior; asientos
3. Características: bonito   grande   pequeño   cómodo   rápido   económico

---

LUCÍA: Rafael has a new car. AMPARO: And what kind of car is it? LUCÍA: I'm not sure. I only know that it's small, but very comfortable. AMPARO: What color is it? LUCÍA: It's yellow and the seats are black. It's very pretty. Look, there's Rafael.

# GRAMÁTICA

## Adjectives

Adjectives are words that describe people, places, and things. Like articles (**el, la, un, una**) and nouns (**chico, chica**), they generally have more than one form. In Spanish an adjective must agree in gender (masculine or feminine) and in number (singular or plural) with the noun or pronoun it describes.

1. Some adjectives end in **-o** when used with masculine words and in **-a** when used with feminine words(**alto/alta**). To form the plural, these adjectives add **-s** (**altos/altas**).

| | | |
|---|---|---|
| SINGULAR | chico alto | chica alta |
| PLURAL | chicos altos | chicas altas |

2. Other adjectives have only two forms, singular and plural. These end in **-e** or a consonant and agree only in number with the noun they describe. To form the plural, these adjectives add **-s** and **-es** respectively.

| | | |
|---|---|---|
| SINGULAR | amigo interesante<br>chico popular | amiga interesante<br>chica popular |
| PLURAL | amigos interesantes<br>chicos populares | amigas interesantes<br>chicas populares |

3. Some adjectives that end in a consonant have four forms, however.

| | | |
|---|---|---|
| SINGULAR | alumno español<br>alumno trabajador | alumna española<br>alumna trabajadora |
| PLURAL | alumnos españoles<br>alumnos trabajadores | alumnas españolas<br>alumnas trabajadoras |

## Position of adjectives

Adjectives that describe a characteristic of a noun usually follow the noun.

Necesito un papel roj**o**.    Es un hombre mal**o**.

**Bueno, malo,** and **grande** may precede nouns. When **bueno** and **malo** precede masculine singular nouns, they are shortened to **buen** and **mal.**

Es un **buen** libro.    Es un **mal** hombre.

**Grande** is shortened to **gran** when it precedes any singular noun. Note, however, that **grande** means *large* when it follows a noun, but *great* or *wonderful* when it precedes.

Es una chica **grande.**    *She's a big girl.*
Es una **gran** chica.    *She's a great girl.*

# ACTIVIDADES

**A  Descripciones.** Usted administra una escuela y necesita unos empleados. Dígale a la agencia de empleos qué clase de persona necesita. Escoja entre las palabras que aparecen más abajo.

**1.** Busco una secretaria...

| atractiva | perezosa | tonta | trabajadora | delgada |
| reservada | vieja | simpática | alta | habladora |

**2.** Necesito un consejero (*advisor*)...

| independiente | pasivo | competente | activo | persistente |
| generoso | callado | interesante | | |

**3.** Deseo emplear una profesora...

| simpática | imparcial | romántica | sincera | rebelde |
| emocional | paciente | inteligente | tonta | importante |

**B  ¿De qué color es (son)...?**

**1.** Pregúntele a un/a compañero/a el color de los siguientes objetos.

*Modelo*    ¿De qué color es tu bolígrafo?
        **Es azul.**

tu auto    tu lápiz    tu diccionario    tus ojos    tu casa (*house*)    tu libro de español

**2. En el salón de clase.** Pregúntele a un/a compañero/a el color de los siguientes objetos de la clase.

la pizarra    el escritorio    la puerta    las ventanas    el reloj    las paredes

**C Descripciones.**

**1.** Usted es el supervisor/la supervisora de una fábrica (*factory*). El dueño/La dueña (*owner*) le hace las siguientes preguntas sobre un empleado. Trabaje con otro/a estudiante y conteste las preguntas.

| | |
|---|---|
| **Dueño/a** | ¿Cómo se llama ese señor? |
| **Usted** | . . . |
| **Dueño/a** | ¿Cómo es? |
| **Usted** | . . . |
| **Dueño/a** | ¿Es un buen trabajador? |
| **Usted** | . . . |
| **Dueño/a** | Muchas gracias. |
| **Usted** | . . . |

**2.** Usted es el/la gerente (*manager*) de una compañía. Usted desea tener (*to have*) más información sobre una empleada y habla con el supervisor/la supervisora.

| | |
|---|---|
| **Usted** | ¿Cómo se llama esa señora? |
| **Supervisor/a** | . . . |
| **Usted** | ¿De dónde es? |
| **Supervisor/a** | . . . |
| **Usted** | ¿Cómo es ella? |
| **Supervisor/a** | . . . |
| **Usted** | Gracias. |
| **Supervisor/a** | . . . |

**D ¿Cómo es usted?** Use dos adjetivos para explicar cómo es usted con las siguientes personas o situaciones.

*Modelo*   con su amiga
   **Con mi amiga soy simpático/a y alegre.**

1. con el profesor/la profesora
2. en el trabajo
3. en público
4. en la clase
5. con sus compañeros
6. con sus padres (*parents*)

**E Las diferencias.** Mirta y Ángel son hermanos (*brother and sister*), pero son muy diferentes. Describa a Mirta y a Ángel.

Mirta es. . . , pero Ángel es. . .

Mirta tiene. . . , pero Ángel tiene. . .

# EN CONTEXTO

## El mundo hispano

## ACTIVIDAD

**¿De dónde es?**

Lupe Villegas    Diana Samper    César Gómez    Carlos Arias
Arturo Mejía     Sara Rivero

## GRAMÁTICA

### Present tense of the verb *ser*; uses of *ser*

|  | **ser** | *to be* |  |
|---|---|---|---|
| yo | soy | nosotros/as | somos |
| tú | eres | vosotros/as | sois |
| él, ella, usted | es | ellos/as, ustedes | son |

1. **Ser** is used with adjectives to describe persons, places, or things. For example, we can express our first impression of someone or something with **ser** and an adjective.

¿Cómo es?

Ella es bonita.

La casa es grande.

El auto es viejo.

2. **Ser** is used to express the nationality of a person; **ser** + **de** is used to express the origin of a person.

| *Nationality* | *Origin* |
|---|---|
| Luis es chileno. | Luis es de Chile. |
| Ana es boliviana. | Ana es de Bolivia. |

Indígenas con sus llamas en Cuzco, Perú. La ciudad del Cuzco era la antigua capital del Imperio de los Incas.

**3. Ser + de** is also used to express possession.

| | |
|---|---|
| La casa es de Marta. | *The house is Marta's.* |
| Los libros son de José. | *The books are José's.* |

**De + el** contracts to **del. De + la(s)** or **los** does not contract.

el auto **del** estudiante

el auto **de** { **la** señora / **las** señoras / **los** señores

**4. Ser** is used to express the location and time of an event.

*Location*

| | |
|---|---|
| El baile es en la universidad. | *The dance is at the university.* |
| El examen es en el gimnasio. | *The exam is at the gymnasium.* |

*Time*

| | |
|---|---|
| La fiesta es a las 9:00 de la noche. | *The party is at 9:00 P.M.* |
| El examen es a las 3:00. | *The exam is at 3:00 P.M.* |

### *Ser* and *estar* with adjectives

**Ser** and **estar** can be used with many of the same adjectives. However, the choice of verb determines the meaning of the sentence. They are not interchangeable. The use of **ser** or **estar** is determined by the person's perception of the situation.

1. **Ser** + adjective expresses what is considered to be the norm for a person or a thing.

| | | |
|---|---|---|
| Manolo es delgado. | *Manolo is thin.* | (He is a thin boy.) |
| Mirta es morena. | *Mirta is a brunette.* | (She has dark skin, hair, and eyes.) |
| La casa es pequeña. | *The house is small.* | (It's a small house.) |

2. **Estar** + adjective expresses a change from the norm and/or a person's feelings.

| | | |
|---|---|---|
| Manolo está gordo. | *Manolo is fat.* | (He's gained weight recently.) |
| Mirta está rubia. | *Mirta is blond.* | (She dyed her hair.) |
| La casa está pequeña. | *The house is small.* | (The family has grown; the house has become small for them.) |

3. More adjectives that can be used with **ser** or **estar** with the meanings described in sections 1 and 2 are

   alegre    nervioso/a    tranquilo/a    triste    feliz (*happy*)

4. The adjective **contento/a** *happy, glad* is always used with **estar.**

   Ella está muy contenta hoy.

5. Some adjectives have two meanings; one with **ser** and another with **estar.**

| | |
|---|---|
| Ese señor es malo. | *That man is bad.* (evil) |
| Ese señor está malo. | *That man is sick.* (not well) |
| El chico es listo. | *The boy is clever.* |
| El chico está listo. | *The boy is ready.* |
| La manzana es verde. | *The apple is green.* (color) |
| La manzana está verde. | *The apple isn't ripe.* |

Jóvenes puertorriqueños en el desfile del Día de Puerto Rico en Nueva York. En esta ciudad viven cerca de un millón de puertorriqueños.

## ACTIVIDADES

**A** **Contexto.** Use la forma apropiada de **ser** o **estar** para describir una norma (*norm*) o un cambio (*change*).

1. Fernando is a good boy. *He is nice.* ___ simpático.
2. In New Mexico it rains very little in summer and the grass is always brown. This year it rained a lot. *The grass is green.* La hierba ___ verde.
3. You have seen coal before. *It is black.* ___ negro.
4. The sky over Los Angeles is usually brownish-gray. Today the wind is blowing and *it is blue.* ___ azul.
5. Everybody agrees about the color of snow. *It is white.* ___ blanca.
6. Marta is always in a good mood. *Marta is happy.* Marta ___ feliz.
7. Today Marta received a D and she is not herself. *Marta is sad.* Marta ___ triste.
8. Martín is an awful child. He always misbehaves. *He is terrible.* ___ terrible.

**B** Salude a su compañero/a. Dígale de dónde es usted y pregúntele de dónde es él/ella. Después salude a varios compañeros. Dígales de dónde es usted y pregúnteles de dónde son ellos.

**C** Dígale a su compañero/a cómo usted se siente (*you feel*) en las siguientes situaciones y pregúntele como se siente él/ella.

| *Modelo* | en la clase | **Usted** | **Estoy contento/a ¿Y tú?** |
| | | **Compañero/a** | **Yo estoy contento/a también** o **Yo estoy triste.** |

1. en la carretera (*highway*)
2. en la clase de inglés
3. antes de un examen
4. en la universidad

5. en el trabajo
6. con muchas personas
7. en una fiesta
8. los lunes

**D** **Otros.** ¿Cómo describen otros a su...?

mamá    hermana (*sister*)    profesor/a    amigo/a    jefe (*boss*)
compañero/a de cuarto (*roommate*)

**E** **Primera impresión.** Usted ve (*see*) a estas personas por primera vez (*time*). ¿Cuál es su impresión?

**F** Otra persona ve lo siguiente por primera vez. ¿Cuál es la reacción de esta persona?

1. su casa                          Es... y...
2. su auto (o motocicleta)          Es... y...
3. su salón de clase                Es... y...
4. su universidad                   Es... y...

**G** **En la oficina del departamento de lenguas extranjeras (*foreign languages*).** Dígale a un estudiante nuevo quiénes son las siguientes personas y describa a estas personas.

*Modelo*   Olga / morena / Bolivia
           **Es Olga. Es morena y es boliviana.**

1. Renée / alta / Francia              5. Keiko / elegante / Japón
2. Helmut / rubio / Alemania           6. Alicia / inteligente / Colombia
3. Ian / simpático / Inglaterra        7. Fernando / simpático / Puerto Rico
4. Orieta / delgada / Italia           8. Yo / ... / ...

**H** **Posesiones.** Señale y además identifique algunos de los objetos de la clase. Su compañero/a debe decir (*should say*) de quién es.

*Modelo*        **Usted**   **Es un lápiz.**
          **Compañero/a**   **Es de Marcia.**

**I** **Eventos.** Usted está a cargo (*in charge*) de la caseta (*booth*) de información en su universidad. Dígales a los visitantes dónde tienen lugar (*take place*) los siguientes eventos.

*Modelo*   **Visitante**   **¿Dónde es el examen de español?**
               **Usted**   **Es en la biblioteca.**

la fiesta     la conferencia (*lecture*)     el concierto     la manifestación (*demonstration*)
el banquete     el concurso (*contest*)

Ahora dígales a los visitantes dónde están los siguientes lugares y edificios.

la biblioteca     el salón de clase     el gimnasio     la librería     el teatro
la oficina     el estadio     la cafetería

# ═══ EN CONTEXTO ═══

**Preguntas y respuestas**

¿Quién es?
¿Cuándo es el examen?

Viviana Domínguez

¿Qué hora es?
¿Quiénes están en la clase?

¿Cuántos estudiantes hay?
¿Dónde están?

Yolanda

¿Cuál es el libro de español?
¿De quién es el libro?

Miguel

¿Cómo se llama? ¿Cómo es?
¿Cuánto papel hay?

## ACTIVIDAD

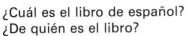

Conteste las preguntas sobre cada uno de los dibujos anteriores.

## GRAMÁTICA

### Question words

| | | | |
|---|---|---|---|
| **cómo** | *how/what* | **cuál/es** | *which* |
| **dónde** | *where* | **quién/es** | *who* |
| **qué** | *what* | **cuánto/a** | *how much* |
| **cuándo** | *when* | **cuántos/as** | *how many* |

1. Question words ask for specific information about someone or something. Most question words have only one form (**cuándo, cómo**), some have two (**cuál, cuáles**), and one has four (**cuánto, cuánta, cuántos, cuántas**).

**2.** In an information question, question words generally come first, but in some cases another word may precede them.

> ¿**Qué** hora es?    ¿**A qué** hora es la clase?
>
> ¿**Quién** es él?    ¿**De quién** es el libro?

**3.** Use **por qué** to express *why.* The equivalent of *because* is **porque.**

> —¿**Por qué** está Pepe en la biblioteca?    —**Porque** necesita estudiar.

**4.** If the question can be answered affirmatively or negatively—with **sí** or **no**—do not use a question word. Subjects, if used, normally follow the verb, as in information questions.

> —¿**Estudian ustedes** español?    —Sí, estudiamos español.

**5.** Another way of asking a question is by placing an interrogative tag after a declarative statement.

> Estudias español, ¿**verdad**?    *You study Spanish, don't you?*
>
> El es mexicano, ¿**no**?    *He's Mexican, isn't he?*

## *ACTIVIDADES*

**A** Escoja entre las siguientes palabras para completar estas preguntas: **dónde, por qué, cuándo, cuál, quién, cuántos.**

1. —¿\_\_\_\_ estudian ustedes? —En la Universidad Nacional.
2. —¿\_\_\_\_ son tus clases? —Por la mañana.
3. —¿\_\_\_\_ es tu profesor favorito? —El profesor Jiménez.
4. —¿\_\_\_\_ es tu materia favorita? —El español.
5. —¿\_\_\_\_ estudias español? —Porque es una lengua muy importante.
6. —¿\_\_\_\_ alumnos hay en tu clase de español? —Veinticinco.

**B** **Entrevista.** Su amigo/a tiene muchas cosas (*things*). Usted desea saber (*to know*) cuántas cosas tiene. Use la forma correcta de **cuánto** en sus preguntas.

> *Modelo*    calculadoras    —¿**Cuántas calculadoras tienes?**
>                               —**Tengo diez.**

> autos    computadoras    grabadoras    relojes    bolígrafos

**C** **Información.** Use las siguientes preguntas para entrevistar (*interview*) a su compañero/a. Comparta (*Share*) la información con la clase.

1. ¿Cómo te llamas?
2. ¿Cómo estás?
3. ¿Dónde trabajas?
4. ¿Cuántas clases tienes?
5. ¿Cuál es tu clase favorita? ¿Por qué?
6. ¿Cuándo estudias?
7. ¿Quién es tu mejor (*best*) amigo/a?
8. ¿Cómo es él/ella?

**D La publicidad** (*Advertising*).
Lea el siguiente anuncio (*ad*) y
hágales tres preguntas sobre
el anuncio a sus compañeros.

**E** Haga preguntas sobre el siguiente dibujo a su compañero/a.

# PRONUNCIACIÓN

**1.  l**

At the beginning of a syllable, Spanish **l** and English *l* are pronounced alike. At the end of a syllable, Spanish **l** has, for all practical purposes, the same sound, but the pronunciation of English *l* changes. Compare the following words: **Lucas,** *Lucas;* **hotel,** *hotel.*

lápiz    libro    mal    papel    español    alto

**2.  m, n**

Spanish and English **m** are pronounced the same way.

mamá    malo    amable    moreno    mesa    mexicano

At the beginning of a syllable, Spanish and English **n** are pronounced the same way. At the end of a syllable, Spanish **n** may vary according to the next consonant. Before **p, b,** and **v,** Spanish **n** is pronounced like an **m;** before **q, g, k, j, ca, co,** and **cu,** Spanish **n** is pronounced like **ng.**

japonés    un bolígrafo    un viejo    inglés    un casete

**3.  ñ**

Spanish **ñ** is similar to the pronunciation of *ni* in the English word *onion* or *ny* in *canyon.*

español    señora    mañana    pequeño    tamaño

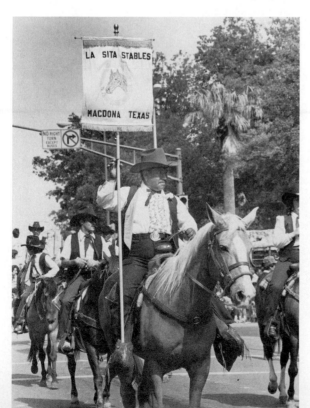

Un desfile hispano en Texas. La influencia hispana, especialmente mexicana, ha sido muy importante en el Suroeste de los Estados Unidos. En muchas zonas de esta región existen numerosas palabras y costumbres hispanas.

# LECTURA

## Los estereotipos

### Escena 1

Es el primer día de clases y Michael Smith entra en la clase de español. La profesora es de Colombia y Michael espera ver° a una señora morena y baja, pero la señora que está en el salón es una señora alta, delgada y rubia.

espera... *expects to see*

### Escena 2

Laura Villegas entra en su clase de inglés. El profesor es de Chicago y Laura espera ver a un señor alto, rubio y de ojos azules. El profesor es bajo, moreno y tiene ojos negros.

Estas dos escenas ocurren con frecuencia, pues los estereotipos son muy comunes cuando pensamos en° las personas de otras culturas. Para muchos norteamericanos, todos° los hispanos tienen ojos negros y son morenos y bajos. Para muchos hispanos, los norteamericanos tienen ojos azules y son altos y rubios. Estos estereotipos no representan la realidad. En los Estados Unidos, Hispanoamérica y España hay muchas personas morenas y bajas, y también hay muchas personas altas y rubias.

pensamos... *we think of*
all

También hay estereotipos relacionados con la comida°. Muchos piensan que todos los hispanos comen° tortillas, tacos y enchiladas, cuando en realidad ésa es sólo una parte de la comida típica de México y no es popular en España y otros países°. Algunos hispanos piensan que todos los norteamericanos comen hamburguesas° y perros calientes° con mucha salsa de tomate°.

*food*
*eat*

*countries*
*hamburgers* / perros... *hot dog*
  salsa... *catsup*

Los estereotipos sólo presentan una parte de la realidad. Cuando estudiamos una lengua podemos ir más allá de° estos estereotipos superficiales, ver la realidad total y apreciar y comprender mejor° otra cultura.

ir... *we can go beyond*
comprender... *better understand*

## Preguntas

**1.** Complete los siguientes cuadros (*charts*) de acuerdo con la lectura.

Los hispanos según muchos norteamericanos

| tamaño (*size*) | ojos | pelo | comida |
|---|---|---|---|
|  |  |  |  |

Los norteamericanos según muchos hispanos

| tamaño | ojos | pelo | comida |
|--------|------|------|--------|
|        |      |      |        |

**2.** ¿Cómo son en realidad los hispanos y los norteamericanos?

**3.** ¿En qué país son populares las tortillas, los tacos y las enchiladas?

**4.** Según algunos hispanos, ¿qué comen los norteamericanos?

**5.** ¿Qué pasa (*happens*) cuando estudiamos una lengua?

## SITUACIONES

1. You are interviewing applicants for a job in your company. You want to get the following information: name, where they are from, what they are studying, a self-description, and where they work now.

2. Think of a famous person or place. Your partner must ask you up to ten questions to determine who or what it is. You will answer **sí** or **no** until your partner guesses correctly.

3. Describe your room (**cuarto**) to a friend. Tell (a) what color it is, (b) if it is small or big, (c) what you need for it, and (d) what you have in it. Have your friend give you the same information about his/her room. You may need some additional vocabulary: **cama** (*bed*), **mesa de noche** (*nightstand*), **televisor** (*television set*), **radio.**

4. Talk to a classmate about your hometown. Greet him/her by telling your name and where you are from. Then tell as much as you can about the town (size, location, etc.). Your classmate should give you the same type of information about his/her hometown.

5. A new student has just joined your class. Ask the student next to you who the new student is. Your classmate should give you as much information as possible about him/her.

6. Go around the room and ask your classmates the following questions. For each question, be sure to get a signature on a separate sheet of paper from all students who answer affirmatively. Create your own question for *f.*

   a. ¿Trabajas en la biblioteca?
   b. ¿Estudias química?
   c. ¿Tienes cuatro clases?
   d. ¿Eres alto/a y amable?
   e. ¿Es Historia Moderna tu clase favorita?
   f. ¿————————?

7. Tell your friend that there is a party on Saturday. Your friend should (a) find out where the party will take place and (b) the time it will begin.

# VOCABULARIO

## colores

| | | | |
|---|---|---|---|
| amarillo | *yellow* | moreno | *brunet* |
| anaranjado | *orange* | nervioso | *nervous* |
| azul | *blue* | nuevo | *new* |
| blanco | *white* | oscuro | *dark* |
| café | *brown* | perezoso | *lazy* |
| castaño | *brown* | pobre | *poor* |
| gris | *gray* | rico | *rich, wealthy* |
| morado | *purple* | rubio | *blond* |
| negro | *black* | simpático | *nice, charming* |
| rojo | *red* | soltero | *single* |
| rosado | *pink* | tonto | *silly, foolish* |
| verde | *green* | trabajador | *hardworking* |
| | | tranquilo | *calm, tranquil* |
| | | triste | *sad* |
| | | viejo | *old* |

## descripción

| | |
|---|---|
| alegre | *happy, glad* |
| alto | *tall, high* |
| antipático | *unpleasant* |
| bajo | *short, low* |
| bonito | *pretty* |
| buen | *good* |
| callado | *quiet* |
| casado | *married* |
| claro | *light* |
| cómodo | *comfortable* |
| contento | *happy, glad* |
| débil | *weak* |
| delgado | *thin* |
| feliz | *happy* |
| feo | *ugly* |
| fuerte | *strong* |
| gordo | *fat* |
| gran | *great* |
| guapo | *good-looking, hand-some* |
| hablador | *talkative* |
| inteligente | *intelligent* |
| joven | *young* |
| listo | *smart, ready* |
| mal | *bad* |
| malo | *bad, evil, sick* |

## el cuerpo — *body*

| | |
|---|---|
| el bigote | *moustache* |
| los ojos | *eyes* |
| el pelo | *hair* |

## en la clase

| | |
|---|---|
| el compañero/la compañera | *classmate* |
| la nota | *grade* |

## hispanos

| | |
|---|---|
| argentino | *Argentinian* |
| boliviano | *Bolivian* |
| colombiano | *Colombian* |
| cubano | *Cuban* |
| chileno | *Chilean* |
| mexicano | *Mexican* |
| panameño | *Panamanian* |
| peruano | *Peruvian* |
| puertorriqueño | *Puerto Rican* |
| salvadoreño | *Salvadorian* |
| venezolano | *Venezuelan* |

## vehículos

| | |
|---|---|
| el auto | *car* |
| el asiento | *seat* |

**verbos**

| | |
|---|---|
| mirar | *to look at* |
| sacar | *to get* |
| ser | *to be* |
| tengo | *I have* |
| tiene | *he/she has, you have (formal)* |
| sé | *I know* |

**palabras interrogativas**

| | |
|---|---|
| cuál/cuáles | *which (one/s)* |
| cuándo | *when* |
| cuánto/cuánta | *how much* |
| de quién/de quiénes | *whose* |
| por qué | *why* |

**palabras útiles**

| | |
|---|---|
| allí | *there* |
| de | *from* |
| del | *(contraction of* **de** + **el**) *of the* |

| | |
|---|---|
| no... ni | *neither . . . nor* |
| porque | *because* |
| que | *that* |
| seguro | *sure* |
| sólo | *only* |
| también | *also, too* |

**palabras adicionales**

**verbos**

| | |
|---|---|
| comparta | *share* |
| describa | *describe* |
| escoja | *choose* |
| explique | *explain* |

**otras palabras**

| | |
|---|---|
| abajo | *below* |
| arriba | *above* |
| apropiado | *appropriate* |
| opuesto | *opposite* |
| todos | *all* |

Los diseños de estos malacates *(clay spindle weights)* precolombinos, encontrados en excavaciones arqueológicas en México, muestran gran imaginación y originalidad.

**In** Lección 3 **you will**
a. **discuss and inquire about daily activities.**
b. **order food.**
c. **ask for and give addresses and telephone numbers.**
d. **count from 100 to 1,000.**
e. **solve simple problems using those numbers.**
f. **make suggestions and future plans.**

# Lugares y actividades

cronómetro

entrenador

**en el estadio**

Amelia trota en el estadio de la universidad.
Alberto corre. Él practica para una competencia (*meet*).

# Lección 3
# Las actividades de los estudiantes

Marta busca un libro en el estante. Manolo saca unos libros para su clase.

**en la biblioteca**

discos

estéreo

**en una fiesta**

Rafael toca la guitarra. Elvira canta una canción (*song*) popular. Unos muchachos y muchachas bailan y otros hablan.

# ACTIVIDADES

**A** **¿Cuántos/as. . . hay en la biblioteca?** Hágales preguntas a sus compañeros/as usando (*using*) las siguientes palabras.

estudiantes    computadoras    diccionarios    libros    estantes

**B** **En la biblioteca.** Usted está en la biblioteca de su universidad. Dígales a sus compañeros/as lo que usted hace en la biblioteca y las cosas que hay allí.

*Modelo*    **Yo saco unos libros de historia. Hay veinte alumnos y dos computadoras.**

**C** Complete las siguientes oraciones con las palabras a la derecha.

1. Amelia trota en el. . . de la universidad.
2. Alberto practica para una. . .
3. Él. . . toma el tiempo con el. . .
4. Alberto desea ser el. . . nacional.

entrenador
estadio
competencia
cronómetro
campeón

**D** Usted es un/a corredor/a (*sprinter*). Diga quién es usted y hábleles de su entrenamiento (*training*) a sus compañeros completando el siguiente párrafo.

Me llamo ____. Practico ____. Mi entrenador/a es muy bueno/a. Se llama ____. Yo ____ todos los días en el ____ de la universidad. Cuando yo practico, mi entrenador/a toma el ____ con el ____. Yo deseo ganar (*win*) la ____ para ser el campeón/la campeona.

**E** Complete las siguientes oraciones con las palabras a la derecha.

1. Teresa toca la. . .
2. Elvira canta una. . .
3. El. . . está al lado de Elvira.
4. Elvira prefiere (*prefers*) la. . .
5. Hay tres. . . sobre el estéreo.

discos
guitarra
música moderna
estéreo
canción

**F** Háblele sobre usted a su compañero/a escogiendo (*choosing*) las palabras apropiadas. Después su compañero/a debe hacer lo mismo (*the same*).

1. Yo (no) toco la guitarra.   (el piano, el violín, el saxofón)
2. Yo (no) canto muy bien.   (canto mal, canto regular)
3. Yo (no) escucho música moderna.   (música clásica, rock)
4. En mi dormitorio (no) hay un estéreo y unos discos.   (un radio, una grabadora)
5. En las fiestas yo (no) bailo.   (canto, escucho música, hablo mucho)

# Cultura

## Student life in the Hispanic countries

Although there are similarities between student life in the Hispanic countries and in the United States, there are also differences. Some of the principal ones are in study programs, living arrangements, and social life.

Since very few universities have dormitories, students whose families reside near the university live at home while attending classes. Those who come from other cities or towns normally live in guest houses. Fraternities and sororities are not a part of Hispanic universities. Sports programs, which usually play an important role on campuses in the United States, are not generally included in Hispanic universities. Students who participate in sports do so at clubs and neighborhood parks.

Because there is less emphasis on campus life, students tend to maintain close contact with former friends. And although friendships do develop at the university, the ties to family and old friends remain strong.

In general, students are very politically aware and active, following both national and international events. When students disagree with the conditions at the university or in the country, they organize demonstrations and even strikes.

Cafés are very popular meeting places for people of all ages in Hispanic countries, and those that are close to schools or universities are often filled with students before and after classes. Students may have **café** (strong black coffee similar to *café espresso*), **café con leche** (strong coffee with hot milk), beer, soda, or sandwiches while they sit at a table and socialize with their friends, sometimes for hours on end.

Hispanic students have a great interest in North American culture. Modern American music is very popular, especially at parties and dance clubs. American films and television programs, while also popular, tend to give students a somewhat distorted idea of life in the United States.

Unas estudiantes conversan en una de las zonas verdes de la UNAM en México. El intercambio de ideas con sus compañeros y amigos es un aspecto muy importante en la vida de los estudiantes hispanos.

# EN CONTEXTO

### En un café

Las chicas están en un café. Nancy lee el menú y Lola y Olga miran a las personas que caminan por la acera. El camarero llega para tomar la orden.

| | |
|---|---|
| **Camarero** | Buenas tardes, señoritas. ¿Qué desean? |
| **Nancy** | Para mí, un sándwich de jamón y queso. |
| **Camarero** | ¿Y para beber? |
| **Nancy** | Un té, por favor. |
| **Camarero** | ¿Frío o caliente? |
| **Nancy** | Frío. |
| **Lola** | ¿Qué pasteles hay? |
| **Camarero** | De pollo, de jamón y de manzana. |
| **Lola** | Un pastel de pollo. |
| **Nancy** | ¿Y qué tomas? |
| **Lola** | Un refresco de limón. |
| **Camarero** | (Escribe la orden.) ¿Y usted, señorita? |
| **Olga** | Sólo un jugo de naranja. |
| **Lola** | ¿Sólo un jugo? ¿Por qué no comes algo? |
| **Olga** | No debo comer. Estoy a dieta. |

### Para completar

Complete las oraciones con la información que se da en el diálogo.

1. Las chicas están en...
2. Nancy desea un sándwich de jamón y queso y un...
3. En el café hay pasteles de...
4. Lola desea un pastel de...
5. Olga bebe sólo un...
6. Olga no debe comer porque está a...

---

The girls are at a café. Nancy reads the menu and Lola and Olga are looking at the people walking on the sidewalk. The waiter arrives to take the order.
WAITER: Good morning, ladies. What would you like? NANCY: For me, a ham and cheese sandwich. WAITER: Anything to drink? NANCY: Tea, please. WAITER: Hot or iced tea? NANCY: Iced tea. LOLA: What kind of pies do you have? WAITER: Chicken, ham, and apple. LOLA: Chicken pie. NANCY: And what are you going to drink? LOLA: Lemon soda. WAITER: (Writes the order) And you, Miss? OLGA: Just orange juice. LOLA: Just juice? Why don't you eat something? OLGA: I shouldn't eat. I'm on a diet.

## Más comidas y bebidas

**el desayuno**

el café — el cereal — la leche

los huevos fritos — las tostadas / el pan tostado

**el almuerzo**

la ensalada de lechuga y tomate

la hamburguesa

las frutas

el sándwich de atún

las papas fritas

**la comida (o cena)**

el pescado — los vegetales

el arroz

la sopa

el helado

# ACTIVIDADES

**A** **¿Qué platos desea?** Escoja un plato de cada grupo y dígale a su compañero/a cuáles son. Después él/ella debe decirle qué platos desea.

1. sopa de tomate, sopa de vegetales, sopa de pollo
2. espaguetis, pollo frito, pescado
3. vegetales, ensalada, pizza
4. helado de chocolate, banana, pastel de manzana

**B** Usted es el dueño/la dueña de un café. Prepare un menú. Compare su menú con el menú de su compañero/a.

**C** Usted tiene un amigo/una amiga en su casa. Pregúntele qué desea desayunar.

   *Modelo*   —¿Qué deseas desayunar? o —¿Qué deseas para el desayuno?
   —Jugo de naranja, cereal y leche.

**D** **En el restaurante.**

1. Es la hora del almuerzo. Usted es el camarero/la camarera en un restaurante. Pregúnteles a dos clientes qué desean.
2. Es la hora de la cena. Su compañero/a es el camarero/la camarera y le pregunta qué desea cenar.

Jóvenes mexicanos disfrutando de la música en una discoteca de la ciudad de México. La música moderna es muy popular entre los jóvenes hispanos.

## GRAMÁTICA

### Present tense of regular *-er* and *-ir* verbs

| comer | | vivir *to live* | |
|---|---|---|---|
| yo | com**o** | yo | viv**o** |
| tú | com**es** | tú | viv**es** |
| él, ella, usted | com**e** | él, ella, usted | viv**e** |
| nosotros/as | com**emos** | nosotros/as | viv**imos** |
| vosotros/as | com**éis** | vosotros/as | viv**ís** |
| ellos/as, ustedes | com**en** | ellos/as, ustedes | viv**en** |

1. The endings for **-er** and **-ir** verbs are the same, except for the **nosotros** and **vosotros** forms.
2. Some common **-er** and **-ir** verbs are **leer, deber, beber, correr, vender** (*to sell*), **escribir, abrir** (*to open*).
3. The verb **ver** (*to see*) has an irregular **yo** form.

   ver: **veo,** ves, ve, vemos, veis, ven

# ACTIVIDADES ▬▬▬▬▬

**A** ¿Qué no debe hacer (*do*) usted en los siguientes lugares?

1. En un café: hablar / correr / beber un refresco
2. En un gimnasio: trotar / tomar ron / practicar con el entrenador
3. En una discoteca: ver televisión / bailar / escuchar música
4. En una fiesta: tocar la guitarra / cantar / escribir
5. En la biblioteca: comer / buscar un libro / estudiar

**D** **Lugares y actividades.** ¿Qué hace usted en estos lugares? ¿Y otras personas?

en el dormitorio     en un restaurante     en el estadio     en el laboratorio
en la clase          en la librería

**C** Cambie (*Change*) el sujeto (*subject*) de cada párrafo por el sujeto entre parentesis. Haga los cambios necesarios.

1. (**Yo**) María es una chica muy activa. Ella corre por la mañana. Después bebe un jugo, come cereal y toma una taza (*cup*) de café.
2. (**Ellos**) Ernesto es un chico liberado. Según Ernesto, los hombres deben trabajar en la casa. Por eso él limpia (*cleans*) la casa también.
3. (**Nosotros**) Marisel trabaja en un salón de belleza (*beauty parlor*). Ella vende cosméticos. Los viernes ella está en el salón a las ocho y media porque ese día hay muchos clientes.
4. (**Miriam**) Por la noche yo estudio, hablo por teléfono y veo televisión. A las diez y media, más o menos, bebo un vaso (*glass*) de leche con unas galletitas (*cookies*). Después leo un buen libro o escucho las noticias (*news*).

**D** Su compañero/a está a dieta. Dígale lo que debe y no debe comer o beber.

*Modelo*   **Debes comer ensaladas. No debes beber refrescos.**

**E** Usted es un alumno/una alumna nuevo/a en la universidad y le hace las siguientes preguntas a otro/a alumno/a.

1. ¿Vives en el dormitorio?               4. ¿Desayunas en la cafetería?
2. ¿Trotas en el gimnasio?                5. ¿A qué hora abren la cafetería?
3. ¿A qué hora abren el gimnasio?

**F** Hágale a su compañero/a las siguientes preguntas. Después comparta la información con la clase.

1. ¿Cuántos libros lees al mes?
2. ¿Cuántos libros debe leer una persona?
3. ¿Cuál es tu libro preferido?
4. ¿Lees revistas (*magazines*) o periódicos (*newspapers*)? ¿Cuáles?

# EN CONTEXTO

## En la Facultad de Ciencias

| | | |
|---|---|---|
| **Sara** | ¿Cuál es la dirección° de Marta? | *address* |
| **Dulce** | Creo° que vive en la calle° Manzanares, número 425. | *I believe / street* |
| **Sara** | Debo ir° a su casa después a repasar° álgebra para el examen del jueves. | *go / review* |
| **Miriam** | Yo también necesito repasar. | |
| **Dulce** | Pues ven° con nosotras. | *come* |
| **Miriam** | Está bien, pero debemos llamar por teléfono antes de ir. | |
| **Sara** | Sí, yo llamo ahora°. ¿Cuál es su número de teléfono? | *now* |
| **Dulce** | Es el 544-3318. | |

## Para completar

Complete las siguientes oraciones con la información que se da en el diálogo.

1. La dirección de Marta es...
2. Sara debe ir a casa de Marta a...
3. El examen de álgebra es...

4. Antes de ir las chicas deben...
5. El número de teléfono de Marta es el...

## GRAMÁTICA

### Numbers 100 to 1,000

| | | | | | |
|---|---|---|---|---|---|
| 100 | cien/ciento | 400 | cuatrocientos/as | 800 | ochocientos/as |
| 101 | ciento uno | 500 | quinientos/as | 900 | novecientos/as |
| 200 | doscientos/as | 600 | seiscientos/as | 1.000 | mil |
| 300 | trescientos/as | 700 | setecientos/as | | |

Una manifestación estudiantil en Madrid, España. Muchas veces los estudiantes protestan o expresan sus opiniones por medio de una manifestación.

1. Spanish uses **cien/ciento** to say 100.
2. Use **cien** when no other number follows 100.

   | | |
   |---|---|
   | 100 chicos | cien chicos |
   | 100 chicas | cien chicas |

3. Use **ciento** with numbers from 101 to 199.

   | | |
   |---|---|
   | 105 profesores | ciento cinco profesores |
   | 120 profesoras | ciento veinte profesoras. |

4. **Uno** becomes **un** before a masculine noun and **una** before a feminine noun.

   | | |
   |---|---|
   | 131 entrenadores | ciento treinta y un entrenadores |
   | 131 entrenadoras | ciento treinta y una entrenadoras |

5. The numbers 200 through 900 agree in gender with the noun they modify.

   | | |
   |---|---|
   | 200 escritorios | doscientos escritorios |
   | 200 sillas | doscientas sillas |

6. Spanish normally uses a period instead of a comma when writing one thousand (**1.000**) and numbers greater than one thousand.

## ACTIVIDADES

**A** Su profesor/a va a leer un número de cada grupo. Indique cuál es el número.

| | | | | | | | |
|---|---|---|---|---|---|---|---|
| 114 | 360 | 850 | 524 | 667 | 777 | 984 | 534 |
| 213 | 330 | 919 | 490 | 215 | 550 | 260 | 620 |
| 818 | 414 | 723 | 514 | 490 | 650 | 770 | 1.000 |

**B** Lea los siguientes números.

181  347  238  673  879  591  435  221  115  913  1.000  799

**C** Lea los siguientes números y palabras.

| | | |
|---|---|---|
| 939 discos | 486 estantes | 71 camareras |
| 765 grabadoras | 870 entrenadores | 627 pollos |
| 693 canciones | 621 cronómetros | 1.000 casas |
| 379 guitarras | 538 pasteles | 789 refrescos |

**D** Lea los problemas siguientes y dé el resultado.

| 437 | 731 | 893 | 237 |
|---|---|---|---|
| + 83 | + 72 | + 15 | +863 |

**E** Pregúntele a un/a compañero/a su (a) dirección (b) número de teléfono. Comparta esta información con la clase.

**F** **¿Cuánto cuesta(n). . . ?** Pregúntele a su compañero/a cuánto cuestan los siguientes objetos.

1  2  3

4  5  6

**G** Ésta es una información que generalmente se pide (*is requested*) en una entrevista. Use el siguiente diálogo como modelo para entrevistar a su compañero/a.

| | |
|---|---|
| **Entrevistador/a** | Su nombre, por favor. |
| **Compañero/a** | . . . |
| **Entrevistador/a** | ¿Estado civil (*marital status*)? |
| **Compañero/a** | . . . |
| **Entrevistador/a** | ¿Cuál es su dirección? |
| **Compañero/a** | . . . |
| **Entrevistador/a** | ¿Cuál es su número de teléfono? |
| **Compañero/a** | . . . |

# EN CONTEXTO

## La agenda de Laura

| lunes | martes | miércoles | jueves | viernes | sábado | domingo |
|---|---|---|---|---|---|---|
| 6 | 7 | 8 | 9 | 10 | 11 | 12 |
| biblioteca 8:30 A.M. | llamar a María 9:00 A.M. | terminar° proyecto 10: A.M. | estudiar en casa de Teté A.M. | ir al° laboratorio 8:00 A.M. | ir a la playa° 11:00 A.M. | iglesia° 11:00 A.M. |
| examen 5:00 P.M. | trabajar librería 4:00 P.M. | programa televisión 7:00 P.M. | película° T.V. 10:00 P.M. | fiesta de Pablo 9:00 P.M. | | café 1:00 P.M. cine° 5:00 P.M. |
| | | (finish) | (movie) | (go to the) | (beach) | (church) (movies) |

# ACTIVIDADES

**A** Complete las siguientes oraciones según la agenda de Laura.

**Modelo**   El día 7 por la mañana Laura va a (*is going to*) **llamar a María.**

1. El día 7 por la tarde Laura va a...      3. El día 9 por la mañana Laura va a...
2. El día 8 por la mañana Laura va a...      4. El día 11 Laura va a...

**B** Conteste las siguientes preguntas sobre las actividades de Laura.

1. ¿Qué día va a ir Laura a la biblioteca? ¿A qué hora? ¿Qué tiene Laura por la tarde?
2. ¿Con quién va a estudiar Laura? ¿Qué día?
3. ¿Qué va a hacer Laura el día 10?
4. ¿Dónde va a estar Laura el sábado?
5. ¿Cuándo va a ir Laura a la iglesia? ¿A qué hora?
6. ¿Qué días va a mirar televisión?

# GRAMÁTICA

## Present tense of *ir*

|  | **ir** *to go* |  |  |
|---|---|---|---|
| yo | voy | nosotros/as | vamos |
| tú | vas | vosotros/as | vais |
| él, ella, usted | va | ellos/as, ustedes | van |

1. Use **a** to introduce a noun after the verb **ir.** Whenever **a** is followed by the article **el,** they contract to form **al.**

   Voy **a la** fiesta de María.      *I'm going to Maria's party.*
   Vamos **al** gimnasio.      *We're going to the gymnasium.*

2. Use **adónde** when asking a question with the verb **ir.**

   **¿Adónde** vas?      *Where are you going?*

## Some ways to express the future: present; *ir + a +* infinitive

1. To express future time use the present tense of **ir + a +** infinitive.

   Ellos van a correr después.      *They're going to run later.*
   ¿Vas a ir a la fiesta?      *Are you going to go to the party?*

Unos estudiantes conversan y toman unos refrescos en un café de la Plaza Mayor de Madrid. Los cafés constituyen un aspecto muy importante en la vida social de muchos hispanos.

2. You may also express future time by using the present tense of the verb, especially when referring to a not too distant future. The context shows whether you are referring to the future or to the present time.

| | |
|---|---|
| Vamos mañana. | *We're going tomorrow.* |
| ¿Estudiamos esta noche? | *Are we going to study tonight?* |

3. Some additional expressions that denote future time are

| | |
|---|---|
| pasado mañana | *the day after tomorrow* |
| la semana próxima | *next week* |
| el mes próximo | *next month* |
| el año próximo | *next year* |
| el próximo fin de semana | *next weekend* |

## ACTIVIDADES

**A** Diga que usted va a hacer lo siguiente.

> **Modelo** ver televisión / esta noche
> **Voy a ver televisión esta noche.**

1. ir al café / esta tarde
2. hablar con mis amigos / el fin de semana
3. terminar la tarea / después
4. comer pescado / mañana
5. estudiar / pasado mañana
6. bailar/ /esta noche

**B** Hay un examen de español mañana. Diga las cosas que van a hacer los estudiantes antes del examen.

**C** Su amigo y usted van a ir a su restaurante favorito esta noche. Diga qué van a comer y beber.

**D** Yolanda desea perder peso (*lose weight*). Diga qué va a hacer Yolanda.

**E** Los dibujos muestran lo que Maribel va a hacer el próximo sábado. Diga lo que ella va a hacer y después diga lo que usted va a hacer.

**F** **Entrevista.** Pregúntele a su compañero/a sobre sus próximas vacaciones. Use las siguientes preguntas.

1. ¿Adónde vas a ir?   2. ¿Con quién vas a ir?   3. ¿Cuántos días vas a estar allí?   4. ¿Cuándo vas a ir?   5. ¿Qué lugares vas a visitar?   6. ¿A quién vas a visitar?   7. ¿Qué vas a comer y beber?

# PRONUNCIACIÓN

**1.** **ll, y**

In most parts of the Spanish-speaking world, **y** and **ll** are pronounced like English *y* in the word *yoke,* but with more friction. At the end of a word, **y** sounds very similar to **i,** but if the next word begins with a vowel, **y** is pronounced like English *y* in *yoke.*

yo    llamo    ella    estoy    muy bien    muy alto    voy allí

**2.** **x**

Before a consonant, **x** is pronounced in Spanish as **s** or **ks.**

experiencia    explicación    experimento    texto    extensión

Between vowels, **x** is pronounced like English *ks* or Spanish **gs.** It is never pronounced like English *x.*

examen    sexo    existir    exacto    éxito

## LECTURA

These suggestions for a successful party were taken from *Coqueta*, a Mexican magazine for young people. You may need the following words to understand the chart better.

| exitosa | *successful* | las verduras | *vegetables* | la limpieza | *cleaning* |
|---------|-----------|--------------|-------------|-------------|-----------|
| elegir | *to choose* | colocar | *to put* | | |
| la bandeja | *tray* | el vaso | *glass* | | |

### ¿Vas a dar una fiesta?

### PLANIFICACION

**El plan maestro:** El secreto para planificar una fiesta exitosa es: ¡organización!

| | 2 DIAS ANTES | 1 DIA ANTES | EL DIA DE LA FIESTA | DESPUES DE LA FIESTA |
|---|---|---|---|---|
| **VIVIAN** | Comprar la comida. | Preparar la bandeja de verduras, pastas, tortas, etc. | Colocar la comida en la mesa y hacer el ponche. | *LIMPIEZA* |
| **MELISSA** | | | | |
| **MARTA** | Decorar la casa. | Preparar ensaladas de pollo o papas, la bandeja de quesos, etc. | Preparar los platos, vasos, etc. | |
| **NELSON** | Elegir la música y buscar el estéreo. | | Hacer de disc jockey (DJ) | |

### ¡Vámonos de fiesta!

### Preguntas

1. ¿Qué deben hacer Vivian y Melissa dos días antes?
2. ¿Quién está a cargo del estéreo?
3. ¿Cuándo deben preparar las ensaladas?
4. ¿Quiénes están a cargo de las ensaladas?

5. ¿Qué clases de ensalada van a preparar?
6. ¿Qué van a hacer Vivian y Melissa un día antes de la fiesta?
7. ¿Cuándo van a hacer el ponche?
8. ¿Qué van a hacer todos después de la fiesta?

## Los viajes° de estudio

*trips*

Una de las actividades más interesantes y populares entre los estudiantes de muchas universidades españolas es el viaje de estudio, que generalmente se organiza en el tercer año de la carrera.

Algunos de los estudiantes del curso son las personas que están a cargo de la organización del viaje. Estos estudiantes deben averiguar° los precios de los boletos°, excursiones, hoteles y hostales, el itinerario, etc. Además es necesario conseguir° precios bajos pues los jóvenes no pueden gastar° mucho.

*find out*
*tickets*
*to get / no… cannot spend*

Para cubrir los gastos° del viaje los alumnos venden durante todo el curso boletos para rifas°, bolígrafos, dulces° típicos, camisetas°, etc. a amigos y parientes°. También organizan fiestas y venden las entradas°. De esta forma cada alumno puede ahorrar° durante varios meses el dinero° que va a necesitar para el viaje.

*Para… To cover the expenses*
*raffles / sweets / T-shirts*
*relatives / tickets*
*save / money*

Para los estudiantes, el viaje de estudio es una oportunidad excelente para estar con buenos amigos y divertirse°, y también para visitar otro país, aprender° cosas nuevas y estar en contacto con otra cultura.

*have a good time / learn*

## ¿Verdadero o falso?

Diga si las siguientes oraciones son verdaderas o falsas de acuerdo con la lectura.

1. Los alumnos hacen el viaje de estudio en el primer año.
2. Los profesores organizan el viaje.
3. Los estudiantes venden diferentes artículos para conseguir dinero para el viaje.
4. Sólo van al viaje los alumnos que sacan buenas notas.
5. En el viaje de estudio los estudiantes aprenden y también se divierten.

Unos alumnos en un viaje de estudio en las Islas Canarias. Estas islas españolas, situadas muy cerca de la costa oeste del Africa, ofrecen una variedad extraordinaria de paisajes.

## SITUACIONES

1. You are a waiter/waitress at a café. Two of your classmates will play the part of the customers. Greet your customers and ask what they would like to eat and drink. Be prepared to answer any questions they may have.

2. You have ordered soup at a restaurant, but it is cold. Call the waiter and explain that the soup is cold. The waiter should apologize.

3. One of your friends is asking for your advice. He/She wants to be in shape for a track meet. Tell him/her what to do.

4. Itemize your expenses for next week. You are going to do the following: go to the movies, spend the day at the beach, eat at a restaurant, and go dancing. Tell your partner how much you are going to spend (**gastar**) for each of the things you plan to do.

5. Your friend is planning to go to a concert. Find out where and when the concert is, who is going to sing, and who is going to play the guitar. Then tell your classmates what you found out.

6. Tell your partner about your plans for tonight. Tell him/her (a) where you are planning to go, (b) with whom, and (c) what you are planning to do. Inquire about his/her plans.

7. Think about the great weekend you are going to have. Tell your partner about it.

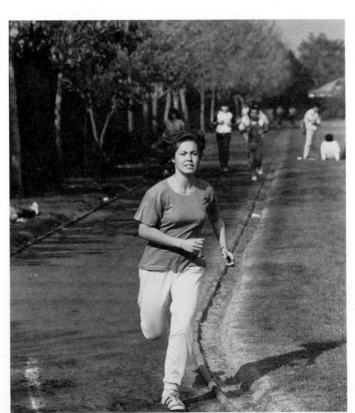

Una joven trota en un parque de Santiago de Chile para mantenerse en buenas condiciones físicas.

Un coro de estudiantes
practica en la
Universidad de
Guadalajara en México.

# VOCABULARIO[1]

**comunicación**
el teléfono — *telephone*
la televisión — *television*

**deportes** — *sports*
la competencia — *meet*
el cronómetro — *stop watch*

**direcciones** — *addresses*
la calle — *street*
el número — *number*

**diversiones** — *entertainment*
la canción — *song*
el disco — *record*

el estéreo — *stereo*
la fiesta — *party*
la guitarra — *guitar*
la película — *film*
el programa — *program*

**lugares**
la acera — *sidewalk*
el café — *café*
la casa — *house*
el cine — *movies*
el estadio — *stadium*
la iglesia — *church*
la playa — *beach*

---

[1] See page 90 for numbers 100–1,000.

**muebles** — *furniture*
el estante — *bookshelf*

**personas**
el camarero/la camarera — *waiter/waitress*
el entrenador/la entrenadora — *trainer, coach*

**en un café o restaurante**
el almuerzo — *lunch*
el arroz — *rice*
el atún — *tuna*
el café — *coffee*
la cena — *dinner, supper*
el cereal — *cereal*
la comida — *dinner, supper, food*
el desayuno — *breakfast*
la ensalada — *salad*
la fruta — *fruit*
la hamburguesa — *hamburger*
el helado — *ice cream*
el huevo — *egg*
el jamón — *ham*
el jugo — *juice*
la leche — *milk*
la lechuga — *lettuce*
el limón — *lemon*
la manzana — *apple*
el menú — *menu*
la naranja — *orange*
la orden — *order*
el pan — *bread*
   el pan tostado — *toast*
la papa — *potato*
   las papas fritas — *French fries*
el pastel — *pie*
el pescado — *fish*
el pollo — *chicken*
el queso — *cheese*
el refresco — *soda*
el sándwich — *sandwich*
la sopa — *soup*

el té — *tea*
el tomate — *tomato*
la tostada — *toast*
el vegetal — *vegetable*

**descripción**
caliente — *hot*
frío — *cold*
frito — *fried*

**las clases**
la agenda — *agenda, calendar*
el álgebra — *algebra*
el examen — *examination*
el proyecto — *project*

**verbos**
abrir — *to open*
bailar — *to dance*
beber — *to drink*
caminar — *to walk*
cantar — *to sing*
comer — *to eat*
correr — *to run*
creer — *to believe, to think*
deber — *should, ought to*
escribir — *to write*
ir — *to go*
leer — *to read*
llamar — *to call*
llegar — *to arrive*
repasar — *to review*
sacar — *to check out, to take out*
terminar — *to finish*
tocar — *to play, to touch*
tomar — *to drink, to take*
trotar — *to jog*
vender — *to sell*
ver — *to see*
vivir — *to live*

**tiempo**

| | |
|---|---|
| ahora | *now* |
| antes | *before* |
| el año próximo | *next year* |
| después | *after* |
| el fin de semana | *weekend* |
| mañana | *tomorrow* |
|   pasado mañana | *the day after to-morrow* |

**palabras útiles**

| | |
|---|---|
| al | *(contraction of* **a** + **el***) to the* |

**expresiones útiles**

| | |
|---|---|
| algo | *something* |
| estar a dieta | *to be on a diet* |
| ven | *come* |

Porque Pulco es limón exprimido.

Te presentamos el primer zumo concentrado de limón: PULCO.

NATURAL.
Sin conservantes. Sin colorantes. Sin azúcar. Porque es auténtico limón.

ECONOMICO.
UNA BOTELLA DE PULCO EQUIVALE A 6 LITROS DE LIMONADA.

COMODO.
Porque PULCO es limón exprimido y lo tienes siempre a mano. Listo para usar en cualquier momento.

**In** Lección 4 **you will**

a. **identify and describe family members.**
b. **describe physical and emotional states.**
c. **provide information about a person's age and abilities.**
d. **ask about and express ownership.**
e. **express preferences and desires.**

don José
el abuelo

doña Olga
la abuela

los abuelos

Jorge
el tío

Elena (esposa)
la tía

los tíos

Ana

Elenita

las primas

# La familia

## La familia de Eduardo

Eduardo es el hijo de María y Jaime. Él es el nieto de don José y doña Olga, y es el sobrino de Jorge, Elena, Rita y Juan.

María
la madre

Jaime (esposo)
el padre

los padres

Rita
la tía

Juan (esposo)
el tío

los tíos

Eduardo

Inés
la hermana

Juanito

Diego

los primos

## ACTIVIDADES

**A** Complete las siguientes oraciones de acuerdo con el árbol genealógico (*family tree*) de Eduardo.

1. La hermana de Eduardo se llama ____.
2. Don José y doña Olga son los ____ de Eduardo. Ellos tienen ____ hijas y ____ hijo.
3. Eduardo es el ____ de Jaime.
4. Jaime es el ____ de Eduardo, y María es la ____.
5. Juanito y Eduardo son ____.
6. Inés y Ana son ____.
7. Don José y doña Olga tienen ____ nietos y ____ nietas.
8. Eduardo es el ____ de Juan y Rita.
9. Inés es la ____ de Jorge y Elena.
10. María y Jaime son los ____ de Elenita.

**B** Escoja una persona de la familia de Eduardo. Su compañero/a debe decir cuál es su parentesco (*family relationship*) con Eduardo.

*Modelo*    —¿Quién es Ana?
            —**Es la prima de Eduardo.**

**más parientes**

| | |
|---|---|
| el cuñado | *brother-in-law* |
| la cuñada | *sister-in-law* |
| el suegro | *father-in-law* |
| la suegra | *mother-in-law* |
| el yerno | *son-in-law* |
| la nuera | *daughter-in-law* |

Un reunión familiar de varias generaciones en Bogotá, Colombia.

| **otras relaciones** | *other relationships* |
|---|---|
| el esposo, el marido | *husband* |
| la esposa, la mujer | *wife* |
| el novio | *fiancé, boyfriend* |
| la novia | *fiancée, girlfriend* |
| el ahijado | *godson* |
| la ahijada | *goddaughter* |
| el padrino | *godfather* |
| la madrina | *godmother* |

## ACTIVIDADES

**A** Asocie los parientes de la columna de la izquierda con los de la columna de la derecha.

| 1. nieto | a. hijo |
|---|---|
| 2. padrino | b. tío |
| 3. madre | c. abuela |
| 4. marido | d. ahijado |
| 5. sobrina | e. suegro |
| 6. nuera | f. esposa |

**B** Complete las siguientes oraciones con la palabra apropiada.

1. La esposa de mi hijo es mi...
2. El hermano de mi esposo/a es mi...
3. La madre de mi esposo/a es mi...
4. Los hijos de mis hijos son mis...
5. Yo soy la madrina/el padrino de Roberto. Él es mi...

**C** **¿Quién es?** Describa a un miembro de su familia. Su compañero debe identificar a ese pariente.

*Modelo*  —No es muy vieja. Es la hermana de mi padre.
—Es tu tía.

**D** **Entrevista.** Hágale las siguientes preguntas sobre su familia a su compañero/a. Él/ella le debe hacer las mismas preguntas a usted.

1. ¿Vives con tu familia?
2. ¿Cuántas personas hay en tu familia?
3. ¿Cuántos hermanos tienes? ¿Cómo se llaman?
4. ¿Cuántos tíos tienes? ¿Dónde viven?
5. ¿Tienes muchos primos?
6. ¿Cómo se llama tu primo/a favorito/a?

# Cultura

## Families in the Hispanic world

In the Hispanic world, the word **familia** generally refers not only to one's mother, father, and children but to other relatives as well. It is not unusual to have three generations living in the same house, and it is instilled in children at an early age that they should respect and help the elderly. Because Hispanic societies do not have the mobility that characterizes American society, most families tend to remain in the same city or town, maintaining close ties with one another.

However, industrialization and urbanization have had their effects on Hispanic societies, too. As they come of age, many young people leave small towns, hoping to find better-paying jobs in cities or in other countries. More women have entered the work force, and smaller families with one or two children are becoming common, especially in urban centers.

In Hispanic countries people use two last names (**apellidos**) following their given name. A person's first surname is the father's last name, and the second is the mother's maiden name. For example, if you see the name **Jorge Fernández Campos,** you know that **Fernández** is the first surname of Jorge's father and **Campos** is the first surname of Jorge's mother. Sometimes **y** is used between the two last names: **Jorge Fernández y Campos.** A married woman generally retains her maiden name followed by **de** and her husband's surname. Mrs. Fernández (Jorge's mother) would be known as **María Campos de Fernández** or **señora de Fernández.** Nevertheless, in legal documents, she would not use her husband's last name but her own.

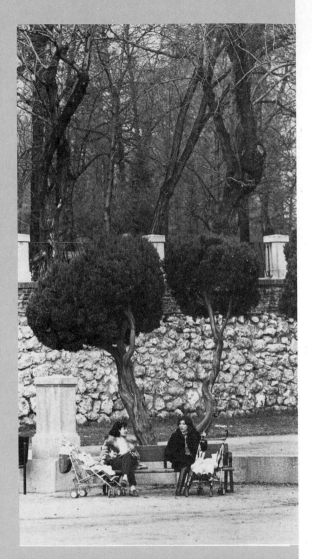

Dos madres con sus hijos en el parque del Buen Retiro en Madrid. Este parque, conocido generalmente como el Retiro, es muy popular entre las familias madrileñas.

# EN CONTEXTO

## Las vacaciones de la familia Villegas

El Sr. Villegas quiere° visitar la ciudad de México donde tiene unos parientes. *wants*
La Sra. de Villegas quiere visitar Guadalajara, pero los hijos prefieren ir a la
playa. Joaquín quiere ir a Acapulco pues unos amigos van a pasar° sus vaca- *spend*
ciones allí. Beatriz prefiere ir a Cancún. Ella lee muchos artículos sobre viajes
en las revistas° y los periódicos°, y según estos artículos Cancún es un lugar *magazines / newspapers*
maravilloso.

Además hay otro problema para este viaje: el perro y la gata de la familia.
Según los padres, Sansón puede° ir a una guardería de perros° y Fifí a casa de *can / guardería... kennel*
la abuela. Joaquín prefiere dejar° el perro con su abuela. La Sra. Villegas piensa° *leave / thinks*
que su madre está muy vieja para cuidar° dos animales y que Sansón va a estar *take care of*
muy bien en la guardería.

Las vacaciones de los Villegas empiezan° la semana próxima. ¿Adónde cree *begin*
usted que van a ir? ¿Dónde van a dejar los animales?

## Para completar

Complete las siguientes oraciones sobre los Villegas.

1. El padre quiere ir a...
2. La madre prefiere ir a...
3. Acapulco es la ciudad que prefiere...

4. El hijo quiere visitar...
5. Fifí es...
6. Sansón es...

Una familia hispana en los Estados Unidos disfruta de una tarde al aire libre. Las familias hispanas tratan de mantener muchas de las costumbres y tradiciones de su país de origen.

## GRAMÁTICA

### Present tense of *e* ⟶ *ie* and *o* ⟶ *ue* stem-changing verbs

| **pensar** *to think* | | **volver** *to return* | |
|---|---|---|---|
| yo | pienso | yo | vuelvo |
| tú | piensas | tú | vuelves |
| él, ella, usted | piensa | él, ella, usted | vuelve |
| nosotros/as | pensamos | nosotros/as | volvemos |
| vosotros/as | pensáis | vosotros/as | volvéis |
| ellos/as, ustedes | piensan | ellos/as, ustedes | vuelven |

**1.** These verbs change the stem vowel **e** to **ie** and **o** to **ue** except in the **nosotros** and **vosotros** forms.

**2.** Other common verbs and their vowel changes are[1]

| **e** ⟶ **ie** | | **o** ⟶ **ue** | |
|---|---|---|---|
| empezar | *to begin* | almorzar | *to have lunch* |
| perder | *to lose* | contar | *to count* |
| preferir | *to prefer* | costar | *to cost* |
| querer | *to want, to love* | dormir | *to sleep* |
| | | poder | *to be able to, can* |

---

[1] Stem-changing verbs will be identified in vocabularies with **ie** or **ue** in parentheses: e.g., **pensar (ie); volver (ue).**

**3. Tener** (*to have*) and **venir** (*to come*), in addition to changing **e ⟶ ie,** have a completely irregular **yo** form.

**tener:** ten**go,** t**ie**nes, t**ie**ne, tenemos, tenéis, t**ie**nen

**venir:** ven**go,** v**ie**nes, v**ie**ne, venimos, venís, v**ie**nen

**4.** When the verb **pensar** is followed by an infinitive, it means *to plan to.*

¿Adónde **piensas ir** mañana? *Where are you planning to go tomorrow?*

**5.** The verb **jugar** (*to play—a game or a sport*) has the change **u ⟶ ue.**

Mario j**ue**ga muy bien, pero nosotros jugamos regular.

## ACTIVIDADES

**A** Diga a qué hora empiezan y a qué hora terminan las siguientes actividades.

> *Modelo* las clases
>
> **Las clases empiezan a las ocho. Terminan a las cuatro.**

1. la clase de español
2. la música en una discoteca
3. las noticias (*news*)
4. su programa favorito de televisión
5. los juegos de béisbol (*baseball games*)

**B** Las personas prefieren diferentes actividades. Diga lo que las siguientes personas prefieren hacer de acuerdo con el dibujo.

> *Modelo* **María**
>
> **María prefiere correr.**

Carlos

el Sr. Pérez

Pablo    Alberto

Marisa

nosotros

yo

**C** Usted es un hombre/una mujer de negocios (*businessman/woman*) que hace las siguientes transacciones. Diga si (*if*) usted gana (*make money*) o pierde.

> **Modelos**   Compro un estéreo por $100. Vendo el estéreo por $150.
> **Gano $50.**
> Compro un radio por $250. Vendo el radio por $220.
> **Pierdo $30.**

1. Compro un teléfono por $60. Vendo el teléfono por $40.
2. Compro un diccionario por $30. Vendo el diccionario por $60.
3. Compro una computadora por $850. Vendo la computadora por $1000.
4. Compro 50 casetes por $200. Vendo los casetes por $160.

**D** ¿Qué cree usted que piensan hacer las siguientes personas?

> **Modelo**   María desea estar delgada.
> **María piensa correr mucho,** o **estar a dieta,** o **comer poco.**

1. Alberto tiene un examen mañana.
2. Mi tía está muy enferma.
3. Mis primos están de vacaciones.
4. Nosotros queremos ver una película española.
5. Yo voy a ir a México.

**E** Hágale las siguientes preguntas a su compañero/a. Después comparta esta información con la clase.

1. ¿A qué hora almuerzas? ¿Con quién? ¿Dónde?   2. ¿Qué prefieres almorzar?   3. ¿Qué bebes a la hora del almuerzo?   4. ¿Duermes la siesta (*Do you take a nap*) después del almuerzo?

**F** Usted organiza una fiesta para celebrar el cumpleaños (*birthday*) de su hermano. Conteste las preguntas que él le hace sobre la fiesta.

1. ¿Cuántas personas vienen?   2. ¿A qué hora van a venir?   3. ¿Viene Arturo? ¿Y Ángeles y Rosa?   4. ¿Quién no puede venir?   5. ¿Qué discos tienes para la fiesta?

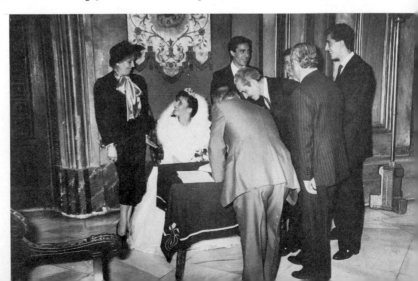

Una boda en Madrid. En los países hispanos es muy común que los amigos íntimos de las dos familias firmen como testigos (*sign as witnesses*) en la ceremonia.

# EN CONTEXTO

## ¿Qué tienen estas personas?

Pablo tiene frío.

Carlos tiene hambre.

Pilar tiene calor.

agua

Susana tiene
mucha sed.

El bebé tiene
mucho sueño.

Eugenio tiene miedo.

## GRAMÁTICA

### Special expressions with tener

Spanish uses **tener** + noun in many cases where English uses *to be* + adjective. These expressions always refer to people or animals and never to things.

| tener | hambre | to be | *hungry* |
|---|---|---|---|
| | sed | | *thirsty* |
| | sueño | | *sleepy* |
| | miedo | | *afraid* |
| | calor | | *hot* |
| | frío | | *cold* |
| | suerte | | *lucky* |
| | razón | | *right* |
| | cuidado | | *careful* |
| | prisa | | *in a hurry* |

1. Use **mucho/mucha** for *very* with these expressions.

Tengo **mucho** miedo.          Tienen **mucha** hambre.

2. **Estar equivocado/a** means *to be wrong.*

Juana **está equivocada.** Los Villegas no     *Juana is wrong. The Villegas are not*
vuelven mañana.                         *coming back tomorrow.*

3. Use **tener. . . años** *to be . . . years old* to express age.

Jorge **tiene 21 años.**            *Jorge is twenty-one years old.*

4. Use **tener ganas de** + infinitive to express that you feel like doing or are eager to do something.

**Tengo ganas de ir** al cine.        *I feel like going to the movies.*

5. Use **tener** + **que** + infinitive to express obligation.

**Tengo que repasar** para el examen.    *I have to review for the test.*

## ACTIVIDADES

**A** Escoja la expresión correcta de acuerdo con la situación.

1. Mario va a comer mucho.      Tiene sed. / Tiene miedo. /
Tiene sueño. / Tiene hambre.

2. Asunción va a dormir 10 horas.    Tiene calor. / Tiene cuidado. /
Tiene prisa. / Tiene sueño.

3. Ellos van a tomar 6 refrescos.    Tienen razón. / Tienen sed. /
Tienen frío. / Tienen miedo.

4. Yo necesito llegar a la         Tengo prisa. / Tengo suerte. /
clase a las ocho.            Tengo 20 años. / Tengo frío.

**B** Complete las siguientes oraciones con la expresión apropiada con **tener.**

1. Si no comemos bastante, después vamos a. . .
2. La película empieza a las 9:00 y son las 8:55. Por eso Juan. . .
3. En el desierto los turistas. . ., pero en el Polo Norte. . .
4. El león es muy valiente; nunca (*never*). . .
5. Son las dos de la mañana y nosotros. . .
6. Necesito beber agua porque. . .
7. Cuando Luis juega a la lotería siempre gana; él. . .

**C** **Entrevista.** Use las siguientes preguntas para entrevistar a un/a compañero/a. Después comparta esta información con la clase.

1. ¿Cuántos años tienes?    2. ¿Tienes hermanos o hermanas? ¿Cuántos años tienen?
3. ¿Qué comes cuando tienes hambre?    4. ¿Qué prefieres tomar cuando tienes sed?

La abuela mira los trabajos que sus nietos hacen en la escuela. Las horas de las comidas les ofrecen a las familias la oportunidad de reunirse y conversar.

**D** La familia Menéndez quiere lograr (*achieve*) ciertas cosas. Diga lo que tienen que hacer.

> *Modelo*   Magdalena quiere hablar francés muy bien.
> **Ella tiene que estudiar mucho** o **Tiene que practicar más** o **Tiene que vivir un año en Francia.**

1. El padre quiere estar más delgado.
2. La madre quiere ver la película *Carmen*.
3. Los primos necesitan unos libros.
4. El tío Paco quiere ser doctor en medicina.
5. Amparo quiere jugar (al) tenis muy bien.

**E** Mire los siguientes dibujos y explique lo que pasa (*is happening*).

**F** **Entrevista.** Usted quiere saber lo que su compañero/a tiene que hacer esta noche (o mañana, o el próximo fin de semana) y lo que tiene ganas de hacer. Hágale las siguientes preguntas y comparta la información con la clase.

|  |  |
|---|---|
| **Usted** | ¿Qué tienes que hacer ___? |
| **Compañero/a** | . . . |
| **Usted** | ¿Y qué tienes ganas de hacer? |
| **Compañero/a** | . . . |

# EN CONTEXTO

## Una conversación entre dos niños

## Para completar

Complete el siguiente cuadro según la conversación de los dos niños.

**Opiniones diferentes**

Según Lucila
su mamá es...
su papá es...
sus hermanos son...
su familia es...
Cuquito es...

Según Cuquito
su mamá es...
su papá es...
sus hermanos son...
su familia es...

**Mis opiniones**

Lucila es una niña...
Cuquito es un niño...
Yo prefiero a... porque...

## GRAMÁTICA

### Possessive adjectives

| | |
|---|---|
| **mi, mis** | *my* |
| **tu, tus** | *your* |
| **su, sus** | *his, her, its, your (formal), their* |
| **nuestro, nuestra** | *our* |
| **vuestro, vuestra** | *your (familiar plural)* |

**1.** These possessive adjectives always precede the noun they modify.

    **mi** mamá    **tu** hermana

**2.** Possessive adjectives change number (and gender in the case of **nuestro** and **vuestro**) to agree with *the thing possessed,* not with the possessor.

    **mi** casa, **mis** casas
    **nuestro** padre, **nuestros** padres, **nuestra** familia, **nuestras** primas

**3.** **Su, sus** has multiple meanings. To ensure clarity, you can use **de** + the name of the possessor, or the appropriate pronoun, instead of the possessive adjective.

possible meanings

su madre
{
    la madre de ella (la madre de Elena)
    la madre de él (la madre de Jorge)
    la madre de usted
    la madre de ustedes
    la madre de ellos (la madre de Elena y Jorge)
    la madre de ellas (la madre de Elena y Olga)
}

## *ACTIVIDADES*

**A** Lea los siguientes párrafos usando los adjetivos posesivos correspondientes a las palabras subrayadas (*underlined*).

1. <u>Roberto</u> vive con ____ padres en la ciudad de México. De lunes a viernes él trabaja con ____ tío Miguel por las mañanas y por las tardes estudia en la universidad. Marisa, la novia de Roberto, vive en Cuernavaca y los fines de semana Roberto va a casa de ____ futuros suegros para visitar a ____ novia. Él piensa terminar ____ estudios el año próximo y buscar trabajo en Cuernavaca. El tío está muy contento con el trabajo de ____ sobrino y cree que ____ futuro está en la ciudad de México y no en Cuernavaca.

2. Diego y Alfredo viven en los Ángeles. _____ familia es mexicana y ellos hablan español con _____ padres, tíos y primos; pero Diego y Alfredo quieren vivir un tiempo en un país hispano. _____ abuelos viven en Mérida, la capital de Yucatán. Ellos van a hablar por teléfono con _____ abuelos para ver si pueden visitar Yucatán y estar en _____ casa durante dos meses.

3. Mi hermano y yo pensamos visitar Guadalajara el mes próximo. _____ compañero Félix Montaña va a estudiar este año allí y nosotros podemos estar en su apartamento. Nosotros queremos ir en auto, pero _____ auto es muy viejo. _____ amigos creen que no vamos a tener problemas pues en Guadalajara hay mecánicos excelentes.

**B** Su compañero/a le va a hacer preguntas sobre las cosas que usted tiene. Después usted le hace las preguntas a él/ella.

1. ¿Tienes auto? ¿Es pequeño tu auto? ¿De qué color es? 2. ¿Tienes perro? ¿Sacas a tu perro por la noche? ¿Dónde dejas tu perro cuando vas de viaje? ¿Cómo es tu perro? 3. ¿Tienes novio/a? ¿Cómo se llama? ¿Cuántos años tiene? ¿Cómo es?

**C** Usted le va a hacer preguntas a su compañero/a sobre sus hermanos. Comparta la información con la clase.

1. ¿Cuántos hermanos tienes? 2. ¿Viven en tu casa? 3. ¿Cómo se llama tu hermano mayor (*older*)? 4. ¿Y tu hermano menor (*younger*)? 5. ¿De qué color son los ojos de tu hermano mayor? ¿Y el pelo? 6. ¿De qué color son los ojos de tu hermano menor? 7. ¿Cuántos años tiene tu hermano menor? 8. ¿Son simpáticos tus hermanos?

## PRONUNCIACIÓN

### Stress and the written accent mark

Word stress is meaningful in both English and Spanish. Normally all words in both languages have one stressed syllable. If a person changes the stress to another syllable, the meaning of the word changes.

In English words like *permit* and *present* illustrate this very well. When the first syllable is stressed, these words are nouns; when the second syllable is stressed, they become verbs.

| *Nouns* | *Verbs* |
|---------|---------|
| *per*mit | per*mit* |
| *pres*ent | pres*ent* |

Differences in meaning due to stressing one syllable rather than another are more common in Spanish. One effect is to change the tense of a verb. Sometimes stress is indicated by a written accent mark.[2]

---

[2] In this lesson and in **Lecciones 5** and **6** you will learn the rules for accentuation.

| *Present* | *Past* |
|-----------|--------|
| **ha**blo | ha**bló** |
| es**tu**dio | estu**dió** |

If you know how to pronounce a word you can determine if it needs a written accent mark by applying a few simple rules. By the same token, if you see an unknown word, the presence or absence of a written accent mark will tell you where to place the stress.

Some rules for accentuation follow.

**1.** Interrogative and exclamatory words have a written accent mark on the vowel of the stressed syllable.

¿**Có**mo es tu primo?     ¡**Qué** va!

**2.** Some one-syllable words have a written accent mark to distinguish them from words with the same spelling but different meaning.

| el *the* | tu *your* | si *if* | te *(to) you* |
|----------|-----------|---------|---------------|
| él *he* | tú *you* | sí *yes* | té *tea* |

**3.** All words stressed on the third from the last syllable have a written accent mark.

**fí**sica   **sá**bado   sim**pá**tico   gra**má**tica   mate**má**ticas

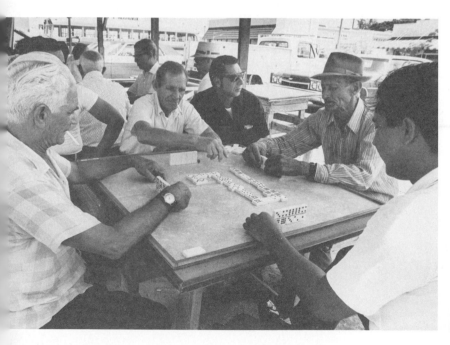

Jugadores de dominó en la Pequeña Habana, Miami. El dominó es un juego muy popular en muchos de los países hispanos.

# LECTURA

## Las familias hispanas

Las familias hispanas, en general, son muy unidas y mientras° los hijos están solteros viven con sus padres. En muchos casos viven varias generaciones en la misma casa: los abuelos, los padres y los hijos. Los días de fiesta° o los fines de semana es común ver a dos o tres generaciones de la misma familia en un restaurante, en un café o en un parque.

En general, las relaciones con otros parientes son muy cordiales. Las personas mayores° (tíos, cuñados, primos) salen juntos o van a casa de uno de ellos para conversar o comer algo. Los primos jóvenes se reúnen con frecuencia, tienen amigos comunes, y van a fiestas, al cine o a un café.

Muchas familias hispanas que viven en los Estados Unidos mantienen° o quieren mantener estas costumbres° aquí. Esto causa a veces° conflictos en la familia. Hay jóvenes hispanos que prefieren la independencia que tienen los jóvenes norteamericanos y quieren vivir solos° o con algún amigo o amiga.

*while*

*días... holidays*

*adults*

*maintain/customs / a... sometimes*

*by themselves*

Los padres y los padrinos con el bebé el día del bautizo en Napa, California. Las relaciones entre los padrinos, los ahijados y sus padres son muy importantes en la cultura hispana.

## Preguntas

1. En general, ¿dónde viven los hijos solteros de las familias hispanas?
2. ¿Salen juntas dos o tres generaciones de una familia en los países hispanos?
3. ¿Cómo son las relaciones con otros parientes?
4. ¿Adónde van los jóvenes de las familias hispanas?
5. ¿Por qué hay conflictos a veces en las familias hispanas que viven en los Estados Unidos?
6. ¿Vive usted solo/a o con su familia? ¿Qué prefiere usted?

### La tercera edad°

tercera... *senior citizens*
(literally, the third age)
Hoy... *Nowadays*
*outside (the home)* / *difficult*
*elderly*
*rooms*

Hoy en día°, especialmente en las ciudades, hay más mujeres que trabajan fuera°, y como los hijos estudian o trabajan, resulta difícil° cuidar a los ancianos° en la casa. Por este motivo existen residencias para la tercera edad que ofrecen servicios médicos y habitaciones° cómodas a los ancianos, pero el costo puede ser bastante alto para la familia.

Éste es un tipo de servicio relativamente nuevo en el mundo hispano, pues por tradición y costumbre los ancianos permanecen el la case de sus familiares. A continuación pueden ver un anuncio de un periódico donde se explica lo que ofrece una residencia para la tercera edad.

---

# TERCERA EDAD

- Estancias permanentes y temporales.
- Servicio médico interno las veinticuatro horas.
- Habitaciones individuales y dobles, con baño y terraza, vídeo, televisión y parabólica, restaurante, amplias zonas de estar y jardines.

## REGERSA

**Información:**
URBANIZACIÓN PARQUE ROZAS
**Avenida de Atenas, s/n.
Carretera Coruña, km. 23,800**
(vía de servicio junto Punta Galea).

**LAS ROZAS
Teléfono 630 33 22** (ocho líneas)

---

### ¿Verdadero o falso?

Diga si las siguientes oraciones son verdaderas o falsas de acuerdo con la lectura y el anuncio.

1. Las residencias para la tercera edad son bastante nuevas en el mundo hispano.
2. Las residencias para la tercera edad cuestan muy poco.
3. En la residencia del anuncio no hay servicio médico de noche.
4. Los ancianos pueden ver televisión y vídeos.
5. Los ancianos deben comer en la habitación.
6. Si una persona desea recibir información debe llamar a las ocho.

## SITUACIONES

1. You are doing some research regarding immigrants in this country. Diagram your partner's family tree as he/she describes it to you. Find out the country of origin of the various family members.

2. You are getting information for a census. Working with a partner, find out (a) how many members of his/her family live in the same house or apartment, (b) their ages, and (c) their marital status.

3. Find out (a) what city your partner wants to visit, (b) why, (c) when he/she is planning to go, and (d) with whom.

4. You are a very busy person. Tell your partner all you have to do on a typical day.

5. Find out your classmates' preferences. In a group of five or six classmates one of you will be in charge and act as secretary (**secretario/a**). Each person should rank the following kinds of movies according to preference. The student in charge will report the results to the class.

   ____ cómicas      ____ de aventuras
   ____ dramáticas      ____ de detectives
   ____ musicales      ____ de misterio
   ____ románticas      ____ de ciencia ficción
   ____ documentales      ____ del oeste (*western*)

6. You are a law student (**estudiante de derecho**) who wants to quit school. Tell your mother/father that (a) you are not happy in school, (b) you want to quit school (**no quiero estudiar más**), (c) you don't have any friends, and (d) you prefer to work and have money. Your mother/father will try to persuade you not to quit.

## VOCABULARIO[3]

**animales**

| | | | |
|---|---|---|---|
| el gato | *cat* | el hermano | *brother* |
| la guardería de perros | *kennel* | la hija | *daughter* |
| | | el hijo | *son* |
| el perro | *dog* | la nieta | *granddaughter* |
| | | el nieto | *grandson* |
| **la familia** | *family* | la nuera | *daughter-in-law* |
| la abuela | *grandmother* | los padres | *parents* |
| el abuelo | *grandfather* | el papá | *dad* |
| la cuñada | *sister-in-law* | el pariente/la parienta | *relative* |
| el cuñado | *brother-in-law* | | |
| la hermana | *sister* | el primo/la prima | *cousin* |

[3] See page 111 for expressions with **tener** + noun.

la sobrina — *niece*
el sobrino — *nephew*
la suegra — *mother-in-law*
el suegro — *father-in-law*
la tía — *aunt*
el tío — *uncle*
el yerno — *son-in-law*

## otras relaciones

la ahijada — *goddaughter*
el ahijado — *godson*
la esposa/mujer — *wife*
el esposo/marido — *husband*
la madrina — *godmother*
la novia — *fiancée, girlfriend*
el novio — *fiancé, boyfriend*
el padrino — *godfather*

## las vacaciones — *vacation*

la ciudad — *city*
el dinero — *money*
el lugar — *place*
el problema — *problem*
el viaje — *trip*

## personas

el bebé — *baby*
la estrella — *star*
el genio — *genius*
el millonario — *millionaire*
el niño/la niña — *child*

## bebidas

el agua[4] — *water*

## las publicaciones

el artículo — *article*
el periódico — *newspaper*
la revista — *magazine*

## conceptos

la imaginación — *imagination*
la mentira — *lie*
la verdad — *truth*

## descripciones

enorme — *enormous*
maravilloso — *marvelous*

## verbos

almorzar (ue) — *to have lunch*
contar (ue) — *to count*
costar (ue) — *to cost*
cuidar — *to take care of*
dejar — *to leave*
dormir (ue) — *to sleep*
empezar (ie) — *to begin, start*
jugar (ue) — *to play (game, sport)*
pasar — *to spend*
pensar (ie) — *to think*
   pensar + *inf.* — *to plan to + verb*
perder (ie) — *to lose*
poder (ue) — *to be able to, can*
preferir (ie) — *to prefer*
querer (ie) — *to want, to love*
tener (g, ie) — *to have*
venir (g, ie) — *to come*
visitar — *to visit*
volver (ue) — *to return*

## expresiones

estar equivocado/a — *to be wrong*
tener... años — *to be . . . years old*
tener ganas de + *inf.* — *to feel like + pres. part.*
tener que + *inf.* — *to have to + verb*

## posesión

mi, mis — *my*
tu, tus — *your*
su, sus — *his, her, your, its, their*
nuestro(s), nuestra(s) — *our*

## palabras útiles

muchos — *many*
según — *according to*

---

[4] Although **agua** is feminine, it uses **el** and not **la** in the singular whenever the article is required. This happens when an article directly precedes a singular feminine noun beginning with stressed **a** or **ha: el agua, el hambre.**

# La casa de la familia Estévez

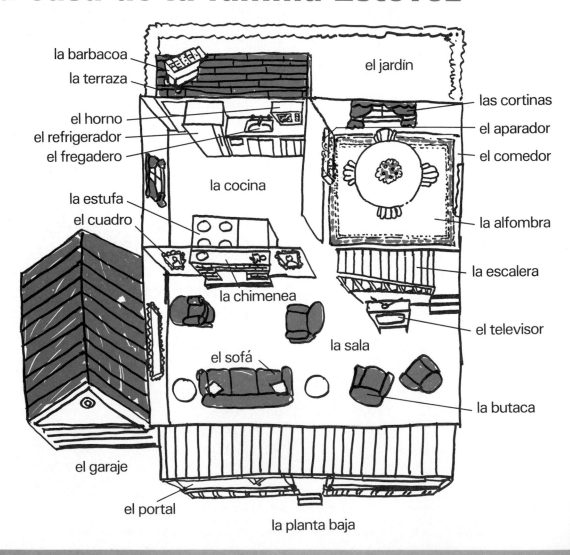

la barbacoa
la terraza
el jardín
las cortinas
el horno
el refrigerador
el fregadero
el aparador
el comedor
la cocina
la estufa
el cuadro
la alfombra
la chimenea
la escalera
la sala
el televisor
el sofá
la butaca
el garaje
el portal
la planta baja

# Lección 5
# La casa y los muebles

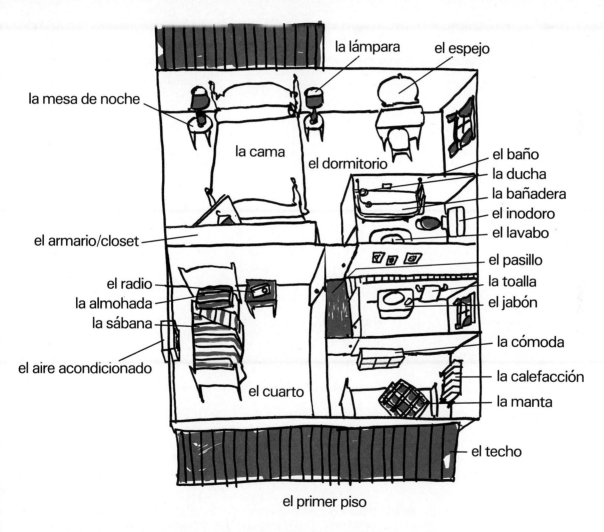

la lámpara

el espejo

la mesa de noche

la cama

el dormitorio

el baño
la ducha
la bañadera
el inodoro
el lavabo

el armario/closet

el pasillo

el radio
la almohada
la sábana

la toalla
el jabón

el aire acondicionado

la cómoda

la calefacción
la manta

el cuarto

el techo

el primer piso

La casa de los Estévez está en las afueras° de la ciudad. Está lejos° del centro, *outskirts / far*
pero cerca° de los padres de la Sra. de Estévez. Ellos no alquilan° la casa; la *near / rent*
casa es de ellos.

| electrodomésticos | electrical appliances |
|---|---|
| la batidora | mixer |
| la lavadora | washing machine |
| el lavaplatos | dishwasher |
| la licuadora | blender |
| el (horno) microondas | microwave |
| la plancha | iron |
| la secadora | drier |

## ACTIVIDADES

**A** **¿Dónde?** Asocie las siguientes actividades con las partes de la casa donde normalmente tienen lugar.

1. dormir
2. ver televisión
3. dejar el auto
4. preparar la comida
5. correr y jugar
6. almorzar

a. sala
b. comedor
c. cocina
d. garaje
e. cuarto
f. jardín

**B** ¿En qué parte de su casa están generalmente estos objetos y muebles?

1. la estufa
2. la barbacoa
3. el sofá y las butacas
4. la licuadora
5. la mesa de noche
6. el jabón y las toallas
7. el aparador
8. la cómoda
9. las almohadas y las sábanas

a. la cocina
b. el baño
c. la sala
d. el dormitorio
e. el comedor
f. la terraza

**C** Usted es una persona muy curiosa y quiere saber cómo es la casa o apartamento de su compañero/a. Hágale las siguientes preguntas. Después él/ella va a hacerle las preguntas a usted.

1. ¿Vives en una casa, un apartamento o un condominio?   2. ¿Está cerca o lejos de la universidad?   3. ¿Es grande?   4. ¿Cuántos cuartos tiene?   5. ¿Tiene aire acondicionado y calefacción?   6. ¿Qué muebles tienes en la sala?   7. ¿Y en tu cuarto?   8. ¿Qué electrodomésticos hay en la cocina?

# Cultura

## Housing in the Hispanic world

Although the architectural style of houses varies somewhat from one Hispanic country to the next, houses are built to last a long time. Homes in urban areas are generally constructed of bricks or blocks; thus it is not unusual, especially in Spain, to find examples of those that have been inhabited for the last two or even three centuries.

A comparison of Hispanic and American homes shows that Hispanic homes tend to be smaller and closer together, but spacious homes can be found in affluent neighborhoods. A characteristic feature of middle-class homes and apartments, especially in Latin America, is the living quarters for domestic help. A fence or wall usually surrounds the property of the house, and wrought-iron grillwork covers the windows. Central air conditioning or heating is not common. Homes tend to lack many modern conveniences, but the current trend is to modernize the kitchen area by equipping it with electrical appliances.

The contrast in economic conditions between an average American family and a Hispanic one accounts for a lower percentage of home owners in the Hispanic world. The upper and middle classes in most Hispanic countries enjoy the privilege of owning a home. Because of the small proportion of upper and middle classes, however, much of the population does not have that privilege. Banks also present obstacles to the potential homeowner. They do not offer thirty-year mortgage loans as in the United States. Due to unstable economic conditions, the typical loan period is no more than ten years, resulting in very high monthly payments.

Since it is difficult for families or individuals to buy a house or apartment, most have to rent. Many people want housing that is close to the downtown area, where they can take advantage of public transportation, convenient shopping areas, and proximity to the workplace.

La casa Batló en Barcelona, España, es una de las construcciones más conocidas del gran arquitecto catalán Antonio Gaudí (1852–1926).

# EN CONTEXTO

## A la hora de la cena

Irma y Augusto son un matrimonio° joven. Los dos trabajan fuera y en la casa comparten las tareas domésticas°.

*(married) couple*
*tareas… house chores*

| | | |
|---|---|---|
| **Augusto** | Ya son casi° las siete. ¿Pongo° la mesa? | *almost / Shall I set* |
| **Irma** | Sí, por favor. Tengo que hacer° dos o tres cosas° en la cocina. | *do/ things* |
| **Augusto** | Bueno, pero es temprano°. | *early* |
| **Irma** | Sí, pero si comemos tarde° no salgo° de la cocina hasta las nueve. | *late / leave* |
| **Augusto** | Irma, no salimos de la cocina, porque yo sí ayudo°. | *I do help* |
| **Irma** | Es verdad. Por cierto°, ¿puedes sacar la basura°? | *By the way/ garbage* |

## Preguntas

1. ¿Trabaja Irma fuera de la casa?
2. ¿Ayuda Augusto en las tareas domésticas?
3. ¿Va a poner Irma la mesa?
4. ¿Dónde va a trabajar Irma?
5. ¿Es tarde o temprano?
6. ¿Por qué quiere comer temprano Irma?
7. ¿Quién va a sacar la basura?
8. Y usted, ¿trabaja mucho en su casa?

Los grandes edificios modernos de Caracas, la capital de Venezuela, contrastan con las casas de los barrios pobres de la ciudad.

Unas amigas conversan
mientras lavan y secan los
platos en un apartamento en
Madrid.

### otras tareas domésticas

| | |
|---|---|
| barrer | *to sweep* |
| limpiar | *to clean* |
| pasar la aspiradora | *to vacuum* |
| sacudir | *to dust* |
| preparar la comida/cocinar | *to cook* |
| lavar/secar los platos | *to wash/to dry the dishes* |
| colgar(ue)/doblar la ropa | *to hang/to fold the clothes* |
| planchar | *to iron* |
| tender (ie)/hacer la cama | *to make the bed* |

## ACTIVIDADES

**A** Usted tiene que trabajar mucho en su casa hoy. ¿En qué orden va a hacer usted las siguientes tareas domésticas?

____ cocinar la cena      ____ preparar el desayuno
____ tender la cama      ____ planchar la ropa
____ pasar la aspiradora      ____ lavar la ropa

**B** Pregúntele a su compañero/a qué tareas domésticas hacen las siguientes personas en su casa. Comparta esta información con el resto de la clase.

papá     mamá     hermano     hermana     tú

## GRAMÁTICA

### Present tense of *hacer, poner,* and *salir*

> **hacer:** **hago,** haces, hace, hacemos, hacéis, hacen
> **poner:** **pongo,** pones, pone, ponemos, ponéis, ponen
> **salir:** **salgo,** sales, sale, salimos, salís, salen

1. The **yo** form of these verbs is irregular; the other forms are regular.
2. **Poner** normally means *to put.* With electrical appliances, **poner** means *to turn on.*

   Ella va a **poner** los platos en el fregadero.     *She's going to put the plates in the sink.*
   Yo **pongo** la televisión por la tarde.     *I turn on the TV in the afternoon.*

3. **Salir** can be used with several different prepositions.

   **a.** To state that you are leaving a place, use **salir de.**

   **Yo salgo de mi cuarto ahora.**     *I'm leaving my room now.*

   **b.** To state your destination, use **salir para.**

   **Salgo para tu casa.**     *I'm leaving for your house.*

   **c.** To state with whom you go out or the person you date, use **salir con.**

   Ella **sale con** Mauricio.     *She goes out with Mauricio.*

## ACTIVIDADES

**A** **¿Cuándo salen?** El curso termina el viernes. Sus compañeros y usted van a salir a horas diferentes. Diga a qué hora salen.

> *Modelo*   Juan / 8 A.M.
> **Juan sale a las ocho de la mañana.**

See IM, **Lección 5,** for suggestions.

1. Alicia / 9 A.M.
2. Pedro y Julio / 11:00 A.M.
3. mi amigo Luis / 3:00 P.M.
4. tú / 2:30 P.M.
5. yo / 1:00 P.M.
6. Mirta y Elda / 10:00 A.M.

**B** **¿Qué haces en la clase de español?** Su compañero/a le va a decir las cosas que su hermano hace en la clase de español. Conteste diciendo si usted hace esas cosas o no.

> *Modelo*   Mi hermano tiene la clase por la mañana. ¿Y tú?
> **Yo tengo la clase por la tarde** o **Yo también tengo la clase por la mañana.**

1. Él hace la tarea por la noche. ¿Y tú?
2. Llega a la clase a las nueve. ¿Y tú?
3. Pone la tarea sobre el escritorio del profesor. ¿Y tú?
4. Habla español en la clase. ¿Y tú?
5. Sale de la clase a las diez. ¿Y tú?

**C** Diga dónde ponen las personas de la columna A las cosas de la columna B. Los lugares están en la columna C.

*Modelo* **Compañero/a** mi mamá / las toallas / el baño
**Usted** **Mi mamá pone las toallas en el baño.**

| A | B | C |
|---|---|---|
| mi mamá | las sillas | la cocina |
| mi papá | la lámpara | el armario |
| mis hermanos | la batidora | el dormitorio |
| mi hermano y yo | el jabón | el pasillo |
| yo | el televisor | el garaje |
|  | el gato y el perro | el comedor |
|  | la barbacoa | la terraza |
|  | el auto | el jardín |
|  | la plancha | el baño |
|  | los platos | la sala |

**D** Complete el siguiente párrafo de acuerdo con el dibujo usando la forma correcta de **salir + de, para** o **con**.

1. Javier y Marcelo son hermanos. Ellos ___ ___ su casa. ___ ___ el cine. Javier siempre ___ ___ Marcelo los domingos por la tarde.

Ahora complete el siguiente párrafo de acuerdo con sus actividades.

2. Yo ___ ___ casa a las ___ de la mañana. ___ ___ la universidad. Llego a la universidad a las ___. Las clases terminan a las ___. A esa hora yo ___ ___ casa. Por las noches ___ ___ mi novio/a.

**E** **Entrevista.** Usted quiere saber qué hace su compañero/a en su tiempo libre. Hágale las siguientes preguntas.

1. ¿A qué hora sales de la universidad?   2. ¿Sales para tu casa o para el trabajo?   3. ¿Qué haces cuando llegas a tu casa?   4. ¿Pones la televisión por las noches?   5. ¿Qué programa prefieres?   6. ¿Cuándo limpias la casa?   7. ¿Con quién sales los fines de semana? 8. ¿Adónde van?

# EN CONTEXTO

## ¿Qué hacen estas personas?

Juan lava **el auto.**
↓
Juan **lo** lava.

Alicia saca **la basura.**
↓
Alicia **la** saca.

Alfonso lava **los platos.**
↓
Alfonso **los** lava.

Ana tiende **las camas.**
↓
Ana **las** tiende.

Ella ayuda **al niño.**
↓
Ella **lo** ayuda.

Ramón ayuda **a las niñas.**
↓
Ramón **las** ayuda.

## GRAMÁTICA

### Direct object nouns and pronouns; the personal *a*

**1.** A direct object is a noun or pronoun that receives the action of the verb. In Spanish direct object nouns follow the verb. When direct object nouns refer to a specific person or group of

Vista de la Alhambra, residencia de los reyes árabes en Granada, España. Según muchos, la Alhambra es el palacio árabe más bello (*beautiful*) del mundo.

persons, or to a pet, the word **a** must precede them. This is called the personal **a** and has no equivalent in English.

| | |
|---|---|
| Amanda seca **los platos.** | *Amanda dries the dishes.* |
| Amanda seca **a la niña.** | *Amanda dries the girl.* |

2. Since the question word **quién(es)** refers to people, use the personal **a** when **quién(es)** is used as a direct object.

—¿**A quién** vas a ver? —Voy a ver a Pedro.

3. Direct object pronouns may refer to people, animals or things.

| | | |
|---|---|---|
| me | *me* | |
| te | *you* | *(familiar, singular)* |
| lo | *you* | *(formal, singular), him, it (masculine)* |
| la | *you* | *(formal, singular), her, it (feminine)* |
| nos | *us* | |
| os | *you* | *(familiar, plural)* |
| los | *you* | *(formal & familiar, plural), them (masculine)* |
| las | *you* | *(formal & familiar, plural), them (feminine)* |

**4.** To avoid repetition use direct object pronouns when the direct object noun has already been mentioned. Place the direct object pronoun before the conjugated verb form and after the word **no** when it appears.

—¿Quieres mucho **a tu perro**? —Sí, **lo** quiero mucho.
—¿Magdalena prepara **la comida**? —No, **no la** prepara.

**5.** When there are both a conjugated verb form and an infinitive, a direct object pronoun can be placed before the conjugated verb form or be attached to the dependent infinitive.

—¿Vas a visitar a **Rafael**? —Sí, **lo** voy a visitar.
　　　　　　　　　　　　 —Sí, voy a visitar**lo**.

## ACTIVIDADES

**A** Conteste las siguientes preguntas sobre sus responsabilidades en la casa. Use pronombres en sus respuestas.

*Modelo*　　¿Sacas la basura?
　　　　　　**Sí, la saco** o **No, no la saco.**

1. ¿Limpias tu cuarto?　2. ¿Limpias la cocina? ¿y el garaje?　3. ¿Lavas los platos?
4. ¿Secas los platos?　5. ¿Lavas la ropa?　6. ¿Cuelgas la ropa o secas la ropa en la secadora?

**B** Conteste las siguientes preguntas sobre las actividades de sus compañeros en la clase. Use pronombres en sus respuestas.

*Modelo*　　¿Hablan español en la clase?
　　　　　　**Sí, lo hablan.**

1. ¿Contestan las preguntas?　2. ¿Leen revistas?　3. ¿Hacen la tarea?　4. ¿Escriben los diálogos?　5. ¿Estudian el vocabulario?

**C** Su hermanita le hace las siguientes preguntas. Conteste usando pronombres.

*Modelo*　　¿Me ayudas ahora?
　　　　　　**Sí, te ayudo ahora** o **No, no te ayudo ahora.**

1. ¿Me quieres?　2. ¿Me vas a cuidar este fin de semana?
3. ¿Me extrañas (*miss me*) cuando no estoy aquí?

**D** Complete el siguiente diálogo con su compañero/a.

|  |  |
|---|---|
| **Usted** | ¿Dónde haces la tarea? |
| **Compañero/a** | . . . |
| **Usted** | ¿Cuándo la haces? |
| **Compañero/a** | . . . |
| **Usted** | ¿Quién te ayuda con la tarea? |
| **Compañero/a** | . . . |

**E** Dígale a su compañero/a lo que usted va a hacer en su cuarto esta tarde. Él/Ella debe decir si lo va a hacer también o no.

> *Modelo* limpiar mi cuarto
> **Usted** Voy a limpiar mi cuarto.
> **Compañero/a** Yo lo voy a limpiar (voy a limpiarlo) también o Yo no lo voy a limpiar (no voy a limpiarlo).

sacudir los muebles     pasar la aspiradora     tender la cama     doblar la ropa
colgar la ropa

**F** **Entrevista.** Pregúntele a su compañero/a sobre sus relaciones con otras personas.

1. ¿Quién te comprende en tu casa?
2. ¿Quién te quiere?
3. ¿Quién te llama por teléfono?
4. ¿A quién ayudas tú?
5. ¿A quién saludas en la clase?
6. ¿A quién(es) quieres mucho?
7. ¿A quién(es) quieres un poco?

# EN CONTEXTO

## Las actividades de Rafael

### *Por la mañana*

Rafael se despierta.

Se levanta.

Se lava los dientes.

Se afeita.

Se baña.

Se seca.

Se peina.

## Por la noche

Rafael se sienta a ver la tele.

Se quita la ropa y
los zapatos.

Se pone la piyama.

Se acuesta.

Se duerme.

### Preguntas

1. ¿A qué hora se despierta Rafael?
2. ¿Dónde duerme Rafael?
3. ¿A qué hora se levanta?
4. ¿Dónde se afeita?
5. ¿Con qué se seca Rafael?
6. ¿Dónde se peina?
7. Por la noche, ¿se sienta a ver la tele en la cocina?
8. ¿Qué ropa se pone Rafael para dormir?
9. ¿Dónde se acuesta Rafael?
10. ¿A qué hora se duerme?

## ACTIVIDADES

**A** ¿Cuál es la expresión opuesta?

1. se despierta
2. se levanta
3. se quita la ropa
4. se lava

    a. se pone la ropa
    b. se acuesta
    c. se seca
    d. se duerme

**B** Su profesor/a va a hablar sobre sus actividades, cuándo las hace, etc. Conteste diciendo lo que usted hace.

*Modelo*  Yo me despierto a las siete.
  **Y yo (me despierto) a las ocho.**

1. Yo me levanto a las siete y media.  2. Yo me lavo los dientes.  3. Yo me baño por la tarde.  4. Yo desayuno muy poco por las mañanas.  5. Yo llego a la universidad a las nueve.  6. Yo salgo a las cuatro.  7. Yo me acuesto a las once.  8. Yo me duermo a las doce más o menos.

## GRAMÁTICA

### Reflexive verbs and pronouns

| | | |
|---|---|---|
| yo | me lavo | *I wash myself* |
| tú | te lavas | *you wash yourself* |
| usted | se lava | *you wash yourself* |
| él | se lava | *he washes himself* |
| ella | se lava | *she washes herself* |
| nosotros/as | nos lavamos | *we wash ourselves* |
| vosotros/as | os laváis | *you wash yourselves* |
| ustedes | se lavan | *you wash yourselves* |
| ellos/ellas | se lavan | *they wash themselves* |

**1.** Spanish uses reflexive pronouns and verbs to express what people do to or for themselves, that is, the subject does the action and the action is reflected back to the subject.

*Non–reflexive*
Margarita acuesta a su hijo. (Margarita is the doer; the son is the receiver.)

*Reflexive*
Margarita **se acuesta.** (Margarita is both the doer and the receiver.)

**2.** A reflexive pronoun refers to the same person as the subject. In English this is expressed by pronouns ending in *-self* or *-selves* (e.g., *myself, themselves*). Spanish uses reflexives in many cases where English does not (e.g., afeitarse, *to shave*).

**3.** Place reflexive pronouns before the conjugated verb and after the word **no** when it is used. Reflexive pronouns may precede the conjugated verb or be attached to the infinitive.

Yo (no) **me** voy a acostar a las diez.
Yo (no) voy a acostar**me** a las diez.

4. When referring to parts of the body and articles of clothing, use definite articles, and not possessives, with reflexive verbs.

   Me lavo **los** dientes.    Me pongo **la** ropa.

5. The pronoun **se** attached to the end of an infinitive shows that the verb is reflexive.

   lavar *to wash*    lavarse *to wash oneself*

6. Some verbs change meaning when used reflexively.

| | | | |
|---|---|---|---|
| acostar | *to put to bed* | acostarse | *to go to bed, to lie down* |
| dormir | *to sleep* | dormirse | *to fall asleep* |
| ir | *to go* | irse | *to go away, to leave* |
| levantar | *to raise, to lift* | levantarse | *to get up* |
| llamar | *to call* | llamarse | *to be called* |
| quitar | *to take away* | quitarse | *to take off* |

## ACTIVIDADES

**A** Usted y su hermano tienen diferentes horarios. Diga las cosas que ustedes hacen y a qué hora las hacen.

*Modelo*    despertarse    mi hermano    yo
                              8:00            7:00
**Mi hermano se despierta a las ocho.**
**Yo me despierto a las siete.**

| | mi hermano | yo |
|---|---|---|
| levantarse | 8:15 | 7:05 |
| afeitarse | 8:20 | 7:10 |
| bañarse | 8:30 | 7:15 |
| peinarse | 8:45 | 7:20 |

**B** Describa las actividades de la familia Menéndez los lunes por la mañana.

*Modelo*    la mamá / levantarse / 6:30
            **La mamá se levanta a las seis y media.**

1. el papá / despertarse / 6:30
2. la mamá / peinarse
3. el papá / afeitarse / bañarse
4. el papá / despertar a los niños
5. los niños / lavarse los dientes
6. la mamá / preparar el desayuno
7. los niños / ponerse los zapatos
8. la familia / desayunar en el comedor

Una señora y su hija miran televisión en Bogotá, Colombia. La televisión, igual que en los Estados Unidos, es parte de la vida diaria en los países hispanos.

**C** Usted quiere saber cuánto tiempo necesita su compañero/a para hacer ciertas cosas. Hágale las siguientes preguntas. Después usted debe decir el tiempo que usted necesita.

*Modelo*    **Usted   ¿Cuánto tiempo necesitas para lavarte?**
          **Compañero/a   Necesito diez minutos para lavarme.**
          **Usted   Y yo necesito quince minutos.**

1. ¿Cuánto tiempo necesitas para bañarte?   2. ¿Y para afeitarte (o maquillarte *to put on makeup*)?   3. ¿Y para peinarte?

**D** Usted y su mejor amigo/a están de vacaciones en Madrid. Diga las cosas que van a hacer mañana.

*Modelo*   levantarse a las ocho
         **Nos vamos a levantar a las ocho** o **Vamos a levantarnos a las ocho.**

bañarse    ponerse zapatos cómodos    desayunar en un café    visitar el Museo del Prado
almorzar en un restaurante típico    ir al teatro    cenar con unos amigos
acostarse a la una

**E** Lea la siguiente selección sobre un día típico de Marcela Gracia. Después su compañero/a y usted van a hablar de las actividades de Marcela usando la tabla que sigue.

*Modelo* | nombre | Se llama Marcela Gracia. |

Me llamo Marcela Gracia y vivo en Caracas. Soy locutora de televisión (*TV announcer*) y siempre estoy muy ocupada.

Me despierto a las 6:00 y hago ejercicio (*exercise*). A las 6:30 me baño, me peino, me maquillo (*put on makeup*) y luego desayuno. Me voy al trabajo a las 7:30.

Empiezo a trabajar a las 8:00. Tengo una reunión con mi jefe a las 9:30. Después hago muchas llamadas por teléfono entre 10:00 y 11:30. A veces tengo que salir para hablar con otras personas. Almuerzo a la 1:00 y vuelvo a los estudios a las 2:30. A esa hora me lavo los dientes, me peino y me maquillo otra vez. Mi programa empieza a las 3:30 y tengo que estar lista a las 3:15.

| ¿dónde vive? | |
| --- | --- |
| profesión | |
| 6:00 a 6:30 | |
| 6:30 a 7:30 | |
| 8:00 | |
| 9:30 | |
| 10:00 a 11:30 | |
| 1:00 a 2:30 | |
| 2:30 a 3:15 | |
| 3:30 | |

**F** Dígale a su compañero/a todo lo que usted hace desde (*since*) que se despierta hasta que llega a la universidad. Después su compañero/a va a decirle a usted todo lo que hace los sábados por la mañana.

# PRONUNCIACIÓN

## Stress and the written accent mark (*continuation*)

**1.** Words that are stressed on the next to the last syllable

    **a.** do not have a written accent mark if they end in **n, s,** or a vowel.

       examen    casas    padre    hermana    sobrino

    **b.** have an accent mark if they end in any other letter.

       lápiz    útil    débil    mártir    Félix

**2.** Words that are stressed on the last syllable

  **a.** have a written accent mark if they end in **n, s,** or a vowel.

    está**n**    está**s**    est**á**    in**glés**    ale**mán**

    Those that end in **n** or **s** do not require an accent mark in the plural form since they then stress the next to the last syllable.

    japo**nés** ⟶ **japone**se**s**    ale**mán** ⟶ ale**ma**ne**s**

  **b.** do not have a written accent mark if they end in any other letter

    ha**blar**    ver**dad**    espa**ñol**    fe**liz**    borra**dor**

Para una reunión en Bogotá, Colombia, unos amigos preparan parte de la comida mientras un niño los ayuda. Hoy en día los hombres hispanos están participando un poco más en las tareas domésticas.

A la hora del almuerzo en casa de una familia en Bogotá, Colombia.

## LECTURA

### Buscando apartamento

You are in Madrid looking for an apartment and you read the following ads in a newspaper. Choose one apartment telling why you prefer it. You may need the following words to better understand the ads.

| | |
|---|---|
| lujo | *luxury* |
| vistas | *views* |
| Retiro | *a famous park in Madrid* |
| calidad | *quality* |
| entrega | *occupancy* |
| propio | *same* |
| c/ | *abbreviation for* calle |
| desde | *from* |
| pts. | *abbreviation for* pesetas |
| piscina | *swimming pool* |
| entrada | *down payment* |
| obra | *construction (site)* |
| millón | *million* |

Pisos de Lujo de 1 y 2 dormitorios. Junto Arturo Soria-López de Hoyos.

COMUNIDADES PARQUECONDE c/ Carril del Conde

desde 5.590.000 pts. piscina, tenis, zonas ajardinadas.

Infórmese en: Propia obra, y Oficina principal: c/ Aranjuez, 25-Tel. 233 79 76

Para vivir en comunidad VYCSA

APARTAMENTOS C/. Echegaray, 22

13 Apartamentos de lujo Totalmente exteriores 1.000.000 pts. de entrada Resto 10 años

GAVIAR

C/ Velázquez, 100. Tel. 276 20 00-09. Madrid

CALLE SERRANO, N.º 5 APARTAMENTOS DE LUJO

- Apartamentos de dos dormitorios.
- Dos cuartos de baño.
- Vistas al Retiro.
- Edificio señorial remodelado.
- Calidades de primer orden.
- Próxima entrega.

INFORMACION:

En el propio edificio, de lunes a sábado, de 11 a 14 horas y de 17 a 20 horas

### Bueno, bonito y barato°    *inexpensive*

El edificio de apartamentos donde viven Rafael Sotomayor y su mujer Juana es bastante nuevo, con un pequeño jardín y garaje para los autos de los inquilinos°.    *tenants*
Está en Insurgentes Sur, una zona o colonia de la ciudad de México. El apartamento de los Sotomayor es cómodo y bonito, pero pequeño. El problema principal es que no está cerca del metro° y Rafael tiene que manejar° casi una    *subway / to drive*
hora todos los días para ir a su trabajo. Además, Juana va a empezar a trabajar en una oficina del centro el mes próximo y ellos prefieren alquilar un apartamento cerca de esta zona y así poder usar el metro para ir al trabajo.
   Todos los días los Sotomayor leen el periódico para ver si encuentran° un    *find*

buen apartamento. Según Rafael, ellos buscan las tres «bes»: bueno, bonito y barato. Esto no es fácil° porque en las zonas que ellos prefieren los alquileres son bastante altos.

*easy*

Hoy Juana va a ir a ver un apartamento en la colonia Irrigación, que está relativamente cerca del centro. Muchos de los edificios de esa colonia son más viejos que en otras zonas, pero los apartamentos son más grandes. Un problema es que generalmente no tienen garaje y en esa zona es difícil conseguir° uno.

*get*

### Preguntas

1. ¿Cómo es el edificio de apartamentos de los Sotomayor?
2. ¿Dónde está?
3. ¿Cómo es el apartamento donde viven?
4. ¿Por qué quieren mudarse?
5. ¿Dónde va a empezar a trabajar Juana?
6. ¿Dónde quieren vivir los Sotomayor?
7. ¿Cómo es el apartamento que ellos quieren?
8. ¿Adónde va a ir Juana hoy?
9. ¿Cómo son los apartamentos de esta colonia?
10. ¿Qué problema pueden tener los Sotomayor en esa zona?

### La división del trabajo en la casa

The following selection was taken from *Telva,* a very popular Spanish magazine, showing with percentages the division of household chores among men and women in Spain. You may need the following vocabulary to better understand the selection.

| | | |
|---|---|---|
| | tiende | = cuelga |
| coser  *to sew* | alimentos | = comida |
| | fregar | = lavar platos |

### Preguntas

1. ¿Quiénes trabajan más, los hombres o las mujeres?
2. ¿Qué porcentaje de mujeres cocina siempre?
3. ¿Qué porcentaje de hombres plancha o cose la ropa?
4. ¿Cree usted que estos porcentajes son más o menos como los porcentajes en los Estados Unidos?

**Encuesta.** ¿Qué porcentaje de las siguientes tareas domésticas cree usted que hace el hombre en este país: cocinar, lavar los platos, planchar, pasar la aspiradora, coser? Compare sus porcentajes con los de sus compañeros/as.

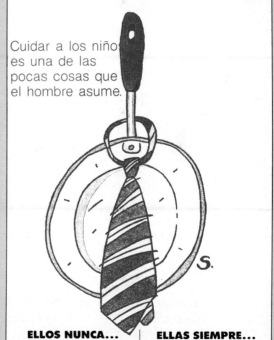

Cuidar a los niños es una de las pocas cosas que el hombre asume.

**ELLOS NUNCA...**

El 95 por ciento de los hombres **NUNCA** plancha ni cose un botón; el 85 por ciento **NUNCA** pone la lavadora ni tiende a secar la ropa; el 82 por ciento **NUNCA** pasa el aspirador; el 74 por ciento **NUNCA** se hace la cama y el 70 por ciento **NUNCA** cocina en casa y el 71 por ciento de ellos **NUNCA** se ocupa de comprar los alimentos.

**ELLAS SIEMPRE...**

El 81 por ciento de las mujeres españolas **SIEMPRE** prepara la comida; el 80 por ciento **SIEMPRE** cose toda la ropa de su casa; el 82 por ciento **SIEMPRE** plancha las prendas de su familia; el 75 por ciento **SIEMPRE** friega o pone el lavaplatos y el 70 por ciento de ellas **SIEMPRE** hacen la compra semanal o diaria.

## SITUACIONES

1. You want to sell your house/apartment. Explain to a real-estate agent what it is like.

2. You are talking to a prospective roommate. Tell him/her what he/she can and cannot do or have.

3. You are looking for an apartment to rent. You saw one that you like. Explain to a friend that the apartment (a) is near the university, (b) is on the ground floor, (c) has a big kitchen, (d) doesn't have a dining room, and (e) has a garage. He/She will ask you how much it is, and you will answer the question.

4. Ask your partner (a) what time he/she gets up on weekdays (**entre semana**), (b) what he/she has for breakfast, (c) what time he/she leaves for school, (d) what time he/she returns, and (e) what time he/she goes to bed.

5. You are at a furniture store. Your partner will play the part of the salesperson. Tell him/her that (a) you are looking for a desk and chair for your room, (b) the chair has to be big and comfortable, and (c) you don't want to spend (**gastar**) much money. The salesperson should tell you about the desks and chairs they have. Say that you want to see them.

6. You visited the home of a famous actor/actress. Tell your partner whose house it was and describe it.

# VOCABULARIO[1]

**en una casa**

| | | | |
|---|---|---|---|
| el aire acondicionado | *air conditioning* | el techo | *roof* |
| el armario/closet | *closet* | la terraza | *terrace* |
| el baño | *bathroom* | | |
| la calefacción | *heating* | **muebles y** | **furniture and** |
| la cocina | *kitchen* | **accesorios** | **accessories** |
| el comedor | *dining room* | la alfombra | *carpet, rug* |
| el cuarto/dormitorio | *bedroom* | el aparador | *china cabinet* |
| la chimenea | *fireplace* | la butaca | *armchair* |
| la escalera | *stairs* | la cama | *bed* |
| el garaje | *garage* | la cómoda | *dresser* |
| el pasillo | *hall* | la cortina | *curtain* |
| el piso | *floor* | el cuadro | *picture* |
| la planta baja | *first floor* | el espejo | *mirror* |
| el portal | *porch* | la lámpara | *lamp* |
| la sala | *living room* | la mesa de noche | *night stand* |
| | | el sofá | *sofa* |

---

[1] See pages 130–132 and 135–136 for direct object and reflexive pronouns.

| **electrodomésticos** | *electrical appliances* |
|---|---|
| la aspiradora | *vacuum cleaner* |
| la batidora | *mixer* |
| la lavadora | *washing machine* |
| el lavaplatos | *dishwasher* |
| la licuadora | *blender* |
| el (horno) microondas | *microwave oven* |
| la plancha | *iron* |
| el/la radio | *radio* |
| el refrigerador | *refrigerator* |
| la secadora | *drier* |
| el televisor | *TV set* |

**para la cama**

| la almohada | *pillow* |
|---|---|
| la manta | *blanket* |
| la sábana | *sheet* |

**en el baño**

| la bañadera | *tub* |
|---|---|
| la ducha | *shower* |
| el inodoro | *toilet* |
| el jabón | *soap* |
| el lavabo | *washbowl* |
| la toalla | *towel* |

**en la cocina**

| la estufa | *stove* |
|---|---|
| el fregadero | *sink* |
| el plato | *dish, plate* |

| **en el jardín** | *yard, garden* |
|---|---|
| la barbacoa | *barbecue* |
| la basura | *garbage* |

**personas**

| el matrimonio | *(married) couple* |
|---|---|

| **el cuerpo** | *body* |
|---|---|
| los dientes | *teeth* |

| **la ropa** | *clothes* |
|---|---|
| el/la piyama | *pajamas* |
| los zapatos | *shoes* |

**verbos**

| acostar (ue) | *to put to bed* |
|---|---|
| acostarse | *to go to bed, to lie down* |

| afeitar | *to shave* |
|---|---|
| alquilar | *to rent* |
| ayudar | *to help* |
| bañar | *to bathe* |
| barrer | *to sweep* |
| cocinar | *to cook* |
| colgar (ue) | *to hang* |
| compartir | *to share* |
| despertar (ie) | *to wake up* |
| doblar | *to fold* |
| dormirse (ue) | *to fall asleep* |
| hacer | *to do, to make* |
| irse | *to go away, to leave* |
| lavar | *to wash* |
| levantar | *to raise* |
| levantarse | *to get up* |
| limpiar | *to clean* |
| pasar la aspiradora | *to vacuum* |
| peinar | *to comb* |
| planchar | *to iron* |
| poner | *to put, to turn on* |
| preparar | *to prepare* |
| quitar | *to take away, to remove* |
| quitarse | *to take off* |
| sacudir | *to dust* |
| salir | *to go out, to leave* |
| secar | *to dry* |
| sentarse (ie) | *to sit down* |
| tender (ie) la cama | *to make the bed* |

**lugares**

| las afueras | *outskirts* |
|---|---|
| el centro | *downtown, center* |
| cerca (de) | *near* |
| fuera | *outside* |
| lejos (de) | *far* |

**tiempo**

| tarde | *late* |
|---|---|
| temprano | *early* |

**palabras útiles**

| casi | *almost, hardly* |
|---|---|
| la cosa | *thing* |

**expresiones útiles**

| por cierto | *by the way* |
|---|---|
| las tareas domésticas | *house chores* |

**In** Lección 6 **you will**
a. ask and answer questions concerning weather conditions.
b. express/describe physical abilities.
c. express on-going actions.
d. use numbers from 1,000 to 2,000,000.
e. express sequence and order.
f. express dates.

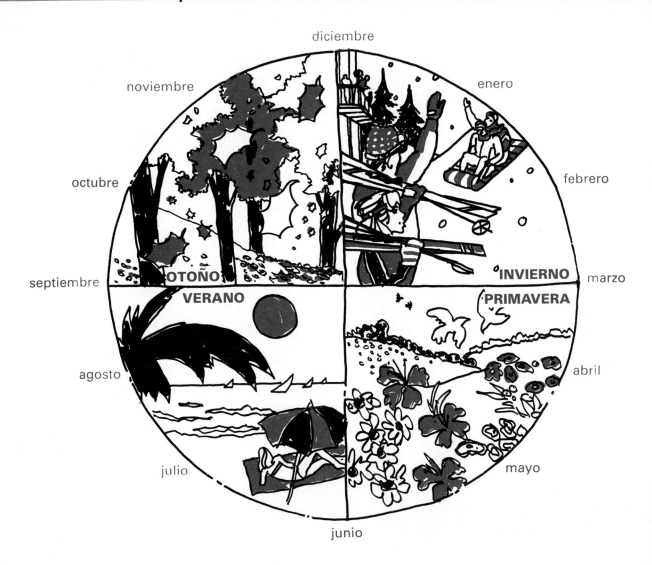

# Lección 6

# Los deportes

## Las estaciones y los meses del año

Paco juega (al) fútbol con sus amigos.

Alicia esquía cuando hay mucha nieve.

Alicia monta (en) bicicleta y Paco patina.

Paco nada en la piscina.

Unas personas esperan el autobús en San Sebastián, un famoso lugar de veraneo en la costa norte de España. Esta zona del norte de España es un lugar de mucha lluvia.

### el tiempo

| ¿Qué tiempo hace? | *How's the weather?* |
|---|---|

Hace { buen / mal } tiempo.  The weather is { *fine.* / *bad.* }

Hace (mucho) { frío. / calor. / fresco. / viento. / sol. }  It's (*very*) { *cold.* / *hot.* / *cool.* / *windy.* / *sunny.* }

Está (muy) { claro/despejado. / nublado/nuboso. }  It's (*very*) { *clear.* / *cloudy.* }

**Nieva. / Está nevando.** }  *It's snowing.*
**Llueve. / Esta lloviendo.** }  *It's raining.*

1. Use the verb **hacer** to ask about and to express weather conditions. With the adjectives **claro/despejado** and **nublado/nuboso,** use **estar.**
2. To express *very,* use **mucho** with **hace** and **muy** with **está.**

   Hace **mucho** frío y está **muy** nublado.

3. Hispanic countries use the Centigrade system to measure temperature. The thermometer below shows both the Centigrade and Fahrenheit systems so you can compare them.

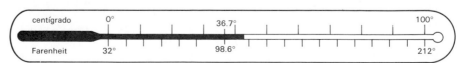

## ACTIVIDADES

**A** Asocie las estaciones de la columna de la izquierda con los meses y las condiciones del tiempo de la columna de la derecha.

1. primavera
2. verano
3. otoño
4. invierno

a. hace frío
b. abril y mayo
c. octubre
d. hace mucho calor
e. hace fresco
f. los días son más cortos
g. hay muchas flores ( *flowers* )
h. los días son más largos

**B** Diga en qué meses del año ocurren estas cosas.

1. Empiezan las clases en la universidad.
2. Nieva en Vermont.
3. Llueve aquí.

4. Es el Día de la Independencia.
5. Empieza el año.
6. Termina el año.

**C** Éstas son las temperaturas máximas y mínimas de diferentes ciudades de España. Escoja una ciudad y complete el siguiente diálogo con su compañero/a. Para convertir del sistema centígrado a Fahrenheit, debe multiplicar por (*multiply by*) 1.8 y añadir (*add*) 32. (e.g., $10°C \times 1.8 = 18$; $18 + 32 = 50°F$)

| **España** M. m. | | **España** M. m. | | **España** M. m. | |
|---|---|---|---|---|---|
| Albacete | 29 12 | Huelva | 35 18 | Palma | 29 12 |
| Algeciras | 23 17 | Huesca | 29 15 | Pamplona | 29 13 |
| Alicante | 25 17 | Ibiza | 23 16 | Pontevedra | 22 12 |
| Almería | 30 23 | Jaén | 30 15 | Salamanca | 28 13 |
| Ávila | 25 13 | Jerez | 30 19 | S. Sebastián | 18 15 |
| Badajoz | 35 17 | La Coruña | 17 13 | Santander | 18 14 |
| Barcelona | 22 17 | Lanzarote | 25 19 | Santiago | 18 11 |
| Bilbao | 17 14 | Las Palmas | 25 19 | Segovia | 26 12 |
| Burgos | 26 12 | León | 27 13 | Sevilla | 32 20 |
| Cáceres | 32 19 | Lérida | 28 14 | Soria | 25 10 |
| Cádiz | 26 14 | Logroño | 24 12 | Tarragona | 25 15 |
| Castellón | 29 16 | Lugo | 19 10 | Tenerife | 24 20 |
| Ceuta | 23 19 | Mahón | 24 16 | Teruel | 26 11 |
| C. Real | 32 15 | Málaga | 28 19 | Toledo | 29 18 |
| Córdoba | 35 18 | Melilla | 21 19 | Valencia | 26 17 |
| Cuenca | 28 13 | Murcia | 27 15 | Valladolid | 27 13 |
| Gerona | 27 14 | Orense | 23 13 | Vitoria | 14 12 |
| Granada | 32 16 | Oviedo | 16 13 | Zamora | 30 14 |
| Guadalajara | 30 14 | Palencia | 29 12 | Zaragoza | 30 16 |

**ABREVIATURAS.**—M.: Temperatura máxima.—m.: Temperatura mínima.—

| | |
|---|---|
| **Usted** | ¿Qué temperatura hace en ___? |
| **Compañero/a** | Unos ___ grados más o menos. |
| **Usted** | ¿Por el día o por la noche? |
| **Compañero/a** | Por ___. |
| **Usted** | ¿Cuánto es eso en Fahrenheit? |
| **Compañero/a** | . . . |

**D** Piense en el lugar donde usted quisiera (*would like*) pasar sus vacaciones. Su compañero/a le va a hacer las siguientes preguntas sobre el clima en ese lugar y sus actividades allí. Después usted le debe hacer las mismas preguntas a su compañero/a.

1. ¿Adónde quieres ir?  2. ¿Qué tiempo hace allí en el invierno? ¿y en el verano?
3. ¿Nieva allí?  4. ¿Cuándo llueve?  5. ¿Cuándo piensas ir?  6. ¿Qué vas a hacer allí?

**E** Usted está a cargo del pronóstico ( *forecast*) del tiempo en un canal de televisión. Explique qué tiempo va a hacer mañana según los siguientes mapas.

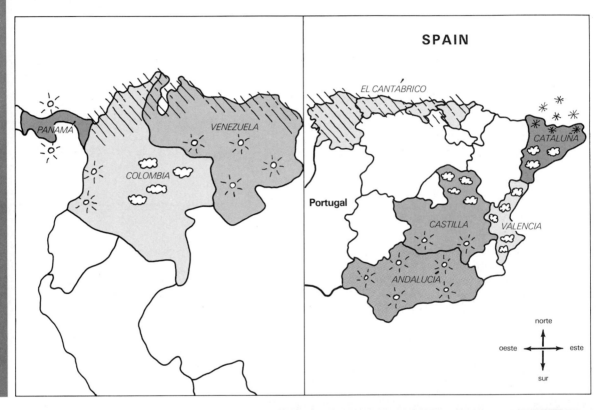

Un partido de fútbol en
las afueras de Bogotá, Colombia.

# Cultura

## Sports in the Hispanic world

Sports are important events for both participants and spectators in the Hispanic world, as they are in the United States. However, differences exist between Hispanic countries and the United States in the kinds of sports traditionally popular, in those newly popular, in the fans, and in sports heroes.

In the United States no one sport captures the heart and attention of the majority of the citizens; there are three major ones, baseball, basketball, and football. In Hispanic countries, soccer dominates; it is even the national sport of many of these nations. Most children grow up playing soccer and everyone has a favorite local team. In some countries a national team is selected from the best players of different teams around the country. This team then represents the country in annual international tournaments, and every fourth year plays for the World Cup (**la Copa del Mundo/la Copa Mundial**) which truly determines who is the world champion.

The predominance of one sport as local and national pastime helps to explain the fervor of the sports fan in Spanish-speaking countries. Virtually everyone has played and likes soccer. Teams and players have ardent supporters who are extremely loyal—or critical when their team does not play well. During international competitions fans see their team as an extension of their country. Thus, the national honor and pride are at stake when teams compete. For this reason and others, fans become very vocal and involved when their teams are playing.

Although soccer is easily the dominant sport, baseball also enjoys a large following, especially in the Caribbean and the Gulf of Mexico. The caliber of players from this area is such that many are drafted by the major leagues in the United States and go on to win top awards in baseball.

Boxing has also been popular for many years and numerous world champions have come from Argentina, Cuba, Mexico, Nicaragua, and Puerto Rico. Cuba, where athletes are not regarded as professional, continues to be a perennial powerhouse in amateur boxing.

There are a number of sports not traditionally associated with Hispanic countries that have attracted many followers. Basketball has been growing in appeal; Spain now has a professional basketball league with Spanish and American players and knowledgeable fans. In addition, students from the Dominican Republic, Venezuela, and Argentina are now playing for top college teams in the United States. Tennis, golf, Grand Prix racing, skiing, cycling, men's and women's volleyball, and weightlifting are other sports which have become popular.

Sports heroes in Hispanic countries take on different dimensions from those in the United States. Due to the diversity of sports interests of Americans, no one game or player dominates. However, in countries where there are only a handful of star athletes, they get tremendous national coverage and attention, which results in the creation of sports heroes. A recent article about Gabriela Sabatini, a young Argentine tennis star, states that she is already as famous and revered as the world-known writer Jorge Luis Borges and closing in on the liberator Simón Bolívar. It would be difficult for a U.S. sports star to achieve that kind of fame.

# EN CONTEXTO

## Un partido de béisbol

Nuestro equipo de béisbol es excelente. Los jugadores practican todos los días. En estos momentos

ellos están jugando.

Si ganamos este partido, ganamos el campeonato. Los aficionados están muy emocionados y ahora

están aplaudiendo.

Algunos aficionados no están de acuerdo con una decisión del árbitro. Uno de los jugadores y el árbitro

están discutiendo.

| P | 1 2 3 4 5 6 7 8 9 10 |
|---|---|
| 46 LEONES | 0 2 0 2 |
| 41 TIGRES | 1 0 3 |

Es un partido muy reñido. El equipo contrario es también muy bueno, pero

nuestro equipo está ganando.

Un partido de béisbol en el Estadio de Béisbol de Caracas, Venezuela. El béisbol es el deporte más popular en toda el área del Caribe.

Unos jóvenes juegan al vólibol, pasatiempo popular en las playas de Perú.

## Para completar

Complete las siguientes oraciones de acuerdo con la información correcta.

1. Nuestro equipo de béisbol es
   a. bueno.
   b. regular.
   c. muy bueno.
2. En estos momentos los jugadores están
   a. aplaudiendo.
   b. jugando.
   c. practicando.
3. En el estadio hay
   a. pocas personas.
   b. mucho público.
   c. muchos árbitros.

4. El árbitro y uno de los jugadores están
   a. bailando.
   b. conversando.
   c. discutiendo.
5. El equipo contrario está
   a. ganando.
   b. corriendo.
   c. perdiendo.

### otros deportes y actividades

| | | | |
|---|---|---|---|
| el baloncesto/básquetbol | *basketball* | la natación | *swimming* |
| el boxeo | *boxing* | el tenis | *tennis* |
| el esquí | *skiing* | el vól(e)ibol | *volleyball* |
| el golf | *golf* | bucear | *to skin/scuba-dive* |
| el judo/yudo | *judo* | pescar | *to fish* |

## *ACTIVIDADES*

**A** En grupos de cuatro estudiantes haga la siguiente encuesta. Compare los resultados de su grupo con los de otro grupo.

1. deporte favorito
2. jugador/a favorito/a
3. asistencia (*attendance*) a los partidos
   a. todos
   b. casi todos
   c. algunos
   d. ninguno (*none*)
4. ver los partidos por televisión
   a. todos
   b. casi todos
   c. algunos
   d. ninguno

**B** Hágale las siguientes preguntas sobre deportes a su compañero/a. Después él/ella va a hacerle las mismas preguntas a usted. Comparta la información con la clase.

1. ¿Qué deporte practicas?
2. ¿Dónde lo practicas? ¿Con quién? ¿Cuándo?
3. ¿Ves los partidos de fútbol? ¿y los de béisbol?
4. ¿Cuál es tu jugador favorito?

## GRAMÁTICA

**Present progressive:** *estar + -ndo*

|  | PRESENT **estar** | PRESENT PARTICIPLE **-ndo** |
|---:|---|---|
| yo | estoy | |
| tú | estás | hablando |
| él, ella, usted | está | comiendo |
| nosotros/as | estamos | escribiendo |
| vosotros/as | estáis | |
| ellos/as, ustedes | están | |

**1.** Form the present progressive with the present of **estar** and the present participle (**-ndo**).

2. To form the present participle, add **-ando** to the stem of **-ar** verbs and **-iendo** to the stem of **-er** and **-ir** verbs.

> hablar ⟶ hablando
> comer ⟶ comiendo
> escribir ⟶ escribiendo

3. When the verb stem of an **-er** or an **-ir** verb ends in a vowel, add **-yendo.**

> leer ⟶ leyendo
> creer ⟶ creyendo

4. The **-ir** verbs that change the stem vowel **o** to **ue** in the present (**dormir** ⟶ **duermo**), have the change **o** ⟶ **u** in the present participle.

> Ellos están durmiendo.

5. Place reflexive and direct object pronouns before the conjugated form of **estar** or attach them to the present participle. Notice that when the pronoun is attached to the present participle, an accent mark is needed on the stressed syllable.

> Pedro **se** está peinando.    Pedro está pein**á**ndo**se**.
> Arturo **lo** está mirando.    Arturo está mir**á**ndo**lo**.

6. Use the present progressive to emphasize an action in progress at the moment of speaking.

> Marcela estudia mucho. (normally)
> Marcela está estudiando. (at this moment)

7. Contrary to English, Spanish does not use the present progressive to refer to a time in the near future. The present is used instead.

> Salgo esta noche.                    *I'm leaving tonight.*

El esquí se practica en algunas zonas de los Andes como en el Club Andino Boliviano.

## ACTIVIDADES

**A** Diga lo que las siguientes personas están haciendo de acuerdo con la situación.

1. Andrés tiene un examen esta tarde. Por eso, él
   a. está repasando con un compañero.
   b. está jugando tenis con su novia.
   c. está conversando con sus amigos en un café.
2. Mañana hay una competencia muy importante y los atletas
   a. están bailando en la fiesta.
   b. están practicando en el estadio.
   c. están sacudiendo los muebles.
3. Es la hora del desayuno y los niños
   a. están jugando en el parque.
   b. están montando bicicleta en la calle.
   c. están comiendo el cereal en el comedor.
4. Esta noche vienen unos amigos a cenar a casa de los Gorostiza. Por eso la señora
   a. está comprando un coche grande.
   b. está cocinando un plato especial.
   c. está nadando en la piscina.
5. Uno de los jugadores de béisbol no está de acuerdo con la decisión del árbitro. Ellos
   a. están conversando.
   b. están discutiendo.
   c. están pescando.

**B** **¿Qué están haciendo?** Estudie los dibujos y diga lo que están haciendo las personas.

1

2

3

4

5

6

**C** **Lugares y actividades.** Usted está en los siguientes lugares. ¿Qué actividades observa?

la clase de español      su casa      la biblioteca      un estadio de béisbol
una discoteca            la playa

**D** **El parque.** Estudie el siguiente dibujo y determine lo que están haciendo las personas.

**E** **Pantomimas.** Piense en una actividad (leer, cantar, dormir, etc.). Usted debe imitar esa actividad y sus compañeros deben decir lo que está haciendo usted.

## EN CONTEXTO

### Escuelas de deportes

TENIS

**SPORT** *Club*

ESCUELA
ANDRES
GIMENO

- Alumnos de 10 a 18 años.
- Internos o externos.
- Cursos semanales
del 25 de Julio al 15 Agosto.
- En Castelldefels.

Desde: **50.000** ptas.

GOLF

**SPORT** *Club*

ESCUELA
DE GOLF
MARBELLA

- Cursos semanales Julio
y Agosto.
- Aprendizaje y práctica
en circuitos de 4 campos
por cursillo.

Desde: **67.200** ptas.

BALONCESTO

**SPORT** *Club*

CAMPUS
RAFAEL
RULLAN EN
NAVACERRADA

- Alumnos de 9 a 15 años.
Internos y externos.
1.er turno: del 1 al 9 de Julio.
2.º turno: del 11 al 19 de Julio.
3.er turno: del 22 al 30 de Julio.

Desde: **37.500** ptas.

## ¿Verdadero o falso?

Diga si las siguientes oraciones son verdaderas o falsas de acuerdo con los anuncios de las escuelas de deportes.

1. Un chico de 19 años puede ir a la escuela de tenis.
2. Las clases en la escuela de tenis empiezan el 25 de julio.
3. Los cursos en la escuela de tenis cuestan 50.000 pesetas.
4. La escuela de tenis está en Marbella.
5. En la escuela de golf hay cursos en el invierno.
6. Los cursos de golf cuestan 67.200 pesetas.
7. Los alumnos de los cursos de básquetbol pueden tener de 9 a 15 años.
8. Los cursos en la escuela de básquetbol cuestan 20.000 pesetas.

## GRAMÁTICA

### Numbers 1,000 to 2,000,000

| | | | |
|---|---|---|---|
| 1.000 | mil | 10.000 | diez mil |
| 1.001 | mil un(o)/una | 100.000 | cien mil |
| 1.100 | mil cien(to) | 150.000 | ciento cincuenta mil |
| 2.000 | dos mil | 500.000 | quinientos mil |
| | | 1.000.000 | un millón (de) |
| | | 2.000.000 | dos millones (de) |

1. Use **mil** for *one thousand.*
2. Use **cien mil** for *one hundred thousand,* but use **ciento** with any number greater than 100,000 up to 199,000.

   | | |
   |---|---|
   | 100.000 | cien mil |
   | 101.000 | ciento un mil |
   | 130.000 | ciento treinta mil |

3. Use **cientos/as** with numbers greater than two hundred thousand.

   | | |
   |---|---|
   | 200.000 (libros) | doscien**tos** mil libros |
   | 350.000 (niñas) | trescien**tas** cincuenta mil niñas |
   | 500.000 (mesas) | quinien**tas** mil mesas |

4. Use **un millón** to say *one million.* Use **un millón de** when a noun follows.

   | | |
   |---|---|
   | 1.000.000 | un millón |
   | 1.000.000 (sillas) | un millón **de** sillas |

# ACTIVIDADES

**A** Su profesor/a va a leer un número de cada grupo. Indique cuál es el número.

| | | | |
|---|---|---|---|
| 4.000 | 6.000 | 7.500 | 10.200 |
| 15.000 | 20.300 | 32.000 | 40.100 |
| 100.000 | 400.000 | 600.000 | 900.000 |
| 340.000 | 460.000 | 880.000 | 750.000 |
| 670.000 | 275.000 | 296.000 | 1.000.000 |
| 530.000 | 315.000 | 775.000 | 995.000 |

**B** Lea los siguientes números y palabras.

| | | | |
|---|---|---|---|
| 1.000 clases | 12.531 cuadernos | 1.000.000 de autos | 1.001 árbitros |
| 60.000 aficionados | 400.000 pesos | 1.100 jugadores | 101.000 casas |
| 720.000 casetes | 5.000 discos | 170.000 personas | 950.000 dólares |

**C** **Entrevista.** Determine quién nació (*was born*) en los siguientes años. Consiga (*get*) su firma (*signature*) en una hoja de papel. Si algún (*any*) estudiante no nació en uno de estos años, debe decir cuándo nació.

**Modelo**   1940       ¿Naciste (*were you born*) en 1940?

*Carlos Viramontes*

| | | |
|---|---|---|
| 1963 _____ | 1969 _____ |
| 1964 _____ | 1970 _____ |
| 1965 _____ | 1971 _____ |
| 1966 _____ | 1972 _____ |
| 1967 _____ | 1973 _____ |
| 1968 _____ | 1974 _____ |

**D** **Eventos futuros.** Diga en qué año van a ocurrir los siguientes hechos.

**Modelo**   Brasil va a ir a la luna (*moon*)
           **En 1998.**

1. Los Yankees van a participar en la Serie Mundial (*World Series*).
2. Un inglés va a ser el campeón mundial de boxeo.
3. Una mujer va a ser la presidenta de los Estados Unidos.
4. Vamos a tener paz (*peace*) en todo el mundo.
5. Los astrónomos van a descubrir otro planeta.
6. Van a descubrir una cura (*cure*) para el cáncer.
7. Vamos a tener una depresión mundial.
8. No vamos a tener más petróleo.
9. El inglés, el chino y el español van a ser las lenguas oficiales del mundo.
10. Van a descubrir vida (*life*) en otros planetas.

**E Casas y precios.** Describa estas casas y diga cuánto cuestan.

*Modelo*

**Nueva Orleans, Luisiana**
2 cuartos, 1 baño, sala, cocina
moderna, jardín, garaje. Precio:
$115.000

**La casa está en Nueva Orleans. Tiene dos cuartos y sólo un baño. La sala es grande. No tiene comedor, pero la cocina es muy moderna. Tiene un jardín detrás y un garaje para un auto. Cuesta ciento quince mil dólares.**

**Phoenix, Arizona**
3 cuartos, sala, cocina, comedor,
2 baños, piscina, jardín grande,
garaje para 2 autos. Precio:
$455.000

**Beverly Hills, California**
5 cuartos, 5 baños, sala, biblioteca, comedor, cocina, piscina,
jardín, garaje para 3 autos.
Precio: $2.000.000

**Pasadena, California**
3 cuartos, cocina, sala, 2 baños,
comedor, jardín, garaje. Precio:
$247.000

**Miami, Florida**
4 cuartos, sala, cocina, 2½
baños, terraza, garaje. Precio:
$150.000

## GRAMÁTICA

### Ordinal numbers

Point out: **sétimo** is also used.

| | | | | |
|---|---|---|---|---|
| primero/a | *first* | | sexto/a | *sixth* |
| segundo/a | *second* | | séptimo/a | *seventh* |
| tercero/a | *third* | | octavo/a | *eighth* |
| cuarto/a | *fourth* | | noveno/a | *ninth* |
| quinto/a | *fifth* | | décimo/a | *tenth* |

1. Ordinal numbers agree in gender and number with the nouns they modify.

   segundo edificio   cuarta casa

2. **Primero** and **tercero** drop the **-o** before masculine singular nouns.

   **primer** partido   **tercer** partido

## ACTIVIDADES

**A** Conteste las preguntas de acuerdo con el siguiente cuadro.

| Fila 3 | Carlos | Carolina | Gabriela | Lorenzo | Jaime | Javier | Alma |
|---|---|---|---|---|---|---|---|
| Fila 2 | Elena | Ester | Elías | Melisa | Lupe | Linda | Ana |
| Fila 1 | Pedro | Ninfa | Lidia | Lucía | José | Clara | Paz |
| Asientos | 1 | 2 | 3 | 4 | 5 | 6 | 7 |

(Asiento 4, Fila 1: usted)

1. ¿Quién está en la primera fila, en el segundo asiento?
2. ¿Quién está en la tercera fila, en el sexto asiento?
3. ¿Quiénes están en la segunda fila?
4. ¿Quién está en la tercera fila, en el primer asiento?
5. ¿Dónde está Lupe? ¿Y Javier?
6. ¿Dónde están Gabriela y Linda? ¿Y usted?

**B Orden de los días.** Conteste las preguntas que su compañero/a le va a hacer sobre el orden de los días de la semana.

*Modelo*   ¿Qué día de la semana es el lunes?
   **El lunes es el primer día de la semana.**

## GRAMÁTICA

### Dates

1. To express the date in Spanish, use cardinal numbers (**dos, trece**), except for the first day of the month (**primero**).

   —¿Cuál es la fecha?
   —¿Qué fecha es hoy?   —Es el 14 de febrero (de 1991).

2. Use **el** for *on* when referring to dates.

   La fiesta es **el** cuatro de mayo.   *The party is on May fourth.*

## ACTIVIDADES

**A** Asocie los acontecimientos (*events*) de la columna de la izquierda con las fechas de la columna de la derecha.

| | |
|---|---|
| 1. Día de la Independencia | a. 12 de octubre de 1492 |
| 2. Descubrimiento de América | b. 4 de julio de 1776 |
| 3. John F. Kennedy muere | c. 21 de mayo de 1927 |
| 4. Lindbergh cruza el Atlántico | d. 22 de noviembre de 1963 |

**B** Complete las siguientes oraciones con la fecha del cumpleaños de las personas.

1. Mi cumpleaños es...
2. El cumpleaños de mi novio/a (o mejor amigo/a) es...
3. El cumpleaños de mi padre (o madre) es...
4. El cumpleaños de mi hermano/a es...

**C** Pregúnteles a cuatro de sus compañeros cuándo es su cumpleaños.

## EN CONTEXTO

### Un partido muy importante

**1**

Arturo quiere conseguir una entrada para el partido.

**2**

Arturo sigue la flecha para ir a la taquilla.

**3**

El empleado dice que no hay entradas.

**4**

José tiene dos entradas y lo invita para el partido.

**5**

Los amigos se ríen y Arturo pide dos cervezas.

**6**

El camarero sirve las cervezas mientras los amigos conversan.

## Preguntas

1. ¿Qué quiere comprar Arturo?
2. ¿Adónde va para comprarla?
3. ¿Por qué está triste Arturo?

4. ¿Quién tiene entradas para el partido?
5. ¿Por qué está contento Arturo?
6. ¿Qué sirve el camarero?

## ACTIVIDAD

**Una invitación.** Complete el siguiente diálogo con su compañero/a.

| | |
|---|---|
| **Usted** | Tengo dos entradas para el partido del sábado. ¿Quieres ir? |
| **Compañero/a** | Sí, ... |
| **Usted** | El partido es a las ____. Yo puedo estar en tu casa a las ____ más o menos. ¿Está bien? |
| **Compañero/a** | ____. Y después yo te invito a cenar. ¿De acuerdo? |
| **Usted** | ... |

## GRAMÁTICA

**Present tense of** $e \longrightarrow i$ **stem-changing verbs**

| **pedir** *to ask for, to order* | |
|---|---|
| yo | **pido** |
| tú | **pides** |
| él, ella, usted | **pide** |
| nosotros/as | **pedimos** |
| vosotros/as | **pedís** |
| ellos/as, ustedes | **piden** |

**1.** These verbs change the stem vowel **e** to **i** except in the **nosotros** and **vosotros** forms.

**2.** Other common **e** $\longrightarrow$ **i** verbs are

| | |
|---|---|
| conseguir | *to get* |
| decir | *to say* |
| reír(se) | *to laugh* |
| sonreír(se) | *to smile* |
| servir | *to serve* |
| seguir | *to continue, to follow* |
| vestir | *to dress* |
| vestirse | *to get dressed* |

3. The verbs **seguir** and **conseguir** also have the orthographic change **gu** ⟶ **g** in the **yo** form to maintain the same **g** sound.

  **seguir**: si**g**o, si**gu**es, si**gu**e, se**gu**imos, se**gu**ís, si**gu**en

4. The verb **decir,** in addition to changing **e** ⟶ **i,** has an irregular **yo** form.

  **decir**: di**g**o, dices, dice, decimos, decís, dicen.

5. These stem-changing verbs also change the stem vowel **e** to **i** in the present participle.

  El camarero está s**i**rviendo el vino.

## ACTIVIDADES

**A** ¿Qué comida sirven en los siguientes lugares?

*Modelo*  en un restaurante chino
    **Sirven arroz frito y pollo con vegetales.**

1. en un restaurante mexicano
2. en un restaurante francés
3. en un restaurante de servicio rápido
4. en un restaurante italiano
5. en la cafetería de la universidad

**B** ¿Qué piden las siguientes personas cuando van a un restaurante o a una cafetería?

*Modelo*  **Piden sopa, sándwiches y leche.**

Olga y Pedro

**1**

Alicia

**2**

nosotros

**3**

tú

**4**

mis padres

**C** **¿Sí o no?** ¿Cómo contestan las siguientes personas estas preguntas?

> *Modelo*  (su padre)  ¿Tiene una familia grande?
> **Él dice que sí. o Él dice que no.**

1. (su profesor)  ¿Tiene usted buenos estudiantes?
2. (usted)  ¿Habla usted dos lenguas?
3. (sus amigos)  ¿Estudian mucho?
4. (su madre)  ¿Cocina usted todos los días?
5. (usted)  ¿Tiende su cama y barre su cuarto?

**D** **¿Qué sigue?** Diga lo que sigue en las siguientes secuencias.

> *Modelo*  1, 2, 3, . . .  ¿Qué sigue?
> **Sigue el (número) 4.**

1. 10, 20, 30, 40, 50, . . .
2. lunes, miércoles, . . .
3. alto, bajo; gordo, delgado; rubio, . . .
4. 3, 6, 9, . . .

5. bebé, niño, joven, . . .
6. ¿Cómo estás? . . .
7. 200, 400, 600, . . .
8. enero, febrero, marzo, . . .

**E** **¿Quién sigue a quién?** Explique lo que ocurre en los siguientes dibujos. Debe usar dos o tres oraciones para cada dibujo.

**Entrevistas sobre ropa y programas de televisión.** Usted le debe hacer una de las entrevistas a su compañero/a. Él/Ella le va a hacer la otra entrevista a usted.

1. ¿Cuánto tiempo necesitas para vestirte?
   ¿Cómo te vistes, con ropa moderna o clásica?
   ¿Te pones la misma ropa para la universidad y para una fiesta?
   ¿Crees que las personas gastan demasiado (*too much*) en la ropa?
2. ¿Cuáles son tus tres programas favoritos de televisión?
   ¿Con cuál programa te ríes más?
   ¿Puedes hablar sobre lo que pasa en uno de estos programas?

## PRONUNCIACIÓN

### Stress and the written accent mark (*continuation*)

1. The combination of unstressed **u** or **i** with another vowel forms a dipthong which is pronounced as one syllable.

   b**ai**le    f**ie**sta    b**ue**no    beb**ie**ndo

2. When an accent mark is needed, place it over the **a, e,** or **o,** not over the **i** or **u.**

   Dios adi**ó**s        bien tambi**é**n        seis diecis**é**is

3. If the **i** or **u** is stressed, a diphthong is not formed: the vowels form two syllables. A written accent mark is required over the the **i** or **u.**

   cafeter**í**a    pa**í**s    fr**í**o    Ra**ú**l

The combination of **i** and **u** forms a diphthong.

   ciudad    cuidado    jesuita

| POR QUE HACE DEPORTE EL ESPAÑOL | 1985 | 1980 |
|---|---|---|
| Por hacer ejercicio fisico | 65 | 58 |
| Porque me gusta el deporte | 53 | 47 |
| Por diversión y pasar el tiempo | 52 | 51 |
| Por encontrarse con amigos | 28 | 25 |
| Por mantener la linea | 28 | 15 |
| Por evasión (escaparse de lo habitual) | 14 | 14 |
| Porque le gusta competir | 7 | – |
| Por hacer carrera deportiva | 2 | 2 |
| Ostros motivos | 5 | 2 |

| DEPORTES PRACTICADOS | % práctica semanal |
|---|---|
| Fútbol | 18,8 |
| Carrera a pie | 13,0 |
| Baloncesto | 10,8 |
| Ciclismo | 10,4 |
| Tenis | 9,5 |
| Natación | 8,8 |
| Danza y gimnasia | 8,5 |
| Fútbol sala | 8,0 |
| Atletismo | 6,7 |
| Artes marciales | 4,1 |
| Pelota (frontón) | 3,6 |
| Tenis mesa | 3,4 |
| Voleivol | 3,2 |
| Tiro y caza | 3,1 |
| Balonmano | 1,9 |
| Montañismo | 1,3 |

# LECTURA

## Un deporte muy popular entre la juventud (*young people*)

The following selection was taken from *Blanco y negro,* a Sunday supplement of the prestigious Spanish newspaper *ABC.* From it you can see how popular professional American basketball is in Spain. You may need the following words to better understand the selection:

| | | | |
|---|---|---|---|
| a partir de | *beginning at* | se conoce | *is known* |
| presenciar | *to see, to watch* | mitad | *half* |
| encuentros | *games* | subir | *to increase* |
| extranjera | *foreign* | campos | *fields* |

LOS viernes, a partir de las once y media de la noche, entre un millón ochocientas mil y dos millones de personas conectan la Segunda Cadena de Televisión Española. Lo hacen para presenciar encuentros de baloncesto, que no es el primer deporte en España. Pero además son partidos de una competición extranjera, la profesional de los Estados Unidos, donde no actúa un solo jugador español y donde no se conoce «en vivo» a uno solo de sus participantes. La cosa tiene aún más importancia si se sabe que más de la mitad de los espectadores de estos encuentros de la NBA están entre los diez y los veinte años. Los periódicos dan ya información diaria de los resultados de esta competición y hay varias revistas especializadas que viven tanto de hablar del baloncesto norteamericano como del español. La audiencia tiene tendencia a subir en todos los campos. El director del programa televisivo «Cerca de las estrellas», Ramón Trecet, no se quiere apuntar ningún mérito en este fenómeno multitudinario:

—El baloncesto tiene ya implantación importante en España. Por otra parte, es muy televisivo y espectacular. En todo caso, está claro que es el deporte de la juventud.

## ¿Verdadero o falso?

Diga si las siguientes oraciones son verdaderas o falsas de acuerdo con la lectura.

1. Los aficionados al básquetbol pueden ver los partidos de la NBA en la televisión española.
2. El baloncesto es el deporte más popular en España.
3. Los espectadores ven los partidos por la tarde.
4. La mayor parte de los espectadores son muy jóvenes.
5. Hay publicaciones especializadas en el baloncesto.
6. Los periódicos dan los resultados de los partidos de la NBA.

7. Ramón Trecet es un jugador español de baloncesto.
8. «Cerca de las estrellas» es un programa de la televisión española.

The next reading selection explains two sports that originated in the Hispanic world.

## Dos deportes de origen hispano

Entre los muchos deportes que se practican en los países hispanos hay dos que tienen su origen allí: el pato y el jai-alai o pelota vasca. El primero es de la Argentina y el segundo, de España.

Hoy en día° muy pocas personas juegan al pato. Es un deporte muy rudo° que tiene su origen en el campo° argentino. Hay cuatro jugadores en cada equipo y todos montan a caballo°. La pelota que usan tiene asas° y los jugadores tratan de agarrarla° por una de las asas. Después tienen que pasar la pelota por un aro° con una red°. Muchos dicen que es más o menos un juego de básquetbol a caballo, pero los jugadores de pato dicen que este deporte es mucho más difícil y violento.

El pato es el deporte nacional de la Argentina. Los gauchos° argentinos son los primeros que juegan al pato. Al principio° no usaban° una pelota; usaban un pato vivo° dentro de una bolsa de cuero°. Por eso este deporte se llama pato.

El jai-alai es un deporte muy rápido y dinámico. Los jugadores o pelotaris usan un guante° que tiene una cesta° larga y curva. Allí reciben la pelota y la

*nowadays / rough*
*countryside*
*horse / handles*
*grab it*
*ring / net*

*Argentine cowboys*
*Al...At the beginning /*
*no...didn't use*
*pato...live duck /*
*bolsa...leather bag*

*glove / basket*

Jugadores de jai-alai en Guernica, España. Este deporte vasco es muy popular en muchos países hispanos.

lanzan° contra una de las paredes de la cancha donde juegan. El jugador del   *throw*
otro equipo contesta y el juego continúa hasta que un jugador pierde. Este
deporte es muy peligroso° porque la pelota es muy dura° y va a una velocidad   *dangerous / hard*
muy grande. En estos partidos muchas personas del público apuestan° y es   *bet*
muy interesante ver cómo las apuestas cambian° durante el partido. En los   *change*
Estados Unidos juegan al jai-alai en Las Vegas, en la Florida y en Bridgeport,
Connecticut.

## Preguntas

1. ¿Qué dos deportes tienen su origen en el mundo hispano?
2. ¿De qué países son estos deportes?
3. ¿Cómo es la pelota que usan hoy en día para jugar al pato?
4. ¿Quiénes juegan primero al pato?
5. ¿Qué usan estas personas al principio?
6. ¿Quiénes son los pelotaris?
7. ¿Qué usan para recibir la pelota?
8. ¿Cómo es la pelota que usan?
9. ¿Qué hacen muchas personas del público durante los partidos de jai-alai?
10. ¿Dónde juegan al jai-alai en los Estados Unidos?

## SITUACIONES

1. You want to take a trip to New Mexico. Ask your friends (a) what the weather is like in the fall and the spring, (b) about the temperature, because you cannot be there if it is very hot, (c) about the rain, and (d) what people do when they visit New Mexico.

2. Find out where your partner is from. Then ask four questions about the weather in his/her hometown and state.

3. Introduce yourself to a student in class. Find out about his/her sports interests. You may want to know what sports he/she plays, where, with whom, if he/she plays well, and so on. Finish the conversation and thank the student.

4. You are living in a dormitory on campus. Your mother/father calls. Another student will play the part of your parent. He/She asks what you are studying, what you are doing right now, if you are eating well, if you are washing your clothes, if you are studying a lot, and other questions related to school and your social life.

5. You are being questioned about your activities on Saturdays. Tell step by step (e.g., **Primero**..., **Segundo**...) what you do on Saturdays. Be thorough in your narration.

6. You and your partner will play the roles of a newspaper reporter and a well-known athlete. Interview this athlete and try to find out as much as possible about his/her (a) family, (b) activities, (c) plans for the future, and so on. Share this information with the class.

# VOCABULARIO[1]

**deportes** — *sports*
el baloncesto/básquetbol — *basketball*
el béisbol — *baseball*
la bicicleta — *bicycle*
el boxeo — *boxing*
el campeonato — *championship*
el equipo — *the team*
el esquí — *skiing*
el fútbol — *soccer*
el golf — *golf*
el judo/yudo — *judo*
el tenis — *tennis*
el vól(e)ibol — *volleyball*

**en el estadio**
la decisión — *decision*
la entrada — *ticket*
la flecha — *arrow*
el partido — *game*
la taquilla — *ticket office*

**estaciones** — *seasons*
el invierno — *winter*
el otoño — *autumn*
la primavera — *spring*
el verano — *summer*

**bebidas** — *beverages*
la cerveza — *beer*

**lugares**
la escuela — *school*
la piscina — *pool*

**personas**
el aficionado — *fan*
el árbitro — *umpire, referee*
el empleado — *employee*
el jugador/la jugadora — *player*

**tiempo** — *weather*
la nieve — *snow*
el sol — *sun*
el viento — *wind*
claro/despejado — *clear*
fresco — *cool*
nublado/nuboso — *cloudy*

**descripción**
contrario — *opposite, contrary*
emocionado — *excited*
importante — *important*
reñido — *close (game)*

**verbos**
aplaudir — *to applaud*
bucear — *to skin/scuba-dive*
conseguir (i) — *to get*
conversar — *to converse, to talk*
decir (g, i) — *to say*
discutir — *to argue*
esquiar — *to ski*
ganar — *to win*
invitar — *to invite*
llover (ue) — *to rain*
montar — *to ride*
nadar — *to swim*
nevar (ie) — *to snow*
patinar — *to skate*
pedir (i) — *to ask for, to order*
pescar — *to fish*
reírse (i) — *to laugh*
seguir (i) — *to follow*
servir (i) — *to serve*
sonreírse (i) — *to smile*
vestir (i) — *to dress*
vestirse (i) — *to get dressed*

---

[1] See pages 144, 156, and 158 for the months of the year and the numbers.

**palabras útiles**

| | | | |
|---|---|---|---|
| algunos | *some* | en estos momentos | *right now, at this moment* |
| mientras | *while* | estar de acuerdo | *to agree* |
| si | *if* | ¿Qué tiempo hace? | *What's the weather?* |
| | | todos los días | *everyday* |

**expresiones útiles**

¿Cuál es la fecha? — *What's the date?*

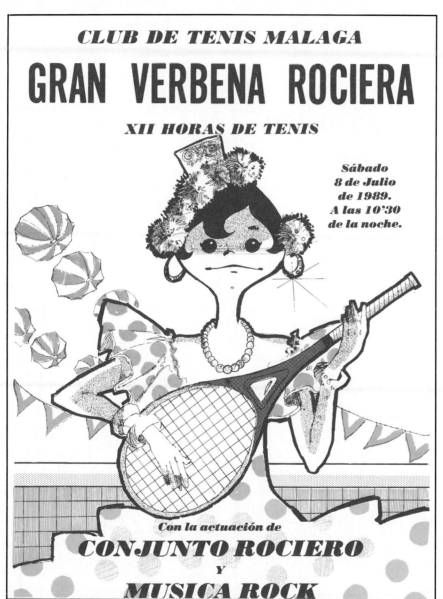

**In** Lección 7 **you will**

a. **talk about and describe clothing.**

b. **make and answer telephone calls.**

c. **ask for and tell prices.**

d. **express needs.**

e. **express likes and dislikes.**

f. **express satisfaction and dissatisfaction.**

# El escaparate de una tienda

**más ropa**

| | |
|---|---|
| el abrigo | *coat* |
| la blusa | *blouse* |
| la bufanda | *scarf* |
| los calcetines | *socks* |
| la camiseta | *T-shirt* |
| la chaqueta | *jacket* |
| el impermeable | *raincoat* |
| las medias | *stockings* |
| el sombrero | *hat* |
| el traje | *suit* |
| el traje de baño | *bathing suit* |
| los vaqueros/jeans | *blue jeans* |
| el vestido | *dress* |

el suéter $45,00

la falda $39,95

las botas $99,50

# De compras

El escaparate de un almacén de Madrid. En los últimos años la moda española ha adquirido mucha importancia en los países europeos.

## ACTIVIDADES

**A** **¿Cuánto cuesta(n)?** Usted quiere saber (*know*) el precio de la ropa que está en el escaparate. Pregúntele a su compañero/a.

> *Modelo* —**¿Cuánto cuesta el suéter?**
> —**Cuesta $45,00.**
> —**¿Cuánto cuestan los zapatos tenis?**
> —**Cuestan $35,00.**

**B** Usted quiere saber dónde compra la ropa su compañero/a y cuánto paga (*pays*).

> *Modelo* —**¿Dónde compras las camisas?**
> —**Las compro en...**
> —**¿Cuánto pagas por una camisa?**
> —**Pago...**

**C** Pregúntele a su compañero/a qué ropa lleva (*wears*) cuando

> hace frío    hace calor    llueve    va a una fiesta    practica deportes
> va a la playa    está en su casa

**D** **¿Quién es?** Describa la ropa que lleva un/a compañero/a sin decir su nombre. Sus compañeros deben tratar de adivinar (*guess*) quién es esa persona.

> *Modelo*    **Usted** Lleva una falda roja, una blusa blanca y un suéter gris.
> **Compañero/a** Es Amelia.

# Cultura

## Shopping in the Hispanic world

See IM, **Lección 7, Cultura.**

Shopping in the Hispanic world offers many choices. Very popular among tourists as well as the local people are the markets (**mercados**), where one can find a wide range of items, from food supplies to beautiful handicrafts. In the **mercados,** a common practice is for buyers to bargain (**regatear**) for a better price. In many cases, the final price is substantially lower than the asking price.

Although department stores (**almacenes**) and shopping malls (**centros comerciales**) are not very common in the Hispanic world, there are some notable examples: **El Corte Inglés,** a chain department store in the principal cities of Spain; **Unicentro** shopping mall in Bogotá, Colombia; and the **Centro Ciudad Comercial Tamanaco, Plaza Las Américas,** and **Concresa** in Caracas, Venezuela. Small stores (**tiendas**) that specialize in certain merchandise are more common. In these places, prices are fixed and people do not bargain.

In some Hispanic cities, such as Buenos Aires, Santiago, and Madrid, one can find streets that are closed to traffic, allowing people to shop with ease. They are similar to the pedestrian malls in the United States.

Shopping hours vary among the different countries. In many cities, stores close at lunch time (which may be as late as one thirty) and reopen in the afternoon (usually between four and five). Stores also close on Saturday afternoon. However, these customs are slowly changing in order to accommodate shoppers.

A typical sight in Hispanic countries are street vendors. They sell all kinds of merchandise, including food, clothing, toys, and handicrafts. In some countries they perform varied services such as sharpening knives and scissors, repairing or cleaning cars right on the street, and fixing up buildings.

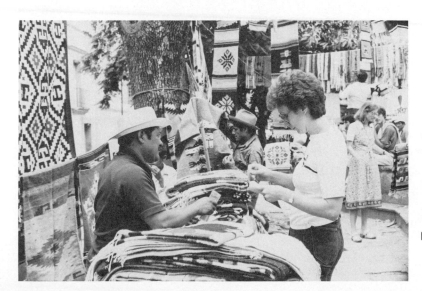

Una turista compra un poncho en un mercado de Oaxaca en México. La belleza (*beauty*) de los diseños y los colores brillantes son características de los chales, sarapes y otros artículos tejidos (*woven*).

# EN CONTEXTO

## Una conversación por teléfono

Josefina está en su casa. El teléfono suena y ella contesta.

**Josefina** ¡Aló!

**Paula** Josefina, te habla Paula. ¿Cómo estás?

**Josefina** Bien, ¿y tú?

**Paula** Muy bien. Mira, Josefina, te llamo porque hay unas rebajas° muy buenas en el Centro Comercial° Tamanaco. Yo pienso ir esta tarde. ¿Quieres venir?

**Josefina** Yo, encantada. El sábado es el cumpleaños de Pilar y quiero comprarle un regalo°.

**Paula** ¿Qué piensas regalarle°.

**Josefina** Todavía° no sé. Ella siempre lleva° ropa muy bonita. Quizás una pulsera°, un cinturón°...

**Paula** Allá seguramente encuentras algo. Entonces paso por ti° a las dos y media. ¿Te parece bien°?

**Josefina** Perfecto. Te espero° a las dos y media.

**Paula** Hasta la tarde.

**Josefina** Hasta entonces.

*sales* / Centro...
*Shopping Center*

comprarle... *buy her a present*
*to give her*
*still* / *wears*
Quizás... *Perhaps a bracelet / belt*
paso... *I'll pick you up*
¿Te... *Is it OK with you?*
Te... *I'll wait for you*

## Preguntas

1. ¿Quién llama a Josefina?
2. ¿Qué dice Josefina cuando contesta el teléfono?
3. ¿Adónde va a ir Paula esta tarde?
4. ¿Por qué va a ir allí?
5. ¿Qué quiere comprar Josefina?
6. ¿Cuándo es el cumpleaños de Pilar?
7. ¿Qué piensa regalarle Josefina?
8. ¿A qué hora van a ir a las tiendas?

# ACTIVIDADES

**A** Hágale las siguientes preguntas a su compañero/a. Comparta la información con la clase.

1. ¿Hablas mucho por teléfono? ¿Con quién hablas más? 2. ¿Compras cosas por teléfono? ¿Qué compras? 3. ¿Usas el directorio telefónico? ¿Cuándo?

**B** Usted llama a un amigo/una amiga para ir a un centro comercial. Debe decirle a qué centro comercial va a ir, qué piensa hacer allá y a qué hora puede pasar por él/ella.

## GRAMÁTICA

### Indirect object nouns and pronouns

| | | | | |
|---|---|---|---|---|
| me | *(to), (for) me* | | nos | *(to), (for) us* |
| te | *(to), (for) you (fam.)* | | os | *(to), (for) you (fam.)* |
| le | *(to), (for) you (formal), him, her, it* | | les | *(to), (for) you (formal), them* |

**1.** Indirect object nouns and pronouns tell to or for whom an action is done.

El profesor **me** explica la lección.     *The professor explains the lesson to me.*

**2.** Indirect object pronouns have the same form as direct object pronouns except in the third person: **le** and **les.** Place the indirect object pronoun before the conjugated verb form. It may be attached to an infinitive or to a present participle when these are together with a conjugated verb.

**Te** voy a comprar un regalo.⎫     *I'm going to buy you a present.*
Voy a comprar**te** un regalo.⎬
Juan **nos** está preparando la cena.⎫     *Juan is preparing dinner for us.*
Juan está preparándo**nos** la cena.⎬

**3.** When the indirect object is a noun, the corresponding indirect object pronoun is normally used as well.

Yo **le** compro un regalo a **Victoria.**     *I'm buying Victoria a present.*

Unos jóvenes hablan por teléfono en Guadalajara, México.

4. Since **le** and **les** have several meanings, **le** is often clarified with the preposition **a** + **él, ella,** or **usted,** and **les** with **a** + **ellos, ellas,** or **ustedes.**

> **Le** hablo a **usted.**        *I'm talking to you.* (not to him)
> Siempre **les** compro algo a **ellos.**        *I always buy them something.*

5. For emphasis, use **a** + **mí, ti, nosotros/as,** and **vosotros/as** in addition to the indirect object pronouns **me, te, nos,** and **os** respectively.

> Juan **me** escribe **a mí.**        *Juan writes to me.* (not to you)
> Pedro **te** habla a **ti.**        *Pedro is talking to you.* (not to someone else)

**The verb *dar* to give**

> **dar:**    doy, das, da, damos dais, dan

This verb is almost always used with indirect object pronouns. Notice the difference between **dar** (*to give*) and **regalar** (*to give as a gift*).

> Ella le **da** el casete a Pedro.        *She gives Pedro the cassette.*
> Ella le regala el casete a Pedro.        *She gives Pedro the cassette.* (as a gift)

## ACTIVIDADES

**A** Usted está cuidando a un niño en su casa. Diga las cosas que usted hace.

> *Modelo*    preparar la comida
>          **Yo le preparo la comida.**

> dar la comida     poner la piyama     poner la televisión     lavar la cara
> quitar los zapatos     leer un cuento (*story*)

**B** Usted quiere ir a esquiar a las montañas (*mountains*) este fin de semana. Su compañero/a de cuarto no quiere ir. Trate de convencerlo/la (*Try to convince him/her*) diciendo todo lo que usted va a hacer por él/ella la semana próxima.

> *Modelo*    lavar el auto
>          **Si vas conmigo, te voy a lavar (voy a lavarte) el auto.**

> preparar el desayuno     planchar la ropa     servir el desayuno en la cama
> pasar la aspiradora     hacer la tarea     regalar un/a...

**C** Diga todas las cosas que su profesor/a hace o no hace por ustedes.

*Modelo*    hacer preguntas
           **Nos hace preguntas.**
           limpiar la casa
           **No nos limpia la casa.**

hablar en español    dar la tarea    preparar el almuerzo    explicar las lecciones
dar buenas notas     regalar entradas

**D** Usted está en Venezuela de vacaciones. Diga quién(es) le escribe(n) a usted. Después, diga a quién(es) le(s) escribe usted.

*Modelo*   **Mi hermano me escribe todas las semanas.**
           **Le escribo a mi profesor de español.**

**E** Usted quiere vivir una vida sana (*healthy life*). Pregúntele a su compañero/a qué le recomienda. Su compañero/a puede usar algunas de las sugerencias (*suggestions*) que están más abajo o darle sus propias (*own*) sugerencias.

*Modelo*        **Usted**    ¿Qué me recomiendas?
           **Compañero/a**   Te recomiendo hacer ejercicio.
                **Usted**    ¿Qué más me recomiendas?
           **Compañero/a**   Te recomiendo dormir ocho horas.

1. comer pescado                    5. comer frutas y vegetales
2. caminar                          6. no tomar mucha cerveza
3. beber mucha agua                 7. no comer papas fritas
4. nadar en la piscina              8. ir al gimnasio

**F** Este mes es el cumpleaños de varias personas. Diga qué les va a regalar usted y qué les va a regalar su amigo Pedro.

*Modelo*   María Cristina
           **Yo le voy a regalar (voy a regalarle) una bufanda.**
           **Pedro le va a regalar un libro.**

nuestro entrenador    mi hermana    Ricardo    Silvia

**G** ¿Qué les dice usted a las diferentes personas en estas situaciones?

*Modelo*   Es el cumpleaños de su prima y usted va a verla.
           **Le digo: «Feliz cumpleaños» («Felicidades»).**

1. Sus padres le regalan un auto deportivo.
2. Usted tiene dos entradas para un concierto y llama a un/a amigo/a.
3. Usted está en un café y viene el camarero.
4. Su novio/a quiere ir a esquiar a las montañas, pero hace mal tiempo.
5. Un amigo lo/la invita para ir al cine, pero usted tiene un examen mañana.

Un moderno almacén
de la ciudad de México.

## EN CONTEXTO

### En una tienda

| | | |
|---|---|---|
| **Josefina** | Paula, ¿qué te parece esa billetera°? | *wallet* |
| **Paula** | Es bonita. Y ésta es muy bonita también. | |
| **Josefina** | ¿Cuánto cuesta ésa? | |
| **Paula** | Setecientos bolívares[1]. | |
| **Josefina** | Está un poco cara°. | *expensive* |
| **Paula** | ¡Ay, Josefina! No está cara. | |
| **Josefina** | Pues yo creo que sí. Mira, allá hay unos cinturones rebajados°. | cinturones... *marked down belts* |
| **Paula** | Vamos a verlos. (Las chicas miran los cinturones) | |
| **Josefina** | Este cinturón es precioso°. Y aquél también. | *beautiful* |
| **Paula** | Además están muy baratos°. | *inexpensive* |
| **Josefina** | Sí, y muy de moda. No pierdo más tiempo. Le compro este cinturón a Pilar. | |
| **Paula** | Entonces vamos a pagar° a la caja°. | *pay / cash register* |

### Preguntas

1. ¿Qué miran las chicas primero?
2. Según Josefina, ¿son baratas o caras? ¿y según Paula?
3. ¿Qué otras cosas ven las chicas?
4. ¿Cómo son los precios?
5. ¿Qué le va a comprar Josefina a Pilar?
6. ¿Por qué va a ir a la caja?

---

[1] Monetary unit in Venezuela. In 1989 a dollar was the equivalent of about 40 **bolívares.**

**más accesorios**

| | |
|---|---|
| el anillo | *ring* |
| los aretes | *earrings* |
| la bolsa | *purse* |
| la cadena | *chain* |
| el collar | *necklace* |
| los guantes | *gloves* |
| el pañuelo | *handkerchief* |

## *ACTIVIDADES*

**A** A usted le van a regalar ciertas cosas. Dígale a su compañero/a lo que usted prefiere de cada grupo. Después su compañero/a le debe decir qué prefiere él/ella.

1. una pulsera, un anillo, una cadena
2. un suéter, una sudadera, una camisa
3. una billetera, un cinturón, un pañuelo
4. un abrigo de visón (*mink*), un impermeable, una chaqueta
5. una camiseta, un traje de baño, unos zapatos tenis

**B** Dígale a su compañero/a qué cosas tiene usted en su billetera o en su bolsa.

## GRAMÁTICA

### Demonstrative adjectives and pronouns

Demonstrative adjectives agree in gender and number with the noun they modify. Whereas English has two sets of demonstratives (*this, these* and *that, those*), Spanish has three.

| | | | |
|---|---|---|---|
| *this* | este vestido<br>esta blusa | *these* | estos vestidos<br>estas blusas |
| *that* | ese abrigo<br>esa bufanda | *those* | esos abrigos<br>esas bufandas |
| *that*<br>(*over there*) | aquel anillo<br>aquella tienda | *those*<br>(*over there*) | aquellos anillos<br>aquellas tiendas |

1. Use **este, esta, estos,** and **estas** when referring to people or things that are close to you in space or time.

   **Este** señor no está de acuerdo.
   **Esta** tarde vamos de compras.

   *This gentleman doesn't agree.*
   *We're going shopping this afternoon.*

2. Use **ese, esa, esos,** and **esas** when referring to people or things that are not close to you. Sometimes they are close to the person you are addressing.

   **Esa** blusa que llevas es muy bonita.

   *The blouse you're wearing is very pretty.*

3. Use **aquel, aquella, aquellos** and **aquellas** when referring to people or things that are more distant.

   **Aquella** tienda es muy cara.

   *That store (over there) is very expensive.*

4. Demonstratives can be used as pronouns. Add a written accent mark to the stressed vowel to distinguish demonstrative pronouns from demonstrative adjectives.

   Compran **esta** billetera y **ésa.**
   ¿Qué anillo prefieres, **éste** o **aquél**?

   *They buy this wallet and that one.*
   *What ring do you prefer, this one or that one?*

5. To refer to a general idea or concept and to ask for the identification of an object, use **esto, eso** or **aquello.**

   Ellos trabajan mucho y **eso** es muy bueno.
   ¿Qué es **esto**? Es un collar.
   ¿Qué es **aquello**? Es un cinturón.

   *They work a lot and that's very good.*
   *What's this? It's a necklace.*
   *What's that (over there)? It's a belt.*

## ACTIVIDADES

**A** Escoja el demostrativo correcto según cada situación.

**este     ese     aquel**

1. Yo tengo un libro a mi lado. Yo digo: «____ libro es muy interesante».
2. Mi hermana lleva un impermeable muy bonito. Yo le digo: «____ impermeable es muy elegante».
3. Mi amigo dice que el auto rojo que está allá es de Pepe. Yo le digo: «____ auto no es de Pepe».

**estas     esas     aquellas**

4. Yo le estoy hablando a mi amiga sobre dos chicas que están cerca. Yo le digo: «____ chicas salen con mis hermanos».
5. Tú estás hablando de las botas que llevas y dices: «____ botas son viejas».
6. Mi amigo está mirando unas casas que están un poco lejos. Él dice: «Ofelia vive en una de ____ casas».

**B** Complete el siguiente diálogo usando los demostrativos correctos de acuerdo con el dibujo.

Adela                    Carmen

|          |                                                      |
|----------|------------------------------------------------------|
| **Adela**  | ___ blusa es bonita, pero ___ vestido está muy feo. |
| **Carmen** | Es verdad, y también ___ botas.                     |
| **Adela**  | ¿___ sombrero y ___ abrigo están rebajados?         |
| **Carmen** | No, pero ___ cinturón sí está rebajado.             |

**C** Usted va a quitarles varios objetos a sus compañeros y los va a poner en diferentes lugares del salón de clase. Después llama a un compañero y él/ella debe decir de quién es cada objeto usando la forma correcta de **ese, este** o **aquel.**

*Modelo*   **Este bolígrafo es de Alberto.**
           **Esos cuadernos son de David.**

**D** Conteste las siguientes preguntas sobre diferentes personas y objetos de la clase usando la forma correcta de los pronombres **éste, ése** o **aquél,** de acuerdo con la distancia.

*Modelo*   ¿Prefieres esta silla?
           **No, prefiero ésa (aquélla).**

1. ¿Lees ese cuaderno?
2. ¿Escribes estas palabras?
3. ¿Estudias con ese estudiante?
4. ¿Necesitas este lápiz? ¿y ese bolígrafo?
5. ¿Abren ustedes aquella ventana?

**E** Complete cada situación de la columna de la izquierda con un comentario lógico de la columna de la derecha.

1. Los jugadores hacen ejercicio todos los días.
2. No hay comida en este café.
3. Piensan visitar el Amazonas.
4. Mi nombre no está en la lista de esta clase.

a. Esto es absurdo.
b. Aquello es muy interesante.
c. No entiendo esto.
d. Eso es muy bueno.

**F** **¿Qué es esto (eso, aquello)?** Señale (*Point to*) diferentes objetos de la clase y pídales a sus compañeros que los identifiquen. Use el pronombre correspondiente según la distancia.

## EN CONTEXTO

### En un almacén°

| | | |
|---|---|---|
| | | *department store* |
| **Dependienta** | Buenas tardes. ¿En qué puedo servirles°? | *¿En... May I help you?* |
| **Josefina** | Me gusta° este vestido de rayas°, pero no encuentro mi talla°. | *Me... I like / de... striped size* |
| **Dependienta** | ¿Qué talla usa usted? | |
| **Josefina** | La treinta². | |
| **Dependienta** | Aquí hay uno. Los probadores° están allá, a la derecha. (Josefina se prueba° el vestido y sale.) | *fitting rooms se... tries on* |
| **Paula** | Te queda° muy bien. Además la tela° es preciosa. | *Te... It fits / material* |
| **Josefina** | A mí me gusta, pero está un poco caro. | |
| **Paula** | ¡Otra vez!° Mira, yo te puedo prestar° dinero si lo necesitas. | *¡Otra... again! / lend* |
| **Josefina** | No, es que tú gastas° mucho y yo no, especialmente en un vestido. | *spend* |
| **Dependienta** | Yo le puedo mostrar° otros que son muy bonitos y no son tan caros. | *show* |

### Preguntas

1. ¿Qué vestido le gusta a Josefina?
2. ¿Qué talla usa?
3. ¿Quién le consigue un vestido de su talla?
4. ¿Dónde están los probadores?

5. ¿Cómo le queda el vestido a Josefina?
6. ¿Por qué no lo quiere comprar?
7. ¿Qué le dice Paula a Josefina?
8. ¿Qué va a mostrarle la dependienta a Josefina?

---

² This chart shows the approximate equivalents of various sizes.

| U.S.A. | 8 | 10 | 12 | 14 | 16 | 18 | 20 |
|---|---|---|---|---|---|---|---|
| Spain | 38 | 40 | 42 | 44 | 46 | 48 | 50 |
| Some other Hispanic countries | 28 | 30 | 32 | 34 | 36 | 38 | 40 |

Un mercado cerca de la catedral en una calle de Barcelona, España. En muchas ciudades hispanas se levantan pequeños mercados al aire libre ciertos días de la semana.

**expresiones útiles en las tiendas**

| | |
|---|---|
| Me queda grande. | *It's too big.* |
| Me queda ancho. | *It's too wide.* |
| Me queda estrecho. | *It's too narrow.* |
| Me gustaría cambiar esto. | *I'd like to exchange this.* |
| Combinan muy bien. | *They go together.* |
| de cuadros | *plaid, checked* |
| de color entero | *solid* |

## ACTIVIDADES

**A** Escoja la contestación adecuada para cada situación.

1. La blusa de rayas rojas y la falda azul son muy bonitas.
2. Este vestido es talla 32 y yo uso la talla 34.
3. Esta blusa es preciosa, pero muy cara.
4. Me gustaría probarme esta chaqueta.
5. Los zapatos son 38 y yo uso el número 37.

a. Sí, te queda muy estrecho.
b. Y combinan muy bien.
c. El probador está allí.
d. Aquí hay otras más baratas.
e. Te quedan grandes.

**B** Usted está de compras en un almacén. Su compañero/a es el/la dependiente/a. Usted le debe explicar qué ropa necesita. Su compañero/a debe hacerle preguntas y explicarle lo que tienen en el almacén.

**C** Usted es el/la dependiente/a de una tienda. Su compañero/a se está probando ropa, pero no le queda bien. Él/Ella debe explicarle por qué no le queda bien y usted debe tratar de solucionar el problema.

183

# GRAMÁTICA

## The verb *gustar*

**1.** Spanish uses the verb **gustar** to express likes and dislikes. However, **gustar** is not used the same way as the English verb *to like*. **Gustar** is more similar to the expression *to be pleasing (to someone)*.

Me gusta ese vestido.    *I like that dress. (That dress is pleasing to me.)*

**2.** In this construction, the person or thing liked is the subject. The indirect object pronoun shows to whom something is pleasing.

| | | | |
|---|---|---|---|
| Me | | *I* | |
| Te | | *You (fam.)* | |
| Le | gusta el traje. | *He, She, You (formal)* | *like(s) the suit.* |
| Nos | | *We* | |
| Os | | *You (fam.)* | |
| Les | | *They, You (formal)* | |

**3.** Generally, only two forms of **gustar** are used: **gusta, gustan.** If one person or thing is liked, use **gusta.** If two or more persons or things are liked, use **gustan.**

Me **gusta** ese collar.            *I like that necklace.*
No me **gustan** esos anillos.     *I don't like those rings.*

**4.** To express what people like or do not like to do, use an infinitive after **gustar.**

Me gusta caminar por la mañana.    *I like to walk in the morning.*
No me gusta correr.                  *I don't like to run.*

**5.** To emphasize or clarify the indirect object pronoun, use **a** + noun or pronoun.

A Marina le gusta el abrigo.
A ella le gusta esa tienda.

**6.** Other Spanish verbs that follow the pattern of **gustar** are **encantar** (*to delight, to love*), **interesar** (*to interest*), **parecer** (*to seem*), and **quedar** (*to fit, to have something left*).

## ACTIVIDADES

**A Reacciones.** Diga si a usted le gustan o no los siguientes lugares, personas o actividades. Trabaje con un compañero/a.

*Modelo*    **Compañero/a  California.**
                 **Usted  Me gusta (No me gusta) California.**
           **Compañero/a  las fiestas**
                 **Usted  Me gustan (No me gustan) las fiestas.**

| lugares | personas | actividades |
|---------|----------|-------------|
| esta universidad | el presidente | esquiar |
| las tiendas | Julio Iglesias | nadar |
| las cafeterías | los niños | estudiar |
| la playa | Gloria Estefan | los conciertos |

**B  Reportando reacciones.** ¿Qué le gusta o no le gusta a su mejor amigo/a?

*Modelo*    los jugadores      el entrenador
**Le gustan los jugadores, pero no le gusta el entrenador.**

| | | |
|---|---|---|
| esos almacenes | jugar al tenis | nadar |
| los deportes | la comida china | ir de compras |
| dormir tarde | bailar | la ropa moderna |
| esa canción | las clases | beber Coca-Cola |
| la música popular | los conciertos | los programas de radio |

**C**  Hable con tres compañeros/as y diga lo que le gusta de ellos/as (*what you like about them*).

*Modelos*   **Me gusta tu blusa. Me gustan tus zapatos (de) tenis.**

**D**  ¿Qué le(s) encanta a estas personas?

*Modelo*    **A mi hermano le encantan los partidos de béisbol.
A mis tíos les encanta ver televisión.**

| personas | actividades |
|----------|-------------|
| a mis amigos/as | leer novelas románticas |
| a mi novio/a | bailar salsa |
| a mi entrenador | ir al cine |
| a los estudiantes | ver partidos de fútbol |
| a los jugadores | gastar dinero |

**E  ¿Qué te gusta hacer?** Pregúntele a su compañero/a qué le gusta hacer. Debe averiguar (*find out*) por lo menos tres cosas y compartir la información con la clase.

*Modelo*              Usted    **¿Qué te gusta hacer?**
            Compañero/a    **Me gusta esquiar.**
                 Usted    **¿Y qué más te gusta hacer?**
            Compañero/a    **Me gusta bailar.**

**F** Preséntele estos problemas a su compañero/a. Él/Ella debe darle la respuesta correcta.

| *Modelo* | **Usted** | Pilar tiene $50,00. Paga $20,00 por un suéter. ¿Cuánto dinero le queda? |
|---|---|---|
| | **Compañero/a** | Le quedan $30,00. |

1. Ernesto tiene $75,00. Le presta $20,00 a su hermano. ¿Cuánto dinero le queda?
2. Erica tiene $20,00. Ella va al cine y a cenar con una amiga. El cine cuesta $5,00 y la cena $12,00. ¿Cuánto dinero le queda?
3. Yo tengo $40,00. Compro un suéter por $39,00. ¿Cuánto dinero me queda?

**G** **¿Es usted un/a comprador/a** (*buyer*) **compulsivo/a?** Este cuestionario va a darle la respuesta. Compare sus resultados con un compañero/a.

| | | | |
|---|---|---|---|
| 1. | Le doy mucha importancia a la ropa. | sí | no |
| 2. | Me fijo° en la ropa que llevan las personas. | sí | no |
| 3. | Les pido solicitud° de crédito a todas las tiendas. | sí | no |
| 4. | Cuando voy a una tienda siempre compro algo. | sí | no |
| 5. | Les recomiendo a mis amigos tiendas y almacenes nuevos. | sí | no |
| 6. | Cuando tengo dinero siempre voy de compras. | sí | no |
| 7. | Si no tengo dinero, uso las tarjetas° de crédito. | sí | no |

Sí = 2 puntos
No = 0 puntos
De 8 a 14 puntos.  Usted es un/a comprador/a compulsivo/a.
De 4 a 7 puntos.  Usted es un/a comprador/a normal.
De 0 a 3 puntos.  Usted es un poco tacaño/a. Le recomendamos renovar su ropa.

I notice

application

cards

Frente a El Corte Inglés,
la cadena más
importante de
almacenes de España.

# LECTURA

## Unos regalos

Usted necesita comprar ciertas cosas. Lea los siguientes anuncios y diga a qué tienda iría usted (*would you go*) para comprarlas.

1. Es el cumpleaños de su sobrino de cinco años.
2. Usted necesita ropa informal.
3. Busca un regalo para el Día de las Madres.

## La ropa

La ropa que se usa en las ciudades de los países hispanos y las ciudades de los Estados Unidos es muy similar. Sin embargo°, la ropa que llevan las personas mayores es, en general, más conservadora y formal que la que llevan las personas de su misma edad en los Estados Unidos. Por ejemplo, en una playa o en un club una señora puede llevar una camiseta y unos pantalones cortos o *shorts,* pero si esa misma señora tiene que ir a otro lugar, como el supermercado que está cerca de su casa, se pone un vestido, o una blusa con una falda o unos pantalones largos.

En los lugares calurosos°, especialmente en el verano, los hombres usan mucho la guayabera en vez de° una camisa. Las guayaberas son muy frescas y prácticas, y además pueden ser muy elegantes y bonitas. En algunos países como México, las guayaberas pueden llevar bordados° al frente.

Entre los jóvenes, la moda norteamericana es muy popular. Antes, para ir a la universidad, los jóvenes llevaban° traje o una chaqueta. Hoy en día, llevan

*Nevertheless*

*hot*

*en... instead of*

*embroidery*

*used to wear*

jeans con camisas o camisetas y zapatos tenis a casi todas partes. Sin embargo, en general, la ropa que llevan es un poco más conservadora que la que llevan los jóvenes norteamericanos.

Una de las cosas que más les gusta a los turistas que visitan los mercados de Hispanoamérica es la ropa típica que pueden comprar allí. Como es natural, esta ropa varía de un país a otro. Los dibujos, la combinación de colores y los bordados hechos a mano° son la admiración de los compradores. Los indígenas° que normalmente hacen estos bordados no han seguido° cursos de diseño o de combinación de colores, y sin embargo sus trabajos son, en la gran mayoría de los casos, verdaderas obras° de arte. Muchas veces las modas norteamericana y europea se inspiran en estos trajes típicos.

bordados... *hand–made embroidery / Indian*
no... *have not taken*

*works*

## Para completar

Complete las siguientes oraciones con la respuesta correcta de acuerdo con la información que se da en la selección.

1. Si comparamos la ropa que llevan las personas mayores en los países hispanos y en los Estados Unidos, podemos decir que en los países hispanos la ropa es más
   a. informal.
   b. cómoda.
   c. tradicional.
2. En general, las señoras no van a las tiendas con
   a. pantalones cortos.
   b. vestidos.
   c. faldas.
3. La guayabera es una especie de
   a. camiseta
   b. corbata.
   c. camisa.
4. Hoy en día para ir a la universidad, los jóvenes llevan
   a. traje y corbata.
   b. vaqueros.
   c. trajes típicos.
5. En los mercados de Hispanoamérica los turistas compran
   a. vaqueros a buenos precios.
   b. ropa de diseño español.
   c. trajes con bordados a mano.

## SITUACIONES

1. You are in your favorite clothing store:
   (a) tell the clerk what you need (e.g., pants, shoes, and so on),
   (b) ask for the price of each item,
   (c) say if you like each one or not, and
   (d) decide if you will buy it/them.

2. You find the item to the right advertised in a newspaper. Tell a classmate
   (a) what it is,
   (b) what its features are,
   (c) what it costs, and
   (d) when you can start to pay.

3. You are going to take some friends to your favorite place (**una playa, una ciudad,** and so on). Tell them what you like about it and what you will show them. Your friends should ask some pertinent questions about this place.

   *Modelo*   **Los voy a llevar a la universidad. A mí me gusta mucho la piscina. También me gusta la biblioteca. Yo les voy a mostrar la cafetería, el estadio y la piscina.**

4. You need to borrow money to buy a jacket. You are going skiing Saturday and you don't have a nice jacket. Explain the situation to a friend and ask him/her to lend you some money.

5. You are trying on some clothes; (a) tell the salesperson that they don't fit you, (b) ask for a bigger (or smaller) size, and (c) thank the salesperson.

6. You are a salesperson at a clothing store and a client has bought a sweater. You should (a) ask the client to go to the cash register, (b) tell him/her how much it is, and (c) ask if he/she is going to pay cash (**en efectivo**) or with a credit card.

# VOCABULARIO[3]

**los accesorios**

| | |
|---|---|
| el anillo | *ring* |
| los aretes | *earrings* |
| la billetera | *wallet* |
| la bolsa | *purse* |
| la cadena | *chain* |
| el cinturón | *belt* |
| el collar | *necklace* |
| los guantes | *gloves* |
| el pañuelo | *handkerchief* |
| la pulsera | *bracelet* |

**las compras** *shopping*

| | |
|---|---|
| el almacén | *department store* |
| la caja | *cash register* |
| el centro comercial | *shopping center* |
| el dependiente, la dependienta | *store clerk* |
| el escaparate | *store window* |
| el probador | *fitting room* |
| las rebajas | *sales* |
| la talla | *size* |
| la tela | *material* |
| la tienda | *store* |

**el cumpleaños** *birthday*

| | |
|---|---|
| el regalo | *present* |

**la ropa**

| | |
|---|---|
| el abrigo | *coat* |
| la blusa | *blouse* |
| las botas | *boots* |
| la bufanda | *scarf* |
| los calcetines | *socks* |
| la camisa | *shirt* |
| la camiseta | *T-shirt* |
| la corbata | *tie* |
| la chaqueta | *jacket* |
| la falda | *skirt* |

| | |
|---|---|
| el impermeable | *raincoat* |
| las medias | *stockings* |
| los pantalones | *pants* |
| el sombrero | *hat* |
| la sudadera | *jogging suit, sweat shirt* |
| el suéter | *sweater* |
| el traje | *suit* |
| el traje de baño | *bathing suit* |
| los vaqueros/jeans | *jeans* |
| el vestido | *dress* |
| los zapatos (de) tenis | *tennis shoes* |
| de color entero | *solid color* |
| de cuadros | *plaid* |
| de rayas | *striped* |

**descripción**

| | |
|---|---|
| ancho | *wide* |
| barato | *inexpensive, cheap* |
| caro | *expensive* |
| estrecho | *narrow, tight* |
| perfecto | *perfect* |
| precioso | *beautiful* |
| rebajado | *marked down* |

**verbos**

| | |
|---|---|
| cambiar | *to change, to exchange* |
| contestar | *to answer* |
| dar | *to give* |
| encantar | *to delight, to love* |
| encontrar (ue) | *to find* |
| esperar | *to wait for* |
| gastar | *to spend* |
| gustar | *to like, to be pleasing to* |
| interesar | *to interest* |
| llevar | *to wear* |

[3] For indirect object pronouns and demonstratives, see pages 175–176 and 179 respectively.

| | | | | |
|---|---|---|---|---|
| mostrar (ue) | *to show* | | entonces | *then* |
| pagar | *to pay* | | especialmente | *especially* |
| parecer | *to seem* | | quizá(s) | *perhaps, maybe* |
| pasar por | *to pick up* | | seguramente | *for sure* |
| prestar | *to lend* | | todavía | *still* |
| probarse (ue) | *to try on* | | | |
| quedar | *to fit, to have something left* | | | |

**expresiones útiles**

| | |
|---|---|
| regalar | *to give (a present)* |
| sonar (ue) | *to ring* |
| usar | *to wear, to use* |

| | |
|---|---|
| a la derecha | *on the right* |
| Creo que sí. | *I think so.* |
| ¿En qué puedo servirle(s)? | *May I help you?* |
| estar de moda | *to be fashionable* |
| perder (ie) el tiempo | *to waste time* |

**palabras útiles**

| | |
|---|---|
| aló | *hello* |
| allá | *over there* |

El mercado de Guanajuato en México, donde se pueden comprar artesanías y toda clase de vegetales frescos.

In Lección 8 **you will**
a. **talk about the workplace and professions.**
b. **express opinions.**
c. **give orders.**
d. **give and follow directions.**
e. **express knowledge of facts.**
f. **express and ask for acquaintance of people.**

# Las profesiones y los oficios

En el hospital

el médico

En el bufete

la abogada

En la peluquería

la peluquera

# El trabajo

**En el taller**

el mecánico

**En la cocina**

el cocinero

**En el banco**

la cajera

Un mecánico examina un auto en Jerez de la Frontera. En esta ciudad española se produce el vino de Jerez *(sherry)* y hay una Escuela de Arte Ecuestre donde se entrenan los famosos caballos andaluces *(Andalusian horses).*

### otras profesiones, oficios y ocupaciones[1]

| | |
|---|---|
| el actor | *actor* |
| la actriz | *actress* |
| el ama de casa[2] | *housewife, homemaker* |
| el arquitecto | *architect* |
| el/la astronauta | *astronaut* |
| el bombero | *fireman* |
| el/la dentista | *dentist* |
| el enfermero | *nurse* |
| el hombre/la mujer de negocios | *businessman/businesswoman* |
| el ingeniero | *engineer* |
| el obrero | *worker* |
| el/la piloto | *pilot* |
| el plomero | *plumber* |
| el policía/la (mujer) policía | *policeman/policewoman* |
| el/la recepcionista | *receptionist* |
| el secretario | *secretary* |
| el (p)sicólogo | *psychologist* |
| el/la (p)siquiatra | *psychiatrist* |
| el veterinario | *veterinary* |

---

[1] The feminine form of masculine singular nouns ending in **-o** or a consonant follows the general rule (final **o**→**a**; final consonant + **a**), except in the cases indicated. In professions where women have been latecomers, some Spanish speakers may still use the masculine form, but this is changing. Example: **Ella es arquitecto/arquitecta.**

[2] Although **ama de casa** is feminine, it uses **el** and not **la** in the singular because it begins with a stressed **a**.

## *ACTIVIDADES*

**A**  Asocie una o más profesiones con los siguientes lugares de trabajo.

el hospital     el aeropuerto     la clase     el bufete     la cocina     la peluquería
el taller     el banco     un estudio de Hollywood

**B**  Dígale a su compañero/a cuál es la ocupación de cada miembro de su familia.

**C**  Usted quiere saber cuál es la ocupación actual de su compañero/a y qué quiere ser en el futuro. Complete el siguiente diálogo y comparta la información con la clase.

| | |
|---|---|
| **Usted** | ¿Dónde trabajas? |
| **Compañero/a** | ——. Soy ——. |
| **Usted** | ¿Qué quieres ser en el futuro? |
| **Compañero/a** | ——. |

**D**  Exprese su opinión sobre cómo deben ser estas personas para tener éxito (*to be successful*).

**Modelo**  un piloto  ¿inteligente?  ¿joven?  ¿perezoso?  ¿ . . . ?
**Debe ser inteligente y serio. No debe ser perezoso.**

1. un/a (p)siquiatra

   ¿valiente?  ¿romántico/a?  ¿irónico/a?
   ¿antipático/a?  ¿inteligente?  ¿ . . . ?

2. un actor/una actriz

   ¿guapo/a?  ¿atractivo/a?  ¿simpático/a?
   ¿delgado/a?  ¿alto/a?  ¿ . . . ?

3. un hombre/una mujer de negocios

   ¿autoritario/a?  ¿serio/a?  ¿perezoso/a?
   ¿viejo/a?  ¿responsable?  ¿ . . . ?

Ahora su compañero/a y usted van a decir cómo debe ser

un/a recepcionista   un/a astronauta   un ama de casa

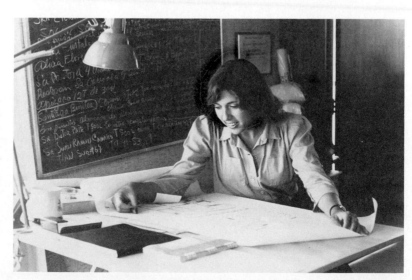

Una arquitecta examina unos planos en México. Poco a poco las mujeres comienzan a ocupar puestos que antes estaban reservados para los hombres.

# Cultura

## Work and economic environment in the Hispanic countries

Unemployment (**desempleo, paro**) is a major problem in the Hispanic world. In May 1988, official figures placed unemployment at 19.85% in Spain; in other countries, such as Bolivia and Peru, it can run even higher. However, these figures do not give an accurate picture of the economic environment in each country because they do not take into account the "underground economy"—the often large numbers of people who buy and sell goods or offer services without paying taxes or following government regulations.

In countries with political instability, there is usually less investment activity, resulting in fewer opportunities for employment. Many workers therefore emigrate to the United States in hopes of finding jobs and better living conditions. The controversial Immigration Reform and Control Act of 1986 seeks to legalize the status of the many men and women who came to the United States without the necessary documentation before January 1, 1982, allowing them to emerge from a "phantom society." These workers have made significant contributions to the United States economy.

Another serious problem in the Hispanic countries is inflation (**inflación**). In Argentina, wartime inflation ran higher than 1,000% in 1982 after the Falkland Islands War (**Guerra de las Malvinas**), a conflict between Great Britain and Argentina over the sovereignty of the Falkland Islands. Inflation brings spiraling prices, and in order to keep up, many workers take on more than one job (**pluriempleo**). This extra income is seldom reported.

Technological advances have been introduced in the Hispanic world, but they are generally much less widespread than in the more industrialized countries. This factor, together with a poor job market, has brought many technicians and professionals to the United States to look for further opportunities to advance their careers. This "brain drain" (**fuga de cerebros**) is a serious problem for Hispanic countries, which are losing the human resources necessary for continued development.

Some of these countries face an additional serious problem in the lack of a middle class. It is indeed difficult for any country to form a strong economic base and sustain a period of progress without a sizable middle class. The tremendous difference between the very small elite and rich ruling class and the very large and poor lower socio-economic masses is painfully obvious.

Spain, which has a middle class, has shown what a country can do to improve itself and the future of its people. While restoring the monarchy in 1975, Spain also reestablished a democratic government just two years later. This strengthened political, legal, and economic institutions throughout the country, enabling Spain to join the European Common Market. As a result, unemployment is decreasing, and Spain has experienced marked improvement in the standard of living, increased productivity, and achieved lower rate of inflation.

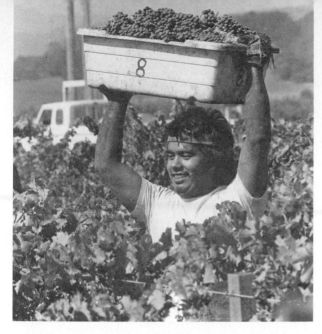

Un trabajador hispano recoge uvas en el valle de Napa en California. La importante industria del vino en California depende en gran parte de estos hombres y mujeres que trabajan en el campo.

# EN CONTEXTO

## Anuncios[3]

**1**

### SE NECESITA
### DIRECTOR

● Para hotel de 3 estrellas con más de 150 habitaciones.
● Situado en el sur de España.

**Enviar** solicitudes con *curriculum vitae* y pretensiones económicas al apartado de Correos de Madrid número 46.283.

**2**

### SE NECESITAN
### VENDEDORES DE MUEBLES
#### CON EXPERIENCIA

Solicitar entrevista con el Sr. Alonso. Tel. 697 54 06.

## Preguntas

1. ¿Qué se necesita en el primer anuncio?
2. ¿Cómo es el hotel?
3. ¿Dónde está?
4. ¿Adónde se deben enviar las solicitudes?
5. ¿Qué se necesita en el segundo anuncio?
6. ¿Deben tener experiencia?
7. ¿A quién deben llamar para una entrevista?
8. ¿Cuál es el número de teléfono?

---

[3] *Ads*

**1.** enviar *to send*   la solicitud *application*   pretensiones económicas *desired salary*   apartado de Correos *P.O. Box*
**2.** vendedor *salesperson*   solicitar *to apply* (*for a job*)

## *ACTIVIDADES*

**A** Usted está buscando trabajo. Diga en qué orden ocurren las siguientes cosas.

Me llaman de la Compañía Rosell para una entrevista.
Leo los anuncios del periódico.
Voy a la compañía para la entrevista.
Envío mi curriculum a la Compañía Rosell.
Me ofrecen (*offer*) el puesto de vendedor/a.

**B** Hágale las siguientes preguntas a su compañero/a. El trabajo puede ser real o imaginario. Comparta la información con la clase.

| | |
|---|---|
| **Usted** | ¿Dónde trabajas? |
| **Compañero/a** | . . . |
| **Usted** | ¿A qué hora llegas al trabajo? |
| **Compañero/a** | . . . |
| **Usted** | ¿A qué hora sales del trabajo? |
| **Compañero/a** | . . . |
| **Usted** | ¿Cuántas personas trabajan allí? |
| **Compañero/a** | . . . |
| **Usted** | ¿Qué haces en tu trabajo? |
| **Compañero/a** | . . . |

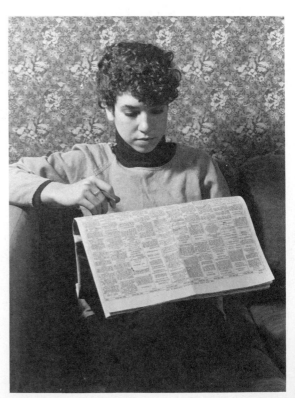

Una joven puertorriqueña lee la sección de anuncios clasificados en busca de trabajo en Nueva York.

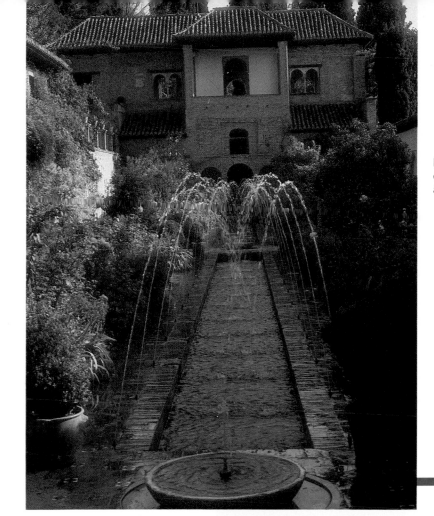

El Generalife, residencia de campo de los reyes árabes, en Granada.

*La españa árabe y cristiana*

El Alcázar de Segovia.

Un paisaje de la provincia
de Carchi en Ecuador.

En las afueras de Tulum,
ciudad maya de México.

*Paisajes*
*del mundo*
*hispano*

Bariloche en la Argentina.

El salto de Hacha en Canaima, Venezuela.

Vista de
los Andes
en el Perú.

La Plaza Mayor
de Madrid, España.

Casas en Montevideo,
Uruguay.

Un mercado al aire libre
en Montevideo, Uruguay.

**Pueblos
y ciudades**

La ciudad colonial
de Guanajuato en México.

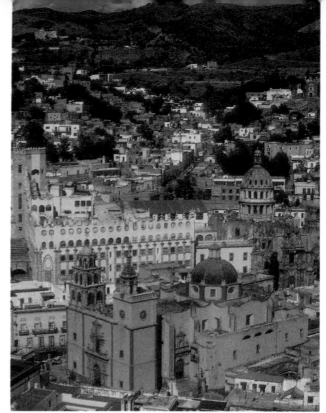

Vista de la ciudad de México.

Semana Santa
en Caracas,
Venezuela.

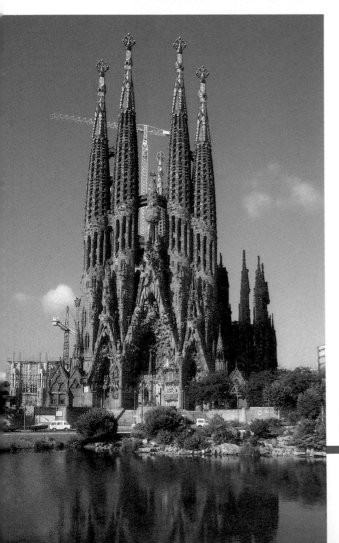

Una corrida de toros en España.

La Iglesia de la Sagrada Familia
en Barcelona, España.

La ciudad inca
de Machu Picchu
en Perú.

Las ruinas mayas
de Tikal en Guatemala.

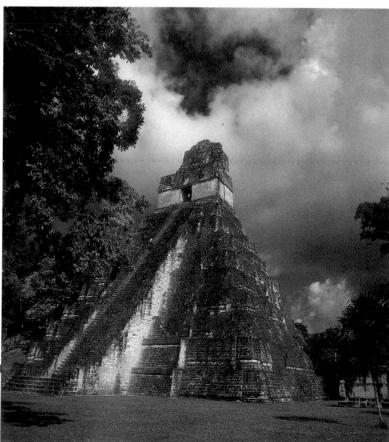

*Fiestas
tradicionales
y joyas
arquitectónicas*

Edificios antiguos
y modernos
de la ciudad
de Caracas.

**El Nuevo
Mundo**

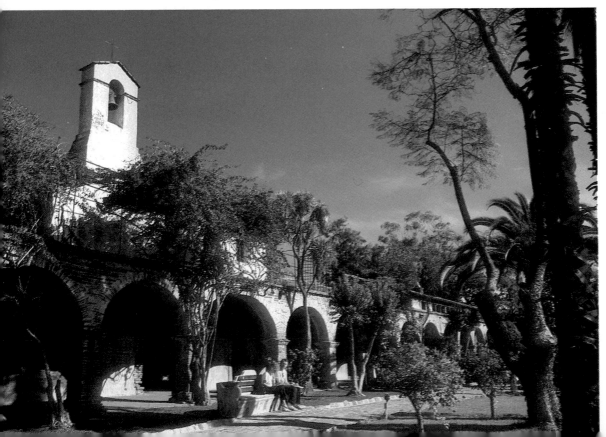

La Misión de
San Juan
Capistrano,
una de las
construcciones
hispanas de
California.

# GRAMÁTICA

**Se + verb**

| | |
|---|---|
| Se habla español. | *Spanish is spoken.* |
| Se necesitan enfermeros. | *Nurses (are) needed.* |
| Se vende (un) auto en buenas condiciones. | *Car in good condition for sale.* |
| Se venden libros aquí. | *Books (are) sold here.* |

**1.** Spanish uses the **se** + verb construction when emphasis is on the action and not on the person(s) responsible for the action.
**2.** The subject usually follows the verb.
**3.** The verb is the **él, ella, usted** verb form or the **ellos, ellas, ustedes** verb form depending on the subject.
**4.** **Se** followed by the **él, ella, usted** verb form is also used to express English indefinite *one*.

**Se come** muy bien aquí.        *One eats very well here.*

## ACTIVIDADES

**A** Diga en qué orden se preparan unos espaguetis. Trabaje con un compañero/a.

Se pone salsa de tomate sobre los espaguetis.
Se hierve (*boil*) el agua con un poco de sal.
Se ponen los espaguetis en el agua que está hirviendo.
Se escurren (*drain*) los espaguetis.
Se pone queso rallado (*grated*) sobre los espaguetis y la salsa.
Se cocinan los espaguetis unos ocho minutos.

**B** Asocie las actividades de la columna de la izquierda con los lugares de la derecha.

| actividades | lugares |
|---|---|
| 1. Se baila y se canta. | a. un centro comercial |
| 2. Se vende ropa. | b. un estadio |
| 3. Se habla español. | c. una discoteca |
| 4. Se juega fútbol. | d. mi auto |
| 5. Se sirve vino. | e. una cama grande |
| 6. Se duerme bien. | f. Nueva York |
| 7. Se necesita mucho dinero. | g. mi dormitorio |
| 8. Se bebe cerveza. | h. la América Latina |
| 9. Se vive bien. | i. un restaurante italiano |

**C** Usted es el/la director/a de un drama. Un empleado le pregunta dónde se ponen unos muebles en el escenario (*stage*). Trabaje con su compañero/a y contéstele de acuerdo con el siguiente dibujo.

*Modelo*    ¿Dónde se pone la butaca?
            **Se pone al lado de la chimenea.**

1. ¿Dónde se pone la mesa redonda?
2. ¿Dónde se pone el sofá?
3. ¿Dónde se ponen las mesas cuadradas?
4. ¿Dónde se pone la silla?
5. ¿Y la alfombra? ¿Y la mesa rectangular?

**D** **Anuncios locos.** Con un/a compañero/a, lea estos anuncios «locos» y diga cuáles les gustan más.

1. Se vende un loro (*parrot*) porque habla mucho.
2. Se busca un/una esposo/a leal (*loyal*).
3. Se necesita urgentemente un robot para hacer todas las tareas de español.
4. Se busca un/a compañero/a de cuarto que no ronque (*snore*).
5. Se compra un fantasma para aterrorizar a mi suegro/a. También se acepta un Drácula o un Frankenstein.
6. Se necesitan tres extraterrestres para organizar un club de baile.

Ahora prepare con un/a compañero/a dos anuncios locos para compartir con la clase.

# EN CONTEXTO

## En la oficina del señor Macía

Pedro Domínguez solicita trabajo en una compañía. Hoy tiene la entrevista y toca a la puerta de la oficina del gerente.

## Preguntas

1. ¿A quién quiere ver Pedro?
2. ¿Qué le dice el gerente cuando toca a la puerta?
3. ¿Es Pedro el programador de computadoras?
4. ¿Qué puesto solicita Pedro?
5. ¿A quién van a despedir?

## ACTIVIDADES

**A** ¿Qué haría usted (*would you do*) en las siguientes situaciones. Escoja la respuesta adecuada.

1. Usted toca a la puerta de una oficina y le dicen: «Pase».
   a. Digo adiós.
   b. Cierro la puerta.
   c. Entro en la oficina.

2. Su jefe (*boss*) lo llama y le dice que tienen que despedir a veinte empleados, que usted está entre ellos y que siente mucho darle la noticia (*news*). Usted le contesta:
   a. «¡Qué bueno!»
   b. «Estoy muy contento con la noticia».
   c. «Yo también lo siento».

3. Usted está trabajando en su oficina y un cliente viene a verlo. Usted le dice:
   a. «Siéntese, por favor».
   b. «Yo no quiero hablar con usted».
   c. «¿Quién es usted?»

4. Usted trabaja en la Compañía de Teléfonos. Un cliente se queja (*complains*) de un error en su cuenta (*bill*). Usted le contesta:
   a. «Estoy muy contento con esa información».
   b. «No se preocupe. Vamos a rectificar el error en la computadora».
   c. «Hoy no tengo ganas de trabajar».

**B** Usted va a entrevistar a una persona que solicita trabajo en su compañía. Complete el siguiente diálogo con su compañero/a.

| | |
|---|---|
| **Usted** | Su nombre, por favor. |
| **Compañero/a** | . . . |
| **Usted** | ¿Dónde trabaja usted y qué hace allí? |
| **Compañero/a** | . . . |
| **Usted** | ¿Por qué quiere trabajar en nuestra compañía? |
| **Compañero/a** | . . . |

La filmación de unas escenas para una película en una calle de Barcelona, España. Una de las zonas más interesantes de esta ciudad es la parte antigua, conocida como el Barrio Gótico por los numerosos edificios de este estilo.

# GRAMÁTICA

## Formal commands

1. Commands are the verb forms used to tell others to do something. Use formal commands with people you address as **usted** or **ustedes.** To form these commands, drop the final **-o** of the **yo** form of the present tense and add **e** for **-ar** verbs and **a** for **-er** and **-ir** verbs.

| | | | | |
|---|---|---|---|---|
| **hablar:** | hablo | ⟶ hable (usted) | hablen (ustedes) | *speak* |
| **comer:** | como | ⟶ coma (usted) | coman (ustedes) | *eat* |
| **escribir:** | escribo | ⟶ escriba (usted) | escriban (ustedes) | *write* |

Verbs that are irregular in the **yo** form of the present tense will maintain the same irregularity in the command.

| | | | | |
|---|---|---|---|---|
| **pensar:** | pienso | ⟶ piense (usted) | piensen (ustedes) | *think* |
| **dormir:** | duermo | ⟶ duerma (usted) | duerman (ustedes) | *sleep* |
| **poner:** | pongo | ⟶ ponga (usted) | pongan (ustedes) | *put* |

2. The use of **usted** and **ustedes** is optional. When used, they normally follow the command.

   Pase.   Pase usted.    *Come in.*

3. To make a negative command, place **no** before the affirmative command.

   **No salga** ahora.    *Don't leave now.*

4. Verbs ending in **-car, -gar, -zar,** and **-guir** have orthographic changes.

| | | |
|---|---|---|
| **sacar:** | saco | ⟶ saque, saquen |
| **jugar:** | juego | ⟶ juegue, jueguen |
| **almorzar:** | almuerzo | ⟶ almuerce almuercen ~eat lunch |
| **seguir:** | sigo | ⟶ siga, sigan _ follow |

5. Formal commands of the verb **estar** have written accent marks (**esté, estén**). The **usted** form of **dar** has a written accent mark (**dé**) to distinguish it from the preposition **de.**

6. Object and reflexive pronouns follow and are attached to an affirmative command. Note the written accent mark over the stressed syllable.

   Cómprela.    Háblele.    Siéntese.

7. Object and reflexive pronouns precede a negative command.

   No **la** compre.    No **le** hable.    No **se** siente.

8. The verbs **ir, ser,** and **saber** (*to know*) have irregular command forms.

   **ir:** ⟶ vaya, vayan    **ser:** ⟶ sea, sean    **saber:** ⟶ sepa, sepan

## ACTIVIDADES

**A** Usted está hablando con su secretario/a y le dice las cosas que debe hacer en la oficina. Use mandatos formales.

**Modelo** llamar al Sr. Palma
**Llame al Sr. Palma.**

1. contestar esta carta (*letter*)
2. buscar la carta del Sr. Vega
3. llamar a la Sra. Narváez
4. pedir más información al banco
5. cerrar la puerta
6. terminar el proyecto

**B** Usted es el/la entrenador/a de un equipo de vólibol. Dígales a los jugadores las cosas que deben hacer. Use mandatos formales.

**Modelo** practicar todos los días
**Practiquen todos los días.**

1. comer bien
2. tomar mucha agua
3. acostarse temprano
4. dormir ocho horas
5. llegar temprano a la práctica
6. correr todas las mañanas

**C** Usted es el/la profesor/a. Uno de los estudiantes le va a preguntar si tiene que hacer ciertas cosas. Conteste usando mandatos formales y los pronombres correspondientes.

**Modelo** ¿Estudio esta lección?
**Sí, estúdiela.**

1. ¿Contesto estas preguntas?
2. ¿Escucho el casete?
3. ¿Escribo estas palabras?
4. ¿Leo la lección ocho?
5. ¿Hago la tarea?

**D** Ahora dígale lo que no debe hacer.

**Modelo** ¿Contesto las preguntas en inglés?
**No, no las conteste en inglés.**

1. ¿Escucho canciones americanas en la clase?
2. ¿Escribo los anuncios en inglés?
3. ¿Termino la tarea en la clase?
4. ¿Hablo francés con mis compañeros?
5. ¿Ayudo a mi compañero en el examen?

**E** Dígales a estas personas lo que deben hacer de acuerdo con las situaciones. Use mandatos formales.

**Modelo** El Sr. Álvarez no está contento en su trabajo.
**Busque otro trabajo.**

1. El Sr. Jiménez necesita un vendedor en su compañía.
2. Una persona está tocando a la puerta de su oficina.
3. Sus amigos quieren hablar con el profesor Gómez.
4. El Sr. Peña quiere saber qué película van a poner en la televisión esta noche.
5. La Sra. Hurtado no quiere vivir en una casa y está buscando un apartamento.
6. Su hermano quiere comprarle un regalo a su novia.

**F** Usted tiene mucho dinero y tiene varias personas que hacen todo el trabajo en su casa. Dígale a cada una de esas personas lo que deben hacer. Use mandatos formales.

   *Modelo*   **Lave el Rolls-Royce azul, por favor.**

# EN CONTEXTO

## Una reunión de ventas°

   La Srta. Marta Vázquez trabaja en la Compañía Garzón en Córdoba, una importante ciudad argentina. Su sueldo° no es muy bueno, pero espera ganar° más muy pronto. Hoy la Srta. Vázquez está en Buenos Aires para asistir° a una reunión de ventas. Ella sabe que el edificio de la compañía está muy cerca de su hotel, pero como no conoce° bien la ciudad, le pregunta a un policía.

| | |
|---|---|
| **Srta. Vásquez** | Perdón, ¿sabe usted dónde está la calle Posadas? |
| **Policía** | Sí, cómo no. Está muy cerca, a unas cinco cuadras°. |
| **Srta. Vázquez** | Por favor, me puede usted indicar... |
| **Policía** | Con mucho gusto. Mire, siga derecho° por esta calle hasta la próxima esquina°. Allí doble° a la izquierda. Camine tres cuadras más y cruce° la plaza. Ésa es la calle Posadas. |

*Glosses (right margin):*
reunión... *sales meeting*
sueldo° *salary* / ganar° *earn*
asistir° *attend*
no... *doesn't know*
cuadras° *blocks*
siga... *go straight ahead*
esquina° *corner* / doble° *turn*
cruce° *cross*

## Preguntas

1. ¿Dónde trabaja la Srta. Vázquez?
2. ¿Gana mucho dinero en su trabajo?
3. ¿Por qué está en Buenos Aires?
4. ¿Qué calle busca la Srta. Vázquez?
5. ¿A quién le pregunta la Srta. Vázquez?
6. ¿Dónde tiene que doblar a la izquierda?
7. ¿Cuántas cuadras más tiene que caminar?
8. ¿Qué tiene que cruzar?

La Bolsa del Mercado *(stock market)* de Buenos Aires, Argentina.

## ACTIVIDADES

**A** ¿Qué hace usted en estas situaciones?

1. Usted está montando bicicleta por la calle. A su derecha hay un perro enorme que empieza a ladrar (*bark*).
   a. Doblo a la derecha.
   b. Empiezo a cantar.
   c. Sigo derecho.

2. Usted está caminando en la playa y ve a su mejor amigo enfrente de usted.
   a. Doblo a la izquierda.
   b. Sigo derecho y no lo miro.
   c. Saludo a mi amigo.

3. Usted tiene una entrevista en una sucursal (*branch*) del Banco de Comercio y no sabe dónde está.
   a. Voy al cine.
   b. Busco la dirección en la Guía Telefónica.
   c. Miro un programa de entrevistas en la tele.

4. Esta tarde usted tiene una entrevista para un trabajo muy importante y tiene que decidir qué ropa se va a poner.
   a. Me pongo un buen traje.
   b. Llevo mi traje de baño.
   c. Me pongo zapatos tenis.

**B** Preséntele a su compañero/a las siguientes situaciones.

1. Quieres ir a esquiar, pero no tienes dinero. ¿Qué haces?
2. Quieres ver un programa de televisión y tu televisor no funciona (*works*). ¿Qué haces?
3. Necesitas buscar trabajo para el verano. ¿Qué haces?

**C** Usted está caminando en la ciudad de Alcalá de Henares en España. Varios turistas le preguntan dónde están algunos lugares. De acuerdo con el siguiente plano, dígales cómo llegar. Trabaje con su compañero/a y cambien de papel (*change roles*).

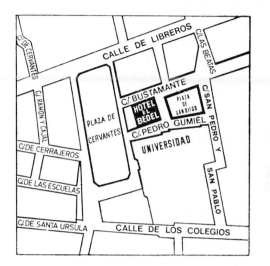

1. Usted está en
   a. la calle Libreros esquina a la calle Las Beatas
   b. La calle Cervantes
   c. la calle Las Escuelas

2. Instrucciones para llegar
   a. a la Plaza de Cervantes
   b. a la Universidad de Alcalá
   c. al Hotél El Bedel

## GRAMÁTICA

### *Saber* and *conocer*

|  | **saber** | **conocer** |
|---|---|---|
| yo | sé | conozco |
| tú | sabes | conoces |
| él, ella, usted | sabe | conoce |
| nosotros/as | sabemos | conocemos |
| vosotros/as | sabéis | conocéis |
| ellos/as, ustedes | saben | conocen |

**1.** Both **saber** and **conocer** mean *to know,* but they are not used interchangeably. The **yo** form of these verbs is irregular; the other forms are regular.

**2.** Use **saber** to express knowledge of facts or pieces of information.

Él sabe dónde está el banco.　　　　　*He knows where the bank is.*

**3.** Use **saber** + infinitive to express that you know how to do something.

Yo sé cocinar.                                    *I know how to cook.*

**4.** Use **conocer** to express that you are acquainted with someone or something. **Conocer** also means *to meet.* Remember to use the personal **a** when referring to people.

Yo conozco a Pedro Rivas.          *I know Pedro Rivas.*
No conozco esa compañía.           *I don't know that company.*
Ella quiere conocer a Luis.         *She wants to meet Luis.*

## ACTIVIDADES

**A  ¿Sabe usted quién es?**

*Modelo*   Es una chica muy pobre que va a un baile. Allí conoce a un príncipe, pero a las 12:00 de la noche ella debe volver a su casa.
**Sí, sé quién es. Es Cenicienta** (*Cinderella*).

1. Es un gorila gigante con sentimientos (*feelings*) humanos.
2. Es un hombre de otro planeta con una doble personalidad. Trabaja como empleado en una oficina, pero cuando lleva una ropa azul especial puede volar (*fly*).
3. Es un hombre joven, blanco, fuerte, educado por unos monos (*monkeys*) en la jungla.
4. Es un detective privado. Es inglés, alto y delgado. Su asistente es un médico.
5. Es un jugador de baloncesto muy famoso. Es negro, alto y lleva gafas (*glasses*).

**B  Preguntas**

1. ¿Conoce usted a tres personas en esta clase? ¿Quiénes son?
2. ¿Conoce usted a otros profesores? ¿Cómo se llaman?
3. ¿Conoce usted a un actor o una actriz de Hollywood? ¿Quién es?
4. ¿Conoce a alguna persona famosa?
5. ¿Desea usted conocer a alguna persona famosa? ¿A quién? ¿Por qué desea conocerla?

**C  ¿Qué sabes hacer?** Pregúntele a su compañero/a si sabe hacer las siguientes cosas. Después pregúntele qué otras cosas sabe hacer. Comparta esta información con la clase.

*Modelo*   bailar música rock
**—¿Sabes bailar música rock?**
**—Sí, sé bailar música rock** o **No, no sé bailar música rock.**

tocar guitarra      planchar bien      jugar tenis      trabajar con computadoras
nadar      usar el microondas      hacer tacos      (otras cosas)

**D** Complete este pequeño diálogo con un/a compañero/a. Use las formas correctas de **saber** o **conocer.**

| | |
|---|---|
| **Usted** | ¿_____ a esa chica? |
| **Compañero/a** | ¡Sí, cómo no! Yo _____ a todas las chicas aquí. |
| **Usted** | Entonces _____ dónde vive. |
| **Compañero/a** | No, no lo _____. |
| **Usted** | Pero _____ su número de teléfono, ¿verdad? |
| **Compañero/a** | No, tampoco lo _____. |
| **Usted** | Y ¿_____ cómo se llama? |
| **Compañero/a** | Pues, la verdad es que no lo _____. |
| **Usted** | ¿Cómo dices que la _____? Tú no _____ dónde vive, tú no _____ su nombre. |
| **Compañero/a** | Es que yo tengo muy mala memoria. |

## GRAMÁTICA

### Pronouns after prepositions

**1.** After a preposition (e.g., **a, de, para, sin** *without*), Spanish uses the subject pronouns except for **mí** and **ti.** In **Lección 7,** you used **a** + pronoun to clarify or emphasize the indirect object pronoun.

Juan **me** habla **a mí,** no **te** habla **a ti.**
**Le** va a prestar el auto a **ella.**
**A nosotros nos** gusta esquiar.

**2.** Do not use **mí** and **ti** after the following prepositions:

**a.** after **con,** use **conmigo** and **contigo.**          **b.** after **entre,** use **yo** and **tú.**

—¿Vas **conmigo?**     —Sí, voy **contigo.**          **Entre tú** y **yo** terminamos el trabajo.

## *ACTIVIDADES*

**A** La familia Rivas está en un restaurante. ¿Qué le piden al camarero?

*Modelo*   El Sr. Rivas quiere pescado. ¿Qué dice?
**Para mí, pescado y papas fritas.**

1. Las dos chicas quieren pollo frito y vegetales. ¿Qué dicen?
2. La Sra. Rivas quiere espaguetis y ensalada. ¿Qué dice?
3. El niño pequeño quiere sopa. ¿Qué dice la Sra. Rivas?
4. La niña pequeña quiere pizza. ¿Qué dice el Sr. Rivas?

**B** Usted está organizando una excursión a la playa. De acuerdo con la siguiente lista, diga con quién va a ir cada una de las personas.

> *Modelo*    nosotros: Pedro, Magdalena
> **Pedro y Magdalena van a ir con nosotros.**

1. yo: Alicia, Marta, Consuelo
2. tú: Carmen, Alberto, Carlos
3. él: Jorge, Javier, Arturo
4. ellos: Mónica, Rafael

**C** Usted va a ir a un concierto con unos amigos. Complete el siguiente diálogo con su compañero/a usando pronombres.

| | |
|---:|:---|
| **Usted** | ¿Vas conmigo? |
| **Compañero/a** | No, no voy ＿＿. |
| **Usted** | ¿Con quién vas a ir? |
| **Compañero/a** | Voy a ir con ＿＿. |
| **Usted** | ¿Dónde te vas a sentar? |
| **Compañero/a** | Entre ＿＿ y ＿＿. |

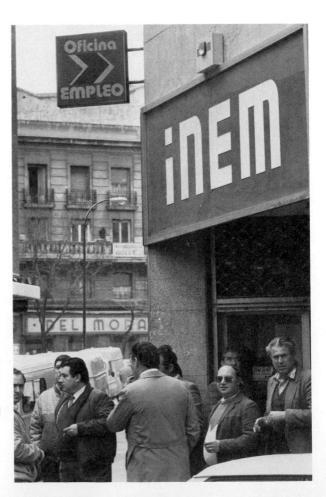

Una oficina de empleo en Madrid. El paro o desempleo ha disminuido en España, pero todavía hay muchas personas sin trabajo.

# LECTURA

## Buscando trabajo

Las siguientes personas están buscando trabajo y leen en el periódico los anuncios que aparecen más abajo. ¿Cuál de los anuncios debe contestar cada una de las personas y por qué?

## Personas

1. Pedro Heredia Solís, 35 años
   graduado universitario
   experiencia como cajero y administrador de un supermercado
   habla español y francés

2. Adela Sánchez Toraño, 28 años
   graduada universitaria
   experiencia de cuatro años en el bufete de un abogado
   habla español, inglés y algo de francés

3. Juan Gómez Machado, 20 años
   dos años de estudios universitarios
   experiencia como camarero en un café.

## Anuncios

Lea ahora los anuncios para captar (*to get*) la idea general y poder asociar el anuncio con la persona apropiada.

**FABRICANTE DE ALIMENTOS PARA ANIMALES DE COMPAÑIA**
PRECISA
**JEFE DE VENTAS**
Imprescindible experiencia sector alimentación. Preferible con estudios Comerciales y Marketing. Residencia en Madrid
**Apartado Correos n.º 14.724**
**28080 MADRID. Referencia 196**

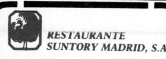

**RESTAURANTE SUNTORY MADRID, S.A**

Perteneciente a la cadena Internacional de restaurantes de lujo **SUNTORY,** busca personal con motivo de su próxima inauguración:

**COCINEROS**

con o sin experiencia hasta 25 años de edad
Enviar historial detallado con datos personales y fotografía reciente a:
c/ Ayala, 20 - 3.º E. 28001 MADRID
**RESTAURANTE SUNTORY**

**JOVEN LICENCIADO/A EN DERECHO**
Con buen conocimiento de inglés necesita empresa de servicios para interesante trabajo jurídico administrativo, jornada completa. Se valorará positivamente conocimiento de alemán o francés
Enviar oferta detallada manuscrita al **número 190688, Apartado de Correos 40, 28080 Madrid**

Lea ahora los anuncios con más cuidado para poder contestar las preguntas. Las siguientes palabras pueden ayudarlo/la a entender mejor los anuncios.

| | |
|---|---|
| fabricante | *manufacturer* |
| precisa | *needs* |
| jefe de ventas | *sales manager* |
| imprescindible | *essential* |
| lujo | *first class, (luxury)* |
| licenciado en derecho | *lawyer* |
| jornada completa | *full-time* |

## Preguntas

1. ¿Qué necesitan en el anuncio número 1?
2. ¿Es necesario tener experiencia para contestar este anuncio?
3. ¿Qué clase de comida vende la compañía?
4. ¿Qué necesitan en el anuncio número 2?
5. ¿Puede contestar el anuncio una persona sin experiencia?
6. ¿Qué se debe enviar para contestar el anuncio número 2?
7. ¿Adónde se debe enviar?
8. ¿Qué buscan en el anuncio número 3?
9. ¿Puede solicitar la plaza una persona de 50 años?
10. ¿Qué otras lenguas es necesario saber para solicitar la plaza?

## El empleado o empleada ideal

El siguiente perfil del empleado o empleada ideal es el resultado de una encuesta° realizada entre hombres y mujeres de negocios.　　　　　　　　　*survey*

### ASÍ DEBE SER EL/LA EMPLEADO/A IDEAL

1. trabajador/a
2. responsable
3. honrado/a°　　　　　　　　　　　　　　　　　　　　　　　　　*honest*
4. inteligente
5. tener iniciativa
6. mostrar una actitud positiva

Todos los encuestados están de acuerdo en que el empleado que nadie°　*no one*
quiere en su empresa es el chismoso°. Según los encuestados, este tipo de　*gossiper*
persona sólo crea problemas y un mal ambiente° en la oficina o la fábrica°. «Es　*atmosphere/factory*
como un cáncer que crece° y acaba° con las buenas relaciones que deben　*grows/ends*
existir en los lugares de trabajo», dijo° uno de los encuestados haciéndose eco　*said*
de la opinión general.

Después de expresar sus opiniones sobre los empleados, los encuestados debían decir las cualidades que debe tener el jefe o jefa ideal. Aquí hay más diferencias entre sus opiniones, pero todos coinciden en que debe ser trabajador, inteligente y justo.

## ¿Verdadero o falso?

Diga si las siguientes oraciones son verdaderas o falsas de acuerdo con la información que se da en el artículo.

1. Las personas que toman parte en esta encuesta tienen experiencia para contestar bien las preguntas.
2. Los encuestados creen que los empleados deben obedecer (*obey*) siempre al jefe o jefa.
3. El chismoso es una persona simpática que ayuda a los empleados a pasar mejor las horas de trabajo.
4. En esta encuesta sólo se expresan opiniones sobre el empleado o empleada ideal.

## El trabajo

El trabajo es una parte muy importante de nuestra vida. No sólo nos proporciona° los medios económicos para mantenernos, sino que° también puede producir mucha satisfacción si podemos escoger el oficio o profesión que nos gusta. Esto resulta muy importante pues hay momentos en que tenemos que dedicarle muchas horas extras al trabajo y abandonar otras actividades que nos interesan. Si no nos gusta el trabajo que realizamos, estas horas extras de trabajo intenso nos pueden hacer muy infelices.   *offers*/sino... *but*

Según muchos psicólogos y expertos, el exceso de trabajo puede ser bueno cuando es temporal, pues nos ayuda a eliminar energía acumulada, quemar° calorías y hasta olvidar° algunos de los problemas que todos tenemos en la vida. Pero hay otros casos en que el exceso de trabajo es permanente debido a° necesidades económicas o psicológicas. A veces estas necesidades económicas (gastos por enfermedades o accidentes, deudas, etc.) son tan importantes que la situación nos obliga a trabajar para satisfacerlas y no tenemos otras opciones.   *burn* / *forget* / debido... *due to*

Cuando el exceso de trabajo se debe a necesidades psicológicas la situación es diferente pues existen otras opciones. Para estas personas «trabajomaníacas» el descanso° es como un pecado°, y el trabajo es una obsesión. Estas personas que tienen que estar ocupadas todo el día necesitan ayuda para poder establecer prioridades en su vida y comprender que también es muy importante disfrutar° de otras cosas como la compañía de los amigos, el teatro, la televisión, los deportes, etc.   *rest* / *sin* / *enjoy*

El siguiente dicho°, que es muy antiguo y popular en el mundo hispano, presenta una filosofía con respecto al trabajo que podría° ayudar mucho a las personas que no saben descansar: «Hay que trabajar para vivir, no vivir para trabajar».   *saying* / *could*

## ¿Verdadero o falso?

Diga si las siguientes oraciones son verdaderas o falsas de acuerdo con la lectura.

1. Una persona puede ser feliz cuando tiene un trabajo que le gusta.
2. Según los psicólogos, el trabajo intenso es siempre malo para las personas.
3. Un efecto del trabajo intenso temporal es que la persona no piensa en sus problemas personales.

4. A veces las personas trabajan mucho por problemas económicos o psicológicos.
5. Las personas que necesitan trabajar todo el tiempo no saben disfrutar de la vida.
6. La idea que expresa el dicho hispano de esta lectura es que tenemos que trabajar todos los días para ser felices.

## Opiniones

Ponga en orden de importancia los siguientes aspectos de la vida. Diga cuál es el más importante para usted y por qué. Compare sus respuestas con las de otros estudiantes.

| | | |
|---|---|---|
| ____ objetos materiales | ____ trabajo | ____ deportes |
| ____ dinero | ____ familia | ____ salud (health) |
| ____ casa | ____ amigos | |
| ____ viajes | ____ estudios | |

## SITUACIONES

1. You are the president of an important company that is going to start a new advertising campaign (**campaña de publicidad**). Bring in two ads that you like and show them to the person in charge of advertising. He/She should ask you (a) why you like them and (b) where you want to place them.
2. You are going to take a trip to Chile for one month. A neighbor is housesitting for you during this time. Tell your neighbor what to do and what not to do while you are gone. You may use the following verbs in your instructions: **limpiar, lavar, barrer, llamar, preparar, cerrar, abrir, hablar, invitar, apagar** (turn off).
3. Tell a student who is new to this country how to write a check step by step. Explain the following: (a) where to put the date, (b) where to write the payee's name, (c) where to write the amount (**cantidad**) in numbers, (d) where to write the amount in words, and (e) where to sign (**firmar**) the check.

| Banco Comercial | |
|---|---|
| | No. 775 |
| | Fecha _____ |
| Páguese a la orden de _____ | $ _____ |
| la suma de _____ | |
| _____ | |

‹:0 2 l0000 2 l‹: 0 25 l l 3 2 7 6 7‹‹ 0 2 8 5 ‹‹000000 l l00‹‹

4. You are standing in front of your house. A car stops and the driver asks for directions to go downtown. Give him/her the directions.
5. You are interviewing a prospective employee for your company. Ask him/her (a) where he is working, (b) why he/she wants to change jobs, (c) what salary he/she wants, and (d) why he/she wants to work for your company.

# VOCABULARIO

## profesiones y oficios

| | |
|---|---|
| el abogado | *lawyer* |
| el actor | *actor* |
| la actriz | *actress* |
| el ama de casa | *housewife, home-maker* |
| el arquitecto | *architect* |
| el/la astronauta | *astronaut* |
| el bombero | *fireman* |
| el cajero | *cashier* |
| el cocinero | *cook* |
| el/la dentista | *dentist* |
| el director | *director, manager* |
| el/la electricista | *electrician* |
| el enfermero | *nurse* |
| el gerente | *manager* |
| el hombre/la mujer de negocios | *businessman/businesswoman* |
| el ingeniero | *engineer* |
| el mecánico | *mechanic* |
| el médico | *medical doctor* |
| el obrero | *worker* |
| el peluquero | *hairdresser* |
| el/la piloto | *pilot* |
| el plomero | *plumber* |
| el policía/la (mujer) policía | *policeman/policewoman* |
| el programador | *programmer* |
| el (p)sicólogo | *psychologist* |
| el/la (p)siquiatra | *psychiatrist* |
| el/la recepcionista | *receptionist* |
| el secretario | *secretary* |
| el vendedor | *salesman* |
| el veterinario | *veterinary* |

## lugares

| | |
|---|---|
| el banco | *bank* |
| el bufete | *lawyer's office* |
| la compañía | *company* |
| la cuadra | *city block* |
| la esquina | *corner* |
| la habitación | *room* |
| el hospital | *hospital* |
| el hotel | *hotel* |
| la oficina | *office* |
| la peluquería | *beauty salon, barber-shop* |
| el taller | *shop* |

## trabajo

| | |
|---|---|
| el anuncio | *ad* |
| la entrevista | *interview* |
| la experiencia | *experience* |
| la plaza | *position* |
| el puesto | *position* |
| la reunión de ventas | *sales meeting* |
| la solicitud | *application* |
| el sueldo | *salary* |

## verbos

| | |
|---|---|
| asistir | *to attend* |
| cerrar (ie) | *to close* |
| conocer (zc) | *to know, to meet* to know people |
| cruzar (c) | *to cross* |
| despedir (i) | *to dismiss, to fire* |
| doblar | *to turn* |
| entender (ie) | *to understand* |
| entrar | *to enter, to come in* |
| enviar | *to send* |
| indicar (qu) | *to indicate* |
| ganar | *to earn* |
| pasar | *to come in* |
| preguntar | *to ask (a question)* |
| saber | *to know* |
| seguir derecho | *to go straight ahead* |
| tocar (qu) (a la puerta) | *to knock* |

## pronombres

| | |
|---|---|
| conmigo | *with me* |
| contigo | *with you (fam.)* |

## palabras útiles

| | |
|---|---|
| izquierda | *left* |
| pronto | *soon* |
| tampoco | *neither, not either* |

## expresiones útiles

| | |
|---|---|
| cómo no | *of course* |

In Lección 9 **you will**
a. **talk about and describe body movements.**
b. **give orders informally.**
c. **give advice informally.**
d. **give and follow instructions.**
e. **express weight and measurements.**
f. **make comparisons.**

# Las partes del cuerpo

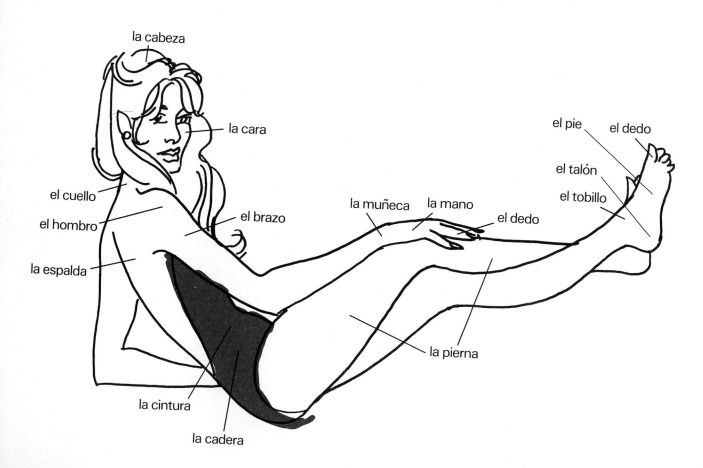

la cabeza

la cara

el pie  el dedo

el talón

el cuello

el tobillo

el hombro

el brazo

la muñeca  la mano  el dedo

la espalda

la pierna

la cintura

la cadera

# Lección 9
# El cuerpo y los ejercicios

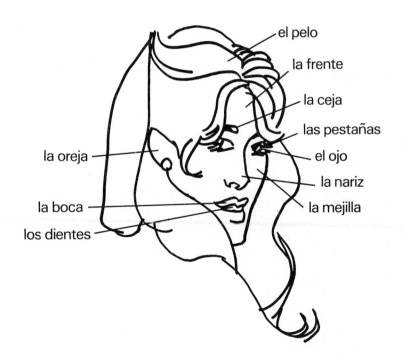

el pelo

la frente

la ceja

las pestañas

el ojo

la nariz

la mejilla

la oreja

la boca

los dientes

## ACTIVIDADES

**A** Asocie las partes del cuerpo con las siguientes acciones.

| las partes del cuerpo | acciones |
|---|---|
| 1. la boca | a. tocar el piano |
| 2. los ojos | b. comer algo |
| 3. los dedos | c. pensar |
| 4. el oído | d. caminar |
| 5. la cabeza | e. tocar a la puerta |
| 6. los pies | f. leer un libro |
| 7. la mano | g. escuchar música |

**B** Asocie la ropa y los accesorios con las partes del cuerpo.

| la ropa | las partes del cuerpo |
|---|---|
| 1. las calcetines | a. la muñeca |
| 2. el anillo | b. el dedo |
| 3. los guantes | c. el cuerpo |
| 4. la blusa | d. las orejas |
| 5. el collar | e. el cuello |
| 6. los aretes | f. la cabeza |
| 7. el reloj | g. los pies |
| 8. el sombrero | h. las manos |

**C** Señale diferentes partes del cuerpo preguntando **¿Qué es esto?** Sus compañeros/as deben identificar las partes del cuerpo.

# Cultura

## Physical fitness and exercise in the Hispanic world    See IM, **Lección 9, Cultura.**

Physical fitness and exercise have always been of interest in the Hispanic world. In recent years, as in the United States and Europe, this interest has grown, affecting many aspects of Hispanic life.

Nowadays, it is not unusual to see office workers, business people, senior citizens, students, and others setting aside time for some kind of physical activity. As a result, there are more and more places for people to meet and pursue their interest in exercise and fitness. Most large cities have **gimnasios** as well as public and private health clubs and spas. In cities like Buenos Aires, Bogotá, Mexico City, Madrid, and Barcelona, for example, you can find health clubs or spas with names such as **Gimnasio del Presidente, Club Gimnástico Bilbao,** and **Casa del Deporte.** And for those staying closer to home, television and radio programs focus on fitness and good nutrition. You can pick up the newspaper of almost any major Hispanic city and find such programs listed.

This interest in developing healthy bodies is also reflected in the number of advertisements and articles dealing with this topic in Hispanic publications. Popular magazines such as **Vanidades, Cambio 16, Gente** (*People*), and **Muy interesante** quite often have articles devoted to the subject. Specialized magazines like **Salud y belleza** (*Health and beauty*) and **Corredores** are published regularly. Bookstands have special sections filled with books on fitness and nutrition.

At the same time, health food stores are increasingly popular. They are known by several names, among them **almacén de salud, centro naturista,** or **herboristería.** All kinds of natural and exotic health foods can be purchased at these stores.

Many people who are interested in fitness and health are similarly concerned with maintaining proper body weight.

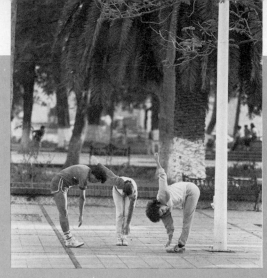

Unos jóvenes hacen unos ejercicios de calentamiento en un parque de Oaxaca, México.

They may consult charts such as the following one taken from the book **Salud y nutrición,** which indicates the ideal weight for men and women according to their height. Since the metric system is used throughout the Hispanic world, weight is measured in kilos instead of pounds (1.6 pounds per kilo), and height in meters instead of feet (3.3 feet per meter).

**PESO IDEAL**

HOMBRES

| Estatura (con zapatos) metros | Talla pequeña kilogramos | Talla mediana kilogramos | Talla grande kilogramos |
|---|---|---|---|
| 1,58 | 51-54 | 53-58 | 57-64 |
| 1,60 | 52-55 | 55-60 | 59-65 |
| 1,63 | 54-56 | 56-65 | 60-67 |
| 1,65 | 55-58 | 58-63 | 61-70 |
| 1,68 | 57-60 | 60-65 | 63-71 |
| 1,70 | 58-62 | 61-67 | 64-73 |
| 1,73 | 60-64 | 63-69 | 67-75 |
| 1,75 | 62-66 | 64-71 | 69-77 |
| 1,78 | 63-68 | 67-74 | 70-79 |
| 1,80 | 65-70 | 69-75 | 72-81 |
| 1,83 | 68-72 | 70-77 | 74-83 |
| 1,85 | 69-73 | 73-80 | 76-86 |
| 1,88 | 71-76 | 74-82 | 78-88 |
| 1,90 | 73-78 | 75-83 | 81-90 |
| 1,93 | 75-80 | 78-86 | 83-92 |

MUJERES

| Estatura (con zapatos) metros | Talla pequeña kilogramos | Talla mediana kilogramos | Talla grande kilogramos |
|---|---|---|---|
| 1,47 | 42-44 | 43-48 | 47-54 |
| 1,50 | 43-46 | 44-50 | 48-55 |
| 1,52 | 43-47 | 46-51 | 49-57 |
| 1,55 | 45-48 | 47-53 | 51-58 |
| 1,58 | 46-50 | 48-54 | 52-59 |
| 1,60 | 48-51 | 50-55 | 53-61 |
| 1,63 | 49-53 | 51-57 | 55-63 |
| 1,65 | 50-54 | 53-59 | 57-64 |
| 1,68 | 52-56 | 54-61 | 58-66 |
| 1,70 | 53-58 | 56-63 | 60-68 |
| 1,73 | 55-59 | 58-65 | 62-70 |
| 1,75 | 57-61 | 60-67 | 64-72 |
| 1,78 | 59-63 | 62-68 | 66-74 |
| 1,80 | 61-65 | 63-70 | 68-76 |
| 1,83 | 63-67 | 65-72 | 69-78 |

# EN CONTEXTO

## El calentamiento° y los ejercicios

Antes de correr, saltar°, levantar pesas° o hacer ejercicio es importante dedicar unos cinco o diez minutos para calentar los músculos y así evitar° accidentes. Los siguientes dibujos muestran algunos de los movimientos que puedes hacer antes de una sesión de ejercicios. Estos movimientos no son difíciles°, al contrario, son muy fáciles°. Debes hacer cada movimiento diez veces° por lo menos°.

*warm-up*

*jump* / levantar... *lift weights*
*avoid*

*difficult*
*easy* / *times*
por... *at least*

1. Levanta los brazos.

2. Respira por la nariz.
   No respires por la boca.

3. Sube y baja los hombros.

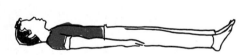

4. Acuéstate.

5. Mueve los dedos.

6. Dobla la rodilla derecha.

## ¿Verdadero o falso?

Diga si las siguientes oraciones son verdaderas o falsas de acuerdo con la selección anterior.

1. Se recomienda hacer movimientos de calentamiento antes de una sesión de actividad fuerte.
2. Es importante dedicar unos treinta minutos a los movimientos de calentamiento.
3. Los movimientos o ejercicios de calentamiento les evitan problemas a las personas.
4. Debes hacer estos movimientos por la mañana y por la noche.
5. Los movimientos de calentamiento son difíciles de hacer.

## *ACTIVIDADES*

**A** Su profesor/a le va a pedir que haga ciertos movimientos. Siga sus instrucciones.

**B** Hágale las siguientes preguntas a su compañero/a. Comparta la información con la clase.

1. ¿Cuándo haces ejercicio?  2. ¿Dónde haces ejercicio?  3. ¿Cuánto tiempo dedicas a los ejercicios?  4. ¿Haces ejercicios de calentamiento?  5. ¿Prefieres hacer ejercicio solo/a (*alone*) o con otras personas? ¿Por qué?

## GRAMÁTICA

### Informal commands

**1.** Use informal commands with persons you address as **tú.** To form the affirmative **tú** command, use the present indicative **tú** form without the final **s.**

|  | PRESENT INDICATIVE | TÚ AFFIRMATIVE COMMAND |
|---|---|---|
| **llamar:** | (tú) llamas ⟶ | llama (tú) |
| **leer:** | (tú) lees ⟶ | lee (tú) |
| **abrir:** | (tú) abres ⟶ | abre (tú) |

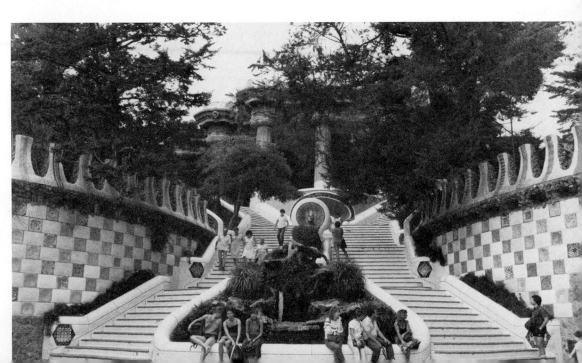

El Parque Güell en Barcelona, diseñado por el famoso arquitecto Antonio Gaudí, donde se puede caminar al aire libre y descansar de las presiones de la vida en una gran ciudad.

**2.** To form the negative **tú** command, use the **usted** command + **s.**

|  | USTED COMMAND | TÚ NEGATIVE COMMAND |
|---|---|---|
| **llamar:** | llame (usted) ⟶ | no llames (tú) |
| **leer:** | lea (usted) ⟶ | no leas (tú) |
| **abrir:** | abra (usted) ⟶ | no abras (tú) |

**3.** The use of **tú** is optional. When used, it normally follows the command.

**4.** Some **-er** and **-ir** verbs have shortened affirmative **tú** commands, but their negative command takes the long form like that of other verbs.

| | | | |
|---|---|---|---|
| **poner:** | pon, no pongas | **hacer:** | haz, no hagas |
| **salir:** | sal, no salgas | **decir:** | di, no digas |
| **tener:** | ten, no tengas | **ir:** | ve, no vayas |
| **venir:** | ven, no vengas | **ser:** | sé, no seas |

**5.** Placement of object and reflexive pronouns with **tú** commands is the same as with **usted** commands.

**a.** Affirmative

Cómprala.
Háblale.
Siéntate.

**b.** Negative

No la compres.
No le hables.
No te sientes.

**6.** The plural of **tú** commands in Spanish America is the **ustedes** command.[1]

Escribe (tú).   Escriban (ustedes).

---

[1] The plural of **tú** in Spain is **vosotros.** To form the affirmative **vosotros** command, change the **r** of the infinitive to **d:** **hablar** ⟶ **hablad; comer** ⟶ **comed; escribir** ⟶ **escribid.**

To form the negative **vosotros** command, use the stem of the infinitive (except stem-changing **-ir** verbs) and add **-éis** for **-ar** verbs and **-áis** for **-er** and **-ir** verbs: **hablar** ⟶ **no habléis; comer** ⟶ **no comáis; escribir** ⟶ **no escribáis.**

Stem-changing **-ir** verbs change the **e** or **o** of the stem to **i** and **u** respectively: **preferir** ⟶ **no prefiráis; pedir** ⟶ **no pidáis; dormir** ⟶ **no durmáis.**

## ACTIVIDADES

**A** Escoja el consejo (*advice*) adecuado que usted debe dar de acuerdo con la situación.

1. Su compañero saca notas muy bajas en la clase de química.
   a. Mira más programas de televisión.
   b. Practica en el laboratorio.
   c. Ve al cine con tu novia.

2. Su hermano quiere estar más delgado.
   a. No comas hamburguesas.
   b. No hagas ejercicio.
   c. No bebas té.

3. Su amiga quiere organizar una fiesta.
   a. Ve al cine por la noche.
   b. Repasa la lección.
   c. Invita a un grupo simpático.

4. A su amiga le gusta una sudadera que ve en una tienda.
   a. Cómprala.
   b. Préstala.
   c. Contéstala.

5. Su compañero quiere ir a un partido de fútbol muy importante.
   a. Saluda a tus amigos.
   b. Compra la entrada hoy.
   c. Practica con el entrenador.

Una madre besa a su hija en Oaxaca, México. El cuidado y el cariño que se les da a los niños es muy importante para que puedan ser adultos sanos física y mentalmente.

**B** Un estudiante extranjero quiere hacer unas compras en la tienda La Elegante del Centro Comercial Continente y no sabe dónde está. Déle las siguientes instrucciones para llegar allá.

*Modelo*   salir de la Facultad de Ciencias
**Sal de la Facultad de Ciencias.**

1. doblar a la derecha
2. seguir derecho hasta la calle Príncipe
3. tomar el autobús 32
4. bajarse en la Plaza San Martín
5. cruzar la plaza
6. doblar a la izquierda en la calle Real
7. caminar tres cuadras y allí está el centro comercial

**C** Usted está cuidando a un niño de seis años. Dígale todas las cosas que debe hacer.

*Modelo*   despertarse     **Despiértate.**

1. levantarse
2. lavarse la cara y los dientes
3. vestirse
4. ponerse las medias y los zapatos
5. venir a desayunar
6. beber el jugo de naranja
7. comer el cereal
8. salir a jugar

**D** Usted está a cargo de una clase de ejercicios. Sus alumnos están haciendo mal algunos ejercicios. Dígales lo que deben hacer.

*Modelo*   Magdalena respira por la boca.
**Magdalena, no respires por la boca.**

1. Juan dobla las rodillas.
2. Berta mueve las caderas.
3. Alfonso baja los brazos.
4. Irma sube los hombros.
5. Francisco salta.
6. Rafael levanta los pies.

**E** Su compañero/a tiene una entrevista esta tarde. Dígale qué debe hacer y qué no debe hacer para causar una buena impresión.

*Modelo*   **Llega temprano. No hables demasiado.**

**F** Piense en alguna actividad y dígale a su compañero/a que la haga. Su compañero/a debe hacerla.

*Modelo*   **Pon la mano derecha sobre el hombro izquierdo.**

# EN CONTEXTO

**El peso** (*weight*)

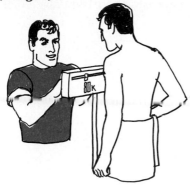

Eduardo pesa 80 kilos.
Eduardo pesa menos que Álvaro.

Álvaro pesa 95 kilos.
Álvaro pesa más que Eduardo.

**La estatura**

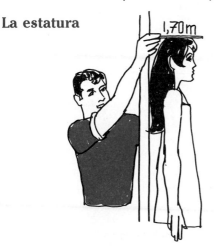

Juliana mide 1 metro 70.
Juliana es más alta que Adela.

Adela mide 1 metro 57.
Adela es más baja que Juliana.

## *ACTIVIDADES*

**A** Preguntas

1. ¿Cuánto mide la pizarra? ¿y el salón de clase? ¿y la puerta?
2. ¿Cuánto mide su habitación?
3. ¿Cuál es más grande, el salón de clase o su habitación?
4. ¿Cuál es más pequeño, el libro o el lápiz?

**B** Pregúntele a su compañero/a cuánto mide en metros y cuánto pesa en kilos. Después su compañero/a debe hacerle las mismas preguntas a usted (no es necesario decir la verdad). Use la siguiente tabla con las equivalencias aproximadas para las conversiones. Si su peso o su estatura no aparece en la tabla, dé un número aproximado basándose en los números de la tabla.

| ESTATURA | | PESO | |
|---|---|---|---|
| *PIES* | *METROS* | *LIBRAS* | *KILOS* |
| 5 | 1,52 | 90 | 41 |
| 5,1 | 1,55 | 100 | 45,5 |
| 5,2 | 1.58 | 110 | 50 |
| 5,3 | 1,60 | 120 | 54,5 |
| 5,4 | 1,62 | 130 | 59 |
| 5,5 | 1.65 | 140 | 63,5 |
| 5,6 | 1,68 | 150 | 68 |
| 5,7 | 1,70 | 160 | 72,5 |
| 5,8 | 1,73 | 170 | 77 |
| 5,9 | 1,75 | 180 | 81,5 |
| 5,10 | 1,78 | 190 | 86 |
| 5,11 | 1,80 | 200 | 91 |
| 6 | 1,83 | 210 | 95 |
| 6,1 | 1,85 | 220 | 100 |
| 6,2 | 1,88 | 230 | 104,5 |

## GRAMÁTICA

### Comparisons of inequality

**1.** Use **más. . . que** or **menos. . . que** to express unequal comparisons.

> Ella es { más / menos } activa que él.
>
> *She is { more / less } active than he.*
>
> El doctor tiene { más / menos } pacientes que el especialista.
>
> *The doctor has { more / fewer } patients than the specialist.*

**2.** Use **de** instead of **que** before numbers.

Humberto tiene **más de** veinte años.
Jorge pesa **menos de** 80 kilos.

**3.** The following adjectives have regular and irregular comparative forms.

| | | |
|---|---|---|
| bueno | más bueno/mejor | *better* |
| malo | más malo/peor | *worse* |
| pequeño | más pequeño/menor | *smaller* |
| joven | más joven/menor | *younger* |
| grande | más grande/mayor | *bigger* |
| viejo | más viejo/mayor | *older* |

**Menor** and **mayor** normally refer to a person's age.

La doctora es $\begin{Bmatrix} \text{mayor} \\ \text{menor} \end{Bmatrix}$ que la enfermera.

Este gimnasio es $\begin{Bmatrix} \text{mejor} \\ \text{peor} \end{Bmatrix}$ que aquél.

## ACTIVIDADES

**A** Compare a estos dos estudiantes usando los adjetivos que aparecen más abajo.

*Modelos*   **Felipe es más activo que Gloria.**
**Gloria es menos activa que Felipe.**

| **Gloria López Reyes** | **Felipe Saura Torres** |
|---|---|
| Edad: 19 años | Edad: 20 años |
| Estatura: 1, 60 m. | Estatura: 1, 80 m. |
| Peso: 50 kilos | Peso: 84 kilos |
| Promedio: A | Promedio: B |
| Actividades: Club de Latín | Actividades: Club de Baile |
|    Presidenta del Club de Ciencias |    Redactor (*editor*) del periódico |
| Honores: Beca (*scholarship*) | Honores: Premio (*prize*) por sus editoriales |
|    de matemáticas | Intereses: deportes, baile, música popular, |
| Intereses: lectura, arte, música clásica |    guitarra |

| | |
|---|---|
| serio | simpático |
| delgado | trabajador |
| atlético | popular |
| inteligente | joven |
| alegre | interesante |
| fuerte | alto |

**B** Compare estas dos clínicas.

> *Modelo*  **La Clínica Villalón tiene menos camas que la Clínica El Bosque.**

| **Clínica Villalón** | **Clínica El Bosque** |
|---|---|
| 18 camas | 80 camas |
| 8 doctores | 30 doctores |
| 10 enfermeras | 50 enfermeras |
| 12 cuartos | 50 cuartos |
| farmacia y cafetería | farmacia y cafetería |
| salón de cirugía (*surgery*) | 2 salones de cirugía |
| laboratorio | 2 laboratorios |
| servicio de ambulancia | servicio de ambulancia |
| médico residente 24 horas | 2 médicos residentes 24 horas |

**C** Compare a las siguientes personas.

1. Woody Allen y Robert Redford
2. Madonna y Cher
3. Fernando Valenzuela y Don Mattingly
4. Julio Iglesias y Plácido Domingo

**D** Con un compañero/a compare los precios de las oficinas más caras del mundo.

> *Modelo*  **Las oficinas de Chicago son más caras que las de Madrid.**

**LAS OFICINAS DE ALQUILER MAS CARAS DEL MUNDO**

| | |
|---|---|
| Tokio | 16.690 ptas. m² |
| Londres | 14.989 ptas. m² |
| New York | 6.674 ptas. m² |
| París | 6.633 ptas. m² |
| Hong Kong | 6.493 ptas. m² |
| Chicago | 4.207 ptas. m² |
| Los Angeles | 4.177 ptas. m² |
| Madrid | 3.734 ptas. m² |
| San Francisco | 3.573 ptas. m² |
| Frankfurt | 3.543 ptas. m² |
| São Paulo | 2.848 ptas. m² |
| Barcelona | 2.637 ptas. m² |
| Bruselas | 2.335 ptas. m² |
| Amsterdam | 1.912 ptas. m² |

## EN CONTEXTO

### En una clase de ejercicios aeróbicos

Hay tantas chicas como chicos en la clase de ejercicios.
Felipe es tan fuerte como Arturo.
Ana es tan alta como Lucía.
Carlos pesa tanto como Arturo.

### Preguntas

1. ¿Dónde están estas personas?
2. ¿Qué están haciendo?
3. ¿Cuántos hombres hay? ¿y mujeres?
4. ¿Quién pesa tanto como Carlos?
5. ¿Quién salta tanto como Marcia?
6. ¿Quién es más baja, Ana o Lucía?

## ACTIVIDADES

**A** Diga qué cosas se hacen y no se hacen en un gimnasio.

> *Modelo*   ver televisión
> **No se ve televisión.**

bailar          saltar       levantar los brazos       tocar el piano       correr       dormir
hacer la tarea   cocinar      hablar

**B** Llame por teléfono a su amigo/a para ir al gimnasio. Complete el siguiente diálogo con su compañero/a.

| | |
|---|---|
| **Amigo/a** | ¡Aló! |
| **Usted** | ____, te habla ____. ¿Cómo estás? |
| **Amigo/a** | ____. ¿Y tú? |
| **Usted** | ____. Te llamo porque ____. ¿Quieres venir? |
| **Amigo/a** | ____. |
| **Usted** | Paso por ti a ____. |
| **Amigo/a** | Te espero ____. |

## GRAMÁTICA

### Comparisons of equality

| | |
|---|---|
| tan... como | *as ... as* |
| tantos/as... como | *as many ... as* |
| tanto/a... como | *as much ... as* |
| tanto como | *as much as* |

1. Use **tan. . . como** to express equal comparisons with adjectives.

   Él es **tan** alto **como** ella.                    *He is as tall as she.*

2. Use **tanto(s)/tanta(s). . . como** to express equal comparison with nouns.

   Cristina tiene **tanto** trabajo **como** su amiga.                    *Christina has as much work as her friend.*
   Hay **tanta** leche **como** café.                    *There is as much milk as coffee.*
   Hay **tantos** chicos **como** chicas.                    *There are as many boys as girls.*
   Hay **tantas** enfermeras **como** técnicos.                    *There are as many nurses as technicians.*

**3.** Use **tanto como** to express equal comparison of activities.

La enfermera trabaja **tanto como** el doctor.     *The nurse works as much as the doctor.*

## ACTIVIDADES

**A** Complete las siguientes oraciones. Trabaje con un/a estudiante.

    1. Soy tan inteligente como...
    2. Un tigre come tanto como...
    3. Mi novio/a es tan guapo/a como...
    4. En Nueva York hay tantos teatros como...
    5. Los Ángeles es tan bonito como...
    6. King Kong es tan feo como...

**B** Use las cinco características que aparecen en la tabla para comparar a los estudiantes.

  *Modelo*   **Vilma tiene tantos hermanos como Marta o Vilma tiene más hermanos que Ricardo.**

|  | **Pedro** | **Vilma** | **Marta** | **Ricardo** |
|---|---|---|---|---|
| clases | 5 | 5 | 4 | 6 |
| dinero | $15 | $8 | $15 | $8 |
| hermanos | 3 | 4 | 4 | 3 |
| discos | 225 | 253 | 253 | 309 |
| casetes | 45 | 38 | 56 | 56 |

Unos jóvenes levantan pesas en un gimnasio de México.

**C** El Dr. López y la Dra. Garcés son unos cirujanos (*surgeons*) excelentes. Compárelos usando las siguientes palabras.

> *Modelos*    famoso     **El Dr. López es tan famoso como la Dra. Garcés.**
>               ganar dinero   **La Dra. Garcés gana tanto dinero como el Dr. López.**

| | | | |
|---|---|---|---|
| bueno | tener pacientes | inteligente | enfermeras |
| trabajar | tener libros | viajar | saber |

**D** **Opiniones.** Exprese su opinión comparando las siguientes personas o cosas. Puede usar las palabras que aparecen entre paréntesis o usar otras palabras.

> *Modelo*    comida china y comida italiana (buena)
> **La comida china es tan buena como la comida italiana** o **La comida china es mejor/peor que la comida italiana.**

1. Tina Turner y Liza Minelli
   (famosa / rica / simpática / alta)
2. autos norteamericanos y autos japoneses
   (bueno / grande / caro / cómodo / fuerte)
3. dos ciudades (e.g., Nueva York y San Francisco)
   (teatros / cines / restaurantes / habitantes / hoteles)
4. dos programas de televisión
   (triste / largo / bueno / simpático / malo)

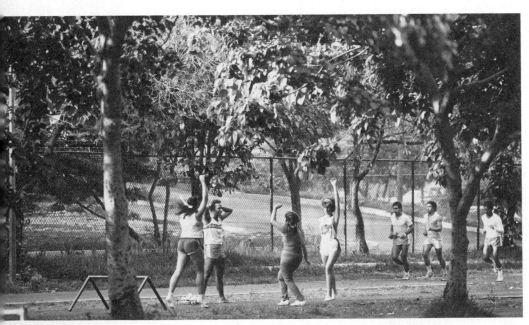

Unos estudiantes venezolanos hacen ejercicio y trotan en los terrenos de la Universidad de Caracas.

# LECTURA

Esta selección sobre los ejercicios aparece en el libro *Salud y nutrición*. Las siguientes palabras pueden ayudarlo/la a entender mejor la selección y la tabla.

| | |
|---|---|
| rato | *while* |
| aire libre | *open air* |
| desarrollar | *develop* |
| montañismo | *(mountain) trekking, hiking* |
| la respiración se entrecorta | *breathing becomes short* |
| con cuidado | *carefully* |
| parar | *to stop* |
| sin olvidar | *without forgetting* |

**¿Existe el deporte ideal?**

Se dice que el mejor deporte es caminar un buen rato todos los días y, a ser posible, al aire libre lejos de la contaminación urbana. Este ejercicio, como todos aquellos que más se acercan a los movimientos naturales, que en su día practicaban los hombres primitivos, son los ideales para desarrollar armónicamente el cuerpo humano: la natación, el montañismo, la marcha, el salto...

La marcha, tan de moda hoy día, es un buen deporte, pero hay que realizarlo de manera progresiva y con cuidado. Lo mejor es adoptar un trote rítmico, respirando adecuadamente, de tal manera que te permita hablar con facilidad a la persona que está a tu lado. Si no es así, y la respiración se entrecorta en exceso, es mejor parar y proseguir al cabo de un rato.

El gráfico siguiente da una idea aproximada de las actividades que pueden influir en cada uno de los factores resistencia, flexibilidad y fuerza, sin olvidar la forma en que contribuyen a liberar la tensión y la ansiedad.

| Actividad | Resistencia | Flexibilidad | Fuerza | Relajación |
|---|---|---|---|---|
| Atletismo | ** | **** | *** | ** |
| Baile | *** | **** | * | **** |
| Ciclismo | **** | ** | *** | **** |
| Fútbol | *** | *** | *** | * |
| Golf | * | ** | * | **** |
| Jogging | **** | ** | ** | **** |
| Marcha | ** | * | * | **** |
| Montaña | *** | * | ** | ** |
| Natación | **** | **** | **** | **** |
| Squash | *** | *** | ** | ** |
| Subir escaleras | *** | * | ** | * |
| Tenis | ** | *** | ** | ** |
| Trabajos domésticos | * | ** | * | * |
| Yoga | * | *** | * | **** |

   \* *Muy poco útil*     \*\*\* *Bastante útil*
\*\* *Útil*     \*\*\*\* *Muy útil*

## ¿Verdadero o Falso?

Diga si las siguientes oraciones son verdaderas o falsas de acuerdo con la lectura.

1. El mejor deporte es trotar.
2. Es muy bueno hacer ejercicios de movimientos naturales.
3. Es mejor caminar en las ciudades.
4. Para caminar es una buena idea empezar poco a poco.
5. Los ejercicios ayudan a eliminar las tensiones.

## Preguntas

Para contestar las siguientes preguntas consulte la tabla de actividades.

1. ¿Cuáles son los ejercicios que son muy útiles para la resistencia?
2. ¿Qué ejercicio es más útil para la flexibilidad, el tenis o la natación?
3. ¿Qué ejercicio le da más fuerza a la persona, subir escaleras o el ciclismo?
4. ¿Qué ejercicios ayudan menos a la relajación?
5. Según la tabla, ¿cuáles son los mejores ejercicios?

**¿Cuál es?** Escoja una de las actividades que aparecen en la tabla. No le diga a su compañero/a cuál es. Sólo le debe decir cuántos asteriscos tiene en una categoría. Su compañero/a debe tratar de adivinar cuál es.

| *Modelo* | |
|---|---|
| **Usted** | **Tres asteriscos en flexibilidad.** |
| **Compañero/a** | **El fútbol.** |
| **Usted** | **No. Dos asteriscos en relajación.** |
| **Compañero/a** | **El tenis.** |
| **Usted** | **Muy bien.** |

Lea el siguiente anuncio sobre un lugar llamado Pardiñas 50 y conteste después las preguntas.

1. ¿Es grande o pequeño este lugar?
2. ¿Quiénes atienden al público?
3. ¿Qué pueden hacer las personas allí?
4. ¿Por qué se llama Pardiñas 50?
5. ¿Por qué dice el anuncio que este lugar es «algo más que un gimnasio»?
6. ¿Qué le interesa a usted más de este gimnasio? ¿Por qué?

## SITUACIONES

1. You are expecting company for the weekend. Your friend has come to help you with the housework. Tell your friend to (a) open the windows, (b) vacuum the living room, (c) put towels in the bathroom, and (d) prepare a salad.
2. You are organizing a surprise party for a friend. Two of your classmates are going to help. Tell them (a) what they should do, (b) what they should bring, (c) whom they should call, and so on. Your classmates should give you some ideas about the party.
3. Compare your university with a rival school. You may use the following elements to compare them: (a) athletic teams (e.g., football, basketball), (b) size, (c) number of students, (d) tuition, (e) professors, (f) departments, (g) . . .
4. Imagine you are a foreign student. You want to go someplace on campus. Ask your partner where it is located. Your partner will give you directions to get there.
5. Your best friend tells you that he/she is feeling very depressed (**deprimido/a**). Tell him/ her (a) to go out with friends, (b) to talk to other people, (c) to call you, and (d) to do some exercise. Add any other advice you may deem necessary.
6. Compare two sports with respect to activity, players, interest, and so on, telling why you prefer one over the other. Ask your partner about his/her favorite sport.
7. Select two cars you are familiar with and compare them with respect to size, speed, price, appearance, shape, prestige, weight, and any other characteristic you can think of.

8. You are "lucky" today. Everyone is asking you for directions. Look at the map below and tell each person how to get to his/her destination.

| You are at | Person wants to go to |
|---|---|
| a. Torre Europa | El Corte Inglés |
| b. Palacio de los Deportes | Plaza de toros |
| c. Plaza de M. Becerra | Torre España |

# VOCABULARIO[2]

**ejercicios**

| | |
|---|---|
| el accidente | *accident* |
| el calentamiento | *warm-up* |
| los ejercicios aeróbi-cos | *aerobics* |
| el movimiento | *movement* |
| el músculo | *muscle* |
| el peso | *weight* |
| la sesión | *session* |

| | |
|---|---|
| **estatura** | *height* |
| el metro | *meter* |
| el pie | *foot* |

| | |
|---|---|
| **peso** | *weight* |
| el kilo | *kilo* |
| la libra | *pound* |

**descripciones**

| | |
|---|---|
| difícil | *difficult* |
| fácil | *easy* |
| mayor | *bigger, older* |
| mejor | *better* |
| menor | *smaller, younger* |
| peor | *worse* |

| | |
|---|---|
| **tiempo** | |
| el minuto | *minute* |

**verbos**

| | |
|---|---|
| bajar | *to lower, to bring down* |
| calentar (ie) | *to warm up* |
| dedicar (qu) | *dedicate* |
| doblar | *to bend* |
| evitar | *to avoid* |
| medir (i) | *to measure* |
| mover (ue) | *to move* |
| pesar | *to weigh* |
| respirar | *to breathe* |
| saltar | *to jump* |

**palabras útiles**

| | |
|---|---|
| cada | *each* |
| el dibujo | *drawing* |
| siguiente | *following* |
| vez | *time* |

**expresiones útiles**

| | |
|---|---|
| al contrario | *on the contrary* |
| más... que | *more . . . than, adj. + est than* |
| menos... que | *less . . . than, fewer . . . than* |
| por lo menos | *at least* |
| tan... como | *as . . . as* |
| tanto/a... como | *as much . . . as* |
| tantos/as... como | *as many . . . as* |

---

[2] For parts of the body, see pages 216–217.

In Lección 10 **you will**
a. **plan menus.**
b. **order food.**
c. **express wishes and hope.**
d. **make requests.**
e. **express opinions.**
f. **express doubt.**
g. **express fear and worry.**
h. **express joy and satisfaction.**

# Supermercado La Cubanita

zanahorias
0,48 kilo

espinacas
0,50 1/2 kilo

pimiento verde
1,00 kilo

vinagre
1,20 1/2 litro

aceite
2,29 1/2 litro

salsa de tomate
0,23 lata

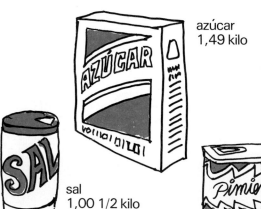

azúcar
1,49 kilo

sal
1,00 1/2 kilo

pimienta
0,50 2 gramos

mostaza
1,35

mayonesa
1,89

arroz
1,19 kilo

# La comida

## Su mercado latino

aguacates
0,50 cada uno

limones
0,60 docena

papas
1,00 2 kilos

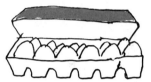

huevos
1,09 docena

pavo
1,99 1/2 kilo

lechuga
0,40

ajo
0,90 1/4 kilo

cebollas
0,50 kilo

tocino
1,98 1/2 kilo

carne molida
2,79 1 kilo

## ACTIVIDADES ━━━━━━━━━━━━━

**A** Pregúntele a su compañero/a el precio de algunos de los comestibles en el Supermercado La Cubanita.

| *Modelo* | **Usted** | **¿Cuánto cuestan las zanahorias?** |
|---|---|---|
| | **Compañero/a** | **Cuestan 48 centavos el kilo.** |

**B** Con un/a compañero/a haga una lista de la comida que tienen en el refrigerador y en la despensa (*pantry*). Después otros/as compañeros/as les van a preguntar qué tienen ustedes.

| **Refrigerador** | **Despensa** |
|---|---|
| leche | cereal |
| tomates | azúcar |
| carne | salsa de tomate |

| *Modelo* | **Compañero/a** | **¿Qué tienen en el refrigerador?** |
|---|---|---|
| | **Usted** | **Tenemos leche, tomates y carne.** |
| | **Compañero/a** | **¿Qué tienen en la despensa?** |
| | **Usted** | **Tenemos cereal, azúcar y salsa de tomate.** |

**C** La señora García está preparando su lista de compras para la semana. Prepare la lista según las comidas que quiere servir.

*Quiere servir*

fruta
vegetales
ensalada
2 clases de carne
comida para el desayuno
una cena italiana

*Lista de compras*

**D** En grupos de tres personas decidan lo que van a cenar. Preparen un menú y una lista de lo que tienen que comprar. Después las personas de otro grupo les van a hacer las siguientes preguntas.

1. ¿Cuál es el menú?
2. ¿Qué tienen que comprar?
3. ¿A cuántas personas van a invitar?
4. ¿Cuánto va a costar la cena?

# Cultura

## Food in the Hispanic world

When shopping for food in Hispanic countries, people generally go to specialty stores (**panadería,** bakery; **carnicería,** meat market; **heladería,** ice-cream shop; **dulcería,** or **pastelería,** pastry shop; **frutería,** fruit store; **pescadería,** fish market). However, many people who live in the cities find it more convenient and sometimes more economical to shop at supermarkets.

Hispanic cuisine varies not only from country to country but also from region to region. Some of the more popular dishes throughout the Hispanic countries are **la paella,** a Spanish dish made of rice, seafood, and chicken; **el arroz con pollo,** which may be cooked in water, chicken broth, white wine, or beer; and the Mexican **enchiladas** and **tacos,** made with **tortillas** (corn or wheat dough shaped like a very thin pancake) filled with meat or chicken. Many Hispanic dishes are becoming increasingly popular in the United States, especially in the Southwest and in cities like Miami, Chicago, and New York, where the necessary ingredients can be easily found in supermarkets and Latin stores.

Mealtimes in Hispanic countries differ from those in the United States. People typically eat breakfast (**el desayuno**) at around 7:00 or 8:00 A.M. Breakfast normally consists of **café con leche** or **chocolate caliente** with bread, a sweet roll, and sometimes juice or fruit. This is a light breakfast, so people sometimes have a snack in the late morning.

The main meal of the day is lunch (**el almuerzo** or **la comida**), eaten between 1:00 and 3:00 P.M., depending on the country. Normally the entire family can eat together, because children return from school around 1:00 and many businesses close at lunchtime. This is changing, however, especially in cities, due to the distances, traffic, and time involved. Lunch consists of soup or beans, rice and/or potatoes, salad, and a fish or meat dish. After the dessert, adults usually drink coffee.

Supper (**la cena** or **comida**) is served after 7:00 or 8:00 P.M., sometimes as late as 10:00 or 11:00 in Spain. Dinner is generally lighter than lunch. Because it is eaten rather late, many Hispanics have an afternoon snack (**la merienda**), which may consist of pastries or small sandwiches and tea, coffee, or a soft drink.

Dining etiquette differs somewhat from that in the United States. In Hispanic countries, it is a custom that people place both forearms on the table while eating. In Spain and other countries, people eat with the fork in the left hand and the knife in the right. Fruits are generally peeled and eaten with a knife and fork.

Una frutería de Buenos Aires.

# EN CONTEXTO

### Una invitación a cenar

La Sra. Ochoa tiene invitados esta noche y está muy ocupada. Tiene que sacar
la vajilla° y las copas°, poner la mesa y preparar la cena. Ella está en la cocina      *china / glasses*
hablando con su hija Petra.

| | |
|---|---|
| **Sra. Ochoa** | Necesito ir al supermercado. Esta noche los Morales vienen a cenar. |
| **Petra** | ¿Quieres que vaya? Yo no tengo clases hasta las once. |
| **Sra. Ochoa** | Me alegro° que puedas ir. Tengo tanto que hacer. |
| **Petra** | Tú te preocupas mucho, mamá. Los Morales son casi de la familia. |
| **Sra. Ochoa** | Sí, pero a mí me gusta que todo quede° perfecto. |
| **Petra** | Bueno, ¿qué necesitas? |
| **Sra. Ochoa** | Necesito que traigas° medio kilo de mantequilla°, pan, dos kilos de camarones° y helado de vainilla. |
| **Petra** | ¿Tienes verduras°? |
| **Sra. Ochoa** | Espero que haya en el refrigerador. (Abre el refrigerador.) Sí, hay suficientes°. |
| **Petra** | ¿Algo más? |
| **Sra. Ochoa** | No, eso es todo. Aquí tienes el dinero. |

*Me... I'm glad*

*to be*

*bring / butter*
*shrimp*

*vegetables*

*enough*

### Para completar

Complete las siguientes oraciones según el diálogo

1. Los invitados de esta noche son...
2. La mamá tiene que poner...
3. Para ayudar a su madre Petra va a ir...

4. Para la cena la mamá necesita...
5. En el refrigerador hay...
6. Para las compras, la mamá le da a Petra...

Un moderno supermercado
en Caracas, Venezuela.

## Vamos a poner la mesa

la botella de vino
el vaso   la taza
el tenedor
la cucharita
la servilleta   el plato   el cuchillo   la cuchara
el mantel

## *ACTIVIDADES*

**A** Usted es el administrador/la administradora de un restaurante y está entrenando a un camarero. Dígale dónde debe poner cada cosa de acuerdo con el dibujo.

*Modelo*   **Ponga el cuchillo a la derecha del plato.**

**B** Usted necesita comprar los ingredientes de su receta favorita. Dígale a su compañero/a cuáles son los ingredientes que necesita.

**C** Usted está muy ocupado/a porque tiene invitados esta noche. Dígale a su compañero/a todas las cosas que tiene que hacer.

## GRAMÁTICA

### Indicative versus subjunctive

In previous lessons you have used the present tense of the indicative mood (**Yo sé que Pepe estudia español.**). The indicative is used to state facts (what is happening, happens regularly, has happened), or is certain to happen. Thus, in the above sentence, I am stating the fact that I know something (**sé**) and also the fact that Pepe studies Spanish (**estudia**).

You have also learned commands (**usted** or **ustedes**), which are forms of the subjunctive. Spanish uses the subjunctive to express what we want to happen (**Quiero que vayas al supermercado.**), hope will happen (**Espero que vuelvas pronto.**), and in situations in which there is an emotional reaction (**Me alegro que vayas.**).

## Present subjunctive

|  | **hablar** | **comer** | **vivir** |
|---|---|---|---|
| yo | hable | coma | viva |
| tú | hables | comas | vivas |
| él, ella, usted | hable | coma | viva |
| nosotros/as | hablemos | comamos | vivamos |
| vosotros/as | habléis | comáis | viváis |
| ellos/as, ustedes | hablen | coman | vivan |

**1.** To form the present subjunctive use the **yo** form of the present indicative, drop the final **o**, and add the subjunctive endings. Notice that as with **usted/ustedes** commands, **-ar** verbs change the **a** to **e**, and **-er** and **-ir** verbs change the **e** and **i** to **a**.

**2.** The present subjunctive forms of verbs with irregular indicative **yo** forms are

| **conocer:** | conozca, conozcas... | **tener:** | tenga, tengas... |
|---|---|---|---|
| **decir:** | diga, digas... | **traer:** | traiga, traigas... |
| **hacer:** | haga, hagas... | **venir:** | venga, vengas... |
| **poner:** | ponga, pongas... | **ver:** | vea, veas... |
| **salir:** | salga, salgas... | | |

Una antigua dulcería de la ciudad de México. En los pueblos y ciudades hispanas hay numerosas dulcerías donde se pueden comprar los dulces típicos de la región.

**3.** The following verbs have irregular forms:

   **ir:**  vaya, vayas...       **saber:**  sepa, sepas...       **ser:**  sea, seas...

**4.** The verbs **dar** and **estar** require written accent marks.

   **dar:**      dé, des, dé, demos deis, den
   **estar:**   esté, estés, esté, estemos, estéis, estén

**5.** Stem changing **-ar** and **-er** verbs follow the same pattern as in the present indicative.

   **pensar:**   piense, pienses, piense, pensemos, penséis, piensen
   **volver:**   vuelva, vuelvas, vuelva, volvamos, volváis, vuelvan

**6.** Stem-changing **-ir** verbs follow the pattern of the present indicative, but have an additional change in the **nosotros** and **vosotros** forms.

   **preferir:**   prefiera, prefieras, prefiera, prefiramos, prefiráis, prefieran
   **dormir:**    duerma, duermas, duerma, durmamos, durmáis, duerman

## The subjunctive used to express wishes and hope

**1.** When the verb of the main clause expresses wanting or hoping, use a subjunctive verb form in the dependent clause.

main clause    dependent clause

| La jefa quiere | que (él) **haga** el trabajo. | *The boss wants him to do the work.* |
| Yo espero | que **termine** temprano. | *I hope he'll finish early.* |

Notice that there is a different subject in each clause. If there is no change in subjects, use an infinitive instead of a clause with the subjunctive.

| Yo **espero terminar** temprano. | *I hope to finish early.* |
| La jefa **quiere hacer** el trabajo. | *The boss wants to do the work. (herself)* |

**2.** Common verbs that express wanting and hoping are **desear, esperar, necesitar, pedir, preferir, permitir** (*to permit*), **prohibir** (*to prohibit or forbid*), and **querer.** With the verbs **pedir, permitir,** and **prohibir,** Spanish may use an indirect object.

| **Me** prohíbe que (yo) entre. | *He forbids me to go in.* |
| **Les** permite que salgan esta noche. | *He allows them to go out tonight.* |

**3.** With the verb **decir,** use the subjunctive in the dependent clause when expressing a wish or an order. Use the indicative when reporting something.

| Dice que los niños **duermen.** | *She says (that) the children are sleepi⌐* |
| | *(reporting)* |
| Dice que los niños **duerman.** | *She says (that) the children should sl⌐* |

## The subjunctive used with verbs of emotion

**1.** When the verb of the main clause expresses emotion (fear, happiness, sorrow, and so on), use a subjunctive verb form in the dependent clause.

Sentimos que no **puedan** venir.      *We're sorry (that) they can't come.*
Me alegro de que **estés** aquí.      *I'm glad (that) you're here.*

**2.** Common verbs that express emotions are **alegrarse (de), sentir, gustar,** and **temer** (*to fear*).

## ACTIVIDADES

**A** Usted está organizando una reunión del club de español. Dígales a sus compañeros lo que usted quiere que hagan para la reunión.

*Modelo*    Marta / traer los vasos
       **Quiero que Marta traiga los vasos.**

   1. Alberto / invitar a los profesores
   2. Julia y Ángeles / preparar la ensalada
   3. Vilma / comprar los refrescos
   4. Roberto / traer el estéreo
   5. Juan y Berta / poner la mesa

**B** Ustedes piensan ir de excursión el sábado y reciben esta nota de su amigo David. ¿Qué dice David que ustedes deben hacer para la excursión?

*Modelo*    preparen unos sándwiches
       **David dice que preparemos unos sándwiches.**

> Llamen a Federico.
> Pasen por María.
> Desayunen bien antes de salir.
> Salgan temprano.
> Traigan refrescos.

**C** Usted tiene invitados a cenar esta noche. Diga qué cosas quiere usted que pasen.

*Modelo*    Deseo que... **Deseo que vengan temprano.**

   1. Quiero que...      3. Prefiero que...
   2. Espero que...      4. Necesito que...

**D** Unos amigos van a venir a su casa esta noche y usted tiene que cuidar a su hermanito. Dígale las cosas que usted no quiere que él haga.

*Modelo* **No quiero que salgas a la calle.**

**E** Los amigos de Arturo quieren que él haga las siguientes cosas este sábado. Diga que él no quiere hacerlas o que él quiere hacer otras cosas.

*Modelo* Quieren que se levante temprano.
**Pero él no quiere levantarse temprano** o **Pero él quiere levantarse tarde.**

1. Quieren que vaya a la playa con ellos.
2. Quieren que juegue vólibol en la playa.
3. Quieren que invite a su hermana.
4. Quieren que vaya al cine después.
5. Quieren que cene en el centro con ellos.

**F** Usted va a tener una entrevista para un trabajo. Diga todas las cosas que usted espera o necesita hacer ese día.

*Modelo* **Necesito (Espero) salir temprano.**

**G** Usted va a visitar a un amigo que está en la clínica. ¿Qué le dice usted a su amigo?

1. Siento que...
2. Me alegro de que...
3. Espero que...
4. Deseo que...

**H** En grupos de tres estudiantes hagan una lista de las actividades que permiten o prohíben en una fábrica o en una oficina.

*Modelo* **Permiten que salgan temprano para ir al médico.**
**Prohíben que beban cerveza en la cafetería.**

Unos clientes esperan a que los atiendan en una charcutería de Madrid. Los jamones serranos que están colgados al fondo son típicos de España.

# EN CONTEXTO

## En un restaurante

Ana Celia y Margarita quieren perder peso. Están en un restaurante que sirve comida sana y con pocas calorías.

---

**RESTAURANTE SU SALUD¹**

Comida sana a buenos precios

*Menú*

| Sándwiches | | Sopas | |
|---|---|---|---|
| Sándwich de aguacate y tomate | 2,50 | Sopa de tomate | 2,50 |
| Sándwich de pavo y lechuga | 3,80 | Sopa de cebolla | 2,50 |
| Sándwich de atún | 3,80 | Sopa de pollo | 3,00 |
| Sándwich de pollo | 4,00 | Sopa de papas | 2,50 |
| Sándwich de alfalfa y requesón | 2,50 | Sopa de zanahoria | 2,50 |

Platos combinados

| $6,50 | $7,50 |
|---|---|
| Pavo asado | Pescado al horno |
| Puré de papas | Papas hervidas |
| Ensalada de lechuga y tomate | Espinacas |
| Yogur de fresa | Sorbete de naranja |

| Postres | | Bebidas | |
|---|---|---|---|
| Frutas de la estación | 2,00 | Leche descremada | 1,50 |
| Yogur | 1,50 | Jugo de naranja | 2,00 |
| Gelatina | 1,50 | Té | 1,00 |
| | | Café descafeinado | 1,00 |
| | | Agua mineral | 1,00 |

Gracias por su visita y conserve su salud.
No se admiten propinas.

---

| | |
|---|---|
| **Ana Celia** | ¿Crees que a Gilberto le guste esta comida? |
| **Margarita** | No, yo no creo que le guste. A él le encantan las salsas, la carne, los postres… |
| **Ana Celia** | Bueno, ¿por qué no lo invitamos y así la prueba? Quizás le guste. |
| **Margarita** | Si lo invitas a un restaurante francés o español, seguro que acepta. Pero aquí, dudo que acepte. |

## Preguntas

1. ¿Cómo se llama el restaurante?
2. ¿Qué tipo de comida sirven?
3. ¿Por qué van a ese restaurante Ana Celia y Margarita?
4. ¿A quién quiere invitar Ana Celia?
5. ¿Qué clase de comida prefiere Gilberto?
6. ¿Cree Ana Celia que él va a aceptar la invitación?

---

¹ *key* requesón *cottage cheese* asado *roast* hervidas *boiled* descremada *nonfat* propina *tip*

## ACTIVIDADES

**A** Usted y su compañero/a están en el restaurante Su Salud. Lean el menú y decidan qué van a pedir.

**B** Usted es vegetariano/a. Diga qué platos puede usted comer de cada grupo.

| grupo 1 | grupo 2 | grupo 3 |
|---|---|---|
| sopa de pollo y vegetales | sándwich de jamón y queso | carne asada, papas fritas y ensalada |
| sopa de zanahoria | sándwich de ensalada de pollo | espaguetis con salsa de tomate y ensalada de espinacas |
| sopa de cebolla | sándwich de tomate, alfalfa y aguacate | pescado frito, arroz y verduras |

**C** Prepare con su compañero/a dos clases de menú: un menú normal y un menú vegetariano.

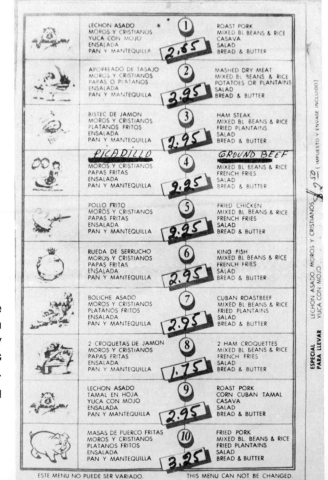

El menú de un restaurante de Miami, donde la comida cubana es también muy popular entre muchos norteamericanos.

## GRAMÁTICA

### The subjunctive used with verbs and expressions of doubt

**1.** When the verb in the main clause expresses doubt or uncertainty, use a subjunctive verb form in the dependent clause.

Dudo que ella **conozca** a Amanda.        *I doubt that she knows Amanda.*

**2.** When doubt is implied with the verbs **creer** and **pensar** in questions or in the negative, use a subjunctive verb form in the dependent clause. If no doubt is implied, use the indicative.

¿Crees que $\left\{ \begin{array}{l} \textbf{lleguen} \\ \textbf{llegan} \end{array} \right\}$ hoy?        *Do you think they'll arrive today?*

No, no creo que **lleguen** hoy.        *No, I don't think they'll arrive today.*

**3.** Since the expressions **tal vez** (*perhaps*) and **quizá(s)** convey doubt, the subjunctive is normally used.

$\left. \begin{array}{l} \text{Tal vez} \\ \text{Quizá(s)} \end{array} \right\}$ ella **pruebe** el postre.        *Perhaps she'll try the dessert.*

## ACTIVIDADES

**A** **¿Qué cree usted?** Diga su opinión sobre las cosas que se afirman más abajo.

*Modelo*    Hay vida en Marte.
          **Creo que hay vida en Marte** o **Dudo/no creo que haya vida en Marte** o **Tal vez/Quizá(s) haya vida en Marte.**

1. Los Yankees tienen los mejores jugadores.
2. El yogur tiene muchas calorías.
3. Todos debemos beber mucha agua.
4. Los amigos son más importantes que el dinero.
5. Los médicos visitan a los enfermos en su casa.
6. El pescado es mejor que la carne para la salud.
7. Es importante hacer ejercicio regularmente.
8. La comida afecta nuestra personalidad.

**B** Su compañero/a dice muchas mentiras. Él/Ella va a decir las cosas que hace, las personas que conoce, etc. y usted le va a decir a otro/a compañero/a que usted lo duda.

*Modelo*    —**Hablo todos los días con Eddie Murphy.**
          —**Dudo que él hable todos los días con Eddie Murphy.**

**C** Usted tiene una cita (*date*) con una persona muy especial. Diga lo que usted espera que pase en esa cita y lo que usted duda que pase.

**Modelo**  **Espero que me invite a comer.**
**Dudo que vayamos a un restaurante elegante.**

**D** En grupos de cuatro estudiantes determine la opinión de sus compañeros/as sobre los siguientes temas.

**Modelo**  las vacaciones
**Usted**  **Creo que las vacaciones son importantes para todos. ¿Y tú qué crees?**
**Compañero/a**  **Dudo que las vacaciones muy cortas sean buenas para todos.**

la lotería   la televisión   la música popular   la universidad   los doctores
la vida en los Estados Unidos

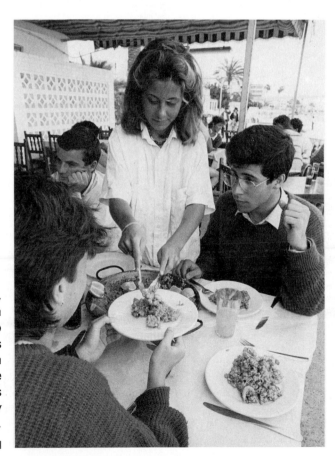

En un restaurante de Málaga, España, una pareja observa cómo les sirven paella, uno de los platos más populares en el mundo hispano. La paella se hace básicamente con arroz, carne, mariscos *(seafood)*, cebolla, ajo y azafrán *(saffron)*.

Unos jóvenes en uno de los muchos restaurantes y cafeterías que sirven comida cubana en Miami.

## EN CONTEXTO

### Miami

Miami es la ciudad más famosa de la Florida. Hay muchísimos hoteles grandes, especialmente en las playas. Tiene el mayor número de cubanos de cualquier° *any* ciudad de los Estados Unidos, tal vez porque está cerca de Cuba y porque el clima es como el de Cuba.

La Pequeña Habana es la zona más hispana de Miami. Mide unos seis kilómetros cuadrados y está cerca del centro comercial de Miami. Además es una de las zonas más antiguas° de la ciudad. *old*

La Calle Ocho está en la Pequeña Habana. En esta calle hay muchas tiendas y negocios y también están allí los mejores restaurantes de comida cubana. Los platos típicos como los frijoles° negros y el arroz, los plátanos fritos, el *beans* cerdo° asado, el picadillo (carne molida cocinada con cebolla, pimiento verde *pork* y ajo) y el café cubano se encuentran en todos los menús. Se habla español en todas partes y las personas que visitan estos lugares reciben la impresión de estar en un país hispano.

### ¿Verdadero o falso?

Diga si las siguientes oraciones son verdaderas o falsas, de acuerdo con la selección leída.

1. El clima de Miami es diferente del clima de Cuba.
2. Miami tiene más cubanos que otros lugares de los Estados Unidos.
3. La Pequeña Habana está lejos del centro de los negocios de Miami.
4. Los restaurantes cubanos están cerca de la Pequeña Habana.
5. El pavo asado es un plato típico cubano.
6. En la Calle Ocho se habla español en las tiendas y los restaurantes.

252

**Preguntas**

1. ¿Cuál es la ciudad más famosa de la Florida?
2. ¿Dónde hay muchos hoteles grandes?
3. ¿Qué platos típicos sirven en los restaurantes cubanos?
4. Describa la Pequeña Habana.

## GRAMÁTICA

### The superlative

**1.** To form the superlative use a definitive article + noun + **más/menos** + adjective. To express *in* or *at* with the superlative use **de.**

Es **el** traje $\begin{Bmatrix} \text{más} \\ \text{menos} \end{Bmatrix}$ caro (**de** la tienda).    *It is the* $\begin{Bmatrix} \text{most} \\ \text{least} \end{Bmatrix}$ *expensive suit (in the store).*

**2.** Do not use **más** or **menos** with **mejor, peor, mayor,** and **menor.**

Son **los mejores** alumnos de la clase.    *They're the best students in the class.*

**3.** You may leave out the noun when using the superlative.

Es el más caro de la tienda.    *It's the most expensive (one) in the store.*
Son los mejores de la clase.    *They're the best in the class.*

### Superlative with *-ísimo*

**1.** To express the idea of *extremely* add the ending **-ísimo(-a, -os, -as)** to the adjective. If the adjective ends in a consonant, add **-ísimo** directly to the singular form. If it ends in a vowel, drop the vowel before adding -**ísimo.**

fácil    El examen es **facilísimo.**    *The exam is extremely easy.*
grande   La casa es **grandísima.**    *The house is extremely big.*
bueno    Los jugadores son **buenísimos.**    *The players are extremely good.*

**2.** The following orthographic changes occur when **-ísimo** is added.

c → q    poco → poquísimo
g → gu    largo → larguísimo
z → c    feliz → felicísimo

## ACTIVIDADES

**A La universidad.** Complete la información con un compañero/a.

> *Modelo* **Compañero/a   el edificio más alto**
> **Usted   *La biblioteca* es el edificio más alto.**

1. el edificio más grande
2. la clase más interesante
3. el/la mejor profesor/a
4. el libro más caro

5. la peor comida de la cafetería
6. el/la estudiante menor (edad)
7. el deporte más popular
8. la materia menos difícil

**B Preguntas personales.** Hágale las siguientes preguntas a su compañero/a. Comparta la información con la clase.

1. ¿Quién es tu mejor amigo/a?
2. ¿Cuál es el peor día de la semana para ti?
3. ¿Cuál es la clase más fácil este semestre/trimestre?
4. ¿Quiénes son los mejores profesores?
5. ¿Dónde venden la mejor pizza? ¿y la mejor hamburguesa?
6. ¿Cuál es la mejor película de este año?
7. ¿Cuál es el peor programa de televisión este año?
8. ¿Cuál es el mejor equipo de béisbol este año? ¿y el peor?
9. ¿Cuáles son los mejores jugadores?
10. ¿Quién es el mejor entrenador?

**C Opiniones.** Usted y su compañero/a están en el teatro. Él/ella le da su opinión y usted está de acuerdo con todo lo que dice. Use el adjetivo terminado en la forma apropiada de **-ísimo.**

> *Modelo* **Compañero/a   Este drama es muy interesante.**
> **Usted   Sí, es interesantísimo.**

1. Las entradas son muy caras.
2. Los actores son buenos.
3. Los asientos son cómodos.
4. El programa es muy largo.
5. El actor principal es muy viejo.
6. La actriz principal es muy simpática.

**D** Haga oraciones sobre los diferentes estudiantes de la clase usando los siguientes adjetivos.

> *Modelo* alto   **Pedro es el estudiante más alto de la clase.**

| | | | | |
|---|---|---|---|---|
| simpático | inteligente | fuerte | serio | paciente |
| elegante | listo | trabajador | optimista | popular |

**E Un concurso.** Usted está a cargo de anunciar (*announce*) los/las ganadores/as de un concurso de aficionados al arte. Escoja a los ganadores/as entre sus compañeros/as y anúnciele a la clase en qué categoría van a recibir el premio. Anuncie primero los premios principales y después los premios de consolación.

*Modelo*   **La mejor diseñadora es la Srta. Asunción Benítez.**

| Premios principales | Premios de consolación |
|---|---|
| mejor cantante (*singer*) | más creativo |
| mejor actor/actriz | más ingenioso |
| mejor bailarín/bailarina (*dancer*) | más rápido |
| mejor pianista/violinista | más sensitivo |

Ahora piense en otras categorías posibles y anuncie a los ganadores/as.

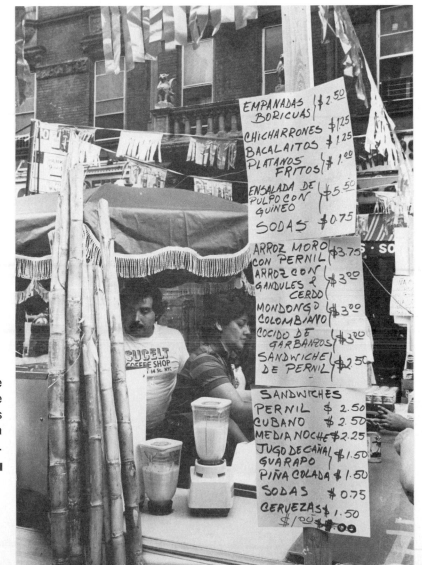

Un puesto en una calle de Nueva York donde se pueden probar muchos platos típicos de la cocina hispana.

# LECTURA

## Un verdadero banquete

Los alumnos extranjeros están organizando una fiesta para celebrar el final del curso. Cada uno va a llevar° un plato típico de su país. Todos quieren que sus compañeros norteamericanos prueben diferentes platos. De esta forma pueden conocer mejor la cocina hispana.

*to take*

José María es un estudiante español y él va a llevar una tortilla española. David, un estudiante norteamericano, le pregunta dónde va a comprar las tortillas de maíz para su plato. José María le explica que la tortilla española se prepara con huevos y patatas° y que es una *omelette*.

*potatoes (in Spain)*

Guadalupe, una chica de México, dice que su mamá hace los mejores chiles rellenos° de México y que le va a pedir que prepare unos.

*chiles... peppers filled with cheese*

Mercedes, que es cubana, dice que ella va a llevar el arroz y los frijoles negros. Vivian, su compañera de cuarto, es puertorriqueña y dice que sin arroz con gandules° la comida no va a estar completa y que ella lo va a preparar.

*peas (in Puerto Rico)*

Todos están seguros que esta fiesta va a ser un verdadero banquete.

## ¿Verdadero o falso?

Diga si las siguientes oraciones son verdaderas o falsas de acuerdo con la lectura.

1. Los alumnos van a llevar platos típicos de los países hispanos.
2. La tortilla española se prepara con maíz.
3. Los chiles rellenos son típicos de México.
4. La madre de la estudiante mexicana hace unos chiles rellenos muy buenos.
5. El arroz con gandules es típico de Cuba.
6. La chica cubana va a llevar arroz y frijoles negros.

## Preguntas

1. ¿Qué están organizando los estudiantes extranjeros?
2. ¿Qué va a llevar cada estudiante extranjero?
3. ¿De dónde es Ana María?
4. ¿Qué plato va a llevar?
5. ¿Qué se necesita para hacer una tortilla española?
6. ¿Quién va a preparar el plato mexicano?
7. ¿Qué plato típico cubano va a llevar Mercedes?
8. Según Vivian, ¿qué plato necesitan?

## Una fruta excelente

La siguiente lectura está tomada de un anuncio donde se describe una fruta y sus características. Al leerla trate de determinar cuáles son estas características y quiénes deben comer esta fruta. Los siguientes palabras le pueden servir para entender mejor la selección.

| | |
|---|---|
| alimenta | *nourishes* |
| no debe faltar | *should not be missing* |
| hierro | *iron* |
| aporta | *supplies* |
| crecimiento | *growth* |

# El plátano alimenta mucho

Generalmente, lo que les gusta a los niños no les alimenta.
Y lo que les alimenta, no les gusta.

El plátano es una excepción.
Alimenta mucho y les encanta.

Por su gran valor nutritivo, el plátano no debe faltar nunca en la dieta infantil. El plátano contiene más proteínas, calcio y hierro que ninguna otra fruta fresca. Por eso es tan bueno para los niños. Porque les aporta una buena cantidad de sustancias indispensables para el crecimiento, de la forma más sencilla.

¿A que nunca tiene problemas cuando le da un plátano a su hijo?

**Plátano de Canarias**
**el Rey de la Fruta**

## ¿Verdadero o falso?

Diga si las siguientes oraciones son verdaderas o falsas de acuerdo con la lectura.

1. En general a los niños les gusta la comida que alimenta.
2. El plátano alimenta a los niños y además les gusta.
3. El plátano contiene muchas proteínas y minerales.
4. Los niños pueden ser más saludables si comen plátanos.

## Preguntas

1. En general, ¿qué les gusta a los niños?
2. ¿Por qué es el plátano una excepción?
3. Explíquele a su compañero/a por qué debe comer plátano.

## SITUACIONES

1. Ask a classmate which Hispanic foods he/she likes the best. Also ask him/her about other ethnic foods.
2. Find out about the food that your partner buys every week: (a) where he/she buys it, (b) how much it costs, and (c) who cooks the meals.
3. You and a friend are at a restaurant in a Spanish-speaking country. You will do the talking for the two of you. Another student will be the waiter/waitress. Tell the waiter/waitress (a) that you want to be far from the door, (b) that you want menus, (c) ask what the special for the day **(plato del día)** is, (d) say that you want two specials with wine for your friend and a large Coca-Cola for you, and (e) ask if you can pay with a credit card **(tarjeta de crédito).**
4. You are unable to go to the market this week because you were in an accident. Call a friend and ask him/her to go for you. Tell your friend over the phone what you want him/her to buy. You will need some items from the following categories: (a) **carne,** (b) **verduras,** (c) **frutas,** and (d) **para beber.**
5. Go to your local market and find the section where they have Hispanic foods. Write down the names of the foods you can find, the prices, and if possible, what they are used for. During the next class meeting, interview a classmate about what he/she discovered. Then he/she will interview you. Report your findings to the class.

## VOCABULARIO

**comida**

| | |
|---|---|
| el aceite | oil |
| el aguacate | avocado |
| el ajo | garlic |
| la alfalfa | alfalfa |
| el/la azúcar | sugar |
| el camarón | shrimp |
| la carne molida | ground meat |
| la cebolla | onion |
| el cerdo | pork |
| la espinaca | spinach |
| la fresa | strawberry |
| los frijoles | beans |
| la gelatina | gelatin |
| la mantequilla | butter |
| la mayonesa | mayonnaise |
| la mostaza | mustard |
| el pavo | turkey |
| la pimienta | pepper |

| | |
|---|---|
| el pimiento verde | green pepper |
| el puré de papas | mashed potatoes |
| el requesón | cottage cheese |
| la sal | salt |
| la salsa de tomate | tomato sauce |
| el sorbete | sherbet |
| el tocino | bacon |
| la vainilla | vanilla |
| la verdura | vegetable |
| el vinagre | vinegar |
| el yogur | yogurt |
| la zanahoria | carrot |

**en el restaurante**

| | |
|---|---|
| la botella de vino | bottle of wine |
| la copa | (stemmed) glass |
| la cuchara | spoon |
| la cucharita | teaspoon |
| el cuchillo | knife |

el mantel — *tablecloth*
el plato — *plate, dish*
   plato combinado — *combination plate*
el postre — *dessert*
la propina — *tip*
la servilleta — *napkin*
la taza — *cup*
el tenedor — *fork*
la vajilla — *china*
el vaso — *glass*

### en el supermercado
la docena — *dozen*
el gramo — *gram*
la lata — *can*
el litro — *liter*

### la salud — *health*
las calorías — *calories*
descafeinado — *decaffeinated*
descremado — *nonfat*
hervido — *boiled*
sano — *healthy*

### lugares
el país — *country*
el supermercado — *supermarket*
la zona — *zone*

### una cena
la invitación — *invitation*
el invitado — *guest*

### descripciones
antiguo — *old*
asado — *roast*
famoso — *famous*
latino — *Latin*

### verbos
aceptar — *to accept*
admitir — *to admit, to allow*
alegrarse — *to be glad*
conservar — *to conserve, to keep*
dudar — *to doubt*
esperar — *to hope, to expect*
permitir — *to permit, to allow*
preocuparse — *to worry*
prohibir — *to prohibit, to forbid*
quedar — *to be, to remain*
sentir (ie) — *to be sorry*
temer — *to fear*
traer — *to bring*

### palabras útiles
cualquier — *any*
quizá(s)/tal vez — *maybe*
suficiente — *enough*

### expresiones útiles
en todas partes — *everywhere*
eso es todo — *that's all*

In Lección 11, **you will**
a. **describe health conditions.**
b. **express opinions.**
c. **express attitudes.**
d. **express expectations and wishes.**

# Lección 11
## La salud y los médicos

## El cuerpo humano por dentro

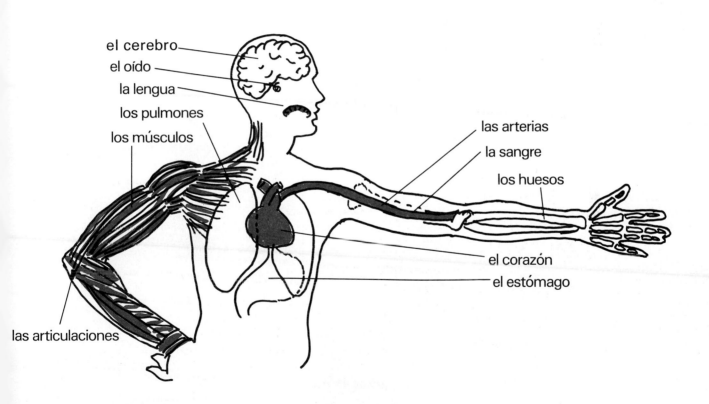

el cerebro
el oído
la lengua
los pulmones
los músculos
las articulaciones
las arterias
la sangre
los huesos
el corazón
el estómago

## ACTIVIDADES

**A** Asocie las actividades de la izquierda con las partes del cuerpo de la derecha.

| | |
|---|---|
| 1. escuchar | a. el corazón |
| 2. respirar | b. la lengua |
| 3. mover la sangre | c. el estómago |
| 4. hablar | d. el oído |
| 5. pensar | e. el cerebro |
| 6. digerir (*digest*) la comida | f. la sangre |
| 7. circular por las arterias | g. los pulmones |
| 8. permitir movimientos | h. las articulaciones |

**B Entrevista.** Use las siguientes preguntas para entrevistar a un/a compañero/a. Comparta la información con la clase.

1. ¿Vas al médico con frecuencia?   2. ¿Cómo se llama tu médico?   3. ¿Dónde está su consultorio?   4. Si estás enfermo/a (*sick*), ¿va tu médico/a a tu casa?   5. ¿Cómo es tu médico/a?

Una farmacia de Miami. Muchas de las farmacias hispanas ofrecen el servicio de enviar medicinas a otros países.

### Farmacias de guardia

**De nueve y media de la mañana a diez de la noche:** Puerta Nueva, 3 (esquina a Carretería). Gallito, 1 (junto ambulatorio Los Girasoles, sector Carretera Cádiz) frente a barriada La Paz. Avenida Juan Sebastián Elcano, 123 (Pedregalejo, junto cochera de autobuses). Capitán Huelin, 11 (Haza de Cuevas, detrás del Cine Cayri). Arroyo de los Angeles, Bl. Venus (frente Colegio Gibraljaire). Urbanización Parque del Sur, Bl. 16 (Ciudad Jardín). Alemania, 3-7 (junto antiguo mercado de mayoristas).

**De diez de la noche a nueve y media de la mañana:** Larios, 8, teléfono 211915. Serrato, s/n (barriada Santa Isabel), teléfono 333345.

**TORREMOLINOS-BENALMADENA**

**De nueve y media de la mañana a diez de la noche:** Arroyo de la Miel, Avda. de la Concepción, Bloque I (a 80 metros centro salud), Benalmádena. Montemar, calle Aladino, 19, Torremolinos.

**De diez de la noche a nueve y media de la mañana:** Arroyo de la Miel, Avda. de la Concepción, Bloque I (a 80 metros centro salud), Benalmádena.

# Cultura

## Doctors, hospitals, and pharmacies in the Hispanic world

Although there have been many advances in medical care in Hispanic cities, the majority of doctors and hospitals cannot afford the latest technological equipment. Modern health care is even less available in rural areas. In general, there are no hospitals in small towns or farming areas. People depend on first-aid centers (**casas de socorro**), the town doctor, the midwife (**comadrona**), and even on healers (**curanderos**), who use herbs and objects, such as shells, believed to have healing powers.

In many Hispanic countries, medical–school graduates are often obliged to spend one year working in rural areas. This gives them experience in diagnosing and treating patients and in turn offers those patients much needed health care.

A distinction exists in the Hispanic world between a **clínica** and a **hospital.** A **clínica** is privately run and charges fees. A **hospital** is operated by the government or by a religious or charitable organization, and usually provides free medical care. In many cases, relatives may stay at the **hospital,** sometimes in the patient's room. Relatives can relieve some of the nurses' duties as well as contribute to the patient's well–being.

American medicines are available in Hispanic countries, though sometimes under a different name. Prescriptions are not necessary in many cases, and pharmacists have more freedom in advising patients than in the U.S. Pharmacists may also give injections and take the patient's blood pressure. Neighborhood pharmacies rotate night and holiday duty (**farmacias de turno/de guardia**), thereby providing 24-hour service. Local newspapers print lists showing pharmacy schedules, such as the one on page 262.

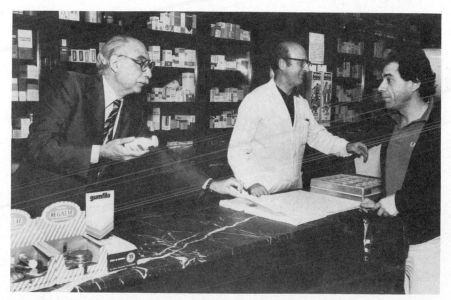

Una farmacia en Barcelona. El contacto personal que se establece con el farmacéutico es muy importante en la cultura hispana.

# EN CONTEXTO

## En el consultorio° de la doctora Suárez

*office*

La Sra. Muñoz está enferma. Tiene catarro° y un poco de fiebre.

*cold*

| | |
|---|---|
| **Dra. Suárez** | ¿Cómo se siente, Sra. Muñoz? |
| **Sra. Muñoz** | Me siento muy cansada°. Además, me duele la garganta° y también me duelen los oídos. |

*tired / me... I have a sore throat*

| | |
|---|---|
| **Dra. Suárez** | ¿Usted fuma°? |
| **Sra. Muñoz** | No, doctora. |

*smoke*

| | |
|---|---|
| **Dra. Suárez** | Bueno, vamos a examinarle la garganta y los oídos. Abra la boca, por favor. Diga «Ah». (Examina a la Sra. Muñoz.) Tiene una infección en los oídos. No es muy seria, pero es necesario que se cuide. ¿Es usted alérgica a los antibióticos? |
| **Sra. Muñoz** | No, doctora. |
| **Dra. Suárez** | Entonces le voy a recetar° unos antibióticos. Es importante que tome las pastillas° cada° cuatro horas. Además, descanse° y beba mucho líquido. (Le da una receta a la Sra. Muñoz.) |

*prescribe*
*pills / every*
*rest*

| | |
|---|---|
| **Sra. Muñoz** | ¿Y para la fiebre, doctora? |
| **Dra. Suárez** | Puede tomar aspirinas. Pero con los antibióticos es probable que la fiebre le baje muy pronto. |

## ¿Verdadero o falso?

Diga si las siguientes oraciones son verdaderas o falsas de acuerdo con el diálogo.

1. A la Sra. Muñoz le duele la garganta.
2. La Dra. Suárez está muy cansada.
3. La Sra. Muñoz tiene una infección en los pulmones.
4. La Sra. Muñoz es alérgica a la aspirina.
5. Ella debe tomar los antibióticos cada cuatro horas.
6. Ella debe descansar y tomar líquidos.

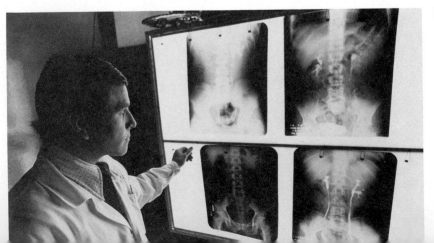

Un médico examina unas radiografías en Bogotá, Colombia.

**expresiones útiles para hablar con los médicos**

| | | | |
|---|---|---|---|
| guardar cama | *to stay in bed* | el análisis | *analysis* |
| hacer gárgaras | *to gargle* | la inyección | *injection* |
| tener gripe | *to have the flu* | una fractura | *fracture* |
| tener dolor de... | *to have a(n) . . . ache* | la presión/la tensión | *pressure* |
| tener tos | *to have a cough* | la radiografía | *x-ray picture* |
| toser | *to cough* | los síntomas | *symptoms* |

## ACTIVIDADES

**A** Usted es el médico/la médica. ¿Qué recomienda usted en los siguientes casos?

1. Su paciente tiene una infección en los ojos.
   a  Nadar en la piscina.
   b  Tomar antibióticos.
   c  Leer mucho.

2. A su paciente le duele mucho la espalda.
   a  Ir a la playa.
   b  Beber mucho líquido.
   c  No hacer ejercicio.

3. Su paciente tiene fiebre y le duele el cuerpo.
   a  Descansar y tomar aspirinas.
   b  Comer mucho y caminar.
   c  Ir a su trabajo y después al cine.

4. Estamos en primavera y su paciente es alérgico al polen de muchas plantas.
   a  Ir al campo (*countryside*) para respirar el aire.
   b  Dormir en una habitación con aire acondicionado.
   c  Trabajar en el jardín.

5. A su paciente le duele la garganta y tiene tos.
   a  Hacer gárgaras.
   b  Ir a esquiar.
   c  Salir y hablar con sus amigos.

6. Su paciente se siente muy mal. Usted no sabe lo que tiene.
   a  Enviarlo a la casa.
   b  Hacerle unos análisis.
   c  Decirle que no se preocupe.

7. Su paciente tiene un pie fracturado.
   a  Correr tres kilómetros todos los días.
   b  Tomar clases de baile.
   c  Hacer una radiografía.

**B** ¿A quién debo llamar? Explíquele a su compañero/a sus síntomas o lo que usted necesita. Su compañero/a le va a decir a quién debe llamar de acuerdo con los anuncios.

> *Modelo*        **Usted**    **Necesito un examen médico para un nuevo trabajo.**
> **Compañero/a**   **Llama a la Dra. Corona López.**

1. Me da dolor de cabeza cuando leo o miro televisión.
2. Siempre me siento triste y deprimido/a y no puedo dormir.
3. Mi hermano pequeño está enfermo y tiene fiebre.
4. No puedo respirar bien y tengo la piel (*skin*) irritada.
5. Me duelen mucho los dientes cuando como.
6. Necesito una operación.

---

SEGUNDO PISO

**Dr. Fco. Javier Amador Cumplido**
CIRUGÍA Y ENFERMEDADES DE LOS OJOS
**86-43-57**
*CONSULTORIO 204*

**Dr. Héctor Molina Oviedo**
PSIQUIATRA
**86-51-49**
*CONSULTORIO 102*

**Dra. Silvia Corona López**
MEDICINA INTERNA
**86-51-49**
*CONSULTORIO 102*

**Dr. Jaime A. Rodríguez Peláez**
PEDIATRA NIÑOS Y ADOLESCENTES
**86-17-15**
*CONSULTORIO 212*

---

**CLÍNICA DE ASMA Y ALERGIAS**
Dr. Rubén Shturman

AMSTERDAN 219-A 2° PISO
**294-3866  584-0153**

---

**Dra. Gabriela Jacobo de Alcaraz**
CIRUJANO DENTISTA
**86-48-44**
*CONSULTORIO 314*

---

**Dr. Raúl Elguezábal R.**
MEDICINA FAMILIAR Y CIRUGÍA
**86-34-73 EU. 428-4846**
*CONSULTORIO 309*

---

**C** Complete el siguiente diálogo con otro/a estudiante. Usted debe ser el/la doctor/a.

| | |
|---|---|
| **Doctor/a** | ¿Cómo te sientes, _____? |
| **Estudiante** | ... |
| **Doctor/a** | Tienes un poco de fiebre. ¿Te duele la cabeza? |
| **Estudiante** | ... |
| **Doctor/a** | ¿Qué otros síntomas tienes? |
| **Estudiante** | ... |
| **Doctor/a** | ¿Eres alérgico/a a la penicilina? |
| **Estudiante** | ... |
| **Doctor/a** | Te voy a recetar _____. Si no te sientes bien mañana, me llamas. |

## GRAMÁTICA

### Indicative and subjunctive after impersonal expressions

**1.** Use the indicative after impersonal expressions that denote certainty.

Es verdad que Ana fuma mucho.     *It's true that Ana smokes a lot.*

Other expressions that require the indicative are: **es cierto que, es evidente que, es obvio que,** and **es seguro que.**

**2.** In the negative, these expressions normally take the subjunctive.

No es cierto que fume tanto.     *It's not true that she smokes a lot.*

**3.** Use the subjunctive with expressions that denote possibility, probability, importance, or other value judgments.

Es probable que venga hoy.     *It's probable that he will come today.*

Other expressions that require the subjunctive are: **es posible que, es importante que, es bueno que, es mejor que** and **es lógico que.**

## *ACTIVIDADES*

**A** Complete las siguientes oraciones con las formas correctas del verbo entre paréntesis.

1. Es cierto que Auerlio (trabajar) en esa oficina. Él llega todos los días a las nueve de la mañana, luego es probable que (estar) allí ahora.
2. Es evidente que las personas que (fumar) tienen más problemas del corazón. Según los médicos, es importante que las personas (saber) esto.

**B** Usted es un/a médico/a y le da instrucciones a un paciente que tiene gripe. Use las expresiones **es importante que** o **no es bueno que** con las siguientes frases para darle las instrucciones.

*Modelo*     beber bastante líquido     **Es importante que beba bastante líquido.**
             salir de la casa           **No es bueno que salga de la casa.**

dormir bastante                    hacer ejercicio
comer mucho                        trabajar mucho
tomar la medicina                  mirar televisión
ir a la universidad                abrir la ventana
bañarse con agua fría

**C** ¿Qué les sugiere a sus amigos/as cuando no se sienten bien? Escoja el consejo y trabaje con varios/as estudiantes.

*Modelo*   **Amigo/a**   **Tengo dolor de estómago.**
            **Usted**    **Es necesario que descanses.**

| amigos/as | usted |
|---|---|
| dolor de cabeza | hacer ejercicio |
| fiebre | acostarse |
| dolor de estómago | tomar bastante jugo |
| tos | descansar |
| ojos irritados | dormir bastante |
| una alergia | tomar té con limón |
| dolor de muelas (*toothache*) | tomar dos aspirinas |
| dolor de espalda | llamar al médico |
| dolor de garganta | ir al dentista |
| estar nervioso/a | hacer gárgaras |

**D** **¿Por qué se sienten mal?** Usted es médico/a. Varios/as amigos/as vienen a su consultorio a decirle cómo se sienten. Usted les hace una pregunta y les dice lo que deben hacer.

*Modelo*   dolerle la cabeza      mirar televisión
           **Amigo/a**   **Me duele la cabeza.**
           **Usted**    **¿Miras mucha televisión?**
           **Amigo/a**   **Sí, tres o cuatro horas.**
           **Usted**    **Pues es importante que no mires televisión.**

| sus amigos/as | usted |
|---|---|
| dolerle la garganta | hablar mucho |
| dolerle el estómago | comer a horas irregulares |
| dolerle los ojos | leer con poca luz (*light*) |
| dolerle los pies | caminar mucho |
| dolerle la espalda | trabajar en el jardín |

**E** **Situaciones.** Complete las siguientes oraciones de acuerdo con la situación.

1. La Sra. Ortiz va al médico porque no se siente bien. Ella trabaja más de diez horas todos los días y no duerme bien. Además come muchos dulces y no toma vitaminas ni hace ejercicio. Usted es el médico/la médica. ¿Qué le dice usted a la Sra. Ortiz?

   Es obvio que...     Es natural que...     Es necesario que...

2. Julia estudia español en la universidad. Ella quiere trabajar en un país hispano después de su graduación. ¿Qué le dice usted a Julia?

   Es cierto que...     Es importante que...     Es mejor que...

3. El mes próximo es el cumpleaños de Martita. Ella quiere celebrar su cumpleaños con una fiesta. ¿Qué le dice usted?

Es posible que... Es verdad que... Es muy importante que...

# EN CONTEXTO

**En el hospital**

termómetro

Ojalá que te mejores pronto.

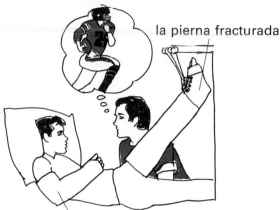

la pierna fracturada

el brazo fracturado

Ojalá que puedas jugar muy pronto.

**Preguntas**

1. ¿Dónde está la chica enferma?
2. ¿Qué tiene en la boca?
3. ¿Qué quiere su amiga?
4. ¿Por qué está el chico en cama?
5. ¿Qué quiere su amigo?

# ACTIVIDADES

**A** Diga si usted se cansa (*get tired*) o no se cansa con las siguientes actividades.

*Modelo* ver televisión
**Yo (no) me canso cuando veo televisión.**

| | | |
|---|---|---|
| estudiar español | jugar fútbol | ir a la playa |
| hacer ejercicio | trabajar | escuchar música |

**B** Pregúntele a su compañero/a si hace ejercicio, cuándo y dónde lo hace. Si su compañero/a no hace ejercicio explíquele por qué debe hacerlo.

## GRAMÁTICA

### The subjunctive after *ojalá*

The expression **ojalá (que),** which originally meant *may Allah grant that . . .,* is always followed by the subjunctive. Its equivalent in English is *I/we hope.* The word **que** is optional after **ojalá.**

Ojalá que ellos vengan temprano.     *I hope they'll come early.*
Ojalá (que) pueda ir al gimnasio.     *I hope I can go to the gym.*

## *ACTIVIDADES*

**A** Su hijo/a va a estudiar en otra ciudad y usted está preocupado/a. Exprese lo que usted desea usando **Ojalá que. . .**

*Modelo*    lavar la ropa todas las semanas
           **Ojalá que laves la ropa todas las semanas.**

1. dormir ocho horas todos los días
2. estudiar mucho
3. comprar una buena calculadora
4. ser feliz allí
5. aprender mucho
6. no gastar mucho dinero
7. comer regularmente
8. llegar temprano a clase
9. estar contento
10. leer muchos libros
11. recibir buenas notas
12. escribir frecuentemente

ora exprese lo que usted desea para usted el próximo semestre/trimestre.

**B** Su mejor amiga va a tener un bebé. ¿Cómo quiere usted que sea el bebé? Use **Ojalá que. . .** y los siguientes verbos en sus oraciones.

*Modelo*    ser      **Ojalá que sea saludable.**

tener     estar     pesar     medir     venir

**C** Usted tiene sus propias ideas de cómo debe ser su primer puesto. Use **Ojalá que. . .** para hablar de sus ideas.

*Modelo*    **Ojalá que el sueldo sea bueno.**

**D** Usted tiene muchas ganas de ir a la fiesta más importante del año en su club. Su amigo/a le va a hacer unas preguntas acerca de la fiesta. Contéstelas usando **Ojalá que. . .**

*Modelo*    Amigo/a    **¿Qué van a servir en la fiesta?**
          Usted    **Ojalá que sirvan comida mexicana.**

1. ¿Con quién vas a ir?   2. ¿Qué vas a hacer en la fiesta?   3. ¿Quiénes van a estar allí?
4. ¿Qué tipo de música van a tocar?   5. ¿A qué hora va a terminar?

## GRAMÁTICA

### The equivalents of English *let's*

**1. Vamos** + **a** + infinitive is commonly used in Spanish to express English *let's* + verb.

Vamos a empezar ahora.                    *Let's begin now.*

**2.** Use **vamos** by itself to mean *let's go.* The negative *let's not go* is **no vayamos.**

Vamos al gimnasio.                    *Let's go to the gym.*
No vayamos al gimnasio.               *Let's not go to the gym.*

**3.** There is another equivalent for *let's* + verb in Spanish; it is the **nosotros** form of the present subjunctive.

Hablemos de la cena.                  *Let's talk about supper.*
No hablemos de la cena.               *Let's not talk about supper.*
Corramos.                             *Let's run.*
No corramos.                          *Let's not run.*
Abramos esta botella.                 *Let's open this bottle.*
No abramos esta botella.              *Let's not open this bottle.*

**4.** Remember that stem-changing **-ir** verbs change from **e→i** and **o→u** in the **nosotros** form of the present subjunctive.

Sirvamos el vino ahora.               *Let's serve the wine now.*
No durmamos en ese cuarto.            *Let's not sleep in that room.*

**5.** The final **-s** of reflexive affirmative commands is dropped when the pronoun **nos** is attached.

Levantemos    +    nos    ⟶    Levantémonos.
Sirvamos      +    nos    ⟶    Sirvámonos.

## *ACTIVIDADES*

**A** Usted y su mejor amigo/a van a cambiar su vida totalmente porque quieren ser más saludables. Su amigo/a le dice lo que deben hacer y usted le contesta reafirmando lo que él/ella dice.

> *Modelo*   comer más verduras
> **Su amigo/a   Vamos a comer más verduras.**
> **Usted   Sí, comamos más verduras.**

1. comer menos comida frita
2. tomar leche descremada
3. ver menos televisión
4. levantarse a las 6:00

5. correr más
6. beber más jugo
7. dormir ocho horas
8. acostarse temprano

9. hacer ejercicio
10. comprar más fruta
11. nadar más
12. jugar golf

**B** Usted y unos/as amigos/as van a ir a San Francisco por una semana. Diga lo que usted quiere que todos/as hagan en la ciudad cada día.

*Modelo* comer en Fisherman's Wharf
**Comamos en Fisherman's Wharf el domingo por la noche.**

1. ir a la ópera
2. visitar el Hotel St. Francis
3. ir a Sausalito
4. descansar
5. montar en un tranvía (*streetcar*)

6. ver el puente Golden Gate
7. cenar en el Hyatt Regency
8. almorzar en el barrio chino
9. ver un partido de béisbol
10. caminar por el Parque Golden Gate

|  | lunes | martes | miércoles | jueves | viernes | sábado |
|---|---|---|---|---|---|---|
| mañana |  |  |  |  |  |  |
| tarde |  |  |  |  |  |  |
| noche |  |  |  |  |  |  |

Un anuncio en contra del uso del tabaco en el metro de Madrid.

**C** Usted y sus compañeros van a tener una fiesta fantástica y ahora mismo están haciendo los preparativos (*plans*). Con dos compañeros usen los siguientes verbos para determinar cómo va a ser la fiesta.

**Modelo** **Invitemos a Carlota, Lucía, Pablo y Marcos.**

| invitar | servir | empezar | terminar | tomar | comprar | comer |
|---------|--------|---------|----------|-------|---------|-------|
| preparar | decorar | tocar | bailar | hablar | traer | tener |

## EN CONTEXTO

### El campo y la ciudad

La vida en el campo es muy diferente a la vida en las ciudades, pero todos los lugares, ya sean rurales o urbanos, tienen sus aspectos buenos y malos.

Las personas que viven en el campo tienen muchas ventajas°. El ritmo de la vida es más lento y tranquilo y se siente menos presión. El aire es más puro y hay poca contaminación porque no hay tantos vehículos ni tantas fábricas°. Por estas razones es muy sano vivir en el campo.

Pero la vida rural no es ideal, ni mucho menos. En el campo hay que° trabajar mucho para ganarse la vida°. No hay muchas actividades sociales en estas zonas para las personas que desean una vida activa. A veces no se tienen los mismos servicios públicos que en las áreas urbanas. Un problema perenne es el desempleo. Por eso muchas familias dejan el campo y se van a las ciudades.

Para las personas que viven en los pueblos°, la ciudad representa una manera de mejorar su vida. Allí esperan obtener una educación mejor o un buen trabajo y tener un nivel de vida° más alto. Hay servicios públicos, atención médica, buenas comunicaciones y toda clase de actividades sociales, culturales y deportivas.

Las personas que llegan a la ciudad muy pronto se dan cuenta de° que no todo es bueno allí. La vida urbana no es lenta y tranquila como en el campo; el individuo siente mucha más presión. El número de habitantes, autos y fábricas produce un alto índice de contaminación. La salud de la persona sufre en todos los aspectos.

El campo y la ciudad tienen ventajas y desventajas y el individuo tiene que escoger dónde quiere vivir.

*advantages*

*factories*

hay... *it's necessary*
ganarse... *earn a living*

*towns*

un nivel... *standard of living*

se... *realize*

### Para completar

Complete las oraciones según la selección anterior.

1. Las ventajas de vivir en el campo son...
2. Las personas que viven en el campo...
3. Las ventajas de la ciudad son...
4. Un problema en la ciudad es...

## *ACTIVIDADES*

**A** Use la expresión **hay que** + infinitivo para decir todas las cosas que se deben hacer para ser saludables.

*Modelo* **Hay que comer muchas verduras.**

**B** Con un/a compañero/a haga una lista de las ventajas y desventajas de vivir en un pueblo. Compartan su lista con la clase.

**C** Complete el siguiente diálogo con un/a compañero/a. Después su compañero/a debe hacerle las mismas preguntas a usted.

| | |
|---:|---|
| **Usted** | ¿Dónde prefieres vivir? |
| **Compañero/a** | . . . |
| **Usted** | ¿Por qué? |
| **Compañero/a** | . . . |
| **Usted** | ¿Qué ventajas tiene vivir en ese lugar? |
| **Compañero/a** | . . . |

## GRAMÁTICA

### Relative pronouns

1. The relative pronouns **que** and **quien(es)** are used to combine two sentences into one. They refer to an antecedent (a noun or pronoun that has been previously mentioned) and introduce a subordinate clause.

| | |
|---|---|
| Las personas son tranquilas. | *The persons are calm.* |
| Las personas viven en el campo. | *The persons live in the country.* |

Las personas **que** viven en el campo son tranquilas.
    \   / \          /
   antecedent    subordinate clause

2. **Que** is the most commonly used relative pronoun. It may refer to persons or things.

Las vitaminas **que** yo tomo son excelentes.
Ése es el doctor **que** me receta las vitaminas.

3. **Quien(es)** only refers to persons; it may replace **que** in a clause set off by commas.

Los Márquez, $\left\{ \begin{array}{c} \textbf{quienes} \\ \textbf{que} \end{array} \right\}$ viven en la ciudad, prefieren el campo.     *The Márquezes, who live in the city, prefer the country.*

**4.** Use **quien(es)** after a preposition when referring to a person or personas.

Allí está la persona **a quien** le debes dar
el dinero.

*There is the person to whom you should
give the money.*

## *ACTIVIDADES*

**A** Primero estudie los dibujos y después hable de la ciudad y el campo.

La ciudad y el campo

*Modelos* **La ciudad es un lugar que tiene muchos autos.**
**El campo es un lugar que es muy limpio.**

**B** **¿Cómo son?** Estudie los dibujos y después diga cómo es la persona de la ciudad y cómo
es la del campo.

*Modelos* **Es una persona que trabaja en una oficina.**
**Es una persona que trabaja al aire libre.**

**C** **Mi ciudad o pueblo.** Dígale a la clase cómo es su ciudad/pueblo. Mencione por lo menos tres o cuatro características.

*Modelos* **Vivo en una ciudad que. . .**
**Vivo en un pueblo que. . .**

**D** Complete las siguientes selecciones con el pronombre relativo **que** o **quien** según convenga.

**1.** Una telenovela (*soap opera*)

*Mi corazón* es la telenovela ____ tiene más público. El actor principal es Álvaro
                                    1
Montalvo. Él es el actor de ____ todos hablan. La crítica cree que este año va
                              2
a ganar el premio Talía ____ es el equivalente del Oscar norteamericano. El 90
                          3
por ciento de las chicas dice que Álvaro es el actor con ____ les gustaría salir.
                                                          4
Silvina Bosque es la actriz principal. En la telenovela ella está enamorada de
(*is in love with*) Álvaro, pero Álvaro no la quiere. Esmeralda del Valle es la
chica a ____ él quiere, pero Esmeralda no es buena. A ella sólo le interesa el
        5
dinero de Álvaro. La telenovela es muy melodramática y siempre hay problemas
____ mantienen el interés del público.
6

**2.** Una conversación entre dos amigos

La fiesta es mañana y Jorge no tiene compañera. Él está en la cafetería con
Evaristo, ____ es su mejor amigo. En esos momentos entra una chica muy guapa.
          1

| | |
|---|---|
| **Jorge** | Ésa es la chica a ____ voy a invitar para la fiesta. |
| | 2 |
| **Evaristo** | ¿Conoces a Angélica? |
| **Jorge** | No, no la conozco, pero no importa. |
| **Evaristo** | ¡Por favor, Jorge! Angélica Domínguez es la chica a ____ todos |
| | 3 |
| | quieren invitar. Es simpática, inteligente y bonita. Además |
| | tiene novio. |
| **Jorge** | No importa. Mi corazón me dice que ésa es la chica con |
| | ____ voy a pasar el resto de mis días. |
| | 4 |
| **Evaristo** | Estás tan ridículo como las telenovelas. No te voy a presentar |
| | a Angélica. Te voy a presentar al siquiatra ____vive cerca de |
| | 5 |
| | casa. |

| **SÁBADO    8** | | |
|---|---|---|
| **PRIMERA CADENA** | **9.10.**—La Rosa Amarilla. | **20.30.**—Telediario fin de se- |
| | **10.00.**—Cajón desastre. | mana. |
| **0.50.**—Clásicos en blanco y | **13.15.**—Lotería. | **21.05.**—Informe semanal. |
| negro. *Cadenas rotas.* | **13.30.**—Suplementos 4. | **22.20.**—Sábado cine. *¿Qué* |
| **2.45.**—La luna (repeti- | **14.30.**—Sábado revista. | *me pasa, doctor?* |
| ción). | **15.00.**—Telediario fin de se- | **0.10.**—Rokambole. |
| **3.45**—★ Documentos TV. | mana. | |
| **4.45.**—★ Corrupción en | **15.30.**—El tiempo. | **SEGUNDA CADENA** |
| Miami. | **15.35.**—Ferdy. | |
| **5.35.**—La buena música. | **16.05.**—Primera sesión. *Los* | **13.30.**—Objetivo 92. |
| **6.30.**—★ De película. | *conquistadores de Atlantis.* | **15.00.**—Estadio 2. |
| **7.30.**—Largometraje. *Los* | **17.45.**—Rockopop. | **23.00.**—Buscando el arco |
| *amantes crucificados.* | **19.35.**—McGyver. | iris. |
| | | **0.40.**—Andalucía abierta. |

# LECTURA

## ¿Lleva usted una forma de vida sana?

El siguiente examen o test, tomado de la publicación semanal *Blanco y negro,* le puede ayudar a determinar si usted va a tener una vida larga y saludable. Las preguntas son fáciles y usted puede contestarlas rápidamente. Después de anotar sus respuestas en una hoja de papel, vea la solución para saber cómo vive usted. Las siguientes palabras le pueden ayudar a entender mejor las preguntas y la solución.

| | |
|---|---|
| repercute | *reflects* |
| bienestar | *well–being* |
| descuidada | *careless* |
| excedido de peso | *overweight* |
| ingiere | *drinks* |
| promedio | *average* |
| ansiedad | *anxiety* |
| cotidianas | *daily* |
| conduce | *drive* |
| ligero | *slight* |
| avance | *improvement* |
| compromiso | *commitment* |
| riesgos | *dangers* |

## Test

### ¿Lleva usted una forma de vida sana?

Su salud y su longevidad dependen mucho de la forma de vida que usted lleva. Lo que usted hace día tras día es parte de su estilo de vida. Y éste repercute sobre su bienestar físico. La conducta descuidada en cualquier campo puede llevar a serios problemas de salud. Conteste cada pregunta en alguna de las variantes marcadas, y fíjese después en la solución.

**(1)** ¿Con qué frecuencia hace usted ejercicios físicos?

a) Cuatro o cinco veces por semana.
b) Tres veces por semana.
c) Una vez por semana.
d) Rara vez.

**(2)** ¿Con qué frecuencia prefiere usted subir escaleras, aunque haya ascensores o escaleras mecánicas?

a) Casi siempre.
b) Frecuentemente.
c) Ocasionalmente.
d) Rara vez.

**(3)** ¿Cuántas horas diarias dedica a ver la televisión?

a) Menos de una hora.
b) Una o dos horas.
c) Dos o cuatro horas.
d) Cuatro o más horas.

**(4)** ¿Está usted excedido de peso?

a) No.
b) Sí, un par de kilos.
c) Sí, de tres a diez kilos.
d) Sí, más de diez kilos.

**(5)** ¿Cuántas copas de bebidas alcohólicas —cerveza, vino o licores— ingiere usted como promedio en la semana.

a) Nada.
b) Una a siete copas.
c) Ocho a quince copas.
d) Más de quince.

**(6)** ¿Cuántos cigarrillos fuma por día?

a) Ninguno.
b) Menos de cinco.
c) Entre cinco y diez.
d) Más de diez.

**(7)** ¿Fuma usted marihuana o usa alguna otra droga ilegal?

**(8)** ¿Ingiere bebidas alcohólicas en las seis horas siguientes a píldoras tranquilizantes, barbitúricos, antihistamínicos o alguna droga?

a) No.
b) Rara vez.
c) Ocasionalmente.
d) Frecuentemente.

**(9)** ¿Utiliza usted drogas como el valium y similares?

a) No.
b) Rara vez.
c) Ocasionalmente.
d) Frecuentemente.

**(10)** ¿Con qué frecuencia se siente deprimido?

a) Casi nunca.
b) Rara vez.
c) Ocasionalmente.
d) Frecuentemente.

**(11)** ¿La ansiedad o la tensión interfieren con sus actividades cotidianas?

a) Casi nunca.
b) Rara vez.
c) Ocasionalmente.
d) Frecuentemente.

**(12)** ¿Consigue usted dormir en forma satisfactoria?

a) Siempre.
b) Habitualmente.
c) Ocasionalmente.
d) Rara vez.

**(13)** ¿Conduce usted su automóvil a mayor velocidad que los límites fijados?

a) No.
b) Sí, pero con un exceso de cinco kilómetros por hora.
c) Sí, entre cinco a quince kilómetros por hora.
d) Sí, a más de quince kilómetros de exceso.

**(14)** ¿Usa usted el cinturón de seguridad en el automóvil?

a) Siempre.
b) Habitualmente.
c) Rara vez.
d) Nunca.

**(15)** ¿Conduce usted alguna vez bajo la influencia del alcohol, las drogas o alguna medicación?

a) Nunca.
b) Rara vez.
c) Ocasionalmente.
d) Con frecuencia.

### SOLUCIÓN

Marque un punto por cada respuesta en a), dos por cada b), tres por cada c), cuatro por cada d).

**Entre 16 y 25 puntos:** Usted tiene un excelente estilo de vida, basado en costumbres sensatas y mostrándose alerta sobre su salud personal.

**Entre 26 y 35 puntos:** Posee usted un muy buen estilo de vida, y con un ligero avance llegará a la categoría de excelentes.

**Entre 35 y 45 puntos:** Usted tiene una buena comprensión de los principios generales de la salud, pero necesita un poco más de firmeza y de compromiso para alcanzar un estilo de vida más sano.

**Entre 46 y 55 puntos:** Usted está incurriendo en riesgos innecesarios con su salud y debería fijarse como objetivo el mejorar su estilo de vida.

**Más de 55 puntos:** Son la indicación de que usted ignora los hábitos de la buena salud o que ha resuelto ignorarlos. Está en la zona de peligro y debería comenzar hoy mismo a mejorar su estilo de vida.

## Preguntas

1. Después de determinar cuántos puntos usted tiene, diga cuál es su estilo de vida según la solución.
2. ¿Cómo puede mejorar su forma de vida?
3. ¿Cuál es su punto más débil?
4. ¿Cuál es su punto o cuáles son su puntos más fuertes?
5. Si su estilo de vida puede mejorar, ¿qué va a hacer usted para tener una forma de vida más sana?

## ¿Te quieres o no te quieres?

Éste es un anuncio del Ministerio de Sanidad y Consumo animando a las personas a que se cuiden. Después de leer el anuncio, conteste las siguientes preguntas.

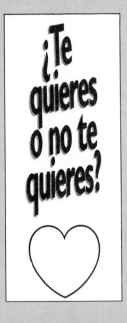

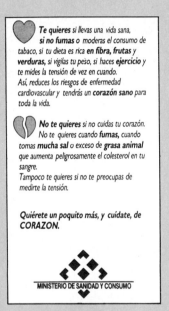

**Te quieres** si llevas una vida sana, **si no fumas** o moderas el consumo de tabaco, si tu dieta es rica **en fibra, frutas y verduras**, si vigilas tu peso, si haces **ejercicio** y te mides la tensión de vez en cuando. Así, reduces los riesgos de enfermedad cardiovascular y tendrás un **corazón sano** para toda la vida.

**No te quieres** si no cuidas tu corazón. No te quieres cuando **fumas**, cuando tomas **mucha sal** o exceso de **grasa animal** que aumenta peligrosamente el colesterol en tu sangre. Tampoco te quieres si no te preocupas de medirte la tensión.

Quiérete un poquito más, y cuídate, de **CORAZON.**

MINISTERIO DE SANIDAD Y CONSUMO

1. ¿Cuál es la idea principal de este anuncio?
2. Según el anuncio, ¿qué hace una persona que se quiere?
3. ¿Y qué hace una persona que no se quiere?

## ¿Me quiero o no me quiero?

Dígale a su compañero/a si usted está entre las personas que «se quieren» o entre las que «no se quieren» y explíquele qué hace usted para estar entre esas personas. Después su compañero/a le debe decir en qué grupo está él/ella y qué hace para estar en ese grupo.

## SITUACIONES

1. Your friend is a heavy smoker: (a) ask your friend how many cigarettes (**cigarrillos**) he/she smokes a day, then (b) tell him/her to cut down (**fumar menos**), and (c) give some good advice such as going to the gym, walking, chewing gum (**masticar chicle**), and so on.

2. You are at the dentist's office. Tell the dentist (a) that you have a toothache, and (b) that you are afraid. The dentist will tell you (a) not to be afraid, (b) that it is not going to hurt, and (c) that he/she will give you some anesthesia (**ponerle anestesia**).

3. Play the part of a patient. One of your classmates will play the part of a doctor. Describe all your symptoms. The doctor should ask pertinent questions and prescribe some medication. You should also ask the doctor some questions.

4. You are visiting your friend at a hospital: (a) tell your friend that he/she looks fine, (b) ask when he/she is leaving the hospital, (c) tell him/her that you are giving a party for your birthday, and (d) that you hope he/she will be able to come.

5. You have the flu and you call your doctor. Tell him/her that you (a) feel very tired and (b) have a headache, a fever, and a sore throat. Your doctor should tell you what to do.

6. Read the following cartoon about an uncooperative patient. What do you think the doctor and the wife will ask the patient? You may need the word **adivinar** (*to guess*) to better understand the situation.

© Mr. Keraz

# VOCABULARIO[1]

**el cuerpo humano**

| | |
|---|---|
| la arteria | *artery* |
| la articulación | *joint* |
| el cerebro | *brain* |
| el corazón | *heart* |
| el estómago | *stomach* |
| la garganta | *throat* |
| el hueso | *bone* |
| la lengua | *tongue* |
| el músculo | *muscle* |
| el oído | *(inner) ear* |
| el pulmón | *lung* |

**la salud**

| | |
|---|---|
| el catarro | *cold* |
| la fiebre | *fever* |
| la fractura | *fracture* |
| la gripe | *flu* |
| la infección | *infection* |
| el síntoma | *symptom* |
| la tensión/la presión | *pressure* |

**tratamiento médico**

| | |
|---|---|
| el análisis | *analysis* |
| el antibiótico | *antibiotic* |
| la aspirina | *aspirin* |
| la inyección | *injection* |
| el líquido | *liquid* |
| la pastilla | *pill* |
| la radiografía | *X ray picture* |
| la receta | *prescription* |

**lugares**

| | |
|---|---|
| la fábrica | *factory* |
| el pueblo | *town* |

**la ciudad y el campo**

| | |
|---|---|
| la comunicación | *communication* |
| la contaminación | *air pollution* |
| el desempleo | *unemployment* |
| la desventaja | *disadvantage* |
| la educación | *education* |
| los servicios públicos | *public services* |
| la ventaja | *advantage* |
| la vida | *life, living* |

**personas**

| | |
|---|---|
| el habitante | *inhabitant* |
| el individuo | *individual* |

**descripciones**

| | |
|---|---|
| alérgica | *allergic* |
| cansado | *tired* |
| cultural | *cultural* |
| deportivo | *sport* |
| enfermo | *sick* |
| fracturado | *fractured, broken* |
| lento | *slow* |
| puro | *pure* |
| rural | *rural* |
| serio | *serious* |
| social | *social* |
| urbano | *urban* |

**verbos**

| | |
|---|---|
| descansar | *to rest* |
| doler (ue) | *to hurt* |
| escoger (j) | *to choose* |
| examinar | *to examine* |
| fumar | *to smoke* |
| guardar cama | *to stay in bed* |
| hacer gárgaras | *to gargle* |
| mejorar | *to improve* |
| obtener (ie) | *to obtain* |
| recetar | *to prescribe* |
| sentirse (ie) | *to feel* |
| sufrir | *to suffer* |
| toser | *to cough* |

[1] See page 267 for words used in impersonal expressions.

**palabras útiles**

| | |
|---|---|
| el aspecto | *aspect* |
| ojalá | *I (we) hope* |

**expresiones útiles**

| | |
|---|---|
| ganarse la vida | *earn a living* |

| | |
|---|---|
| hay que + *inf.* | *it's necessary to + verb* |
| nivel de vida | *standard of living* |
| tener dolor de... | *to have a(n) . . . ache* |
| tener tos | *to have a cough* |

Una doctora española le toma la tensión a su paciente.

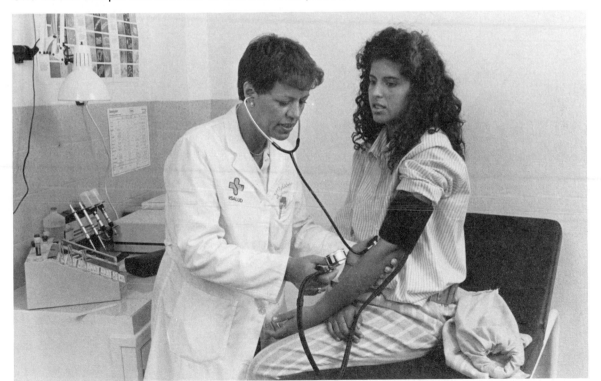

# En el aeropuerto

Los pasajeros hacen cola frente al mostrador de la aerolínea.

# Lección 12
# *Los viajes*

## En la estación de ferrocarril

el tren

Ella va a viajar en tren
porque no le gusta manejar.

## En el puerto

el barco

el mar

Él va a viajar en barco.

Va a tomar un crucero.

## la carretera

la gasolinera/
la estación de
servicio

el autobús

el camión

el coche/
carro deportivo

la motocicleta

la gasolina

A otras personas les gusta manejar y prefieren viajar por carretera.

El aeropuerto de Cali en Colombia.

## más vocabulario para viajeros

| | |
|---|---|
| la aduana | *customs* |
| el inspector de aduana | *customs inspector* |
| el cheque de viajero | *traveler's check* |
| el pasaje de ida y vuelta | *round-trip ticket* |
| la tarjeta de embarque | *boarding pass* |
| la hora de llegada | *arrival time* |
| el pasaporte | *passport* |
| la visa/el visado | *visa* |
| el metro | *subway* |
| facturar/chequear el equipaje | *to check the luggage* |
| hacer la maleta/empacar | *to pack* |
| revisar el equipaje | *to inspect the luggage* |

## ACTIVIDADES

**A** **Entrevista.** Hágale las siguientes preguntas a su compañero/a. Después él/ella le debe hacer las mismas preguntas a usted. Comparta la información con la clase.

1. ¿Prefieres viajar en tren, en avión o en barco? ¿En autobús o en automóvil? ¿Por qué?
2. ¿Te gusta viajar de día o de noche? ¿Por qué?   3. ¿Qué aerolínea te gusta más? ¿Por qué?

**B** Su compañero/a y usted van a visitar Chile. Hagan una lista de cinco cosas que deben hacer antes del viaje. Comparen su lista con la lista de otros estudiantes.

**C** Diga cómo va a viajar cada persona.

**el viaje**

1. Julia va a tomar un crucero por el Mediterráneo. Va a visitar varios puertos y muchas ciudades interesantes.
2. Arturo va a ir de Málaga a Madrid. Va a viajar por tierra (*land*). Su medio de transporte tiene comedor, bar y camas.
3. Margarita quiere visitar a sus parientes en Buenos Aires. Su medio de transporte no tiene camas, pero es muy rápido y va por el aire.
4. Carmen quiere visitar las pirámides de Teotihuacan cerca de la ciudad de México. A ella no le gusta manejar, pero quiere ir por carretera.
5. Diego va a visitar a sus abuelos. Él no tiene que comprar un pasaje; sólo necesita comprar gasolina.

**medio de transporte**

a. Viaja en avión.
b. Viaja en barco.
c. Viaja en auto.
d. Viaja en autobús.
e. Viaja en tren.

**D** **¿Qué piden estas personas?** Asocie la situación con la respuesta correcta.

1. El Sr. Vargas tiene mucho dinero y le gusta estar muy cómodo en el viaje.
2. La Srta. Marcela Armenteros es alérgica a los cigarrillos.
3. Al Sr. Venegas le gusta mirar el paisaje (*landscape*).
4. Joaquín Torres tiene poco dinero y quiere gastar muy poco.
5. El Sr. Gabriel Méndez es vegetariano.
6. La Sra. Luz María López sale para Caracas hoy y vuelve el mes próximo.

a. un asiento de ventanilla
b. la sección de no fumar
c. una comida especial
d. un asiento en primera
e. un asiento en la clase turista
f. un pasaje de ida y vuelta

# Cultura[1]

## Los viajes en los países hispanos

Los países hispanos le ofrecen al viajero una gran variedad de escenarios y de culturas. En ellos se pueden encontrar restos de antiguas civilizaciones, ciudades cosmopolitas con todas las comodidades de la vida moderna, pueblos donde parece que el tiempo se ha detenido°, y playas, montañas, selvas° y paisajes de una belleza extraordinaria.

Para viajar entre ciudades importantes en España, hay personas que usan el avión, pero el tren y los autobuses se usan más. El sistema de ferrocarril se llama RENFE (Red° Nacional de Ferrocarriles Españoles). Los trenes son buenos, especialmente el Talgo que es el más rápido. Este tren hace muy pocas paradas° y le ofrece muchas comodidades al viajero. Otros trenes como los expresos y los rápidos viajan a menos velocidad que el Talgo y son menos cómodos. La mayor parte de los trenes en España tienen servicio de primera y de segunda clase; además, algunos tienen coches cama° y los viajeros pueden escoger entre departamentos privados, donde pueden dormir hasta cuatro personas, o departamentos de seis literas° donde uno comparte el departamento con otras personas a quienes probablemente no conoce.

Las carreteras en España son buenas, pero la mayoría son de sólo dos vías°. Hay algunas autopistas° que son similares a las carreteras interestatales de los Estados Unidos, pero para viajar por ellas es necesario pagar peaje°. La mayor parte de los autobuses que comunican

Una parada de autobuses en Tegucigalpa, Honduras. El bus es el medio de comunicación que más se usa en la mayoría de las ciudades hispanas.

las ciudades importantes son muy cómodos, tienen baño y vídeo, y en algunos casos si el viaje es muy largo les sirven comida a los pasajeros.

En España el número de automóviles ha aumentado° mucho en los últimos años—alrededor° de dos millones de autos entre 1987 y 1988—a pesar de que° la gasolina es muy cara. La gente joven normalmente usa el transporte público o las motocicletas para trasladarse de un lugar a otro en las ciudades.

---

[1] Beginning with this lesson, the culture sections will be in Spanish.  se ha detenido *has stopped*  selvas *jungles*  Red *Network*  paradas *stops*  coches cama *sleeping cars*  literas *berths*  dos vías *two lanes*  autopistas *freeways or superhighways*  peaje *toll*  ha aumentado *has increased*  alrededor *around*  a pesar de que *in spite of*

El metro de Caracas. En algunas de las estaciones de este moderno metro se encuentran unos bellos vitrales *(stained glass)* de la artista venezolana Mercedes Pardo.

En Hispanoamérica las montañas, especialmente los Andes en la América del Sur, las selvas, los ríos y los desiertos hacen que la construcción de carreteras y de vías de ferrocarril sea muy cara y complicada. La estación de las lluvias en el trópico dificulta todavía más la construcción. A pesar de todos estos problemas, se construyó la Carretera Panamericana que comunica a Norteamérica con Centro y Suramérica. Esta carretera es un importante medio de comunicación y una extraordinaria obra de ingeniería.

La aviación fue° una solución para el transporte en Suramérica. Hoy en día hay muchos vuelos de carga y de pasajeros entre las diferentes ciudades, pero el costo resulta muy alto para la mayor parte de la población, y los autobuses y trenes son los medios de transporte que más se usan entre ciudades y pueblos. Hay autobuses modernos, pero también hay muchos que son viejos y hacen numerosas paradas.

En las ciudades del mundo hispano la población normalmente depende del transporte público. El metro ha ayudado° a mejorar la situación del tráfico al mismo tiempo que ofrece un medio de transporte económico en ciudades como Madrid y Barcelona en España, y Santiago, Buenos Aires, Caracas y la ciudad de México en Hispanoamérica.

fue *was*   ha ayudado *has helped*

# EN CONTEXTO

### Un accidente

Arturo está caminando por la acera cuando ve a su amigo Juan. Juan tiene
un tobillo vendado° y camina con muletas°.

*bandaged / crutches*

| | | |
|---|---|---|
| **Arturo** | ¿Qué te pasó°, Juan? | *happened* |
| **Juan** | Ayer° choqué° con un taxi. El chofer no frenó° porque no | *yesterday / I collided /* |
| | vio la luz° roja y le dio° a mi carro. Gracias a Dios° | *didn't brake* |
| | yo sólo me torcí° un tobillo. | *light / hit / Gracias. . .* |
| | | *Thank God* |
| **Arturo** | ¿Te llevaron° al hospital? | *twisted* |
| **Juan** | Sí, me llevaron en ambulancia. | *did they take* |
| **Arturo** | ¿Y tu carro? | |
| **Juan** | Pues tengo que cambiarle una puerta y un guardabarros°, | *fender* |
| | pero el seguro° del taxi cubre° todo. | *insurance / covers* |

### Para completar

Complete las siguientes oraciones de acuerdo con el diálogo.

1. Arturo ve a su amigo Juan en. . .
2. Juan no puede caminar bien porque. . .
3. El chofer del taxi no vio. . .
4. Juan fue al hospital en. . .
5. Quien paga todo es. . .

### Partes de un coche

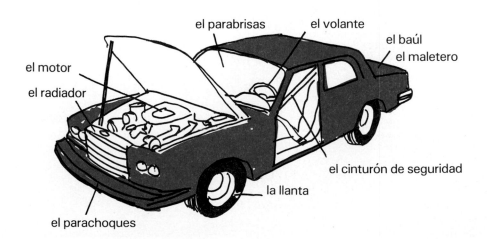

**más palabras útiles**

| | |
|---|---|
| la licencia de manejar | *driver's license* |
| la multa | *fine* |
| el semáforo | *traffic light* |
| estacionar | *to park* |
| parar/hacer alto | *to stop* |

## ACTIVIDADES

**A** Asocie las descripciones de la columna de la izquierda con las palabras de la columna de la derecha.

1. Las personas que viajan en un auto deben usarlo como protección.
2. Lugar donde se pone el equipaje.
3. Lugar donde se pone agua para que no se caliente el motor.
4. Sirve para proteger (*protect*) el carro delante y detrás.
5. Está delante del chofer y sirve para doblar o ir derecho.
6. Documento necesario para manejar un coche.
7. Una señal de tráfico que tiene luz roja, verde y amarilla.
8. Pago que debe hacer una persona cuando no sigue las regulaciones de tránsito.

a. el maletero/el baúl
b. el volante
c. el cinturón de seguridad
d. el radiador
e. el parachoques
f. la multa
g. la licencia, de manejar
h. el semáforo

**B** Complete el siguiente diálogo sobre un accidente con su compañero/a.

| | |
|---|---|
| **Usted** | ¿Qué te pasó, ___? |
| **Compañero/a** | Choqué con ___. |
| **Usted** | ¿Te llevaron al hospital? |
| **Compañero/a** | . . . |
| **Usted** | ¿Cómo te sientes ahora? |
| **Compañero/a** | . . . |
| **Usted** | ¿Y qué le pasó a tu carro? |
| **Compañero/a** | Tengo que cambiarle ___. |
| **Usted** | ¿Quién va a pagar los gastos? |
| **Compañero/a** | . . . |

**C Entrevista.** Hágale las siguientes preguntas a su compañero/a.
Después él/ella le debe hacer las mismas preguntas a usted. Comparta la
información con la clase.

1. ¿Te gusta manejar? 2. ¿Te gustan los autos grandes o pequeños?
3. ¿Qué autos prefieres, los americanos, los japoneses o los europeos?
4. ¿Cuál es tu auto favorito? ¿Y tu color favorito?

## GRAMÁTICA

### Preterit tense

Spanish has two simple tenses to express the past: the preterit and the imperfect (**el pretérito,
el imperfecto**).[2] Use the preterit to express actions initiated or completed in the past.

|  | **hablar** | **comer** | **vivir** |
|---|---|---|---|
| yo | habl**é** | com**í** | viv**í** |
| tú | habl**aste** | com**iste** | viv**iste** |
| él, ella, usted | habl**ó** | com**ió** | viv**ió** |
| nosotros/as | habl**amos** | com**imos** | viv**imos** |
| vosotros/as | habl**asteis** | com**isteis** | viv**isteis** |
| ellos/as, ustedes | habl**aron** | com**ieron** | viv**ieron** |

1. Note the accent mark in the **yo** and the **él, ella, usted** forms. These forms of the verb **ver** do
   not have accent marks because they have only one syllable: **vi, vio.**
2. The **nosotros** preterit form of **-ar** and **-ir** verbs is the same as the present. Context will indicate
   whether it is present or past.

   Llegamos temprano. } *We arrive early.*
   *We arrived early.*

3. Stem-changing **-ar** and **-er** verbs do not change in the preterit.

   **pensar:** pensé, pensaste, pensó, pensamos, pensasteis,
   pensaron
   **volver:** volví, volviste, volvió, volvimos, volvisteis, volvieron

---

[2] The preterit is presented in **Lecciones 12, 13,** and **14;** the imperfect is presented in **Lección 15.**

**4.** Verbs ending in **-car, -gar,** and **-zar** have a spelling change in the **yo** form.

| | |
|---|---|
| **sacar:** | sa**qué,** sacaste, sacó, sacamos, sacasteis, sacaron |
| **llegar:** | lle**gué,** llegaste, llegó, llegamos, llegasteis, llegaron |
| **empezar:** | empe**cé,** empezaste, empezó, empezamos, empezasteis, empezaron |

**5.** The verb **dar** uses the endings of **-er** and **-ir** verbs.

    **dar:**   di, diste, dio, dimos, disteis, dieron

**6.** Some time expressions that you can use with the preterit to denote past time are

| | |
|---|---|
| anoche | *last night* |
| anteayer | *the day before yesterday* |
| anteanoche/antenoche | *the night before last* |
| la semana pasada | *last week* |
| el mes pasado | *last month* |

ayer
el año pasado

Las autopistas y los pasos a diferentes niveles hacen de Caracas una de las ciudades más modernas de Hispanoamérica.

## ACTIVIDADES

**A** Ponga en orden las actividades de Manuel el lunes pasado.

Se despertó a las siete.
Estudió con un compañero por la tarde.
Asistió a sus clases por la mañana.
Salió con un amigo y cenaron en un café.
Se acostó a dormir.
Se levantó, se lavó los dientes y se bañó.
Su padre lo llevó a la universidad.
Volvió a la casa para almorzar.
Desayunó con sus padres.

**B** Su compañero/a le va a decir que las siguientes personas siempre llegan a tiempo al trabajo. Usted le va a contestar que hoy llegaron tarde.

*Modelo*   Juan   **Compañero/a   Juan siempre llega a tiempo.**
**Usted   Pero hoy llegó tarde.**

Amanda   los inspectores   nosotros   ellas   yo   tú

**C** Ayer usted manejó de su casa a la universidad. Diga las cosas que pasaron desde que salió de su casa hasta que almorzó en la cafetería.

*Modelo*   salir de casa a las...
**Salí de casa a las ocho.**

1. manejar media hora
2. estacionar en la calle...
3. llegar a la biblioteca a las...
4. estudiar con... una hora
5. caminar a la Facultad de Humanidades
6. hablar con la profesora...
7. entrar en la clase de sicología a las...
8. salir de la clase a las...
9. comer una hamburguesa en la cafetería
10. beber un refresco

**D** Usted viajó en avión la semana pasada. Diga las cosas que pasaron en el vuelo cambiando los infinitivos al pretérito.

La azafata (saludar) a los pasajeros, les (explicar) el uso de los cinturones de seguridad y les (indicar) las salidas de emergencia. El avión (salir) a las once y poco después el piloto (hablar) sobre el vuelo. Después yo (tomar) una cerveza y mi hermano (tomar) un jugo de naranja. El señor de al lado (comer) mucho y (beber) tres copas de vino. Detrás de nosotros unos amigos (conversar) todo el tiempo. Después del almuerzo nosotros (ver) una película. El avión (llegar) a Miami a su hora.

**E  Los trabajos de un ama de casa.** Lea el siguiente párrafo cambiando los verbos al pretérito.

*[levantó]* *[tomó]* *[empezó]*
La Sra. Campos se levanta temprano, toma el desayuno y empieza a *[limpió]* *[pasó]* trabajar. Primero limpia los baños y pasa la aspiradora en la sala y las *[lavó]* *[preparó]* *[comió]* habitaciones. Después lava la ropa y prepara el almuerzo. A la una come un sándwich y una ensalada y bebe una taza de café. Después de al- *[bebió]* *[escribió]* muerzo habla por teléfono con una amiga y le escribe una carta a su *[planchó]* *[preparó]* hermana. Por la tarde plancha la ropa, se baña y prepara la comida para *[llegaron]* *[ayudaron]* *[pusieron]* la familia. Sus hijos llegan a eso de las cinco y la ayudan a poner la *[llegó]* *[descansó]* *[bañó]* mesa. Su marido llega a las seis y media, descansa un rato y se baña *[sentaron]* antes de la cena. A las ocho se sientan a la mesa para cenar. Después *[lavaron]* *[secaron]* de la cena el Sr. Campos y sus hijos lavan y secan los platos. A eso de las nueve todos miran uno o dos programas de televisión y después se *[miraron]* acuestan. *[acostaron]*

**F**  Pregúntele a su compañero/a sobre sus actividades de ayer. Después él/ella le va a hacer las mismas preguntas a usted.

*Modelo*    levantarse temprano
            —¿**Te levantaste temprano?**
            —**Sí, me levanté temprano** o **No, no me levanté temprano.**

1. desayunar en casa
2. tomar vitaminas
3. manejar a la universidad
4. estudiar en la biblioteca
5. asistir a la clase de español
6. comer en la cafetería
7. beber leche
8. correr por la tarde
9. bañarse después
10. ver televisión por la noche

**G**  Usted va a entrevistar a dos actores famosos que trabajaron en la misma película y les hace las siguientes preguntas sobre sus experiencias durante la filmación. ¿Qué contestan ellos?

*Modelo*    —¿Cuántos meses trabajaron en África?
            —**Trabajamos dos meses.**

1. ¿En qué país trabajaron?
2. ¿Dónde vivieron durante esos dos meses?
3. ¿Se enfermaron (*Did you get sick*) durante la filmación?
4. ¿Cuándo terminaron la filmación en África?
5. ¿Qué otros países visitaron en África?
6. ¿Cuándo empezaron a filmar en España?
7. ¿Cuánto tiempo filmaron en España?
8. ¿Creen ustedes que la película va a ganar un Oscar?

**H**  Dígale a su compañero/a las cosas que usted hizo (*did*) el domingo pasado. Después él/ella le va a decir lo que hizo.

# EN CONTEXTO

## En la agencia de viajes

| | |
|---|---|
| **Cliente** | Quisiera° hacer una reservación para ir a Guadalajara el día 15. |
| **Agente de viajes** | ¿Por la mañana o por la tarde? |
| **Cliente** | Prefiero por la mañana. |
| **Agente de viajes** | Un momento, por favor. Lo siento, señor. El vuelo que sale por la mañana está lleno°. No hay ningún asiento disponible°. Puedo ponerlo en la lista de espera. |
| **Cliente** | ¿Y el de la tarde? |
| **Agente de viajes** | Déjeme ver°. Hay muchos asientos vacíos°, pero ese vuelo hace escala° en Mazatlán. Si a usted no le importa°... |
| **Cliente** | A nadie° le gusta hacer escala, pero si no hay ningún otro vuelo... |
| **Agente de viajes** | ¿Por qué no reserva un asiento en este vuelo y lo pongo en la lista de espera para el otro? Siempre hay alguien° que cancela. |
| **Cliente** | Está bien. |
| **Agente de viajes** | ¿Cómo va a pagar, en efectivo° o con tarjeta de crédito? |
| **Cliente** | Con tarjeta de crédito. |

*I'd like*

*full*

ningún... *any seats available*

Déjeme... *Let me see / empty*
hace... *makes a stopover*
Si... *If you don't mind*
*No one*

*someone*

*cash*

## Para completar

Complete las siguientes oraciones de acuerdo con el diálogo.

1. El cliente quiere ir a...
2. Él prefiere ir por...
3. El vuelo de la mañana está...
4. En el vuelo que sale por la tarde hay...
5. El vuelo de la tarde hace...
6. El cliente va a reservar un asiento en...
7. Para el vuelo de la mañana él va a estar en...
8. El cliente va a pagar...

# ACTIVIDADES

**A** Usted quiere saber qué planes tiene su amigo/a para sus vacaciones. Hágale las siguientes preguntas y comparta la información con la clase.

1. ¿Adónde vas a ir?
2. ¿Cómo vas a ir?
3. ¿Cuánto tiempo vas a estar allí?
4. ¿Qué vas a hacer allí?
5. ¿Vas a llevar tu cámara?
6. ¿Dónde vas a comprar los pasajes?
7. ¿Vas a pagar en efectivo o con tarjeta de crédito?

1. llegar temprano al aeropuerto
2. facturar el equipaje
3. dormir durante el vuelo
4. conocer a otros pasajeros
5. no llevar mucha ropa
6. pedir un asiento en el pasillo
7. no ver la película
8. no gastar mucho dinero

**F** Diga qué cosas le gustan o no le gustan de la lista que aparece más abajo. Su compañero/a debe decir si le gustan o no.

*Modelo*      los postres de chocolate

| | |
|---|---|
| **Usted** | **A mí me gustan los postres de chocolate.** |
| **Compañero/a** | **A mí también** o **A mí no.** |

viajar en avión

| | |
|---|---|
| **Usted** | **A mí no me gusta viajar en avión.** |
| **Compañero/a** | **A mí tampoco** o **A mí sí.** |

1. tener un coche nuevo
2. levantarme temprano
3. hacer ejercicio
4. ir al médico
5. los coches deportivos
6. sacar malas notas
7. la ropa deportiva
8. sentirme mal

**G** Usted está en la aduana y el inspector le hace las siguientes preguntas. Trabaje con un/a compañero/a.

| | |
|---|---|
| **Inspector** | ¿Tiene algo que declarar? |
| **Usted** | No,... |
| **Inspector** | ¿Trae usted alguna planta? |
| **Usted** | No,... |
| **Inspector** | ¿Tiene usted más de $10.000? |
| **Usted** | No,... |
| **Inspector** | Por favor, abra el equipaje. |
| **Usted** | ... |

**H** Usted y un amigo están en una fiesta en casa de Luisa. Ella viene adonde están ustedes y les hace estas preguntas. Trabajen en grupos de tres personas y completen el siguiente diálogo.

| | |
|---|---|
| **Luisa** | ¿Quieres comer algo? |
| **Usted** | ... |
| **Luisa** | Y tú, ¿quieres que te sirva algo? |
| **Su amigo** | ... |
| **Luisa** | ¿Quieren probar algunos postres? |
| **Usted** | ... |
| **Su amigo** | ... |
| **Luisa** | ¿Desean beber algo? |
| **Usted** | ... |
| **Su amigo** | ... |

# EN CONTEXTO

**La imaginación y la realidad**

## ACTIVIDADES

**A** Usted compró un carro (o una moto). Su compañero/a quiere saber cómo es y le va a hacer las siguientes preguntas. Después él/ella debe compartir la información con la clase.

1. ¿De qué color es?   2. ¿Es grande?   3. ¿Consume mucha gasolina?   4. ¿Cuánto costó?
5. ¿Dónde lo/la compraste?   6. ¿De qué marca es?

**B** Su compañero/a va a hacer un viaje en moto. Hágale preguntas para obtener la siguiente información: (a) adónde va a ir, (b) qué piensa hacer allí, (c) si va a ir solo o con un/a compañero/a, y (d) cuánto tiempo va a estar fuera.

# GRAMÁTICA

## Indicative and subjunctive in adjective clauses

**1.** An adjective clause is a dependent clause that is used as an adjective.

Hay algunos estudiantes **trabajadores.**
\_____/
adjective

Hay algunos estudiantes **que son trabajadores.**
\_____/
adjective clause

The word that the adjective clause modifies (**estudiantes**) is the antecedent.

**2.** Use the indicative in an adjective clause that refers to a person, thing, or place (antecedent) that exists or is known or specific.

| | |
|---|---|
| Hay alguien que **habla** 34 lenguas. | *There is someone who speaks 34 languages.* |
| Quiero viajar en el tren que **sale** por la mañana. | *I want to travel on the train that leaves in the morning. (you know there is such a train)* |

**3.** Use the subjunctive in an adjective clause that refers to a person, thing, or place that does not exist or is not known or not specific.

| | |
|---|---|
| No hay nadie que **hable** 34 lenguas. | *There isn't anyone who speaks 34 languages.* |
| Quiero viajar en un tren que **salga** por la mañana. | *I want to travel on a train that leaves in the morning. (any train as long as it leaves in the morning)* |

**4.** When the antecedent is a specific person and functions as a direct object, use the personal **a** and the indicative. If the antecedent is not a specific person, use the subjunctive and no personal **a.**

Busco { **a una** / **a la** } estudiante que **trabaja** aquí.
Busco una estudiante que **trabaje** aquí.

*I'm looking for { a / the } student who works here.*
*I'm looking for a student who works here. (any student)*

**5.** In questions you may use the indicative or the subjunctive; nevertheless, if you are not sure about the existence of the antecedent use the subjunctive.

¿Hay alguien que { **entiende** / **entienda** } esto?

*Is there anyone who understands this?*

## *ACTIVIDADES*

**A** Usted sabe que hay una agencia de viajes muy buena en Acapulco. Déle información sobre la Agencia Las Hamacas a su compañero/a de acuerdo con el siguiente anuncio.

*Modelo* **Hay una agencia que planea viajes al extranjero.**

TURISMO

○ **Las Hamacas** ○

**SERVICIO DE VIAJES**
**LE PLANEAMOS SU VIAJE A CUALQUIER PARTE**
**DE MÉXICO Y DEL EXTRANJERO**
BOLETOS DE AVIÓN, DE BARCO, RENTA DE AUTOS, VIAJES TODO
PAGADO, RESERVACIONES A HOTELES, LOBBY HOTEL ACAPULCO IMPERIAL
**521-24**          **528-59**
**5-22-79**     LLAME LE ENVIAMOS
SUS BOLETOS

COSTERA M. ALEMÁN N° 251, ACAPULCO, GRO.

**B** Diga que ninguna agencia ofrece los siguientes servicios.

*Modelo*     regalar pasajes
**No hay ninguna agencia que regale pasajes.**

1. vender aviones
2. cambiar cheques
3. abrir el 25 de diciembre

4. servir comidas
5. vender pasajes a Marte
6. comprar autos

**C** Conteste las siguientes preguntas sobre los alumnos de la clase de español. Si la respuesta es afirmativa diga quién es.

*Modelo*     ¿Hay alguien que lleve una sudadera blanca?
**Sí, hay alguien que lleva una sudadera blanca. Marta.**
¿Hay alguien que hable cuatro lenguas?
**No, no hay nadie que hable cuatro lenguas.**

1. ¿Hay alguien que sea alto y delgado?
2. ¿Hay alguien que mida ocho pies?
3. ¿Hay alguien que sea moreno y tenga el pelo corto?
4. ¿Hay alguien que sepa contar en español?
5. ¿Hay alguien que conozca al Presidente?
6. ¿Hay alguien que tenga un avión?
7. ¿Hay alguien que estudie para ser médico?
8. ¿Hay alguien que quiera vivir en Madrid durante un año?

**D** Usted quiere ir a Villa de Leiva, un pueblo colonial de Colombia. Usted le hace las siguientes preguntas a su agente de viajes. Trabaje con un/a compañero/a.

> **Usted** ¿Hay algún vuelo que vaya a Villa de Leiva?
> **Agente** No,. . .
> **Usted** ¿Hay algún autobús que pueda tomar?
> **Agente** Sí,. . .
> **Usted** ¿Hay algún buen hotel allí?
> **Agente** Sí,. . .

**E** Usted tiene que hacer un trabajo urgente y muy importante en su oficina y necesita unos empleados que lo ayuden. Dígale a su jefe/a qué clase de empleado necesita. Él/ella le va a decir si hay o no hay un empleado así en la compañía.

*Modelo*    Necesito a alguien que programe la computadora.
> **Sí, hay alguien que programa la computadora** o
> **No, no hay nadie que programe la computadora.**

1. Necesito a alguien que sepa usar mi computadora.
   Sí, hay. . .
2. Necesito un empleado que hable inglés, japonés y español.
   No, no hay. . .
3. Necesito un empleado que pueda trabajar esta noche.
   No, no. . .
4. Entonces, un empleado que pueda trabajar este fin de semana.
   Sí, hay. . .
5. Necesito un empleado que lleve estos documentos al banco ahora.
   Sí, hay. . .

**F** Usted quiere saber si su compañero/a conoce a ciertas personas. Hágale las siguientes preguntas. Si la respuesta es afirmativa, su compañero/a debe decir quién es esa persona y cómo es.

*Modelo*    vivir en Panamá
> **Usted** ¿Conoces a alguien que viva en Panamá?
> **Compañero/a** Sí, conozco a alguien que vive en Panamá.
> Uno de mis primos. Es un chico muy simpático
> o No, no conozco a nadie que viva en Panamá.

1. tener un Rolls Royce
2. hablar ruso
3. viajar a Europa este año
4. trabajar en el aeropuerto
5. saber canciones mexicanas

**G** Complete la oraciones de la columna de la izquierda con la información de la columna de la derecha.

> *Modelo*   Vamos a tomar un vuelo       sale a las tres.
> **Vamos a tomar un vuelo que sale a las tres.**

| | |
|---|---|
| Me gustan los vuelos | es interesante. |
| Compramos unas blusas | no hacen escala. |
| Conozco varias ciudades | tiene buenas comidas. |
| Alquilaron una casa | tienen buen clima. |
| Conozco un hotel | son pequeños y bonitas. |
| | tiene piscina. |
| | es elegante. |
| | salen y llegan a tiempo. |
| | no cuestan mucho. |

**H** Lea el siguiente anuncio y diga cómo es el Hotel Rubens.

> *Modelo*   **Es un hotel que está en Barcelona.**

SU HOTEL EN BARCELONA
★★★ **HOTEL RUBENS** ★★★
Zona residencial y tranquila, junto Plaza Lesseps. Todas las Habitaciones con TV color, vídeo, ambiente musical, calefacción. Parking, Restaurante, solárium, etc.

| **Individual** | **Doble** | **Cama Supl.** |
|---|---|---|
| 3.600 | 4.300 | 1.000 |

ESTANCIAS SUPERIORES A 1 SEMANA, GRANDES DESCUENTOS

Pº Ntra. Sra. del Coll, 10 (Barcelona 08023)
Reservas: Tel. 93 / 219 12 04. Tx. 98.718

**I** Usted y su compañero están hablando con un agente de viajes. Díganle cómo debe ser el hotel que ustedes desean en San Cristóbal, una pequeña ciudad de México. Cada uno debe decir por lo menos dos cosas que esperan encontrar en el hotel.

> *Modelo*   **Agente**   **¿Qué tipo de hotel desea?**
> **Usted**   **Queremos un hotel que sea tranquilo.**
> **Compañero/a**   **Queremos un hotel que esté cerca del centro.**

**J** Describa a las personas en la tabla y después describa a un/a amigo/a.

> *Modelo*   **Compañero/a**   **¿Cómo es Olivia?**
> **Usted**   **Es una muchacha que tiene 24 años.**

| NOMBRE | EDAD | DIRECCIÓN | OJOS | PELO | NACIONALIDAD | PROFESIÓN |
|---|---|---|---|---|---|---|
| Olivia | 24 | Pío Pico 34 | negros | negro | española | abogada |
| Danilo | 28 | San Luis 18 | verdes | rubio | colombiano | contador |
| amigo/a | | | | | | |

**K** Usted es un idealista y siempre busca las cosas o las personas ideales. Describa cómo espera usted que sean estas personas o cosas.

*Modelo*  la casa ideal
> **Busco una casa que esté frente al mar, que sea grande y que tenga cinco cuartos.**

1. el amigo/la amiga ideal
2. el profesor/la profesora ideal
3. el novio/la novia ideal

4. la cocina ideal
5. el carro ideal
6. el viaje ideal

Un tranvía en una calle de Asunción, Paraguay. Los tranvías han desaparecido de la mayor parte de las ciudades hispanas.

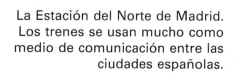

La Estación del Norte de Madrid. Los trenes se usan mucho como medio de comunicación entre las ciudades españolas.

# LECTURA

### Evite accidentes

Este anuncio de la Secretaría de Comunicaciones y Transportes de México les da consejos (*advice*) muy importantes a las personas que manejan. El anuncio es fácil de leer, pues hay muchos cognados y usted sabe el resto de las palabras, excepto «ingerir» que quiere decir «beber».

> Antes de salir a carretera revise su vehículo
> No ingiera bebidas alcohólicas antes o durante su viaje
> No maneje con exceso de velocidad
> Use el cinturón de seguridad
> Antes de cruzar la vía del tren... haga alto total
>
> # EVITE ACCIDENTES
>
>  SECRETARIA DE COMUNICACIONES Y TRANSPORTES

### Para completar

**A** Complete las siguientes oraciones con la información que se da en el anuncio anterior.

1. Antes de empezar el viaje usted debe...
2. Las personas que manejan no deben...
3. Todas las personas que van en el auto deben usar...
4. Los choferes deben parar...

**B** Usted y su compañero/a deben pensar en otros consejos para evitar accidentes. Comparta sus consejos con los otros estudiantes.

### Puerto Rico

El anuncio de la siguiente página es de Iberia, la línea aérea española. La forma del cupón de la derecha imita una parte de El Morro, la fortaleza que está a la entrada de la bahía de San Juan. Esta parte de El Morro es un símbolo de Puerto Rico y se ve también abajo a la izquierda, entre el nombre de Iberia y el de Puerto Rico. El Morro es uno de los edificios coloniales más interesantes que hay en San Juan, la capital de Puerto Rico. La parte antigua de la ciudad es el Viejo San Juan. Allí no se puede construir ningún edificio moderno para mantener su aspecto colonial.

Las siguientes palabras le pueden ayudar a entender mejor el anuncio.

| | |
|---|---|
| se mezcla | *combines* |
| sabor | *flavor* |
| disfrutar | *to enjoy* |
| rincones | *places, corners* |
| a pleno sol | *full sun* |
| D.P. (distrito postal) | *zip code* |

**Puerto Rico: 9 días desde 149.900 Pts.**

Al sol del Caribe. En invierno y en verano, así es Puerto Rico. Una isla donde las playas no acaban nunca. Donde la naturaleza más exótica se mezcla con el sabor de sus construcciones coloniales. Una isla donde la palabra clave es disfrutar. Con sus gentes, su folklore y los mil rincones que usted puede descubrir a pleno sol. Incluso en invierno. Iberia pone a su alcance el atractivo de Puerto Rico desde 149.900 Ptas.

Incluyendo viaje en vuelo regular ida y vuelta, 9 días de estancia en un magnífico hotel, traslados aeropuerto-hotel-aeropuerto, Tour por el viejo San Juan y visita a St. Thomas. También podrá disfrutar de la magia de tres espectáculos folklóricos y el regalo de ron del país.

Infórmese en Iberia, en su agencia de viajes o en la Oficina de Turismo del Estado Libre Asociado de Puerto Rico en Madrid.

Para mayor información, envíe este cupón a la Oficina de Turismo de Puerto Rico. Pedro Texeira, 8, 4º 28020 Madrid.

Nombre _____
Dirección _____
Población _____ D.P. _____

**ESTADO LIBRE ASOCIADO DE PUERTO RICO OFICINA DE TURISMO**

**IBERIA IB**
LINEAS AEREAS DE ESPAÑA

BN

**A** Conteste las siguientes preguntas con la información que se da en el anuncio.

1. ¿Cuánto cuesta el viaje a Puerto Rico?
2. ¿Qué incluye ese precio?
3. ¿Qué tiempo hace en Puerto Rico en invierno y en verano?
4. ¿Dónde está la Oficina de Turismo de Puerto Rico en Madrid?
5. ¿En qué otros lugares le pueden dar información sobre este viaje?
6. ¿Qué puede decir usted sobre San Juan?

**B** Usted y su compañero/a están planeando un viaje a San Juan. Hagan una lista de las cosas que necesitan para el viaje y todo lo que piensan hacer allí.

## Al Andalus Expreso

El siguiente anuncio es de un tren muy elegante, Al Andalus Expreso, que visita distintos lugares de Andalucía. Al Andalus fue el nombre que los árabes le dieron a la región que está al sur de España, lo que hoy en día conocemos como Andalucía. Los árabes permanecieron en España desde el año 711 d.C.[3] hasta el año 1492 y su influencia, especialmente en la arquitectura, se nota más en Andalucía que en otras regiones españolas. Granada, una de las provincias de Andalucía, fue el último reino (*kingdom*) árabe en España. El mapa en la siguiente página muestra las ciudades que están incluidas en este viaje.

En español, la palabra tren se usa en algunas expresiones que no tienen que ver con los trenes. En este anuncio se usan las expresiones **a todo tren** (*complete luxury*) y **tren de vida** (*way of life*). Otras palabras que le pueden ayudar a entender mejor el anuncio son

| | | | |
|---|---|---|---|
| el placer | *pleasure* | alcance | *reach* |
| bello | *beautiful* | escribir a máquina | *to type* |
| mayúsculas | *capital letters* | C.P. (código postal) | *zip code* |
| inolvidable | *unforgettable* | | |

---

[3] En español **d.C.** es la abreviatura para «después de Cristo». Su equivalente en inglés es A.D.

**A** Conteste la siguientes preguntas sobre el anuncio.

1. ¿Qué ciudades visita el tren Al Andalus Expreso?
2. ¿Cuánto cuesta el pasaje?
3. ¿Qué clase de tren es Al Andalus Expreso?
4. ¿Qué recibe usted si envía el cupón?

**B** Usted y sus compañeros/as deben pensar en las ventajas de viajar en tren, avión, autobús o coche. Divídanse en grupos de cinco o seis personas. Cada grupo debe escoger un medio de transporte. Después deben tratar de convencer a los otros grupos de que su medio de transporte es el mejor.

## SITUACIONES

1. You are at a train station in Madrid. Tell the employee (a) you need a round–trip ticket to Valencia, (b) the day of departure and return, (c) ask him/her how much it is, and (d) find out what time the train leaves.

2. You visited a friend over the weekend and had a great time. Tell your partner (a) whom you visited, (b) what you did on Saturday, and (c) when you returned.

3. You witnessed an accident. Your partner will be the policeman/woman and will ask you several questions about the accident: (a) when it happened, (b) where it happened, and (c) how many injured people (**heridos**) you saw.

4. You are the owner of a travel agency and you are looking for a young person to help you in the afternoon and on weekends. With a classmate write an ad including the following: (a) salary, (b) hours, and (c) any other pertinent information.

5. You are at a travel agency and you want to take a trip to Puerto Rico. Your partner will play the part of the travel agent. Find out the following information: (a) how much the ticket is, (b) when the plane leaves and arrives, (c) if you need a passport, (d) what hotel they can recommend, (e) how much the hotel is, and (f) if you can pay with a credit card.

6. You want to visit a Spanish-speaking country, but you haven't made up your mind which. A travel agent is going to help you plan your vacation. He/She is going to ask you several questions. Answer them so that he/she can recommend where to go.

| | |
|---|---|
| **Agente** | Buenos días. Bienvenido a Viajes Marina. |
| **Usted** | . . . |
| **Agente** | ¿En qué puedo servirle? |
| **Usted** | . . . |
| **Agente** | ¿Prefiere España, México, el Caribe, Centroamérica o Sudamérica? |
| **Usted** | . . . |
| **Agente** | ¿Entiende y habla español? |
| **Usted** | . . . |
| **Agente** | ¿Prefiere las playas o las ciudades? |
| **Usted** | . . . |
| **Agente** | ¿Prefiere un hotel de primera clase o un hotel más económico? |
| **Usted** | . . . |
| **Agente** | ¿Cómo le gusta viajar? |
| **Usted** | . . . |
| **Agente** | Bueno, creo que usted debe ir a ____ porque. . . ¿Qué le parece? |
| **Usted** | . . . |

7. You need to buy a car. Tell the salesperson (a) what kind of car you want, (b) ask what car he/she has. The salesperson will tell you the advantages of the cars they sell, such as price, gas consumption (**consumo**), and features.

# VOCABULARIO[4]

**el aeropuerto**

| | |
|---|---|
| la aerolínea | *airline* |
| el mostrador | *counter* |
| la puerta | *gate* |
| la sala de espera | *waiting room* |
| el vuelo | *flight* |

**en un avión**

| | |
|---|---|
| la sección de (no) fu-mar | *(no) smoking section* |
| la ventanilla | *window* |

**lugares**

| | |
|---|---|
| la aduana | *customs* |
| la carretera | *highway* |
| la estación de ferro-carril | *railroad station* |
| la estación de gaso-lina/gasolinera | *service station* |
| el mar | *sea* |
| el puerto | *port* |

**medios de trans-porte**

| | |
|---|---|
| el autobús | *bus* |
| el avión | *plane* |
| el barco | *ship* |
| el camión | *truck* |
| el carro/coche | *car* |
| el metro | *subway* |
| la moto(cicleta) | *motorcycle* |
| el taxi | *taxi* |
| el tren | *train* |

**personas**

| | |
|---|---|
| el/la agente de viajes | *travel agent* |
| el cliente/la clienta | *client* |
| el/la chofer | *driver* |
| el inspector | *inspector* |
| el pasajero | *passenger* |

**viajes**

| | |
|---|---|
| la agencia de viajes | *travel agency* |
| el boleto/pasaje | *ticket* |
| el boleto de ida y vuelta | *round–trip ticket* |
| el crucero | *cruise* |
| el cheque de viajero | *traveler's check* |
| el destino | *destination* |
| el equipaje | *luggage* |
| la gasolina | *gas* |
| la hora de llegada/ salida | *arrival/departure time* |
| la licencia de mane-jar | *driver's license* |
| la lista de espera | *waiting list* |
| la maleta | *suitcase* |
| el maletín | *attaché case* |
| la mochila | *backpack* |
| el pasaje | *ticket* |
| el pasaporte | *passport* |
| la reservación | *reservation* |
| la tarjeta de crédito | *credit card* |
| la tarjeta de em-barque | *boarding pass* |
| la visa/el visado | *visa* |

**partes de un coche**

| | |
|---|---|
| el baúl/maletero | *trunk* |
| el cinturón de seguri-dad | *safety belt* |
| el guardabarros | *fender* |
| la llanta | *tire* |
| el motor | *motor* |
| el parabrisas | *windshield* |
| el parachoques | *bumper* |
| el radiador | *radiator* |
| el volante | *steering wheel* |

---

[4] For affirmative and negative expressions, see page 296.

**el accidente**

| | |
|---|---|
| la ambulancia | *ambulance* |
| la muleta | *crutch* |
| el seguro | *insurance* |

**el tráfico**

| | |
|---|---|
| la luz | *light* |
| la multa | *fine* |
| el semáforo | *traffic light* |

**descripción**

| | |
|---|---|
| deportivo | *sports* |
| disponible | *available* |
| lleno | *full* |
| vacío | *empty* |
| vendado | *bandaged* |

**verbos**

| | |
|---|---|
| cancelar | *to cancel* |
| cubrir | *to cover* |
| chequear/facturar | *check (luggage)* |
| chocar | *to collide* |
| dejar | *to let, to permit* |
| empacar/hacer la maleta | *to pack* |
| estacionar | *to park* |
| frenar | *to brake* |
| importar | *to mind, to matter* |

| | |
|---|---|
| manejar | *to drive* |
| parar/hacer alto | *to stop* |
| pasar | *to happen* |
| reservar | *to make a reservation* |
| revisar | *to examine, to inspect* |
| torcer (ue) | *to twist* |
| viajar | *to travel* |
| volar (ue) | *to fly* |

**tiempo**

| | |
|---|---|
| anoche | *last night* |
| anteanoche/antenoche | *the night before last* |
| anteayer | *the day before yesterday* |
| ayer | *yesterday* |
| pasado/a | *last* |

**expresiones útiles**

| | |
|---|---|
| en efectivo | *cash* |
| gracias a Dios | *thank God* |
| hacer cola | *to stand in line* |
| hacer escala | *to make a stopover* |
| quisiera | *I would like* |

**In** Lección 13 **you will**
a. **interpret and compose telegraphic messages.**
b. **communicate by phone, postcard, and letter.**
c. **report past events.**
d. **describe actions.**

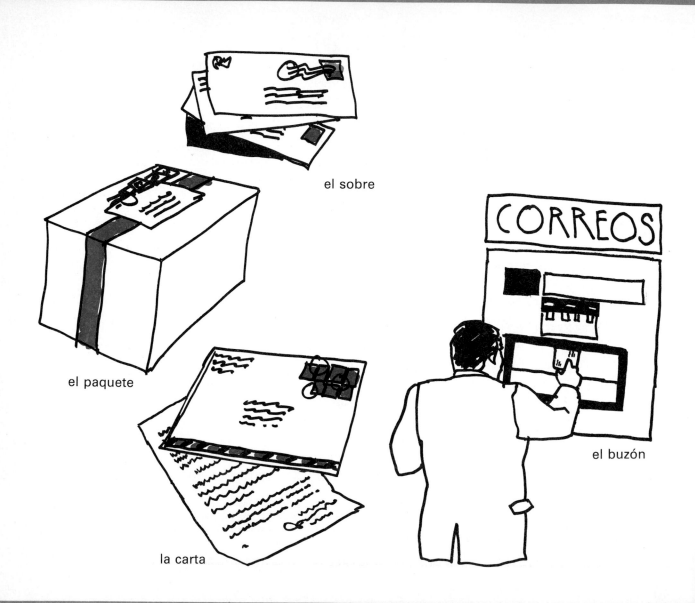

el sobre

el paquete

la carta

el buzón

## Un telegrama

FORMA DGTN-81

## TELEGRAFOS NACIONALES

### SECRETARIA DE COMUNICACIONES Y TRANSPORTES
### DIRECCION GENERAL DE TELEGRAFOS NACIONALES

T.G.N.

TELEGRAMA PARA TRANSMITIR CON ABSOLUTA SUJECION AL REGLAMENTO EN VIGOR.

| NUM. | PALABRAS | VALORES | H.D. |
|------|----------|---------|------|

(ANOTE USTED AQUI CLASE DE SERVICIO QUE DESEE UTILIZAR) *urgente*

PROCEDENCIA *Guadalajara*  EL *10* DE *marzo*  19 *90*

SR. *Aurelio Montalvo*

DOMICILIO *Calle 86 nº 96-11*  TELEFONO NUM. *257-4698*

DESTINO *Bogotá, D.E. Colombia*

*Llego marzo 14 8:30 a.m. vuelo 418*

*Cariños*

*Emilia*

*Andrés Terán #1553*
*Colonia Chapultepec, Guadalajara*

DOMICILIO DEL SIGNATARIO UNICAMENTE PARA CASOS DE ACLARACION

**más palabras útiles**

| | |
|---|---|
| el sello/la estampilla | *stamp* |
| la oficina de correos/el correo | *post office* |
| el cartero | *mailman* |
| mandar | *to send* |
| recibir | *to receive* |

REPUBLICA ARGENTINA

CAMINITO (Buenos Aires)
CASA DE MONEDA          J. CANNELLA Pin.
₳5

# ACTIVIDADES

**A** Complete las siguientes oraciones con la palabra adecuada.

1. El lugar donde las personas recogen la correspondencia y compran sellos es el . . .

   cartero

2. Para mandar una carta la ponemos dentro de un. . .

   sobre

3. La persona que reparte (*delivers*) cartas, tarjetas, etc. es el. . .

   correo

4. El depósito que generalmente está en la acera para poner las cartas es el. . .

   sello

5. No se puede mandar una carta sin escribir la dirección y ponerle un. . .

   buzón

**B** Preguntas

1. ¿Cuándo manda usted un telegrama?
2. ¿Adónde se debe ir para mandar un telegrama?
3. ¿Se puede mandar un telegrama desde la casa?
4. ¿Qué es más caro, un telegrama, una carta o una llamada telefónica?

**C** Hágale las siguientes preguntas a su compañero/a. Después él/ella debe hacerle las mismas preguntas a usted.

1. ¿A quién le escribes?
2. ¿Cuándo le escribes?
3. ¿Cómo son tus cartas?
4. ¿Prefieres escribir o llamar por teléfono?

## Cultura

### El teléfono, las cartas y el servicio postal en los países hispanos

El sistema de comunicaciones en el mundo hispano es muy similar al de este país, aunque existen algunas diferencias. Como en los Estados Unidos, el teléfono es una parte esencial de la vida diaria en una ciudad; sin embargo, en algunas ciudades hispanas resulta muy difícil conseguir un teléfono en ciertas zonas, especialmente en las afueras. Siempre se puede encontrar un teléfono público para hacer una llamada, pero no hay tantos como en los Estados Unidos. En algunas ciudades como Buenos Aires es necesario tener una ficha° para poder usar un teléfono público. Generalmente se pueden conseguir estas fichas en una tienda o quiosco cerca del teléfono. A veces existen problemas en el servicio telefónico debido a diversos factores como la falta de capital para invertir en mejoras, el rápido crecimiento° de algunas ciudades y aun°, en algunas zonas, la lluvia.

La expresión que se usa para contestar el teléfono varía entre los países hispanos: **diga** o **dígame** en España, **hola** en la Argentina y el Perú, **oigo** o **qué hay** en Cuba. **Aló** también se usa mucho. Cuando una persona hace una llamada telefónica es común que le pidan que se identifique con una de estas preguntas: **¿Quién habla?, ¿Con quién hablo?** o **¿De parte de quién?** En Colombia también se acostumbra° preguntarle **¿Con quién hablo?** a la persona que contesta el teléfono. Esto generalmente no se hace en otros países.

En inglés, en una carta familiar o comercial se usa la palabra *dear* para dirigirse° a la persona a quien le escriben la

Unos jóvenes hablan por teléfono en Buenos Aires.

carta. En español se usan palabras diferentes según el tipo de carta. La palabra **querido/a** tiene una connotación afectiva y sólo se usa entre familiares o personas muy amigas. La palabra **estimado/a** es más formal; se usa en las cartas comerciales o entre personas que no son tan amigas. En las cartas fami-

ficha *token*   crecimiento *growth*   aun *even*   se acostumbra *it is customary*   dirigirse *to address.*

liares en inglés se pone una coma después de la palabra *dear* y el nombre de la persona; en las cartas comerciales se usan dos puntos°. En español se usan dos puntos en las cartas familiares y en las comerciales.

Los sobres se dirigen de la misma forma en las dos lenguas, pero en español el número de la zona postal°, también conocido como código postal o distrito postal, generalmente se pone antes del nombre de la ciudad. El equivalente de *P.O. Box* es **apartado.**

Los sellos o estampillas se pueden comprar en correos, en quioscos o en algunas papelerías. Para escribir al extranjero, muchas personas usan un **aerograma** en vez de papel de carta y sobre. El aerograma es una hoja de papel que ya tiene un sello impreso y que cuando se dobla y se cierra se convierte en el sobre. No está permitido poner nada dentro de los aerogramas, pero se usan bastante porque son más económicos.

dos puntos *colon*   zona postal *zip code*

Para que la carta llegue en el menor tiempo posible, debe enviarse **urgente** o **entrega especial.** Cualquier cosa de valor debe mandarse por correo certificado°. Los telegramas se pueden mandar desde un correo, pero en algunos países es necesario ir a una oficina de la compañía de teléfonos.

A continuación pueden ver una selección de un folleto° publicado por la Dirección de Correos y Telégrafos de España donde se explican algunos de sus servicios.

certificado *registered*   folleto *brochure*

---

## Dirección General de Correos y Telégrafos

Porque el Servicio de Telégrafos dispone de los medios más modernos y sofisticados, podemos afirmar que

LAS COMUNICACIONES TELEGRÁFICAS SON LAS COMUNICACIONES DEL FUTURO

SERVICIO DE TELEGRAMAS Y RADIOTELEGRAMAS

Los telegramas.

¿Dónde y cómo pueden depositarse?

Recuerde que Vd. puede poner *sus telegramas*

— *personalmente* en nuestra red de Oficinas

— *a través del teléfono* desde su domicilio, o

— *a través del télex,* desde su posición de abonado, si Vd. tiene condición de tal.

Los telegramas pueden ser:

NACIONALES, e

INTERNACIONALES, y éstos, a su vez,

— *Continentales* si van dirigidos a países europeos y a los asiáticos y africanos de la cuenca mediterránea, e

— *Intercontinentales,* los destinados al resto del mundo.

Todos estos telegramas pueden cursarse con carácter ORDINARIO y, también, con carácter URGENTE, previo abono de la tasa reglamentaria

---

Una de las oficinas de correos de la ciudad de México. En las oficinas de correos de los países hispanos siempre hay un continuo movimiento de público.

# EN CONTEXTO

## Una conversación por teléfono

| | |
|---|---|
| **Sirvienta** | ¡Aló! |
| **Jorge** | ¿La casa de los señores Ávila? |
| **Sirvienta** | Sí, señor. ¿Con quién desea hablar? |
| **Jorge** | Con la Srta. Ávila, por favor. |
| **Sirvienta** | ¿De parte de quién? |
| **Jorge** | De Jorge Bermúdez. |
| **Sirvienta** | Un momento, por favor. Señorita Emilia, la llaman por teléfono de parte de Jorge Bermúdez. |
| **Emilia** | ¡Hola, Jorge! ¿Cómo estás? |
| **Jorge** | Muy bien, ¿y tú? |
| **Emilia** | Bien. Ayer fui a Monserrate con mis primos y lo pasamos muy bien.° |
| **Jorge** | Emilia, te oigo° muy mal. ¿Puedes hablar más alto°? |
| **Emilia** | Es que hay mucho ruido°. Mi primito se cayó° y está llorando°. ¿Me oyes ahora? |
| **Jorge** | ¡Aló, aló! No te oigo nada. Creo que se cayó la comunicación°. |
| **Emilia** | Yo sí te oigo, pero tenemos una conexión muy mala. |
| **Jorge** | Cuelga°. Te vuelvo a llamar enseguida°. |

*lo... we had a great time*

*hear / más... louder*

*noise / se... fell*

*crying*

*se... we were cut off*

*Hang up / Te... I'll call you right back*

## ¿Verdadero o falso?

Diga si las siguientes oraciones son verdaderas o falsas, de acuerdo con la conversación telefónica.

1. La sirvienta quiere saber quién llama.
2. Emilia no se siente muy bien hoy.
3. Emilia fue a casa de unos amigos ayer.
4. Emilia se cayó en casa de sus amigos.
5. Jorge le pide a Emilia que hable más bajo.
6. La comunicación telefónica es mala.
7. Emilia cuelga porque no quiere hablar con Jorge.
8. Jorge va a llamar a Emilia otra vez.

### vocabulario útil para hablar por teléfono

| | |
|---|---|
| el indicativo/el prefijo | *area code* |
| la operadora | *operator* |
| la guía telefónica/de teléfonos | *telephone directory* |
| llamada de cargo revertido/a cobrar | *collect call* |
| llamada de larga distancia | *long–distance call* |
| marcar/discar | *to dial* |

## ACTIVIDADES

**A** Usted está en Santiago de Chile y tiene que hablar con un amigo que está en otra ciudad de Chile. Diga en qué orden ocurren las siguientes cosas.

Marco el O.
Hablo con mi amigo.
Cuelgo el teléfono.
Le doy a la operadora el indicativo, el número y el nombre de la persona.
La operadora me comunica.

**B** Éste es un anuncio de la guía telefónica de Bogotá sobre los teléfonos públicos. Observe el anuncio con cuidado y conteste después las preguntas sobre el dibujo y el mensaje del anuncio. Las siguientes palabras le pueden ayudar a entenderlo mejor.

| | | | |
|---|---|---|---|
| dañado | *out of order, damaged* | recordar | *to remember* |
| E.T.B. | Empresa de Teléfonos de Bogotá | avisar | *to notify* |

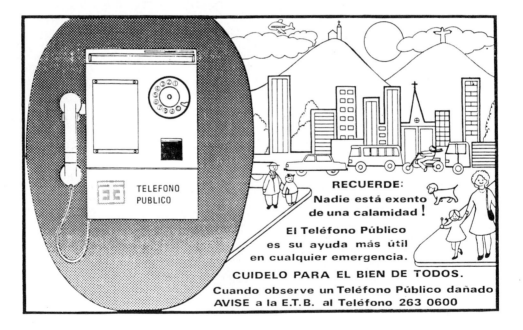

1. ¿Qué hay detrás de los edificios?
2. Describa los edificios.
3. ¿Qué vehículos ve usted?
4. ¿Qué tiempo hace?
5. Describa a las personas.
6. ¿Cuáles son los puntos importantes que hay en el mensaje de este anuncio?

**C** Complete la siguiente conversación telefónica con su compañero/a.

| | |
|---|---|
| **Usted** | ¡Aló! |
| **Compañero/a** | ____, te habla ____. ¿Cómo estás? |
| **Usted** | ... ¿Y tú qué tal? |
| **Compañero/a** | ... Te llamo porque esta noche hay una fiesta de sorpresa en casa de Carmen Ferrándiz. ¿Puedes ir? |
| **Usted** | Sí,... ¿A qué hora es? |
| **Compañero/a** | ... Me alegro que puedas ir. Te veo esta noche. |
| **Usted** | ... |

## GRAMÁTICA

### Preterit of *ir* and *ser*

| ir, ser | |
|---|---|
| fui | fuimos |
| fuiste | fuisteis |
| fue | fueron |

**Ir** and **ser** have identical forms in the preterit.

### Preterit tense of stem-changing *-ir* verbs (*e→i*) (*o→u*)

| preferir | | dormir | |
|---|---|---|---|
| preferí | preferimos | dormí | dormimos |
| preferiste | preferisteis | dormiste | dormisteis |
| prefirió | prefirieron | durmió | durmieron |

1. The preterit endings of stem-changing **-ir** verbs are the same as those used for regular **-ir** verbs.
2. All **-ir** verbs whose stem vowel **e** changes to **ie** or **i** in the present tense change the same vowel to **i** in the **él, ella, usted** form and the **ellos, ellas, ustedes** form.
3. Other verbs which follow the **preferir** pattern are **pedir, despedir, seguir,** and **servir.**
4. **Dormir** and **morir** (*to die*), whose stem vowel **o** changes to **ue** in the present tense, change the same vowel to **u** in the **él, ella, usted** form and the **ellos, ellas, ustedes** form.

## Preterit of -er and -ir verbs whose stem ends in a vowel

| leer | | oír[1] | |
|------|------|------|------|
| leí | leímos | oí | oímos |
| leíste | leísteis | oíste | oísteis |
| leyó | leyeron | oyó | oyeron |

1. The preterit endings of verbs whose stem ends in a vowel are the same as those of regular **-er** and **-ir** verbs, except for the **él, ella, usted** form and the **ellos, ellas, ustedes** form which end in **-yó** and **-yeron** (**leyó, oyeron**).
2. Other verbs like **leer** and **oír** are **caer, creer,** and **construir** (*to build*).

## ACTIVIDADES

See IM, **Lección 13,** for additional activities.

**A** **Encuesta.** Usted quiere saber cuántas personas hicieron ciertas cosas ayer. Hágales las siguientes preguntas a un grupo de sus compañeros/as y cuente las respuestas afirmativas. Después cada grupo debe compartir la información con los otros grupos.

1. ¿Quiénes leyeron el periódico ayer?
2. ¿Quiénes oyeron las noticias?
3. ¿Quiénes fueron al cine?
4. ¿Quiénes miraron televisión?
5. ¿Quiénes durmieron siete horas o más?
6. ¿Quiénes durmieron menos de seis horas?

**B** Estudie la siguiente tabla y pregúntele a un/a compañero/a qué hizo cada una de estas personas.

| *Modelo* | Usted | ¿Qué hizo Raquel por la tarde? |
|------|------|------|
| | Compañero/a | Fue a un café. |

| | Carlos | Raquel | Susana y Mirta |
|------|------|------|------|
| Por la mañana | leer el periódico | dormir hasta las diez | ir a la oficina de correos |
| Por la tarde | construir un avión de papel | ir a un café; pedir ensalada | leer un libro |
| Por la noche | oír un programa de música | preferir estar en casa con sus amigas | invitar a unos amigos a cenar; servir espaguetis |

---

[1] The forms of the present tense of **oír** are: **oigo, oyes, oye, oímos, oís, oyen.**

**C** Ahora usted debe decirle a su compañero/a todo lo que usted hizo el sábado pasado. Después su compañero/a le debe decir lo que él/ella hizo.

**D** Entreviste a un/a compañero/a acerca de su vida en la escuela secundaria. Después comparta la información con la clase.

> *Modelo*  **Usted** ¿Dónde estudiaste la secundaria?
> **Compañero/a** Estudié la secundaria en San Antonio.

1. ¿Practicaste muchos deportes en la secundaria? ¿Cuáles?  2. ¿Conociste a muchos/as muchachos/as?  3. ¿Te gustó la secundaria? ¿Por qué?  4. ¿Te dormiste en una clase alguna vez? ¿En cuál?  5. ¿Leíste muchos libros? ¿Cuáles?

**E** Usted fue a una oficina de correos. Dígale a un/a compañero/a que usted hizo lo siguiente.

1. ir a la oficina de correos a las 9:30
2. leer las noticias en el tablero (*notice board*)
3. ir a la ventanilla donde venden estampillas
4. pedir 20 estampillas de 25 centavos
5. pagar las estampillas
6. escribir la dirección en el sobre
7. depositar la carta en el buzón

> Variation: **Dígale a la clase lo que su compañero/a hizo.**

**F Situaciones locas.** Lea estas situaciones locas con su compañero/a y diga cuál le parece más loca o más simpática.

1. Ayer recibí un telegrama de mil quinientas palabras.
2. Ayer mi gato le ganó una pelea (*fight*) al elefante de mi vecina.
3. Ayer empecé un programa de ejercicios aeróbicos y bajé quince kilos.
4. Ayer cené en un restaurante francés muy elegante y sólo pagué quince centavos.
5. Ayer choqué con un autobús. Mi moto está perfecta, pero el autobús está destruido.

Ahora trabaje con su compañero/a y prepare dos situaciones locas sobre lo que usted hizo o le pasó para compartir con la clase.

**G Personajes importantes.** Piense en un personaje importante. Sus compañeros le van a hacer preguntas para tratar de saber quién es el personaje. Abajo se ofrecen algunas posibilidades, pero pueden usar sus propios personajes y además deben hacer más preguntas.

| **Preguntas posibles** | **Personajes posibles** |
|---|---|
| 1. ¿Fue usted hombre o mujer? | Adán |
| 2. ¿Cuándo murió usted? o ¿Está usted vivo? (*Are you alive?*) | Romeo o Julieta |
| | Albert Einstein |
| 3. ¿Fue Ud. músico (científico, artista, político, etc.)? | Margaret Thatcher |
| | Shakespeare |
| 4. ¿Dónde vivió usted? | Marilyn Monroe |

# EN CONTEXTO

## Una tarjeta postal

Emilia le mandó la siguiente tarjeta a su amiga Ana Luisa Amescua, quien la recibió una semana después. Emilia está pasando unos días en casa de unos primos en Bogotá. Éste es su primer viaje a Bogotá y ella no está acostumbrada° a la altura de esa ciudad (unos 2.600 metros[2]). Aunque° Bogotá está relativamente cerca del ecuador°, debido a la altura la temperatura es más bien fresca y de noche puede hacer bastante frío. Sin embargo, en «tierra caliente», a una hora u[3] hora y media de Bogotá por carretera, la temperatura es mucho más alta.

*no… is not used*
*Although*
*equator*

---

**BOGOTA. COLOMBIA.**

Cerro de Monserrate, importante centro turístico que se encuentra localizado al oriente de Bogotá, altura 10.000 pies sobre el nivel del mar.
Monserrate Hill, an important tour center which is located at the East of Bogotá, with a 10.000 Feet height on the level of the sea.

F.180

*17 de marzo*

Querida Ana Luisa:
  El martes llegué a Bogotá después de un vuelo muy bueno. El miércoles mis primos me llevaron a conocer la parte antigua de la ciudad. Es preciosa. Ayer hicimos una excursión a Ibagué, en tierra caliente. Hizo muchísimo calor. Vinieron varios amigos de mis primos y lo pasamos muy bien.
  Muchos recuerdos a tu familia, y para ti un abrazo y un beso de
  Emilia

**Fotoroma** APARTADO AEREO NO. 20053 BOGOTA 2, D. E. COLOMBIA S. A.
Tel. 2457453

Srta. Ana Luisa Amescua
Calle Encanto N° 47
Colonia Florida
México, D. F.
México

Ejemplar de Colección

---

[2] 8.600 pies

[3] In Spanish, **o** changes to **u** before a word beginning with **o** or **ho: ocho o siete,** but **siete u ocho.** Also, **y** changes to **e** before a word beginning with **i** or **hi: Isabel y Alicia,** but **Alicia e Isabel.**

Una vista de Bogotá, la capital de Colombia, donde se observan los modernos edificios de la ciudad y la cordillera de los Andes al fondo.

## Para completar

Complete las siguientes oraciones de acuerdo con la información que se da en la explicación sobre el viaje de Emilia y la tarjeta postal.

1. Ana Luisa recibió...
2. Emilia llegó a Bogotá...
3. El vuelo de Emilia fue...

4. El miércoles Emilia visitó...
5. Ayer Emilia fue a...

## Preguntas

Ahora conteste las siguientes preguntas sobre Ibagué y Bogotá.

1. ¿Por qué hace frío en Bogotá?
2. ¿Dónde hace más frío, en Bogotá o en Ibagué?
3. ¿Cuánto tiempo tiene que manejar una persona para ir de Bogotá a tierra caliente?
4. ¿Cómo es el clima de Ibagué?

# ACTIVIDADES

**A** Usted y su compañero/a están preparando un viaje a Colombia. Piensan visitar Bogotá y también otras ciudades como Ibagué. Hagan una lista de la ropa que necesitan para este viaje.

**B** Usted está en una oficina de correos de Colombia para enviar un paquete a unos amigos. Complete el siguiente diálogo con su compañero/a.

| | |
|---|---|
| **Usted** | ¿Cuánto pesa el paquete? |
| **Empleado** | ... |
| **Usted** | ¿Cuánto cuesta si lo mando por vía aérea? |
| **Empleado** | ... |
| **Usted** | ¿Y si lo mando por correo ordinario? |
| **Empleado** | ... |
| **Usted** | Bueno, lo voy a mandar por ___. |

## GRAMÁTICA

### Irregular preterits

The following verbs have irregular preterit forms. All of them have an **i** in the stem and do not stress the last syllable in the **yo** and **él, ella, usted** forms.

| INFINITIVE | NEW STEM | PRETERIT FORMS |
|---|---|---|
| **hacer:** | hic | hice, hiciste, hizo, hicimos, hicisteis, hicieron |
| **querer:** | quis[4] | quise, quisiste, quiso, quisimos, quisisteis, quisieron |
| **venir:** | vin | vine, viniste, vino, vinimos, vinisteis, vinieron |

The verbs **decir, traer,** and all verbs ending in **-ducir** (e.g., **traducir** *to translate*) have a **j** in the stem and use the ending **-eron** instead of **-ieron. Decir** also has an **i** in the stem.

| INFINITIVE | NEW STEM | PRETERIT FORMS |
|---|---|---|
| **decir:** | dij | dije, dijiste, dijo, dijimos, dijisteis, dijeron |
| **traer:** | traj | traje, trajiste, trajo, trajimos, trajisteis, trajeron |
| **traducir:** | traduj | traduje, tradujiste, tradujo, tradujimos, tradujisteis, tradujeron |

---

[4] The verb **querer** in the preterit normally means *to try,* in the sense of wanting but failing to do something.

# ACTIVIDADES

**A** Diga lo que Emilia y sus primos hicieron durante el viaje de Emilia a Colombia.

> **Modelo**   ver la Plaza Bolívar
> **Vieron la Plaza Bolívar.**

| | |
|---|---|
| lunes | ir a una corrida de toros (*bullfight*) |
| | visitar el Museo Colonial |
| | traducir unos anuncios para unos turistas |
| martes | hacer un viaje a Ibagué |
| | comprar unas cosas en Ibagué |
| | traer regalos de Ibagué |
| miércoles | querer entrar en el Museo del Oro |
| | hacer cola para entrar en el museo |
| | venir a la casa con unos amigos |
| jueves | perder los cheques de viajero |
| | ir a la estación de policía |
| | decirle al policía el problema |
| viernes | buscar los cheques todo el día |
| | no encontrar los cheques |
| sábado | ir a la estación de autobuses |
| | volver a la parte antigua de la ciudad |
| | mandar un telegrama a los padres de Emilia |

**B** **De vacaciones en Puerto Rico.** Usted y su amigo/a están de vacaciones en Puerto Rico por dos semanas. Dígale a un/a compañero/a qué trajeron y qué no trajeron ustedes.

> **Modelo**   sombrero
> **Traje un sombrero** o **No traje sombrero.**
> **Mi amigo trajo un sombrero** o **No trajo sombrero.**

| | | | |
|---|---|---|---|
| calcetines | impermeable | licencia de manejar | ropa formal |
| zapatos tenis | cheques de viajero | piyama | vaqueros |
| traje de baño | cámara | aspirinas | ropa interior |

**C** Las siguientes personas quisieron hacer ciertas cosas ayer pero fue imposible. Con un/a compañero/a determine qué quisieron hacer.

> **Modelo**   tu entrenador
> **Mi entrenador quiso cambiar la fecha del partido (pero fue imposible).**

| | | |
|---|---|---|
| tu novio/a | tus compañeros/as | tu profesor/a |
| tu mejor amigo/a | tu perro | |

**D La historia de una tarjeta postal.** Lea los siguientes párrafos cambiando los verbos al pretérito.

Dos de mis mejores amigos (ir) al Perú en agosto. Desde allí me (mandar) una tarjeta postal, pero ellos no (escribir) el número de la zona postal. (Volver) a los Estados Unidos en noviembre. Enseguida me (llamar) y (venir) a verme a mi apartamento. Ellos me (traer) un suéter precioso y me (decir) que el viaje (ser) magnífico. Los tres (hablar) mucho del Perú y yo les (hacer) muchas preguntas.

Después ellos me (preguntar) por la tarjeta postal. Yo les (contestar): «¿Qué tarjeta?» En ese momento el cartero (tocar) a la puerta con la tarjeta de mis amigos.

**E Mis actividades.** Conteste las siguientes preguntas sobre sus actividades. Trabaje con un/a compañero/a y después hágale las mismas preguntas a él/ella.

*Modelo*   **Compañero/a   ¿Qué hiciste ayer?**
           **Usted   Vine a la universidad a estudiar.**

1. ¿Qué hiciste en la casa esta mañana?
2. ¿Qué hiciste ayer en la clase? ¿después de la clase?
3. ¿Qué hiciste el fin de semana? ¿anoche? ¿el jueves?

El Museo del Oro en Bogotá. En este museo existe la mejor colección de objetos precolombinos de oro del mundo.

# EN CONTEXTO

## ¿Cómo escriben y hablan?

Sofía escribe a máquina rápidamente.

Pepito escribe lentamente.

La entienden fácilmente.

Lo entienden difícilmente.

## *ACTIVIDADES*

**A** Diga qué cosas hace usted rápidamente y qué cosas hace usted lentamente.

**Modelo** subir las escaleras
**Subo las escaleras lentamente (rápidamente).**

hablar inglés   escribir a máquina   limpiar la casa   manejar   caminar   comer   leer

**B** Hay cosas que podemos hacer fácilmente (o con facilidad) y hay otras cosas que podemos hacer difícilmente (o con dificultad). Usted y su compañero/a deben completar las siguientes oraciones de acuerdo con su manera de ser (*the way you are*).

**Modelo** Yo entiendo los problemas...
**Yo entiendo los problemas fácilmente (con facilidad, difícilmente, con dificultad).**

1. Yo aprendo bailes nuevos...
2. Hablo con personas desconocidas...
3. Les presto cosas a mis amigos...
4. Les doy consejos a otras personas...
5. Escribo cartas...
6. Hablo en público...
7. Monto en bicicleta...
8. Devuelvo (*I return*) cosas en las tiendas...

## GRAMÁTICA

### Adverbs

You have used many common Spanish adverbs when expressing time (**ayer, mañana, anoche, siempre**), place (**aquí, allí, debajo**), degree (**más, menos, tanto como**), how things are done (**bien, mal, regular**), and so on. Spanish also uses adverbs ending in **-mente** to qualify how things are done.

1. To form these adverbs add **-mente** to the feminine form of the adjective (**rápida → rápidamente**), or to adjectives ending in a consonant (**difícil → difícilmente**), or the vowel **-e** (**alegre → alegremente**).

| | |
|---|---|
| El carro pasó **rápidamente.** | *The car went by rapidly.* |
| Habló **fácilmente.** | *She spoke easily.* |
| Pagaron **amablemente.** | *They paid courteously.* |

2. When two or more adverbs are together, the suffix **-mente** need only be attached to the last one.

| | |
|---|---|
| Contestaste **clara** y **lentamente.** | *You answered clearly and slowly.* |

3. Other commonly used adverbs ending in **-mente** are

| | | |
|---|---|---|
| generalmente | normalmente | frecuentemente |
| realmente | básicamente | simplemente |
| tranquilamente | regularmente | perfectamente |
| relativamente | tradicionalmente | lógicamente |

4. Instead of an adverb Spanish may use some adjectives or **con** + noun to qualify how things are done.

Leyó { **rápidamente.** / **rápido.**     Leyó **con rapidez.**
Habló **fácilmente.**     Habló **con facilidad.**

5. Place an adverb that modifies a verb as close as possible to the verb.

| | |
|---|---|
| El Sr. Urrutia caminó lentamente por la acera. | *Mr. Urrutia walked slowly along the sidewalk.* |
| Ellos explicaron claramente el problema. | *They explained the problem clearly.* |

When expressing what generally or normally happens with an adverb ending in **-mente,** the adverb is commonly placed at the beginning of the sentence.

| | |
|---|---|
| Generalmente salimos los viernes. | *We generally go out on Fridays.* |

## Comparison of adverbs

**1.** Use the following structures to make comparisons with adverbs:

tan *adverb* como (comparison of equality)

más
menos } *adverb* que (comparison of inequality)

Ofelia escribe **tan bien como** Andrés.     *Ofelia writes as well as Andrés.*
Un avión viaja **más rápidamente que** un     *An airplane travels faster than a bus.*
  autobús.

**2.** The following adverbs have irregular forms for comparisons of inequality

bien → mejor     Yo canto **mejor** que Héctor.
mal → peor     Héctor canta **peor** que yo.
mucho → más     El cartero camina **más** que usted.
poco → menos     Ese niño come **menos** que tu hijo.

**3.** To express the idea of *extremely* you may add the suffix **-ísimo** to an adverb. Adverbs ending in **-mente** do not normally add **-ísimo**.

Llegaron muy tarde.     Llegaron **tardísimo.**

# ACTIVIDADES

**A** ¿Cómo hace su compañero/a las siguientes actividades? Escoja verbos de la columna de la izquierda para sus preguntas. Su compañero/a debe contestar con un adverbio apropiado de las dos columnas de la derecha.

   *Modelo*   caminar     rápidamente

             **Usted**   **¿Cómo caminas?**
      **Compañero/a**   **Camino rápidamente.**

| | | | |
|---|---|---|---|
| escribir a máquina | bailar salsa | lentamente | claramente |
| trabajar | manejar | tranquilamente | perfectamente |
| cantar | jugar béisbol | normalmente | fácilmente |
| hablar español | tocar el violín | alegremente | terriblemente |

**B** Complete las oraciones de acuerdo con sus actividades.

   *Modelo*   Yo quiero... independientemente.
          **Yo quiero vivir en mi apartamento independientemente.**

  1. Me gusta... tranquilamente.       4. Voy a... regularmente.
  2. Prefiero... lentamente.            5. Puedo... perfectamente.
  3. No viajo... diariamente.

**C** Usted y su familia están de vacaciones en una playa y reciben una carta de un/a amigo/a que quiere saber cómo es el lugar y qué se puede hacer allí. ¿Cómo contestan ustedes las preguntas?

**Modelo** ¿Qué hacen normalmente por las tardes?
**Normalmente vamos a la playa.**

1. ¿Adónde salen regularmente?
2. ¿Adónde van por la noche generalmente?
3. ¿Pueden conversar tranquilamente en la playa?
4. ¿El lugar es relativamente tranquilo?
5. Básicamente, ¿qué les gusta más de ese lugar?

**D** Usted es un/a reportero/a para el periódico de su universidad y quiere saber más detalles (*details*) acerca de un campamento (*camp*) en las montañas. Hágale las siguientes preguntas a un/a compañero/a y después comparta la información con la clase.

**Modelo** **Usted** ¿Vienes regularmente a este lugar?
**Compañero/a** **Sí, vengo todos los veranos.**

1. Generalmente, ¿qué hacen por las mañanas?
2. Normalmente, ¿qué actividades tienen para las muchachas?
3. ¿Sirven las comidas puntualmente?
4. ¿Cuesta más el campamento este año?
5. Básicamente, ¿hay un ambiente sano?
6. Honestamente, ¿qué piensas de este lugar?

**E** Usted va a una fiesta con un/a estudiante nuevo/a que le hace muchas preguntas acerca de las personas que están allí. Su compañero/a va a hacer el papel del estudiante y usted va a contestar sus preguntas.

**Modelo** **Compañero/a** ¿Quién baila tan bien como ella?
**Usted** **Yo bailo tan bien como ella.**

1. ¿Quién canta mejor que él?
2. ¿Llegó alguien más tarde que nosotros?
3. ¿Quién es aquella muchacha que tocó la guitarra mejor que Eva?
4. ¿Quién salió más temprano que la muchacha del vestido azul?
5. ¿Alguien baila mejor que tú?

**F** **Opiniones.** Usted y su compañero/a deben decir si están de acuerdo o no con las siguientes ideas. Expliquen por qué.

1. Generalmente los programas de televisión tienen mucha violencia.
2. Básicamente los carros japoneses son mejores que los norteamericanos.
3. Realmente los alumnos de la escuela secundaria estudian poco.
4. Tradicionalmente los mejores jugadores de fútbol de los equipos de las universidades pasan a ser profesionales.

# LECTURA

## *Antes de leer:* the future tense

You have learned and used several verb tenses since you began to study Spanish. To express what is going on or happens normally you use the present indicative tense; to emphasize what is actually in progress you use the present progressive; to express your wishes, hopes, or doubts you use the present subjunctive; to report past events you use the preterit; and to express future plans you use the present tense or the construction **ir** + **a** + infinitive.

English uses two verb forms to express future time (*they are going to read; they will read*). In addition to the two ways mentioned in the previous paragraph, Spanish also has a future tense. You do not have to use this future tense in order to communicate in Spanish, but you should be able to recognize it when reading or listening.

The future tense is formed by the infinitive plus the future endings: **-é, -ás, -á, -emos, -éis, -án.** These endings are the same for **-ar, -er,** and **-ir** verbs.

|  | hablar | comer | vivir |
|---|---|---|---|
| yo | hablaré | comeré | viviré |
| tú | hablarás | comerás | vivirás |
| él, ella, usted | hablará | comerá | vivirá |
| nosotros/as | hablaremos | comeremos | viviremos |
| vosotros/as | hablaréis | comeréis | viviréis |
| ellos/as, ustedes | hablarán | comerán | vivirán |

Few verbs are irregular in the future, and their irregularities are only found in the stem. An easy way to remember these irregular forms is to divide them into three groups. The first group (-**er** verbs) drops the **e** from the infinitive ending.

| INFINITIVE | NEW STEM | FUTURE FORMS |
|---|---|---|
| **haber:** | habr | habré, habrás, habrá, habremos, habréis, habrán |
| **poder:** | podr | podré, podrás, podrá, podremos, podréis, podrán |
| **querer:** | querr | querré, querrás, querrá, querremos, querréis, querrán |
| **saber:** | sabr | sabré, sabrás, sabrá, sabremos, sabréis, sabrán |

The second group (-**er** and -**ir** verbs) replaces the **e** or **i** of the infinitive ending with a **d.**

| INFINITIVE | NEW STEM | FUTURE FORMS |
|---|---|---|
| **poner:** | pondr | pondré, pondrás, pondrá, pondremos, pondréis, pondrán |
| **tener:** | tendr | tendré, tendrás, tendrá, tendremos, tendréis, tendrán |
| **salir:** | saldr | saldré, saldrás, saldrá, saldremos, saldréis, saldrán |
| **venir:** | vendr | vendré, vendrás, vendrá, vendremos, vendréis, vendrán |

The third group consists of two verbs (**decir, hacer**) that do not follow the previous patterns.

| INFINITIVE | NEW STEM | FUTURE FORMS |
|---|---|---|
| **decir:** | dir | diré, dirás, dirá, diremos, diréis, dirán |
| **hacer:** | har | haré, harás, hará, haremos, haréis, harán |

The use of the future in Spanish is similar to the use of the construction *will* (or *shall*) + verb in English. The only difference is that Spanish may also use the future tense to express probability in the present.

| | |
|---|---|
| **Mandaré** la carta mañana. | *I'll send the letter tomorrow.* |
| **Saldremos** la semana próxima. | *We'll leave next week.* |
| **Serán** las tres de la tarde. | *It's probably three in the afternoon.* |

## COMPRENSIÓN E IDENTIFICACIÓN ▬▬▬▬▬

Lea el siguiente párrafo sobre los planes de unos estudiantes para el próximo fin de semana.

Nosotros pensamos salir el viernes después del almuerzo para la casa que tienen los padres de Jacinto en el campo. Iremos en mi auto, y si no tenemos ningún problema, llegaremos a la casa a eso de las siete. Allí estaremos en contacto con la naturaleza y podremos descansar sin ruidos y sin teléfono.

También podremos leer y dormir bastante. Probablemente caminaremos por las mañanas y comeremos muchas frutas y vegetales que cultivan allí. No veremos televisión porque gracias a Dios no la tienen. Será un cambio fabuloso que nos vendrá muy bien después de esta semana de exámenes.

Diga si las siguientes oraciones son verdaderas o falsas de acuerdo con la información del párrafo.

1. Los estudiantes piensan salir a eso de las siete.
2. Van a ir en el carro de los padres de Jacinto.
3. Van a pasar unos días muy tranquilos en el campo.
4. Van a comer comida sana durante el fin de semana.
5. Trabajaron mucho y necesitan descansar.

Ahora lea el párrafo otra vez identificando las formas del futuro.

Una joven compra una revista en uno de los muchos quioscos que venden revistas y periódicos en Santiago de Chile.

## Los horóscopos

Los horóscopos son muy populares en las revistas y los periódicos hispanos. El primer horóscopo que van a leer, tomado de la revista española *Blanco y negro,* es muy sencillo. Sólo presenta cuatro aspectos muy importantes de la vida: el amor (*love*), la salud, el trabajo y el dinero. Usted y su compañero/a deben buscar sus signos y compararlos. Después deben contestar las siguientes preguntas y compartir la información con la clase.

# Horóscopo
## Optimista Leo

Óptimo ★★★    Regular ★
Bueno ★★       Pésimo ●

### Signos afortunados de la semana

LEO (23-7 al 23-8)
Amor ★★★    Trabajo ★★★
Salud ★★★    Dinero ★★★

LEO:
ARIES (21-3 al 20-4)
Amor ★★★    Trabajo ★★★
Salud ★★★    Dinero ★★

### Signos favorables de la semana

SAGITARIO (23-11 al 21-12)
Amor ★        Trabajo ★★
Salud ★★      Dinero ★★

LIBRA (24-9 al 23-10)
Amor ★★       Trabajo ★★
Salud ★★      Dinero ★★

### Signos indiferentes de la semana

CÁNCER (22-6 al 22-7)
Amor ★        Trabajo ★
Salud ★        Dinero ★

CAPRICORNIO (22-12 al 20-1)
Amor ★        Trabajo ★
Salud ★        Dinero ★

### Signos desfavorables de la semana

TAURO (21-4 al 20-5)
Amor ★        Trabajo ★
Salud ★        Dinero ★

ACUARIO (21-1 al 19-2)
Amor ★        Trabajo ★
Salud ★        Dinero ●

VIRGO (24-8 al 23-9)
Amor ●        Trabajo ★
Salud ★        Dinero ●

GÉMINIS (21-5 al 21-6)
Amor ★        Trabajo ★
Salud ★        Dinero ★

PISCIS (20-2 al 20-3)
Amor ★        Trabajo ★
Salud ★        Dinero ★

### Signo pésimo de la semana

ESCORPIO (24-10 al 22-11)
Amor ●        Trabajo ●
Salud ★        Dinero ●

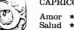
Por NIRAK ARYEVLIS

1. ¿Cuál es tu signo?
2. ¿Cómo es tu signo esta semana? (afortunado, favorable, etc.)
3. ¿Quién es más afortunado en el amor?
4. ¿Quién va a tener mejor salud esta semana?
5. ¿Cómo va a estar el trabajo esta semana para los dos? ¿y el dinero?

En la página siguiente está el horóscopo para todo el año publicado en *Vanidades*[5], una revista muy popular en Hispanoamérica y entre los hispanos que viven en los Estados Unidos. El tiempo futuro se usa mucho en los horóscopos, pero como pueden reconocerlo no tendrán dificultad en entender las predicciones para el año.

Primero busque su horóscopo de acuerdo con su signo. Después anote cuáles son las predicciones que usted considera más importantes. Su compañero/a le va a preguntar cuáles son. Después usted le debe preguntar lo mismo a su compañero/a.

Las siguientes palabras le podrán ayudar a entender mejor su horóscopo y el de su compañero/a.

Aries:          fijarse *to set*
Taurus:         asunto *matter;* pareja *partner*
Géminis:        nacidos *those born;* tener presente *to keep in mind;* aprovechar *to take advantage*
Cáncer:         alcanzar *to obtain*
Leo:            herir *to hurt*
Virgo:          apoyo *support;* jugar un papel *to play a part*
Libra:          contratiempo *disappointment;* aprovechar *to take advantage*
Escorpión:      alcanzar *to obtain;* atareado *busy*
Sagitario:      no ha logrado *you have not achieved;* alejado *far away*
Capricornio:    brillar *to shine;* nubarrones *dark clouds;* encarar *to face*
Acuario:        alcanzar *to obtain;* esfuerzo *effort;* empeño *persistence;* rechazar *to reject*
Piscis:         perseguir *to pursue;* desde hace *for;* herramienta *tool*

[5] Leonor Andrassy, "Horóscopo" © Editorial América, S.A., Vanidades Continental #1, 8 de enero de 1988.

# horóscopo

**Por Leonor Andrassy**

## ARIES

**Marzo 21
- a -
Abril 19**

Para Aries, los primeros días del año serán ideales para fijarse un plan a seguir. En el trabajo tendrá la oportunidad de mejorar si se lo propone. Nuevas ideas, nuevos métodos pueden ser especialmente valiosos. Si no es necesarió, nó viaje en estos días. El momento es muy favorable para tratar con personas influyentes. Evite las discusiones. Sea más prudente y diplomático . . .

## CÁNCER

**Junio 22
- a -
Julio 22**

Los primeros días de este año son magníficos para entrevistas de todo tipo. Si fuera más discreto se evitaría problemas. Si se lo propone, los planes del año pasado, que no hizo realidad, pueden llegar a un final feliz. Viaje corto con algunas sorpresas. Las circunstancias se han combinado de tal manera que puede alcanzar triunfos en su trabajo, siempre que usted sea más positivo.

## LIBRA

**Septiembre 22
- a -
Octubre 22**

Este año que comienza traerá a Libra un poco de todo: mucha felicidad y algunos contratiempos. Exceso de energía mental, en los primeros días, que debe aprovechar para llevar adelante todas las ideas que tiene acumuladas. El momento es bueno para los asuntos que requieren negociaciones. Si piensa entrevistarse con alguna persona importante, es conveniente que lo haga el 8.

## CAPRICORNIO

**Diciembre 22
- a -
Enero 19**

Este año será, para los nacidos bajo este signo, en general bueno. El sol brillará, aunque a veces surgirán pequeños nubarrones. Gran habilidad en la forma de encarar la realidad. En el trabajo, algunos conflictos por haber mezclado la amistad con los negocios. Cierta confusión en materia económica. Emplee todo su encanto en reconquistar a la persona que es el centro de su vida.

## TAURO

**Abril 20
- a -
Mayo 20**

A Tauro se le presenta un año muy movido con pequeños triunfos que traerán momentos de felicidad inmensa. Los primeros días del año se presentan con mucha actividad. Los intelectuales tendrán grandes sorpresas. Si tiene que resolver algún asunto de tipo personal debe hacerlo ahora. Pueden surgir diferencias de criterio con su pareja. Alguien llega a su vida inesperadamente . . .

## LEO

**Julio 23
- a -
Agosto 22**

El año en general no tendrá grandes complicaciones para los hijos de Leo. Una cosa debe tener muy presente: controlar su carácter, a veces demasiado impetuoso, que puede herir a los que están cerca de usted, especialmente al hombre o mujer con quien comparte su vida. Su gran creatividad será reconocida. Para los más jóvenes, nuevos romances. Posibilidad de cambios en el trabajo.

## ESCORPIÓN

**Octubre 23
- a -
Noviembre 21**

Lo que no ha logrado el año pasado podrá alcanzarlo este año, si se lo propone. Los primeros días de este período seguirán siendo extremadamente atareados, sobre todo en lo relacionado con los asuntos personales. Su energía y vitalidad serán muy altas, lo que será una ventaja, pero debe tener cuidado con los excesos. Domine su carácter, a veces un poco agresivo. Vida social activa.

## ACUARIO

**Enero 20
- a -
Febrero 19**

Los acuarianos alcanzarán este año lo que se propongan, todo depende del esfuerzo y empeño que pongan en sus planes. Los primeros días serán especialmente útiles y agradables para enriquecer su círculo de amistades. Invitaciones a diferentes lugares que no debe rechazar, puede hacer muy buenos contactos en estas reuniones. ¡Sorpresas en la vida sentimental de Acuario!

## GÉMINIS

**Mayo 21
- a -
Junio 21**

Los nacidos bajo este signo tendrán grandes oportunidades en este año, especialmente en los primeros días; tiene que tener muy presente que las oportunidades se presentan, pero usted tiene que saber aprovecharlas. Debe ponerse al día en los asuntos pendientes. ¿Por qué no hace un análisis de los fallos del año pasado? Es la mejor forma de no cometer los mismos errores en este año . . .

## VIRGO

**Agosto 23
- a -
Septiembre 21**

Este año será muy positivo para Virgo. Personas influyentes continuarán ayudándolo. La habilidad artística que caracteriza a este signo le impulsará a mejorar su casa. Podrá contar con el apoyo de su familia. Preocupación por problemas de salud de personas que están cerca de usted. Los primeros días serán muy positivos para el amor. Los amigos jugarán un papel muy importante.

## SAGITARIO

**Noviembre 22
- a -
Diciembre 21**

El año que comienza seguirá con el mismo ritmo del año pasado aunque con algunas sorpresas. . . Los primeros días de este período serán los más felices para los sagitarianos. Tendrá las mejores oportunidades para llevar adelante sus proyectos personales y conseguir lo que no ha logrado el año pasado. Personas alejadas adquieren importancia en sus proyectos. Dedíquele tiempo al amor. . .

## PISCIS

**Febrero 20
- a -
Marzo 20**

Para Piscis, las cosas mejorarán este año. Durante los primeros días, el ambicioso pisciano debe centrar su atención y esfuerzos en sus asuntos profesionales, ya que le será más fácil que nunca antes obtener lo que está persiguiendo desde hace tanto tiempo. Debe cuidarse de no humillar a las personas que están cerca de usted. Cuidado si tiene que trabajar con herramientas.

Bogotá, 20 de marzo

Querida Dulce:

Estoy pasando unos días maravillosos en Colombia. Mis tíos son un encanto y mis primos, ni hablar. Salimos todos los días y siempre tienen planes pues quieren que conozca todas las cosas interesantes que hay aquí.

Ayer me llevaron al Museo del Oro. Allí tienen más de 25.000 objetos precolombinos de oro. Es algo increíble. Hay una sala que sólo se abre a ciertas horas y que tiene todas las paredes cubiertas de objetos de oro. Por fuera uno no se da cuenta que hay una sala allí, pues sólo ve una pared, pero esa pared es la puerta. Antes de ir al museo mis primos me explicaron todo esto, pero así y todo me sorprendí cuando la pared se movió. Después que entramos en la sala oscura, la puerta se empezó a cerrar lentamente y de repente se encendieron las luces. Yo tuve que cerrar los ojos por todo el brillo del oro. Tú tienes que venir a conocer esto. Como quieres estudiar un año fuera, ¿por qué no vienes a Bogotá? Aquí hay universidades muy buenas y además están mis primos que tienen muchas ganas de conocerte y que te pueden ayudar y presentar a sus amigos.

Este fin de semana vamos a ir a Cartagena. Dicen que es una ciudad preciosa. Además allí podremos disfrutar de la playa.

Dentro de dos semanas estaré de nuevo con ustedes y les contaré con más detalles. Recibe un abrazo y un beso de

Emilia

## Una carta

A la izquierda está la carta que Emilia le mandó a su amiga Dulce contándole de sus vacaciones en casa de sus tíos en Bogotá. En esta carta ella le escribe sobre sus experiencias en el Museo del Oro° de Bogotá. Este museo pertenece al Banco de la República y tiene la colección de objetos precolombinos de oro más grande del mundo. Además tiene una colección extraordinaria de esmeraldas°. Colombia es el mayor productor de esmeraldas del mundo, con más del 80 por ciento de la producción mundial.

Emilia también le cuenta sus planes para ir a Cartagena, una de las ciudades más interesantes de la América del Sur. Está situada en la costa norte de Colombia, y es famosa por sus playas y su arquitectura colonial, especialmente las fortalezas° que defienden su bahía. La más conocida de éstas es el Castillo de San Felipe, que se considera la mejor obra de arquitectura militar que construyeron los españoles en América. El Castillo de San Felipe fue terminado en 1667 y está a un lado de la ciudad. Tiene galerías subterráneas que lo conectan con el centro. El sistema de ventilación y el de acústica son impresionantes obras de ingeniería.

Museo... *Gold Museum*

*emeralds*

*fortresses*

## ¿Verdadero o falso?

Diga si las siguientes oraciones son verdaderas o falsas de acuerdo con la introducción a la carta.

1. El Museo del Oro está en Bogotá.
2. Los objetos de oro del museo son muy modernos.
3. Cartagena es famosa por sus esmeraldas.
4. En Cartagena hay edificios muy interesantes de la época colonial.
5. Hay túneles que comunican una de las fortalezas de Cartagena con el centro de la ciudad.

## Preguntas

Conteste las siguientes preguntas sobre la carta de Emilia.

1. ¿Qué fecha tiene la carta?
2. ¿Está contenta Emilia en Bogotá?
3. ¿Por qué se sorprendió Emilia en el Museo del Oro?
4. ¿Qué ventajas puede tener Dulce si va a estudiar a Bogotá?
5. ¿Cuándo se va a ir Emilia de Bogotá?

## SITUACIONES

1. You need stamps to mail some letters and you go to the post office to buy them: (a) tell the employee that you want to send two letters air mail to the United States, (b) ask him/her to weigh them for you, and (c) ask him/her how much it is.

2. You want to mail a package to a friend. You take the package to the post office and ask the employee to (a) weigh it for you, (b) tell you how much it is to send it air mail or regular mail (**correo ordinario**). Then, (c) decide how you will send it and tell the employee.

3. Call a friend's house and ask to talk to him/her. The person who answers the phone says that your friend is not in. Ask the person to tell your friend (a) that you called, and (b) that you need to talk to him/her. Leave your telephone number, thank the person, and say good-by. Your partner will write down your message.

4. You call a friend and he/she answers the phone. Identify yourself and greet your friend. Then (a) say that you and some friends are going to the movies this afternoon, (b) give the name of the film, and (c) ask if he/she would like to go. If the answer is yes, give the time and place you are going to meet. If the answer is no, say that you are sorry he/she cannot come.

5. You are talking to your friend about your last trip. Tell (a) where and when you went, (b) how you went, (c) what you did there, and (d) if you liked it or not. Then try to find out the same information from your friend.

6. You are the director of a school play. Tell one of the actors that he/she should (a) walk slowly on the stage (**escenario**), (b) speak clearly, (c) look at the audience (**público**), and (d) leave rapidly.

7. You are in Bogotá and need to make a long-distance telephone call to your mother. Give the operator (a) your mother's full name, (b) the city and country, (c) the area code and telephone number, and (d) the number you are calling from.

8. You are helping a friend make a telephone call. Find out if (a) it is a local or a long-distance call, and (b) if it is a collect call. Make the call and tell your friend (a) that it is busy, and (b) to call later.

**CONTESTADOR CASSETTE**

Asociado al teléfono, facilita la contestación y recepción de las llamadas telefónicas.

*Cuota de conexión . . . . . . 6.000 pts.*
*Cuota de abono mensual . 1.381 pts.*

# VOCABULARIO[6]

**el correo** — *post office*
el buzón — *mail box*
la carta — *letter*
la estampilla/el sello — *stamp*
el paquete — *package*
el sobre — *envelope*
la tarjeta postal — *post card*
el telegrama — *telegram*

**el teléfono**
la conexión — *connection*
la guía telefónica/de teléfonos — *telephone directory*
el indicativo/el prefijo — *area code*
llamada de cargo revertido/a cobrar — *collect call*
llamada de larga distancia — *long–distance call*
el ruido — *noise*

**geografía**
la altura — *height, elevation*
el ecuador — *equator*
la temperatura — *temperature*
la tierra — *land*

**las personas**
el cartero — *mailman*
la operadora — *operator*
el sirviente/la sirvienta — *servant, maid*

**expresiones de afecto**
el abrazo — *embrace*
el beso — *kiss*
el cariño — *love, affection*
querido/a — *dear*
recuerdos — *regards*

**verbos**
caerse — *to fall*
colgar (ue) — *to hang up*
escribir a máquina — *to type*
llorar — *to cry*
mandar — *to send*
marcar/discar — *to dial*
oír — *to hear*
recibir — *to receive, to get*
traducir — *to translate*

**palabras útiles**
aunque — *although*
enseguida — *immediately*

**expresiones útiles**
¿de parte de quién? — *who's calling?*
debido a — *due to*
estar acostumbrado/a — *to be used to*
hablar más alto — *to speak louder*
pasarlo bien — *to have a good time*
se cayó la comunicación — *we were cut off*
volver a + infinitivo — *verb + again*

---

[6] For a list of commonly used adverbs ending in **-mente,** see page 328.

**In** Lección 14 **you will**
a. **explain needs.**
b. **describe and get hotel accommodations.**
c. **report past events.**
d. **express possession (emphatic).**

# La ciudad y la playa

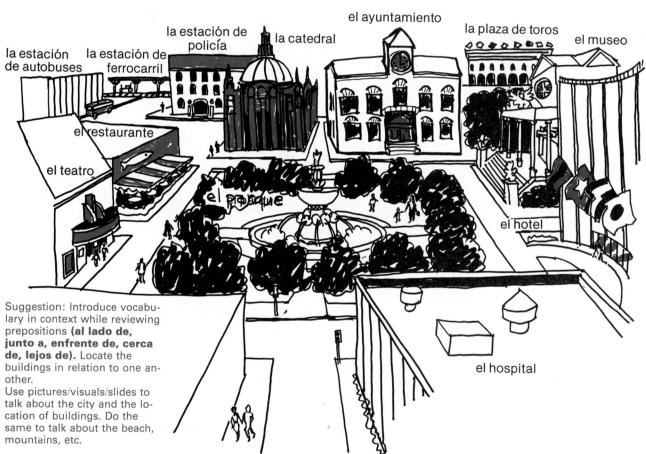

la estación
de autobuses

la estación de
ferrocarril

la estación de
policía

la catedral

el ayuntamiento

la plaza de toros

el museo

el restaurante

el teatro

el parque

el hotel

el hospital

Suggestion: Introduce vocabulary in context while reviewing prepositions **(al lado de, junto a, enfrente de, cerca de, lejos de).** Locate the buildings in relation to one another.
Use pictures/visuals/slides to talk about the city and the location of buildings. Do the same to talk about the beach, mountains, etc.

**Muchas personas prefieren pasar las vacaciones en una ciudad porque allí pueden ver muchas cosas interesantes.**

# Lección 14

# De vacaciones

las montañas

los árboles

la arena

las flores

Otras personas prefieren pasar sus vacaciones en la playa donde pueden descansar y olvidar las presiones de la vida moderna.

La playa de Luquillo,
una de las playas más
famosas de Puerto Rico.

## ACTIVIDADES

**A** Hágale las siguientes preguntas a su compañero/a. Comparta la información con la clase.

1. ¿Dónde pasas normalmente tus vacaciones?   2. ¿Con quién vas?   3. ¿Cuánto tiempo pasas allí?   4. ¿Adónde fuiste el año pasado?   5. ¿Te gustó el lugar? ¿Por qué?

**B** Escoja la ciudad, las montañas o el campo y dígale a su compañero/a por qué prefiere pasar sus vacaciones allí.

**C** Usted quiere que su amigo/a pase las vacaciones con usted en una playa. Dígale cinco cosas que pueden hacer allí para tratar de convencerlo/la.

Las ruinas de Palenque
en México muestran los
extraordinarios
adelantos que había
logrado la cultura maya
antes de la llegada de
los españoles.

**D** Éste es un anuncio de un periódico español sobre campamentos de verano. Trabaje con un/a compañero/a y (a) dígale qué actividades del anuncio le interesan a usted y (b) pregúntele cuáles le interesan a él/ella. Después comparen estas actividades con las que ofrecen los campamentos que ustedes conocen.

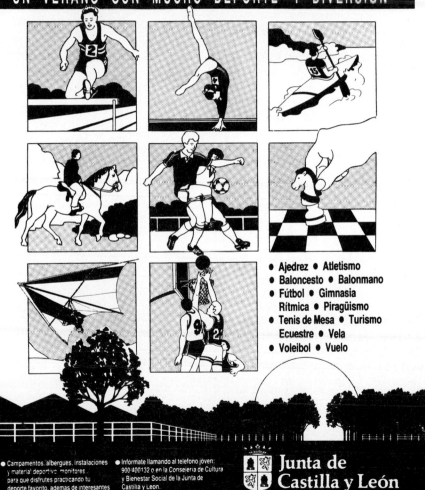

# Cultura

## El turismo en los países hispanos

Las atracciones turísticas de España están a la par con° las de cualquier país europeo, y su clima, playas, museos, castillos y monumentos atraen a visitantes de todo el mundo. Según la Secretaría General de Turismo, en 1987 llegaron a España, que tiene unos 38 millones de habitantes, más de 59 millones de turistas que le dejaron al país unos 15 mil millones de pesetas[1].

Madrid, la capital de España, les ofrece a los turistas tantas atracciones como cualquiera de las ciudades europeas más conocidas: museos, especialmente el Museo del Prado que tiene una de las mejores colecciones de pintura del mundo; el Palacio Real; conventos, parques y bibliotecas; conciertos, obras de teatro; excelentes restaurantes y pequeños cafés.

Como España tiene tanto que ofrecerles a los turistas, el gobierno ha tratado de facilitarles su estancia en el país. En 1926, siendo Comisario Regio de Turismo el Marqués de la Vega–Inclán, se inició en España el sistema de paradores. Estos son hoteles que ofrecen todas las comodidades del mundo moderno en castillos antiguos, palacios y monasterios a través de° todo el país. Hoy en día los paradores son muy populares tanto entre los españoles como los extranjeros.

Además de los paradores, el gobierno ha creado hosterías, que son restaurantes que están decorados según el estilo de la región y que sirven platos típicos, y refugios, que son hoteles que

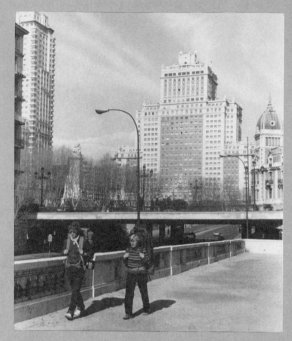

Unos turistas caminan frente a la Plaza de España en Madrid. En esta plaza están las esculturas de Don Quijote y Sancho Panza, los inmortales personajes de la novela de Miguel de Cervantes.

están fuera de las ciudades en zonas donde se puede esquiar, cazar° o pescar.

México es otro país donde el turismo constituye una industria muy importante. En 1987, según la Secretaría General de Turismo, unos cinco millones y medio de turistas visitaron México y gastaron más de dos mil millones de dólares. Esto crea puestos de trabajo y ayuda a mejorar la situación de desempleo en ese país.

[1] **Mil millones** is the Spanish equivalent of an English billion. The Spanish **billón** is the equivalent of the English trillion.  a la par con *equal to*  a través de *throughout*  cazar *hunt*

Los turistas se maravillan al visitar las ruinas de las ciudades mayas en Yucatán, Monte Albán en Oaxaca o las pirámides de Teotihuacan cerca de la ciudad de México y ver los adelantos° que existieron en esas culturas. El Museo Antropológico y los nuevos descubrimientos del Templo Mayor de los aztecas en la ciudad de México son pruebas del progreso y desarrollo° que alcanzaron las culturas indígenas antes de la llegada de los españoles.

México tiene playas famosas como Cancún en el Caribe y Acapulco en la costa del Pacífico, donde se puede descansar lejos de las tensiones de las ciudades. Hay muchos hoteles en todo el país, desde los más económicos hasta los más caros y lujosos, para satisfacer los gustos de cualquier viajero.

España y México son los países que atraen más turismo en el mundo hispano y es lógico que estén orgullosos° de su herencia° cultural y de su riqueza° artística. Sin embargo°, los otros países también tienen mucho que ofrecerles a los turistas. Para los que tienen interés en la arquitectura precolombina, una visita a las ruinas mayas de Copán en Honduras o a las fortalezas y ciudades incas del Perú es una experiencia inolvidable°. Aquellos que prefieren ver objetos precolombinos de oro pueden encontrar excelentes colecciones en Colombia, Perú y Costa Rica. Y los que prefieren la cerámica o la artesanía antigua o moderna pueden encontrarlas en todos los países hispanos.

La arquitectura colonial, con sus iglesias, edificios de gobierno, palacios y fortalezas, es uno de los aspectos más

Unos turistas en la recepción de un hotel en Oaxaca, México. Cerca de esta ciudad están las maravillosas ruinas de Monte Albán, centro ceremonial de los zapotecas, otra de las grandes culturas precolombinas.

interesantes de las ciudades hispanoamericanas. El estilo de muchos de estos edificios es un buen ejemplo de la unión del arte español e indígena.

Argentina y Chile tienen excelentes zonas montañosas para esquiar. Como estos países están situados en el hemisferio sur, su invierno corresponde al verano en el hemisferio norte y algunos atletas europeos y norteamericanos viajan a estos países para practicar el esquí durante los meses de julio, agosto y septiembre.

adelantos *advances*  desarrollo *development*  orgullosos *proud*  herencia *heritage*  riqueza *wealth*
Sin embargo *However*  inolvidable *unforgettable*

# EN CONTEXTO

## En la recepción del hotel

| | |
|---|---|
| **Empleado** | Buenas tardes, señores. |
| **Sr. García Urrutia** | Buenas tardes. Hicimos una reservación para una habitación doble para esta noche. |
| **Empleado** | ¿A nombre de quién? |
| **Sr. García Urrutia** | A nombre de los Sres. García Urrutia. |
| **Empleado** | Un momento, por favor. Lo siento, pero no la puedo encontrar. |
| **Sr. García Urrutia** | Yo tengo la confirmación. Creo que la puse° en mi maletín. |
| **Empleado** | No se moleste°, señor. Aquí está. La pusieron bajo el nombre de Urrutia. Perdone. |
| **Sr. García Urrutia** | No se preocupe. Nosotros estuvimos° en este hotel el año pasado y nos gustó mucho. Por eso quisimos regresar. |
| **Empleado** | Gracias. Es usted muy amable. Llene y firme° esta tarjeta, por favor. ¿Me puede dar su pasaporte? |
| **Sr. García Urrutia** | Aquí lo tiene. |
| **Empleado** | Gracias. Su habitación es la 612. El botones° los va a acompañar°. |

*I put*

*No. . . Don't bother*

*were*

*sign*

*bellboy*
*accompany*

## Para completar

Complete las siguientes oraciones según la información que se da en el diálogo.

1. Los Sres. García Urrutia están en. . .
2. Ellos tienen una reservación para. . .
3. El empleado no puede encontrar. . .
4. En el hotel pusieron la reservación bajo el nombre de. . .
5. Los Sres. García Urrutia estuvieron en ese hotel. . .
6. El Sr. García Urrutia le da su pasaporte al. . .
7. La habitación de los Sres. García Urrutia es. . .
8. La persona que los va a acompañar es el. . .

### vocabulario útil en un hotel

| | | | |
|---|---|---|---|
| el ascensor | *elevator* | la lavandería | *laundry* |
| el bar | *bar* | la llave | *key* |
| la cuenta | *bill* | el mensaje | *message* |
| el estacionamiento | *parking* | la tintorería | *cleaners* |
| la habitación sencilla | *single room* | | |

# *ACTIVIDADES*

**A** Asocie las siguientes palabras.

| | |
|---|---|
| 1. la llave | a. el teléfono |
| 2. la tintorería | b. la habitación |
| 3. el botones | c. el equipaje |
| 4. la cuenta | d. la ropa |
| 5. el mensaje | e. el dinero |

**B** Hágale las siguientes preguntas a su compañero/a. Después comparta la información con la clase.

1. ¿Vas a un motel o a un hotel cuando viajas?
2. ¿Qué hoteles conoces?
3. ¿Haces reservaciones antes de ir a un hotel o motel?
4. ¿Las haces por teléfono o escribes al hotel/motel?
5. ¿Por qué es importante hacer reservaciones?

## GRAMÁTICA

### More irregular preterits

The following irregular verbs have a **u** in the preterite stem. As in the group of verbs presented in **Lección 13,** the **yo** and **él, ella, usted** forms do not stress the last syllable.

| INFINITIVE | NEW STEM | PRETERIT FORMS |
|---|---|---|
| **estar:** | estuv | estuve, estuviste, estuvo, estuvimos, estuvisteis, estuvieron |
| **tener:** | tuv | tuve, tuviste, tuvo, tuvimos, tuvisteis, tuvieron |
| **poder:** | pud | pude, pudiste, pudo, pudimos, pudisteis, pudieron |
| **poner:** | pus | puse, pusiste, puso, pusimos, pusisteis, pusieron |
| **saber[2]:** | sup | supe, supiste, supo, supimos, supisteis, supieron |

---

[2] **Saber** in the preterit normally means *to learn* or *to find out.* Supe que llegaron anoche. *I learned that you arrived last night.*

# ACTIVIDADES

**A** La semana pasada los estudiantes de su clase organizaron una excursión. Cada estudiante trajo algo y lo puso en una de las cestas. Dígale a su compañero/a qué pusieron las siguientes personas.

**Modelo** Alicia / las servilletas
**Alicia puso las servilletas.**

1. Julio / la ensalada
2. Alberto y Beatriz / los manteles
3. Margarita / los sándwiches

4. La profesora / el postre
5. Ustedes / los refrescos
6. Tú / . . .

**B** Las siguientes personas no pudieron hacer la tarea. Diga qué excusa dieron estas personas y después diga cuál es su excusa.

**Modelo** Irma. . . se sintió mal anoche.
**Irma no pudo hacer la tarea porque se sintió mal anoche.**

1. Esperanza. . . tuvo que ir al médico.
2. Norma y Elvira. . . tuvieron un examen ayer.
3. Fermín y Cecilia. . . estuvieron ausentes.
4. Tú. . . perdiste el libro.
5. Aurelio. . . no supo hacerla.
6. Yo. . .

**C** **Sus vacaciones el año pasado.** Pregúntele a su compañero/a dónde estuvo el año pasado. Él/ella debe usar uno de los anuncios para contestar sus preguntas. Después usted va a compartir la información con la clase.

| AEROPERÚ | AEROLÍNEAS ARGENTINAS | IBERIA |
|---|---|---|
| Visite Machu Picchu; dos días en Cuzco, cinco días en Lima en el Hotel El Inca. Todo de primera. Desayuno incluido $1.259,00 | 7 días en Buenos Aires, dos días en Bariloche, dos días en Iguazú. Hoteles de lujo. Servicio especial. Un viaje inolvidable $1.987,00 | Una semana en la Costa del Sol y otra en Madrid Hoteles Meliá $1.750,00 |

1. ¿Adónde fuiste en tus vacaciones?
2. ¿Cuánto costó el viaje?
3. ¿En qué aerolínea fuiste?
4. ¿En qué hotel te pusieron?

5. ¿Cuánto tiempo estuviste allí?
6. ¿Qué pudiste hacer allí?
7. ¿Pudiste hablar español con otras personas?
8. ¿Tuviste alguna experiencia inolvidable?

**D** **El robo del año.** Alguien entró anoche en el Banco Internacional y se llevó un millón de dólares. Hay varias personas investigando el robo. Todos están de acuerdo en que el ladrón (*thief*) es el gerente del banco y van a decir por qué lo supieron.

*Modelo* la secretaria... el gerente recibió una llamada misteriosa
**La secretaria lo supo porque el gerente recibió una llamada misteriosa.**

1. el detective... escuchó un mensaje en el contestador automático (*answering machine*)
2. los policías... llegó a su casa en un coche nuevo
3. su cuñado... lo oyó hablar con un banco suizo
4. los empleados... compró una casa de medio millón de dólares
5. tú... encontraste un maletín lleno de dinero en su oficina
6. yo...

**E** Sus amigos/as estuvieron de vacaciones la semana pasada. Usted quiere saber dónde estuvieron, qué hicieron, qué visitaron, y muchas cosas más. Hágales las preguntas necesarias a dos de sus compañeros/as para obtener la siguiente información.

*Modelo* dinero que gastaron
        **Usted** **¿Cuánto dinero gastaron?**
  **Compañero/a** **Gastamos $800.**

1. ciudad(es) donde estuvieron
2. medio de transporte que usaron
3. nombre del hotel donde estuvieron
4. tiempo que estuvieron
5. lugares y personas que conocieron
6. platos típicos que probaron
7. otras cosas que pudieron hacer

**F** Usted fue a una fiesta cuando estuvo de visita en casa de unos primos. Su compañero/a quiere saber más de la fiesta. Conteste sus preguntas.

*Modelo* **Compañero/a** **¿Cuántas personas fueron a la fiesta?**
        **Usted** **Fueron unas 50 personas.**

1. ¿Conociste a alguien?
2. ¿Con quién fuiste?
3. ¿Pudiste bailar?
4. ¿Qué comiste?
5. ¿Qué bebiste?
6. ¿Qué te pusiste para la fiesta?

# EN CONTEXTO

### En la taquilla

Antonio llegó al teatro a las 8:20.
Varias personas están haciendo cola frente a la taquilla.

Antonio está en la cola hace 20 minutos.

Antonio llegó hace media hora.
La función empieza a las nueve.
¡Por fin compró los boletos!

## ACTIVIDADES

**A  Encuesta.** Usted quiere saber qué obras de teatro prefieren sus compañeros/as. En grupos de seis o siete, cada uno/a debe decir cuál prefiere. Determine el resultado y comparta la información con la clase.

cómicas    clásicas    musicales    dramáticas    infantiles    de misterio

**B  Entrevista.** Su compañero/a fue al teatro cuando estuvo en Nueva York. Hágale las siguientes preguntas para saber qué hizo ese día.

1. ¿Cuándo fuiste al teatro?    2. ¿Fuiste solo/a?    3 ¿Hiciste cola para comprar los boletos?
4. ¿Cuánto tiempo estuviste en la cola?    5. ¿Cuánto costaron los boletos?    6. ¿A qué hora empezó la obra?    7. ¿Qué obra viste? Háblame de la obra.    8. ¿Qué hiciste después de la función?

## GRAMÁTICA

*Hace* **with expressions of time**

**1.** To state that an action began in the past and continues into the present, use **hace** + the length of time + **que** + the present tense of the verb.

**Hace** dos horas **que** trabajan.         *They've been working for two hours.*

If you begin the sentence with the present tense of the verb, do not use **que.**

Trabajan **hace** dos horas.

**2.** To indicate the time that has passed since an action started or was completed, use **hace** + length of time + **que** + the preterit tense of the verb. **Hace** is the equivalent of *ago.*

**Hace** dos horas **que** llegaron.         *They arrived two hours ago.*

If you begin the sentence with the preterit tense of the verb, do not use **que.**

Llegaron **hace** dos horas.

## *ACTIVIDADES*

**A** Complete las siguientes oraciones de acuerdo con sus experiencias. Después su compañero/a debe completarlas.         See IM, **Lección 14, Gramática.**

    1. Estudio español hace... Hablé español por primera vez hace...
    2. Tengo un auto (una moto, una bicicleta) hace...
       Mi auto (moto, bicicleta) es... Yo lo/la compré hace...
    3. Conozco a mi novio/a (mejor amigo/a) hace... Él/ella es...
    4. Mi programa favorito de televisión es... Yo veo ese programa hace...

**B** Éstas son las actividades de diferentes personas que están de vacaciones. Diga cuánto tiempo hace que estas personas están ocupadas.

    *Modelo*    Los turistas llegaron a la agencia de viajes a las diez. Son las once.
               **Hace una hora que están en la agencia.**

    1. El niño empezó a nadar a las once. Son las once y media.
    2. El Sr. Matos empezó a mirar televisión a las nueve. Son las doce.
    3. Las jóvenes entraron al museo a las cuatro. Son las seis.
    4. Margarita llegó al aeropuerto a las doce de la noche. Son las tres de la mañana.
    5. Usted está en Lima, Perú. Llegó a... y son las...

**C** Los Molina estuvieron de vacaciones la semana pasada. Diga cuánto tiempo hace que hicieron lo que aparece en los dibujos.

*Modelo*

**Salieron (Tomaron el tren) hace. . . días.**

**1** sábado

**2** lunes   **3** martes

**4** miércoles

**5** jueves

**6** sábado

**D** **Entrevista.** Hágale las siguientes preguntas a su compañero/a. Comparta la información con la clase.

1. ¿Dónde vives? ¿Cuánto tiempo hace que vives allí?   2. ¿Cuánto tiempo hace que estudias en esta universidad? ¿Y por qué estudias español?   3. ¿Practicas algún deporte? ¿Cuánto tiempo hace que lo practicas? ¿Juegas mucho mejor ahora?

**E** Usted hizo un viaje hace algún tiempo. Su compañero/a le va a hacer preguntas sobre ese viaje.

1. ¿Adónde fuiste?   2. ¿Cuánto tiempo pasaste allí?   3. ¿Qué hiciste?   4. ¿Te gustaría volver? ¿Por qué?

# EN CONTEXTO

## Un problema serio

| | |
|---|---|
| **Ernesto** | ¿Dónde están mis maletas? |
| **Ángel** | ¿No las trajo el botones? |
| **Ernesto** | No, mira, trajo las maletas tuyas pero no las mías. |
| **Ángel** | Pero ésas no son las mías. Deben ser de otra persona. |
| **Ernesto** | Pues enseguida llamo a la recepción. ¡Ojalá que las maletas nuestras estén allí! ¿Tienes tu cámara? |
| **Ángel** | Sí, está en mi mochila. ¿Y la tuya? |
| **Ernesto** | Está en mi maleta. |
| **Ángel** | Bueno, pero tienes el dinero. |
| **Ernesto** | Sí, aquí, en el bolsillo°. ¡Ay, pero no está! Ahora sí que tenemos un problema. |

*pocket*

## ¿Verdadero o falso?

Diga si las siguientes oraciones son verdaderas o falsas de acuerdo con el diálogo.

1. Ernesto busca sus maletas.
2. Ángel trajo las maletas.
3. El botones trajo las maletas de Ángel y Ernesto.
4. Los chicos van a llamar a la recepción.
5. Las cámaras de los chicos están en la habitación.
6. Ernesto tiene el dinero en el bolsillo.

Unas personas frente a la taquilla de un multicine en Sevilla, España.

## *ACTIVIDADES*

**A** Hágale las siguientes preguntas a su compañero/a. Comparta la información con la clase.

1. ¿Sacas buenas fotos?
2. ¿Cuándo sacas fotos generalmente?
3. ¿Qué cámara tienes?
4. ¿Pones las fotos en un álbum?
5. ¿Les muestras las fotos a tus amigos?

**B** Lea los siguientes consejos para antes y después del revelado (*developing*). Dígale a su compañero/a qué consejos sigue o no sigue usted cuando toma fotos. Las siguientes palabras pueden ayudarle a entender mejor los consejos.

| | |
|---|---|
| polvo | *dust* |
| archivador | *filing jacket* |
| colecciónelos | *keep them* |

**CONSEJOS IMPORTANTES PARA HACER BUENAS FOTOS Y CONSERVARLAS:**

**\* ANTES DEL REVELADO**
— Mantener limpia y cuidada la cámara.
— Evite el polvo, el calor y la humedad.
— No deje mucho tiempo el rollo en la cámara y envíelo rápidamente a revelar.

**\* DESPUÉS DEL REVELADO**
— No saque los negativos del archivador.
— No corte los negativos.
— No toque los negativos con los dedos.
— Colecciónelos en una carpeta o álbum igual que las fotos.
Si sigue estas indicaciones, conseguirá mejores fotos y sus negativos estarán siempre dispuestos para hacer nuevas ampliaciones.

*Rob*
FOTOCOLOR

# GRAMÁTICA

## Stressed possessive adjectives

| | | | | |
|---|---|---|---|---|
| mío | mía | míos | mías | *my, (of) mine* |
| tuyo | tuya | tuyos | tuyas | *your (fam.), (of) yours* |
| suyo | suya | suyos | suyas | *his, her, its, your (formal)* |
| | | | | *their, (of) his, hers* |
| nuestro | nuestra | nuestros | nuestras | *our, (of) ours* |
| vuestro | vuestra | vuestros | vuestras | *your (fam.), (of) yours* |

The stressed possessive adjectives follow the noun they modify and agree with it in gender and number. An article or demonstrative usually precedes the noun.

| | |
|---|---|
| El cuarto **mío** es grandísimo. | *My room is very big.* |
| La maleta **mía** está en la recepción. | *My suitcase is at the front desk.* |
| Esos primos **míos** llegan mañana. | *Those cousins of mine arrive tomorrow.* |
| Las llaves **mías** están en la puerta. | *My keys are in the door.* |

## Possessive pronouns

| | SINGULAR | | | PLURAL | | |
|---|---|---|---|---|---|---|
| | MASCULINE | FEMININE | | MASCULINE | FEMININE | |
| el { | mío | mía | los { | míos | mías | |
| | tuyo | tuya | | tuyos | tuyas | |
| | suyo | la { suya | | suyos | las { suyas | |
| | nuestro | nuestra | | nuestros | nuestras | |
| | vuestro | vuestra | | vuestros | vuestras | |

**1.** Possessive pronouns have the same form as stressed possessive adjectives.

**2.** The definite article precedes the possessive pronoun and they both agree in gender and number with the noun they refer to.

| | |
|---|---|
| ¿Tienes la mochila suya? | *Do you have his backpack?* |
| Sí, tengo **la suya.** | *Yes, I have his.* |

**3.** After the verb **ser,** the article is usually omitted.

| | |
|---|---|
| Esa ropa es mía. | *Those clothes are mine.* |

4. To be more specific and clear, the following structures may be used to replace any corresponding form of **el suyo.**

la mochila suya ⟶ la suya
- la de él   *his*
- la de ella   *hers*
- la de usted   *yours (sing.)*
- la de ellos   *theirs (masc.)*
- la de ellas   *theirs (fem.)*
- la de ustedes   *yours (pl.)*

## ACTIVIDADES

**A** Usted y su compañero/a deben identificar los siguientes objetos y decir de quién son.

*Modelo*

**La bicicleta es mía (tuya, suya, nuestra)**

 1
 2
3
 4

 5
 6
 7
 8
 9

 10
11
 12

**B** Es el fin del año escolar y un/a amigo/a está ayudando a empacar las cosas de usted y de su compañero/a de cuarto. Conteste sus preguntas.

*Modelo*   esta lámpara
**Compañero/a**   **¿De quién es esta lámpara?**
**Usted**   **Es suya** o **Es mía.**

| | | | |
|---|---|---|---|
| esos casetes | los cuadernos | las revistas | el afiche (*poster*) |
| estos discos | el radio | esta toalla | este mapa |

**C** Usted tiene exámenes la semana próxima y va a estudiar con un/a compañero/a. Hágale las siguientes preguntas. Él/ella debe contestar usando pronombres posesivos.

*Modelo*    —¿Quieres ir en mi auto o en el tuyo?
    —**Quiero ir en el tuyo.**

1. ¿Prefieres estudiar en mi casa o en la de Marta?
2. ¿Quieres mi cuaderno o el de Pedro?
3. ¿Hablaste con mi profesor o con el tuyo?
4. ¿Leíste mi proyecto o el de Arturo?
5. ¿Quieres mis apuntes (*notes*) o los de mis hermanos?

**D** Su compañero/a va a hablarle de sus cosas. Contéstele explicando cómo son las suyas.

*Modelo*    —**Mi apartamento es pequeño y cómodo.**
    —**Y el mío es grande y viejo.**

mi perro    mis amigos    mis compañeras    mi bicicleta    mi cuarto
mi novio/a

**E** Usted va a hablarle a su compañero/a sobre su casa y su familia usando la forma correcta de **nuestro.**

*Modelo*    cocina
    **Nuestra cocina es muy moderna.**

familia    vecinos (*neighbors*)    abuelos    casa    auto    padres

# LECTURA

## *Antes de leer:* the past subjunctive

In **Lecciones 10, 11,** and **12,** you studied the forms and uses of the present subjunctive. In this lesson you are going to learn the past subjunctive, also called the imperfect subjunctive. The emphasis will be on knowing how the past subjunctive is formed and on recognizing it when reading or listening.

All past subjunctive verb forms, regular and irregular, are based on the **ellos/as, ustedes** form of the preterit. Drop the **-on** preterit ending, and substitute the past subjunctive endings. The following chart will help you see how the past subjunctive is formed.

| INFINITIVE | ELLOS/AS, USTEDES PRETERIT FORM | PAST SUBJUNCTIVE |
|---|---|---|
| **hablar:** | hablaron | hablara, hablaras, hablara, habláramos, hablarais, hablaran |
| **comer:** | comieron | comiera... |
| **vivir:** | vivieron | viviera... |
| **estar:** | estuvieron | estuviera... |
| **hacer:** | hicieron | hiciera... |
| **poder:** | pudieron | pudiera... |
| **poner:** | pusieron | pusiera... |
| **querer:** | quisieron | quisiera... |
| **saber:** | supieron | supiera... |
| **tener:** | tuvieron | tuviera... |

The same general rules that determine the use of the present subjunctive also apply to the past subjunctive, with a few exceptions. The present subjunctive is oriented to the present or future while the imperfect subjunctive focuses on the past.

Quiere que **preparemos** la comida para las ocho. (hoy ⟶ present subjunctive)
Quería que **preparáramos** la comida para las ocho. (ayer ⟶ past subjunctive)

## Unas vacaciones en Chile

Lea los siguientes párrafos sobre lo que Adriana hizo antes de sus vacaciones en Chile. Adriana es una esquiadora excelente y piensa salir la semana próxima para Portillo, uno de los centros de esquí más importantes de la América del Sur.

Antes de mis vacaciones en Portillo fui a ver al Dr. Sánchez Hurtado. Él me dijo que tuviera mucho cuidado al esquiar este año. Desde que me caí hace dos años siempre me dice lo mismo. Es verdad que el año pasado tuve algunos problemas con el tobillo derecho, pero ya me siento muy bien. Como yo quiero ir a las Olimpiadas de Invierno tengo que practicar mucho para poder clasificar entre los atletas mejores. El doctor me dijo además que siempre hiciera ejercicios de calentamiento antes de esquiar. Eso es tan elemental que casi me reí en su cara. El pobre doctor es muy amigo de mis padres y me conoce hace muchos años así que todavía me trata como una niña. Me pidió que llamara a un doctor amigo de él y que lo saludara de su parte. Además me pidió que le trajera de Chile alguna revista de medicina.

Después de la consulta fui a la agencia de viajes para buscar mi boleto. Según el agente mi asiento está en la sección de fumar. Yo le dije que el entrenador nos prohibió que estuviéramos entre los fumadores y le pedí que me cambiara de asiento. Me dijo que quizás pudiera reservar varios asientos. Yo le pedí que reservara uno para mí y dos para mis amigos. Así podremos hacer el viaje juntos y pasarlo mejor.

## ¿Verdadero o falso?

Diga si las siguientes oraciones son verdaderas o falsas de acuerdo con la selección anterior.

1. Adriana va a practicar su deporte favorito en Chile.
2. Ella tuvo un accidente este año.
3. El médico es un amigo de la familia.
4. El médico le dijo que no fumara.
5. El doctor no conoce a ningún médico en Chile.
6. Adriana quiere competir en las Olimpiadas.
7. Adriana cambió su asiento en la agencia de viajes.
8. Ella va a hacer el viaje sola.

## Un hotel diferente

Este anuncio se refiere a un hotel diferente. Después de leerlo debe contestar las preguntas. El siguiente vocabulario le podrá ayudar a entender mejor la selección.

| | |
|---|---|
| cuestión | *a matter* |
| hacer noche | *spend the night* |
| próximo | *near* |
| asearse | *to tidy oneself* |

# PARA CUANDO VIAJAR ES CUESTION DE HORAS

Cuando viaje en tren por cuestiones de trabajo y no necesite hacer noche, usted podrá disponer durante el día de una habitación con baño en un hotel de lujo próximo a la estación.

Así, tendrá un lugar donde poder descansar, asearse, preparar sus reuniones o trabajar. Por un precio muy especial y con sólo presentar su billete de viaje en la recepción del hotel, disfrutará de un hotel de día.

Haga sus reservas llamando al propio teléfono del hotel.

**RENFE**

**MEJORA TU TREN DE VIDA.**

## Para completar

Complete las oraciones de acuerdo con la información que se da sobre el hotel en la selección.

1. Este hotel es diferente porque...
2. Es para personas que...
3. Está...
4. En este hotel las personas...
5. Se hace una reserva...
6. La compañía... ofrece este servicio.

## Programa comercial

Esta selección explica los beneficios que varios hoteles le ofrecen al hombre de negocios. Las siguientes palabras pueden ayudarle a entender mejor el anuncio.

| | |
|---|---|
| lanzar | *start* |
| el alojamiento | *lodging* |
| la tarifa | *cost* |
| hospedarse | *to stay, lodge* |
| encaminado a lograr | *designed to provide* |
| agilizar | *to speed up* |
| la disposición | *availability* |
| el enjuague | *rinse* |
| rastrillo desechable | *disposable razor* |

# 17 Grandes beneficios de hotel en una gran tarjeta

## Programa Comercial

★ ★ ★ ★ ★

Hoteles Fiesta Americana, Fiesta Inn, Holiday Inn y Holiday Inn Crowne Plaza, tienen el gran placer de lanzar su ''PROGRAMA COMERCIAL'', el más rico en beneficios para los hombres de negocios, como usted.

1. Su reservación le garantiza una magnífica habitación sin necesidad de depósito ni límite para su hora de llegada.

2. En caso de llegar sin reservación y que el hotel esté lleno, nos encargaremos de todos los detalles, para conseguirle alojamiento en la mejor habitación de otro hotel.

3. Descuento mínimo garantizado del 25% en habitación sobre la tarifa al público.

4. Centro Ejecutivo: Todos los servicios de una oficina dentro del hotel.

5. Plan de Incentivos Vacacionales: Usted puede ganar cortesías y descuentos en nuestros hoteles (incluyendo los de playa) al ir acumulando las noches que se hospede con nosotros.

6. Salida Express agilizando ampliamente los trámites de pago y salida del hotel.

7. Disposición de efectivo hasta por $ 25,000 M.N. con cargo a su cuenta.

8. Llamada de despertador con café o jugo y periódico a su elección en su habitación.

9. Derecho a extender la hora de salida hasta por 4 horas sin cargo extra.

10. Cortesías en su baño: shampoo, enjuague, rastrillo desechable, jabón perfumado y gorra de baño.

11. Preregistro para ahorrarle tiempo en su llegada al hotel.

12. Preasignación de una magnífica habitación de acuerdo a sus gustos particulares.

13. Bebida Nacional de bienvenida a su elección.

14. Media botella de vino nacional de cortesía en comida o cena.

15. Dulce o chocolate y flor en habitación como cortesía nocturna diaria.

16. Facilidades de cortesía para aseo de calzado.

17. Promoción especial en renta de autos.

Entonces son diecisiete beneficios verdaderamente grandes, encaminados a lograr la total satisfacción de un hombre de negocios como usted...

AHORA SOLO FALTA SU SOLICITUD: Llame usted al (91-5) 570-81-22 extensiones 770, 771, 785 y recibirá en breve las formas necesarias para que, llenándolas, pueda usted gozar de las extraordinarias ventajas de nuestro PROGRAMA COMERCIAL. Por supuesto, en la recepción de cada uno de nuestros hoteles, que se muestran en la parte inferior, puede solicitar dichas formas.

 HOTELES **FIESTA** AMERICANA ®     FIESTA INN    ❄ Holiday Inn     HOLIDAY INN CROWNE PLAZA ®

---

Conteste las siguientes preguntas de acuerdo con la selección.

1. ¿Qué beneficios tienen que ver con la habitación?
2. ¿Qué beneficios se relacionan con el aseo?
3. ¿Qué beneficios tienen como fin ahorrarle tiempo al hombre de negocios?
4. ¿Qué beneficios tienen que ver con algo para beber o comer?
5. En su opinión, ¿cuál es el mejor beneficio para un hombre de negocios?

## SITUACIONES

1. You have to make a reservation for a hotel: (a) explain that you need a double room, (b) find out the price per night, (c) ask if it includes breakfast, and (d) check if they have transportation to and from the airport.

2. Tell a friend where you spent your vacation last year. Try to persuade him/her to go there. Tell him/her (a) where this place is, (b) what you can do there, (c) what it costs (a bargain), and (d) how long you stayed.

3. You are a clerk in a hotel. Help a family who wants to stay in your hotel. First greet the family and ask them if you can help them. Then find out if they have a reservation, and ask (a) how many rooms they need, (b) how many single or double rooms, (c) how long they need the rooms, and (d) how they want to pay (cash, traveler's checks, or credit card). Then ask them to fill out a form and thank them.

4. You are not completely satisfied with your room and you go talk with the clerk. Greet the clerk and tell him/her that (a) you don't have hot water or heat, (b) you need soap and towels. Then ask him if you can have another room, and say that you would like a room on the tenth floor.

5. You and two friends are going to spend your vacation in the mountains and already have your basic supplies. From the following list of extra items, choose three you are going to take and tell your friends why: **un periódico, un walkman, un televisor portátil, dos libros, un despertador** (*alarm clock*), **un traje de baño, una canoa, una linterna** (*flashlight*), **fósforos** (*matches*), **un radio.**

6. You and some friends are trying to decide what to do for a three-day weekend. Each one will choose one of the following places and explain why you should all go there. Use the following reasons to convince your friends.

   **Lugares: la playa, el campo, una ciudad grande, las montañas**

   **Motivos: la comida, la tranquilidad, el aire puro, la música, las fiestas, el teatro, los bailes, los museos, el sol, las noches, la naturaleza, el silencio**

7. You have had a busy week in Mexico doing many things. Tell your friend (a) what places you visited, (b) what you saw, (c) what you were able to do, (d) what you bought, and (e) what and where you ate. Your friend will ask you some pertinent questions.

**KH** Gran Rex Hotel ✶✶

*HABITACIONES Y DEPARTAMENTOS
CON BAÑO Y TELEFONO PRIVADO
DESAYUNO, ESTACIONAMIENTO
A DOS CUADRAS DE LA PLAYA*

AVENIDA MITRE 805
TELEFONOS 20942 - 20783
(7607) MIRAMAR

# VOCABULARIO[3]

**lugares**

| | |
|---|---|
| el ayuntamiento | *city hall* |
| la catedral | *cathedral* |
| la estación de policía | *police station* |
| el museo | *museum* |
| el parque | *park* |
| la plaza de toros | *bullring* |
| el teatro | *theater* |

**la naturaleza** — *nature*

| | |
|---|---|
| el árbol | *tree* |
| la arena | *sand* |
| la flor | *flower* |
| la montaña | *mountain* |
| la ola | *wave* |

**el hotel**

| | |
|---|---|
| el ascensor | *elevator* |
| el bar | *bar* |
| el botones | *bellboy* |
| la confirmación | *confirmation* |
| la cuenta | *bill* |
| el estacionamiento | *parking* |
| la habitación doble/ sencilla | *double/single room* |
| la lavandería | *laundry* |
| la llave | *key* |
| el mensaje | *message* |
| la recepción | *reception* |
| la tintorería | *cleaners* |

**el teatro**

| | |
|---|---|
| la función | *show* |
| la cámara | *camera* |

**la ropa**

| | |
|---|---|
| el bolsillo | *pocket* |

**descripciones**

| | |
|---|---|
| amable | *nice* |

**verbos**

| | |
|---|---|
| acompañar | *accompany* |
| firmar | *to sign* |
| llenar | *fill out* |
| molestar(se) | *to bother* |
| olvidar | *to forget* |
| regresar | *to come back* |
| sacar fotos | *take pictures* |

**expresiones útiles**

| | |
|---|---|
| ¿a nombre de quién? | *under whose name?* |
| bajo el nombre de... | *under . . .'s name* |

## Los toros de hoy

| Nombre | Num. | Capa | Kilos |
|---|---|---|---|
| «Gacetrillo» | 10 | Negro | 542 |
| «Caracolillo» | 21 | Negro | 531 |
| «Carazul» | 37 | Negro | 552 |
| «Manzanito» | 33 | Negro | 536 |
| «Pintadito» | 31 | Negro | 584 |
| «Cañurino» | 8 | Negro | 539 |

---

[3] See page 355 for possessive adjectives and pronouns.

**In** Lección 15 **you will**
a. talk about and describe holiday activities.
b. express on–going actions in the past.
c. extend an invitation.
d. accept or decline an invitation.
e. express goals and purposes.
f. express intense reactions.
g. ask for and give a definition or an explanation.

# Fechas importantes

el último jueves de noviembre
el Día de Acción de Gracias

En los Estados Unidos las familias se reúnen para celebrar este día.

el 14 de febrero
el Día de los Enamorados o
el Día de Amor y la Amistad

Laura y Jorge están enamorados y van a salir esta noche.

# Lección 15
# Fiestas y tradiciones

el 4 de julio
el Día de la Independencia

Hay desfiles con bandas y muchas personas
ponen banderas al frente de su casa.

el 31 de octubre
el Día de las Brujas

En los Estados Unidas los niños se disfrazan y se divierten mucho.

Unos niños junto a unos Reyes Magos en la ciudad de México. El Día de los Reyes Magos es una fiesta muy importante para los niños hispanos.

**más días y fechas importantes**

| | |
|---|---|
| la Nochevieja | *New Year's Eve* |
| el Año Nuevo | *New Year's Day* |
| el Día de la Independencia | *Independence Day* |
| la Nochebuena | *Christmas Eve* |
| la Navidad | *Christmas* |
| el Carnaval | *Mardi gras* |
| la Pascua | *Passover, Easter* |
| la Semana Santa | *Easter week* |
| el Día de los Muertos/Difuntos | *All Souls' Day* |
| el Día de la(s) Madre(s) | *Mother's Day* |

## ACTIVIDADES

**A** Asocie las descripciones de la izquierda con las fiestas de la derecha.

1. Empieza el año.
2. Los niños salen y piden dulces.
3. Les damos regalos a los amigos y parientes.
4. Las personas bailan en la calle y se divierten mucho.
5. Termina el año.

a. el Día de las Brujas
b. la Navidad
c. el Año Nuevo
d. la Nochevieja
e. el Carnaval

**B** **Entrevista.** Hágale a su compañero/a las siguientes preguntas. Después él/ella le debe hacer las mismas preguntas a usted.

1. ¿Qué fiestas celebra tu familia?   2. ¿Qué días son esas fiestas?   3. ¿Quiénes van a tu casa para celebrarlas?   4. ¿Qué hacen para celebrarlas?

**C** Complete las siguientes oraciones.

1. Mi fiesta favorita es...   2. Es mi fiesta favorita porque...   3. Para celebrar ese día yo...

# Cultura

## Días de fiesta y tradiciones en el mundo hispano

Muchos de los días de fiesta y fechas importantes que se celebran en los Estados Unidos también se celebran en los países hispanos, pero con ciertas diferencias. Por ejemplo, la Navidad es una fecha muy importante en ambas° culturas; en los Estados Unidos ése es el día que Santa Claus les lleva regalos a los niños, mientras que en algunos países hispanos es Papá Noel o el Niño Dios. En otros países hispanos los Reyes Magos° son quienes les llevan regalos a los niños el 6 de enero, conocido en el mundo hispano como el Día de los Reyes Magos.

El Día de Acción de Gracias no existe en los países hispanos, pero las familias generalmente se reúnen en Nochebuena y cenan juntos ese día. Los platos que se sirven en esa cena varían de un país a otro. Después de la cena muchas familias van a la misa de medianoche o **Misa del Gallo.**

Las fiestas religiosas son muy importantes en la cultura hispánica. Cada pueblo o ciudad tiene su santo patrón (o santa patrona) y observan su día con ceremonias religiosas, procesiones y, a veces, ferias. Muchos de los hispanos también celebran el día de su santo; por ejemplo, un chico que se llama José celebra su santo el día de San José, o sea° el 19 de marzo. Ese día sus familiares y amigos lo felicitan y algunos le regalan algo, tal como° se hace en los Estados Unidos por el cumpleaños. Algunos calendarios y periódicos muestran los nombres de los santos para cada día.

La Semana Santa es extremadamente importante en los países hispanos. En

Una de las procesiones durante la Semana Santa en Sevilla.

general las oficinas cierran los jueves al mediodía y no vuelven a abrir hasta el lunes por la mañana. En Andalucía, la región del sur de España, se celebra la Semana Santa de una manera impresionante, especialmente en las ciudades de Sevilla, Granada y Málaga. Durante toda la semana hay procesiones que comienzan por la tarde, casi siempre después de las seis. Algunas no termi-

---

ambas *both*   Reyes Magos *Wise Men*   o sea *that is*   como *as*

Estas carretas adornadas «hacen el camino» para llegar al Rocío, un pequeño pueblo de Huelva, donde está la ermita de la Virgen del Rocío. En este pueblo se reúnen cerca de un millón de personas para celebrar la fiesta de la Virgen del Rocío.

nan hasta la madrugada°. Las imágenes religiosas se colocan° en unas andas (plataformas decoradas con plata°, oro, bronce, etc.) que se llevan por las calles. Algunas de estas andas pesan más de tres toneladas y se necesitan más de doscientos hombres para cargarlas°. La combinación del fervor religioso, la música, los miles de velas° y los penitentes encapuchados°, hacen de estas procesiones un espectáculo inolvidable.

Otras ceremonias religiosas, como los bautizos y la primera comunión, son también eventos sociales y para celebrarlos se invita a los parientes y a los amigos más íntimos. Generalmente los invitados le llevan un regalo al niño o niña que bautizan o celebra su comunión.

Los cumpleaños son también importantes en el mundo hispano. En las fiestas de niños frecuentemente hay una piñata. La forma de ésta puede variar (una estrella, un toro°, un payaso°), pero todas tienen caramelos° o dulces y a veces frutas o pequeños regalos. La piñata se cuelga y cada niño trata de romperla con un palo°. Para hacerlo más difícil le cubren los ojos al niño y le dan vueltas° para que no sepa exactamente dónde está la piñata. A veces uno de los adultos mueve la cuerda° donde está colgada la piñata para que los niños no la puedan alcanzar. Cuando finalmente se rompe la piñata caen al suelo todos los caramelos y cada niño trata de conseguir tantos como pueda. En algunos países la piñata tiene un fondo de cartón° con cintas° de colores y cada niño tira° de una para que el fondo caiga.

Cuando una joven cumple los quince años generalmente se celebra esta fecha con **la fiesta de quince** o **quinceañera,** similar a los bailes de *Sweet Sixteen.* Muchas familias hispanas que viven en los Estados Unidos celebran los quince años con una fiesta muy elaborada y formal.

hasta la madrugada *until early morning* se colocan *are placed* plata *silver* cargarlas *carry them* velas *candles* encapuchados *hooded* toro *bull* payaso *clown* caramelos *candies* palo *stick* dan vueltas *spin around* cuerda *cord* carton *cardboard* cintas *ribbons* tira *pulls*

# EN CONTEXTO

## La abuela recuerda° otros tiempos

*remembers*

En mi época la vida de la gente° joven era° diferente. No teníamos° la libertad ni las comodidades° que tiene la juventud° hoy en día, pero tampoco teníamos el problema de las drogas y la inconformidad de hoy. Era una vida más tranquila y más sana. Nos reuníamos° en casa de amigos, escuchábamos música, organizábamos fiestas y excursiones, salíamos en grupo y nos divertíamos° mucho. Creo que éramos más felices.

*people / was / No... We didn't have comforts / youth*

*Nos... We used to get together*
*nos... we had a great time*

Entonces, como no existía la televisión, las familias tenían más tiempo para hablar y los niños no veían esos programas donde hay tanta violencia y sexo. Se respetaba a las personas mayores y había° más seguridad en las calles.

*there was*

Hasta la música era diferente. Tenía melodía y era más suave y romántica. Además, no tocaban tan alto como hoy en día, ni la gente se movía tanto para bailar. Definitivamente, eran otros tiempos.

## ¿Verdadero o falso?

Diga si las siguientes oraciones son verdaderas o falsas, según las ideas de la abuela.

1. Antes la gente joven lo pasaba muy bien.
2. Las muchachas no salían de excursión.
3. En esa época el problema de las drogas era serio.
4. Las familias veían buenos programas de televisión.
5. La gente era más conforme entonces.
6. La orquestas de antes tocaban muy alto.
7. Los jóvenes eran más felices.
8. La gente se sentía más segura.

Una familia en el cementerio el Día de los Muertos en la ciudad de México.

## *ACTIVIDADES* ▬▬▬▬▬▬▬▬▬▬▬▬▬▬▬▬▬▬▬▬▬▬▬▬

**A** Complete las siguientes oraciones para describir cómo eran ciertas cosas antes.

> *Modelo*  Los aviones eran más... y no tenían...
> **Los aviones eran más pequeños y no tenían tantos asientos.**

1. Las ciudades eran... y tenían...
2. Las casas eran... y no tenían...
3. La gente joven era más... y...
4. Los automóviles eran... y no tenían...
5. La vida era...

**B** La vida moderna tiene muchas ventajas. Con su compañero/a haga una lista de cinco.

## GRAMÁTICA

### Preterit and imperfect

English has one past tense, but Spanish, as mentioned in **Lección 12,** has two: the preterit and the imperfect.

|  English |  Spanish |  |
| --- | --- | --- |
| PAST TENSE | PRETERIT | IMPERFECT |
| *I did* | (yo) hice | (yo) hacía |

The preterit and imperfect are not interchangeable. When talking about the beginning or end of an event, the Spanish speaker will use the preterit. To talk about (a) the middle or on–going part of an event or (b) customary or habitual actions in the past, the speaker will use the imperfect.

In the preceding monolog, the grandmother used the imperfect because she was explaining what used to happen (on–going or habitual actions) when she was young. If she had been talking about what she did yesterday (terminated action), she would have used the preterit.

Some time expressions that are normally used with the imperfect are **mientras, a veces, siempre, generalmente,** and **frecuentemente.**

### Imperfect of regular and irregular verbs

|  | hablar | comer | vivir |
| --- | --- | --- | --- |
| yo | hablaba | comía | vivía |
| tú | hablabas | comías | vivías |
| él, ella, usted | hablaba | comía | vivía |
| nosotros/as | hablábamos | comíamos | vivíamos |
| vosotros/as | hablabais | comíais | vivíais |
| ellos/as, ustedes | hablaban | comían | vivían |

1. Note that the endings for **-er** and **-ir** verbs are the same and that every verb form has an accent mark over the **í** of the ending.
2. The Spanish imperfect has several English equivalents.

Mis amigos estudiaban mucho.

$$\left\{\begin{array}{l} \textit{My friends studied a lot.} \\ \textit{My friends were studying a lot.} \\ \textit{My friends used to study a lot.} \\ \textit{My friends would study a lot.} \\ \qquad \text{(implying a repeated action)} \end{array}\right.$$

3. Stem-changing verbs do not change in the imperfect.

   Ella no **duerme** bien ahora, pero antes **dormía** muy bien.

4. Only three verbs are irregular in the imperfect.

   **ir:**  iba, ibas, iba, íbamos, ibais, iban
   **ser:** era, eras, era, éramos, erais, eran
   **ver:** veía, veías, veía, veíamos, veíais, veían

5. The imperfect form of **hay** is **había** (*there was, there were, there used to be*).

## Uses of the imperfect

Use the imperfect to

1. express habitual or repeated actions in the past.

   Nosotros **íbamos** a la playa todos los días.

2. express an action that was in progress in the past.

   En esos momentos Agustín **hablaba** con su hermana.

   You may also use the imperfect of **estar** + present participle (imperfect progressive) to emphasize the on-going activity.

   En esos momentos Agustín **estaba hablando** con su hermana.

3. describe characteristics and conditions in the past.

   La casa **era** blanca, con techo rojo, y **tenía** dos dormitorios.

4. tell time in the past.

   **Era** la una, no **eran** las dos.

5. tell age in the past.

   Ella **tenía** dieciocho años entonces.

## ACTIVIDADES

**A** Diga qué cosas hacía o no hacía usted cuando tenía cinco años.

*Modelo*  vivía cerca de mis primos
**Yo vivía (no vivía) cerca de mis primos.**

1. vivía con mis padres
2. estudiaba español
3. montaba bicicleta
4. jugaba con mis amigos
5. miraba televisión
6. ayudaba a mi mamá
7. tenía un perro grande
8. iba al cine
9. me acostaba temprano

**B En la escuela secundaria.** Diga con qué frecuencia hacían usted y sus amigos estas cosas.

*Modelo*  organizar excursiones
**Frecuentemente (o nunca, o a veces) organizábamos excursiones.**

siempre     frecuentemente     a veces     casi nunca     nunca

1. estudiar mucho
2. tener fiestas
3. nadar en la piscina
4. hacer la tarea
5. ir a los partidos de fútbol
6. salir con los amigos
7. almorzar juntos
8. hablar por teléfono

**C** Hoy en día hacemos muchas cosas que antes no se hacían o no hacemos cosas que antes se hacían. Lea cada oración y diga cómo era la vida antes.

*Modelo*  Hoy en día se viaja mucho en avión.
**Antes no se viajaba (mucho) en avión** o **Se viajaba poco en avión,** o **Se viajaba en tren.**

1. Hoy en día muchas mujeres trabajan en oficinas.
2. Ahora las chicas salen solas.
3. Ahora se practican muchos deportes.
4. Hoy en día manejamos coches muy rápidos.
5. Ahora muchas personas compran comida congelada (*frozen*).
6. Ahora hay mujeres astronautas.
7. Hoy en día se venden muchos productos japoneses.
8. Hoy en día hay mucha violencia en las películas.

**D** Lea las siguientes oraciones y decida si debe usar el pretérito o el imperfecto.

1. (Fueron, Eran) las dos de la mañana cuando ellos (llegaron, llegaban) al hotel.
2. La fiesta de quince años que mis padres le (dieron, daban) a mi hermana (fue, era) algo muy especial.
3. Cada Navidad (fuimos, íbamos) a casa de mis abuelos y Papá Noel nos (trajo, traía) muchos regalos.

4. Recuerdo que un año mis padres no le (compraron, compraban) una piñata a mi hermano.
5. Mientras Ernesto (cantó, cantaba) los muchachos (escuchaban, escucharon) con mucha atención.
6. Durante el Carnaval todos (fueron, iban) a la plaza a ver los bailes.
7. El Día de las Madres (llevé, llevaba) a mi mamá a un concierto de rock.
8. Todos los años para la Nochevieja Ester y Martín (fueron, iban) a casa de los Solís y allí (bailaron, bailaban) hasta las dos o las tres de la mañana.

**E** Lea los siguientes párrafos y complételos con el pretérito o el imperfecto de los verbos entre paréntesis.

La semana pasada Enrique —(1)— una fiesta e —(2)— a todos sus amigos. —(3)— una fiesta sorpresa para celebrar el cumpleaños de su amiga Carmen que —(4)— con él en la universidad. Carmen —(5)— en su tercer año y —(6)— bastante porque las clases —(7)— difíciles.

Enrique —(8)— todos los arreglos (*planning*) desde la comida hasta la música. Cuando Carmen —(9)— a la casa de Enrique todo —(10)— oscuro, pero en el momento en que ella —(11)— a la puerta se —(12)— todas las luces y —(13)— la fiesta. —(14)— una verdadera sorpresa para Carmen.

1. (tener)
2. (invitar)
3. (ser)
4. (estudiar)
5. (estar)
6. (trabajar)
7. (ser)
8. (hacer)
9. (llegar)
10. (estar)
11. (tocar)
12. (encender)
13. (empezar)
14. (ser)

**F** **Entrevista.** Usted quiere saber cómo era la vida de su compañero/a cuando era pequeño/a. Hágale las siguientes preguntas y comparta la información con la clase.

1. ¿Dónde vivías? 2. ¿Estaba tu casa (apartamento) en el centro o en las afueras? 3. ¿Cómo era tu casa (apartamento)? 4. ¿Dormías solo/a o con algún miembro de tu familia? 5. ¿A qué escuela ibas? 6. ¿Cómo se llamaba tu profesor/a favorito/a? ¿Cómo era? 7. ¿Quién era tu mejor amigo/a? ¿Cómo era? 8. ¿Qué deportes practicabas/ 9. ¿Qué programas de televisión veías/ 10. ¿Qué te gustaba hacer los fines de semana?

**G** Piense en las vacaciones cuando usted era pequeño/a y dé la mayor información posible siguiendo el siguiente esquema.

Lugar: nombre, descripción
Personas que iban: número, parientes, amigos
Actividades: día, noche
Actividad favorita: descripción

# EN CONTEXTO

### El cumpleaños de Amparo

Salen para comprar el vestido.

Caminan por la calle para llegar a la tienda.

Amparo paga 10.000 pesos por el vestido.

Las amigas de Amparo vienen para felicitarla por su cumpleaños. Todos estos regalos son para Amparo.

### Preguntas

1. ¿Qué quiere comprar Amparo?
2. ¿Para qué día lo necesita?
3. ¿Para dónde van las chicas?
4. ¿Cuánto paga Amparo por el vestido?
5. ¿Para qué van los amigos a casa de Amparo?
6. ¿Para quién son los regalos?

## ACTIVIDADES

**A** Su compañero/a y usted están organizando una fiesta de sorpresa para celebrar el cumpleaños de una amiga. Hagan una lista de las cosas que tienen que hacer antes de la fiesta.

**B** Su compañero/a quiere saber las cosas que usted y sus amigos hacían en las fiestas cuando eran pequeños. Conteste las siguientes preguntas.

    1. ¿Dónde eran las fiestas?
    2. ¿Eran por la tarde o por la mañana?
    3. ¿Qué hacían en las fiestas?
    4. ¿Cuál era el juego más popular?
    5. ¿Qué comían?
    6. ¿Adónde iban después de las fiestas?

## GRAMÁTICA

### *Por* and *para*

**Por** and **para** are often translated as *for* or *by,* depending on the context, but they are not interchangeable. Choosing one or the other will affect the meaning of the sentence.

**1.** Use **por** to

    **a.** indicate exchange or substitution.

| | |
|---|---|
| Venden la casa **por** $50.000. | *They sell the house for $50,000.* |
| Cambió ese suéter **por** éste. | *He changed that sweater for this one.* |
| Andrés va a trabajar **por** mí. | *Andrés is going to work for (instead of) me.* |

    **b.** express unit or rate.

| | |
|---|---|
| Yo camino 5 kilómetros **por** hora. | *I walk 5 kilometers per hour.* |
| El interés es diez **por** ciento. | *The interest is ten per cent.* |
| Se vende el pescado **por** kilo. | *Fish is sold by the kilo.* |

    **c.** express means of transportation.

| | |
|---|---|
| Lo mandaron por avión. | *They sent it by plane.* |

    **d.** indicate general or imprecise location in space or time.

| | |
|---|---|
| Está **por** allá. | *It's around there.* |
| Llegan **por** la noche. | *They'll arrive at (during the) night.* |

**2.** Use **para** to express judgment.

| | |
|---|---|
| **Para** nosotros, ésta es la mejor tienda. | *For us, this is the best store.* |

## *Por* and *para* contrasted

**1.** To express movement and destination

| **por** | **para** |
|---|---|
| passing through or by a place | going toward a place |
| Caminan **por** la playa. | Caminan **para** la playa. |
| *They walk along the beach.* | *They walk towards the beach.* |
| Maneja por el túnel. | Maneja para el túnel. |
| *He drives through the tunnel.* | *He drives towards the tunnel.* |

**2.** To express time

| **por** | **para** |
|---|---|
| time during which an action takes place | deadline |
| Lo necesitamos **por** tres meses. | Lo necesitamos **para** el martes. |
| *We need it for three months.* | *We need it for Tuesday.* |

**3.** With actions

| **por** | **para** |
|---|---|
| a. cause or reason why something is done | a. for whom something is intended or done |
| Compró la casa **por** ella. | Compró la casa **para** ella. |
| *He bought the house because of her.* | *He bought the house for her.* |
| b. followed by a noun to express the object of an errand | b. followed by an infinitive to indicate intention or purpose |
| Fueron **por** gasolina. | Fueron **para** comprar gasolina. |
| *They went for gas.* | *They went to buy gas.* |

## ACTIVIDADES

**A** Usted necesita pintar su apartamento y le dice a su amigo cuándo van a estar listas las diferentes partes de la casa.

*Modelo*   cocina / el lunes
           **La cocina va a estar lista para el lunes.**

1. mi dormitorio / el martes
2. la sala / el sábado
3. el baño / el jueves
4. el pasillo / el domingo

**B** Mire los siguientes dibujos y diga hacia (*towards*) dónde va cada persona y por dónde pasa para llegar allí.

*Modelo*

**El alumno camina por el pasillo.**
**Él va para su clase de español.**

1

2

3

**C** Las siguientes personas van a diferentes lugares. Use su imaginación y diga para qué van a esos lugares.

*Modelo*    El Sr. Martínez va a la estación de gasolina.
            **Va para comprar gasolina.**

1. Juan va al cine.
2. Mónica y Laura van al gimnasio.
3. Adolfo va a la piscina.

4. Joaquín va al supermercado.
5. Magdalena va al Centro Comercial Los Arcos.
6. Alejandro va a la farmacia.

**D** Complete el párrafo con **por** o **para** según el contexto.

Pasado mañana es el 24 de septiembre y es el santo de Mercedes. Su madrina, la Sra. de Ortiz, compró un regalo muy bonito ___ Mercedes. La Sra. de Ortiz vive en otra ciudad y quiere que Mercedes reciba el regalo ___ el 24. Ella decide mandarlo ___ avión. ___ la mañana prepara el paquete y sale ___ el correo. Cuando llega al correo va ___ la ventanilla de los paquetes. El empleado lo pesa y le dice que tiene que pagar 500 pesos ___ el paquete.

**E** Complete cada oración de acuerdo con sus propias experiencias.

1. Para mí, el mejor programa de televisión es... porque...
2. El mes próximo salgo de vacaciones. Voy para... Pienso ir por... Voy a estar allá por...
3. Yo quiero comprarme... Voy a pagar... por...
4. Para el sábado yo tengo que... No sé si voy a hacerlo el viernes por la tarde o...
5. Yo (no) camino... kilómetros por hora. A mí (no) me gusta caminar porque...
6. Mañana es el santo de mi novio/a. Para comprarle un regalo voy a ir a... No quiero pagar más de... por el regalo.
7. Para las Navidades yo quiero que me regalen... Yo prefiero ese regalo porque...
8. Esta noche vamos a celebrar el aniversario de mis padres. Para tener todo listo, por la mañana voy a... y por la tarde voy a...

# EN CONTEXTO

## Una invitación para una fiesta

| | |
|---|---|
| **Alfonso** | ¡Qué bueno que las veo! Las iba a llamar esta noche. El sábado es el santo de Antonio, y Magdalena y yo estamos organizando una fiesta en casa. |
| **Josefina** | ¿Este sábado? |
| **Miriam** | ¿En qué mundo vives, Josefina? Por supuesto° que sí. Este sábado es 13 de junio. |
| **Josefina** | ¡Qué barbaridad°! El tiempo vuela. |
| **Alfonso** | Queríamos invitarlas. ¿Creen que puedan ir? |
| **Josefina** | Yo, encantada. ¿Y tú, Miriam? |
| **Miriam** | Lo siento mucho, Alfonso, pero este sábado quedé° en ir a la finca° con mis primos. De todas formas°, gracias por la invitación. |
| **Alfonso** | Por favor, no le digan nada a Antonio. Va a ser una sorpresa. ¿Te imaginas la cara que va a poner°? |
| **Miriam** | ¡Qué pena° no poder verlo! |

*Por... Of course*

*It's amazing!*

*I agreed*
*farm / De... Anyway*

*la... his face*
*Qué... What a pity*

## Preguntas

Conteste las siguientes preguntas con la información que se da en el diálogo.

1. ¿Por qué quería Alfonso hablar con las chicas?
2. ¿Para quién es la fiesta?
3. ¿Dónde va a ser?
4. ¿Por qué se organiza la fiesta?
5. ¿Quiénes organizan la fiesta?
6. ¿Puede ir Josefina? ¿y Miriam?
7. ¿Adónde va a ir Miriam este sábado?
8. ¿Por qué no pueden decirle nada a Antonio?

## ACTIVIDADES

**A** ¿Qué dice usted en estas situaciones? Escoja la expresión correcta para cada situación.

1. Lo/La invitan a una fiesta y usted no puede ir.
2. El auto de su amigo no funciona. Él le pregunta si lo puede llevar a su casa y usted va a hacerlo.
3. Lo/la invitan a una fiesta y usted acepta la invitación.
4. Es el santo de una amiga y usted la saluda en una fiesta en su casa.

a. Por supuesto.
b. Lo siento.
c. Felicidades.
d. Encantado/a.

**B** Su compañero/a lo/la invitó a un concierto, pero usted tiene muy mala memoria y no recuerda la fecha, la hora y el lugar. Pregúntele a su compañero/a y comparta la información con la clase.

**C** Complete el siguiente diálogo con su compañero/a.

**Compañero/a**  ¡Hola, ____! Te iba a llamar esta noche. Mañana nos vamos a reunir en casa de ____ después del partido de ____. ¿Puedes ir?

**Usted**  No, ____. Quedé en ir a ____. Gracias por la invitación.

Una niña trata de romper una piñata en Matagalpa, Nicaragua.

# GRAMÁTICA

## Exclamatory *qué*

**1.** Use **qué** + noun as an equivalent of *what* + *a* + noun.

¡Qué fiesta!                        *What a party!*

**2.** When the noun is modified by an adjective, add **tan** or **más.**

¡Qué fiesta $\begin{Bmatrix} \text{tan} \\ \text{más} \end{Bmatrix}$ buena!          *What a great party!*

**3.** Use **qué** + adjective as an equivalent of *how* + adjective.

¡Qué lindo!                        *How pretty!*
¡Qué raro!                         *How odd!*

## Interrogative *qué* and *cuál(es)* with *ser*

**1.** Use **qué** + **ser** when you want to ask for a definition or an explanation.

—¿Qué es la Nochevieja? —Es el último día del año.

**2.** Use **cuál(-es)** + **ser** when you want to ask *which one(s).*

—¿Cuál es tu asiento? —Es éste.
—¿Cuáles son tus boletos? —Los dos que están sobre la mesa.

# ACTIVIDADES

**A** Escoja la expresión adecuada de acuerdo con la situación.

1. Hay un león enorme en la clase.
   a. ¡Qué lindo!
   b. ¡Qué horrible!
   c. ¡Qué divertido!

2. Sus tíos van a pagarle un viaje a Europa.
   a. ¡Qué bueno!
   b. ¡Qué pena!
   c. ¡Qué miedo!

3. Usted ve el edificio Empire State por primera vez.
   a. ¡Qué edificio tan feo!
   b. ¡Qué edificio tan alto!
   c. ¡Qué edificio más viejo!

4. Usted conoció a una estudiante encantadora.
   a. ¡Qué simpática!
   b. ¡Qué trabajadora!
   c. ¡Qué rara!
5. Su hermano ganó $5.000.000 en la lotería.
   a. ¡Qué dolor!
   b. ¡Qué suerte!
   c. ¡Qué malo!

**B** **¿Qué es?** o **¿Cuál es?** Haga las preguntas adecuadas. Uno de sus compañeros/as debe contestar su pregunta.

> *Modelo*    la definición de la palabra **Carnaval**
> **Usted**   **¿Qué es el Carnaval?**
> **Compañero/a**   **Es una fiesta muy importante y divertida.**
> el nombre del mejor hotel
> **Usted**   **¿Cuál es el mejor hotel?**
> **Compañero/a**   **Es el Ritz.**

1. el número de teléfono de su compañero/a
2. la definición de la palabra **teléfono**
3. la explicación de **habitación doble**
4. el número de la habitación doble
5. la definición de **postre**
6. el postre más caro

**C** Complete el siguiente diálogo con su compañero/a.

> **Compañero/a**   ¡Hola, ____! ¿Sabes que ganamos el campeonato de fútbol?
> **Usted**   ¡Qué ____! ¿Dónde vamos a celebrarlo?
> **Compañero/a**   No lo vamos a celebrar hoy. Juan se cayó en el partido y se torció un tobillo.
> **Usted**   ¡Qué ____! ¿Y cómo está?
> **Compañero/a**   ...

# LECTURA

## *Antes de leer:* the conditional

Since **Lección 7,** you have used the expression **me gustaría. . .** to express what you would like to do. **Gustaría** is a form of the conditional. It is an easy tense to recognize because it is formed by adding the endings **-ía, ías, ía, íamos, íais, ían** to the infinitive.

| | hablar | comer | vivir |
|---|---|---|---|
| yo | hablar**ía** | comer**ía** | vivir**ía** |
| tú | hablar**ías** | comer**ías** | vivir**ías** |
| él, ella, usted | hablar**ía** | comer**ía** | vivir**ía** |
| nosotros/as | hablar**íamos** | comer**íamos** | vivir**íamos** |
| vosotros/as | hablar**íais** | comer**íais** | vivir**íais** |
| ellos/as, ustedes | hablar**ían** | comer**ían** | vivir**ían** |

Few verbs are irregular in the conditional. They are the same verbs that are irregular in the future and they have the same stem.

| INFINITIVE | NEW STEM | CONDITIONAL FORMS |
|---|---|---|
| **haber:** | habr | habría, habrías, habría, habríamos, habríais, habrían |
| **poder:** | podr | podría, podrías, podría, podríamos, podríais, podrían |
| **querer:** | querr | querría, querrías, querría, querríamos, querríais, querrían |
| **saber:** | sabr | sabría, sabrías, sabría, sabríamos, sabríais, sabrían |
| **poner:** | pondr | pondría, pondrías, pondría, pondríamos, pondríais, pondrían |
| **tener:** | tendr | tendría, tendrías, tendría, tendríamos, tendríais, tendrían |
| **salir:** | saldr | saldría, saldrías, saldría, saldríamos, saldríais, saldrían |
| **venir:** | vendr | vendría, vendrías, vendría, vendríamos, vendríais, vendrían |
| **decir:** | dir | diría, dirías, diría, diríamos, diríais, dirían |
| **hacer:** | har | haría, harías, haría, haríamos, haríais, harían |

The use of the conditional in Spanish is similar to the use of the construction *would* + verb in English.[1] The only difference is that Spanish may also use the conditional to express probability in the past.

| | |
|---|---|
| Yo **saldría** temprano. | *I would leave early.* |
| **Serían** las diez de la mañana. | *It was probably ten in the morning.* |

The conditional and the imperfect subjunctive are used in *if* sentences expressing a condition that is unlikely to happen or contrary to fact in the present.

| | |
|---|---|
| Si yo consiguiera el dinero, pagaría la cuenta. | *If I were to get the money I would pay the bill.* (It is unlikely that I get the money.) |
| Si yo tuviera el dinero, pagaría la cuenta. | *If I had the money, I would pay the bill.* (I don't have the money.) |

# IDENTIFICACIÓN

Identifique el condicional en las siguientes oraciones.

1. Debería comer más frutas y verduras.
2. Iría a México si tuviera dos semanas de vacaciones.
3. Nosotros vendíamos boletos para los conciertos de rock.
4. Andrés vivía y trabajaba cerca de su casa y por eso no tenía que viajar largas distancias.
5. Dijo que escribiría desde Madrid.

# COMPRENSIÓN

### Un joven indeciso

Lea la siguiente selección sobre Jorge Hermida, un joven que nunca está muy seguro de lo que debe hacer.

A Jorge le encantaban las fiestas y también le gustaba viajar, pero no tenía mucho dinero. Un día estaba caminando por la calle y pasó por un quiosco donde vendían billetes de lotería. Era el sorteo° más importante del año con un premio de cien millones de pesos. A Jorge le gustó uno de los números y pensó que sería una buena idea comprarlo y probar su suerte.

Por su mente° pasaron todas las cosas que podría hacer con el dinero del primer premio. ¿Iría a la India o a Egipto? ¿Visitaría la Antártida o Australia? ¿Cuánto tiempo estaría en la América del Sur? ¿Invitaría a sus amigos a una

*drawing*

*mind*

---

[1] When *would* implies *used to,* the imperfect is used. Yo salía temprano.     *I would (used to) leave early.*

fiesta en su yate o en un hotel? ¿Qué orquesta tocaría en su fiesta? ¿Se compraría una casa en la playa o un apartamento de lujo en la ciudad? ¿Qué auto deportivo compraría? ¿Qué les regalaría a sus padres? ¿Y a su novia? ¿Cuánto dinero daría a obras de caridad°? ¿Viviría parte del año en Europa o en Hawaii? ¿Cuánto tendría que pagar de impuestos°?

*charity*
*taxes*

Todo esto le pareció muy complicado y no compró el billete. Era más fácil vivir con poco dinero y sin complicaciones.

## Preguntas

1. ¿Es Jorge rico o pobre?
2. ¿Dónde vio Jorge los billetes de lotería?
3. ¿Cuánto dinero podía ganar?
4. ¿Qué lugares pensaba visitar?
5. ¿Qué prefería Jorge, una casa o un apartamento?
6. ¿Compró Jorge el billete? ¿Por qué?
7. ¿Está usted de acuerdo con lo que hizo Jorge? ¿Por qué?
8. ¿Qué haría usted con cien millones de dólares?

## Unos regalos para los novios

En este anuncio se ofrecen ciertas ventajas a los novios que celebren su boda (*wedding*) en un hotel. El anuncio menciona a los padrinos de la boda. En los países hispanos el padrino es la persona que acompaña a la novia al altar. Generalmente es el padre de la novia. La madrina de la boda está en el altar con el novio y generalmente es su madre.

Las siguientes palabras le podrán ayudar a entender mejor el anuncio.

| | |
|---|---|
| traslado | *transportation* |
| Dpto. | *abbreviation for* departamento |

## ¿Verdadero o falso?

Diga si las siguientes oraciones son verdaderas o falsas de acuerdo con el anuncio.

1. El hotel invita a comer sólo a los novios.
2. El menú más barato del hotel cuesta 4.500 pesos.
3. Si los novios celebran la boda en el hotel, reciben un auto de regalo.
4. El hotel les ofrece a los novios una habitación muy elegante sin pagar.
5. Los novios pueden pasar una semana en el hotel.

## Las corridas de toros

La siguiente selección es sobre las corridas de toros, un espectáculo emocionante y muy popular en algunos países hispanos.

Se cree que hay que buscar el origen de las corridas de toros en la isla de Creta hace unos 6.000 años y que los gladiadores de Julio César lidiaban° toros en el Coliseo de Roma en el siglo I a.C°. Poco a poco este enfrentamiento de hombre y fiera° fue cambiando hasta llegar a la corrida o fiesta brava tal como existe hoy en día en España y en cinco países hispanoamericanos: México, Perú, Ecuador, Colombia y Venezuela. Portugal y Francia también tienen corridas, pero en estos países no se mata° al toro.

*fought*
siglo... *1st century B.C.*
*beast*

no... *is not killed*

Una corrida de toros en la ciudad de México.

Las corridas empiezan puntualmente a la hora que indica el programa—a las cuatro y media, cinco o seis de la tarde, para que el sol no sea tan fuerte—y duran° unas tres horas. Generalmente participan tres toreros y cada uno lidia dos toros. Éstos son de una raza agresiva y fuerte que se cría° únicamente para las corridas. — *last* / *se... is bred*

La entrada de los toreros con sus cuadrillas°, el ritmo alegre y vibrante de la música, la emoción de los aficionados y el duelo entre el torero y el toro crean un ambiente° por completo diferente al que existe en una competencia deportiva. — *teams* / *atmosphere*

La fiesta brava tiene sus aficionados y detractores. Para los aficionados, el toreo no es un deporte. Es un arte donde el hombre se enfrenta a la fiera demostrando su destreza° y su valor ante la muerte°. Para sus detractores, es un acto bárbaro e inhumano, donde se tortura y se mata a un animal. Según ellos, deberían prohibirse las corridas pues sólo sirven para mostrar los peores instintos del ser humano y no deberían ser un espectáculo de países civilizados. — *dexterity / death*

## ¿Verdadero o falso?

Diga si las siguientes oraciones son verdaderas o falsas según la selección anterior.

1. La corrida de toros existe hace muchos años.
2. Los romanos lidiaban toros.
3. Hay corridas en todos los países hispanos.
4. En una corrida generalmente hay seis toros.
5. Puede usarse cualquier toro en una corrida.
6. Las corridas son por la mañana.
7. Los aficionados creen que la corrida es el mejor deporte.
8. Los detractores de la fiesta brava quieren que no haya corridas.

## Para completar

Complete las siguientes oraciones según la información que se da en la selección sobre las corridas.

1. Las corridas de toros empezaron en...
2. En las corridas de Portugal y Francia...
3. Los países hispanos donde hay corridas de toros son...
4. Los toros que se usan en las corridas son...
5. Los aficionados creen que la corrida de toros es...
6. Los detractores creen que la corrida de toros es...

Éste es un pequeño artículo periodístico sobre un día muy especial que se celebra en Madrid. Las siguientes palabras le podrán ayudar a entenderlo mejor.

meta = objetivo      lucha *fight*

### El domingo se celebra la XI fiesta de la bicicleta

La organización de esta fiesta deportiva espera que participen alrededor de trescientos mil ciclistas. Los aficionados al deporte del pedal ocuparán las calles de Madrid durante tres horas y media, en una fiesta que es ya muy popular entre los madrileños. No se trata de obtener meta alguna, sino de luchar, al menos durante un día, contra el ruido y la contaminación, promover el ejercicio físico y afirmar que la ciudad puede ser una ciudad habitable y solidaria.

Durante estas tres horas, los organizadores recomiendan no utilizar los automóviles por las calles por las que pasará el pelotón deportivo, que recorrerá un total de veintiocho kilómetros.

### Preguntas

Conteste las siguientes preguntas sobre el artículo.

1. ¿Cuándo va a ser la fiesta?
2. ¿Cuánto tiempo dura?
3. ¿Cuál es el objetivo de esta fiesta?
4. ¿Cuántas personas van a tomar parte?
5. ¿Qué le piden los organizadores al público?
6. ¿Qué le parece esta fiesta a usted? Explique por qué.

## SITUACIONES

1. Invite your partner to a party: (a) give date, time, and location, and (b) say that he/she can bring a friend. Your partner should accept and ask some pertinent questions.
2. Invite your partner to go to a concert. Your partner should decline and explain why.
3. Tell your partner what you used to do for Halloween when you were a child and what you liked the most. Then your partner should tell you about the way he/she celebrated Halloween.
4. You are going to have a party. Tell your partner (a) whom you will invite, (b) the food and drinks you will serve, (c) the music you will have, and (d) what you are going to do afterward.
5. A recent immigrant wants to find out what Thanksgiving is. Explain to that person (a) when it is celebrated, (b) why it is celebrated, (c) how people celebrate it, and (d) what the traditional foods are for that occasion.
6. You don't know what **el Día de los Reyes Magos** is. Ask your partner (a) what it is, (b) when it is celebrated, and (c) where.
7. You were invited to a party. Explain to your partner that you don't want to go because (a) your former girl/boyfriend is going to be there, (b) you don't like to dance, and (c) you have a test the following day. Your partner will try to convince you by telling you that (a) many of your friends are going to be there and (b) you are going to have a good time.

El ''Cortijo Bacardi''
tiene el honor de invitarle al
concierto de canto que
ofrecerá la soprano

## M.ª José González
acompañada del pianista

## Manuel del Campo
que tendrá lugar el
próximo viernes 25 de
Septiembre a las 20,30 h.

''Cortijo Bacardi''
Bacardí y Cía., S. A., España
Polígono Industrial Santa Teresa

### Málaga, 1987

Confirmar asistencia
al teléfono 33 02 00

# VOCABULARIO[2]

**las fiestas**

| | |
|---|---|
| la banda | *band* |
| la bandera | *flag* |
| el desfile | *parade* |
| la sorpresa | *surprise* |

**las personas**

| | |
|---|---|
| el grupo | *group* |
| la juventud | *youth* |

**en el mundo moderno**

| | |
|---|---|
| la comodidad | *comfort* |
| la droga | *drug* |
| la inconformidad | *dissatisfaction* |
| la libertad | *liberty, freedom* |
| el sexo | *sex* |
| la violencia | *violence* |

**la música**

| | |
|---|---|
| la melodía | *melody* |

**en el campo**

| | |
|---|---|
| la finca | *farm* |

**tiempo**

| | |
|---|---|
| la época | *time, epoch* |
| hoy en día | *nowadays* |

**descripciones**

| | |
|---|---|
| horrible | *horrible* |
| suave | *soft* |
| terrible | *terrible* |

**verbos**

| | |
|---|---|
| celebrar | *to celebrate* |
| disfrazarse | *to wear a costume* |
| divertirse (ie, i) | *to have a good time* |
| existir | *to exist, to be* |
| felicitar | *to congratulate* |
| había | *there was, there were* |
| imaginarse | *to imagine* |
| mover (ue) | *to move* |
| organizar | *to organize* |
| recordar (ue) | *to remember, to remind* |
| respetar | *to respect* |
| reunirse | *to get together* |

**palabras útiles**

| | |
|---|---|
| definitivamente | *definitely* |
| felicidades | *congratulations* |
| hasta | *even* |

**expresiones útiles**

| | |
|---|---|
| de todas formas | *anyway* |
| estar enamorado/a | *to be in love* |
| por supuesto | *of course* |
| ¡qué barbaridad! | *it's amazing!, good grief!* |
| ¡qué pena! | *what a pity!* |
| quedar en + inf. | *to agree to + verb* |

---

[2] See pages 364, 365, and 366 for holidays.

**In** Lección 16 **you will**
a. describe physical conditions and the environment.
b. report facts in the present and past.
c. express disappointment.
d. give opinions.

# Los efectos de un terremoto

un fuego/incendio

el humo

un herido
una camilla

la Cruz Roja

## ¿Una ciudad moderna o un infierno?

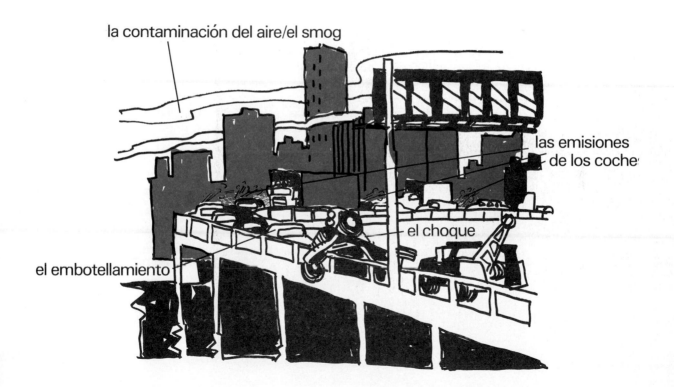

la contaminación del aire/el smog

las emisiones de los coches

el choque

el embotellamiento

## *ACTIVIDADES*

**A** Complete las siguientes oraciones de acuerdo con el primer dibujo.

1. Si la tierra se movió y se cayeron algunos edificios tuvimos un...
2. Llamamos a los bomberos cuando hay...
3. Una organización que ayuda en casos de emergencia es la...
4. Después de un accidente acuestan a los heridos en...
5. El vehículo que generalmente se usa para llevar a los heridos al hospital es la...

**B** Complete las siguientes oraciones de acuerdo con el segundo dibujo.

1. Muchas personas se enferman y no pueden respirar bien por...
2. Cuando hay muchos autos que casi no se pueden mover decimos que hay un...
3. A veces las personas tienen dolor de oídos por...
4. Es necesario inspeccionar los autos para controlar...
5. Si un auto le da a otro hay un...

**C** Diga qué cosas debe hacer o no debe hacer usted en caso de un fuego.

usar el ascensor / abrir todas las puertas interiores / tocar una puerta interior antes de abrirla / si la puerta está caliente, tratar de buscar otra salida / abrir una ventana y pedir ayuda / llamar a los bomberos / poner la televisión para ver un buen programa / si entra humo por debajo de la puerta, poner una toalla húmeda / llamar a los amigos para decirles lo que está pasando / si no puede salir, ponerse en una ventana

**D** Prepare con su compañero/a una lista de cosas que se deben hacer para evitar la contaminación del aire. Comparen su lista con la de otros compañeros.

*Modelo* **usar menos el auto**

San Juan, igual que casi todas las ciudades importantes, tiene problemas de tráfico.

## Cultura

### Catástrofes y problemas ambientales en el mundo hispano

Los países hispanos ocupan grandes extensiones de tierra con diferentes climas y características geográficas. En muchos de estos países existen los mismos problemas ambientales y catástrofes, pero debido a sus diferentes características geográficas, los problemas también varían.

En la América del Sur, la cordillera° de los Andes se extiende a lo largo de la costa oeste y sus montañas dificultan las comunicaciones entre las diferentes regiones. En algunas el desarrollo agrícola resulta imposible debido a la altura. Pero además los Andes son una zona sísmica muy activa y los terremotos han° afectado extensas zonas de la América del Sur. En 1946, un terremoto destruyó Lima, la capital del Perú, y en 1970 otro terremoto y un alud° causaron unos 50.000 muertos° en este país. En Ecuador, unas 6.000 personas murieron en el terremoto de 1949 y en Colombia, en 1985, la erupción del volcán Nevado del Ruiz causó inundaciones y la ciudad de Armero quedó cubierta por el lodo° con la pérdida° de más de 20.000 vidas. Las imágenes de dolor y muerte que presentó la televisión afectaron a todos los que las vieron al mostrar la destrucción que pueden causar estas catástrofes.

En la América Central y México existe una situación similar. Los terremotos han destruido gran parte de la ciudad de Managua tres veces, en 1885, en 1931 y en 1972. En Guatemala, en 1773, un terremoto destruyó la antigua° capital y en 1976 otro terremoto dejó más de 22.000 muertos y 74.000 heridos. El terremoto de 1985 de la ciudad de México causó

Una de las muchas casas y edificios que destruyó el terremoto de 1985 en la ciudad de México.

unos 4.000 muertos y destruyó muchos edificios dejando sin hogar° a numerosas familias.

Además de las catástrofes mencionadas anteriormente, hay también serios problemas ambientales que afectan a muchas ciudades hispanas. Según los expertos, la ciudad de México tiene el peor caso de contaminación del aire del mundo. Hoy en día hay un programa vo-

cordillera *mountain range*   han *have*   alud *landslide*   muertos *dead*   lodo *mud*   pérdida *loss*   antigua *former*
hogar *home*

luntario para que las personas no usen el automóvil un día a la semana, pero se necesitan medidas más estrictas para proteger la salud de la población y la riqueza° artística y arquitectónica de esta ciudad. Un plan que se propone es la prohibición del tráfico por algunas zonas del centro como el Zócalo (la plaza cen-tral) y sus alrededores°, donde se encuentran la catedral, muchos edificios coloniales y los últimos descubrimientos del Templo Mayor de los aztecas. Las Naciones Unidas declararon esta área como patrimonio de la humanidad y debe conservarse para las generaciones futuras.

riqueza *wealth*   alrededores *surrounding areas*

Dos hombres socorren a una joven que estuvo enterrada en el lodo, en la ciudad de Armero en Colombia como resultado de la erupción del volcán Nevado del Ruiz.

# EN CONTEXTO

## Las últimas noticias°

| | | |
|---|---|---|
| **Bernardo** | ¿Han oído° las últimas noticias? | |
| **Margot** | No, no hemos oído nada. | |
| **Bernardo** | Hubo° un terremoto en San Salvador. Parece que ha sido muy fuerte. | |
| **Teresa** | ¡Qué horror! ¿Hay muchos muertos y heridos? | |
| **Bernardo** | Todavía no se sabe, pero por lo menos doscientos. | |
| **Margot** | ¡Dios mío! Y como siempre los más afectados van a ser los pobres. | |
| **Bernardo** | Hay muchos edificios destruidos. La Cruz Roja ha mandado tiendas de campaña°. Además están pidiendo donaciones en efectivo, pero se pueden mandar mantas, ropa, medicinas... | |
| **Teresa** | Dentro de un rato° empieza el noticiero° de la tarde. ¿Por qué no vamos a casa a verlo? | |

Las... *The latest news*

Han... *Have you heard*

Hubo° *There was*

ha... *has sent tents*

Dentro... *in a while/newscast*

## Preguntas

1. ¿Han oído Margot y Teresa las últimas noticias?
2. ¿Quién les da las noticias?
3. ¿Qué noticias les da?
4. ¿Hay muertos y heridos?
5. ¿Quiénes son siempre los más afectados en los terremotos?
6. ¿Qué ha mandado la Cruz Roja?
7. ¿Qué otras cosas piden?
8. ¿Cuándo va a empezar el noticiero de la tarde?

## otras catástrofes

| | |
|---|---|
| el huracán | *hurricane* |
| la inundación | *flood* |
| la lluvia ácida | *acid rain* |
| la sequía | *drought* |
| el tornado | *tornado* |

La cordillera de los Andes, Chile

## *ACTIVIDADES*

**A** Asocie las catástrofes y problemas ambientales de la columna de la izquierda con las acciones de la columna de la derecha.

1. un huracán
2. un terremoto
3. una inundación
4. una sequía
5. un tornado

a. cerrar puertas y ventanas
b. ir al sótano (*cellar*)
c. no gastar mucha agua
d. buscar lugares altos
e. ponerse debajo de una mesa o del marco de una puerta

**B** ¿Qué debemos hacer durante un terremoto? Prepare una lista con su compañero/a y compárela con la de otros/as estudiantes.

**C** **Entrevista.** Hágale las siguientes preguntas a su compañero/a para saber su opinión sobre los noticieros de la televisión.

1. ¿A qué hora ves el noticiero?   2. ¿En qué canal de la televisión?   3. ¿Ves el noticiero los fines de semana?   4. ¿Crees que los noticieros de la televisión son imparciales y objetivos?   5. ¿Qué harías para mejorar los noticieros?

## GRAMÁTICA

**The past participle**

| INFINITIVE | PAST PARTICIPLE |
|------------|-----------------|
| hablar | hablado (*spoken*) |
| comer | comido (*eaten*) |
| vivir | vivido (*lived*) |

**1.** All past participles of **-ar** verbs end in **-ado.**
**2.** Past participles of **-er** and **-ir** verbs end in **-ido,** except the following:

| | | | |
|---|---|---|---|
| hacer | hecho | abrir | abierto |
| poner | puesto | escribir | escrito |
| romper (*to break*) | roto | cubrir | cubierto |
| ver | visto | decir | dicho |
| volver | vuelto | morir | muerto |

**3.** Compounds of verbs with irregular past participles normally have the same irregularity.

describir → descrito    posponer → pospuesto

**4.** If the stem of an **-er** or **-ir** verb ends in **a, e,** or **o,** place a written accent mark over the **i** of **ido** to indicate that no diphthong is formed.

traer → traído    creer → creído    oír → oído

## The present perfect

Form the present perfect of the indicative by using the present tense of **haber** (*to have*) as an auxiliary verb with the past participle of the main verb. **Tener** is never used as auxiliary verb in forming the perfect tenses.

| PRESENT TENSE | | |
|---|---|---|
| | **haber** | PAST PARTICIPLE |
| yo | he | |
| tú | has | hablado |
| él, ella, usted | ha | comido |
| nosotros/as | hemos | vivido |
| vosotros/as | habéis | |
| ellos/as, ustedes | han | |

(+ between haber and past participle columns)

**1.** In general, you can use the present perfect in Spanish in the same instances that you would use the present perfect in English.

**2.** Normally no word intervenes between the auxiliary verb **haber** and the past participle.

Yo nunca **he estado** aquí.                *I have never been here.*

**3.** Place object and reflexive pronouns before the auxiliary verb **hacer.**

—¿Has visto a Juan? —No, no **lo** he visto.
—¿**Se** han lavado? —Sí, ya **nos** hemos lavado.

**4.** The present perfect of **hay** is **ha habido.**

**Ha habido** mucha contaminación          *There has been a lot of smog lately.*
últimamente.

**5.** Use the present tense of **acabar** + **de** + infinitive, not the present perfect, to state that something *has just* happened.

**Acabo de oír** las noticias.              *I've just heard the news.*

## ACTIVIDADES

**A** Dígale a su compañero/a las cosas que usted no ha hecho de cada grupo. Después su compañero/a debe decirle a usted las cosas que él/ella no ha hecho.

1. Yo nunca he estado en
   a. un terremoto.
   b. un tornado.
   c. un huracán.

2. Yo nunca he montado en
   a. bicicleta.
   b. avión.
   c. un elefante.

3. Yo nunca he corrido en
   a. las Olimpiadas.
   b. el estadio de la universidad.
   c. un parque.

4. Yo nunca he visto
   a. una jirafa.
   b. un cocodrilo.
   c. una llama.

5. Yo nunca he roto
   a. un plato.
   b. un vaso.
   c. un estéreo.

6. Yo nunca he dicho
   a. una mala palabra.
   b. una mentira.
   c. palabras en chino.

**B** Usted ha estado muy ocupado/a hoy. Diga que usted ha hecho todo lo que sigue.

***Modelo*** preparar el desayuno
**He preparado el desayuno.**

1. terminar la tarea
2. escuchar un casete
3. limpiar la casa
4. correr por el parque
5. oír las noticias
6. ir al mercado
7. leer el periódico
8. ver televisión
9. escribirle a una amiga
10. lavarse los dientes dos veces

**C** Pregúntele a su compañero/a si ha hecho lo siguiente.

***Modelo*** estudiar las lecciones
**Usted ¿Has estudiado las lecciones hoy?**
**Compañero/a Sí, ya he estudiado las lecciones** o **Sí, ya las he estudiado** o **No, no las he estudiado todavía.**

1. ir a la biblioteca
2. comer
3. hablar con tu profesor
4. hacer ejercicio
5. comprar los libros nuevos

**D** Joaquín es un atleta excelente. Dígale a su compañero/a cinco cosas que ha hecho para ser tan buen atleta.

***Modelo*** **Joaquín ha practicado todos los días.**

**E** Usted y un/a amigo/a van a hacer un viaje, pero no han organizado nada. Su compañero/a le va a hacer las siguientes preguntas. Conteste diciendo que no lo han hecho todavía.

*Modelo*   Compañero/a   **¿Han hecho las reservaciones?**
    Usted   **No las hemos hecho todavía.**

1. ¿Han ido a la agencia de viajes?
2. ¿Han llamado a la línea aérea?
3. ¿Han hecho las maletas?
4. ¿Han comprado los cheques de viajero?
5. ¿Qué han hecho entonces?

**F** Usted es el jefe/la jefa de una oficina y quiere saber si sus empleados han hecho las siguientes cosas. Su compañero/a va a hacer el papel de su secretario/a.

*Modelo*   terminar el proyecto
        Usted   **¿Terminaron el proyecto?**
    Secretario/a   **Sí, ya lo terminaron** o **Todavía no lo han terminado.**

1. traer el papel de cartas
2. programar la computadora
3. hacer las fotocopias

4. llamar a los clientes
5. invitar al Sr. Alonso
6. pedir los programas

**G** Dígale a su compañero/a todo lo que usted ha hecho esta mañana.

**H** Ha habido un terremoto y su padre le pide que haga varias cosas. Dígale que Ud. acaba de hacerlas.

*Modelo*   Padre   **Hijo/a, llena la bañera de agua.**
    Usted   **Acabo de llenarla, papá.**

1. Desconecta la electricidad.
2. Apaga el gas.
3. Llama a tus abuelos.
4. Pregúntales a los vecinos si necesitan algo.
5. Pon a los animales en el garaje.
6. Revisa (*check*) la casa.

**I** Sus amigos salen de diferentes lugares. ¿Qué cree usted que acaban de hacer?

*Modelo*   Juan sale del estadio.
        **Acaba de ver un partido de fútbol.**

1. Maricarmen sale de una discoteca.
2. Pedro sale de un café.
3. Mercedes y Paula salen de la biblioteca.
4. Humberto sale de la cocina.
5. Jorge y Ricardo salen de una tienda.

# EN CONTEXTO

## Los efectos de un huracán

El huracán va a pasar por la ciudad. Los vecinos están asustados y se están preparando.

A las cinco el huracán había pasado por la ciudad. El supermercado está destruido. Las calles están inundadas. Los cristales de algunas ventanas están rotos.

## ACTIVIDADES

**A** Usted está de vacaciones en casa de unos amigos en Miami. Según las últimas noticias, es probable que un huracán pase esa noche por la ciudad. Para estar preparados, diga qué cosas de la siguiente lista deben o no deben hacer.

> **Modelo**   poner al gato en la terraza
> **No debemos poner al gato en la terraza.**

1. comprar comida
2. sacar el auto del garaje
3. tener una linterna (*flashlight*)
4. dejar al perro en el jardín
5. cubrir las ventanas
6. ir al cine
7. cerrar bien las puertas
8. tener agua en la casa
9. comprar pilas (*batteries*)
10. sacar la basura a la acera

**B** Piense en una experiencia o momento difícil de su vida (accidente, terremoto, etc.). Dígale a otro/a estudiante (a) cuál fue su experiencia, (b) cuándo ocurrió, (c) dónde ocurrió y (d) qué hizo usted.

# GRAMÁTICA

## The past perfect

Form the past perfect with the imperfect tense of **haber** as an auxiliary verb and the past participle of the main verb.

| IMPERFECT | | |
|---|---|---|
| | **haber** | PAST PARTICIPLE |
| yo | había | |
| tú | habías | hablado |
| él, ella, usted | había | comido |
| nosotros/as | habíamos | vivido |
| vosotros/as | habíais | |
| ellos/as, ustedes | habían | |

With a `+` sign between the haber column and the past participle column.

1. In general, you can use the past perfect in Spanish as you would use the past perfect in English.
2. The past perfect describes an action completed in the past before another event.

| | |
|---|---|
| La fiesta **había terminado** cuando llegamos. | *The party had ended when we arrived.* |
| Todos **se habían ido** a las dos. | *Everyone had left at two.* |

## Past participles used as adjectives

1. When a past participle is used as an adjective, it agrees with the noun it modifies.

| | |
|---|---|
| un apartamento **alquilado** | *a rented apartment* |
| una puerta **cerrada** | *a closed door* |
| los libros **abiertos** | *the open books* |
| las ventanas **rotas** | *the broken windows* |

2. Spanish uses **estar** + the past participle to express a state or condition resulting from a prior action.

| ACTION | RESULT |
|---|---|
| El huracán destruyó el edificio. | El edificio está **destruido.** |
| El terremoto asustó a la gente. | La gente estaba **asustada.** |

**3.** Use **estar** + past participle to describe a position. In this case English uses an -*ing* verb.

El señor está **parado.**  *The man is standing.*
La gente estaba **sentada.**  *The people were sitting.*

## ACTIVIDADES

**A** Usted llega tarde a una fiesta. Diga qué habían hecho los invitados antes de que usted llegara.

*Modelo*  bailar salsa
Ya habían bailado salsa.

1. escuchar a Julio Iglesias
2. comerse toda la comida
3. irse muchas personas
4. hablar de los exámenes
5. cantar canciones cubanas
6. tomarse todos los refrescos
7. ver un vídeo
8. contar chistes (*tell jokes*)

**B** Pregúntele a su compañero/a lo que había hecho antes de 1990.

*Modelo*  **Usted**  **¿Habías ido a Europa?**
**Compañero/a**  **Sí, ya había ido en 1989.**

1. vivir en tu propio apartamento
2. estar en un terremoto
3. comprar un auto
4. estudiar una lengua extranjera
5. viajar en avión
6. hacer un viaje largo
7. ganar mucho dinero
8. jugar vóleibol
9. visitar otros estados
10. tomar buenas fotos

**C** Ayer fue un día muy feliz para la Sra. Jiménez. Cuando ella volvió a su casa después del trabajo encontró que no tenía que hacer nada en la casa. Diga qué habían hecho los diferentes miembros de la familia.

*Modelo*  su esposo / cocinar para toda la familia
**Su esposo había cocinado para toda la familia.**

1. su madre / lavar la ropa sucia
2. su hija Carmen / limpiar la casa
3. su hijo mayor / poner la mesa
4. su hijo menor / sacar al perro
5. su hija Diana / hacer su postre favorito

**D** Ayer fue un día terrible para usted. Diga las cosas que habían pasado cuando llegó a su casa.

1. Mi perro...
2. Mi vecino...
3. Mi hermano/a...
4. El cartero...
5. Mi novio/a...

**E** Usted entra en el cuarto de su mejor amigo/a y observa que está muy desordenado (*messy*). Diga cómo están los objetos de la columna de la izquierda usando **(no) está(n)** y la forma correcta de los participios de la columna de la derecha.

*Modelo*    la puerta del armario    abierto
            **La puerta del armario está abierta**

| | |
|---|---|
| el espejo del armario | roto |
| la cama | tendido |
| los libros de las clases | abierto |
| la ropa | colgado |
| el televisor | encendido |
| las ventanas | cerrado |

**F** Un huracán terrible pasó por la ciudad. Usted llega al día siguiente y ve los efectos del haracán. Descríbale a un/a amigo/a lo que usted vio.

*Modelo*    Inundó las calles.
            Las calles estaban inundadas.

1. Rompió las ventanas de las casas.
2. Destruyó muchos edificios.
3. Tumbó (*knocked down*) muchos árboles.
4. Interrumpió las comunicaciones.
5. Asustó a los animales.
6. Dañó (*damaged*) muchos autos y camiones.

**G** Usted le va a describir una fiesta a su compañero/a. Trate de usar algunos participios en su descripción.

*Modelo*    **Hay tres chicos parados al lado del estéreo.**

## EN CONTEXTO

### Peligro° de incendio                                                      *Danger*

| | | |
|---|---|---|
| **Guardia** | Lo siento mucho, pero tienen que apagar° el fuego. | *put out* |
| **Miguel** | Está bien, pero siempre hemos encendido el fuego aquí. | |
| **Guardia** | Sí, pero no llueve hace varios meses y el bosque° está muy seco°. Por eso se prohíbe hacer fuegos aquí. Es muy peligroso porque todo esto se puede quemar° fácilmente. | *forest* *dry* *burn* |
| **Hugo** | ¡Qué pena! ¿Y qué vamos a hacer con toda esta carne? | |
| **Guardia** | Se la pueden llevar° a un lugar un poco más arriba°. Allí hay barbacoas y se puede cocinar sin peligro. | Se... *You can take it /* más... *higher up* |
| **Mariana** | Pues a guardar° la comida y recoger° los platos. | *put away / pick up* |
| **Hugo** | Y yo apago el fuego. | |
| **Guardia** | Disculpen la molestia°. | Disculpen... *Sorry for the inconvenience* |
| **Miguel** | No se preocupe. Hay que evitar los incendios. | |

## Para completar

Complete las siguientes oraciones con la información que se da en el diálogo.

1. Los jóvenes están...
2. El guardia les dice que deben...
3. Hace varios meses que...
4. El bosque está...
5. Las barbacoas están...
6. Allí se puede cocinar sin...
7. Los muchachos van a guardar...
8. Ellos quieren evitar...

## ACTIVIDADES

**A** Usted y su compañero/a van a hacer una excursión a un bosque. Hagan una lista de las cosas que van a llevar.

**B** Cuando usted era pequeño/a usted pertenecía a los niños/as exploradores/as (*Boy/Girl Scouts*). Diga las cosas que ustedes hacían.

**C** Usted está a cargo de una casa muy antigua que está abierta al público. En la casa no se permite fumar, pero uno de los visitantes está fumando. Complete el siguiente diálogo con su compañero/a.

| | |
|---|---|
| **Usted** | Lo siento, pero ____. |
| **Visitante** | Perdone, no lo sabía. ¿Dónde ____? |
| **Usted** | Se puede fumar en ____. |
| **Visitante** | ¿Dónde está ____? |
| **Usted** | ... |

Unos niños exploradores en la ciudad de Mérida en Yucatán. En esta región de México se pueden visitar muchas de las ciudades que los mayas construyeron antes de la llegada de los españoles.

# GRAMÁTICA

## Direct and indirect object pronouns

1. When both a direct and an indirect object pronoun are used in the same sentence, the indirect object pronoun precedes the direct object pronoun.

   **a.** Place double object pronouns before conjugated verbs and negative commands.

   Ella me da el libro.  ⟶  Ella **me lo** da.
   No me des el libro.  ⟶  No **me lo** des.

   **b.** Place them after and attach to affirmative commands, infinitives, and present participles. Note the written accent over the stressed syllable.

   Dame el libro.  ⟶  Dá**melo**.
   Él quiere darme el libro.  ⟶  Él quiere dár**melo**.
       Él **me lo** quiere dar.
   Está comprándote el libro.  ⟶  Está comprándo**telo**.
       **Te lo** está comprando.

2. This combination of direct and indirect object pronouns is often used when the direct object noun has already been mentioned.

   —¿**Me** prestas **el libro**? —Sí, **te lo** presto.      *"Would you lend me the book?" "Yes, I'll lend it to you."*

   —¿Va a dar**te la mesa**? —Sí, va a dár**mela.**      *"Is he going to give you the table?" "Yes, he's going to give it to me."*

   —¿**Le** pido **un taxi**? —Sí, pída**melo,** por favor.      *"Shall I call you a taxi?" "Yes, call it for me, please."*

3. **Le** or **les** cannot be used with **lo, los, la,** or **las**. Change **le** or **les** to **se**.

   **Le** da **un regalo.**  ⟶  **Se lo** da.      *He gives it to her.*
   **Les** voy a mandar **una tarjeta.**  ⟶  **Se la** voy a mandar.      *I'm going to send it to them.*

4. You may use the prepositional phrase **a** + pronoun to clarify or emphasize the indirect object pronoun.

   —Alfredo **me lo** dio a **mí.**      *"Alfredo gave it to me."*
   —No, él **se lo** dio a **ella**.      *"No, he gave it to her."*

5. When a direct object pronoun and a reflexive pronoun are together, the reflexive pronoun precedes the direct object pronoun.

   **Me** lavo **las manos.**  ⟶  **Me las** lavo.
   Juan **se** lava **la cara**.  ⟶  **Se la** lava.

## *ACTIVIDADES*

**A** Unas personas necesitan varias cosas que Agustín tiene. Usted debe decir si Agustín se las presta o no, escogiendo la respuesta adecuada entre las que se dan en la columna de la derecha.

> *Modelo*   Juan necesita unos discos.
> **Sí, se los presta** o **No, no se los presta.**

1. Alfredo necesita una chaqueta.
2. Nuria necesita seiscientas pesetas.
3. Sus hermanos necesitan un diccionario.
4. Narciso necesita diez dólares.

a. Sí, se lo presta. No, no se lo presta.
b. Sí, se la presta. No, no se la presta.
c. Sí, se los presta. No, no se los presta.
d. Sí, se las presta. No, no se las presta.

**B** Ha habido un terremoto muy fuerte en la ciudad de Guatemala. Su compañero/a le pregunta si la Cruz Roja va a mandar ciertas cosas. Conteste usando los pronombres de objeto directo e indirecto.

> *Modelo*   **Compañero/a**   ¿La Cruz Roja les va a mandar camillas?
> **Usted**   **Sí, se las va a mandar** o **No, no se las va a mandar.**

1. ¿La Cruz Roja les va a mandar mantas?
2. ¿Les va a mandar dinero?
3. ¿Les va a mandar antibióticos?
4. ¿Les va a mandar tiendas de campaña?
5. ¿Les va a mandar ropa?
6. ¿Les va a mandar zapatos?

**C** Conteste las siguientes preguntas de acuerdo con los dibujos.

> *Modelo*
> ¿Le explica la lección al director?
> **No, no se la explica a él.**
> ¿Les explica la lección a los alumnos?
> **Sí, se la explica a ellos.**

1. ¿Le da un regalo a su madre?
   ¿Le da un regalo a su profesor?
   ¿Le da un regalo a su novia?

2. ¿Les escribe una carta a sus padres?
   ¿Le escribe una carta a su mejor amiga?
   ¿Le escribe una carta a su novio?

3. ¿Les sirve la comida a sus amigas?
   ¿Les sirve la comida a los clientes?
   ¿Les sirve la comida a sus hijos?

**D** **Diálogo.** Usted trabaja de guía de turismo en Buenos Aires. Su jefe/a le va a hacer las siguientes preguntas.

| | |
|---|---|
| **Jefe/a** | ¿Les mostró la ciudad a los turistas? |
| **Usted** | Sí, _____. |
| **Jefe/a** | ¿Les explicó la historia de la ciudad? |
| **Usted** | ... |
| **Jefe/a** | ¿Les contestó las preguntas? |
| **Usted** | ... |
| **Jefe/a** | ¿Les llevó el equipaje al hotel? |
| **Usted** | ... |

**E** Usted está en un hotel muy elegante. El botones lo/la ha llevado a su habitación y le hace las siguientes preguntas.

> *Modelo*   ¿Le dejo la llave sobre la cómoda?
> **Sí, déjemela allí, por favor.**

1. ¿Le abro la ventana?
2. ¿Le enciendo el aire acondicionado?
3. ¿Le pongo el equipaje aquí?
4. ¿Le traigo el periódico?

**F** Su amigo/a está enfermo/a y usted va a su apartamento para ayudarlo/a. Complete el siguiente diálogo con su compañero/a.

> **Usted**   ¿Te tiendo la cama?
> **Amigo/a**   . . .
> **Usted**   ¿Te traigo agua?
> **Amigo/a**   . . .
> **Usted**   ¿Te preparo algo de comer?
> **Amigo/a**   . . .

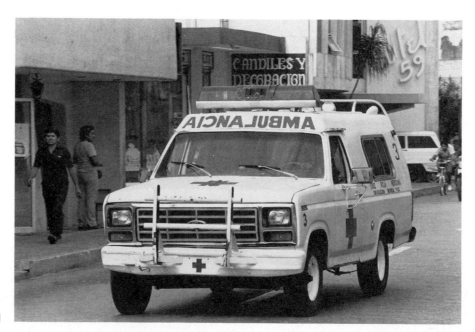

Una ambulancia en
una calle de Mérida.

# LECTURA

*Antes de leer:* **the passive voice**

In the following reading selection, you will encounter the passive voice, which is formed with any tense of the verb **ser** + past participle.

El humo **era producido** por las fábricas. *The smoke was produced by the factories.*

**1.** Use the preposition **por** when telling who performs the action.

El bosque fue destruido.       (*who or what did it is not expressed*)
El bosque fue destruido **por** el fuego.       (*the fire did it*)

**2.** The past participle agrees in gender and number with the subject.

**Los árboles** fueron **destruidos** por la lluvia ácida.
**La casa** fue **construida** el año pasado.

**3.** The passive voice is more common in English than in Spanish. It is found in written Spanish, especially in newspapers and formal writing. However, in conversation, Spanish speakers normally use other constructions.

Vendieron el edificio.                    *They sold the building.*
Se vendió el edificio.                    *The building was sold.*

## IDENTIFICACIÓN

Identifique la voz pasiva en las siguientes oraciones.

1. Las fábricas producen mucho humo.
2. La contaminación es estudiada por los científicos.
3. Los países fueron afectados seriamente.
4. El muchacho se fue a estudiar.
5. Los atletas son entrenados por expertos.

**Murió víctima de un sabotaje**

La siguiente selección fue tomada de una noticia sobre un accidente aéreo que apareció en el periódico español *ABC*. Como usted podrá ver, las oraciones que se usan en los periódicos hispanos son generalmente más largas que las que se usan en los periódicos escritos en inglés.

Las siguientes palabras le podrán ayudar a entender mejor el artículo.

| | |
|---|---|
| dictamen | *opinion* |
| mediante | *by means of* |
| descarta | *rejects* |
| escombros | *debris* |

## Murió víctima de un sabotaje

Éste es el dictamen de la comisión investigadora que ayer hizo público su informe en el que deja completamente claro que el accidente aéreo fue provocado mediante un acto de sabotaje por una persona o grupo desconocidos.

El informe descarta el error humano, señala que el aparato no fue alcanzado por ningún misil, y en base a los restos de antimonio, sodio y potasio encontrados en cantidades anormales entre los escombros del avión dictamina que la única probabilidad que explique el suceso es un sabotaje.

### ¿Verdadero o falso?

Diga si las siguientes oraciones son verdaderas o falsas de acuerdo con la selección.

1. La comisión investigadora ya sabe quién atacó al avión.
2. Un error humano fue la causa del accidente.
3. Los restos de sodio y potasio ayudaron a descubrir la causa del accidente.

## LA ECOLOGÍA

En los últimos años ha aumentado notablemente el interés en la ecología y muchas personas en diferentes países se preocupan ante la situación alarmante que se observa en algunas partes de este planeta.

Durante muchos años, los seres humanos han vivido sin preocuparse por el medio ambiente°. Los ríos, los lagos y el aire que respiramos son contaminados por las industrias. Los derrames de petróleo han causado la muerte de peces° y aves°, especialmente en las costas. Además se han cortado árboles y se han dejado zonas extensas sin replantar, lo que ha aumentado la erosión y ha disminuido las lluvias. Como consecuencia, las tierras° áridas y los desiertos han aumentado en muchos lugares. Por ejemplo, hoy en día en España, se considera que el 25% de su superficie es desierto, mientras que antes las zonas desérticas sólo ocupaban el 8%.

Los grupos ecologistas piensan que todo esto, unido a la lluvia ácida que ha afectado a diversas zonas, es un problema que tenemos que resolver ahora, pues hemos vivido muchos años sin hacer nada para mejorar° la situación.

*environment*

*fish / birds*

*land*

*improve*

## La ecología

### Preguntas

1. ¿Quiénes se preocupan mucho por el medio ambiente?
2. ¿Qué han hecho muchas industrias?
3. ¿Por qué han muerto muchos peces y aves?
4. ¿Qué pasa cuando se cortan muchos árboles y no se replantan?
5. ¿Ha aumentado la zona de desierto en España?
6. Según los grupos ecologistas, ¿cuándo debemos resolver estos problemas?

## OPINIONES

Complete las siguientes oraciones dando su opinión sobre los diferentes temas.

1. Yo creo que es importante tener parques nacionales porque...
2. Es necesario mejorar el aire en las ciudades porque...
3. Todos debemos cuidar los árboles porque...
4. Yo creo que en los aviones (no) se debe prohibir que las personas fumen porque...

### The present perfect subjunctive

Another tense that you should recognize is the present perfect subjunctive. It is formed with the present subjunctive of the verb **haber** + past participle.

| PRESENT SUBJUNCTIVE | | |
|---|---|---|
| **haber** | | PAST PARTICIPLE |
| haya | | |
| hayas | | hablado |
| haya | + | comido |
| hayamos | | vivido |
| hayáis | | |
| hayan | | |

Use this tense to express a completed action in sentences which require the subjunctive. Its English equivalent is normally *have* + past participle, but it may vary according to the context.

| | |
|---|---|
| Ojalá que **haya nevado.** | *I hope it has snowed.* |
| Me alegro que **hayan llegado** temprano. | *I'm glad they arrived early.* |
| Es posible que **hayas ganado.** | *It's possible you may have won.* |

# IDENTIFICACIÓN ▬▬▬▬▬

Identifique el presente perfecto de subjuntivo en las siguientes oraciones.

1. Es necesario que haya más información sobre terremotos.
2. Ojalá que hayan venido a vernos.
3. Han dicho que es un problema serio.
4. Es posible que haya visitado ese lugar.
5. Dudo que haya visto el derrame.

La siguiente selección trata sobre los terremotos y sus efectos físicos y sicológicos.

## Los efectos de un terremoto

Las personas que no han experimentado un terremoto piensan básicamente en la destrucción física que éste ocasiona. Los noticieros de la televisión y las fotos que ven en periódicos y revistas les muestran los edificios destruidos, las familias sin hogar°, las personas heridas o muertas. El impacto, como es natural, es muy fuerte, pero pronto olvidan lo que han visto. En cambio°, cualquier persona que haya estado en un terremoto nunca olvidará la experiencia, pues los terremotos, además de la destrucción física, también pueden causar muchos trastornos° sicológicos.

    Aunque hoy en día existen edificios diseñados para resistir un temblor°, la destrucción causada por un terremoto puede adquirir proporciones catastróficas. Caminos, carreteras, puentes°, en fin, toda la infraestructura necesaria para las comunicaciones sufre serios daños°.

    Probablemente es imposible determinar todos los efectos de un terremoto en las personas. Los niños que hayan experimentado un sismo° pueden sufrir de una variedad de síntomas: no pueden dormir, no quieren ir al baño solos, tienen alguna erupción en la piel o sufren crisis emocionales. En cambio, hay otros niños que no muestran ningún efecto, pero cuando hay otro temblor experimentan síntomas parecidos a los de los primeros. Cuando se pueda saber con anticipación el momento en que va a ocurrir un terremoto se podrán evitar efectos tanto físicos como sicológicos.

*sin... homeless*
*En... On the other hand*

*disorders*
*earthquake*

*bridges*
*damages*

*earthquake*

## ¿Verdadero o falso?

Diga si las siguientes oraciones son verdaderas o falsas, de acuerdo con la selección.

1. Las personas que han estado en un terremoto pueden olvidar esta experiencia fácilmente.
2. Los periódicos, las revistas y la televisión muestran los daños físicos que producen los temblores.
3. Los terremotos pueden afectar sicológicamente a las personas.
4. La destrucción física es más seria que la psicológica.
5. Todos los niños presentan los mismos síntomas después de un terremoto.
6. Hay niños que sólo muestran trastornos sicológicos después de estar en un segundo temblor.

ORENSE, 38 -Suites-

Estimado Cliente:

¡ Bienvenido a ORENSE, 38 -Suites- !

La Dirección de este establecimiento junto con su equipo queremos agradecerle su confianza al elegir nuestro Hotel.

Permítanos Recomendarle:

**EN CASO DE INCENDIO**

Si descubre un incendio:

1.—Comunique rápidamente a Recepción la situación del fuego.

2.—Mantenga la calma, no grite ni corra.
Si se prende su ropa, tiéndase en el suelo y ruede.
Si hay humo abundante gatee.

3.—Abandone su habitación CERRANDO LA PUERTA.
Sitúese en el cuadro indicativo de situación y localice la escalera más próxima.

4.—No utilice los ascensores.

5.—Si los pasillos están bloqueados ponga ropa húmeda en todas las ranuras de su habitación, puerta, aire acondicionado, etc.

6.—Hágase ver por la ventana si es posible sin abrir ésta.

Si usted fuma, no deje el cigarro encendido al acostarse, puede ocasionar un incendio involuntariamente.

Estamos a su entera disposición en cualquier momento de su estancia en esta, SU CASA, o en esta su CIUDAD. No dude en ponerse en contacto con NOSOTROS en cualquier situación anómala.

La Dirección

# SITUACIONES

1. Tell the person sitting next to you (a) that he/she cannot smoke in this area, (b) point out where smoking is permitted, and (c) apologize for the inconvenience.
2. You have been asked to submit a list of things that can be done to improve the environment. Prepare a list with your partner and share it with the class.
3. You are interviewing a famous Spanish writer who lives in the United States. Ask (a) how long ago he/she wrote the first novel, (b) how many he/she has written, (c) how long he/she has been living here, and (d) what his/her favorite book is.
4. You have noticed a fire across the street from your house. You should (a) call the Fire Department, (b) explain what you see, and (c) give them the address. Your partner will answer the phone and ask you some pertinent questions.
5. Some visitors have lit a fire in an area of the forest where fires are prohibited. You will play the part of the forest ranger, and two of your classmates will play the part of the visitors. You should (a) greet the visitors, (b) tell them that fires are prohibited in that area, (c) explain why, (d) ask them to put out the fire, and (e) apologize for the inconvenience and say goodbye. Your classmates should answer accordingly.
6. Tell your partner about an earthquake: (a) when it happened, (b) where you were, and (c) what the condition of the streets, buildings, and people was. Your partner should ask some pertinent questions.

7. You are a client of Banco de Bilbao in Spain and you have been asked to answer a survey regarding the bank's services. Answer the survey according to your experiences at the bank. Then tell your partner (a) what the bank or employees have done to deserve your rating and (b) your suggestions for improvement. You may need the following words to better understand the questionnaire.

| | |
|---|---|
| atender | *to take care of* |
| asunto/gestión | *matter, business* |
| tramitación | *transaction* |

**Rellene, por favor, el siguiente cuestionario, señalando con una X la casilla correspondiente.**

REFIRIENDOSE, CONCRETAMENTE, A LA GESTION O CONSULTA QUE HA REALIZADO HOY EN ESTA OFICINA.

1. ¿Cómo le hemos atendido?
   - Mal (1)
   - Regular (2)
   - Bien (3)
   - Muy bien (4)

2. ¿Hemos sido rápidos en dar respuesta a su necesidad, problema o consulta?
   - Nada (1)
   - Poco (2)
   - Normal (3)
   - Mucho (4)

3. ¿Hemos sido amables al atenderle en su problema o necesidad?
   - Nada (1)
   - Poco (2)
   - Bastante (3)
   - Mucho (4)

4. ¿Ha encontrado facilidades en la tramitación de los asuntos que le han traído a esta oficina?
   - No (1)
   - A medias (2)
   - Sí (3)

5. ¿Ha resuelto las gestiones que le han traído hoy a esta oficina del Banco de Bilbao?
   - No (1)
   - A medias (2)
   - Sí, totalmente (3)

OFICINA DEL BB DONDE HA HECHO LA GESTION

Municipio .......... Agencia ..........
Fecha .......... Hora ..........

MUCHAS GRACIAS POR SU COLABORACION. DEPOSITE EL CUESTIONARIO CUMPLIMENTADO EN EL BUZON MAS PROXIMO. NO NECESITA FRANQUEO.

# VOCABULARIO[1]

**las catástrofes** — *disasters*
el derrame de petró-leo — *oil spill*
el huracán — *hurricane*
la inundación — *flood*
la lluvia ácida — *acid rain*
la sequía — *drought*
el terremoto — *earthquake*
el tornado — *tornado*

**la atención médica** — *medical care*
la camilla — *stretcher*
el herido — *injured person*

**los incendios** — *fires*
el fuego — *fire*
el humo — *smoke*
el peligro — *danger*

**la ayuda** — *aid*
la Cruz Roja — *Red Cross*
la donación — *donation*
la tienda de campaña — *tent*

**la información** — *information*
el noticiero — *newscast*

**el tráfico**
la contaminación del aire/el smog — *smog*
el choque — *accident*
el embotellamiento — *traffic jam*
las emisiones de los coches — *car emissions*

**personas**
guardia — *guard*
vecino — *neighbor*

**descripciones**
ambiental — *environmental*
peligroso — *dangerous*
seco — *dry*

**verbos**
acabar — *to finish*
 acabar + de + inf. — *to have just + past participle*
afectar — *to affect*
apagar — *to put out, to turn off*
destruir — *to destroy*
encender (ie) — *to light, to turn on*
guardar — *to put away*
hubo — *there was, there were*
inundar — *to inundate, to flood*
prepararse — *to get ready*
quemar — *to burn*
recoger — *to put away, to pick up*
romper — *to break, to tear*

**expresiones útiles**
dentro de un rato — *in a while*
disculpe la molestia — *sorry for the inconvenience*

---

[1] For irregular past participles see page 396.

In Lección 17 **you will**
a. **talk about and describe social customs.**
b. **describe customary actions.**
c. **project goals and purposes.**
d. **express conjecture.**
e. **talk about and express unexpected occurrences.**

# ¿Qué ha cambiado y qué no ha cambiado?

Los jóvenes tienen más libertad en muchos aspectos de su vida y esto se refleja en su forma de vestir y en sus relaciones con el otro sexo. Poco a poco se han hecho más independientes de la familia y de los valores tradicionales.

# Lección 17
# Los cambios de la sociedad

Los adelantos técnicos han afectado a la sociedad y se han creado puestos de trabajo para las personas capacitadas. Más mujeres siguen estudios universitarios y hoy en día tienen más oportunidades en campos como la medicina, la contabilidad, las ciencias y las leyes que antes estaban dominados por los hombres.

No ha cambiado el problema del desempleo en el campo y la ciudad para los que no están preparados. Tampoco ha cambiado la pobreza ni la falta de oportunidades y atención médica para muchas personas.

## ACTIVIDADES

**A** En grupos de cuatro o cinco estudiantes hagan una lista de los cambios que han ocurrido en la sociedad de este país en los últimos años. Comparen su lista con las de otros grupos de la clase.

**B** Usted ha ganado el Premio Nobel por su contribución en un campo importante (física, medicina, literatura o paz). Diga qué hizo usted para recibir ese premio y por qué es importante lo que usted hizo para la sociedad.

**C** **¿Qué debe cambiar en nuestra sociedad?** Usted y su compañero/a van a escoger tres cosas que deben cambiar en la sociedad. Después compartan sus ideas con la clase.

# Cultura

## Cambios en la sociedad hispana

Los últimos veinte años representan una época de muchos cambios en todo el mundo y en particular en los países hispanos. La migración, el alto índice de natalidad° y las modificaciones en la estructura social han afectado a la sociedad hispanoamericana. En España también han ocurrido muchos cambios, pero éstos son diferentes a los de Hispanoamérica.

La estructura social de la mayoría de los países hispanos no es igual a la de los Estados Unidos, pues aunque en ambos existen tres clases sociales (alta, media y baja), su distribución y tamaño son diferentes. En Hispanoamérica la clase más numerosa es la baja, pero el poder y la riqueza están concentrados en la clase alta, que es muy reducida. A pesar

*birth rate*

de los cambios políticos de Hispanoamérica, esta realidad social ha cambiado muy poco. Sin embargo, en los últimos años se ha notado un ligero aumento en la clase media, lo que le ha ofrecido mayores oportunidades a parte de la población. Si esto continua, se podrá hablar de una verdadera modificación de la estructura social de estos países.

En España la clase media ha aumentado mucho más que en Hispanoamérica. Con la entrada de España en la Comunidad Económica Europea y su total participación en 1992, se espera un mayor crecimiento de esta clase.

En Hispanoamérica, debido a la falta de empleos en el campo, existe una migración interna de las zonas rurales a las urbanas. Esto ha contribuido al crecimiento de muchas ciudades y ha creado numerosos problemas. Con la concentración de gran número de personas en las áreas metropolitanas, las ciudades no han podido darles los servicios necesarios para cubrir sus necesidades. El resultado ha sido el aumento del desempleo en las ciudades, el descenso en la calidad de los servicios y el aumento de las enfermedades, la pobreza y la contaminación. Además de la migración interna existe el problema de la emigración de los que buscan fuera, especialmente en los Estados Unidos, las oportunidades que no han podido encontrar en su país.

Los fenómenos de la migración interna y la emigración también han existido en España en los últimos veinte años, pero sin llegar a alcanzar las proporciones que tienen en Hispanoamérica. En España, las zonas más industrializadas están al norte del país y como consecuencia la migración interna se produce básicamente del sur hacia el norte. Los que emigran van a otros países europeos o a América.

El alto índice de natalidad también ha contribuido a los cambios en Hispanoamérica. En los últimos treinta años la población hispanoamericana ha aumentado más del doble y el número de nacimientos es dos veces el de los Estados Unidos. En España la situación es diferente, pues el aumento de la población es mucho menor. La siguiente tabla muestra el aumento de la población en los Estados Unidos y en algunos países hispanos desde 1970.

| | 1970 | 1980 | 1985 | % aumento |
|---|---|---|---|---|
| Argentina | 23.362.204 | 27.947.446 | 30.563.833 | 30,8% |
| Bolivia | 4.930.000 | 5.600.00 | 6.429.226 | 30,4% |
| Chile | 8.884.786 | 11.100.00 | 12.121.678 | 36,4% |
| Colombia | 20.053.000 | 25.890.000 | 27.867.326 | 39% |
| Ecuador | 6.050.000 | 8.020.000 | 9.377.980 | 55% |
| Guatemala | 5.250.000 | 6.920.000 | 7.963.356 | 51,7% |
| México | 48.225.238 | 66.846.833 | 77.938.288 | 61,6% |
| Venezuela | 10.210.000 | 14.000.000 | 17.316.741 | 69,6% |
| España | 33.750.000 | 37.540.000 | 38.600.000 | 14,4% |
| Estados Unidos | 203.302.031 | 217.000.000 | 238.741.000 | 17,4% |

## EN CONTEXTO

### La mujer en la sociedad hispana

*Las mujeres trabajadoras españolas ganan por término medio un 22,6% menos que los hombres, y en las jefaturas administrativas y de taller la diferencia supera al 40%. Así lo indica un amplio estudio del Ministerio de Economía y Hacienda que aporta nuevos datos sobre la discriminación femenina*[1].

Desgraciadamente la mujer en México ha estado marginada, ocupando siempre un lugar detrás del esposo. Pero este concepto, por fortuna, ha comenzado a cambiar en los tiempos actuales[2].

La situación de las mujeres no es igual en la ciudad y el campo y tampoco es igual en todos los países hispanos. Aunque ha mejorado en los últimos años, especialmente en las ciudades donde hay mujeres que ocupan puestos de importancia, todavía falta mucho para que las mujeres tengan las mismas oportunidades que los hombres.

Hoy en día existen en casi todos los países grupos feministas que trabajan activamente a favor de la mujer. Uno de sus objetivos básicos es la igualdad de salarios. No es justo que la mujer gane menos que el hombre cuando ambos realizan el mismo trabajo. Hasta que no cambie este dualismo sexual en la economía la mujer va a ocupar un puesto inferior en la sociedad.

---

[1] *El pais,* 4 de abril de 1988.
[2] Niní Trevit, *Visión,* 8 de agosto de 1988.

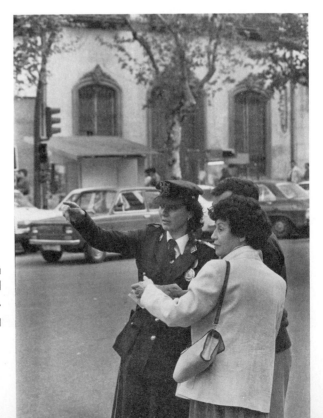

Una mujer policía ayuda a unos turistas en la ciudad de Sevilla.

## Preguntas

Conteste las siguientes preguntas con la información que se da en el artículo sobre la mujer.

1. ¿Qué problema existe en cuanto a salario con las trabajadoras españolas?
2. ¿Qué por ciento de diferencia hay entre los salarios de las mujeres y los hombres en España?
3. En general, ¿qué puesto ocupa la mujer mexicana con respecto al hombre dentro de la sociedad?
4. ¿Cuál es uno de los objetivos principales que quieren conseguir los grupos feministas?
5. El artículo habla del dualismo sexual en la economía. ¿Cree usted que existe ese dualismo en la economía de este país? ¿En qué áreas?

# ACTIVIDADES

**A** Con su compañero/a haga una lista de los cambios que han ocurrido con respecto a la mujer en la sociedad de este país en los últimos años.

**B** Usted y su compañero/a están a cargo de un programa para buscarle una solución al problema de las personas sin hogar. Infórmenle a la clase qué piensan hacer para mejorar la situación de estas personas.

## GRAMÁTICA

**Adverbial conjunctions that always require the subjunctive**

| | | | |
|---|---|---|---|
| para que | *so that* | antes (de) que | *before* |
| con tal (de) que | *provided that* | sin que | *without* |
| a menos que | *unless* | | |

**1.** A dependent clause introduced by these conjunctions always requires the use of the subjunctive.

| | |
|---|---|
| Van a la ciudad para que sus hijos **puedan** tener una vida mejor. | *They go to the city so their children can have a better life.* |
| Vamos a salir temprano con tal que **lleguen** a tiempo. | *We're going to leave early provided they arrive on time.* |
| No vayas a menos que te **paguen**. | *Don't go unless they pay you.* |
| Voy a terminar antes que **empiece** el programa. | *I'm going to finish before the program begins.* |
| Sal de la casa sin que te **oigan**. | *Leave the house without them hearing you.* |

**2.** The use of **de** is optional in **antes (de) que** and **con tal (de) que**.

Box A

## Adverbial conjunctions that use the subjunctive or the indicative

| | | | |
|---|---|---|---|
| cuando | *when* | en cuanto | *as soon as* |
| hasta que | *until* | aunque | *although* |
| después (de) que | *after* | donde | *where, wherever* |
| mientras | *while, as long as* | según | *according to* |
| tan pronto (como) | *as soon as* | como | *as* |

1. **Cuando, hasta que, después (de) que, mientras, tan pronto (como), en cuanto,** and **aunque** require the subjunctive when the event in the adverbial clause has not yet occurred. Note that the main clause expresses future time.

| | |
|---|---|
| Ella me va a llamar cuando **venga** a Nueva York. | *She's going to call me when she comes to New York.* |
| Va a estudiar hasta que **empiece** el programa. | *She's going to study until the program begins.* |
| Llámalo tan pronto como **llegue** la carta. | *Call him as soon as the letter arrives.* |
| Voy a salir a comer aunque **sea** tarde. | *I'm going out to eat although it may be late.* |

2. They require the indicative when the event in the adverbial clause has taken place, is taking place, or usually takes place.

| | |
|---|---|
| Ella me llamó cuando **vino** a San Juan. | *She called me when she came to San Juan.* |
| Ellos hablan mientras ustedes **trabajan.** | *They talk while you work.* |
| Siempre estudio hasta que **empieza** el programa. | *I always study until the program begins.* |

3. The use of **de** in **después (de) que** and **como** in **tan pronto (como)** is optional.

4. **Donde, según,** and **como** require the indicative when they refer to something definite or known, and the subjunctive when they refer to something indefinite or unknown.

| | |
|---|---|
| Vamos a donde ella **dice.** | *We're going where she says.* |
| Vamos a donde ella **diga.** | *We're going wherever she says.* |

5. **Aunque** also requires the subjunctive when it introduces a condition not regarded as fact.

| | |
|---|---|
| Lo compro aunque **es** caro. | *I'll buy it although it is expensive.* |
| Lo compro aunque **sea** caro. | *I'll buy it although it may be expensive.* |

# ACTIVIDADES

**A** Usted les va a explicar a sus amigos lo que va a determinar si se muda o no se muda a otra ciudad. Complete la oración **(No me voy a mudar. . .** usando las expresiones de la columna de la izquierda y la mejor selección de la columna de la derecha.

> *Modelo*   a menos que                              me suban el sueldo aquí
> **Me voy a mudar a menos que me suban el sueldo aquí.**

| | |
|---|---|
| a menos que | tenga un buen trabajo |
| para que | hable con todos los amigos |
| con tal que | pueda vender la casa |
| sin que | vayan otros amigos conmigo |
| antes de que | pueda llevar a mi familia |
| | me despida de mis padres |
| | pueda tener una vida mejor |
| | mi esposo/a esté más cerca del trabajo |

**B** Jorge Rivera no sabe si debe dejar sus estudios universitarios para seguir una carrera profesional en el mundo del deporte. Complete la oración **Jorge (no) va a dejar la universidad. . .** diciendo qué factores van a determinar su decisión. Use frases adverbiales (**para que, sin que,** etc.) en sus oraciones.

> *Modelo*   ganen el campeonato
> **Jorge no va a dejar la universidad antes de que ganen el campeonato.**

1. le ofrezcan un buen contrato
2. le paguen muy bien
3. termine el año
4. sus notas mejoren
5. le den un buen seguro médico
6. le ofrezcan la oportunidad de anunciar productos

**C** Usted y su compañero/a quieren irse a vivir a otro lugar (el campo, otra ciudad, otro país). Deben decir (a) dónde piensan vivir, (b) por qué quieren ir allí y (c) qué tiene que ocurrir para que vayan. Compartan después sus ideas con la clase.

**D** Usted y su compañero/a deben decir lo que van a hacer después de la clase de hoy. Completen las oraciones de la columna de la izquierda con una frase apropiada de la columna de la derecha o de acuerdo con sus propios planes.

> *Modelo*   Voy a estudiar hasta que. . .     tenga tiempo
>                                               empiecen las noticias
>                                               sea la hora de cenar
>
> **Usted**   **Voy a estudiar hasta que empiecen las noticias.**
> **Compañero/a**   **(Y yo) voy a estudiar hasta que sea la hora de cenar.**

| | |
|---|---|
| Voy a trabajar hastá que. . . | vaya a la tienda. |
| Voy a comer después de que. . . | tenga tiempo. |
| Voy a jugar básquetbol tan pronto como. . . | termine la tarea. |

Una oficina del periódico El Diario en Nueva York, donde las computadoras y el teléfono son elementos indispensables.

Voy a ver mi programa favorito cuando...    lleguen mis amigos.
Voy a dormir aunque...    sea temprano.
Voy a llamar a mi novio/a en cuanto...    sean las 7:00.
    no pueda ver.
    tenga un examen de física.
    me duerma.

**E** Cuando Esperanza López tiene problemas en una clase siempre habla con el profesor o la profesora bajo ciertas condiciones.

*Modelo*   **Habla con él/ella tan pronto puede.**

1. No habla con el profesor/la profesora hasta que...
2. Va a su oficina cuando...
3. Habla de los exámenes aunque...
4. Cree que es difícil hablar después de que...
5. Le gusta hablar con él/ella tan pronto como...
6. Quiere hablar con él/ella en cuanto...

**F** Con un/a compañero/a hable de sus planes para después que terminen las clases este año.

*Modelo*   Me voy a casar en cuanto...
       **Usted**  **Me voy a casar en cuanto consiga el dinero.**
      Me voy a ir a México tan pronto...
    **Compañero/a**  **Pues yo me voy a ir a México tan pronto pueda.**

1. Quiero dormir hasta que...
2. No voy a abrir los libros aunque...
3. Tengo que trabajar para que...
4. Me voy de vacaciones cuando...

5. No voy a hacer nada mientras...
6. Voy a ir a la playa todos los días a menos que...
7. Voy a nadar para que...
8. Quiero visitar a mis parientes antes de que...

**G** Usted y su compañero/a tienen planes para hacer ciertas cosas juntos/as después que se gradúen en la universidad (empezar un negocio, viajar, trabajar, seguir estudios de posgrado). Explíquenles a sus compañeros/as cuáles son sus planes. Traten de usar las expresiones adverbiales que han estudiado.

## EN CONTEXTO

### Problemas actuales° en una ciudad grande

*present*

Se le apagaron
las luces.

Se les descompuso
el teléfono.

Se les acabó el
trabajo.

## ACTIVIDADES

**A** Estudie los dibujos anteriores. Use su imaginación y explique por qué tienen problemas esas personas.

**B** Con su compañero/a haga una lista de los problemas que pueden encontrar las personas que vienen del campo a la ciudad.

**C** Usted y su compañero/a deben explicar las posibilidades de trabajo en una ciudad grande (a) para una persona que ha terminado sus estudios universitarios y (b) una persona que sólo tiene estudios primarios. Compartan la información con la clase.

## GRAMÁTICA

*Se* for unplanned occurrences

| | |
|---|---|
| Se me perdió el libro | *I lost the book.* |
| Se les apagaron las luces. | *Their lights went out.* |
| A él se le acabó el dinero. | *He ran out of money.* |
| Se nos olvidó el número. | *We forgot the number.* |
| A Paz se le rompió la blusa. | *Paz's blouse got torn.* |

1. **Se** + indirect object pronoun + verb is used to express unplanned or accidental events. This construction emphasizes the event in order to show that no one is responsible.
2. Use the indirect object pronoun (**me, te, le, nos, os, les**) to indicate whom the unplanned or accidental event affects. Place it between **se** and the verb.
3. The indirect object pronoun may be clarified or emphasized by **a** + noun/pronoun.
4. If the subject of the sentence (what is lost, forgotten, and so on) is plural, the verb must also be plural.

| | |
|---|---|
| Se me **quedó el dinero** en el hotel. | *I left the money in the hotel.* |
| Se me **quedaron los boletos** en casa. | *I left the tickets at home.* |

## ACTIVIDADES

**A** A las personas de cada grupo les pasó lo mismo. Diga lo que les pasó.

*Modelo*  Se nos acabó el vino. (a Evita)
**Se le acabó el vino.**
A Pilar se le olvidaron las direcciones. (a ti)
**A ti se te olvidaron las direcciones.**

1. Se me descompuso el tocadiscos. (a Carlota, a Pedro y a Paco, a Armando y a mí)
2. A Rodolfo se le perdieron las notas. (a Marta y a Carlos, a nosotros, a mí)
3. Se nos acabó el dinero. (a ti, a Leticia, a ellos)

**B** Hágale las preguntas de la columna de la izquierda a su compañero/a. Él/ella debe contestar completando las oraciones de la columna de la derecha.

*Modelo*  Usted  ¿Dónde está la cámara de Pedro?
Compañero/a  Se me perdió **en la universidad.**

1. ¿Qué pasó anoche?            Se nos apagaron...
2. ¿Por qué llegaste tarde?     Se me descompuso...
3. ¿Por qué no almorzaron?      Se nos olvidó...

4. ¿Qué le pasó a Marta?      Se le cayó...
5. ¿Dónde está tu libro?      Se me quedó...
6. ¿Dónde están los boletos?      Se nos quedaron...

**C** Explique con las sugerencias a la derecha lo que ha pasado en las siguientes situaciones.

    *Modelo*    Carlos no puede comprar el libro.     olvidarse el dinero
             **Se le olvidó el dinero.**

    1. Anita está preocupada.            romperse el vestido
    2. La profesora no vino hoy.        enfermarse un hijo
    3. Ellos llegaron tarde a clase.      acabarse la gasolina
    4. No salió en ese vuelo.           olvidarse los boletos
    5. Ellas no pudieron entrar en la casa.   perderse las llaves

**D** Ayer usted tuvo en día terrible. Diga qué pasó usando **se** + pronombre.

    Antes de levantarme...      Cuando desayunaba...      No hice la tarea porque...
    No almorcé porque...       Cuando iba a la casa en la autopista...

# EN CONTEXTO

## Letreros°                          *signs*

En una sociedad hay que respetar las leyes. Muchos ciudadanos recuerdan sus
derechos, pero olvidan sus deberes°. Los letreros les recuerdan algunas de sus    *duties*
obligaciones como miembros de la sociedad.

## Preguntas

    1. ¿Cree usted que son importantes los letreros? ¿Por qué?
    2. Explique por qué se debe obedecer cada uno de los letreros que aparecen en los dibujos
         anteriores.
    3. ¿Cuáles son algunos de los derechos y los deberes de los ciudadanos de esta sociedad?

## *ACTIVIDADES*

**A** Diga en qué lugares se pueden encontrar letreros como éstos.

1. No correr
2. Prohibido entrar con comida
3. Usar el cinturón de seguridad
4. Favor de apagar la luz

5. Usar cascos (*helmets*) en esta zona
6. Favor de cerrar la puerta
7. No traer vasos de cristal

**B** Usted y su compañero/a deben preparar unos letreros y decir dónde los pondrían.

## GRAMÁTICA

### The infinitive as subject of a sentence

| | |
|---|---|
| (El) Estudiar es importante. | *Studying is important.* |
| (El) Trotar es buen ejercicio. | *Jogging is good exercise.* |
| Me interesa saber eso. | *I'm interested in know-ing that.* |

1. When an infinitive is the subject of a sentence, it corresponds to an English noun ending in *-ing,* or gerund.
2. The article **el** may be used to introduce an infinitive at the beginning of a sentence. It is seldom used in spoken Spanish.

### The infinitive as the object of a preposition

| | |
|---|---|
| Al llegar, Cuando llegó } llamó a su tío. | *Upon arriving, he called his uncle.* |
| Vino sin avisarles. | *She came without letting them know.* |
| Antes de venir, habla con él. | *Before coming, talk to him.* |

1. When an infinitive is the object of a preposition, it corresponds to an English noun ending in *-ing* (gerund).
2. **Al** + infinitive is the equivalent of **cuando** + verb.
3. No article is used with other prepositions.

# ACTIVIDADES

**A** Trabaje con un/a compañero/a y escoja una frase con infinitivo para decir lo que es o no es importante (necesario, malo, terrible) para cada uno.

> *Modelo*    hacer ejercicio
>            **Usted**    **Hacer ejercicio es necesario para mí.**
>      **Compañero/a**    **Hacer ejercicio es terrible para mí.**

1. ir a las fiestas
2. escuchar música
3. no tener trabajo
4. ir de compras
5. tener un auto bonito
6. sacar una F
7. vivir en una ciudad grande
8. llegar tarde a los lugares
9. estar enfermo/a
10. jugar básquetbol
11. bailar salsa
12. tener amigos
13. comer bien
14. dormir bastante

**B** Hágale las siguientes preguntas a su compañero/a. Él/Ella debe contestar con una frase con infinitivo. Después él/ella le debe hacer las preguntas a usted.

> *Modelo*            **Usted**    ¿Qué es difícil para ti?
>      **Compañero/a**    **Nadar es difícil para mí.**

1. ¿Qué es divertido para ti?
2. ¿Qué es interesante para ti?
3. ¿Qué es fácil para ti?
4. ¿Qué es importante para ti?
5. ¿Qué es difícil para ti?

**C** Su compañero/a quiere saber qué va a hacer usted en ciertas situaciones. Conteste usando **al** + infinitivo.

> *Modelo*    cuando llegues a tu casa
>            **Usted**    **¿Qué vas a hacer cuando llegues a tu casa?**
>      **Compañero/a**    **Al llegar a mi casa, me voy a quitar los zapatos.**

1. cuando termines la clase de español
2. cuando salgas de la universidad
3. cuando hables español perfectamente
4. cuando te levantes mañana
5. cuando llegues a viejo/a *(become old)*

**D** Dígale a su compañero/a todo lo que usted hace en estas situaciones.

> *Modelo*    antes de dormir
>          **Antes de dormir, yo hago la tarea y miro televisión.**

1. antes de comer
2. después de tomar los exámenes finales
3. después de salir de un concierto
4. antes de ir a un partido de baloncesto
5. después de despertarse
6. antes y después de bañarse

**E** Usted no sale de su casa sin hacer ciertas cosas. Dígale a su compañero/a cuáles son estas cosas. Después su compañero/a le debe decir a usted qué cosas hace él/ella.

> *Modelo*    **No salgo sin llevar la llave.**

## LECTURA

**Antes de leer:** the conditional perfect; the pluperfect subjunctive

In this section, you will learn two new verb tenses: the conditional perfect and the pluperfect subjunctive. You should be able to recognize them when reading.

The conditional of **haber** + past participle is the *conditional perfect* and the past subjunctive of **haber** + past participle is the *pluperfect subjunctive.*

The conditional perfect usually corresponds to English *would have* + past participle.

| | |
|---|---|
| Sé que le habría gustado esta casa. | *I know she would have liked this house.* |

The pluperfect subjunctive corresponds to English *might have, would have,* or *had* + past participle. It is used in structures where the subjunctive is normally required.

| | |
|---|---|
| Dudaba que hubiera venido más temprano. | *I doubted that he might have come earlier.* |
| Esperaba que hubieran comido en casa. | *I was hoping that they would have eaten at home.* |
| Ojalá que hubieran visto ese letrero. | *I wish they had seen that sign.* |

The conditional perfect and pluperfect subjunctive are also used in contrary-to-fact *if* sentences.

| | |
|---|---|
| Si hubieras venido, te habría gustado la comida. | *If you had come, you would have liked the food.* |

Unos indocumentados pasan el río Bravo para llegar a El Paso.

The following charts show the forms for the conditional perfect and the pluperfect subjunctive respectively.

| CONDITIONAL PERFECT | | |
|---|---|---|
| yo | habría | |
| tú | habrías | |
| él, ella, usted | habría | hablado/comido/vivido |
| nosostros | habríamos | |
| vosotros | habríais | |
| ellos/as, ustedes | habrían | |

| PLUPERFECT SUBJUNCTIVE | | |
|---|---|---|
| yo | hubiera | |
| tú | hubieras | |
| él, ella, usted | hubiera | hablado/comido/vivido |
| nosostros | hubiéramos | |
| vosotros | hubierais | |
| ellos/as, ustedes | hubieran | |

## *Identificación*

Identifique el condicional perfecto o el pluscuamperfecto de subjuntivo en las siguientes oraciones.

1. No creía que hubiera llegado a esa hora.
2. Habría estado muy contento si hubiera sacado una A.
3. Hubiera preferido viajar a Santiago.
4. Lo habría comprado, si hubiera tenido lugar en mi apartamento.
5. Si hubiéramos empezado a las diez, habríamos terminado a las doce.
6. Sentí que no hubieran venido ayer.

En la siguiente selección hay varias oraciones con los tiempos perfectos que acaba de estudiar. Estas oraciones le pueden parecer algo largas o complicadas. No se preocupe por esto y lea la selección tratando de entender la ideas básicas que se presentan.

## Eusebio Manrique recuerda su vida

A Eusebio Manrique le parecía mentira que hubieran pasado cuarenta años. Y sin saber ni cómo ni por qué, los diferentes acontecimientos° de su vida pasaron en breves° minutos ante sus ojos como en una película. Recordaba el primer día en la compañía. Él, un chico del campo que hacía unos años había llegado a la ciudad para estudiar y ganarse la vida, sólo había podido conseguir un puesto de mensajero. Sus aspiraciones eran otras, pero la realidad era diferente y decidió aceptarlo ya que «por algo se empieza». ¿Habría hecho algo diferente si pudiera volver a vivir esos momentos de necesidad? ¿Qué otra cosa hubiera podido hacer? No encontró respuesta a estas preguntas y pensó en los primeros años en la compañía. El sueldo era bajo y el trabajo muy duro, pero su voluntad de triunfar era más fuerte. Y así pasaron los años y poco a poco fue ascendiendo y dejó de ser Eusebio el mensajero, a quien mandaban de un lugar a otro, para pasar a ser don Eusebio. ¿Quién hubiera dicho que todo esto iba a ocurrir? Si alguien lo hubiera pensado, él habría dicho que eran sueños. Pero en la vida los sueños a veces se convierten en realidad y hoy, después de cuarenta años, rodeado° de compañeros y amigos, el Presidente de la Compañía Trébol, don Eusebio Manrique, se despedía de todos ellos para disfrutar de un buen descanso después de tantos años de trabajo.

*events*
*en... a few short*

*surrounded*

## ¿Verdadero o falso?

Diga si las siguientes oraciones son verdaderas o falsas de acuerdo con la selección anterior.

1. Eusebio Manrique es un hombre mayor.
2. Él siempre vivió en una ciudad.
3. Ganaba un buen sueldo en su primer puesto.
4. Eusebio trabajó en varias compañías.
5. Eusebio Manrique es un hombre importante hoy en día.

## Preguntas

Conteste las siguientes preguntas de acuerdo con la selección.

1. ¿Qué puesto ocupa Eusebio Manrique hoy en día?
2. ¿Cuál fue su primer puesto?
3. ¿Por qué se han reunido los amigos y compañeros de Eusebio?

## Los hispanos en los Estados Unidos

La presencia hispana en los Estados Unidos data de la llegada de los españoles a América. Desde entonces y a través de los años, distintos grupos de hispanos han llegado a este país. Con mucho esfuerzo esta minoría compuesta de mexicanos, puertorriqueños, cubanos, colombianos, nicaragüenses y otros han hecho sentir su presencia en los Estados Unidos y han influido en la sociedad del país.

Según el último censo, en 1980 la población hispana representaba un total de más de 14 millones de habitantes. En 1986, según cifras no oficiales, el número de hispanos llegaba ya a 18 millones, y para el año 2000 se cree que sobrepasará los 20 millones. Aunque todos los hispanos tienen muchos rasgos culturales comunes, hay una gran diversidad entre ellos debido a su país de origen, historia, y a la influencia de otras culturas y costumbres.

La presencia hispana es obvia en muchos aspectos de la vida norteamericana, como por ejemplo en la lengua. Se usan palabras españolas o derivadas del español en los nombres de estados (Colorado, California, Montana), y de ciudades (Los Ángeles, San Francisco, Albuquerque, San Antonio), en los términos rancheros (*ranch, lasso, buckaroo*), en los nombres de calles y en muchos otros aspectos de la vida norteamericana.

En la comida la influencia hispana es muy notable y muchas personas disfrutan de la cocina típica de los diferentes países hispanos. Palabras como **tortillas, salsa picante, fritos, chile, pollo** y otras forman parte del vocabulario de muchas personas.

Los nombres de los hispanos que se han destacado en diversos campos artísticos son ya muy conocidos: María Conchita Alonso, Ricardo Montalbán, Bárbara Carrera, Oscar de la Renta, Julio Iglesias, Luis Valdés, Rita Moreno, Fernando Bujones y otros. En el deporte se han distinguido individuos como José Canseco, Fernando Valenzuela, Lee Treviño y Nancy López.

Cada día se ven más hispanos en las universidades, aunque su número debería ser mayor. Se especializan en diversas carreras como medicina, física, matemáticas, derecho, negocios y pedagogía y esperan poder participar en las decisiones de la sociedad.

Se puede notar la importancia de los hispanos por la atención que los medios de comunicación les prestan en los últimos años. Hay cada vez más estaciones de radio y televisión en español. En las ciudades donde hay grandes números de hispanos hay periódicos en español como *La opinión, La voz libre* y *Noticias del mundo* en Los Ángeles, *El Diario/La Prensa* en Nueva York y *El diario de las Américas* en Miami. También se encuentran revistas como *Américas 2001, Geomundo, Buenhogar, Miami mensual, Hispanics* y otras. Algunos periódicos en inglés como el *Miami Herald* tienen secciones en español para los hispanos de su ciudad.

Las compañías grandes y pequeñas se dirigen al público hispano. No es raro ver campañas de publicidad en español para casi cualquier producto y los hogares hispanos reciben cupones en español para toda clase de artículos. Estas compañías ven la importancia del mercado hispano y no quieren perder esta oportunidad.

La influencia que han tenido en la vida norteamericana y el éxito que muchos hispanos han logrado en la educación y los negocios son indicaciones positivas del progreso de los hispanos en los Estados Unidos.

## Preguntas

1. ¿Qué grupos de hispanos viven en los Estados Unidos?
2. ¿Son todos los hispanos iguales? Explique.
3. ¿En qué aspectos de la vida norteamericana se nota la influencia hispana?
4. ¿Qué estados y ciudades tienen nombres en español?
5. ¿Qué productos de comida vienen de los hispanos?
6. ¿Quiénes son Ricardo Montalbán y José Canseco?
7. Nombre tres periódicos y dos revistas en español que se publican en este país.
8. ¿Qué hacen algunas compañías ahora para venderle productos al mercado hispano?

## La Guardia Civil marcan el paso en Baeza

La Guardia Civil fue fundada a mediados del siglo XIX en España. Durante esos años ha tenido sus defensores y detractores que la ven como representante del orden y el respeto o como órgano de la represión. Pero tanto unos como otros la han considerado una organización eminentemente masculina donde muchos jóvenes «se hacían hombres». En 1988 esto cambió radicalmente cuando entraron las primeras mujeres a la Guardia Civil. El siguiente artículo tomado de *Blanco y negro* da más detalles sobre este grupo de pioneras que se entrenaron en la ciudad española de Baeza.

Las siguientes palabras le podrán ayudar a entender mejor el artículo.

| | |
|---|---|
| trato | *treatment* |
| tocar diana | *play reveille* |
| pocilga | *pigpen* |
| aseo | *washing* |

### España

# Los ángeles de la Guardia Civil marcan el paso en Baeza

DOSCIENTOS de los mil setecientos «cetmes» de la Academia de Guardias de la Benemérita de Baeza, en la provincia de Jaén, se sienten diferentes desde que a primeros del pasado mes de septiembre otras tantas mujeres ingresaron en el Centro tras aprobar las pruebas de acceso, que sólo se diferenciaron con las del sector masculino en insignificantes detalles físicos.

Los dos centenares de mujeres que soportan con soltura los 940 kilos del mismo número de «cetmes» (cada uno pesa cuatro kilos setecientos gramos), se han convertido en las pioneras de una renovación en los tradicionales esquemas de la Guardia Civil. Con un ligero toque femenino en el pelo y algo de maquillaje, «aquí como en el resto de los trabajos se pide un poco de discreción—señala el general jefe de Enseñanza de la Benemérita, Arturo Lafuente—, porque no sería lógico que fueran con los pelos a lo *punkie*», las futuras guardias civiles han conseguido, incluso, superar a muchos de sus compañeros.

Y es que entre ellas y ellos no hay diferencias en el trato ni en las obligaciones que impone el duro régimen de la Academia. A las siete de la mañana el corneta toca diana y ellas acuden a la primera formación del día. Lo hacen con la misma rapidez que sus compañeros, pero con la notable diferencia del estado en que dejan la compañía. «No es que la de los hombres sea una pocilga, pero ellas lo tienen todo más ordenado y con un aroma distinto», comenta el director de la Academia, el coronel Pedro Moreno Muñoz.

#### Nueve casadas

Tras el aseo, disponen de media hora para el desayuno . . . Un café con leche, un «donuts», mortadela, pan y mantequilla, ayudarán a aguantar las dos horas de instrucción que dan paso a las clases teóricas hasta las dos de la tarde.

Después de dos horas de siesta se reanudan las clases y, tras un descanso de sesenta minutos, se encierran para estudiar hasta las nueve de la noche.

Una hora más tarde estarán acostadas y acostados, cada uno en su compañía, para respetar el toque de silencio. Cualquier arresto reduciría la puntuación con la que comienza el curso, un diez, la cifra mágica que les permitiría elegir un destino cercano al de sus familiares.

Este es el caso de Concepción Viyuela, de veintiséis años, casada con un taxista de Madrid y con un hijo de cuatro años. «Sé que será un problema si me destinan fuera de Madrid, porque allí tengo a mi marido y a mi hijo. Por eso voy a hacer todo lo posible para estar entre las primeras de la promoción.»

Además de Concepción, hay otras ocho casadas, una de ellas con un guardia civil, además de cinco separadas y una divorciada. El resto, solteras con y sin compromiso, niegan que exista cualquier tipo de noviazgo en la Academia. «Tampoco hemos tenido problemas con nuestros novios, ya que han entendido muy bien nuestro nuevo papel». No obstante, en otros casos la situación ha sido diferente: una de las mujeres que llegó a Baeza tras aprobar las pruebas abandonó las instala-

ciones con lágrimas en los ojos después de que su marido viniera a buscarla . . .

Sobre la posibilidad de que Cupido visite las instalaciones de Baeza, el general Lafuente se muestra comprensivo, «ya que entra dentro de las posibilidades de las relaciones humanas y no lo vamos a prohibir, aunque no parece lógico que dos guardias civiles vayan agarrados de la mano por la calle, aunque los dos formen una pareja».

### «Somos iguales»

Esta el frase que más se escucha entre las guardias civiles cuando se les pregunta por las posibles diferencias de trato con los mandos. Nuria Latorre, de veintiún años, piensa pedir un destino muy especial. «A mí lo que me gustaría es ir destinada a una unidad de desactivación de explosivos o incorporarme a la lucha contra el terrorismo». Para ello piensa pedir destino en el País Vasco, aunque como el resto de sus compañeras y compañeros, tendrá que esperar un año para conseguirlo. «Sé que voy a correr un riesgo. pero me atrae».

Miguel Berrocal

María del Carmen Zarauza, ex «Miss Asturias», es una de las doscientas mujeres que cada mañana forman en el patio de la Academia de Baeza

## ¿Verdadero o falso?

Diga si las siguientes oraciones son verdaderas o falsas de acuerdo con la información del artículo.

1. Las mujeres y los hombres reciben el mismo trato.
2. Los guardias civiles se despiertan a las seis.
3. Los dormitorios de las mujeres están tan ordenados como los de los hombres.
4. Los guardias civiles asisten a clase por la mañana y por la tarde.
5. Los guardias civiles se acuestan a las nueve.
6. Cuando empieza el curso todos los guardias civiles tienen diez puntos.
7. Si no siguen las regulaciones pierden puntos.
8. Todas las mujeres que empezaron el curso lo terminaron.
9. No hay mujeres divorciadas entre las guardias civiles.
10. Está prohibido que haya novios o matrimonios entre los guardias civiles.

## Opiniones

Usted y su compañero/a van a estar a favor o en contra de que las mujeres formen parte de las Fuerzas Armadas. Deben decir en qué se basan para tener esta opinión.

La calle Olvera en Los Angeles, California, es parte del centro antiguo de esta ciudad que fue fundada por familias mexicanas y españolas en 1781.

## SITUACIONES

1. Your best friend has just moved to town. He/She sounds very unhappy and you want to help. You should (a) determine what the problem is, (b) sympathize with his/her situation, and (c) suggest some solution.

2. You're watching TV with a friend at his/her house. You've been watching the newscast which mentions the following problems: (a) bad telephone service, (b) unemployment, and (c) lack of opportunities for women. Choose one of these areas (or another of your choice) and tell your friend your opinion about this situation. Your friend should ask you two or three questions about it.

3. You are approached by a homeless person on the street. Listen to his/her questions and react accordingly. The homeless person will ask for such things as money, food, shelter, or another type of help.

4. You are a woman and want to interview for a job normally held by men in your country. Tell your partner what the job is. Your partner will tell you that you should not interview for this job. Tell your partner (a) why you want to get it, and (b) your qualifications.

5. You need to make an urgent call and your phone is out of order. You don't know your neighbor, but you go to his/her home and try to convince him/her to let you use the phone.

6. You are going to donate money to four different institutions: a university, a hospital, a museum, and a church. Your partner should ask you how much you want to donate to each. Answer that question and also tell for what purpose the money should be used.

# VOCABULARIO[3]

**la sociedad**

| | |
|---|---|
| el adelanto | *advance* |
| el cambio | *change* |
| el ciudadano | *citizen* |
| los datos | *data* |
| el deber | *duty* |
| la diferencia | *difference* |
| la discriminación | *discrimination* |
| el dualismo | *dualism* |
| la igualdad | *equality* |
| la ley | *law* |
| el miembro | *member* |
| el objetivo | *objective* |
| la oportunidad | *opportunity* |
| la pobreza | *poverty* |
| las relaciones | *relations* |
| el salario | *salary* |
| los valores tradicionales | *traditional values* |

**en el parque**

| | |
|---|---|
| el césped | *lawn* |
| el letrero | *sign* |

**descripciones**

| | |
|---|---|
| actual | *present* |
| capacitado | *prepared, qualified* |
| feminista | *feminist* |
| igual | *equal, the same* |
| independiente | *independent* |
| inferior | *inferior* |
| justo | *just* |
| marginado | *not fully accepted* |
| sexual | *sexual* |
| técnico | *technical* |

**verbos**

| | |
|---|---|
| comenzar | *to begin* |
| crear | *to create* |
| descomponer | *to break down* |
| dominar | *to dominate* |
| faltar | *to lack, to be necessary* |
| indicar | *to indicate* |
| ocupar | *to occupy* |
| pisar | *to step on* |
| realizar | *to perform, to accomplish* |
| reflejar | *to reflect* |
| tirar | *to throw* |

**expresiones útiles**

| | |
|---|---|
| a favor de | *in favor of* |
| en voz baja | *softly, in a soft voice* |
| poco a poco | *little by little* |
| por fortuna | *luckily* |

---

[3] For a list of adverbial conjunctions, see pages 421 and 422.

# *Verb Tables*

## I. REGULAR VERBS

|  | **-ar** | **-er** | **-ir** |
|---|---|---|---|
| *Infinitive* (*Infinitivo*) | **hablar** | **comer** | **vivir** |
| *Present participle* (*Gerundio*) | hablando | comiendo | viviendo |
| *Past participle* (*Participio pasivo*) | hablado | comido | vivido |

### Simple Tenses

#### INDICATIVE MOOD (MODO INDICATIVO)

| | -ar | -er | -ir |
|---|---|---|---|
| *Present* (*Presente*) | hablo | como | vivo |
| | hablas | comes | vives |
| | habla | come | vive |
| | hablamos | comemos | vivimos |
| | habláis | coméis | vivís |
| | hablan | comen | viven |
| *Imprefect* (*Imperfecto*) | hablaba | comía | vivía |
| | hablabas | comías | vivías |
| | hablaba | comía | vivía |
| | hablábamos | comíamos | vivíamos |
| | hablabais | comíais | vivíais |
| | hablaban | comían | vivían |

| | | | |
|---|---|---|---|
| *Preterit* | hablé | comí | viví |
| *(Pretérito)* | hablaste | comiste | viviste |
| | habló | comió | vivió |
| | hablamos | comimos | vivimos |
| | hablasteis | comisteis | vivisteis |
| | hablaron | comieron | vivieron |
| *Future* | hablaré | comeré | viviré |
| *(Futuro)* | hablarás | comerás | vivirás |
| | hablará | comerá | vivirá |
| | hablaremos | comeremos | viviremos |
| | hablaréis | comeréis | viviréis |
| | hablarán | comerán | vivirán |
| *Conditional* | hablaría | comería | viviría |
| *(Condicional)* | hablarías | comerías | vivirías |
| | hablaría | comería | viviría |
| | hablaríamos | comeríamos | viviríamos |
| | hablaríais | comeríais | viviríais |
| | hablarían | comerían | vivirían |

**IMPERATIVE MOOD[1] (MODO IMPERATIVO)**

| | | | | |
|---|---|---|---|---|
| *Affirmative* | **tú** | habla | come | vive |
| | **vosotros** | hablad | comed | vivid |

**SUBJUNCTIVE MOOD (MODO SUBJUNTIVO)**

| | | | |
|---|---|---|---|
| *Present* | hable | coma | viva |
| *(Presente)* | hables | comas | vivas |
| | hable | coma | viva |
| | hablemos | comamos | vivamos |
| | habléis | comáis | viváis |
| | hablen | coman | vivan |
| *Past (-ra)* | hablara | comiera | viviera |
| *(Imperfecto)* | hablaras | comieras | vivieras |
| | hablara | comiera | viviera |
| | habláramos | comiéramos | viviéramos |
| | hablarais | comierais | vivierais |
| | hablaran | comieran | vivieran |
| *Past (-se)* | hablase | comiese | viviese |
| *(Imperfecto)* | hablases | comieses | vivieses |
| | hablase | comiese | viviese |
| | hablásemos | comiésemos | viviésemos |
| | hablaseis | comiescis | vivieseis |
| | hablasen | comiesen | viviesen |

[1] For the negative **tú** and **vosotros** command forms, and for both affirmative and negative **usted** and **ustedes** command forms, see the corresponding subjunctive verb forms.

# Compound Tenses

## INDICATIVE MOOD (MODO INDICATIVO)

|  |  | **-ar** | **-er** | **-ir** |
|---|---|---|---|---|
| *Present perfect* (*Pretérito perfecto*) | he has ha hemos habéis han | hablado | comido | vivido |
| *Past perfect*[2] (*Pretérito pluscuamperfecto*) | había habías había habíamos habíais habían | hablado | comido | vivido |
| *Future perfect* (*Futuro perfecto*) | habré habrás habrá habremos habréis habrán | hablado | comido | vivido |
| *Conditional perfect* (*Condicional perfecto*) | habría habrías habría habríamos habríais habrían | hablado | comido | vivido |

[2] The second past perfect, rarely used today, is:

| hube hubiste hubo hubimos hubisteis hubieron | hablado | comido | vivido |
|---|---|---|---|

SUBJUNCTIVE MOOD (MODO SUBJUNTIVO)

| *Present perfect*<br>(*Pretérito perfecto*) | haya<br>hayas<br>haya<br>hayamos<br>hayáis<br>hayan | hablado | comido | vivido |
|---|---|---|---|---|
| *Past perfect* (**-ra**)<br>(*Pretérito pluscuamperfecto*) | hubiera<br>hubieras<br>hubiera<br>hubiéramos<br>hubierais<br>hubieran | hablado | comido | vivido |
| *Past perfect* (**-se**)<br>(*Pretérito pluscuamperfecto*) | hubiese<br>hubieses<br>hubiese<br>hubiésemos<br>hubieseis<br>hubiesen | hablado | comido | vivido |

# II. STEM-CHANGING VERBS

**A.** Stressed **e** changes to **ie** and stressed **o** changes to **ue** throughout the singular and in the third-person plural of the present indicative and in the present subjunctive of some **-ar, -er,** and **-ir** verbs.

## 1. Stressed e → ie

pensar            perder            sentir

PRESENT INDICATIVE                                      PRESENT SUBJUNCTIVE

| **pienso** | **pierdo** | **siento** | **piense** | **pierda** | **sienta** |
|---|---|---|---|---|---|
| **piensas** | **pierdes** | **sientes** | **pienses** | **pierdas** | **sientas** |
| **piensa** | **pierde** | **siente** | **piense** | **pierda** | **sienta** |
| pensamos | perdemos | sentimos | pensemos | perdamos | sintamos |
| pensáis | perdéis | sentís | penséis | perdáis | sintáis |
| **piensan** | **plerden** | **sienten** | **piensen** | **pierdan** | **sientan** |

*Other verbs whose stem vowel* **e** *changes to* **ie** *are:* atravesar, calentar, cerrar, comenzar, defender, despertar, divertirse, empezar, entender, nevar, preferir, querer, recomendar, sentar, sugerir.

## 2. Stressed o → ue

contar           volver           morir

PRESENT INDICATIVE                                    PRESENT SUBJUNCTIVE

| | | | | | |
|---|---|---|---|---|---|
| **cuento** | **vuelvo** | **muero** | **cuente** | **vuelva** | **muera** |
| **cuentas** | **vuelves** | **mueres** | **cuentes** | **vuelvas** | **mueras** |
| **cuenta** | **vuelve** | **muere** | **cuente** | **vuelva** | **muera** |
| contamos | volvemos | morimos | contemos | volvamos | muramos |
| contáis | volvéis | morís | contéis | volváis | muráis |
| **cuentan** | **vuelven** | **mueren** | **cuenten** | **vuelvan** | **mueran** |

*Other verbs whose stem vowel* **o** *changes to* **ue** *are:* acostar, almorzar, contar, costar, doler, dormir, encontrar, llover, poder, probar, recordar, resolver.

**Jugar** *is the only verb that changes* **u** *to* **ue**.

**B.** Unstressed **e** changes to **i** and unstressed **o** changes to **u** in the third-person singular and plural of the preterit; in the present participle; in the first and second persons plural of the present subjunctive; and throughout the two versions of the past subjunctive.[3]

## 1. Unstressed e → i

sentir

| PRETERIT | PRESENT SUBJUNCTIVE | PAST SUBJUNCTIVE | |
|---|---|---|---|
| sentí | sienta | **sintiera** | **sintiese** |
| sentiste | sientas | **sintieras** | **sintieses** |
| **sintió** | sienta | **sintiera** | **sintiese** |
| sentimos | **sintamos** | **sintiéramos** *or* | **sintiésemos** |
| sentisteis | **sintáis** | **sintierais** | **sintieseis** |
| **sintieron** | sientan | **sintieran** | **sintiesen** |

PRESENT PARTICIPLE

**sintiendo**

*Other* **-ir** *verbs whose stem vowel* **e** *changes to* **i** *are:* divertirse, preferir.

---

[3] These verbs belong in the preceding section **A** as well because of their other stem change, stressed **e** to **ie** and stressed **o** to **ue** in the present indicative and present subjunctive.

## 2. Unstressed o → u

**morir**

| PRETERIT | PRESENT SUBJUNCTIVE | PAST SUBJUNCTIVE | | |
|---|---|---|---|---|
| morí | muera | **muriera** | | **muriese** |
| moriste | mueras | **murieras** | | **murieses** |
| **murió** | muera | **muriera** | *or* | **muriese** |
| morimos | **muramos** | **muriéramos** | | **muriésemos** |
| moristeis | **muráis** | **murierais** | | **murieseis** |
| **murieron** | mueran | **murieran** | | **muriesen** |

PRESENT PARTICIPLE

**muriendo**

*Another* **-ir** *verb whose stem vowel* **o** *changes to* **u** *is* dormir.

**C.** The change **e → i** occurs throughout the singular and in the third-person plural of the present indicative, in the third-person singular and plural of the preterit, in the present participle, and throughout the present and past subjunctive of some **-ir** verbs.

**e → i**

**pedir**

| PRESENT INDICATIVE | PRETERIT |
|---|---|
| **pido** | pedí |
| **pides** | pediste |
| **pide** | **pidió** |
| pedimos | pedimos |
| pedís | pedisteis |
| **piden** | **pidieron** |

| PRESENT SUBJUNCTIVE | PAST SUBJUNCTIVE | | |
|---|---|---|---|
| **pida** | **pidiera** | | **pidiese** |
| **pidas** | **pidieras** | | **pidieses** |
| **pida** | **pidiera** | *or* | **pidiese** |
| **pidamos** | **pidiéramos** | | **pidiésemos** |
| **pidáis** | **pidierais** | | **pidieseis** |
| **pidan** | **pidieran** | | **pidiesen** |

PRESENT PARTICIPLE

**pidiendo**

*Other* **-ir** *verbs whose stem vowel* **e** *changes to* **i** *are:* competir: conseguir, despedir, medir, repetir, seguir, vestir.

# III. ORTHOGRAPHIC-CHANGING VERBS ▬▬▬▬▬▬▬

**A.** Verbs ending in **-car: c → qu** before **e**
The change **c → qu** occurs in the first-person singular preterit and throughout the present subjunctive.

**chocar**

*Preterit*　　　　　　　　choqué, chocaste, chocó, chocamos, chocasteis, chocaron

*Present subjunctive*　　choque, choques, choque, choquemos, choquéis, choquen


**B.** Verbs ending in **-gar: g → gu** before **e**
The change **g → gu** occurs in the first-person singular preterit and throughout the present subjunctive.

**llegar**

*Preterit*　　　　　　　　llegué, llegaste, llegó, llegamos, llegasteis, llegaron

*Present subjunctive*　　llegue, llegues, llegue, lleguemos, lleguéis, lleguen


**C.** Verbs ending in **-zar: z → c** before **e**
The change **z → c** occurs in the first-person singular preterit and throughout the present subjunctive.

**comenzar**

*Preterit*　　　　　　　　comencé, comenzaste, comenzó, comenzamos, comenzasteis, comenzaron

*Present subjunctive*　　comience, comiences, comience, comencemos, comencéis, comiencen


**D.** Verbs ending in **-ger** and **-gir: g → j** before **a** and **o**
The change **g → j** occurs in the first-person singular of the present indicative and throughout the present subjunctive.

**recoger**

*Present indicative*　　　recojo, recoges, recoge, recogemos, recogéis, recogen

*Present subjunctive*　　recoja, recojas, recoja, recojamos, recojáis, recojan


**E.** Verbs ending in **-guir: gu → g** before **a** and **o**
The change **gu → g** occurs in the first-person singular of the present indicative and throughout the present subjunctive.

**seguir**

*Present indicative*　　　sigo, sigues, sigue, seguimos, seguís, siguen

*Present subjunctive*　　siga, sigas, siga, sigamos, sigáis, sigan

**F.** Verbs ending in **e** + **er**: unstressed **i** → **y**
The change **i** → **y** occurs in the third-person singular and plural of the preterit, the present participle, and throughout the past subjunctive.

| | **leer** |
|---|---|
| *Preterit* | leí, leíste, leyó, leímos, leístes, leyeron |
| *Past subjunctive* | leyera, leyeras, leyera, leyéramos, leyerais, leyeran |
| *Present participle* | leyendo |

**G.** Verbs ending in a consonant + **cer** or **cir**: **c** → **z** before **a** and **o**
The change **c** → **z** occurs in the first-person singular of the present indicative and throughout the present subjunctive.

| | **torcer**  *to twist, to turn* |
|---|---|
| *Present indicative* | tuerzo, tuerces, tuerce, torcemos, torcéis, tuercen |
| *Present subjunctive* | tuerza, tuerzas, tuerza, torzamos, torzáis, tuerzan |

## IV. IRREGULAR VERBS

**A.** Verbs ending in a vowel + **cer** or **cir**: **c** → **zc** before **a** and **o**
The letters **zc** occur in the first-person singular of the present indicative and throughout the present subjunctive.

| | **conocer** |
|---|---|
| *Present indicative* | conozco, conoces, conoce, conocemos, conocéis, conocen |
| *Present subjunctive* | conozca, conozcas, conozca, conozcamos, conozcáis, conozcan |

**B.** Verbs ending in **-uir** (except **-guir**): insert **y** before **a** and **o**[4]
The letter **y** is inserted in all singular forms and in the third-person plural and of the present indicative and throughout the present subjunctive.

| | **construir** |
|---|---|
| *Present indicative* | construyo, construyes, construye, construimos, construís, construyen |
| *Present subjunctive* | construya, construyas, construya, construyamos, construyáis, construyan |

---

[4] These verbs also have an orthographic change: unstressed **i** changes to **y** in the third-person singular and plural of the preterit (**construyó, construyeron**), throughout the past subjunctive (**construyera, construyeras,** etc.), and in the present participle (**construyendo**).

## C. Other irregular verbs[5]

**andar**   *to walk, to go*

| | |
|---|---|
| *Preterit* | anduve, anduviste, anduvo, anduvimos, anduvisteis, anduvieron |
| *Past subjunctive* | anduviera, anduvieras, anduviera, anduviéramos, anduvierais, anduvieran |

**caer**   *to fall*

| | |
|---|---|
| *Present indicative* | caigo, caes, cae, caemos, caéis, caen |
| *Preterit* | caí, caíste, cayó, caímos, caísteis, cayeron |
| *Present subjunctive* | caiga, caigas, caiga, caigamos, caigáis, caigan |
| *Past subjunctive* | cayera, cayeras, cayera, cayéramos, cayerais, cayeran |
| *Present participle* | cayendo |

**dar**   *to give*

| | |
|---|---|
| *Present indicative* | doy, das, da, damos, dais, dan |
| *Preterit* | di, diste, dio, dimos, disteis, dieron |
| *Present subjunctive* | dé, des, dé, demos, deis, den |
| *Past subjunctive* | diera, dieras, diera, diéramos, dierais, dieran |

**decir**   *to say, to tell*[6]

| | |
|---|---|
| *Present indicative* | digo, dices, dice, decimos, decís, dicen |
| *Preterit* | dije, dijiste, dijo, dijimos, dijisteis, dijeron |
| *Present subjunctive* | diga, digas, diga, digamos, digáis, digan |
| *Past subjunctive* | dijera, dijeras, dijera, dijéramos, dijerais, dijeran |
| *Future* | diré, dirás, dirá, diremos, diréis, dirán |
| *Conditional* | diría, dirías, diría, diríamos, diríais, dirían |
| *Affirmative* **tú** *command* | di |
| *Present participle* | diciendo |
| *Past participle* | dicho |

[5] Only the tenses in which irregularities occur are shown.
[6] Compounds of **decir** (**contradecir, predecir**) have the same irregularities.

**estar**   *to be*

| | |
|---|---|
| *Present indicative* | estoy, estás, está, estamos, estáis, están |
| *Preterit* | estuve, estuviste, estuvo, estuvimos, estuvisteis, estuvieron |
| *Present subjunctive* | esté, estés, esté, estemos, estéis, estén |
| *Past subjunctive* | estuviera, estuvieras, estuviera, estuviéramos, estuvierais, estuvieran |

**haber**   *to have* (auxiliary)

| | |
|---|---|
| *Present indicative* | he, has, ha, hemos, habéis, han |
| *Preterit* | hube, hubiste, hubo, hubimos, hubisteis, hubieron |
| *Present subjunctive* | haya, hayas, haya, hayamos, hayáis, hayan |
| *Past subjunctive* | hubiera, hubieras, hubiera, hubiéramos, hubierais, hubieran |
| *Future* | habré, habrás, habrás, habremos, habréis, habrán |
| *Conditional* | habría, habrías, habría, habríamos, habríais, habrían |

**hacer**   *to do, to make*

| | |
|---|---|
| *Present indicative* | hago, haces, hace, hacemos, hacéis, hacen |
| *Preterit* | hice, hiciste, hizo, hicimos, hicisteis, hicieron |
| *Present subjunctive* | haga, hagas, haga, hagamos, hagáis, hagan |
| *Past subjunctive* | hiciera, hicieras, hiciera, hiciéramos, hicierais, hicieran |
| *Future* | haré, harás, hará, haremos, haréis, harán |
| *Conditional* | haría, harías, haría, haríamos, haríais, harían |
| *Affirmative* **tú** *command* | haz |
| *Past participle* | hecho |

**ir**   *to go*

| | |
|---|---|
| *Present indicative* | voy, vas, va, vamos, vais, van |
| *Imperfect* | iba, ibas, iba, íbamos, ibais, iban |
| *Preterit* | fui, fuiste, fue, fuimos, fuisteis, fueron |
| *Present subjunctive* | vaya, vayas, vaya, vayamos, vayáis, vayan |
| *Past subjunctive* | fuera, fueras, fuera, fuéramos, fuerais, fueran |
| *Affirmative* **tú** *command* | ve |
| *Present participle* | yendo |

**oír**   *to hear*

| | |
|---|---|
| *Present indicative* | oigo, oyes, oye, oímos, oís, oyen |
| *Preterit* | oí, oíste, oyó, oímos, oísteis, oyeron |
| *Present subjunctive* | oiga, oigas, oiga, oigamos, oigáis, oigan |
| *Past subjunctive* | oyera, oyeras, oyera, oyéramos, oyerais, oyeran |
| *Affirmative* **tú** *command* | oye |
| *Present participle* | oyendo |


**poder**   *to be able to, can, may*

| | |
|---|---|
| *Present indicative* | puedo, puedes, puede, podemos, podéis, pueden |
| *Preterit* | pude, pudiste, pudo, pudimos, pudisteis, pudieron |
| *Present subjunctive* | pueda, puedas, pueda, podamos, podáis, puedan |
| *Past subjunctive* | pudiera, pudieras, pudiera, pudiéramos, pudierais, pudieran |
| *Future* | podré, podrás, podrá, podremos, podréis, podrán |
| *Conditional* | podría, podrías, podría, podríamos, podríais, podrían |
| *Present participle* | pudiendo |


**poner**   *to put*[7]

| | |
|---|---|
| *Present indicative* | pongo, pones, pone, ponemos, ponéis, ponen |
| *Preterit* | puse, pusiste, puso, pusimos pusisteis, pusieron |
| *Present subjunctive* | ponga, pongas, ponga, pongamos, pongáis, pongan |
| *Past subjunctive* | pusiera, pusieras, pusiera, pusiéramos, pusierais, pusieran |
| *Future* | pondré, pondrás, pondrá, pondremos, pondréis, pondrán |
| *Conditional* | pondría, pondrías, pondría, pondríamos, pondríais, pondrían |
| *Affirmative* **tú** *command* | pon |
| *Past participle* | puesto |

[7] Compounds of **poner** (**componer, disponer, proponer**) have the same irregularities.

**querer**  *to want*

| | |
|---|---|
| *Present indicative* | quiero, quieres, quiere, queremos, queréis, quieren |
| *Preterit* | quise, quisiste, quiso, quisimos, quisisteis, quisieron |
| *Present subjunctive* | quiera, quieras, quiera, queramos, queráis, quieran |
| *Past subjunctive* | quisiera, quisieras, quisiera, quisiéramos, quisierais, quisieran |
| *Future* | querré, querrás, querrá, querremos, querréis, querrán |
| *Conditional* | querría, querrías, querría, querríamos, querríais, querrían |
| *Affirmative* **tú** *command* | quiere |

**saber**  *to know*

| | |
|---|---|
| *Present indicative* | sé, sabes, sabe, sabemos, sabéis, saben |
| *Preterit* | supe, supiste, supo, supimos, supisteis, supieron |
| *Present subjunctive* | sepa, sepas, sepa, sepamos, sepáis, sepan |
| *Past subjunctive* | supiera, supieras, supiera, supiéramos, supierais, supieran |
| *Future* | sabré, sabrás, sabrá, sabremos, sabréis, sabrán |
| *Conditional* | sabría, sabrías, sabría, sabríamos, sabríais, sabrían |

**salir**  *to go (come) out, to leave*

| | |
|---|---|
| *Present indicative* | salgo, sales, sale, salimos, salís, salen |
| *Present subjunctive* | salga, salgas, salga, salgamos, salgáis, salgan |
| *Future* | saldré, saldrás, saldrá, saldremos, saldréis, saldrán |
| *Conditional* | saldría, saldrías, saldría, saldríamos, saldríais, saldrían |
| *Affirmative* **tú** *command* | sal |

**ser**  *to be*

| | |
|---|---|
| *Present indicative* | soy, eres, es, somos, sois, son |
| *Imperfect* | era, eras, era, éramos, erais, eran |

| Preterit | fui, fuiste, fue, fuimos, fuisteis, fueron |
| Present subjunctive | sea, seas, sea, seamos, seáis, sean |
| Past subjunctive | fuera, fueras, fuera, fuéramos, fuerais, fueran |
| Affirmative **tú** command | sé |

### tener   *to have*[8]

| Present indicative | tengo, tienes, tiene, tenemos, tenéis, tienen |
| Preterit | tuve, tuviste, tuvo, tuvimos, tuvisteis, tuvieron |
| Present subjunctive | tenga, tengas, tenga, tengamos, tengáis, tengan |
| Past subjunctive | tuviera, tuvieras, tuviera, tuviéramos, tuvierais, tuvieran |
| Future | tendré, tendrás, tendrá, tendremos, tendréis, tendrán |
| Conditional | tendría, tendrías, tendría, tendríamos, tendríais, tendrían |
| Affirmative **tú** command | ten |

### traducir   *to translate*[9]

| Present indicative | traduzco, traduces, traduce, traducimos, traducís, traducen |
| Preterit | traduje, tradujiste, tradujo, tradujimos, tradujisteis, tradujeron |
| Present subjunctive | traduzca, traduzcas, traduzca, traduzcamos, traduzcais, traduzcan |
| Past subjunctive | tradujera, tradujeras, tradujera, tradujéramos, tradujerais, tradujeran |

### traer   *to bring*

| Present indicative | traigo, traes, trae, traemos, traéis, traen |
| Preterit | traje, trajiste, trajo, trajimos, trajisteis, trajeron |
| Present subjunctive | traiga, traigas, traiga, traigamos, traigáis, traigan |
| Past subjunctive | trajera, trajeras, trajera, trajéramos, trajerais, trajeran |
| Present participle | trayendo |

[8] Compounds of **tener** (**contener, retener**) have the same irregularities.
[9] Verbs ending in **-ducir**, besides changing **c → zc** before **a** and **o**, change **c → j** throughout the preterit and the past subjunctive.

**valer**   *to be worth*

| | |
|---|---|
| *Present indicative* | valgo, vales, vale, valemos, valéis, valen |
| *Present subjunctive* | valga, valgas, valga, valgamos, valgáis, valgan |
| *Future* | valdré, valdrás, valdrá, valdremos, valdréis, valdrán |
| *Conditional* | valdría, valdrías, valdría, valdríamos, valdríais, valdrían |
| *Affirmative* **tú** *command* | val *or* vale |

**venir**   *to come*[10]

| | |
|---|---|
| *Present indicative* | vengo, vienes, viene, venimos, venís, vienen |
| *Preterit* | vine, viniste, vino, vinimos, vinisteis, vinieron |
| *Present subjunctive* | venga, vengas, venga, vengamos, vengáis, vengan |
| *Past subjunctive* | viniera, vinieras, viniera, viniéramos, vinierais, vinieran |
| *Future* | vendré, vendrás, vendrá, vendremos, vendréis, vendrán |
| *Conditional* | vendría, vendrías, vendría, vendríamos, vendríais, vendrían |
| *Affirmative* **tú** *command* | ven |
| *Present particple* | viniendo |

**ver**   *to see*

| | |
|---|---|
| *Present indicative* | veo, ves, ve, vemos, veis, ven |
| *Imperfect* | veía, veías, veía, veíamos, veíais, veían |
| *Present subjunctive* | vea, veas, vea, veamos, veáis, vean |
| *Past participle* | visto |

[10] Compounds of **venir** (**intervenir**) have the same irregularities.

# *Vocabulary*

This vocabulary includes all the active and passive words presented in the **pasos** and **lecciones,** except for proper nouns spelled the same in Spanish and English, diminutives with literal meanings, and certain words encountered only in the pronunciation exercises. The **pasos** are identified as P1, P2, and so forth.

Numbers indicate the lesson in which each word first appears. Italic numbers indicate that the word is passive vocabulary. Words presented in the introduction (dialogs, ads, and so on) of the **pasos** and **lecciones** and those explained in the grammar sections are considered active. All other vocabulary is considered passive. If a word is followed by two numbers, the italic one shows when it appears as passive vocabulary; the other shows when it becomes active.

The following abbreviations are used:

| | | | | |
|---|---|---|---|---|
| *adj* | adjective | | *n* | noun |
| *fam* | familiar | | *part* | participle |
| *fem* | feminine | | *pl* | plural |
| *inf* | infinitive | | *pron* | pronoun |
| *masc* | masculine | | *sing* | singular |
| | | | *v* | verb |

## SPANISH-ENGLISH VOCABULARY

A

**a** at, to P4
**a.C.** B.C. (before Christ) *15*
**abajo** below *2*

**abandonar** to abandon *8*
el **abogado,** la **abogada** lawyer 8
el **abrazo** embrace 13
el **abrigo** coat 7
**abril** April 6

**abrir** to open *P1,* 3
**absoluto/a** total *13*
**absurdo/a** absurd 7
la **abuela** grandmother 4
el **abuelo** grandfather 4
los **abuelos** grandparents 4

**453**

**acabar** to end, to terminate *8*; to finish *16*; **acabar de** + *inf* to have just + *past part* *16*

el **accessorio** accessory *7*

el **accidente** accident *8, 9*

la **acción: el Día de Acción de Gracias** Thanksgiving *15*

el **aceite** oil *P3, 10*

**aceptar** to accept *8, 10*

la **acera** sidewalk *3*

**acercar (qu)** to move closely, to approximate *9*

**ácido/a** acid *16*

la **aclaración** clarification *13*

**acompañar** to accompany *4*

**acondicionado: el aire acondicionado** air conditioning *5*

el **acontecimiento** event *6*

**acostar (ue)** to put to bed *5*; **acostarse (ue)** to go to bed, to lie down *5*

**acostumbrar: se acostumbra** it's customary *13*

**acostumbrado/a** accustomed, used to *13*

la **actitud** attitude *8*

**activamente** actively *17*

la **actividad** activity *P1, 3*

**activo/a** active *P2*

el **acto** action *15*

el **actor** actor *8*

la **actriz** actress *8*

**actual** present *8*

**actuar** to act, to play *6*

**acudir** to go *17*

**acuerdo: de acuerdo con** according to *1*; **estar de acuerdo** to agree *5*

**acumulado/a** accumulated *8*

**acústica** acoustics *13*

**adecuadamente** adequately *9*

**adecuado/a** adequate *1*

**adelante** forward *13*

el **adelanto** advance *14, 17*

**además** besides *1*

**adiós** good-bye *P1*

la **adivinanza** riddle, guessing game *P3*

**adivinar** to guess *7*

el **administrador, la administradora** administrator, manager *8*

**administrar** to administer, to direct *2*

**administrativo/a** administrative *8*

la **admiración** admiration *7*

**admitir** to allow, to admit *10*

el/la **adolescente** adolescent, teenager *11*

**adónde** where (to) *3*

**adoptar** to assume, to follow *9*

**adquirir** to get, to acquire *16*

la **aduana** customs *12*

**adverbial** adverbial *17*

**aéreo/a** *adj* air *12*

**aeróbico/a** aerobic *9*

el **aerograma** aerogram *13*

la **aerolínea** airline *12*

el **aeropuerto** airport *P4, 12*

**afectar** to affect *17*

**afectado/a** affected *16*

**afectivo/a** affectionate *13*

**afeitar** to shave *5*

el **aficionado, la aficionada** fan *6*

el **afiche** poster *14*

**afirmar** to assert, to declare *15*

**afirmativo/a** affirmative *13*

**afortunado/a** fortunate *13*

las **afueras** outskirts *5*

**agarrado** holding; **agarrados de la mano** holding hands *17*

**agarrar** to grab *6*

la **agencia** agency *2, 12*; la **agencia de viajes** travel agency *12*

la **agenda** agenda *3*

el **agente, la agente** agent *12*

**agilizar** to speed up *14*

**agosto** August *6*

**agresivo/a** aggressive *P2*

el **agua** *fem* water *4*

el **aguacate** avocado *P3, 10*

**aguantar** to endure *17*

la **ahijada** goddaughter *4*

el **ahijado** godson *4*

**ahora** now *3*

**ahorrar** to save *3*

el **aire** air *5*; el **aire libre** open air *9*

el **ajedrez** chess *14*

el **ajo** garlic *10*

**al** (*contraction of* ***a*** + ***el***) to the *3*; **al lado de** next to *P3*

el **ala** *fem* wing *12*

**alarmante** alarming *16*

el **álbum** album *14*

el **alcance** reach *12*

**alcanzado/a** hit *16*

**alcanzar (c)** to obtain *13*; to reach *14*

el **alcohol** alcohol *P3*

**alcohólico/a** alcoholic *11*

**alegrarse** to be glad *10*

**alegre** happy, glad *2*

**alejado/a** far away *13*

**alemán, alemana** German *1*

la **alergia** allergy *11*

**alérgico/a** allergic *11*

**alerta** aware *11*

la **alfalfa** alfalfa *10*

la **alfombra** carpet, rug *5*

el **álgebra** *fem* algebra *P3, 3*

**algo** something, anything *1*; **algo más** anything else, something else *1, 3*

**alguien** someone, somebody, anyone *12*

**algún** some *4, 12*; any *12*

**alguno/a** any, some *P3, 12*

**algunos/as** some, several *1, 6*

la **alimentación** food *8*

**alimentar** to nourish *10*

el **alimento** food *5*

el **almacén** department store *7*

la **almohada** pillow *5*

**almorzar (ue, c)** to have lunch *1, 4*

el **almuerzo** lunch *P4, 3*

**aló** hello *7*

el **alojamiento** lodging *14*

**alquilar** to rent *5*

**alrededor** around *12*; los **alrededores** surrounding areas *16*

**alto/a** tall *2*; **hacer alto** to stop *12*; **más alto** louder *P4, 13*

la **altura** height, elevation *13*

el **alud** landslide, avalanche *16*

el **alumno,** la **alumna** student *1*

**allá** there *7*; **más allá** beyond *2*

**allí** there *1, 2*

el **ama:** el **ama de casa** *fem* housewife, homemaker *8*

**amable** kind, nice *2, 14*

**amablemente** cheerfully, kindly *13*

**amarillo/a** yellow *2*

**ambicioso/a** ambitious *P2*

**ambiental** environmental *16*

el **ambiente** atmosphere *8*; background *12*; el **medio ambiente** environment *16*

**ambos/as** both *15*

la **ambulancia** ambulance *9, 12*

el **ambulatorio** emergency center *11*

**americana:** la **hora americana** precise time *P4*

el **amigo,** la **amiga** friend *P2*

la **amistad** friendship *13*

el **amor** love *13*

**amplio/a** ample *4*

**añadir** to add *6*

el **análisis** analysis *11*

**anaranjado/a** orange *2*

el **anciano,** la **anciana** old, elderly person *4*

**ancho/a** wide *7*

las **andas** platform *15*

la **anestesia** anesthesia *11*

el **ángel** angel *17*

el **anillo** ring *7*

el **animal** animal *1, 4*

**animar** to urge *11*

el **aniversario** anniversary *15*

el **año** year *1, 3*

**anoche** last night *12*

**anormal** abnormal *16*

**anotar** to write down *13*

la **ansiedad** anxiety *9*

**ante** before *17*

**anteanoche** the night before last *12*

**anteayer** the day before yesterday *12*

**antenoche** the night before last *12*

**anterior** previous *1*

**anteriormente** previously *16*

**antes** before *1, 3*; **antes (de) que** before *17*

el **antibiótico** antibiotic *11*

la **anticipación: con anticipación** beforehand *16*

**antiguo/a** old *10*; former *16*

**antihistamínico/a** antihistaminic *11*

el **antimonio** antimony *16*

**antipático/a** unpleasant *2*

la **antropología** anthropology *1*

**antropológico/a** anthropological *14*

**anunciar** to announce *10*

el **anuncio** ad *1, 8*

**apagar (gu)** to turn off *8*

el **aparador** china cabinet *5*

el **aparato** airplane *16*

**aparecer (zc)** to appear *2*

el **apartado** P.O. box *8*

el **apartamento** apartment *5*

el **apellido** last name *1*

**aplaudir** to applaud *6*

**aportar** to supply *10*

**apostar (ue)** to bet *6*

el **apoyo** support *13*

**apreciar** to appreciate *2*

**aprender** to learn *3*

el **aprendizaje** apprenticeship *6*

**aprobar (ue)** to pass *1*

**apropiado/a** appropriate *2*

**aprovechar** to take advantage of *13*

**aproximado/a** approximate *9*

**apuntar** to take credit *6*

los **apuntes** notes *14*

**aquel, aquella** *adj* that (over there) *7*; **aquél, aquélla** *pron* that one (over there) *7*

**aquellos/as** *adj* those *7*; **aquéllos/as** *pron* those (ones) (over there) *7*

**aquí** here *4*

**árabe** Arab *12*

el **árbitro** umpire, referee *6*

el **árbol** tree *4, 14*

el **área** *fem* area *16*

la **arena** sand *14*

el **arete** earring 7
**árido/a** arid 16
el **armario** closet 5
**armónicamente** harmoniously 9
el **aro** ring 6
el **aroma** aroma 17
el **arquitecto,** la **arquitecta** architect 8
**arquitectónico/a** architectonic 16
la **arquitectura** architecture 13
los **arreglos** planning 15
el **arresto** arrest 17
el **arroz** rice 3
**arriba** high 16
el **arte** art 1
la **arteria** artery 11
la **artesanía** handicraft 14
la **articulación** joint 11
el **artículo** article 1, 4
el/la **artista** artist 13
**artístico/a** artistic 13
el **asa** *fem* handle 6
el **asado** roast 10
**ascender** to rise 17
**ascender (ie)** to promote, to be promoted 17
el **ascensor** elevator 11, 14
**asearse** to tidy oneself 14
el **aseo** washing 17
**así** this way 5; like this 8
el **asiento** seat 2
la **asistencia** attendance 6
el **asistente,** la **asistenta** assistant 8
**asistir** to attend 8
el **asma** *fem* asthma 11
la **asociación** matching 2
**asociado** associated 12
**asociar** to associate 1
el **aspecto** aspect 11
la **aspiración** aspiration 17
la **aspiradora/**el **aspirador** vacuum cleaner 5
la **aspirina** aspirin 11

el **asterisco** asterisk 9
el/la **astronauta** astronaut 8
el **astrónomo** astronomer 6
el **asunto** matter 13, 16
**asustado/a** frightened 16
**asustar** to frighten 16
**atacar (qu)** to attack 16
**atareado/a** busy 13
la **atención** attention 11
**atender (ie)** to take care of 16
**atendido/a** staffed 9
**aterrorizar (c)** to frighten 8
el/la **atleta** athlete 16
el **atletismo** athletics 9
la **atracción** attraction 14
**atractivo/a** atrractive 2
**atraer (g)** to attract 14
el **atún** tuna 3
la **audiencia** public 6
**aumentar** to increase 11
el **aumento** increase 17
**aun** even 13
**aunque** although 11, 13
**ausente** absent P3
el **auto** car 2
el **autobús** bus 2, 12
la **autodescripción** self-description 2
**automático:** el **contestador automático** answering machine 14
el **automóvil** car 12
la **autopista** freeway, superhighway 12
**autoritario/a** authoritarian 8
el **avance** improvement 11
el **ave** *fem* bird 16
la **avenida** avenue 4
la **aventura** adventure 4
**averiguar** to find out 3
la **aviación** aviation 12
el **avión** plane 12
**avisar** to notify 13
**ayer** yesterday 12

la **ayuda** help 1
**ayudar** to help 5
el **ayuntamiento** city hall 14
la **azafata** stewardess 1
**azteca** Aztec 14
el/la **azúcar** sugar 10
**azul** blue 2

## B

el **bachillerato** high school curriculum 1
la **bahía** bay 12
**bailar** to dance 3
el **bailarín,** la **bailarina** dancer 10
el **baile** dance 8
**bajar** to lower, to bring down 9
**bajo/a** short, low 2; under 14
el **baloncesto** basketball 6
el **balonmano** handball 14
la **bañadera** tub 5
la **banana** banana 3
**bañar** to bathe 5
el **banco** bank 8
la **bandeja** tray 3, 17
el **baño** bathroom 4, 5; el **traje de baño** bathing suit 7
el **banquete** banquet 2
el **bar** bar 14
**barato/a** inexpensive, cheap 5, 7
la **barbacoa** barbecue 5
la **barbaridad: ¿qué barbaridad!** good grief!, it's incredible! 15
**bárbaro/a** barbarian 15
el **barbitúrico** barbituric 11
el **barco** ship 12
**barrer** to sweep 5
la **barriada** neighborhood 11
**basado/a** established, set 11
**basarse** to be founded 9

la **base: en base a** based on
   *16*
**básicamente** basically *13*
**básico/a** basic *17*
el **básquetbol** basketball *6*
**bastante** enough *P1*
la **basura** garbage *5*
la **batidora** mixer *5*
el **baúl** trunk *12*
**bautizar (c)** to baptize *15*
el **bautizo** christening *15*
el **bebé** baby *4*
**beber** to drink *3*
la **bebida** drink, beverage *3,*
   *10*
la **beca** scholarship *9*
el **béisbol** baseball *4, 6*
la **belleza** beauty *3;* el **salón**
   **de belleza** beauty par-
   lor *3*
**bello/a** beautiful *12*
el **beneficio** benefit *14*
el **beso** kiss *13*
la **biblioteca** library *1*
la **bicicleta** bicycle *6*
**bien** well, fine *P1*
el **bienestar** well-being *11*
el **bigote** moustache *2*
el **billete** ticket *17*
la **billetera** wallet *7*
la **biología** biology *1*
**blanco/a** white *2*
la **blusa** blouse *7*
la **boca** mouth *9*
la **boda** wedding *15*
el **boleto** ticket *P4, 12;* el
   **boleto de ida y vuelta**
   round-trip ticket *12*
el **bolígrafo** ballpoint pen *P3*
el **bolívar** monetary unit of
   Venezuela *7*
**boliviano/a** Bolivian *2*
la **bolsa** bag *6;* purse *7*
el **bolsillo** pocket *14*
el **bombero** fireman *8*
**bonito/a** pretty *2*
el **bordado** embroidery *7*

el **borrador** eraser *P3*
el **bosque** forest *16*
la **bota** boot *7*
la **botella** bottle *10*
el **botón** button *5;* el **bo-**
   **tones** bellboy *14*
el **boxeo** boxing *6*
**brava: la fiesta brava**
   bullfight *15*
el **brazo** arm *9*
**brillar** to shine *13*
el **brillo** shine *13*
el **bronce** bronze *15*
la **bruja: el Día de las Bru-**
   **jas** Halloween *15*
**bucear** to skin/scuba dive
   *6*
**buen** good *2;* bueno/a
   good *P1*
la **bufanda** scarf *7*
el **bufete** lawyer's office *8*
**buscar (qu)** to look for *1*
la **butaca** armchair *5*
el **buzón** mail box *13*

## C

la **cabeza** head *9*
el **cabo: al cabo de** after *9*
**cada** each, every *P4, 9*
la **cadena** chain *6, 7*
la **cadera** hip *9*
**caerse** to fall *13*
**café** brown *2;* café *1, 3;*
   coffee *3;* el **café con**
   **leche** strong coffee with
   hot milk *3*
la **cafetería** cafeteria *1*
la **caja** cash register *7*
el **cajero,** la **cajera** cashier *8*
la **calamidad** calamity *13*
el **calcetín** sock *7*
el **calcio** calcium *10*
la **calculadora** calculator *1*
el **cálculo** calculus *1*
la **calefacción** heating *5*
el **calendario** calendar *P4*

el **calentamiento** warm–up *9*
**calentar (ie)** to warm up
   *9*
la **calidad** quality *5*
**caliente** hot *2, 3*
el **calor: hace calor** it's hot
   *6;* **tener calor** to be hot
   *4*
la **caloría** calorie *10*
**caluroso/a** hot *7*
**callado/a** quiet *2*
la **calle** street *3*
la **cama** bed *2, 5;* **coche**
   **cama** sleeper *12;* **guar-**
   **dar cama** to stay in bed
   *11*
la **cámara** camera *12, 14*
la **camarera** waitress *3*
el **camarero** waiter *3*
el **camarón** shrimp *10*
**cambiar** to change, to exchange *3, 7*
el **cambio** change *1, 17;* **en**
   **cambio** on the other
   hand *16*
la **camilla** stretcher *16*
**caminar** to walk *3*
el **camión** truck *12*
la **camisa** shirt *5*
la **camiseta** T-shirt *3, 7*
el **campamento** camp *14*
la **campaña** campaign *8;* la
   **tienda de campaña** tent
   *16*
el **campeón** la **campeona**
   champion *3*
el **campeonato** championship *6*
el **campo** country, countryside *6, 11;* field, area *6,*
   *11;* el **campo de golf**
   golf course *6*
el **canal** channel *6*
**cancelar** to cancel *12*
el **cáncer** cancer *6*
la **canción** song *3*
la **cancha** court *6*

la **canoa** canoe *14*
**cansado/a** tired *11*
**cansarse** to get tired *11*
el/la **cantante** singer *10*
**cantar** to sing *3*
la **cantidad** amount *8*
**capacitado/a** prepared, qualified *17*
la **capital** capital *P4*
la **cara** face *5*
el **carácter** temper *13*
la **característica** characteristic *9*
**caracterizar (c)** to characterize *13*
el **caramelo** candy *15*
**cardiovascular** cardiovascular *11*
la **carga** cargo *12*
**cargar (gu)** to carry *15*
el **cargo: estar a cargo** to be in charge *2*; la **llamada de cargo revertido** collect call *13*
la **caridad** charity *15*
el **carnaval** Mardi Gras *15*
la **carne** meat *10*
la **carnicería** meat market *10*
**caro/a** expensive *7*
la **carrera** career *1*; studies *3*
la **carretera** highway *2, 12*
el **carro** car *12*
la **carta** letter *8, 13*
el **cartero** mailman *13*
el **cartón** cardboard *15*
la **casa** house *1, 3*; la **casa de socorro** first-aid center *11*
**casado/a** married *2*
**casarse** to get married *17*
el **casco** helmet *17*
la **caseta** booth *2*
el **casete** cassette *1*
**casi** almost *5*
la **casilla** box *16*
el **caso** case *1*

**castaño/a** brown *2*
**castellano/a** Castilian *P3*
el **castillo** castle *13*
el **catarro** cold *11*
la **catástrofe** (natural) disaster *16*
**catastrófico/a** catastrophic *16*
la **catedral** cathedral *14*
la **categoría** category *9*
**catorce** fourteen *P4*
la **causa** cause *16*
**causado/a** caused *16*
**causar** to cause *4*
**cazar (c)** to hunt, to go hunting *14*
la **cebolla** onion *10*
la **cebra** zebra *2*
la **ceja** eyebrow *9*
**celebrar** to celebrate *4, 15*
la **cena** supper *3*
**cenar** to have dinner, supper *3, 10*
el **censo** census *17*
el **centavo** cent *P4*
el **centígrado** centigrade *6*
**central** central *1*
**centrar** to focus *13*
el **centro** downtown, center *5*; el **centro comercial** shopping center *7*
la **cerámica** ceramics *14*
**cerca** near *1, 5*
**cercano/a** near, close *17*
el **cerdo** pork *10*
el **cereal** cereal *3*
el **cerebro** brain *8, 11*
la **ceremonia** ceremony *15*
**cero** zero *P3, P4*
**cerrar (ie)** to close *P1, 8*
**certificado/a** registered *13*
la **cerveza** beer *6*
el **césped** lawn *17*
la **cesta** basket *6*
el **cesto** basket *P3*
el **ciclismo** cycling *9*
el/la **ciclista** cyclist *15*

**cien** one hundred *3*
la **ciencia** science *1*
el **científico,** la **científica** scientist *13*
**ciento** one hundred *3*
**cierto** true *11*; certain *13*; **por cierto** by the way *5*
la **cifra** figure, number *17*
el **cigarrillo** cigarette *11*
**cinco** five *P4*
**cincuenta** fifty *P4*
el **cine** movies *3*
la **cinta** tape *1*; ribbon *15*
la **cintura** waist *9*
el **cinturón** belt *7*; el **cinturón de seguridad** safety belt *11, 12*
el **circuito** tour *6*
**circular** circular *11*
el **círculo** circle *13*
la **circunstancia** circumstance *13*
la **cirugía** surgery *9*
el **cirujano,** la **cirujana** surgeon *9*
la **cita** date *10*
la **ciudad** city *P4, 4*
**ciudadano/a** citizen *17*
**civil** civil *17*; el **estado civil** marital status *3*
la **civilización** civilization *12*
**civilizado/a** civilized *15*
**claramente** clearly *13*
**claro/a** light *2*; clear *6*
la **clase** class *P1, P3*
**clásico/a** classic *3*
**clasificar (qu)** to classify *14*
**clave** *adj* key *12*
el **cliente,** la **clienta** client *3, 12*
el **clima** climate *6, 10*
la **clínica** clinic, hospital *9*
el **closet** closet *5*
el **club** club *7*
**cobrar:** la **llamada a cobrar** collect call *13*
la **cocina** kitchen *5*

cocinar to cook 5

el cocinero, la cocinera cook 8

el cocodrilo crocodile 16

el coche car 12; el coche cama sleeping car 12

la cochera garage 11

el código code 1; el código postal zip code 13

el cognado cognate P2

coincidir to coincide 8

la cola line 12; hacer cola to stand in line 12

la colaboración collaboration 12

la colección collection 13

el colegio school 1

el colesterol cholesterol 11

colgar (ue) to hang 5; to hang up 13

el coliseo coliseum 15

colocar (qu) to put, to place 3

colombiano/a Colombian 2

la colonia house development, neighborhood 5

colonial colonial 12

el color color 2; de color entero solid color 7

la columna column 1

el collar necklace 7

la coma comma 13

la comadrona midwife 11

la combinación combination 7

combinado: el plato combinado combination plate 10

combinar to combine 13; combinar bien to go together 7

el comedor dining room 5

el comentario commentary 7

comenzar (ie, c) to begin 11, 17

comer to eat 1, 3

comercial adj business 8; el centro comercial shopping center 7

el comestible food 10

cómico/a funny 4

la comida food 2; dinner, supper 3

el comisario commissioner 14

la comisión commission 16

como as 3, 9; since 4; like 8

cómo how P1; cómo no of course 8

la cómoda dresser 5

la comodidad comfort 12, 15

cómodo/a comfortable 2

el compañero, la compañera classmate P1, 2

la compañía company 2, 8

comparar to compare 3

compartir to share 2

la competencia meet 3

competente competent P2

la competición competition 6

competir (i) to compete 14

completamente completely 16

completar to complete 1

completo/a: la jornada completa full time 8; por completo completely 15

la complicación complication 13

complicado/a complex 12

la compra shopping 5, 7

el comprador, la compradora buyer 7

comprar to buy 1

comprender to understand P3

la comprensión understanding 11

comprensivo/a comprehensive 17

el compromiso commitment 11

compulsivo/a compulsive 7

la computadora, el computador computer 1

común common 2

la comunicación communication 11

comunicar (qu) to communicate, to link 12

la comunidad community 5

la comunión communion 15

con with 1; con permiso excuse me P1; con tal (de) que provided that 17

la concentración concentration 17

concentrado/a concentrated 17

el concepto concept 17

el concierto concert 2

concretamente specifically 16

el concurso contest 2

la condición condition 6

el condominio condominium 5

conducir (zc) to drive 11

la conducta behavior 11

conectar to turn on 6; to connect 13

la conexión connection 13

la conferencia lecture 2

la confirmación confirmation 14

el conflicto conflict 4

conforme agreeable 15

la confusión confusion 13

congelado/a frozen 15

conmigo with me 8

la connotación connotation 13

conocer (zc) to know 8

**conocido/a** known *13*

el **conocimiento** knowledge *8*

la **consecuencia** consequence *16*

**conseguir (i)** to get, to obtain *3, 6*

el **consejero,** la **consejera** advisor *2*

el **consejo** advice *9*

**conservador/a** conservative *7*

**conservar** to conserve, to keep *10*

**considerar** to consider *13*

la **consolación** consolation *10*

la **consonante** consonant *P2*

**constituir** to make up *14*

la **construcción** construction, building *12*

**construido/a** built *16*

**construir (y)** to construct, to build *12*

la **consulta** consultation, visit to the doctor *14*

**consultar** to consult *1*

el **consultorio** doctor's office *8*

**consumir** to use *12*

el **consumo** consumption *11*

la **contabilidad** accounting *1*

el **contacto** contact *3*

la **contaminación** pollution *9, 11*

**contaminado/a** contaminated *16*

**contar (ue)** to count *P4, 4*; to tell *13*

**contener (g, ie)** to contain *10*

**contento/a** happy, glad *2*

el **contestador:** el **contestador automático** answering machine *14*

**contestar** to answer *P1, 7*

el **contexto** context *2*

**contigo** with you *fam 8*

la **continuación: a continuación** below *4*

**continuar** to continue *6*

**contra** against *6*

**contrario/a** opposite, contrary *6*; **al contrario** on the contrary *9*

el **contratiempo** disappointment *13*

**contribuir (y)** to contribute *9*

**controlar** to control *13*

**convencer (z)** to convince *7*

**conveniente** convenient *13*

el **convento** convent *14*

la **conversación** conversation *4*

**conversar** to talk, to converse *1, 6*

**convertir (ie, i)** to convert *6*

la **copa** (stemmed) glass *10*

el **corazón** heart *11*

la **corbata** necktie *7*

**cordial** cordial *4*

la **cordillera** mountain range *16*

el **corneta** bugler *17*

el **coronel** colonel *17*

**correcto** correct *1*

el **corredor,** la **corredora** sprinter *3,* runner *9*

el **correo** post office *13*; el **apartado de correos** P.O. box *8*; la **oficina de correos** post office *13*

**correr** to run *3*

la **correspondencia** correspondence *13*

**corresponder** to correspond *14*

**correspondiente** corresponding *4*

la **corrida (de toros)** bullfight *13*

**cortado/a** cut *16*

la **cortesía** courtesy *P1*

la **cortina** curtain *5*

**corto/a** short *P3*

la **cosa** thing *2, 5*

**coser** to sew *5*

**cosmético/a** cosmetic *3*

**cosmopolita** cosmopolitan *12*

la **costa** coast *14*

**costar (ue)** to cost *P4,* 1

el **costo** cost *4*

la **costumbre** custom *4*

**cotidiano/a** daily *11*

al **coyote** coyote *P3*

**crear** to create *8, 17*

la **creatividad** creativity *13*

**creativo/a** creative *P2*

**crecer (zc)** to grow *8*

el **crecimiento** growth *10*

el **crédito** credit *7, 12*; la **tarjeta de crédito** credit card *12*

**creer** to believe *3*; **creer que sí** to think so *7*

**criar** to breed *15*

la **crisis** crisis *16*

el **cristal** glass *16*

el **criterio** judgment *13*

la **crítica** criticism *11*

el **cronómetro** stop watch *3*

el **crucero** cruise *12*

la **cruz** cross *16*; la **Cruz Roja** Red Cross *16*

**cruzar (c)** to cross *6, 8*

el **cuaderno** notebook *P3*

la **cuadra** city block *8*

**cuadrado/a** square *P3*

la **cuadrilla** team (in bullfighting) *15*

el **cuadro** chart *2*; picture *5*; **de cuadros** plaid, checked *7*

**cuál** which (one) *P4, 2*

la **cualidad** quality *8*

**cualquier** any *10*

**cuándo** when *2*

**cuando** when *2*

**cuanto: en cuanto** as soon as *17*

**cuánto/a** how much *P4, 1*

**cuántos/as** how many P4

**cuarenta** forty P4

el **cuarto** quarter P4; room *2, 5*; fourth *6*

**cuatro** four P4

**cuatrocientos** four hundred *3*

**cubano/a** Cuban *2*

**cubierto/a** covered *13*

**cubrir** to cover *3, 16*

la **cuchara** tablespoon *10*

la **cucharita** teaspoon *10*

el **cuchillo** knife *10*

el **cuello** neck *9*

la **cuenta** bill *8, 14*; **darse cuenta (de)** to realize *11*

el **cuento** story *7*

la **cuerda** cord *15*

el **cuero** leather *6*

el **cuerpo** body *5, 9*

el **cuestionario** questionnaire *16*

el **cuidado: con cuidado** carefully *9*; **tener cuidado** to be careful *4*

**cuidar** to take care of *4*

**cultivar** to grow, to cultivate *13*

la **cultura** culture *P1*

**cultural** cultural *11*

el **cumpleaños** birthday *4, 7*

la **cuñada** sister–in–law *4*

el **cuñado** brother–in–law *4*

la **cuota: la cuota inicial** down payment *12*

**Cupido** Cupid *17*

el **cupón** coupon *12*

la **cura** cure *6*

el **curandero,** la **curandera** healer *11*

el **curso** course *1,* school year *3*

**curvo/a** curved *6*

## Ch

el **champán** champagne *15*

la **chaqueta** jacket *7*

el **cheque** check *12*

**chequear** to check (luggage) *12*

la **chica** girl *P2*

el **chicle** chewing gum *11*

el **chico** boy *P2*

el **chile** green pepper *10*

**chileno/a** Chilean *2*

la **chimenea** fireplace *5*

**chino/a** Chinese *1*

**chismoso/a** gossiper *8*

el **chiste** joke *16*

**chocar (qu)** to collide *12*

el **chocolate** chocolate *P3*

el **chofer** driver, chauffeur *12*

el **choque** (car) accident *16*

## D

**d.C.** A.D. (after Christ) *12*

**dañado/a** out of order, damaged *13*

**dañar** to damage *16*

el **daño** damage *16*

la **danza** dance, dancing *9*

**dar** to give *P4, 7*; to hit *12*; **darse cuenta (de)** to realize *11*

**datar** to date *17*

los **datos** data *8, 17*

**de** of *P3*; from *2*; **de nada** you're welcome *P1*; **de quién** whose *2*

**debajo** under *P3*

**deber** ought to, should *1, 3*; *n masc* duty *17*

**debido: debido a** due to *8, 13*

**débil** weak *2*

**decidir** to decide *8*

**décimo** tenth *6*

**decir (i)** to say, *2, 6*; **diga** say *P3*

la **decisión** decision *6*

**declarar** to declare *12*

**decorado/a** decorated *15*

**decorar** to decorate *3*

**dedicar (qu)** to dedicate *8, 9*

el **dedo** finger *9*

**defender (ie)** to defend *13*

el **defensor,** la **defensora** defender *17*

la **definición** definition *15*

**definido/a** definite *1*

**definitivamente** definitely *15*

**dejar** to leave *4*; **dejar +** *inf* to let + *verb 12*

**delgado/a** thin *2*

**demasiado/a** too much *6*

**demostrar (ue)** to show, to prove *15*

**demostrativo/a** demonstrative *7*

el/la **dentista** dentist *8*

**dentro (de)** inside *6, 11*; **dentro de un rato** in a while *16*

el **departmento** department *2*

**depender** to depend *P4*

el **dependiente,** la **dependienta** clerk *1*

el **deporte** sport *6*

**deportivo/a** *adj* sport *9, 11*

**depositar** to deposit *13*

el **depósito** container, box *13*

la **depresión** depression *6*

**deprimido/a** depressed *9*

la **derecha: a la derecha** to the right *1, 7*

el **derecho** law *4*; right *17*; **seguir derecho** to go straight ahead *8*

**derivado/a** derived *17*

el **derrame** spill *16*

la **desactivación** defusing *17*

**desarrollar** to develop *9*

el **desarrollo** development *14*

**desayunar** to have breakfast *3*

el **desayuno** breakfast *3*

**descafeinado/a** decaffeinated *10*

**descansar** to rest *8*, 11

el **descanso** rest *8*

**descartar** to reject *16*

el **descenso** descent, decline *17*

**descomponer (g)** to break down 17

**desconectar** to disconnect *16*

**desconocido/a** unknown *13*

**descremado/a** nonfat *10*

**describir** to describe *2*

la **descripción** description P3

**descrito/a** described *16*

el **descubrimiento** discovery *14*

**descubrir** to discover *6*

el **descuento** discount *12*

**descuidado/a** careless *11*

**desde** from *P4*; since *12*

**desear** to wish, to want 1

**desechable** disposable *14*

el **desempleo** unemployment *8*, 11

el **deseo** wish *11*

**desértico/a** *adj* desert *16*

**desfavorable** unfavorable *13*

**desgraciadamente** unfortunately *17*

el **desierto** desert *4*

**desordenado/a** messy *16*

**despacio** slow *P3*

la **despedida** leave taking, farewell *P1*

**despedir (i)** to dismiss, to fire 8

**despejado/a** clear *6*

la **despensa** pantry *10*

el **despertador** alarm clock *14*

**despertar (ie)** to wake up 5

**después** later, after *3;* then *1*, 3

**destacado/a** distinguished *17*

**destinar** assign *17*

el **destino** destination 12

la **destreza** dexterity *15*

la **destrucción** destruction *16*

**destruido/a** destroyed *13*, 16

**destruir (y)** to destroy 16

la **desventaja** disadvantage 11

**detallado/a** detailed *8*

el **detalle** detail *13*

el/la **detective** detective *4*

**detener (g, ie)** to stop *12*

**determinar** to determine *11*

el **detractor**, la **detractora** detractor *15*

**detrás (de)** behind P3

la **deuda** debt *8*

**devolver (ue)** to return *13*

el **día** day P4; **buenos días** good morning P1; el **día de fiesta** holiday *4;* **todos los días** every day 5

el **diálogo** dialogue *1*

la **diana** reveille *17*

**diariamente** daily *13*

**diario/a** daily *5*

el **diario** newspaper *17*

el **dibujo** drawing *1*, 9

el **diccionario** dictionary P3

**diciembre** December 6

el **dictamen** opinion, judgment *16*

**dictaminar** to consider *16*

el **dicho** saying *8*

**diecinueve** nineteen P4

**dieciocho** eighteen P4

**dieciséis** sixteen P4

**diecisiete** seventeen P4

el **diente** tooth 5

la **dieta** diet *3*

**diez** ten P4

la **diferencia** difference *2*, 17

**diferente** different *1*; *pl* various

**difícil** difficult *1*, 9

**difícilmente** with difficulty 13

la **dificultad** difficulty *12*

**dificultar** to make difficult *12*

**difunto/a** deceased *15*; el **Día de los Difuntos** All Soul's Day 15

**diga** hello *13*; **dígame** hello *13*

**digerir (ie)** to digest *11*

**dinámico/a** dynamic *6*

el **dinero** money *3*, 4

**Dios** God 12

**diplomático/a** diplomatic *13*

la **dirección** address *P4*, 3

**directamente** directly *12*

el **director**, la **directora** director, manager 8

el **directorio** directory 7

**dirigirse (j)** to address 13

**discar (qu)** to dial 13

el **disco** record 3

la **discoteca** discotheque *4*

**discreto/a** discreet *P2*

la **discriminación** discrimination 17

**disculpar: disculpe(n) la molestia** sorry for the inconvenience 16

la **discusión** argument *13*

**discutir** to argue *6*

**diseñado/a** designed *16*

el **diseñador**, la **diseñadora** designer *10*

el **diseño** design 7

**disfrazarse (c)** to wear a costume 15
**disfrutar** to enjoy 8, 12
**disminuido/a** diminished 16
**disponer (g)** to have 17
**disponible** available 12
la **disposición** disposal 9; availability 14
la **distancia** distance 7, 13
**distinguido/a** distinguished 17
la **distribución** distribution 17
el **distrito** district 13; el **distrito postal** zip code 13
la **diversidad** diversity 17
la **diversión** entertainment 14
**diversos/as** several 13
**divertido/a** amusing, funny 15
**divertirse (ie, i)** to have a good time 3, 15
la **división** division 5
**divorciado/a** divorced 17
**doblar** to fold 5; to turn 8; to bend 9
el **doble** double 4, 14
**doce** twelve P4
la **docena** dozen 10
el **doctor**, la **doctora** doctor P1, 11
el **dólar** dollar P4, 1
**doler (ue)** to hurt 11
el **dolor** ache, pain 11
**doméstico/a** adj house 5
el **domicilio** address 13
**dominar** to dominate 17
el **domingo** Sunday P4
**don** title of respect P1, P2
**doña** title of respect P1, P2
la **donación** donation 16
**donde** where 1
**dónde** where P3
el **donut** doughnut 17

**dormir (ue, u)** to sleep 4; **dormirse** to fall asleep 5
el **dormitorio** bedroom 3, 5
**dos** two P4
**doscientos** two hundred 3
el **drama** drama 8
**dramático/a** dramatic 5
la **droga** drug 11, 15
el **dualismo** dualism 17
la **ducha** shower 5
**dudar** to doubt 10
el **duelo** duel 15
el **dueño**, la **dueña** owner 2
el **dulce** sweet, candy 3
la **dulcería** pastry shop 10
**durante** during 3
**durar** to last 15
**duro/a** hard 6

## E

**e** and 13
el **eco: hacerse eco** to repeat, to reflect 8
la **ecología** ecology 16
el/la **ecologista** ecologist 16
la **economía** economics 1
**económico/a** economical 2; economic 17; la **pretensión económica** desired salary 8
el **ecuador** equator 13
**ecuatorial** equatorial 12
**ecuestre** equestrian 14
la **edad** age 7; la **tercera edad** senior citizenhood 4
el **edificio** building 1
la **educación** education 11
**educado/a** raised 8
el **efectivo: en efectivo** cash 7, 12
el **efecto** effect 16
**eficiente** efficient P2
el **ejemplo** example 7
el **ejercicio** exercise 5, 9

**el** the P1, P3
**él** he P2
**elaborado/a** elaborate 15
la **electricidad** electricity 16
el/la **electricista** electrician 8
el **electrodoméstico** electrical appliance 5
el **elefante** elephant 2
**elegante** elegant P2
**elegir (i, j)** to choose 3
**elemental** elementary 14
el **elemento** element 1
**eliminar** to eliminate, to get rid of 8
**ella** she P2
**ello** it, this 9
**ellos/as** they 1
**embargo: sin embargo** nevertheless 1
el **embarque** boarding 12
el **embotellamiento** traffic jam 16
la **emergencia** emergency 13
la **emigración** emigration 17
**eminentemente** basically 17
la **emisión** emission 16
la **emoción** emotion, excitement 15
**emocionado/a** excited 6
**emocional** emotional 2
**empacar (qu)** to pack 12
el **empeño** persistence 13
**empezar (ie, c)** to begin, to start 1, 4
el **empleado**, la **empleada** employee 2, 6
**emplear** to employ 2
el **empleo** employment 2, 11
la **empresa** corporation 1
**en** in P1, P3, at 1
**enamorado/a: el Día de los Enamorados** Saint Valentine's Day 15; **estar enamorado (de)** to be in love with 11, 15

**encaminado/a** designed *14*

**encantado/a** delighted *P1*

**encantador/a** charming *15*

**encantar** to delight, to love *7*

el **encanto** charm, delight *13*

**encapuchado/a** hooded *15*

**encarar** to face *13*

**encender (ie)** to turn on *13, 16*; to light *16*

**encerrar (ie)** to lock in, to confine *17*

**encontrar (ue)** to find *5, 7*

el **encuentro** game *6*

la **encuesta** survey *4*

el **encuestado**, la **encuestada** person surveyed *8*

la **enchilada** tortilla filled with meat covered with sauce *2*

la **energía** energy *13*

**enero** January *6*

**enfermarse** to get sick *12*

la **enfermedad** sickness *8*

el **enfermero**, la **enfermera** nurse *8*

**enfermo/a** sick *11*

el **enfrentamiento** confrontation *15*

**enfrentar** to face, to confront *15*

**enfrente (de)** in front (of) *P3*

el **enjuague** rinse *14*

**enorme** enormous, huge *4*

**enriquecer (zc)** to enrich *13*

la **ensalada** salad *3*

**enseguida** immediately *13*

**enseñar** to teach *1*

**entender (ie)** to understand *8*

**entero: de color entero** solid color *7*

**entonces** then *7*

la **entrada** ticket *3, 6*; down payment *5*; entrance *12*; entry *15*

**entrar** to enter, to come in *2, 8*

**entre** between *P3*; among *1*; **entre semana** week days *5*

**entrecortar** to become short *9*

la **entrega** possession *5*; la **entrega especial** special delivery *13*

**entrenado/a** trained *16*

el **entrenador**, la **entrenadora** trainer, coach *3*

el **entrenamiento** training *3*

**entrenar** to train *10*

la **entrevista** interview *P2, 8*

el **entrevistador**, la **entrevistadora** interviewer *3*

**entrevistar** to interview *2*

**enviar** to send *8*

la **época** time, epoch *15*

el **equilibrio** balance *9*

el **equipaje** luggage *12*

el **equipo** team *6*

la **equivalencia** equivalency *9*

**equivalente** equivalent *11*

**equivocado/a** wrong *4*

la **erosión** erosion *16*

el **error** error, mistake *8*

la **erupción** eruption *16*

la **escala: hacer escala** to make a stopover *12*

la **escalera** stairs *5*; la **escalera mecánica** escalator *11*

el **escaparate** store window *7*

la **escena** scene *2*

el **escenario** stage *8*

**escoger (j)** to choose *2, 11*

**escolar** *adj* school *14*

el **escombro** debris *16*

**escribir** to write *P2, 3*; **escribir a máquina** to type *12, 13*

el **escritorio** desk *P3*

**escuchar** to listen to *1*

la **escuela** school *1, 6*

**escurrir** to drain *8*

**ese, esa** *adj* that *P2*; **ése, ésa** *pron* that one *7*

el **esfuerzo** effort *13*

la **esmeralda** emerald *13*

**eso** that *P3*

**esos/as** *adj* those *7*; **ésos/as** *pron* those (ones) *7*

el **espagueti** spaghetti *3*

la **espalda** back *9*

**español** Spanish *P3, 1*; *n* Spaniard *1*

**especial** special *6*

**especializado/a** specializing *6*

**especializarse (c)** to major *17*

**especialmente** especially *4*

**específico/a** specific *1*

**espectacular** spectacular *6*

el **espectáculo** show *12*; spectacle *15*

el **espectador**, la **espectadora** spectator *6*

el **espejo** mirror *5*

la **espera: la sala de espera** waiting room *12*

**esperar** to expect *2, 10*; to hope *10*

la **espinaca** spinach *10*

la **esposa** wife *4*

el **esposo** husband *4*

el **esquema** pattern *15*

el **esquí** ski *6*

el **esquiador**, la **esquiadora** skier *14*

**esquiar** to ski 6
la **esquina** corner 8
**establecer (zc)** to establish 8
la **estación** season 6; station 14; la **estación de gasolina** service station 12
el **estacionamiento** parking 14
**estacionar** to park 12
el **estadio** stadium 2, 3
el **estado: estado civil** marital status 3; **estado** state; el **estado libre asociado** associated commonwealth 12
la **estampilla** stamp 13
la **estancia** stay 4
**estar** to be P1, 1; **estar a cargo** to be in charge 2
la **estatura** height 9
**este, esta** adj this 1; **éste, ésta** pron this one 7; n east 6; **esta noche** tonight 3
el **estéreo** stereo 3
el **estereotipo** stereotype 2
el **estilo** style 9
**estimado/a** dear 13
**esto** this P3
el **estómago** stomach 11
**estos/as** adj these 2, 7; **éstos/as** pron these (ones) 7
**estrecho/a** narrow, tight 7
la **estrella** star 4
**estricto/a** strict 16
la **estructura** structure 17
el/la **estudiante** student P3
**estudiar** to study 1
los **estudios** studies 1
la **estufa** stove 5
**europeo/a** European 7
el **evento** event 2
**evidente** evident 11
**evitar** to avoid 9

**exactamente** exactly 15
el **examen** examination 3
**examinar** to examine 11
**excedido/a: excedido de peso** overweight 11
**excelente** excellent 1
la **excepción** exception 10
el **exceso** excess 8
**exclusivo/a** exclusive 9
la **excursión** tour, excursion 3, 13
la **excusa** excuse 14
**exento/a** exempt 13
**existir** to exist, to be 4, 15
el **éxito: tener éxito** to be successful 8
**exitoso/a** successful 3
**exótico/a** exotic 12
la **experiencia** experience 8
**experimentar** to experience 16
el **experto, la experta** expert 8
**explicar (qu)** to explain 2
**explorador/a: los niños exploradores** Boy Scouts; las **niñas exploradoras** Girl Scouts 16
**explosivo/a** explosive 17
**expresar** to express 1
la **expresión** expression 1
el **expreso** express train 12
la **extensión** extension 16
**extenso/a** extended, vast 16
**exterior** exterior 2
**externo** day (student) 6
**extra** extra 8
**extranjero/a** foreign 2; el **extranjero** abroad 13
**extraordinario/a** extraordinary 12
**extraterrestre** extraterrestrial 8
**extremadamente** extremely 13

el **extremo** end 6
**extravertido/a, extrovertido/a** extroverted P2

**F**

la **fábrica** factory 2, 8, 11
el/la **fabricante** manufacturer 8
**fabuloso/a** fabulous, great 13
**fácil** easy 5, 9
la **facilidad: con facilidad** easily 9, 13; las **facilidades** cooperation 16
**facilitar** to facilitate, to make easier 14
el **factor** factor 13
**facturar** to check (luggage) 12
la **facultad** college, school 1
la **falda** skirt 7
**falso/a** false P3
la **falta** lack 11
**faltar** to be missing 10; to lack, to be necessary 17
el **fallo** error 13
la **familia** family 4
el **familiar** relative 4; adj familiar 13
**famoso/a** famous 8, 10
el **fantasma** phantom 8
**fantástico/a** fantastic P2
la **farmacia** pharmacy 9; la **farmacia de turno/ guardia** pharmacy that takes turns attending customers during holidays and Sundays 9
el **favor: a favor de** in favor of 17; **por favor** please P1
**favorable** favorable 13
**favorito/a** favorite 1
**febrero** February 6
la **fecha** date 6
la **felicidad** happiness 13; pl congratulations 15

**felicitar** to congratulate 15
**feliz** happy 2
el/la **feminista** feminist 17
el **fenómeno** phenomenon 6
**feo/a** ugly 2
la **feria** fair 15
el **ferrocarril** railroad 12
el **fervor** fervor 15
la **ficción** fiction 4
la **ficha** token 13
la **fiebre** fever 11
la **fiera** beast 15
la **fiesta** party 2, 3
**fijado/a** set 11
**fijarse** to notice 7; to set 11
la **fila** row 6
la **filmación** filming 12
la **filosofía** philosophy 8
el **fin: en fin** in short 16; el **fin de semana** weekend 3; **tener como fin** to have as a goal 14
el **final** end 10
la **finca** farm 15
la **firma** signature 2
**firmar** to sign 8, 14
la **firmeza** resolution 11
**física** physics P4, 1
**físico/a** physical 15
la **flecha** arrow 6
la **flexibilidad** flexibility 9
la **flor** flower 6, 14
el **folklore** folklore 12
**folklórico/a** folkloric 12
el **folleto** pamphlet, brochure 13
la **forma** shape 1; way 9; **de esta forma** this way 3; **de todas formas** anyway 15
la **formación** formation 17
**formal** formal 7
**formar: formar pareja** to be a couple 17;

**formar parte de** to be part of 17
la **fortaleza** fortress 12
la **fortuna: por fortuna** luckily 17
la **foto** photo, picture 14
la **fotografía** photograph, picture 8
la **fractura** fracture 11
**fracturado/a** fractured, broken 11
**francés/a** French 1
la **frase** phrase 11
la **frecuencia: con frecuencia** frequently 2
**frecuentemente** frequently 11, 13
el **fregadero** sink 5
**fregar (gu)** to wash dishes 5
**frenar** to brake 12
la **frente** forehead 9
la **fresa** strawberry 10
**fresco/a** cool 6; fresh 10; **hace fresco** it's cool 6
los **frijoles** beans 10
**frío/a** cold 3; **hace frío** it's cold 6
**frito/a** fried 3; las **papas fritas** French fries 7
la **fruta** fruit 3
la **frutería** fruit store 10
el **fuego** fire 16
**fuera** outside 4, 5
**fuerte** strong 2
la **fuerza** strength, force 9
la **fuga: la fuga de cerebros** brain drain 8
**fumar** to smoke 11
la **función** show 14
**funcionar** to work 8
**fundado/a** established, founded 17
el **fútbol** football, soccer 6
el **futuro** future 1

## G

las **gafas** glasses 8
la **galería** gallery 13
la **galletita** cookie 3
el **gallo: la Misa del Gallo** midnight mass on Christmas Eve 15
el **ganador, la ganadora** winner 11
**ganar** to win 3, 6; to earn 8; **ganarse la vida** to earn a living 11
las **ganas: tener ganas de** to feel like 4
los **gandules** peas (in Puerto Rico) 10
el **garaje** garage 5
la **garganta** throat 11
las **gárgaras: hacer gárgaras** to gargle 11
la **gasolina** gasoline 12
la **gasolinera** service station 12
**gastar** to spend 3, 7; to waste 16
el **gasto** expense 3
el **gato, la gata** cat 4
el **gaucho** Argentine cowboy 6
la **gelatina** gelatin 10
**genealógico/a: el árbol genealógico** family tree 4
la **generación** generation 4
**general** general 4
**generalmente** generally 3, 13
**generoso/a** generous P2
el **genio** genius 4
la **gente** people 9, 15
la **geografía** geography 1
**geográfico/a** geographic 16
el/la **gerente** manager 2, 8

la **gestión** matter, business *16*

**gigante** giant *8*

la **gimnasia** gymnastics *P1*

el **gimnasio** gymnasium *1*

el **gladiador** gladiator *15*

el **golf** golf *6*

**gordo/a** fat *2*

la **grabadora** tape recorder *1*

**gracias** thank you *P1;* el **Día de Acción de Gracias** Thanksgiving Day *15*

la **graduación** graduation *1*

**graduado/a** graduate *8*

**graduarse** to graduate *17*

**gráfico/a** graphic *9*

la **gramática** grammar *1*

el **gramo** gram *10*

**gran** great *2*

**grande** big *P3*

la **grasa** fat *11*

**gratis** gratis, free *15*

la **gripe** flu *11*

**gris** gray *2*

el **grupo** group *P4, 15*

el **guante** glove *6, 7*

**guapo/a** handsome, pretty *2*

el **guardabarros** fender *12*

**guardar** to put away *16;* **guardar cama** to stay in bed *11*

la **guardería de perros** kennel *4*

el/la **guardia** guard *16;* la **farmacia de guardia/de turno** pharmacy that takes turns attending customers during holidays and Sundays *11*

la **guayabera** shirt made of light material *7*

la **guerra** war *8*

la **guía** directory *8, 13;* el/la **guía** guide *16*

la **guitarra** guitar *3*

**gustar** to like, to be pleasing to *7*

el **gusto: mucho gusto** pleased to meet you *P1*

## H

**haber** to have *16*

**había** there was, there were *15*

la **habilidad** ability *13*

**habitable** livable *15*

la **habitación** room *4, 8*

el/la **habitante** inhabitant, resident *11*

el **hábito** habit *11*

**habitualmente** habitually *11*

**hablador/a** talkative *2*

**hablar** to speak *1*

**hace: hace** + *time expression* + *preterit* ago *14*

**hacer** to do, to make *3, 5;* **hacer cola** to stand in line *12;* **hacer el papel** to play the part *1;* **hacer escala** to make a stopover *12;* **hacer gárgaras** to gargle *11;* **hacer la maleta** to pack *12;* **hacer una pregunta** to ask a question *1*

**hacia** towards *15*

**hacerse** to become *17*

el **hambre** *fem:* **tener hambre** to be hungry *4*

la **hamburguesa** hamburger *2, 3*

**hasta** until *P1;* up to *8;* even *15*

**hay** there is, there are *P4;* **hay que** + *inf* it's necessary to + *verb 8, 11*

el **hecho** event *6;* **hecho a mano** hand made *7*

la **heladería** ice-cream shop *10*

el **helado** ice cream *3*

el **hemisferio** hemisphere *14*

la **herboristería** health food store *9*

la **herencia** heritage *14*

el **herido** injured person *12, 16*

**herir (ie, i)** to hurt *13*

la **hermana** sister *2, 4*

el **hermano** brother *4*

los **hermanos** brothers, brother and sister *2, 4*

la **herramienta** tool *13*

**hervido/a** boiled *10*

**hervir (ie)** to boil *8*

la **hierba** grass *2*

el **hierro** iron *10*

la **hija** daughter *P4*

el **hijo** son *4*

**hispánico/a** Hispanic *15*

**hispano/a** Hispanic *2*

**hispanoamericano/a** Hispanic American *14*

la **historia** history *1*

el **historial** resumé *8*

el **hogar** home *16*

**hola** hello, hi *P1*

el **hombre** man *4, 8*

el **hombro** shoulder *9*

**honrado/a** honest *8*

la **hora** time *P4*

el **horario** schedule *P4*

el **horno** oven *5*

el **horóscopo** horoscope *13*

el **horror: ¡qué horror!** how horrible! *16*

**hospedarse** to stay, to lodge *14*

el **hospital** hopital *1, 8*

el **hostal** hostal *3*

la **hostería** inn *14*

el **hotel** hotel *3, 8*

**hoy** today P4; **hoy en día** nowadays *4,* 15
**hubo** there was, there were 16
el **hueso** bone 11
el **huésped** guest *1*
el **huevo** egg 3
las **humanidades** humanities 1
**humano/a** human 11
**húmedo/a** wet, humid *16*
**humillar** to humiliate *13*
el **humo** smoke 16
el **huracán** hurricane 16

**I**

la **ida:** el **boleto de ida y vuelta** round-trip ticket 12
la **idea** idea *1*
**ideal** ideal *8,* 11
el/la **idealista** idealist *P2*
la **identificación** identification *P2*
**identificar (qu)** to identify *1*
el **idioma** language *1*
la **iglesia** church 3
**ignorar** not to know *11*
**igual** equal, same 17
**igualdad** equality 17
**igualmente** likewise P1
**ilegal** illegal *11*
la **imagen** image *15*
la **imaginación** imagination 4
**imaginario/a** fictitious *8*
**imaginarse** to imagine 15
**imitar** imitate *6*
el **impacto** impact *16*
**imparcial** impartial *2*
**imperfecto/a** imperfect *12*
el **impermeable** raincoat 7
**impetuoso/a** impetuous *13*

la **implantación** introduction *6*
**imponer (g)** to demand, to order *17*
la **importancia** importance *1,* 17
**importante** important *P2,* 6
**importar** to mind, to matter 12; **no importa** it doesn't matter *11*
**imprescindible** necessary, essential *8*
la **impresión** impression *2*
**impresionante** impressive *15*
**impreso/a** printed *13*
el **impuesto** tax *15*
**impulsar** to move *13*
**impulsivo/a** impulsive *P2*
la **inauguración** inauguration *8*
**inca** Inca *14*
el **incendio** fire 16
**incluido/a** included *14*
**incluir** to include *12*
la **inconformidad** dissatisfaction 15
**incorporarse** to join *17*
**increíble** unbelievable, incredible *13*
**incurrir** to take on *11*
**indeciso/a** undecided *15*
**indefinido/a** indefinite *1*
la **independencia** independence *4,* 15
**independiente** independent *2,* 17
la **indicación** indication *17*
**indicar (qu)** to indicate *P4,* 8
el **indicativo** area code 13
el **índice** index, rate 11
**indiferente** indifferent *13*
el/la **indígena** Indian *7;* indigenous *14*
**indiscreto/a** indiscrete *P2*

**indispensable** indispensable *10*
**individual** individual *4,* 11
el **individuo** individual *17*
la **industria** industry *14*
**industrializado/a** industrialized *17*
**inesperadamente** unexpectedly *13*
**infantil** *adj* children's *14*
la **infección** infection 11
**infeliz** unhappy *8*
**inferior** inferior *17*
el **infierno** hell 16
**infinitesimal** infinitesimal *1*
el **infinitivo** infinitive *11*
la **inflación** inflation *8*
la **influencia** influence *11*
**influir** to affect *9*
**influyente** important *13*
la **información** information *P4*
**informal** informal, causal 7
**informar** to inform *12*
la **informática** computer science 1
el **informe** report *16*
la **infraestructura** infrastructure *16*
la **ingeniería** engineering *12*
el **ingeniero,** la **ingeniera** engineer 8
**ingenioso/a** ingenious *10*
**ingerir (ie, i)** to drink, to eat *11*
**inglés, inglesa** English 1; la **hora inglesa** precise time *P4*
el **ingrediente** ingredient *10*
**inhumano/a** inhuman *15*
**inicial:** la **cuota inicial** down payment *12*
**iniciar** to begin, to initiate *14*

la **iniciativa** initiative, drive *8*

**ininterrumpido/a** uninterrupted *1*

**inmediato/a** immediate *12*

**inmenso/a** immense *13*

el **inodoro** toilet *5*

**inolvidable** unforgettable
*12*

el **inquilino,** la **inquilina**
tenant *5*

**inspeccionar** to inspect
*16*

el **inspector,** la **inspectora**
inspector *12*

**inspirar** to inspire *7*

la **instalación** installation *9*

el **instinto** instinct *15*

el **instituto** institute, high
school *1*

la **instrucción** training *17;*
las **instrucciones** directions *8*

**integral** complete *9*

**intelectual** intellectual *13*

**inteligente** intelligent *P2,*
*2*

**intenso/a** intense *8*

el **interés** interest *11*

**interesante** interesting *P2*

**interesar** to interest *7*

**interestatal** interstate *12*

**interior** interior *13;* la
**ropa interior** under-
wear *13*

**internacional** international *8*

**interno/a** in–house *4;*
boarder *6;* internal *17;* la
**medicina interna** internal medicine *11*

**interrumpir** to interrupt
*16*

**íntimo/a** intimate *1*

**introvertido/a** introverted
*P2*

la **inundación** flood *16*

**inundado/a** flooded *16*

**inundar** to inundate *16*

**invertir (ie, i)** to invest
*13*

**investigador/a** *adj* investigating *16*

**investigar (gu)** to investigate *14*

el **invierno** winter *6*

la **invitación** invitation *10*

el **invitado,** la **invitada** guest
*10*

**invitar** to invite *6*

la **inyección** injection *11*

**ir** to go *1,* 3; **irse** to go
away, to leave *5*

**irónico/a** ironic *8*

**irregular** irregular *11*

**irritado/a** irritated *11*

**irse** to go away, to leave *5*

la **isla** island *12*

**italiano/a** Italian *1*

el **itinerario** itinerary *3*

la **izquierda** left *1, 8*

## J

el **jabón** soap *5*

el **jai alai** jai alai *6*

el **jamón** ham *3*

**japonés/japonesa** Japanese *1*

el **jardín** yard, garden *4,* 5

la **jefatura** headquarters *17*

el **jefe,** la **jefa** boss *2*

la **jirafa** giraffe *16*

la **jornada:** la **jornada completa** full time *8*

**joven** young *2*

el **judo** judo *6*

el **juego** game *4*

el **jueves** Thursday P4

el **jugador,** la **jugadora**
player *6*

**jugar (ue)** to play (game
or sport) *4*

el **jugo** juice *3*

**julio** July *6*

la **jungla** jungle *8*

**junio** June *6*

la **junta** council *12*

**junto** next *4:* **juntos** together *4*

**jurídico/a** legal *8*

**justo/a** just, fair *8, 17*

la **juventud** youth *6, 15*

## K

el **kilo** kilo *9*

el **kilogramo** kilogram *9*

el **kilómetro** kilometer *11*

## L

**la** the *P1,* P3; you (*formal,
sing*), her, it (*fem*) *5*

el **laboratorio** laboratory *P4,*
1

el **lado: al lado (de)** next
(to) P3

**ladrar** to bark *8*

el **ladrón** thief *14*

la **lágrima** tear *17*

la **lámpara** lamp *5*

**lanzar (c)** to throw *6:* to
start *14*

el **lápiz** pencil P3

**largo/a** long P3; **a lo
largo de** along *16*

**las** the *1*; you *formal, fam,
pl* them *fem* *4*

la **lata** can *10*

**latino/a** Latin *10*

el **lavabo** washbowl *5*

la **lavadora** washing machine
5

la **lavandería** laundry *14*

el **lavaplatos** dishwasher *5*

**lavar** to wash *5*

**le** (to) you (*formal*) P2;
(to) him, her, it *7*

**leal** loyal *8*

la **lección** lesson *1*

la **lectura** reading *1*
la **leche** milk 3
la **lechuga** lettuce 3
**leer** to read *P2,* 3
**lejos** far 5
la **lengua** language *1*; tongue 11
**lentamente** slowly 13
**lento/a** slow 11
el **león** lion *4*
**les** (to) you (*formal pl*), them 7
el **letrero** sign 17
**levantar** to raise 5; **levantarse** to get up *P2,* 5
la **ley** law 17
**liberado/a** liberated 3
**liberal** liberal *P2*
**liberar** to release *9*
la **libertad** freedom, liberty 15
la **libra** pound 9
**libre** free *5*: el **aire libre** open air *9*
la **librería** bookstore 1
el **libro** book P3
la **licencia** license 12; la **licencia de manejar** driver's license 12
el **licenciado en derecho** lawyer *8*
el **liceo** high school *1*
el **licor** liquor *11*
la **licuadora** blender 5
**lidiar** to fight *15*
**ligero/a** slight *11*
el **límite** limit *11*
el **limón** lemon *2,* 3
**limpiar** to clean *3,* 5
la **limpieza** cleaning *3*
**limpio/a** clean *11*
la **línea** line *4*
la **linterna** flashlight *16*
el **líquido** liquid 11
la **lista** roll *P1*; list *1,* 12
**listo/a** smart 2
la **litera** berth *12*

la **literatura** literature 1
el **litro** liter 10
**lo** the 3; you (*formal, sing*), him, it (*masc*) 5; **lo siento** I'm sorry P1
**loco/a** crazy *8*
el **locutor,** la **locutora** announcer *5*
el **lodo** mud *16*
**lógicamente** logically 13
**lógico/a** logical *P2,* 11
**lograr** to achieve *4*; to provide *14*
la **longevidad** longevity *11*
el **loro** parrot *8*
**los** the *P4, 1*; you (*formal & fam, pl*), them (*masc*) 5
la **lotería** lottery *4*
la **lucha** fight *15*
**luchar** to fight *15*
**luego** so *11*; **hasta luego** so long P1
el **lugar** place *1,* 4
el **lujo** luxury; **de lujo** first class 5
la **luna** moon *6*
el **lunes** Monday P4
la **luz** light *11,* 12

## Ll

la **llama** llama *16*
la **llamada** call *5,* 13
**llamar** to call 3; **llamarse** to be called, to be named P1
la **llanta** tire 12
la **llave** key 14
la **llegada** arrival 12
**llegar (gu)** to arrive 3
**llenar** to fill out *2*
**lleno/a** full *P3,* 12
**llevar** to wear 7; to take *10,* 12
**llorar** to cry 13
**llover (ue)** to rain 7
la **lluvia** rain *12, 16*

## M

la **madre** mother 4
**madrileño/a** from Madrid *15*
la **madrina** godmother 4
la **madrugada** early morning *15*
**maestro/a** master *3*
**magia** magic *12*
**mágico/a** magical *17*
**magnífico/a** magnificent, great *12*
**magos:** los **Reyes Magos** the three Wise Men *15*
el **maíz** corn P3
**mal** not well, sick P1; bad 2
la **maleta** suitcase 12
el **maletero** trunk 12
el **maletín** attaché case 12
**malo/a** bad 2; la **mala palabra** dirty word *16*
la **mamá** mother P4
**mañana** tomorrow P1; la **mañana** morning P4
**mandar** to send 13
el **mandato** command *8*
el **mando** assignment 17
**manejar** to drive *5,* 12
la **manera** way, manner *9*
la **manifestación** demonstration *2*
la **mano** hand *P3,* 9
la **manta** blanket 5
el **mantel** tablecloth 10
**mantener (ie, g)** to maintain *4*
el **mantenimiento** upkeep *9*
la **mantequilla** butter 10
**manuscrito/a** hand written *8*
la **manzana** apple 3
el **mapa** map 1
**maquillarse** to put on makeup 5

la **máquina: escribir a máquina** to type *12, 13*

el **mar** sea *12*

**maravillarse** to marvel *14*

**maravilloso/a** marvelous *4*

la **marca** brand, make *2*

**marcado/a: variantes marcadas** (multiple choice) answers *11*

**marcar (qu)** to dial *13*; to mark *17*; **marcar el paso** to mark time *17*; **marcar un punto** give a point *13*

el **marco** atmosphere *9*; frame *16*

la **marcha** walking *9*

**marginado/a** not fully accepted *17*

el **marido** husband *4*

la **marihuana** marijuana *11*

el **marqués** marquis *14*

el **martes** Tuesday *P4*

**marzo** March *6*

**más** more *P2, P4*; **más allá** beyond *2*

**masculino/a** masculine *17*

**masticar (qu)** to chew *11*

**matar** to kill *15*

las **matemáticas** mathematics *P4, 1*

la **materia** subject *1*; la **materia económica** business matters *13*

el **material** material *8*

**materialista** materialistic *P2*

el **matrimonio** married couple *5*

**máximo/a** high, maximum *6*

**mayo** May *6*

la **mayonesa** mayonnaise *10*

**mayor** older *4, 9*; oldest *10*; la **persona mayor** adult, older person *4*

la **mayoría** majority *12*

el/la **mayorista** wholesaler *11*

la **mayúscula** capital letter *12*

**me** myself *P1*; me *5*; (to) me *7*

el **mecánico** mechanic *4, 8*

**media** half *P4*; *n* stocking *7*; la **clase media** middle class *17*

**mediados: a mediados de** about the middle of *17*

**mediano/a** medium *9*

la **medianoche** midnight *15*

**mediante** by means of *16*

la **medicación** medication *11*

la **medicina** medicine *4*; la **medicina familiar** general practice *13*

**médico/a** medical *4, 17*; *n* doctor *8*

la **medida** measure *16*

el **medio** means *8*; el **medio ambiente** environment *16*; el **término medio** average *17*

el **mediodía** noon *15*

**medir (i)** to measure *9*

la **mejilla** cheek *9*

**mejor** better, *2, 9*; best *2, 10*

la **mejora** improvement *13*

**mejorar** to improve *11*

la **melodía** melody *15*

**melodramático/a** melodramatic *11*

la **memoria** memory *8*

**mencionar** to mention *15*

**menor** younger *4, 9*; youngest *10*

**menos** to (in telling time) *P4*; minus *P4*; less, fewer *9*; **a menos que** unless *17*; **por lo menos** at least *9*

el **mensaje** message *13, 14*

el **mensajero,** la **mensajera** messenger *17*

**mental** mental *13*

la **mente** mind *15*

la **mentira** lie *4*

el **menú** menu *3*

el **mercado** market *7, 10*

la **merienda** snack in the afternoon *10*

el **mérito** merit *6*

el **mes** month *P4*

la **mesa** table *P3*; la **mesa de noche** nightstand *2, 5*

la **meta** goal, objective *15*

el **método** method *13*

el **metro** subway *5, 12*; meter *9*

**metropolitano/a** metropolitan *17*

**mexicano/a** Mexican *2*

**mezclar** to combine, to mix *12*

**mí** (to) me *7*

**mi(s)** my *P2, 4*

el **microondas** microwave *5*

el **miedo: tener miedo** to be afraid *4*

el **miembro** member *4, 17*

**mientras** while *4, 6*

el **miércoles** Wednesday *P4*

la **migración** migration *17*

**mil** thousand *3*

**militar** military *13*

el **millón** million *5, 6*

**millonario/a** millionaire *4*

**mineral** *adj* mineral *10*

el **minidiálogo** minidialog *P1*

**mínimo/a** low, minimum *6*

la **minoría** minority *17*

el **minuto** minute *9*

**mío (-a, -os, -as)** (of) mine *14*

**mirar** to look at *1, 2*

el **misil** missile *16*

la **misión** mission *1*

**mismo/a** same *3*
el **misterio** mystery *4*
**misterioso/a** mysterious *14*
la **mitad** half *6*
la **mochila** backpack *12*
la **moda** fashion *7;* **estar de moda** to be fashionable *7*
el/la **modelo** model *P4*
**moderno/a** modern *P2*
la **modificación** modification, change *17*
**molestar** to bother *14*
la **molestia** inconvenience *16*
**molido/a** ground *10*
el **momento** moment *6:* **en estos momentos** right now, at this moment *6*
el **monasterio** monastery *14*
el **monólogo** monolog *15*
la **montaña** mountain *7, 14*
el **montañismo** (mountain) trekking, hiking *9*
**montañoso/a** mountainous *14*
**montar** to ride *6*
el **monumento** monument *14*
**morado/a** purple *2*
**moreno/a** brunet(te) *2*
**morir** to die *13*
la **mortadela** mortadella *17*
la **mostaza** mustard *10*
el **mostrador** counter *12*
**mostrar (ue)** to show *3, 7*
el **motivo** reason *4*
la **moto(cicleta)** motorcycle *2, 12*
el **motor** motor *12*
**mover (ue)** to move *9*
**movido/a** lively *13*
el **movimiento** movement *9*
la **muchacha** girl *3*
el **muchacho** boy *3*
**mucho** much, a lot *1;* **mucho gusto** nice to meet you *P1*

**muchos/as** many *1, 4*
**mudarse** to move *17*
el **mueble** furniture *5*
la **muela: dolor de muelas** toothache *11*
la **muerte** death *15*
**muerto/a** dead *16:* el **Día de los Muertos** All Soul's Day *15*
la **mujer** wife *4;* woman *4, 8*
la **muleta** crutch *12*
la **multa** fine *12*
**multiplicar (qu)** to multiply *6*
**multitudinario/a** multifaceted *6*
**mundial** *adj* world *6*
el **mundo** world *1*
la **muñeca** wrist *9*
el **músculo** muscle *11*
el **museo** museum *7, 14*
la **música** music *9*
**musical** musical *4*
el **músico** musician *13*
**muy** very *P1*

# N

**nacer (zc)** to be born *6*
**nacido/a** born *13*
el **nacimiento** birth *17*
**nacional** national *6*
**nada** nothing *12;* **por/de nada** you're welcome *P1*
**nadar** to swim *6*
**nadie** no one, nobody *8, 12*
la **naranja** orange *3*
la **nariz** nose *9*
la **natación** swimming *9*
la **natalidad** birth rate *17*
**nativo** native *1*
**natural** natural *7*
la **naturaleza** nature *12*
**naturista:** el **centro naturista** health food store *9*

la(s) **Navidad(es)** Christmas *15*
**necesario/a** necessary *3, 11*
la **necesidad** need *8*
**necesitar** to need *1*
**negar (ie)** to deny *17*
**negativamente** negatively *12*
la **negociación** discussion *13*
el **negocio** business *4, 8*
**negro/a** black *2*
**nervioso/a** nervous *2*
**nevar (ie)** to snow *6*
**ni** nor *2;* **ni . . . ni** neither . . . nor *12*
**nicaragüense** Nicaraguan *17*
la **nieta** granddaughter *4*
el **nieto** grandson *4*
la **nieve** snow *6*
**ningún** no, not any *12*
**ninguno/a** none, not any, *6, 12*
el **niño,** la **niña** child *1, 4*
el **nivel:** el **nivel de vida** standard of living *11*
**no** no *P2*
la **noche** evening, night *P1;* **esta noche** tonight *3*
la **Nochebuena** Christmas Eve *15*
la **Nochevieja** New Year's Eve *15*
el **nombre** name *P1*
la **norma** norm *2*
**normal** normal *10*
**normalmente** normally *5, 13*
el **norte** north *4*
**norteamericano/a** American *1*
**nos** us *5;* (to) us *7*
**nosotros/as** we *1*
la **nota** grade *1, 2;* note *10*
**notable** noteworthy, notable *17*

**notablemente** noticeably *16*

**notarse** to be noticeable *12*

la **noticia** news *3*, 16

el **noticiero** newscast 16

**novecientos** nine hundred 3

**noveno/a** ninth 6

**noventa** ninety P4

la **novia** fiancée, girlfriend 4

el **noviazgo** engagement, courtship *17*

**noviembre** November 6

el **novio** fiancé, boyfriend 4

el **nubarrón** dark cloud *13*

**nublado/a** cloudy 6

**nuboso/a** cloudy 6

la **nuera** daughter–in–law 4

**nuestro (-a, -os, -as)** our 4

**nueve** nine P4

**nuevo/a** new 2

el **número** number P4

**numeroso/a** numerous 12

**nunca** never *4*, 12

la **nutrición** nutrition *9*

**nutritivo/a** nourishing *10*


## O

**o** or *P3*, P4; **o . . . o** either . . . or 12

**obedecer (zc)** to obey *8*

el **objetivo** objective, goal 11, 17

el **objeto** object *1*

la **obligación** obligation, duty *17*

**obligar (gu)** to force *8*

la **obra** (construction) site *5*; work *7*; la **obra de teatro** play *14*

el **obrero,** la **obrera** worker 8

**observar** to observe, to see *6*

la **obsesión** obsession *8*

**obstante: no obstante** however, nevertheless *17*

**obtener (g, ie)** to obtain *1*, 11

**obvio** obvious 11

**ocasionalmente** occasionally *11*

**ocasionar** to cause *16*

**octavo** eighth 6

**octubre** October 6

la **ocupación** occupation *8*

**ocupado/a** busy 1

**ocupar** to cover, to extend over *16*; to occupy, to hold 17; to take over *15*; **ocuparse** to attend to *5*

**ocurrir** to occur *2*

**ochenta** eighty P4

**ocho** eight P4

**ochocientos** eight hundred 3

**oeste** *adj* western *4*; *n* west *6*

**oficial** official *1*

la **oficina** office *2*, 8

el **oficio** occupation 8

**ofrecer (zc)** to offer *4*

el **oído** (inner) ear 11

**oír** to hear 13

**ojalá** I/we hope 11

el **ojo** eye 2

la **ola** wave 14

las **Olimpiadas** Olympic Games *14*

**olvidar** to forget *8*, 14

**once** eleven P4

la **opción** option *8*

la **operación** operation *11*

la **operadora** operator 13

la **opinión** opinion *4*

la **oportunidad** opportunity *3*, 17

**optimista** optimistic *P2*

**óptimo/a** optimum, best *13*

**opuesto/a** opposite *2*

la **oración** sentence *1*

la **orden** order 3

**ordenado/a** tidy *17*

la **oreja** ear 9

la **organización** organization *3*

el **organizador,** la **organizadora** organizer *15*

**organizar (c)** to organize *3*, 15

el **órgano** body *17*

**orgulloso/a** proud *14*

el **origen** origin *6*

el **oro** gold *13*

la **orquesta** orchestra *15*

**os** you (*fam pl*) 5; (to) you 7

**oscuro/a** dark 2

el **otoño** autumn 6

**otro/a** other, another *1*; **otra vez** again *P4*, 7

el **oxígeno** oxygen *1*


## P

**paciente** patient *P2*

el **padre** father 1

los **padres** parents *2*, 4

el **padrino** godfather 4

la **paella** paella *10*

**pagar (gu)** to pay for 7

la **página** page *P3*

el **país** country *2*, 10

el **paisaje** landscape *12*

el **pájaro** bird *4*

la **palabra** word *P1*; la **mala palabra** dirty word *16*

el **palacio** palace *14*

el **palo** stick *15*

el **pan** bread 3

la **panadería** bakery *10*

**panameño/a** Panamanian 2

los **pantalones** slacks 7

la **pantomima** pantomime *6*

el **pañuelo** handkerchief 7

la **papa** potato 3; las **papas fritas** French fries 3

el **papá** father 4

el **papel** paper 1; role 17; **hacer el papel** to play the part 8

la **papelería** stationery store 13

el **paquete** package 13

el **par** pair 11; **a la par con** equal to 14

**para** for 1; to 3; towards, in order to 15; **para que** so that 15, 17

la **parabólica** satellite dish antenna 4

el **parabrisas** windshield 12

el **parachoques** bumper 12

la **parada** stop 12

**parado/a** standing 16

el **parador** hotel 14

**parar** to stop 9, 12

**parcial** partial P2

**parecer (zc)** to seem 7

**parecido/a** similar 16

la **pared** wall P3

la **pareja** partner 13; couple 17

el **parentesco** relationship 4

el **paréntesis** parenthesis 15

el **pariente** relative 3, 4

el **paro** unemployment 8

el **parque** park 4, 14

el **párrafo** paragraph 1

la **parte** part 2, 9; **¿de parte de quién?** who's calling? 13; **en todas partes** everywhere 10; **por otra parte** on the other hand 6

la **participación** participation 17

el/la **participante** participant 6

**participar** to participate 12

**particular: en particular** particularly 17

el **partido** game P4, 6

**partir: a partir de** beginning at 6

**pasado/a** last 12; **pasado mañana** the day after tomorrow 3

el **pasaje** ticket 12; el **pasaje de ida y vuelta** round-trip ticket 12

el **pasajero**, la **pasajera** passenger 12

el **pasaporte** passport 12

**pasar** to happen 2, 12; to spend 4; to come in 8; **pasar la aspiradora** to vacuum 5; **pasar la lista** to call roll P1; **pasarlo bien** to have a good time 13; **pasar por** to pick up 7

la **Pascua** Passover 15

el **pasillo** hall 5

**pasivo/a** passive P2

el **paso** step P1; **dar paso a** to open way to 17

el **pastel** pie 3

la **pastelería** pastry shop 10

la **pastilla** pill 11

la **patata** potato (in Spain) 10

**patinar** to skate 6

el **pato** duck, Argentine sport 6

el **patrimonio** patrimony 16

el **patrón**, la **patrona** patron 15

el **pavo** turkey 10

el **payaso** clown 15

la **paz** peace 6

el **peaje** toll 12

el **pecado** sin 8

la **pedagogía** pedagogy 17

el **pedal** pedal 15

el/la **pediatra** pediatrician 11

**pedir (i)** to request 3, 6; to ask for, to order 6

**peinar** to comb 5

la **pelea** fight 13

la **película** film 3

el **peligro** danger 11

**peligroso/a** dangerous 6, 16

el **pelo** hair 2

la **pelota** ball 6

el **pelotari** jai alai player 6

el **pelotón** crowd 15

la **peluquería** beauty salon, barber shop 8

el **peluquero**, la **peluquera** hairdresser 8

la **pena: ¡qué pena!** what a pity! 15

**pendiente** pending 13

el/la **penitente** penitent 15

**pensar (ie)** to think 2, 4; **pensar** + *inf* to plan to + *verb* 4

la **pensión** boarding house 1

**peor** worse 9; worst 10

**pequeño/a** small P3

**perder (ie)** to lose 3, 4; **perder el tiempo** to waste time 7

la **pérdida** loss 16

**perdón** excuse me P1

**perezoso/a** lazy 2

**perfectamente** perfectly 13

**perfecto/a** perfect 7

el **perfil** profile 8

el **periódico** newspaper 3, 4

el **período** period 13

**permanecer (zc)** to remain, to stay 4

**permanente** permanent 4

**permanentemente** permanently 9

**permiso: con permiso** excuse me P1

**permitir** to permit, to allow 9, 10

**pero** but 1

el **perro**, la **perra** dog 2, 4

**perseguir (i)** to pursue
*13*

**persistente** persistent *P2*

la **persona** person P1

el **personaje** person of importance *13*

**personal** *adj* personal *8*;
el **personal** personnel,
staff *8*

la **personalidad** personality
*8*

**pertenecer (zc)** to belong
*13*

**perteneciente** part of, belonging *8*

**peruano/a** Peruvian *2*

**pesar** to weigh *9*; **a pesar
de** in spite of *12*

la **pescadería** fish market
*10*

el **pescado** fish *3*

**pescar (qu)** to fish *6*

**pesimista** pessimistic *P2*

**pésimo/a** terrible, very
bad *13*

**peso** peso *1*; weight *3, 9*

el **pez** (*pl* peces) fish *4*

la **pestaña** eyelash *9*

el **petróleo** oil, petroleum *6,
16*

el/la **pianista** pianist *10*

el **piano** piano *3*

el **picadillo** ground meat
cooked with onions,
garlic, and green pepper
*10*

**picante** hot, spicy *17*

el **pie** foot *9*

la **piel** skin *11*

la **pierna** leg *9*

la **pila** battery *16*

el/la **piloto** pilot *8*

la **pimienta** pepper *10*

el **pimiento** green pepper *10*

**pintar** to paint *15*

la **pintura** painting *14*

la **piñata** clay pot or card-

board container covered
with tissue paper and
filled with candy, nuts,
and other treats *15*

el **pionero,** la **pionera** pioneer *17*

el **piragüismo** canoeing *14*

la **pirámide** pyramid *12*

**pisar** to step *17*

la **piscina** pool *5, 6*

el **piso** floor *5*

el/la **piyama** pajama *5*

la **pizarra** blackboard *P2, P3*

la **pizza** pizza *3*

el **placer** pleasure *12*

el **plan** plan *3*

la **plancha** iron *5*

**planchar** to iron *5*

**planear** to plan *12*

el **planeta** planet *6*

**planificar (qu)** plan *3*

el **plano** map *8*

la **planta** plant *2*; floor *5*

la **plata** silver *15*

la **plataforma** platform *15*

el **plátano** banana *3, 10*

el **plato** dish, plate *3, 5*; el
**plato combinado** combination plate *10*

la **playa** beach *3*

la **plaza** position *8*; plaza *8*;
la **plaza de toros** bullring *14*

**pleno: a pleno** full *12*

el **plomero** plumber *8*

**plural** plural *1*

el **pluriempleo** moonlighting
*8*

la **población** population,
people *12*

**pobre** poor *2*

la **pobreza** poverty *17*

la **pocilga** pigpen *17*

**poco: poco a poco** little
by little *17*; **un poco** a
little *1*

**poder (ue)** to be able to,

can *2, 4*; el **poder**
power *17*

el **polen** polen *11*

el **policía** policeman; la **(mujer) policía** policewoman *8*

el **político** politician *13*; *adj*
political

el **polo** pole *4*

el **pollo** chicken *3*

el **ponche** punch *3*

**poner (g)** to put *5*

**popular** popular *1*

**por** about *1*; for *4*; by *11*;
by, per, around, through,
because of *15*; **por
cierto** by the way *5*; **por
ciento** per cent *5*; **por
eso** that's why *1*; **por
favor** please P1; **por lo
menos** at least *9*; **por
qué** why *2*

el **porcentaje** percentage *5*

**porque** because *2*

el **portal** porch *5*

**portátil** portable *14*

**portugués, portuguesa**
Portuguese *1*

**poseer** to have *11*

la **posesión** possession *2*

**posgrado** postgraduate *17*

la **posibilidad** possibility *1*

**posible** possible *9, 11*

**positivamente** postively *8*

**positivo/a** positive *8*

**posponer (g)** postpone
*16*

**pospuesto** postponed *16*

**postal** postal *13*; la **tarjeta postal** post card *13*

el **postre** dessert *10*

el **potasio** potassium *16*

la **práctica** practice *1*

**practicar (qu)** to practice
*1*

el **precio** price *1*

**precioso/a** beautiful *7*

**precisar** to need *8*
**precolombino/a** pre-Columbian *13*
la **predicción** prediction *13*
**preferible** preferable *8*
**preferido/a** favorite *3*
**preferir (ie, i)** to prefer *3, 4*
el **prefijo** area code *13*
la **pregunta** question *P3*, P4
**preguntar** to ask (a question) *P1, 8*
el **premio** prize *9*
la **prenda (de ropa)** clothes *5*
la **prensa** press *17*
la **preocupación** preoccupation *13*
**preocupado/a** preoccupied *11*
**preocuparse** to worry *10*
**preparar** to prepare *3, 5*; **preparar la comida** to cook *5*; **prepararse** to get ready *16*
el **preparativo** plan, preparation *11*
la **preparatoria** college preparatory *1*
la **presencia** presence *17*
**presenciar** to watch, to see *6*
la **presentación** introduction *P1*
**presentar** to introduce P2; to present *2*
**presente** here, present *P3*; **tener presente** to keep in mind *13*
el **presidente,** la **presidenta** president *9*
la **presión** stress *11*
**prestar** to lend *7*; **prestar atención** to pay attention *17*
la **pretensión:** la **pretensión económica** desired salary *8*

el **pretérito** preterit *12*
**primario/a** elementary *17*; la **primaria** elementary school *1*
la **primavera** spring *6*
**primer** first *P1,* 6
**primero/a** first *6*
**primitivo/a** primitive *9*
el **primo,** la **prima** cousin *4*
**principal** principal, main *5*
el **príncipe** prince *8*
el **principio** beginning *6*; principle *11*
los **principios** principles *11*
la **prioridad** priority *8*
la **prisa: tener prisa** to be in a hurry *4*
**privado/a** private *12*
la **probabilidad** probability *16*
**probable** probable *11*
**probablemente** probably *12*
el **probador** fitting room *7*
**probar (ue)** to try *7*; **probarse (ue)** to try on *7*
el **problema** problem *P4, 4*
la **procedencia** origin *13*
la **procesión** procession *15*
la **producción** production *13*
**producido/a** produced *16*
**producir (zc)** to produce *8*
el **producto** product *17*
el **productor,** la **productora** producer *13*
la **profesión** profession *8*
**profesional** professional *6*
el **profesor,** la **profesora** professor P3
el **programa** program *1*
la **programación** programming *1*
el **programador,** la **programadora** programmer *8*
**programar** to program *12*

**progresivo/a** progressive *9*
el **progreso** progress *14*
la **prohibición** prohibition *16*
**prohibir** to prohibit, to forbid *10*
el **promedio** average *11*
la **promoción** graduating class *17*
**promover (ue)** to promote *15*
el **pronombre** pronoun *1*
el **pronóstico** forecast *6*
**pronto** soon *8*
la **pronunciación** pronunciation *P1*
la **propina** tip *10*
**propio** same *5*; own *7*
**proponer (g)** to propose *16*; **proponerse** to set oneself to do to something *13*
la **proporción** proportion *16*
**proporcionar** to offer *8*
**proseguir (i)** to continue *9*
la **protección** protection *12*
**proteger (j)** to protect *12*
la **proteína** protein *10*
la **provincia** province *12*
**próximo** next *3*; near *14*; **próxima entrega** immediate possession *5*
el **proyecto** project *3*
**prudente** wise *13*
la **prueba** proof *14*
la **psicología** psychology *1*
**psicológico/a** psychological *8*
el **psicólogo,** la **psicóloga** psychologist *8*
el/la **psiquiatra** psychiatrist *8*
**psiquiátrico/a** psychiatric *12*
**Pts.** abbreviation for pesetas
**publicado/a** published *13*

la **publicidad** advertising *2*
**público/a** public *2*, 11
el **pueblo** town 11
el **puente** bridge *16*
la **puerta** door *P3*; gate 12
el **puerto** port 12
**puertorriqueño/a** Puerto Rican *2*
**pues** well *P4*; since *2*
el **puesto** position 8
el **pulmón** lung 11
la **pulsera** bracelet 7
el **punto** point *7*; **dos puntos** colon *13*; **en punto** sharp *P4*
la **puntuación** punctuation *17*
**puntual** punctual *P2*
**puntualmente** punctually *13*
el **pupitre** desk *P3*
el **puré:** el **puré de papas** mashed potatoes 10
**puro/a** pure 11

## Q

**qué** what *P3*; **¿qué hay?** hello *13*; **¡qué va!** no way!, of course not 1
**que** that 2; **lo que** what, that which *1*; **ya que** since *17*
**quedar** to fit, to have something left *7*; to be, to remain 10; **quedar en + *inf*** to agree on + *present participle* 15
**quejarse** to complain 8
**quemar** to burn *8*, 16
**querer (ie)** to want, to love 4
**querido/a** dear 13
el **queso** cheese 3
**quién** who *P2*
**quien** who 11
la **química** chemistry 1
**quince** fifteen *P4*
la **quinceañera** celebration of a girl's fifteenth birth-

day, fifteen year-old girl *15*
**quinientos** five hundred 3
**quinto** fifth 6
el **quiosco** kiosk *13*
**quitar** to take away, to remove 5; **quitarse** to take off 5
**quizá(s)** maybe 7

## R

el **radiador** radiator 12
**radicalmente** radically *17*
el/la **radio** radio *2*, 5
la **radiografía** X-rays 11
**rallado/a** grated *8*
**rápidamente** rapidly, fast 13
la **rapidez** speed *17*; **con rapidez** rapidly, fast 13
**rápido/a** fast *2*, 13
**raro/a** odd *15*; **rara vez** seldom *11*
el **rasgo** characteristic, trait *17*
el **rastrillo** razor (in Mexico and other countries) *14*
el **rato** while *9*, 16; **dentro de un rato** in a while 16
la **raya: de rayas** striped 7
la **raza** race, breed *15*
la **razón: por estas razones** that's why 11; **tener razón** to be right 4
la **reacción** reaction *2*
**real** real *8*; royal *14*
la **realidad** reality *2*; **en realidad** really *2*
**realista** realistic *P2*
**realizado/a** carried out *8*
**realizar (c)** to do, to perform *8*, 17; to accomplish 17
**realmente** really 13
**reanudar** to resume *17*
la **rebaja** sale 7

**rebajado/a** marked down 7
**rebelde** rebellious *P2*
la **recepción** reception 14
la **recepcionista** receptionist 8
el **receso** break *P4*
la **receta** recipe *10*; prescription 11
**recetar** to prescribe 11
**recibir** to receive *6*, 13
**reciente** recent *8*
**recoger (j)** to pick up *13*, 16
**recomendar (ie)** to recommend 7
**reconocer (zc)** to recognize 13
**reconocido/a** recognized *13*
**reconquistar** to win back *13*
**recordar (ue)** to remember *13*, 15; to remind 17
**recorrer** to travel *15*
**rectangular** rectangular *P3*
**rectificar (qu)** rectify *8*
los **recuerdos** regards 13
**rechazar (c)** to turn down, to refuse *13*
la **red** net 6
el **redactor,** la **redactora** editor *9*
**redondo/a** round *P3*
**reducido/a** small *17*
**reducir (zc)** to reduce *17*
**referir (ie, i)** to refer *16*
**reflejar** to reflect 17
el **refresco** soda 3
el **refrigerador** refrigerator 5
el **refugio** country/mountain resort *4*
**regalar** to give (a present) 7
el **regalo** present 7

**regatear** to bargain, to haggle 7
el **régimen** system 17
**regio/a** royal 14
la **región** region 12
el **reglamento** regulation, law 13
**regresar** to come back 14
la **regulación** regulation, rule 12
**regular** so, so P1
**regularmente** regularly 11, 13
el **reino** kingdom 12
**reír(se) (i)** to laugh 6
la **relación** relation 1, 17; relationship 4
**relacionado/a** related 2, 13
la **relajación** relaxation 9
**relativamente** relatively 4, 13
**religioso/a** religious P2
el **reloj** clock, watch P3
**relleno/a** filled 10; el **chile relleno** green pepper filled with cheese 10
**remodelar** to remodel 5
**renovar (ue)** to renew 7
la **renta** rent 12
**reñido/a** close (game) 6
**repartir** to deliver 13
**repasar** to review 3
**repente: de repente** suddenly 13
**repercutir** to reflect 11
**repetir (i)** to repeat P1
**replantar** to replant 16
**reportar** to report 9
el/la **representante** representative 17
**representar** to represent 2
la **represión** repression 17
la **república** republic 13
el **requesón** cottage cheese 10

la **reservación** reservation 12
**reservado/a** reserved 2
**reservar** to make a reservation 12
la **residencia** residence, home 4
**residencial** residential 12
el/la **residente** resident 9
la **resistencia** resistance 9
**resistir** to resist, to withstand 16
**resolver (ue)** to solve 13
**respecto: con respecto a** with respect to 8
**respetar** to respect 15
el **respeto** respect 17
la **respiración** breathing 9
**respirar** to breathe 9
la **responsabilidad** responsibility 5
**responsable** responsible 8
la **respuesta** answer 1
el **restaurante** restaurant 3, 10
el **resto** rest 5; pl traces 16
el **resultado** result 4
**resultar** to be 4
la **reunión** meeting 8
**reunirse** to get together 1, 15
el **revelado** development 14
**revertido/a: la llamada de cargo revertido** collect call 13
**revisar** to inspect, to examine 12
la **revista** magazine 3, 4
el **rey: los Reyes Magos** the three Wise Men 15
**rico/a** rich 2
**ridículo/a** ridiculous 11
el **riesgo** danger, risk 11
la **rifa** raffle 3
el **rincón** place, corner 12
el **río** river 12
la **riqueza** wealth 14

**rítmico/a** rhythmic 9
el **ritmo** rhythm 11
el **robo** theft 14
el **robot** robot 8
el **rock** rock 3
**rodeado/a** surrounded 17
**rojo/a** red 2
el **romance** romance 13
**romántico/a** romantic P2
**romper** to break, to tear 16
el **ron** rum 3
**roncar** to snore 8
la **ropa** clothes 5; la **ropa interior** underwear 13
la **rosa** rose 2
**rosado/a** pink 2
**roto/a** broken, torn 16
**rubio/a** blond 2
**rudo/a** rough 6
el **ruido** noise 13
las **ruinas** ruins 14
**rural** rural 11
**ruso/a** Russian 1

## S

el **sábado** Saturday P4
la **sábana** sheet 5
**saber** to know P3, 8; **sé** I know P3, 2
el **sabor** flavor 12
el **sabotaje** sabotage 16
**sacar (qu)** to get 1, 2; to check out, to take out 3; **sacar fotos** to take pictures 14
**sacudir** to dust 5
**sagitariano/a** Sagittarian 13
la **sal** salt 8, 10
la **sala** living room 5; la **sala de espera** waiting room 12
el **salario** salary 17
la **salida** departure P4, 12; exit 16

salir (g) to leave *1*; to go out, to leave *5*

el salón (de clase) classroom P3

la salsa sauce *2*, 10; type of music *13*

saltar to jump *7*

el salto jumping *9*

la salud health *8*, 10

saludable healthy *7*

saludar to greet *2*

el saludo greeting P1

salvadoreño/a Salvadoran *2*

el sándwich sandwich *3*

la sangre blood *11*

la sanidad: Ministerio de Sanidad Health Department *11*

sano/a healthy *7*, 10

el santo, la santa saint *15*

la satisfacción satisfaction *8*

satisfacer (g) to satisfy *8*

satisfactorio/a satisfactory *11*

la sauna sauna *9*

el saxofón saxophone *3*

se yourself P1; himself *3*, 5; herself, itself, yourselves, themselves *5*; (to) him, her, you, it *16*

sea: o sea that is *15*

la secadora drier *5*

secar (qu) to dry *5*

la sección section *12*

seco/a dry *16*

la secretaría department *12*

el secretario, la secretaria secretary *4*, 8

el secreto secret *3*

el sector area *8*

la secundaria high school *1*

la sed: tener sed to be thirsty *4*

seguir (i) to follow P2, *6*; seguir cursos to take courses *7*;

seguir derecho to go straight ahead *8*

según according to *P4*, 4

segundo second *P2*, 6

seguramente for sure *7*

la seguridad security *11*; cinturón de seguridad safety belt *11*, 12

seguro/a sure *2*; el seguro insurance *12*

seis six P4

seiscientos six hundred *3*

la selección selection *13*

selecto/a select *9*

el sello stamp *13*

la selva jungle *12*

el semáforo traffic light *12*

la semana week P4

semanal weekly *5*

el semestre semester *1*

sencillo/a simple, easy *13*; single *14*

sensato/a sensible *11*

sensitivo/a sensitive *10*

sentarse (ie) to sit down *P2*, 5

sentimental sentimental P2

el sentimiento feeling *8*

sentir (ie, i) to be sorry *10*; lo siento I'm sorry P1; sentirse (ie) to feel *2*, 11

la señal signal *12*; señal de tráfico traffic signal *12*

señalar to point to *7*

señor Mr P1

señora Mrs. P1

señorial stately *5*

señorita Miss P1

separado/a separated *17*

se(p)tiembre September *6*

séptimo/a seventh *6*

la sequía drought *16*

ser to be P2; el ser being *15*

la serie series *6*

serio/a serious P2

el servicio service *4*, 11

la servilleta napkin *10*

servir (i) to serve *6*; ¿en qué puedo servirle(s)? may I help you? *7*

sesenta sixty P4

la sesión session *9*

setecientos seven hundred *3*

setenta seventy P4

el sexo sex *15*

sexto sixth *6*

sexual sexual *17*

sí yes P2

si if *4*, 6

la sicología psychology *1*

el sicólogo, la sicóloga psychologist *8*

siempre always *1*

la siesta nap *4*

siete seven P4

el siglo century *15*

el signatario person who signs *13*

el signo sign *13*

siguiente next *P4*, 9

la silla chair P3

el símbolo symbol *12*

similar similar *7*

simpático/a nice, charming *2*

simplemente simply *13*

sin without *7*, 8; sin embargo nevertheless *1*; sin que without *17*

sincero/a sincere *P2*

sino but *8*

el síntoma symptom *11*

el/la siquiatra psychiatrist *8*

sísmico/a seismic *16*

el sismo earthquake *16*

el sistema system *6*

la situación situation *16*

situado/a situated *8*

el smog smog *16*

sobre on, above P3; el sobre envelope *13*

**sobrepasar** to surpass *17*

la **sobrina** niece *4*

el **sobrino** nephew *4*

**social** social *11*

la **sociedad** society *17*

**socorro: casa de socorro** first-aid center *11*

el **sodio** sodium *16*

el **sofá** sofa *5*

el **sol** sun *6*; **hace sol** it's sunny *6*

**solicitar** to ask for *8*

la **solicitud** application *7*, *8*

**solidario/a** solidary *15*

**sólo** only *2*

**solo/a** alone *4*; **solos/as** by themselves *4*

**soltero/a** single *2*

la **solución** answer *P4*

el **sombrero** hat *7*

**sonar (ue)** to ring *7*

**sonreír(se) (i)** to smile *6*

la **sopa** soup *3*

el **sorbete** sherbet *10*

**sorprenderse** to be surprised *13*

la **sorpresa** surprise *13*, *15*

el **sorteo** drawing *15*

el **sótano** basement *16*

**Sr.** abbreviation for **señor** *P1*

**Sra.** abbreviation for **señora** *P1*

**Srta.** abbreviation for **señorita** *P1*

**su(s)** his *P1*, *4*; her, your, its, their *4*

**suave** soft *15*

**subir** to increase, to go up *6*; to raise, to go up *9*

**subrayado/a** underlined *4*

**subterráneo/a** underground *13*

el **suceso** event, happening *16*

**sucio/a** dirty *16*

la **sucursal** branch *8*

la **sudadera** sweat shirt, jogging suit *7*

la **suegra** mother–in–law *4*

el **suegro** father–in–law *4*

el **sueldo** salary *8*

el **sueño: tener sueño** to be sleepy *4*

la **suerte: tener suerte** to be lucky *4*

el **suéter** sweater *7*

**suficiente** enough *10*

**sufrir** to suffer *11*

la **sugerencia** suggestion *7*

**sugerir (ie, i)** to suggest *11*

la **suite** suite *15*

**suizo/a** Swiss *14*

la **sujeción** subordination *13*

el **sujeto** subject *3*

la **suma** amount *8*

**superar** to surpass *17*

**superficial** superficial *2*

la **superficie** surface, area *16*

el **supermercado** supermarket *7*, *10*

el **supervisor,** la **supervisora** supervisor *2*

**supuesto: por supuesto** of course *15*

el **sur** south *8*

**surgir (j)** to appear *13*

la **sustancia** element, substance *10*

**suyo (-a, -os, -as)** your, (of) yours, (of) his/her, (of) hers, (of) its, their, (of) theirs *14*

**T**

la **tabla** chart *5*

el **tablero** notice board *13*

**tacaño/a** stingy *P3*

el **taco** rolled or folded tortilla filled with meat, beans, etc. *2*

**tal: con tal (de) que** provided that *17*; **qué tal** how are you *P1*; **tal como** as *15*; **tal vez** perhaps *10*

el **talón** heel *9*

la **talla** size *7*

el **taller** shop *8*

el **tamaño** size *2*

**también** also, too *2*

**tampoco** neither, not either *8*

**tan** so *1*; as *9*

**tanto** as much *9*

**tantos** as many *9*

la **taquilla** ticket office *6*

**tarde** late *5*; **la tarde** afternoon *P1*

la **tarea** homework *P2*, *1*; la **tarea doméstica** house chore *5*

la **tarifa** tariff *14*

la **tarjeta** card *7*, *12*

el **taxi** taxi *12*

el/la **taxista** taxi driver *17*

la **taza** cup *3*, *10*

**te** yourself *P1*; you (*fam sing*) *5*; (to) you *7*

el **té** tea *3*

el **teatro** theater *2*, *14*

**técnico/a** technical *17*

la **tecnología** technology *1*

el **techo** roof *5*

la **tela** material *7*

la **tele** television *5*

**telefónico/a** *adj* telephone *7*, *13*

el **teléfono** telephone *P4*, *3*

el **telégrafo** telegraph *13*

el **telegrama** telegram *13*

la **telenovela** soap opera *11*

la **televisión** television *3*

**televisivo/a** *adj* television, telegenic *6*

el **televisor** television set *2*, *5*

el **tema** theme, topic *10*

el **temblor** earthquake *16*

**temer** to fear *10*

la **temperatura** temperature
6, 13

el **templo** temple 14

**temporal** temporary 4

**temprano** early 5

la **tendencia** tendency 6

**tender (ie)** to hang 5;
**tender la cama** to make
the bed 5

el **tenedor** fork 10

**tener (g, ie)** to have P3,
4; **tener presente** to
keep in mind 13; **tener
que** + inf to have to +
verb 4

el **tenis** tennis P4, 6

la **tensión** pressure, stress
11

**teórico/a** theoretic, theoretical 17

**tercer** third P3, 6

**tercero** third 6

**terminado/a** finished 13

**terminar** to finish, to end
1, 3

el **término** term 17; el **término mcdio** average 17

el **termómetro** thermometer
11

la **terraza** terrace 4, 5

el **terremoto** earthquake 16

**terrible** terrible P2, 15

el **terrorismo** terrorism 17

**ti** (to, for) you (fam sing)
7

la **tía** aunt 4

el **tiempo** weather 6; time
15; **a tiempo** on time
12; **hace buen/mal
tiempo** the weather is
fine/bad 6; **¿qué tiempo
hace?** how's the weather
6

la **tienda** store 7; la **tienda
de campaña** tent 16

la **tierra** land 12

el **tigre** tiger 2

**tímido/a** timid P2

la **tintorería** cleaners 14

el **tío** uncle 4

**típico/a** typical 2, 10

el **tipo** type 4; kind 17

**tirar** to pull 15; to throw
17

la **tiza** chalk P3

la **toalla** towel 5

el **tobillo** ankle 9

**tocar (qu)** to play (an instrument) 3; to knock 8

el **tocino** bacon 10

**todavía** still 7

**todo** everything 12; **eso
es todo** that's all 10

**todos** all 2, 12; **en todas
partes** everywhere 10;
**todos los días** everyday
6

**tomar** to drink, to take 3

el **tomate** tomate P3, 3

la **tonelada** ton 15

**tonto/a** silly, foolish 2

el **toque** sound to signal an
activity 17

**torcer (ue, z)** to twist 12

el **torero** bullfighter 15

el **tornado** tornado 16

el **toro** bull 13; la **corrida de
toros** bullfight 13; la
**plaza de toros** bullring
13

la **torta** sandwich (in Mexico)
3

la **tortilla** thin cornmeal or
flour cake 2; omelette 10

la **tortura** torture 15

la **tos** cough 11

**toser** 11

la **tostada** toast 3

**tostado/a: pan tostado**
toast 3

**total** total 2

**totalmente** totally 15

**trabajador/a** hard working
2

**trabajar** to work 1

el **trabajo** work 1, 8

el **trabajomaníaco, la trabajomaníaca** workaholic 8

la **tradición** tradition 4, 15

**tradicional** traditional 7

**tradicionalmente** traditionally 13

**traducir (zc)** to translate
13

**traer** to bring 10

el **tráfico** traffic 12

el **traje** suit 7; el **traje de
baño** bathing suit 7

la **tramitación** transaction
16

**tranquilamente** calmly 13

el **tranquilizante** tranquilizer
11

**tranquilo/a** calm P2, 2

la **transacción** transaction 4

el **tránsito** transit 12

**transmitir** to transmit 13

el **transporte** transportation
12

el **tranvía** streetcar 11

**tras** after 11

**trasladarse** to move, to
transport 12

el **traslado** transportation 12

el **trastorno** disorder 16

**tratar (de)** to try to 6; to
treat 14

el **trato** treatment 17

**través: a través de**
throughout 14

**trece** thirteen P4

**treinta** thirty P4

el **tren** train 12

**tres** three P4

**trescientos** three hundred
3

**triste** sad 2

**triunfar** to succeed 17

el **triunfo** victory 13

el **trópico** tropics 12

**trotar** to jog 3

el **trote** gait *9*
**tu(s)** your *4*
**tú** you (*fam sing*) P1
**tumbar** to knock down *16*
el **turismo** tourism *12*
el/la **turista** tourist *4*
**turístico/a** *adj* tourist *14*
**turno** session *6*; la **farma-cia de turno** pharmacy that takes turns attending customers holidays and Sundays *11*
**tuyo (-a, -os, -as)** (of ) yours *14*

## U

**u** or *13*
**últimamente** lately *16*
**último/a** last *1*
**un/a** a, an P3; one P4
**únicamente** only *15*
la **unidad** unit *17*
**unido/a** united *4*
la **unión** union *9*
la **universidad** university *1*
**universitario/a** *adj* university *8*
**uno** one P4
**unos** some *1*
la **urbanización** housing development *4*
**urbano/a** urban *9*, 11
**urgente** urgent *12*
**urgentemente** urgently *8*
**usar** to use *P4*
**usted** you (*formal sing*) P1
**ustedes** you (*formal pl*) 1
**útil** useful *P1*
**utilizar (c)** to use *13*

## V

**va: ¡qué va!** of course not, no way *1*
las **vacaciones** vacation *3, 4*
**vacío/a** empty *12*

la **vainilla** vanilla *10*
la **vajilla** china *10*
**valiente** valiant, brave *P2*
**valioso/a** useful *13*
**valor** value *10*, 17; courage *15*
**valorar** to value *8*
los **vaqueros** jeans *7*
**variante** (multiple choice) answer *11*
**variar** to vary *7*
la **variedad** variety *12*
**varios/as** several *3*, 14
**vasco/a** Basque *6*
el **vaso** glass *3, 10*
**vecino/a** neighbor *13*, 16
el **vegetal** vegetable *3*
**vegetariano/a** vegetarian *10*
el **vehículo** vehicle *11*
**veinte** twenty P4
**veinticinco** twenty-five P4
**veinticuatro** twenty-four P4
**veintidós** twenty-two P4
**veintinueve** twenty-nine P4
**veintiocho** twenty-eight P4
**veintiséis** twenty-six P4
**veintisiete** twenty-seven P4
**veintitrés** twenty-three P4
**veintiún/veintiuno** twenty-one P4
la **vela** sail, sailboat *14*; candle *15*
la **velocidad** speed *6*
**vendado/a** bandaged *12*
el **vendedor,** la **vendedora** salesperson *8*
**vender** to sell *3*
**venezolano/a** Venezuelan *2*
**venir (g, ie)** to come *4*
la **venta** sale *8*
la **ventaja** advantage *11*

la **ventana** window P3
la **ventanilla** window (car, train, etc.) *12*
las **ventas** sales *8*
la **ventilación** ventilation *13*
**ver** to see *2, 3*
el **verano** summer *6*
el **verbo** verb *1*
la **verdad** truth *4*
**verdadero/a** true *P3*
**verde** green *2*
la **verdura** vegetable *3, 10*
el **vestido** dress *7*
**vestir (i)** to dress *6*; **vestirse** to get dressed *6*
la **vez** (*pl* **veces**) time *2, 9*; **alguna vez** sometime *12*; **en vez de** instead of *7*; **otra vez** again *P4, 7*; **tal vez** perhaps *10*; **una vez** once *12*; **a veces** sometimes, at times *4, 12*; **algunas veces** sometimes *12*
la **vía** lane *12*; (railroad) track *12*
**viajar** to travel *14*
el **viaje** trip *3, 4*
**vibrante** vibrant *15*
la **víctima** victim *16*
la **vida** life *6*, 11; living *11*
el **vídeo/video** video *4*
**viejo/a** old *2*
el **viento** wind *6*; **hace viento** it's windy *6*
el **viernes** Friday P4
**vigilar** to watch *11*
**vigor: en vigor** in force *13*
el **vinagre** vinegar *10*
el **vino** wine *10*
la **violencia** violence *13*, 15
**violento/a** violent *6*
el **violín** violin *3*
el/la **violinista** violinist *10*
la **visa** visa *12*
el **visado** visa *12*

la **visita** visit 10
el/la **visitante** visitor 2
**visitar** to visit 3, 4
el **visón** mink 7
la **vista** view 5
la **vitalidad** vitality 13
**vivir** to live 3
**vivo/a** adj live 6; alive 13
el **vocabulario** vocabulary P1
la **vocal** vowel P1
el **vól(e)ibol** volleyball 6
el **volante** steering wheel 12
**volar (ue)** to fly 8, 12
el **volcán** volcano 16
**voluntario/a** voluntary 16

**volver (ue)** to come 4
**vosotros/as** you (fam pl) 1
la **voz: en voz baja** softly 17
el **vuelo** flight 12
la **vuelta: dar vueltas** to spin around 15; el **pasaje de ida y vuelta** round trip ticket 12
**vuestro/a(s)** your (fam pl) 4

### Y

**y** and P1
**ya** already 1; **ya que** since 17

el **yerno** son–in–law 4
**yo** I P2
el **yoga** yoga 9
el **yogur** yogurt 10
el **yudo** judo 6

### Z

la **zanahoria** carrot 10
el **zapato** shoe 5; los **zapatos (de) tenis** tennis shoes 7
la **zona** zone 4, 10

—————————— ENGLISH-SPANISH VOCABULARY ——————————

**A**

**A.D. (after Christ)** d.C.

**a** un/a

to **abandon** abandonar

**ability** la habilidad

**able: to be able to** poder (ue)

**abnormal** anormal

**about the middle of** a mediados de

**above** sobre

**abroad** en el extranjero

**absent** ausente

**absurd** absurdo/a

to **accept** aceptar

**accessory** accesorio/a

**accident** (*car*) el choque, el accidente

to **accompany** acompañar

to **accomplish** realizar (c)

**according to** según, de acuerdo con

**accounting** la contabilidad

**accumulated** acumulado/a

**ache** el dolor

to **achieve** lograr

**acid** ácido/a

**acoustics** la acústica

to **act** actuar

**action** el acto

**active** activo/a

**actively** activamente

**activity** la actividad

**actor** el actor

**actress** la actriz

**ad** el anuncio

**add** añadir

**address** la dirección; el domicilio; *v* dirigirse

**adequate** adecuado/a

**adequately** adecuadamente

to **administer** administrar

**administrative** administrativo/a

**administrator** el administrador, la administradora

**admiration** la admiración

**adult** la persona mayor

**advance** el adelanto

**advantage** la ventaja

**adventure** la aventura

**adverbial** adverbial

**advertising** la publicidad

**advice** el consejo

**advisor** el consejero, la consejera

**aerobic** aeróbico/a

**aerogram** el aerograma

to **affect** influir (y), afectar

**affected** afectado/a

**affectionate** afectivo/a

**affirmative** afirmativo/a

**afraid: to be afraid** tener miedo

**after** al cabo de; tras; después

**afternoon** la tarde

**again** otra vez

**against** contra

**age** la edad

**agency** la agencia; **travel agency** la agencia de viajes

**agenda** la agenda

**agent** el/la agente

**ago** hace + *time expression* + *preterit*

to **agree** estar de acuerdo; to **agree on** + *pres part* quedar en + *inf*

**agreeable** conforme

**aggressive** agresivo/a

**ahead: to go straight ahead** seguir derecho

**air** el aire; *adj* aéreo/a; **air conditioning** el aire acondicionado; **open air** el (al) aire libre

**airline** la aerolínea

**airplane** el avión, el aparato

**airport** el aeropuerto

**alarm clock** el despertador

**alarming** alarmante

**album** el álbum

**alcohol** el alcohol

**alcoholic** alcohólico/a

**alfalfa** la alfalfa

**algebra** el álgebra

**alive** vivo/a

**all** todo, todos; **that's all** eso es todo

**allergic** alérgico/a

**allergy** la alergia

to **allow** admitir; permitir

**almost** casi

**alone** solo/a

**along** a lo largo de

**already** ya

**also** también

**although** aunque

**always** siempre

**ambitious** ambicioso/a

**ambulance** la ambulancia

**American** norteamericano/a

**among** entre

**amount** la cantidad, la suma

**ample** amplio/a

**amusing** divertido/a

**an** un/a

**analysis** el análisis

**and** y, e

**anesthesia** la anestesia

**angel** el ángel

**animal** el animal

**ankle** el tobillo

**anniversary** el aniversario

to **announce** anunciar

**announcer** el locutor, la locutora

**another** otro/a

to **answer** contestar; *n* la contestación, la solución, la respuesta; **answer (multiple choice)** la variante; **answering machine** el contestador automático

anthropological antropológico/a

anthropology la antropología

antibiotic el antibiótico

antihistaminic el antihistamínico

antimony el antimonio

anxiety la ansiedad

any alguno/a; algún; cualquier

anyone alguien

anything algo; anything else? ¿algo más?

apartment el apartamento

to appear aparecer (zc); surgir (j)

to applaud aplaudir

apple la manzana

application la solicitud

to appreciate apreciar

apprenticeship el aprendizaje

appropriate apropiado/a

approximate aproximado/a

April abril

Arab árabe

architect el arquitecto, la arquitecta

architectonic arquitectónico/a

architecture la arquitectura

area el sector, el área fem; area code el indicativo, el prefijo; surrounding areas los alrededores

Argentine cowboy el gaucho

to argue discutir

argument la discusión

arid árido/a

arm el brazo

armchair la butaca

aroma el aroma

around alrededor

arrest el arresto

arrival la llegada

to arrive llegar (gu)

arrow la flecha

art el arte

artery la arteria

article el artículo

artist el/la artista

artistic artístico/a

as como; tal como; as much as tanto como; as many as tantos/as como; as soon as en cuanto

to ask (a question) preguntar; hacer (g) una pregunta; to ask for pedir (i), solicitar

aspect el aspecto

aspiration la aspiración

aspirin la aspirina

to assert afirmar

to assign destinar

assignment el mando

assistant el asistente, la asistenta

to associate asociar

associated commonwealth el estado libre asociado

to assume adoptar

asterisk el asterisco

asthma el asma

astronaut el/la astronauta

astronomer el astrónomo, la astrónoma

at a; en; at least por lo menos

athlete el/la atleta

athletics el atletismo

atmosphere el ambiente; el marco

attaché case el maletín

to attack atacar (qu)

to attend asistir; to attend to ocuparse de

attendance la asistencia

attention la atención; to pay attention prestar atención

attitude la actitud

to attract atraer

attraction la atracción

attractive atractivo/a

August agosto

aunt la tía

authoritarian autoritario/a

autumn el atoño

availiability la disposición

available disponible

avenue la avenida

average el promedio, el término medio

aviation la aviación

avocado el aguacate

to avoid evitar

aware alerta

Aztec azteca

## B

B.C. (before Christ) a.C.

baby el bebé

back la espalda

background el marco; el ambiente

backpack la mochila

bacon el tocino

bad mal, malo/a; very bad pésimo

bag la bolsa

bakery la panadería

balance el equilibrio

ball la pelota

ballpoint pen el bolígrafo

banana la banana, el plátano

bandaged vendado/a

bank el banco

banquet el banquete

to baptize bautizar (c)

bar el bar

barbarian bárbaro/a

barbecue la barbacoa

barber shop la peluquería

barbituric barbitúrico

to bargain regatear

to bark ladrar

baseball el béisbol

based on en base a

basement el sótano

basic básico/a

**basically** básicamente; eminentemente
**basket** el cesto; la cesta
**basketball** el baloncesto, el básquetbol
**Basque** vasco/a
to **bathe** bañar(se); **bathing suit** el traje de baño
**bathroom** el baño
**battery** la pila
**bay** la bahía
to **be** estar; ser; resultar; to **be a couple** formar pareja; to **be able to, can** poder (ue); to **be afraid** tener miedo; to **be born** nacer; to **be called,** to **be named** llamarse; to **be careful** tener cuidado; to **be founded on** basarse en; to **be glad** alegrarse; to **be hot** tener calor; to **be hungry** tener hambre; to **be in a hurry** tener prisa; to **be in charge** estar a cargo; to **be in love** estar enamorado/a (de); to **be lucky** tener suerte; to **be missing** faltar; to **be necessary** hacer falta; to **be noticeable** notarse; to **be part of** formar parte de; to **be right** tener razón; to **be sleepy** tener sueño; to **be sorry** sentir (ie, i); to **be successful** tener éxito; to **be surprised** sorprenderse; to **be thirsty** tener sed; to **be used to** estar acostumbrado/a
**beach** la playa
**beans** los frijoles
**beast** la fiera
**beautiful** precioso/a; bello/a
**beauty** la belleza; **beauty parlor (beauty salon)** el salón de belleza, la peluquería

**because** porque
to **become** hacerse; to **become short** entrecortar
**bed** la cama; to **go to bed** acostarse; to **put to bed** acostar; to **stay in bed** guardar cama
**bedroom** el dormitorio
**beer** la cerveza
**before** antes; antes (de) que; ante
**beforehand** con anticipación
to **begin** empezar (ie, c), comenzar (ie, c), iniciar
**beginning** el principio; **beginning at** a partir de
**behavior** la conducta
**behind** detrás (de)
**being** el ser
to **believe** creer
**bellboy** el botones
to **belong** pertenecer (zc); **belonging to** perteneciente a
**below** abajo; a continuación
**belt** el cinturón; **safety belt** el cinturón de seguridad
to **bend** doblar
**benefit** el beneficio
**berth** la litera
**besides** además
**best** mejor; óptimo
to **bet** apostar (ue)
**better** mejor
**between** entre
**beyond** más allá (de)
**bicycle** la bicicleta
**big** grande
**bill** la cuenta
**biology** la biología
**bird** el pájaro, el ave
**birth** el nacimiento
**birthday** el cumpleaños
**birthrate** la natalidad
**black** negro/a
**blackboard** la pizarra
**blanket** la manta
**blender** la licuadora
**blond** rubio/a

**blood** la sangre
**blouse** la blusa
**blue** azul
**boarder** el interno, la interna
**boarding** el embarque; **boarding house** la pensión; **boarding pass** tarjeta de embarque 12
**body** el cuerpo; el órgano
to **boil** hervir (ie, i)
**boiled** hervido/a
**bolívar (monetary unit of Venezuela)** bolívar
**Bolivian** boliviano/a
**bone** el hueso
**book** el libro
**bookstore** la librería
**boot** la bota
**booth** la caseta
**born: to be born** nacer
**boss** el jefe, la jefa
**both** ambos/as
to **bother** molestar
**bottle** la botella
**box** la casilla
**boxing** el boxeo
**boy** el chico, el muchacho; **Boy Scouts** niños exploradores
**boyfriend** el novio
**bracelet** la pulsera
**brain** el cerebro; **brain drain** la fuga de cerebros
to **brake** frenar
**branch** la sucursal
**brand** la marca
**brave** valiente
**bread** el pan
**break** el receso; *v* romper; to **break down** descomponer(se) (g)
**breakfast** el desayuno
to **breathe** respirar
**breathing** la respiración
to **breed** criar
**bridge** el puente
to **bring** traer (g)
**brochure** el folleto
**broken** roto/a; fracturado/a

**bronze** el bronce
**brother** el hermano;
   **brother–in–law** el cuñado;
   **brothers, brother and
   sister** los hermanos
**brown** café, castaño/a
**brunette** moreno/a
**bugler** el corneta
to **build** construir (y)
   **building** el edificio, la construcción
**built** construido/a
**bull** el toro
**bullfight** la corrida (de toros), la fiesta brava
**bullfighter** el torero
**bullring** la plaza de toros
**bumper** el parachoques
to **burn** quemar
**bus** el autobús
**business** *adj* comercial; *n* el
   negocio; **business matters**
   la materia económica
**busy** ocupado/a, atareado/a
**but** pero; sino
**butter** la mantequilla
**button** el botón
**buy** comprar
**buyer** el comprador, la compradora

## C

**café** el café
**cafeteria** la cafetería
**calamity** la calamidad
**calcium** el calcio
**calculator** la calculadora
**calculus** el cálculo
**calendar** el calendario
to **call** llamar; to **call roll** pasar
   (la) lista; *n* la llamada; **collect call** la llamada a cobrar, la llamada de cargo
   revertido; to **be called** llamarse; **who's calling?** ¿de
   parte de quién?
**calm** tranquilo/a

**calmly** tranquilamente
**calorie** la caloría
**camera** la cámara
**camp** el campamento
**campaign** la campaña
**can** la lata; *v* poder (ue)
**cancel** cancelar
**cancer** el cáncer
**candle** la vela
**candy** el caramelo, el dulce
**canoe** la canoa
**canoeing** el piragüismo
**capital** la capital; **capital
   letter** la mayúscula
**car** el auto, el automóvil, el
   coche, el carro; **sleeping
   car** coche cama
**card** la tarjeta
**cardboard** el cartón
**cardiovascular** cardiovascular
**career** la carrera
**careful: to be careful** tener
   cuidado
**carefully** con cuidado
**careless** descuidado/a
**cargo** la carga
**carpet** la alfombra
**carried out** realizado/a
**carrot** la zanahoria
to **carry** cargar (gu)
**case** el caso; **attaché case** el
   maletín
**cash** en efectivo; **cash register** la caja
**cashier** el cajero, la cajera
**cassette** el casete
**Castilian** castellano/a
**castle** el castillo
**casual** informal
**cat** el gato, la gata
**catastrophic** catastrófico/a
**category** la categoría
**cathedral** la catedral
to **cause** causar, ocasionar; *n* la
   causa
**caused** causado/a
to **celebrate** celebrar

**census** el censo
**cent** el centavo
**center: shopping center** el
   centro comercial
**centigrade** centígrado
**central** central
**century** el siglo
**ceramics** la cerámica
**cereal** el cereal
**ceremony** la ceremonia
**certain** cierto/a
**chain** la cadena
**chair** la silla
**chalk** la tiza
**champagne** el champán
**champion** el campeón, la
   campeona
**championship** el campeonato
**change** cambiar; *n* el cambio
**channel** el canal
**characteristic** el rasgo, la
   característica
to **characterize** caracterizar (c)
**charge: to be in charge** estar a cargo
**charity** la caridad
**charm** el encanto
**charming** encentador/a; sim-
   pático/a
**chart** la tabla, el cuadro
**cheap** barato/a
to **check (luggage)** chequear,
   facturar; *n* el cheque; to
   **check out** sacar (qu)
**checked** de cuadros
**cheek** la mejilla
**cheerfully** amablemente
**cheese** el queso
**chemistry** la química
**chess** el ajedrez
to **chew** masticar (qu); **chewing
   gum** el chicle
**chicken** el pollo
**child** el niño, la niña
**children** *adj* infantil; *n* los
   niños, las niñas
**Chilean** chileno/a

**china** la vajilla; **china cabinet** el aparador
**Chinese** chino/a
**chocolate** el chocolate
**cholesterol** el colesterol
to **choose** escoger (j), elegir (j)
**chore: house chore** la tarea doméstica
**christening** el bautizo
**Christmas** la(s) Navidad(es); **Christmas Eve** la Nochebuena
**church** la iglesia
**cigarette** el cigarrillo
**circle** el círculo
**circular** circular
**circumstance** la circunstancia
**citizen** el ciudadano, la ciudadana
**city** la ciudad; **city block** la cuadra; **city hall** el ayuntamiento
**civil** civil
**civilization** la civilización
**civilized** civilizado/a
**clarification** la aclaración
**class** la clase; **first class** de lujo
**classic** clásico/a
to **classify** clasificar (qu)
**classmate** el compañero, la compañera
**classroom** el salón (de) clase
to **clean** limpiar; *adj* limpio/a
**cleaners** la tintorería
**cleaning** la limpieza
**clear** despejado/a; claro/a
**clearly** claramente
**clerk** el dependiente, la dependienta
**client** el cliente, la clienta
**climate** el clima
**clinic** el hospital, la clínica
**clock** el reloj
to **close** cerrar (ie); *adj* (game) reñido/a

**closet** el armario, el closet
**clothes** la ropa, la prenda (de ropa)
**cloud (dark)** el nubarrón
**cloudy** nublado/a, nuboso/a
**clown** el payaso
**club** el club
**coach** el entrenador, la entrenadora
**coast** la costa
**coat** el abrigo
**code** el código; **zip code** código postal
**coffee** el café
**cognate** el cognado
to **coincide** coincidir
**cold** el frío; el catarro; **it's cold (weather)** hace frío
**coliseum** el coliseo
**collaboration** la colaboración
**collect call** llamada a cobrar, llamada de cargo revertido
**collection** la colección
**college** la facultad; **college preparatory** la preparatoria
to **collide** chocar (qu)
**Colombian** colombiano/a
**colon** dos puntos
**colonel** el coronel
**colonial** colonial
**color** el color; **solid color** color entero
**column** la columna
to **comb** peinar
**combination** la combinación; **combination plate** el plato combinado
to **combine** combinar
to **come** venir (g, ie); to **come back** volver (ue), regresar; to **come in** entrar, pasar
**comfort** la comodidad
**comfortable** cómodo/a
**comma** la coma
**command** el mandato
**commentary** el comentario

**commission** la comisión
**commissioner** el comisario
**commitment** el compromiso
**common** común
to **communicate** comunicar (qu)
**communication** la comunicación
**communion** la comunión
**community** la comunidad
**company** a compañía
to **compare** comparar
to **compete** competir (i)
**competent** competente
**competition** la competencia, la competición
to **complain** quejarse
to **complete** completar; *adj* integral
**completely** completamente, por completo
**complex** complicado/a
**complication** la complicación
**comprehensive** comprensivo/a
**compulsive** compulsivo/a
**computer** la computadora, el computador; **computer science** la informática
**concentrated** concentrado/a
**concentration** la concentración
**concept** el concepto
**concert** el concierto
**condition** la condición
**condominium** el condominio
**confirmation** la confirmación
**conflict** el conflicto
**confrontation** el enfrentamiento
**confusion** la confusión
**congratulations** felicidades
to **congratulate** felicitar
to **connect** conectar
**connection** la conexión
**connotation** la connotación

**consequence** la consecuencia

**conservative** conservador/a

to **consider** considererar

**consolation** la consolación

**consonant** la consonante

**construction** la construcción

to **consult** consultar

**consultation** la consulta

**consumption** el consumo

**contact** el contacto

to **contain** contener (g, ie)

**contaminated** contaminado/a

**contest** el concurso

**context** el contexto

to **continue** continuar, proseguir

**contrary** contrario/a; **on the contrary** al contrario

to **contribute** contribuir (y)

to **control** controlar

**convenient** conveniente

**convent** el convento

**conversation** la conversación

to **convert** convertir (ie, i)

to **convince** convencer (z)

to **cook** cocinar, preparar la comida; *n* el cocinero, la cocinera

**cookie** la galletita

**cool** fresco/a; **it's cool (weather)** hace fresco

**cord** la cuerda

**cordial** cordial

**corn** el maíz

**corner** la esquina; el rincón

**corporation** la empresa

**correct** correcto/a

to **correspond** corresponder

**correspondence** la correspondencia

**corresponding** correspondiente

**cosmetic** el cosmético

**cosmopolitan** cosmopolita

**cost** el costo; *v* costar (ue)

**cottage cheese** el requesón

to **cough** toser; *n* la tos

**council** la junta

to **count** contar (ue)

**counter** el mostrador

**country** el país; el campo

**couple** la pareja; to **be a couple** formar pareja

**courage** el valor

**course** el curso; **of course** por supuesto; **of course not** ¡qué va!; to **take courses** seguir cursos

**court** la cancha

**courtesy** la cortesía

**cousin** el primo, la prima

to **cover** cubrir

**covered** cubierto/a

**coyote** el coyote

**crazy** loco/a

to **create** crear

**creative** creativo/a

**creativity** la creatividad

**credit** crédito; **credit card** la tarjeta de crédito

**crisis** la crisis

**criticism** la crítica

**crocodile** el cocodrilo

to **cross** cruzar (c); *n* la cruz; **Red Cross** la Cruz Roja

**crowd** el pelotón

**cruise** el crucero

**crutch** la muleta

to **cry** llorar

**Cuban** cubano/a

to **cultivate** cultivar

**cultural** cultural

**culture** la cultura

**cup** la taza

**Cupid** Cupido

**cure** la cura

**curtain** la cortina

**curved** curvo/a

**custom** la costumbre

**customary: it's customary** se acostumbra

**customs** la aduana

**cut** cortado/a

**cycling** el ciclismo

**cyclist** el/la ciclista

## D

**daily** diario/a; cotidiano/a; *adv* diariamente

to **damage** dañar; *n* el daño

**damaged** dañado

to **dance** bailar; *n* el baile, la danza

**dancer** el bailarín, la bailarina

**danger** el peligro

**dangerous** peligroso/a

**dark** oscuro/a

**data** los datos

**date** la fecha; la cita; *v* datar

**daughter** la hija; **daughter–in–law** la nuera

**day** el día; **All Souls' Day** el Día de los Muertos/Difuntos; **day student** el externo; **everyday** todos los días; **holiday** día de fiesta; the **day after tomorrow** pasado mañana; the **day before yesterday** anteayer; **weekdays** entre semana

**dead** muerto/a

**dear** estimado/a; querido/a

**death** la muerte

**debris** el escombro

**debt** la deuda

**decaffeinated** descafeinado

**deceased** difunto/a

**December** diciembre

to **decide** decidir

**decision** la decisión

to **declare** declarar; afirmar

to **decorate** decorar

**decorated** decorado/a

to **dedicate** dedicar (qu)

to **defend** defender (ie)

**defender** el defensor

**definite** definido/a

**definitely** definitivamente

**definition** la definición
**defusing** la desactivación
to **delight** encantar
**delighted** encantado/a
to **deliver** repartir
**delivery: special delivery**
entrega especial
to **demand** imponer (g)
**demonstration** la manifestación
**demonstrative** demostrativo
**dentist** el/la dentista
to **deny** negar (ie)
**department** el departamento;
la secretaría; **department
store** el almacén
**departure** la salida
to **depend** depender
to **deposit** depositar
**depressed** deprimido/a
**depression** la depresión
**derived** derivado/a
**descent** el descenso
to **describe** describir
**described** descrito/a
**description** la descripción
**desert** el desierto; *adj* desértico/a
**design** el diseño
**designed** encaminado/a; diseñado/a
**designer** el diseñador, la diseñadora
**desired salary** pretensión
económica
**desk** el escritorio, el pupitre
**dessert** el postre
**destination** el destino
to **destroy** destruir
**destroyed** destruido/a
**destruction** la destrucción
**detail** el detalle
**detailed** detallado/a
**detective** el detective
to **determine** determinar
**detractor** el detractor
to **develop** desarrollar

**development** el desarrollo;
el revelado
**dexterity** la destreza
to **dial** marcar (qu), discar (qu)
**dialogue** el diálogo
**dictionary** el diccionario
to **die** morir (ue, u)
**diet** la dieta
**difference** la diferencia
**different** diferente
**difficult** difícil
**difficulty** la dificultad; **with
difficulty** difícilmente
to **digest** digerir (ie, i)
**diminished** disminuido/a
**dining room** el comedor
**dinner** la comida, la cena
**diplomatic** diplomático/a
to **direct** administrar
**directions** las instrucciones
**directly** directamente
**director** el director, la directora
**directory** el directorio, la
guía
**dirty** sucio/a; **dirty word**
mala palabra
**disadvantage** la desventaja
**disappointment** el contratiempo
**disaster** la catástrofe
to **disconnect** desconectar
**discoteque** la discoteca
**discount** el descuento
to **discover** descubrir
**discovery** el descubrimiento
**discreet** discreto/a
**discrimination** la discriminación
**discussion** la negociación
**dish** el plato
**dishwater** el lavaplatos
**disorder** el trastorno
**disposable** desechable
**disposal** la disposición
**dissatisfaction** la inconformidad

**distance** la distancia
**distinguished** distinguido/a,
destacado/a
**distribution** la distribución
**district** el distrito; **zip code**
el distrito postal
**diversity** la diversidad
**division** la división
**divorced** divorciado/a
to **do** hacer (g); realizar (c)
**doctor** el doctor, la doctora;
**doctor's office** el consultorio
**dog** el perro, la perra
**dollar** el dólar
to **dominate** dominar
**donation** la donación
**door** la puerta
**double** doble
to **doubt** dudar
**doughnut** el donut
**down payment** la cuota inicial, la entrada
**downtown** el centro
**dozen** la docena
to **drain** escurrir
**drama** el drama
**dramatic** dramático/a
**drawing** el dibujo; el sorteo
to **dress** vestir (i); to **get
dressed** vestirse; *n* el vestido
**dresser** la cómoda
to **drink** beber, tomar; *n* la bebida
to **drive** manejar, conducir (zc)
**driver** el chofer
**drought** la sequía
**drug** la droga
**dry** seco/a; *v* secar (qu)
**dryer** la secadora
**dualism** el dualismo
**duck (Argentine sport)** el
pato
**due to** debido a
**duel** el duelo
**during** durante

to **dust** sacudir
**duty** el deber
**dynamic** dinámico/a

## E

**each** cada
**ear** la oreja; **(inner) ear** el oído
**early** temprano/a; **early morning** la madrugada
to **earn** ganar; to **earn a living** ganarse la vida
**earring** el arete
**earthquake** el terremoto, el temblor, el sismo
**easily** con facilidad
**easy** fácil, sencillo
to **eat** comer, ingerir (ie, i)
**ecologist** el/la ecologista
**ecology** la ecología
**economical** económico/a
**economics** la economía
**editor** el redactor, la redactora
**education** la educación
**effect** el efecto
**efficient** eficiente
**effort** el esfuerzo
**egg** el huevo
**eight** ocho; **eight hundred** ochocientos
**eighteen** dieciocho
**eighth** octavo
**eighty** ochenta
**either: not either** tampoco 8
**elaborate** elaborado/a
**electrical appliance** el electrodoméstico
**electrician** el/la electricista
**electricity** la electricidad
**elegant** elegante
**element** el elemento; la sustancia
**elementary** elemental; primario/a; **elementary school** la primaria
**elephant** el elefante

**elevation** la altura
**elevator** el ascensor
**eleven** once
**eliminate** eliminar
**embrace** el abrazo
**embroidery** el bordado
**emerald** la esmeralda
**emergency** la emergencia; **emergency center** el ambulatorio
**emigration** la emigración
**emission** la emisión
**emotional** emocional
**emotion** la emoción
to **employ** emplear
**employee** el empleado, la empleada
**employment** el empleo
**empty** vacío/a
to **end** acabar, terminar; *n* el extremo; el final
to **endure** aguantar
**energy** la energía
**engagement** el noviazgo
**engineer** el ingeniero, la ingeniera
**engineering** la ingeniería
**English** inglés, inglesa
to **enjoy** disfrutar (de)
**enormous** enorme
**enough** bastante, suficiente
to **enrich** enriquecer (zc)
to **enter** entrar
**entertainment** la diversión
**entrance** la entrada
**environment** el medio ambiente
**environmental** ambiental
**equal** igual; **equal to** a la par con
**equality** la igualdad
**equator** el ecuador
**equatorial** ecuatorial
**equestrian** ecuestre
**equivalency** la equivalencia
**equivalent** equivalente
**eraser** el borrador

**erosion** la erosión
**error** el error; el fallo
**eruption** la erupción
**escalator** la escalera mecánica
**especially** especialmente
**essential** imprescindible
to **establish** establecer (zc)
**established** basado/a; fundado/a
**European** europeo/a
**even** aun; hasta
**evening** la noche
**event** el evento, el acontecimiento, el suceso, el hecho
**every** cada; **every day** todos los días
**everything** todo
**everywhere** en todas partes
**evident** evidente
**exactly** exactamente
**examination** el examen
to **examine** examinar; revisar
**example** el ejemplo
to **exceed** sobrepasar
**excellent** excelente
**exception** la excepción
**excess** el exceso
to **exchange** cambiar
**excited** emocionado/a
**excitement** la emoción
**exclusive** exclusivo/a
**excuse** la excusa; **excuse me** con permiso, perdón
**exempt** exento/a
**exercise** el ejercicio
to **exist** existir
**exit** la salida
**exotic** exótico/a
to **expect** esperar
**expense** el gasto
**expensive** caro/a
**experience** la experiencia; *v* experimentar
**expert** el experto, la experta
to **explain** explicar (qu)
**explosive** el explosivo

to **express** expresar; **express train** el expreso
**expression** la expresión
**extended** extenso/a
**extension** la extensión
**exterior** el exterior
**extra** extra
**extraordinary** extraordinario/a
**extraterrestial** extraterrestre
**extremely** extremadamente
**extroverted** extrovertido, extravertido/a
**eye** el ojo
**eyebrow** la ceja
**eyelashes** las pestañas

**F**

**fabulous** fabuloso/a
**face** la cara; *v* encarar, enfrentar
to **facilitate** facilitar
**factor** el factor
**factory** la fábrica
**fair** la feria; *adj* justo/a
to **fall** caer(se)
**false** falso/a
**familiar** familiar
**family** la familia
**famous** famoso/a
**fan** el aficionado, la aficionada
**fantastic** fantástico/a
**far** lejos (de); **far away** alejado/a
**farewell** la despedida
**farm** la finca
**fashion** la moda; to **be fashionable** estar de moda
**fast** rápidamente, con rapidez
**fat** gordo/a; *n* la grasa
**father** el padre, el papá; **father–in–law** el suegro
**favor: in favor of** a favor de
**favorable** favorable; **favorable conditions** la facilidad

**favorite** favorito/a, preferido/a
to **fear** temer
**February** febrero
to **feel like** tener ganas de
**feeling** el sentimiento
**feminist** el/la feminista
**fender** el guardabarros
**fervor** el fervor
**fever** la fiebre
**fewer** menos
**fiancé** el novio
**fiancée** la novia
**fiction** la ficción
**fictitious** imaginario/a
**field** el campo
**fifteen** quince; **fifteen year-old girl** la quinceañera
**fifth** quinto
**fifty** cincuenta
**fight** la pelea, la lucha; *v* lidiar, luchar
**figure** la cifra
to **fill out** llenar
**filled** relleno/a
**film** la película
**filming** la filmación
to **find** encontrar (ue); to **find out** averiguar
**fine** la multa; *adv* bien
**finger** el dedo
to **finish** terminar, acabar
**finished** terminado/a, acabado/a
**fire** el fuego, el incendio; *v* despedir (i)
**fireman** el bombero
**fireplace** la chimenea
**first** primer, primero/a; **first–aid center** la casa de socorro; **first class** de lujo
to **fish** pescar (qu); *n* el pescado; el pez (los peces); **fish market** la pescadería
to **fit** quedar; **fitting room** el probador
**five** cinco; **five hundred** quinientos

**flashlight** la linterna
**flavor** el sabor
**flexibility** la flexibilidad
**flight** el vuelo
**flood** la inundación
**flooded** inundado/a
**floor** el piso; la planta
**flower** la flor
**flu** la gripe
to **fly** volar (ue)
to **focus** centrar
to **fold** doblar
**folklore** el folklore
**folkloric** folklórico/a
to **follow** seguir (i)
**food** la comida, el alimento; la alimentación; el comestible
**foolish** tonto/a
**foot** el pie
**football** el fútbol
**for** para
to **forbid** prohibir
to **force** obligar (gu); *n* la fuerza
**forecast** el pronóstico
**forehead** la frente
**foreign** extranjero/a
**forest** el bosque
to **forget** olvidar
**fork** el tenedor
**formal** formal
**formation** la formación
**former** antiguo/a
**fortress** la fortaleza
**fortunate** afortunado/a
**forty** cuarenta
**forward** adelante
**founded: to be founded on** basarse en
**four** cuatro; **four hundred** cuatrocientos
**fourteen** catorce
**fourth** cuarto/a
**fracture** la fractura
**fractured** fracturado/a
**free** libre; gratis
**freedom** la libertad

**freeway** la autopista
**French** francés, francesa
**frequently** con frecuencia, frecuentemente
**fresh** fresco/a
**Friday** el viernes
**fried** frito/a; **French fries** las papas fritas
**friend** el amigo, la amiga
**friendship** la amistad
**frighten** aterrorizar (c); asustar
**frightened** asustado/a
**from** de; desde
**frozen** congelado/a
**fruit** la fruta; **fruit store** la frutería
**full** lleno/a; **full–time** jornada completa
**funny** cómico/a; divertido
**furniture** los muebles
**future** el futuro

## G

**gait** el trote
**gallery** la galería
**game** el partido, el juego; el encuentro
**garage** el garaje, la cochera
**garbage** la basura
**garden** el jardín
to **gargle** hacer gárgaras
**garlic** el ajo
**gasoline** la gasolina
**gate** la puerta
**gelatin** la gelatina
**general** general; **general practice** la medicina familiar
**generally** generalmente
**generation** la generación
**generous** generoso/a
**genius** el genio
**geographic** geográfico/a
**geography** la geografía
**German** alemán/a

to **get** conseguir (i); adquirir (ie, i); sacar (qu); to **get married** casarse; to **get ready** prepararse; to **get sick** enfermarse; to **get tired** cansarse; to **get together** reunirse; to **get up** levantarse
**giant** el gigante
**giraffe** la jirafa
**girl** la chica, la muchacha; **Girl Scouts** niñas exploradoras
**girlfriend** la novia
**give** dar; to **give a present** regalar
**glad** contento/a; to **be glad** alegrarse
**gladiator** el gladiador
**glass** el cristal; el vaso; **stemmed glass** la copa
**glasses** la gafas
**glove** el guante
to **go** ir; acudir; to **go away** irse; to **go straight ahead** seguir derecho; to **go to bed** acostarse; to **go together** combinar bien; to **go up** subir; aumentar
**goal** la meta, el objetivo; to **have as a goal** tener como fin
**God** Dios
**goddaughter** la ahijada
**godfather** el padrino
**godmother** la madrina
**godson** el ahijado
**gold** el oro
**golf** el golf; **golf course** el campo de golf
**good** bueno/a; buen; **good–bye** adiós; **good grief!** ¡qué barbaridad!
**gossiper** el chismoso, la chismosa
**grab** agarrar
**grade** la nota
**graduate** el graduado, la graduada; *v* graduar(se);

**graduating class** la promoción
**graduation** la graduación
**gram** el gramo
**grammar** la gramática
**granddauther** la nieta
**grandfather** el abuelo
**granddaughter** la nieta
**grandparents** los abuelos
**grandson** el nieto
**graphic** gráfico/a
**grass** la hierba
**grated** rallado/a
**gratis** gratis
**gray** gris
**great** gran; fabuloso
**green** verde; **green pepper** el pimiento, el chile
to **greet** saludar
**greeting** el saludo
**ground** molido/a
**group** el grupo
to **grow** crecer (zc); cultivar
**growth** el crecimiento
**guard** el/la guardia
to **guess** adivinar
**guest** el invitado, la invitada; el huésped
**guide** el/la guía
**guitar** la guitarra
**gymnasium** el gimnasio
**gymnastics** la gimnasia

## H

**habit** el hábito
**habitually** habitualmente
**hair** el pelo
**hairdresser** el peluquero, la peluquera
**half** medio/a; *n* la mitad
**hall** el pasillo
**Halloween** el Día de las Brujas
**ham** el jamón
**hamburger** la hamburguesa
**hand** la mano; **on the other**

**hand** en cambio, por otra parte
**handball** el balonmano
**handicraft** la artesanía
**handkerchief** el pañuelo
**handle** el asa *fem*
**handmade** hecho a mano
**handsome** guapo/a
**handwritten** manuscrito/a
to **hang** colgar (ue); tender (ie); to **hang up** colgar
to **happen** pasar
**happiness** la felicidad
**happy** alegre, contento/a, feliz
**hard** duro/a; **hard working** trabajador/a
**harmoniously** armónicamente
**hat** el sombrero
to **have** haber; poseer; disponer de (g); tener (g, ie); to **have a good time** divertirse (ie, i), pasarlo bien; to **have as a goal** tener como fin; to **have breakfast** desayunar; to **have dinner, supper** cenar; to **have lunch** almorzar (ue); to **have to** + *verb* tener que + *inf*
**he** él
**head** la cabeza
**headquarters** la jefatura
**healer** el curandero, la curandera
**health** la salud; la sanidad, **health food store** la herboristería, el centro naturista
**healthy** saludable; sano/a
to **hear** oír
**heart** el corazón
**heating** la calefacción
**heel** el talón
**height** la estatura; la altura
**hell** el infierno
**hello** hola; aló, diga, dígame, ¿qué hay?

**helmet** el casco
to **help** ayudar; *n* la ayuda
**hemisphere** el hemisferio
**her** ella; *adj* su(s); suyo/a
**here** aquí; presente
**heritage** la herencia
**high** arriba; alto/a; **high school** la escuela secundaria, el liceo; **high school curriculum** el bachillerato
**highway** la carretera
**hiking** (*mountain*) el montañismo
**hip** la cadera
**his** su(s); suyo/a
**Hispanic** hispano/a, hispánico/a; **Hispanic American** hispanoamericano/a
**history** la historia
**hit** alcanzado/a; *v* dar
**holding** agarrado/a; **holding hands** agarrados de la mano
**home** el hogar
**homework** la tarea
**honest** honrado/a
**hooded** encapuchado/a
to **hope** esperar; **I/we hope** ojalá (que)
**horoscope** el horóscopo
**hospital** el hospital
**hostal** el hostal
**hot** *adj* caluroso/a; caliente; picante; to **be hot** tener calor
**hotel** el hotel; el parador
**house** la casa; *adj* doméstico/a; **house chore** la tarea doméstica
**housewife** el ama de casa *fem*
**housing development** la colonia; la urbanización
**how** cómo; **how are you?** ¿qué tal?; **how horrible!** ¡qué horror!; **how many** cuántos/as; **how much** cuánto/a

**however** no obstante
**huge** enorme
**human** humano/a
**humanities** las humanidades
**humid** húmedo/a
to **humiliate** humillar
**hungry: to be hungry** tener hambre
to **hunt** cazar
**hurricane** el huracán
**hurry: to be in a hurry** tener prisa
to **hurt** doler (ue); herir (ie, i)
**husband** el esposo, el marido

## I

**I** yo
**ice cream** el helado; **ice–cream shop** la heladería
**idea** la idea
**ideal** ideal
**idealist** el/la idealista
**identification** la identificación
to **identify** identificar (qu)
**if** si
**illegal** ilegal
**image** la imagen
**imagination** la imaginación
to **imagine** imaginarse
to **imitate** imitar
**immediate** inmediato/a; **immediate possession** próxima entrega
**immediately** enseguida
**immense** inmenso/a
**impact** el impacto
**impartial** imparcial
**imperfect** imperfecto/a
**impetuous** impetuoso/a
**importance** la importancia
**important** importante; influyente
**impression** la impresión
**impressive** impresionante
to **improve** mejorar

**improvement** el avance; la mejora
**impulsive** impulsivo/a
**in** en; **in force** en vigor; **in front (of)** enfrente (de); **in–house** *adj* interno/a
**inauguration** la inauguración
**Inca** inca
to **include** incluir (y)
**included** incluido/a
**inconvenience** la molestia
to **increase** subir; aumentar; *n* el aumento
**incredible** increíble
**indefinite** indefinido/a
**independence** la independencia
**independent** independiente
**index** el índice
**Indian** *n* el/la indígena
to **indicate** indicar (qu)
**indication** la indicación
**indifferent** indiferente
**indiscrete** indiscreto/a
**indispensable** indispensable
**individual** *adj* individual; *n* el individuo
**industrialized** industrializado/a
**industry** la industria
**inexpensive** barato/a
**infection** la infección
**inferior** inferior
**infinitesimal** infinitesimal
**infinitive** el infinitivo
**inflation** la inflación
**influence** la influencia
to **inform** informar
**informal** informal
**information** la información
**infrastructure** la infraestructura
**ingenious** ingenioso/a
**ingredient** el ingrediente
**inhabitable** liveable
**inhabitant** el/la habitante
**inhuman** inhumano/a

**initiative** la iniciativa
**injection** la inyección
**injured person** el herido
**inn** la hostería
**inside** dentro (de); en
to **inspect** revisar; inspeccionar
**inspector** el inspector, la inspectora
to **inspire** inspirar
**installation** la instalación
**instead of** en vez de
**instinct** el instinto
**institute** el instituto
**insurance** el seguro
**intellectual** intelectual
**intelligent** inteligente
**intense** intenso/a
to **interest** interesar; *n* el interés
**interesting** interesante
**interior** interior
**internal** interno/a; **internal medicine** la medicina interna
**international** internacional
to **interrupt** interrumpir
**interstate** interestatal
to **interview** entrevistar; *n* la entrevista
**interviewer** el entrevistador, la entrevistadora
**intimate** íntimo/a
to **introduce** presentar
**introduction** la presentación; la implantación
**introverted** introvertido/a
to **inundate** inundar
to **invest** invertir (ie, i)
to **investigate** investigar (gu)
**investigating** *adj* investigador/a
**invitation** la invitación
to **invite** invitar
to **iron** planchar; *n* la plancha; *n* el hierro
**ironic** irónico/a
**irregular** irregular
**irritated** irritado/a

**island** la isla
**it** ello
**Italian** italiano/a
**itinerary** el itinerario
**its** su(s); suyo/a

## J

**jacket** la chaqueta
**jai alai** jai alai; **jai alai player** el pelotari
**January** enero
**Japanese** japonés, japonesa
**jeans** los vaqueros
to **jog** trotar
to **join** incorporarse
**joint** la articulación
**joke** el chiste
**judgment** el criterio; el dictamen
**judo** el judo
**juice** el jugo
**July** julio
to **jump** saltar
**jumping** el salto
**June** junio
**jungle** la jungla; la selva
**just** justo/a

## K

to **keep** conservar; to **keep in mind** tener presente
**kennel** la guardería de perros
**key** *adj* clave; *n* la llave
to **kill** matar
**kilo** el kilo
**kilogram** el kilogramo
**kilometer** el kilómetro
**kind** amable; *n* el tipo
**kindly** amablemente
**kingdom** el reino
**kiosk** el quiosco
**kiss** el beso
**kitchen** la cocina
**knife** el cuchillo
to **knock** tocar (qu); to **knock down** tumbar

to **know** conocer (zc); saber; **I know** sé
**knowledge** el conocimiento
**known** conocido/a

## L

**laboratory** el laboratorio
**lack** la falta; *v* faltar
**lamp** la lámpara
**land** la tierra
**landscape** el paisaje
**landslide** el alud
**lane** la vía
**language** el idioma, la lengua
to **last** durar; *adj* último/a; pasado/a; **last night** anoche
**late** tarde
**lately** últimamente
**later** después
**Latin** latino/a
to **laugh** reír(se) (i)
**laundry** la lavandería
**law** el derecho, la ley
**lawn** el césped
**lawyer** el abogado, la abogada; el licenciado en derecho; **lawyer's office** el bufete
**lazy** perezoso/a
to **learn** aprender
**least: at least** por lo menos
**leather** el cuero
to **leave** irse; salir; dejar; **leave taking** la despedida
**lecture** la conferencia
**left** izquierdo/a
**leg** la pierna
**legal** jurídico/a
**lemon** el limón
to **lend** prestar
**less** menos
**lesson** la lección
to **let** + *verb* dejar + *inf*
**letter** la carta
**lettuce** la lechuga
**liberal** liberal

**liberated** liberado/a
**liberty** la libertad
**library** la biblioteca
**license** la licencia; **driver's license** licencia de manejar
**lie** la mentira; to **lie down** acostarse (ue)
**life** la vida
**light** claro/a; *n* la luz; *v* encender (ie)
**like** como
to **like** gustar
**likewise** igualmente
**limit** el límite
**line** la cola; la línea; to **stand in line** hacer cola
**lion** el león
**liquid** el líquido
**liquor** el licor
**list** la lista
to **listen** escuchar
**liter** el litro
**literature** la literatura
**little** poco; un poco; **a little bit** un poquito/a; **little by little** poco a poco
to **live** vivir; *adj* vivo/a
**lively** movido/a
**living: to earn a living** ganarse la vida; **living room** la sala
**llama** la llama
to **lock in** encerrar (ie)
to **lodge** hospedarse
**lodging** el alojamiento
**logical** lógico/a
**logically** lógicamente
**long** largo/a
**longevity** la longevidad
to **look (at)** mirar; to **look for** buscar (qu)
to **lose** perder (ie)
**loss** la pérdida
**lottery** la lotería
**louder** más alto
**love** el amor; to **be in love** estar enamorado/a (de)

**low** bajo/a
to **lower** bajar
**loyal** leal
**luckily** por fortuna
**lucky: to be lucky** tener suerte
**luggage** el equipaje
**lunch** el almuerzo
**lung** el pulmón
**luxury** lujo

## M

**machine: answering machine** el contestador automático
**magazine** la revista
**magic** la magia
**magical** mágico/a
**magnificent** magnífico/a
**mail box** el buzón; el depósito
**mailman** el cartero
**main** principal
to **maintain** mantener (g, ie)
to **major** especializarse (c)
**majority** la mayoría
to **make** hacer; to **make a reservation** reservar; to **make a stopover** hacer escala; to **make difficult** dificultar; to **make up** constituir
**man** el hombre
**manager** el/la gerente
**manufacturer** el/la fabricante
**many** muchos/as
**map** el mapa; el plano
**March** marzo
**Mardi Gras** el carnaval
**marijuana** la marihuana
**marital status** el estado civil
to **mark** marcar (qu); **marked down** rebajado/a; to **mark time** marcar el paso
**market** el mercado
**marquis** el marqués

**married** casado/a; **married couple** el matrimonio
to **marvel** maravillarse
**marvelous** maravilloso/a
**masculine** masculino/a
**mashed potatoes** el puré de papas
**master** el maestro
**matching** la asociación
**material** la tela; el material
**materialistic** materialista
**mathematics** las matemáticas
**matter** la gestión; el asunto; *v* importar; **business matters** la materia económica; **it doesn't matter** no importa
**maximum** máximo/a
**May** mayo
**maybe** quizá(s)
**mayonnaise** la mayonesa
**me** mí; me
**means** medios; **by means of** mediante
to **measure** medir (i); *n* la medida
**meat** la carne; **ground meat** la carne molida; **meat market** la carnicería
**mechanic** mecánico/a
**medical** médico/a
**medication** la medicación
**medicine** la medicina
**medium** mediano/a
**meet** la competencia; *v* conocer (zc); **nice (pleased) to meet you** mucho gusto
**meeting** la reunión
**melodramatic** melodramático/a
**melody** la melodía
**member** el miembro
**memory** la memoria
**mental** mental
to **mention** mencionar
**menu** el menú
**merit** el mérito

**message** el mensaje
**messenger** el mensajero, la mensajera
**messy** desordenado/a
**meter** el metro
**method** el método
**metropolitan** metropolitano/a
**Mexican** mexicano/a
**microwave** el microondas
**middle class** la clase media
**midnight** la medianoche; **midnight mass** la Misa del Gallo
**midwife** la comadrona
**migration** la migración
**military** militar
**milk** la leche
**million** el millón
**millionaire** millonario/a
**mind** la mente
**mine** mío(-a, -os, -as)
**mineral** mineral
**minidialog** el minidiálogo
**minimum** mínimo/a
**mink** el visón
**minority** la minoría
**minus** menos
**minute** el minuto
**mirror** el espejo
**Miss** señorita, Srta.
**missile** el misil
**missing: to be missing** faltar
**mission** la misión
to **mix** mezclar
**mixer** la batidora
**model** el/la modelo
**modern** moderno/a
**modification** la modificación
**moment** el momento, el momentito; **at this moment** en estos momentos
**monastery** el monasterio
**Monday** el lunes
**money** el dinero
**monologue** el monólogo
**month** el mes

**monument** el monumento
**moon** la luna
**moonlighting** el pluriempleo
**more** más
**morning** la mañana; **early morning** la madrugada
**mortadella** la mortadela
**mother** la mamá, la madre; **mother–in–law** la suegra
**motor** el motor
**motorcycle** la moto(cicleta)
**mountain** la montaña; **mountain range** la cordillera
**mountainous** montañoso/a
**moustache** el bigote
**mouth** la boca
to **move** mover(se) (ue); trasladarse; impulsar; mudarse; to **move close** acercarse (qu)
**movement** el movimiento
**movies** el cine
**Mr.** señor, Sr.
**Mrs.** señora, Sra.
**much** mucho/a
**mud** el lodo
**multifaceted** multitudinario/a
**multiply** multiplicar (qu)
**muscle** el músculo
**museum** el museo
**music** la música
**musical** musical
**musician** el músico
**mustard** la mostaza
**my** mi(s)
**myself** me
**mysterious** misterioso/a
**mystery** el misterio

## N

**name** el nombre; to **be named** llamarse
**nap** la siesta
**napkin** la servilleta
**narrow** estrecho/a

**national** nacional
**native** nativo/a
**natural** natural
**nature** la naturaleza
**near** cerca; *adj* cercano/a
**necessary** necesario/a; **it's necessary to** + *verb* hay que + *inf*; to **be necessary** hacer falta
**neck** el cuello
**necklace** el collar
**necktie** la corbata
to **need** necesitar, precisar; *n* la necesidad
**negatively** negativamente
**neighbor** el vecino, la vecina
**neighborhood** la barriada; la colonia; la urbanización
**neither** tampoco
**nephew** el sobrino
**nervous** nervioso/a
**net** la red
**never** nunca
**nevertheless** sin embargo
**new** nuevo/a
**news** la(s) noticia(s)
**newscast** el noticiero
**newspaper** el periódico, el diario
**next** próximo/a; *n* el siguiente; **next to** al lado de, junto a
**Nicaraguan** nicaragüense
**nice** simpático/a; amable; **nice to meet you** mucho gusto
**niece** la sobrina
**night** la noche; the **night before last** antenoche, anteanoche
**nightstand** la mesa de noche
**nine** nueve; **nine hundred** novecientos
**nineteen** diecinueve
**ninety** noventa
**ninth** noveno/a
**no** no; **no one** nadie

**nobody** nadie
**noise** el ruido
**none** ninguno/a
**nonfat** descremado/a
**noon** el mediodía
**nor** ni; **neither . . . nor** ni . . . ni
**norm** la norma
**normal** normal
**normally** normalmente
**north** el norte
**nose** la nariz
**not** no; **not to know** ignorar; **not fully accepted** marginado/a
**notably** notablemente
**note** la nota; **notes** los apuntes
**notebook** el cuaderno
**noteworthy** notable
**nothing** nada
to **notice** fijarse; **notice board** el tablero
**noticeable: to be noticeable** notarse
to **notify** avisar
to **nourish** alimentar
**nourishing** nutritivo/a
**November** noviembre
**now** ahora; **right now** en estos momentos
**nowadays** hoy en día
**number** el número
**numerous** numeroso/a
**nurse** el enfermero, la enfermera
**nutrition** la nutrición

## O

to **obey** obedecer (zc)
**object** el objeto
**obligation** la obligación
to **observe** observar
**obsession** la obsesión
to **obtain** obtener (g, ie); alcanzar (c); conseguir (i)

**obvious** obvio/a
**occasionally** ocasionalmente
**occupation** el oficio; la ocupación
to **occupy** ocupar
to **occur** ocurrir
**October** octubre
**odd** raro/a
**of** de; **of course** por supuesto; **of course not** ¡qué va!
to **offer** ofrecer (zc); proporcionar
**office** la oficina
**official** oficial
**oil** el aceite; el petróleo
**old** viejo/a; antiguo/a; **old person** el anciano, la anciana
**older** mayor
**Olympic Games** las Olimpiadas
**omelette** la tortilla
**on** sobre; en
**once** una vez
**one** uno/a, un; **one hundred** ciento, cien
**onion** la cebolla
**only** sólo, únicamente
to **open** abrir; to **open the way to** dar paso a
**operation** la operación
**operator** la operadora
**opinion** la opinión
**opportunity** la oportunidad
**opposite** opuesto/a
**optimistic** optimista
**optimum** óptimo/a
**option** la opción
**or** o, u; **either . . . or** o . . . o
**orange** anaranjado/a; *n* la naranja
**orchestra** la orquesta
**order** la orden; *v* pedir (i); **in order to** para
**organization** la organización
**organize** organizar (c)

**organizer** el organizador, la organizadora
**origin** el origen, la procedencia
**other** otro/a; **on the other hand** en cambio, por otra parte
**ought to** deber
**our** nuestro/a
**out of order** dañado/a
**outside** fuera
**outskirts** las afueras
**oven** el horno
**overweight** excedido de peso
**own** propio/a
**owner** el dueño, la dueña
**oxygen** el oxígeno

P

**P. O. Box** el apartado (de correos)
to **pack** empacar (qu), hacer la maleta
**package** el paquete
**paella** la paella
**page** la página
**pain** el dolor
to **paint** pintar
**painting** la pintura
**pair** el par
**pajama** el/la piyama
**palace** el palacio
**pamphlet** el folleto
**Panamanian** panameño/a
**pantomime** la pantomima
**pantry** la despensa
**paper** el papel
**paragraph** el párrafo
**parenthesis** el paréntesis
**parents** los padres
to **park** estacionar; *n* el parque
**parking** el estacionamiento
**parrot** el loro
**part** la parte; to **be part of** formar parte de; to **play the part** hacer el papel

**partial** parcial
**participant** el participante, la participante
to **participate** participar
**participation** la participación
**particularly** en particular
**partner** la pareja
**party** la fiesta
to **pass** aprobar (ue)
**passenger** el pasajero, la pasajera
**passive** pasivo/a
**Passover** la Pascua
**passport** el pasaporte
**pastry shop** la dulcería, la pastelería
**patient** paciente
**patrimony** el patrimonio
**patron** el patrón, la patrona
**pattern** el esquema
to **pay (for)** pagar (gu); to **pay attention** prestar atención
**peace** la paz
**peas** (*Puerto Rico*) los gandules
**pedagogy** la pedagogía
**pedal** el pedal
**pediatrician** el/la pediatra
**pen: ballpoint pen** el bolígrafo
**pencil** el lápiz
**pending** pendiente
**penitent** el/la penitente
**people** la gente
**pepper** la pimienta; **green pepper** el chile, el pimiento
**percentage** el porcentaje
**perfect** perfecto/a
**perfectly** perfectamente
**perhaps** tal vez, quizá(s)
**period** el período
**permanent** permanente
**permanently** permanentemente
to **permit** permitir

**persistence** el empeño
**persistent** persistente
**person** la persona; **person from Madrid** madrileño/a; **person of importance** el personaje; **person surveyed** el encuestado, la encuestada; **person who signs** el signatario
**personal** personal
**personality** la personalidad
**personnel** el personal
**Peruvian** peruano/a
**peso** el peso
**pessimistic** pesimista
**phantom** el fantasma
**pharmacy** farmacia
**phenomenon** el fenómeno
**philosophy** la filosofía
**photo** la foto
**photograph** la fotografía
**phrase** la frase
**physical** físico/a
**physics** la física
**pianist** el/la pianista
**piano** el piano
to **pick up** recoger (j); pasar por
**picture** el cuadro
**pie** el pastel
**pigpen** la pocilga
**pill** la pastilla
**pillow** la almohada
**pilot** el/la piloto
**pink** rosado/a
**pioneer** el pionero, la pionera
**pizza** la pizza
**place** el lugar
**plaid** de cuadros
**plan** el plan; *v* planificar (qu); planear; to **plan to** + *verb* pensar + *inf*
**plane** el avión
**planet** el planeta
**planning** los arreglos
**plant** la planta

**plate** el plato; **combination plate** el plato combinado
**platform** las andas; la plataforma
to **play** (*game or sport*) jugar (ue); (*an instrument*) tocar (qu); *n* la obra de teatro; to **play the part** hacer el papel
**player** el jugador, la jugadora
**please** por favor; **pleased to meet you** mucho gusto
**pleasure** el placer
**plumber** el plomero
**plural** plural
**pocket** el bolsillo
**point** el punto; to **give a point** marcar un punto; to **point to** señalar
**pole** el polo
**policeman** el policía
**policewoman** la mujer policía
**political** político/a
**politician** el político
**pollen** el polen
**pollution** la contaminación
**pool** la piscina
**poor** pobre
**popular** popular
**population** la población
**porch** el portal
**pork** el cerdo
**port** el puerto
**portable** portátil
**Portuguese** portugués/portuguesa
**position** el puesto, la plaza
**positive** positivo/a
**positively** positivamente
**possession** la posesión; **immediate posession** próxima entrega
**possibility** la posibilidad
**possible** posible
**post card** la tarjeta postal
**post office** el correo, la oficina de correos

**postal** postal
**poster** el afiche
**postgraduate** posgrado
**postpone** posponer
**postponed** pospuesto/a
**potassium** el potasio
**potato** la papa; (*Spain*) la patata
**pound** la libra
**poverty** la pobreza
to **practice** practicar (qu); *n* la práctica; **general practice** la medicina familiar
**pre-Columbian** precolombino/a
**precise time** hora americana, hora inglesa
**prediction** la predicción
to **prefer** preferir (ie, i)
**preferable** preferible
**preparation** el preparativo
to **prepare** preparar
**prepared** capacitado/a
to **prescribe** recetar
**prescription** la receta
**presence** la presencia
**present** actual; *n* el regalo; *v* presentar
**president** el presidente, la presidenta
**press** la prensa
**pressure** la presión, la tensión
**preterit** el pretérito
**pretty** bonito/a
**previous** anterior
**previously** anteriormente
**price** el precio
**primitive** primitivo/a
**prince** el príncipe
**principal** principal
**principle** el principio
**printed** impreso/a
**priority** la prioridad
**private** privado/a
**prize** el premio
**probability** la probabilidad

**probable** probable
**probably** probablemente
**problem** el problema
**procession** la procesión
to **produce** producir (zc)
**produced** producido/a
**producer** el productor, la productora
**product** el producto
**production** la producción
**profession** la profesión
**professional** profesional
**professor** el profesor, la profesora
**profile** el perfil
to **program** programar; *n* el programa
**programmer** el programador, la programadora
**programming** la programación
**progress** el progreso
**progressive** progresivo/a
to **prohibit** prohibir
**prohibition** la prohibición
**project** el proyecto
to **promote** ascender (ie); promover (ue)
**pronoun** el pronombre
**pronunciation** la pronunciación
**proof** la prueba
**proportion** la proporción
to **propose** proponer (g)
to **protect** proteger (j)
**protection** la protección
**protein** la proteína
**proud** orgulloso/a
to **provide** lograr; **provided that** con tal (de) que
**province** la provincia
**psychiatrist** el/la (p)siquiatra
**psychologist** el (p)sicólogo, la (p)sicóloga
**psychology** la (p)sicología
**peseta** (*monetary unit of Spain*) la peseta

**public** público/a; *n* la audiencia
**published** publicado/a
**Puerto Rican** puertorriqueño/a
to **pull** tirar
**punch** el ponche
**punctual** puntual
**punctually** puntualmente
**punctuation** la puntuación
**pure** puro/a
**purple** morado/a
**purse** la bolsa
to **pursue** perseguir (i)
to **put** poner (g), colocar (qu); to **put away** guardar; to **put on makeup** maquillarse; to **put to bed** acostar (ue)
**pyramid** la pirámide

Q

**qualified** capacitado/a
**quality** la calidad; la cualidad
**quarter** el cuarto
**question** la pregunta
**questionnaire** el cuestionario
**quiet** callado/a

R

**race** la raza
**radiator** el radiador
**radically** radicalmente
**radio** el radio
**raffle** la rifa
**railroad** el ferrocarril
**rain** la lluvia; *v* llover (ue)
**raincoat** el impermeable
to **raise** levantar
**raised** educado/a
**rapid** rápido/a
**rapidly** rápidamente, con rapidez
**razor** (*Mexico and other countries*) el rastrillo

**reach** el alcance; *v* alcanzar (c)
**reaction** la reacción
to **read** leer
**reading** la lectura
**ready** listo/a; **to get ready** prepararse
**real** real
**realistic** realista
**reality** la realidad
to **realize** darse cuenta (de)
**really** realmente, en realidad
**reason** el motivo
**rebellious** rebelde
to **receive** recibir
**recent** reciente
**reception** la recepción
**receptionist** el/la recepcionista
**recipe** la receta
to **recognize** reconocer (zc)
**recognized** reconocido/a
to **recommend** recomendar (ie)
**record** el disco
**rectangular** rectangular
to **rectify** rectificar (qu)
**red** rojo/a
to **reduce** reducir (zc)
to **refer** referir (ie, i)
**referee** el árbitro
to **reflect** repercutir; reflejar
**refrigerator** el refrigerador
to **refuse** rechazar (c)
**regards** los recuerdos
**region** la región
**registered** certificado/a
**regularly** regularmente
**regulation** la regulación; el reglamento
to **reject** descartar
**related** relacionado/a
**relation** la relación
**relationship** el parentesco; la relación
**relative** el pariente, la parienta; el familiar
**relatively** relativamente

**relaxation** la relajación
**release** liberar
**religious** religioso/a
to **remain** permanecer (zc), quedar(se)
to **remember** recordar (ue)
to **remind** recordar (ue)
to **remodel** remodelar
to **remove** quitar
to **renew** renovar (ue)
to **rent** alquilar; *n* el alquiler, la renta
to **repeat** repetir (i); hacerse eco
to **replant** replantar
to **report** reportar; *n* el informe
to **represent** representar
**representative** el/la representante
**repression** la represión
**republic** la república
to **request** pedir (i)
**reservation** la reservación
**reserved** reservado/a
**residence** la residencia
**resident** el/la residente
**residential** residencial
to **resist** resistir
**resistance** la resistencia
**resolution** la firmeza
**resort** (*country/mountain*) el refugio
to **respect** respetar; *n* el respeto; **with respect to** con respecto a
**responsibility** la responsabilidad
**responsible** responsable
**rest** el descanso; el resto; *v* descansar
**restaurant** el restaurante
**result** el resultado
**resumé** el curriculum, el historial
to **resume** reanudar
to **return** devolver (ue)
**reveille** la diana

to **review** repasar
**rhythm** el ritmo
**rhythmic** rítmico/a
**ribbon** la cinta
**rice** el arroz
**rich** rico/a
**riddle** la adivinanza
to **ride** montar
**ridiculous** ridículo/a
**right** derecho/a; *n* el derecho; **right now** en estos momentos, to **be right** tener razón; **to the right** a la derecha
**ring** el aro; el anillo; *v* sonar (ue)
**rinse** el enjuague
**rising** ascendiendo
**risk** el riesgo
**river** el río
**roast** asado/a
**robot** el robot
**rock** el rock
**role** el papel
**roll** la lista; to **call roll** pasar (la) lista
**romance** el romance
**romantic** romántico/a
**roof** el techo
**room** la habitación, el cuarto, el dormitorio; **dining room** el comedor; **living room** la sala; **waiting room** la sala de espera
**rose** la rosa
**rough** rudo/a
**round** redondo/a; **round–trip ticket** el boleto/pasaje de ida y vuelta
**row** la fila
**royal** regio/a, real
**rug** la alfombra
**ruins** las ruinas
**rule** la regulación
**rum** el ron
to **run** correr
**runner** el corredor, la corredora

**rural** rural
**Russian** ruso/a

## S

**sabotage** el sabotaje
**sad** triste
**Sagittarian** sagitariano/a
**sail** la vela
**saint** el santo, la santa
**salad** la ensalada
**salary** el sueldo, el salario; **desired salary** la pretensión económica
**sale** la rebaja; la venta
**salesman** el vendedor
**saleswoman** la vendedora
**salt** la sal
**Salvadoran** salvadoreño/a
**same** mismo/a; igual
**sand** la arena
**sandwich** el sándwich; (*Mexico*) la torta
**satellite dish antenna** la parabólica
**satisfaction** la satisfacción
**satisfactory** satisfactorio/a
**satisfy** satisfacer (g)
**Saturday** el sábado
**sauce** la salsa
**sauna** la sauna
to **save** ahorrar
**saxophone** el saxofón
to **say** decir (g, i)
**saying** el dicho
**scarf** la bufanda
**scene** la escena
**schedule** el horario
**scholarship** la beca
**school** el colegio; la escuela; la facultad; *adj* escolar; **school year** el curso
**science** la ciencia
**scientist** el científico, la científica
**Scout: Boy Scouts** niños exploradores; **Girl Scouts** niñas exploradoras

**sea** el mar
**season** la estación
**seat** el asiento
**second** segundo/a
**secret** el secreto
**secretary** el secretario, la secretaria
**section** la sección
**security** la seguridad
to **see** ver
to **seem** parecer (zc)
**seismic** sísmico/a
**seldom** rara vez
**select** selecto/a
**selection** la selección
**self–description** la autodescripción
to **sell** vender
**semester** el semestre
to **send** enviar, mandar
**senior citizenhood** la tercera edad
**sensible** sensato/a
**sensitive** sensitivo/a
**sentence** la oración
**sentimental** sentimental
**separated** separado/a
**September** septiembre
**series** la serie
**serious** serio/a
to **serve** servir (i)
**service** el servicio; **service station** la gasolinera, la estación de gasolina
**session** la sesión
**set** fijado/a; *v* fijar; to **set oneself to do something** proponerse
**seven** siete; **seven hundred** setecientos
**seventeen** diecisiete
**seventh** séptimo
**seventy** setenta
**several** varios/as; diversos/as
to **sew** coser
**sex** el sexo
**sexual** sexual
**shape** la forma

to **share** compartir
**sharp** en punto
to **shave** afeitar(se)
**she** ella
**sheet** la sábana
**sherbet** el sorbete
**shine** el brillo; *v* brillar
**ship** el barco
**shirt** la camisa; la guayabera
**shoe** el zapato; **tennis shoes** zapatos (de) tenis
**shop** el taller
**shopping** la compra; **shopping center** el centro comercial
**short** corto/a; bajo/a; **in short** en fin
**should** deber
**shoulder** el hombro
to **show** mostrar(se) (ue); demostrar; *n* la función, el espectáculo
**shower** la ducha
**shrimp** el camarón
**sick** enfermo/a; mal
**sickness** la enfermedad
**sidewalk** la acera
to **sign** firmar; *n* el signo; el letrero
**signal** la señal; **traffic signal** señal de tráfico
**signature** la firma
**silly** tonto/a
**silver** la plata
**similar** similar, parecido/a
**simple** sencillo/a
**simply** simplemente
**sin** el pecado
**since** ya que; como; desde; pues
**sincere** sincero/a
to **sing** cantar
**singer** el/la cantante
**single** soltero/a; sencillo
**sink** el fregadero
**sister** la hermana; **sister–in–law** la cuñada
to **sit down** sentarse (ie)
**site (construction)** la obra

**situated** situado/a
**situation** la situación
**six** seis; **six hundred** seiscientos
**sixteen** dieciséis
**sixth** sexto
**sixty** sesenta
**size** la talla; el tamaño
to **skate** patinar
to **ski** esquiar; *n* el esquí
**skier** el esquiador, la esquiadora
**skin** la piel
to **skin/scuba dive** bucear
**skirt** la falda
**slacks** los pantalones
to **sleep** dormir (ue, u); to **fall asleep** dormirse (ue)
**sleeper (car)** coche cama
**sleepy: to be sleepy** tener sueño
**slight** ligero/a
**slow** *adv* despacio; *adj* lento/a
**slowly** lentamente, despacio
**small** pequeño/a; reducido/a
**smart** listo/a
to **smile** sonreír(se) (i)
**smog** el smog, la contaminación del aire
to **smoke** fumar; *n* el humo
**snack** la merienda
to **snore** roncar (qu)
**snow** la nieve; *v* nevar (ie)
**so** tan; luego; **so long** hasta luego; **so–so** regular; **so that** para que
**soap** el jabón; **soap opera** la telenovela
**soccer** el fútbol
**social** social
**society** la sociedad
**sock** el calcetín
**soda** el refresco
**sodium** el sodio
**sofa** el sofá
**soft** suave
**softly** en voz baja

**solid color** de color entero
**solidary** solidario/a
to **solve** resolver (ue)
**some** alguno/as; algún; unos
**somebody** alguien
**someone** alguien
**something** algo; **something else** algo más
**sometime** alguna vez
**sometimes** a veces
**son** el hijo; **son–in–law** el yerno
**song** la canción
**soon** pronto
**sorry: sorry for the inconvenience** disculpe(n) la molestia; to **be sorry** sentir (ie, i)
**sound** (*to signal an activity*) el toque
**soup** la sopa
**south** el sur
**spaghetti** el espagueti
**Spaniard** el español, la española
**Spanish** el español
to **speak** hablar
**special** especial; **special delivery** entrega especial
**specializing** especializado/a
**specific** específico/a
**specifically** concretamente
**spectacle** el espectáculo
**spectacular** espectacular
**spectator** el espectador, la espectadora
**speed** la rapidez, la velocidad; to **speed up** agilizar (c)
to **spend** gastar; pasar
**spill** el derrame
to **spin around** dar vueltas
**spinach** la espinaca
**spite: in spite of** a pesar de
**sport** el deporte; *adj* deportivo/a
**spring** la primavera
**square** cuadrado/a
**stadium** el estadio

**staff** el personal
**staffed** atendido/a
**stage** el escenario
**stairs** la escalera
**stamp** la estampilla, el sello
**standard of living** el nivel de vida
**standing** parado/a
**star** la estrella
to **start** empezar (ie, c); comenzar (ie, c)
**stately** señorial
**station** la estación; **service station** la estación de gasolina, la gasolinera
**stationery store** la papelería
**status: marital status** el estado civil
**stay** la estancia; *v* quedar(se), permanecer
**steering wheel** el volante
to **step** pisar; *n* el paso
**stereo** el estéreo
**stereotype** el estereotipo
**stewardess** la azafata
**stick** el palo
**still** todavía
**stingy** tacaño/a
**stocking** la media
**stomach** el estómago
to **stop** detener(se) (g, ie), parar(se); hacer alto; *n* la parada
**stopover: to make a stopover** hacer escala
**stopwatch** el cronómetro
**store** la tienda; **store window** el escaparate
**story** el cuento
**stove** la estufa
**straight: to go straight ahead** seguir derecho
**strawberry** la fresa
**street** la calle
**streetcar** el tranvía
**strength** la fuerza
**stress** la presión, la tensión

**stretcher** la camilla
**strict** estricto/a
**striped** de rayas
**strong** fuerte
**structure** la estructura
**student** el/la estudiante; el alumno, la alumna
**studies** los estudios
to **study** estudiar
**style** el estilo
**subject** la materia; el sujeto
**subordination** la sujeción
**subway** el metro
to **succeed** triunfar
**successful** exitoso/a; **to be successful** tener éxito
**suddenly** de repente
to **suffer** sufrir
**sugar** el/la azúcar
to **suggest** sugerir (ie, i)
**suggestion** la sugerencia
**suit** el traje; **bathing suit** el traje de baño
**suitcase** la maleta
**suite** la suite
**summer** el verano
**sun** el sol; **it's sunny** hace sol
**Sunday** el domingo
**superficial** superficial
**supermarket** el supermercado
**supervisor** el supervisor, la supervisora
**supper** la cena, la comida
to **supply** aportar
**support** el apoyo
**sure** seguro/a
**surface** la superficie
**surgeon** el cirujano
**surgery** la cirugía
to **surpass** superar, sobrepasar
**surprise** la sorpresa; **to be surprised** sorprenderse
**surrounded** rodeado/a
**surrounding areas** los alrededores

**survey** la encuesta
**sweater** el suéter
**sweatshirt** la sudadera
**sweep** barrer
**sweet** dulce
to **swim** nadar
**swimming** la natación
**Swiss** suizo/a
**symbol** el símbolo
**symptom** el síntoma
**system** el sistema; el régimen

T

**T-shirt** la camiseta
**table** la mesa
**tablecloth** el mantel
**tablespoon** la cuchara
to **take** llevar; tomar; **to take advantage of** aprovechar; **to take away** quitar; **to take care of** cuidar, atender (ie); **to take courses** seguir cursos; **to take credit** apuntar; **to take off** quitarse; **to take on** incurrir; **to take out** sacar; **to take pictures** sacar fotos
to **talk** conversar
**talkative** hablador/a
**tall** alto/a
**tape** la cinta
**tape recorder** la grabadora
**tariff** la tarifa
**tax** el impuesto
**taxi** el taxi; **taxi driver** el/la taxista
**tea** el té
to **teach** enseñar
**teacher** el maestro, la maestra
**team** el equipo; (*in bullfighting*) la cuadrilla
**tear** la lágrima; *v* romper, romperse
**teaspoon** la cucharita
**technical** técnico/a
**technology** la tecnología
**teenager** el/la adolescente

**telegram** el telegrama
**telegraph** el telégrafo
**telephone** el teléfono; *adj* telefónico/a
**television** la televisión, la tele; **television set** el televisor
**telegenic** *adj* televisivo/a
to **tell** contar (ue)
**temper** el carácter
**temperature** la temperatura
**temple** el templo
**temporary** temporal
**ten** diez
**tenant** el inquilino, la inquilina
**tendency** la tendencia
**tennis** el tenis
**tent** la tienda de campaña
**tenth** décimo
**term** el término
**terrace** la terraza
**terrible** terrible
**terrorism** el terrorismo
**thank you** gracias
**Thanksgiving Day** Día de Acción de Gracias
**that** aquel, aquello/a; esa, ese, eso; que; **that is** o sea; **that one** aquél, aquélla; ésa, ése; **that which** lo que
**the** el, la, los, las; lo
**theater** el teatro
**theft** el robo
**their** su(s); suyo/a
**them** ellos; les; los
**theme** el tema
**themselves** se
**then** entonces; después
**theoretical** teórico/a
**there** allí, allá; **there is, there are** hay; **there was, there were** hubo; había
**thermometer** el termómetro
**these** estos, estas
**they** ellos, ellas
**thief** el ladrón
**thin** delgado/a

**thing** la cosa
to **think** pensar (ie); to **think so** pensar que sí
**third** tercero/a; tercer
**thirsty: to be thirsty** tener sed
**thirteen** trece
**thirty** treinta
**this** esto; este, esta; *n* east; **this way** así
**those** aquellos/a; esos/as; aquéllos/as; ésos/as
**thousand** mil
**three** tres; **three hundred** trescientos
**throat** la garganta
**throughout** a través de
to **throw** lanzar (c), tirar
**Thursday** el jueves
**ticket** el boleto, el billete, el pasaje; la entrada; **round–trip ticket** boleto (pasaje) de ida y vuelta; **ticket office** la taquilla
**tidy** ordenado/a; to **tidy oneself** asearse
**tiger** el tigre
**tight** estrecho
**time** la hora; la época; la vez; el tiempo; **full–time** jornada completa; to **have a good time** pasarlo bien; **on time** a tiempo; **precise time** hora americana/inglesa; to **waste time** perder (el) tiempo
**timid** tímido/a
**tip** la propina
**tire** la llanta
**tired** cansado/a
**to** a; para
**toast** el pan tostado, la tostada
**today** hoy
**together** juntos/as; to **go together** combinar bien
**toilet** el inodoro

**token** la ficha
**toll** el peaje
**tomato** el tomate
**tomorrow** mañana; **the day after tomorrow** pasado mañana
**ton** la tonelada
**tongue** la lengua
**tonight** esta noche
**too** también; **too much** demasiado
**tool** la herramienta
**tooth** el diente
**toothache** el dolor de muelas
**topic** el tema
**torn** roto/a
**tornado** el tornado
**tortilla** la tortilla
**torture** la tortura
**total** absoluto/a; total
**totally** totalmente
**tour** la excursión; el circuito
**tourism** el turismo
**tourist** el/la turista; *adj* turístico/a
**toward(s)** hacia, para
**towel** la toalla
**town** el pueblo
**track** (*railroad*) la vía
**tradition** la tradición
**traditional** tradicional
**traditionally** tradicionalmente
**traffic** el tráfico; **traffic jam** el embotellamiento; **traffic light** el semáforo
**train** el tren; *v* entrenar
**trained** entrenado/a
**trainer** el entrenador, la entrenadora
**training** el entrenamiento; la instrucción
**trait** el rasgo
**tranquilizer** el tranquilizante
**transaction** la transacción; la tramitación

**transit** el tránsito
to **translate** traducir (zc)
to **transmit** transmitir
**transportation** el traslado, el transporte
to **travel** recorrer, viajar
**tray** la bandeja
to **treat** tratar
**treatment** el trato
**tree** el árbol; **family tree** el árbol genealógico
**trip** el viaje
**tropics** el trópico
**truck** el camión
**true** verdadero/a; cierto/a
**trunk** el baúl, el maletero
**truth** la verdad
to **try** probar (ue); to **try on** probarse (ue); to **try to** tratar (de)
**tub** la bañadera
**Tuesday** el martes
**tuna** el atún
**turkey** el pavo
to **turn** dar vueltas; doblar; to **turn down** rechazar (c); to **turn off** apagar (gu); to **turn on** conectar, encender (ie)
**twelve** doce
**twenty** veinte; **twenty–eight** veintiocho; **twenty–five** veinticinco; **twenty–four** veinticuatro; **twenty–nine** veintinueve; **twenty–one** veintiuno, veintiún; **twenty–seven** veintisiete; **twenty–six** veintiséis; **twenty–three** veintitrés; **twenty–two** veintidós
to **twist** torcer (ue, z)
**two** dos; **two hundred** doscientos
**type** el tipo; *v* escribir a máquina
**typical** típico/a

**U**

**ugly** feo/a
**umpire** el árbitro
**unbelievable** increíble
**uncle** el tío
**undecided** indeciso/a
**under** debajo, bajo
**underground** subterráneo/a
**underlined** subrayado/a
**understand** comprender, entender (ie)
**understanding** la comprensión
**underwear** la ropa interior
**unemployment** el desempleo, el paro
**unexpectedly** inesperadamente
**unfavorable** desfavorable
**unforgettable** inolvidable
**unfortunately** desgraciadamente
**unhappy** infeliz
**uninterrupted** ininterrumpido/a
**union** la unión
**unit** la unidad
**united** unido/a
**university** la universidad; *adj* universitario/a
**unknown** desconocido/a
**unless** a menos que
**unpleasant** antipático/a
**until** hasta; (*when telling time*) menos
**upkeep** el mantenimiento
**urban** urbano/a
to **urge** animar
**urgent** urgente
**urgently** urgentemente
**us** nos; nosotros/as
to **use** usar, consumir, utilizar (c); to **be used to** estar acostumbrado/a
**useful** útil

**V**

**vacation** las vacaciones
to **vacuum** pasar la aspiradora; **vacuum cleaner** la aspiradora/el aspirador
**Valentine's Day** el Día de los Enamorados
**valuable** valioso/a
**value** el valor; *v* valorar
**vanilla** la vainilla
**variety** la variedad
**various** diferentes
to **vary** variar
**vast** extenso/a
**vegetable** la verdura, el vegetal
**vegetarian** vegetariano/a
**vehicle** el vehículo
**Venezuelan** venezolano/a
**ventilation** la ventilación
**verb** el verbo
**very** muy
**vibrant** vibrante
**victim** la víctima
**victory** el triunfo
**video** el vídeo/video
**view** la vista
**vinegar** el vinagre
**violence** la violencia
**violent** violento/a
**violin** el violín
**violinist** el violinista, la violinista
**visa** el visado, la visa
to **visit** visitar; *n* la visita
**visitor** el/la visitante
**vitality** la vitalidad
**vocabulary** el vocabulario
**volcano** el volcán
**volleyball** el vól(e)ibol
**voluntary** voluntario/a
**vowel** la vocal

**W**

**waist** la cintura
**waiter** el camarero

**waiting room** la sala de espera
**waitress** la camarera
to **wake up** despertar(se) (ie)
to **walk** caminar
**walking** la marcha
**wall** la pared
**wallet** la billetera
to **want** querer (ie); desear
**war** la guerra
**warm up** el calentamiento; *v* calentar (ie)
to **wash** lavar; to **wash dishes** fregar (ie, gu)
**washbowl** el lavabo
**washing** el aseo; **washing machine** la lavadora
to **waste** gastar; to **waste time** perder (el) tiempo
to **watch** presenciar; vigilar
**water** el agua *fem*
**wave** la ola
**way** la manera, la forma; **anyway** de todas formas; **by the way** por cierto; to **open the way to** dar paso a; **this way** de esta forma
**we** nosotros/as
**weak** débil
**wealth** la riqueza
to **wear** llevar; to **wear a costume** disfrazarse (c)
**weather** el tiempo; **how's the weather?** ¿qué tiempo hace?; **the weather is fine/bad** hace buen/mal tiempo
**wedding** la boda
**Wednesday** el miércoles
**week** la semana
**weekdays** entre semana
**weekend** el fin de semana
**weekly** semanal
to **weigh** pesar
**weight** el peso
**welcome: you're welcome** de nada

**well** bien; pues; **well–being** el bienestar
**west** oeste
**wet** húmedo/a
**what** qué; lo que; **what a pity!** ¡qué pena!
**when** cuándo; cuando
**where** dónde; donde; **where to** adónde
**which** cuál(es); **which one(s)** cuál(es)
**while** mientras; *n* el rato; **in a while** dentro de un rato
**white** blanco/a
**who** quién(es); **who's calling?** ¿de parte de quién?
**wholesaler** el mayorista
**whose** de quién
**wide** ancho/a
**wife** la esposa, la mujer
to **win** ganar; to **win back** reconquistar
**wind** el viento; **it's windy** hace viento
**window** la ventana; (*car, train, etc.*) la ventanilla
**windshield** el parabrisas
**wine** el vino
**winner** el ganador, la ganadora
**winter** el invierno
**wise** prudente; **the Three Wise Men** los Reyes Magos
to **wish** desear; *n* el deseo
**with** con; **with difficulty** difícilmente; **with me** conmigo; **with you** *fam* contigo
**without** sin; sin que
**woman** la mujer
**word** la palabra; **dirty word** la mala palabra
**work** el trabajo, la obra; *v* trabajar, funcionar

**workaholic** el trabajomaníaco, la trabajomaníaca
**worker** el obrero, la obrera
**world** el mundo; *adj* mundial
**worried** preocupado/a
to **worry** preocuparse; *n* la preocupación
**worse** peor
**worst** peor
**wrist** la muñeca
to **write** escribir; to **write down** anotar
**wrong** equivocado/a

## X

**X-ray** la radiografía

## Y

**yard** el jardín
**year** el año; **New Year's Eve** la Nochevieja; **school year** el curso
**yellow** amarillo/a
**yes** sí
**yesterday** ayer; **the day before yesterday** anteayer
**yoga** el yoga
**yogurt** el yogur
**you** tú; usted, Ud.; vosotros/as; ustedes, Uds.; te; os; lo, la, los, las; le, les, ti
**young** joven
**younger** menor
**your** tu; su; vuestro/a
**yours** tuyo/a; suyo/a; vuestro/a
**yourself** te; se; os
**youth** la juventud

## Z

**zebra** la cebra
**zero** el cero
**zone** la zona

# *Index*

**a**
  after **ir,** 93
  personal, 130, 297, 301
abbreviations
  for **don** and **doña,** 10
  for **señor, señora** and **señorita,** 10
  for **usted** and **ustedes,** 42
**acabar de** + infinitive, 397
accentuation, 116–117, 138, 139, 164
adjectives
  agreement of, 65
  comparisons of equality of, 230–231
  comparisons of inequality of, 226–227
  demonstrative, 179–180
  ending in **-ísimo,** 253
  gender of, 65
  number of, 65
  of nationality, 69
  past participles used as, 401
  position of, 66
  possessive, 115
  regular and irregular comparative forms of certain, 226
  shortened forms of, 66
  stressed possessive, 355
  superlative of, 253
  with **ser** and **estar,** 70–71
**adónde,** 93
adverbial conjunctions

requiring the subjunctive, 421
  followed by the subjunctive or the indicative, 422
adverbs, 328
  comparison of, 329
  **con** + noun instead of, 328
  ending in **-mente,** 328
  ending in **-ísimo,** 329
affirmative and negative expressions, 296–297
**al,** 93
  + infinitive, 428
alphabet, 8
articles
  definite (singular), 46–47
  indefinite (singular), 46–47
  plural forms of, 49
  singular feminine nouns with masculine, 194 *n* 2
  use of definite, 49, 136
  with dates, 159
  with infinitives, 428

cardinal numbers. See numbers.
Centigrade system, 146
cognates, 13
commands
  formal, 203

  informal, 221–222
  **nosotros,** 271
  of **ir, saber,** and **ser,** formal, 203
  of verbs ending in **-car, gar, zar,** and **-guir,** formal, 203
  shortened affirmative **tú,** 221
  object and reflexive pronouns used with, 203, 222
  **vosotros,** 222 *n* 1
**cómo,** 74
comparisons
  of equality, 230–231
  of inequality, 226–227
conditional
  of **gustar,** 183, 382
  in *if* clauses, 383
  perfect, 431
  tense, 382
  use of the, 383
**conmigo,** 209
**conocer**
  present tense of, 207
  and **saber,** 207–208
consonants
  pronunciation of, 15, 23, 33, 77
**contigo,** 209
**cuál(es)**
  as a question word, 74
  **ser** used with the interrogative, 380
**cuándo,** 74
**cuánto (a, -os, -as),** 74

culture
attitudes concerning time in the
Hispanic world, 34
doctors, hospitals, and pharmacies in the Hispanic world, 263
**cambios en la sociedad his-
pana,** 418–419
**catástrofes y problemas am-
bientales en el mundo hispano,** 393–394
**días de fiesta y tradiciones en
el mundo hispano,** 367–368
education in the Hispanic world,
40
families in the Hispanic world,
106
food in the Hispanic world, 241
general awareness, titles, and
some social customs, 10
the Hispanics, 63
housing in the Hispanic world,
125
physical fitness and exercise in
the Hispanic world, 218–219
shopping in the Hispanic world,
173
social customs when greeting
and body language, 17
student life in the Hispanic countries, 85
Spanish language, 24
sports in the Hispanic world, 149
**el teléfono, las cartas y el ser-
vicio postal en los países
hispanos,** 315–316
**el turismo en los países hispa-
nos,** 344–345
**los viajes en los países hispa-
nos,** 286–287
work and economic environment
in the Hispanic countries, 196

**dar**
present tense of, 176
dates, 159
days of the week, 29

**de**
after **ser** to express origin, 69
after **ser** to express possession,
70
and noun or pronoun to replace
**su,** 115
and noun or pronoun to replace
**el suyo,** 356
indicating possession, 70, 115
instead of **que** in comparisons of
inequality, 226
**decir**
present tense of, 161–162
indicative or subjunctive after,
245
definite articles. See articles.
**del,** 70
demonstrative adjectives. See adjectives.
demonstrative pronouns. See pronouns.
diphthongs, 52, 164
direct object nouns. See nouns.
direct object pronouns. See pronouns.
**dónde,** 74

**e** in place of **y,** 322 *n* 3
**el** with feminine singular noun, 194
*n* 2
**estar**
for location, 20, 51
for states of health, 51
present tense of the verb, 51
or **ser** with adjectives, 70–71
some uses of, 20, 51
used with past participle, 401–402
used with present participle, 152–
153
with expressions of weather, 146

future
tense, 331–332
uses of the, 332
using the present of **ir** + **a** +
infinitive to express, 93

using the present tense to express, 94

gender
of nouns, 46–47
of adjectives, 65
**gustar,** 184
verbs that follow the pattern of,
184

**haber**
as an auxiliary verb, 397, 401
**había,** 371
**hacer**
present tense of, 128
with weather expressions, 146
+ expressions of time, 351
present tense of, 128
**hay,** 27

*if* clauses, 383
imperfect tense
and preterit, 370
of regular and irregular verbs,
370–371
of **hay,** 371
of **ir, ser,** and **ver,** 371
uses of the, 371
impersonal expressions, indicative
and subjunctive after, 267
indefinite articles. See articles.
indicative
after impersonal expressions, 267
and subjunctive in adjective
clauses, 301
or subjunctive, adverbial conjunctions followed by, 422
versus subjunctive, 243
See also individual tenses.
indirect object nouns. See nouns.
indirect object pronouns. See pronouns.
infinitive
as the object of a preposition,
428

as subject of a sentence, 428
instead of subjunctive, 245
**ir**
+ **a** + infinitive, 93
present tense of, 93
preterit tense of, 319
**-ísimo,** 253

**jugar,** 109

last names
paternal and maternal, 106
*let's,* equivalents of English, 271
linking, 52

**más de,** 226
**más. . . que,** 226–227
**menos de,** 226
**menos. . . que,** 226–227
months, 144–145
**mucho** with weather expressions, 146

negative, 44
and affirmative expressions, 296–297
nominalization of adjective, 253
nouns
comparisons of equality of, 230–231
comparisons of inequality of, 226–227
direct object, 130
gender of, 46
indirect object, 175
number of, 48
numbers
cardinal, 26–27, 90, 156
ordinal, 158–159

**o** replaced by **u,** 322 *n* 3
object pronouns. See pronouns.

**oír**
present tense, 320 *n* 1
preterit tense, 320
**ojalá,** 270
ordinal numbers. See numbers.
orthographic-changing verbs, 161, 203, 291

**para**
and **por,** 375
and **por** contrasted, 376
passive voice, 409
other constructions instead of the, 409
**por** used with the, 409
past participle
as adjective, 401
forms of the, 396–397
in perfect tenses, 397, 401, 431
used where English uses present participle, 402
used with **estar,** 401–402
used with **ser,** 409
past perfect (indicative), 401
past subjunctive. See subjunctive.
**pensar** + infinitive, 109
**poner**
present tense of, 128
preterit tense of, 347
personal **a,** 130–131, 297, 301
personal pronouns. See pronouns.
**por**
and **para,** 375
and **para** contrasted, 376
used with the passive voice, 409
**¿por qué?,** 75
**porque,** 75
possessive adjectives. See adjectives.
possessive pronouns. See pronouns.
prepositions
infinitives as the object of, 428
pronouns after, 209
present participle
forms of, 152–153
past participle in Spanish where English uses, 402

present perfect (indicative), 397
object and reflexive pronouns used with, 397
present perfect subjunctive. See subjunctive.
present subjunctive. See subjunctive.
present tense (indicative)
English equivalents of Spanish, 43
irregular verbs in the first-person singular of the, 128, 207
of **e** → **ie** and **o** → **ue** stem-changing verbs, 108, 109
of **e** → **i** stem-changing verbs, 161–162
of **decir,** 162
of **hacer, poner,** and **salir,** 128
of regular **-ar** verbs, 43
of regular **-er** and **-ir** verbs, 88
of **saber** and **conocer,** 207
of **seguir** and **conseguir,** 162
of **tener** and **venir,** 109
of **ver,** 88
to express future, 94
preterit tense
irregular, 324, 347
of **dar,** 291
of **ser,** and **ir,** 319
of regular **-ar, -er,** and **-ir** verbs, 290
of **-er** and **-ir** verbs whose stem ends in a vowel, 320
of verbs ending in **-car, -gar,** and **-zar,** 291
of verbs ending in **-ducir,** 324
of stem-changing **-ar** and **-er** verbs, 290
of stem-changing **-ir** verbs, 319
verbs with special meanings in the, 324 *n* 4, 348 *n* 1
use of the, 291
and imperfect, 371
probability
future of, 332
conditional of, 383
progressive tenses
present, 152–153

progressive tenses *(Continued)*
  reflexive and object pronouns used with the, 153
  uses of the present, 153
pronouns
  after prepositions, 209
  commands using object and reflexive, 203
  demonstrative, 179–180
  direct object, 131
  direct and indirect object pronouns, 405
  direct object and reflexive, 405
  indirect object, 175
  position of direct object, 130, 131, 153
  possessive, 355
  preceded by **a** to clarify or emphasize indirect object pronoun, 176, 405
  progressive tenses using reflexive and object, 153
  reflexive, 135
  relative, 274–275
  subject, 42
  use of reflexive, 135
  use of subject, 42–43
pronunciation
  consonants, 15, 23, 33, 77
  linking, 52
  stress and the written accent mark, 116–117, 138–139, 164
  vowels, 7–8

**que**
  as a relative pronoun, 274
  in comparisons of inequality, 226
**qué**
  as a question word, 74–75
  exclamatory, 380
  **ser** used with the interrogative, 380
**¿qué tal?,** 5
question
  with question word, 74–75
  with interrogative tag, 75
  without a question word, 75

question words, 74–75
**quien(es)** as a relative pronoun, 274–275
**quién(es)** as a question word, 75
reflexive pronouns. See pronouns.
reflexive verbs, 135–136
  change in meaning of, 136

**saber**
  and **conocer,** 207–208
  present tense of, 207
  preterit tense of, 347
**salir**
  present tense of, 128
  + prepositions, 128
**se**
  for unplanned occurrences, 426
  + verb construction, 199
  + verb to express English indefinite *one,* 199
  reflexive pronoun, 135–136
  replacing **le** and **les,** 405
seasons, 144–145
**ser,** 14
  and **estar** with adjectives, 70–71
  and the time of day, 30–31
  for identification and description, 14, 22
  present tense of, 69
  preterit tense of, 319
  some uses of, 69–70
  used with past participle, 409
shortened forms. See adjectives.
stem-changing verbs, 108–109, 161–162, 203, 245
stress, 116–117, 138–139, 164
subject pronouns. See pronouns.
subjunctive
  adverbial conjunctions always followed by the, 421
  after indefinite and non specific antecedents, 301
  after **decir,** 245
  after **dudar,** 250
  after impersonal expressions, 267
  after **ojalá,** 270
  imperfect, 358

  in adjective clauses, 301
  in adverbial clauses, 422
  in noun clauses, 245, 246, 250, 267
  infinitive instead of, 245
  or indicative, adverbial conjunctions followed by, 422
  past, 358
  past, of **querer** for a softened request, 294
  pluperfect, 431
  present, 244–245
  present perfect, 411
  sequence of tenses with, 358
  to express wishes and hope, 245
  versus the indicative, 243
  with verbs and expressions of doubt, 250
  with verbs of emotion, 246
superlative
  of adjectives, 253
  with **-ísimo,** 253, 329
syllabication, 52, 164

**tan. . . como,** 230
**tanto/a. . . como,** 230–231
**tener**
  + **que** + infinitive, 112
  present tense of, 109
  preterit of, 347
  special expressions with, 111–112
  to express age in the past, 371
time of day, 30–31
**tú,** 5, 42

**u** in place of **o,** 322 *n* 3
useful expressions in the classroom, 10, 16, 24, 33
**usted,** 5, 42
**ustedes,** 42

**vamos a** + infinitive
  to express English *let's* + verb, 271
  to express future, 94

**venir**
    present tense of, 109
    preterit tense of, 324
verbs
    reflexive, 135–136
See also individual tenses.

voice
    passive, 409
**vosotros/as,** 42
vowels
    stressed, 8
    unstressed, 8

weather, 146

**y** replaced by **e,** 322 *n* 3

# Illustration Acknowledgments

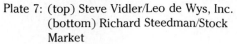

Plate 7: (top) Steve Vidler/Leo de Wys, Inc.
(bottom) Richard Steedman/Stock Market
Plate 8: (top) Peter Menzel
(bottom) Howard Dratch/The Image Works

**Realia**

**Lección 1:** 44, ad, Idiomas Serrano, Madrid, Spain; 53, ad, courtesy of Linguacenter, S.A., Caracas, Venezuela. **Lección 2:** 76, courtesy of Instituto Mexicano de televisión. **Lección 3:** 96, chart with illustration, *Revista Coqueta,* Bogotá, Colombia; 101, ad, Pulco. **Lección 4:** 119, ad, Regersa, Urbanización Parque Rozas, Las Rozas. **Lección 5:** 140, 3 ads, VYCSA, Madrid, Spain; 141, extract of article "Solo ante el peligro" with art, courtesy Ediciones Conica, S.A., *Revista Telva,* Madrid, Spain. **Lección 6:** 155, 3 ads, Sport Club; 164, 2 charts, *Cambio;* 165, extract of article on basketball, *Blanco y negro,* courtesy Luis María Anson, ABC, Prensa Española. **Lección 7:** 187 (left), Blusa's, Madrid, Spain, (center) Donjota, Madrid, Spain, (right), Felix Saenz. **Lección 9:** 219, 233, extracted text of and charts from *Salud y nutrición* by Virginia Diez del Moral, courtesy Editorial Tiempo Libre S.A.; 234, ad, courtesy Pardiñas 50, S.A., Madrid, Spain; 235, ad, from Spanish newspaper, ABC. **Lección 10:** 257, Comunidad Autónoma de Canarias, Gabinete de Prensa, Spain; 259, Restaurante Cueva del Tesoro. **Lección 11:** 276, extracted TV guide, *Tiempo;* 277, *Blanco y negro,* courtesy Luis María Anson, ABC, Prensa Española; 278, ad, Gabinete de Prensa, Madrid, Spain; 279, cartoon, courtesy Mr. Kiraz. **Lección 12:** 285, boarding pass, Iberia Airlines of Spain; 295, ad, Latitud 4, Cunard Lines, Spain; 296, ad, Eastern airlines; 302, ad, courtesy Turismo Las Hamacas, S.A.; 307, ad, courtesy Iberia Airlines of Spain; 308, ad, courtesy, Al-Andalus Expreso, RENFE; 311, ad, Sedeco, Servicio del Conductor, S.A., Málaga, Spain. **Lección 13:** 334, ad, *Blanco y negro,* courtesy Luis María Anson, ABC, Prensa Española; 335, ad, courtesy *Vanidades* Continental; 338, ad, Telefónica. **Lección 14:** 343, ad, Conserjería de Cultura y Bienestar Social, Junta de Castilla y León; 349, ad, Grebol electrónica, Caracas, Venezuela; 354, ad, Ros Fotocolor, Madrid, Spain; 357, ad, La silla, Madrid, Spain; 360, ad, Red Nacional de Ferrocarriles Españoles; 361, ad, Hotel Crown Plaza, Mexico; 362, ad, Gran Rex Hotel, Miramar. **Lección 15:** 381, lottery ticket, ONCE; 384, ad, Hotel El Dorado; 387, ad, Plaza de Toros de Málaga; 388, ad, Bacardi y Cia, S.A., España. **Lección 16:** 410, article, "Murió víctima de un sabotaje," *Blanco y negro,* Luis María Anson, ABC, Prensa Espanola; 413, extracted ad, Orense, Madrid, Spain. **Lección 17:** 434–435, extracted article "Los Ángeles de la Guardia Civil marcan el paso en Baeza," *Blanco y negro,* courtesy Luis María Anson, ABC, Prensa Española.

MAR DEL CARIBE

Barranquilla
Cartagena
Maracaibo • Caracas
Mérida
GUYANA
Río Orinoco
SURINAM
Medellín
VENEZUELA
GUAYANA FRANCESA
Bogotá
Cali
COLOMBIA
ECUADOR
ECUADOR
Quito
Manaus
Belém
Río Amazonas
Guayaquil
Iquitos

OCÉANO

PERÚ
Lima
Cuzco
BOLIVIA
Brasilia
Arequipa
La Paz
BRASIL
Arica
Sucre
Iquique

OCÉANO ATLÁNTICO

TRÓPICO DE CAPRICORNIO
PARAGUAY
São Paulo
Río de Janeiro
Antofagasta
Asunción
Santos

PACÍFICO
Tucumán
CHILE
Córdoba
Valparaíso
Mendoza
URUGUAY
Santiago
Rosario
Montevideo
Concepción
Buenos Aires
Río de la Plata
ARGENTINA
La Plata
Bahía Blanca
Puerto Montt
Bariloche

ANDES

**América del Sur**

0      600      1200
Kilómetros

Estrecho de
Magallanes
Islas Malvinas
Punta Arenas
TIERRA DEL FUEGO
Cabo de Hornos